B53 032 898 X

ROTHERHAM LIBRARY & INFORMATION SERVICE

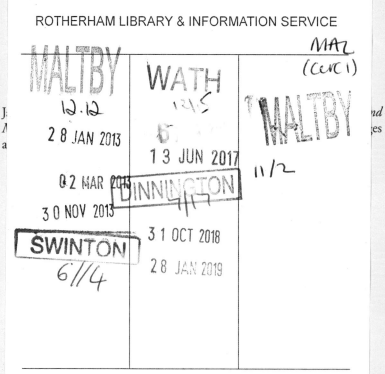

MALTBY
12.12
2 8 JAN 2013
02 MAR 2013
30 NOV 2013
SWINTON
6/14

WATH
12.5
1 3 JUN 2017
DINNINGTON
4/17
3 1 OCT 2018
2 8 JAN 2019

MAZ
(CENCI)
MALTBY
11/2

This book must be returned by the date specified at the time of issue as
the DATE DUE FOR RETURN.
The loan may be extended (personally, by post, telephone or online) for
a further period if the book is not required by another reader, by quoting
the above number / author / title.

Enquiries: 01709 336774

www.rotherham.gov.uk/libraries

Spencer Tracy

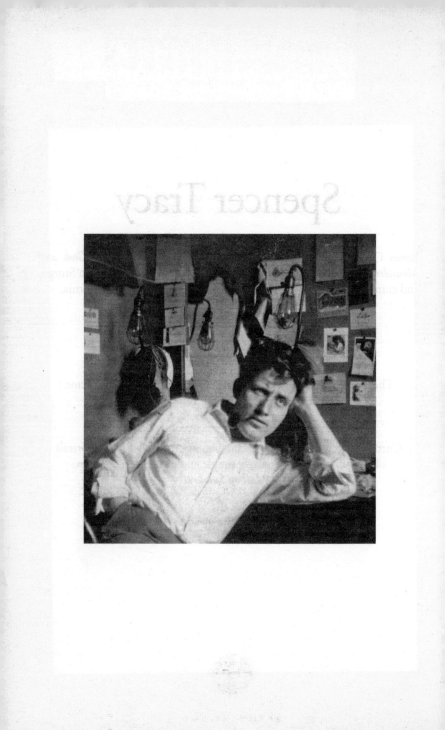

Spencer Tracy

A Biography

JAMES CURTIS

arrow books

Published by Arrow Books 2012

2 4 6 8 10 9 7 5 3 1

Copyright © James Curtis 2011

James Curtis has asserted his right under the Copyright, Designs
and Patents Act 1988 to be identified as the author of this work

This book is a work of non-fiction.

This book is sold subject to the condition that it shall not,
by way of trade or otherwise, be lent, resold, hired out,
or otherwise circulated without the publisher's prior
consent in any form of binding or cover other than that
in which it is published and without a similar condition,
including this condition, being imposed
on the subsequent purchaser

First published in the United States by Alfred A. Knopf, Inc.

First published in Great Britain in 2011 by Hutchinson

Arrow Books
Random House, 20 Vauxhall Bridge Road,
London SW1V 2SA

www.rbooks.co.uk

Addresses for companies within The Random House Group Limited can be found at:
www.randomhouse.co.uk/offices.htm

The Random House Group Limited Reg. No. 954009

A CIP catalogue record for this book
is available from the British Library

ISBN 9780099547297

The Random House Group Limited supports The Forest Stewardship Council (FSC®), the
leading international forest certification organisation. Our books carrying the FSC label are
printed on FSC® certified paper. FSC is the only forest certification scheme endorsed by
the leading environmental organisations, including Greenpeace. Our paper procurement
policy can be found at www.randomhouse.co.uk/environment

Printed and bound by CPI Group (UK) Ltd, Croydon, CR0 4YY

Frontispiece: Actor George Fleming snapped Tracy, at age twenty-four, in his dressing room at
the Montauk Theatre during the Christmas week run of *Uncle Tom's Cabin.* (SUSIE TRACY)

This one is for Kim.
On the level.

ROTHERHAM LIBRARY SERVICE	
B53032898	
Bertrams	29/10/2012
AN	£10.99
BSU	920 TRA

Being Irish, he had an abiding sense of tragedy, which sustained him through temporary periods of joy.

—WILLIAM BUTLER YEATS

Contents

Acknowledgments		xiii
1	General Business	3
2	A Born Actor	25
3	A Sissy Sort of Thing	50
4	The Best Goddamned Actor	75
5	Dread	102
6	The Last Mile	122
7	Quick Millions	143
8	The Power and the Glory	168
9	The Amount of Marriage We've Experienced	202
10	And Does Love Last?	236
11	That Double Jackpot	258
12	The Best Year	290

13 The New Rage   314

14 Enough to Shine Even Through Me   343

15 A Buoyant Effect on the Audience   370

16 Someone's Idea of Reality   393

17 Woman of the Year   424

18 I've Found the Woman I Want   448

19 Not the Guy They See Up There on the Screen   476

20 The Big Drunk   502

21 The Rugged Path   518

22 State of the Union   535

23 Adam's Rib   561

24 Father of the Bride   581

25 Rough Patch   605

26 At Loose Ends   628

27 A Granite-like Wedge of a Man   652

28 The Mountain   690

29 The Last Hurrah   719

30 Our Greatest Actor   746

31 The Value of a Single Human Being   777

32 Something a Little Less Serious   804

33 A Lion in a Cage   827

34 A Humble Man   865

Author's Note: The Biographies of Katharine Hepburn   879

Appendix I: Stage Chronology   885

Appendix II: Film Chronology   889

Notes and Sources   907

Selected Bibliography   965

Index   971

Acknowledgments

"I'm too trusting," Spencer Tracy lamented. "I always believe the best of people and often get fooled." In vetting any statement or proposition put to him, Tracy would often do no more than lock eyes with the other person and ask, "Is this on the level?" It's one of the first things his daughter ever recalled to me, and it's a question I've repeatedly asked myself as I've worked on this book. As so much has been written about Spencer Tracy that is either careless, foolish, or downright malicious, there would be no valid reason to spend six years on a biography of him that merely culled the misinformation printed elsewhere. Finding the truth and nuance in a life as maligned as Tracy's wasn't easy, and it would have been impossible without the help of a great many people.

This book wouldn't exist at all without the good faith and persistence of Susie Tracy, the daughter of Spencer and Louise Tracy, who wanted it written and was a fierce advocate for seeing it done properly. I first approached her through Dr. James Garrity, then the executive director of John Tracy Clinic, convinced a thorough and balanced biography of her father needed to be written, and that the time to talk to the people who knew him was running out. Susie demurred at first, as another biography had long been in the works. A few months later, I had an e-mail message from the Emmy-winning makeup artist and author Michael Blake, passing along word from producer William Self. Was I still interested in writing a biography of Spencer Tracy? If so, Susie Tracy would like to meet.

Bill Self knew Spencer Tracy for nearly twenty-five years and, as it turned out, was familiar with my work. Over a three-hour lunch, Bill, Susie, and I discussed the challenges of doing a subject as notoriously difficult and complex as Tracy, and how I would propose to go about it. I also learned the situation was complicated on a variety of levels, and that it would take time to clear the way for me to begin, were all the elements to fall into place. Well, it did take time—nearly two years passed before I was formally able to assume the task of researching and writing the book. Susie made everything in her possession—datebooks, scrapbooks, letters, and manuscripts—available for my use, and cleared the way for my work at John Tracy Clinic. I also began the task of interviewing Tracy's friends, family members, and coworkers, some of whom agreed to talk with me only because I had Susie's approval.

It should be stressed that at no time did Susie Tracy attempt to influence content or act in any way as a barrier to primary materials. She always cheerfully and without reservation signed any forms necessary to release confidential records—medical records, school records, business records. Nor at any time during the many hours of talks we had did she ever duck a question or stonewall on a answer. I found that, like her mother, she was incapable of lying or coloring the truth to suit a predetermined outcome. Unlike her mother, she declared no subjects off limits and plumbed the depths of her memory for whatever shards of detail she could muster. At length, I learned her motivation was surprisingly simple: She had missed great portions of her father's life, had known Katharine Hepburn only after his death. There was much she wanted—needed—to understand, and the only way she could do so was to see his life documented as thoroughly and as truthfully as possible.

Toward that goal, I could benefit from no greater resource than Selden West, who in 1977 began interviewing people who had known and worked with Spencer Tracy, and who, over the course of twenty-five years, amassed the single greatest archive of materials relating to Tracy and his life. The extreme value of her work was most vividly apparent in her interviews with figures long since dead—Lorraine Foat, Joseph L. Mankiewicz, Dore Schary, and publicist Eddie Lawrence being just a few. Moreover, Selden had gained access to the M-G-M archives in Atlanta, held by the Turner organization and, alas, unavailable during the period in which I found myself researching the Tracy story. Her notes from Atlanta proved invaluable, as did her frequent and generous takes on numerous aspects of Tracy's life and work. Her reactions were always vibrant and splendidly lucid. It must be emphasized, however, that her help and cooperation came with no strings attached, and in no way should one presume her endorsement of this book or the conclusions contained herein. She has, nevertheless, influenced its quality immeasurably, and I owe her a debt of gratitude I can never adequately repay.

I owe a similar debt of gratitude to Katharine Houghton, whom I met through Susie Tracy and who has always been forthcoming in matters regarding her aunt, Katharine Hepburn. Katharine's spirited input has been critical in shaping my understanding of the woman millions have come to know as Kate, yet at no time have I found her to be defensive or overly protective of the Hepburn image. Indeed, her knowledge of family history is formidable, and she has consistently proven herself a fierce advocate of the truth, no matter where it may lead. Her help has been one of the best breaks I have had in tackling this decidedly difficult subject, and my appreciation to her is boundless.

My understanding of the Tracy family, and particularly of John and Carrie Tracy, was helped immensely by my talks with the late Jane Feely Desmond, who was the last remaining family member of Spencer Tracy's generation. Jane's remarkable memory and her wry insights gave me a vivid and unanticipated window on the world of Spencer and Louise Tracy and the forces that shaped their relationship. In Freeport, Bertha Calhoun provided valuable memories of Carroll and Dorothy Tracy, and of Emma Brown, Carroll and Spencer's venerable "Aunt Mum." From Chicago, further details of the Tracy family and its history were provided by Sister Ann Willitts, O.P.

John Tracy Clinic in Los Angeles maintains an astonishing archive representing its history—as nothing appears ever to have been thrown away. It is possible to visit the basement in the main building on Adams Boulevard and find the original enrollment cards to the clinic's first summer session filed neatly in the appropriate cabinet. For complete and unfettered access to the clinic's records, I am grateful to Mary Ann Bell, Jack Cooper, and Dottie Blake. Mrs. Mary Wales, one of the clinic's original mothers, spent several hours on the phone with me from Arkansas, describing the early days in the cottage on West 37th Street and the evolution of the clinic over the ensuing years. For giving me a vivid understanding of what it was like to be a child in those early days at the clinic, I am grateful also to Carol Lee Barnes, Mrs. Wales' daughter, and to Chuck Watson.

Jane Kesner Ardmore was a veteran freelancer for such national magazines as *McCall's* and *Good Housekeeping* and the author or coauthor of several books, among them Eddie Cantor's memoir *Take My Life*. In 1972 she began interviewing Louise Tracy and her associates for a ghosted autobiography proposed by M-G-M's erstwhile publicity chief Howard Strickling. When that project died a quiet death, Louise refusing to discuss her husband's relationship with Katharine Hepburn, Ardmore's notes and inter-view transcripts were filed away and subsequently donated, along with her other papers, to the Margaret Herrick Library in Beverly Hills. I am grateful to Barbara Hall, who, with the able assistance of Jenny Romero, made these transcripts, as well as materials from a number of other special collections, available to me during the early days of this project.

From Seattle, Robert B. Edgers supplied a copy of his parents' unpublished 1968 memoir, "The Spencer Tracy We Knew." Bob and his late wife, Terry, were also wonderful hosts on a visit to the Emerald City, during which he shared data and photographs from his father's Ripon scrapbooks and his own detailed memories of Northwestern Military and Naval Academy. Joan Kramer and David Heeley, the award-winning documentarians responsible for, among many others, *Katharine Hepburn: All About Me,* generously allowed me to view unedited interview footage shot in 1985 for *The Spencer Tracy Legacy.* In Moraga, California, Larry Swindell was a gracious host, discussing work on his groundbreaking 1969 Tracy biography. From England, Kevin Brownlow kindly supplied me with excerpts from Sidney Franklin's unpublished autobiography regarding the aborted filming of *The Yearling.* By phone from Mequon, Wisconsin, John Ehle shared his boyhood memories of Daisy Spencer. And in New York, Gino Francesconi took me on an unforgettable backstage tour of Carnegie Hall, showing me the spaces likely occupied by the American Academy of Dramatic Arts during Tracy's tenure there in 1922 and 1923.

Ned Comstock, as usual, came through way beyond the call of duty in identifying and locating files from the indispensable M-G-M and 20th Century-Fox script collections at the University of Southern California's Cinematic Arts Library. Ned's expert help, his interest and enthusiasm, have long been essential to me and countless others during his lengthy tenure at USC. In Florida, Patricia Mahon generously made her incomparable collection of photographs of Spencer and Louise Tracy available to me, as well as letters and clippings dating back to the early 1970s. Marvin Paige was unfailingly helpful in getting me to several people who had memories of working with Spencer Tracy, most significantly the late Jean Simmons. Karl Thiede, as he has with past books, opened the files of his singular research library, providing reliable profit-and-loss data I could never have found anywhere else. At the Hollywood facilities of the UCLA Film and Television Archive, Jere Guldin ran the archive's nitrate print of *Society Girl* for Susie Tracy and me. And in Milwaukee, David Tice permitted me to tour and photograph the Tracys' 1910 residence on what was then Kenesaw, a house that he and his family were in the process of expertly restoring.

Eugene Cullen Kennedy was a constant source of inspiration, sharing not only his memories of Spencer Tracy and Katharine Hepburn, but his deep understanding of the Irish experience and the role the Roman Catholic Church played in the lives of many first-generation Americans. Gene was kind enough to review the manuscript of this book, making suggestions and offering thoughts that were always well considered and immensely valuable. It's been my great fortune to enjoy both his counsel and his friendship.

For various assists, courtesies and nudges, I am also indebted to A. Scott Berg, Ralph Blumenthal, Diana Caldwell, Don Cannon, David E. Cote, Dr. Dean Cromwell, Lee Ehman, Mike Germain, Erik Hanson, Charles Higham, Christy Hughes, Dan Ford, Karen Fyock, Robert Gitt, Ronnie James, Carmen Johnson, Tracey Johnstone, Christopher Knopf, Betty Lasky, Mindy Lu, Patrick McGilligan, Leonard Maltin, Judy Samelson, Sherry Sauerwine, Stephanie Shih, Anthony Slide, Michael Sragow, Gilbert Thiede, Kerrie Tickner, Susan Updike, Toni Volk, and Jordan Young.

A number of libraries and institutions held parts of the Tracy story, often through related collections, and I am grateful to the librarians and administrators who made that aspect of my work so rewarding.

Margaret Herrick Library, Academy of Motion Picture Arts and Sciences, Beverly Hills: Stacey Behlmer. American Academy of Dramatic Arts: Betty Lawson. Louis B. Mayer Library, American Film Institute: Caroline Cisneros. Archdiocese of Milwaukee Archives: Shelly Solberg. Bay View Historical Society: Greg Bird, Ronald Winkler.

Hall of History, Boys Town: Thomas Lynch. Cathedral of St. John the Evangelist, Milwaukee: Barbara Kowalewski. Rare Book and Manuscript Library, Columbia University: Tara C. Craig. Freeport Public Library: Cheryl Gleason. Fullerton Public Library: Janet Melton, Cheri Pape. Special Collections, Georgetown University: Heidi Rubenstein.

Library of Congress: Dr. Alice Birney, Josie Walters-Johnston. Marquette University High School: Dan Quesnell. Midwest Jesuit Archives: Dr. David P. Miros. Milwaukee High School of the Arts: Eugene Humphrey, Chris Wszalek. Milwaukee Public Library: Brian Williams–Van Klooster. Museum of the City of New York: Marty Jacobs. Film Study Center, Museum of Modern Art, New York: Charles Silver. New York Public Library for the Performing Arts: Barbara Knowles, Karen Nickenson. Fales Library, New York University: Ann Butler.

Ripon College: Rev. Dr. David Joyce, Richard Damm, Valerie Viers. Rockhurst High School, Kansas City: Theresa Fessler, Laurence W. Freeman. St. Bonaventure University: Dennis Frank. St. John's Northwestern Military Academy: Anita Kopaczewski, Chuck Moore. Shubert Archive: Maryann Chach. Regional History Collection, University of Southern California: Dace Taube. UCLA Film and Television Archive: Mark Quigley.

Trowbridge Elementary School of Discovery and Technology, Milwaukee: Montina Nelson. 20th Century-Fox Archive, Arts Library, University of California, Los Angeles: Lauren Buisson (with a special tip of the hat to David F. Miller of the 20th Century-Fox Legal Department). Special Collections, University of Arizona, Tucson: Bonnie Travers. Warner Bros. Archive: Haden Guest, Sandra Joy Lee. White Plains Public Library: Miriam Berg Varian.

The core of this book was formed from interviews conducted with those who knew and worked with Spencer and Louise Tracy (and, in many cases, with Katharine Hepburn) and were gracious enough to share their memories. My heartfelt thanks go to Donna Anderson, James Arness, Lauren Bacall, Leah Bernstein, Betsy Blair, Pat Bolliger, Ernest Borgnine (courtesy Scott Eyman), Jimmy Boyd, David Caldwell, June Caldwell, Harry Carey, Jr., Edie Carr, Esme Chandlee, June Dally-Watkins, Lewis W. Douglas, Jr., Jean Porter Dmytryk, Betsy Drake, June Dunham, Gene Eckman, John Ericson, Joel Freeman, Anthony Harvey, Dr. Robert Hepburn, Darryl Hickman, Clifford Jones, Robert C. Jones, Fay Kanin, Marvin Kaplan, Richard Kline, Karen Kramer, Philip Langner, Jack Larson, Joan Marie Lawes, Jimmy Lydon, A. C. Lyles, Abby Mann, Alice Mannix, Kerwin Mathews, Dina Merrill (courtesy Scott Eyman), Diane Disney Miller, Colleen Moore, Patricia Morison, Joseph Newman, Hugh O'Brien, Carol Holmes Phillips, Dorothy Provine, Luise Rainer, Elliott Reid, Gene Reynolds, Marshall Schlom, William Self, Jean Simmons, Charles R. Sligh III, Tina Gopadze Smith, Lynn Stalmaster, Sandy Sturges, Margaret Tagge, Ruthie Thompson, Patti Ver Sluis, Robert Wagner, and Jean Wright.

The late Millard Kaufman was an indefatigable champion of this book long before the first lines were written, and he followed its progress closely. Besides sharing his own memories of Spencer Tracy, Dore Schary, and the making of *Bad Day at Black Rock,* Millard put me in touch with several important figures from the period, and was always at the ready with both help and advice. The same can be said in spades for Scott Eyman, who was with me throughout the difficult period when it looked, at first, as if this book would happen, and then again when it seemed for sure that it would not. I'm certain his ready presence at the other end of the phone kept me sane on the long road to this book's completion, and, as always, he has my deepest appreciation.

Victoria Wilson, senior editor and associate publisher, cleared the way at Knopf for this book to be written, and was always intensely interested in its development. I could not ask for a more supportive or knowledgeable editor, and that this book exists at all is a testament to her judgment and determination. My agent, Neil Olson, has likewise been a rock-solid source of support and advice, and shall always have my thanks for taking this on.

Most of all, my wife, Kim Geary, made it possible for me to take the time to research and write this book. She has my gratitude for the essential role she played in its development, and my love for the essential role she plays in my life.

James Curtis
Brea, California
November 2010

Spencer Tracy

CHAPTER I

General Business

The first time she saw him was in profile. He was seated halfway back in the car and she noticed him as he stood. His was a strong Irish face, lined and ruddy, jaw square, eyes blue, hair sandy brown, thick and jostled by the movement of the train.

There was no clue as to who he was, the work he did, or exactly what he was doing on the nearly empty Westchester bound for White Plains, the last stop on an electric line that began at the Harlem River and glided northward through the Bronx, Mount Vernon, and New Rochelle on a fifty-minute trip to the suburbs.

She collected her things from the seat beside her and was depositing her ticket in the chopper box when it occurred to them both that they were the only two people on the platform. He asked if she'd care to share a cab. And when he told her that he was headed for the Palace Theatre on Main Street, she knew at once that she had not only made an acquaintance but met a colleague as well.

The Palace was six blocks west of the station, a big barn of a place that had opened promisingly but fallen on hard times. It started with stock and traveling shows and event recitals, went through two name changes and a spell as a movie emporium, and was now home to the freshly minted stock company of one Leonard Wood, Jr.

Wood was something of a local celebrity in that he bore the name of his father, military governor of Cuba, army chief of staff, and current governor-general of the Philippines. He had worked a deal for the theater on a percentage basis, brought in Kendal Weston, the "Belasco of stock," to direct, but then lost his leading woman to a contract dispute before the dusty seats of the Palace could be warmed by paying customers. With the company's opening set for April 9, 1923, Weston was sent scrambling, and it was then that he put in a call for Louise Treadwell.

Louise had appeared under Weston's direction in Manchester, where her long brown hair, expressive face, and dancer's body enabled her to play both ingenues and character parts with equal conviction. She had a flair for comedy and a nice singing voice, and although her engagement was only for a week or two, she needed the job. Rehearsals for the four-act comedy *Nice People* began promptly, Louise taking the Francine Larrimore part, and Wood—who could never seem to get her name right—pronounced himself duly impressed with what he saw. "Louise Treadway," he declared in a newspaper ad, "is a delightfully cultured girl whose personality goes right over the footlights and makes you wish you knew her personally." As soon as *Nice People* opened, daytime rehearsals began on the following week's play. She made a quick trip home to gather more clothes; stock actresses furnished their own wardrobes, and Louise, like most, was an accomplished seamstress.

The man she met on the ride back to White Plains also needed the job. Having just turned twenty-three, he had no credits to speak of, save a four-line bit in *R.U.R.* and six months of student productions at the American Academy of Dramatic Arts. He wasn't a lead, so Weston had never seen him act, but it soon dawned on Louise that she, in fact, had. It was some two months earlier in an afternoon performance at New York's Lyceum Theatre. "My friend was very apologetic," she remembered. "It was a student play and she promised someone she'd come and would I come too?" The play was *Knut at Roeskilde,* a tragedy set in the year 1027. In the cast that day were West Phillips, Olga Brent, Bryan Lycan, and the young man she now knew to be Spencer Tracy.

Kendal Weston had expanded the company to fourteen players for the second week. The play was Jules Eckert Goodman's *The Man Who Came Back,* a lurid tale of redemption in the opium dens of Shanghai. Louise would play the drug-addled Marcelle opposite Ernest Woodward, an alumnus of the American Academy who was cast in the title role. Engaged for general business, Tracy was assigned two minor parts in the show, one played almost completely out of sight of the audience. He soon disappeared, and when Louise again saw him, it was at the tiny Nut and Coffee House around the corner on Mamaroneck Avenue, where he was taking a meal that consisted in its entirety of chocolate cake and chocolate ice cream, the combination dripping with chocolate sauce. It became a familiar scene: "If you saw him twice on one day, one time or the other he was sure to be eating cake or ice cream or chocolate sauce, or all three." At first she noticed him only during breaks, when a small group would go around the corner for doughnuts and buttermilk. They fell easily into conversation, but there was little time for more than an occasional glance.

Louise lacked formal training, but compensated with long hours and a dancer's instincts. She moved expressively, absorbing the part as she learned her lines. Weston nurtured her over the course of a tense and uncertain week, helping her master a showy but difficult part while leaving Tracy, who had little to do, much to his own devices.

The actors were expected to learn an act a day, with Fridays given over to hair, wardrobe, and nails. On Saturday morning they played the whole thing straight through, one of only two chances they would get before opening on Monday night. The company performed *Nice People* eight times that week, and those who weren't yet working ran lines, did their laundry, enjoyed the brief luxury of having their evenings to themselves. The rehearsal on Monday was particularly chaotic. Actors huddled in the lounge of the theater, mumbling their lines, while stagehands hammered the sets together and aimed the lights, a cracked canvas backdrop shimmering with wet paint. It was only after supper that they were briefly allowed onstage to try out props, find their entrances, sit in chairs. Then came time for the stage manager to call, "Half hour!"

The performance that night was before an audience that consisted chiefly of die-hards—those who wanted to be among the first to see the new play and sadists who hoped to see the actors flub their lines. The pit band offered brassy renditions of everything from "Flower of Araby" and Irving Berlin's "Dearest" to selections from *Blossom Time.* Since most of the Palace's 1,200 seats were empty, the room's acoustics contributed a noticeable ring to the dialogue.

Taking the part created by Mary Nash in the original New York production, Louise tore into Marcelle's big scene in Sam Shew Sing's dingy opium joint. The dead center of the stage was defined by a circular radiance of yellow light and the walls were comprised of tattered bunks. Cornered by the man she had followed in vain from San Francisco to Shanghai, she called out to Tracy, now a dope fiend thrashing helplessly on one of the bunks: "Where are you now, Binksie?"

And from the shadows he wailed, "I've looked through most every star and I can't find her! I can't find her!"

Louise leveled a bone-chilling stare at Woodward. "Binksie there made a fool of himself over a girl—a girl who wasn't anything or anybody until Binksie came along and taught her. Then he grew tired of her, or he wanted to reform or something, and he went to her to let her know. There was a quarrel. He was nasty and perhaps she was nastier. He started to go. She swore he'd never leave her, that she'd follow him wherever he went, and he . . . he only laughed."

Woodward stood frozen at the edge of the light. "Go on—," he said softly.

"She told the truth," Louise continued. "She took strychnine there before him and—" A strange smile came over her. "Did you ever see anyone die of strychnine poisoning? It's a nasty way to die—body all shook to pieces, eyes grinning—and she died that way in Binksie's arms."

A slight pause to let the image sink in.

"Well, she followed him all right. Even the dope won't help him to forget her, and wherever she is—in Heaven or Hell—she's got the laugh on Binksie."

Louise picked a bottle of rye whiskey up off the floor. "Do you mind?" she asked matter-of-factly, not really caring if he did or he didn't. But he did mind, and gently he took it from her.

Her face turned hard, defiant. "If a man ever did a thing like that to me, I'd never kill myself that way—it's too painful, too quick. No, I'd live . . . live to let him see her dying slow . . . body and soul rotting before his eyes . . ."

When the performance came to an end, the crowd gave her a rousing ovation—the loudest of the evening—and Weston came to her afterward and said, "We're going to keep you here."

Business improved as the week progressed, and Wood, who rarely came down from his office, took to haranguing the locals with quarter-page ads in the *Daily Reporter*.

Ticket sales jumped for *It's a Boy,* the company's offering for the week of April 23, but it was the musical comedy *Buddies* that brought the people out in droves. Louise sang Julie, the part made famous by Peggy Wood on Broadway, and the theater was nearly full on a Saturday night when kids whistled and catcalled from the balconies and seats ranged from twenty-five cents to a dollar twenty-five, plus war tax.

Tracy played a peripheral part each week, inhabiting the background while Louise drew the crowd's attention and acclaim. His projection was good and his diction clear, and from the very start he showed he could deliver the most innocuous of lines with a startling intensity. He took the stage just ahead of Marcelle in *The Man Who Came Back,* and as the pipe-smoking Captain Gallon his exit line was "To hell with him!" Louise, immersed in her own role, took particular notice: "The way he did it was so effective he always got a nice little round of applause, and I remember thinking, 'That boy has got something there.' "

She naturally gravitated to Tracy, whose experience was nowhere near her own, but whose enthusiasm was infectious and whose natural gifts as an actor were plain to see. She found him a fast study with an almost photographic memory. Lines were much harder for her to absorb, and he would feed her cues during breaks and prompt her when the words wouldn't come. She, in turn, taught him how to use makeup, since he had learned in school and tended to overdo it. "You aren't the Great Lover type," she told him, "but you have a nice stage presence and a good voice. Some day you'll find your particular niche and you'll click." Spence took to calling her "Weeze," the pet name her mother had given her.

Louise was staying at the Gedney Farm Hotel, a three-hundred-acre resort just outside of town, and she returned there most days for dinner. Wood traded courtesies with Edward H. Crandall, the hotel's general manager, whose handsome son fancied himself an actor. In exchange for an occasional bit or a walk-on for Eddie Jr., the principal players of Wood's company could rub elbows with bankers, stockbrokers, and international celebrities at boardinghouse prices.

And so one Sunday, Louise invited Spence to dinner at the nautically themed dining room of the Gedney.

Louise Ten Broeck Treadwell was born in 1896 in New Castle, Pennsylvania, where her grandfather, George Edwards Treadwell, had founded the *New Castle News.* Her father, Allienne Treadwell, practiced law and owned the Treadwell News Company, an agency for out-of-town newspapers. Louise was a serious, bookish child whose greatest pleasure was the company of adults. She matured into a classic beauty, milky complexion, chestnut hair, soft gray-blue eyes, one of the most popular girls in high school, a suffragist and a varsity basketball star.

Her mother, Bright Smith, was a tiny woman of high ideals who sold baked goods to make ends meet when Allienne deserted the family in 1913. The following year, Bright's eighteen-year-old daughter announced her intention to go to New York. "Mother loved the theatre and was torn," Louise said. "She didn't really want me to go into the theatre, but if this was what I had to do . . . And it *was* what I had to do. Never any question. From the time I was ten, or even earlier, I was saving photos and old programs. My mother took me to the nickelodeon and to any number of good plays . . . touring companies of *The Merry Widow* and *The Red Mill* . . . I saw Elsie Janis and Montgomery and Stone . . . New Castle was on a good theater circuit, along the route to Chicago."

Bright had been the soprano soloist at an Episcopal church in Pittsburgh and was afraid Louise wouldn't get work in New York unless she knew how to sing. Loath to say anything herself that could be construed as discouraging, she consulted the local rector, an infinitely practical man, and asked him to make the case instead. "Louise has a small voice," she confided, ticking off the challenges, both economic and moral, a young girl would surely face alone in the big city. The rector listened gravely and commiserated and did indeed speak to Louise, but, sensing her determination, couldn't say very much to sway her.

"What it must have cost my mother to let me go!" Louise marveled. "She and my father were divorced, so it was doubly her decision. I was so naive—she knew that—and I had virtually no experience, just one little musical show in high school." She stayed with cousins on Long Island, had her first ride on the elevated, and almost immediately got a job in vaudeville. "I could sing and I could dance, and there I was in some old theater down around Fourteenth Street singing, 'By the sea, by the sea, by the beautiful sea . . .' The leading lady said, 'Honey, have you ever put on makeup?' and since I never had, she showed me how. I made quite an entrance: I tripped and fell flat at the first matinee performance, but I got up and went right on."

The show lasted a week, then Louise's luck dried up. Her cousins thought she should go home and teach dancing, so they staked her to a series of lessons with the Castles, where she learned the fox-trot and the two-step. Once she had a diploma, she returned to New Castle to teach ballroom dancing. She staged some children's shows, the mothers making the costumes themselves, then enrolled in the Lake Erie College for Women. "I really had no desire to go to college," she admitted, "but I'm glad I did. There was, for example, an excellent course in English composition, and I learned to do a little writing." She developed an interest in art, took part in a couple of plays, and performed an interpretive dance program at commencement, subsequently touring under the management of Southard Harris.

Actress Henrietta Crosman was a distant cousin. "I'd heard Grandma speak of her, and I found some of her old programs. When she played Cleveland, I wrote and went to see her." Crosman was touring *Cousin Eleanor* in vaudeville, and Louise was a little frightened of her. "Henrietta was sixty by then, a buxom woman, but you could see what she had been.* She'd been a beauty, and she'd tell anyone anything with a candor that floored me. A fine old-time actress. I told her I was going to New York again, and she said frankly she had no idea what she'd be doing in the fall, but I was to let her know when I got there."

Louise did indeed let her know and found that Crosman was about to

* Actually, Crosman was fifty when Louise met her, but must have seemed older.

Louise Treadwell (*foreground*), circa 1916.
(PATRICIA MAHON COLLECTION)

take out a play called *Erstwhile Susan.* She saw the producer and the director, read, and was assigned a couple of small parts: a Mennonite girl and a
debutante. When relatives offered the use of an apartment in the Bronx,
Louise and her mother went off to New York. They went to visit Crosman
at her estate in the country. She was gracious, but Louise was aware that she
was taking stock of her. "You have nice hands," she told Louise. "Use
them."

They went across the country with *Erstwhile Susan,* making two stops
in each state they crossed. Once they reached Seattle, they traveled down
the coast to Portland, San Francisco, San Jose, Los Angeles, and San Diego.
"You've got to learn to talk," the actress told Louise one day on the train.
"Avoid Pennsylvaniaisms." Louise did a lot of listening—to Crosman, to an
Englishman in the cast, to the young leading lady who spoke with a South-
ern lilt. "I listened, practiced, and began to realize how totally unprepared
I was."

After America entered the war in the spring of 1917 things got tough
just about everywhere. Stock companies closed in record numbers. Louise
hung on as long as she could, sharing quarters with four other girls she'd
known in college, then she went home again in June 1918. "I went home
only to reconnoiter and get some money." She spent eight weeks working

on the *New Castle News,* then her mother died suddenly at the age of fifty-four.

The pains came without warning sometime around midnight, and Louise summoned an ambulance. On the bumpy road to the hospital Bright's appendix burst. Louise couldn't go with her—no room—so she took the streetcar instead and wasn't able to see her mother again until after the surgery, when there was really nothing more to be done. She stayed at her bedside—Bright lived several days—then, in something of a daze, she pulled together what was left of her life in New Castle. Her grandmother was still there, but her younger sister was away at school and her father had remarried and was living in California. She sold the house on Highland Avenue, keeping the third floor and furnishing it with the things that most meant home to her. She took a job teaching third grade and made plans to return to the stage.

Louise played stock in Chicago, making an impression with a small part in a play called *Happiness.* After a lean period, she landed a role with Eva Le Gallienne in *Not So Long Ago,* a romantic period piece that had only a short stay at the Booth Theatre. Late in 1920 she again wrote Henrietta Crosman, who had settled in California where her husband, Maurice Campbell, was directing the Bebe Daniels comedies for Realart. She asked what Crosman thought about her working in pictures, and Crosman replied that if she wanted to come to Los Angeles, she would find her a place to live and maybe something to do. So Louise came west in February 1921, taking a room with some people who lived next door to the Campbells on Carlos Avenue in Hollywood. Maurice Campbell gave her work as an extra, but she didn't much care for the monotony of moviemaking. The other extras on the set were friendly and helpful, but she kept to herself, writing poetry, as she had since high school, and reading prodigiously. She got a bit part as a chorus girl in a feature directed by William DeMille, but it wasn't fun or satisfying, and after a few months she went back to New York.

In December the iconoclastic editors of the *Smart Set,* George Jean Nathan and H. L. Mencken, bought one of her poems for publication and asked to see others. Before she could reply, she landed a key role in Edward Goodman's revival of the John Galsworthy fantasy *The Pigeon.* The show started in Greenwich Village, then moved uptown to the Frazee. The part wasn't her kind of part—a "goody-goody" as she put it—and Goodman was a rigid disciplinarian, demanding and excessively precise. She frankly thought herself "lousy" in *The Pigeon,* but it led to *Chains of Dew* for the Provincetown Players and a few weeks of stock in New Hampshire.

Emboldened by the *Smart Set* sale, she tried her hand at humor and sold a boardinghouse piece called "Top Floor Pests" to the *New York Times.*

By summer, she had allowed herself to be seduced into a Chautauqua tour that took her on a string of one-nighters through Oklahoma, New Mexico, Texas, Kansas, Colorado, and Nebraska, most of the audiences seeing the one play, in all probability, they would see all year. The applause, she wrote, would "shame even a Belasco opening" and the experience resulted in another piece for the *Times*. She laid off the remainder of the year, thinking she might go to Europe, but by the time of Kendal Weston's call, she was not only ready and willing but desperate to work.

Louise Treadwell could have been a journalist, written a book, or published more of her poems, but all she ever really wanted to be was an actress, and despite being such a hard study when it came to learning her lines, she was working with the best director she had ever had, playing some of the best things she had ever played, and at the age of twenty-six there was no place in the world she would rather be.

The company continued with *Up in Mabel's Room* for the week of May 6, then Kendal Weston quarreled with Leonard Wood over the cuts Wood was making to cover expenses. He left, taking a pair of actors with him. Ray

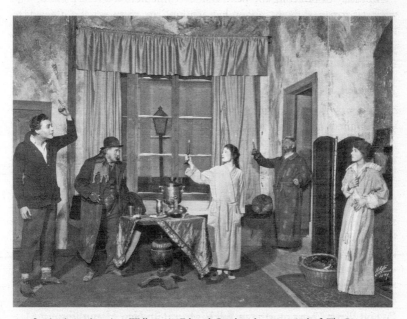

Louise (center) as Ann Wellwyn in Edward Goodman's 1922 revival of *The Pigeon*. Whitford Kane, who headed the original production at London's Royalty Theatre, can be seen at the doorway. (NEW YORK PUBLIC LIBRARY)

Capp, another actor-director of similar vintage, took over from Weston and the show went on as planned. The Elks Lodge attended as a body, showering the ladies of the cast with floral tributes, and the players, still basking in the success of *Buddies,* were guests of honor at the monthly ball of the White Plains Club. It was at such a party, on a Sunday night at the Gedney, just after Tracy had graduated to the role of Jimmy Larchmont in *Mabel's Room,* that he worked up the courage to ask Louise to marry him.

She had been in love before, but never with an actor, and no one had ever proposed. She always described herself as a romantic, someone who preferred to dream of the perfect mate rather than actually go out and pursue him. Having come from a broken home, she also knew a man's devotion could be mysterious and fleeting, and the institution of marriage as much a trap as a blessing. "My father wasn't a man you ever came to know well," she said. "He was a shy man who tried to make up for that with this reserve. I never felt I could talk to him."

Tracy, she observed, was a lot like her father, brusque and painfully shy around strangers, but with a joy for the art of acting that was something quite different from anything she had ever before observed in a man. They both found it easier to talk about the work than to talk about each other, since both came from families where feelings were rarely expressed. The silences between them could be deafening, but there was an urgency to everything they had to say to one another. Tracy didn't handle the matter of proposing very well, having condescended to dance with her even though he hated dancing. Then, not being terribly romantic either, he wondered if she would marry him without his embellishing the words or setting the scene in the slightest. "I'm *asking* you to," he finally said, mustering some of the intensity he could unleash onstage.

Louise was mindful of what actresses always said about marrying actors, that their egos were too huge to contain, and that no woman could ever love an actor as much as he undoubtedly loved himself. She didn't think of Spence as an actor, though. He lacked the ego, the pose, the artifice. She couldn't think of another one even remotely like him, and so there, amid the rolling green hills of White Plains on a crisp spring evening in May 1923, Louise Treadwell said yes.

Weston's departure signaled a decline in the company and the quality of its productions. Business fell off, and Wood concluded that White Plains was too small to support a company of its own. In late May he announced the Wood Players were moving to Fall River, a mill town in southeastern Massachusetts known for the Lizzie Borden ax murders, and anyone who didn't care to go had his or her two weeks' notice. Nobody wanted to go to Fall

River, but only three cast members said as much. The Wood Players gave their final performance in White Plains on June 1, 1923, and decamped the next day.

In Fall River, Wood worked the local papers, building anticipation for the town's first season of summer stock, and when the company opened with *Getting Gertie's Garter* on June 11, 1923, all 1,900 seats were filled and some two hundred people were turned away. The town's goodwill didn't extend much past opening night, and Wood switched from comedies to thrillers. By the third week, the Players were performing four matinees a week with a two-for-one admission policy on Monday nights. Louise grew to loathe the place: "Nobody was interested in the theatre. I don't know how in the world they ever thought they could make it go there, and it didn't go."

When Wood moved the company to the Fulton Opera House in Lancaster, Pennsylvania, he promoted Tracy to second business and bumped his rate to fifty dollars a week. Louise went along, but only for a couple of days and with no intention of playing there. Spence wired his parents in Milwaukee, and almost immediately his older brother arrived to give Louise the once-over. Carroll Tracy was the same age as Louise, a bigger, beefier version of his younger brother, infinitely more quiet. He didn't ask many questions, so Louise volunteered the things she thought he'd want to know. "I had no intention in the world of giving up the theatre," she said. She talked about her people, her education, her writing. "Apparently he decided I was all right . . . I was invited to go to Milwaukee."

Tracy stayed in Lancaster, intent on finding something better, while Louise returned to New Castle to tell what family she still had there—her grandmother and a few cousins—that she was going to get married. Wood's company churned continuously, but Tracy, easily the most opinionated member of the company, was out of favor. It wasn't a good time to be looking for work, and it took the better part of a month to land a job with a company in Cincinnati. Stuart Walker's renowned stock company was a considerable step up in prestige, if not necessarily in compensation. Elated, Tracy gave notice in Lancaster and advised his fiancée they could be married in September.

Louise traveled to Chicago in late August, and Spence's father, John Edward Tracy, met her at the station. A small but powerfully built man with shimmering white hair and blue-gray eyes, John Tracy was vice president and general manager of the Parker Motor Truck Company. His son Carroll towered over him, but it was John Tracy's solid demeanor and ready smile that instantly drew Louise into the family. "He was just so natural and so easy," she remembered, "the nice little light in his eyes, the humor . . ."

In Milwaukee, the Tracys' comfortable wood frame house stood on a tree-lined street on the upper East Side. Down the block was Lake Park and a spectacular view of the Lake Michigan shoreline. Spence's mother welcomed Louise with a warmth and generosity she had never known in her own family. Carrie Tracy was, at age forty-nine, a beautiful woman who was indulged in every possible way by her doting husband. "She was the kind of person who'd give you anything," Louise said. "I was very fond of her, and I quickly felt much closer to him than I had ever felt toward my own father. He was a very warm, dear man . . . You couldn't help but like them, you couldn't help feeling you'd known them all your life."

The Gypsy Trail would mark Spencer Tracy's first appearance in Cincinnati—not that there was much for him to rehearse. He had been cast in the utilitarian role of the house man, Stiles, and the extent of his duties was to appear occasionally, answer the phone or open the door, and say things like "Who is speaking, please?" and "I will inquire."

Walker's roster now consisted of sixty-seven players, among them Blanche Yurka, Albert Hackett, Spring Byington, and Beulah Bondi. His civilized practice of resting his actors from week to week made a slot in Cincinnati one of the most coveted in stock.

Louise had hopes of joining the Walker company, but her immediate goal was to make a good impression on the Tracys. She feared an awkward silence over the matter of religion, as she was an Episcopalian while Spence embraced his father's Catholicism. Then she learned that Spence's mother was a Presbyterian and all her anxieties fell away. John Tracy, in fact, laughed out loud when she confessed her fear of being asked to convert. "There's no use in doing that!" he exclaimed, and Louise, relieved, chimed in, "No, no use at all!" The next thing she knew, Spence's dad was taking her downtown to pick out a ring. "There was nothing like the present," she said of his direct, almost impulsive nature. "You don't wait around for anything—you do it now." When Spence called to ask what they thought of her, his father was typically plainspoken: "If you don't marry this girl, you're a bigger fool than I thought you were when you went on the stage!"

Tracy opened at the George B. Cox Memorial Theatre on September 10, 1923, and while he rated a mention in the lukewarm review that appeared the next day in the *Post*, the display ads accounted for his presence in the cast with the words ". . . and others." Louise and the Tracys arrived by train on Tuesday afternoon, John and Carrie taking a room at the Hotel Gibson on Fountain Square, Louise putting up at the elegant Sinton a block away. The next afternoon, Spence played the Wednesday matinee, finishing just after 4:30 p.m. He then grabbed a cab to St. Xavier, a neighborhood parish some five blocks to the east, where he met his parents, his brother, and his bride-to-be.

Louise was wearing a dark blue suit over a patterned silk blouse with matching hat and shoes. The pastor of the church, Father Joseph P. De Smidt, had agreed to marry them, but there would be no mass with the ceremony. "I was lucky to get in the back door," Louise commented. "We had a special dispensation and got married in the Priest's study." There were readings from the Old and New Testaments, a homily of sorts (considering the priest didn't know either one of them), and the vows were exchanged. Carroll, the best man, stepped forward and handed Louise's ring to the priest, who blessed it and passed it to the groom, who placed it on her finger in the name of the Father, and of the Son, and of the Holy Spirit. After the Lord's Prayer and a blessing, they returned to the Gibson, where Stuart Walker joined them for a quick celebratory dinner. At 7:30 p.m., Walker and the newest member of his esteemed company took a cab back to the Cox, where the evening performance of *The Gypsy Trail* got under way at 8:20 p.m.

Walker went easy on Tracy during his brief stay in the Queen City. He did not cast him in *Time,* the following week's play, which meant that Spence had his days free to roam the city with his new wife. Then rehearsals got under way for *Seventeen,* a perennial for Walker, and this time Tracy had a showier part in the boisterous George Cooper, the thickheaded nineteen-year-old who has designs on Miss Lola Pratt. His key scene, an awkward exchange of rings toward the end of the third act, brought an audible hush from the audience, but it was Walker's newest discovery, William Kirkland, who, as Willie Baxter, dominated the show. The role of Willie had made a Broadway star of Gregory Kelly, and when *Seventeen* ended Walker's twenty-eight-week season at the Cox, it was Kirkland who was announced as one of the leads when Walker took *Time* to Broadway.

Louise, moving up to the role of Spence's booster, understood Walker's reasoning, given Kirkland's tenure with the company, but she also knew that her new husband was infinitely more talented, and she was all for the move when the fuss over Kirkland inspired Tracy to take a crack at Broadway himself. Walker, who believed it took an actor four or five years to fully develop, advised against it. But Tracy knew a place on the Upper West Side where he had lived with an old friend. "Come on," he said to Weeze. "Mrs. Brown will give us a room. I can talk her into anything."

Despite a steep, gloomy interior, Mrs. Brown's had the benefit of a landlady who genuinely liked and admired struggling actors. She greeted Spence like a wayward son and made his wife feel as if she were an established star. Louise set her electric stove up in the bathroom and proceeded to familiarize her husband with the vegetables he had never before regarded as food. She cooked ground round occasionally, and when they were feeling flush they would get a couple of lamb chops.

Fifteen shows were casting, and Tracy figured a big star vehicle offered the best chance for a long run and maybe even a tour. He missed out on Walter Hampden's revival of *Cyrano de Bergerac,* which had more than fifty parts to fill, but got word that producer Arthur Hopkins was casting a new comedy for Ethel Barrymore at the Plymouth. The play had sixteen speaking parts, two given over to the star and her leading man, Cyril Keighley, and three requiring the services of children. Of the eleven remaining, the four that meant anything had already been filled with Beverly Sitgreaves, Jose Alessandro, Edward G. Robinson, and Virginia Chauvent. Only the bits remained, and Tracy landed the least of those, the character of a newspaper photographer named Holt. And that night, the Tracys' room at Mrs. Brown's modest walk-up smelled of lamb.

Rehearsals for the Barrymore play, *A Royal Fandango,* were unlike anything Tracy had ever witnessed. "Arthur Hopkins," said Edward G. Robinson, "pulled his usual stunt of leaving the actors alone for a week to find their own places and get the play on its feet. I soon discovered that Miss Barrymore—and why not?—did what came naturally to her: took the stage, filled it, and left the rest of us to stage rear."

The actors began referring to the production as *A Royal Fiasco,* and when Hopkins finally appeared, Robinson asked to be let out. "I know I'm a supporting actor and Miss Barrymore's a great star," he told the producer, "but the way the play is staged, all the values are distorted." Hopkins listened and understood and set about restaging the scenes, and although his improvements gave the play more vitality and pace, the production was doomed, doomed, doomed, and everyone, excepting perhaps Ethel Barrymore herself, seemed to know it.

They opened in Washington on November 6 before a capacity house that included Commander and Mrs. W. W. Galbraith and Secretary of Commerce Herbert Hoover. Tracy, whom Robinson remembered as "an intense young man," had only to walk on with a paper, but the weight of doing so while Ethel Barrymore held the stage was almost too much for him to bear. "He had one line to say," Barrymore recalled in her autobiography, "and I saw he was very nervous, so I said to him, 'Relax. That's all you have to do—just relax. It'll all be the same in a hundred years.'"

Tracy got through the night, as did the rest of the cast, but the man from *Variety* said playwright Zoë Akins had made "without a doubt the most impossible and ridiculous attempt at a satire that this scribe has seen in a long time." The New York opening on the twelfth wasn't much better received, and only two of the sixteen Manhattan dailies saw any future to it at all. The closing notices went up by the beginning of the second week, and Miss Barrymore was, according to Robinson, "indignant."

Tracy began using his days to smoke out another engagement, casually at first, then more keenly as the holiday lull settled in and the only shows casting were musicals like *Kid Boots.* Counting their pennies, he and Louise (who wasn't working) allotted thirty-five cents a day for food. "I went on a rice pudding diet because it was filling," Tracy remembered. "I could tell you every restaurant from the Bowery to the Bronx that served the stuff and tell you which gave the most cream with it and which the most raisins."

Combing the trade papers, he used the cachet of the Barrymore name to land an interview with the Proctor Players, a struggling stock enterprise located across the Hudson in Elizabeth, New Jersey. They were short a character man for a production of *Within the Law.* "Can you play an old man?" the director asked. "I'm an actor," Tracy replied. "I can play anything."

The Proctors were on a grueling "matinees daily" policy. Hired for general business at fifty dollars a week, Tracy wasn't permitted to draw against his salary until the play had actually opened. After rehearsing a full week, he and Louise (who was three months pregnant at the time) were reduced to splitting an egg sandwich for dinner. On opening night, December 3, he came offstage after his first scene and made a sprint to the cashier's office. Nearly missing his second cue, he resolved to get out of the place as quickly as possible.

He remained through Christmas, and was playing a minor role in *Mrs. Wiggs of the Cabbage Patch* when a wire from Kendal Weston found him. The Belasco of Stock was inaugurating a company in Winnipeg, taking on the longest-running stock company in North America, the very aptly named Permanent Players. Tracy dropped Louise in Milwaukee and was in Manitoba by New Year's Day. "The first week," Tracy said, "we weren't paid because the manager said he had to pay off the local firms to which he owed money. We got through the second week, and after the Saturday night performance we looked for the manager and found he had absconded with the two weeks' receipts."

They began operating on the commonwealth plan, divvying up the box office in lieu of salaries. Tracy was second man in *What's Your Wife Doing?* when the leads gave notice, suddenly elevating him, after just nine months, to the status of leading man. Given the company's rattling condition, there was only one viable choice for leading woman, and it was a done deal when the wire grandly offering her the job reached Louise in Milwaukee. "I went up," she said, "and found the company was really on the rocks."

Knowing she could only play a few weeks before her pregnancy would begin to show, Louise opened January 28, 1924, in Eugene Walters' *The Flapper* and, in the words of the critic for the *Winnipeg Free Press,* "took the house by storm." With nothing to lose and her husband playing opposite, she abandoned herself to the role in a way she might otherwise have found difficult. "Miss Treadwell made her Winnipeg debut in rather a light part," the *Press* observed, "to which, nevertheless, she brought a vast amount of honest talent and evidently a good deal of careful preparation. Of her future popularity there can be no question. Her performance Monday night not only popularized her, but came very near endearing her to her auditors." Spence's work as her long-suffering husband, the first lead he had ever played as a professional actor, was "a rare exhibition of restraint in what might have been a frothy and wrathful role."

When they opened in the grim crime melodrama *The Highjacker* on the fourth of February, they knew it would be their last week in Winnipeg. "They called us up to the office and talked," Louise recalled, "and of course they were going to close. Then they let down their hair and said they'd like to see us get back safe." They paid Louise's fare back to Milwaukee and Spence's to New York City—the only cast members accorded such a courtesy. Five weeks later, several members of the company were still in town, reportedly working as day laborers to earn their fares back to the States.

Nineteen twenty-four wasn't starting out well for stock. There weren't more than a hundred companies nationwide, and only about two dozen of those were making money. One of the managers whom Tracy was following in the pages of *Variety* was William Henry Wright, the man in charge of Pittsburgh's Lyceum Stock Company. Wright had been a press agent for Klaw & Erlanger, Henry W. Savage, and George Broadhurst, among others, and knew how to get people into a theater—a critical talent lacking in the vast majority of stock managers.

Emboldened by a successful summer of stock in Grand Rapids, Michigan, Wright had taken a lease on the Bijou, an old vaudeville house, renamed it the Lyceum, and opened Thanksgiving week with a policy of high-class fare at a one-dollar top scale. It was a hopeless strategy for a place like Pittsburgh, and some nights there was less than one hundred dollars in the box office when the curtain rang up. Finally coming to the realization he was playing class stuff in the wrong neighborhood, Wright closed the company on January 7, 1924, having dropped $14,000 in the space of seven weeks.

There were, however, a lot of people rooting for "Papa" Wright, a beloved figure who, in another time, had managed the lecture tours of Mark Twain, Arthur Conan Doyle, and James Whitcomb Riley. He had, in fact, touched virtually every facet of show business, from playwriting to movie work, and was known for promptly paying his bills in even the darkest of hours. He took just two weeks to regroup in Pittsburgh, building a new policy on hokey melodramas at a fifty-cent top, and was open again by the end of January. "We'll give him credit," commented one stock executive. "It's either guts or idiocy."

The agent who handled Tracy's booking with Wright told him it was "the world's worst stock company" and that he should therefore "fit in fine."

When Wright got a look at his new leading man, Tracy was clad in the same serge suit he had worn since college. "You've got to get yourself a new suit," Wright told him, and Tracy, in no position to argue the point, touched him for an advance. That next week, he began rehearsals for a topical play called *The Bootleggers* in a snappy blue pinstripe.

The Bootleggers was the first effort of a young drama critic named William Page, formerly of the *Baltimore American,* later of the *Washington Post.* Wright's staging at the Lyceum constituted its stock debut and, typical for a Wright company, no reasonable expense was spared. Tracy took the part of Rossmore, the mastermind of a prosperous smuggling ring, and Wright's leading lady, Marguerite Fields, took the role of Rossmore's daughter.

The show was under the direction of John Ellis, a classically trained actor who had been with Wright since his first stock enterprise in Schenectady. Tracy proved adept at handling the comedy in the play as well as its tragedy, and the Monday performance played to a sizable crowd that included the playwright himself.

Wright followed *The Bootleggers* with a more intimate, though no less sensationalistic, drama called *Her Unborn Child,* and scheduled brief talks on birth control during Tuesday and Thursday "ladies only" matinees.

A splendid production of *The Shepard of the Hills* was followed by *The Love Test,* and then Wright lost his lease on the theater just as he was starting to make a little money. The house management was flooded with letters and a petition to retain the company, but it was rumored a deal had gone over to give the theater to a burlesque syndicate and there was nothing more to be done about it. The *Gazette Times* reported the opening performance of *The Girl Who Came Back,* Wright's selection for the final week, played to "one of the largest audiences ever assembled in the Lyceum Theatre." Floral tributes sent to the ladies each night threatened to swamp the stage, and favorites like Arthur Mack, Cliff Boyer, and Ernest Ganter were accorded standing ovations. "They used to put chairs on the stage," Tracy recalled. "That's how much business we did. Couldn't get the people in the theater."

The Lyceum closed its doors on May 9, 1924, and the Tracys left for Milwaukee the next morning.

There was much about Grand Rapids that made it a good place for stock. It was laid out on an orderly grid, the streets running east and west and the avenues north and south. There was plenty of work, Grand Rapids being known as Furniture City for the woodworking plants that clustered just north and south of the city center—Berkey & Gay, Luce, John Widdicomb, American Seating, Sligh, Robert W. Irwin. The city bustled with skilled workers and a society class comprised of the owners of the mills and furniture factories and the descendants of the Baptist missionaries and land brokers who settled the area. It was a stable, educated population with money and taste and an appreciation of good theatrics. When W. H. Wright installed his Broadway Players there in the spring of 1923, he found he had stumbled onto a largely untapped audience for middlebrow fare.

The 1924 season began on April 14 at the Powers Theatre just as Wright was opening *Her Unborn Child* in Pittsburgh. *Honors Are Even,* the first attraction, was a shaky affair, not up to the standards of the previous season, and it was to Wright's advantage that the loss of the Lyceum freed him to focus his attention more fully on Grand Rapids. As soon as the Pittsburgh company had closed, Wright moved Halliam Bosworth, a solid character man, and director John Ellis to the Powers, and began shuffling the calendar of plays.

The Bootleggers had done extraordinarily well in Pittsburgh and was, in fact, one of the few Lyceum plays Wright thought would go over in Grand Rapids. He cabled Tracy in Milwaukee, offering him the lead in *Bootleggers* and the balance of the season under less specific terms, but Spence, with Louise now eight months pregnant, hesitated, not wanting to be on the other side of Lake Michigan when the baby was born. It was only at Louise's insistence that he went, bolstered as he was by the knowledge that she was in his mother's able care and that nothing at all could possibly go wrong.

Tracy officially joined the Broadway Players on June 10, 1924, when he began rehearsals for *The Meanest Man in the World,* a comedy George M. Cohan had played a few seasons back. The title role fell to Kenneth Daigneau, an able comedian and the company's de facto leading man, leaving Tracy to the part of Carlton Childs, an idealistic young businessman. In publicity, Wright dutifully acknowledged Tracy's status as a "well-known leading man" who would nevertheless be "classed as a juvenile" for his present engagement. Mary Remington, the critic for the *Grand Rapids Press,* found Tracy "convincing, well poised . . . natural" in a somewhat thankless part. The *Herald*'s Clarence Dean reported "generous applause frequently rippling through the audience and breaking out into a salvo." Tracy, he concluded, had "captured the approval of the first night audience."

The Meanest Man in the World continued through Sunday, June 22, and Tracy was back in Milwaukee the following Wednesday. John Tracy was now president of George H. Lutz, Inc., one of the Midwest's leading suppliers of paving machinery, and he and Carrie had relocated to a spacious two-bedroom apartment on Prospect Avenue in the city's historic First Ward. The Tracys fussed endlessly over Louise, who was due at any moment and miserable in the summer heat and humidity. Spence didn't quite know what to say or do with fatherhood so close at hand, and when Louise went into labor late on the evening of June 25, it was Father Tracy who got her to St. Mary's Hospital on North Lake Drive, some two miles away, and then stayed with his son until an eight-pound boy was delivered at 2:30 on the morning of the twenty-sixth.

The baby was named John Ten Broeck Tracy, Ten Broeck being the maiden name of Louise's maternal grandmother, Louisa Smith. "I was very much afraid of him at first," Louise admitted. "What do you do when you give him a bath? How [do] you hold him in there? I hadn't been around a small baby, well, in years and years. I just didn't know anything about it." And Spence, of course, wasn't any help. "He was crazy about him, but he didn't know what to do with a small baby either." Home from the hospital, Louise was installed in the guest room on Prospect, where the new grand-parents could scarcely get their fill of little Johnny. Spence stayed as long as he could—ten days, through the Independence Day festivities—then took the ferry back across Lake Michigan to Muskegon, his father having staked him to the fare, and then the twenty-five miles inland by bus to Grand Rapids.

Wright's makeover of the Broadway Players hadn't ended with the addition of Spencer Tracy. Actress Geneva Harrison made her final Grand Rapids appearance in *Meanest Man in the World,* and the following week saw the arrival of a new leading lady, a genuine star of both stock and Broadway named Selena Royle. The nineteen-year-old daughter of play-wright Edwin Milton Royle, she was just in from New York, where she had played the previous week alongside Helen Hayes, Elsie Ferguson, and Pauline Lord in a Players Club staging of *She Stoops to Conquer.* Landing her for the Broadway Players was something of a coup, but John Ellis had known her since she was a baby. In 1905, when she was less than a year old, Ellis had appeared in the first English production of her father's most famous play, *The Squaw Man,* and the two men had remained friends over the years.

For Selena's debut at the Powers, Ellis and Wright selected the Harvard Prize drama *Common Clay,* an evergreen in stock that gave Jane Cowl one of her signature roles. A statuesque blonde, Royle towered over the men in the cast, and as Ellen Neal, a poor girl wrongly accused of murder, she com-manded the stage. "She is beautiful, she is youthful, she has a rich, low-pitched voice that chimes like sweet bells," Clarence Dean raved in the *Herald.* "She has depth of feeling that gets right under the skin, and she is perfectly natural, easy and unaffected. There is no effort apparent, no straining for effect, but a sure touch that misses no points."

Selena Royle was a hit with Grand Rapids audiences, and Wright vowed to hang on to her as long as he possibly could. For her second week, he indulged her with the stock premiere of the Vincent Lawrence comedy

In Love with Love, which had run three months on Broadway with Lynn Fontanne, and for which Wright paid the highest royalty he had ever paid for a play. Those facts, which were widely reported in the press, and solid word-of-mouth for Selena Royle brought the Broadway Players their strongest week to date. Royle was playing Maugham's *Too Many Husbands* the week Tracy returned and managed to fill all 1,400 seats for both the Friday and Saturday evening performances. She was considered a surefire asset for *The Bootleggers,* which had both Tracy and William Laveau repeating their roles from Pittsburgh, and hopes were high for yet another hit.

Tracy was ready to settle in with a good company—at least for a while—and knew a good week for *The Bootleggers* would put him in line for a lead by the end of the season. The production was, in some ways, better than in Pittsburgh, Selena bringing undeniable star power to the role of Nina. But the gritty realism and violence of the play didn't go in a town that routinely turned out for comedy and romance and whose entertainment choices were made chiefly by women. *The Bootleggers* wasn't a disaster but it ended the week in the red, and the following week Tracy found himself demoted to general business. Demoralized and homesick, he withdrew from the Broadway Players, insisting he would play only leads in the future, and left for Milwaukee to spend time with his wife and his month-old son.

The respite lasted all of three weeks.

Charley's Aunt with Selena Royle and Ken Daigneau proved so popular that a Friday matinee was added to accommodate the demand. *Cornered* and *Mary's Ankle* proved equally popular, but then Daigneau gave notice to go into a play on Broadway. Wright, with just three weeks left to the season, lacked a leading man. "A lack," Royle said, "which could not be corrected in Grand Rapids, which could hardly be said to abound in theatrical talent. It was an expensive thing to send to New York for another actor, pay his fare both ways, and give him a salary commensurate with his two weeks' expenses."

A month earlier, Clarence Dean had watched Tracy play the bootlegger king alongside Selena Royle and suggested that Tracy "would indeed be a fitting man to play opposite so fine an actress as Miss Royle." After conferring with his new star and John Ellis, who thought Tracy talented but cocky, Wright cabled Milwaukee and asked Tracy to come back in the role he wanted—as Selena Royle's leading man.

Tracy quit a job selling pianos—something he admittedly wasn't any good at—and returned to Grand Rapids with Louise and Johnny. They set up housekeeping at the Browning, an apartment hotel about seven blocks from the theater. Spence and Selena played a classic farce, *Are You a Mason?,* for their first week as a team, and although the pacing flagged on opening night and more than a few cues got dropped amid all the horseplay, a natu-

Selena Royle, circa 1923.
(NEW YORK PUBLIC LIBRARY)

ral chemistry—the sheer fun of performing together—won the crowd over, and the week finished in the black.

A far better test of the Tracy-Royle combination came the week of September 1. The company performed the intimate George Broadhurst drama *Bought and Paid For,* with Selena in the role of the social-climbing Virginia and Tracy as Stafford, the alcoholic millionaire she marries not for love, but status. The play was old (1911) but potent in its simplicity and its quiet moments, and both Tracy and Royle attacked their roles with subtlety and intelligence. The cast had the luxury of a matinee for the first performance—it was Labor Day—and had settled into their roles when Louise witnessed the 8:30 performance that evening.

The play gripped her as few did, with Stafford's drunken rages reflected in Virginia's desperation and terror. Tracy was chilling at the bottom of the second act when Selena locked herself in her bedroom and Spence, bent on spousal rape, grabbed the poker from the fireplace and beat the door in like a madman. A troubled hush fell over the auditorium.

The third act was devoted to Virginia's determination to leave her husband, now sober and remorseful, and Tracy's performance, all eagerness and resolve with a shading of doom, found a poignance largely missing in the text. Ignoring all his promises and his extravagant gifts, Selena placed her ring on the table at the end of the act and exited for good. Louise sat mesmerized as Spence at first stood motionless, unable to comprehend what had finally and inevitably happened to his marriage, and then, after what seemed an eternity, he picked the ring up and read the inscription softly to himself: "From Robert to Virginia with eternal love."

His silences were astonishing in their power. No artificiality, no grand gestures, no playing to the gallery. He scarcely moved; it was all in his eyes and the way he held himself. Subdued, natural, he was the character in all of its subtle shadings. He demanded the crowd's attention, dared them not to feel what he was feeling, not to think what he was thinking. He was unlike any actor they had ever seen before, not merely because he underplayed a fragile moment that could easily have drawn groans, but because he did it all from within.

"I suppose it might have taken two minutes," Louise said, thinking back on the scene, "but the whole thing, the expression, the way he looked . . . was so moving. It was a beautiful moment, and I could see the lights on the marquee. And in my mind I said, 'He is going to be a star. A really great star.' "

CHAPTER 2

A Born Actor

It was an enclave, insular and, in a city known for brewing and bratwurst, predominantly Irish; a company town in some respects, working-class but by no means poor. The Catholic parish, St. Rose of Lima, counted nineteen millionaires, including the Millers of brewing fame, among its congregants, and its charismatic pastor, Father Patrick H. Durnin, was one of the city's best-connected and most effective fund-raisers. Along West Clybourn Street were dentists, barbers, a cobbler, a druggist, four grocery stores, a plumber, hardware, and a men's shop. The names on the businesses spoke for themselves: Corrigan, Curley, O'Leary.

Merrill Park didn't start out that way. The original plat fell south of the estates along Grand Avenue at the west end of Milwaukee. Sherburn S. Merrill, general manager of the Chicago, Milwaukee & St. Paul Railroad, built his Victorian mansion on Grand at Thirty-third Street, then gathered up the land along three sides, from Thirtieth to Thirty-fifth Streets and back to the edge of the Menomonee Valley. Merrill's company, meanwhile, acquired nearly half a square mile of marshland in the valley itself, and in 1879 began work on the Shops of West Milwaukee, where the rolling stock of the state's largest railroad would be manufactured and maintained.

By 1900 the railroad was the city's largest employer, and many of the men who worked there—blacksmiths, woodworkers, painters, machinists—found a vibrant neighborhood of cottages, single-family frame houses, and spacious duplexes just up the steps in Merrill Park. Mostly they were Germans and Poles, first- and second-generation Americans who brought their skills with them from Europe. The Irish influx started in 1892, after a disastrous fire in the Third Ward left many of them homeless. The Irish were the men on the trains—the engineers, firemen, brakemen, switchmen—and soon they came to dominate. Merrill Park wasn't entirely Irish, but by the turn of the century it sure seemed that way.

So it was to Merrill Park that John Tracy naturally came in 1899, installing his young family on the first floor of a modest duplex at 3003 St. Paul Avenue, just a block from the Clybourn business district and two from St. Rose's. Like a lot of other people in the neighborhood, he worked for the St. Paul, but he wasn't in the shops nor on the trains either. Rather, he clerked in offices contained in a nondescript brick building around the corner from Union Depot, where he could gaze out the window at almost any hour of the day or night and watch freight and passenger stock roll gracefully across Second Street, arcing to the west toward Fourth. It was a factory district, the heart of the original village, where boots and soap and stoves got made, and where ironworks and hardware companies sat alongside packing plants and warehouses.

John Edward Tracy was born into railroading. His father, John D. Tracy, emigrated from Galway during the Great Famine and went to work for the Vermont Central at the age of fifteen. In 1854 he moved to Wisconsin and joined the Milwaukee & St. Paul as a section foreman. He made roadmaster in Savanna, Illinois, then settled in Freeport, in 1870, where he was in charge of the track to Rock Island. He had four sons, three of whom worked for the line. John, born in 1873, had a head for numbers and became a bookkeeper. His brother Andrew, born in 1883, held a similar position with the Illinois Central.

The Tracys were unusually prominent for a railroad family. J.D. was treasurer of the building committee for St. Mary's Catholic Church, which anchored a section of town that became known as Piety Hill. He contributed a pillared altar of marble and onyx, and for years was one of the directors of St. Mary's School. He was also one of the organizers of the State Bank of Freeport, and one of its directors from the very beginning. It could be said the Tracys lived on the right side of the tracks, if only just barely. Liberty Division abutted the easements, which ran roughly parallel to the Pecatonica River. John D. Tracy shared a four-bedroom wood frame house with his wife Mary, their daughter Jenny, and their sons John, William, and Andrew. Two daughters by his first wife, Letitia, became nuns, and a son, Frank, a journalist and newspaper editor. Letitia died in childbirth in 1865, and John wed Mary Guhin, from County Kerry, the following year.

John D. Tracy was honest, industrious, charitable, a pillar of the community, but the Tracys were still lace curtain Irish, devoutly Catholic in a town that was largely Methodist and Presbyterian. Freeport was known for its Henney Buggies, its Stover windmills and bicycles, and the coffee mills and cast iron toys manufactured by Arcade. Rail service was the landbound city's lifeline, but when John Tracy, the younger, began courting the twenty-year-old daughter of Edward S. Brown, son of the late Caleb Wescott Brown of the Browns of Rhode Island, John's upright father couldn't begin to pass muster with the merchant miller of Stephenson County.

According to family lore, Caleb Brown was directly descended from the famous mercantile family of Providence, specifically Nicholas Brown, who entered the family business at an early age and whose son was the Brown after whom Brown University was named. Caleb Brown came to Freeport by way of Buffalo, Oneco, Cedarville, and Silver Creek. In 1857 he built a flouring mill on the banks of the Pecatonica, which, starting in 1865, supplied a grain-and-feed store he opened on Galena Avenue. He bought the Prentice house, a ponderous brick showplace on West Stephenson Street, and joined the First Methodist Church. Gradually, the operation of both Brown's Mill and the store fell to his eldest son, Ed, a Civil War veteran who was also town supervisor and a member of the First Presbyterian Church. Ed Brown married Abigail Stebbins of Silver Creek in 1867, and the couple had three children who lived to adulthood: Emma, Caroline, and Frank.

Exactly how John Tracy made the acquaintance of Carrie Brown is unknown, but it is unlikely that they met socially. John attended school at St. Mary's and the University of Notre Dame, while Carrie graduated from Freeport High and spent only a short time in college. It may be that they met through the family business, or perhaps at the bank, where John had been a teller. She was one of the most beautiful girls in Freeport, a "down easterner" who didn't lack for proper suitors. When word got around she was seeing an Irish Catholic from Liberty Street, the town was properly scandalized. Ed Brown, in fact, may well have had a word with Tracy Sr. on the matter, for J.D. imposed a strict curfew on his two eldest boys.

"This door will be locked at ten o'clock," he declared, "and nobody will be allowed in after ten o'clock!" Both John and Will appealed to their sister Jenny for help. "I would sit up on the stairs or at the upstairs window and wait for those two to come home," Jenny later told her daughter Jane. "I would sneak down and open the door so that they would be able to come in the house, and God knows sometimes it was two or three o'clock in the morning and I would have sat there all night. My nerves were ruined when I was a very young girl."

There was little love lost between the Tracy boys and their rigid old man, but Jenny adored her father and faithfully went to Benediction with him every Sunday night. J.D. wasn't any happier about his son's relationship with a Protestant girl than were Ed Brown and his family, but John and Carrie were the real thing, a genuine love match at a time when arranged marriages were still common among the Irish. Amid much gnashing of teeth, the union was made legal on the evening of August 29, 1894. The Browns opened their home on upper Stephenson for the event, and Father W. A. Horan of St. Mary's agreed to officiate. "In accordance with the wishes of the bride and groom the wedding was a very quiet and informal affair," the *Daily Journal* reported, "no attempt at display being made excepting that the parlors were very prettily decorated for the occasion." Only a week earlier, the groom had traveled to LaSalle to accept the position of assistant cashier with a new bank, and so after the formalities of "a bountiful feast" had played themselves out, the newlyweds left town, putting a good one hundred miles between them and Freeport and their painfully incompatible families.

It was in LaSalle that Carrie Tracy first sensed the physical intolerance her husband displayed toward alcohol, a characteristic passed to both John and his brother Will through the Guhin line of the family. Carrie herself never drank and her husband rarely did so at home, but when he did the results were immediate and profound. There is no evidence that John Tracy

The home of John D. Tracy and family, Freeport, Illinois.
(SUSIE TRACY)

was a mean or even a disagreeable drunk. Drink, in fact, may well have brought out his genial side, but he was prone to disappear, leaving Carrie at home alone, sometimes for days, with no word as to where he was. Without the sobering influence of his father at hand, John developed a reputation at the bank as being unreliable. Then there was a whispered story within the family that he had been caught with his hand in the till. Within a year they were back in Freeport, where John's father had gotten his son his first job out of college as a teller at the State Bank, and where he now settled him as a bookkeeper with the St. Paul.

Living in the same house with John and Mary and Jenny and Will and Andrew was trying for the two of them—especially Carrie, who was used to grander things—and the close quarters got downright stifling with the birth of a ten-pound boy on the morning of June 15, 1896. The baby was baptized Carroll Edward Tracy, with his aunt and uncle serving as godparents. Shortly thereafter, John and Carrie moved in with the Browns, where there was considerably more room and staff, but where the atmosphere was no less strained or uncomfortable. On the whole, it was a better arrangement than before, but the Browns were a starchy bunch, sociable but distant, and John's occasional binges didn't endear him to his in-laws. When a job opening presented itself in Milwaukee, John Tracy pursued it with all the charm and resolve he could muster, and when the time came to again say goodbye to Freeport, the relief all around was palpable.

It wasn't long after the Tracys' arrival in Milwaukee that Carrie learned she was once again with child. Merrill Park was a vast improvement over Freeport, a modern neighborhood with conveniences and open space and plenty of kids. It was just far enough from the center of town to offer a pleasurable blend of urban and rural living. There were no saloons or livery stables, Sherburn Merrill having thoughtfully placed deed restrictions on such enterprises (as well as any other businesses "detrimental to the interests of a first class residence neighborhood"). The city center was just minutes away, yet one could stroll due east a block and gaze down into the Menomonee Valley, four miles long and a half mile wide, and see virtually every kind of industrial operation, from breweries to grain elevators to tanneries, stockyards, and flour mills. Carrie's pregnancy took her through a relatively mild winter, and although she was hoping for a girl, the result delivered by Dr. O'Malley on Thursday, April 5, 1900, was another boy. Carrie made no effort to hide her disappointment, and found it impossible to come up with a name for the child.

As the unmarried girl in the family, it fell to Jenny Tracy to ensure the baby got baptized, and it was on Sunday, April 22, that she and her brother prepared to take the seventeen-day-old boy to St. Rose's for the sacrament.

"What are we going to name him?" she asked Carrie.

"I'm so disappointed that he's a boy," Carrie moaned. "He was supposed to be 'Daisy' after my good friend Daisy Spencer."*

"Why don't you call him Spencer and honor Daisy that way?"

"Well . . ." said Carrie in a dispirited tone, "that'll be all right."

Jenny was so relieved to have a name for the baby that the matter of a
baptismal name didn't occur to her until she and her brother were already
on their way to Mass. "John," she said, "you know that this child has got to
have a saint's name. We can't present him without a saint's name. What do
you want to call him?"

"I don't know," said John. "What do you think?"

"Why don't we honor Bonnie?" Catherine Tracy, the younger daughter
of John and Letitia Tracy, had become Bonaventure, Mother General of the
Sinsinawa Dominicans.

John smiled and nodded his agreement. "That's all right with me," he
said.

When they brought the baby, swaddled in white, up to the font, Father
Durnin said, "What is the name?"

Jenny said, "Spencer Bonaventure."

And the priest asked, "Boy or girl?"

When Carrie Tracy learned her new son had been given "Bonaventure"
as a middle name, she was unhappy, as much for the baby's sake as her own.
(She may have learned that Bonaventure was the patron saint of those
afflicted with bowel disorders.) When the certificate of birth was filed on
June 4, 1900, the boy's name was given as "Spencer Bernard Tracy" and it
remained that way for the rest of his mother's life.

The only industrial enterprise to rival the West Milwaukee Shops in terms
of size and employment was a rolling mill that occupied nearly thirty acres
at the southeastern corner of the city where the Kinnickinnic River flowed
into Lake Michigan. As the shops had given birth to Merrill Park, the iron
and steel mill founded in 1867 by the Milwaukee Iron Company begat the
similarly self-contained village of Bay View.

Initially, the neighborhood was populated with iron and steel workers
imported from Great Britain, but as factories sprang up to the west of the
mill complex and the need for support services grew, the ethnic makeup of
the area became considerably more diverse. By the time John Tracy moved
his family to Bay View in 1903, there were Irish mill hands, a sizable Italian
colony, and significant numbers of Poles and Germans. The architecture

* Daisy Spencer (1873–1963) and Carrie Brown attended Evansville Seminary and were subsequently roommates at Milwaukee College (later Milwaukee-Downer).

was a pleasing mix of Queen Anne, Italianate, and Greek Revival, with a few Civil War–era farmhouses remaining. New single-family frame houses were built alongside duplexes, and the dense woods on the lakeshore were only a short walk from the compact business district along Kinnickinnic Avenue.

The mill itself employed 1,600 men, transforming ore from Dodge County and the Lake Superior region into steel and iron bars, tracks, billets, rails, and the square-cut nails that held much of Bay View together. Then there were the companies that sprang up around the mill, producing products for the building and transportation industries.

One such enterprise was the Milwaukee Corrugating Company, which took its first orders for galvanized roofing shingles in 1902. Over time, the line expanded to include pressed-tin ceilings, wall tiles, skylights, and ventilators for barns and creameries. Milwaukee Corrugating was a prosperous, growing concern when John Tracy joined the company. Exactly why he left the St. Paul isn't clear, but his promotion to general foreman in late 1901 would likely have put him in closer proximity to the numerous saloons that served the men of the shops, and a stop on the way home would not only have led to calamity but a clash with the abstentious culture so carefully shaped by Sherburn Merrill. In little more than a year, John was out at the railroad and glad to land yet another clerk's position in the factory district north of Lincoln Avenue.

The move to Bay View coincided with Carroll Tracy's start in school and Spencer's emergence as a hyperactive terror. Not long after the family's relocation to a roomy duplex on Bishop Avenue, the younger boy took a firm grip on a cast iron fire engine and brained his older brother with it. He watched calmly as his mother ministered to the screaming seven-year-old, then settled into a soothing and sympathetic chant: "Poor Ca'l, poor Ca'l . . ." Carroll Tracy was a good son, his mother's favorite, but Spencer was something else again, and his aunt Emma predicted John and Carrie would have their hands full with the boy she ominously referred to as "that one." Said Emma, "He's a throwback. I dare say he is part Indian."

Bay View was full of young working-class families. Rowdy kids were everywhere, yet Spencer stood out. In an early picture he radiates energy, his deep-set eyes suggesting not so much a thoughtful, well-behaved child as a malevolent raccoon. "He was in dresses when I first saw him," said Mrs. Henry Disch, an early neighbor. "He was bubbling with life. I don't believe he ever sat still. I can't remember him sitting down in a chair or reading a book. His brother Carroll was a quiet boy. He liked to stay inside and listen to the talk of his elders, but Spence was always outside with the boys." When the kids were cleaned up and brought to dinner, Spencer sat restlessly as the adults talked, kicking the legs of the chairs on either side of him and methodically peeling the enamel dots off Mrs. Disch's new salt and pepper shakers.

It was in Bay View that Spencer's spiritual development began with his weekly attendance at Mass, his mother remaining at home while his father walked the boys to Immaculate Conception, the Catholic parish that served the neighborhood. The sacred rite was a pageant of spectacle and wonder to an impressionable three-year-old—the singing, praying, kneeling, the nourishment of the Divine Liturgy and Holy Communion. However close he was to his indulgent mother, Spencer grew closer still to his father in those early years, the shared experience of worship a powerful bond that would hold firm in the years to come. It became Carroll's job to corral his kid brother like a gentle sheepdog, hovering over him before and after while greetings were exchanged between their father and the neighbors on the steps in front of the church. And when it came time to put Spencer in kindergarten in 1906, it too became Carroll's job to lead him the eight blocks to District 17 School #2 on Trowbridge Street.

School widened Spencer's social circle and encouraged a tendency to disappear. "I began to show signs of wanderlust at seven," he later admitted. "I wandered completely out of the neighborhood and struck up an acquaintance with two delightful companions—'Mousie' and 'Rattie.' Their father owned a saloon in a very hard-boiled neighborhood. It was a lot more fun playing with them than it was going to school." Mousie and Rattie were nine and eleven, respectively, and incorrigible truants. "Being sentimentally Irish," Spencer said, "that common-enough episode in a kid's life was to have a lasting effect on my future. For the first time I saw my mother cry over me. I resolved in an immature way never to make her cry again. I don't mean to intimate that I became a model boy. I didn't."

The family's pattern of movements during these years suggests they were as much a result of Spencer's abysmal attendance record as they were for reasons of economics. In 1907 the Tracys moved closer to the school, cutting three blocks off the daily commute. In their next relocation, the family settled within sight of the building, where the route home was a short walk through a brick-paved alley. Just beyond the schoolyard was dairy pasture, forest, and, at a gravel road called Oklahoma Avenue, the Milwaukee city limits.

Spence seemed to prefer the rougher neighborhoods to Bay View proper, and frequently he would return home with a band of scruffy-looking kids who seemed as if they hadn't eaten in a week. Invariably Mrs. Tracy would fix sandwiches—cheese on buttered bread—only to discover that Spencer had sent one or more of them home with clothes from his own closet. "I can honestly say that back of every one of Spencer's exploits was something fine like sympathy, generosity, affection, pride, or ambition," she

The Tracy family, Bay View, circa 1908.
(SUSIE TRACY)

said in 1937. "There was not a mean bone or thought in him. True, he broke windows with the same alarming and expensive regularity boys do today. And he would get embroiled in fights to help a friend—fights, incidentally, from which Carroll invariably would have to rescue him because he was so thin and sickly a child until he was 14 that he could never finish on his own what he was quick to start or join in . . . Even though it meant added work for me and bigger bills for John to pay at the stores, neither of us could find it in our hearts to punish or discourage him from such a fine philosophy."

With its hundreds of mill and factory workers, there was no shortage of saloons in Bay View, many of which, called "tied houses," were exclusive (or "tied") to the output of a particular brewery. The Globe Tavern on St. Clair Street was built of the same Cream City brick as the Romanesque school on Trowbridge, and it proudly displayed the belted globe of the Schlitz Brewing Company atop its turreted entryway. Vollmer's Grocery Store and Saloon was due west of the Globe on Lenox. Kneisler's White House Tavern stood boldly at the corner of Ellen and Kinnickinnic Avenue, and yet another Schlitz tavern was under construction just outside the walls of the rolling mill on South Superior. The walk to and, especially, from work became an obstacle course of temptations for a man of John Tracy's cravings, and he didn't always negotiate the route with complete success. An eminently convivial man, John honored the Irish tradition of the saloon as a center of the community, and he often found it impossible to pass one without stopping to pay his respects. At other times he walked a tortured path that purposely avoided all licensed establishments, a not altogether easy task, in that saloons, like stores and churches, were part of the fabric of a residential neighborhood and stood side by side with new homes, parks, and schools.

Despite the daily challenges he faced, John Tracy won favor with Louis Kuehn, the president of Milwaukee Corrugating, and found himself promoted to traffic manager within the space of a year. Even so, he would, on occasion, fall spectacularly off the wagon and disappear without a trace. The boys had no clear understanding of what was happening; their father worked long hours and it was only their mother's tears that told them something was dreadfully wrong. Carroll did what he could to comfort their mother, but Spencer withdrew, possibly wondering, as the children of alcoholics often do, if his father had gone off because of something his younger boy had said or done.

What they couldn't have known was that alcoholism ran in their grandmother's side of the family, and that their Uncle Will Tracy was even more severely afflicted with "the creature" than was their own father. It was never discussed, a matter of unspoken shame, a sin against wife and family, a good man's weakness. At times like these there was little Carrie could do, and a call would go out to Andrew Tracy, John's genuinely abstentious brother, who would come to Milwaukee, find his elder sibling, clean him up, and bring him back. The process took its toll on John, whose genial nature hid a prematurely lined face and whose hair, in his mid-thirties, was already beginning to gray at the temples. It took a toll on his brother as well, for there was genuine terror in the fact that Guhin blood also ran through Andrew Tracy's veins. "Uncle Andrew was paralyzed, afraid, of liquor," said his niece, Jane Feely. "He just wouldn't touch it. Not because he wouldn't want it, but because he was so terribly afraid of it."

Summers for the boys were spent in Freeport, where they divided their time between the Tracy house in Liberty Division and the Brown house on upper Stephenson. Grandfather Brown's asthma was bad, aggravated by the summer dust, and the shades were always pulled. It was dark and hot inside, all stiff and lifeless with a horsehair sofa in the sitting room and a five-octave square piano that nobody ever played. Spencer escaped whenever he could—to the circus, to the moving pictures, to the Stebbins house on Walnut Street. Warren Stebbins was the younger brother of Abbie Brown, but the family never looked forward to Spencer's visits. "He was terrible," said Warren's granddaughter, Bertha Calhoun. "He was just into everything."

Bertha's father, Clarence Forry, once described him, without affection, as "one big ugly freckle."

When there weren't any horse races or baseball games at Taylor's Park, and no kids were swimming in the river, the storefront theaters along Stephenson Street offered the best respite from the heat. The Majestic was a favorite hangout when Spencer could cadge a nickel, as was the Superba across the street. When there wasn't money he would stand and stare at the displays out on the sidewalk, sighing extravagantly, or fix the box office with a woeful gaze until the woman at the window, a friend of his Aunt Mame's, would say, "Oh, Spencer, go on in!" His Aunt Emma once refused him the money to see a movie about Jesse James. "You've got enough wild ideas without going to see those things." He thought hard a moment, then announced *The Life of Christ* was playing at the other theater. "You wouldn't want to keep me from seeing that, would you?" He got the nickel, but Emma Brown had little doubt as to which film he saw.

John Tracy sent a dollar a week to be split between the boys. What Carroll did with his share was a mystery, but Spencer, noting the economic divide between the Tracy and Brown households, always seemed to be broke. "At that time you could buy a bag full of candy for ten cents," said Frank Tracy, the son of Andrew and Mary Tracy. "My mother said that very often, Spence would come home with a loaf of bread and give it to his grandma. 'That's for us.' Probably eight or nine cents a loaf at that time. Another time he was helping Grandma Tracy in the kitchen, and she had a paring knife and it was dull, wasn't working right. So the next time he got his fifty cents, he went over to Woolworth's and he bought a paring knife for his grandmother. My mother was telling me this and she said, 'He was always very generous.' He did other little things like that around the house, things Carroll would never think of doing."

Spencer hated the tradition of the Saturday night bath, and the task of getting him to take one fell to his Aunt Mary. "She'd try to round him up and get him in the tub," Frank said. "Spencer was always pretty hard to find. She'd literally have to push him to the bathroom, and then she wouldn't hear anything. She'd ask Spencer, 'Are you taking a bath in there?' He'd say yes, but he'd be sitting on the floor fully clothed—even his hat still on his head—splashing the water with his hands." Even when he actually got into the tub, he wouldn't shampoo his hair, and his grandmother would invariably say, "Your hair stinks!" Finally, it was decided the boys would do better under the no-nonsense supervision of Grandmother Brown, and Spencer wore a collection of scapular medals for the occasion.

"What are all these things?" she demanded, yanking at them.

"Don't take 'em off my neck!" he exclaimed. "You can't take those off!

They're holy!" Her expression must have told him she thought he was crazy, for he took them out and started to explain: "Well, this is so you won't get drowned . . . and this is so you won't get killed . . . and this one is so you won't commit a sin . . ."

"You certainly won't drown in that bathtub!"

Thoroughly scrubbed, his hair washed and teeth brushed, Spencer and his brother would be returned to Grandma Tracy so that they could serve Mass at St. Mary's the next morning. With her husband dead and her daughter Jenny now married, Mary Guhin Tracy sought the solace of the bottle ("a drop o' th' cratur"), and her son-in-law's gift to her each Christmas was a case of beer and a jug of good Irish whiskey. "She would always specify that it be delivered after dark," her granddaughter Jane remembered, "so the neighbors wouldn't see."

"From the time Spencer was a tiny lad," recalled Carrie Tracy, "Carroll appointed himself as special guardian. He worried more about Spencer than the rest of the family put together." Carroll had an almost pathological fixation on his brother, as if hovering over him and getting him out of scrapes was in some way compensation for their father's absences. He had the example of Andrew Tracy and his palliative visits to Milwaukee when times got bleak, the sober brother who could always be relied upon in times of distress. Try as he might, Carroll's dogged oversight was never much of a substitute for a father's attention, and the family's proximity to the Trowbridge Street campus did little to improve the boy's performance. "I never would have gone back to school," Spencer once said, "if there had been any other way of learning to read the subtitles in the movies."

He discovered the Comique, a storefront theater that showed split-reel movies on Kinnickinnic Avenue. "Spencer was always punished by depriving him of things he liked," Carrie said. "Motion pictures formed a great type of discipline, because refusing to allow him to attend broke his heart." It was impossible to keep his clothes clean, he rarely wiped his nose, and there were the usual schoolyard fights. "A tough kid," said Joe Bearman, who lived down the street, "but a good one. Ran with the hard-boiled gang of the neighborhood."

They tried sending him to Freeport, where he was put to work in the family feed store and enrolled for a short time at the Union Street School. Spencer was kept on a short leash, working at the store before and after class, and it was the structured life in Freeport that likely convinced John and Carrie he would benefit from a more disciplined educational environment. Sometime around 1909—the records no longer go back that far—

they turned him over to the Dominican nuns at St. John's Cathedral, where the consequences of a wayward disposition would carry considerably more weight. He had, by then, started going to Confession and fasting before receiving Holy Communion, and understanding what sin, repentance, and forgiveness were all about. He had also come to see his father's disappearances as something to emulate, an old suitcase in hand, food, such as it was, filched from the ice box when nobody was looking. He'd get a few blocks out and get hungry, then go a few more blocks and suddenly realize he was out of food.

The school was directly behind the historic church near downtown Milwaukee, a no-nonsense structure of native brick with floor-to-ceiling windows facing east toward the lake. The commute from Bay View was three miles by streetcar, and missing opening prayers would have been unthinkable. *Come, O Holy Ghost, enlighten the hearts of the faithful . . .* the Lord's Prayer, the Angelical Salutation, the Apostle's Creed. Glory be to the Father. *O Mary, conceived without sin, pray for us who have recourse to thee.* Two hundred minutes a week were devoted to the study of Christian doctrine and Bible history; only reading, as a subject, was accorded more time. Geography, arithmetic. Penmanship. Composition and recitation, phonics and hymns. There were prayers before and after meals, prayers at the end of the day. *O Mother of the Word Incarnate, despise not my petitions, but graciously hear and grant my prayer . . .* "He remembered this nun," said his cousin Frank. "He said, 'If you did anything wrong, out with the ruler—bang!—across your hands. If you said anything, you'd get another one. You feared those nuns. They were tough.'"

He made no secret of his love for the movies, but it was the church that gave him his first taste of performance. Serving Mass, the phonetic Latin and ritual movements of the altar boy, donning costume in the sacristy, starched collar and lace surplice. "I couldn't keep an unlit taper in the house," Carrie Tracy told an interviewer. "Directly after school, Spencer would race home and arrange the candles in every room. Then he would practice lighting and extinguishing them for hours." He caught the five-cent show at the Union Theater, where the proprietor seated his patrons on ordinary chairs and the ticket girl sang and played the piano. At a capacity of 275, the Union, which offered "high class vaudeville" and a change of program every Monday and Friday, was intimate enough for card tricks and coin manipulations, and it may well have been at one of the Union's hour-long shows that young Tracy got his first exposure to the art of magic.

"He was a great magician as a child," his cousin Jane said. "Whenever anyone went to Milwaukee, Spencer did his magic act. Always in the family you did your number, and then you went to your bedroom. He was very

Spencer, age twelve.
(AUTHOR'S COLLECTION)

good, according to my mother." He began staging shows in the cramped basement of the family's rented duplex on Estes, admitting audience members through the cellar door and seating them among the coal bins, the furnace, and the laundry. "Admission was a few pins," said Forrest McNicol, whose mother ran a grocery store at the corner of Ellen and East Russell. "I guess you'd have to say that was the beginning of the little theater movement in Bay View." Over time, Spence learned how to manage an audience's expectations, usually by downplaying the impact of a particular illusion. One safety pin, Carrie Tracy remembered, had the same value as two straight pins, and ofttimes Spencer was accused of overcharging.

Soon the wonders of downtown Milwaukee no longer seemed so distant. The grandest of the new movie emporiums was the Princess on North Third Street, which boasted private boxes, a $5,000 pipe organ, and seating for nine hundred patrons. Ads offered a variegated program of comedies and dramas, accompanied by travel talks, scenic views, illustrated songs, and a five-piece pit band billed as "the famous Princess orchestra." Movies were going uptown and so were the admission prices: the Princess was the first of the Milwaukee movie theaters to charge ten cents' admission. The following year, the Butterfly—so known because of the huge terra cotta butterfly that loomed over Grand Avenue—went the Princess one better, installing a $10,000 pipe organ and a ten-piece house orchestra. Fortunately, most of Milwaukee's picture parlors were still nickelodeons, dark and primitive, and it wasn't hard to find a chase picture or some crude knockabout at half the price the fancy places were charging.

Carroll would soon be starting high school, and John's bouts with the bottle were growing less frequent. Obsessed with kicking the habit for the good of the marriage as well as his own health, John Tracy moved the family to a duplex on Kenesaw, scarcely two blocks from work, where the floorplan offered no more room than any of their previous locations—two bedrooms, front sitting room, dining area, commodious kitchen—but where the stroll to Bay Street was mercifully unimpeded by the presence of a saloon. Just to the north were wetlands where kids would hang out, marshlands that surrounded an old European-style fishing village at Jones Island. The mill whistles blew at seven and nine-thirty in the morning, noon, twelve-thirty, and five in the evening, and the entire sky lit up when the furnaces were charged.

Over the summer of 1910, Spencer was sent to Aberdeen, South Dakota, where his Aunt Jenny had married a gentle Irishman named Patrick Feely. "He went and played with the wrong kids," said his cousin Jane, who was Pat and Jenny's daughter. "He got on the wrong side of the tracks, so it was good to get him away." Spencer was a spindly kid, delicate and undersized from not eating well. Stepping down from the train, he was greeted by his aunt and her son Bernard, not quite three, who was wrapped around a lamppost and intently staring up at him. "Oh, Mama," he exclaimed, "he ain't so homely!"

Over the summer, he also spent time in Ipswich, a one-street town roughly thirty miles due west of Aberdeen, where Frank J. Tracy was editor of the *Edmunds County Democrat.* Not long after Spencer's return from Aberdeen, the Tracys moved yet again, this time to lower Bay View. Immaculate Conception was just a block north, at the intersection of Russell and Kinnickinnic, and Humbolt Park, with its playground and clay tennis courts and pond for boating, was four blocks to the west.

The years on Logan Avenue were among the most memorable of Spencer's childhood, and practically the only ones of which he spoke in later years. He joined the Boy Scouts ("I made a good one") and kept to his studies. Winters were spent skating, summers playing marbles and baseball. John's work at Milwaukee Corrugating was secure and valued, and the binges came to a complete halt with the brutal realization that he could never drink moderately. The need never openly manifested itself, but John was always waging the battle, cut off as he was from the society of the tavern. He tried limiting himself to a pint, nursing it as one would a highball, but it was never enough, and all too easy to fall for another. So he cut himself off entirely, strictly limiting himself to work and family and indulging an accelerated taste for sweets. It was a restrictive yet necessary way to live. At times a furious pacing of the floor betrayed the struggle within, and not even Carrie could find a way to comfort him.

Performance, by now, had become routine for Spencer, something absorbing and fun and as natural as breathing. He was involved with the Christmas show at St. John's in 1911, and at home in Bay View the magic act gave way to more elaborate entertainments "enacting scenes I'd seen in movies." He staged his first play—a murder mystery—before an audience of neighbors in the living room of the house on Logan in 1912. Having lost himself at the movies, watching the same subjects over and over, he now put himself in the hero's shoes and imagined himself in the middle of the action. In his own childish way, he was becoming the character he had seen on the screen, and the representation came forth without effort or artifice. "How many times we have told people of that show," one of Carrie's friends enthused in a 1931 letter, "proving Spencer was a born actor starting as a child."

Tracy rarely spoke of these early performances, and although he freely admitted to being fascinated by moving pictures, it is impossible to say just how much live drama he consumed as a kid. Neither of his parents was a dedicated theatregoer, and the legitimate playhouses—the Shubert and the Davidson—charged as much as $1.50 a ticket to see the likes of Ethel Barrymore and Otis Skinner in weeklong stands. The Pabst Theatre, designed on the order of a European opera house, offered German-language programming almost exclusively. The Crystal, Empress, and Majestic were all vaudeville houses, although it was possible to see someone like Mme. Bertha Kalich headlining in a one-act play. The Gaiety was given over to burlesque, leaving the Saxe, Juneau, and Columbia to the ten-twenty-thirty tradition of stock. The plays were things like *The Little Homestead* and *Mrs. Temple's Telegram* and *Caught with the Goods,* blood-and-thunder melodramas where a seat in the balcony could be had for a dime.

Spencer welcomed his twelfth birthday with particular enthusiasm because it made him eligible for a permit to engage in street trades. Most kids distributed handbills or sold newspapers—the *Milwaukee Journal,* the *Evening Wisconsin,* the *Leader*—but sensing, perhaps, too much competition in the hustling of papers, he managed instead to snag a lamplighter's route when he was, as his brother put it, "scarcely tall enough to reach the lamps with a burning taper." Using the tip of a five-foot pole to open the valve on a light, he would hold a match aloft to ignite the gas. "He had about 50 lamps to light each night and to extinguish each morning," Carroll said. "He also had to see to it that the wicks were in good order, and on Saturdays he had to clean the globes with old newspapers. For this job he received around $3.50 a week, if I remember correctly."

After ten years of service, John Tracy left Milwaukee Corrugating sometime over the summer of 1913, and the family departed Bay View for Milwaukee proper. The move must have been for the better, for the family relocated to a fashionable stretch of Grand Avenue, almost directly across from the Pabst Mansion and within blocks of the old parish at St. Rose's, where Spencer would now return for his last two years of grade school. He had to relinquish the lamplighting job, but found work as a towel boy at the Milwaukee Athletic Club, where his father held a membership and where he would learn to box from Wisconsin middleweight Gus Christie. These were, in some ways, the most unsettled years of his young life. The household theatrics ceased, but he never lost that childlike quality, the eagerness to inhabit another skin.

By 1916 the family was renting a Colonial Revival on a tree-lined street in the Story Hill section of Wauwatosa, a bedroom community just west of the Menomonee River. John Tracy had gone into sales as a representative for the Sterling Motor Truck Company, whose plant and offices were nearby in West Allis. The house on Woodlawn Court had three bedrooms, cherrywood floors, and a formal dining room where the Tracys did a lot of entertaining. Spence saw little of Carroll, who had finished high school and was doing clerical work for the Milwaukee Road. He entered Wauwatosa High in the fall of 1915, where, freed from the strict discipline of the Dominican nuns, he failed spectacularly. His only arguments with his father, he later confirmed, were over school. "I might have enjoyed school if I had been doing the thing I wanted to do. My trouble was not having a definite ambition or goal on which to concentrate. I wanted to be doing something that would hold my interest, but I had no idea what it would be."

He displayed an entrepreneurial streak, and at one point hatched a scheme with a neighbor boy to sell the water they got from a spring under the Grand Avenue viaduct at a nickel a bottle. Significantly, he was returned to St. John's in the fall, and when his father was asked to take over the Sterling Truck office in Kansas City, Missouri, his only hesitation was over what to do about Spencer. After some inquiries, John enrolled the boy at St. Mary's Academy, a Jesuit boarding school twenty-five miles west of Topeka, where there would be no distractions from a regimen of study, sports, and the sacraments. Life on the tall-grass prairie must have come as a shock after the comparative excitement of downtown Milwaukee. Separated from his family and friends and limited to just one movie a month, he may well have been tempted to join the boys caught gambling or flagging down cars at the edge of campus, hoping for a ride into town. He lasted just five weeks at St. Mary's, and no credits accrued as a result of the experiment.

In Kansas City, Spencer was placed at the Rockhurst Academy, another Jesuit institution, where he could go home to his parents at night and where, as he later acknowledged, they took the "badness" out of him "almost immediately." The Rev. Michael P. Dowling, the school's founder, named it Rockhurst because the grounds were stony and there was a grove of forest nearby. "I remember Rockhurst as a big building," Tracy later told the *Kansas City Star,* "and I remember pursuing to the best of my capabilities the study of Latin and geometry . . . I also remember that there were some boys at Rockhurst and in Kansas City who were mighty good fighters."

Official transcripts show he passed first-year Latin, as he did English, Algebra, and Ancient History, and that he did B-level work in Religion and Bookkeeping. The Jesuits were admirable men, spiritual and rigorously educated, and there were few boys who came under their influence who weren't inspired at some point to consider the priesthood. There was also the bustle of Union Station, fairly new at the time, and Electric Park, with its primitive thrill rides. Most important, he was "almost positive" he saw Lionel Barrymore for the first time onstage, truly a signal event, for Barrymore impressed him as no other actor ever had. He seemed, in fact, to be adapting well to Kansas City when the decision was made to close the Sterling office in the spring of 1917. The semester ended in June and the Tracys eventually returned to Story Park, where they took another house on the same block as before.

The way he remembered it, Tracy first met Bill O'Brien when the two were employed at a Milwaukee lumber yard. "I started for two bucks and a half a week, piling lumber after school," he said. O'Brien, on the other hand, thought they had met as students at Marquette Academy, and that they stacked wood only on Saturdays. "One of the clearest recollections I have of Spence is of the two of us in dirty overalls and jumpers sitting in the dining room of what was, in those days, Milwaukee's swankiest apartment hotel. We were stowing away a modest breakfast of grapefruit, ham and eggs, toast, jelly, and milk. At the end of the meal, Spence airily scrawled his signature across the bill and we left." The Tracys, back from Kansas City, were stopping at the Stratford Arms Hotel, adjacent to the campus of Marquette University. "We worked in a lumber yard to pick up a couple of iron men so we could roister around on Saturday nights. Our breakfasts usually cost more than we made during the day, but Spence's father paid for them."

The academy stood on a hill at Tenth and State Streets. It was a block over from the massive Pabst brewing complex, and the smell of hops hung in the air. The location led to the students being referred to as "hilltoppers," a name that has stuck ever since. "All of us Catholics wanted to enter Marquette Academy," O'Brien wrote in his autobiography, "but the cost made our parents sigh." Bill, on a scholarship, was five months older than Spence, taller, darker, rounder, more of a match for Carroll Tracy than for his younger brother. But O'Brien, like Tracy, was "infected" with a love of the stage, and they found time to see such beloved figures as Jane Cowl, David Warfield, Otis Skinner, Lenore Ulric, James O'Neill, and Maude Adams— usually from high in peanut heaven. The great vaudeville attractions of the day came through Milwaukee by way of Chicago—McIntyre and Heath, Harry Houdini, Bert Williams, whose expressive pantomimes were models of economy. A particular thrill came in May 1918 when Madame Sarah Bernhardt headlined at the Majestic and necessitated multiple visits by playing *Du théâtre au champ d'honneur* during the week and *La dame aux camélias* on the weekend.

Spence held on to the things that comforted and excited him, and although he was fascinated by vaudeville, his interest in the stage wasn't reawakened until he and Bill met and they started seeing plays together. The boys may even have arranged their own performances, for E. R. Moak, then city editor on the *Milwaukee Free Press* (and later a *Variety* staffer) remembered the first time he met Tracy was when the two of them came to enlist the paper's support for an "amateur dramatic enterprise" they were promoting. Though Spencer's grades weren't as stellar as they had been at Rockhurst, O'Brien was unquestionably a good influence. "Spence and I were a combination," he said. "He was an introvert and I was an extrovert." O'Brien went out for sports—baseball, football, basketball—and carried a full load of classes. Tracy worked, played some casual baseball, and eventually took on a class load equal to what Bill himself was tackling. O'Brien went to Mass each Sunday, an acolyte when Spence had long since given it up. Both were restless young men with a war going on, and however much the academy meant to their parents, they had a hard time keeping their minds on their studies.

"I was itching for a chance to go and see some excitement," Tracy said, and he tried enlisting when the school year was scarcely half over. "I knew very well where there was a U.S. Marines recruiting station, for I'd seen it lots of times before." He walked up and down Wells Street a dozen times, then went inside. "I want to join the Marines," he told the gray-haired officer behind the desk, his voice cracking. The man took down his name, address, the answers to a few questions, then asked his age. "I'd been all ready to say, 'Twenty, sir.' But he was looking me right in the eye. I stammered out, 'Seventeen years and eight months, sir.' The recruiting officer put the form aside, stood, and held out his hand. "Thanks for trying, youngster," he said.

Spence left the office, as he later put it, "feeling like a chump," and he said nothing to his family about it. When he celebrated his eighteenth birthday, he was immersed in Greek, Latin, third-year English, History, and Geometry. On April 13, 1918, a hundred thousand spectators lined the curbs as a three-hour parade in support of the third Liberty Loan marched down the center of America's most German city. The next day, the Whitehouse Theatre on Third Street began a week-long engagement of *The Kaiser—The Beast of Berlin* ("The Photoplay That Made New York Cheer Like Mad"), kicking off a naval recruitment competition with Chicago that was, by early May, delivering seventy-five recruits a day. The campaign reached its zenith on Mother's Day weekend, when Lieutenant John Philip Sousa arrived in town with his 250-member "Jackie" band from the Great Lakes Naval Training Station. The city seemed to be crawling with sailors, and a half-page ad in the Sunday paper bore the headline: THE NAVY NEEDS YOU! YOU NEED THE NAVY! As Bill O'Brien put it, "The bands played, the drill parades started, the Liberty Bond drives were on, and Spence and myself and some others left school one afternoon and went downtown to the enlistment headquarters of the Navy."

They didn't join that day, but they came plenty close. In the O'Brien household on Fourteenth Street, cooler heads prevailed and Bill was persuaded to finish the school year before enlisting. Spence, however, had no wish to continue at Marquette, and the prospect of losing an entire semester's credits didn't seem to bother him in the least. That night, as Carroll remembered it, he marched into the kitchen, wearing "that crooked one-sided grin" that had become something of a trademark, and said to his mother, "I've enlisted in the Navy." Carrie instantly burst into tears, but John Tracy "was sort of proud of the kid." As for Carroll: "I was out of the house and down the street before anyone could stop me. I enlisted too, not so much for patriotic motives, mind you, but because of my desire to be near Spence and to keep an eye on him." It was Monday, May 13, and naval records show that Carroll Edward Tracy, in one of the few impulsive acts of his life, did indeed sign up for service that day. What he didn't know was that his brother was merely floating the idea, eager to gauge their parents' reaction, and that he hadn't yet done what he said he had done. Once Carroll made his move, though, Spence's bluff had been called, and he quietly and somewhat sheepishly joined the navy the following day, Tuesday, May 14, 1918.

Navy seaman, age eighteen.
(SUSIE TRACY)

Enrolled as a "Landsman for Electrician (Radio)," he went straight to school and bypassed boot camp. After vaccinations for cowpox and typhoid, he was sent to the Naval Training Station in North Chicago, where he gallantly spent the rest of the war in a classroom. "The training, the discipline, and the healthy life not only did me good physically," he said, "but mentally as well. I realized for the first time that a man must make his own way in life, that he must assume certain responsibilities, and that a man can't receive too much education, because the Navy demands alert minds."

On the rare weekend when he could get away on leave, Tracy headed home to Woodlawn Court, where, on at least one occasion, he was accompanied by "six of the toughest-looking sailors" Carrie had ever seen. "They were decidedly not what you would call polite specimens of manhood. They apparently were so stunned by our mode of living that they asked Spencer if Mr. Tracy was a bootlegger, and each of them ended up the weekend visit by borrowing $25 from Mr. Tracy. In fact, John used to say it cost him $100 a month, as well as the government its share, to keep Spencer in the service." After the Armistice, he was sent to Hampton Roads, where Carroll, who spent most of his stretch in Detroit, thought he had some sort of an ordnance job. "I didn't sleep very well at night because of worrying about him, until I heard through a mutual friend that Spence was doing okay; he was acting as an aide or some such cushy job for an officer." Bill O'Brien, who waited until August to enlist, never made it out of training.

"When I got into the Navy," Tracy said, "the least I expected was to see the world through a porthole. As it was, I wound up in a training station at Norfolk, Virginia, looking eastward to the sea and considering myself lucky if they let me go cruising in a whaleboat." He once made a veiled reference to wild liberties in Norfolk, but remembered the people there with considerable fondness. "They turned that city over to a group of young men who had traveled thousands of miles from home. They made us feel that it was our home. It got us into a couple of rows with authorities, but they understood that it was all in good spirit and never complained. The difficulties weren't serious, but they would have meant demerits if the Naval authorities had heard of them. They never did."

Having achieved the rank of seaman second class, Tracy was released from active duty on February 19, 1919, given a sixty-dollar discharge bonus, and sent home to Milwaukee. He later remembered going to work for his father, who was still with Sterling Truck at the time, and it is known that he drove in truck convoys before and probably after the war. "He was a handful when he was a teenager and a little bit older," his cousin Jane said,

and that was when he was driving these caravans of trucks across the country . . . He came to Aberdeen the summer I was born, 1917. He said this on many occasions: "If it wasn't for me she wouldn't be alive." Because my mother couldn't feed me and [when] it was found that I couldn't tolerate formula, I was sent to the wet nurse. My father had bought a Mitchell car in celebration [of my birth]—because we had all this money from the farms that later collapsed—but nobody could drive the car and he refused to learn. (Eventually, I guess, he figured my mother would learn to drive.) Somehow, they got ahold of Spencer and he came. Of course, he was the car driver and the truck driver in the family. Spencer would drive me to the wet nurse every four hours to be fed.

Neither Tracy nor Bill O'Brien would return to Marquette in the fall of 1919. O'Brien tried law school, but found football more engaging. Spence seemed perfectly happy ferrying trucks across the country, and could have done so indefinitely had his father not wanted a college degree for at least one of his boys. Carroll's career had ended abruptly in 1917 when he dropped out of Dartmouth, but Spencer, who had excelled in radio school at Great Lakes, still had to get through high school before he could even think of college. He applied to Northwestern Military and Naval Academy with the intention of completing his senior year, and the fact that Dr.

Henry H. Rogers, the school's principal, was willing to take on such an indifferent student was a testament to the academy's declining enrollment.

Spencer made the connection between Milwaukee and Springfield by rail, traveling on to the city of Lake Geneva via stage. The first look he got of Davidson Hall, the neoclassical edifice which fronted the lake, was from the steamer that connected the city to the academy's wooded grounds on the opposite shore.

The academic year began on the afternoon of September 24, 1919, as Dr. Rogers began the hellish task of gathering credits from the other schools Tracy had attended. The returns were not heartening. And Rogers was getting conflicting accounts of what exactly the plan was to be after high school. Spencer told him his father had left the "college question" entirely up to him, while John told him he wanted Spencer to go to the University of Wisconsin "at least for the first year." John, Carrie, and Carroll came for Thanksgiving dinner, but the topic of college was scrupulously avoided. The Christmas furlough was similarly harmonious. Still, Spencer's grades, while not exemplary, were the best of his life, and after the first of the year, his father was encouraged to aim higher than Madison. He applied to Marquette for war credits to cover the semester left incomplete when his son enlisted in the navy, then wrote Colonel Royal Page Davidson, superintendent of the academy: "Assuming that Spencer applies himself diligently until June and then remains at Northwestern for the summer course, would he be able to establish enough credits to enter the Wharton course at Pennsylvania University?"

At the end of the 1919–20 school year, he had only ten credits toward the sixteen necessary for graduation. John pulled him out of Northwestern and brought him back to Milwaukee, where he arranged for him to do some work at St. Rose's. What happened that summer is no longer a matter of record, but when Spencer entered Milwaukee's West Division High School in September, scarcely three months later, he had acquired two additional credits. That fall, he began his senior year in English and Economics, took a Sales course, and excelled at Public Speaking.

By all accounts, Tracy emerged from Northwestern an adult, confident and disciplined. The academy's geographical isolation and its twin emphases on personal responsibility and scholastic achievement hastened the maturing process. As with Bill O'Brien, he also responded to the influence of a close friend, in this case his roommate, a slender kid from Seattle named Ken Edgers. Two years younger than Spence, Kenny was a friendly sort, uncomplicated and funny, a good student whose interests and habits rubbed off on the more rough-hewn Tracy. The two went ice skating on the mirrorlike surface of the lake, played basketball, spent long hours in study hall. Kenny, a tenor, went out for glee club, while Spence played bass tuba

Northwestern Military and
Naval Academy, 1919.
(SUSIE TRACY)

in the school band. Neither was heavy enough for football, although Tracy
managed some time in uniform as a substitute. John and Carrie met Ken
for the first time when they came to campus on Thanksgiving and were so
impressed they invited him to spend the Christmas holidays in Milwaukee.

Since Seattle was five long days away by train, Carrie told Kenny she
would like to be his Wisconsin mother. John was equally impressed, convinced Ken was one of the reasons Spencer got such good grades at Northwestern. He wanted the two boys to continue into college together, but
Spencer was, by Dr. Rogers' reckoning, a full year and a half behind when
Kenny graduated in June 1920. So the elder Tracy went looking for schools
that would grant war credits, generously and immediately. "During the
summer," Ken said, "Spence's father wrote to my father suggesting a small
college might be advantageous for our college education. It might, he felt,
require us to pay more attention to the academic than to the extracurricular
activities. He sent information about Ripon College. He felt that Spence
would be more anxious to go if I did. So, after considerable investigation
and correspondence, our fathers made arrangements for our entrance."

Kenneth Barton Edgers entered Ripon in September 1920, and Tracy,
with an allowance of nine quarter-hours for military service, followed in
February 1921. Ripon wasn't as small as Northwestern and lacked the dra-

matic lakeside setting, but it was similarly isolated, some ninety miles
northwest of Milwaukee on the western edge of the Fox River Valley. The
campus was dotted with intimate limestone residence halls, and Spence
shared a room with Kenny (who gave him "a tremendous build-up") on the
third floor of West Hall—one of the buildings dating from the time of the
school's first commencement in 1867. He signed up for courses in English
Language, History, and Zoology, declaring his major to be Medicine.

"The idea of doing something with my hands appealed to me," he said,
"and I think I might have gone into plastic surgery if something hadn't happened to make me change my mind."

CHAPTER 3

A Sissy Sort of Thing

Public Speaking was the course Tracy liked best at West Division, and he perfected a direct, almost conversational way of addressing an audience. At Ripon, the class satisfied the requirement for three quarter-hours of English, which made it doubly attractive. Henry Phillips Boody, the professor of English Composition who taught the class, emphasized the structure of persuasive material as well as its delivery, and Tracy quickly learned that he could, in Boody's words, "control the minds and emotions of a group." Tracy threw himself into the preparation and rehearsal of his speeches with a zeal that Boody, for one, found fascinating: "I remember very vividly the occasions when we were working on problems of impression [and] his speeches would actually leave the class in tears. His dramatic instinct was shown in his surpassing ability in telling a story. There was always the proper sequence of events, the gradual rise to a climax, the carefully-chosen ending."

Soon he was keeping steady company with Lola Schultz, an Education major who found him spellbinding. "He was the most popular man I ever met," she said shortly before her death in 1992. "He could make the birds sing in the trees. He could tell you black was white, and even if you thought he was wrong, pretty soon he'd have you believing him . . . Of course, he was as homely as a mud fence."

Spence had never been particularly conscious of his looks until he hit puberty—a late event, he once implied—and took a sudden and fervent interest in girls. Then his freckled face, lined and ruddy, became a torment when he discovered it was tough to get dates. He wasn't movie-star handsome nor even Midwestern good-looking. Girls generally found him earnest and amusing, but callow and not the least bit romantic. Worse still, he didn't dance. "We went on dates," Lola Schultz allowed, "but it was not a serious romance."

Tracy was more popular among the men, who responded to the Irish charm his father had in such abundance. Socially, he always seemed to be around, though invariably on his own terms. Ken Edgers had a dance band called the Crimson Orchestra, and Spence took an administrative title to justify his traveling with the group to parties, dances, and proms. "[He] enjoyed the trips and bull sessions between dances and during intermissions," Edgers said. "On our Crimson Orchestra business card it said I was 'Business Manager' and Spence was 'Financial Manager.' That probably is a fair amount of 'management' for a group of five musicians."

The money from the Crimson gigs came in handy as the month wore on. Both Spence and Kenny were on allowances from their parents, which made them flush the first couple of weeks. They'd dine at the City Lunch Room—invariably referred to as the "downtown beanery" or "the greasy spoon"—and proprietor Emil Reinsch was delighted to see them when they had real money in their pockets. Kenny always suggested big steaks and, knowing Spence's Catholicism, was sometimes able to trick him into ordering one on a Friday. When he could see the plates making their way to the table, he'd casually mention something about "the game tomorrow" and then watch with undisguised glee as Tracy would dissolve into a slow burn. "You dirty dog," he'd growl. "You knew it was Friday and you just wanted my steak!" After a flash of inner struggle, Tracy would order fish and then sit morosely and watch as Kenny devoured his steak before moving on to his own.

Generally, they'd continue to splurge until the money ran low, sometime around the third week of the month. Then they'd start going through their laundry bags, separating out the most presentable specimens and scrubbing the cuffs and the collars clean in order to make them suitable for another day's wear. "We wore each other's clothes," Kenny said, "and in our case the old wheeze of 'the first one up is the best dressed' was true."

It was John Davies, one of the West Hall gang, who picked up on Spence's interest in theatre. Davies was part of the Mask and Wig, the honors society responsible for the school's annual commencement play. He had appeared in *The Witching Hour* the previous winter and was planning to audition for *The Truth* when Tracy got wind of it. Cornering Davies one evening at West Hall, Tracy wanted to know all about the auditions—how they were conducted, who was in charge of them, whether they were open to anyone who wanted to read. Davies told him what he could, then got on the phone to Clark Graham, the faculty adviser who directed the plays.

"There's a fellow in our house who is interested in acting," Davies told the professor. "I believe he has real talent. He would like to try out for our next play. Could I bring him over?" Graham, a sort of utility man in the English Department, had them at his door in a matter of minutes. "Tracy was a fine looking lad," he later recalled of the meeting, "more mature in appearance than the average freshman. I noted especially a certain decisiveness in his speech, a clipped firmness of expression indicating poise, self-control, and confidence. I was impressed and invited him to try out for our next play."

The Truth is famously a woman's showcase, the lead part being that of Becky, a compulsive liar whose relentless embroidery threatens her marriage to the agreeable, unquestioning Tom Warder. Taking the part of Becky would be Ethyl Williams, a star around campus who was president of Theta

Carrie and John Tracy, circa 1922.
(ROBERT B. EDGERS)

Alpha Phi, the dramatic fraternity, and was, by general agreement, the best actress the school had ever produced. Both Davies and Tracy read for the role of Tom, an easy skate of a part except for a tense confrontational scene at the bottom of the second act, and Tracy, to everyone's surprise, landed it effortlessly. Ken Edgers, who covered the tryouts for the school paper, acknowledged that Tracy was new to the Ripon stage "but should prove to be one of the strongest actors in the cast if the ability revealed last Tuesday may be taken as a sample of his future work." Edgers mercifully refrained from reporting Tracy's first line onstage a few days later, when, focused on the playscript clutched in his hand, he backed out from the wings and tripped over a pile of band instruments, tumbling into the middle of a bass drum. "Gosh!" came the historic words. "I busted Foam Lueck's drum!"*

Faced with the daunting task of acting the male lead in the first full-length play he had ever tackled, Tracy threw himself into the rehearsal process with an all-consuming dedication that forced him to drop all of his third-quarter classes. "He didn't always see the sense in 'education,'" Professor Boody wrote, "and in some courses he was more or less of a problem. The Dean frequently had to jack him up on attendance. But when it came to anything on the stage he was right there." He also spent so much time running lines with Ethyl Williams, his moon-faced leading lady, that Kenny came to consider her "one of Spence's flames."

Tracy made his stage debut at the Ripon Municipal Auditorium on the night of June 21, 1921. The performance began promptly at 8:15, Ethyl taking the stage within a couple of minutes and exhibiting, in the words of Professor Boody, "real ability and a high degree of technique." Spence appeared about ten minutes later, "straightforward and lovable" as the text required. As Becky schemed and manipulated, Tom steadfastly remained his trusting old self, a model of contented domesticity, completely oblivious to the web of deceit being spun around him.

Then came the second act, where Becky covered a man's visit with a cascade of falsehoods that not even Tom could ignore. Tracy, his jaw taut, his voice getting lower, listened with mounting fury as Ethyl continued to trip herself up. "Lies!" he erupted, blowing like a long-dormant volcano. "All of it! Every word a lie. And another and another and another!"

"Tom!"

"You sent for him!"

Too frightened to speak, she frantically shook her head in a desperate attempt at denial.

"Don't shake your head! I know what I'm talking about and for the first time with you, I believe!"

---

* Clemens E. "Foam" Lueck was the college bandmaster.

She put her hands up helplessly and backed away from him.

"I saw your note to him!" he jabbed, moving in on her. "I read it here in this room! He gave it to me before you came down!"

"The beast!"

"You're going to misjudge him too!"

"No, Tom, I'll tell you the truth, and all of it."

"Naturally," he said, spitting the words. "Now you've *got to!*"

Ethyl later confessed that Spence had truly frightened her that night, and that she had been able to channel the terror she felt into the performance she gave. "Mr. Tracy proved himself a consistent and unusually strong actor in this most difficult straight part," the Ripon paper said in its review. "His steadiness, his reserve strength and suppressed emotion were a pleasant surprise to all who heard him as Warder." The applause was strong and genuine, the exhilarating reward for two months of the most sustained work he had ever done in his life.

And from that night forward, his college career would be a shambles.

That summer Ethyl Williams returned to her family in Green Bay, where she would eventually give up acting and become a teacher. Spence and Kenny went west by way of the Canadian Rockies, stopping over in Banff and Lake Louise on their way to Seattle, where they spent time at Dr. and Mrs. Edgers' cottage on Fox Island. "As we left Milwaukee," said Kenny, "at the train station Mr. Tracy slipped me $20 so I would not run short. As we left Seattle at the end of the summer, *my* father said to Spence, 'Here is an extra $20 in case you run short.' We called it even."

At Fox Island they swam, dug clams, fished. There were side trips by boat to Mount Rainier and out into the ocean. Spence, fired by the triumph of his performance in *The Truth,* spent long hours at a portable typewriter transcribing a one-act play he had found in a copy of *McClure's* called *The Valiant.* After a week on Fox Island, they ditched their overalls and took the S.S. *Rose City* from Portland to San Francisco (where Spence had an aunt) and spent several days motoring around the peninsula cities of Palo Alto, Monterey, and Carmel. They returned to Wisconsin via the Grand Canyon, arriving back at Ripon in time for the campuswide mixer the Crimson Orchestra always played at the end of registration.

The "walk-around" was the first social event of the year, the ritual introduction of incoming students to the faculty, and it was customary for the upperclassmen to escort them. The best friend of Lorraine Foat, a Mask and Wig stalwart, was entering Ripon, and Lorraine prevailed upon Spence, who hated dancing, to be her friend's escort that night. Lois Heberlein, as it turned out, was well connected: her father had attended Ripon, where one of his classmates was Silas Evans, the current president of the college. As they made their way down the reception line, Spence was complimented repeatedly on the excellence of his commencement performance, while Lois was welcomed warmly as the daughter of an active alumnus.

"My God," Tracy said to her as they made their way to the dance floor, "I'm glad your father went to school here and that I was in that play. We at least had something to talk about to the faculty." He danced her over toward the bandstand where Kenny was holding forth with his saxophone and nodded. "There's my roommate," he said, "Kenny Edgers." Lois and Kenny exchanged glances, each taking careful note of the other. "She must be a good date if she can get you to dance," Kenny said to Spence as they disappeared back into the crowd.

Soon they were a foursome—Kenny and Lois, Spence and Lorraine. Tracy was obsessive about acting to the degree that he talked about little else. He signed up for another quarter of Zoology, but otherwise filled his

Transcribing *The Valiant*, Fox Island, Washington, 1921.
(ROBERT B. EDGERS)

schedule with speech and drama classes. Most girls would have found him hard to take, but Olive Lorraine Foat, the petite brunette who played the flamboyant Mrs. Crespigny—all bracelets and bangles and rouge and wax pearls—in *The Truth,* was known campuswide as a deft comedienne who loved the theater. "I was very fond of Spence," she said, "but not in a romantic way. He just was . . . I admired him so for his ability. I loved to play opposite him because you were playing against someone who was solid. I knew the things he believed in, I knew the things he had no patience with . . . I think some of the girls who tried out for plays that he was in hoped that he would pay attention . . . but I don't remember anyone."

Tracy involved himself with the Prom Committee and was elected premier of Alpha Phi Omega, the house fraternity at West Hall. Then Professor Boody urged him to come out for debate: "Spencer, you get in and out of more arguments than any student in this school. You belong on the debating team." The Mask and Wig produced only two plays a year—winter and spring—and each play was good for only one or two performances. Both Spence and Lorraine wanted to do a play a month, but the others weren't sure they could afford the time away from their studies. When they forged ahead with plans for two performances of an obscure one-act called *The Dregs,* the backlash wasn't entirely unexpected.

William Vaughn Moody's *The Great Divide* had been announced as the fall play, but the director would be Professor H. H. Allen, new to Ripon and not at all familiar with Tracy's work. Spence and Lorraine made a pact: they would both try out for the leads, but if one got the lead and the other did not, then neither would do the play. Casting was announced on October 17, 1921. As expected, Lorraine got the part of Ruth Jordan, the female lead in Moody's perennial favorite, but Spence drew only a supporting role, that of Ruth's brother, Philip. Lorraine promptly resigned her part, a calculated act of loyalty to Spence that roiled the Mask and Wig and got everyone talking. "The Dean called me in to question my refusal, and suggested that perhaps the reason Spence didn't get the part was because he had been neglecting his studies. That didn't satisfy me, although I knew that Spence wasn't too enthusiastic about studying. That was when we decided we'd have our own acting company with rehearsals at my house, and we called ourselves The Campus Players."

The following day, the school paper carried the announcement that *The Dregs* had been put aside in favor of *The Valiant.* The latter would be performed by Spencer Tracy and Lorraine Foat at the Municipal Auditorium on Thursday and Friday evenings, October 27 and 28. Working from Tracy's own hunt-and-peck transcription, the Players began the process of nightly rehearsal. *The Valiant* was simple enough to stage, all the action taking place in a prison office, the warden and the chaplain trying to confirm the condemned man's identity just as he is about to die. A girl comes to see him, thinking he may be her long lost brother, but he sends her back to her mother convinced that her brother had died a war hero. The girl's part was meaty enough, laden as it was with stark emotion, but the play really belonged to the actor playing the mysterious prisoner who called himself Dyke.

As a boy Tracy had learned the trick of immersing himself in a part. The hours he spent in the nickelodeon were the equivalent of study, and once he had it, he could replay it in performance—not strictly as the character but the character as filtered through his own set of experiences. He now did the same with the text of the play, imprinting it so thoroughly on his memory he'd never have to reach for a line, a thought, an action. "Because possibly of his military training, perhaps through natural instinct, Tracy always manifested unusual poise," Professor Boody said. "He could stand still, remain in character, and do nothing *but act.*"

Although the theater wasn't filled to capacity as it had been for *The Truth,* the advance word bolstered the crowd considerably from the several hundred who typically turned out for Tom Mix and William S. Hart on Thursday nights. The set was minimal: a desk, a few straight-backed chairs, a water cooler. Jennings Page and Jack Davies, in their respective roles as the warden and the prison chaplain, provided the somber setup, Tracy making his entrance about five minutes into the action. He was calm and cynical, unashamedly guilty of the murder for which he was about to hang. ("The man deserved to be killed; he wasn't fit to live. It was my duty to kill him, and I did it.") And he was steadfast in his refusal to give them his true identity. Then Lorraine appeared, a seventeen-year-old girl thinking the condemned prisoner might be her long lost brother Joe, the man with whom she exchanged long passages of Shakespeare as a child.

Doing his best to convince her that he was not Joe, Tracy launched into his big speech, the concocting of a heroic death in France for a man who bore the name of her brother, selling it with all the conviction and force he could muster. ". . . The Jerries were getting ready for a raid of their own, so they were putting down a box barrage with light guns and howitzers and a few heavies. This officer was lying right in the middle of it. Well, all of a sudden a young fellow dashed out of a trench not far from where I was, and went for that officer . . . The chances were just about a million to one against him, and he must have known it, but he went out just the same . . . Afterward, we got what was left . . . the identification tag was still there . . . and that was the name . . . Joseph Anthony Paris!"

It was a vaudeville moment, pat and heavy-handed, but Tracy managed real conviction where another actor—especially a student—might well have chewed the scenery. Lorraine tearfully withdrew, convinced (as now was the audience) that the man who was about to die was not her brother after all. He waited, and once she was out of earshot, he brought a gasp from the audience by answering from memory the verses she had just spoken to him:

> *Of all the wonders that I yet have heard,*
> *It seems to me most strange that men should fear;*
> *Seeing that death, a necessary end,*
> *Will come when it will come.*

And then, reaching for the lines:

> *Cowards die many times before their death;*
> *The valiant never taste death but once.*

And with head held "proud and high," he walked offstage to his date with the gallows.

The applause was generous. "He loved to do this play," Lorraine said, "because he was trying to keep me from finding out who he was . . . I did cry in [it] and they were real tears, because he was marvelous, just marvelous." The *Days* review on November 1, 1921, described the attendance as "large and appreciative," and Tracy, it said, played the part of the prisoner "in such a masterful way that the audience felt with him the emotions he portrayed." Lorraine, it went on, "added another triumph to her long list of stage successes."

Abandoning any pretense of a medical career, Tracy flunked Zoology that quarter while pulling solid Bs in his English and Speech classes. Clark Graham directed the Mask and Wig productions, but it was Professor Boody who taught Dramatics at Ripon and who introduced him to the mechanics of performance. Boody gave him the process of getting into a part, the analysis of action and character, and the understanding of a play's structure and purpose. He taught the use of the eyes as exhibited in the best motion picture acting and maintained the brow was the actor's chief asset.* "The response of those not talking," he said, "is vastly more important than the actions of the person who holds the stage." Boody's great failing as a teacher of acting was an emphasis on imitation rather than immersion, the notion that a character was assembled from a toolbox of characteristics

---

* Tracy, headstrong, went his own way when Boody's admonitions failed to suit him. "He never used make-up," Ken Edgers remembered, "because of the deep lines in his forehead, even at 20. Also, his eyebrows did not seem to be in the right place for eyebrow accent."

rather than acquired from within. "Never be yourself on stage," he warned. "You are taking a part."

Boody's suggestion that Spence and Lorraine start the Campus Players resulted in an ambitious plan to revive *The Truth* for a statewide tour over the Christmas recess. Elmer "Red" Wagner, functioning as the group's road manager, laid out an itinerary of eleven towns over the space of two weeks, starting in Plymouth on December 22 and finishing up in Berlin on the evening of January 6, 1922. Rehearsals at Lorraine's house were under way by Thanksgiving with first-year student Anna Klein serving as understudy for Ethyl Williams (who was teaching school in Neenah and could only rehearse on weekends). Lorraine remembered Spence eating his way through the entire holiday season: "He liked to go out in our kitchen to talk with my mother and eat all her doughnuts." Mrs. Foat thought Spence likable enough, but puzzling in some respects. "Why does he always come over to go over lines at meal time?" she would ask.

Bad weather dogged the intrepid company most nights, and they arrived in Princeton during a raging blizzard. The tour broke for Christmas, and Spence and Kenny drove down to Milwaukee, where Bill O'Brien, who was attending the Marquette College of Economics, met them. They

On tour with the Campus Players of Ripon College, 1921. Left to right: Evelyn Engelbracht, Ken Edgers, Lorraine Foat, Tracy, Meta Bohlman. Seated: Ethyl Williams. (ROBERT B. EDGERS)

A sampling of the West Hall gang, Ripon College, 1922. Tracy's arm is around his pal Kenny Edgers. (ROBERT B. EDGERS)

regrouped at Ripon on the morning of the twenty-sixth and traveled to Wautoma, where Red Wagner met them at the hotel. Jim Gunderson, father of West Hall officer Coleman Gunderson, treated the cast to supper after the show. "I saw *The Truth* in the movies once," he told Spence by way of a compliment, "and I think you imitated them real swell."*

The next night, at Daly's Theatre in Wisconsin Rapids, the mechanism supporting the curtain broke. It failed to drop at the climax of the play, and the actors had to improvise a graceful way of getting offstage. In Marshfield, the lights failed, throwing the house into an uproar. Tomahawk and Merrill came next, and Ken Edgers noticed that even the smallest of audiences unnerved his pal. "I remember Spence asking the person nearest him as he went on stage for his first appearance in any play to hit him hard between the shoulder blades to get him over his initial stage fright." New Year's Eve was spent in Antigo, the second in Wausau, the fifth in Fond du Lac. By the time they finished up on the sixth, they were no longer a group of amateurs, but

---

* The moving picture version of *The Truth* was filmed in 1920 by Samuel Goldwyn. Madge Kennedy played the part of Becky Warder and Tom Carrigan played Tom.

the seasoned veterans of a whirlwind Chautauqua tour. "I found," Tracy said of the experience, "that acting was good hard work as well as play."

There was one final performance of *The Truth* to be mounted on January 16, a benefit for the American Legion. Anticipation ran high—those who had only heard about the commencement performance wanted to see the play for themselves, while others who were there wanted to see it again. Then there was Red Wagner's announcement in the paper that Ethyl Williams would be making her final appearance before a Ripon audience. The show at the Armory that Monday night sold out, and while the *Ripon Commonwealth* dutifully found Ethyl's performance "masterly," it went on at length about what Tracy had done: "His quiet manner of portraying the deceived husband was characterized by such an air of strong reserved force as to be quite remarkable. If his work in other productions has not already done so, the acting he displayed Monday night deservedly places him as a leader in the dramatic circles of the present student generation."

John and Carrie Tracy arrived for the play in their Wisconsin-built Kissel coupe and found their son talking excitedly about dramatic school. "He wants to be an actor," John said to Kenny Edgers, barely containing his disgust. "Can you imagine that face ever being a matinee idol?" Subsequently there was a family conference with Professor Graham presiding. "As a result," he said, "I wrote Mr. Sargent of the American Academy of Dramatic Arts in New York and he suggested that Tracy appear for a tryout."

The timing couldn't have been better, for the final performance of *The Truth* also marked the last time Spence and Lorraine would share a stage. Directly after the performance, Lorraine left for Boston, where she would spend a year at the Emerson School of Oratory. In later years she would downplay her relationship with Tracy, maintaining it was their love of theatre that had so inexorably glued them together. "He took me to a dance once in a while," she acknowledged, never forgetting how distracted and self-absorbed he could be. "We'd dance once, and he'd say, 'Let's go in the balcony,' and we'd go up there and sit and watch everybody else dance. He wouldn't dance. It was too much effort. And he'd say, 'Let's go down to the greasy spoon and get some food.' And I put up with that because I liked to be in the plays with him. But I didn't date him; I dated other people—boys who danced!"

Clearly there was more to the relationship than just acting; in Lorraine's old age (she lived to be ninety-three) the spark was still there. She was pretty, smart, and Protestant—three things that would always attract him—and she was serious about acting. "I think Spence thought that I was talented," she allowed, "and he liked to play opposite me because we were both very intense about it. He was always Spence, but he also never steered off the track."

She and Tracy had real potential together, but he was never focused on girls so much as his work, and the excitement of finding something he could do well and with unbridled enthusiasm was greater than any sexual attraction. He was also careless in his manner of dress and oblivious to the interests of others. "He had a sweater," she said, "and I think it was the same sweater that he wore all the time—it was always out in the elbows. He didn't look very tidy on campus. He didn't need [to look like that], but he was so independent . . . He didn't care whether anyone else liked him or not. He really didn't ever seem to crave the attention of people there in college."

It wasn't Spence her parents objected to so much as the idea of his being an actor. Lorraine's father was a carryover from the days when boarding-houses routinely posted signs reading NO ACTORS and traveling theatrical companies were regarded as if they were roving bands of Gypsies. Certainly the stage was no place for a respectable young woman, and Spence, it was feared, would drag her in that direction. Then Lorraine got to the meat of it: "My family had a very strong feeling . . . we were not Catholics, and my dad wouldn't feel that it was a proper marriage. At that time there were very few people who crossed over. You think nothing of it now, but . . ."

And so it was. A week after Lorraine's departure for Emerson, Spencer Tracy was elected to Theta Alpha Phi and simultaneously called an end to the Campus Players. He never acted on a Ripon stage again.

Though he came to Ripon as a "flunk-out"—arriving two or three weeks into the second quarter—Tracy quickly earned a reputation as a ringleader of sorts, taking a key role in West Hall initiation rites and bolstering the school's well-earned reputation for hazing. ("Frosh! Go upstairs and warm a toilet seat for me!") As premier of Alpha Phi Omega, he once put the owner of a pet rabbit on trial for paternity. Another time, he indulged a newfound taste for cigars by proposing a series of "smokers" between rival houses, permitting freshmen to provide both eats and smokes while upperclassmen feted the likes of Silas Evans and Clark Graham. He generally spoke on such occasions, ribbing the guests, deadpan, and picking arguments with some of the more academically talented students.

Tracy's zeal for one-upmanship found a constructive outlet in Professor Boody's debate class, where it soon dawned on him that debate was just another facet of performance. He joined Pi Kappa Delta, and when tryouts were announced for the intercollegiate season, he went after a spot on the Eastern team as aggressively as he would pursue the lead in a play. "There were two places to be filled," Curtis MacDougall, a West Hall journalism major, recalled, "and competition was quite severe. The candidates were grouped into teams of three, and there was really a tournament with judging. My team had on it Tracy and Newton Jones, another fraternity brother. We won. We went undefeated, we beat everybody else. And I'm sure a great deal of the reason was Tracy's platform performance."

Boody had come to the college in 1915 with a mandate to raise its forensic profile. He did so by quadrupling the number of annual debates and building an admirable record of "strong colleges met." He needed three men for a home team, but the most coveted slots were those for a tour of Eastern campuses, debating the Veterans' Adjusted Compensation Bill then before Congress. Given the press attention the team would draw, they were also the slots in which he wanted his most able performers. On December 2, 1921, Boody announced his choices: J. Harold Bumby, who had been opener for Ripon the previous two seasons, Curtis MacDougall, and Tracy, whose "forceful presentation" and complementary stage experience won him a place on the team despite the dean's concerns over his grades.

Deep into rehearsals for *The Truth,* Tracy took his selection for the team in stride until Clark Graham's letter to Franklin Sargent of the American Academy brought forth the offer of an audition in New York. At once the tour took on a whole new significance, and it was Graham who encouraged Tracy to use Sada Cowan's two-character dialogue *Sintram of Skagerrak* as his tryout piece. Spence and Ethyl Williams had performed the brief one-act as a benefit for the Harwood Scholarship Fund over the Christmas holidays. Sintram's lyrical effusions of love for the sea struck Graham as ideal for showcasing the way his student could handle difficult dialogue while managing the build in intensity that brings the play to its tragic conclusion.

On February 21, 1922, chapel period was given over to a kind of pep rally for the college debaters, Tracy earnestly urging the student body to "keep the home fires burning" while three of their number were "clashing verbally" with Eastern collegians. They left the next day in the midst of a terrific snowstorm and stopped at the Auditorium Hotel in Chicago. Lionel Barrymore was appearing in *The Claw,* and they all went to see it. "I remember that night Tracy emphatically saying that he was going to go on the stage," MacDougall said. "He wanted to be an actor."

The next morning they were off for Bloomington, where they would face Illinois Wesleyan at Amie Chapel in "Old Main," the university's Hedding Hall. A reception committee met them at the train and were genuinely solicitous over the course of their stay. The Wesleyan team failed to establish a case and Tracy, in his first intercollegiate debate appearance, helped win a two-to-one decision over Illinois with a strong rebuttal. "He never spoke a line that somebody, usually me, hadn't written for him," MacDougall said. "I wrote his main speech, and we wrote out his potential rebuttal pieces, short answers to points which we were almost certain the opposition would bring up. And, during the debate, we'd sit at the platform, and when one of

Lionel Barrymore in *The Claw.*
(AUTHOR'S COLLECTION)

those matters came up, that we thought Spence could well handle, we'd toss a slip of paper over to him as a reminder and he'd go to it brilliantly."

The team headed for Boston, passing through Cleveland, Buffalo, and Niagara Falls on their way to Hamilton, Ontario, where Spence and "Mac" went to church that Sunday while Bumby visited some relatives in Burlington. They spent the twenty-seventh in Montreal, their last stop before Portland, and Tracy, MacDougall remembered, "asked Bumby and me to wait while he went into the big cathedral there, where we waited and we waited and we waited. He finally came out, and he announced that the result was in the bag, that he had spent the time praying that we would win the debate at Bowdoin [College]. We went on blithely to Maine."

The team met Bowdoin at Brunswick on March 1 and lost the decision two to one. Tracy, despite the loss, was ranked first in excellence by the judges and received special mention in the Portland newspapers. The next night they met Colby College at Waterville, where they were royally received but handed a nondecision by the judges.

Fittingly, Mac and Harold both picked up colds at Brunswick and spent a full day in Boston without leaving the hotel. Spence took in the city, walking off nervous energy, anxious and impatient to get on to New York. He caught up with Lorraine Foat, told her of the American Academy audition and all it meant to him. "I know at the time his father thought it was disgusting. A sissy sort of thing to do . . . [But] Spence was so determined to do it, even if he didn't have a cent. He was going to go to New York, he was going to make something [of himself] . . . He wanted to get ahead."

Tracy's first glimpse of New York City was the cavernous interior of Grand Central Terminal and the vaulted blue ceiling of the main concourse. Stepping out into the crisp night air at Forty-second and Vanderbilt, he could see the electric white glow of the Times Square theater district four blocks to the west. Marilyn Miller was in *Sally* at the New Amsterdam that night. *Six Cylinder Love* was at the Sam H. Harris, and Helen Hayes was appearing in *To the Ladies* at the Liberty. Other theaters on other streets held Roland Young, Estelle Winwood, Alice Brady, Blanche Yurka, Frank Fay, Laurette Taylor, Florence Eldridge, Lenore Ulric, Fred Astaire, Lynne Overman, Violet Heming, and Henry Hull.

At Spence's insistence, the boys took a four-dollar room at the Waldorf-Astoria and got directions to a nearby speakeasy. The fare was Italian, the air stifling, the service poor. Spence delighted in the widened eyes of his small-town teammates, neither of whom had ever been outside the state of Wisconsin. It was the first time Mac, for instance, had ever seen a woman smoke a cigarette, and he was so scandalized by the experience he couldn't enjoy his meal. A lot of walking got done that weekend amid the orange juice and hot dog stands that populated Broadway in the wake of Prohibition, the off-the-arm cafeterias, the phony auction parlors, the medicine shows and two-bit photographers, the cut-rate haberdasheries, the drugstores and bookstores that lined both sides of the street between Forty-second and Fifty-third. Through it all, Tracy's mind was never far from his appointment with Franklin Sargent on Monday, and he insisted that Bumby accompany him.

The entrance to the American Academy of Dramatic Arts was at the northeast corner of Carnegie Hall, Fifty-seventh Street and Seventh Avenue, a modest portal alongside the grand Italianate entrance to America's preeminent concert hall. The president's office was on the first floor, as it had been since the academy's move to the hall in 1896. Franklin Haven Sargent had founded the AADA as the Lyceum School of Acting in 1884, the first institution in the United States created expressly for the purpose of dramatic instruction. Now sixty-six, Sargent was still at the helm, personally passing on all admissions and teaching the course in Classic Drama that was the cornerstone of the school's curriculum. A taciturn man, Sargent asked Tracy if he had brought "anything like a skit." Tracy produced his copy of *Sintram,* and when he suggested the passage would work best with two actors, Sargent agreed to read the lines of Gunhilde. Bumby settled back to watch as Tracy assumed the posture of the brooding Sintram, frail and listless.

I have always lived here, as you know, little comrade . . . In that old house just the other side of the cliff, I was born; weighed down with riches and an untarnished name. My people had intermarried closely . . . no strong, vital peasant's blood ran through my veins . . . My mother's bedroom faced the ocean, so the first sound which reached my ears was the moan of the sea. My mother died when I was born, so the sea became my mother and sang her lullabies to me until I fell asleep, stilled by her soft crooning . . .

As Tracy spoke, Sargent scribbled notes on an evaluation form: Personality "sensitive & masculine" . . . Stage Presence "good (not technically)" . . . Voice "untrained but natural" . . . Pronunciation "Fair" . . . Reading "a little declamatory yet sincere" . . . Spontaneity "good" . . . Versatility and Characterization "passable" . . . Distinction "good" . . . Pantomime "crude but manly" . . . Dramatic Instinct "fair underdeveloped" . . . Intelligence "good" . . . Imagination "good." When he finished, Sargent gave Tracy a long piercing look and said, "Yes, yes, yes."

He initiated a discussion of finances: tuition for the Academy's Junior Course was $400, playbooks and makeup extra. Board in the immediate area would cost ten to twenty dollars a week, maybe more. Tracy said his father disapproved of his becoming an actor and was unlikely to cover the cost. Sargent, in turn, suggested a scholarship might be possible, something he rarely offered a first-year student. Tracy, he noted, was medium-dark in coloring, well proportioned, and in "very good" physical condition—a very masculine applicant for a program where such types were rare. At the bottom of the sheet he wrote "Acceptable Oct. Junior F.H.S."

There were four days left to the recreational end of the trip, but they weren't days to be wasted in New York or Washington, D.C. Back at Ripon, Kenny Edgers had fallen desperately ill, and Tracy seized the excuse to return home at once. He found Kenny recovering, and they started walking to build up his strength, five miles a day. Spence told him about Sargent and the academy and the offer of the scholarship, as if that might swing some weight when it came to his father. And, in the end, Lorraine thought that it might: "His father, I know, finally said, 'You can go for a year, and if at the end of that time you haven't hit it off big, then you will come back and go into business with me.' Spence spoke of it as something that he was being indulged in, and he was determined to show his father that he was going to be a success."

Tracy presided over his last fraternity meeting on March 14, 1922, and returned to Milwaukee that same day. His six months as premier had left Alpha Phi Omega with new bylaws, new ceremonials, a new constitution, and thirteen new members.

A month after he left, Tracy won the degree of proficiency, order of debate, in Pi Kappa Delta. The announcement of his departure in *Ripon College Days* concluded with the words: "His ability will be sorely missed next fall."

Spencer Tracy entered the American Academy of Dramatic Arts during its thirty-eighth year. The junior class consisted of 142 pupils, the majority women who fancied themselves stageworthy and who, more importantly, had the tuition and wherewithal to keep the academy going. Only a small portion of its graduates ever went professional, but those who did enjoyed long and distinguished careers. Among the academy's past students, William Powell '13 was appearing in *Bavu* at the Earl Carroll Theatre, and Edward G. Robinson (also '13) was at the Plymouth in *The Deluge.* Howard Lindsay, who staged *To the Ladies,* was an academy graduate, as was Dale Carnegie '12, who developed his famous course immediately upon leaving the school. In England, Marion Lorne '04 was starring in the plays of her husband, Walter C. Hackett. In California, Cecil B. DeMille '00 was directing movies for Famous Players.

On the faculty were playwright-director Edward Goodman; actors Lemuel Josephs, Joseph Adelman, and Philip Loeb; and actor-director Edwin R. Wolfe. George Currie taught Physical Training, Pantomime, and Life Study; Wellington Putnam, Vocal Training; James J. Murray, Fencing and Stage Dueling. All were presided over by the redoubtable Charles Jehlinger, who directed the senior plays and gave an occasional lecture. "Jehli," as he was known to nearly everyone, had been with Franklin Sargent from the beginning in that he was in the school's very first graduating class. Twelve years later, Jehlinger returned as faculty, concurrent with the school's move to Carnegie Hall. He didn't teach any of the junior classes, but his presence was felt throughout the academy, a martinet of sorts where Sargent could be gloomy and reclusive.

Tracy found a room on West Seventy-sixth Street, around the corner from the New-York Historical Society, and reported for classes on the morning of April 3, 1922. He found himself plunged almost immediately into an intensive regimen of vocal and physical training, covering everything from hygiene and makeup to dancing, fencing, and diction. Defects in speech, projection, and posture were identified and corrective exercises prescribed. Control and resonance of the voice came next, breathing, word colorings, and accents; physical presence and poise, terminology and workmanship; the mechanics of business—standing, walking, listening.

The building itself was a stimulating environment, Andrew Carnegie having poured $2 million—roughly nine-tenths of the total cost—into what was conceived as New York's finest concert venue. The Main Hall was accompanied by two smaller auditoriums—a recital hall underneath and a chamber music hall adjacent. After its opening in 1891, Carnegie added two wings of studio offices and apartments above and around the structure, removing the original roof and building over it. The spaces were typically tall, with enormous windows and skylights; some studios (which often doubled as living spaces) ran the entire length of the building. Artists, such as Frederick E. Church and Edwin Blashfield, shared the building with architects, writers, photographers, dance studios, voice coaches, and the academy, which occupied the first floor of the northeast tower and parts of three upper floors. There was a large room with a raised platform on which the students were taught dancing, fencing, and how to fall gracefully down the steps. The doors to the rooms were usually left open, especially in the summer, and the sounds of piano lessons, recitals, dance workshops, and play rehearsals mingled in the hallways. Spaces were constantly being vacated and upgraded; the walls were eight feet thick in some places.

Two months into the term, Tracy embarked on a campaign to lure Lorraine Foat to New York. He had the academy send her a catalog, then followed up with a letter: "This really is quite the place, the only place, in fact, for one who wishes to follow the stage. Look over the catalog and if there is anything you wish to know further, let me know and I'll try to give you the dope. You had better come here, Lorraine—you won't be sorry. The school is recognized by all theatrical people, and nearly all the present stars of the stage are graduates. I have been working mighty hard but enjoy it very much, and I have been encouraged very greatly since coming here."

Lorraine responded that she'd come in the fall, hesitant to risk her father's disapproval. Of course, there was no shortage of girls at the school, and acting, if only in character, had become Tracy's way of relating to them. Sorting through the choices, he took up with a red-haired Texan named Olga Goodman. She was more serious than a lot of the other girls, certainly more talented, but Spence, as she remembered him, was "a very ambitious student" who "actually had little time for fun, and little money." Their dates consisted of "sandwiches made up at a delicatessen near Carnegie Hall and rides atop a Fifth Avenue bus."

The matter of money was a sensitive subject, Spence having no real talent for either making or preserving it. His father had agreed to cover his housing costs—no mean concession—and Carroll, who had embarked on a sales career, slipped a little "happy cabbage" into the letters he wrote. It was, however, Bill O'Brien who knew that Wisconsin legislators had authorized cash bonus payments to Badger State veterans, and that they had created an education option that paid up to $1,080 if a vet wanted to continue in school. "We began pulling wires, told the Board we couldn't get the training we wanted in Wisconsin," O'Brien said. Bill had played both football and *Charley's Aunt* at Marquette, and when his uncle Charlie (who managed Manhattan's Union Club) invited both him and his mother to spend the summer of 1920 in New York City, he did so gladly and with an eye toward finding work as an actor. "I remained in New York and managed to get on in the merry-merry (a musical comedy chorus), but, after all, I knew that hipping the ballet was not going to teach me to be a Booth or a Barrett."

That fall, while Spence was working to complete high school at West Division, Bill auditioned for Franklin Sargent and was accepted into the program. Then, shortly after his twenty-first birthday, Bill's father fell ill and he was forced to return to Milwaukee before taking a single day of instruction. O'Brien entered the Marquette School of Economics instead, but when he heard of Tracy's own audition and acceptance at the academy, he finished out the semester with the intention of joining Spence in New York.

The money from the state was doled out at the rate of thirty dollars a month, which would enable the two men to survive only if they shared a room. "We darn near starved there several times," O'Brien said. "Spence wouldn't take any more from his family than mine could send me because he wanted us to be on an equal footing." Bill arrived during the summer of 1922, aiming to start at the academy in October. To commemorate the occasion, he assumed the name of his paternal grandfather and became, for purposes of the stage, Pat O'Brien.

They found quarters on West End Avenue between Ninety-eighth and Ninety-ninth, one block over from Broadway on the Upper West Side. "It was two steep shaky flights up," O'Brien wrote, "but as Spencer said, 'It has a ceiling.'" Tracy took Pat to a tearoom where the students met for lunch, and in short order Pat was seeing one of Spence's classmates, a blue-eyed gal from San Francisco named Dolores Graves.

At the academy, Tracy progressed to dramatic analysis, life study, pantomime, and vocal interpretation, playing scenes in the middle of the classroom with other hopeful and impossibly earnest young actors. The term would end with "examination plays" that would give each student at least three good opportunities before faculty to show, after twenty-four weeks of hard work, what he or she could do with a straight part, a comedy part, and a character part. The glut of one-acts came in late August, the students taking full charge of lights, makeup, and costuming, and continued unabated through the first week of September. To nobody's surprise, Tracy was judged fit to enter the senior class and thereby join the academy stock company, as were fifteen others, among them Sterling Holloway, Kay Johnson, Muriel Kirkland, George Meeker, Monroe Owsley, Ernest Woodward, and Thelma Ritter.

The senior course was the intensive and continuous production of plays, and every week brought a new text, a new part, a new audience of students, instructors, and invited guests. The first three months were spent in the Carnegie Lyceum, the choral space under the Main Hall that Franklin Sargent commandeered upon his arrival in 1896. Seating eight hundred on two levels, it was blasted out of some of the hardest rock on earth. There were no flies, so the scenery had to be slid into place from the wings, but the Carnegie Lyceum had an intimacy few New York theaters could match. When full (which was seldom), the exchange of energy between the actors and the audience—"that breathing, panting mass creature," as O'Brien referred to it—was extraordinary. The last three months were given over to the mounting of the best of the productions as matinees at Daniel Frohman's Lyceum Theatre on Forty-fifth Street, where the students could get the experience of working in a major commercial theater, and where the audience would be composed of members of the general public.

In charge of it all was Jehlinger, a flinty old man with large piercing eyes and a voice that could slice through masonry. His vociferous criticisms inspired both awe and terror in his students, and occasionally even murderous impulses. (After a particularly stinging tirade, Edward G. Robinson is said to have heaved a table at him, knocking him flat.) Jehli unnerved almost everyone, yet he never got to Tracy—at least to the point where Tracy would admit as much.

There was, in fact, much in Jehlinger's teachings that confirmed Tracy's own instinctive technique, principal among them Jehli's insistence that the character and the actor must always be one and the same. ("You can't have two brains in one head or you are a monster!") The actor was the servant of the character, Jehlinger taught, and it was up to the character to run things, to make the performance inevitable. His mantra was "give in" and he repeated it again and again: "Don't worry, just yield. It will all handle itself if you surrender . . . Human impulse is the only thing that counts, not stage directions . . . Give in to your instincts. Instinct must rule in performance, not judgment . . . So long as your mind is on *acting* instead of the thoughts of the character, you make no progress . . . *Obey your impulses* . . . It is better to be crude by overdoing than to be negative. Obey your impulses at any cost. Don't fear mistakes. *Be fearless!* Yield! Obey!"

Tracy's first appearance before a New York audience took place on October 20, 1922, when he acted in a curtain-raiser called *The Wedding Guests* at the Carnegie Lyceum. Three days later, on October 23, Lorraine came for her tryout and found that he was still keyed up: "Here was Spence, pacing up and down in front, watching. Why was I late? 'You can't afford to miss this time that was all set up for you.' And when I got out of this taxi, 'It must have cost you a fortune! You should have come on the streetcar!' So we went right up and had the audition. I remember where I sat . . . I was kind of nervous about that. And then [Mr. Sargent] said, 'Do this scene,' and we did the whole play." The play, of course, was *The Valiant,* and once again came the tension and the desperate seeking, and once again came the tears. Sargent didn't have to pretend; he was genuinely impressed. He wrote "good" for most every line item on Lorraine's audition sheet. It was, in fact, an altogether better evaluation than Tracy himself had received some seven months earlier. She was acceptable for the January course, Sargent affirmed, and he said, in fact, that he would like to meet the man who trained such outstanding prospects.

Tracy was relieved, even jubilant, and to celebrate they joined up with Pat and Dolores and went to 790 West End for hot dogs. "We didn't have anything very fancy," Lorraine recalled. "We had to climb a flight of stairs to get to this apartment these two boys were living in, and they did use the gas flame in the gas lights to cook their hot dogs. They didn't have a regular stove. I was so impressed with these two fellows trying to cook a meal for us. We had a wonderful time talking; Pat was fun to be with."

They took her back to the train with the expectation that she would be back after the first of the year, when she would see Spence onstage at the Lyceum and aspire to the same thing for herself. Pat started at the academy just as Spence was rehearsing *The Wooing of Eve,* a full-length play in which he had been assigned the second male lead. In quick succession, he did *The Importance of Being Earnest* (with Sterling Holloway in the lead); Milne's *Wurzel-Flummery,* a whimsical one-act; and *Knut at Roeskilde,* a two-act tragedy. O'Brien, meanwhile, immersed himself in the junior course, drawing on Spence's prior experience and his availability to run lines. "Pat and I used to read lines to each other, rearrange the furniture and pace back and forth doing bits of business as if we were in front of the footlights," Tracy recounted. "The other roomers used to yell at us to shut up."

The total immersion demanded by the program was only intensified by a profound lack of money. "That $30 a month didn't go very far," Tracy said. "I was broke several days before the end of each month. So I studied dramatics as I'd never studied anything before in my life. Always in the back of my mind was the idea that I'd never have enough money to finish the course, and that I'd better learn all I could as fast as possible."

Times became especially desperate toward Christmas, when Pat and Spence made the decision to forgo food altogether in order to see John Barrymore in *Hamlet*. They went a total of four times. "Dear God," said Pat, "what an actor!" Tracy once told actor Robert Ryan he would wait near the stage door of the Broadhurst Theatre just to watch Lionel Barrymore leave at the end of the evening. "He couldn't afford to see him act on stage," as Ryan remembered it, "but at least he could watch and see him walk out of the theater."

After missing eight meals in a row, Tracy decided he had to do something. "I didn't know how to go about getting a stage job, though I'd have taken anything. I hit every agent on Broadway, and just about every showhouse in town. Then, the afternoon of the third day, I went down to the Theatre Guild and applied for a job. I must have looked like a deserving cause, for the directors gave me a chance. I was to be a $15 a week robot in the play *R.U.R.* and I drew $1 eating money in advance. I went out and bought the thickest steak I could find."

Tracy made his professional debut on the night of January 1, 1923, when he stepped onstage at the Frazee Theatre and wordlessly decorated the third act of *R.U.R.,* a fantasy of mechanized society whose title stood for "Rossum's Universal Robots." Within days, Pat had become a super as well: "Spence and I were two of the guys who just stood there in the play while some other guy cried out in stentorian tones, 'We are the masters of the world.' And then he said, 'March,' and that's all we did." After a few weeks, Tracy was given a line to read and his salary was raised to twenty dollars a week. "This was a definite step up to wealth," said Pat. "It sure aided the exchequer."

Baseball and theater entrepreneur Henry H. Frazee had assumed management of *R.U.R.* when it moved to his eponymous theater on Forty-second Street in November 1922, and he planned to tour it on the subway circuit after it had played itself out. There was, however, still life in the show when Frazee was forced to close on February 17, 1923, to make way for another play. With a $9,000 week in the till—the Frazee was a small house—*R.U.R.* began weeklong stands at theaters such as the Bronx Opera House and Teller's Shubert, where popular prices and daily matinees enabled him to wring every last remaining dollar from the play. Cast changes were inevitable, and when Domis Plugge stepped away from his role as the first robot, Tracy moved up, garnering four lines and a twenty-five-dollar increase in salary. "Boy, I thought I was really hot stuff when I got that first

Graduation portrait, American
Academy of Dramatic Arts.
(AADA)

raise," he said. "I gave the doorman of the theater a dollar tip on the way out that night. Many times later I wished I could get my hands on it."

There was a matinee in Queens to play the day the academy's graduation exercises took place, and Tracy regretfully missed the experience of having his diploma personally handed him by Franklin Sargent. The scholarship Sargent had arranged for Tracy had brought a young man from promising amateur to trained professional, someone who was now prepared to earn a shaky living on the stage and who, with time, luck, and development, might one day become a star. Some forty years later, when asked to sum up what the AADA had done for him, Tracy responded with the following: "I shall always be grateful to the American Academy for what I was taught there—by Mr. Jehlinger and the other teachers—the value of sincerity and simplicity, unembellished and unintellectualized."

Pat O'Brien was still at the academy, the junior course having another month yet to run, when Spence began scanning the papers on a daily basis. *R.U.R.* was a job, but it was hardly acting, and Tracy needed to consider his next move. Time and again he had been told the best education for a young actor was to land a spot in a stock company, mastering a play a week and acting all manner of roles. It was demanding, unforgiving, lowly paid work, but those who could do it and flourish and eventually rise above it were literally ready for anything. March was early for summer companies, which usually got under way in June, but the trades were carrying items about a new company going into White Plains, a mere thirty miles outside of New York City, where the long-shuttered Palace Theatre had been taken by Leonard Wood, son of the famous general. As *R.U.R.* began its last week on the subway circuit, Tracy took the bold step of wiring the new manager—collect.

"I will always have a soft spot in my heart for Leonard Wood, Jr.," he later said. "He is the only man I ever knew who would answer a collect telegram, and one asking for a job at that. He wired me back to report at White Plains, New York, and started me at $20."

CHAPTER 4

The Best Goddamned Actor

It was to Michigan that Spencer Tracy returned as Selena Royle's leading man in the summer of 1924. But his ultimate destination, the one always front and center in his mind, was New York. Playing with actors of Selena's caliber kept him on his game, and, happily, Mr. Wright had plans to sustain the Broadway Players during the winter hiatus in Grand Rapids when the Powers Theatre was given over to touring shows and holiday pageants.

In the days just after the turn of the century, when Wright was press agent for Henry W. Savage, the New York borough of Brooklyn had a reputation as an extraordinarily good stock town, supporting as it did both the Spooner family of actors at the Park Avenue Theatre and Corse Payton's renowned company, which originated the ten-twenty-thirty scale of pricing and gave two shows a day at Payton's Lee Avenue theater. The Spooners and Payton were long gone by 1924, but the reputation lingered and attracted Wright to the notion of leasing the Montauk Theatre on Livingston Street and moving his company to Brooklyn until the Powers was once again available.

In recent times, the Montauk had housed road attractions and actor Walter Hampden in repertory. Two competing companies, the Alhambra Players (at the Loew's house of the same name) and the James Carroll Players at the Fifth Avenue, were already established, but Wright was banking on Selena Royle's undeniable appeal to trump the competition. He limited his initial commitment for the shuttered Montauk to four weeks, but held an option on the balance of the season if Selena and the company got over as hoped.

The Broadway Players closed in Grand Rapids on September 15, 1924, ending their twenty-one-week season with a net loss of about $7,000—half of which was borne by Harry G. Sommers, who held the long-term lease on the theater. Tracy, Selena Royle, Arthur Kohl, and the other remaining players left for New York the next morning, where they would have less than a week to get the first play of the new season on its feet.

Renamed the Montauk Players, the company opened on Monday, September 22, but it wasn't until the second week of the stand that they got much attention. Selena took star billing in *Anna Christie* opposite Frank Shannon (from the original Broadway production) and Tracy played the relatively minor role of a longshoreman in Johnny the Priest's waterfront saloon. As was now typical for a Wright company, the production was exemplary ("a credit to dramatic stock," as *Billboard* put it) and Selena's handling of the part was everything it was supposed to be, widely praised and fervently applauded.

After a couple of weeks, Louise, who had stopped off in New Castle, arrived in Brooklyn with the baby. She found Spence, used to lead roles, biding his time as Wright did everything possible to draw patrons to the Montauk.

Selena signed on to a Broadway tryout as Wright knew she might, given that she had refused to play the winter in Grand Rapids (or any stock for that matter) and his choice of Brooklyn had been in part an accommodation in creating for her a New York showcase. The crowds weren't there as they had been in Grand Rapids, though, and so when her four-week guarantee expired, she stepped away under the most diplomatic of terms, promising to return if the new play failed to work out as she hoped.

The following week, Tracy was back playing leads, first in *Chicken Feed,* which had been a modest hit on Broadway the previous season, then in *Seven Keys to Baldpate,* the old George M. Cohan warhorse, and finally in *The Bat,* which proved so popular it was held a second week, all opposite Selena's replacement, actress Georgia Backus. As the season wore on, the Tracys grew to appreciate Brooklyn as a place were they could live as a family, Spence working long hours but without the travel and the financial insecurities that were routinely part of a young actor's life. They were, in fact, so contented in Brooklyn they never once crossed the bridge into Manhattan the entire time they were there. Louise stayed home with Johnny, just coming to the theater on Mondays to see the new play. "I [was] a hard critic," she said. "At night when he was in stock, after we were married, he'd go through scenes at home. I'd cue him and I was always honest. I had to be. I'd tell him what I didn't like and why. His reaction? He'd get mad, but I know I helped him in many instances, [because] he'd change a characterization. I was ahead of him in experience, but he went up very fast."

Thanksgiving week, when most companies were playing "old boys" (*Way Down East* and *The Old Homestead* and other cheap or royalty-free properties), Wright gamely programmed *The First Year*, Frank Craven's hit comedy, then followed it with Cohan's *A Prince There Was* and *The Breaking Point*, a new play by Mary Roberts Rinehart, the author of *The Bat*. For Christmas, he revived *Uncle Tom's Cabin*, augmenting the production with "pickaninnies, jubilee singers, and dancers," all of whom paraded daily down Livingston Street. Nothing in the way of ballyhoo seemed to work for very long though, and by the first week of January, Wright was papering the town with twofers and looking ahead to March and the company's return to Grand Rapids.

In all, it was a bruising season, costly and unprofitable, but when the Montauk Players closed on March 7, 1925, they had played all twenty-two weeks of their commitment, something of which everyone in the company was justifiably proud. *Variety* subsequently ran an item summarizing the extraordinary season and its various participants under the headline BROOKLYN NO LONGER MECCA FOR STOCK.

Mercifully, there was considerably more time to make the jump back to Grand Rapids, Wright having set their opening at the Powers for Easter week, giving his company a well-earned interval after forty-three weeks of continuous work. The Tracys went back to Milwaukee, where they could stop with John and Carrie and go easy on their finances. "I don't think either of us were too good with the money," Louise admitted, thinking back on that period. "If I have a dollar, I can live on it. If I have a dollar to spend, I'll spend it . . . We were always broke after a run. There was never enough." Moreover, salaries were flat in Grand Rapids, where another company had entrenched itself during Wright's six-month absence.

The Washington Players specialized in broad melodramas at popular prices, but it was beginning to look as if the Wright company was facing a cruel replay of the Brooklyn debacle on their home turf, and prices were held to a top of $1.10 to counter the competition. There was also the matter of Selena Royle, who demanded a "general utilitywoman" as part of her deal for another season with Papa Wright. To hold the line on costs, the first few shows would be repeats of the most popular plays of the Montauk season, all using scenery trucked in from Brooklyn. The Tracys settled back in at the Browning, and Spence, now officially leading man for the company, was looking forward to a relatively carefree summer. "My salary was steady," he said, "and it seemed things had opened up for us at last." He was in rehearsals for the first play of the new season the day Louise, having put the baby down for a nap, made a horrifying discovery.

She and Spence were going out that night, and after a while it occurred to her that if Johnny napped too long, the babysitter might have trouble getting him to sleep. "I went out on the sleeping porch, calling to him," she said. "Accidentally as I went through, the door slammed. John never moved. I stopped right where I was and called him again. Took a few steps closer. Called again." She couldn't say what prompted her, for at other times she had touched his crib, gently, unconsciously, or him, and watched him awaken. Now she stood motionless beside his crib, and purposely she did not touch it. "Johnny," she said softly, soberly. No response. "Johnny," she said, now with more volume and intensity. Again no response. "Johnny!" she shouted, and still no movement. "Then I touched him and he opened his eyes and smiled at me.

"I knew, of course, our child was deaf."

She was, she said, terror-stricken at first, then a curious wave of relief swept over her. "It was rather like awakening from a nightmare," she wrote.

Such a thing could not be. There was no reason. One reads about such things, but they did not happen to people one knew. I knew of no deafness ever having existed in either my husband's family or my own. More substantial arguments rushed to mind. John had a perfectly natural laugh and cry. I remembered he had had all the tiny baby's first cooing, chirping sounds—those heavenly little early morning sounds. He would lie there, gurgle, wiggle his whole body ecstatically after each effort, then suddenly burst forth again, adding an extra note or quaver in an effort to top the last one. And, as I looked down now into those clear, bright blue eyes and that smiling little face, it did not seem possible that he could not hear. But I could not still the cold, dispassionate voice within me which replied, "All these are but hopes, the straws at which drowning people clutch. He *is* deaf."

Over the next few days she tested him incessantly, and each day strengthened her conviction that he heard nothing. She didn't tell Spence, wanting to spare him the news as long as possible. Besides, she could think of no gentle way of telling him. "Perhaps, when it became necessary to do so, I would know of something that could be done—some treatment, an operation. At least I hoped to have more control over my emotions and some philosophy worked out which might help to soften for him that first shock."

The Broadway Players began their third season at the Powers on the night of April 12, 1925, the house "packed as it has been packed but few times the past season." Tracy was greeted warmly as he took the stage in the title role of *The Nervous Wreck,* as were William Laveau, Halliam Bosworth, and Herbert Treitel, all favorites from the 1924 season. (Director John Ellis, familiar from numerous character parts, slipped so seamlessly into his role that he went completely unnoticed.) Reporting that Tracy had the audience in "constant roars" from his first entrance, Clarence Dean went on to suggest that twenty-two weeks in Brooklyn had knocked the rough edges off a particularly promising newcomer: "Mr. Tracy has gained in poise, in ease, and natural utterance since last seen here, and is therefore more convincing. It is plain to be seen that Mr. Tracy is going to be a big favorite." The same issue of the *Grand Rapids Herald* carried an item that said the Washington Players were initiating a policy at the Isis Theatre of giving away "groceries and things."

Spence unwound after the show, usually at the Greek's, a little coffee place that served exquisite popcorn, or occasionally at the local speakeasy, a blind pig near Campau Square that kept him out long past midnight. "No amount of arguing could get him into the Pantland Hotel, then the town's top-ranking after-theatre spot," said his friend Al Rathbone, who went by "A.D." and who, along with actor George Fleming, formed the nucleus of a group. "He hated the idea of walking into a public place and having people point him out as their leading man." Going out was a way of connecting with other men; it was fun, routine, a release after the pressure of a demanding performance. A drink made him more comfortable around other people—women especially—but he was the son of an alcoholic, the grandson of another.

Growing up, alcohol, like sex, was never part of the family discussion, and both held a mysterious allure. There was no rite of passage when Spence had his first pint in his dad's company. And then, of course, in being Irish—even half-Irish—drinking was expected, part of the identity of all adult males. If one indulged to the point of drunkenness, it was not so much frowned upon as thought natural and, to a degree, celebrated. Where Spence got in trouble was when he drank before a performance, when sociability wasn't a motivating factor but steadying the nerves was—and what little drinking he did made him wildly unpopular. "I think the naughtiest thing he ever did was take Halliam Bosworth's toupee off onstage one time," said Emily Deming, newly installed as Selena Royle's nineteen-year-old dresser. "Of course, it was supposed to be an accident, but I saw him do it. Halliam never forgave him . . . That was one of the times when he'd had a little too much to drink."

His cutting up onstage embarrassed Louise, who couldn't abide unprofessional behavior. She also wanted him home at night after the show, though it was typically hours before he could get to sleep. "I remember once when he was really drunk on stage," said Deming, recalling the opening performance of *Grounds for Divorce,* the second play of the season. "He and Louise had a flaming row, and he got blind drunk, really. He was good with his lines, but he blew up that night a couple of times." Selena, Deming remembered, was boiling mad "because he 'went up' and spoiled her lines. Once badly. That was one of the times I was pressed in as cue." The Powers was an old opera house dating from the 1870s, and Emily had to throw cues from the prompter's box down front of the stage. The crowd noticed, as did Dean, the *Herald*'s unfailingly diplomatic reviewer, who said Tracy had made much of his role of an eminent divorce lawyer "in spite of a very inconvenient indisposition."

Louise confided her fear of Johnny's deafness to Emily, who occasionally babysat for the Tracys and who urged her to have him examined at the Blodgett Home for Children, an orphanage in the East Hills neighborhood of Grand Rapids. The pediatrician who saw the boy was unwilling to say much—the baby was only ten months old—and suggested she take him to a specialist. Louise made frequent trips across Lake Michigan so the Tracys could dote on their new grandchild, and she realized it would be hard to get Johnny examined in Milwaukee without Mother Tracy knowing about it. ("She was with us almost constantly.") Then, unexpectedly, within days of her discovery, Carrie solved the problem herself. She was feeding the baby his lunch—one of her favorite things to do—and Louise was sitting just inside the next room. "I don't believe John hears very well," she said quietly.

Louise's heart raced. "No," she said, "I don't think he does. I have been thinking I would take him to some specialist here."

"Yes," said Carrie. "Do."

"I'm sure she knew that afternoon as well as I knew," Louise wrote. "Perhaps she had suspected longer. I never asked her. We never talked about it much at first. It was easier." Carrie gave her the name of a prominent otologist, and Louise made an appointment.

The doctor wasn't encouraging. He listened to Louise's story, asked a few questions, examined the baby's ears for abnormalities. Then he made a few simple tests, trying to attract Johnny's attention with a variety of noises, including those made by a bell and a tuning fork. Finally, he said he couldn't be sure because Johnny was too young to test conclusively.

"But," Louise persisted, "if he *is* deaf, what could be the cause? What could be done?"

"It would be nerve deafness from an indeterminable cause. If the nerve merely has been impaired it may come back, but if it has been killed, it cannot come back. In either case, there is nothing we can do about it."

But there was something she still had to know. "And if he is deaf," she asked, "will he ever be able to talk?"

The question hung in the air a moment. "Well," he slowly replied, "I don't see how. While apparently there is nothing wrong with his vocal apparatus, a baby learns to talk through hearing, by imitation." He tried to be cheery, and told Louise of a deaf boy who lived near him who was about twelve years old and got along very well. He often saw him riding his bicycle around the neighborhood and he seemed perfectly happy. After all, he said, John was still very young, and she really couldn't take anything for granted just yet.

"I did not seem to hear much of what he said at the time," Louise later wrote, "though I remembered most of it afterwards, I think. Then, the words that kept pounding in my brain were, 'He will never talk, he will never talk, never talk, never talk—' Somehow, I got out of the office and home."

In the weeks that followed, Louise made a desperate effort to be cheerful and natural when Spence was around, but she was clearly distracted, depressed, obsessed with the baby in a way that she had not been before. She remembered a time when, as a little girl, she saw two people crossing in front of her house. It looked as if they were conversing with their hands, and she turned to her grandmother and asked who they were and what they were doing. "Oh, they're deaf and dumb, poor things," her grandmother said, and Louise played that fleeting image from childhood over and over in her mind.

"There was nothing in life except Johnny," said Emily Deming. "And that wasn't quite fair to Spencer either, because he knew he came second, and with Spencer that would not have been easy to take." Not talking somehow seemed worse to Louise than not hearing, and where before she had merely lacked the words to tell Spence that his son was deaf, she now contemplated the unfathomable—that he would never speak, either. "She was afraid to tell him," Deming said. "She talked to me about it. She didn't think Spencer would accept it . . . that was one of the few times I ever saw her weep." Louise's English, Scotch, and Dutch ancestry helped her keep her emotions in check, and she always remembered what her father had once told her as a child, that if she had tears she should save them for her own pillow. "I saw her with tears in her eyes many times, but I never saw her weep except that one time. She'd have him in her arms or put him down in the crib, or when she came back [and] I'd been taking care of him, she'd go and pick him up and her eyes [would be] red."

The season at the Powers was going wonderfully well. The theater was often full on weekends and the matinees were packed with kids—little girls with starry eyes who came with their families and sat in reserved boxes holding

violets they'd picked for Selena Royle. Spence got his share of attention, but
it was Selena they all came to see, and although he wasn't a small man, he
always wore lifts in his shoes when he played opposite her. He worked so
well with her and spent so much time at the theater—morning rehearsals,
matinees, evening performances stretching to eleven o'clock or later—that
rumors of an affair began to circulate.

"The dressing rooms were appalling," Emily Deming said.

The stairwell was a circular thing with little narrow steps, and then
the dressing rooms were horrid little rooms up on the upper levels,
which meant that you had to race up and down to do costumes,
and their dressing rooms were close together. Which was very con-
venient a number of times and was used a good deal. [Spencer and
Selena] didn't necessarily stay in one room. They spent a lot of
time together. And when there were quick changes and we had to
put a dressing room on the main floor to be close enough for me
to get her dressed for the next scene, he generally stepped in for
a minute or two one way or the other, not necessarily when she
was fully clothed . . . I think Louise had a good deal of difficulty
with it.

As Selena admitted in a 1969 interview: "I was in love with Spence, and
I believe he was in love with me." Yet she denied having ever slept with him.
Selena considered Louise a friend, and had pushed John's perambulator
along the streets of Brooklyn during their days together at the Montauk.
"Acting gave us everything we needed," she said, "without the usual playing
around."

When Wright tried extending the season into the fall, proposing to
continue well into 1926, he learned that Harry G. Sommers' twenty-year
lease on the theater was coming to an end. Meanwhile, the million-dollar
Regent, a new brick-and-stone palace on Crescent Street, had been given
over to moving pictures. William Wurzburg, the Regent's managing director, coveted the stability and prestige of a resident stock company, and had
been thinking of starting one of his own when Sommers' abandonment of
the Powers lease got out and he was able to make a deal for Papa Wright's
company instead. The significance of the move to the new theater for Tracy
and the other cast members was that the Regent could continue playing
movies on Sundays and, with the addition of a Friday matinee, the Broadway Players could finally afford the luxury of a six-day work week.

Unfortunately, the move to the Regent came concurrently with the
announcement of Selena Royle's departure. *The Green Hat* was playing a
shakedown engagement in Chicago prior to Broadway, and Selena had

been offered the chance to replace Ann Harding in the role of Venice Pollen opposite Katharine Cornell. Leaving was something she regarded with mixed emotions. The audiences and the new surroundings were wonderful, yet Spence was becoming a constant irritant with his ad-libs and his willingness to break character when something suddenly struck him as funny.

As the hysterical Annabelle in *The Cat and the Canary*, the last play of her engagement, Selena was required to step behind a screen and change into nightclothes toward the end of the second act. Emily, who had fashioned a lovely pair of black satin pyjamas for the occasion, wanted to put elastic in the waist, but Selena, in thinking through the dialogue and physical business that would attend the change, decided on a drawstring instead. One night, she made the change, tied the drawstring, and played the rest of the scene as written, fainting dead away when a body came tumbling out of a hidden panel at curtain. She began the third act with Spence placing her on a couch, still clad in the pyjamas, the other cast members surrounding them. "As I came out of the faint and arose to walk across stage, I heard an audible gasp from the audience. Spence, who could break up on stage over any small deflection, started to grin and giggle, and I looked down. My pyjamas had dropped around my feet.

"Thank goodness, having changed on stage, I was fully underclothed. So hissing at Spence, 'Shut up, you damn fool!' I reached down, pulled up the pyjamas, retied them, and went on with the scene to a resounding round of applause." The audience clapped and clapped; Selena took bows, Spence took bows, they bowed to each other. Yet it was hard to stay mad at him when he misbehaved so. "There was no one I wanted to act with so much as Spence, and I know he felt the same way. We had our ups and downs, of course, but they were always resolved by good sense and the pride we both had in doing the best job possible."

She may also have been aware that Spence was involved with the company's ingenue, a pretty brunette named Betty Hanna, and that when Louise sensed an affair, she mistakenly assumed that Selena was the culprit. Having Sundays off gave him more time to spend at home, but getting Weeze out of the apartment was a chore. "I think if she had been the emotionally 'in-love' type, he would have driven her stark staring mad," Emily Deming said. "Once, when I was babysitting, when they came back they were arguing. And I got out as fast as I could. But I think I was changing Johnny . . . I had to stay for a few minutes . . . I was upset by what was happening, and I thought as I went out the door, 'I'd smash a plate over your head if you were my husband.' That was the only time I ever heard him [yell at her]. I didn't hear her voice at all."

There was an amusement park at Reed's Lake on the east side of town, and Spence liked to spend Sunday evenings there, munching popcorn and riding the rides. There was a skating rink, a Ferris wheel, bumper cars, a shooting gallery, and a huge carousel whose riders were serenaded by a trio of band organs. A trip on the Derby Racer, the park's roller coaster, cost a dime. "He used to love all the crazy things," Louise said. "If he went crazy, he really went crazy."

Weeze did her best to be a spirited companion, but the burden of her secret and the certainty that Spence could never accept Johnny's deafness had, after three long months, grown intolerable. "She seemed to have lost her interest in everything except the baby," Spence recounted. "But even that was not a happy interest. She would sit and watch him and brood. For weeks I kept asking her to tell me what was the matter. But it was always the same answer, 'Nothing.' One Sunday morning I went in the baby's room and found her sobbing as though her heart would break. I insisted that she tell me. She didn't answer at first. She went and bathed her eyes and straightened her hair and then came back and sat down in a rocker. She sat there a minute, staring into space, rocking and rocking. I've never seen such tragedy on a human face. Suddenly she said, very quietly, 'Johnny can't hear. He's deaf.'"

The news hit him like nothing else he had ever heard in his life. As Louise remembered it, "he just broke down." He buried his face in his hands, and then, after a moment, he said brokenly, "He'll never be able to say Daddy." At that, Louise was suddenly able to do for him what she had been unable to do for herself. "Words of encouragement came tumbling out. Thoughts of which I had never before been conscious rushed into speech. How much closer he would be to us, how much more we could do for him, how much more we had to work for, the miracles of science doctors constantly were performing, what was unheard of today might in twenty years be as simple as breathing. Hope, hope, hope, I poured into his ears, and hope crept into my heart, never to leave. We wept uncontrollably for a few moments and were strangely comforted."

They decided at last that they couldn't let it spoil all three of their lives, and Spence said, "Let's see if we can get Emily to sit with John. Let's go down to the park." They spent that night convincing themselves that Johnny's deafness didn't matter, that he was still an intelligent, happy baby who was otherwise in perfect health, and that they would somehow find a way to see that he lived a normal life. But privately, spiritually, Spence needed to make sense of it, what had happened to his son and why. "You could never pin him down to just what he believed," Louise said. "He never liked to talk about the church, but he *believed* it. He had grown up that way, and he [was] settled [in his faith] . . . I felt that [his father] was more flexible in some ways, that he had a little broader [interpretation] where my husband took it as it was and didn't discuss it. And what he thought, I don't know. He never talked about those things, excepting the general thing that he didn't see how anybody could say there wasn't a God."

Tracy had committed adultery—emotionally, if not carnally, with Selena, and physically, it would seem, with Betty Hanna. And possibly with others over the long months of Louise's pregnancy. It was not something he could ever take lightly, given his Catholic upbringing, and he may, in fact, have given some account of his behavior in confession. The guilt he felt was corrosive in its effect on his mind and his sense of well-being. It was something he couldn't discuss with Louise, something he couldn't let out of himself, something he carried with him at all times. The Irish stream of Catholicism being so severe and demanding, he was keenly aware of how easily the gifts of God could be forsaken, their goodness traduced through the ever-present threat of sin. But that the greatest gift of all, his son, could be so afflicted was something he could never understand or justify, and something for which he could never forgive himself.

Spence passed the rest of the season in alternating fits of acceptance and denial, convinced Johnny would never speak and yet blindly hopeful that a miracle of either science or faith would somehow intervene. Lacking guidance, or even a definitive diagnosis, he and Louise settled into a pattern of treating Johnny as if he were perfectly normal in every respect. "We talked to him," Louise said, "just exactly as we would have done if he had heard . . . I told him nursery rhymes, I sang to him, we did everything which, of course, was just right, but I just fell into that because I couldn't imagine doing anything else."

Selena left *The Green Hat* at the end of its Chicago run, unhappy with the part, and returned to Grand Rapids to holiday at Camp Lake, north of town, with her parents and her sister, the actress Josephine Royle. It was there the idea was hatched to premiere her father's new play, a tragedy of modern Washington titled *Set Free,* at the Regent with Spence in the role of an idealistic young senator and Selena as the political operative he loves but can never marry. Tracy put off a tonsillectomy to do the show, and Selena saw that a change had come over him in the six weeks since she had last seen him. His sober mood suited the dark circumstances of *Set Free* (which ended with the suicide of Selena's character) and the opening on August 3rd was a major event. The house was sold out, quite a stunt for a 1,700-seat theater on a Monday night. Several New York producers were in town to see the play, among them Earle Boothe, who was riding high as producer of the big Broadway comedy success *Is Zat So?* Boothe didn't think much of *Set Free,* and although Selena was the recipient of all the floral tributes—great banks of flowers draped over the footlights to honor her homecoming—it was Tracy's earnest performance as the straight-arrow politico that impressed him.

After the show they talked; Boothe and his partners, actors James Glea-son and Ernest Truex, were unhappy with the work of Paul Kelly, who was set to play the juvenile lead in a new Broadway-bound western called *The Sheepman*. It wasn't the material that appealed to Tracy, even though the play had emerged from Harvard's famed 47 Workshop. It was the stark val-idation of a Broadway role that excited him, and the chance to get off the treadmill of stock, where, for the sake of security, a lot of good actors frit-tered their best years away in places like Pittsburgh and Grand Rapids. The two men shook hands, and Tracy went off to Milwaukee to have his tonsils removed. Upon his return to work a week later, he tendered his notice.

They left Johnny with his grandparents and made their way east to New York, where rehearsals for *The Sheepman* were already in progress. The announcement of Tracy's resignation did not sit well with the Broadway Players. "It shook everybody up," said Emily Deming. "It was a scene you could remember for a long time. Nobody was very happy except Spencer. Of course, he was leaving to do what he wanted to do. He had no consider-ation for the person who had given him his start, looked after him, kept him on." Louise would always remember Papa Wright's reaction: "That good-for-nothing! I took him practically out of the gutter with his one blue suit—which he is still wearing!"

The Sheepman wasn't worth the trouble. The playwright was a first-time author named Charlotte Chorpenning, who would later find her drama-tist's voice as the author of children's plays. Her only work for adults was overlong, obvious, dull, and when Louise was finally able to read the thing—too late to talk Spence out of it—she thought it very poor indeed. The first break-in performance took place in Stamford, Connecticut, on October 9, 1925, and ran upwards of three hours. The reviewer in the *Stam-ford Advocate* found it "gripping" and Tracy "likable" as the sheepman's sup-posed son, Jack Roberts, but a more savvy notice in *Variety* thought it dreadful. Drastic surgery and a week's stand in New Haven failed to improve it, and after twelve performances the new producing team of Boothe, Gleason, and Truex summarily pulled the plug.

Back in New York—"close to bedrock" as Louise put it—they landed stock leads in companies under the management of New Jersey theater magnate Walter Reade—Spence in Trenton, Louise in Plainfield. The arrangement wasn't ideal—fifty miles separated them—but there was no economic incentive to be picky, and they figured they could see each other on Sundays, train schedules permitting. His leading lady was Ethel Remey, who had spent her entire stage career in stock and bonded instantly with Louise. When Louise left for Plainfield, Spence began taking his meals at the boardinghouse where Ethel was living, the home cooking infinitely preferable to hotel fare.

The Trent Stock Company opened its winter season on November 3 with the David Gray–Avery Hopwood comedy *The Best People,* and continued on the ninth with George M. Cohan's *The Song and Dance Man.* It was the Cohan play that showed local audiences what Spencer Tracy could do with a dramatic role, albeit one as hokey as the "hick trouper" created on Broadway by Cohan himself. Ethel thought he acted the part "magnificently" and the *Trenton Times* reported an "exactness that several times brought him rounds of applause from a fair-sized first night audience."

There followed the usual jumble of stock titles, some of which he had played before (*Buddies, The First Year, The Mad Honeymoon*) and many of which were new, if not particularly challenging. "I never saw any evidence of a temper at all," said Ethel Remey, who found him a joy to play with. "He was very placid, and very easy to get along with. And no drinking, no drinking at all, possibly because he had too much responsibility."

Once Louise was settled in Plainfield, the Tracys and a nurse brought Johnny east, and Spence came up on a Sunday so that they could all be together. Louise wrote: "Fortunately for John and for us, in those days, despite our constantly broke condition, there was always help in the offing. Spencer's father thought, and with reason, that selling trucks was a much more substantial occupation than acting." It was in Plainfield that Johnny had his tonsils and adenoids out because a doctor in Milwaukee had told Carrie Tracy their removal occasionally helped hard-of-hearing children. "The doctor who did it was not optimistic," Louise said, "but he said he would remove them if we wished it."

Not long after Christmas, when Spence found himself playing a gimmicky show called *Shipwrecked,* he heard from Mr. Wright, who was in the process of setting up new companies in Saginaw and Flint, and who said, as Louise remembered it, "Come on out to Grand Rapids again. We need you out here." He didn't need much persuading. It was practically impossible to get between Trenton and Plainfield by rail on a Sunday, and he only saw Louise and Johnny when he could persuade someone to drive him. Louise was fed up as well: "It was no kind of a life. We might as well have been 300 miles apart."

Tracy played his final week opposite Ethel Remey in *The Family Upstairs,* and she mourned his loss to Trenton as few others did:

Spencer wasn't the average stock leading man. He wasn't the clotheshorse. He was a very fine actor, but I think a lot of people, because he wasn't a clotheshorse, didn't appreciate him. They didn't know anything about acting. They didn't realize what a gem they had as an actor, because he wasn't the average matinee idol of that time . . . When Spence left, it affected me no end. They got this average stock leading man, good looking—I suppose one would call him the matinee idol sort—but he couldn't compare with Spencer as an actor. Yet the matinee girls thought he was totally wonderful, so there you are. It was maddening.

Louise's father, having had a classmate at Yale who was an ear specialist in New York, wrote and urged her to go see him. One snowy morning during her last week in Plainfield—the only day she had neither a rehearsal nor a matinee to play—Louise, Johnny's nurse, and Johnny took the train into New York. It proved to be a courtesy call, Allienne's friend having nothing new to say about the case and no real information to add to the comparatively little she had already. However, Louise had made a second appointment with a Dr. John Page, whom she understood to be one of the best-known and most highly rated men on the East Coast.

I felt that here was to be my last stand. We were there for almost an hour. He took John's history in minute detail. He made by far the most thorough examination ever made. Then he sat me down and talked to me. His findings were practically those of everybody else: It was nerve deafness, cause undetermined, for which there was no known treatment or cure. But, for the first time, I was told something to do about it. He told me to whom I should go [and] the names of the schools—the Wright Oral School and the Lexington Avenue School for the Deaf, both in New York City, happened to be the ones he mentioned—where I could get the information I should have. He told me some of the wonderful things [the] schools were doing. He told me that one day John would be able to talk.

It seemed as I went out that at least half the weight over my heart was gone. For the moment, at least, our troubles were negligible. I walked on air. *Now* I had something I could *do*. And one day John would talk!

Tracy rejoined the Broadway Players on February 2, 1926, when rehearsals began for *Seven Keys to Baldpate*. The new leading woman of the company was Helen Joy, a competent actress who would go on to a brief career in New York. Tracy didn't fill the theater for his homecoming, but was grandly received nevertheless, a respectable crowd braving snow flurries to see him. Business was tepid the first eight weeks. Radio was cutting into stock audiences nationwide, and it was only *What Price Glory*—with Papa Wright's solemn curtain speeches the week before, warning the easily shocked to stay away, and Tracy's star turn as the battle-weary Captain Flagg—that filled the Regent on a Monday night. The following week, convinced the smaller theater would make for happier audiences, Wright announced his company's move back to the Powers, as well as the return of Selena Royle, who would manage the transition, appearing the last week at the Regent in her father's play *The Struggle Everlasting* and the first week at the Powers in an import called *Stolen Fruit.*

Selena raced onstage the night of April 5, her hair streaming wildly, and had to wait several minutes for the applause to subside enough for her to speak her first lines. She was, as usual, the center of the play, and when the flowers went over the footlights at the close of the third act, she was buried in them and Spence and Bill Laveau held the surplus over her head. The allegorical play—Selena played "Body" to Tracy's "Mind" and Clifford Dunstan's "Soul"—didn't do well, but the Royles stayed another two weeks in Grand Rapids, Selena inaugurating a new "guest star" policy at the Powers that brought William Faversham to town the following week in her father's greatest stage success, *The Squaw Man.* The move back to the Powers restored Sunday performances to the company, and Wright, hoping to get the drop on a competing troupe, moved opening nights to Sundays, something not often done in stock because of the difficulty of scaring up last-minute props and supplies on the Sabbath.

With guest stars playing one-week stands at the Powers, both Helen Joy and Tracy were relegated to supporting roles, making neither of them happy. Drag comic Tommy Martelle was followed by Nance O'Neil, Harry Beresford, Edmund Breese, and actor-playwright J. C. Nugent. Joy left after O'Neil's two-week stay and was replaced by Peggy Conway, late of the *Garrick Gaieties.* Together, Tracy and Conway filled a hole in the schedule with the popular character comedy *The Family Upstairs,* Spence serving as the company's "guest star" for that particular week. Edith Taliaferro came to the Powers the following week with *Polly of the Circus,* and when she was asked by the Sligh Furniture Company to pose for a picture with a prize-winning bedroom set, she agreed to do so only if Spence could be in the shot with her.

The photo was the idea of Charles R. Sligh, Jr., the twenty-year-old scion to the famous furniture builder, who had joined the firm just out of college and was looking for ways to pump up sales. Edith and Spence went out to the factory, where Taliaferro slipped between the satin sheets and Tracy, in a three-piece business suit, sat on an adjoining stool, book in hand, pretending to read to her. Chuck Sligh and Spence hit it off immediately, the Tracys not having made many friends in Grand Rapids. "He was a very nice young man," Louise said of Chuck, who was both affable and unabashed. "They took us out to the country club and we met quite a few people." When Wright announced a ten-week break for the Players, Spence stepped away from the company early to spend time at a cottage the Slighs had rented for the summer at Gun Lake.

Louise helped arrange Spence's absence by stepping into the final two weeks of the season herself. The first week's attraction was *Happiness,* which she had once played in Chicago, and in which she would now take the role of Jenny, the little dressmaker's apprentice created by J. Hartley Manners for his wife, the great Laurette Taylor. The part was a formidable one—110 sides—and Taylor had played it practically in monologue. The audience wasn't huge on opening night, but Louise so completely disappeared into the character that Clarence Dean (whose notice in the *Herald* ran under the headline LAURETTE TAYLOR HAS WORTHY FOLLOWER) was astonished at how someone as tall and athletic could suggest a girl so small and winsome.*

Emily, who had never before seen Louise onstage, pronounced her "an infinitely better actress" than Selena Royle. "Selena was a very pretty woman," she said, "and she had good stage sense and a good voice and used it well, but she was not a 'depth' actress. Louise was. She wasn't as pretty by any manner or means, and Selena projected herself well and Louise did not. Selena sparkled; Louise had no sparkle. She was solid business." But like Laurette Taylor, Louise could place a whisper in the back row of the top-most gallery. "I used to have to check the house to see whether they could be heard," Emily said. "It had a balcony beyond the balcony like all the old opera houses did. They sold the seats then . . . every matinee was sold out. I used to have to go check, and I never had to check her. Her voice carried."

Louise's second week—the company's last—was as Peggy Fairfax, the sporty and palpitating heroine of the farce steeplechase comedy *Hottentot.* She was so good—and had such fun—that Papa Wright asked her to consider playing a full season opposite Spence in one of his new companies.

The Tracys relinquished their tiny apartment at the Browning, where Johnny had celebrated his second birthday, gone to his first party, tasted his first ice cream cone. They took their son to Lake Delavan, Wisconsin, where John and Carrie Tracy had a summer cottage, and where, surrounded by his grandmother, grandfather, a grandaunt, and a number of their friends, he would be spoiled shamelessly while his parents enjoyed the first genuine vacation of their married life.

It lasted all of a week.

Spence spent most of it either in the lake or on it, piloting a decrepit speedboat that seemed to absorb him endlessly. Then a telegram arrived:

---

* Laurette Taylor was five feet five—a good height for the stage, she said, because she could make herself look tall or short as a part required. Louise was an inch shorter.

Selena Royle had landed a role in a new play for George M. Cohan called *Yellow,* and it now looked as if there might be a part for Spence as well. This would be his third shot at Broadway. "It was a reprieve," he said, "a message from Garcia." And if it didn't work out, he told Louise, he wouldn't be going back to stock—he'd get into some "regular" business instead. "It was by far the best opportunity he had had," Louise said, "and he was off immediately. John and I stayed on at Delavan."

Yellow was a modernized version of *Within the Law,* the work of a first-time playwright named Margaret Vernon. The Shuberts, who owned the script, had just done a complicated deal with Cohan that involved the exclusive booking of all his future shows, and they reportedly invited him on as a partner for, as *Variety* put it, "purposes of prestige and Cohanesque treatment." Despite a well-known flair for melodrama, Cohan had thus far limited his involvement with *Yellow* to casting, having assigned direction of the show to actor-playwright John Meehan. "I was over at the Lambs Club one day," remembered Tracy, "and they called me and told me to come over. [T]hey had let a fellow go. Chester Morris was the star. Marjorie Wood and Hale Hamilton. Harry Bannister. And there was this wonderful part for a young husband in the thing . . . Hale lied to George—he told him he had seen me. But Selena went for me. She was the one who got me the job."

Tracy joined rehearsals on September 9, 1926, the day he signed an Equity contract with Eddie Dunn, Cohan's longtime press agent and general factotum, calling for a salary of $175 a week. "I rehearsed; John Meehan directed it. And it was about a week before George M. came in." The first public performance was scheduled for the night of September 13. "George would never fully direct his shows," actor-playwright Jack McGowan said. "Sam Forrest or Julian Mitchell or Johnny Meehan would block them out and then George would take over, sometimes as late as two days before the opening, and give it his special touch."

Tracy had performed six Cohan plays in stock—and had actually played Cohan's parts in two of them—but the mere thought of shaking hands with the greatest living figure in American theater had him terrified. One morning, Cohan strolled onto the stage and greeted all twenty-two members of the cast individually. When he came to Tracy, he turned to Meehan, grinned, and said, "I don't believe I have met this gentleman." Then, said Tracy, came the "terrible moments" when they rehearsed for him. Cohan didn't say a lot; his manner was curt and snappy. "Taught me to keep my hands out of my pockets. Oh, yes. Don't be a lazy actor. Don't start hiding your hands, so you'll never know what to do with them."

Louise left Johnny in Milwaukee and met the company in Buffalo, where *Yellow* was set to open a week's stand at the Shubert-Teck Theatre. "I was scared to death," Tracy said. "Christ, I thought I was going to get canned any minute. In those days they could fire you anytime up to ten days." Tracy's character, Jimmy Wilkes, was obvious business, a newlywed who serves as Chester Morris' best friend, getting him out of scrapes long after the audience has given up on him. He had only two good scenes in the entire play, only one of which really gave him the chance to make an impression. In stock, he could simply "glance through his lines" (as Louise put it) and then run through them a couple of times with the rest of the cast. He was, in other words, used to holding back in rehearsal, but now with Cohan out front, that was no longer an option. The final dress— practically an all-nighter—took place in Buffalo, and the mood was decid- edly tense. Cohan had a reputation for knowing all of the parts in all of his plays, and Tracy had somehow convinced himself that the Prince of Broad- way would only use him up until opening and then go on in his place.

"During rehearsals," said Selena Royle, "George M. sat in the front row of the orchestra pit, his feet high in the air crossed on the railing in front of him, his mouth down to one side in its perpetual characteristic lopsided grin, and as he gave you a direction his upper foot pointed the way he wished you to go . . . Spencer was rehearsing a scene when suddenly George M.'s feet came down from the railing with a bang and he sat up straight. Through his tight lips out of the side of his mouth he barked, 'Tracy, you're the best goddamned actor I've ever seen! Go ahead!' His feet went back to their crossed blades position and he relaxed again on the tip of his spine."

As an actor, Cohan had grown up admiring the amiable Nat Goodwin, whose expressive face and dry manner of delivery had taken him from vaudeville to light comedy and eventually to Shakespeare. Then he saw the versatile French actor Lucien Guitry: "I couldn't imagine any actor better than Nat Goodwin, but here he was. The same ease and command of pres- ence Nat had, but something else. A deeper reserve. Guitry never opened up, but you always knew he had plenty to open up with if he so wanted. I don't understand a word of French, but I knew everything Guitry was say- ing because he was saying it with his eyes and his posture and the way he lis- tened to his fellow actors."

And now Cohan saw the same qualities in Spencer Tracy, whose big scene that Sunday night came toward the end of the third act. Figuring he had nothing to lose, Tracy invested a tight, almost negligible exchange between himself and Marjorie Wood with all the animation and gravity he could muster, holding nothing back but remaining at all times in absolute command of the role. Tracy's young husband, boisterous and lusty, gave Cohan a lift toward the end of a particularly long and grueling night, and George M. may well have overreacted. Certainly Tracy thought as much. "Spencer looked startled," as Selena recounted it, "and, to us who were watching, turned slightly pale. After the scene was over, he came over to me

With Marjorie Wood in George M. Cohan's production of *Yellow,* 1926.
(PATRICIA MAHON COLLECTION)

and said, 'What did he mean?' I laughed. It's like an actor never to believe
or remember the good notices. You can't forget the bad. 'You silly fool,' I
explained, 'he meant it.' "

Spence played the rest of the rehearsal in something of a daze. "That
was a wonderful night," Louise recalled. "He didn't get back to the hotel
until very late—four or five in the morning. I was in bed. He just couldn't
get over it. He sat on the bed and said, 'Listen what happened . . .' He told
me all about it . . . [He said,] 'I thought I was going to be sacked.' He
always thought that. I think it was one of the highlights of his career."

For its out-of-town opening, *Yellow* was accorded a warm reception by
what Louise described as a "Cohan-minded audience." The advance notice
in *Variety* was an outright rave: "Loaded with nervous theatrical dynamite,
it sent the hard-boiled local first-nighters out raving with frazzled nerves,
wet handkerchiefs, and wilted collars." In New York the show was ham-
pered by the fact that the street out front of the National Theatre was under
construction, as were the avenues at each end of its block. Patrons had to
drive over loose planks or stumble through muddy, unpaved walkways,
unlighted and treacherous, to reach the lobby. Consequently, *Yellow* was

reviewed almost exclusively by the second-string critics, only a couple of whom truly liked it. Most thought it convoluted, poorly structured, and overlong.

"It is easy to perceive the role that delighted the heart of George M.," L.W. M'Laren wrote perceptively in the *New York Journal.* "It is that of the bank clerk with a small flat and a wife, played well by Spencer Tracy. One suspects that Cohan broadened it considerably. Certain it is that his smile of satisfaction was broad as Tracy went through the part last night."

John Tracy was proud of his grandson and rarely missed an opportunity to show him off. Johnny was a beautiful child, with long auburn curls, exquisite skin, and, in Louise's words, "a sweetly grave expression" that rarely failed to attract attention. While at Lake Delavan, the elder Tracy frequently ran "errands" to a particular drugstore known for its malted milks, and he generally found an excuse to take the boy with him. It was on one such expedition that a woman spoke to Johnny. She remarked on what a handsome child he was, but he did not turn. She spoke again, then looked at John: "He is hard of hearing, isn't he?"

As he hesitated, not knowing quite what to say, the woman introduced herself as Matie E. Winston, a teacher for the Wright Oral School in New York City. A native of Wisconsin, Miss Winston was home on vacation when she noticed all the obvious signs and concluded that Johnny must be either very hard of hearing or completely deaf. Then, when she heard the name "Tracy," she remembered having answered Louise's recent letter to the school.

The following day, Louise and Johnny called on Miss Winston. "As I rang the doorbell and waited for someone to appear, my heart thumped against my ribs, my hands were clammy, and I felt the same quivering in the pit of my stomach that I always felt on an opening night. In a moment, I would be able to talk to someone who, not in the vernacular, but in reality, knew all the answers. All the questions I had been carrying around for so long, I thought in a moment were to be exchanged for facts. How will he talk? When will he talk? How will his voice compare with ours? Will he be able to carry on a conversation? Now I would *know.* It was almost like meeting God."

Matie Winston was a cheerful, forthright woman in her mid-forties, enthusiastic and knowledgeable. She asked all the basic questions and wanted to know what Louise and her husband were doing for their son. She listened intently as Louise told her, in as much detail as she could muster. Then she said, "Fine, as far as it goes, but you ought to do more. He is old enough to start sense training." She meant differences and likenesses—

colors to start. She suggested blocks of two different colors, separating them by color, letting him do it, making a game out of it. Then, once he caught on, adding more colors to the pile. It sounded too simple. "I craved something hard," Louise said. When Spence left for New York, she continued working with the blocks, and by the time she left to join him in Buffalo, Johnny was walking unaided, finally mustering the courage—and the balance—to try it alone.

It was exciting for Spence and Louise to be back in New York, especially at a time when neither one of them had to look for work. They could see old friends, shop, and take in an occasional show. After the first night, ticket sales were respectable, if not spectacular, and although *Yellow* was not a genuine hit, there was enough demand to keep it running awhile—which meant Louise had to find an apartment. "Eventually we went to a small 'family' hotel in the West Seventies, and, with the permission of the management, my well-worn electric stove of pre-marriage date—the same which more than once had put out the hotel lights in Detroit and points west—came out of the bottom drawer of my trunk and went on duty in the bathroom."

Johnny arrived the last of September, his grandparents taking a temporary apartment not far from the hotel. Father Tracy had been ill and, prior to coming east, had resigned his position as president and treasurer of the Frankenberg Refrigerating Machinery Company. "I think he knew he might not be here long," Louise said, "and he wanted to spend as much of the time as possible near his namesake."

Spence's relationship with Johnny had always been tentative, conflicted, but the boy and his grandfather were utterly devoted to one another and their example seemed to ease his burden. "I saw Spencer with Johnny when I visited their apartment," Ethel Remey said, "and he was very affectionate and tender with the little boy. And very relaxed." Tracy, however, always clung to the notion that Johnny's condition could somehow be fixed, and that he could not truly bond with his son until he had undone the horrible thing he had wrought. "He was very disturbed one minute," said Louise, "the next minute he was reassuring me that everything was going to be fine. I was the one who could do it. But I didn't know enough. And he didn't know how to talk to John. He did antics, he put on makeup, all sorts of silly things. He loved to show off what John could do, but he couldn't get down to the brass tacks of what the learning problem was."

Tracy didn't tell many people about Johnny's deafness, and Pat O'Brien found out only when he could no longer hold it in. "I think," said Pat, "he was like any father, you know? You're trying to solve a problem and you want to blame yourself for it. And I imagine Spence probably blamed himself for John's trouble." O'Brien was in *Henry—Behave* at the Nora Bayes at the same time Tracy was appearing in *Yellow.* "We'd meet every night after the theatre and walk to a restaurant for griddle cakes and coffee. Well, this particular night I noticed he was under some emotional strain, and he actually started to cry." Did they close the show? Had he been fired? Finally O'Brien stopped and asked, "What's the matter?"

"Billy," said Spence, "I've got to tell you," and he went on to relate how Johnny would wait up for him at night, standing patiently in his crib, his hands gripping the rails, his eyes wide with anticipation. The previous day had been a matinee day, a long day, and when Spence came trudging through the door at a little before midnight, he went straight to bed. "I don't know what happened," he said. "It was one of those things . . . In the middle of the night—God knows what time it was—I awoke, and I always leave the door open into the little room with the crib, and I looked in and Johnny was standing in his crib. I'd forgotten to kiss him goodnight." The ordinary child, he explained, would call "Daddy," but Johnny couldn't. "You see, Billy, Johnny can neither hear nor speak."

Spence scooped the baby up in his arms, hugged him and kissed him extravagantly, handed him his teddy bear and put him back in his crib, where he fell promptly and soundly to sleep. The image stayed with him though, haunted him through the rest of the night.

"God knows," he said, "how long he'd been standing there."

Yellow continued through the rest of the year, averaging houses of around $14,000 a week—pretty good considering the discouraging location. (By way of comparison, *Broadway,* the big nonmusical hit of the season, was averaging $23,000 a week at a theater almost exactly the same size and at the same top price of $3.30 a seat.) Sales began to drop off toward Christmas, then word came down in January that the show would close after a respectable run of seventeen weeks. Having been cast in a Cohan play, Tracy picked up an agent, a Harvard-educated producer and sometime actor named Chamberlain Brown.* It was Brown who not only saw to it that Tracy had another job within the space of a week, but that he made considerably more money than Cohan would ever pay.

Ned McCobb's Daughter was the work of the Pulitzer Prize–winning playwright Sidney Howard, a shrewd comedy frankly designed as a vehicle for Howard's wife, the actress Clare Eames. The Theatre Guild was playing it in repertory with *The Silver Cord* when actor-manager John Cromwell

---

* Chamberlain Brown, together with Wales Winter and the Packard Agency, handled most of the casting for stock companies nationwide. As a rule, however, Tracy got jobs in stock through referrals or by making his own contacts.

With Florence Johns in the Chicago company of *Ned McCobb's Daughter*, 1927. (AUTHOR'S COLLECTION)

(who had staged *The Silver Cord*) set about establishing a second company in Chicago. The plum part of Carrie Callahan, the dowdy sea captain's daughter, fell to actress Florence Johns, with Cromwell himself taking the part of Babe, the genial bootlegger who also happens to be Carrie's brother-in-law. Tracy found himself cast in the role of Carrie's thieving, dim-witted husband George, a part played in New York by Earle Larimore. Commanding the princely rate of $225 a week, Tracy dutifully mailed Chamberlain Brown a twenty-five-dollar money order the first Monday after the opening, enthusing over the quality of the material and making note of the reviews in the Chicago dailies. "I was very happy over mine," he wrote Brown, "because of the vast difference in this part and the one I played in *Yellow*. It should mean something for me."

As in New York, the play drew considerably more critical than commercial attention. "Business is only fair," Tracy advised his agent the following week, "and I do not look for a long engagement. Cromwell is very much discouraged and disgusted. It would be too bad to flop in face of the splendid notices we received."

With Spence in Chicago, Louise was again approached by W. H. Wright, who had the idea of hiring the two of them as leads in one of his nine companies. "He never believed in this before, but he said, 'I'll try it.' Would the two of us come to Lima and play?" Lima was 230 miles east of Chicago in northwest Ohio, a center of agriculture and heavy industry and, for a brief while, oil. On the circuits, its Klan-cheering populace was known as one of the toughest audiences in vaudeville, and the old joke "First prize, one week in . . . / Second prize, two weeks in . . ." was supposedly coined about Lima. Spence hated the idea of going back to stock again—the longer hours and shorter pay—and held off giving an answer. Then Wright sweetened the offer with a percentage just as *Ned McCobb's Daughter* took a dive at the box office. The third week's gross was a paltry $6,000 and it looked as if they would close when Cromwell, emboldened by the emphatic critical support, announced an extension—another three weeks—with the cast taking a 25 percent cut.

"I have decided to accept Wright's proposition for the summer," Tracy advised Chamberlain Brown, "which is a good one. Louise and I playing joint leads, and in addition he is giving me ten percent of the gross over $4000. He claims we will do as high as $5000 nearly every week. I am doing this to get on my feet. Cromwell thinks I am wise to do it, and has definitely set me for his new play and also Sidney Howard's for next season. I should return in August with a nice little bankroll and get out of the financial rut in which I have been." He added: "I hope this will be the last time I'll have to do this, but feel it won't hurt me any and I need the money."

When Louise arrived with Johnny to read for a part with Cromwell, Spence had a small apartment waiting near Lincoln Park, having abandoned a room at the swanky Allerton Club when the salary cut took effect. There was a Murphy bed (one of the hardest Louise ever slept on), a room scarcely large enough for Johnny's crib, a bath, a tiny kitchen, and something akin to a breakfast nook. It was in the kitchen that Johnny's habitual jabbering filled the air. "One evening," Louise said, "while I was cooking the dinner and he was playing near me, out of a ribbon of meaningless sounds came suddenly, 'Mama, mama, mama' over again, sing-song fashion. He had hit upon the combination—strange he had not done so before, as it is one of the most natural—and, perhaps liking the feel of it, continued to say it. A perfectly clear and beautiful 'mama.' "

Louise immediately dropped what she was doing and grabbed him. He smiled up at her. "Yes, yes!" she said, trembling with excitement. "Mama, mama!"

As he watched my moving lips, realization slowly dawning on his face, he repeated with me, "Mama, mama." At last he knew that something went with those strange movements we made with our lips, movements of which he was growing more and more aware, movements requiring him to wave his hand when he or someone else went away—he even took it upon himself occasionally to do this now without waiting for the lips—to drink his milk, to wipe his mouth, and lots of other things. He did not know what he had done, or how he had done it, but he found he could do it again and again; he did not know what it meant, but he knew it pleased that person who seemed so very necessary to him, and somehow her laughing and dancing around and kissing him created a very pleasant feeling inside him, and I am sure, from a certain something in his expression, and from the renewed gusto and assurance with which he attacked what he was doing, he felt as though he had done something pretty smart.

Spence closed in *Ned McCobb's Daughter* after six discouraging weeks, and he and Louise arrived in Lima on April 9, 1927. The calm and methodical Miss Krause accompanied them, caring for Johnny again as she had in Plainfield. They settled into a large apartment at Moreland Manor, within walking distance of the theater, and rehearsals for the first play of the season, the raucous *Laff That Off,* began the following Monday. Papa Wright had a habit of moving players around like pieces on a chessboard, and he assembled from his various companies a wildly uneven supporting cast of nine, the only familiar face from Grand Rapids being the dour character man Porter Hall. The schedule was weighted heavily with plays Spence had already done; director Harry Horne's habit of starting the week with a full read-through of the script—unusual in stock—struck him as unnecessary.

Having not worked since August, Louise enjoyed Lima. Horne's quiet style ("I try," he said, "to avoid thunder and lightning interference and dogmatism") suited her, and she liked the idea of the weekly read-throughs around the table. She sat for an interview with the *Lima News* on her first Tuesday in town, trim and tailored in a brown velvet frock, and dismissed the widely held notion that the theater wasn't a proper vocation for a career-minded young woman. "How many bankers, lawyers, physicians, and other professional men become known outside of their home town or state?" she reasoned.

The profile ran that same day, stimulating matinee sales for *Laff That Off,* but Louise fell ill toward the end of the week and was unable to open with Spence the following Sunday (which happened to be Easter). Her understudy, Geraldine Browning, went on in her place, and the *News* reported "large audiences" in its notice the next evening. Browning played out the week, Louise focusing on rehearsals for *The Patsy* instead and spending as much time as possible with Johnny. She loved the stimulation and challenge of a lead character, and the wisecracking Patsy became one of her favorites.

"Miss Louise Treadwell, leading lady of the company, makes her debut to Lima audiences this week in the title role," a notice in the *News* reported. "She possesses charm, vivacity, and ability seldom found on the stock stage." Playing opposite Spence was fun, too, especially in a spirited comedy, and it was a great help to be onstage with someone so thoroughly in command of the text. "[E]very once in a while he threw me a line," she said. "He knew lines were difficult for me to learn in stock, especially, [and] once in a while I would go blank when he was on stage. All I had to do was look at him and he'd mumble something that would give me a clue."

Louise had started the Wright Oral School's correspondence course in November, but had little time to devote to Johnny and his lessons with rehearsals most every morning, three matinees a week, and nightly performances. Miss Krause carried on as best she could, adding skeins of colored yarn to the blocks he had gotten so good at separating, and commencing with lipreading lessons. In time, he not only knew what to do when he saw his mother say, "Wipe your mouth," but he also came to know what the individual words *wipe, your,* and *mouth* meant. Auricular exercises—ear training—were less productive, for, unlike most children who were hard of hearing to varying degrees, Johnny was as close to stone deaf as it was possible to get, and no amount of testing would ever suggest otherwise.

The 1,200-seat Faurot Opera House was rarely filled to capacity, effectively negating Spence's percentage, but the $300 a week the Tracys pulled down as a team helped pay off a lot of old bills. By the middle of May, Tracy was able to send Chamberlain Brown all the back commissions he owed, a total of seventy-five dollars. "Things are running along here as well as could be expected," he said, "but frankly I don't like it and would like to break away in about six more weeks. Next season my plans remain the same as far as I know. I am to begin rehearsals August first with John Cromwell's new play, and Sidney Howard's is to be done later. All of which is fine, but at the same time I don't want to let anything slip by. Something better might come up in the meantime. I have hopes of doing something for George Cohan. If he or anyone else should want me, or if anything good comes up, please let me know and I will give my notice."

Toward the end of the month, a contract arrived from Cromwell which specified $175 a week for the juvenile lead in *What the Doctor Ordered,* a farce comedy set to open mid-August. Lacking anything else in the way of offers, Tracy impulsively signed the contract and returned it. Less than a week later, a wire arrived from Cohan, offering him a "specially written part" in his new play, *The Baby Cyclone*. Spence and Louise opened *The Cat and the Canary* that Sunday—Memorial Day weekend—and the house, for a change, was sold out for both performances. Tracy played the show in a miasma of exhilaration and dread, delighted to have the Cohan offer in hand but now worried as to how Cromwell might react.

Brown settled the contract with Cohan at the end of the following week. "It is the lead in his new play and written for himself," Brown advised his client. "You've never heard of such a wonderful part. It has everything. He is giving $200 which is the best he will do, but worth it. He thinks a lot of you and you are surrounded by a great cast. I am very happy over it all. Rehearsals are July 11th and the opening is August 4th in Atlantic City . . . You will have to finish there July 9th and then we can take up all the details about Cromwell on your return."

Tracy thought the news wonderful, more than he had dared to hope for. "It means the big chance," he told Brown, "and if we make good, both of us should benefit."

CHAPTER 5

Dread

"I am sure Cromwell will be the first to tell me to go ahead and good luck," Tracy said in a letter to Chamberlain Brown. "He seems genuinely interested in me and would be glad for my chance. But, he has been very nice to me and I wouldn't want to hurt him—that's why I wanted the Cohan thing settled so I could let him know." Cromwell, Tracy assured Brown, would understand and know that to pass up an offer from George M. Cohan would be crazy. "If necessary," he added, "I will pay Cromwell two weeks salary, which will break any contract, but I know that won't be necessary. Cromwell isn't that kind." Mr. Wright, he said, felt that as long as he was leaving Lima so early, he would rather have him go right away so that he could save some money by bringing over a man from his company in Pontiac, which would be closing the following week. "Mrs. T. is going on a visit, and I shall come right into N[ew] Y[ork]."

Not realizing his client had actually signed a contract with John Cromwell, Brown advised Tracy not to inform Cromwell of their deal with Cohan. "I sent your wire to Cohan," Brown explained, "and he did not want Cromwell to hear of this, so that's why I said so in the wire. He feels it might cause a lot of trouble for him, so be sure you don't mention it. Of course, there is nothing set with Cromwell so you are protected." By the time Brown more fully understood the situation, the damage had been done. Tracy was keeping quiet, as instructed, when an item in one of the New York dailies announced the casting of Grant Mitchell, a Cohan favorite, as the star of *The Baby Cyclone*. "By the way," Tracy wrote Brown, "this clipping also mentioned me, so I hope Mr. Cromwell doesn't see it and wonder why I haven't notified him. However, guess I can explain."

As it turned out, he couldn't explain. Cromwell was furious when he saw the news and threatened actions against both Tracy and Cohan. Tracy was unable to mollify him and blamed Brown for the falling out. "After the terrible mess of this year's contract, which has upset me terribly, lost me one man's friendship, and nearly lost both jobs, I feel you have too much to do to handle all my troubles exclusively," he told Brown, distancing himself. "I should like and hope to do business with you as an agent—and will pay [the] same commission as in [the] past."*

Louise and Johnny boarded the night train to New Castle, Miss Krause seeing them off at the depot. "Well, I guess it's a good thing you are through," the nurse told her bluntly. "John will be glad to have you. He needs his mother." Johnny had just turned three. When they pulled away from the station and it dawned on him that he had his mother to himself once again, his face lit up with both understanding and delight, and Louise figured she had played her final engagement.

Rehearsals for *The Baby Cyclone* commenced immediately, its first performance scheduled for Atlantic City on August 8, 1927. In the cast were Grant Mitchell as Joseph Meadows, a hapless banker, Natalie Moorhead, his fiancée, and Nan Sunderland, a newlywed named Jessie. Tracy played Gene Hurley, Jessie's pugnacious husband, a man who buys his wife a Pekingese and then watches helplessly as it quickly takes first position in their marriage. One day, Hurley takes the dog for a walk and gives it away to the first woman who admires it. The ensuing argument between him and Jessie draws in Meadows, a complete stranger, and Hurley gives him a black eye for his trouble. Meadows bundles the hysterical Jessie off to his house, where he learns the woman Hurley gave the dog to was in fact Lydia, the girl he is planning to marry. And, as did Jessie, Lydia babies the dog, whose name is Cyclone because he was born in a storm.

Cohan wrote Hurley as another side of Jimmy Wilkes, the peripheral character Tracy had played so vividly in *Yellow*. As was Wilkes, Hurley is an accountant, newly married, but where Wilkes' challenges were desperate and peculiar to a newlywed, Hurley's are patently ridiculous, and over the

---

* Despite all the unpleasantness with Cromwell, Tracy made the right decision in going with Cohan. The Cromwell show, *What the Doctor Ordered*, would have paid less and lasted just twenty performances.

course of the play they afflict three generations of households. Hurley was the kind of character Cohan always took for himself—cocky, talented, bound for great things. Sam Forrest was the credited director on *Baby Cyclone,* but both he and Cohan were concurrently staging *The Merry Malones,* an elaborate musical in which Cohan was also starring, and the two men worked as a tag team throughout the rehearsal process.

"I've forgotten what exactly I did," Tracy said some thirty years later. "[I] cocked my head over or limped or some goddamn thing, and George M. said, 'What are you doing? What have you got your head over for?'

"I said, 'Well, I, ah, Mr. Cohan, I thought I'd sort of, ah, characterize it.'

"He said, 'You'd thought you'd *what*?'

"I said, 'I thought I'd, you know, kind of characterize it.' "

"Oh, oh . . ." said Cohan, now nodding wisely.

"Then he took me aside and said, 'Now you cock your head back where it was before—when I wrote this part for you. And quit walking with that club foot.' Or whatever the hell I did. 'If I want an actor like that I can go out on the street and get five-hundred of them for twelve dollars!' "

Once Cohan had Tracy's attention, he showed him how he himself would play the part, restlessly pacing the stage, his hat cocked down over his right eye, throwing out lines as if they were wisecracks. Mastering the text was easy for Tracy, and although he had the most lines in the play, he considered Grant Mitchell's part the more difficult of the two. "Listening, to me, is the great art in acting," he said in an interview.

In five seasons of stock I've played a lot of leading men who talked most of the time, but never had to listen. It's a lot easier to talk than to listen. In this play I talk a lot. Grant Mitchell does the listening . . . Do you think that I could possibly put over some of my long speeches if Grant Mitchell were not really listening to me? Suppose he let his mind dwell on football games, the horse races, or his supper engagement? Do you think for a moment that I would not feel it and let down unconsciously? And believe me, it would not take an audience many seconds to slump in its chairs and produce a mild bronchitis from first row to gallery top.

Both Spence and Louise grew close to Grant Mitchell, who expressed an uncommon interest in Johnny, and who revealed one night over dinner that his own sister was deaf. "He gave us her latest letter to read," Louise remembered. "Newsy, humorous, grammatically perfect, it obviously could not have been written by any other than an intelligent, well-educated, and altogether delightful person. I am sure he must have been amused at our amazement and, yes, excitement. To us, still so ignorant of what the future could hold, still so hungry for concrete examples and comparisons, it was manna from Heaven."

Louise and Johnny went down to Atlantic City for the first performance of *The Baby Cyclone* and stayed the entire week. The new show brought forth "gales of laughter and storms of applause," but Cohan nevertheless decided it was too long. The next morning, he was back in the theater "before the janitor" (as Tracy recalled it) and had the entire play revised in the space of six hours. "If an actor didn't 'feel' his lines," said Tracy, "[Cohan] crossed 'em out and re-wrote them on the spot."

From Atlantic City the company moved to Boston for four weeks, and Louise and Johnny followed. When Allienne Treadwell learned his daughter and grandson were going to be there, he insisted they see Dr. Harvey Cushing, a noted brain specialist and another of his Yale classmates. Dr. Cushing made a cursory examination of the boy and said he was quite sure there was no brain tumor or other condition he could possibly treat. He did, however, minister to Louise's spirit, and one thing he said to her would stay with her for the rest of her life: "You are blessed above all mothers. Yours can be a very interesting life."

The New York opening of *The Baby Cyclone* took place on September 12, 1927, the show packing snugly into Henry Miller's 950-seat theater on West Forty-third Street. No construction crews impeded the flow of traffic, and Pat O'Brien, in the midst of a dry spell, was hard-pressed to afford a seat in the balcony. Then, having forgone the expense of a shave, he found it almost impossible to get past the backstage doorman after the show. "And I'll admit I did look like a bum," he said.

> So [the doorman] wouldn't pay any attention to me. But finally, he turned his back and I sneaked in. I had heard the doorman telling the boys in the tuxedos and the tails that Spencer's dressing room was on the second floor, so I went up. But his dressing room wasn't all I found. I discovered that the son-of-a-gun had a Japanese dresser. This Jap was posted outside the dressing room door, and when I told him to tell Mr. Tracy his pal was outside, he held up his hand in horror. "No—no—go 'way. Room full of nice mans—you go 'way." I told him I'd start yelling "fire" if he didn't take my message. So he went inside, shaking his head and muttering. And then you should have seen those "nice mans" come out of there. You

With Grant Mitchell in *The Baby Cyclone*.
(AUTHOR'S COLLECTION)

never saw so many stiff shirts pouring out of one place in your life. When Spence heard I was there, he told them someone had called that he had to talk business with, and he herded 'em all out. Then he rushed out and grabbed me. He pulled me in and said: "Listen, you mick, what did you think of it? It's your opinion I want to hear."

Pat's opinion was the same as everyone else's: the show was a scream, an expert farce in which the spirit of George M. Cohan loomed large over the entire affair—his words, his cast, and, in many respects, his presence in the form of an actor named Spencer Tracy. With *The Baby Cyclone* a hit on Broadway, Cohan brought *The Merry Malones* in just behind it. A trademark pastiche of sentiment, flag waving, and pure unadulterated hokum, it was crowd-pleasing, if not revolutionary, theater from a master showman. Tracy came to regard Cohan as a kind of spiritual father, a man who recognized his gifts when his own father could not, and who applauded them, at the same time helping to nurture them. "He thought the world of George M. Cohan," Chuck Sligh said. "He was his sort of hero."

Tracy marveled at Cohan's energy and stamina, watching him sit at the piano for five or six hours a day, poking out tunes with one finger, playing a performance in the evening, holding court in his dressing room afterward, and then going home to draft an act in yet another new play. And Tracy's feelings for Cohan were reciprocated; when Cohan inscribed a picture to him, he wrote, "To Spencer Tracy, A guy after my own heart."

Deciding they needed more of a home than a hotel room could ever be, Louise persuaded Spence to take a four-room apartment on East Ninety-eighth Street at the southern edge of Harlem—the first they had ever had. For help in furnishing the place, she appealed to the elder Tracys, who had some of their things shipped out from Milwaukee, and to Chuck Sligh, their one lasting friend from the furniture metropolis of Grand Rapids. They moved into their new home on October 10, and presently took delivery of a sturdy new Sligh bedroom set, Chuck having given them the wholesale price—$200. Still, they had to break up the payments to manage the purchase.

Tracy entered radio about this time, for he mentioned working as an announcer for Standard Oil in a couple of early interviews. Radio money would have come in handy, for concurrent with the New York opening of *The Baby Cyclone,* they enrolled Johnny—at the age of three years and three months—in the toddlers' program at the Wright Oral School. In the morning session, he joined a group of four other children who were learning to lace and tie their shoes and to sort colored yarn. That same month, Louise made a list of thirty-three words the boy was able to lip-read, among them *arm, ball, hat, shoe, soap, pillow, chair,* and *mouth.* A spelling list included nineteen words, and after a little time in school, a list of words he could actually say began with *mama, thumb,* and *lamb.* She watched as he would stroke his arm from shoulder to wrist and say *arm,* then stretch it out toward the coffeepot, withdrawing it suddenly, his eyes full of mischief as he shouted "*ot!*" (The *h* would come later.) Over time, *pineapple* became a favorite word (although it sounded a lot like *apple pie*). The word *fish* came out sounding like *foosh,* and on Fridays Spence took to murmuring, "Ah, foosh for dinner!"

In February 1928 Johnny developed a bad case of the measles, and Spence, upon his recovery, suggested that Weeze take him to Florida. "Florida!" she exclaimed. "He's in school and he shouldn't miss any."

"You can teach him," he said, urging her along. "He's so young. The change will do John good and his health comes first. Besides, you should have a trip."

Louise and John spent most of their days at Miami Beach. "John was crazy about the water," she said, "and had we stayed another week or two, I think he would have been swimming."

As his namesake was growing and learning to talk and understand spoken English, John Tracy was slowly fading away. The curious illness that had overtaken him in Milwaukee had been diagnosed as rectal cancer, and the crude radiation treatments of the day were taking their toll on a vibrant and generous man. He worried endlessly about money and his ability to make ends meet. In New York he took a position with General Motors, assigned to the National Account Division, but he suffered bouts of weakness and fatigue, and they were as unhappy with him as he was with them. At the same time he grew enormously proud of his son's success in New York and his association with the great George M. Cohan. ("He was a long time coming around," Spence marveled, "but—") Now practically a Broadway insider, he would stand at the back of Henry Miller's Theatre every night at 8:25 and count the house. And after the performance the two men would go to supper, arm in arm.

Cohan sold the movie rights to *The Baby Cyclone* and sent the play out on the road, first to Boston, then to Philadelphia. John regarded Spencer's absence with melancholy, but Carrie seized the opportunity to fix up the kids' new place. "I suppose Mother is up at your apartment by this time," he wrote one morning in a letter. "No doubt she will be busy there for a while, and you won't know the place . . . Am going to keep off my feet as much as possible today. I have rather an uncomfortable sensation where the trouble is, and it may be due to too much walking or a reaction from the treatments I have taken recently." He added: "Don't forget your Easter duty while in Boston."

The play's return to Boston lasted only a week, but Spence took advantage of Louise's absence to bring Lorraine Foat backstage on opening night. Lorraine had last heard from him in the days leading up to his marriage, when he urged her to come to Cincinnati and apply for a spot with the Stuart Walker company. ("Spence told me to get some pictures and send them along . . . My grandmother, my darling little grandmother, thought I should have gone, but I didn't.") Now Mrs. John Foster Holmes, Lorraine was proud of Spence's success and anxious to see him.

They talked for a long time—about Cohan, about the theater, about the separate paths their lives had taken. "He adored this son," Lorraine said, "but felt terribly about it. He *suffered* over that, feeling that somehow or other he had failed." Chuck Sligh came to Boston, and comments Spence made to him suggest Louise's trip to Florida may have been arranged for less than completely altruistic motives. "I think," said Chuck, "Spence, at that time, probably was . . . upset . . . Louise had given over her life to John . . . He gave me the feeling that she wasn't too attentive to his needs . . . I don't like to put words in his mouth, but the feeling I got was that, 'Gosh, I don't know, but Louise is so cold.' Something like that . . ."

Tracy came from a tradition, a teaching within the church, that sex within a marriage was solely for procreation, and that recreational sex—the act without the intent or possibility of reproduction—was immoral. "I really believe that it was a very separate part of their lives," his cousin Jane remarked. "It wasn't part of the warp and woof of their existence. It was not a natural, normal thing accepted with joy. And I do think, too, that the first result of the sexual act with Spencer and Louise, nine months later, was John—now I think that must have been tremendously traumatic to people of that generation with that kind of background." Johnny's birth had come almost nine months to the day after their marriage in Cincinnati. ("Very fast!" Johnny said one day in 1937. "You bet it was fast!" Louise agreed.) "I think that trauma must have led to: 'Let's not do this anymore.' And let's just not do THIS anymore—not let's prevent a birth."

That Spence and Louise still loved and respected and needed each other was obvious to the small circle of friends who knew them both, but the energies and urges normal to people in their twenties and thirties were sublimated, ignored, channeled into other avenues of thought and deed. Louise always tried to be there for him. ("When Spencer played out of town," she once said, "he needed us with him.") But Johnny's schooling made it difficult, if not impossible, to pull up and go, and Spence's work separated them for weeks at a stretch.

From Philadelphia, where blue laws prohibited Sunday performances, Tracy was able to come home for a day. John looked drawn and tired and anxious to get out of GM. Later, when he was in Chicago and Carroll was with him, John wrote the two of them about a job he was pursuing, concerned his salary demands would discourage an offer. "But I am desperate and nervous and worried so am going to work fast . . . I haven't said a word to Mother yet, [but will] tell her in a few days when I know a little more."

John Tracy, however, was too weak to work, and when Louise and Johnny left to join Spence in Chicago, they did so reluctantly. ("He was a very brave man," Louise said of her father-in-law. "You would never have known that he suffered at any time.") *The Baby Cyclone* enjoyed an eight-week stand at the Blackstone, and from there they went to Cleveland, where Spence would spend most of July playing stock. He returned to New York in late July, where he found himself assigned to the Chicago company of Cohan's newest play, a turgid comedy called *Whispering Friends*. His father was wasting away, the cancer by now having metastasized to his liver, and he hated the prospect of being stuck in Chicago. Frank Tracy, John's half brother, had died the previous month in Aberdeen at the age of sixty-seven, and the dark knowledge of John's condition enveloped his sister Jenny. "John will be the next one," she told her daughter Jane.

"He got sick," Tracy said of his father. "And then he got sicker. Weak. And scared. He'd look at me beggingly—as though I could help if I wanted to. I'd see him wince. Once, visiting, I heard him crying out in the other room . . . Nothing to do but wait and suffer and wait and wait." Prior to opening in Chicago, *Whispering Friends* played a six-night stand in Newark, and Spence made the commute into town by rail. Saturday being a matinee day, he was at the theater between performances when advised of his father's imminent passing. The news also reached Cohan in Monroe, where his own mother was near death, and at once he came, spending an entire hour alone with Spence, his hand on his shoulder, the call boy pounding insistently on the door. Back in Manhattan, Louise stayed with Mother Tracy at their hotel on East Eighty-sixth Street, stroking her hand. She spent a couple of minutes with John—he was conscious but did not speak—and then left the two of them alone. The end came peacefully at 6:15 in the evening, just as Cohan was racing to Spence's side.* Tracy played the performance that night as usual, and afterward found a taxi waiting outside to take him to the station.

They brought John's body back to Freeport the following Monday, and a viewing was held in the evening at the Wiese & Temple Funeral Church on Main Street. The funeral mass was celebrated at 9:30 the next morning at St. Mary's on Piety Hill, where John had served Mass as a child and where his father's altar still stood. Although she and her cousin Frank didn't have to go to the Rosary, Jane Feely would remember the awful sadness of the place, the black veils all the women wore and the crush of people, the prayers, the eating, the drinking. The cemetery was in the process of being expanded, and there was no space for John in the Tracy plot. Andrew Tracy managed to arrange a temporary grave in the middle of the grounds, and it was there that John Edward Tracy, aged fifty-four years, seven months, and five days, was buried. There would be time for laughter and remembrance afterward, but not for Spence, who had to catch up with the *Whispering Friends* company in Chicago and give a performance that evening.

It was a blessing for him not to have to go straight back to New York, with its familiar terrain and its constant reminders of his father's absence. The following day, Andrew Tracy's wife, Spence's aunt Mame, brought Aunt Jenny and Cousin Jane in on the train to see the matinee performance of *Whispering Friends*. Jane was eleven at the time and thought Spence's tiny

* Cohan's mother, Helen Costigan "Nellie" Cohan, died the following day—August 26, 1928.

dressing room, with its makeup mirror bordered in lightbulbs, nothing short of magnificent. "Did you really think I was any good?" he pressed the women, almost childlike in his need for reassurance, and they both told him he was just wonderful. "Talent isn't all that you have to have," he said sagely, echoing one of Cohan's admonitions. "You have to have personality. That's the thing that's important. A good personality." They talked about the future and where he would go next and how his life had inexorably changed with the death of his father. And then they all sat in his dressing room at the Illinois Theatre and wept.

At length he told them about the previous day, when, arriving at the theater, he saw his name in lights for the first time in his life. At considerable expense, Cohan had wired ahead and ordered star billing, which involved tearing down all the posters around town and putting up new ones that displayed the name of Spencer Tracy in ten-inch letters. The press notices and programs all had to be changed—all in tribute to John Tracy and the tradition that the show must go on and to the fact that his son was now, despite all prognostications to the contrary, a big shot.

To four generations of actors, dramatists, composers, producers, managers, scenic designers, librettists, and press agents, the heart of the Times Square theater district wasn't Forty-second and Broadway or the Winter Garden or even the stretch of pavement between Forty-fourth and Forty-fifth Streets known as Shubert Alley, but rather a six-story facade of red brick and limestone on West Forty-fourth Street, across from the Hudson and Belasco Theatres, that marked the marble-columned fold of the Lambs. In 1927 the membership numbered some 1,700 individuals—an all-time high—and the clubhouse served as both home and office to virtually every major name associated with the stage—Irving Berlin, Al Jolson, W. C. Fields, Fred Astaire, Eddie Foy, Douglas Fairbanks, William S. Hart, Will Rogers, David Belasco, and John Philip Sousa, to name but a few.

When actor John Cumberland offered to propose Pat O'Brien for membership in the fall of 1926, the mere suggestion of the honor caught him up short. "I thought you had to spend at least five to ten years on Broadway before this happened," he said. And when O'Brien, in turn, proposed his pal Tracy little more than a year later, the gesture was no less a matter of gravity. Spence had been Pat's guest at the clubhouse, had entered the grillroom with its stone floor, its rough-hewn oak tables, its dark-paneled walls, and its huge marble fireplace, and had sensed what it was like to be, in Pat's words, "A club man, an actor among fellow actors." He became a duly elected member of the Lambs on December 15, 1927, and managed to scrape together the $200 entrance fee, semiannual dues of

$23.33, and 10 percent war tax only with considerable difficulty and Louise's patient indulgence. And so it was not by virtue of his performance in *The Baby Cyclone* that Spencer Tracy "arrived" as a Broadway player, but rather by his acceptance into the Lambs as a member, professional class.

When the Midwest tour of *Whispering Friends* petered out, Tracy returned to New York. Louise was now immersed in Johnny's studies at the Wright Oral School, so Spence retreated to the Lambs, where he spent his days writing letters and working the phones, a bank of which lined the north wall of the reception corridor. By edict of incorporation, the Lambs never closed. The bar officially served tea and apple juice, but the premium stuff—whiskey, sherry, champagne—was always around, tucked away in someone's locker or available for purchase from the night doorman. "Dry times or wet, the bar of the Lambs was never raided," Pat O'Brien said, recalling that the mayor of the city of New York, the honorable James J. Walker, was a loyal member. "We had political power."

Idle in the midst of a new season, Tracy's natural bent toward melancholia deepened to the point where he suffered wicked bouts of depression. His self-loathing over his son's deafness surged at times of inactivity, and his grief over the loss of his father swept over him in waves. One weekday afternoon it took hold of him as he began a routine note to his mother. "Mother dear," he wrote, "your lovely wire made us so happy, dear. We were going to wire you—thought of it several times—but didn't know where to send it . . . We had a dandy dinner and a wonderful time at Ray's. Spoke of you & dear Dad so much." And then the pen began to race—page after page—as the pent-up feelings suddenly spilled over.

> O Mother dear—I never let you know and never will again how much I miss my wonderful dad. I have come home at night and stood and cried before his picture in our front room. I talk to him many times. He was so good to me—and I know you won't mind—nor will Carroll—but I always felt he was closer to me than anyone—except you, of course, Dear. He understood me so well, and was so kind and always forgave. Sometimes I want to go with him—I know I'd be all right where he is—and when that time comes, I'll hate to leave anyone behind but I won't be afraid, and I'll be glad because I'm going to see my dad. But we must be cheerful—and I will, Dear. Forgive me for writing this letter, but sometimes I feel I just gotta see Pop—or I'll go crazy.

It was as naked an expression of inner feelings as he ever permitted himself, but talk of suicidal grief and going crazy could well frighten his mother, and he obviously fought to control the words he was now putting down on the page. "But he is happy now," he continued, reining himself in, "and he is watching us and taking care of us, and he wants us to do our best and be happy—and we will, Dear. We have lots to live for. Excuse all this, darling Mother, but I guess I'm still yours and Pop's little boy, and sometimes I get sad—and cry—just like my little boy."

John Tracy had found such joy in his four-year-old grandson, his little victories and pleasures and the sounds he made to represent words. Around the house, Johnny had names for the people he loved, vocal labels that derived from the words he could say. *Mumum* was his name for Grandmother Tracy, *Mum* (pronounced "Moom") for his grandaunt Emma. *One* was his teddy bear. His nurse came again in November, the one who had been with him in Grand Rapids and at Lake Delavan, and although her name was Eleanor Lystad, she became *Sss* at first, then *Sis*.

Eleanor's arrival, along with the costs of the Wright Oral School, put yet another burden on the family finances. Spence scared up a week of stock on Long Island, but was forced to borrow $1,000 from his mother until he could find steadier work. He gave her an IOU at 6 percent interest, but the whole matter upset Carrie so greatly she worried that Spencer would be unable to support his family. Then Johnny broke his leg, the result of a fall while playing in the park, and was in the hospital for six straight weeks. Arrangements had to be made for one of his teachers to go to his bedside for a short period each day to keep up his speech and lipreading, which otherwise would have suffered sharp relapses.

Pat O'Brien saw enough of Spence at the Lambs—too much, for he too was out of work—to know the spiritual toll unemployment was taking on his old friend. "An unemployed actor becomes a different person," he said. "His morale sags, he wears a haunted look. The burden of the ages sits on his shoulders as he gossips with other unemployed actors." When Lester Bryant, a brother Lamb who was married to actress Edna Hibbard, announced one day that he was going to organize a new stock company, Pat walked him around the clubhouse until he had engaged practically his entire company—William Boyd, Frank McHugh, O'Brien himself, Tracy, of course. Spence had sworn he wouldn't play stock again that winter—had, in fact, turned down a season with the George Cukor company in Rochester—but he was plainly out of options and desperate for income. O'Brien, McHugh, and he performed in the Lambs Kid Gambol on December 16, then passed the hat for traveling money and entrained to Baltimore, where the Auditorium Players would open Christmas Eve in a gangster melodrama called *Tenth Avenue*.

Nineteen twenty-eight had been a rough year, but 1929 would be rougher still. The run of the Auditorium Players lasted just three weeks. ("But," said Frank McHugh, "it was a rip-roaring three weeks!") Leaving

With Albert Van Dekker in *Conflict,* 1929.
(AUTHOR'S COLLECTION)

Baltimore put Tracy on a seemingly endless rotation of two- and three-week stands, unsure of where his next job would come from, breathing life into mediocre material and occasionally making it sing. Returning home to New York, he wired his mother in Freeport and said that he had "several things in view," and did in fact land a part in a play called *Scars* on February 6.

Backed by New York retailer Hiram Bloomingdale and authored by Warren Lawrence, the brother of Boston golf crack and playwright Vincent Lawrence, *Scars* ran the arc of an American serviceman's career from draftee to flight commander to peacetime has-been. Out of town, the lead actor had been a toothy twenty-seven-year-old named Clark Gable. He was well received, giving, in the words of one critic, "a true-to-life picture of a man who hit heights of glory and then slid to the bottom of the pile." The play was choppy, though, full of awkward stage waits that undercut the psychology of the piece. "I didn't like my part," Gable later said. "I hadn't been able to get anything out of it. In Springfield I handed in my notice; I wanted to leave just as soon as they could get another actor up from New York to take my place—and it couldn't be too soon to please me." Tracy stepped into the role of Richard Banks with little rehearsal and suddenly the play, no masterpiece but with flashes of near-brilliance, began working as never before.

Retitled *Conflict,* it was brought to the Fulton Theatre on March 6, where critics saw an uneven but sincere piece of work, elevated by Tracy's masterful performance and supported by an exceptionally capable cast consisting of Edward Arnold, Frank McHugh, George Meeker, and Albert Van Dekker. "The final impression," J. Brooks Atkinson wrote in the *Times,* "is of a genuine character portrait surrounded with disenchanting chromoes. What Mr. Lawrence and Mr. Tracy have done with Richard Banks deserves a more harmonious setting."

No one thought the play a disaster, but the fact that it needed work was indisputable. Tracy thought Banks the strongest part he had yet played before a New York audience, and when the author announced his intention to revise the play over a Holy Week recess, Spence joined him in making the rounds of the various dailies, going from one drama critic to the next, notices in hand. *Conflict* hit the boards again on Monday, April 1, and the critics were invited to come take another look. Regrettably, the play wasn't much better than before, but virtually every critic gave it a kinder notice. Trade improved slightly, but the company managed to survive only on cut rates.

Conflict closed on April 27, 1929, and Tracy went almost immediately into rehearsals for an ill-fated comedy titled *Salt Water.* They tried it out in Mamaroneck, where it was well received, then moved it to Atlantic City, where, despite sterling reviews, the play's coauthor, actress Jean Dalrymple, concluded her lead actor had "no sense of comedy." She pushed director John Golden to replace him with actor Frank Craven. "So there we all were, down in Atlantic City, and the show went very well. But, of course, Tracy was really heavy in the part, and afterwards Frank Craven said, 'Oh, I could really play that part. I could play the hell out of that part.' So Golden closed the show and let Spencer go."

Smarting from such a summary dismissal, Tracy returned to Manhattan in a surly mood. Broadway had suffered its worst season in nine years, due largely to the proliferation of talking pictures. Dramatic stock wasn't doing any better against the onslaught of amplified dialogue. Two years earlier Tracy had advised Chamberlain Brown he was playing Lima strictly for the money. "Next season," he said, "I should have a nice bankroll, and I hope this will be the last time I have to do stock—unless it's a real good one." Now, miraculously, a real good one presented itself, almost on cue.

Selena Royle had settled into a pattern of playing summers with the Albee stock of Providence, Rhode Island, one of the top two or three companies in all of North America. When the company's leading man, Walter Gilbert, quit early in the season, she naturally thought of Spence. "By this time," she said, "we had played together so often that we automatically knew what to expect of the other on stage—a great advantage in stock,

Spencer Tracy
of the
Albee Players
- Season 1929 -

Albee Theatre
Providence, R. I.

(SUSIE TRACY)

especially in Providence, where we played five matinees a week . . . So, on my recommendation, Spencer was sent for." Tracy settled in for the remainder of the season, taking a house for the summer that would give Johnny the experience of having a yard of his own. His debut at Providence was in a four-act mystery called *The Silent House,* and while he was universally well received, nobody mistook him for a traditional leading man.

"There is nothing stagy about him," the critic for the *Providence Journal* declared. "No makeup—none to speak of—no tricks whatever; just an unassuming, easy manner that gets him about the stage without your quite knowing how he does it. He belongs to that school of acting—if it is a school—which doesn't want you to think it is acting. It is acting, though, of a very high order, forceful, reserved, artistic."

It looked as if the season at Providence would be a triumph, and Louise happily settled into the relaxing routine of managing her own house. "Upstairs and down, outdoors and in, John would trot. The freedom of it all was a constant wonder and delight after hotels and apartments and Central Park, with its KEEP OFF signs dotting its hundreds of acres of grass and its policemen whose main job seemed to be to enforce those warnings." The ensuing weeks brought *The Second Man* and *Night Hostess* and *Skidding,* and while Tracy was always a hit with both audiences and reviewers, an uneasiness crept into the atmosphere of the company, as if there was a subtle malfunction that nobody could quite place a finger on. It was likely Tracy's spoof of John Barrymore in *The Royal Family* that sealed his fate.

Tracy blamed Albee's general manager—a man called Foster Lardner—whose sense of material was seemingly infallible but whose ideas of what actors were suited to what parts were rigidly traditional. Tracy was a fine actor, Lardner acknowledged, but lacked the profile of a leading man. "The

women don't want to come to see you at the matinee," he told Tracy in letting him go, "but it wouldn't surprise me if someday you became a great
motion picture star."

"How the hell can I do that," Tracy responded, "if I don't have any sex
appeal?"

He was terminated with two weeks' salary and spent much of August at
liberty, waiting for the new season to come together in New York. He spent
his afternoons at the Lambs, saw Johnny principally at dinner and on Sundays. All sorts of projects took shape at the club—ideas for plays, songs that
needed writing, schemes to keep working. A year earlier, Jack McGowan
had formed a loose partnership with Joe Santley, who was secretary of the
club, and Theodore Barter, to produce their own plays and the plays of
brother Lambs. In October they had signed Tracy to appear in a postwar
tragicomedy McGowan was writing called *Nigger Rich*. Spirits ran high
until the first production of Santley, Barter & McGowan hit the boards, a
melodrama from Johnny Meehan titled *The Lady Lies*. It lasted twenty-four
performances, putting a quick end to plans for the McGowan play until Lee
Shubert embraced it the following summer.

Retitled *Parade*, it had a week at Greenwich, where Chamberlain
Brown had a stock company. Shubert thought the play had potential, but
butted heads with the author over its provocative original title. Unilaterally,
Shubert changed the title to *True Colors*, a move which so incensed
McGowan that he threatened to withdraw it. Shubert backed down, but
the staging of the play by its headstrong author was, by common agreement, careless at best. After one invitation-only preview, during which the
crowd's mood went from hope to despair, it premiered at the Royale to
largely negative reviews and was yanked after eight days—something of a
record for the distinguished members of Cohan's inner circle.

Tracy had plans to step away from *Nigger Rich* before the white slip
appeared on the call board, as Sam Harris had contracted him for a play
called *Dread*. The work of Owen Davis, the Pulitzer Prize–winning author
of nearly a hundred plays, *Dread* was the aptly titled study of a young man's
disintegration into madness, a graphic look at how the caustic effects of fear
and a guilty conscience can do both emotional and physical damage to a
man. Tracy, with the highest of hopes for the role, began rehearsals under
the author's direction on September 30, Madge Evans, Miriam Doyle, and
Frank Shannon working in support. The first performance took place at
Washington's Belasco Theatre on the night of October 20.

There were no real heroes in *Dread*, only the amoral Perry Crocker and
a pair of willing victims. On the eve of Crocker's wedding to the frail Olive
Ingram, he declares his love for Olive's younger sister, Marion. Then
Crocker's wife appears at the door and tells Olive of her son by him and his

subsequent desertion of the family. The shock of it all brings on a heart attack. Olive's dying words to Perry: "You'll—never—have—my—sister—living or dead. I'll stop you—some way—some how—you—can't—have—Marion!" Then, clutching his wrist, she falls back in the chair, her fingers locked in a death grip, Perry unable to pry himself free. He lies to Marion, tells her Olive has blessed their union, but Marion knows better. "When I go with you—and I am going—I will be as degraded as you are." Perry is tormented by Olive's death, her vow to him, the memory of her cold, rigid hand refusing to let him go. He flinches at sounds in the house, sees Olive's form in the shadows, deteriorates into a pale, quivering shadow of his former self.

Great things were expected of *Dread,* the most ambitious play Davis had written since *Icebound,* the one that had won him the Pulitzer. The *Post's* John Daly hailed the playwright's return to melodrama, the boldness of his contrivances, the stunning fact that the old master's theatrics "spit fire and cause squirmings in the orchestra chairs just as his earlier works did when they played on the old Stair and Haviland circuit in the 'ten-twent-thirt' days . . . Mr. Tracy stands up nobly under the punishment, a villain who makes you want to shoot him in the back or kick him in the trousers every time he turns around—so that by the end of the night you expect to hear hisses."

Harris had planned to move the company to Philadelphia, but a musicians' strike intervened and the play landed instead in Brooklyn. Stopping at the Lambs, Tracy was asked by Ring Lardner, the renowned author of *Alibi Ike* and *Haircut,* what he was doing. "I told him," said Tracy, "I was going to Brooklyn with *Dread* and he said, 'Is there any other way?' "

Lardner's disdain notwithstanding, *Dread* managed to fill the 1,700-seat Majestic on a Monday night. "In the parlance of the stage," said the notice in the *Brooklyn Standard Union,* "overplaying a part means 'taking it big,' mostly concerned where grief and semi-madness are the expressive emotions. *Dread* calls for both emotions in a large measure. Spencer Tracy and Miss Madge Evans play the two important characters with proper reserve. Others might have 'taken it big' and ruined what is now a most thrilling piece of drama . . . The audience called for ten final curtains, which speaks for itself."

The strong responses in both Washington and Brooklyn would have assured a place for *Dread* on Broadway but for the fact that the play opened in Brooklyn on October 28, 1929. The next day—October 29—would go down in history as Black Tuesday, the day when huge blocks of stock were thrown on the plummeting market, and paper millionaires were rendered penniless in the space of a few hours. Sam Harris, his funding uncertain, sent both *Dread* and the promising *Swan Song* (by the surefire team of Ben

Hecht and Charles MacArthur) to the storehouse, hinting the Davis play "may be rewritten" but ultimately allowing only one Broadway production to go forth under his management in the year following the crash. The Brooklyn performance of *Dread* on the night of November 2 was the last ever given anywhere. Louise disliked the play, its obvious hokum, and thought it deserved to close, but Spence was bitterly disappointed and always carried the lingering suspicion it would have made him a star. In May 1940 he lamented its disappearance to Halsey Raines of the *New York Herald Tribune,* saying that the property he was "most enthusiastic" about, the one he was sure would have been "a box office sensation" had it come to Broadway, was an obscure but singularly nerve-racking play called *Dread.*

"Now we sometimes laugh about *Dread,*" Louise later wrote, "and Spencer will relate with great gusto how the family nearly was broken up, of how his mother demanded that he leave the stage and get a job whereby he could be sure of supporting his wife and child, and how his wife said if he left the stage she would leave him. But at that time it was not so funny." In the wake of the stock market crash, Mother Tracy took note of the fact that her son had worked eight jobs in the fifteen months since the close of *The Baby Cyclone.* An actor wasn't paid for up to five weeks of rehearsal, and during the first two weeks of performance a show could close without any notice, making it very possible to earn just two weeks' salary for six or seven weeks' work. There was also the traveling, and even among the luckiest of actors there were periods before and after when no money at all was coming in. "Even to approximate foresight to any degree," Louise said, "an actor should divide his weekly salary into tenths, living on one-tenth and banking the other nine to fortify those unproductive ones."

When playing, Spence was earning as much as $400 a week, but with layoffs and rehearsals factored in, his earnings came closer to $150 a week. So when Mother Tracy raised the subject as forcefully as she could, the best answer her son could give her was "Louise said she'd leave me if I quit the theatre." Late in life, Louise wasn't so sure she had ever put it exactly that way. "I don't remember saying quite that," she said, "but I might have, because I felt that Spence must do the thing he could do so well." In 1942 Pat O'Brien recalled witnessing the exchange, which was sparked, as he remembered it, by his suggestion, during a particularly lean period, that both he and Spence call it quits and go back home to Milwaukee and settle down.

> Louise flamed. She was always a good actress, but she never put as much emotion into any role as she did in her reply to my suggestion. "No!" she blazed to Spence, ignoring me. "If you give up the theatre I'll leave you. You're not a good actor, you're a *great* actor! I don't mind going hungry. I don't mind doing our laundry. I don't

mind *any* sacrifice because you have something not one actor in ten-thousand has, and the day will come when you'll be acclaimed the finest actor on the stage! I'm not only willing but *eager* to do anything I can to help you toward that day. But DON'T QUIT. You CAN'T." It isn't often a man finds someone with that much confidence in him.

After the folding of *Dread,* Tracy was out of work a full three weeks before he picked up a job replacing Henry Hull in a Jazz Age tragedy titled *Veneer.* Hull, the nominal star, had decided to leave the show in favor of A. A. Milne's new comedy *Michael and Mary;* Tracy stepped into the role of a smooth-talking braggart with less than a week's rehearsal. Nobody expected it to last very long, but a deal was afoot for the Shuberts to buy in and take the show to Chicago, where fresh casting, slick staging, and a new title might possibly save it. Louise, who read all of Spence's plays, thought *Veneer* "an unpleasant play, though very moving at times." It gave Tracy a chance to wear—and pay for—the expensive wardrobe he had bought for *Dread.* It was a star part, and for the first time in New York his name would appear in lights on a theater marquee. Most important, it was a job at a time when nearly a third of all the theaters on Broadway were dark, and the new slogan along the big street was "Got change for a match?"

Hull played his final performance on Saturday, November 30, and Tracy stepped into the role of Charlie Riggs two days later. He played a week, then followed the show into an Equity-approved layoff, the Shuberts guaranteeing salaries while they moved the physical production to Chicago's Garrick Theatre. It opened there on December 20 under the title *Blue Heaven* and was largely savaged by the critics.

Back in New York, things were particularly grim, with nearly a score of houses lacking legitimate plays. The few genuine hits—*Strictly Dishonorable, June Moon, It's a Wise Child, Berkeley Square*—were gobbling up much of the available business, and the holiday spirit was so lacking along the street that the "merchandise" men who supplied wet goods to the Times Square theater district were forced to accept installment payments to move inventory. That Tracy was able to get himself cast in a new play titled *All the World Wondered* was something of a miracle. The play wasn't promising— an all-male cast in a decidedly raw portrait of life on death row. They played three days in Hartford, where the audiences were, in Tracy's words, "as cold as the Yukon." He wasn't in a particularly hopeful mood when his pals at the Lambs next saw him, glum and sagging. "He was a pretty disconsolate guy," Pat O'Brien remembered. They were all sitting at the round table in the grill.

"Boys, I'm in one hell of a flop!" Tracy announced to the group. "I'd like to pull out, but I have a run-of-the-play contract."

"What do you mean pull out?" someone said. "Stay with it."

"It's to have a week of doctoring," Tracy told them, "and then open on Tuesday."

"Maybe you'll get a break," another suggested helpfully, "and the theater will burn down."

CHAPTER 6

The Last Mile

In the years prior to 1924, Texas counties with inmates convicted of capital crimes conducted their own executions, generally by hanging. Then the legislature consolidated all such business at the State Penitentiary in Huntsville, establishing a death row at the birthplace of Sam Houston. Its centerpiece, at the end of a brief corridor adjacent to nine holding cells, was a handsome new electric chair, built of solid oak by prison craftsmen. They did their work well; over the next forty years, "Old Sparky" would become the final unpadded resting stop for 361 men and women on their way to court-mandated eternity. One such prisoner, a condemned killer called Robert Blake, was dispatched on April 19, 1929—but not before having set down on paper a taste of life in the Texas death house called "The Law Takes Its Toll."

When the *American Mercury* posthumously published the sketch in July of that year, it attracted a lot of attention, including that of a twenty-two-year-old actor and playwright named Ely John Wexley. Blake's account, in the form of a one-act play, covered the eighteen hours leading up to the execution of Number Six, one of a handful of condemned men—five white, one Mexican—at Huntsville. Number Seven breaks into verse more often than not, Number Nine has gone mad, howling "Jo-------nes!" at all hours. The talk among the others centers on clemency, then the banter turns grim as the details of the condemned man's ritual play themselves out—the last meal, the slitting of the trouser legs, the shaving of the head, and the ceremonial reading of the death warrant.

"Wonder how it will feel," Six muses. "I hope it won't take long. Wonder if a fellow knows anything after the first shot hits him . . . You know, it's funny. I was worse at my trial than I am here. I almost broke down there at the trial. I lost 15 pounds when my trial was going on." The guard, having some difficulty opening the door to the death chamber, yanks at the lock and rattles it. Number Seven tells Six to take the keys and open the door himself. "I'd stay here until next Christmas before I'd open that door for 'em," Six declares. "Well, the door is open. I'll say goodbye to everybody again."

These lines, Blake notes, were written while Six was being strapped into the chair. "I hope I am the last one that ever sits in this chair," Six calls out. "Tell my mother that my last words were of her." The lights go dim as they hear the whine of a motor. The others cry out, and then the lights go dim again and yet again.

"They're giving him the juice again!" shouts Number Five. "Wonder what they're trying to do, *cook* him?"

Wexley saw the basis of a full-length play in "The Law Takes Its Toll," but struggled with the problem of expanding it to three acts until the events of October 3, 1929. The attempted escape of two prisoners at the Colorado State Penitentiary in Cañon City went awry when a guard was killed while grappling over a set of keys. Knowing they'd hang for his death and, consequently, had nothing to lose, the convicts began taking hostages. In the bloody standoff that followed, eight guards and five inmates were killed and another ten were wounded. Wexley plumbed the New York dailies for details of the riot, and his play took shape within a couple of weeks.

The first act was Blake's sketch almost verbatim, Wexley's chief liberty being to change Blake's Mexican prisoner to a black man. The second and third acts portrayed an opportunistic escape attempt patterned on the events at Cañon City. In the end, the matter of a title was more vexing than the structure; Wexley had inserted bits of Tennyson's "Charge of the Light Brigade" amid the machine gun bursts of his play's final moments ("Oh, the wild charge they made! All the world wondered!") and so he decided to call it *All the World Wondered.* Inexplicably, his agent sent the play to producer Herman E. Shumlin, a onetime reporter and press agent whose track record was 0–4, his last play having tanked just two days prior to the onset of Black Tuesday. Shumlin, who was used to seeing only "the bottom of the barrel," was astonished at the raw power of Wexley's play and managed to scare up the money to produce it at a time when "all the backers anybody could think of were jumping out of high windows."

"It was one o'clock when I finished reading it," Shumlin recalled, "and

I went all the way out to Brooklyn and woke up Sam Golden, the printer, and read it to him.* He gave me a check for $500 to buy an option on the play, I think maybe because he wanted to go back to bed. After that, my troubles began, raising the money to put the show on. I borrowed from a bank. I squeezed my relatives dry." The title was the first thing to go, but it would be nearly a month before the play had the title under which it would see its Broadway debut: *The Last Mile.*

To direct, Shumlin selected Chester Erskine, who had earlier had a hand in staging *The Criminal Code,* a similarly themed prison drama that was one of the season's few genuine hits. Briefly an actor but too tall and pale for anything but character work, Erskine knew the success of Wexley's play would depend on its casting and the ability of its actors to inhabit their characters to the point of morbidity. Skeptical of Spencer Tracy from the outset, Erskine regarded their meeting as a courtesy at first, not the urgent mating dance that comes with the ideal match of actor and role.

"I had seen a few of his performances," Shumlin said, "and was not overly impressed by him as a candidate for the lead in *The Last Mile.* I was just about to dismiss him when something about our too-brief casting interview stayed with me. Since it was getting on to dinnertime, I invited him to join me at a theatrical haunt. There, in a less strained atmosphere, I was suddenly made aware as we were talking that, beneath the surface, here was a man of passion, violence, sensitivity, and desperation: no ordinary man, and just the man for the part."

Wexley's play was intense, grim, uncompromising; hard to take over the course of three acts. And there were no women in the cast, an anomaly on Broadway, where the ticket-buying decisions were often made by wives and girlfriends and where the matinee trade was crucial to the success of a show.† Louise, as was her habit, read the script and told Spence she thought it "pretty bad." There was little that jumped off the page, other than the unusually coarse language tossed between the prisoners. "It was so *violent,*" she said, grimacing. "That was the kind of part I never liked him in."

Tracy's contract for *All the World Wondered,* signed on January 14, 1930, called for his now standard price of $400 a week, payable Saturdays, and weekly bonuses of $50 and $100 if the gross hit $8,000 and $10,000, respectively. Rehearsals began the following day, Tracy meeting his fellow prisoners for the first time: James Bell, who would play the gutsy Richard Walters, Cell 7, whose execution is imminent as the curtain rises; Howard Phillips,

---

* Sam Golden was the owner of the Artcraft Litho and Printing Company, which produced most of the programs and window cards seen on Broadway.
† The rare exception to the rule was *Journey's End,* a British war drama with an all-male cast that was a hit in New York and Chicago as well as in London.

whose hot-tempered Fred Mayor, Cell 3, would be next in rotation; Hale Norcross, who, as "Red" Kirby, Cell 9, would be the graybeard, the senior member of the group; Ernest Whitman, the muscular black man engaged to play the superstitious Vincent Jackson, Cell 13; George Leach, chosen by Erskine to play Eddie Werner, Cell 11, Wexley's crazy man, a poet of sorts; and Joseph Spurin-Calleia, the Maltese actor and singer who would be playing the dapper Tom D'Amoro, Cell No. 1. All took their places alongside the men who would be their captors: Don Costello, Herbert Heywood, Orville Harris, Ralph Theodore, Richard Abbott, Henry O'Neill, Clarence Chase, Allen Jenkins, Albert West.

"The sixteen were seated in a straight line across the stage," Herman Shumlin recalled, "and when they read their parts for the first time, it was clear they meant business . . . Maybe (in part, at least) the absence of women in the cast had something to do with it too. With no good-looking actress to make them feel self-conscious, they seemed to forget they were actors of long experience, with all kinds of past performances and position to live up to. Instead, they gave themselves up completely to the emotional fury of the play and into the guiding hands of the director."

"Tracy was perfect. Tracy made the show. But then Tracy got worried and he said he wouldn't do it. He had to shoot a priest in the play and he said he'd rather not." Henry O'Neill, the actor playing Father O'Connors and a fellow Catholic, could see that Tracy's torment was deep and genuine and not simply a dodge, and he took him downtown to see a priest. As Shumlin remembered it, "The father told Tracy he need have no scruples," but then Wexley fixed the problem by writing the priest's death out of the script altogether, finding the mere threat of his shooting more effective in sustaining the tension than the act itself.

Erskine quickly got the show on its feet, marking out the individual cells—each just two and a half steps wide—on the floor with a piece of chalk. Tracy spent a lot of time miming the window in the back of his cell, looking out to such an exaggerated degree that Erskine, three years his junior, made a memorable comment: "Spence, I didn't tell you to break the window, I told you to look through it." His point, which Tracy took to heart, was that a good actor didn't look out the window—he let the *audience* look out the window.

"He was," said Erskine, "cooperative and disciplined, and set an attitude for the other performers who followed his lead. He was the kind of actor whom a director leans on for just such behavior." They spent such long hours at it that Tracy took a room at the Lambs Club, three blocks from the theater, to avoid traveling all the way home to Ninety-eighth Street. Tensions ran high, rehearsal being a thoroughly emotional process, and there were more than the usual flashes of temper.

"I cannot remember," wrote Tracy, "when I have spent so much time with other members of the cast outside of the theater, discussing the story of the play back and forth. And I don't think any of us can ever forget the first dress rehearsal inside the completed prison set. It had been all very well to pretend to be clutching at bars on bare and dingy stages—but now, confined within a four-by-nine cell, chafing at real cold steel—well, it was a sensation! The end of the first act found us rushing out into the wings, desperate for cigarettes. Nobody had any intention of staying in the cell longer than necessary."

Never before had Tracy immersed himself so deeply in a part, and never had he felt so completely drained by one. "As Killer Mears he had to expose a less-winning phase of his personality," Erskine said, "one which might unlock secrets of his inner self and which he would have preferred to remain hidden. It is a choice many actors have to make but which only the artists can survive."

Tempting fate, Shumlin set the New York opening of the play, still titled *All the World Wondered,* for February 13, pointing out that the numerals in "1930" added up to thirteen. Tryouts took place at Parsons' Theatre in Hartford beginning on the sixth, and the cast, to a man, was dubious. "They all felt that the play was a good one, an unusual one," Shumlin said, "but they were almost all a little doubtful of its chances for success. This was hardly astonishing since it departed to such a great extent from the traditional rules of what a successful play should be."

That first performance was a ragged affair, the set being insubstantial compared to what they would have in New York, but Tracy as Mears was letter perfect. "Tracy fought the role through rehearsal—not the doing of it, but the surrendering to it," Erskine said. "When, however, he finally did surrender to it, it was total, absolute, and frightening. He did not simulate anger and violence, he *was* anger and violence. In one night—at the out-of-town opening—he changed from a presentable juvenile and a hopeful leading man to an artist, a true artist. He had crossed the threshold into that area where he could submerge himself in a role to the point of eliminating himself completely, to the point where he could no longer tell which was which himself."

All the World Wondered brought forth a mixed reaction from the Hartford audience. One man was overheard to say to his wife, "It ain't so pleasant to see *Romeo and Juliet* either." Another, putting a brighter spin on the evening, said, "Well, it's kinda good to see a show without any wimmen in it, ain't it?" The notices were similarly conflicted, recognizing the power of the material but wondering just how much the general public could take. "One would call it rank melodrama," said the reviewer for the *Hartford Times,* "if it were not so truthful a report of what all the world knows has happened at least three times in our large American prisons within the past six months . . . Either this show will be a dismal failure or it will pack them in."

Erskine and Wexley set about doctoring the play, shaping the dialogue to accommodate the needs and characteristics of its individual actors. ("Some individuals simply cannot say things in a certain way," Erskine explained, "no matter how splendid an actor or actress they may be. Expressing the same thought in another way is the director's only alternative.") About one thing both men were adamant: All six of the condemned men would stay guilty as sin—no cheap points for making one of the characters unjustly convicted. Erskine noted that of the three basic appeals in the theatre—eye, ear, and instinct—the oldest and strongest was instinct, and that his best chance for success would be to strive for "sympathy for a situation rather than for the people who are in that situation."

The camaraderie of the cast was infectious, and when the company manager, in his line of duty, went through the group, asking which of them wanted Pullmans on the way back to New York, they decided en masse to take the midnight train instead and sit up in the coach together. "Hearing this," said Shumlin, "the management (Erskine and myself) gave up our 'sumptuous' drawing room and all rode back together, playing poker (which cost me $26) eating sandwiches and in general having one swell time."

The following Thursday night, Wexley's revision, titled *The Last Mile,* opened at the Sam H. Harris Theatre before an audience that had only the vaguest idea of what they were about to see. At 8:50 p.m. the curtain rose on a stark row of identically configured cells, each but one inhabited by the pale gray figure of a condemned prisoner. Erskine had told the cast he didn't want anyone wearing makeup, and it was Henry Dreyfus' lighting scheme that took the place of greasepaint and eyebrow pencil. A slab of concrete had been poured to stabilize the iron bars, and the harsh acoustics lent a cold authenticity to the prison set. A steel door at stage right led to offices and the outside world. A green door at stage left opened into the bright white light of the death chamber.

Actor Howard Phillips, clutching the bars, spoke first: "Nine o'clock, Walters."

"How do you know?" asked James Bell.

"Just heard the whistle blow."

"Funny," mused Bell. "I didn't hear it. You've got good ears, Three."

"Sure I got good ears. Nothin' to do but listen, is there?"

"Nothin' to do but listen," Bell repeated listlessly. "Well, fellers, this is my last coupla hours . . ."

The words took on a forlorn, obligatory cadence, as if governed by a

With James Bell in Chester Erskine's staging of *The Last Mile*.
(AUTHOR'S COLLECTION)

weary piece of machinery. Then George Leach, as the ghostly Werner, broke
into a crude verse about the chair they all called the Midnight Special:

> *The death house's where they come and go,*
> *They linger just a little time,*
> *Before they give you the electric chair,*
> *Sentenced for some awful crime . . .*

And suddenly Tracy, his words erupting like rifle shots, appeared at the
bars of his cage: "Shut up, you crazy bastard!"

Unminding, Leach continued on.

"Drake!" hollered Tracy. "Why don't you stop him?"

"Stop him yerself," returned the guard, played with surly intransigency
by Don Costello. "I like it."

"Bitch!"

And so it went, the panic of impending doom informing every glance,
every line, every nuance of posture. Hardened prisoners awkwardly reassured and comforted each other as one among them sat trembling and
hopeless, the preparations for execution going forth as mandated by law.

"No detail is missed," Burns Mantle, the veteran critic, wrote for the *New York Daily News*. "For half an hour you sit, tense and miserable, through the visits of the prison priest for the last prayers; the visit of reporters for the last messages of the condemned; the visits of the guards to cut the trousers leg, moisten the hair of the head, and shave the temples of the man to go. You hear the reading of the death warrant and finally you grip the arms of your chair as the march to the chair begins and the mumbling, shaken voice of Richard Walters is heard, assuring his cell mates that he will be game, that he will meet them, he hopes, somewhere, sometime."

And through the green door he staggered: "I wish I'm the last one who ever sits in that goddamn bastard chair!" After a moment's silence, as the other condemned men waited, tightly gripping the bars, there came a deep, reverberating hum from the dynamos, and the lights went dim. Then a pause as they came back up. Howard Phillips as Fred Mayor, Number Three, broke down and sobbed. Then again the whine of the motors and again the lights went low. And then Tracy delivered his curtain line, an echo straight from the Texas death house. "They're givin' him the juice again!" he erupted in a burst of animal fury. "What the hell are they tryin' to do? *Cook* him??"

And from that moment forward, Spencer Tracy, with both truth and passion as his twin weapons, dominated the play. Chet Erskine was at the back of the auditorium: "I suddenly saw him, after a hesitant start, realize his power as he felt the audience drawn into the experience of the play and respond to the measure of his skill and the power of his personality. I knew that he had found himself as an actor, and I knew that he knew it."

At intermission the audience sat in stunned silence at first, and then the conversation and the milling about was unusually subdued. Some people left the theater and never came back. There was a report that one woman got physically ill. Burns Mantle could remember no other experience "as emotionally upsetting" and fought an impulse to bolt from the room. "Nothing this season," said Gilbert Gabriel of the *American,* "has crossed the footlights with such unregenerate savagery. Nothing, I'll witness, has left its house so shaken and stirred as the first act of *The Last Mile* did." The performances in Hartford hadn't gone like this, and the cast took their cigarette break in utter silence.

When the curtain rose on the second act, the scene was the same, except that Walters had been replaced by Jackson, the black man, in Cell 7. Two weeks had passed, and now it was time for Mayor to die. The banter and the action were familiar from the events of the first act, and then the guard Drake got too close to Mears' cell while pushing the condemned's last meal through the aperture. In a flash, Mears had his arm around the guard's throat, and the other convicts watched motionless, their eyes popping in disbelief, as he choked him into unconsciousness.

Tracy was so keyed up—as were they all—that, as Herman Shumlin remembered it, he "so far forgot he was only acting that when he grabbed the guard from whom he obtains the keys of his cell and choked him, he actually choked him so relentlessly that the curtain of the third act had to be deferred three minutes before the guard, Don Costello, regained full consciousness and sufficient strength to go on with the play."

As Tracy told it, "I was supposed to grab the guard to get the keys to unlock the cell, but that night the keys flew into the footlights. So I choked the guard a little more, grabbed his gun, and said, 'Now get those keys, you son of a bitch!' The poor guy crawled down and got the keys and, afterward, when I saw the marks on his neck, I realized I'd *really* choked him. He was damn near dead."

The tension mounted from there. The prisoners rounded up all the guards they could find, making their intentions clear they'd start shooting them—one at a time—if their demands weren't met.

Hale Norcross cut his right hand so badly breaking out a pane of glass at the back of a cell that blood streamed down the sleeve of his costume. And when the curtain rang down five minutes early, a series of backstage signals having gone temporarily awry, the cast "almost massacred" the poor stagehand blamed for the mistake. But such was the intensity of the performance that no one in the audience seemed to notice, and when Tracy exulted, "Well men, it's on! The war's begun! Shoot, you bastards! Shoot!!" and the curtain again came down—this time legitimately—there was a palpable sense of relief all around.

The third act built to a nerve-racking barrage of explosions and machine gun fire, Tracy savagely murdering two of the hostages before stepping himself into the line of fire, the searchlight catching him in its glare, the bursts coming as the priest intones Latin and the two remaining convicts stand motionless amid the dust and the fury. "Let 'em wonder out there," he shouts. "Let all the world wonder. *Let the whole goddamn world wonder!*" And then slowly, quietly: "I'm goin' out into the open air . . ."

Curtain.

At first the audience wasn't sure what to do, and the curtain rose on the first of the calls to only tepid applause, but then it built, quickly, forcefully, as the crowd as one came to the full realization of what it had just witnessed, a numbing, heart-pounding, ear-shattering performance torn straight from the pages of their daily newspapers. By the time Tracy, drenched in perspiration, came to the fore, his arms limp, summoning every ounce of strength he still had within him, they were shouting and stomping and on their feet, and the ovation continued solidly through the cast bow, through the second calls, and kept up until he had taken fourteen curtain calls for himself. And he knew, as did the critics cheering in the stalls, that something extraordinary had just happened, and that he finally had what he had pursued so relentlessly over the past seven years—the lead in a hit play on Broadway.

Herman Shumlin had spent the entire performance in an advanced state of agitation, fidgeting and nervously walking in and out of the building. When the play was over, someone came running up to him and said that Alexander Woollcott was looking for him backstage. "I told him to say I was gone. I couldn't think of going backstage." Minutes later, Woollcott, in his usual opening night costume—dark blue cape and black felt hat, oversized and flopping—found him. "This is one of the most extraordinary experiences of my life," he said, his voice trembling with feeling. "I can't begin to tell you how important this play is to me. I'm not a critic anymore, so I can't write a review of it in the newspaper, but if there is anything I can do for you, just tell me." Shumlin considered the offer, then asked if he might write a short letter that could be used as an advertisement.

Woollcott's demonstration was a bellwether, for the notices the next day were universally positive, some extraordinarily so. "A prison play that is so relentless that it lacerates you, so anguishing that it tears your heart with pity, so real that you feel you cannot face another of its terrific brutalities, so grimly compelling that you follow it with a breathless sickened interest, and so superbly done that cheers are constantly rising in your parched throat, arrived last evening at the Harris," John Mason Brown heralded in the *New York Evening Post*.

The Last Mile drew the most consistently favorable notices a nonmusical had gotten in months, and was far and away the critical favorite of the nine Broadway shows that opened that week. "*The Last Mile*," wrote Whitney Bolton, "is a play of desperation and fury with the power and sweep to drive the blood from your heart and leave you frozen before the granitic spectacle of the condemned. It is a ferment of steel and stone and the withering frost of terror, a restless working force to fasten the mind and nerves and hold them resolutely." Brooks Atkinson called it "taut, searing drama with a motive" and Richard Lockridge described it as "grimly effective."

To all, the play was memorably acted, and the ensemble cast was praised as widely as the play itself. Robert Littell in the *World* said that Tracy had made Killer Mears into "a thrillingly savage and icy rebel." The whole fire and grandeur of the play, as Bolton put it, was encompassed in Tracy's masterful portrayal of Mears, "a murderer of brutality and an imprudent but iron-hearted man, a man for the gods to wonder upon as he thrashes through the redoubtable, inexorable application of doom." Richard Dana Skinner, critic for the *Commonweal,* declared that Tracy had put "the final seal on his qualifications as one of our best and most versatile young actors—a position he has been headed for ever since his outstanding work in that trivial little comedy, *The Baby Cyclone*."

The Harris was practically sold out the following evening, and the gross for the first full week of performances was about $11,000—moderate, given the exceptional reviews, but predictable given the weak matinee trade. Woollcott's letter arrived, thanking Shumlin for the most satisfactory evening in the theater that any new play had given him that season. "Mr. Erskine's direction was brilliant in its imaginativeness and in its resourcefulness," he wrote. "After having been told that all the good actors have deserted to the talkies, it is mystifying to find a cast packed with good ones. Perhaps, after all, it does help to have intelligence, intuition, and energy employed in casting." The next day, under the headline ALEXANDER WOOLLCOTT GOES TO THE PLAY, Shumlin ran it as a two-column ad in every newspaper in the city.

The drama's appeal was completely lost on women, and there was talk of eliminating the Wednesday matinee altogether. One critic actually recorded some of the comments he overheard from female audience members as he sat "enthralled by the terrible intensity and realism" of the thing: "For goodness sakes! What did you ever pick out such a thing as this for?" And: "My dear, this is simply terrible. Let's go someplace and dance." And: "Why in Heaven's name did the critics rave about this melodrama?" Playing Killer Mears wouldn't make a matinee idol of Spencer Tracy, but the name gained new prominence in the minds of theatergoers, and new respect on the parts of producers and critics. By Lent, when business everywhere was typically slow, the box office had leveled off at around $13,000, putting *The Last Mile* on a par with *Street Scene* and *Death Takes a Holiday*.

For Tracy the timing was right, for unlike *Baby Cyclone,* which had opened when most movies were still free of voice, *The Last Mile* came at a time when Broadway was vigorously being scouted for actors, directors, and writers who could manage dialogue. Within a month he had made his screen debut in a lively Vitaphone short called *Taxi Talks*.

Tracy had already made two tests, one for Metro-Goldwyn-Mayer and one for Fox at that company's Tenth Avenue studio. Nothing had come of either of them. "Nobody ever said a word—they never even called to tell me I was lousy. In those days they loaded you with makeup for a screen test. I wasn't exactly pretty anyway, so I probably ended up looking like a gargoyle. They most likely threw the film in the ashcan, but I didn't care very much because I never thought I'd be a movie actor; I had no ambition in that direction and was perfectly happy on the stage."

The Tracys' movie consumption had leveled off with the coming of talkies. The action pictures Spence liked so much had slowed to a crawl, and Louise genuinely disliked the static musicals that, at least for a while, seemed to be all Hollywood was turning out. "The first sound movie that we saw, we thought that, well, they've got to do better than this," she said. "I can't remember that we were very impressed." She wrote her sister after the second audition: "Spencer doesn't photograph well . . . we don't think there is much chance for enough salary to make it worthwhile to leave the stage. So for the present we are just forgetting about the talkies."

Neither company came back for a second look when *The Last Mile* hit big, but Warner Bros. scooped him up as a matter of course. The company was making a point of filming practically anyone they could get in a car to its Vitaphone studio complex, a rambling group of gray stone buildings at Avenue M and East Fourteenth Street in the heart of Flatbush. Since each voice and screen test required a crew of eight and about two hours to make, it made better economic sense to put an actor in a releasable one- or two-reeler and apply the $300-to-$500 cost of a test to the production of a short picture. Initially, Vitaphone subjects drew heavily from the concert stage and vaudeville, committing more than one hundred specialties to film in a single year. By 1928, vaudeville playlets, one-act dramas, and comedies were being integrated into the schedule, and the ever-expanding Vitaphone release index consisted of several hundred individual films.

Taxi Talks, which came from the husband-and-wife team of Frederick and Fanny Hatton, was an exercise in modern slang as observed in the back seat of a taxi cab. The Hattons wrote it for producer Rosalie Stewart, who subsequently released it to vaudeville. Vitaphone paid $2,000 for the picture rights—absolute top dollar for a fourteen-minute short—and cast it with Broadway luminaries Katherine Alexander (currently in *The Boundary Line* at the 48th Street Theatre), Mayo Methot (who had just closed in Sidney Howard's *Half Gods*), Roger Pryor (of the hit comedy *Apron Strings*), and Tracy, none of whom had ever before appeared in a film.

The process of making *Taxi Talks* was relatively painless. For Tracy, it involved traveling to Brooklyn on March 3, 1930. The action took place almost entirely in the cab, Alexander, as a gangster's moll, slipping in beside him just as it pulls away from the curb. Tracy's role, a "gunman" as specified in his contract, was opposite his old girl, the only dramatic segment of an otherwise smart and breezy comedy. "What have I done to make you want to leave me?" the girl implores. "Me, that would die for you?"

"You ain't done nothin'," he tells her. "I'm just tired of you, that's all. I want to get me a new gal . . . and I'm going to get me one with some spunk and class."

She threatens to "fix" the other woman. "I'll put her where she won't run after you . . . I know a lot about her . . . Plenty to put her in hock, and I'll do it too!"

"You never meant a thing to me," he tells her finally. "I'd given you up a long time ago, only you were useful. Yeah, and cut out all the talk about suicide, too. Say listen, I never cared for you the way I do for this woman—she's the only woman in the world I ever wanted, see? Yeah, and she's mine . . ."

Unable to take it anymore, the moll grabs a knife and shoves it deep into his stomach. "You got me!" he gasps. "Well . . . do something . . . can't you? I'm dizzy . . . I'm . . . you dirty little hell cat, you've croaked me! You'll . . . you . . ."

"Joe . . ." she calls frantically. "I didn't mean to do it . . . Joe . . . Joe . . . Oh . . . Oh God! Joe! I didn't mean to do it—I didn't mean to do it! Stop this taxi . . . stop it I say!"

The driver looks back over his shoulder, apparently not having noticed any of it. "What's the matter? HOLY—GEE!"

"You better drive to the nearest police station," she somberly tells him. "I just killed a man."

Covered by two elaborately blimped cameras, the scene consumed roughly four minutes of screen time, and it is unlikely that Tracy and Alexander, even allowing for false starts and technical malfunctions, needed more than an hour or two to complete it. "It was all strange and new and uncomfortable and rather embarrassing," Alexander said, "but, honestly, playing even the shortest scene with [Tracy] there was simply no question that he was a brilliant actor." For an afternoon's work Tracy collected $150 and was back at the Lambs by nightfall. The thing he would remember most vividly about the experience was the makeup they made him wear, as he was by then used to wearing none at all in his role as Killer Mears. Perversely, the only cast member signed as a result of *Taxi Talks* was Evelyn Knapp, a young actress who had no Broadway credits whatsoever.

The Last Mile continued to be an important show, outlasting *The Criminal Code* and seemingly set for the balance of the season. (Even the ticket brokers eventually came around and made an eight-week buy on seats.) In Hollywood, the success of both plays did not go unnoticed. The picture rights were snapped up, and M-G-M began filming its own prison melodrama, *The Big House,* with Martin Flavin, author of *The Criminal Code,* on hand to punch up the dialogue. John Wexley was similarly courted by Universal, and at Fox, generally the most derivative of the major studios, an original screenplay was commissioned from Maurine Watkins, author of the racy Jazz Age satire *Chicago.* Based in New York, Watkins naturally chose Sing

Sing as the backdrop for her story, the nineteenth-century prison at Ossining—on the Hudson some forty miles north of Manhattan—being famous for the progressive policies of Warden Lewis E. Lawes, an author, lecturer, and death penalty opponent who had just recently made the cover of *Time* magazine. Unlike Wexley, Watkins had a firm and obvious title before writing a single word: *Up the River.*

John Ford, assigned to direct the film, was brought in from Los Angeles to "assess the new plays and scout young actors." The next picture on his schedule being a prison yarn, he naturally arranged to see *The Last Mile* on his first night in town. "I liked it so much," he remembered, "that I went back the next night and was tantalized by Spence. I began to see that he had it all—the consummate power of an actor. So, hell, I went a third time, and introduced myself to Spence backstage. He took me to the Lambs Club for what turned out to be quite an evening. We stayed until about four o'clock, when I think they threw us out. Most of the time we only talked baseball, but I liked Spence so much I knew I had to have him in my next picture, whether it was *Up the River* or something else. The way it turned out, I was supposed to see six plays in six nights, but I saw *The Last Mile* every night I was there."

Ford, a crusty Irishman, was directing Harry Carey westerns when Tracy was still cadging dimes from his father to go see them. "I'd meet Spencer after the show and we'd go over to the Lambs Club and drink ale. In those days we could both drink pretty well after a fashion." The management at Fox, Ford discovered, did not share his enthusiasm for Spencer Tracy. As Tracy described the scene: "Ford said, 'I'd like to have him,' and the Fox guy said, 'Well, we made tests of him. They're not very good. He looks lousy in makeup.' Ford said, 'Makeup? He's not going to wear any makeup in my picture. He's the guy I want.' When we got out of the office, he told me how much money to ask for."

While all the head scratching was taking place over on Tenth Avenue, Sam Sax, the newly appointed production chief at Vitaphone, took the opportunity to contract with Tracy for a second short. In the six weeks since they had filmed *Taxi Talks,* staffing at Warners' Brooklyn studio had been beefed up to the point where it constituted the largest production force in the nation devoted solely to one- and two-reelers. Sax now had four directors and a staff of five writers churning out playlets, flash acts, musical comedies, and miniature revues in a general attempt to escape the old stigma of vaudeville. Sax had a story called *The Hard Guy,* a seriocomic sketch with a trick finish, and he doubled Tracy's original fee to get him to do it. There was an element of brinkmanship in the offer, for *The Hard Guy* was filmed under Arthur Hurley's direction on Monday, May 5, 1930, with the supposition that an offer from Warner Bros. would soon be forthcoming. Fox signed Tracy to a one-picture contract the very next day.

Tracy, Valli Roberts, and Katherine Alexander in *The Hard Guy*.
(PATRICIA MAHON COLLECTION)

Ford had persuaded Winfield R. Sheehan, general manager of the Fox studio, to take a flyer on Tracy. Sheehan, aligned with AT&T and the banking interests that controlled Fox, was locked in a protracted litigation with founder William Fox over leadership of the company, and was stuck in New York while the battle played itself out. He may well have seen *The Last Mile* for himself, for he had plenty of opportunity, and it would have been the experience of seeing Tracy live—and not in his abortive Movietone test— that convinced him to let Ford have his way.* Fox was adding stage-trained actors to the payroll at a furious rate, and during Sheehan's six-month stay at the Hotel Savoy, Humphrey Bogart, George Brent, Robert (later Bob) Burns, Larry Fine, Ted Heeley, Rose Hobart, Harry (later Moe) Howard, Shemp Howard, Elizabeth and Helen Keating, Nat Pendleton, Tyrone Power, John Swor, Ruth Warren, and Charles Winninger were all signed to contracts. That Tracy was practically an afterthought, engaged just days before Sheehan's return to California, is supported by the somewhat bewildering way in which he was approached.

"The producer," said Tracy,

* The fact that Sheehan was also negotiating a new two-year contract with Ford couldn't have hurt.

was well known, the theater was well known, and I was sufficiently well known so that nobody could possibly have had any difficulty in getting in touch with me. They could have reached me through the producer, they could easily have found out where I lived, they could have reached me at the Lambs Club, or by the simple process of coming back stage after the show. But what they did was to get hold of an agent. They told him they wanted me for a part in *Up the River* and *he* called me up on the telephone. When I went over to the Fox offices, everything was cut and dried. Jack Ford was determined to have me for the part, and they had decided exactly what contract they would offer me. The agent sat in the next room while I talked to them. He had nothing whatever to do with the negotiations.

The agent was one Leo Morrison, late of the United Booking Office, a powerful presence in vaudeville who brought the first large contingent of New York stage actors to talking pictures in 1928. Morrison had offices in both New York and Hollywood (where he occupied the mezzanine level at the Roosevelt Hotel) and vague ties to Winnie Sheehan, who, with his Tammany background, would have expected him to play ball. Morrison later claimed to have seen Tracy in *The Last Mile,* and he may well have been the one who first alerted Fox to Tracy's nascent appeal. It is just as possible, however, that Tracy was delivered to Morrison in payment for a favor of some kind, or that Morrison would be paying someone a kickback on the commission.

Morrison had other clients at Fox, notably Mae Clarke, Beatrice Lillie, Ruth Warren, Rose Hobart, and Leo Carrillo. The contract Tracy signed employed him for a period of six weeks, commencing June 16, 1930, at a rate of $600 a week. It included a six-month option on his further services and an acknowledgment that Herman Shumlin expected him back in New York no later than August 21 "AS SHOW MUST OPEN CHICAGO SEPTEMBER FIRST."

Up the River had a rocky time making its way to the screen. Warden Lawes was famous for his stewardship of prison baseball, grooming a field, building grandstands, and busing in teams from other facilities. They played tennis at Sing Sing, handball and miniature golf, too. Lawes was shaved every morning by a convict who had slashed a man's throat, and trustees cared for his three children. Ford had visited Sing Sing and, having observed her interaction with the prisoners, asked the warden if his eight-year-old daughter, Joan Marie, known to just about everyone as Cherie, would like to come to Hollywood.

Ford liked the idea of working against the hellhole cliché of other prison pictures—Paramount's *Thunderbolt* comes immediately to mind—but Watkins' story lacked the vigor and cynicism of *Chicago*, written as it was by someone who had no direct knowledge of prison life and scarcely six months' experience as a newspaperwoman. (Frances Marion, the veteran screenwriter who took scenario credit on *The Big House*, was reputed to have been fronting for Robert Tasker, who spent nearly six years in San Quentin.) Tentative casting had Tracy teamed with Warren Hymer, a comic heavy, leaving the love story to the film's juvenile lead, Humphrey Bogart, and Broadway actress Claire Luce. Fox had an oversupply of contract players, and there was a push to use as many as possible: Robert Burns and John Swor, Goodie Montgomery, Elizabeth and Helen Keating. With the exception of Hymer, none had ever before appeared in a feature.* Others proposed for the cast were Ilka Chase, Lee Tracy, Mitchell Harris, Stepin Fetchit, and Willie Collier, the American stage institution who would also be serving as Ford's dialogue director.

"Sheehan wanted to do a great picture about a prison break," Ford told Peter Bogdanovich, "so he had some woman write the story and it was just a bunch of junk. Then he went away for a while, and day by day Bill Collier, who was a great character comedian, and I rewrote the script. There was so much opportunity for humor in it that eventually it turned out to be a comedy—all about what went on inside a prison; we had them playing baseball against Sing Sing, and these two fellows broke back *in* so they'd be in time for the big game."

Tracy was set to leave *The Last Mile* on May 26 when actor Lawrence Leslie, his replacement, fell ill with grippe. He remained with the play another week as Herman Shumlin monitored Leslie's worsening condition, then stayed yet another week as Thomas Mitchell was brought in to replace him.† He was finally able to step away on Saturday, June 7, and left immediately for the West Coast. Despite the rush to get him to Los Angeles, where he arrived late Monday evening, Tracy found there was absolutely nothing for him to do.

The release of *The Big House* on June 21 validated Ford's determination to take the picture in a different direction. M-G-M's movie was well received, grim as it was, graphic and utterly devoid of comedy. Ford and Collier worked nearly two months on *Up the River*, joking it up, giving Watkins detailed notes and edits, and stalling production until the end of

---

* Due to a delay in starting *Up the River*, Bogart was put into *A Devil With Women* and ended up shooting both films simultaneously. The Ford picture was released on October 12, 1930, making it Bogart's feature debut. *A Devil With Women* was released a month later.
† Leslie died on July 15, 1930. He was twenty-two years old.

July. Tracy rented a Ford roadster, and every Tuesday afternoon he drove down to the Fox lot and drew $600. "I'm in Hollywood all alone, nothing to do," he told his cousin Frank. "I'd call up once in a while. 'No, we're still working on the script.' I was hoping someone would give me something to memorize, something to do. Nothing. Absolutely zilch. John Ford was working on another film, waiting for this one to get together. He was busy."

The plan at first had been for Spence to go to California alone, since the film wouldn't take long to shoot and the studio would cover only his own expenses. Then, after a week of sitting around and waiting for something to happen, he called Louise and asked her to come and to bring Johnny out with her. Louise, who had just had her appendix out, hobbled down to the bank and drew out the last of their savings to make the trip. They arrived in time to celebrate Johnny's sixth birthday, and it was on that day that they went and had his hair cut. As the auburn curls and bangs fell to the floor, Spence and his boy cavorted in front of the mirror and made fun of Weeze's long face. They found a tiny bungalow on Franklin Avenue where they could live until Spence had finished his scenes. They spent Sundays with the Fords at their beachfront home and had time to drive down to San Diego to visit Louise's father and sister. They also renewed some old friendships; Grant Mitchell was in town making a picture and Frank McHugh was under contract to Warner Bros.

It was an idyllic summer, marred only by the terrible news that Mother Tracy had broken her back in Chicago. Spence was frantic; she had been riding in a taxi with Carroll when they were broadsided at an intersection. Carroll escaped with minor injuries, but Carrie cracked a vertebra and would be laid up for months. Stuck in California waiting for the picture to start, Spence could do nothing more than call and wire and send money and gifts. Then Louise saw an ominous squib in one of the papers: the number of infantile paralysis cases was on the decline. It was her first inkling that there had been an epidemic. "That's all John needs," she muttered to her sister. "If we had known this, we wouldn't have come." It would have been silly to go back to New York, so they decided they would just have to be careful, keeping Johnny away from crowds and other children. She combed the papers daily for news, saw the infection rate drop to only one or two cases a day for all of Los Angeles. Gradually, playgrounds and public pools reopened; in time she practically forgot about it.

Eventually, the people at Fox got around to making the picture. "[Ford] called us to the studio at long last to inform us that the drama was now going to be filmed as a comedy," Claire Luce recalled. "We all groaned inwardly but somehow got through it." It wasn't all comedy, though. Ford and Collier had supplied a new frame to the story, turning the prison into a kind of coed country club, but a lot of Watkins' material remained. The result was an awkward blend of farce and melodrama, a tall order for a newcomer like Tracy, who was called upon to play low comedy one minute, deliver a tense monologue on death row the next. Ford set the tone by opening the film with a nighttime prison break, Tracy and Hymer rendezvousing with a stolen vehicle. "Look at this!" Tracy mutters. "A roadster—and the gang promised me a limousine and a chauffeur!" He tells the dim-witted Hymer to get out and fix a flat, then cheerfully drives off without him. "I don't see no flat tire!" Hymer shouts. "No?" calls Tracy as he pulls away. "Well, buy a mirror!"

At last there was something to do, and the California summer seemed to energize the whole family. Every morning, after his father had inched the Ford out of the little garage on Franklin, Johnny would race the car down to the corner as Louise watched. "Then, after Spencer had stepped on the gas and disappeared down the street, he would come tearing back again, up and down the sidewalk, brimming with sheer animal spirits, until panting, like a little puppy, he would throw himself down on the grass to rest."

Up the River got under way on August 1, the company working nonstop to close with Tracy as scheduled. Joan Marie Lawes, who had turned nine while waiting for work on the film to begin, appreciated Tracy's businesslike attitude toward the process of making the picture: "It was interesting at first, but it was a lot of time, a lot of hot lights and makeup. I couldn't wait to get home." Spence did his best to put her at her ease, gently joking with her between shots, and as one of the first actors to play a scene with him on film, she found him to be thoroughly in command of the material. "Playing a scene with him was just talking. That's all. It was so impressive what he could convey with just his expression."

As per Ford's dictate, Tracy wore no makeup, and the wax face of the Vitaphone shorts gave way to a wizard's grid of lines and crevices, the sort of landscape that told more about a character than a dozen lines of dialogue.* The script called for as many exteriors as interiors, and a traveling shot atop a train was made using the relatively new Dunning process, where background action was filmed independently of dialogue and married with studio footage in the laboratory. "*Up the River* turned out all right," Ford acknowledged, "and Spence was perfect. Unlike most stage-trained actors, he instinctively subdued himself before a camera. And he was as natural as

---

* Fortunately, Tracy tanned well in the California sun. According to author and makeup artist Michael Blake, he would have needed a good, even color to work without makeup. "Perhaps some base color under the eyes to 'even him out' as we put it." Blake is certain he would have needed powder. "No doubt the oils in his skin would make him appear 'shiny' under the lights, and he would need powder to dull the shine down or he'd be too bright under the lights."

With Claire Luce, Humphrey Bogart, and Warren Hymer in *Up the River* (1930).
(SUSIE TRACY)

if he didn't know a camera was there." According to Claire Luce, no one was particularly happy with the bizarre experience. "We made bets as to who could break our contract first."

Tracy made his last shot on Sunday, August 17, at around five in the afternoon, and was on a train bound for New York by eight that same evening. Before he left, the terms of a new contract were discussed, but he told Sol Wurtzel, the superintendent of production under Winfield Shee-han, he had given his word he'd return to *The Last Mile* and was honor-bound to do so. Louise and Johnny went back to San Diego for a few days and then left for home. In Chicago, they stopped to see Mother Tracy, who was still in the hospital. While there, Johnny showed signs of fatigue and nausea and was registering a slight fever. The symptoms would fade and then return, and just before it was time to leave, they worsened.

Louise called the general practitioner who was overseeing Carrie's recovery, but it never occurred to her to call the orthopedist who was in charge of her broken back. The doctor came to the hotel, gave the child a cursory examination, and said he thought that Johnny was probably just upset from all the travel and the change in his eating habits, and that he didn't think it was anything serious or a reason to delay the rest of their trip.

Despite his assurances, Louise felt a certain undercurrent of dread: "I knew I must get home as quickly as possible before whatever I felt was going to happen did so." That night on the train, she slept in the berth with her son, and his body felt very hot. He tossed relentlessly, moaning in his sleep, and occasionally he would cry out sharply, partially awaken, and then draw his legs up and point to them. And Louise, by that point, knew exactly what was happening.

CHAPTER 7

Quick Millions

As planned, Spencer Tracy rejoined *The Last Mile* on September 1, 1930—in New York, however, not Chicago, Herman Shumlin having extended the Broadway run on the promise of Tracy's return. Curiously, his absence hadn't made much of a difference in terms of ticket sales, and Wexley, the author, actually liked Thomas Mitchell's work as Mears better than Tracy's—though his was certainly a minority report. ("Poor Tommy," said Chester Erskine, "he just couldn't get into that part.") Mitchell played the role five weeks, then went on one night stewed to the gills, heaving and snorting and stumbling into the footlights. Erskine replaced him with Allen Jenkins, Mitchell's understudy, and it was Jenkins who played the role—superbly, as one cast member recalled—until his predecessor had completed *Up the River*.

Tracy's return to New York coincided neatly with the release of *The Hard Guy*, which showed up on a bill at the Strand and drew favorable comment from *Variety*. ("Well acted and directed, short is very worthwhile subject for any house.") He wired Chicago:

THOUGHT OF DEAR DAD TONIGHT AND THE THRILL HE
WOULD HAVE HAD COULD HE HAVE WALKED UP BROAD-
WAY WITH ME TONIGHT AND IN BLAZING LIGHTS ON

GREAT   BROADWAY   ASTOR   STRAND   THEATRE   SEEN
"SPENCER TRACY IN VITAPHONE PRODUCTION."

In Los Angeles, Jack Gardner, the Fox casting director, was penciling out the best offer he could make on a fifty-two-week contract. Sol Wurtzel had offered $500 a week to start, but Tracy was noncommittal, citing his obligation to Shumlin and his need to get back to New York. It wasn't just a ploy; Tracy was genuinely conflicted about taking the Fox offer. Louise disliked movie work and thought the only real pleasure an actor had was in developing a part over a number of performances, each audience bringing something new to the experience. Spence had spent nearly a decade building up to the point where he could command serious critical and commercial attention, and now he was being asked to chuck it all for the gossamer of a Hollywood contract.

Chuck Sligh was in town, and Spence raised the subject with him.

We were walking down Park or Fifth Avenue one day. He was telling me about it. "I've got this offer," he said. "I never liked the thought of going in the movies. You've got a line on the floor, you can't go past it, you've got to stand that way and look this way."

"Gee, I don't think I'd like that."

He said, "They're offering me $500 a week. God, I don't know. I just don't know what to do."

I said, "Why don't you tell them [that] if they'll pay you a thousand dollars a week, you'll take it and give it a try and see how you like it?"

"Well, I think maybe I'll do that."

Gardner's offer, the best he could do, was $750 a week for the first year and $1,000 a week for the second, graduating to $2,500 a week in the fifth year of the contract. A night letter went out on September 4, 1930:

FORWARDING YOU TODAY LETTER EXERCISING OPTION
IN YOUR CONTRACT LETTER GIVES FULL DETAILS STOP
VERY HAPPY TO HAVE YOU WITH US

KINDEST REGARDS
SOL M WURTZEL

Louise arrived back in New York the following morning. Johnny, by then, was running a fever and showing signs of stiffness as well as severe muscle pain. Over the next few days, a total of six doctors saw him, including three pediatricians who agreed he was showing the classic symptoms of spinal meningitis. Two different neurologists attempted spinal punctures, neither with the benefit of anesthetic. Johnny lost consciousness one afternoon, his face assuming a strange pinched look and his body stiffening slightly but unmistakably, his head pulling backward as if suddenly possessed. A third neurologist put him in the hospital—not St. Luke's where he had been before but a newer, fancier place—and a furor was sparked when the doctor wrote on the admitting card "Poliomyelitis."

Spence and Louise had to don aprons to see him—large coveralls of stiff white linen—and scrub up afterward, turning the taps on and off with their elbows. Nothing could be done for him, they were told. The disease would have to run its course, then either Johnny would get better or he wouldn't. Tracy endured the nightmare of *The Last Mile,* channeling his confusion and fury into a performance actor Dore Schary remembered as both "magnificent and terrifying." What no one could possibly have known was the emotional price he paid, conjuring the reality of Killer Mears while grappling with the knowledge that his child was hovering near death in a crosstown hospital room, his chances for part of one week, as cousin Frank Tracy recounted, "about zilch."

By the twelfth they knew that Johnny would live, but beyond that there were no assurances. The level of paralysis would take months to know, perhaps even years, and the care he would need, how much and for how long, was unknowable as well. All that was certain was that the cost would be stratospheric. Tracy went to the Lambs Club that day and wrote out a long-delayed reply to Sol Wurtzel:

> *My Dear Mr. Wurtzel:*
>
> > *Enclosed please find signed letter.*
> > *I am very happy that you should want me to return and will do my best to warrant your confidence.*
> > *We are still doing fair business here. Looks like perhaps four or five more weeks and then Chicago. I will keep you informed at all times.*
> > *Hope "Up the River" proves a big hit.*
> > > *My thanks and sincere regards.*
> > > > *Spencer T.*

A few days later, Johnny was discharged from the hospital as "cured," but the use of that word became a cruel hoax when he was urged by a nurse to try and stand on his own and had to pull himself around on the floor. "Mrs. Tracy," one of the doctors said to Louise, "you must think we doctors are a pack of fools. John is getting well, but certainly not because of anything we have done." When they brought Johnny home, the two doctors on the case assured Louise that they did not believe he had any paralysis at all, despite the fact that he could move only one leg slightly and the other almost not at all. All he needed was rest, she was told—rest and sunshine.

"For two weeks he stayed in bed and got the rest," Louise said, "but all the sunshine he could get in the apartment was in the form of viosterol capsules. At the end of two weeks, he seemed no better. He had no appetite, was listless and uninterested. He would lie hour after hour, moving only his eyes as they followed his [toy] autos whizzing down the ironing board stretched from bed to floor. The family living below us deserved a medal for their uncomplaining patience."

They decided the best medicine for Johnny would indeed be rest and sunshine, and with the doctor's approval they stretched him out on pillows and blankets on the back seat of the car and took off for Silvermine, in Connecticut, where they would have a rustic inn pretty much to themselves. The weather was warm and John began to grow stronger, his left leg gradually improving. Spence came out on Sundays and Mondays and oft-times on Tuesdays and Thursdays, days when he had no matinees to play. He and Louise spent time visiting some of the local kennels—everyone seemed to own at least one dog—and although there were a number of very sound reasons why they shouldn't want the responsibility of keeping one in the city, he suddenly said one day, "I think John should have a dog—now."

And so they got a dog, a six-month-old Irish setter. Louise got the inn's permission to let him sleep in her room on the promise that she would pay for any damage. They named the dog Pat—an easy word for John to say.

Maurine Watkins saw so little of her original story that she proposed splitting the writing credit for *Up the River* with Willie Collier and Jack Ford. Both executed releases on their material, but it was Watkins who bore the brunt of Winfield Sheehan's disappointment when he saw how his gritty prison yarn had ripened into low comedy. "Sheehan refused to go to the preview," Ford recalled, "but just at that time all the exhibitors were out here for one of their meetings, and they all went to see it, and they fell out of their chairs. One guy actually *did* fall out of his chair—they had to bring him to. A very funny picture—for those days. I kept ducking the woman who wrote the original script, but she went to another studio on the success of *Up the River* and got three times her salary per script."

Up the River opened at New York's Roxy Theatre on October 18, 1930, and proved "violently funny" to the thousands who filled the auditorium that first afternoon. Regina Crewe of the *American* celebrated the film's absurdist aspects as if they came straight from the Marx Brothers: "Can you imagine the roars of laughter greeting the scene where the 'important guy' of the underworld arrives to do his bit and is welcomed by the prison band and as big a turnout as an oceanic flier gets at City Hall? Or where the manager of the baseball team bewails the fact that he has lost the jail series by having a pitcher electrocuted just before the final game? Or that sequence in which the convicts, with bared heads and reverential attitudes, sing the 'varsity song' of their alma mater?"

The picture was a surprise hit, opening as it did between two much fancier Fox productions, the $2 million widescreen epic *The Big Trail* and the futuristic musical *Just Imagine*. Louise thought the film terrifically funny—particularly a safecracking scene with Warren Hymer loafing and listening to the radio while Tracy did the dirty work—but Spence's reaction was sharper, more critical, and he couldn't quite fall into the lighthearted mood of the crowd. "I thought I was the worst actor I had ever seen on the screen," he later said of the experience. "I was surprised that Ford and the Fox officials didn't remake the picture."

The Last Mile ended its New York run after thirty-six weeks, and Tracy left for Chicago on November 1. Johnny's left leg had improved steadily—he could now sit on the floor and hitch himself along—and he was back to taking short lessons at home from one of his teachers at the Wright Oral School. Both Spence and Louise thought the play would have a decent run at Chicago's Harris Theatre, and that there would be plenty of time to pack before the move to Los Angeles. "We decided to store our furniture until we came back," Louise said. "That we might not come back, except on trips, I do not think ever occurred to either of us."

The Last Mile got off to a slow start in Chicago, and the company manager posted a closing notice the week of November 10. Then there was an urgent message from Fox asking Spence to come immediately, so he wired Louise and asked if she could meet him in Chicago that following week.

The prospect [Louise wrote] of sorting our various possessions, packing those we might need for the next six months or year, arranging for their shipping, and that of the Ford roadster we had bought the preceding spring, as well as the storing of the furniture, all within a week, and transporting an invalid child who could not even stand, as well as a still unbroken Irish Setter puppy across the continent, with an overnight stop in Chicago, and, at the end of the trip, finding a place to live, more doctors, and a teacher for John, well might have filled me with dismay. But, except for a faint picture of myself, telegram in hand, wondering why it was men always happened to be someplace else when there was any moving, and thinking this would be the scramble to end all scrambles, I remember no particular emotion. I knew we would make it somehow. We always did.

In Chicago the closing notice stayed up all of forty minutes, then it was removed on orders from New York. Two days later, a letter from Fox set Tracy's start date at December 1, promising twenty weeks at $750 a week and commencing with a six-week layoff period. He would be expected to report to work in Los Angeles on January 11, 1931. With the play set to move from the Harris to the smaller Princess, he started dickering with both Shumlin and Equity to get out of town on a two-week notice.

When Johnny's doctor heard they were leaving New York, he told Louise he would like an orthopedist to examine the child and it was arranged. After he had carried the boy from the waiting room into his office, the orthopedist asked Louise what she thought the trouble was. She said, "Polio."

He stared at her in disbelief. "Polio!" he exclaimed. "How long ago?"

"Three months."

"And you mean nothing has been done for him up to now?"

She told him her story, ending with the news that they would be leaving for California in a few days. He told her he could do nothing in three days, and that he should have seen the boy when the attack first occurred. He wrote down the name of a doctor in Los Angeles. "He is one of the two finest men on the coast, and, I believe, *the* finest. Don't waste a moment after you reach there before making an appointment. Tell whomever you talk to in his office that it is urgent." The man whose name he wrote on the card was Dr. John C. Wilson, the chief of the orthopedic department at Children's Hospital.

Mother Tracy was only told of her grandson's illness the day before he was due to arrive from New York. In the aftermath of her accident, Carrie had suffered a complete nervous collapse and it was feared the shock of the news might be too great for her. Her orthopedist, Dr. Charles Pease, was present when Spencer broke the news, and he asked if he might drop around and see John the following day. When he did, he confirmed the other doctor's endorsement of Dr. Wilson, but then he went a step further.

"Every day is precious," he said. "It will be another three or four days at least before anything can be done in Los Angeles. If you will stay over one more day here, and allow me to, I will take him to the Children's Memorial Hospital and put a cast on his leg. That, at the moment, is the most important thing to be done."

As the Tracys learned, the affected muscles should have been put in a cast to enforce complete rest immediately after the attack. The fact that

Johnny had instead been encouraged to work the muscles had undoubtedly resulted in permanent damage, though it was impossible to say exactly how much. The next day, the boy's leg was encased in plaster from hip to toe. Then Louise mentioned a persistent weakness in John's back, and Dr. Pease ordered some x-rays of the spine. After they had returned to the hotel, the doctor called and said he would like to make a back cast, too, a removable one. It wouldn't delay their departure; he'd come to the hotel and do the job right there. So that evening, with Louise assisting, he made a half cast for Johnny's back that reached from his shoulder to his hips and around under his arms.

They left Chicago in the midst of a blinding snowstorm and were met in California by Leo Morrison, who had two taxis on hold and promptly hailed a third when he took in the size and breadth of the party. He knew a boarding kennel where they could leave the dog, essentially taking charge of everything. "I feel sure," said Louise, "I must have drawn a long sigh of relief as I sank onto the brown leather seat of the cab, with Pat—no longer carsick—sitting quietly at my feet. We were there! That mad ten days were over and we were *there*. I could have said *home,* but that would not have occurred to me."

When they saw Dr. Wilson, he listened to a history of the case and then walked over to the table on which John was lying and told him to raise his leg—his good one. John did so and moved it easily from side to side.

"Now the other one," he said.

"But he can't—" Louise began, but even as she spoke, and to John's wide-eyed amazement, he raised the leg with its heavy cast almost straight up.

"Well," said the doctor, turning to Louise. "You see what just a few days of immobilization has done for this leg? You fell into good hands in Chicago. I feel sure we can do a lot for this boy."

The Fox Film Corporation was an organization in free fall. William Fox, the visionary head of the empire, had been crippled by the stock market meltdown and forced to sell when some $25 million in short-term notes came due. A company called General Theatres Equipment paid $18 million for Fox's voting shares—a bargain price considering the deal included control of Fox Film, Metro-Goldwyn-Mayer, Gaumont British, and 1,500 theaters in the United States and Great Britain. Fox's cronies, including his two brothers-in-law, were swept from the board, and Fox himself was handed the chairmanship of a newly created "advisory board" that left him with no authority. In charge of the restructured company would be Fox's former secretary and longtime lieutenant, Winfield R. Sheehan.

Winnie Sheehan (as he was known to practically everyone) was a police reporter on the New York *World* when he made the jump to machine politics as secretary to city fire commissioner Rhinelander Waldo. At about the same time, a former cloth sponger named Bill Fox was entering into a partnership with Tammany politicians "Big Tim" and "Little Tim" Sullivan to run the City Theatre on East Fourteenth Street. Fox, of the firm of Fox, Moss & Brill, was struck by the fact that the Sullivans never had any trouble with fire regulations, and the connection he made was to Sheehan. Indeed, when Waldo was moved to the position of police commissioner in 1911, Sheehan followed as general factotum and bagman. He was dragged before a committee of the Board of Aldermen on more than one occasion, but they never could make anything stick until a whorehouse madam testified that she had paid graft to an agent of Sheehan's at the rate of one hundred dollars a month. Forced to resign, Sheehan went to work for Fox, who understood and valued his connections. In 1916 Sheehan attained the position of vice president and general manager of the newly established Fox Film Corporation.

"The Sheehan influence on Fox production began there at the beginning with an approach reminiscent of the New York *World*'s Sunday supplement," the industry's first historian, Terry Ramsaye, later wrote. "The pictures were addressed at the masses with alarming and successful precision, from the vampiring roles of Theda Bara and Virginia Pearson to such classics as *Bertha the Sewing Machine Girl* . . . That did not, however, represent Mr. Sheehan's ceiling of taste or capacity. He was affected both by the market and by William Fox, who was able to cry at his own emotions in the making of *Over the Hill,* his own version of Will Carleton's sad fifth reader poem of 'Over the Hill to the Poor House.' "

Blue-eyed and rosy-cheeked, Sheehan was a supremely cynical little man, an Irishman and a Roman Catholic in an industry dominated by Jews. Fox was a big thinker when it came to exhibition, a man who built the world's most lavish movie theaters and filled them with widescreen and sound. And while it was Fox who gave the world Movietone, the sound-on-film miracle that became the industry standard, it was Sheehan who produced the pictures that made Movietone matter. Winnie Sheehan came west in 1926, assuming charge of the Fox plant on Western Avenue in Los Angeles. *What Price Glory?, 7th Heaven, Mother Machree, Sunny Side Up,* and *The Cock-Eyed World* were all made on Sheehan's watch. Raoul Walsh, Frank Borzage, and John Ford prospered at Fox, as did Janet Gaynor, Warner Baxter, Edmund Lowe, and Victor McLaglen. Sheehan put Will Rogers in talkies, made the first western feature with dialogue, and won five of the first twelve Academy Awards.

Sheehan, who was personally responsible for the company's European distribution network, often seemed more focused on foreign markets—which accounted for roughly 33 percent of Fox's revenue—than he was on the domestic market. Distracted, he could find time for no more than a dozen pictures a year and relied on an ever-shifting group of associate producers to take up the slack—men like Ralph Block, Ned Marin, George Middleton, and James Kevin McGuinness, none of whom had the creative chops to make great or even consistently good movies. All were presided over by Sheehan's superintendent, a tough, humorless character named Sol Wurtzel, who had started with Fox as a stenographer and knew about as well as anyone how to get an incoherent picture shot in twelve days.

Wurtzel tried all genres but rarely did any well. When a good movie got made at Fox, it was more the result of leaving a director like Ford or Borzage or William K. Howard alone. Sheehan announced forty-eight to fifty-two pictures a season, then left it to Wurtzel to figure out how to deliver on the promise. Sheehan himself inhabited a vast Beverly Hills mansion with sunken gardens and a library ceiling imported from Spain. Though he usually had a half-chewed cigar rolling around in his mouth, his meals were grandly served on golden plates with golden goblets at their side. He had the Irish gift of conviviality, but could also be a ruthless son of a bitch.

Louise was taken house hunting by Mary Ford. "I was appalled at the rents," she said, "especially in Beverly Hills. Mary said I now was connected with an industry which, in quite a measure, had been responsible for those rents, and that I must take the bad with the good. I was beginning to realize that the salary which had looked so big, unless we were careful, probably would leave a smaller net income than the one Spencer had been drawing in New York on the stage." The places in Louise's price range were all dreary affairs, obvious rentals, dark inside with cheap oriental rugs cast about. On the second day she took a six-month lease on a plain-looking Spanish stucco on a hill just east of the UCLA campus. It had the requisite red tile roof, a nice rose garden, and a little yard in which Johnny's recovery could take place.

It was wonderful to spread out over a house and a yard again; the weather was warm and sunny and the rains came only at night. There was a wicker chaise longue in the den, and every day it was taken outside. John's nurse would carry him downstairs around ten and he would lie outside, except for lunch, until late afternoon. Mother Tracy arrived with her own nurse in tow, determined not to like anything about California. The roses had none of the size and color of Eastern roses, the fruits and vegetables were flavorless, the weather was downright monotonous. Spence cajoled and charmed her, as he had always been able to do in the past, and she settled in for a stay that would come to be permanent.

Johnny's treatments consisted of putting him in a tub of hot salt water—where he was afraid at first he was going to drown—and giving him foot and leg exercises, all followed by a gentle massage. By the first of the year he was slowly improving, gaining weight and tanning just like his father. Dr. Wilson consented to having his lessons resumed, and a teacher from the Los Angeles School for the Deaf came for half an hour each day after school. Louise wasn't satisfied with the arrangement—the late hour and John's obvious fatigue—but over the short term it was the best option available.

Spence drove to the studio on January 16, 1931, and balked at signing the fourteen-page contract Leo Morrison had negotiated. He wanted the right to quit and return to the stage at the end of the first or second year, and he believed he was entitled to a share of any profit the studio made on a loan-out. Wurtzel held firm. "The remarkable thing about Wurtzel," said the playwright S. N. Behrman, "was his manner of speech, his voice. It had a curious, granulated quality, like an instrument for crushing pebbles. Remarks erupted from him; there was always a fascinating absence of preamble."

With chronic constipation and a facial tic that curled his mouth into a nervous smile, Wurtzel appeared to be both pained and gloating at having his quarry over a barrel. Tracy was certainly trapped, having already accepted $4,500 in salary. In the presence of one of the studio lawyers, whose name also happened to be Tracy, he signed the document, sourly and without ceremony, submitting himself to the meat grinder that was the Fox Film production line. He then left for Palm Springs to study the script to his first picture, *Sky Line,* on which filming was set to commence in ten days.

The author of *Sky Line* was also its director, a former illustrator and sports cartoonist named Rowland Brown. Brown had originally come to Fox as a day laborer, a hefty, hard-drinking Irishman who would work his way up through the ranks. He turned to screenwriting under the auspices of the late Kenneth Hawks, went to Universal for a short while, then sold a grim mob story, "A Handful of Clouds," to Warner Bros.* In collaboration with Courtenay Terrett, a star reporter and author of the racketeering exposé *Only Saps Work,* Brown produced for Sheehan an original screenplay that was a model of economy, an entry for Fox in the gangster sweepstakes at a time when *Little Caesar* was breaking attendance records in New York.

"Terrett knew well the milieu he described," Brown's brother, Sam, told Philippe Garnier, "but the matter of writing scenarios he left to Rowland." Brown had a knack for illuminating character through the sparest of dialogue, and the script gave the actors room to work. Its quality delighted Tracy, its bitter sarcasms unique in a medium still struggling to find its

* Filmed as *The Doorway to Hell* (1930).

voice. Brown proved to be as good a director as he was a writer, moving quickly between setups, eschewing coverage and virtually cutting in the camera. "I had worked for Fox some years," Sam Brown said, "thus it was I who chose his team: Joseph August as cameraman, Harold Schuster, Murnau's editor on *Sunrise*. Even the script girl was the best in the studio; later she became a script writer for [Darryl F.] Zanuck. Happily, he was surrounded, because Rowland shot very little film . . . The heads at Fox when they saw the rushes went crazy. Rowland hadn't covered himself at all. If he had Tom Mix's editor, for example, he would not have known what to do with it. But Schuster knew."

The process of making the film was less chaotic than for *Up the River*, Brown being eager to bring the picture in not only on time but substantially under budget. Tracy was equally anxious to do well, giving "Bugs" Raymond a sort of Cohanesque charm that ran counter to the shakedowns and murders he ordered. What emerged was the most engaging racketeer the talkies had yet produced, an affable crook with a glint of bedbug insanity in his eyes, one who aspired to legitimacy and then let it be his undoing.

With his illustrator's sensibilities, Brown surrounded Tracy with an unusual group of supporting players, many picked as much for their faces as for their acting abilities. Typical was dancer George Raft, whom Brown had seen in vaudeville and who was dining with friends one evening at the Brown Derby when the director came over, introduced himself, and offered him a test. Raft, as it turned out, wasn't good at delivering dialogue, but his pose as a ferret-faced hood was priceless. His dark hair slicked back with pomade, he made an ominous counterpoint to Tracy's genial, offhanded mick. Making liberal use of locations in and around Los Angeles, Brown brought the film, retitled *Quick Millions,* in for a negative cost of $171,000. Everyone at Fox was thrilled with the result, and Sheehan awarded Brown a $1,000 bonus. "All the directors at the studio watched it," Sam Brown remembered, "even Mr. Ford."

Rowland Brown had brought forth a new kind of gangster picture, low-key and artfully composed and less nerve-rattling than the brassy Warner fare. Both he and Tracy were part of a new wave in Hollywood, doing fresh things with old ideas, but the public, with its collective mind on its pocketbook, wasn't necessarily paying attention. Established stars were fading— John Gilbert, Ramon Navarro, Norma Talmadge, Harry Langdon—yet new ones were conspicuously slow in taking their place. And there was always the shared feeling among Irish Catholics that no matter how well something was going, it could all collapse without warning.

Around the house, Spence took to using the phrase "Now when the bubble bursts . . ." to preface any discussions of the future, as if it were a foregone conclusion. In shooting an early scene, he and Raft found them-

The humble beginnings of Daniel J. "Bugs" Raymond in the opening
minutes of *Quick Millions*. (SUSIE TRACY)

selves seated together at a testimonial dinner for Bugs' associate, the vicious
"Nails" Markey. Tracy recognized one of the diners, a dress extra, as King
Baggott, one of the first genuine stars of the movies, an action hero back
when Tracy was still lighting lamps in Bay View. "Look at that man," he
whispered to Raft. "Once a great star and now an extra for a few bucks a day
when he can get the work. That could happen to me. That's what really
scares me."

With all the gladhanding and backslapping attendant on the completion of *Quick Millions,* it came as a letdown that Tracy's next assignment
was a talking remake of *Six Cylinder Love.* William Anthony McGuire's hit
comedy was in its seventh month at the Harris Theatre the night Tracy got
his first look at Manhattan, and Fox had filmed it the following year with
members of the original Broadway cast reprising their stage roles. The
material hadn't aged well, and at a time when American picturegoers were
more concerned about feeding and clothing their families than affording an
expensive car, the choice showed just how desperately out of touch studio
management was with its intended audience. Sheehan then compounded
the goof by putting Lorin Raker, another New York import, in the male
lead. Slight and doll-like, Raker was too old to be playing a newlywed
opposite Sidney Fox, nearly twenty years his junior, and lacked both the
name and the presence of a leading man.

With Raker topping the cast, Tracy found himself relegated to the peripheral part of Donroy, the slick salesman who first sells Gilbert and Marilyn Sterling their neighbors' car, then takes it off their hands at the end of the film when he peddles it to the cash-rich janitor, a bootlegger. Not only was the material stale, but the director was Thornton Freeland, a man who had been around the business a long while, but usually as someone's assistant. Freeland displayed a production manager's flair for camera, his principal credit being the stagebound musical *Whoopie* (in which all the directorial highlights were the work of dance director Busby Berkeley). Having worked with John Ford and Rowland Brown on his first two pictures, Tracy thought Freeland inept and did nothing the director told him to do without arguing bitterly about it. The film took twenty-two days to make, unconscionable given the result.

The virtue of *Six Cylinder Love* was that Tracy himself was required for relatively little of it. He would come home, for he was scarcely ten minutes from the studio, slip quietly into the house, change his clothes and be gone again before Louise had a chance to notice. One day she saw him in a pair of well-worn trousers, and a passing remark drew a vague, evasive answer. The more curious she got, the more mysterious he got. Then he'd joke about it, bringing the subject up himself at dinner, but never to the point of explaining much of anything. Then one Sunday, as he and Louise were motoring out toward the ocean along Sunset Boulevard, he slowed and pointed out a sign:

HOTTENTOT RIDING ACADEMY

HORSES 75 CENTS PER HOUR

"That's it," he said.

"That's what?"

"That's where I've been coming."

"You mean you've been riding?"

"Sure," he said. "Riding. Want to go over and see the horses? Midnight, coal black, that's the one I ride."

He inched the car down a narrow ravine to where there was a rundown barn and some stables and found Midnight. Louise, who had practically grown up on horses, was enchanted. "But you've never been on a horse in your life before," she said. "How in the world did you happen to start?"

"I rode once in Silvermine last fall. Remember? I just thought maybe I'd like it."

"But I thought you said you were scared to death."

"Well, I was . . . but I still think maybe I'd like it."

Louise devoutly hoped that he would. "He never had cared for any sport that I knew of since he was a boy and liked to box (and he boxed very well I have been told). Ever since I had known him, he had taken no exercise except a little walking by fits and starts, and he had no hobbies. His entire interest, and most of his friends, had been in the theatre. This opened up new vistas."

They rode together at the Hottentot a few times, walking and trotting slowly along a little trail that led from the stables through a narrow ravine back of the hills that bordered the boulevard. Then they ran into John Cromwell, who was directing features for Paramount. Somehow the subject got around to horses and riding, and Spence shyly told him what he had been doing.

"Start polo," Cromwell urged. "It's a great way to learn to ride. Go out to Snowy Baker at Riviera. He'll teach you. It's wonderful! Most thrilling thing in the world!"

The third film on Tracy's schedule was another comedy, a talking remake of a Fox silent called *A Girl in Every Port*. Sheehan was following through on a threat to make Tracy and Warren Hymer into the new Edmund Lowe and Victor McLaglen, the team that had played Quirt and Flagg in the popular comedies that followed the colossal success of *What Price Glory?* Tracy liked Hymer, a bright guy with an impressive pedigree, but he was strictly a one-note actor, all bluster and business with no shading of any sort. Six years younger than Tracy, Hymer was the son of playwright John B. Hymer and actress Elsie Kent. Educated at Yale, he was signed by Fox in 1929 and settled into a succession of dummy roles, instantly typed as a talkative moron. Hymer responded to his predicament in time-honored fashion, drinking himself into belligerence both off the set and on. "Oh, God," said John Ford, "what a time I had with him. I threw him into a sanatorium and hospitals . . ."

Goldie, as the film came to be known, seemed designed to showcase the new Fox lot in Beverly Hills, 108 acres of prime California real estate known officially as Movietone City. The story took Tracy and Hymer through a succession of international locales, Russia to Venice to Greece to Rio and finally to a carnival in Calais, where they discover the title character diving into a tub of water from a height of two hundred feet. The principal girl in a picture full of them was Jean Harlow, who was being rented to Fox at the rate of $1,250 a week by producer Howard Hughes. Just twenty, Harlow had risen from extra work and bit parts to the female lead in Hughes' $4 million air spectacle *Hell's Angels*. Having been kept under wraps for nearly a year, Harlow now had three pictures in the can, and their collective impact would make her a star. Her delivery tended to be wooden—more so after speech lessons—but her milky white complexion and platinum hair made the eye go straight to her in any shot she was in. She played tarts, gangsters' molls, and the like, and the script for *Goldie* broke questionable ground when the word "tramp" was applied to her character on four separate occasions. She was sweet-natured, though, earnest and professional, and had a photographic memory to rival Tracy's own. When director Ben Stoloff had to call for another take, it was generally because she mispronounced a word or moved incorrectly, never because she went up.

Spence had two pictures in the queue himself, and the similar circumstances forged a bond between them. Ten days into production on *Goldie*, *Quick Millions* opened at the Roxy in New York while Universal's *Iron Man*, a fight drama from the author of *Little Caesar*, debuted at the Globe with Harlow in the female lead opposite Lew Ayres. The Fox publicity people gave Tracy every support, billing his name above the title in ads that bore the headline "A New Star Shines." The picture garnered generally favorable reviews from a fraternity clearly fed up with racketeer stories, and Tracy's personal notices were uniformly fine. ("Mr. Tracy's performance is forceful and he succeeds in impressing one with his characterization," wrote Mordaunt Hall. "Through his gait and the angle at which he wears his hat, the conception of the truck driver is always in evidence, despite his expensive clothes.") Yet the overnight figures were disappointing.

Harlow's picture did better at the much smaller Globe, where fight and gang subjects often found a warm reception. Filling the 5,886-seat Roxy was a terrific burden to place on a film as modest as *Quick Millions*. Tracy knew it wasn't the breakout hit he had hoped it would be, and no one had to tell him *Six Cylinder Love* would be a stiff. Both Sheehan and Wurtzel cooled, and the film wound up the week with a gate of $62,000—brutally bad for the world's largest movie theater. Then temperatures broke and Warners' *Public Enemy*, featuring Harlow and an equally unknown James Cagney in the leads, moved into the New York Strand. Fueled by a predominantly male audience that liked its gangster pictures loud and violent, *Public Enemy* took in about as much money as *Quick Millions* in a theater less than half the size of the plateresque Roxy. With two successful movies playing simultaneously on Broadway, Harlow was suddenly big news, and M-G-M's *Secret Six* made her even bigger news when it was released nationally on April 25. *Goldie* was completed a week later—May 2, 1931—and Harlow was rushed east for a week of appearances at Chicago's Oriental Theatre.

Jean Harlow's participation in *Goldie* brought Tracy to the attention of Howard Hughes, who, having amassed some two million feet of stunt flying footage for *Hell's Angels*, was looking for stories in which he could incorporate the trims. In the movie business since 1926, Hughes had distinguished himself with a comedy called *Two Arabian Knights,* a buddy picture on the order of *What Price Glory?* that won an Academy Award for its director, Lewis Milestone. Almost immediately there was talk of a sequel, but Hughes got mired in the making of *Hell's Angels* and struggling with the problem of how to release a $2 million silent film when the public was clamoring for talkies. His solution—reshoot it with dialogue—occupied most of his time for another year. He produced just two other pictures in the interim: *The Racket* (again with Milestone) and *The Mating Call.* By the time he got back to the notion of a *Two Arabian Knights* sequel, Louis Wolheim, one of the two original stars, was dead, and William Boyd, the other half of the team, was working at RKO.

Hughes focused on developing a script, a gloss on the original as reimagined by Joseph Moncure March, the author of *Hell's Angels.* The project never really coalesced until Hughes saw Tracy as the bacchanalian seaman of *Goldie* and impulsively made the deal to borrow him for six weeks at a flat rate of $11,187.50. With Tracy set to start with Hughes on May 10, the rest of the package was carelessly thrown together. Veteran comic George Cooper (who was in the shots to be used from the earlier film), George Irving, and actress Lola Lane were all added to the cast. The crucial role of Sergeant Hogan, the Wolheim part, was filled by actor-playwright Sidney Toler, who played cops and comic heavies but was as unlike the gnarled Wolheim as any actor could be.

At first Tracy was glad to be out of Fox, even though the company would be collecting considerably more on the loan-out than he.* Filming on *Ground Hogs* (as the film was to be titled) got under way at the Armory in Culver City on Tuesday, May 19, the company shooting a full day of exteriors and working well into the night. The director Hughes picked for the film was Edward Sedgwick, who had turned out a number of silent comedies but whose experience with sound was limited to Buster Keaton's recent features. Sedgwick was a throwback to the days when a director could talk an actor through a scene while the cameras were cranking, and he apparently had no knowledge or appreciation of Tracy's stage experience. Ridgeway "Reggie" Callow, one of the assistant directors on Hughes' payroll, witnessed a testy exchange between Sedgwick and Tracy: "[Sedgwick] told him to take three steps forward and then turn sideways and reach out—all these meticulous directions—so Spencer said, 'One, two, three, and then I turn, reach out . . . now, what the hell do I do next?' "

---

* During the six-week period Tracy would receive $4,500 from Fox, leaving the studio with a net profit on his services of $6,687.50.

The atmosphere on the set wasn't good at all, and Sedgwick compounded the problem when he refused to show Hughes the rushes, claiming they weren't yet ready for viewing. Tracy worked well with Cooper, wide-eyed and elfin, but the on-screen chemistry between him and Toler was poor, Toler being wholly unsuited for the part of a roughneck sergeant. On Sunday, May 24, they traveled to Riverside, two hours east of Los Angeles, where they roomed at the Mission Inn and spent nine days shooting exteriors at March Field. Away from Louise and Johnny, Tracy recalled his days at Norfolk and behaved much as his character Wilkie would have under similar circumstances. "It was just the role he was playing," said Callow. "You know, he was drinking pretty heavily in those days, particularly with his buddy Warren Hymer . . . But the drinking never interfered with his performance; he always had his lines down."

Once the March Field scenes were in the can, the company returned for studio work on the Metropolitan lot in Hollywood, where Hughes' production company, Caddo, was based. But after just one day of filming, Hughes closed the film down, dismissing both Sedgwick and Toler and scrapping some $250,000 worth of footage. Within a week he had novelist Dashiell Hammett working on a new version of the script to be directed, it was announced, by writer-director Tom Buckingham.

Tracy returned to his home studio with time on his hands. If news of his drinking had gotten back to Louise, it wouldn't have surprised her. In New York, he did most of his imbibing at the Lambs, where he was contained and protected and surrounded by pals like Pat O'Brien and Frank McHugh. The booze was of the highest possible quality, a step above the industrial and grain alcohols served in most speakeasies (where the flavoring could range from prune juice to creosote). In Hollywood, the best stuff—genuine or slightly cut—came from inside the studio walls, where it seemed fully half the mechanics, doormen, chauffeurs, and office boys were dealers. Hymer had no trouble staying sloshed, despite the warnings and entreaties of the studio brass, and he proved a poor influence on Spence, especially when the two were disgruntled at work or away on location.

Louise would take a sherry before dinner, but she never particularly cared about it, and neither, really, did Spence. "It had always been there," she said of his intolerance for alcohol, "[but] I was not [aware of it] . . . there seemed to be no reason. He always liked milk and donuts and buttermilk." The root of his problem, she came to realize, was not his taste for the stuff, but his very genuine awkwardness in social situations and the inability to make small talk: "My husband had a shy side. Many times he was very ill at ease. Actually, the gruffness, the shortness, was a cover-up. I've seen him struggle very hard to relate to others."

An industry journalist, a freelancer from Memphis named S. R. "Dick" Mook, frequented the Fox lot at the time of *Up the River* and observed the struggle firsthand:

> I had seen a few rushes of the opus, and knew both Spence and the film were going to be sensational. Imagine my delight when Robert Montgomery brought him down to Neil Hamilton's beach home one Sunday when I was there. I sat back and confidently waited for the flow of wisecracks to start—wisecracks his film portrayal had led me to believe I might expect from him. I was doomed to disappointment. Beyond "Hello" when he came in and "Bye" when he left, I don't believe Spence uttered a half-dozen words during the afternoon. The meeting was a complete flop. Long afterwards, when I got to know him well, I started jibing him about that day. "I didn't *know* any of you people," Spence muttered uncomfortably. "I just can't give out with strangers."

And so to get through the obligations the industry naturally placed on a contract player of Tracy's standing, he would take a drink to calm himself, make himself more at ease around people he didn't know. "He could drink the least little bit," Louise said, "[and] it simply [went] straight to the brain . . . He couldn't [have drinks before dinner]. He struggled against it . . . [and] I gradually saw that he really shouldn't drink at all."

The closing down of *Ground Hogs* dovetailed neatly with the end of the lease on the house in Westwood. Having gradually discarded his casts, John was now on crutches, vigorously swinging from room to room and up and down the walk in front of the house. Thinking it might benefit him, the Tracys took a little cottage for the months of June and July at Las Tunas, a quiet strip of beach about midway between Santa Monica and Malibu that nestled up against Roosevelt Highway on the back side. Carroll's arrival in California that spring had enabled Mother Tracy to take a house of her own in Los Angeles, leaving Spence, Louise, and John to fit compactly into two relatively small but very livable bedrooms.

After little more than a week at Las Tunas, John's back was entirely well and Dr. Wilson decided he should start walking without the crutches for a half hour each day. His first steps took place in the living room at the beach, and they had trouble convincing him that he could do it. "He just stood there," Louise said, "arms outstretched at either side to balance himself, shaking his head and looking utterly frightened and miserable. For weeks his progress was difficult and slow. He had to conquer that fear and feeling of insecurity each time, and he complained of his legs hurting. Eventually he walked, but only for a few minutes at a time." After a month John was on his feet forty minutes a day, and by August he was standing a full hour. He progressed to two and a half hours without the crutches, and was up to four hours a day by the first of September.

The release of *Goldie* on June 28, 1931, did nothing to alleviate Tracy's growing anxiety over the course of his career. Despite Harlow's newfound prominence, Sheehan and the sales department had so little faith in the picture, chopped to fifty-eight minutes, that they opened it in Brooklyn, where the populace could be found romping in the waters off Coney Island, not packing the theaters. *Variety* labeled it a "direct imitation" of the McLaglen-Lowe series, though not as good. "For general b[ox] o[ffice]," the trade paper concluded, "it's a poor entry."

Tracy now had three pictures in release under the terms of his new contract, all undeniable losers. "They said *Quick Millions* was the most marvelous picture ever made. All of Hollywood said it. I was so excited I didn't know what to do. Then that picture went out and grossed about a dollar and eighty cents." *Six Cylinder Love* brought in more—$327,000 worldwide—but cost more and lost nearly $25,000.

He went back to work in July, starting a picture with actress Joan Bennett called *She Wanted a Millionaire.* The fact that it was a program picture and by definition, therefore, second rate, did not mean it would look noticeably cheaper or less carefully produced than the premium Fox product. The production values on all Fox pictures, regardless of category, were second to none. Some of the top cameramen in the industry—Joe August, Ernest Palmer, John F. Seitz, George Barnes, John J. Mescall—were employed at Fox, as were art directors such as Ben Carré, Duncan Cramer, and Joseph Urban, the legendary designer of the *Ziegfeld Follies.* Even the second-tier Fox directors—Ben Stoloff, Sidney Lanfield, David Butler— were talented and conscientious, a cut above the staff directors at most other studios. The things that most noticeably cheapened the films that came out of Fox were the scripts.

Sheehan flattered himself in thinking he somehow knew the story elements that were guaranteed crowd pleasers, and Wurtzel was fiercely devoted to formula in pictures of all types. Between them, they dictated the structure of Fox films to an unusual degree, almost always to their detriment. Fox screenplays were rigidly plotted and rarely character-driven. The typical Fox picture under the Sheehan regime started out well enough—he favored playwrights who knew how to get a story off the ground—but there was always room for improvement. Where most other producers would

Tracy and his son John, circa 1931.
(SUSIE TRACY)

polish dialogue or bring in a specialist to punch up a particular scene, Shee-han's screenplays often jumped genre in the third act, shifting to a different locale or taking on an entirely different mood or coloring. The climax would be a train wreck of melodrama, hurried and illogical, bringing the film to a perfunctory end at seventy minutes or thereabouts.*

The script for *She Wanted a Millionaire* was no exception. It started out as one of Sheehan's own ideas, a sexy morality tale based on a news story about a beauty contestant wed to a theater magnate twenty-nine years her senior. He set about to make her over, sending her to a private finishing

* Screenwriter Frederica Sagor once described Sheehan's story mind as "unhinged."

school and paying for special tutors. Eventually deeming her perfect, he then grew insanely jealous, certain every young man in the world was after her. The end came on March 11, 1931, when in a drunken rage he tried to strangle her and she shot and killed him. Sheehan clipped the item from the *Los Angeles Evening Herald* and had the story outlined and adapted by a succession of writers: Frank Dolan, Sally Frank, Dudley Nichols, even Hugh Stange, the author of *Veneer.* After six weeks of spinning it out in every conceivable direction, he developed a revised outline with the assistance of Sonya Levien. Days after Levien turned in her version, Sheehan put William Anthony McGuire, the author of *Six Cylinder Love,* on the job. By the time the film was ready to shoot, the screenplay had gone through twelve drafts, four by McGuire alone.

Tracy wasn't happy about *She Wanted a Millionaire,* considered it junk, but as was the case with so many Fox productions, the quality of the filmmakers would far exceed the quality of the material. The supporting cast would include Una Merkel, a fine light comedienne, veteran stage and screen actor James Kirkwood, and Dorothy Peterson, a Broadway contemporary of Tracy's borrowed from First National. Shooting the film would be John F. Seitz, one of the most experienced and respected of all cinematographers. Directing would be John G. "Jack" Blystone, an old hand at fashioning silk purses from the sows' ears he was frequently handed by Wurtzel and Sheehan, for whom he had worked since 1920.

Production began on July 6, Tracy making his initial appearance in the film as a rail engineer shuttling coal to the plant where Bennett works. She's walking home from a bad date, and he gives her a ride. "I remember him as a rather private person," Bennett later wrote of Tracy, "taciturn, though he had a delicious sense of humor." No happier with the script than anyone else, Bennett managed to enjoy the process of making the film, if not the film itself. "I liked the director, John Blystone," she said, "and working with Spencer Tracy was a huge treat." Once he knew that he was in good company, Tracy opened up a bit, relaxing around his costar and ribbing her as he would one of his colleagues onstage. "He teased me unmercifully, and it always pleased him when I rose to the bait, which was most of the time."

Blystone, who also hailed from Wisconsin, had a restrained sense of staging, a good eye, and knew how to highlight an actor's performance. He gave Tracy his head, letting him affect a bit of an accent in his early scenes, remembering all too well the Irish aristocracy aboard the Milwaukee Line. *She Wanted a Millionaire* was Bennett's film, on the ascendancy as she was, younger sister to Constance—one of the industry's top stars—and leading lady to both Ronald Colman and John Barrymore. Tracy, though, had a few flashy moments of his own, none better than when he played a poignant love scene to a simple cape draped over a broom and a chair, dinner for two in his room growing cold, despair settling in as it becomes evident she's not going to show. He goes to Merkel, Joan's randy, wisecracking girlfriend, a reporter for the local paper who is typing up a story. Reciting a monologue of grievances, all worked up, he leaves with her to go out and get drunk.

Filming continued at a steady clip until the morning of July 28, 1931. The company was on location in Stone Canyon, a section of Bel Air threaded with bridle paths. Kirkwood, unsteady on his mount, swapped horses with Bennett, who'd been riding since early childhood, and the horse, skittish and unnerved, promptly headed back to the stables. Bennett pulled her around to go back up the hill when the horse saw a camera car racing toward her and shied.

"A tree stopped my flight," said the actress, "and I ended up in a heap like a discarded rag doll with a hip and three vertebrae broken and a beautiful black eye." Sensing the worst, Jack Blystone gave orders that she not be moved, and Bennett arrived at Cedars of Lebanon Hospital with one leg pushed up two inches shorter than the other. An orthopedic surgeon set her hip the next morning, but it would likely be four to six months before she could return to work, handing her costar his second aborted picture in a row.

By now Tracy was resigned to making movies as a livelihood, stuck needing a salary only Hollywood could afford to pay. Responsible for all of John's care, his mother's support, and Louise's help around the house, there was precious little left from paycheck to paycheck, nothing much to show for a weekly salary more than twice what most families made do with in a month. The circumstances gnawed at him, fueled his occasional rounds with Hymer, Wallace Ford, McHugh, and others in his small circle of friends. He was torn between hoping the studio would drop his next option and knowing not quite what he'd do if they did. Could he pull up stakes so completely as he had before? Move everyone back to New York? Find a play with a chance at a run? Live again without the security of a term contract? When he saw the first rushes on *She Wanted a Millionaire,* Sheehan told him to lose weight, and Tracy dropped eleven pounds without having to be asked twice.

They all loved living on the beach at Las Tunas, but the closing down of *She Wanted a Millionaire* coincided with the end of their lease, and the Tracys moved into Hollywood's Chateau Elysée while they looked for another place to rent. The next day, Spence got word that Hughes had retooled *Ground Hogs* and was set to resume filming under a new title, *Sky Devils,* on August 10. In place of Tom Buckingham, whom Hughes had shifted to another picture, director Eddie Sutherland had taken charge, completely remapping the third act of the script and scuttling an Arabian Nights sequence planned for the film simply because there had been one in the earlier Milestone picture. Sutherland, borrowed from Paramount, was a golfing buddy of Hughes' and a specialist in broad comedy. He first made a name for himself with a largely improvised war farce called *Behind the Front* and continued on with nearly two dozen features, including M-G-M's 1928 picturization of *The Baby Cyclone.*

Congenial and literate, Sutherland recast Sidney Toler's failed part with William "Stage" Boyd, the original Quirt of *What Price Glory?,* and set about reshooting all the material Ed Sedgwick had left behind. Fox agreed to return Tracy for four—but no more than six—weeks at the rate of $1,864.60 a week, the same money they had charged the first time around. He was back at March Field on August 29 when word reached him that his cousin Bernard Feely had died at the age of twenty-three.

Spence had first laid eyes on him in 1910, when Bernard was not yet three, and had kept in touch through the intervening years. Spence's uncle Pat had traveled the state for the Lanpher-Skinner Company of St. Louis, selling hats and furs, and when he retired he had invested in farmland that could be worked by tenants. Then came the droughts and the winds that presaged the Dust Bowl, and as the topsoil blew away, Patrick Feely, by then an invalid, mortgaged the farmsteads one by one. After he died of tuberculosis in September 1926, Spence's aunt Jenny took in boarders, made doughnuts, gave music and dancing lessons in the parlor. Bernard went to work as an usher in a movie theater and began studying chemical engineering at the Northern State Teachers College. One of his professors there told him he should really go to the School of Mines in Rapid City, and a good friend of his parents, a Mrs. Lincoln, paid his tuition. He went for two years, working all the while and following Spence's career in *Billboard* and *Variety.* He had a job lined up, but then a strep infection set in and progressed to pneumonia.

With Bernard now gone, Jenny and her daughter, fourteen-year-old Jane, were without means, and Spence, stuck on a hot, dusty movie set playing low comedy to George Cooper and Stage Boyd, saw yet another purpose to the earning power God had somehow seen fit to give him. And back in town that night he sent off a telegram to his favorite aunt in Aberdeen, South Dakota:

YOU HAVE LOST ONE SON BUT YOU HAVE GAINED ANOTHER.

It was Johnny who first raised the matter of a sibling. "John, one," he would say sadly, accustomed to referring to himself in the third person. Then he'd say, "Two—boy, girl," nodding happily and leveling his hand about chest high. "So big." His parents agreed. John needed a playmate, and they thought—almost reflexively—of adopting. John's need was immediate; he couldn't wait for a little brother or sister to grow to a suitable size.

There was also the thing that had happened to John, the horrible thing with the unknowable cause that could happen again. Spence, particularly, was tormented by the thought, the possibility, that they could have another child so afflicted. Louise, too, although she didn't share his Irish temperament, his deep sense of guilt and foreboding. Where Spence felt the raw burden of sin and dark purpose in Johnny's disability, Louise saw a biological mystery, a circumstance of terrific power. And where Spence bore the blame, all visceral and unspoken, Louise felt only responsibility, the need to do everything she could either to fix their son's deafness or to marginalize it to the point where it would no longer matter. The only constructive thing Spence could do under such circumstances was to earn the money she would need to do what she had to do for John. They both grappled with imperfect thoughts, unjustified feelings of inadequacy and torment.

Louise talked to a woman at the Home Adoption Society, who was plainly dubious of their plan.

When she asked me why we wanted to adopt a child, I answered, naturally, that we wanted a playmate for our son. I went on to explain his deafness and the reason for wishing an older child rather than a baby. She told me that John's deafness created a problem in our household, which constituted an "abnormal" situation and might be a handicap to another child. She said that the Society was averse to placing one of its children in less than a perfect environment . . . She also went on to say that, in any case, she thought we had much better take a boy, as a different sex complicated things still further. She said, however, that I might fill out an application, if I wished, and then, if adoption was thought to be possible at all, the whole situation could be investigated thoroughly.

The friends they brought into the discussion advised against adopting an older child, concerned that habits and attitudes set even before the age of three could somehow hamper John's progress. Spence and Louise continued to bat the idea around, wondering not only what age an adopted child should be but whether they could even get one. As soon as he had finished with Hughes and *Sky Devils,* they moved from the Chateau Elysée to a rented house in the Hollywood Hills where they could spread out again and take full stock of the situation.

Sheehan had no immediate assignment for him, preoccupied as he was with the Chase Bank's pursuit of Harley Clarke, the interim president of

Fox, who had managed to turn a $13 million profit (in William Fox's last year at the helm) into a net loss of nearly $3 million. Spence, as it turned out, would have six glorious weeks off before the start of his next picture. Leaving John in Mother Tracy's able care, he and Louise went off to spend a few days at Arrowhead Springs, a resort in the mountains above San Bernardino. They started riding again, Spence deciding that he really did like it, and reconnected on other levels as well. Perhaps it was nothing more than Louise, for the first time in years, being apart from John and the constant, almost compulsive attention she lavished on him. And perhaps, too, it was Spence being away from the pressures of the studio and the worry that option time typically brought upon a contract player of any stripe. Wurtzel had picked up his option so early on that he was assured a regular paycheck through November 1932—more than a year in the future.

Those few days at Arrowhead were relatively carefree, a throwback to the very earliest days of their marriage, when there were just the two of them and their worries extended no farther than the mastering of next week's part. Not long after they returned home—about the time Spence started shooting a picture called *Disorderly Conduct*—Louise discovered, at the age of thirty-five, that she was once again pregnant.

CHAPTER 8

The Power and the Glory

Tracy followed John Cromwell's advice and looked up Snowy Baker, the rugged Australian sportsman who ran the Riviera Polo Club and Equestrian Center in the Santa Monica Canyon. Reginald Leslie "Snowy" Baker was a genuine legend in his home country, a champion horseman, swimmer, rugby player, oarsman, cricketer, and boxer whose work in movies brought him to the United States. He started coaching on the side, and fell in with the developers of the Riviera Country Club in 1928. With Baker as his mentor, Tracy went headlong into polo, embracing it, as Louise put it, "the way people sometimes go when they have waited so long to find something which they really want to do." He arranged for a horse by the month and lessons, and he took a room at the club so that he would be sure to get in his daily stick-and-ball practice, rising at 6:30 each morning to ride for thirty or forty-five minutes before going to the studio.

As with Tracy's three previous Fox pictures, *Disorderly Conduct* had been designed for other actors. Originally it was to be another Quirt and Flagg comedy with Victor McLaglen and Edmund Lowe. When Lowe failed to come to terms over a new contract, Tracy was promptly dropped in his place. Then McLaglen was shifted to another picture, making room for Ralph Bellamy. With the company hemorrhaging red ink, Sheehan renewed his commitment to building Tracy into a marketable commodity, and one of the men he entrusted with the task was producer John W. Considine, Jr.

At Riviera with Reginald Leslie "Snowy" Baker.
(PATRICIA MAHON COLLECTION)

The son of a noted vaudeville impresario, Johnny Considine was, in the words of Joan Bennett, a "wild, attractive Irishman" who had worked almost exclusively for Joseph M. Schenck, the president of United Artists. He started with Schenck as a script clerk and was line producer on most of Schenck's later productions, *Son of the Sheik, Tempest,* and *Abraham Lincoln* among them. Considine made the jump to Fox in November 1930 and Sheehan gave him his own unit, a move which led to speculation he was grooming the younger man to replace Sol Wurtzel. Considine's third picture at Fox was *Six Cylinder Love,* a project hardly calculated to bond him to Tracy, and when he was subsequently given *She Wanted a Millionaire,* Considine spent an inordinate amount of time haunting the set, convinced that Tracy and Joan Bennett, to whom he would soon propose marriage, were having an affair. His concerns were hardly assuaged after Bennett's accident, when Tracy became a daily visitor to her hospital room.

Disorderly Conduct was again the work of William Anthony McGuire, who was more a hand at comedy than anything approaching melodrama and whose famous technique of seeing the first act of a play in rehearsal before writing the second and third acts did not stand him in good stead as a screenwriter. McGuire's scripts tended to start out well before sputtering out in a fantasia of clichés. *Disorderly Conduct* was no different, a plot-driven muddle that nevertheless gave Tracy his strongest screen character yet. Rather than playing a crook or a con man, Tracy found himself cast as an honest cop disillusioned by the graft and corruption he sees around him. Filming began November 30 with Considine making his directorial debut under Sheehan's supervision. In support were Sally Eilers, Ralph Bellamy, Allan Dinehart, Ralph Morgan, and the ubiquitous faux Swedish comedian El Brendel.

It wasn't an easy picture to make. Tightly wound, Tracy often brought tension to a set and was liable to explode if something went awry. Considine knew next to nothing about directing actors and leaned heavily on cinematographer Ray June, who, in collaboration with William Cameron Menzies, had shot many of his productions for Schenck. Moreover, Tracy had been warned that Considine was laying for him, the two men having developed an intense dislike for one another since discovering their common interest in Joan Bennett.

"Tracy came into my dressing room and wanted a drink," Ralph Bellamy remembered. "My God, he looked awful. I gave him the drink, and somehow he managed to get some more, I guess, because when it came time to shoot he wasn't around. I finally found him passed out in his dressing room. In order to cover for him, I had a doctor friend say he was ill." Bellamy, sure that Tracy was in no condition to drive, insisted that Spence follow behind him in his own car as they drove home. "He was still in the police uniform. In the rear-view mirror I saw him stop, so I turned around and went back. He had pulled over another car, and when I got there he was standing next to it in that uniform, bawling the hell out of a woman driver."

Considine let Tracy have his head with the character of Officer Dick Fay and was rewarded with a performance that far exceeded the limitations of the material. Six pictures into his Fox contract, Tracy was essentially typed as a comedian, the failure of *Quick Millions* having convinced both Sheehan and Wurtzel that audiences wouldn't accept him in a serious role. It was Jack Blystone who saw considerably more depth to him, but Blystone's picture was now on hold and there was no telling if they'd ever get around to finishing it. So Tracy immersed himself in the role of Fay, the good-natured cop on the beat, and brought something extraordinary to it by illuminating the small details the story afforded him.

Demoted after pulling over the daughter of a rich bootlegger, Fay declares himself no longer on the square and takes a bribe in exchange for tipping off a gambling hall of an impending police raid. But turning crooked doesn't suit him, and he wears his newfound notoriety as a prize-fighter might wear an ill-fitting suit of clothes. Suspecting a double cross, the crooks make an attempt on Fay's life, during which his little nephew is shot dead. In the intense reaction scene that follows, Tracy's expression ripens from abject grief to horror as an all-consuming trance of vengeance overtakes him. "I did it," he tells Lucy Beaumont, the distinguished British actress playing his widowed mother, quivering and backing away from her as if dripping with poison. "Just as sure as if I put my own gun to his little body, I killed him, Mom." Instinctively she places her hands on his chest, and he erupts as if suddenly shot through with electricity. "Don't touch me, Mom! I'm crooked! I'm low! I'm everything that you hate! That's why those men were after me, Ma, and that's why he's dead! They killed him, Ma, but I'm the cause of it!" And then he kneels at the side of the bed that holds the body of his nephew and crumples into tears.

In *Disorderly Conduct* (1932). The critic for the *Hollywood Citizen News* likened Tracy's work in the movie to that of "the late and great Lon Chaney in his straight roles." Dickie Moore, who played Tracy's nephew in the picture, remembered him as "warm yet distant." (SUSIE TRACY)

Fay cleans up the gang in a memorably framed shot, his back to the camera, the action visible through the broken glass of an office door. The extreme violence of the last act was at odds with the earlier action, the wise-cracking exchanges with Sally Eilers, the scenes of low comedy with El Brendel, but the character arc somehow managed to play, Tracy finding the humanity in brief vignettes where, for instance, Fay silently caresses the headlamp of his motorcycle after having been demoted from sergeant to patrolman, the machine drawing his affection like a familiar old horse.

Given the vigilantism of the character, Sheehan had two endings prepared and shot, one in which Fay is wounded in the confrontation but survives, the other in which he dies. Tracy appeared in both but favored the latter as the stronger and more dramatically valid way of ending the picture. Sheehan planned to preview the film with each of the endings but never got the opportunity.

All during the production of *Disorderly Conduct,* the Fox lot was crawling with auditors from the east, Chase Bank representatives seeking to limit Sheehan's influence solely to the production of features. They brought new people in for budgeting and scheduling, and Keith Weeks, the former prohibition agent who was Sheehan's handpicked studio manager, was given fifteen minutes to clear out of his office. Harley Clarke had been removed as Fox president—sent back to Chicago by the very people who had put him there in the first place—and replaced with Edward R. Tinker, board chairman of Chase National, a career banker who freely admitted he knew absolutely nothing about running a studio.

Tinker's solution to the Fox problem was the only one he could reasonably be expected to manage. Instead of making better movies—"There is nothing in this business which good pictures cannot cure," Nicholas Schenck, president of Loew's Inc., parent of Metro-Goldwyn-Mayer, had famously said—he elected instead to cut operating costs. All contracts were on the table, and Sheehan, under siege, had the richest one of all, paying $6,000 a week and due to escalate, at each succeeding option period, in $1,000 increments. Sheehan had already accepted a 25 percent cut in pay under Clarke—something Wurtzel had successfully refused—and was facing yet another cut when he disappeared altogether, supposedly ill, his whereabouts unknown and his resignation rumored to be imminent.

She Wanted a Millionaire resumed filming on January 5, 1932, little more than a week after Considine wrapped *Disorderly Conduct.* Joan Bennett had been five months in recovery—having had to learn to walk all over again—but there wasn't much left to do on the picture, other than to film a Grand Guignol finale that hardly fit the rest of the story. Two days into it, news came that Sheehan had suffered a nervous breakdown—an "authentic" one, the trade press reported—brought on, it was construed, by the systematic stripping of his studio authority. While he was reportedly recuperating at a sanitarium near San Francisco, responsibility for the balance of the Fox season fell to Wurtzel, who was charged with bringing the average cost of a Fox feature down to an industry-wide target of $200,000.

While his own productions came nowhere near that target figure—the modest *Disorderly Conduct* cost nearly $300,000—it was hard to argue with the fact that the few profitable pictures Fox had released in recent times had all been personally supervised by Winnie Sheehan. Both *Delicious* and *Daddy Long Legs* were Sheehan productions, as were Frank Borzage's *Bad Girl* and *The Man Who Came Back.* When Sheehan's attorney wired Tinker's office in New York requesting a three-month leave of absence, it was, after due consideration, granted at 50 percent of the production chief's usual salary—a grand gesture given how easy it would have been to remove him altogether had the Fox hierarchy wanted to do so.

Still, in the months to follow, it would be Sol Wurtzel calling the shots, not Sheehan, and Wurtzel's interests were not necessarily those of his boss. New players were significantly cheaper than established ones, and part of Wurtzel's mandate was to bring along the starlets Fox had under contract at $500 a week—girls like Sally Eilers and red-headed Peggy Shannon. Wurtzel had less personal interest in Spencer Tracy than in James Dunn, Eilers' costar in *Bad Girl,* who had been pitchforked over Tracy for his greater (perceived) appeal as a leading man. With *She Wanted a Millionaire* finally in the can, Wurtzel, singularly unimpressed with *Disorderly Conduct,* assigned Tracy a secondary role in *Young America,* a Borzage production due to start in the middle of February.

She Wanted a Millionaire opened at the Roxy Theatre on February 19, 1932, and became the first Tracy picture to hit a Manhattan screen in nine months. With the film's emphasis on Joan Bennett and Fred Waring's orchestra on the surrounding program, he might just as well have stayed off screen altogether. Tracy was much better served by *Sky Devils,* which began limited runs in and around Los Angeles in mid-January and performed on par with or better than *Street Scene, Palmy Days, Tonight or Never,* or any of the other recent United Artists releases. The picture ran two and a half weeks at UA's flagship theater in Los Angeles, which was the longest run the house had seen since Hughes' *Front Page* had played there the previous year.

With *Disorderly Conduct* set for release in mid-April, the unit publicist on *Young America* was able to stir up some press interest in Tracy, principally among the members of the freelance corps who fed the fan magazines. Four took the bait, drawing assignments from the newsstand monthlies that targeted a largely female readership. Dutifully, Tracy spent time with each, opening up as best he could, but of the four men he saw over the course of ten days, only Dick Mook was potentially someone to whom he could really talk. Unlike the others, Mook was a seasoned newspaperman, six years Tracy's senior, who had come west from his native Tennessee with the advent of talkies. He wasn't a press flack, nobody's lap dog, and his stuff differed considerably from the fluff that passed for editorial content in most of the major movie magazines. Low-key and gracious, he was often visible at parties and social events where other journalists were rarely to be found. Mook recalled:

After the preview [of *Disorderly Conduct*], one of the Fox officials sought to introduce the members of the cast. They were all right down in front—where they belonged—and when they were introduced they could rise, face the audience, and bow. That is, they were all down in front except Mr. Tracy. He had waited to come in until after the picture started and then had taken a seat directly in front of the door. When the picture was finished he meant to duck out the door, but another official stood in front of it and blocked him. When he was introduced, he gave an ashamed little bow and ran. Outside, I encountered him again and, in that beneficent manner of mine, bestowed the accolade. "A great performance, Tracy," I said. "Thanks," he came back at me brilliantly and fled.

Intrigued, Mook phoned the studio the next day and made an appointment for lunch. "I came to the conclusion," he said, "that it was not possible for a man to be as brilliant on the screen and as uninteresting off as Tracy had tried to be." As they completed their interview, Tracy leaned forward conspiratorially: "How'd you like to go down to the brewery one day and swill a little beer?"

"I'd like it fine," Mook replied.

"All right," said Tracy. "I'll get hold of Frank Borzage and find out when he can go and then I'll call you. What's your phone number?"

Mook gave it to him but said, "Why do you want to wear yourself out writing it down? You know you'll never call me."

"You think so?" said Tracy. "Well, I'll bet you five to one I'll call you within a week."

Mook left, firmly convinced the next time he'd see Tracy was when he pulled another assignment or happened to catch him on the lot. Good to his word, though, Tracy called him just three days later. "They've closed the brewery up," he said, "but how about coming out to the house for dinner tonight?"

Mook arrived to find that Spence was working late. He ended up dining alone with Louise, his host arriving home only after the table had been cleared. The houseboy, said Mook, had to fix him some bacon and eggs. "As

Samuel Richard "Dick" Mook.
(AUTHOR'S COLLECTION)

he brought them in, he turned to Mrs. Tracy. 'Can he have some cheese?' "
Weeze considered. "I glanced at Spencer. His forehead was wrinkled with
worry, and from the expression on his face you would have thought the fate
of the universe hinged on her decision. 'I suppose so,' she said finally. 'He's
been working hard. But only a little.' She turned to me: 'It's so fattening, I
only let him have it once a week.' "

A few days later, Mook was again lunching with Tracy at the Café de
Paris, the themed commissary on the Fox lot. Spence noticed Doris
Kenyon, his costar in *Young America,* picking at a salad at the far end of the
room. "He knew she was on a diet," Mook said. "As he watched her, a dev-
ilish expression spread over his face." Tracy called over the waitress, ordered
a huge banana split, and had the thing sent over to her. It returned a few
minutes later, untouched but with the following note: "You poor under-
nourished dear. You need this more than I. You must keep your strength
up." Tracy, Mook estimated, weighed at least 180 at the time. "Spence eyed
it longingly, finally threw discretion to the winds, and ate every drop of it
after threatening to kill me if I told Louise."

He finished *Young America* on March 10, happy for the experience of
having worked with Borzage, but aware the film would add nothing to his
standing with audiences. The leads belonged to two young boys, Tommy
Conlon and the director's nephew Ray Borzage, and Tracy was left to play
Kenyon's irascible husband, a busy druggist with no time for the troubled

boy his wife has taken into their home. Derived from an antique play, the script was stiff and artificial, nothing like the social commentary it aspired to be, and Tracy struggled to make an impression in what was essentially a supporting part. Giving his character an ever-present pipe and working it extravagantly, he engaged in some shameless fly-catching.

Within two weeks Wurtzel had him back at work in another supporting role, bolstering James Dunn and Peggy Shannon in the flop Broadway comedy *Society Girl.* Again he had little to work with, and again his performance smacked of gimmickry, all intensity and torn paper, the only member of the cast with any energy to show. A key confrontation between Tracy and Dunn took days to shoot—"ever since they can remember," as one visitor to the set put it—and ended with the pudgy Dunn (who was contractually obligated to stay below 157 pounds) busting his third-billed costar in the nose. "I'm playing telephone repairmen or the hero's best friend who always gets the Dumb Dora blonde," Spence complained to Pat O'Brien.

About the same time, Sheehan was granted a two-month extension on his leave of absence. For the time being, the 1932–33 season would be entirely in Wurtzel's hands. Details were necessarily skimpy, but when the program of features was announced, Tracy was top-lined in three: *Rackety Rax,* a football comedy with Greta Nissen and El Brendel; *Shanghai Madness,* an exotic adventure yarn; and an oft-threatened remake of *What Price Glory?* with Ralph Bellamy now in place of Warren Hymer. By the time he started *After the Rain* in early June, Tracy was plainly demoralized, supporting the unexceptional Peggy Shannon in an obvious knockoff of *Sadie Thompson* and not even making his first appearance until the middle of the third reel. After the read-through, Jack Blystone, who was directing, asked him what he thought of the script. "Great," Tracy replied. "I get six days off."

The release of *Disorderly Conduct* was the one bright spot in an otherwise dismal spring. Despite the happy ending Wurtzel had naturally chosen to go with, Dick Mook thought the role of Officer Fay to be Tracy's finest screen portrayal. "It was the picture that sold me on Tracy," he later said. "I immediately started a one-man campaign for him." In its review, *The Motion Picture Herald* advised exhibitors that Tracy "should be played up strong for future B.O. strength," and the film played to capacity audiences in Los Angeles, where it opened at Loew's State with Raquel Torres and bandleader Eddie Peabody on the supporting bill.

Strong promotional support led to domestic rentals of $427,659, making *Disorderly Conduct* not only the most popular of all of Tracy's pictures for Fox, but also the first since *Up the River* to actually show a profit. Tired of getting stuck almost exclusively in comedies, Tracy hoped the picture's success would encourage Wurtzel to use him in more varied fare. "The last two parts I did in New York—*Conflict* and *The Last Mile*—were heavy dramas," he told Mook by way of explanation. "Everything before that was comedy. I was brought out here and put into a film called *Up the River*. Because it was a prison picture, they figured it was not unlike the two plays mentioned. The picture turned out to be a satire, and the reviews stressed my comedy scenes more than the dramatic ones. Immediately the dramas were forgotten. I played a mugg comedian—a racketeer—in a picture that got good notices and I've been playing those parts ever since . . ."

With *After the Rain* in progress and a baby due, Tracy moved his family to a larger house in Westwood, a sprawling six-bedroom Spanish showplace on a steep rise overlooking Holmby Avenue. "I could not but add up, from month to month, the ever-increasing grand total we had paid out in rent," wrote Louise, "and mentally apply it instead to a house we might have bought and be paying for. But Spencer would not listen to any hints dropped on this subject. Although he had done fairly well and might reasonably hope to work out his contract, he personally never had any feeling of security and refused to obligate himself or to sign a lease for a period longer than the date of the next option."

They were settled in the new house in time to celebrate Johnny's eighth birthday on June 26. The five guests at the party were all girls, since neither John nor his parents knew any boys. Spence and Louise expected the new baby to be a girl, and had been referring to her for the better part of nine months as "Susie." Five days later, on July 1, 1932, a Susie did indeed arrive at Good Samaritan Hospital, a seven-and-a-half-pound baby girl to be christened, at her father's insistence, Louise Treadwell Tracy. Spence was on Catalina Island at the time, making location shots for *After the Rain*. When word came, he caught a speedboat to the mainland and arrived at the hospital early on a Saturday morning, able to stay just long enough to ascertain that everything was going to be all right. "I was so pleased because it was a little girl," Louise said. "That was what he wanted. I thought that would be nice, but he was thrilled to death."

John was especially excited and couldn't wait to see his new sister. His mother had talked to him from time to time, telling him that he would soon have a little brother or sister, and approximately when that would be, but waiting the two weeks it would take to bring her home was almost more than he could stand. On the big day, his father, looking for a distraction, took him for ice cream, roaring eighty miles an hour down Sepulveda Boulevard between Sunset and Wilshire. Returning home, they both sat on the lawn eating their ice cream and waiting. When the car finally arrived,

John rushed up excitedly and saw the baby for the first time. A look of utter bewilderment crossed his face. "He had very little to say," said Louise, "and soon turned his attention to me. That something was wrong was obvious."

The baby's room was done up in pink with voluminous ruffled organdy curtains. After Susie was placed in her crib, John stood beside her for some time, touching her and making tentative efforts at play. "I was disappointed," he said later. "I didn't realize the baby would be so small. I had thought I'd play with her outdoors that afternoon." At last he went to his mother and rendered his verdict. "Too small," he said, again showing her the desired height, his hand about chest high. His mother explained as best she could that this was the way they came and that it wasn't possible to exchange her for a larger size. John, however, was adamant.

"Back," he said. "Too small."

He would have nothing more to do with the baby for several days, and Louise felt that she had somehow lost standing because she could do no better than that. Then, finally, he was drawn back to the little pink room, and eventually he made his peace with her.

"Very sweet," he said.

Sheehan returned to Fox in mid-June, just in time to see *Society Girl* released to scathing reviews and tepid box office. Dunn's pose as a boxer drew laughs from audiences asked to believe he was a lean specimen of welterweight splendor when obviously tipping the scales at 170 or better. "James Dunn seems only a little more absurd as a prizefighter (we knew he was only fooling when he said he didn't eat dessert) than Peggy Shannon does as a social butterfly—and that is something of a record," wrote Helen Klumpf in the *Los Angeles Times*. "It might all have been dismissed as conscious irony if Spencer Tracy had not been there bringing reality and sincerity into the proceedings."

Tracy was mortified by the recent pictures he had been asked to make and said as much to Sheehan when he got the chance. "Sheehan . . . had steadfast faith in Tracy," Dick Mook said, "but he seemed unable to find decent pictures for him." After nine features in the space of two years, Tracy was scarcely noticeable to the 70 million viewers who took in films on a weekly basis. In August, concurrent with the release of *After the Rain* (retitled *The Painted Woman*), *Variety* published the results of a survey conducted by exhibitor Harold B. Franklin in which 133 players were graded according to their marquee value. The biggest moneymakers were Maurice Chevalier, Greta Garbo, George Arliss, and Ronald Colman. Will Rogers and Janet Gaynor, the top Fox draws, were rated as third-tier stars, with Warner Baxter, Jimmy Dunn, and Charles Farrell occupying the fifth tier.

Other Fox personalities to make the list were George O'Brien, Marian Nixon, Sally Eilers, Joan Bennett, El Brendel, Frank Albertson, William Collier, Sr., and Minna Gombel. After ten feature pictures, Tracy didn't rate a mention.

"If pressed, he'll admit that he may be a fair actor," Mook wrote at the time, "but his looks are a source of constant anxiety to him. Once he said to me wildly, 'Look, for Pete's sake, they've got *me* playing *love scenes* with Joan Bennett. I should be playing muggs, because that's what I look like.' " Money was a constant worry. Tracy was pulling down $1,000 a week but seemingly spending it as fast as he was taking it in. "It was nice to see all that money," Louise said. "I don't think we thought it would really last. Of course, when you get more money you find there are many more places to put it. We were just as poor as we had always been."

Upon his return to the studio, Sheehan pretty much laid waste to Wurtzel's plans for the new season, canceling *What Price Glory?* and pulling Tracy out of *Rackety Rax* when a more promising picture came up at Warners. Warden Lewis E. Lawes, who carried warm memories of Tracy from the days of *The Last Mile* and *Up the River,* suggested him for the role of Tommy Connors in the film version of Lawes' best-selling memoir, *Twenty Thousand Years in Sing Sing.* At a price of $10,400 for four weeks, the deal was considerably richer for Fox than the previous loan-outs to Howard Hughes had been, but Tracy didn't mind, given his genuine affection for Lawes and the realization this would likely be the closest he would ever come to playing *The Last Mile* on screen.* "I remember one night he, his wife, and I were going to a picture," said Mook. "He was telling me Warner Bros. had just borrowed him for the lead in *20,000 Years in Sing Sing.* 'If this doesn't put me over,' he said, 'I'll just have to resign myself to playing character parts the rest of my life.' "

The film was originally planned as another pairing of James Cagney and director William Wellman, the team responsible for *Public Enemy,* but when Cagney declared himself a free agent in a contract dispute with the studio, actor George Brent was assigned the role. Lawes, who had script approval, disliked Courtenay Terrett's attempt at flushing a storyline out of the episodic book and kept up a steady correspondence with Jack L. Warner, even as plans went forward for director Ray Enright and a four-man crew to shoot nine days of exteriors at the prison. With Tracy obtained from Fox and a revised screenplay by Wilson Mizner and Brown Holmes (who had contributed to the script of *I Am a Fugitive from a Chain Gang*),

---

* After being purchased by Universal, the film rights to *The Last Mile* passed to producer Sam Bishoff and his partners, who made the film at California Tiffany Studios. Preston Foster played Killer Mears.

Lawes finally got on board, suggesting the film had "every possibility of becoming a masterpiece."

The cast was a notch above the typical assemblage at Fox. Bette Davis, making her seventh film for Warner Bros., was cast as Tracy's girl. Arthur Byron, new to pictures after a long career on the New York stage, was set for the part of the warden. Lyle Talbot, Louis Calhern, and Warren Hymer were in supporting roles, Hymer, billed fifth, now earning just $750 a week on a two-week minimum. Tracy was pleased to have an extended scene with his old friend Grant Mitchell.

Allotted twenty-four days, the filming of *20,000 Years in Sing Sing* got under way at the First National Studios in Burbank on August 15, 1932. Matching close shots with the footage Enright made in Ossining was a tedious process, veteran cinematographer Barney McGill and his crew blocking the action with the help of an on-set Moviola and scores of reference stills. Erected on Burbank's Stage 3 were shower and visiting rooms, the prison's barbershop, machine and shoemaking shops, a mess hall, death row, and a faithful re-creation of Lawes' own office, down to the books on his shelves. Director Michael Curtiz worked the company in twelve-hour shifts, generally getting four to five minutes of usable film a day.

When Davis started work on the twenty-fifth, she found an instant rapport with her leading man. "He was crazy about my performance in a terrible independent potboiler I'd made with Pat O'Brien, *The Menace*," she said. "It was the first picture he'd seen of mine—he thought I was different from any other actress in Hollywood." Davis was only nine days on *Sing Sing*, but could vividly recall Tracy's approach to the job: "Spence didn't have any pretenses, and for an actor that's like saying the Hudson River never freezes over. Most of them are so worried about makeup and camera angles that they don't give you what you must have in a scene: concentration. They just stand there and look beautiful . . . But Tracy had no such conceit. For the run of the picture we had this wonderful vitality and love for each other."

The guts of the picture were the scenes that took place in the old cell block of the prison. Warners arranged to shoot the interiors on M-G-M's Stage 10 in Culver City, where the set built for *The Big House* was still standing. Limited to four days, Curtiz shot eighteen hours at a stretch, driving cast and crew almost to the breaking point. Yet, predictably, the only outburst came from Warren Hymer, who showed up drunk on the second night, appearing nearly three hours late for a 6:30 call. When he refused to don his wardrobe, Hymer, who had been let out of his Fox contract after the debacle of *Goldie*, was sent home and docked accordingly. The next day he was on time but clearly hungover. When Curtiz said something, he responded by saying, "Aw, dry up, or I'll walk out on you."

Tracy immediately got in his face: "If you ever come here like that again, I'll save you the trouble. I'll walk out and refuse to finish the picture as long as you're in the cast. Then they can decide whether they want to re-shoot the whole picture with someone else in my part and keep you, or whether they'll re-shoot the few scenes you're in and keep me!" Hymer sobered up for the balance of the shoot but was late again on two subsequent occasions. Retakes and process work finished *20,000 Years in Sing Sing* on September 14, two days over schedule. Tracy had just a week to study the script for his next picture at Fox, a comedy-romance with Joan Bennett titled *Pier 13*.

That summer, there had been a conference on deaf education at UCLA. The principal of the Clarke School for the Deaf in Massachusetts was attending some of the sessions, and Louise was eager to meet her. The Clarke was the first permanent oral school in the United States, and the first to teach deaf children to speak. John's leg was improving steadily, and Louise knew he would soon be able to go away to school. "He needed more

Bette Davis with Tracy in *20,000 Years in Sing Sing*. The two actors had undeniable chemistry but were never to make another film together. (SUSIE TRACY)

work," she said. "He needed children with their companionship and competition, and there seemed no way he could get this in Los Angeles." There was no school of national standing closer than St. Louis, and Louise didn't like what she had heard of most state schools. "If John must go away to school," she declared, "he must go to the best."

The principal, a Miss Leonard, told Louise that even if she wanted to send John to Clarke—and she hadn't yet said that she did—the enrollment for the coming year was full and only a last-minute cancellation in his age group could create room for him. Moreover, Clarke, although a private school, was obligated to take applicants from Massachusetts before considering kids from out of state. It all sounded pretty hopeless, and Louise secretly breathed a sigh of relief. Then, less than a week before the start of school, a telegram arrived. The unexpected had happened, and there was indeed a place for John. The Tracys were asked to wire their answer immediately.

It was a tough decision. Louise drove with Spence to Burbank the next morning, and the two of them struggled with it. "He was against sending him," she remembered. "He said his leg came first, and that he did not think he should go away from home and Dr. Wilson's care yet. Dr. Wilson, when approached in regard to it, had said that if we felt we must send him, all right, but that he wished, naturally, that we could find something in Los Angeles for a little while longer." In view of their attitudes, it would have been easy to say no, but Louise couldn't bring herself to do it. "It was too easy," she said. "It *couldn't* be right." She told herself she wasn't being fair to John, and that she was shirking her duty. And so she argued with Spence: "I leaned over backward in doing it. I do not think I convinced him, but he said if I really thought it right, to send him." To their surprise, John was delighted. "I think the thing that pleased him most was that he would be with children again."

When she left with John for Northampton, *20,000 Years in Sing Sing* was still in production, and had Bette Davis not just married her high school sweetheart, musician Harmon Nelson, there might have been more than a strictly professional relationship between her and Spence. "Up to the time of *Sing Sing,* only George Arliss had given me encouragement," Davis said. "He was a father figure for me, the kindly, gentle father that I'd never had. My own was a holy terror. But Spence and I were smitten with each other before we knew it. He didn't have to pretend he was strong, because he *was* strong, but, oh, he could be tender too . . . I've often wondered if we'd been at the same studio what would have happened?"

Joan Bennett was also newly married—not to John Considine, as she might have been, but to author and screenwriter Gene Markey. Had there been anything between her and Spence on the first film (and she always denied there had been), there was nothing but genuine friendship between them on this second one. *Pier 13* was the slapdash story of a cop and a gum-chewing waitress, a wisecracking romance marred by a darker element completely out of tone with the rest of the film. The script was the work of no fewer than seven writers, principally Arthur Kober, a scenarist and press agent who invested it with what little heart the thing managed to have on paper. The fact that Spence and Joan could take the script's lines and contrivances and weave them into a credible relationship—something that was clearly impossible on *She Wanted a Millionaire*—made *Pier 13* a memorable experience all around. "I wasn't one of those simpering idiots for a change," Bennett said.

Raoul Walsh, never known for his light touch with comedy, directed with a keen awareness the material was second rate. He allowed the cast to embellish shamelessly—sometimes, as with Will Stanton's interminable drunk routine, to ruinous extremes. "[Spence] joked his way through it," Bennett remembered, "and threw in ad-libbed lines—very funny ones, I might add. And he and Raoul Walsh got along beautifully so that Raoul didn't object to Spence throwing in a thing or two of his own." They finished in just nineteen days—six under schedule—and Tracy went on to his next, *Face in the Sky,* virtually without pause.

Toward the end of the year, *Screenland* turned a few pages over to Dick Mook, who had a Roman holiday "giving medals to everyone I like and razzberries to everyone I don't." He awarded a joint medal to his pal Tracy and Paul Muni for being "the two finest actors on the screen." (Muni had appeared in *Scarface* and *I Am a Fugitive from a Chain Gang* that year.) The nod came as a complete surprise to Tracy, who admired Muni's work and didn't think he was doing anything nearly as good. He called Mook and asked him to lunch. "Dick," he said, "did you really mean what you said in your 'Medals and Birds' or was that out of friendship?"

Mook assured him that he meant every word.

"You see," said Tracy, "I'm not getting anywhere out here. My option is coming up, and I was thinking of asking them to let me out of my contract. I don't want to throw away dirty water until I have clean. But if I'm as good as you say, I should be able to find work at other studios, shouldn't I?"

Mook had been an officer in the army during the war, and Spence seemed to regard him as an older brother, a guy whose advice he could ask. It was, said Mook, "an inviolable rule" of his never to advise anyone on a move that was going to vitally affect his or her life. "I broke it that time to urge Spence to get away if he could."

But there was no getting away. On October 25, the Finance Committee voted to exercise Tracy's next option, bumping his rate to $1,500 a week on

December 1, 1932. With three households to support—his own, his mother's, and now his aunt Jenny's—and John attending the Clarke School for the Deaf in Boston, the extra money would be welcome. Yet he could see no improvement in the material he was being assigned, and Leo Morrison, who saw his commission jump from $100 to $150 a week, was of little help in soliciting offers from other studios. Tracy had little, if any, cachet with the moviegoing public, and the box office performance of his last released film, *The Painted Woman,* was characterized in *Variety* as "an atrocity."

Riviera, with its five turf fields, its quarter-mile training track, its stables and bridle paths, had become a grassy green retreat, a haven where the reality of Tracy's life in a cushy sort of purgatory—not quite a movie star, certainly not the actor he had imagined himself as being—rarely intruded. He kept up his lessons with Snowy Baker and started playing twice a week on the scrub team. The speed, the exhilaration, the fear of riding drained him completely, and he left the field utterly spent, his mind blissfully clear of the problems that almost always preoccupied him whenever he wasn't working. He bought a mount called White Sox, one of the prizes of the Hal Roach stable. "There's something about horses which, once you really become interested in them, just naturally makes you think this is a pretty good world," he said.

The costs were substantial, but no more so than for membership at a first-rate country club like Hillcrest or Wilshire. For the same $1,000 per annum, a player could belong to Riviera and maintain a stable of three ponies. Dick Mook asked Louise if she didn't mind his living at Riviera, seeing so little of him as she did. "No," she said. "He comes home to dinner every night, and I'm glad he's got something that interests him at last . . . He's got the most volatile disposition I've ever seen—up in the clouds one minute and down in the depths the next. And when he's low, he's very, very low. All this exercise absorbs a certain amount of that nervous energy and he isn't so apt to become depressed."

The game itself was quite simple: A team consisted of four riders in numbered jerseys, moving a ball down the field through six periods of play known as "chukkers." When the ball was thrown in by one of two umpires, the field would erupt with the fury of galloping hooves, divots flying, the cracks of mallets connecting with the hard surface of the ball, horses and riders shoving against each other for position.

There was, above all, the camaraderie of the field, nourishing because it had nothing whatsoever to do with the industry. To the fore came Will Rogers, who was one of the prime movers in the establishment of the club, and whose 224-acre ranch—originally a weekend retreat—sat just north of Riviera in an adjoining canyon. Rogers was one of the first people Tracy met when he came to Fox, and it was Rogers who seconded John Cromwell's enthusiasm for the game of polo. Frank Borzage played, as did Dick Powell, Darryl Zanuck, Raymond Griffith, Johnny Mack Brown, Jack Warner, Jimmy Gleason, Charlie Farrell, Frank Lloyd, Jack Holt, and producer Walter Wanger.

Rogers became a role model of sorts, a man of genuine humility whose loyalties and charities were legion. Tracy lunched most days at Rogers' corner table in the Café de Paris, where the Oklahoma-born humorist was surrounded by friends. "Only people he liked were invited to sit at that table," Tracy said, "and no one who sat there ever paid a check." Rogers considered the restaurant his club, and if he wasn't filming, he was there in boots, overalls, maybe a sweater or a leather jacket. "He was first to the café," said Douglas Churchill, who covered Hollywood for the *New York Times,* "and in the parade that paused at his table were some of the great and near-great of the world. Every visitor to the lot, if in the position to demand such a thing, wanted to meet Rogers."

Over the summer of 1932, Riviera played host to the cavalries of the Tenth Olympic Games, and Tracy got to know a few of the participants, particularly Baron Takeichi Nishi, a first lieutenant in the Imperial Japanese Army. Nishi, with his excellent command of English and a taste for sporty convertibles, became a favorite of the Hollywood set. In early June, Tracy played host to the entire Japanese Olympic team at a luncheon on the Fox lot. The next night, he and Louise gave a dinner in honor of Baron Shino, the head of the team, and were present in August when Nishi won the gold medal for show jumping, Japan's only Olympic medal in an equestrian event. Having said goodbye to him aboard the M.S. *Chichibu Maru,* they were surprised to find him back at their door the very next evening. Nishi had forgotten Louise's birthday, and had flown back from San Francisco to present her with a box of candy. He then returned north by plane in time to catch the ship for Yokohama.

Louise was six weeks in the East, first to get John settled at the Clarke School in Northampton, then to New York for three weeks, then back to Clarke for a final check before returning home to California. She found the school's spare, institutional interiors chilling, and sensed the administration's lack of interest in John's special needs—the physical therapy his leg still required and the fact that he was behind most of the other children in vocabulary and comprehension. John liked the idea of rooming with two other boys. ("Three!" he kept chortling as he noted the other pieces of furniture in the room.) For Louise, however, it took some getting used to.

She suppressed her concerns, bothered though she was, and kept quiet when she saw the children on the playground making no effort whatsoever to speak. "Speech had been left in the school building," she wrote, "and in its place were gestures and grimaces. These children, evidently, either never had acquired the speech and lip reading habit at home or had lost it here, for lack of encouragement. A kind of helpless terror engulfed me. I saw John look anxiously from one child to another. He tried to talk to them. He had words or phrases, if not sentences, for some of the haphazard and unsupervised games they were trying to play. They looked as blankly at John as he did at them. He came over to me several times and shook his head at this strange state of affairs."

In Springfield a specialist recommended by Dr. Wilson did a muscle test that showed a slight difference was developing in the boy's two legs. At the time, John's right leg was an eighth- to a quarter-inch shorter—hardly measurable—but with eight or nine years of growth ahead of him, there was no telling how pronounced the difference might become.

It was on the train back to Northampton that it suddenly dawned on John that his mother was returning home. With a wide, dark look of fear in his eyes, he flung himself upon her. Somehow, they got through the rest of the day and that night at the hotel. By morning, when she took him back to school, the storm had passed and he marched off to Sunday school with the other children, gently swaying as he did when he walked, smiling and waving happily, and Louise watched and waved back as they dipped below a hill, two by two, and gradually out of sight.

It was the morning of October 20 when Weeze arrived back in Los Angeles. Spence was finishing *Pier 13* and looking at starting another picture within days. There was a brand-new daughter waiting at home, one Louise hardly knew, and one who wanted, at least at first, nothing to do with her. With Johnny in the East, they tried to make sure he received a letter or at least a card almost every day. Mother Tracy—Mum Mum—did best. "Father and Carroll went to church and Father has gone to ride," she wrote Johnny on October 2 while Louise was still in New York. "We are all fine and Susie is growing very fast. She has three new rattles and can hold one and shake it now. She smiles and can say, 'Goo.' Very funny." Spence, who preferred wires to writing, contributed just a line or two. "Can you see the very small boat in this picture?" he carefully wrote on the illustrated stationery of the Santa Barbara Biltmore. "Show this to Mother so she may see how fine Father writes."

Louise took over when she returned, writing to John every day or two. "Friday, Father and I rode on the horses," she reported in her first letter. "Father rode on the black horse. His name is Whitesocks [*sic*]. I rode on the white horse. His name is White Cloud. They went very fast." Then the next: "Today is Sunday. Father and I rode Whitesocks and White Cloud this morning. We rode up in the mountains. Mum Mum and Carroll are coming to dinner today. Father, Carroll, and I went to a football game yesterday. We had lots of fun." And then: "Father is working. We cannot go for a ride on the horses today. Perhaps tomorrow we shall go. Mum Mum and I shall go to the movies today and see Father. Father says it is very terrible."* And: "Father and I went to a large party Saturday. There were sixty people there."

They went out very little. Spence still didn't mix well with strangers, and the thought of dressing up and going to the Trocadero or the Colony after a full day at the studio was profoundly unappealing. "You know how I feel about nightlife," Spence said to his pal Mook. "I hate it. But I'm at the studio all day and I see a lot of people and have laughs, etcetera. Louise is home all day and never sees anybody. Why don't you take her to these previews with you?" Mook did, and Tracy found that he enjoyed the solitude.

The few days he wasn't working were spent at Riviera, where a game could likely be had on any day but Monday. Large concrete grandstands built alongside Number One Field for the Olympics now held tourists straining to catch sight of their favorites. Women played on the old dirt field, and Louise was asked repeatedly why she didn't play too. She demurred, diplomatically at first, suggesting that, although she rode, she would never be equal to polo. "Spencer had expressed himself vigorously, a number of times, on the subject of women playing," she later explained, "and as long as he felt that way, I had no intention of making an issue of it."

Face in the Sky was the work of a novelist and short-story writer named Miles Connolly, who was joining Fox after stints as a supervisor at both RKO and Columbia. Connolly's story concerned the wanderings of Joe Buck, an itinerant artist who paints lipstick ads on the sides of barns. Buck was a cut above the characters Tracy was used to portraying, a rural philosopher and a bit of a dreamer, happy with his lot in life and proud of his work. "I wouldn't trade jobs with anybody in the world," he says earnestly. "I mean these guys they call the great captains of industry. Why, they're a lot of buck privates. Why do you suppose this country built all the good roads? So people could look at the billboards. Who made Americans snappy dressers? Me and my profession. Who gave the gals all their beautiful figures? I did . . . Say, I keep millions of clerks at work. I make the whistles toot and the factories smoke, and that makes us outdoor artists the greatest salesmen in the world."

The girl in the picture was Marian Nixon, a veteran of more than fifty films who had gained new popularity by taking the role refused by Janet Gaynor in *Rebecca of Sunnybrook Farm*. Nixon gave Tracy some badly

* This would have been *The Painted Woman*.

needed support in terms of name value, as did Stu Erwin, who played his dim-witted sidekick. The principal difference, beyond Connolly's story and the script fashioned from it, lay in its director, Harry Lachman. Born in Illinois, Lachman was, like Rowland Brown, trained as an illustrator, but where Brown fell into the life of a roustabout, Lachman went to Paris to study and became one of Europe's better known Postimpressionist painters. He entered films in 1925, initially working in an advisory capacity with Rex Ingram, later directing pictures of his own in both England and France. One of Sheehan's trophies, Lachman was given a generous schedule on *Face in the Sky* and was able to give Tracy a sense of how a real artist would carry himself.

Meanwhile, *Pier 13,* retitled *Me and My Gal,* played a week's stand at the Roxy in New York and cemented Tracy's reputation as a poor draw. Sold as a "high-speed comedy-melodrama," it got caught in the usual pre-Christmas slump and set an all-time low for the massive theater, a weekend blizzard eliminating virtually all the automobile trade. Whatever business there was in the city seemed reserved for Paramount's *A Farewell to Arms* at the Criterion and Metro's *Flesh* at the Capitol.

In the middle of December, just as *Face in the Sky* was finishing up, Louise went east to bring Johnny home for the holidays. While the sight of fresh snow was exhilarating, the mood at the Clarke School was anything but. Johnny was listless, his face pallid. When she embraced him, he was sullen and unresponsive. Upon investigation, she found his rest period had been combined with his physical therapy, negating the value of each. His digestion was poor, potatoes being part of nearly every meal, and he was beginning to show the symptoms of a chest cold. When the housemother asked what of John's she wanted packed, Louise said, "Everything."

On the train going back, John's cough got worse, and he ran a temperature of 104. By the time they got to Los Angeles, his fever had broken but now Louise had it. She was over it in time for Susie's first Christmas, but Spence had a surprise of his own. On New Year's Day, he and Louise were en route to Havana via the Panama Canal aboard the liner S.S. *Santa Rosa.* They would be gone the better part of a month.

In November 1932, while Tracy was on location shooting *Face in the Sky,* Preston Sturges met writer-producer Hector Turnbull at a party. Sturges, author of the hit play *Strictly Dishonorable,* had fallen into the lucrative business of screenwriting. Universal snapped up his play and, eventually, Sturges as well. Then, unsure of quite what to do with him, they assigned him to a series of workaday projects, the last of which was the script for the H. G. Wells thriller *The Invisible Man.* More attuned to originals than adaptations, Sturges wrote an entirely new story to go with the title and was fired for his trouble. Now, with three flop plays to his credit and his name on exactly the same number of flop movies, Sturges was hustling an original story for the screen that he proposed to write on spec and sell on percentage as he would a play. The title he gave his story was *The Power and the Glory.*

Turnbull, story editor and associate producer to his brother-in-law, Jesse L. Lasky, was intrigued by Sturges' idea, which was inspired by the life of C. W. Post, the cereal king of Battle Creek. Sturges had briefly been married to Post's granddaughter, Eleanor Hutton, and he heard the story of the Postum Cereal Company (later General Foods) in snippets. Post was a restless man who built a sales career in "agricultural implements" into one of the great fortunes of the Gilded Age—a rancher, inventor, and art collector who shot and killed himself at the age of fifty-nine. The life of a self-made man naturally interested Sturges, who was himself an inventor and a businessman, but the screen was full of such stories. It was the death of such a man by his own hand that intrigued Sturges, and his nonlinear telling of the life of Tom Garner, his fictional rail tycoon—which mirrored the way Sturges himself had heard the Post story—would begin with Garner's funeral and move back and forth in time as it depicted his rise from track walker to president. It was a compelling notion with an audacious structure, and Turnbull offered to arrange a conference with Lasky, who had recently joined Fox as an independent producer.

Tracy first heard of *The Power and the Glory* when news of Sturges' percentage deal made the rounds, but it wasn't until he was called back from Cuba that there was serious talk of his doing the picture. Originally, he had been set to appear opposite Clara Bow in *Marie Galante,* but when Bow resisted the assignment—as she did practically all assignments—both Tracy and director William K. Howard were suggested to Lasky. *Face in the Sky* had just been released, and though audiences stayed away in droves, Lasky saw much to like in Tracy's genial performance. It was, in fact, hard to picture another actor on the Fox lot handling a character who aged from twenty to sixty over the course of a film. ("You know, Spencer, I don't think you'll need so very much makeup to play a man of fifty-five," Bill Howard said as he gave Tracy's face a hard look.)

Having declined to produce a treatment, Sturges finished the entire script by mid-January. It took form as a recollection, a give-and-take, between the central character's oldest friend, Henry, and Henry's wife, who clearly hates the man. Henry, it seems, knows the real story behind the death of Tom Garner's first wife, as well as the reason Garner's second marriage ended in tragedy. He and Tom meet as children, then Garner is seen years later bullying his board of directors into purchasing another line—a deal he has, in fact, already consummated. Here Tom is established as a tough and resourceful businessman, clearly where he is through hard work and raw, undeniable talent. From there Sturges pulled the story back in time to the meeting between Tom and his first wife, Sally. He then jumped forward to contrast that scene with Tom's encounter with Eve, the daughter of the president of his new rail subsidiary. Having prodded Tom to success, Sally now regrets it. Tom, a cold shadow of his former self, tells her that he loves the younger Eve. In a daze, Sally leaves his office and steps in front of a streetcar.

Throughout, the vignettes are joined by Henry's sympathetic narration. Tom is an antiunionist whose confrontation with his striking employees is one of the highlights of the picture. But his life goes sour as he becomes old and sedentary. As C. W. Post's health failed, so does Tom Garner's second marriage. His young wife shows her contempt for the old man she has married by falling into bed with his grown son. *The Power and the Glory* was the American success story gone sour; wealth and happiness as the prelude to disaster. It was a tragedy of theatrical quality, thoroughly cinematic in its rhythms and ambitions, and behind it was the echo of great literature. "The manuscript crackled with its originality of conception and craftsmanship," Lasky said. "I was astounded. It was the most perfect script I'd ever seen."

The president of Fox—the company's third in as many years—was Sidney R. Kent, a slick salesman from the ranks of distribution who had been vice president and general manager of Paramount-Publix before having his contract settled. Tall and personable, Kent knew everything there was to know about block booking and the hustling of product; considerably less, it seemed, about the actual making of movies. Having inherited a deficit from Edward R. Tinker, Kent reported a loss of more than $9 million for the thirty-nine weeks ended September 24, 1932. With Sheehan in Europe, he declared the cost of pictures would have to be brought into line with admission prices, which had eroded nearly 50 percent in the space of a year. Only Sheehan's glistening production of *Cavalcade* provided some breathing room for the company when it opened in New York on January 5, 1933, and became the surprise hit of the season.

Normally based in New York, Kent appeared unannounced one day at Movietone City and began making changes. He gave Sol Wurtzel a slate of six pictures to produce and promptly replaced him as superintendent with J. J. Gain, the studio's newly appointed business manager. Salary cuts, Kent indicated, would go into effect within two weeks, and most people under contract would be asked to share the pain. "We will have to predicate all our plans on current conditions and gear ourselves to operate, if not profitably, at least without a loss for the next two years . . . Pictures will be produced here ranging from $225,000 to $240,000 in budget. Now and then we will turn out a *Cavalcade*. That type of picture is necessary for prestige, but the average picture will be cut considerably in cost."

It took some talking on Lasky's part to convince Kent that *The Power and the Glory* had potential as a "prestige" title, especially in light of Sturges' extraordinary contract demands. Having first fixed the arbitrary and heart-stopping price of $62,475 on the property, he then insisted on a percentage of the gross at a time when participation deals of any kind were highly unusual. After struggling through a down year, Kent was out to improve the overall quality of Fox product. "Decided I was to do 'Power and the Glory' for Jesse Lasky," Tracy wrote in his Daily Reminder on February 1, 1933. "Script by Preston Sturges, author of 'Strictly Dishonorable'—great script + great part. Sounds like a winner . . . I hope so."

The day after his meeting with Lasky and Turnbull, Tracy drove to Santa Barbara for a polo tournament with Big Boy Williams. He hadn't slept well in months and hoped the combination of riding and relaxation would make a difference. He had White Sox shipped up on the train and was able to take him around the track the next morning. For ten days he followed the same general routine: a ride in the morning, lunch at the hotel, a game in the afternoon. Then dinner with friends and often a movie at one of the theaters along State Street.

Back at the studio, there were meetings with Lasky, Sturges, and Bill Howard. They discussed story, clothes, and the actress who was to play Garner's wife. Both Irene Dunne and Mary Astor were considered before Lasky, an avowed partisan of industry veterans, settled on Colleen Moore. One of the most popular stars of silent pictures, Moore hadn't played in a film since 1929. Yet she was, at thirty-two, the ideal age to play both younger and older, and she would bring some added name power to the picture. "They sent me the script," she remembered. "Mr. Lasky talked to me and Bill Howard talked to me. Well, the minute I read the script, I couldn't wait to do it." Delays were inevitable. By February 20, nearly two hundred people had been dropped from the Fox payroll and salary cuts were estimated as saving another $10,000 a week.

The film was set to start on Monday, February 27, but then on Saturday they were told it had been postponed three weeks. In the meantime, Lasky and Sturges were drawn into meetings with Dr. James Wingate of the Motion Picture Producers and Distributors of America (MPPDA) over the sexual relationship in the script between Tom Garner, Jr., and his step-mother, Eve. *The Power and the Glory* was unacceptable under the Production Code, even though, as Sturges pointed out, the relationship technically was not incestuous. In a subsequent letter to the filmmakers, Wingate suggested that such an "unfortunate affair" could only be redeemed "if the son kills himself also." Word of the situation reached Sidney Kent through Will Hays, president of the MPPDA, and Kent shot a letter off to Sheehan in California: "If there is in this story a sex relationship such as Mr. Hays mentions, it will have to come out. I think the quicker we get away from degenerates and fairies in our stories, the better off we are going to be and I do not want any of them in Fox pictures."

When Sturges was finally told he could come in and sign his contract, a legal holiday was declared in California. Three days later, on March 4, 1933, Franklin Roosevelt entered the White House, and the following day he issued a presidential proclamation declaring a mandatory four-day bank holiday. No checks could be signed or cashed, and no pictures could be funded. The same day, as a financial pall settled over the entire country, the major studios, with no actors' union—no equivalent of Equity—to oppose them, began instituting a mandatory 50 percent reduction in salary for all contract players. George Bagnall, the Fox studio treasurer, induced Tracy— who could ill afford it—to accept the cut for an eight-week period beginning March 6.*

When it looked as if the negotiations with Sturges had irreparably stalled, Sol Wurtzel stepped in and asked that Tracy be assigned to *The American,* a picture based on the life of Anton Cermak, the first foreign-born mayor of Chicago. Admitting it was a plum part, Tracy nevertheless asked to be let out of the assignment, convinced its similarity to *The Power and the Glory* would freeze him out of the latter picture should it subsequently get made. Fortunately, Sturges' contract was finally signed on March 15, and production began eight days later. "The schedule calls for thirty-three days," Sturges wrote his father on March 27, "but it will probably take a little longer than that. It should be finished by the first of May. We have an excellent cast, an excellent director, an excellent cameraman, and an excellent film editor (cutter). If your son is any good at all as an author, we should have an excellent picture."

It was about this time that Louise began talking to Spence about starting a school for the deaf in Los Angeles. A checkup in January had shown that John's leg had gone back considerably during his time at Clarke and that the food there had tied his stomach in knots. He was put on daily treatments and a strict diet, but Louise thought there must be a better answer. "I felt we might start in a very modest sort of way, say with three or four children.

---

* Perversely, income taxes came due on March 15, with new percentage rates nearly doubling over the previous tax year. With only $750 a week coming in and virtually nothing in the bank, Tracy learned he owed nearly $9,000 in federal taxes.

These should not be hard to find, especially as we were willing to finance the venture, and, for the time being, a tuition fee could be waived. I mentally began to turn our den and patio into school room and play yard. All we needed was one good teacher and some children."

Louise mentioned the idea to John's teacher, Mrs. Payzant, who was plainly appalled by it. The public school system, however overtaxed, needed every student it could get. A loss of even a few would trigger a drop in funding that could result in a teacher losing her job. Louise went to the department of handicapped children at the Board of Education, but they couldn't release any names, nor could they offer any suggestions. Next she tried doctors, talking to Dr. Dietrich, who was their pediatrician, and Dr. Dennis, their family practitioner, both of whom thought her plan quite reasonable, even if they knew of no children who were deaf. She wrote a letter about what she wanted to do, which she thought she could mail to all physicians in the county of Los Angeles, but the head of the medical association didn't think it would do any good. She talked to other physicians and otologists, all of whom assured her they personally knew of no deaf children.

Finally, she called the mother of a deaf girl she knew had been going to Wright Oral. This woman belonged to a prominent Los Angeles family of considerable means, and Louise asked if she would be at all interested in such a venture. "She said she had tried the same thing herself once and had had to give it up. She had been able to get neither cooperation nor interest from anyone." Louise learned later that, according to a survey, there were more than two hundred deaf children of school age in the state of California who were not in school because there were inadequate facilities. While Louise was sputtering over the complete lack of understanding and interest, even in the salons of the state capital, an educator asked her, "Why are *you* interested in the deaf?" She could see his point. "Most people are not interested in the deaf," he went on, "until the problem becomes their own."

The Power and the Glory called for a lot of exteriors, significantly Garner's standoff with striking yard men, the Wobblies vilifying him at the scene of a nighttime rally. Garner wades into them, leaving his bodyguards at the car, completely unfazed by the dangerous mood of the mob. They were shooting out near the rail yards, and Howard drew his extras from the hundreds of men who lived like prairie dogs on a vast stretch of flat land that bordered the eastern edge of downtown Los Angeles. Seeing those men working long hours for a day wage of three dollars and a box lunch mollified whatever hard feelings Tracy was nursing over his temporary cut in pay.

The picture was shot largely on Eastman's new super-panchromatic film stock, enabling cinematographer James Wong Howe to capture interiors with approximately one-third the light normally needed for such scenes. "Super Pan" brought out new subtleties of shadow and texture, permitting makeup artist Ern Westmore to achieve the old-age effects called for in the script with a minimum of fuss. In Tracy's case, the lines naturally present in his face were emphasized with a dusting of powder over a foundation base, while Colleen Moore was aged with a careful orchestration of shadows and highlights. Moore also wore a gray wig, while Tracy had his own hair somewhat less convincingly altered with liquid whitener applied with a toothbrush. Much of the effect was achieved with wardrobe, posture, and, as Charles Dudley, the head of the Fox makeup department, put it, "sincerity—characterization and genuine acting ability."

To Tracy's mind, Bill Howard was just about the best director he had ever worked with, a dark, meticulous Irishman who gave the film tone and nuance without getting in the way of either the script or the performances. "He had none of the flamboyancies of many directors," Colleen Moore remembered. "He never raised his voice. He and I had great rapport. I could tell what he was thinking and do it before we talked about it." Howard, who began directing pictures in 1921, was the ideal man to stage the pantomime scenes in which the actions and words of the characters were simultaneously expressed in voice-over by Garner's friend, Henry.

While the nonlinear structure of the story made the development of his character all the more difficult, Tracy displayed a range he had never before shown on screen, going as he did from the childlike spirit of the early Tom to the burnt-out shell of the rail executive at the end of his days. It was screen acting at its most profound, forceful yet natural, at times quiet to the point of inaudibility. It was as if he was trying to push the conventions of the screen to new levels of subtlety. And yet, whenever anyone asked, he invariably cited the Lunt-Fontanne film version of *The Guardsman* as the ideal convergence of stage and talking picture technique. "Look how the dialogue overlapped in that," he would say. "They never waited for each other to finish talking. It was the most natural thing in the world. When you and I talk or when any two people are chatting they don't wait every time for the other to finish before starting, the way they do in most pictures. People anticipate the last few words each other will say and butt in on them. That's one of the things that makes Alfred Lunt and Lynn Fontanne natural. And it's their naturalness that makes them great."

Colleen Moore, who had played in films with John Barrymore, Fredric March, and Jean Hersholt, thought Tracy the best of the lot. "He was the greatest actor I ever worked with," she said. Fittingly, Tracy's most affecting scene in the film was played opposite Moore in the moments following the birth of their son. In the script, Sally's face is very white, her eyes unusually big and dark. She smiles at him but does not speak. Tom sinks to his knees, takes her hand, and speaks gently: "My son . . . my son. I've got a son. Oh, Sally, they'll never stop me now. Thank you . . ." On the set, Howard trusted his actors' instincts and gave them wide latitude with the unfolding of a scene. Tracy entered in something of a trance, still processing the momentous news that he was now a father. He dropped to his knees at the bed. "Sally, are you all right? I've got a son. You gave me a son." Moore's face was toward the camera, her eyes closed, but as Tracy spoke, she found it impossible to maintain her composure. "We finally had to shoot it with my back towards the camera because every time he did his scene, I cried so hard because he was so good. No actor ever did *that* to me."

When it came time for Tracy to recite the Lord's Prayer, Howard moved in close, keeping Moore's face entirely out of the shot. "Our Father . . . Who art in Heaven . . . ," he began haltingly, sticking to the spirit of the scene if not necessarily the text. "Thank you, God. Thank you for your kindness . . . for Thine is the power and the glory, for ever and ever."

As Tracy later told Clifford Jones, the actor playing his adult son: "This

On location for *The Power and the Glory.* From left: William K. Howard, Colleen Moore, screenwriter Preston Sturges, and Tracy. (PATRICIA MAHON COLLECTION)

isn't a business about making faces. You have to concentrate . . . and listen . . . because the camera is there picking up your thoughts."

"In 1933, I was 21 years old," wrote Lincoln Cromwell,

> and about to graduate from UCLA. I had applied to and been accepted at the medical schools of both the University of Southern California and McGill University in Montreal, Quebec, Canada. McGill was my first choice, but I didn't have the funds to attend either school. At this point, almost miraculously, the man who was to become a patron and sponsor entered my life.
>
> Until then, I had never heard of Spencer Tracy. He was just beginning to become known and I wasn't much of a moviegoer. Yet, one spring morning I found myself sitting on the porch of his house in Westwood, sipping lemonade with Spencer and his wife, Louise. At the end of that conversation, which lasted a couple of hours, Spencer informed me that he would underwrite all expenses for my first year of medical school at McGill and, if I proved successful, would pay for the rest of my medical education. There would be a price, Spencer said. I was to write him a weekly letter, telling him what I was learning and describing my life at McGill. Thus we entered into a pact that was to last five years.

In Brentwood, Cromwell and his family lived next door to a Mrs. Brumadge, who in turn shared the hometown of Enid, Oklahoma, with Dr. Howard Dennis. Concerned a promising student might have to forgo medical school, Mrs. Brumadge boarded a bus one day and rode into town to ask Dr. Dennis if anything could be done. "Denny," as Spence liked to call him, was a good friend, the quiet man with the wavy brown hair and the glass eye who routinely patched him up whenever he was injured at polo. He understood Spence's need to make his good fortune count for something and that he had thought of putting a boy through medical school as if to fill the slot he had himself abandoned when he fell in with the Mask and Wig. Tracy, Cromwell learned, had wanted a son to accomplish the great things in life he knew he never would and was unable to shake the notion that the deep sense of disappointment he felt was the same as what his own father must have felt toward him. "There would be people he would meet," Louise said, "professional people, doctors and so on, and it bothered him. You know—'What do you do?' Of course, most of them knew, but then, an actor. 'What is an actor?' he said. He did belittle it, and he wished he had been something else."

Slowly and somewhat reluctantly, Spencer Tracy was beginning to lay down roots in Los Angeles. It was clear he was to be stuck at Fox, churning out second-rate movies, for the full term of his contract. "I don't believe an actor lives who can make four to eight films a year and survive," he told Mook one day over lunch. "It's expecting too much of audiences to ask them to see you that often and not tire of you. I think Paul Muni has the ideal contract—one which specifies only two pictures a year and which permits him to do stage plays in the interim."

If it was only the stage that could bring him the artistic satisfaction he craved, he needed a different kind of gratification from his work in the movies. The money he made could justify a bad picture only if he could do something meaningful with it. A passage from the Gospel of Luke stayed with him from childhood: "For everyone to whom much is given, from him much will be required; and to whom much had been committed, of him they will ask the more." When Carroll came out at Christmastime, he was, as he later put it, "ogling the poinsettias and the climate" when Spence, with an extra $500 a week at his disposal (his pay cut restored and his new option period having kicked in), proposed that he resign his position with Thompson's Malted Milk in Waukesha and come to live in California as his business manager. Louise was too busy with John to manage the accounts as she once had, and their mother needed more attention than Spence alone could provide. Hesitant at first, Carroll said that he had met a girl he wanted to marry. "Move out," said Spence, "and when I'm finished with my next picture, I'll go back with you to be your best man."

Carroll was present throughout the shooting of *The Power and the Glory,* quietly chain-smoking in the background, and he could see his brother was drinking too much. Apart from dinner at home, Spence was essentially living at the Riviera, especially during the week, and it was easy for him to get diverted on the way back to his room. On nights when he "wanted to go out and get drunk," he would call the driver he kept on salary for his mother's use and the man would accompany him "to various bootlegging and drinking joints around Los Angeles."

At one point during production, Spence disappeared altogether. "To the best of my recollection . . . he was found several days later by (I think it was) Bing Crosby in Tijuana," said Colleen Moore. It fell to Carroll—as it had fallen to their uncle Andrew in the previous generation—to go down and get his brother and bring him back to the set. Bill Howard, who had spent considerable time of his own in the Fox doghouse, covered for Spence and managed to keep the film on schedule. Nothing more was said about it. "He just went on as if it hadn't happened," said Moore.

When *The Power and the Glory* finished on April 24, 1933, Tracy was still committed to *The American,* and he wasn't happy about it. The film would carry a significantly lower budget than the Lasky picture while exploring some of the same themes, and both were likely to be released within a few weeks of each other. The issue came to a head on the twenty-eighth, when the Fox brass decided to hold *The Power and the Glory* for a fall release. It was good news for the picture, but W. R. "Billy" Wilkerson, the crusading publisher of the *Hollywood Reporter,* saw it as a typical case of shortsightedness on the part of the studio and said as much in an editorial. *The American,* Wilkerson noted, would likely be released before *The Power and the Glory,* "[s]o when the latter picture is released, instead of Tracy getting the benefit of his admirable work in an entirely new type of role, he will be playing 'just another old man,' losing all the benefit that would accrue to him from the more carefully-made production."

After a tense few days, the starting date for *The American* was pushed back a couple of weeks and the role reassigned to Preston Foster, arguably a bigger name if not quite the same caliber of actor. *Shanghai Madness,* Tracy's next scheduled picture, was set to start in early June, allowing him time to go east with Carroll. Andrew Tracy met the Los Angeles Limited in Dixon early one Sunday morning and drove the brothers the forty miles to Freeport. They had breakfast at their uncle's cold-water flat, went to Mass at St. Mary's, and stopped at the Calvary Cemetery, where, clad in his overcoat, hat in hand, Spence kneeled at the grave of their father and wept. "We all sort of wandered off and left him alone a long time," said Frank Tracy, Andrew's fourteen-year-old son.

In Milwaukee they stayed at the Schroeder Hotel, and when Carroll was married that following Wednesday, it was at the Cathedral of St. John the Evangelist. His bride was a twenty-nine-year-old schoolteacher named Dorothy Sullivan, a talkative little redhead, not more than five feet or so in height, and Carroll towered over her like a giant. "This may be just what Carroll needs," Spence said to his uncle Andrew on the way to the ceremony. "Carroll needs a job and a wife . . . Carroll needs a life of his own."

Carroll Tracy had always been the forgotten son, the one his father John despaired over. "John thought Carroll was a dud," said Frank Tracy, who heard it from his father. "Oh yeah, Carroll was hopeless. You know—nice guy, never got in trouble, anything like that, but he ain't goin' nowhere." Spence was, admittedly, a troublemaker, but he had energy and drive and was able to make his own way in the world. Carroll had only gotten the job at Thompson's because Sam Thompson was an old friend of the family.

There was a big reception, and the only time Frank ever saw Spence take a drink of hard liquor was at the intimate gathering that followed the main event. The Sullivans were a big Irish family, and there were kids crawling all over the place. "I had the impression that he needed a drink," Frank said. "It was going to go on for several hours. My dad and I left about nine or ten. He stayed." The following morning, with Carroll and Dorothy off on their honeymoon, Spence quietly boarded a train for the West Coast and was back home by Memorial Day.

Although *Shanghai Madness* had been on the Fox schedule for more than a year—always with Tracy's name attached—he rightly saw the film as a comedown after *The Power and the Glory*—as almost any picture would be. "What are you dissatisfied about?" Carroll would say to him, having only his own work at Thompson's to compare it to. "Stick with it. What more can you ask?" The screenplay, by the colorful journalist and short-story writer Austin Parker, was better than for most Fox programmers, and the director once again would be Jack Blystone. "I would have felt more that I was getting somewhere if anyone on the lot had seemed to be taking any particular interest in me," Tracy said. "But I was just another actor, sometimes getting good parts, sometimes bad. I didn't feel I was doing my best work and I was getting a bit cynical about it."

When the shooting script came down from mimeo on May 19, the cast was headed by Ralph Morgan, who had played so well opposite Tracy in *The Power and the Glory*, and actress Claire Trevor, fresh from her Fox debut in a George O'Brien western called *Life in the Raw*. Then someone got the bright idea of putting Trevor in O'Brien's next picture as well, and producer Al Rockett borrowed Elizabeth Allan from M-G-M to replace her. Allan lasted only as long as it took for her to quarrel with Blystone, normally the most agreeable of directors. Marion Burns, who had played Joan Bennett's two-timing sister in *Me and My Gal*, had the part for a few days, then Fay Wray, fresh from the release of *King Kong*, stepped into the role with little more than a week's notice.

Tracy's character, Jackson, is given a general court-martial for firing on a Communist boat that killed two of his men. Found guilty, he can't get a job when he rescues Wildeth Christie from a stranded rickshaw and a near-riot. It's only her second day in Shanghai and he's the only white man she's seen. The subtext is that Wildeth was a wild girl back home and that her father has brought her to Shanghai as an "experiment." She's randy and lonely and virtually throws herself at Jackson. ("I'm lots of fun to play around with," she tells him.) There was a good deal of energy in Wray's lusty performance and considerable chemistry between her and her costar as well. "No nonsense, no pretension," she said of him. "I wanted so to complement his realities that I wore no makeup. Without having a light summer tan and without the artistry of the cameraman, Lee Garmes, I might not have been able to do that."

Where *The Power and the Glory* advanced Tracy's mastery of the art of film acting and would serve to cement his reputation as one of the best young actors in Hollywood, *Shanghai Madness* gave him a rugged sort of sex appeal that came with the frank sensuality of Fay Wray. Where previously he had been a sort of roughneck Lothario, struggling to gin up the chemistry with such nonstarters as Peggy Shannon and Sally Eilers, he now had someone he could connect with as fully as Joan Bennett and Bette Davis, but on a more carnal level, the kind of unspoken appeal that electrifies the screen and registers with audiences. Without saying as much, *Shanghai Madness* would advance his standing with the Fox hierarchy more than would *The Power and the Glory,* and not necessarily in the career-advancing way he might have hoped.

As they progressed with the picture, *The Power and the Glory* was put before a preview audience for the first time on the night of June 18, 1933. Tracy was there, sporting a bruise over one eye and a sprained wrist from having been thrown to the gravel by one of his polo ponies. Billy Wilkerson, who had earlier gone to bat for him over the matter of *The American,* published a review the next morning in which he called the film "the most daring piece of screen entertainment that has ever been attempted since the camera first began to flick." After crediting the author, producer, and director, "the big applause of the picture should go and will go to Spencer Tracy. This sterling performer has finally been given an opportunity to show an ability that has been boxed in by gangster roles, thugs, etc. And how the baby does troupe! And the part is no made-to-order affair; it required great ability and Tracy had every requirement. If *The Power and the Glory* does nothing else, it has introduced (at least to this reviewer) Mr. Tracy as one of the screen's best performers and, as such, he should be given roles befitting that ability, thereby giving additional contribution to better pictures."

Wilkerson's notice made *The Power and the Glory* the talk of the town, and suddenly everyone wanted to see Lasky's daring new film. The clamor was so great that Wilkerson took the unprecedented step of running a follow-up the next day, a sort of review of a review, saying the film had actually "frightened us because of our thoughts that the average audience would not go for it." The challenging structure would nonetheless make it a critics' darling, the most written-about movie in a long, long time. "Mr. Tracy was heard to remark in the lobby after the preview that he hoped the next time the picture was shown it would be heard. For his deserving information, he is wrong. Every softly modulated word or whisper WAS heard. Great actors cannot help being personal. The same with genius. Mr. Tracy is both in this picture."

In the midst of all this, Frank Borzage was preparing a breadline romance at Columbia called *A Man's Castle.* He wanted Tracy for the lead but had not parted with Fox on particularly good terms. When the formal request for a loan-out came through, the answer back to Columbia was no. Borzage considered Ralph Bellamy, then under contract to the studio, but according to Hearst columnist Louella Parsons, the one thing he wanted "most in all the world" was Tracy for his picture. Plainly speaking, *The Power and the Glory* had driven up Fox's asking price for their hot new actor, and Columbia's Harry Cohn, at least at first, wasn't willing to pay it. Wilkerson's item, invoking the word "genius" as it did, likely made the difference, for when the deal was consummated, Sheehan got $3,000 a week for Tracy's services and a $3,600 bonus merely for agreeing to the loan.

As soon as Fay Wray knew that Tracy had been set for *Man's Castle,* she mounted a campaign to land the role opposite him. "I tried to shape events," she said, "by talking to the writer Jo Swerling and asking him to please help me get the lead in that film." Borzage reportedly tested a number of candidates, but the only actresses mentioned publicly for the role were Loretta Young, late of Warner Bros., and Anita Louise. The desirability of the part was only intensified by the buzz surrounding Tracy's work in *The Power and the Glory.* Production on *Shanghai Madness* was, in fact, suspended briefly to make retakes on Lasky's picture.

At the close of *Shanghai Madness,* Spence, as was his habit, asked Fay Wray for her photograph, and she signed it " . . . with my utmost admiration," the same words Cary Grant had chosen when he signed a photograph of himself to her. "And we both hoped," she added, "that I would be in *Man's Castle.*" The very next night, she was in a nightclub with her husband, the writer John Monk Sanders, and Tracy was there also, standing at the bar, completely and obviously blotto. "I stood about two feet from him and said hello. He looked at me but didn't know me or, apparently, even *see* me . . . I didn't get the part in *A Man's Castle.*"

CHAPTER 9

The Amount of Marriage
We've Experienced

Good notices notwithstanding, *20,000 Years in Sing Sing* didn't put Tracy over as he had hoped. After winning the role of Tom Garner in *The Power and the Glory,* he fell back to playing muggs and adventurers. "The situation was not of Tracy's making," Frederick Lewis pointed out in a 1937 profile for *Liberty* magazine. "He was simply the victim of a Hollywood wisdom which let Victor McLaglen go 'because he can't act' and didn't know, until it loaned Shirley Temple to another company, that it had on its payroll—at $150 a week!—the greatest box office moneymaker since the picture learned to talk."

The character of Bill in *Man's Castle* was another mugg, albeit better written than most—a cocky vagabond whose vagrant lifestyle is compromised when he allows the indigent Trina to share his shanty lean-to on the New York riverfront. The screenplay was by Jo Swerling, veteran of a half dozen pictures with director Frank Capra. Based on an unproduced play, its mix of unmarried characters gave the guardians of the Code fits, particularly a plainspoken prostitute named Flossie whose lines had already been considerably toned down before Tracy ever saw a script. The principal attraction was Frank Borzage, with whom Tracy played polo, went drinking, and flew to Agua Caliente occasionally in the director's Waco F2 biplane. When Borzage chose to open the film on an elegant note, Bill in tux, opera cape, and top hat feeding the pigeons on a park bench, Trina seated next to him, a famished stranger envying the birds, he was suddenly wary of the extent to which Borzage, the Academy Award–winning director of *7th Heaven,* aimed to romanticize the story's more sordid elements.

"They had decided that he was to dress up and this was to be a romantic thing," said Lorraine Foat, who saw him not long after the film was released. "He didn't want to do the romances in the beginning. He had the fixation, I think, on his looks, but he never really talked about it. He might laugh. 'Whoa, I couldn't do that sort of thing!' That's what he said about Loretta Young, who was a very pretty, dainty person. They decided . . . that they were going to change his role, and he was not very happy about that. He just had kind of a strict feeling about the way he handled girls or women on the stage . . . [When] he played with Ethyl Williams . . . there was a romantic scene, but he was a very careful distance from her."

Man's Castle did not come together easily. The start of production was delayed two weeks with the advent of a technicians' strike, then actress Helen MacKeller, originally cast as Flossie, fell ill, causing her scenes to be reshot with Marjorie Rambeau. The delays forced out Minor Watson, committed to John Golden for a play in New York, and Arthur Hohl took his place as the lecherous Bragg. Borzage, too, tended to work more deliberately than most directors, preferring rehearsal to speed, mood to stagecraft. "That Frank Borzage had a way with actors," said Loretta Young, who felt she finally "proved she could really act" in *Man's Castle.* "He made you believe your part and this intensity came over on the screen."

The film's centerpiece was Stephen Goosson's spectacular Hoover Flats set, an artful assemblage of old cars and ramshackle huts topped with plywood and corrugated sheet metal and weighed down with bricks, washtubs, cracker boxes, and broken chairs. Crowded into the largest stage on the Columbia lot and set against a cubist mosaic of junk and weeds, it descended in forced perspective to the East River and the Manhattan skyline beyond, a sort of makeshift resort for the downtrodden, at once both vast and intimate.

Production got under way on July 28, 1933, not long after Tracy was observed moving into an apartment at the Chateau Elysée. "Irritable as a bear" when preparing for a role, he had come to relish the advantage of sleeping at Riviera, where he could concentrate on the business of perfecting a character. Away from the chaos of the movie set and the distractions of a home life that included two small children, he could study the script as late as he liked and still get in his stick-and-ball practice.

That all changed when Carroll Tracy came west and moved into the ivy-covered "Grand Hotel of Golf" with his new bride. By the time the

Family portrait, 1932.
(SUSIE TRACY)

boys' aunt Jenny arrived with her daughter, Jane, for the summer, Mother
Tracy was also living at Riviera and taking her meals in the dining room
that overlooked the course. Jenny and Jane Feely took the room next door
to Carrie's, bringing the total number of family members on the property to
five. After wrapping *The Power and the Glory,* Spence retreated to the relative privacy of 712 Holmby, at least temporarily.

Jane's first memory of the house in Westwood was of year-old Susie in
the yard in a playpen. There was a pool and a pair of servants named Felix
and Bessie. Spencer wasn't around much, but Louise was unfailingly solicitous and kindly.

Jane admired Louise's elegance and poise, the way she carried herself
and the way she spoke. "Her diction was so perfect, so beautiful. There was
a little bit of a formality to her that attracted me. She seemed to me to be
kind of an actressy sort of person, and I admired her because I was at that
stage where I thought people in the theatre—actors and actresses—were
kind of superior to the rest of us." Louise was a little taller than Jane, but
they wore the same dress size. "I inherited her clothing, always. We always
got the two big boxes from Aunt Carrie and Louise. I got through high

school and two years of college in her good clothes. And beyond that." A check also arrived each month from the time of Bernard's death in 1931. "Sometimes it would be late and [Mama] would write to Louise because we got to depend on it. And it varied in size; sometimes it was $50 and sometimes $75 and sometimes $100." Jenny Feely tried to tell Louise one time how much their generosity had meant to them. "Aunt Jenny," Louise said calmly, cutting her off, "that's what money is for."

Johnny was a constant presence, delighted to have visitors around. As Jane recalled,

> He practiced speaking and watching you, learning how to read your lips. After a while, it was no problem talking to him because he was pretty good. He was a very sunny, happy little kid. He was lonely, though. There was nobody around to play with. He hadn't gotten into a school where he had any kind of association with children. [Louise] was determined that he would be mainstreamed immediately. He was not going to be placed among deaf children. He was going to be made to speak. All of us were told, "When he comes into the room, we all stop and we speak to John first." When he would come in he would say, "Mother, what talk?" And she would explain what we were talking about. And she would impress on all of us that we should speak slowly and include him in the conversation. I guess you could say she had this overpowering sense of direction and protection, that this was her life's work.

There were no outward signs of trouble; the Tracys were an extraordinarily demonstrative family. "Everybody kissed everybody when they came in and when they left. Much outward affection among all of them then. Carroll and Dorothy and Spencer and Louise would go and kiss Mother Tracy before they left and when they came in. Everybody was very affectionate." Louise and Spencer also seemed perfectly comfortable with one another. "Good-natured. They kind of bantered a little bit. I don't remember there being any harshness or any anger between them at that time. I didn't notice it. I think there probably was an undercurrent; must have been at that time, but it was not evident to me."

When Spence moved to the Chateau, a huge, Normandy-themed castle a few blocks from the Columbia lot, no one seemed to notice. Louise took it in stride, focused as she was on Johnny and her plan to establish a private school for the deaf. The Chateau, however, was a high-profile venue. There were a lot of tenants employed in the industry, so his comings and goings were observed to a degree unthinkable at the Riviera. When he sat down for lunch with a writer from *Modern Screen,* the subject naturally got raised:

two Hollywood divorces had broken that same day, and two others had come to light the previous week—including the headline-grabbing separation of Mary Pickford and Douglas Fairbanks.

"The day Louise and I stood up," Tracy told the man, a freelancer named Carter Bruce, "we were just two half-scared—and also half-starved—young stock actors who had felt mutual attraction, part mental but a greater part sex. Marriage came to us over a period of years during which we shared each other's life. Those years weren't any too fat either. When I married Louise, I thought she was a pretty girl and about the best actress I had ever seen. But I didn't know then that she was the kind who could laugh on an empty stomach, who could kid away the tough sledding and never care that she wore the same dress day in and day out months at a time."

He dismissed the rumors that he and Louise were separating. "They make me laugh. They're too silly to even deny. I don't think anyone could ever say enough words between us to dissolve the amount of marriage we've experienced—long before Hollywood and her standards happened to us."

Ironically, by the time the article appeared, word of a Tracy "separation" was, in fact, old news. The *Examiner* carried an item about it on August 30, the same day *Man's Castle* wrapped at Columbia. "If there is any blame to be attached, it is mine," Tracy told a reporter. "If our friends will only let us alone, I think we can work out our problems." He attributed the separation to growing incompatibility and nothing more. "Mrs. Tracy and I are still excellent friends, and perhaps living apart for a while will lead to a reunion."

Louise made no statement, preferring to let Spence do all the talking, yet it was her idea to publicly confirm a trial separation. "The papers forced us into it," she later explained to their friend Mook. "They found out Spencer had taken an apartment at a local hotel and threatened all sorts of things if we didn't give them some kind of statement, so we decided this was the simplest way out—that it would clarify matters. It isn't what we would have chosen for ourselves, but, under the circumstances, it was simply making the best of a bad bargain." Spence added bitterly: "I gave them a statement of the facts as they are, but that wasn't enough. They wanted a statement with 'hot news' in it."

Four weeks into the matter, it became apparent there was something more to the separation than just "growing incompatibility." *Man's Castle* was made over the hottest days of summer, turning the uncooled soundstage with the Hooverville set into what one visitor described as a blazing inferno. Takes had to be aborted as perspiration beaded on the foreheads of the actors, and more work got done at night than during the oppressive afternoon hours. At the tender age of twenty, Loretta Young already had fifty films, an annulled marriage, and several high-profile relationships to her credit. ("I've always been very susceptible to men," she once commented, "and all of them were gorgeous.") Small and slight, with light brown hair and an underdeveloped figure, her fortune was her face, a tableau of Catholic innocence, soulful blue eyes, and full lips, convincingly virginal, yet old enough to radiate sex appeal, sensual and restrained.

"Spencer and I were such complete strangers that we hadn't even seen one another on the screen previous to our being cast together in *Man's Castle*," she said at the time. "I admired his work so much during rehearsal that I went to see several of his recent pictures. He later flattered me very much by telling me that he had done the same thing." She had worked with some of the screen's finest actors, Walter Huston, John Barrymore, and the late Lon Chaney among them, but she had never met anyone quite like Spencer Tracy. "Such fire, the talent blazed at you." The company worked late one night when the picture was about ten days along. "Spencer asked me if I would care to dine with him and run over some of the dialogue. I accepted and we went to the Victor Hugo restaurant. A columnist saw us there and the next day we read the first of the romantic reports."

Stephen Goosson's Hoover Flats set for *Man's Castle,* which covered 21,000 square feet, lent size and color to an otherwise intimate love story. Here Tracy and Loretta Young, age twenty, pose with director Frank Borzage, 1933. (PATRICIA MAHON COLLECTION)

Young, who went by her given name, "Gretchen," among friends and family, made little secret of her infatuation with Tracy. Borzage, in fact, may have encouraged it, knowing it was helping the film. ("The story was a trifle," she said, "but we *lived* it.") For once she didn't push her scenes, sensing the camera was picking up the underlying emotions between them. It was also picking up what Tracy was thinking, a trickier proposition as he was as cool as the character he was playing. Yet she could whisper in his ear and his expression would speak volumes.

"I believe," he said, "that the first time I ever really became conscious of Loretta as a girl, as a woman, was the first time she noticed me as a man— to feel sorry for. She watched me lunching on the lot. She could see that I was feeling kinda low . . . And so, that day Loretta came over to me and out of the goodness of her heart asked if I would like to drive out to her house and have a glass of beer. We were knocking off early. I told her I would. I did. We sat in the garden two or three hours, Loretta, her mother, and I. We talked and had a lot of laughs. It was pleasant. It was fun. Life seemed sort of decent again."

Tracy took to calling her "little ol' Whoosits," which was what the character of Bill called Trina in the story. His confidence and command of the role played out in stark contrast to his own personal diffidence. Acting was the one thing he could do in which he had unshakable confidence. Cursed with a sensitive nature, he was all too aware of his inadequacies as a husband, as a father, as a son, as a lover. He was homely, overweight, as ill suited to stardom as any actor could possibly be. "The idea," he said, "that such a gorgeous person—so sophisticated, so capable of having any man in the world she wanted—should prefer *me*. It was just too much."

Alarmed, Young's agent, former First National executive Dave Thompson, phoned her mother to advise her that Tracy was widely regarded around town as an alcoholic. "He must have meant *Lee* Tracy, not Spence," Gretchen said when her mother relayed the news. Worse to Gladys Belzer was the fact that Tracy was a Catholic with a wife and two kids. "Don't fall in love with him!" she warned.

"Oh, Mama . . . I think I already have!"

Amid much fanfare, *The Power and the Glory* had its world premiere at New York's Gaiety Theatre on the night of August 16, 1933. Although the film itself drew oddly mixed reviews—the *Times, Variety,* and the *New York American* all according it raves, the *World-Telegram, Herald Tribune,* and *Evening Post* somewhat less emphatic—notices for the actors, Tracy in particular, were exceptionally fine. For the first time, he saw such words as "flawless," "vivid," and "brilliant" applied to one of his movie perfor-

Tracy's off-screen relationship with Loretta Young paid dividends for director Frank Borzage. *Man's Castle* is one of Borzage's best-remembered films. (SUSIE TRACY)

mances. Given the forgettable fare in which he routinely appeared, many of the best reactions were couched in degrees of genuine surprise. Regina Crewe of the *American* marveled at the transformative arc of his work in tones that suggested she never would have thought it possible: "The man grows in stature before our eyes. He develops gradually, logically, inexorably from a rural urchin of the swimmin' hole to the iron man of far-reaching affairs. He becomes a familiar figure, understandable in all his strengths and weaknesses, at once admirable and fearsome. The role dominates the drama. And Spencer Tracy dominates the role." Bland Johannsen of the *Daily Mirror* thought Tracy's performance matchless. "He never has had a more exacting role, or one which he handled with such sure skill and finish." Mordaunt Hall's notice in the *Times* went so far as to declare, "No more convincing performance has been given on the screen than Spencer Tracy's impersonation of Tom Garner."

The Gaiety being a legit house commandeered by Fox for its class product, *The Power and the Glory* became the first roadshow attraction of the new season, a two-a-day reserved-seat event going up against such mass-market favorites as *Tugboat Annie* and RKO's *Morning Glory.* Driven by the reviews as much as the ballyhoo—and more than a little curiosity regarding its "Narratage" technique—*The Power and the Glory* grossed $9,500 for its first seven days, solid business for an eight-hundred-seat theater—better, in fact, than *Cavalcade* had done at the exact same venue. It dipped only slightly for its second week, M-G-M's all-star *Dinner at Eight* giving it the stiffest possible competition. *The Power and the Glory* managed a total of three weeks and five days at the Gaiety and could have stayed even longer had the theater not been committed to the premiere of *Berkeley Square* on September 13. Adroitly, Fox shifted the picture to the new Radio City Music Hall (as it had *Cavalcade*), and it played yet another week at the theater that had supplanted the Roxy as the world's largest.

By all standards, the picture looked like a hit. Fueled again by mostly excellent reviews, it did comparable business in Chicago and Los Angeles (where it was incongruously paired with speakeasy impresario Texas Guinan's torrid stage act). Past its initial showcasings in major metropolitan markets, however, *The Power and the Glory* was a loser, failing to ignite the passions of grassroots moviegoers who knew only vaguely who Spencer Tracy was, who preferred Colleen Moore in her flapper days, and who liked their storytelling straightforward and linear. Subsequent runs drew flat rentals of twenty-five dollars or less in neighborhood houses. According to studio records, the picture ultimately drew $563,323.88 in worldwide rentals—respectable, even exceptional given the average maximum for a picture was in the $400,000 range—but scarcely enough for an A-picture of its stature to break even. It was never reissued. A few years later, largely forgotten, the negative and master lavender were destroyed in a New Jersey fire.

Cousin Jane, early on, could sense there was something amiss: "I remember very vividly going to the set with Carroll, meeting Loretta Young, having her send me back to the Riviera Country Club in her town car with her autographed picture. Later, she came and brought me a prayer book, which I think I still have." The story broke wide open with Louella Parsons' column of September 14: "Her dining tete-a-tete with Spencer Tracy, going to the movies with him, and forgetting all her other admirers has made Hollywood wonder about Loretta Young. The reason for this Tracy interest is given as a plan Miss Young and Mr. Tracy have to star in a stage play together this coming season. Mrs. Tracy insists that Spencer's interest in Loretta has nothing to do with her separation from the actor. She and Spencer agreed to part long before he became interested in Loretta."

Emotionally immature, her hormones at odds with her strict Catholic upbringing, Loretta Young was used to sending mixed signals to the opposite sex, aggressive with men but never quite knowing what to do about the fire once it had been lit. She told a fan magazine she had to feel a "romantic interest" in a leading man in order to give a sincere performance. "I've been in love at least 50 times," she said blithely, frankly admitting she used the word "love" much too lightly. "Spencer heard of that one quote," she later said, "and remarked that he hoped he wasn't just Number Fifty-One in the long line."

They kept a low profile at first, spending a lot of time with the Jo Swerlings and frequenting little restaurants like the Thistle Inn on San Vincente, where they were unlikely to be seen. "I remember Carroll really shadowing me, shadowing us all, when we went to the set," Jane said, "and when there was a break he'd say, 'Let's go have a milk shake.' The four of us. Loretta Young said, 'Are you going to pay, or is Carl [meaning Carroll] going to pay?' And [Spencer] said, 'Carl's going to pay.' She constantly called him 'Carl' and I was a little put off by that. I know afterwards, as I grew older, that Mother and Aunt Carrie had lengthy discussions about it and what they were going to do, and Aunt Carrie would cry a lot." The couple grew bolder, and Loretta wound up spending most Sundays watching Spence on the polo field. One day Johnny came with him and she found him charming. When Johnny turned away, she saw how Spence would stamp the ground twice with his foot to get his attention. "I have never known a man with as much gentleness," she said.

Predictably, the relationship ate at him, as did all his infidelities. The mortal sin of adultery had brought him the burden of a deaf child, a responsibility he was ill-equipped to carry on his own, one he could manage only with the help and support of his wife. It was as if God had placed upon him something that could only be endured within the sacrament of marriage, a strengthening rather than a weakening of the bond between them. But as a sexual being, one for whom the potential for sin was ever-present, he also subscribed to the notion that denial equals permission, that Louise's tacit approval was part and parcel of the distance she placed between them. Madge Evans admitted to having been involved with him at one point, presumably during their time out of town together in *Dread*. Bette Davis, though newly married, took note of the spark between them. Joan Bennett was seemingly available, but broke her hip before things could get very far. (He told Loretta how astonished he had been to see Joan's leg sticking out from under the covers of her hospital bed and observing that there was polish on her toenails.) He talked about other actresses, women who slept around and weren't "ladies"—the kind men wanted to marry.

The relationship with Loretta Young was an almost spiritual melding of two souls, its intensity something Tracy had never before encountered. He talked a lot about his kids—John especially, who was, she decided, the most important person in his life. He talked less about Louise, but always with

Jane Feely (center) could sense there was something between her cousin and his costar.
(JANE FEELY DESMOND)

tremendous feeling and respect. Gretchen was different—more delicate, more beautiful, more sensitive. Seventeen years younger, she wasn't as well educated as Louise, nor was she as good an actress. There was nothing even remotely insightful about her, yet she was pure and magical and full of life. She could give him her complete attention in a way Louise never could, and there was, of course, the common bond of their faith.

"He was not a devout Catholic," his cousin Jane said,

and he was often not a practical one either. I would call him a spiritual Catholic. I would say he understood what the law of love was, what Christianity teaches, what the Catholic Church teaches, and what we live by and what we believe. I can remember one thing that kind of struck me. We were at Louise's, we were at the house, and he and Carroll came home from somewhere—he was living at home at that time—and he said, "You know, Aunt Jenny, I went by this church over in Beverly Hills, and there were all these people. Mass was over, and they brought out the Host in a big monstrance." And my mother said, "Spencer, it's the 40 hours. You remember the 40-hour devotion." And he said, "Forty hours? Oh, yeah . . . I guess I forgot." The point was that he made a big issue about being there, so that she would know he had been to Mass. It was very obvious he knew what they were doing.

When it came time for Jenny and Jane to return to Aberdeen, a veil of sadness descended over the family. Carrie Tracy would miss Jenny's spark, her laugh, her sense of shared experience. Spencer's relationship with Loretta Young had turned into a very public event, and Louise was clearly mortified. "In the family," said Jane, "those were the things you pulled the lace curtains for—not that it wasn't true, but you didn't talk about it. Ever." Before she left, Aunt Jenny broached the subject with Spencer just long enough to say, "I *hope* you're not going to drag the Tracy name through the divorce courts!"

They had talked about marriage, Spence and Gretchen, but she never asked him to get a divorce, partly because she knew they could never marry in the church, and partly because she knew deep in her heart that he would never divorce Louise. "I really don't think I could," Tracy told his friend Bogart. "What could I say to Johnny? How could I make a nine year old little boy understand that I'm leaving his mother?"

His drinking accelerated, and he was arrested for public drunkenness one night while attempting to back out of a driveway in the 8400 block of Sunset Boulevard. The address was on a strip of county land across the street from a clutch of notorious businesses. The House of Francis, an apartment building that housed one of the town's priciest brothels, was at 8439 Sunset, and Milton Farmer's Clover Club, a fancy after-hours restaurant and bar where casino-style gambling was available in the back room, was at 8469. Tracy's private behavior and his public image converged in the press that next day.

"Securely held with handcuffs and leg straps, Spencer Tracy, portrayer of 'he-man' roles on the screen, yesterday spent two hours in the county jail after he had been booked as drunk," began a four-inch item in the *Examiner* that carried the headline SPENCER TRACY BOOKED IN JAIL. "Tracy last year played the starring role in the film *Twenty Years in Sing Sing* [*sic*], a motion picture showing prison life based on actual events in the New York penitentiary."

"You see," Tracy later said by way of explanation,

I'd never known anything of this sort. My life has been so completely different, so distant from this kind of thing. And to be suddenly the center of a group that was brilliant and rich and worldly was fascinating to me. The women were gay and beautiful always— they wore furs and jewels and creations in the evening. We dressed for dinner. I'd never done that. We had cocktails in the afternoon, and champagne with food, and liqueurs afterward, and highballs in the evening . . . I forgot all the precepts upon which I had built my life, accepted all the attitudes and philosophies that I'd despised for so many years.

With the completion of *Man's Castle,* Tracy returned to his home studio and almost immediately was put into a picture called *The Mad Game,* which was being rushed to meet a November 17 release date. Resentment over long hours and salary cuts—not to mention quality of material—ran deep among contract players, many of whom were coming to see the Academy of Motion Picture Arts and Sciences as a tool of the producers and not the impartial arbiter of labor disputes it had proposed to be. With virtually no time off between pictures, Tracy joined the nascent Screen Actors Guild, becoming one of twenty-five directors of the organization alongside such friends and colleagues as Ralph Bellamy, George Raft, Robert Montgomery, Chester Morris, Miriam Hopkins, James Cagney, Ann Harding, Boris Karloff, Edward G. Robinson, Ralph Morgan, and Grant Mitchell.

Within a month, twenty-three major stars would resign from the academy and more than five hundred actors would answer the call to complete SAG membership forms in the first serious blow to the academy since its inception in 1927. *The Mad Game* counted as another regression after the twin experiences of *The Power and the Glory* and *Man's Castle.* It was, like *Shanghai Madness* before it, a formula picture, the sort of gangster melodrama Warner Bros. did better than anyone. It had been a story with the Hammettesque title *Lead Harvest,* but then William Conselman started drafting the screenplay under Winnie Sheehan's supervision and it evolved into a film about the kidnapping game—the "snatch racket" that was emerging with the end of Prohibition.

After the taking of the Lindbergh baby in March 1932, most city and state censor boards discouraged such storylines, fearful the public would take offense. And with the release of First National's *Three on a Match* in October of that year, the industry entered into a gentlemen's agreement not to make any more like it. Sheehan was adamant about *The Mad Game,* however, and agreed to remove actual scenes of kidnapping in order to keep the project alive. In July 1933 the Hays office warned Fox the film would likely encounter problems in New York State, where the son of a prominent politician was being held for ransom. Sheehan left for Europe that same month, confident all problems with the script had been worked out and that the film would start as planned as soon as Tracy had finished at Columbia.

For the girl in *The Mad Game,* Sheehan wanted Tracy teamed with

Claire Trevor, a pairing that had almost taken place for *Shanghai Madness.* Like Tracy, Trevor had studied at the American Academy of Dramatic Arts and then moved on to stock and a string of Vitaphone shorts. She made a genuine Broadway hit for herself in *The Party's Over,* then left to accept Sheehan's offer of a contract, a move she already had reason to regret. "The pictures were so cheesy," she said late in life, "those eighteen-day schedules. And usually directors had full sway—directors who had failed long before and were sort of resurrected to do a picture. Or else we'd have a brand-new guy who had never done anything." The director of *The Mad Game,* Irving Cummings, fell more into the first category than the second, a large, sonorous figure who, like Ed Sedgwick, was a holdover from silent days.

Tracy found himself pleasantly surprised by Trevor's smart work as the newspaper reporter who loves his blustery beer baron and rolls her own cigarettes. "He liked the way I delivered lines, tossed lines away. He really liked my style." He also liked the looks of the twenty-three-year-old hazel-eyed blonde and said as much early on in the shoot. She, of course, had already heard about Loretta (who was in Hawaii with her mother at the time) and responded to his overtures with a prim, "I don't go out with married men." After a loaded pause, Tracy flashed her a big smile. "Stay that way!" he said approvingly.

About this time, Dick Mook asked Louise to sit for an interview. He was one of the first people Spence had told about the separation: "If you think it's necessary to run a story on it, go ahead and write it. It's the only one we'll give out." The news about him and Loretta Young had subsequently made all the papers. Louise hadn't said anything to the press, and Dick thought she should at least have a chance to give her side of the story. "I'd known Louise and Spencer—intimately—almost from the time they first came to Hollywood," he said. "I'd done one of the first stories on him the magazines carried, and from that casual contact have developed two of the few friendships I really prize. The announcement of their separation hurt me as much as though I, myself, had been involved."

The night after the story broke, Louise and Mook sat across from one another in a smoky Los Angeles nightclub. (Mook was still taking her around to industry events and previews, and when Spence saw him, he'd usually ask, "Are you seeing to it that Louise has a good time?") Dick thought her remarkably composed that night.

"There's nothing about it that necessitates your wearing such a long face," she said calmly. "It's just one of those things. It doesn't mean that this is the end. In every marriage, no matter how happy it is, there are bound to come times when some sort of adjustment is necessary. This happens to be one of those times in ours. This 'separation' will simply clarify matters. We're not going to get a divorce. At least, that isn't our present intention.

Nor am I going abroad with the children, as the papers reported. We'll probably be back together by the time your story breaks."

Mook said something about the Hollywood press and how anybody's affairs were everybody's. "Hollywood had nothing to do with it," she said, declining the bait.

I don't feel bitter towards Hollywood because Hollywood has done nothing to us—except give us more money than we've ever had before. This and a chance to have a home of our own. I love this place. So does Spencer. I'll admit that if he had been engaged in any other kind of work in some other city, we could probably have worked things out quietly between ourselves without having to tell the world our troubles, but that would only have been because he wouldn't have been in the public eye. Newspapers are here to give the people news. If he had been news in some other city, it would have been the same thing.

We lead a very close family life. We seldom go out anywhere, and we see few people outside our immediate family. We both felt we were getting into a rut. How many times have I been out alone with you? Can you remember? Hasn't Spencer even urged you on numerous occasions to ask me out so I'd get a different viewpoint, get to talk about different things?

He needs the same change. I've repeatedly told him to go out with other people. Occasionally he's gone out with some of the girls he's worked with. I haven't minded because he always told me about it. One of his recent pictures he worked nights a great deal. His leading lady happened to be single and they had dinner together a few times. Once, one of his other pictures was being pre-viewed. I'd already seen it, so he asked this girl to go with him and people saw them there. Why shouldn't he take a friend who was interested to see it?

Marriage out here may be a little more difficult than elsewhere because everyone knows everyone else—at least by sight—and there's little else to talk about. I can't truthfully say that Spencer and I are still madly, passionately in love with each other. I don't believe that kind of love ever lasts. It burns itself out by its very intensity. But in its place comes a deep, understanding companionship and devotion. That's what we have—and prize.

With Sheehan out of the country, Tracy was loaned to a start-up called 20th Century, which was based on the United Artists lot in Hollywood. Coincidentally, it was the same company Gretchen had just joined, an operation assembled by Joe Schenck and run by the former head of production at Warner Bros., Darryl F. Zanuck. At the moment, 20th Century was just an office, a line of credit, and Zanuck's fabled way with a script. Everything else was rented, including most of the stars they used in their productions. George Arliss, also from Warners, was their big male draw, a distinguished British character actor who specialized in period subjects and biographies. Gretchen feared she would get stuck playing his daughter and tried to have a clause inserted into her contract preventing such a thing. When Zanuck refused, she signed anyway and ended up in her first picture, *House of Rothschild*, playing Arliss' daughter.

Twentieth had a slate of twelve films for the 1933–34 season, *Rothschild* being the seventh. Others on the schedule were *Bulldog Drummond Strikes Back*, *The Affairs of Cellini*, and *The Trouble Shooter*, a story based on the adventures of a telephone repairman that proposed to team Tracy with comedian Jack Oakie, borrowed from Paramount. ("The talk," said Oakie, "was that with his underplaying and my jumping around we were a perfect twosome.") Filming began on October 9, just as *Man's Castle* was being readied for release.

The path to the screen for *Man's Castle* was littered with parsed dialogue, trimmed footage, and the dubious approvals of the Hays office. Borzage flouted the Production Code in several key respects, insisting the lead characters remain unmarried until the very end of the picture, when an unplanned pregnancy forces Bill into an armed robbery from which he escapes unpunished. Flossie, the aging whore, retains most of her unsavory qualities, easy to discern for any adult paying attention, the details investing Borzage's fantasy world with a sordid reality that would not have been possible only a year later.

The problems began in June when Dr. James Wingate of the MPPDA read Jo Swerling's draft screenplay and ordered a number of cuts, including the removal of Bill's climactic action of feeling Trina's stomach and the line, "Geez! It's movin'!" and Trina's response, "Life." It was daring for the time and absolutely essential to the picture as far as Borzage was concerned. Wingate subsequently met with the director, Swerling, and Columbia's Sam Briskin over the proposed changes to the script, and most were eventually agreed to, save those specifically tied to the climax. "The studio believes they can handle this scene in such a way as to make it acceptable," Wingate advised in an internal memorandum. "We are reserving our opinion until we see the picture."

While the film was in production, Briskin, fighting back, reassured Dr. Wingate that "great care" would be used in the scene "and as both people are fully clothed, we see nothing that can be censorable about it." Regarding the brief exchange of dialogue, "It is impossible to eliminate the words requested, as they are the essence of our story." A scene of Bill and Trina skinny-dipping in the East River was similarly filmed with care, although a quick shot of Tracy diving, unclothed, into the water and Young's similarly undressed body passing over his were removed before the film could be passed for release.

The matter was allowed to rest until the movie was ready to be screened in early October. Wingate, clearly under the spell Borzage had cast, saw nothing other than beauty in the way the story unfolded and was effusive afterward in his praise of the film. "It struck us as a fine and tender picture," he wrote Harry Cohn, "treated in such a way as to be satisfactory under the Code. We also trust that it will be free from any serious danger of censorship difficulty." Predictably, after Wingate had offered forth such a bold and authoritative assurance, the New York State Censor Board, which Wingate himself used to head, refused to license the film for exhibition without a number of deletions.

Man's Castle and *The Mad Game* were previewed within days of each other, the latter having had its release moved up so as to avoid the spectacle of two Tracy pictures competing head-on. Fox management needn't have worried, as the two films were designed to appeal to vastly different audiences. *Mad Game* was a gangster picture, perfumed, at the behest of the Hays office, with a lot of indignant dialogue about the kidnapping racket and how it was "the lowest of the low." Tracy was noted largely for his use of makeup, a plot device requiring his character to submit to plastic surgery in order to infiltrate his former gang. He laid it on thick, turning into a cheap Italian hood with curly, permed hair and a putty nose that Cummings emphasized by shooting him mostly in profile.

Man's Castle was another matter entirely, a film made with exquisite care and sensitivity and aimed at a more sophisticated crowd, principally adult females and the men whose moviegoing choices they influenced. The press preview at Los Angeles' Romanesque Forum Theatre took place on a Tuesday night. Most observers thought the picture dragged in places and that judicious tightening was in order, but all were agreed on the splendid work done by both Tracy and Loretta Young, on Borzage's command of the material, and on the film's cumulative effect on an audience.

"Tracy's matter-of-fact sincerity and defensive bluster as Bill kept the character at the right pitch every moment," Billy Wilkerson said in the *Reporter*. "Avoiding any of the ordinary theatrical tricks, he made the character so real that one forgot he was acting. No study of a man at war with himself inside, asking no help from anyone, could carry more conviction than Spencer Tracy gives it here."

When *Trouble Shooter* finished in mid-November, someone—maybe

Loretta—got the idea they should go up to San Francisco for a couple of weeks. They were both between pictures; Loretta's mother would meet them there, and her friend Josephine Wayne would accompany them. (Josie's husband, actor John Wayne, was working and said he would come up on weekends.) Tracy suggested driving to Santa Barbara the first night and got a limousine big enough for the three of them, a driver, and Spence's stand-in at the time, a man named Clarence, whose height and general build approximated Tracy's own and whose job it was to stand patiently on the stage while the camera was positioned and the lighting was set.

Young's attitude toward the relationship, no matter how much she thought she was in love, was that it was a completely impossible thing, dangerous and forbidden, and although she indulged herself as might a frisky teenager, she stopped short of consummation, convinced as she was that any form of birth control was tantamount to murder. She could remember one time when they were to meet the Swerlings in Santa Barbara, and their hosts had conspired to afford them some private time. Spence was perfectly happy with the accommodation, and she managed to stay just barely out of reach until Jo and his wife Flo got in the next day. "Flo," said Fay Wray, "was enchanted with the romance—and happy to be a confidante."

Now Loretta was at it again, planning a two-week vacation in California's most romantic city, chaperoned as if it were a convent field trip. Spence started drinking in Santa Barbara, passing on dinner, and Loretta, who hadn't seen this before, didn't catch on until he was completely and utterly looped. She called Clarence, who was upstairs in his room, and had their bags transferred to the coastal Southern Pacific. She and Josie were gone before Tracy knew what had happened. In San Francisco they checked in at the Mark Hopkins, expecting Spence to show up eventually but not knowing quite when or where. Three days into their stay they were attending an elegant dinner party in the main dining room of the hotel when Tracy slipped into the room, stepping gingerly as he scrutinized every woman at every table, quietly excusing himself and moving on to the next. Loretta could see he was looking for her and hid out in the ladies' room, telling Josie to alert her when he had finally given up. Three days later, he called her at the hotel, sober and contrite. She almost talked herself into imagining that she had dreamed the whole incident.

Back in Los Angeles, Carroll called her late one night and told her that Spence was drinking and refusing to eat. He was sure that she was mad at him, Carroll said, sure he had lost her for good, but if she would come down to the hotel and personally ask him to, Spence said that he would stop.

Loretta was skeptical, unwilling to be seen in the lobby of the Beverly Wilshire at one in the morning asking for Mr. Tracy's room, but Carroll thought it might somehow work. He sent a limo for her and met her at the hotel's basement elevator. Upstairs, she found Spence sitting on the floor, propped in a corner, his pajamas askew and barely coherent. He told her he was sure he wouldn't be this way if only they were able to get married. And as she put her arms around him, he leaned into her and began to cry.

Back at Fox, Tracy went into a musical comedy called *Bottoms Up* and was soon being linked in the gossip columns with the film's leading lady, a petite British import named Pat Paterson. "If the off-set scenes of Pat Paterson, English beauty brought here by Winfield Sheehan, and Spencer Tracy were put into one picture you might see the beginning of a romance," Louella Parsons wrote. "These two are in the same picture, but that doesn't necessitate lunching together, talking together, and seeing each other at every possible moment. Maybe Spence is just trying to make Loretta Young jealous, or maybe it's a lovers' quarrel, but all the Fox studio is agog over his attentions to Pat Paterson, who is as blond as Loretta and the same type." At twenty-three, Paterson was three years older than Loretta, getting used to a new country and clearly on the make. After an initial flurry of attention from Tracy, she met actor Charles Boyer at a studio gathering and was Mrs. Boyer within the space of a few weeks.

Spence and Loretta were back out in public again by the first of the year, going to films together and attending industry functions. On New Year's Eve they went to a movie—"a lousy movie," Tracy emphasized—and stopped at a hamburger stand on the way home. For Loretta's twenty-first birthday they celebrated in grand style with Duke and Josie Wayne. The following weekend, they accompanied the Waynes to Palm Springs. A few years earlier, when Duke was under contract to Fox, there was talk of teaming the two of them. "It's a good thing you're good looking," Spence would say, "because you can't act your way out of a paper bag." The affable Wayne would just laugh and say, "That's right, Fats. I'll catch on, then you watch out!"

The one time Loretta met Mother Tracy, Carrie was as cold as a Milwaukee winter, and it dawned on her that she was regarded by Spence's mother as her son's mistress. Shortly thereafter, Tracy agreed to an interview with journalist Gladys Hall for a piece in *Movie Mirror* magazine "if it would protect Loretta—I want to protect Loretta in this." The assumption around town, of course, was that Loretta Young was responsible for the breakup of the Tracy marriage, when, as Spence always insisted, it in no way concerned her.

How could it? I mean, how could it because—as a matter of recorded and verifiable fact—and the register of the Chateau Elysée plus the starting date of our picture, *Man's Castle,* will bear me out—I was registered at the Elysée here in Hollywood three weeks before I ever set foot on the first set of *Man's Castle.* If anyone is sufficiently interested or sufficiently skeptical to want to check me on this, the data is available. And before I started to work on that picture, I had never done more than lay eyes on Loretta Young a couple of times, here and there around town. I had never exchanged four words with her. I don't suppose that I had ever so much as passed a remark about her.

When Hall asked if he wanted to marry Loretta Young, Tracy looked at her and asked, "What man wouldn't?" The question of a divorce, he said, was completely in Louise's hands. "At the moment, Mrs. Tracy is living at home with the children. I am living at the Town House with my mother. I have dinner at the house with the children every Sunday. I go out there to see them as often as I can. This morning, for instance, I had a late call at the studio. I drove out there to see the kids. Johnny hasn't been told anything about it. Johnny believes that I am working and away, as I've had to be before, on location and so on. When the time comes and everything is settled one way or another, I'll tell him the truth. He is entitled to that."

Then there was, he said, the religious aspect, which would have to be "very seriously" considered.

I am a Catholic, you see. Loretta is a Catholic. And so, on account of all these complications it would honestly be rather ridiculous and wholly untrue for me to attempt to make a definite statement. Our personal emotions have nothing to do with what we *can* do. The way I feel about Loretta must be pretty obvious. We haven't tried to hide or beat around the bush or camouflage anything. We have nothing to be ashamed of. I am free to go with whom I please, at any time I please. If I were just playing around, if this were just another "Hollywood romance," if I were a man, recently separated from his wife and from the bonds of marriage and wanting to have a good time for myself, I would be going out with three or four different girls. There is only the one.

This is profoundly sincere with me. It is serious. It is important. It stands apart from any other experience in my not-very-experienced life. I mean, even before I was married, I was working hard, trying to get a foothold on the footlights, struggling, worrying, no time for play. Loretta is young. That attracts me, of course. I can kid her a lot. I do. We have good times together, by ourselves, in our own way . . . Now and again we go to the Grove or the Beverly Wilshire and dance, but for the most part we take long walks and have long arguments and a lot of fun. Loretta is fun to talk to. I, who have always especially liked and enjoyed the talk and companionship of men, get a kick out of just being with her. We always go to church together on Sunday mornings. I drive out to her place and pick her up and we go. Mrs. Tracy is not a Catholic, and so, of course, this is something I never had before.

This is, honestly, our past and our present—the future is not entirely in our hands. There is nothing we can do about it but wait—and hope.

Bottoms Up was the brainchild of the prolific Tin Pan Alley songwriter and Broadway producer B. G. "Buddy" DeSylva, who had collaborated with director David Butler on three other decidedly oddball musicals for Fox. In an industry notoriously reluctant to laugh at itself, *Bottoms Up* was an anomaly, a satire which not only took aim at Hollywood but specifically at the company producing it. The story concerned a Russian-born studio head, Louie Wolf, who is beholden to an East Coast banker, a Mr. Baldwin. The matinee-handsome movie star, who may well have been inspired by Tracy's own circumstances, is a self-loathing drunkard who considers his latest picture "the most stupendous piece of junk I've ever seen." Tracy's character, a genial cigar-flourishing con man named Smoothie, is down to his last dime and determined, with nothing more than a gardenia in his lapel, to conquer the town: "Now look, Mr. Baldwin, you make 52 pictures a year, don't you, but only twelve of them are hits. Now my idea is only to produce the twelve good ones."

While *Bottoms Up* was being filmed at Fox Hills, Louise was struggling to get Johnny accepted as a morning student at the Hollywood Progressive School. Spence was in touch with her daily and appeared for an admissions conference one morning when he could get away from the set. "The superintendent at first protested that it would be too cruel to enter Johnny in a school where the children were completely normal," he recalled. "She argued he would not be able to keep up with them, and that he would be unhappy as they passed him in grades. This almost broke [Louise's] heart. She said, 'Of course, you understand, we're not begging you to take him. It is really a privilege.' The superintendent, no doubt feeling sorry for her and perhaps a little bit ashamed, suggested that she bring Johnny to school the following morning and she would see how he got along."

Johnny entered the third grade as a "guest," limited to one hour in a single classroom. "The class happened to be doing arithmetic," Louise said. "This was John's meat. He was happy, too, at being with children again and instantly became a part of things. His hand went up with the others as the teacher put a problem in addition on the board. I held my breath, as I felt uncertain John would be given his chance. He was." As John would later write, "I didn't know that being deaf was a great handicap. I just got along beautifully with those boys and girls without realizing it."

It was also during the production of *Bottoms Up* that an extraordinary editorial ran in the pages of the *Hollywood Reporter*. Every Monday, Wilkerson printed a front-page column called "Tradeviews" in which he held forth on some timely aspect of the motion picture business. One week, he might rail over labor practices, the next the bane of nepotism and how it made for worse and costlier pictures. *The Power and the Glory*, the highpoint of Tracy's career, had been followed into release by the thoroughly undistinguished *Mad Game*. Then *Man's Castle* came a week later and was not the hit it should have been, domestic rentals just about covering its cost. When Fox announced that *Bottoms Up* would be followed by something called *The Gold Rush of 1933*, the primary excuse for which would be Tracy's reteaming with Claire Trevor, Wilkerson could see that Tracy's work in *Power and the Glory* and *Man's Castle* hadn't counted for much.

> We'll place the name of Spencer Tracy at the top of any list crediting really fine performances, rating artistic ability, or an instance of one of the greatest prospective draws in this business if given good material. We have never seen Tracy giving anything resembling a bad performance, and we have seen him in some pictures that were so bad that standout ability was almost impossible. But not for Tracy; that boy makes even impossible characters interesting.
>
> Tracy never acts; he rather underplays his parts; you never have a feeling that he is trying to perform and that's what makes him so good. And it's a damned shame that he has to be tied to a studio whose production intelligence does not approach his fine talents. This business is missing one of the best money draws it ever had because of this. Give Tracy two or three GOOD pictures, one after the other, and there is not a male star (or female) who would top him in selling tickets, for he has everything that any audience wants in a screen performer.

Wilkerson's column was required reading throughout the industry, and a light obviously went on somewhere. Two days after its appearance, an item in the paper reported that M-G-M had placed a new talking version of George Kelly's hit comedy *The Show-Off* back on its production schedule. "The picture was temporarily put on the shelf a few weeks ago because the studio was unable to secure a suitable lead at that time. M-G-M now has a lead in mind, but is keeping it quiet for the time being." The next day, January 26, 1934, Metro-Goldwyn-Mayer concluded an agreement to borrow Spencer Tracy for the lead.

Originally, *The Show-Off* had been acquired from Paramount for actor Lee Tracy, whose first work on Broadway was in the original 1924 production. Tracy's five-year contract with the studio was abruptly terminated in the aftermath of an international incident the actor allegedly precipitated during the filming of *Viva Villa* in Mexico.* The project languished for nearly two months with no obvious replacement for the title role until Wilkerson's editorial appeared. Suddenly, Metro made a bid for the services of Spencer Tracy and didn't flinch when Fox specified the breathtaking fee of $5,200 a week—close to double what 20th Century had paid just four months earlier.

Writer-producer Lucien Hubbard was in charge of *The Show-Off* but word was that Irving Thalberg was the real force behind the scenes, and Tracy hoped something larger was at hand than a deal for a single picture. He had never before worked at M-G-M, had never even been on the lot, but to be an M-G-M player was to be among the finest array of acting talent anywhere in the world. The Barrymores were under contract to M-G-M, as were Helen Hayes, Marie Dressler, Robert Montgomery, Joan Crawford, Wallace Beery, Clark Gable, Jean Harlow, and Greta Garbo. Metro pictures had a sheen and a respectability second to none, and the brand definitely meant something at the box office. No studio was as profitable nor had as many resources at its disposal.

The wiry Hubbard, who knew Tracy from the Uplifters Club, had been William Wellman's producer on *Wings* and would later play himself, a midlife war correspondent, in Wellman's *Story of G.I. Joe.* He knew how to make B-pictures quickly, but with the spit and polish of someone who took pride in his work and had an excellent sense of story and casting. His treatment of *The Show-Off* was a model of classy packaging. Tracy's leading lady would be M-G-M contract player Madge Evans, the same actress who had appeared opposite him in Sam Harris' ill-fated production of *Dread.* Grant Mitchell would be in the picture, as would Henry Wadsworth, Lois Wilson, Clara Blandick, and Alan Edwards, solid players all. The script was by Herman J. Mankiewicz, who had adapted a number of plays to film, most recently Rose Franken's *Another Language* and *Dinner at Eight.* James Wong Howe, who shot *The Power and the Glory,* would be in charge of the camerawork, and the director would be Charles F. "Chuck" Riesner, a specialist in

* Lee Tracy, whose drinking was the stuff of legend in Hollywood, was accused of insulting a member of the Mexican Cadet Corps during a Revolution Day parade. Accounts differ as to exactly what he was supposed to have done, but the most common version of the story has him urinating off a hotel balcony. Later it was surmised that the growing strength of organized labor in Mexico had much to do with the resulting uproar over the incident.

comedy who had been eight years with Chaplin and codirected Buster Keaton's spectacular *Steamboat Bill Jr.* Riesner's background—he had been a prizefighter, vaudevillian, song writer, and actor—somehow made him ideal for telling the story of J. Aubrey Piper, the well-meaning rattlebrain of Kelly's classic play.

Tracy began work on January 29, 1934, having taken a corner suite at the Beverly Wilshire. Mastering the carnation-wearing Piper, his boasts and vulnerabilities, was as intense a job of preparation as he had ever undertaken for a film. Blessed with exceptional material and fueled by countless cups of black coffee, he managed one of the most deeply layered performances he had ever given, at once dim and overbearing and yet desperate to the point of near-tragedy. Leavening the character still further was Clara Blandick's acid performance as Ma Fisher, Amy's skeptical mother, who can't stand her daughter's windbag of a boyfriend and makes no attempt to hide it. Aubrey is a big talker who holds down a clerical position with the Mid-Atlantic; all his clothes are castoffs, all his cars are demos. He invades the Fisher family like a backslapping pestilence. Amy's parents are suddenly "Mumsie" and "Popsie-Wopsy." The house rings with forced laughter.

"How do you think your mother's gonna take it?" Aubrey asks Amy, suddenly quiet and pensive when they decide to tie the knot.

"Well, I don't know. You see—"

"Well, I know she's not just as fond of me as she might be, is she?"

"Oh," says Amy, "but it's not that she doesn't approve of you, Aubrey. But . . ."

"It's because I'm not serious enough," he says, now a chastened little boy, all knowing and fidgety. "I joke too much to suit a lot of people. Sometimes I just try to kid 'em, you know, and they think I mean it. You think I'm on the level, don't you Amy?"

They marry, Ma Fisher sourly resigned to the situation as they take their own apartment. Aubrey can't handle money, can't live on thirty dollars a week. He spends everything he makes, fills the apartment with tables and lamps and a fancy record changer he can't afford. ("Plays twelve records without stoppin'," he boasts.) When his salary is attached by creditors, Amy has had enough. Tearfully, she announces they'll have to give up their apartment and move back home with her parents. He resists, grandly at first, then remorsefully, swearing he'll turn over a new leaf. "I'm gonna get down to work," he vows, building up a head of steam. "No more goin' to the office late. Quarter of eight every morning from now on . . . Yeah, and I'm gonna quit watchin' the clock to find out what time I can leave. I'm gonna make 'em promote me. And I'm gonna stop talkin' big until I *am* big! Yessir, you're . . . you're gonna be proud of me, Amy."

Aubrey's newfound zeal for responsibility trips him up in a heartbeat.

He butts into real estate negotiations at the Road and ends up costing them a small fortune. After he's been fired, he's walking a sandwich sign around town when he learns his brother-in-law is ready to accept an outright payment of $5,000 for an invention. ("Why Joe, you must be crazy. Five-thousand for an invention that must be worth millions? Why, they can't do that to you!") He takes it upon himself to go see the lawyer involved and demands $100,000 against 50 percent of the net profits. Shown the door, he's convinced he's queered the deal and that Joe is going to kill him for it.

Aubrey goes home to Amy, comes clean, tells her everything. He's a whipped dog by the time Joe comes in, happy as a lark. After thinking about it, the lawyers had called him with their best offer: $50,000 and 20 percent of the profits. As Joe is excitedly relating it all, Aubrey is peering over Amy's shoulder, timidly at first, and the transformation from Jekyll to Hyde was never more adroitly handled. Wordlessly, the chastened Aubrey, eyes downcast, becomes the Aubrey of old, at once smug and self-satisfied, his tongue rolling extravagantly in his mouth. It's a magnificent shot, both horrifying and hilarious, screen acting at its finest. As Joe shows him the check, Aubrey regards it dismissively. "Joesy," he says, "I think you coulda done better."

Tracy lay low during the filming of *The Show-Off,* keeping his name out of the columns. The film finished on Friday, February 16. Two days later he and Loretta turned heads when they showed up for Mass together at Good Shepherd in Beverly Hills. That evening he was nominated by the membership of the Screen Actors Guild to serve on one of two NRA code administration committees, more than a thousand votes being cast at the Hollywood Women's Club to fill a total of fourteen slots.

"I am still married to Louise," he told Walter Ramsey, who was writing his life story for *Modern Screen.* "There has been no divorce action started. At the present time, there is only one thing of paramount importance, my children, and a bad second best, my screen work. No matter how Louise and I solve our problem, we have mutually agreed that neither of us shall be sidetracked from the children. At the moment, they are staying with my mother. Louise is away on a much-needed rest. Naturally, their custody will remain with their mother, where it should be. But the fact that we have parted with the greatest friendliness means that their home will always be open to me, and, I hope, their hearts." He characterized talk of an engagement between himself and Loretta Young as being in "very poor taste." He paused, then slowly added: "This is really a strange time in my life to be giving my life story. At present, things are muddled and uncertain."

His name once again in the papers, Tracy's fan mail surged, as it usually did when he was considered news. One letter, in pencil, looked not unlike countless others written him and scores of other contract players, the spelling poor, the syntax shaky. It arrived at the house on Holmby, however, and for that reason alone it received special attention. Inspired, perhaps, by the subject matter of his picture *The Mad Game*, it bore a Los Angeles postmark and read as follows:

                                                    Feb. 20, 1934

Spencer Tracy
        this is to let you know you and your friend are
covered. By Rattlesnake. Pete Are Silverton I am give
you a brake We. could have pick you up and carried
you a way But I voted hand of[f] you until you were
warned are quite a contact you will save your Self lots.
of troble. and Serious worry if you obay orders to the
letter you need not worry if not look out we sure get
you are your mother are your baby are Miss Young
going a way wont help you a dam. [But] we get you
[j]ust the same See if you know this car #Lic .36876
[Tracy's LaSalle] and this one #.84838 [his mother's
Cadillac] who cars are these do not run to the law are
try to trick us we have fail Bremar* was warned 14 days
and was only ask $30,000 he refuse it you know the
rest he made his own Bargin when we got him you do
the same if you dont obay orders we want 8,000 of you
and Miss Young this is your. this is your contact 4,000
in 1,000 and the other 4,000 in $50 and 20, and 10.
this must be put in a box mark Mr. Silverton and given
to your negro Buttler he is to deliver to Western Ave.
and Wilshiar Box must be Wrap well he must not.
know. anything. only to deliver. and he must not. be.
follow. my spy on the look. out. he is to start with this
box March 10th at 6.30 PM from your house 712
Holmby Ave
                                    Rattlesnake Pete are Silverton

Don't let us hafter get you don't mark this money if you
do you will regret it.

Louise had gone to New York thinking she might return to the stage but found the East Coast in the midst of its heaviest storm since the famous

---

* Minnesota banker Edward G. Bremer had been kidnapped by the Barker-Karpis gang the previous month. His ransom of $200,000 was one of the largest ever paid.

blizzard of 1888, the city paralyzed under nine inches of snow. She bought a new mink coat, her first in a number of years, and spent her days walking, snow whirling around her, lost in thought, the sounds of scraping shovels, stomping feet, and squeaking wheels everywhere. Unable to reach her, Spence bundled up the children and took them off to the Town House, the fashionable hotel overlooking Westlake Park where Mother Tracy was now residing. Susie was too young to sense that anything was wrong, but Johnny, nearing his tenth birthday, was upset when told he could never be alone anywhere.

"I felt ashamed at the idea," Johnny said, "because I thought I was still being treated as if I were a baby. Eventually, after Father probably noticed my annoyance at being considered 'a baby,' he told me I was not that and explained all about it. He said that I would be taken away by 'a bad man' and would never come back if I went out alone and was found by the man. He tried to make it simple for me to understand. I understood it very well and was shocked and frightened."

Once the children were safe and Loretta—who was shooting *Bulldog Drummond Strikes Back*—had been advised, Tracy called an acquaintance at the Los Angeles Police Department, Detective Lieutenant Frank "Lefty" James, whose unit was known for its investigations of local mob figures. Once the case was established as a "confidential police matter," a detective was posted alongside him and would remain his constant companion until the crisis had passed.

Spence was finally able to reach Louise in Miami Beach, where she had fled after the novelty of the snow had worn off. Though he told her he did not seriously anticipate any trouble, he thought she would want to come home anyway, and she returned to Los Angeles the following morning. All the employees at the Town House were on guard, and despite her strong feelings that the whole business was absurd, Louise found herself grasping Johnny's hand just a little more tightly and stepping just a little more quickly as they negotiated the hotel corridors. Outside of school, where he was guarded by two detectives, the outdoors John saw the most were the garden at the back entrance of the hotel, where Louise was thankful for the company of the gardener and the big doorman was just a few yards away.

While behaving as though there was nothing out of the ordinary, Tracy started one of the oddest pictures he would ever make, a gangster story, fittingly, with the singular title *"Now I'll Tell" by Mrs. Arnold Rothstein*. Rothstein, of course, was the famous bootlegger and gambling czar who so prominently figured in the rigging of the 1919 World Series, the infamous "Black Sox" scandal in which six players for the Chicago White Sox conspired to throw five games to Cincinnati in exchange for a collective payoff of $100,000. Known variously as the Fixer, the Big Bankroll, and Mr. Big,

Rothstein was most closely associated with horse racing, the 1921 Travers Stakes conspiracy being the best known of his alleged capers.

Little about Rothstein's criminal activities could ever be proven, and even the events surrounding his death were in dispute. In 1909 Rothstein married a New York showgirl named Carolyn Green, who, though estranged, was still his wife at the time of his killing in 1928. She claimed to know the inside dope on her husband's various enterprises, including the truth behind his murder. As Mrs. Carolyn Rothstein Behar, she granted Fox Film a $2,500 option on the rights to a memoir she proposed to write on her life with the man Damon Runyon dubbed "The Brain."

Rothstein was a contemporary of Winnie Sheehan's in criminal and political circles, and it was Sheehan's idea not only to make a film about him but to coordinate its release with the publication of the book on which it was supposedly based. The deal with Behar was signed in July 1933, not long before Sheehan was to leave for Europe. It gave her time to write the book on her own but reserved the studio's right to impose a ghostwriter in the event she was unable to finish. The plan was to have the story serialized in a first-class magazine or published in book form no later than March 1, 1934.

When Sheehan left the first week in August, he was accompanied by playwright and scenarist Edwin Burke, who was to spend his time in Paris researching a film on the life of chemist Louis Pasteur. By the time of their return in October, Burke had not only drawn the assignment from Sheehan to write the screenplay based on Behar's memoir, but to direct the film as well. A former actor, alumnus of the American Academy and a fellow Lamb, Burke pressed for the unlikely casting of Spencer Tracy to play America's best-known Jewish gangster.

In New York, Burke stopped off to work with Behar. Looking to punch up the story and fill in a number of blanks, he interviewed some of Rothstein's former associates, and the collaboration resulted in an original story for the screen called "Now I'll Tell." Satisfied the film project was on its way, Sheehan hired novelist Donald Henderson Clarke to bring the book into being. In 1929 Clarke had published his own book on the subject, *In the Reign of Rothstein;* two days after he came aboard, Behar signed a contract with Vanguard Press, Clarke's longtime publisher. Burke now found himself in the position of working ahead of Behar and Clarke, adding in material that would more than likely differ from events described in the book. Behar was surprisingly scrupulous about what she wrote, and although she wouldn't object to Burke's fabrications, neither would she agree to say they were true.

On February 8, 1934, Fox purchased worldwide motion picture rights to the book for $25,000. By that point, Burke had abandoned any pretense of his picture being a literal representation of the book, and when the shooting script was finalized on February 23, the name of Tracy's character, the film's title notwithstanding, had become "Murray Golden." Tracy was tense and withdrawn during the first days of filming, his police guard ever-present, and he seemed to rely on Burke to an unusual degree in character-izing Rothstein.

The film had been in production scarcely a week when a second extor-tion letter arrived: "Rattlesnake has not give orders to take you yet[.] I give you nice chance then I strike if <u>you</u> disobey[.] I am plenty good to you I see mother and baby I see you and your queen . . . I want to see the money with note say that it ok from you and your queen you have my orders."

From March 6 to March 11, two detective lieutenants were stationed at the house on Holmby. On the evening of March 10, a dummy package was prepared as specified in the first letter, and Tracy's black chauffeur, Walter, drove to the intersection of Western Avenue and Wilshire Boulevard with Detective Lieutenant Joseph Filkas concealed in the back seat. Walter was told to expect a man to leap onto the running board of the moving car. The setup went flawlessly, but nobody attempted to board the car, drive along-side it, or otherwise collect the money.

There was no further communication from "Rattlesnake Pete" either, and Tracy could think of no one who might have written the letters, other than possibly Walter's predecessor, whose name he mentioned only because he said that he had been forced to discharge the man. The only handwriting samples he could find—endorsements on the backs of canceled checks—were inconclusive, but police interviewed the man anyway. He denied he had been sacked, told them instead he had quit when Carrie Tracy moved out to Riviera, which was too far for him to go by streetcar. "He further stated that Mrs. Tracy, Sr., was a very nervous woman, highly-strung and hard to please." The case wasn't officially closed, but the police decided either the threat was a hoax or the crooks had gotten cold feet. Newspapers published details of the case on March 24, prompting the local office of the FBI to contact and interview Tracy for their own files.

With the tension surrounding the drop on March 10, the national release of *The Show-Off* passed almost without notice. On his best behavior, Tracy had finished the picture in just seventeen days—something of a record—and it had gone to preview six days after that, playing to a large, appreciative audience at the Fox Uptown Theatre. The *Reporter*, with obvi-ous pride in having influenced the matter, trumpeted Tracy's appeal in its notice the following day: "Spencer Tracy does the impossible in *The Show-Off*. He carries the entire thing on his own shoulders—and the part is ter-rific. *The Show-Off* is, of course, a one-part story, with everyone more or less taking back seats and leaving most of the work to the main character.

And what Tracy does with it! In spite of the fact that the play as a whole is too widely familiar to hold any new excitement for the theatregoer, and that his role is a series of dramatic and emotional peaks that would tax the strength of any actor, Tracy turns in a performance that is all wool and a yard wide."

When the picture opened at New York's Capitol Theatre the following week, business went big, with Jimmy Durante, Polly Moran, and Lou Holtz accompanying it onstage. The entire bill was held a second week, a respectable showing for the 5,400-seat house. The New York critics proved a tougher audience than the public. The play itself had been sixteen months on Broadway in its original run and had just completed a successful revival with Raymond Walburn in the title role. On film, *The Show-Off* had been done twice already, Sennett stalwart Ford Sterling having originated the role for Paramount in 1926, and Hal Skelly having brought it to the talking screen in 1930.* Reviewers wondered, with some justification, why bother?

The answer for Metro was Spencer Tracy, who was so ideal for the role of Aubrey Piper that familiarity with the storyline was immaterial. Mordaunt Hall in the *Times* took pains to detail the various differences between George Kelly's original and Mankiewicz's adaptation, allowing as how the play, in its newest incarnation, lacked "the nimble wit and subtle shadings" of the original. "Mr. Tracy gives a capital performance," he concluded, "and if the picture does not come up to expectations, it is not his fault, for it would be difficult to select another player who can do as well by the part."

Ed Sullivan, the popular columnist for the *New York Daily News,* thought it Tracy's best work yet and suggested he was "in the vanguard of the youngsters upon whom the movies must rely to replace the aging veterans." In England, John Betjeman ranked Tracy in the same class as Eddie Cantor and Chaplin, even as his style of acting was so vastly different: "His appeal is entirely based on dialogue and the wrinkled expression of his enormous Irish face." At the bargain price of $162,000, *The Show-Off* showed a profit of $78,000 on worldwide rentals of $397,000. If the film amounted to nothing more than a feature-length audition for Spencer Tracy, it was spectacularly successful.

Out from under the cloud of the kidnapping threat, Loretta and Spence went dining and dancing with Josie and Duke Wayne in the Beverly Wilshire's exclusive Gold Room, by now a favorite haunt. Loretta was turned out in a white sailor frock—blue collar, white stars, red anchors—and Spence, equally festive, was blasted well before dinner. It fell to Duke to get him past the other diners—Winnie Sheehan, George Burns and Gracie

* In addition, Franklin Pangborn played the title character in *Poor Aubrey* (1930), a Vitaphone short derived from the original one act by George Kelly.

Tracy's first film for M-G-M, 1934.
(AUTHOR'S COLLECTION)

Allen, the scenarist and playwright Edgar Allan Woolf—and up to his suite
without creating too much of a fuss. "Once deposited in the room,"
recalled actor William Bakewell, "Tracy became so violent in his efforts to
get away that big Duke (no teetotaler himself) had no alternative but to
coldcock him with a short right to the jaw, which left Spence draped on the
bed for a sobering night's sleep."

Three days later the annual Academy Awards banquet took place at the
Biltmore Hotel. Loretta had made plans to attend with Spence and the
Waynes, but when the time came for him to appear, Tracy was nowhere to
be found. She went without him, fighting back tears, and it was several days
before she heard from him. "Spence was a darling when he was sober,"
Young later told her daughter, Judy Lewis. "He was absolutely awful when
he was drinking."

Bottoms Up was released the week of March 26, hailed for its sly send-
up of the movie business—the *Motion Picture Herald* called it "a comedy of
values"—even if its musical numbers were of the kind that almost killed off
the genre in the early days of sound. *Now I'll Tell* finished on April 4, and
Tracy took the opportunity to get out of town, going back to New York for

a couple of weeks and finding no peace there either. He descended on Manhattan asking about the prospects of the Giants, wondering whether one of his polo ponies had gotten over the colic and apologizing for having taken on a few pounds since his last visit to the Big Apple. "Hollywood's too easy a burg to live in," he told a reporter for the *American,* trafficking in irony. "Polo, sunshine, fishing, and all the rest drive a guy crazy with happiness. Broadway's good to look at from the back end of an observation car going [to] Hollywood."

Handing a redcap his bag, Tracy passed through the gate at Grand Central and saw a crowd of onlookers being held behind a rope. "What are all these people here for?" he asked. The answer that came back was that they were all there to catch a glimpse of him. He refused to believe it until the group surged past the police line and followed him to his taxi. "Holy Moses!" he said, landing in the back seat of the cab. "I would never have thought it." At the hotel, a telegram was awaiting him from Edwin Burke, reporting on the Pasadena preview of *Now I'll Tell.* Its concluding line: YOU'RE STILL MY FAVORITE ACTOR. "Gee, that's great of Eddie," Tracy said. "He's a swell guy."

When he got back to Los Angeles, Tracy was seen out on the town with Loretta again, dining and dancing and generally behaving himself. Following Sheehan's carefully orchestrated plan, the book *Now I'll Tell* was published by Vanguard Press on May 3, 1934, and the film of the same title opened in theaters on May 11. The movie garnered generally favorable notices, even as it varied wildly from the book on which it was purportedly based. Rothstein became Golden, the Black Sox scandal became a fixed prizefight, the various showgirls with whom Rothstein consorted were rolled into the Peggy Warren character played by the Harlowesque Alice Faye.

Burke's coaching paid off in a forceful performance that, while not Rothstein himself, hued to the spirit of the man. In her book Mrs. Rothstein recorded his first private words to her after their wedding at Saratoga: "Sweet, I had a bad day today, and I'll need your jewelry for a few days." She could tell when he was losing big because his voice went flat, even as his expression remained unchanged. He did not bother to watch the finish of a race on which he won $800,000, so certain he was of the outcome, and he orchestrated Nicky Arnstein's surrender to the police by riding him to headquarters in a touring car pacing the end of a police parade.

In a city where interest in Rothstein still ran high, *Now I'll Tell* filled the Roxy as no Tracy film had been able to do. The film went on to do well in urban centers, less well in rural and neighborhood houses where gangster stories never fully caught on. Fox's efforts to position it as a biographical picture as well as a crime melodrama went nowhere, and it ended up, like so

Tracy and Loretta Young at the Cocoanut Grove, June 14, 1934. Their very public relationship would end later that same evening. (PATRICIA MAHON COLLECTION)

many other Fox titles on Tracy's résumé, posting a loss by the time it was played out.

As the studio readied the oft-delayed *Marie Galante* for Sheehan's latest enthusiasm, a French import named Ketti Gallian, Tracy made the papers by trouncing a producers' polo team 9 to 3 and accepting a handsome trophy from Carole Lombard at Uplifters Field.

He and Loretta took to going to Confession together on Saturday afternoons, and Loretta was shaken when one of the priests at Good Shepherd refused to give her absolution. She was seeing a married man, she was told, a Roman Catholic who had been married in the church. She knew, she later said, that if she left the church that day without absolution, she might never come back. Desperate, she walked across the aisle to the other box and told that priest the whole story. He eventually said that he would give her absolution only if she would agree to come back every Friday thereafter for counseling. When she got outside, she told Spence what had transpired—he apparently never told her if he was given absolution—and he understood her crisis of faith, just as she seemed to understand his and the role it played in his drinking. "I am sure the pressure and the soul-searching had something to do with it," she said, "but gradually we faced the fact that there was nothing we could do."

On June 8, 1934, Loretta went to her regular Friday night counseling session at Good Shepherd. Then, sometime over the next few days, she sat down and composed a handwritten letter that began with the words "My darling" and ended with the word "Me." She admitted that when she was with him she had no logic, common sense, or resistance, and that after prayer and counseling, she knew the only way they could go on would be in an entirely platonic relationship. It would be enough for her, she said, just to be with him and to hear his voice, and they would be without sin, but she knew that she would need his help. He would have to decide if he could handle it, and, were it impossible, she would understand. She signed off with the words "I love you." It reached him in a plain envelope addressed to "Mr. Spencer Tracy."

On June 14, the couple was photographed together at the Cocoanut Grove, Loretta's unseasonable mink coat casually draped over the back of her chair, a wide-brimmed summer hat framing her pale face, Spence's wedding ring still plainly in view.

That night at the Grove was the last time they were seen out on the town together. Within hours Tracy had disappeared into his suite at the Beverly Wilshire, and when he emerged nearly two weeks later, it was to board an ambulance that would take him to a hospital.

CHAPTER 10

And Does Love Last?

I t was a measure of her despair over the winter of 1933–34 that Louise Tracy was willing to leave the children—year-old Susie and, particularly, John, the focus of her life—in Spence's care and go off to New York with no specific plan in mind and no date set for her return. She was obviously hurting, humiliated, and maybe even a bit angry, but to all who saw her, the few friends she allowed into her life, her mother-in-law, the servants, John's therapists and teachers, she was calm, collected, the very picture of reserve and forbearance. She had seen her own father walk away from her parents' marriage in much the same way that Spence now seemed to be walking away from theirs. He put it on her to divorce him if she saw fit, knowing she was perfectly within her rights to do so, knowing that he himself could never take the step of divorcing her. She had never given him any cause to do so, never would. What they said in public was remarkably candid and true; what they said in private is anyone's guess.

Louise had longed to take up polo, but Spence was against it, seemingly jealous of his time alone on the field and disapproving in general of women in the game. Then it became a discussion of Western saddle—which Louise knew—versus the lighter, hornless English saddle used in the game. It would be like learning to ride all over again and entirely too dangerous. "He said, 'You aren't going to do that,' and I said, 'Well, everybody else here is doing it.' " One afternoon Snowy Baker talked her into trying it, and Spence had a fit. "I can't see any harm in stick-and-balling," she said, employing the term for simply working out on a pony. He thought for a moment and then allowed as how he supposed not. She borrowed one of his hardwood mallets, awkward and unwieldy, and began taking lessons, marching past the grooms at the stables with as little self-consciousness as she could manage.

Louise had ridden White Sox on picnics into Mandeville Canyon, on Saturday morning rides with the children, and on moonlit outings up into the hills and across Will Rogers' ranch. She had watched with growing envy the women who played in the mixed games on the dirt field. "Never have I seen women have as much fun at any sport—at anything—as the women I watched at Riviera," she wrote. "There were times when I thought them nothing more than mad, and others, nothing less than goddesses. Grimy goddesses, I grant you—grimy but glowing. One can't leave a dirt field after six or eight chukkers and still hope to resemble 'what the well-dressed sportswoman will wear.' At last, when I could bear it no longer, I determined, if possible, to sit with them—or play with them—upon Olympus."

She was immediately embraced by the women who played the dirt field, who occasionally mixed it up with the men and sometimes even won. She made her best and most lasting friendships at Riviera—Lieutenant and Mrs. Gilbert Proctor, Audrey Caldwell, Walt and Lillian Disney, a Mrs. Chaffey (a full generation older and still playing), Mr. and Mrs. Carl Beal, Audrey Scott, the screenwriter Mary McCall. After a few lessons, a group of them corralled her in the office: there was a mixed handicap tournament starting, and they needed more women.

"Feeling far more mad than goddess-like," she said, "I finally agreed to play. From the moment of the first throw-in when, as No. 1,* I knew just enough to turn and ride toward our goal and heard the thunderous pounding of racing hoofs behind me, to the last gasping moment and I slid from my horse—*Spencer's* horse—at the end of the game, it was more fun than I ever imagined."

Spence was amused and even grudgingly pleased when he learned of Weeze's debut on the field, and soon she had a pony of her own, a little brown horse named Blossom. And where Spence found exhilaration and exercise and release on the field, now so did Louise, and it meant a lot to her when she showed up the day after the news of the separation hit the papers

---

* The players are numbered according to their relative positions on the field. No. 1 ranges closest to the opposing team's goal and spearheads the attack.

Tracy relished his time on the polo field but thought the game too dangerous for women. (SUSIE TRACY)

and not one of her fellow players mentioned it. "No one asked any questions and no one appeared interested."

She played furiously that fall and in January announced that she and Audrey Caldwell, a former actress, like herself, who had married an actor, would give California the first women's polo association in the United States. Teams from San Mateo, Santa Cruz, Santa Barbara, Fullerton, San

Pedro, and Long Beach were expected to throw in, and Snowy Baker opined that the better female players were equal to the one-goal players on the men's teams.*

Louise began writing a play as well, a caustic comedy in three acts about a philandering husband having a very public affair aboard an ocean liner bound for Honolulu. Titled *That Broader Outlook,* it gave her a chance, via the character of Jane Stafford, to explain herself, to show the world what she was up against. It also contained a wry portrait of Mother Tracy, appalled by her son's behavior but sure Jane's mishandling of the situation was part of the problem. When the ship's doctor suggests her son is a great deal like his father, always a good fellow, open and aboveboard, Abigail Stafford replies, "In most ways he is. He'd be more so if . . . if he had been managed differently. There's no use talking, women aren't the wives they used to be."

Assertive and opinionated, Mother Stafford takes Jane to task for sitting "like a bump on a log" while Mrs. Darling beguiles her husband "into all kinds of foolishness without raising your hand to stop it." She warns Jane, "He'll fall in love with her if you're not careful."

JANE

Oh, no, I think not.

ABIGAIL

Well that's all you know about it. He <u>kisses</u> her.

JANE

No doubt. It requires no beguiling for Jack to
kiss pretty women. I don't suppose there is
room on this steamer, steerage and lifeboats
included, to hold all the women Jack has kissed
in the last ten years, and his yearly average is
decidedly on the increase.

Jane is patient because she knows she shares the blame, but not quite in the way her mother-in-law thinks. "I haven't a doubt," she says, "that I've failed in many ways to be a good wife. That is only another reason I do not feel qualified to dictate Jack's code of behavior."

---

* For purposes of handicapping, polo players were rated by "goals." A better player might be a six-goal man, a lesser player a two-goal man. Tommy Hitchcock, one of the best-known players of the 1920s and '30s, was rated ten goals, the highest possible. Will Rogers, known more for his horsemanship than for the shots he made, was a three-goal player. Tracy was a no-goal player; the lowest possible rating was a minus two.

JANE

In the first place, I'm not losing Jack's love, and
I would lose it if I nagged and made scenes.
Jack hates unpleasantness, he simply runs from
it. If I made our relations quarrelsome or
unpleasant, he would begin at once to deceive
me, and I prefer to have his confidence, even
when it hurts, than to be contentedly deceived.

ABIGAIL

Confidence? I guess confidence isn't what it
used to be, any more than love is. Do you
mean to tell me that Jack has confided to you
all the times he has kissed this Darling woman?

JANE

Not in detail, I'll admit. He didn't come down
last night and say, "Well, I kissed Mrs. Darling
thirty-seven times." But he indicated that her
romantic intensity was well sustained. He said,
as I remember, that she was a handful. His
endurance is never alarming. He will be
relieved when she goes on and we stop in
Honolulu. You see, in Jack's code of behavior,
flirting is a pastime and has no bearing on our
real loyalty as man and wife.

To his mother, Jack explains his tomcat ways in terms of compatibility,
much as Louise had put it to Dick Mook.

JACK

Jane and I understand each other all right.
You don't realize people look at things
differently than they used to. Jane's no end
highbrow and prosy. Now don't misunderstand
what I mean—I wouldn't have any other wife
in the world, and she's a wonderful mother;
you know that. But we have each got to
interest ourselves in our own way. We're an
institution, not a jail.

Louise got just twelve single-spaced pages into *That Broader Outlook* before giving up on it, unsure of where she was going and knowing it cut too close to the bone to ever be produced. She put it away, along with her poems and her clippings, but she never destroyed it.

Marie Galante was set to start on Wednesday, June 27, 1934, but calls to Tracy's fourth-floor suite at the Beverly Wilshire went unreturned, and he failed to show for costume fittings and a conference with director Henry King. On the night of the twenty-sixth—Johnny's tenth birthday—Fox legal counsel George Wasson went to the hotel with a letter over the signature of studio manager Jack Gain directing Tracy to report to King at ten o'clock the next morning to begin work on the picture. At suite 412, Wasson was admitted by Wingate Smith and an older man whom Wasson did not identify. Smith was Jack Ford's brother-in-law and longtime assistant, a well-known and well-liked figure around the Fox lot.

"Mr. Tracy at the time was in bed, asleep, and apparently in no condition to be disturbed," Wasson recounted in a memo for record. "Mr. Smith informed me that Mr. Tracy has been suffering from an excess consumption of alcohol, and from a lack of proper food and sleep; Mr. Smith also informed me that he had been in constant attendance upon Mr. Tracy for a period of approximately two weeks and that, although Mr. Tracy was not in a condition of continued unconsciousness, Mr. Tracy was, even in his waking, conscious moments, unable to control his physical and mental coordination."

At the time of Wasson's arrival, Smith had already summoned a doctor, who planned to give Tracy a hypodermic so that he could be removed to the hospital and given the constant care and attention required to "restore him to his normal faculties." Wasson waited until the doctor arrived, approximately twenty minutes, then attempted to speak with the patient.

> When Mr. Tracy awoke, he was apparently conscious, but in a semi-dazed and incoherent condition, being able to speak only a part of a sentence without his mind wandering to some other subject or failing to operate entirely. Mr. Tracy seemed to be laboring under some great mental stress and I endeavored to find the cause but was unsuccessful. I advised Mr. Tracy that it was our desire to have him report to our studio the following day and he informed me that he would not do so. I then told Mr. Tracy that I came to present him with a notice to report and proceeded to read the attached notice to Mr. Tracy.
>
> At the time of this conversation with Mr. Tracy, he had requested the other persons present to leave the room so that he

could talk to me alone. He finally started to tell me what he desired to say and after several unsuccessful attempts he discarded the idea in the middle of a sentence and rolled over and proceeded to go back to sleep, thus ending the conversation.

The doctor tried to get him to take the hypodermic. When he refused, the ambulance attendant was summoned, and it was he who managed to get the patient to his feet and down the elevator to the ambulance, which was waiting in the garage. The doctor assured Wasson that Tracy was in no condition to work and would be unable to work for several days. The next morning, Tracy was removed from the studio payroll.

Marie Galante had the reputation of being a jinxed picture. It had been in the works, off and on, for two years, the book on which it was based being an international best seller. The tale of a shanghaied prostitute making her way across Central America, it seemed to Winnie Sheehan the ideal vehicle for Clara Bow (though no one could reasonably expect her to affect a French accent). They were ready to go with a script by Dudley Nichols, Tracy up front as Crawbett and William K. Howard directing, when Bow, suffering increasingly from the chronic depression that would soon end her career, backed out. The picture was shelved until Sheehan saw actor Miles Malleson's adaptation of the German war drama *The Ace* in London and was taken with the performance of French chanteuse Ketti Gallian. Just twenty, Gallian played her entire role in French and required a translator to converse with the cigar-puffing studio boss. When she arrived in Hollywood on Christmas Eve, 1933, she knew barely half a dozen words of English and had virtually no experience in front of a camera.

Playing opposite Clara Bow, still a big box office name, was a vastly different proposition from propping up a newcomer, and Tracy came to regard *Marie Galante* as a throwback to the days of *Society Girl* and *Painted Woman,* when the purpose of the picture was to showcase the girl and he was kept offscreen until the second or third reel. Sheehan had Sonya Levien and Samuel Hoffenstein do a polish on the Nichols screenplay, revising Marie's lines so that a non-English speaker could handle them, and then Henry King had suggestions when he came aboard as director. Reginald Berkeley, known for his work on *Cavalcade,* did his own version of the script, juggling concerns from the German, Japanese, and Panamanian governments over how their nationals were to be portrayed. Subsequently, Berkeley's work was enhanced and emended by John Zinn, Jack Yellen, and Seton I. Miller. All told, twelve writers had a hand in rendering *Marie Galante* completely unrecognizable by the time it reached the screen.

When Tracy was carted off to the hospital the day before filming was to commence, it was agreed he would be unable to render services until the second week in July and his contract was extended accordingly. The picture was held, even though Henry King had an entire reel's worth of action to shoot with Ketti Gallian before Tracy would be needed. Then, after a week, with Tracy still hospitalized, Sheehan announced that he was replacing him with Edmund Lowe.

Loretta Young, meanwhile, was in the hospital herself, recovering from elective surgery of an unspecified nature and getting the word out, as best she could, that she and Spence were kaput. "Speaking of TRACY," Lloyd Pantages wrote in his column of July 5, "his romance with LORETTA YOUNG is COMPLETELY at the 'Commander Byrd at the Pole' stage— you know, FRIGID." Earlier, Spence had shown up at Loretta's hospital, flowers in hand, wobbling from room to room, and she had locked herself in the bathroom while Josie Wayne got rid of him.

The final scene in the relationship came a few weeks later, during a charity match at the Uplifters Club. Loretta attended with a party of friends, and Eddie Cantor, acting as master of ceremonies, introduced her to the crowd. Tracy was astride his horse in midfield. "At the mention of Loretta's name," said Jack Grant, who was present that day, "Spencer involuntarily rose in his saddle as though shot. He gazed in her direction for a long moment before he was aware that as many eyes were observing him as were looking at Loretta." He trotted his pony off to the sidelines and made himself as inconspicuous as possible. That afternoon, it was reported, he played with particular ferocity.

Marie Galante finally got under way on July 13 with Tracy back heading the cast. Berkeley had just submitted his final version of the script, a loose compendium of everything that had come before, but Henry King still wanted a junior writer on the set, uncertain as to what Ketti Gallian could actually handle in the way of dialogue. "[S]he was not an experienced actor," King explained. "She didn't know how to go from one thing to another and how to create emotions." A lengthy test King shot of her was excellent, and whatever Sheehan thought of Tracy at that particular moment in time, he felt that Ketti Gallian was potentially the biggest of stars and that she deserved the best possible support, which the forty-four-year-old Edmund Lowe decidedly was not.

Tracy felt a grudging affinity to the white-faced Gallian, who was ordered to stop using the American slang she learned from Maurice Chevalier and constantly hounded about her weight. (She was caught bingeing on chocolate bars out behind the stage, and the studio assigned a "secretary" to bird-dog her every move.) One crucial scene required her to cry, and when she told the director she couldn't do it, King took Tracy aside and suggested that he grab her roughly by the shoulders and shake her. "Ketti Gallian had been out the night before and had had a few drinks too many," King remembered. "She didn't feel so great and she was supposed to be doing this scene where she was supposed to cry and beg. She said, 'I can't cry, I can't cry.' I said, 'Spence, give her a shake. Slap her face. Get into the mood of the thing.' Spence looked at me and I looked at her. Spence just couldn't do it himself."

King then caught her by the shoulders and gave her a shake and said, "Here is where you're supposed to break down emotionally and cry and tell this man you're sorry." When again she said, "I can't cry," King slapped her hard across the face and called, "Action!" Crying and running her dialogue in a mixture of French and English, Gallian was suddenly giving the camera everything it needed. "Spence," King urged, "play the scene, play the scene!" Tracy, who had never been witness to such a brazen piece of direction, was dumbfounded. "I never saw a man so embarrassed in my life," King said, "[but] he finally grabbed her by the shoulders and he got warmed up to do it and the scene came off in great shape."

Marie Galante was approximately two-thirds finished when, on Monday, August 13, Tracy again failed to report for work and was again taken off salary. According to Edmund Hartmann, the uncredited writer on the set, he turned up in New York and was returned to Hollywood on a chartered plane. "In the middle of the flight," recalled Hartmann, "he came to and went berserk. The co-pilot had to go in with a monkey wrench and knock him out cold." King shot around him for a week, then the picture was shut down pending his return. "Tracy came back to Fox," said Hartmann, "but he didn't look anything like the man in the footage we already had shot. King was a big, tough guy—but a wonderful man—and he said to Tracy, 'You dirty, yellow son-of-a-bitch. You ruined the lives of all the people working on the picture. They're all fired until we start up again!' "

Sidney Kent, who was running the Westwood and Western Avenue plants while Sheehan was away, threatened to start the picture over again with Edmund Lowe in the part of Crawbett and sue Tracy for $125,000 to cover the costs of the shutdown and all the work that had to be remade. Kent had one of his people call Neil McCarthy, Tracy's attorney, and outline the arrangement: Tracy would pay Fox $25,000 upon resuming the picture and half his $2,000 weekly salary for the remaining seventeen weeks of the year. Further, should the studio choose to exercise the final option on his five-year contract, he would agree to a holdback of 50 percent while making the first picture of the new term, with the balance paid only upon completion of the second picture under the deal.

"I recommended to Spencer that he pay the money and go back to work," McCarthy recalled. "I was impelled to do this largely because I felt that if we could hit his pocketbook hard, it might act as an additional strength to keep him from drinking, and particularly during a picture." On McCarthy's advice, Tracy capitulated and agreed to what *Variety* called "the most severe penalty ever imposed on a film player for holding up production." Chastened, he resumed production the day after Labor Day looking wan and lifeless.

As her anxiety over the kidnapping threat subsided, Louise made preparations to return the children to the house on Holmby. Spence, who was making *Now I'll Tell* at the time, thought that unwise, the writer of the two letters having shown an intimate knowledge of its layout and their habits there. "This was a real blow," said Louise. "We fitted into that house so perfectly. I had hoped we would not move again until we moved into a home of our own, which I continued to believe we sometime would do. I fumed and seethed that a featherweight scamp, in concocting such a crackpot scheme, should be able to upset our whole existence."

They found a new place on Palm Drive in Beverly Hills, a palatial spread on—for a change—flat ground with a large screened-in porch out back. For his tenth birthday, Johnny got a bicycle, something he had long wanted, and, to everyone's surprise, he was quickly able to master the thing, even with his weak leg (which Louise feared would prevent him from ever riding it unaided). "Yes, he fell," said Louise, "but other children fall. If he were to be like other children, he *must* fall sometimes."

Occasionally, she brought him to Riviera, where she would put him on Blossom or White Sox and lead him around the yard in front of the stables. "When I mounted the horse," John wrote, "I held the saddle tightly with both of my hands and wanted to get off. I realized I was so high and was afraid that I'd surely fall off and get hurt." His mother insisted that he keep riding, despite his fear, and gradually he progressed to the ring near one of the polo fields, staying on entirely by balance and still tethered to the lead rope. But he never developed any real confidence on a horse—with only one leg to hold on by—until they got him a Western saddle, which made for a far more comfortable and secure ride.

He reentered Hollywood Progressive School in the fall, attending only the morning sessions (to leave time for his treatments and rest periods), but now, like other children, he was starting off for school each day at 8:30 in the morning. Primarily, he studied arithmetic and made things from clay and wood. "He had needed the companionship of hearing children," Louise wrote, "and began to make adjustments toward life which any child learns to make at school and with other children, and which were more numerous for any handicapped child."

Lincoln Cromwell's first year at McGill University was similarly limited, mostly anatomy and related subjects—lectures, readings, lab dissections, the gruesome humor of students learning everything they can about the composition and workings of the human body. Dutifully, Cromwell kept up a running, if largely one-sided, correspondence with his famous sponsor, reporting on exams and study groups and distinctive members of the faculty, mixing in thumbnail sketches of the other students, accounts of the weather and boardinghouse horseplay, anything that could help portray the color, the drudgery, the genuinely hard work that went with being a medical student. "Immersed as we were in the study of anatomy," he wrote, "it never occurred to me that any descriptions of our dissections would be offensive to Spencer. And, in fact, they were not. He was always highly interested in even the most technical aspects of the study of medicine."

Through the turmoil of that first year—which spanned almost the full extent of the Loretta Young affair, the very public separation of the Tracys, the fights, binges, extortion letters, the mediocre pictures and the loan-outs, the arrest off Sunset, and the hopes, largely dashed, of bigger things to come—Tracy had Cromwell's letters, bright spots in a fast life that was sometimes more than he could handle. "Glad you are getting along so well," Carroll wrote back in October 1933. "Spencer is away on location. He got a big laugh over your letter about the stiffs. Keep us posted on all you are doing."

In December, Cromwell heard from Dr. H. O. Dennis, the man who had originally put the two of them together. Spence had read some of his letters aloud, and Denny was pleased to be able to report that Tracy was "very well satisfied with his bargain up to this time, and that he is as proud of you as you are grateful to have him as a friend." A couple of weeks later, Tracy himself wrote, reiterating in a fatherly tone how much he enjoyed the letters. "Have just signed a new contract [meaning his third option had been taken up at Fox] so you will have no worries as far as your continuing at McGill is concerned." Enclosed with the letter was a check for twenty-five dollars "which I want you to use for a Christmas present for yourself."

Cromwell came home to Los Angeles over the summer of 1934, driving a 1920 Studebaker loaded with paying passengers. A few weeks after his arrival, during the early days of filming *Marie Galante,* Spence invited him to dinner, which turned out to be a formal party at which he was the guest of honor. "After dinner they wanted to go out on the town, but I declined because I had to be at work at Douglas [Aircraft] early in the morning. I recall that Spencer laughed and said something like, 'Well, he seems very conscientious so we'll have to let him go.' " He saw Tracy several more times over the summer, then was horrified when he called Carroll just short of his departure and found that his benefactor had lost his job and that "everything, including me, was on hold." The date was August 26, 1934, and it was doubtless Cromwell's presence—one of the many responsibilities Tracy now carried—that contributed to his going back to Fox the following day and agreeing to Sidney Kent's punitive terms for reinstatement.

"I was ready to start the second year of medical school," Cromwell wrote, "and apparently Spencer would continue my support."

In September Jesse Lasky asked Loretta Young to come to his office. She was making *The White Parade* for him at Fox, and he wanted her for his next picture as well, a tale about modern travelers stranded in a California ghost town called *Helldorado*. She knew the film was set to star Spencer Tracy—had been since the spring—and although she would have loved to have done it, she didn't dare, not wanting to "start the whole thing over again." Lasky was glad he asked, sure there was no good to come from forcing the two of them to work together again, and within a few days had signed Madge Evans for the role of Glenda Wynant, spoiled society girl. The film was set to start on Monday, September 24, but Tracy, who had been seen around town the previous couple of weeks with actress Erin O'Brien-Moore, never showed, and by noon it was obvious he wasn't going to.

"The studio gumshoed all the bars but couldn't find him," Lasky said. "Postponing the scheduled starting date of a picture is sometimes prohibitively costly, if not downright impossible, because of interlocked commitments geared to a timetable. In this case, we couldn't even shoot around our star until he showed up because he had to be in almost all the scenes. We slapped Richard Arlen into the part, which didn't fit him at all, but there was no time to tailor it to his personality. The studio rounded up Tracy a few days later, and I sent word to him that I would never ask him what happened but that it might have happened to me instead of him and I was glad it didn't so I was willing to forget it."

Jack Gain prepared once again to charge Tracy for holding up production, in this case one and a half days of overhead for the idle company. On October 13, 1934, Winfield Sheehan returned to the studio and the matter was placed before him. He talked privately with Tracy and, according to Dick Mook, told him that he knew things hadn't been easy but that he still believed in him. "Forget what's happened," Sheehan said grandly. "Get out of town a few weeks and pull yourself together." Winnie Sheehan, Tracy later told Mook, was, with the exception of Louise and his own mother, "the most understanding person I have ever met."

With a great weight suddenly lifted from his shoulders, at least momentarily, Tracy made plans to go to Hawaii for a week with Carroll. He was within a few days of sailing and unusually relaxed when he met with Gain on the subject of a new contract. "While discussing the contract," Gain later recounted in a memo to Sidney Kent,

> he informed me he wanted to make only four pictures per year—he wanted approval of stories—he wanted the right to do a picture on the outside, in addition to which he wanted much more money than I offered him, none of which were granted . . . In my opinion, the deal was a very good one, considering the offers that Tracy received from other studios, and I am positive that if the discussion has to be re-opened and changed so that we are compelled to make him pay the additional $6000 and keep half his salary as outlined by [studio treasurer Sidney] Towell, that he will definitely walk out on the deal, and the only thing we would have left would be to exercise our option for one year at $2500 weekly, in addition to changing his present frame of mind, which we consider is very good.

Tracy's estrangement from Leo Morrison was a significant factor in the deal's getting made, for it would have been considered improper for another company to have opened talks with Tracy while his contract with Fox was still in force. He likely could have doubled his weekly rate by freelancing, yet he had no clear perception of his position in the marketplace. "Spence's naiveté," his pal Mook once said, "runs second only to his ability as an actor." Competition for established screen personalities was at an all-time high, the flow of new talent from the legitimate stage having slowed considerably.

Tracy returned from Honolulu sunburned but rested and went back on salary on November 5, 1934. The next day he signed a new two-year contract calling for $2,250 a week during the first year and $2,500 a week for the second. Sol Wurtzel, grinding out programmers at the Fox Western Avenue complex, had Tracy's final assignment under the old pact: a high-concept, effects-laden spectacle built around the title *Dante's Inferno*.

Wurtzel, whose commercial instincts ranged from the plebeian to the downright bizarre, had overseen a 1924 feature of the same title. What he proposed to get from a talking version was not much different from the earlier picture, an allegorical tale of damnation and redemption with a fabulous tour of the Inferno as its centerpiece. The idea was first floated back in January, the crown jewel of the seventeen pictures Wurtzel proposed to deliver that season. It was formally announced for the program in June, promising an "amazing drama" depicting the "afterlife fate of ruthless millionaires in lower regions" as envisioned by director Harry Lachman and a small army of artists and technicians.

The original outline by Philip Klein and Rose Franklin proposed a radical break from the plotline of the original film, suggesting a sort of *Cavalcade* of tormented souls: "The drama aims at three separate groups of people—the romance of the so-called flaming youth of today, the middle-age story of a man and wife, and the lonely strength of a financial genius. Each contributes to, and enriches, the other while the pictorial leveler of the Inferno is an integral part of the story development, rather than an illusion of abstract thought." Wurtzel thought the storyline too fussy, and when Robert Yost, onetime head of the Fox story department, got involved, it was reduced to the rise and fall of one principal character, an itinerant carny by the name of Jim Carter. Wurtzel declared he wanted Tracy for the part of Carter, proposing once again to team him with Claire Trevor.

As a junior writer, Eric Knight, the British journalist who would come to be known as the creator of Lassie, was brought in on a story conference. Carter, Wurtzel explained, was to be a stoker on a ship. "He clouts the engineer and swims to shore and lands at a sort of Coney Island, where there's a concession—a sort of side show—called the Inferno. He goes inside and meets the daughter of the man and they get married and have a kid. Then he gets the ambition bug. Before long, he owns the concession—then the whole island—then he builds a great big inferno sideshow on a weak pier that collapses."

So far, so good, but then Wurtzel, Klein, and Lachman proceeded, in true Fox fashion, to bring in a current—and completely unrelated—story, the previous month's disastrous sinking of the S.S. *Morro Castle,* making it the third act of the picture. Bewildered, Knight withdrew, deciding it would be better "to play Achilles and sulk in his tent" than to try and urge Wurtzel and his associates to a more coherent treatment. *Dante's Inferno* entered production the week of December 3, 1934, as did Will Rogers' *Life Begins at 40, George White's Scandals,* and *The Little Colonel,* a musical from the makers of *Bottoms Up* with Fox's newest and most commercially potent star, six-year-old Shirley Temple.

Fox, for a change, was riding high. In the space of two years, Sidney R. Kent had taken a $15 million loser and restored it to profitability, showing a net income of more than $1 million for the first six months of 1934. In gratitude, the Fox board, including the representatives of Chase Bank, the company's biggest stockholder, tore up Kent's old contract and awarded him a new three-year deal. Weakened in the process was Winnie Sheehan, whose rumored departure was always part of the industry grapevine. Kent and Sheehan conferred, posed for pictures, got along for the sake of the com-

Tracy came to terms with Louise's passion for
polo and grew to admire her accomplishments on
the field. (HERALD EXAMINER COLLECTION,
LOS ANGELES PUBLIC LIBRARY)

pany, but Kent was onto bigger things for Fox, and none of them involved
the man who was Spencer Tracy's biggest booster.

Louise, meanwhile, was barnstorming across Texas with a handpicked
group of eight other players, staging exhibition games to "prove to the
unsuspecting public that girls' polo can be good polo." They stopped in
Abilene, Arlington Downs, Austin, and San Antonio, playing to large
crowds and consistently making front-page copy in the sports sections of
the local papers. Louise throughout urged more and better opportunities
for female players. "Our shots are not as long," she acknowledged in the
Abilene Morning News, "but they can be just as good shots, and the players
can master the difficulties encountered in hard riding. Then, too, it is no
harder on women physically than a good game of tennis singles. I've played
both, so I should know."

Spence was plainly fascinated by Weeze's self-styled "missionary tour,"
coming as it did on the heels of the newly organized Pacific Coast Women's
Polo Association. Within days of her return, Harrison Carroll of the
Evening Herald Express ran the following item: "The Spencer Tracy reconciliation is almost complete; Spencer and his wife, guests at a dinner given in

honor of Mr. and Mrs. Winthrop Aldrich (visiting banker) from New York, spent the entire evening dancing together."

Marie Galante opened with scarcely a mention of Tracy from the New York critics, and now he found himself—for the first time in nearly a decade—generating less ink than his crusading spouse. He gave her a diamond-studded wristwatch for Christmas, was seen out on the town with her, dancing at the Beverly Wilshire and the Cocoanut Grove and talking animatedly at the Clover Club. While their reconciliation wasn't yet a done deal, they had come to realize they were greater as a couple than the sum of their individual parts and that nothing could really dissolve all the life they had shared, all the marriage they'd experienced.

Dante's Inferno was hardly an actor's dream. Tracy was not keen on doing it, but could scarcely refuse given the fiscal sword of Damocles that now hung over his head. Claire Trevor was no more enthused with the material, nor with Lachman's handling of it. "They gave him a lot of time and a lot of money," she said, "but it was not an A-picture. Harry Lachman was a dreamer, really a creator, an artist, but crazy, you know? The picture had no boundary, no spine, no foundation. It may have been an A-movie budget, but it was a B-movie script."

The plan originally was to shoot the carnival exteriors at Long Beach or Ocean Park, but Lachman thought the real concessions too drab to use. So an amusement pier was constructed on a stage at Western Avenue and real-life concessionaires given jobs as extras at five dollars a day. The vast set saved the inevitable delays that would otherwise have resulted from winter wind and rain, but also made it possible for Lachman to shoot round the clock, and frequently he did.

Filming crept past the first of the year and eventually encroached on the start date of another picture, a modest comedy titled *It's a Small World*. Rather than delay it, the studio compelled Tracy to begin the second film while still shooting the first, splitting his time between two stages over a period of a couple of weeks. After nearly ten weeks of filming, Lachman had a perfectly serviceable melodrama, the sort of thing Fox normally turned out in eighteen to twenty-four days. Dispensing with his actors in mid-February, Lachman spent the next month—and approximately $200,000— perfecting the Inferno segment, which would occupy an entire reel of footage and employ the services of several prominent illustrators and designers, Willie Pogany and Hubert Julian Stowitts among them.

It was Stowitts, particularly, who was responsible for the conga lines of writhing bodies, oiled and muscular, stripped to within an inch of the Production Code and arrayed along tiered and cavernous pits of fire, their size

Tracy was sometimes dwarfed by the bizarre spectacle of *Dante's Inferno* (1935). Set by unit art director David S. Hall. (SUSIE TRACY)

due, in large part, to the masterly glass paintings of Ben Carré. Nearly naked extras were lined up and sprayed with makeup that gave them a translucent quality, while miniature figures of men were cast in plaster and suspended from a revolving disk to create the illusion of flight. Spun before the lens of a high-speed camera, they appeared to be real bodies floating in slow motion through the sulfurous air of the director's own private Hades. The miniatures were the responsibility of Fred Sersen and his special effects crew, while the fire effects were the work of Lee Zavits, who would later be instrumental in bringing off the burning of Atlanta for *Gone With the Wind*. When production on *Dante's Inferno* came to an end, Lachman and his crew had spent nearly $750,000 and printed an estimated 300,000 feet of film.

"I ran amuck," Tracy admitted in the confessional of the fan magazines,

> that's all. I did all kinds of crazy things. That I have not had to pay a sterner penalty is due to the kindness of Winfield Sheehan, the

head of Fox, who forgave me for not showing up on the set, and to the kindness, the extraordinary kindness of my wife, who took those blows like a thoroughbred and a sportswoman and did the thing only a superwoman can do—nothing. Louise is an extraordinary woman. That is why it is possible for me to go home again. She has never upbraided me nor berated me. She never will. She never used the things most women would use as baits to a man who needed to be reminded—she never pleaded the children nor our years together nor the "rights" that legitimately grow out of such sharing. She asked me to come home, of course, but that was all. And I have learned—my son has taught me—that there are those things in life which are stronger even than memories, than personal desires or lovely idylls.

It was December 1934, that time when he and Louise were seen almost everywhere together. He was still living at the Beverly Wilshire, but there were times at Riviera, especially on Sundays, when they were together more than they were apart. And on the days when Spence knew he would be working late, when Lachman was fussing over shots or script and taking forever to make up his mind, he would look in for breakfast and sit with Louise and the kids. "My going back had been a slow process in a way," he told Gladys Hall in February 1935.

I've been unhappy for a long while, lonely, unsatisfied. Life has seemed thin and reasonless. But it sometimes takes an apparently little thing, a word, to help one make the decision. I was having breakfast last week with Mrs. Tracy and the children. I've never been out of touch with them, as you know. There's never been any legal separation or anything like that.

Well, the other day, at the breakfast table, Johnny was ready for school. He wanted me to take him. I was due at the studio and couldn't. His mother said that she would take him. And then he looked at me with a look that seemed to cut clean through all the painful business of the past months and said, "No. Girls belong with mothers. Boys belong with fathers." I knew right then and there that nothing else mattered, not really. Not by comparison with . . . with this. He was right. Boys do belong with their fathers and, even more, fathers belong with their sons. And fathers have no rights that do not include their sons. I'd been thinking that I had "rights"—that I could lead my own life and all that sort of thing— but actually I foreswore that right the day that Johnny was born. I was responsible for this young life. He has a great many years ahead of him. And they are likely to be difficult years because of his handicap of not hearing. It is up to me to live those years to come with him. His place is with me. Mine is with him.

Dick Mook talked of Tracy's naïveté, which was never more apparent than when he was around other film players. When in 1932 James Cagney told Mook that Tracy was "the finest actor on the American stage," Tracy was nonplussed. He had met Cagney but did not know him. "Did he *really* say that?" Tracy asked incredulously, scarcely able to believe it. The following year, he approached Gary Cooper at a party and took his hand. "I am Spencer Tracy," he said, "and I want to tell you how much I enjoyed your work in *A Farewell to Arms.*" Cooper assured him it was unnecessary to introduce himself, as he had watched Tracy's own work with great interest.

The two men struck up an acquaintance, and when Tracy decided it was time to come home, he and Louise leased a ranch that Cooper owned on Dinsmore Avenue in Van Nuys. "We're going to find out how we like the ranch life, how we like the Valley, and if we do, we'll buy a place of our own there and settle down to some real homesteading. The children are going to have a real home now. We'll have horses and dogs. I've already bought a horse for Johnny and a pony for small Susie. I'll ride with Johnny. I'll take him to school whenever I can. I'll be there when he wants me."

He added, "I suppose there comes a time in the life of almost every man when he wants to go hunting, big-game hunting, love-hunting, crazy-adventure hunting, some such nostalgia. I have had such a trip. And now I've come home again."

In his later years Tracy maintained it was Fox Film Corporation that terminated their relationship in the spring of 1935. The details of the story, however, kept shifting. "They fired me," he told the AP's Bob Thomas in 1952. "Those were in the days when I was still drinking, and I got drunk now and then. But never on a picture—always between. Anyway, they worried. I was all set for a big, expensive picture. But they came to me and asked if I was going to behave. I told them, 'That's a heck of a way to get me to behave! If you're worried about me, why don't you let me go?' That's all they needed. I wasn't a box office star or anything. I was out of the studio the same day." Another version had him showing up drunk at the studio and being fired by an administrative executive, allegedly someone who lacked the authority to do such a thing. Sheehan supposedly raised hell when he found out, but Tracy, by that time, had signed with M-G-M and was completely out of reach.

The actual details are skimpy, but neither the Fox legal files nor Tracy's own records—such as they are—support either account. Tracy did indeed sign a new contract with Fox on November 6, 1934, and Jack Gain's memo to Sidney Kent clearly shows that no agent was in on the deal. Gain was, in fact, vigorously patting himself on the back for moving so quickly and taking advantage of Tracy's good mood in the wake of Sheehan's suggestion that he "get out of town." Had he waited, Gain implied, renewing the pact would have been much more difficult, if not downright impossible. Tracy's services were never shopped to other studios; in fact, he accepted a weekly rate $250 less than would otherwise have been due him under the terms of the old contract. Admittedly, the new pact wiped away all further obligations for the delays incurred on *Marie Galante* and *Helldorado,* but an agent would undoubtedly have driven a harder bargain for a man who was now widely regarded as one of the screen's best actors.

A week later, an item appeared in *Variety* indicating that Fox had given Tracy a straight two-year deal, no options. "Old pact," the paper noted, "was torn up." This must have come as news to Leo Morrison, who was aware of M-G-M's interest in his former client and had an obvious stake in repairing the relationship. Sometime after that item appeared, Morrison got back in touch with Tracy and, subsequently, the two men entered into an oral agreement whereby Morrison would collect a 5 percent commission on all monies received under the deal were he "successful in securing the Metro-Goldwyn-Mayer contract." Morrison, who was close to M-G-M general manager Eddie Mannix, went into action and was apparently in talks by the time Tracy began work on *It's a Small World* on February 2, 1935. Five days into the film, Fox attempted to commence employment under the terms of the new contract, but Tracy, evidently acting under Morrison's advice, never signed and returned the letters agreeing to appear.

Actress Astrid Allwyn could remember the "tremendous tension" on the set of *It's a Small World* more vividly than the film itself. "There is no question in my mind that something was wrong, but I was not that sophisticated to understand the actions of other actors." There was the pressure on Tracy to sign and return the letters activating his new contract, something Allwyn could not possibly have known. He was also shooting two very different pictures simultaneously, one requiring a long introductory sequence played entirely in the rain. Cinematographer Arthur Miller recalled that director Irving Cummings was "half loaded" on the picture, a circumstance which could not have improved his leading man's disposition. Moreover, Tracy was in the process of moving for the sixth time in four years. The result was that he was withdrawn and quiet on the set, a considerable counterpoint to the carefree vacationing lawyer he was playing in the film.

The story itself bore a resemblance to the recent Frank Capra comedy *It Happened One Night,* continuing the proud Fox tradition of cranking out quick and inexpensive knockoffs of the hit pictures of other studios. The mood on the set lightened once *Dante's Inferno* wrapped, but then Tracy got beaned with a dinner plate while shooting a kitchen scene with actress Wendy Barrie. The injury required five stitches over his right eye and was responsible for a week's delay in finishing the picture. Tracy was seen at a lavish cocktail party given by Pat and Eloise O'Brien on Valentine's Day, a two-inch bandage gracing his lower forehead. Sol Wurtzel used the hiatus to make some retakes on *Dante's Inferno,* specifically a new ending in the aftermath of the ship disaster in which Tracy's character looked perfectly natural wearing a bandage. *It's a Small World* closed on March 2, 1935, and Tracy retired to the polo fields at Riviera, where he took a serious spill while practicing a few days later.

Whether it was the fall or the move or simply the stress of outmaneuvering the people at Fox, Tracy dropped from sight in early March and headed east with Hugh Tully, an ostler at Riviera. Hughie, the brother of Jim Tully, the famed author of *Beggars of Life,* knew horses about as well as anyone, and he convinced Tracy that the best polo stock was to be had elsewhere. "Horses out here are no good," he said. "Better go back east—New England, upstate New York. Good horse farms." The two men decided they'd drive back to New York and buy some horses. "They'd go off to Virginia, mosey around," as Frank Tracy remembered it.

They'd be gone a couple of weeks. So before they left, Spence sat down with a stack of cards. Post cards. He wrote about four to his mother, four to Louise, four to Johnny, a couple to Carroll. "Today we did this, and today we did that." He figured that he would probably not be able to handle a correspondence, and people would begin to wonder where the hell he was. So he got all these cards stamped and addressed, and he gave them to Hughie. First mistake. He said, "Hughie, every few days, mail some of these cards." Well, Hughie got drunk and he mailed them all the same day. [Spence's] poor mother and Louise were getting these cards, all of different dates, "Today we saw the Statue of Liberty . . . " It turned out to be quite a laugh, but it took a while for everybody to see the humor in the situation.

Louise caught up with him in Yuma via long distance—the postmarks having given them away—and Tracy got so agitated he began hurling dishes against the wall of his hotel room. The disturbance caused the guests in the adjacent room to alert the manager, and when the police showed up Tracy was charged with being "drunk and resisting an officer, cursing and breaking up things in a hotel room," and summarily dragged off to jail. Spectators described a "beautiful battle" in which one cop was able to take both men down "for the count." As Louise set out for Yuma with Audrey Caldwell's husband, Orville, behind the wheel, Spence and Tully were on ice, but only long enough to make bail of fifteen dollars each. They were back on the road—reportedly to Nogales—by the time she arrived.

Andrew Tracy had taken to writing straighten-up letters whenever he read about his nephew's troubles in the papers. Knowing Andrew would likely read about this incident, Spence sent a long, rambling wire to his uncle before quitting Yuma. It ran several pages and kept returning to a central theme: I LOVE YOU ANDREW. In Freeport, Andrew read the telegram with a heavy heart. "Oh, God," he sighed, putting it down. "He's drunk again."

Tracy's disappearance forced Winfield Sheehan to deny press reports that he had been pulled from the cast of *The Farmer Takes a Wife,* the "big, expensive picture" for which Tracy had been set. The film would pair him for the first time with Janet Gaynor, Fox's top adult draw, and actor Henry Fonda, imported from Max Gordon's Broadway production of the same title. *It's a Small World* was previewed in Glendale on March 25, where it was found, in the words of the *Reporter* review, to be "so sadly lacking in story punch that it could be run backward or forward with very few able to detect the procedure."

Sheehan may well have sensed trouble in Tracy's relationship with the studio, for on Friday, March 29, he voluntarily took him out of *The Farmer Takes a Wife,* not as a disciplinary measure (as some suggested) but in the sincere belief that Spence "should rest before he begins another picture." Sheehan had his own problems with the Fox hierarchy, as Kent was working a deal that would merge Schenck's 20th Century with Fox and bring Darryl F. Zanuck to the studio as its new production head. According to Glendon Allvine, Fox's former publicity chief, it was a move calculated to break Sheehan's contract "by wounding his vanity and dignity and pride in the company he had helped create, and bringing in a man 20 years younger to replace him."

By the end of that day, Sheehan's troubles at Fox no longer mattered to Spencer Tracy, for Leo Morrison had finally settled a deal at M-G-M.

CHAPTER II

That Double Jackpot

Metro-Goldwyn-Mayer was the most structured of the major studios, a machine of an organization that not only ground out a disproportionate share of Hollywood's prestige product but sold it with a sophistication that bordered on the supernatural. Much of what happened within its beaverboard walls was due to the philosophies and dictates of Irving Grant Thalberg, the frail production chief whose tireless cultivation of the studio's star roster did much to establish and sustain the M-G-M brand. The slogan "More stars than there are in Heaven" was more than just an empty boast. While other organizations typically stumbled upon star material, Metro had the fewest surprises in terms of what it had to sell the public at any given moment. "Without stars," Thalberg once said, "a company is in the position of starting over again each year."

It was Thalberg's doing that brought Tracy to M-G-M in the spring of 1935, but not everyone at the studio shared his enthusiasm. Of the nineteen pictures Tracy made for Fox, only *Quick Millions* and *The Power and the Glory* were truly memorable, and even those were considered flops at the box office. Tracy got by playing gangsters, vagabonds, and con men, and although he had genuinely distinguished himself as J. Aubrey Piper in *The Show-Off,* his reputation as a troublemaker was well known.

Metro, however, was in the midst of an initiative to pump up its player ranks, and Tracy would fill a valuable slot in the studio's fabled stock company. In terms of genuine male stars, M-G-M had only Clark Gable and Robert Montgomery as leading men, neither of whom fell comfortably into the mugg category Tracy had so expertly occupied at Fox. William Powell was in his forties, Wallace Beery nearly fifty, Jackie Cooper just twelve. Charles Laughton was strictly a character man, and Maurice Chevalier was, well, Maurice Chevalier. Franchot Tone and the impossibly beautiful Robert Taylor were being brought along, as was Nelson Eddy, who seemingly came out of nowhere. In March alone, nine players were signed to term contracts, Reginald Owen, Edna May Oliver, Robert Benchley, and Charles Trowbridge among them. The studio wasn't above acquiring talent that, by Thalberg's reckoning, had been mismanaged elsewhere—the Marx Brothers and now Tracy being the most recent examples.

A memorandum of agreement between Spencer Tracy and M-G-M was signed on Tuesday, April 2, 1935. It outlined a seven-year deal, calling for five pictures a year at $25,000 a picture to start. The studio would advance $1,250 a week against each film, with the unpaid balance due at the end of production. Tracy was to receive first featured billing after the star or costar, with nobody's name in larger type. The concluding sentence of the document confirmed that Tracy was not yet done at Fox: "We recognize the fact that this contract is binding only if Mr. Tracy secures a release from his Fox contract." That same day a meeting took place at Fox Hills. Calls were exchanged between organizations, and the contract Tracy had signed with Fox on November 6, 1934, was terminated "by mutual consent." Tracy verbally agreed—and M-G-M's Benny Thau concurred—that prior to April 1, 1936, he would make one additional picture for Fox at the rate of $3,000 a week. Papers on both coasts carried the news of the move the following morning.

"It is understood that Tracy received a very flattering offer from M-G-M and was very desirous of accepting it," Edwin Schallert wrote in the pages of the *Los Angeles Times*. "Winfield Sheehan kindly conceded to him and allowed him to go to the other studio." The *Hollywood Reporter* added that Tracy's new contract would take effect on his thirty-fifth birthday. "His first picture there will be *Riffraff,* the Frances Marion waterfront story that had the names of Gloria Swanson and Clark Gable penciled opposite it on the M-G-M assignment sheet for some time. Irving Thalberg declined to state last night whether Miss Swanson is still in line for the female lead."

Louella Parsons bested them all when she said there was a "whisper" that Jean Harlow would be starred in *Riffraff* "and right away because M-G-M is eager to get more of her pictures on the market." Thalberg was no longer in charge of production, his health having forced him to take on a lighter workload, but he was still responsible for the development and casting of seven pictures a year.

"Spencer Tracy," Thalberg told Parsons, "will become one of M-G-M's most valuable stars."

The Tracys were still settling into their new home on the Cooper ranch, with its chickens, its horses, its solitary goat. Louise thought the house too big, but the expanse of land—five acres planted mostly with walnut trees— was exhilarating. "We looked at a number of pieces of property with the idea of building," she said, "but Spencer always shied at the final jump. He blamed this on two hazards: summer heat and the distance from the studio. Luckily, we found a place to rent."

There was a swimming pool, and John at long last learned to swim, as did Susie, who was approaching the age of three. They brought White Sox to the property, and Johnny's riding improved as he cantered up and down the driveway by himself. On Easter Sunday they attended a polo match at Riviera. Then, in May, Spence and Louise had a "second honeymoon" in San Francisco, where Louise took the opportunity to visit the Gough School for the Deaf. When she asked if she could hire someone to come to Los Angeles for a few weeks over the summer and work with John on his voice and speech, an exploratory examination was suggested. A few weeks later she was back with her son, and after a brief interview the woman asked, "How much of a hearing loss has he?"

Louise answered that his loss was complete, but knew it was unusual for a child to be "stone" deaf. John hadn't been tested since he was eight, and there was newer and better equipment now available. They marched him down the hall to the school's 2A Audiometer, where they would be able to tell if he had, at age eleven, any usable hearing.

"Although I dreaded having one more nail driven into the already seemingly well-secured lid," she said, "still, having no hope, I could suffer no real disappointment." He was fitted with the headphones, then sat expectantly through the first part of the test. Suddenly he started, surprised, and then he went still, the unmistakable quality of listening in his wide blue eyes.

"I can hear," he said.

Moving to Metro-Goldwyn-Mayer was like a shot of adrenaline for Spencer Tracy. The care with which he was handled and managed was light-years from the ineptitude he had known at Fox. "Spencer Tracy, looking like a million dollars, is reporting at Metro-Goldwyn-Mayer studios every day," Louella Parsons reported in mid-May. "If Irving Thalberg has his way, Spencer's name will be electric-lighted throughout the world within the next year." When Thalberg's picture got delayed, Tracy was offered to other producers on the lot, specifically Lawrence Weingarten, who had an original story of high finance for him called "Plunder," and Harry Rapf, who was developing a script from writer-director Tim Whelan titled *The Murder Man*.

A newspaper story, *The Murder Man* had been written on spec by Whelan and his collaborator, the British playwright and librettist Guy Bolton. A studio reader, who covered the material just days before Tracy's arrival at M-G-M, thought it a "first-rate yarn, well written, cleverly constructed, full of suspense. Dialogue good and not so snappy as to get under the feet of the swift action." There was one great flaw: the hero of the piece, a well-known reporter who covers murder investigations for a metropolitan daily, turns out to be the perpetrator of one of the murders he has written about so presciently. "If he could be made to kill the man who stole his wife instead of merely the one who stole his money, we could get away with it."

Rapf himself was prone to sentiment and soft edges—*Min and Bill, The Champ, The Sin of Madelon Claudet*—so he was somewhat out of his element with a hardboiled crime melodrama. For the rewrite, he paired Whelan with a junior writer named John C. Higgins, who was working on the studio's *Crime Does Not Pay* series of short subjects. With Higgins contributing dialogue, the two men gave the title character a stronger motivation. Tormented by his wife's suicide and the reason for it, the character was recast in the image of the actor they now knew would be playing the part—a binge-drinking insomniac with a reputation for disappearing for days at a time. Tracy seemed to relish the part as a form of public confessional, a cleansing that signaled an end to his turbulent days at Fox.

He began the picture on May 28 with Virginia Bruce, a pale blonde who had been one of the original Goldwyn girls, as his leading lady. The film was, like *The Show-Off*, a quickie by Metro standards, and production zipped along at a brisk pace. Shooting in Culver City was a different experience from working at Fox Hills, where the atmosphere was decidedly more administrative than creative. Sheehan's shimmering Movietone complex was like a gigantic amusement park, expansive and contiguous. Metro, by comparison, was scattered over six separate lots, cramped and shedded and separated from one another by public thoroughfares. Exteriors at many studios were marred by airplanes and wind noise and the chirping of birds, but at M-G-M there were also Pacific Electric train whistles to contend with and the sounds of traffic just steps away.

Stages, dressing rooms, and administrative offices were concentrated on

With Robert Barrat and Virginia Bruce in *The Murder Man,* Tracy's first assignment under his new M-G-M contract, 1935. (SUSIE TRACY)

Lot 1, where the colonnade along Washington Boulevard was originally designed as frontage for the Triangle Film Corporation, so named because it was conceived as a gathering of three major producers: Thomas Ince, D. W. Griffith, and Mack Sennett. When that fragile alliance failed in 1919, the plant passed to Goldwyn, which based its production activities there until its acquisition by Marcus Loew's Metro Pictures Corporation in 1924. Louis B. Mayer, whose own company was located on the grounds of Colonel William Selig's former studio and zoo in East Los Angeles, came aboard to manage the newly formed company, bringing Irving Thalberg and the dour Harry Rapf with him.

Whelan had been a gag writer for Harold Lloyd, and he kept the action smart and sassy. He held Tracy's first appearance until the second reel, but, unlike at Fox, where Tracy frequently appeared out of nowhere, his character dominated the early action as reporters for the *Star* fanned out over the city in search of Steve Gray, the paper's famed "murder man," missing after one of his legendary benders. In Whelan's fanciful scenario, Gray is found aboard an all-night merry-go-round, snoozing soundly, a long string of tickets draped carelessly around his neck. As with *The Show-Off,* Tracy was on his best behavior, his lines down, his scenes frequently in the can with a single take. Thrown from a horse one Sunday while riding with cameraman Les White, he worked the next day as usual, nursing a back injury and a sprained arm. When a bit player failed to show for a brief exchange in a phone booth at the climax of the picture, Tracy mussed his hair and played the part himself.

It was when *The Murder Man* wrapped after seventeen days of filming that Tracy got a real sense of why M-G-M pictures were a cut above all the others. Where Fox would likely have shipped the film or settled at best for a few trims, Rapf ordered retakes, a new scene, and, ultimately, a completely new finish. When the picture was finally put before a preview audience on the night of July 5, 1935, it unfolded with such impact that the crowd was visibly saddened when Gray was revealed as the guilty party in the picture's closing moments.

Tracy, said the man from *Daily Variety,* played the role with "quiet, compelling conviction." A week later, *The Murder Man* was released nationally, finding its way to Loew's Capitol for the week of July 26. Bolstered by a $10,000 stage show starring Lou Holtz and Belle Baker, it drew $54,000 for the week, excellent despite the common judgment that the picture itself was too modest for a deluxe house. Print critics such as Abel Green objected to Tracy's character as "the criminal reporter type of make-believe city-roomer who dictates his stories into an Ediphone, gets pickled in the time-honored Jesse Lynch Williams tradition, and talks to and insults his managing editor in a manner no star legman ever dreamed of doing without getting the blue slip pronto."

"Despite all this," wrote Leo Mishkin in the *Telegraph,* "*The Murder Man* manages to be a fairly exciting piece of work. This is chiefly due, I suspect, to the acting of Brother Tracy, a man with a keen sense of values and an excellent fund of conviction. As a matter of fact, it is not too much to say that Brother Tracy is one of the finest play actors in Hollywood, and if somebody would only give him a decent story, he would emerge as a star of the first magnitude. He is real, he is convincing, and he seems to know who it's all about. That he makes *The Murder Man* a plausible and believable motion picture is a mighty tribute to his prowess."

There was still, however, the unfinished business of Tracy's last two films for Fox. After a studio showing of *Dante's Inferno* on April 16, George Wasson had persuaded Tracy to waive billing on the picture. *It's a Small World* opened in Los Angeles two days later, essentially dumped by a company no longer invested in the promotion of its star. *Small World* didn't make New York until June, when it graced the bottom half of a double bill at the Times, a small grind house at the edge of the Forty-second Street theater district.

The day after *Murder Man* closed at the Capitol, *Dante's Inferno* opened down the block at the Rivoli over Sol Wurtzel's vehement objection. ("You can't release *Dante's Inferno* in the summertime!" he told playwright S. N. "Sam" Behrman.) At first Wurtzel was proven wrong, the film shattering a five-year attendance record in the midst of a sizzling heat wave. The conclusion of the picture's ten-minute depiction of hell brought forth a burst of applause from an opening day audience, but, with another act yet to come, it was anticlimactic, and the critical consensus was that the rest of the picture was dull. "As you may have gathered," Douglas Churchill said in concluding his notice, "*Dante's Inferno* will be greedily accepted by children and received with mixed emotion by their elders."

It flamed out quickly, word of mouth being poor, and it was a clunk in the playoffs, where the strategy of emphasizing the Inferno sequence, with its writhing bodies and implied nudity, kept small-town audiences away. When the final tally was in, Wurtzel's masterwork posted a loss of more than a quarter-million dollars.

Tracy had just returned from Santa Barbara, where the annual Fiesta Week was in full swing, when, on August 16, 1935, word spread through the film colony that Will Rogers had been killed in a plane crash near Point Barrow, Alaska. Tracy had been aware his pal Bill was off with aviator Wiley Post, but the true purpose of the trip—the opening of an air route between Alaska and Siberia—had not been widely known. Flags were dropped to half staff at public buildings in Beverly Hills, where Rogers had reigned as "honorary mayor" in the 1920s and where city and police officials now gathered to mourn. All municipal court cases were postponed, and the gala premiere of Rogers' newest picture, *Steamboat Round the Bend,* was canceled at Grauman's Chinese. John Ford, who directed the movie, "went to pieces," Rogers having declined to sail with him to Hawaii so as to make the flight with Post. "You keep your duck and float on the water," Rogers had told him. "I'll take my eagle and fly."

Louise hadn't known Rogers well—he called her "Ma Tracy"—but Spence was inconsolable. They attended the simple funeral at Forest Lawn on the afternoon of the twenty-second, where only the four Cherokee Indians in attendance managed to remain stoic. Later, he gave an interview that was spun into a bylined remembrance for *Picture Play* magazine, recounting a time at Bill Howard's house when Rogers came by: "We sat around talking for a while. When he rose to go, Howard urged him to have a nip while waiting for his car to be brought around. 'I ain't got any car.' 'Well, let me have mine brought around to take you home. It's raining.' 'Naw. I walked over. I reckon I kin walk back.' It was eight miles to his home, but walk he did. The last we saw of him he was ambling gayly down the path, cutting at shrubs and bushes with a stick he had picked up."

News of Rogers' death ignited another round of drinking on Tracy's part, and it may well have been a subtle warning when, two days after the news broke, the studio fed an item to Louella Parsons. "Perhaps my sense of humor is distorted," she wrote, "but somehow when they told me at M-G-M that Spencer Tracy would be making a costume picture, I had to smile. I just couldn't picture the virile Spence doing a hand-kissing act. But this picture, I am assured, is going to be different." Parsons went on to report that Tracy was to star in an original story about an Irish captain of the Grenadiers, the action for which would take place in England, France, Italy, and Germany. The title? *Tosspot*... which was—and still is, of course—another word for "drunkard."

Riffraff had been developed specifically for Jean Harlow. "The studio doesn't think so," Thalberg said, "but I think she needs a crack at a dramatic story, and this is it." The actress donned a red wig for the part of Hattie, a feisty cannery worker who's stuck on Dutch, the cocky leader of the tuna fishermen and their union. It was a thankless role for Tracy, and Judith Wood, playing Harlow's friend Mabel, remembered the picture was held several days owing to his "illness." She went over to him when he finally appeared, having known him from *Looking for Trouble* (the eventual title of *Trouble Shooter*): "I said, 'I'm sorry you were sick, Spencer,' and he said, 'Sick! Hell, I was drunk.' "

The picture began shooting on August 29, its script having been given a final polish by Anita Loos, who took screen credit along with H. W. Hanemann and Frances Marion. Tracy kept to himself, and associate producer David Lewis, who was present throughout the course of production, never got to know him. Harlow, who wasn't drinking herself at the time, could see that Tracy was and resented it bitterly. One day, she stalked off the set and makeup artist Layne Britton followed. "What's wrong, Baby?" he asked. "Tracy's gassed," she replied, "and I'm not going to work 'til he gets straightened out."

Tracy was developing a reputation for being testy, and he gave unit publicist Cecil "Teet" Carle more "static, more worries, frets, resentments, frustrations, and ulcer symptoms" than any other performer. "A press agent welcomes consistency. A 100% heel or bitch can be coped with because he never varies. But Spence could be snarly and nasty one day, palsy and helpful the next."

Publicist Eddie Lawrence had his first encounter with Tracy when assigned to write the pressbook for the picture. Tracy was in his dressing

Filming *Riffraff* with Jean Harlow. Director J. Walter Ruben looks on, 1935.
(AUTHOR'S COLLECTION)

room with the door closed. Lawrence knocked, and Tracy "wiped me out. He said, 'Don't you ever, EVER knock on my door when the door is closed!' And I said [in a crushed voice], 'Oh.' And so I went to see [M-G-M's advertising director] Frank [Whitbeck]. And I said, 'Frank, what's this with Spencer?' He said, 'Well, you know, he has this terrible insomnia, and he's resting.' So it was quite understandable. Spence would leave the studio and go get a rubdown and sleep on it."

Riffraff was a major undertaking, much of it shot on M-G-M's Lot 1, where an elaborate wharf had been constructed alongside a man-made lake. The exteriors and the scenes shot on location at San Pedro gave the film size, but also made for an exceptionally long shoot. A total of fifty-six days was spent filming an unexceptional movie that did nothing to enhance the Thalberg legend nor advance Tracy's standing with audiences.

They were a happy pair, Johnny and his mother. They learned in San Francisco that he had some hearing—not much, but some. "I can hear," John proudly announced to just about everyone, confident that he would soon be hearing as well as everyone else. "We could not bring ourselves to disabuse his mind of this completely," Louise said, "and, after all, how did we know, anyway?"

What hearing he had was in the speech range, which suggested the possibility that with the right hearing aid he might acquire a more natural tone of talking and the necessary adjuncts—rhythm, accent, inflection. As soon as possible, he was given an audiometric test at the Western Electric office in Los Angeles. The technician was not able to give them an audiogram, a detailed chart, but thought John had about 15 percent usable hearing and recommended the company's most powerful instrument, a large air-conduction aid of the type used in schools. He was sorry, the man said, but the company didn't let their machines go out on trial. "Of course," said Louise, "we bought his machine."

A woman from the Gough School came to Van Nuys for a month over the summer of 1935 and worked with Johnny for three hours a day. At the end of summer, just as Spence was beginning work on *Riffraff*, she said that she was sure he heard enough to make residual training worthwhile. He had worked hard, and his speech showed considerable improvement. Louise, however, was not convinced the psychological effect had been good.

In the first place, John started out—perhaps we all did—with too much optimism. But, of course, we adults had understood the limitations both of John's hearing and of the instrument, and were experienced in disappointments. John had confidently expected the impossible. He was too young to appreciate the amount of intense and protracted work necessary to gain small results, although I do believe that the long uphill struggle with his leg, and his great patience and cooperation there, had given him an insight and philosophy beyond his years. Still, I am sure the labor must have seemed to him out of all proportion to any apparent gain, and his disappointment, as week followed week and no great change in his hearing took place, must have been keen.

It was a case of overdoing a good thing, and the whole experience, with all its attendant anxieties, left him apathetic and rebellious and unwilling to continue with even the short daily periods his mother attempted into the fall. When Johnny's tutor came back into the picture, she would have none of the hearing aid and consigned it to the closet. She said it was too much to fuss with in the scant ninety minutes they had together each day, and

that John had too little hearing to make any work with a hearing aid worthwhile. When Johnny wrote his autobiography in 1946, he made no mention
of it.

By September they knew that they liked the San Fernando Valley, its open
spaces, its solitude, its decidedly rural way of life. However hot the days
were, the nights were cool enough for blankets. "We also knew," said
Louise, "we wanted a home with more 'outside' than 'inside,' call it a ranch,
farm, or just 'place.' " Spence, now faced with a thirty-mile drive to the stu-
dio, stayed at the Beverly Wilshire during the week, coming home to Van
Nuys on Sundays or whenever he wasn't shooting a picture in Culver City.
They planted a vegetable garden, added three dogs (including a mate for
Pat named Queenie), more chickens, and a thoroughbred mare in foal.
Casually, they also began looking for property to buy.

Having worked in support to Jean Harlow for two solid months, Tracy
was now returned to Harry Rapf for a picture called *Whipsaw*. Again he was
cast in support of a big name, Myrna Loy, who had made a terrific hit as
Nora Charles opposite William Powell in *The Thin Man*. After being paired
again with Powell in a second picture and then loaned very profitably to
both Columbia and Paramount, Loy fled to Europe, feeling exploited and
unwilling to return until her compensation had been brought into line with
that of her costar. The ensuing standoff took almost a year to resolve; when
Loy returned to M-G-M in September 1935, she had been offscreen for nine
months.

Whipsaw was a caper movie, based on a story by James Edward Grant
that had appeared in *Liberty* magazine. Loy was an international jewel thief,
Tracy the undercover G-man trying to win her confidence. The script was
all thrust and parry, the kind of dialogue at which Loy had proven so adept
in her pictures with Powell. Tracy lacked Powell's elegance—the picture was
first conceived with Powell in mind—but made up for it with an earthiness
that played surprisingly well against Loy's composure and poise. Despite
their initial dustup over his drinking—perfectly justified, he later
acknowledged—Tracy had grown immensely fond of Jean Harlow during
the making of *Riffraff* and found Loy, in comparison, somewhat aloof.
"[S]he had me scared," Tracy admitted. "I didn't know how she'd feel about
[working with me]. And what worried me the most was kissing her."

Loy was on her way to becoming a big star, and Tracy covered his nervousness with banter. "He'd keep contrasting me to Jean, telling me what a
good sport she was, what a prima donna I was, and how her Victrola had
cheered them up on the set," the actress said in her autobiography. "In self-
defense, I finally took the hint. That began his long torch-carrying: I was

running and Spence was running after me. He would go out to [Riviera] and call my friend [and stand-in] Shirley Hughes to find out where I was. 'What difference does it make?' Shirley told him. 'She isn't going to see you.' Which I never did. I liked him, but not enough."

They completed *Whipsaw* in twenty-six days, and Tracy went back to polo, from which he had refrained during the course of production. Over the summer, Johnny had started to ride in the gymkhanas held every month at Riviera, entering the trotting and potato races, the flag relays, and the autograph races that required the participants to dismount and sign their names before remounting and galloping off toward the finishing line. He was watching the last chukker of a mixed game on Thanksgiving Day when his father rode up and told him to get out on the field and play. "I was very much surprised, as it seemed to me all of a sudden. I rode nervously onto the field and only trotted along with the players. Finally, about the middle of the chukker, I hit a ball two or three times for the first time while walking. Obviously, other players waited generously and let me do the job. I was very much excited and felt proud."

Tracy's contract with Metro required him to make one radio appearance in support of each film he did for the studio, and his first came up on November 29 when he and Harlow performed scenes from *Riffraff* on Louella Parsons' *Hollywood Hotel.* It was a national hookup, unusual for the time, as most network shows originated in either Chicago or New York City. Parsons used her muscle as columnist for the Hearst syndicate to get the industry's biggest stars to appear for little more in compensation than a case of Campbell's soup. The exposure was usually worth it, but for some film personalities the cost came in the terror of broadcasting live for an audience of some 20 million listeners. Tracy, for one, disliked the experience, but it wasn't what sent him off on another bender in the days that followed.

In the eighteen months since Loretta Young ended their relationship, she had starred or costarred in five motion pictures, including *The Crusades* for Cecil B. DeMille. Prior to making the DeMille picture she had gone on location to Mount Baker, Washington, for a film adaptation of the famed Jack London novel *Call of the Wild.* It was a rugged shoot, made all the more so by the volatile mix of personalities at its core. Jack Oakie was in the cast, as boisterous as he was on *Looking for Trouble,* and directing it, as he had that aforementioned film, was William A. Wellman. Something of a coup for 20th Century was Young's leading man—Clark Gable, borrowed from M-G-M. Then, of course, there was the flirtatious, semivirginal Loretta herself, now all of twenty-two years old.

Gable was married to a wealthy Houston socialite seventeen years his senior. (It was a "step-up" marriage, as his first wife—his acting coach—put

John Tracy on the field at Riviera, circa 1935.
(SUSIE TRACY)

it.) Ria Gable, a matronly fifty-one, was the lingering wife of Hollywood's biggest male star (and one of its most notorious cocksmen). With an Academy Award looming in his immediate future, Gable had already decided to seek a divorce when he left for Bellingham with Wellman's company in January 1935. Immediately, he fixed Loretta in his crosshairs, and the blizzard conditions on location only worked to his advantage. Once they began filming, she entered that dreamy zone she almost always occupied when acting opposite a man of just about any description. Gable had an animal-like quality, sexual and dangerous, and she began to regard him romantically. "I think every woman he ever met was in love with him," she said.

Gable's pursuit of her became an all-consuming goal that bordered on an obsession, and Wellman was so annoyed with his behavior, slowing progress on the picture as it did, that he made a very public issue of it. "I called him for it," Wellman said, "which I shouldn't have done in front of my company." Sometime during the making of the picture, Gable made his move and Loretta soon discovered that she was pregnant. After finishing a role in a minor film called *Shanghai,* she fled to Europe in the company of her mother. It wasn't unusual for an unmarried actress to hide a pregnancy, but it was uncommon to carry one to term and remain unmarried. The common remedy—abortion—wasn't an option for a practicing Catholic, and revealing the father as a married man would have amounted to professional suicide. Upon her return, the actress went into seclusion, illness and fatigue the official reasons.

There was, of course, a lot of talk, and it quickly got through to Tracy that for all the bum publicity he had endured over the course of their ten-month relationship, it was Gable, completely unfettered by Catholic chivalry, who had gotten her into the kip. He called and went to see her, her condition now more or less an open secret. Word of the baby's birth on November 6, 1935, spread like wildfire. With *Whipsaw* in the can, Tracy was seen out on the town, sometimes with Louise but usually stag, most often at Billy Wilkerson's Cafe Trocadero on the Sunset Strip. The food was expensive and not very good, but it was a handy hangout for a good many stars, much like a private club, and he could always count on seeing somebody he knew.

Tracy frequented comedian Frank Fay's Sunday night programs there and could be seen in wire photos greeting thirteen-year-old Judy Garland after her appearance as one of Fay's "undiscovered stars." When John Barrymore emerged from seclusion after fleeing nineteen-year-old Elaine Barrie, it was in Tracy's company at the Troc. And it was at Wilkerson's place on a Tuesday night in early December 1935 where Tracy overheard a reference to Loretta and a "baby with big ears" and shot to his feet. "Who said that?" he demanded and turned to find Wellman, on whose watch Gable's conquest had occurred.

Dottie Wellman was upstairs at the time and heard about the remark her husband made only after the two men had been separated. "He shouldn't have said that," she acknowledged. "Bill had a chip on his shoulder, especially when he was drinking." Tracy delivered a punch to Wellman's ribs, which the director countered, according to news reports, with a left to the ear. "He and I just didn't like each other," Wellman later said of Tracy. "We had a lot of fistfights, and I always beat him because he'd start talking and I didn't talk."*

Mutual friends interceded, and those two punches were the only ones landed that night. By the time their altercation made the papers, they were both minimizing the incident, seemingly bewildered by all the commotion. "We had a little misunderstanding, and the others in the place seem to have made quite a fight out of it," Tracy innocently told the *Examiner.* "There

---

* Wellman's claim to the contrary, this was the only documented fight between the two men.

were no hard feelings, and we've laughed about it since." Added Wellman, laying it on a bit thick: "We've been friends a long, long time and made a couple of pictures together. It was merely a case of misunderstanding which has all been straightened out, and I can't for the life of me understand why so much fuss is being made about it."

Neither would confirm the name of the actress involved, but the story made the wire services and at least one of the New York dailies ran both her name and photo alongside Tracy's and capped them with the headline FAIR LORETTA'S KNIGHT. As columnist Jimmy Starr wrote the next day, "The beaut that caused the fistic row between Bill Wellman and Spencer Tracy is certainly getting more than her share of nasty talk. Why doesn't Hollywood leave her alone?"

Whipsaw, released on December 6, was sold almost entirely on the strength of Myrna Loy's return to the screen. It took a dive in New York, but did better elsewhere, pulling in nearly $1 million in rentals on an investment of $238,000. By pairing him first with Loy, then with Harlow—*Riffraff* hadn't yet been released—Metro was getting audiences used to seeing Tracy with top-tier female stars. The next step would be to put their top male stars alongside him—Gable, Powell, and maybe Beery as well. It was a strategy Tracy could appreciate, one that Fox never could have embarked upon, even had it occurred to somebody to try. For Christmas, everyone in the extended family got a card from Spence and a check for fifty dollars, the studio's return address and Carroll's careful handwriting on the envelope. ("Fifty dollars in the 1930s was a helluva Christmas," said Frank Tracy.) Louise made a pitch of her own for a gift when she suggested that Spence give up drinking altogether. "I just think it would be better for you all around, don't you?"

And so, on December 20, 1935, Tracy took the pledge and declared himself on the wagon.

Norman Krasna was a hot commodity, a balding twenty-five-year-old at work on a slick comedy for Clark Gable when an article in the *Nation* gave him an idea for a play. There had been a lynching in San Jose following the kidnapping of a department store heiress, and Krasna began to wonder what would have happened if the men they hanged had been innocent. "I told my idea to [M-G-M story editor] Sam Marx and [producer] Joe Mankiewicz. They were crazy about it."

Sometime later, after Krasna had left M-G-M, Mankiewicz told the story to Louis B. Mayer. Mayer found the subject distasteful but told Mankiewicz, who had exactly one picture to his credit, that he could do it anyway. "I'm going to let you make this film, young man, and I'm going to spend as much money advertising this picture as Irving Thalberg spends on *Romeo and Juliet*. Otherwise, if it fails, you'll always say we didn't get behind it properly. This way, I'm going to prove to you that this picture won't make a nickel. Now go make it!"

When they phoned Krasna in New York to purchase the story, he said he had pretty much forgotten it. "I had to dictate it as he'd told it to me," Mankiewicz said, "so that he could sell it to M-G-M." The two pages that bagged Krasna a $15,000 payday told the story of Joe Wilson, a young lawyer on his honeymoon in California's Imperial Valley. A sheriff's assistant throws him in jail on the day a kidnapping has taken place. The men of the town decide to lynch the alleged perpetrator and a mob forms around the jail. Word reaches the governor, who dispatches a troop of militia to guard the jail. Unable to get to the prisoner, the angry townspeople set fire to the building instead, burning it to the ground. "The gimmick, the hook, the invention, the *inspiration*," said Krasna, "is that he is still alive." When Joe appears to witness the hangings of the vigilantes who left him for dead, the district attorney stops the executions in the nick of time. As Joe sinks into a chair, he buries his head in his hands and says, "But they killed my dog—didn't they?"

Mankiewicz already had the ideal director for Krasna's story in the person of Fritz Lang. David O. Selznick, Mayer's son-in-law, had brought Lang to the studio in 1934. Selznick put him on a project called *The Journey* and paired him with a writer named Oliver H. P. Garrett, but nothing ever came of it. As a screenwriter, Mankiewicz had been assigned to work with Lang because he could speak German.

"I went over and talked to Fritz a couple of times, and I found it very difficult to work with him because he had his office all rigged up as though it was a German office at UFA. He had drawings—what they call a storyboard today—all around the walls. He was working on a version of an old film he made in Germany called *Dr. Mabuse*. He wanted to make an American version which would involve a crooked district attorney. I got very confused, because I just didn't see stories that way. I wanted to know the characters in the film before we started picking camera angles."

Selznick left the studio to form his own company, and Mankiewicz told the front office he wanted Lang as the director of *Mob Rule*. In America, Lang's reputation was based largely on his brilliant 1931 production of *M*, the story of a man hunted down as a murderer of children. He drew the assignment to direct *Mob Rule* about the same time Tracy encountered Mankiewicz for the first time at the M-G-M commissary.

About to start *Riffraff*, Tracy heard the story in much the same way L. B. Mayer had, but his reaction was much different: "I remember playing *The Baby Cyclone* in Boston the night Sacco and Vanzetti were electrocuted," he later said. "The execution was to take place at midnight, and when I got out of the theater at eleven o'clock, the Boston Common was filled with people protesting the execution. The undercurrent of violence was frightening. It's easy to see, after watching a thing like that, how mob hysteria can whip up riots or lynchings."

Lang and screenwriter Leonard Praskins began work on a script by looking at the story from three different perspectives: the wife ("a typical American girl, married to a man in a very good social position"), the mob ("people in a small town—blacksmiths, gas station men, tailors, uneducated people"), and the man through whose character they decided all three of the stories could most effectively be told.

"Spencer Tracy," wrote Lang,

> is a lawyer, a very idealistic type of man who believes that the man is good, that crime is only a disease, that criminals are unhappy people and that the law is there to help them. He is an idealist, an optimist . . . When this lynching occurs to him his philosophy breaks down . . . This man must be made in black and white, not in color hues. Short scenes can give us this man's character. Need no long dialogue scenes . . . I think his guilt is that this man who always believed that he was an idealist tries to do something for personal revenge. He does not try to understand how everything happened. He does not try to understand what drove these people to this uprising. He now has only one idea. He suffered unbelievably. He wants revenge. This is his guilt.

One of the more memorable characters on the M-G-M lot was a former title writer and gag man named Robert E. "Bob" Hopkins. "Hoppy," as he was known to just about everyone, was the closest thing to a handyman they had when it came to a script, and when he wasn't on a set somewhere, a cigarette dangling from his mouth, he was lurking in the studio commissary or standing on the corner—"the crossroads" they called it—ready to nab a producer and shout an idea at him. Tall and profane, Hoppy was easy to laugh off, but the words that shot out of him sometimes amounted to story gold if anyone bothered to pay attention.*

"I was walking along the street one day on the lot," recalled Jeanette MacDonald,

---

* It was Hopkins who once referred to one of the M-G-M producers as "the asbestos curtain between the audience and the entertainment."

and he yelled across, "Hey Jeanette, I've got a hell of an idea for you and Clark Gable." He came rushing over to me. I said, "Oh you have? What is it?" So we stood there and he talked to me and told me this wonderful idea he had. I must confess it was exciting. But he said, "You know I can't get to first base with the g.d. thing." I said, "What do you mean, Bob?" He said, "Well, I'm getting the run-around. I try to see Eddie Mannix and he's too busy, I've tried to see Thalberg and he's too busy. I've just tried to see everybody and nobody wants to see me. Look, I think you could do something with it. They all like you up there. You go up and tell them you like the idea."

Hoppy's idea had size and punch. According to Gottfried Reinhardt, son of Max Reinhardt and new to the studio, it consisted of just six words: " 'San Francisco—earthquake—atheist becomes religious.' That was his idea."

MacDonald went to Mannix. "You see, at this point I was going pretty strong at Metro, having just done *Naughty Marietta* and *Merry Widow,* which surprised them all. Mannix said, 'Would you like to do it?' I said, 'Yes I would like to do it, providing we get a decent script out of it.' "

The earliest bit of extant writing on *San Francisco* is a draft of the opening sequence by Herman Mankiewicz, Joe's elder brother, dated January 9, 1935. The full screenplay, however, was the work of Anita Loos, the tiny novelist and screenwriter who, like Hopkins, had spent her childhood in San Francisco. According to her, the character she and Hopkins envisioned for Gable was based on the late playwright and scam artist Wilson Mizner, who had once run a gambling house on Long Island. Sometime in April, Loos' progress on the script was halted, presumably when Gable said he would not do the picture.

"I was all for *San Francisco,*" MacDonald said,

because I felt like the mother of it in a way. Since Hoppy had said, "This is a picture for you and Gable," I was stuck with this, this idea had clung to me, and then I found out that Mr. Gable didn't want to do it. The story that came to me from Mr. Mannix was, "Who wants to sit there with egg on his face while she sings? Nobody can do anything while she's singing." (He may not have used that expression then but that's what he meant.) That was primarily his reason for not wanting to be in *San Francisco.*

So they started to mention this one and that one and I kept saying, "No, no, no. It's for Gable and me and I'll wait." They said,

"What do you mean you'll wait? Gable has another commitment. He says he doesn't want to do it anyway." "Will he do it after his other commitment?" "Well, yes, he has to. He doesn't have it in his contract that he can sit back and say no." I said, "All right, I'll wait until this other commitment is finished."

You see, my contract called for so much a picture. I wasn't on a long-term contract but on a picture-to-picture basis. So many pictures and each picture was a certain price and the price rose with each picture, plus a guarantee of so many weeks. After that, I got prorated money if it ran overtime. So when I found I would have to wait another six months in order to do a whole picture, contractually and financially they said, "Either we do it or we don't do it, and how are we going to get around it?" I said, "I'll wait" and they said, "What are you going to do about the pay?" I said, "I'll just forfeit the pay. Just let it go, and I'll sit out the six months that I should be paid for because I want Gable that badly. I think Gable is right for it." Then some stupid person told Gable that I had said I would wait and that I had said I wanted him for my picture. He said, "*Her* picture??" You see? Immediately he was rubbed the wrong way.

Work on the script resumed in the fall, when the film was assigned to producer Bernard H. Hyman, a Thalberg protégé, and W. S. "Woody" Van Dyke, the director of MacDonald's two previous movies for the studio. ("We just seemed to think alike," MacDonald said of Van Dyke.) The genial Hyman initiated a series of story conferences with Hopkins, Loos, her husband John Emerson, and Van Dyke, working not so much on developing the relationship between Gable's character, Blackie Norton, and MacDonald's Mary Blake, a prim country preacher's daughter, but rather the more shaded and complex story of Blackie, the Barbary Coast gambler, and his childhood friend, Father Tim Mullin. It would be Mullin's job, with the help of the 1906 quake, to open up Blackie's spiritual side, and it had to be credible—couldn't be sappy. Quickly, they got down to business: Blackie and Tim clashing over Blackie's exploitation of Mary, Blackie's frantic search for Mary before the hall is dynamited, Blackie thanking God when he finds she's okay. It was, as Loos later described it, "unadulterated soap opera," and the proper casting of the priest became the key to making it work.

Typically, priests in movies were played by character men—Edward Arnold in *The White Sister,* Leo Carrillo in *Manhattan Melodrama,* Walter Connolly in *Father Brown, Detective.* Casting a lead actor as the priest in *San Francisco* would be a bold move, giving the conflict over Mary a sizzling undercurrent of sexual tension. When the idea of playing Father Mullin was first broached to Spencer Tracy (who was anticipating *Mob Rule* as his next picture), he was, as Louise put it, "a little dubious about doing a priest." Not only did he feel a terrific sense of responsibility in representing the church to a mass audience, but there was also a hesitancy that grew from his own conviction that maybe he should never have become an actor in the first place. It was a thing he almost never spoke of, but Pat O'Brien heard him say it on more than one occasion, and he repeated it once to Shakespearean scholar and author John McCabe.

"What was it, do you figure, Pat, that made Tracy such an unhappy man?" McCabe asked O'Brien one night over drinks at the Lambs Club. "It's a real mystery, isn't it?"

"No, it's not," O'Brien replied. "At least three times Spence told me why it was." According to Pat, Tracy had never lost the deeply held nostalgia many Irish Catholic boys felt for the *idea* of being a priest, like one of the bright, enviable Jesuits from their prep school days. "Each time he told me he was pretty much in the bag, but he was telling the truth. I can remember once when he was looking out over the ocean, nuzzling a bottle, when he told me this. His unhappiness—he said—was that always deep down he had the feeling that perhaps he had spurned his real vocation—to the priesthood."

As Tracy once explained it, "I was seventeen, maybe sixteen, and I was going to a Jesuit school—Marquette Academy. And you know how it is in a place like that—the influence is strong, very strong, intoxicating. The priests are all such superior men—heroes. You want to be like them—we all did. Every guy in the school probably thought some—more or less—about trying for the cloth."

Had there, in fact, once been a calling? And was he now being asked to act a role he had spurned in real life? "I was awful scared of playing a priest," he later acknowledged in an interview. "Sure, I couldn't see myself in that part—or other people accepting me. I was afraid people would get mad at me for trying to play something like that." To Van Dyke he put it more bluntly: "I'm a Roman Catholic and you know the thing that happened not long ago [meaning the affair with Loretta Young]. I wouldn't have the *crust* to play a priest." It was Van Dyke, he said, who talked him into it, who told him that he'd make him "eat" those words. "I honestly didn't think I ought to try it. I said I'd go ahead if I had to, but I didn't like the idea one bit."

On January 24, 1936, the decision was announced by Edwin Schallert in the pages of the *Los Angeles Times:* "Instead of two stars of the first magnitude, *San Francisco,* [a] depiction of the old days in the great west coast city, is to have three luminaries. As is known, Clark Gable and Jeanette MacDonald for some time have been assigned to this cast, and yesterday Spencer Tracy was added . . . Start of *San Francisco* is programmed as soon as Gable returns from Mexico, which will be in about a week. Gable and Miss MacDonald have never previously appeared in a picture together, and casting Tracy with the stars is also an innovation."

Tracy had known Gable since 1929, when he replaced him in the troubled play that came to be known as *Conflict*. The following year, Gable was offered the role of Killer Mears in the West Coast production of *The Last Mile*. The offer had come from the husband-wife producing team of Louis MacLoon and Lillian Albertson, for whom Gable had worked off and on since 1925. Albertson caught Gable in New York, where he had just closed in a play at the Eltinge Theatre. Tracy was rounding up guards and executing hostages next door at the Harris, but Gable hadn't yet seen him.

"Here we were," said Gable, "working alongside each other, and I couldn't see his play and he couldn't see mine—while mine lasted—because we worked the same hours, matinees included." Gable and his wife caught *The Last Mile:* "I watched Spence as Killer Mears for two acts, and I said to myself, 'That's for me.' I rushed out and wired the producer I was taking the midnight train."

Gable impressed playgoers at the Majestic Theatre in Los Angeles, where *The Last Mile* had a brief but notable run. John Wexley thought him better in the part of Mears than Tracy ("less self-conscious, more dynamic") and director William Wyler shot a test of him for Universal. By the end of the year, Gable was under contract to M-G-M, while Tracy was similarly committed to Fox. "Hollywood didn't have any Lambs Club where we could bump into each other," Gable said, "but both of us went out more in those days. Every now and then we'd meet at some night club or some party and we'd sit around and take the picture business apart." The two men also occasionally saw each other at Riviera, where Gable briefly tried polo and was, in Tracy's early judgment, pretty good.

They began shooting *San Francisco* on Valentine's Day, 1936, Gable reeking of garlic in a rousing show of contempt for his leading lady. ("Gable is a <u>mess!</u>" she complained to her manager Bob Ritchie. "I've never been more disappointed in anyone in my life.") Tracy did his first work as Father Mullin the following day and surprised some members of the crew with his level of professionalism. "I'd heard all the stories about him at Fox, that he'd go off on drinking sprees," said Joe Newman, Van Dyke's assistant director on the picture. "He didn't on *San Francisco;* he was fine. He was always on time. He was perfect in his lines. Everything I'd heard about him, he erased."

Clad in black cassock and biretta, Tracy played a brief phone exchange with Gable, then presided over a nighttime organ recital at the rescue mission. MacDonald sang "The Holy City" ("Jerusalem, Jerusalem"), then took part in an expository scene in which Tracy provided the backstory on Blackie Norton, "the most Godless, scoffing and unbelieving soul in all San Francisco," and a little on himself as well. "Blackie and I were kids together—born and brought up on the Coast. We used to sell newspapers in the joints along Pacific Street. Blackie was the leader of all the kids in the neighborhood, and I was his pal." He tells her he's tried to do something with Blackie for years, but that "maybe I'm not the right one."

It was one of the most critical movie scenes Tracy had ever played, and he played it as he played all scenes, with simplicity and honesty and a conviction that he was the character in all its natural shadings. The authority he exuded was unalloyed with theatrical tricks or the calculations of a leading man suddenly beyond his depth. If he had any fear, it was the fear of artificiality, the fear that lifelong Catholics would look at Father Tim and see a movie star pretending to be a priest and not the soul of a real priest, with a hardscrabble childhood in his background and wisdom as to the ways of the Barbary Coast.

There was an effort to load Tracy's principal scenes toward the front of the schedule, as the start of *Mob Rule* was looming and no one knew quite what to expect of Fritz Lang. There was tension between Gable and Van Dyke, Gable and the front office. "I like Tracy very much," MacDonald wrote after two weeks on the picture. "There's as much difference between the two as day from nite. Gable acts as tho' he were really too bored to play the scenes with me. Typical <u>ham.</u>"

Mob Rule went into production just six days after *San Francisco,* destined to be as grueling a shoot as Tracy had ever endured. ("2 months on wagon," he noted in his datebook.) Lang, meticulous in his preparation, had taken nearly six months to get the script into shape, and by the starting date had storyboarded the entire film. The girl in the story was Sylvia Sidney, a first-rate actress who had heard about Lang making his American film debut and took a substantial cut in price to be part of it. She respected and admired his work, she said, and thought it important to work for him, to "back him up" after his escape from the Nazis.

San Francisco was a big, boisterous carnival of a film, festooned with balloons and good cheer and enveloped in the kind of candy apple coating that was emblematic of the Metro-Goldwyn-Mayer school of moviemaking. *Mob Rule,* on the other hand, was anything but. Grim and Teutonic, it had none of the high spirits for which the studio was typically known, and Tracy found himself stepping from Father Tim's chapel office, brewing coffee for the chaste Mary Blake, to the opening shots of *Mob Rule,* in which he and Sidney portrayed all the lust and frustration an engaged couple could possibly feel in the hours prior to a long separation. Joe can't keep his eyes off Katherine and she can't keep her hands off him. They munch peanuts, coo words of love, and when they're separated by the window of a Pullman car they press the glass as if electricity were passing between them. Sam Katz, the Chicago theater executive who was Mankiewicz's titular boss, sensed the carnal energy of the rushes and sent Lang a note: "I saw your first day's work and I am delighted. I am leaving today on a trip for about two weeks and I am sorry I will not be here with you during this period. However, I know you are going to give us a great picture."

Tracy was used to making one take, two at the most, and was completely unaccustomed to the multiple takes Lang routinely insisted upon. One of the ways the local sheriff puts his suspect at ease early in the film is by noting the character's fondness for peanuts. ("Some peanuts?" actor Edward Ellis asks during the interrogation scene, casually setting a bowl of salted nuts in front of him.) Tracy had done take after take, accepting a handful of nuts and tossing them into his mouth. "Well, now you're talking my language, Sheriff. I've—." And the line was aborted with an explosive cough.

"Cut," said Lang impassively. "Bring this peanut addict a glass of water, somebody."

Tracy's face reddened as he spat out the chewed remains. "This guy," he said, indicating Lang, "is trying to kill me with salted peanuts—a new variety of murder. So far, I've had to eat fourteen bags in succession."

"Uh, no, Spence," corrected the prop man. "Only thirteen."

After quietly printing what he wanted, Lang kept it up, torturing Tracy until Sylvia Sidney signaled him that the scene was already in the can. "I'll get even," Tracy grinned as he stepped out of camera range. "This picture isn't finished yet by a long shot."

After vigorously pursuing the part of Katherine and turning down another picture to take it, Sylvia Sidney found herself unfazed by Lang's temperament. "Fritz had a big ego, to put it bluntly. When he walked on the set, he was the master of the show. He wasn't that tough on me, because he had to get what he wanted on film. He was rough on men . . . Tracy had a very rough time with him."

Lang seemed to regard his players as graphic elements; his rigidity put him at odds with his lead actor, a man who needed the latitude to inhabit a character and make him breathe. For Tracy, the real trick to *Mob Rule* was managing the transformation from the solid, good-natured Joe Wilson, all-around straight arrow, eyes shining with a kind of textbook virtue, to the grim, vengeful shell of a man on the other side of the fire, a walking corpse animated by the sheer power of hate. It wasn't Lang that gave it to him, yet it's hard to imagine quite the same effect from another director. Given a comfortable forty-eight-day schedule, Lang, completely unaccustomed to

Tracy and Clark Gable shoot their first scene together for *San Francisco,* 1936.
(SUSIE TRACY)

working in a studio where meal breaks were dictated by law, proceeded to direct *Mob Rule* as if he were back at Babelsberg.

"Lang," said Joe Mankiewicz,

would have his secretary, affectionately known as The Iron Butter-fly, bring on a small silver tray—it might have been a vitamin pill or something more horrible. I don't know. And a little shot of cognac which Mr. Lang would have as his lunch and continue working. And the crew started grumbling a bit . . . and the crew came to Spence and said, "Look, what about our lunch?" And so he says, "Yeah, it's getting late." And he looked over at Fritz and said, "Mr. Lang, it's one-thirty and the fellows haven't had their lunch yet. Don't you think we ought to break?" And Lang said, "On my set, Mr. Tracy, I will call lunch when I think it should be called." And Spence took it with that wonderful look, that meek look—and look out when he looked at you meekly—and just took his hand and brushed it across his face, smeared the makeup hopelessly. Take an hour and a half to replace that makeup. And he yelled "Lunch!" and walked, and the crew went with him.

The contrast between *Mob Rule* and *San Francisco* could not have been more stark. Where Lang lingered over a scene, making take after take, Van Dyke got in and out as quickly as possible. "He gained a lot by having the actors fresh," Joe Newman said. "He had that momentum going for him, where he let the actors have sway. If they understood the part, he didn't indulge in a lot of explanation, and he didn't believe in a lot of rehearsal." Though his speed worked largely to the cast's advantage—no heavy breathing or time for second thoughts—Van Dyke's stuff tended to be ragged as it came off the stage, and Hyman was already ordering retakes just three days into the schedule.

Tracy was needed only occasionally and seemed to regard his time on the picture as something of a vacation. Still, where *Mob Rule* was well within his comfort zone as an actor, *San Francisco* decidedly was not. "We were pretty serious all through that picture," Gable recalled. "We both had our worries. He was worried about playing a priest, and I was worried about playing an atheist. I had a scene where I was supposed to hit him. How was the public going to take that—seeing a man strike a priest? It took three real priests to convince me I could do it safely if the script had me reforming in the end, and believing."

The conflict between the two boyhood friends—one who became a roisterer, the other a priest—had been built into the script from the very beginning, when Herman Mankiewicz drafted the first sequence and made notes concerning the general tone and structure of the story. The character of "Father Jim" was introduced during a sparring match with his pal "Aces" Hatfield in which the two traded dialogue between punches. ("No dame's on the level," Aces says, to which Jim responds with a quick jab to the chin.) It was Mankiewicz's idea that the camera reveal Jim as a priest only after he has changed his clothes and emerged from the locker room in the Roman collar. By the time the scene was shot some thirteen months later, Jim had become Tim, Aces had become Blackie, and the scene had been sharpened by Anita Loos with a shot of Tim knocking Blackie clear off his feet, thus establishing that Tim could flatten Blackie if he so wished—a vivid image the audience, in its collective memory, would later call to mind when Blackie socks Tim and the priest, in effect, turns the other cheek.

The heated scene in which Blackie pops Father Tim establishes Mary as the force that comes between the two men. All aglitter in gold braid, black tights, and plumed headdress, she is about to walk out onstage at the Paradise Music Hall, where she will become, in Blackie's words, "Queen of the Coast."

"Are you out of your mind?" Tim asks incredulously as he takes her in.

"Why?" asks Blackie innocently.

"Showing Mary like this to that mob out there."

Mary tells Tim that she loves Blackie.

"It isn't love to let him drag you down to his level."

Blackie tells Tim he's going to marry her, and Tim, with eyes narrowed and jaw set, says, "Not if I can stop you, you're not going to marry her. You can't take a woman in marriage and then sell her immortal soul." He puts out his hand and asks Mary to come with him. The stage manager is knocking, they're striking up the band.

"I've listened to this psalm-singing blather of yours for years and never squawked," says Blackie. "But you can't bring it in here. This is *my* joint!"

"She's not going out there!" Tim says firmly, and Blackie hauls off and socks him—a moment of shock for both the characters and the audience.

Gable, who never warmed up to MacDonald, marveled at Spence's seemingly effortless work as the priest: "I couldn't see what Tracy was worried about. He said he felt like a man walking a tightrope. He had to be human and, at the same time, holy. For my money, he hit the perfect balance between the two from the opening scene."

Tracy observed his thirty-sixth birthday while working on both pictures (*Mob Rule* by that time had acquired the title *Fury*) and he came to regard them as "that double jackpot"—the two best things that had happened to him in his six years on the screen. "When Sylvia Sidney and I put in 21 hours a day on *Fury*, we did it because we knew that Lang had something; that it would be something worthwhile. It was the same with *San Francisco*. It was all the difference between that 'just a job' feeling that I'd once had in pictures and the conviction that we were getting somewhere."

The time Lang took seemed partially rooted in the mistaken notion that he had to wear Tracy down in order to get his best performance. According to Joe Mankiewicz, who felt somewhat responsible for Lang's treatment of the cast and crew ("I put my own personal guarantee that he was great for this movie"), one of the key scenes Lang put into the script was the mob's ghostly pursuit of Joe in the hours leading up to their conviction for murder. "Now figure Spence in an overcoat . . . the overcoat flapping in the wind, at night on the back lot, down a very narrow passage followed by a camera car, running for his life. And Fritz Lang letting the car go faster, faster, faster until Tracy *was* running for his life."

Tracy and Lang grew to hate each other, and cinematographer Joe Ruttenberg found himself in the middle. "Spencer Tracy said, 'I can't stand this any longer,' but it was Spencer's first major part [at M-G-M], you know, so he wouldn't quit. He argued with Lang, and the officers in back of me said, 'You do whatever you think.' Mannix says, 'If they can't get along with Joe, they can't get along with anybody.' " Tracy consistently gave Ruttenberg what he needed, even when he was at odds with Lang. "In shooting, he knew what he had to do, he minded his own business, he did his work,

With actress Sylvia Sidney during production of *Fury*.
(PATRICIA MAHON COLLECTION)

went back to his dressing room. But he fought with Fritz all the time. They were always fighting, always fighting."

San Francisco was a film largely written by committee, producer Bernie Hyman holding story conferences with his key people—Hopkins, Loos, Emerson—every few days while the picture was in production. Retakes continued into the first week of April, when the group turned its collective attention to the problem of putting the great earthquake together. The mechanical effects developed by Arnold "Buddy" Gillespie, one of three associate art directors on the show, formed the nucleus of the sequence, principally the quake as experienced from the interior of Lyric Hall as the annual Chickens' Ball is in progress. The set was built on rockers, with breakaway walls of rubber brick and balsa wood, but much of the effect was achieved with the simple combination of jiggling camera and off-balance actors, inserts showing small details of the devastation, the ominous rumblings of the soundtrack setting the nerves on edge.

With his proud mother on the set of *San Francisco*.
(AUTHOR'S COLLECTION)

Tracy, who observed the shooting of the scene even though he wasn't in it, recalled that it was covered with seven cameras. There were 250 extras on the stage, and Van Dyke was careful to explain what they were to do once he gave them the signal. As soon as the building started to shake, though, everyone panicked and surged to one corner. The balcony collapsed, which wasn't planned, but since no one was injured, the shot stayed in the film. Exteriors—cracking walls, falling debris—were intercut with actors in motion. Whole buildings were crumbled in miniature, bit players fleeing for their lives in front of a process screen. One of the few mechanical effects to incorporate stunt personnel was the splitting of the earth, a shot accomplished with a section of street built on rollers, a hydraulic ram driving rocks and dirt up through the rupture, water spewing through an underground pipe to complete the effect. Tracy didn't have to endure the simulated quake but was called upon to step gingerly through the rubble in its aftermath, calmly leading the dazed and broken Gable through the tent city of survivors and back into the arms of Jeanette MacDonald, who has weathered the experience in fine voice and feathered gown, every hair in place and her makeup perfect.

When *San Francisco* was cut together, the result left Hyman and his colleagues deflated. "The earthquake was flat, impersonal, ineffectual," said John Hoffman, who was brought from Slavko Vorkapich's montage unit to fix the problem. "It didn't touch people." Hoffman set to work giving the picture "a brand new, really convincing quake" as well as a rowdy New Year's Eve celebration to serve as its bookend. He shot new material—a stone Atlas pitching forward and smashing a vegetable wagon, its horse rearing, its stock rolling, a solitary wheel spinning aimlessly being one of his more memorable images—but his contribution principally was in the editing, the juxtaposition of disaster footage with the reactions of the people in danger, the rhythmic cuts giving size and immediacy to otherwise ponderous footage. But all this was after the fact for Tracy, who did his last work in the film on Saturday, April 25, 1936.

The more modestly proportioned *Fury* finished two days later, but there were retakes that kept the film open until May 6. The last days were given over to exteriors, largely night work that convinced Joe Ruttenberg that Lang was genuinely a sadist. "He was hell on everybody—actors, technicians, everybody." The centerpiece of the picture was the mob's storming of the jail, and Ruttenberg remembered it being scheduled for a Saturday night so that the company could go straight through without a break. "We worked like slaves," said Tracy. "One day we worked from nine in the morning until five-thirty the next." Mankiewicz heard that some of the crew members were plotting to drop a piece of equipment on Lang to get him off the picture. "Well, it went from that bad to much worse," he said, "till I was summoned from my house one night about four-thirty in the morning. Tracy said, 'Bring the lamp.' He was going to drop it on Lang."

The sheriff's standoff with the mob began with sharp words and angry demands, then accelerated to the hurling of rocks and bottles. Retreating into the jail, the sheriff's men barricade the doors, firing tear gas out the windows. The ringleaders start battering down the doors, and upstairs Joe Wilson, Lang's everyman, calls out desperately to anyone within earshot: "Jailer! Jailer! Can't anyone hear me? Let me out! I'll talk to 'em! Let me out! Give me a chance!" The mob pushes past the sheriff and his men and overruns the jail, but when they find the keys are beyond their reach, they torch the building instead. Stroking his dog, hard against the corner of his cell, Joe watches helplessly as the smoke thickens and begins to curl around them. "Well, Rainbow, it doesn't look so good for us." And down below, as the mob grotesquely watches the building burn in utter silence, Katherine pushes her way through in time to see Joe's anguished face framed in a barred window and faints dead away.

The last segment, shot midway through production when Tracy and Lang were still on speaking terms, was Joe's appearance in court after Katherine has discovered that he is still alive. He witnesses the conviction of the people responsible for the torching of the jail, then makes his entrance. The mob's de facto leader, Dawson, clambers over the others and is sprinting toward the door when he freezes in midstride, his eyes wide with astonishment. There, in reverse, is the dead man himself, moving purposefully toward the bench, clean-shaven once again, his three-piece suit suggesting the very image of a model citizen. "Your honor," he says, "I am Joseph Wilson." And the court erupts in a roar of disbelief.

> I know by coming here I saved the lives of these twenty-two people. But that isn't why I'm here. I don't care anything about saving them. They're murderers. I know the law says they're not because I'm still alive, but that's not their fault. And the law doesn't know that a lot of things that were very important to me—silly things, maybe—like a belief in justice, and an idea that men were civilized, and a feeling of pride that this country of mine was different from all others—the law doesn't know that those things were burned to death within me that night. I came here today for my own sake. I couldn't stand it anymore. I couldn't stop thinking about them with every breath and every step I took. And I didn't believe Katherine when she said—Katherine is the young lady who was going to marry me. Maybe some day after I've paid for what I did there'll be a chance to begin again. And then maybe Katherine and I—

As Lang envisioned the film's final moments, Joe could be seen fumbling in his pocket, and as he says the last words of his statement, his eyes come to rest on what he has pulled from his pocket, nestled among tobacco crumbs and lint—a solitary salted peanut. "I guess that's about all I can say," he says and pops it into his mouth. Instantly, the scene would cut to a close-up of Katherine. "Her eyes dimmed with tears, her face aglow in recognition of the Joe she fell in love with, she moves toward him, smiling her forgiveness. 'Joe—' She moves closer and closer until her face, smiling with tremendous happiness, blots out everything and the picture fades out."

Lang later blamed Mankiewicz and the administrators of the Production Code for being forced to shoot an alternate ending in which Tracy and Sidney embrace in court and actually kiss at the fade-out. "A man gives a speech that . . . is very well written and extremely well delivered, and then suddenly, for no reason whatsoever—in front of the judge and the audience and God knows who—they turn around and they kiss each other. For me, a perfect ending was when he said, 'Here I stand. I cannot do otherwise. God help me.' You could have shown a closeup of Sylvia Sidney—she's very happy—he could look at her—period."

The idea of the kiss came from somewhere inside M-G-M, as the Production Code Administration's correspondence on the film makes no mention of it. The order to reshoot the close-up of Katherine may well have come from Sam Katz, whose memory of those first desperate rushes would surely have suggested a climactic embrace for the couple. In communicating the order to retake the shot, Mankiewicz told Lang, speaking of the original ending, "Frankly, I agree with you that <u>if this holds up before an audience,</u> it is to be preferred as an ending." Dutifully, both Tracy and Sidney played the scene as prescribed, and *Fury* finished after fifty-five turbulent days.

"It was a horrendous test under fire," Mankiewicz concluded, "particularly for someone like Spencer. It was an important part, an emotional part. And then, of course, to have . . . a finish of which everybody connected with the picture can only be ashamed." It wasn't the clinch that undercut the film's impact when it had its initial showing, though, but rather the scene in which Lang had the voices and images of the convicted men following Joe down those deserted streets of the city. "We had a first preview," said Mankiewicz, "at which the film was literally laughed off the screen because Lang had [that] sequence in which ghosts chased Spencer Tracy through the streets. He turned around and the ghosts would disappear behind trees à la Walt Disney. Obviously, that sequence had to be cut out of the film, but Fritz refused to cut anything. It was Eddie Mannix who fired Fritz off the lot and told me to cut the film.* The subsequent preview was a smashing success, after that one deletion, and the reviews were rapturous."

But with the motivating sequence removed from the picture, Lang was left to flounder when questioned about the surrendering of Joe Wilson. "I've often been asked if Tracy gives himself up because of social consciousness or something like that," he said to Peter Bogdanovich in 1965. "I don't think so. I think this man gives himself up because he can't go on living

---

* "It's all very well for you directors to want to make pictures with messages in them," Lang said he was told, "but just remember that Cinderella paid this company $8 million last year—and $8 million can't be wrong." The Cinderella story on the current schedule, of course, was *San Francisco*.

with an eternal lie—he couldn't go through life with it. It's too easy an explanation to say social consciousness makes me do something. One acts because of emotions, personal emotions."

Fritz Lang left M-G-M a bitter man, blaming Joe Mankiewicz for the cutting of a key sequence and the sweetening of the climax. After the film's release, Mankiewicz approached him at the Hollywood Brown Derby and offered his hand in friendship and congratulation, and Lang, to his later regret, refused it. His dislike of Tracy was more subtle, as he never had anything but praise for Tracy's performance in the film. Yet he told Mankiewicz's biographer, Kenneth L. Geist, that Tracy's alcoholism had indirectly delayed the picture. "My friend Peter Lorre, a former drug addict, explained to me that when people are deprived of a craving, they turn to something else—Lorre to drink, Tracy to whorehouses. I assume that's where he'd disappear after lunch, since he didn't come back till four o'clock. I'd be sitting there with the whole crew, wanting to work, when he'd arrive and say, 'Fritz, I want to invite the crew to have coffee.' "

Tracy's habit was to have a rubdown at lunch—and a brief nap if he could manage it—but he was present throughout for *Fury* and only a conflict with the *San Francisco* company could have deprived Lang of his services. Mankiewicz, furthermore, thought Lang's insinuation ludicrous. "I don't think Spence went to whorehouses!" he erupted when asked to comment on Lang's statement in 1992. "He was much too busy with the ladies! If there ever was an actor who had no reason EVER to go to a whorehouse, it was Spencer Tracy!" He called Lang's statement "the most unbelievable lie" and then went into the business of the three-hour delay. "How can that be? When Clark Gable was late one half-hour, forty minutes late, on a Victor Fleming movie . . . Eddie Mannix showed up on the set. Because the [assistant director's] report goes in: 'Mr. Gable showed up at such-and-such a time . . . ' And they come right down. 'Why were you late?' Clark, forty-five minutes late, and they ate his ass out. Those stories . . . if he didn't show up til four o'clock, what did the crew do? These things are impossible, but they are believed."

Though Tracy thought *Fury* a "great document" and a "powerful movie," he maintained a respectful silence on the subject of its legendary director and vowed never again to work with the man. "Fritz Lang, the director, is a German," he said tartly in his only public comment on the subject, "and has a technique all his own."

CHAPTER 12

The Best Year

Louise Tracy saw little of her husband over the spring of 1936. He was, in fact, in the midst of shooting both *San Francisco* and *Fury* when it came time, after years of renting, to move the family to a place of its own.

The Tracys bought in the rural flatlands of the San Fernando Valley, a sprawling region that encompassed practically everything north of the Cahuenga Pass and south of Santa Barbara. A single-story ranch house with two bedrooms, the residence was modest compared to the Cooper property, eight acres on a two-lane road called White Oak just north of Ventura Boulevard in the residential suburb of Encino. The house was nestled in a grove of orange trees, a long driveway leading up from the road. Dick Mook could remember being routed out of bed one morning to see the property Tracy had just purchased.

"The house could not be plainer or simpler," Spence enthused. "It's the grounds that make it look pretentious. Why, if it weren't for the grounds—if this house were sitting on a small lot—any stock player making $100 a week could own it. It's so small and so plainly furnished that we'll only have to keep a cook and a houseboy." And, Mook added, a field hand to tend the horses, the grove, the chickens, the alfalfa . . .

Tracy had several rooms added—known collectively as "the children's wing"—and broke ground on a swimming pool around the time of his thirty-sixth birthday. On the rare day off he cut alfalfa or tended the horses

On the sidelines at Riviera with Walt Disney, circa 1936.
(AUTHOR'S COLLECTION)

or took in the games at Riviera, where he would watch from the sidelines and count the days until he could get back into the action.* *Fury* was previewed May 18 at the Fox Wilshire, and despite Lang's displeasure over the trims Mankiewicz had been forced to make, the first reviews, as Tracy would note in his datebook, were "marvelous." The man from *Daily Variety* saw a "consummate exhibition of a man whose tolerant, compassionate nature is galled to maniacal vengeance against men who, without justification, sought to burn him in jail." It was, said the *Hollywood Reporter,* the best thing Tracy had ever done. Gratified, he played six relatively carefree periods of polo the day following their publication and celebrated five full months of sobriety. Three days later, he and Louise boarded the famed Matson luxury liner, the S.S. *Lurline,* and sailed for Hawaii.

The crossing took five days and was mercifully free of entreaties from the studio. The weather was beautiful, and Tracy worked on his tan

---

* There was no "hazardous acts" clause in Tracy's M-G-M contract, but the matter was taken up with a number of players after the death of actor Gordon Westcott in October 1935. Tracy informally agreed to refrain from playing polo during the production of a picture, as did Robert Montgomery and Clark Gable. Under pressure from their respective boards, studio executives Jack Warner and Darryl F. Zanuck gave up the game altogether—Zanuck quite reluctantly—and, in time, so did Walt Disney.

between naps, champagne receptions (where he stuck to tea and soft drinks), and movies in the ship's theater. Louise reveled in the social scene, posing for photos, swimming and reading, dancing when she could get Spence out onto the floor. When they docked at Honolulu a crowd was waiting, mostly kids but more than a few adults, and they all surged forward, brandishing notebooks and tablets and pencils sharp enough to draw blood. "Mr. Tracy!" they called. "Please, Mr. Tracy!" Piled high with leis, he would stop, sign, try to move on, stop again, sign again. "It looked hopeless," reported the *Star-Bulletin,* which covered the arrival. "No man could sign all those notebooks. Tracy did his urbane best but the hunters grew." It took a couple of traffic cops to clear the way so that the party, under the guidance of the local M-G-M rep, could get to a waiting car. They took off for the Royal Hawaiian, where they'd be staying for two weeks, maybe longer. Veteran waterfronters said he had drawn more autograph hounds than any passenger since Shirley Temple.

Fury was released nationally while the Tracys were on Oahu, opening at the Capitol Theatre in New York on June 5. Coming at the tag end of the 1935–36 season, it almost looked as if the film were being dumped, as Fritz Lang was fond of claiming. There was, however, very little in the way of competition, and Mayer, convinced it would die like a dog, had promised he would push it. Loew's commandeered the electric sign running over the Astor Theatre, where *The Great Ziegfeld* was still drawing crowds, and pumped *Fury* in a big way.

William Boehnel of the *World-Telegram* devoted nearly half a page to the picture, the headline dubbing it "one of the most courageous in screen history." *Variety*'s Abel Green thought it a "cinch critics' picture" that would do well by word of mouth, a prediction confirmed by the *Enquirer* when it studied the trending at the Capitol box office and concluded that *Fury* was, in movie parlance, a "builder"—a film that was selling progressively more tickets as the week wore on. "Sylvia Sidney and Spencer Tracy until now have been players of secondary stardom, but *Fury* raises them to first magnitude box office popularity with the strength of its story and direction, as well as box office response."

The picture ran up domestic rentals of $685,000, then surprised everyone by doing an almost equal amount in foreign rentals—practically unheard of, apart from the films of Greta Garbo. It may have been a measure of Fritz Lang's international reputation or simply the strength of its subject matter, but *Fury* logged worldwide billings of $1,300,000, surpassing *Riffraff* to make it the most popular of all of Tracy's movies. Producer Walter Wanger, late of M-G-M, jumped at the chance to reassemble a winning package, and Tracy, much to his horror, found upon his return from Hawaii that he had been lent to Wanger for a second picture with Lang and

Tracy logged some of the best reviews of his career as the vengeful Joe Wilson of Fritz Lang's *Fury* (1936). (SUSIE TRACY)

Sylvia Sidney.* With a commitment also under way for Tracy to go into *The Plough and the Stars* at RKO, the only diplomatic solution was to cancel all loan-outs and keep Tracy, suddenly hot and getting hotter, under the protective wing of his home studio.

Where Fox had pretty much left audiences to figure Tracy out for themselves, Metro was in the process of shaping his public image and building him into a top-flight attraction. His first three pictures had been a matter of getting his sea legs. *The Murder Man* was a programmer, *Whipsaw* a vehicle for Myrna Loy, *Riffraff* for Jean Harlow. No longer tethered to one of the studio's big female attractions, Tracy caught fire with *Fury*, and audiences who, just a year earlier, had no clear handle on him, were suddenly turning out to see him. It was a transition that was nothing short of miraculous, but there was something else at work as well, a willingness on the part of the public to embrace a leading man who was not textbook handsome nor bigger than life.

"What the movies need," said actress Carole Lombard, as if speaking

---

* Announced as *Three Time Loser*, the film was ultimately made and released as *You Only Live Once* (1937).

for a whole generation of filmgoers, "are more Clark Gables and Gary Coopers. By that I mean virile men stars. Right now there are three times as many [of] the milder romantic types. This needs to be changed." The actors she included on her personal list of "he-men" were Randolph Scott, James Cagney, Pat O'Brien, Fred MacMurray, Charles Bickford . . . and Spencer Tracy. "Half the leading men today either can't act, look like coal-beavers in dinner clothes, or make love like wrestlers."

If there was one man in the Metro organization responsible for Tracy's rise, it was Edgar J. Mannix, vice president and general manager of the studio. Where Louis B. Mayer was the public face of Metro-Goldwyn-Mayer, Eddie Mannix was often regarded as the private one, the man who supervised the supervisors at M-G-M, a professional Irishman who kept a clutch of shillelaghs outside the door of his office. Born in Fort Lee, New Jersey, Mannix was shanty to the bone, part of a gang of Irish street toughs making trouble for the Schenck brothers, whose Palisade Park extended into Fort Lee from Cliffside to the south. Nicholas Schenck, no less streetwise, heard they were lobbing rocks at the trolleys attempting to enter the park and said, "Find the leader and hire him!"

Mannix started as a ticket taker for Schenck in 1910 and worked his way into management, eventually jumping to film production at the ramshackle studio on East Forty-eighth Street where Nick's brother Joe made feature pictures starring his wife, actress Norma Talmadge. When Nick Schenck became vice president of Loew's Incorporated in 1924, he sent Mannix west as comptroller and special assistant to Irving Thalberg, tasked with keeping an eye on Mayer.

Stocky and rough-hewn, Mannix was a bulldog in both style and appearance, with big jowly cheeks and a powerful jaw. He excelled at labor relations, and when he turned on the charm there was nobody more ingratiating. He was a great storyteller, a man of the people, and he could get anyone on his side with a frank talk, a direct word, a pat on the back. His word was his bond, and more than one relationship was predicated on nothing more than a handshake. "Here," Charles Bickford said to himself upon meeting him for the first time, "is a truthful man. If he were to tell me that he was about to slit my throat, I'd believe him." Mannix could be rough stuff, hard on women and dangerous when crossed, but he was also a standup guy in a town full of weasels and, unlike Mayer, he always meant exactly what he said.

Eddie Mannix took a proprietary interest in Tracy's career, and it may well have been his idea, being a lifelong Catholic, to cast Tracy in the role of the priest in *San Francisco*. Certainly it was the most surprising bit of casting in a film for which casting was a big—if not the biggest—selling point. As the film's release date approached, the mechanism designed to exploit a major picture went into overdrive. On the East Coast, Howard Dietz, general director of publicity, worked out the selling angles, the principal one being the first-ever pairing of Clark Gable and Jeanette MacDonald. The line "They were born to fall in love!" appeared in ads and on posters, targeting the female trade. The title itself suggested the action of the earthquake and the bawdy ways of the old Barbary Coast. And then there was Tracy's presence and the obvious chemistry with Gable. ("It's News When Spencer Tracy, Screen's 'Toughest Guy,' Enacts a Priest!" declared a headline in the film's hefty pressbook.) By design, the picture was a marketer's dream.

After John Hoffman's ministrations put the earthquake right, there were at least two "sneak" (i.e., unannounced) previews of *San Francisco* to gauge unbiased audience reactions and fix a number of small problems—laugh lines that weren't properly covered, dull spots to be excised. By the time of the official or so-called press preview on June 22 at the Fox Village Theatre, all the tinkering was done. There was a roped-off section in the center of the auditorium to which executives, directors, players, technicians, agents, secretaries, and their various guests fled after braving the gauntlet of autograph hounds and lobby lizards typically drawn to such events. Members of the working press surrounded the premium seats, as did claques of studio employees carefully interlarded with excited members of the general public.

At the appointed time, a booming voice announced the evening's "surprise" and a roar of applause went up as the showing began and the studio loyalists made sure the clapping continued until every significant name had rolled across the screen. Applause also greeted the principal members of the cast as they made their first appearances—Gable, MacDonald, Tracy, Jack Holt, Ted Heeley, and the others. MacDonald's rousing song, "San Francisco," was a sensation, and the magnitude 7.8 temblor at the top of the tenth reel handed the crowd a split second of genuine panic. Elizabeth Yeaman, covering the event for the *Hollywood Citizen News,* "peered frantically at the ceiling of the theater and endeavored to restrain an impulse to bolt for an exit." A few spectators actually got to their feet.

The conventions of the press preview were meant to bolster weak pictures and eke better notices out of reviewers who couldn't tell the difference between an ovation and a calculated hullabaloo. But *San Francisco* didn't need the help, and the local trades—the most jaded and the first to publish—described "burst after burst" of spontaneous applause for the spectacle, the music, the sheer excellence of the production. Neither Gable nor MacDonald had ever been better, and Tracy surprised and delighted everyone as the humble young priest. The effects were "amazing," far and away the best ever. The movie delivered on every conceivable level, and the cards in the foyer ("How did you like the picture?") were merely a formality; Hyman and his people had no intention of changing a frame.

Conferring with his brother Carroll on the set of *San Francisco*.
(PATRICIA MAHON COLLECTION)

Some three hundred release prints were struck at a cost of approximately $140 a copy. Fresh from the lab, each "green" reel of positive stock was subjected to a waxing process designed to cut down on friction as it ran through the gate of the projector, minimizing scratches and keeping the prints in presentable shape for as many as 180 showings apiece. Processed, inventoried, and numbered, they were allocated to thirty-one domestic exchanges according to bookings logged by the company's regional salespeople, with initial engagements in the Northeast held to the deluxe theaters of Loew's Incorporated, the parent company of Metro-Goldwyn-Mayer. *San Francisco* opened in Los Angeles, Cincinnati, and New York a few days after the Westwood Village preview. Where *Fury* aspired to a level of art rarely attained in the M-G-M model, *San Francisco* was an unabashed work of commerce, slick and professional.

"Spencer Tracy plays the priest, and it's the most difficult role in the picture," Joe Bigelow, acknowledging the significance of Tracy's achievement, wrote in *Variety*.

It was a daring piece of writing to begin with, and only the most expert and understanding handling could have kept it within the proper bounds. This man of the cloth would not be unusual in real life, but on the screen he's a type never attempted before. His slang—he calls Gable "mugg" and "sucker" good naturedly—is the sort usually associated with men of lesser spiritual quality; in this instance the lingo is casually uttered by a character dressed in the vestments of the church. It's explained that he was born on the Barbary Coast and that he and Blackie were raised together, and that qualifies his "eccentricities." Tracy makes him human and refreshing, and his performance precludes any possibility of offense.

There was hardly a review published anywhere that wasn't a rave, and even in summer, when business was typically slow, the crowds were phenomenal. In New York, *Variety* dubbed it "the smash of the town," going up against a particularly strong slate of competing pictures that included the latest Shirley Temple movie and W. C. Fields' hit comedy *Poppy.* "All signs point to a terrific $60,000 the first week, backed by a campaign that worked hard to push this one to a high peak. It's the best business the Cap[itol] has done in as long as the boys want to remember, and a run of three or four weeks appears assured."

The film, in fact, climbed to nearly $70,000 that first week, and held nicely over the Independence Day weekend. The story was the same in other cities as the release widened, and Tracy dutifully went on the CBS network's *Camel Caravan* to push the picture. Underrehearsed and flat, he performed a scene from *Saturday's Children* with Rosalind Russell and failed to impress the few trade reviewers who managed to catch the show. Radio was building into a bonanza for big-name movie personalities who could command as much as $5,000 an appearance, but it held little attraction for Spencer Tracy, who didn't consider it acting to stand in front of a microphone while holding a script in his hand.

With both *Fury* and *San Francisco* in release simultaneously, network radio made little difference to him. In his review of the latter in the *New York Times,* Frank Nugent pointed to "another brilliant portrayal by Spencer Tracy" as the two-fisted Father Mullin. "Mr. Tracy, late of *Fury,* is heading surely toward an award for the finest performances of the year." And columnist Ed Sullivan, who was actually appearing onstage with *Fury* at Loew's State, filed a story with *Silver Screen* magazine in which he labeled Tracy "The Best Bet of the Year" for true stardom.

"A year ago," Sullivan wrote,

it was Victor McLaglen who won the Academy Award for the year's outstanding performance in *The Informer.* This year, Tracy will be in the forefront of the select group who will fight it out for the premiere award of the celluloid pundits . . . His Father Tim will be recognized in every Catholic parish in America, and perhaps the

original walked the streets of Milwaukee when Spencer Tracy was
going to the public schools there. It was the integrity of the priestly
portrait that Tracy paints which lifted him high among the Hollywood performers. Here is no raucous individual, nor one seeking
your sympathy with obvious hokum—here is no compromise—
Father Tim is as great a feat of make believe as Laughton's Captain
Bligh or the Rothschild who was born in the genius of George
Arliss, or the Juliet of Norma Shearer. This is magnificent work, on
a high plane.

Almost on cue, Tracy was announced as having won the Screen Writers
Guild award for *Fury* and would take the honor again in July for his work in
San Francisco. Life was good and getting better all the time. He played polo
nearly every day at Riviera or on the field of the Will Rogers estate. When
Sol Wurtzel wired him in mid-July, congratulating him on his performance
in the Lang picture, he added that he hoped that he and Mrs. Tracy had
enjoyed their trip to Honolulu. Tracy replied:

HAD WONDERFUL TRIP. MRS. TRACY DID TOO BECAUSE I
STAYED ON WATER WAGON.

Of all Spencer Tracy's early pictures, Ed Sullivan liked *The Show-Off* best.

In fact I was so impressed by it that in the following day's column,
I suggested that he was the brightest possibility among the younger
coast actors . . . And then came *Fury* from the pen of Norman
Krasna. There was plenty of raw meat in this one, meat enough for
a Killer Mears to sink his teeth in, and sufficient shading to establish the contrast of restraint and furious bitterness . . . But *Fury* was
not quite enough. It was reminiscent, you see, of Killer Mears.
Tracy was on the way, but he needed something completely different, a part completely removed from blood-and-thunder. And he
found that as the priest in *San Francisco*, for when he donned the
clergyman's collar, it was Hollywood's benediction.

Tracy later told Sullivan that he was the first writer to come out and
predict full stardom for him at a time when no one else could see it. "You'll
never know how much it meant to me at that particular moment—and
you'll never know how much I hoped you were right."
    If settling something so "completely different" on him had finally made
audiences sit up and take notice, it was a tactic that bore repeating. In lieu

of loan-outs to Wanger and RKO, which would have produced solid pictures but more of the same, Tracy was cast alongside William Powell, Jean Harlow, and Myrna Loy in a screwball comedy called *Libeled Lady.* Comedy, of course, wasn't a stretch for him—it had been his forte in stock—but most moviegoers hadn't seen him in one, and never, for that matter, in the sort of hard-driving part that typified the screwball genre. Powell, Harlow, and Loy were among the biggest draws in the industry, and equal billing in such a powerhouse company could only serve to enhance Tracy's standing with both exhibitors and the general public.

Based on a clever story by Wallace Sullivan, *Libeled Lady* had Tracy back in a newsroom setting as an editor whose paper is threatened with ruination when it mistakenly puts an heiress in the middle of a London scandal and is sued for libel. In short order, Tracy's character, Haggerty, marries off his fiancée (Harlow) to Chandler (Powell), who then sets about to seduce the litigious heiress (Loy). Tracy handled the part with such aplomb that his work appeared effortless. ("Walking on the set, if you didn't know him, you'd take him for one of the workmen," said Sidney Skolsky.) There was, however, tension between Harlow and Powell, who were in a difficult relationship together. The delectable Loy, meanwhile, was newly married to producer Arthur Hornblow, Jr., and Tracy made an elaborate show of his disappointment.

"He moped around pretending to pout, playing the wronged suitor," Loy wrote. "He set up a 'Hate Hornblow Table' in the commissary, announcing that only men I had spurned could sit there. So all these men joined him who were supposed to have crushes on me, which they didn't have at all. It was just a gag, but Spence made his point."

Libeled Lady was being directed by Jack Conway, a restless, red-faced Irishman who would jump to his feet at the slightest provocation and act out a scene as he wanted it played. He knew how the action should look up on the screen, but his way of staging often stifled his actors and kept them from taking flight. *Libeled Lady* would be a perfectly serviceable screwball comedy—that most delicate of movie genres—but would lack the frantic grace of *Twentieth Century* or *My Man Godfrey.*

Tracy did his best to be courteous to the various reporters Howard Strickling's people brought to the set, but he had never grown comfortable talking about himself and, after four years of doing so, felt he had run out of things to say. When one asked, "In what have you found your greatest happiness as an actor?" he answered, "In the cashier's office." As columnist Sheilah Graham, newly arrived in Los Angeles, observed, "he would do his best to smile at me, but I knew he wanted me to ask my questions and be gone."

In Honolulu, Tracy discovered coconut cake and coconut-flavored ice cream and, being on the wagon, ate continuously, particularly sweets. "One day," Louise recalled, "Spencer said, 'I'm beginning to gain weight. You'll have to watch that for me.' And with that he dumped the problem in my lap. In spite of one diet and another of energy-giving but supposedly non-fattening foods, his weight continued to go up. I discovered through a friend that between meals Spencer was downing three chocolate ice cream sodas in one sitting." When he began *Libeled Lady* on July 13, Tracy recorded his weight as 180 pounds. Since he wasn't carrying the picture, there were a lot of days off. On the twenty-first he baled hay and saw his weight drop to 177. On the thirty-first—Louise's birthday—he played polo and tipped the scale at 178.

He went into the picture knowing he'd be doing his next assignment under protest, and when, in July, his commitment for *The Plough and the Stars* was very publicly canceled, it was, the *New York Times* reported, because "an unrevealed script is being rushed that is planned to give Tracy his most impressive role." That role, developed over the preceding six months, was that of the Brava fisherman Manuel in Victor Fleming's planned picturization of the late Rudyard Kipling's only American novel, *Captains Courageous*.

Fleming, forty-eight, had been directing movies, westerns in particular, since 1919, and had previously been a cameraman, first for Allan Dwan and Marshall Neilan, later for the Army Signal Corps. In 1929 he teamed with writer-turned-producer Louis D. "Bud" Lighton to make *The Virginian*. Fleming landed at M-G-M in 1931, and Lighton joined him there four years later. Almost immediately the two men began work on a screen version of the Kipling story. Much of the casting was settled early on: Lionel Barrymore as Disko Troop, the captain of the *We're Here*, Melvyn Douglas as Kipling's rail tycoon, updated to the director of a modern steamship line, Freddie Bartholomew, Metro's David Copperfield and Selznick's Little Lord Fauntleroy, as the spoiled rich boy who is whipped into shape during a summer season on the Grand Banks of the North Atlantic.

The eventual screenplay, the collective work of four men, shifted much of the story burden to Manuel, the simple Portuguese fisherman who, in Kipling's novel, rescues young Harvey from the water. Whoever played the character would need his skin darkened and would have to master an accent. Tracy wanted no part of it. "Fought against it like a steer," he admitted. "Thought the characterization would be phony. Didn't see how the pieces would fit together. Didn't know where I could borrow an accent."

Tracy's only work in dialect had been for *The Mad Game*, and that he had dodged by playing the scene in a hoarse whisper. "I'll be leaping all over the continent with the dialect," he warned Lighton and Fleming, both of whom assured him a character who had lived for years among the Gloucester fishermen could easily have picked up any of a dozen different accents. "I've always played rough-and-tumble parts," Tracy added. "This story's religion or something. Those scenes where he talks about his father— suppose I don't bring 'em off? They'll be horrible—sitting there in the boat, talking about Fisherman's Heaven, a guy 37 years old—you'll have your audiences reaching for bigger and wider hats."

They prevailed upon him to take the script home and read it to Louise, who passed on virtually everything he was asked to do. Louise listened, as she always did, and said that she laughed at the idea that he could ever be anything but on the level. "I was in the stock company where he got his first part," she told Ida Zeitlin of *Modern Sceen* magazine. "He had no tricks, no technique, he didn't know how to make up and looked awful. What carried him through was his great sincerity and naturalness, which he had from the start. If Spence has any fault in acting, it's that he doesn't let himself go. He's always afraid of being 'hammy,' so rather than over-play, he under-acts." Then, echoing George M. Cohan, she said, "Whatever he's done, I've always felt he had more to give, and in this part he'd have to let himself go and give it."

Louise's enthusiasm notwithstanding, Tracy still fretted over the matter of an accent:

I went to see every picture in town where an actor might be found speaking an accent—saw Eddie Robinson, Muni [in *Black Fury*], others. Then we scoured San Diego trying to find a Portuguese sailor to use as a model for Manuel. Finally we found our man. The chap came to the studio to see me. He *was* Manuel. The expression in his eyes, the way he walked, the way he sat, the way he used his hands, his knowledge of boats. Then he began to talk, and . . . he spoke better English than I do. When I asked him what he thought about my calling the kid my "leetle feesh," he looked at me patiently—and a little pityingly—and said, "Do you mean *little fish,* Mr. Tracy?" I gave up.

By August Tracy was thinking of buying a boat. They had talked about it, he and Louise, and he told her he'd give up polo because a yacht would cost "a lot of dough." She said, "So what? You don't spend it in other ways. You may as well have your fun . . . I wish you wouldn't give up polo, either. What's wrong with having two sports?" Not knowing the first thing about navigation, he drove to Newport Beach and tried out a power cruiser, then went sailing the following week on a craft called *Landfall*.

When they decided to experiment with a new school, pulling Johnny out of Hollywood Progressive, he decided a boat would be too much of an added expense and gave up on the idea. Despite a thirty-four-mile drive each way, Johnny and Susie entered Brentwood Town and Country School in September 1936. "Susie," said Louise, "was only four and, ordinarily, I do not think I should have started her to school so young, but she, too, needed companionship, and I learned that there were quite a number of even younger children there in nursery school."

They made three days of tests for *Captains Courageous* in early September, Tracy's skin darkened and his hair curled with an iron. "One day," he remembered, "just after I'd had my hair curled, I walked down the stairs at Metro and heard a scream. I looked up, and Joan Crawford said, 'My God, Harpo Marx!' " Eddie Mannix nearly talked him out of taking the role by warning him not to attempt an accent. "You'll fall on your ass," Mannix predicted. After viewing the test footage, Tracy agreed and urged Fleming to test "a couple of other fellows." Then Sam Katz settled the matter by telling him that if he didn't take the part, they wouldn't make the picture at all. Tracy was still getting used to the idea when word spread on the morning of September 14 that Irving Thalberg had died of pneumonia at the age of thirty-six.

All the good things that had come to Tracy in that last year were the result of Thalberg's faith in him. It bothered him that *Riffraff* hadn't turned out better, but he liked to think that what had come since—*Fury,* especially, and *San Francisco*—had justified the trouble Thalberg had taken in bringing him to the studio. He attended the funeral at Wilshire Temple on the morning of the sixteenth, then drove himself out to Riviera and devoted the rest of the day to polo, as he generally did at times of stress, recording his weight at 180½ pounds.

"I finally talked myself into practicing dialect and putting up with having my hair curled twice a day, but the thought of singing gave me the shudders. I dodged the voice teacher, Arthur Rosenstein, for weeks. After I started taking lessons, I used to duck practice as much as I could. Then I just said, 'Oh, what's the difference?' and let the old baritone rip." He also took lessons in playing the vielle, the ancient stringed instrument—something of a cross between a mandolin and a hurdy-gurdy—on which Manuel accompanies himself.

However daunting the role of Manuel seemed, the project had its compensations. Vic Fleming was inspirational and rugged, tall and natty with a poetic streak. Lionel Barrymore was Tracy's boyhood idol, whom he had first seen onstage in Kansas City at the age of sixteen. Twelve-year-old Freddie Bartholomew was a born actor—untrained but with tremendous screen presence—who had developed enough of a following to merit first-featured billing in a picture that had no stars. Tracy's contract guaranteed him first-featured billing, and he had to sign a waiver in order to make the package work.

Preliminary filming had commenced nearly a year earlier, when a six-man crew left California for Massachusetts to make process backgrounds and incidental shots of the fishing fleet in and around Gloucester. Purchased on the scene was a two-masted schooner called the *Oretha F. Spinney,* which they rechristened the *We're Here* of Kipling's novel. With the M-G-M crew on board, the ship set sail for Newfoundland and Nova Scotia, where, as Fleming described it, "shots of the fishing fleet in every conceivable sort of rough winter weather" were filmed. The men then brought the ship down though the Panama Canal and sailed it up past Monterey and San Francisco to Coos Bay, Oregon, making fog shots along the way. By the time the cast and crew assembled on the morning of September 30, a second schooner, redubbed the *Jennie Cushman,* was moored alongside the *We're Here* in the harbor at Avalon. A company of seventy-five crowded onto the two schooners, the ships trailing barges, water taxis, and speedboats, looking for fog and finding, for the most part, bright sun instead.

Captain J. M. Hersey and his crew got their first look at the actors when they clambered aboard the *We're Here* at 7:30 a.m. "Of the whole bunch of them, Christian Rub looks most like a fisherman," Hersey observed. "Tracy was sore because he had no sooner got aboard than a makeup man wanted to curl his hair." Under the direction of cinematographer Hal Rosson, the morning was spent building a parallel out from the port rail to support a camera platform. Tracy, in a dory, practiced pulling into camera range for the scene in which Manuel scoops young Harvey out of the water. "This would be all right," he said, "except for the hair curling business. It's a wonder they don't use perfume on me. Also, I've got to get in a few more licks on those oars. I handle a dory like a washerwoman."

The fog, which had been thick all morning, began to break, and the afternoon passed without getting a single shot in the can. They dismissed the company at four o'clock, returning to Avalon, and tried again the next morning with only marginally better luck. The fog held long enough to get the scene in three takes, Rosson covering it from the barge, the camera platform, and the deck above. Tracy was impressed by Freddie Bartholomew's dedication to the role, jumping over the side of the boat in order to get what he considered to be sufficiently wet after having been shot with a hose and doused with a bucket of water. "The kid can take it," he said admiringly. "I hand it to him."

Again the fog cleared, and the adult cast spent the rest of the day learning to cut bait. Part of the ship's forecastle had been converted to a schoolroom for Bartholomew, his stand-in Ray Sperry, and sixteen-year-old Mickey Rooney. "We had a full schedule," Rooney recalled, "a long shoot

Tracy hated having his hair curled for *Captains Courageous.* Here he submits to M-G-M stylist Larry Germain, 1936. (MIKE GERMAIN)

every morning, then art, history, social studies, arithmetic, composition, grammar, spelling, botany, physiology, and hygiene in the afternoon."

Fleming wrote: "We had purposely set out in October in order to take advantage of the fog. But for days after we began to work, either the sun would break through or the wind would cause a break in the mist." They cruised over to the Isthmus for a brief scene of dialogue with Bartholomew and Rooney, but then the fog broke there as well. "[A]ll the actors and crew were fishing off the back of the boat," Tracy remembered. "Fleming said, 'Goddamnit, we're going home!' And then we went back to Catalina to get the stuff we had left in the hotel, and Fleming was in such a hurry to get away that he was using a speedboat [while] the rest of us were going to use a big tug. He walked out on the pier to jump into his speedboat, and the speedboat took off and he went into the water—with his white [pants], all dressed up." The *We're Here* and the *Cushman* proceeded to Santa Monica to await further orders.

There was process work to be done, but Tracy's scenes were limited to Harvey's time on the water, and the other material—the boy's school days and his life at home—could go on without him. He spent all day at Riviera on October 4, practicing in the morning and watching a game in the afternoon. Then he attended the riotous preview of *Libeled Lady* in the evening. It was, he liked to tell people, the first picture he had ever had to dress up for, preferring, of course, to "slop around" in his shirtsleeves, uncreased trousers, and an old pair of shoes. As he watched the breakneck comedy unspool, he said he couldn't get over the feeling that he was watching a man "who had just put on a clean shirt." When it was over, he turned to Louise and asked her what she thought of his wardrobe. "Well," she allowed, "they did look pretty new."

However much the picture made Tracy's neck itch, *Libeled Lady* went over big with the press, and the reviews the next day were, in Tracy's estimation, "great." Confident he was in "the best comedy of the year," he touched M-G-M for a $5,000 loan and went off again looking for a boat. He inspected Johnny Weismuller's at Santa Monica and took a demo trip in heavy seas on one named, appropriately enough, *Fury.* The studio took up his option a full six months early, and within a week he had closed on a forty-foot gaff-headed ketch called *Resolute.* Following the example of Frank Borzage, who named his yacht the *Rena B.* after his wife, Tracy christened the boat the *Carrie B* in honor of his mother.

He was back at the studio on October 21, still unsure of his performance and grumbling as they fussed with his hair. ("It took me two hours every blessed day to get my hair curled.") The screenwriters, principally John Lee Mahin, who did the final draft of the script with the knowledge that Tracy would be playing the part, kept Manuel's words in the spirit of those Kipling had given the character, accomplishing the effect with syntax and emphasis. ("Ah ha!" said Manuel, holding out a brown hand. "You are some pretty well now? This time last night the fish they fish for you. Now you fish for fish. Eh, wha-at?")

Said Tracy: "We got an educated Portuguese to advise us.* He told me that if you put an Italian, a Spaniard, and a Portuguese in the same room and listen to them talk with your eyes closed, you can't tell which is the Portuguese, which is the Italian, and which is the Spaniard. So I sort of made up my accent as I went along. Maybe some of it was phony. I don't know."

What became his favorite scene in the picture was also its simplest, Manuel out singing under the stars, Harvey tentatively making his approach. Tired of Harvey's attitude, Manuel wishes he would go away and continues to sing and play his vielle as the boy peppers him with questions.

* This was the Portuguese actor Rodrigo de Medicis.

"What do you keep singing for?" Harvey demands.

"Because I like to sing," Manuel says.

"I never heard that song before."

"Me neither. I just make 'em up."

"You can't write songs."

"I don't write 'em. I just find 'em in my mouth."

"A song can't be any good like that—when you just make it up."

"Say—that best kind songs." He taps his chest. "When you feel good inside—like, like trade wind—she just come out."

"Aw, people learn songs. Songs aren't just inside of people like that."

"Say, sometime a song so big and sweet inside I can't get 'im out. And then I look up at stars and maybe cry, I feel so good." And then he peers searchingly into Harvey's eyes and says, "Don't you ever feel like this?" And when the boy returns the same sullen and belligerent face as before he says, "No, guess you don't."

The challenge with Manuel was to put him across as a genuinely happy man without making him seem like an idiot. Tracy gained his screen effects largely out of the strength of his own personality, as the actor's art, at its most basic level, is the bringing of something of one's self to a role. He wasn't a character actor in the sense that Paul Muni was, yet here he was in makeup with his hair curled, reciting his lines with the suggestion of a Portuguese accent. It was absolutely essential to avoid an air of masquerade in the part, and Tracy portrayed Manuel's strength and good nature as a gift from God. Manuel is curious, philosophical, humble but never subservient. Fleming seemed happy with the attack, but it was Tracy's first time with Fleming and he wasn't so sure he could trust him.

Freddie Bartholomew could sense Tracy's insecurity: "I had warm feelings for Spencer Tracy, but there was—curiously—a sense of competitiveness that he felt towards me. I'm not trying to say that I was wonderful and he wasn't—I don't mean that at all—but I think he felt that, 'Ooh, wait a minute. The kid's running off with the picture and this is not necessarily a good idea.' "

They were back out on the ocean in November, midchannel with the *Cushman,* the *Bluegill,* the *Flying Swan,* the *Elizabeth K. Brown,* and nine other schooners brought down from Seattle and the Alaska halibut fleet, the dories putting overside and pulling away, a storm approaching steadily from the northwest. With a ten-day leave of absence, Tracy pulled alongside the *We're Here* one day to show off the *Carrie B.* "Slick as a whistle," he said proudly. "A forty-footer that will sleep six, and that I can handle myself if necessary. Captain Hersey came over in a dory and I showed him around. He even took the wheel for ten minutes and admitted that she 'wasn't so bad.' "

Tracy wanted everyone to see the new boat, and Dick Mook wrote of one particular Sunday afternoon when he took a group of friends out past the breakwater at Wilmington and had trouble getting back. "There is a drawbridge that must be raised to let sailing vessels into the harbor. We came back late in the afternoon when traffic across the bridge was at its heaviest. Naturally, traffic was held up while the bridge was raised to let us through. But Spence, new to navigation and knowing little about steering, couldn't quite get the boat through." Motorists waiting to cross the bridge grew irate, honking their horns and raining insults down on the captain of the *Carrie B.* One driver caustically advised Tracy that he could get the boat through if only he would turn it on its side. "Spence," said Mook, "flushed a lobster red."

Shots of the dories racing back to the *We're Here* were made on November 20, Harvey falling in as he tries to pass a heavy trawl tub to the deck. Fleming spent at least an hour rehearsing the shot, wanting it on the first try so as not to leave Bartholomew in the cold water any longer than necessary. "Stubby Kruger, out of camera range, was all ready to dive in if Tracy had difficulty hauling Freddie back into the dory," Captain Hersey recorded,

but Freddie was sure everything was going to be all right. The kid has nerve, all right. A second dory was ready to race over if there was any hitch, and Mr. Fleming himself had a leg over the rail and wouldn't have hesitated to drop in. Tracy's dory came up alongside. As he reached for the forward dory hook, Freddie put one foot on the gunwale, started to pass up the trawl tub, and took a backward header. Tracy, quick as a flash, reached over, grabbed him by the collar as he came up, got a grip with his other hand on the lad's trousers, and pulled him in as if he was landing a codfish. It was all over in a few seconds. We hauled up the dory, rushed Freddie below, stripped him, dried him, rubbed him down, and put him between blankets in a bunk where Mr. Barrymore, Charley Grapewin, Tracy and others came down and kidded him about his Olympic high-dive.

After a few days back at the studio, they suspended production while waiting for new backgrounds. Eddie Mannix okayed a two-week vacation on December 1, and the Tracys were on the Super Chief bound for Chicago the following morning. In New York they registered at the Sherry-Netherland and, intent upon catching as many shows as possible, took in *Dead End* on a matinee, followed by the *Ziegfeld Follies* with Fannie Brice and Bobby Clark that evening. After hours at the Cotton Club, they got caught up in a mob of autograph seekers, an experience Spence likened to a scene from *Fury*. With no big-name comedies competing against it, *Libeled Lady* was a big hit at the Capitol, and Metro's New York office had the dailies queuing up to buy Tracy lunch.

He loved the musicals—*Red, Hot and Blue, On Your Toes*. They saw *Idiot's Delight, Tovarich,* then *Stage Door* on the tenth. They would have seen another that evening had Spence not caved—after first having said no—to an appearance on Rudy Vallee's *Royal Gelatin Hour* (as the $1,500 fee would handily cover the cost of the trip). They dined with Noël Coward and Gertrude Lawrence, caught Helen Hayes in *Victoria Regina,* and were back on the train to Chicago the next afternoon. They were home on December 16 after five and a half exhilarating days on the town. Four days later, on the twentieth, Tracy celebrated one full year on the wagon.

Yvonne Beaudry was newly arrived in California, a graduate of the Columbia School of Journalism, when, at the age of twenty-eight, she landed a job at Selznick-International. Beaudry made the daily commute to Culver City with a woman who was one of the top secretaries at nearby M-G-M. Unhappy at Selznick, where she was secretary to a dyspeptic producer, Beaudry was asked by her friend if she cared to work for an actor—"never mind who."

"Did I!" she said. "Anything for release from my present employment. But an actor? 'I hope it's Spencer Tracy,' I blurted out, considering he was the only thespian worthy of my efforts. My companion smiled mysteriously, let me off at Selznick's, and drove on to the Metro-Goldwyn-Mayer studio. An hour later, she phoned me for lunch at the M-G-M commissary, where, I supposed, I'd meet the actor."

Nothing happened over lunch, and Beaudry took the bus back to work in low spirits. About four o'clock, though, she had another call. "Can you come for tea in half an hour? Spencer Tracy will pick you up in his car." Beaudry told her boss she was leaving for a job interview at Metro, and he simply nodded, anxious for the chance to hire somebody with more experience. "Evidently I'd been inspected at lunchtime and passed muster. I still wonder if Tracy hired me for my Hollywood get-up, which resembled his— a loose brown wool coat, a felt hat with the brim pulled down over one eye. Certainly he learned little about my qualifications at tea. He did all the talking, and I basked in the warmth of his presence, his smile."

Since the release of *San Francisco,* Tracy told her, he was getting lots of fan mail and needed a secretary to answer letters, send out autographed photos, paste clippings in a scrapbook. The salary would be twenty-five dollars a week, and she'd be based in his dressing room until an office came available elsewhere on the lot. Her first morning at work, Beaudry opened dozens of letters piled on the floor, on easy chairs, on a large table on which sat a typewriter, stationery, rosaries, and medals sent Johnny by his father's fans. Atheists wrote, describing spiritual awakenings they experienced after watching his work as Father Mullin. (One British reviewer described the picture as "a more powerful, more convincing recall to religion than the cold and stilted one issued by the Archbishop of Canterbury.") Some asked for spiritual advice, others for money.

"You can't live up to an idealistic role," Tracy said. "I'm not competent to advise anyone about their spiritual problems. I'm groping myself. I suppose we all are." After he played a young doctor in a radio adaptation of *Men in White,* an influx of letters came from broken and discouraged medical students who said they had drawn new hope and inspiration from his performance. Again, some asked for advice: "They made me feel pretty helpless. It's no simple thing to advise an earnest youngster who is confused about life. You can't ignore them, either. About all I can do is tell them to keep on trying. It's trite, of course, but at least I believe it myself." Then, of course, there were the usual crackpots that all celebrities hear from— inventors, hustlers, people looking for loans or investment dollars. A few, written in honest desperation, got his attention.

"I think of you many, many times, always look forward to your letters," he wrote Lincoln Cromwell, now in his fourth year at McGill,

but I have been so busy the past year, myself, that I haven't found much time for correspondence. Now I have a very fine secretary, so we hope things will be different . . . You have done beautifully, and I'm proud of you, and I want you to go on. Helping you has been a great source of pleasure and satisfaction, and I'm perfectly willing, even anxious, to have you continue in study for another year or two. How you choose to do this will be left practically to your own judgment. I have even thought of Europe for a year, if you feel that anything could be gained and your service to humanity enhanced by study there. I am anxious to see you this summer, when we will talk all these things over. May I tell you, Lincoln, the past year has been wonderful for me, too. It has been the best year that I have ever had in my work, besides being by far the best physically and mentally. We have a lovely farm in [the Valley], and Mrs. Tracy and the children are all well and happy. I have also a nice 40-foot sailboat which has given me a lot of pleasure, and I hope that this summer you and I can have a little cruise in it together. Enclosed please find [a] check, which I'm sure you can use.

Vic Fleming was ill, in the hospital for kidney stones, and *Captains Courageous* was on hold pending his recovery. Tracy went to the races, painted the barn, gave interviews focusing on the hard times he had seen before joining Metro-Goldwyn-Mayer. "As everyone knows, no actor is any better than his last picture," he said in a by-lined article for the *Oakland Tribune*. "And it isn't reasonable to expect that every one of your pictures is going to be a smash hit. You may get two in a row or even three, or you may hit a jackpot consisting of *Fury, San Francisco, Libeled Lady,* and *Captains Courageous,* but not often."

He gave the studio full credit for salvaging his career ("I was well on my way to being a tough heavy for keeps") and he gave Louise credit for his sobriety. "The fact that I'm alive today, that I'm capable of any work or success—I owe to her. She's the most wonderful person I've ever known."

Fleming's two-day stint in the hospital stretched to three weeks, and filming resumed with Jack Conway at the helm. The production was plagued by illness: John Lee Mahin, Barrymore, Charley Grapewin all came down with the flu. Then Tracy, during a routine checkup, was told he had a goiter. He had noticed his thyroid gland was "a bit swollen"; although it wasn't toxic, he was told that it could, in time, obstruct his breathing. Dr. Dennis thought he should have it out "sometime." Tracy was just out of the hospital—more tests—when he learned that he had been nominated for an Academy Award.

The Academy of Motion Picture Arts and Sciences was at a low ebb in 1936, so many actors and writers having resigned during the formation of their respective guilds that neither the nominations nor the actual awards were considered representative of the industry at large. A nominating committee appointed by the academy president, director Frank Capra, came up with the contenders, which, for Best Actor, were Gary Cooper (in Capra's *Mr. Deeds Goes to Town*), Walter Huston (in *Dodsworth*), William Powell (*My Man Godfrey*), Paul Muni (*The Story of Louis Pasteur*), and Tracy, who took the nomination for his work in *San Francisco*.

It was astonishing. Having resigned from the academy, Tracy hadn't considered the possibility of a nomination, much less in the company of men like Huston and Muni, both of whom he regarded as better actors. Moreover, he had managed the trick with a mere seventeen minutes of screen time in a picture that ran just shy of two hours. Given the general antipathy toward the academy on the part of the Screen Actors Guild membership—which had boycotted the Oscars the previous year—he seemed a little embarrassed by the whole thing.

Fleming was back in time to shoot Tracy's last and most difficult scene, the death of Manuel in the icy waters off Gloucester. Tangled in the broken topmast of the *We're Here,* his legs and chest crushed, Manuel is as good as dead and he knows it. ("He's got about five hundred pounds of wire stay cuttin' and stretchin' him down," a crew member gasps, working the line.) Manuel calls out to the crew in Portuguese so that young Harvey won't know what he is saying. To the tearful boy he is his usual carefree self, says he's tired and that he's going to ask Disko to let him go. "I want to go, little fish. I no good anymore fishing here. I go fish with my father. You . . . 'member I say he keep seat for me in his boat?"

On the morning of February 12, 1937, Tracy, with a philosophical grin, slipped down from the mast and into the studio tank, tangling himself in the wreckage, his wetsuit hidden under the water, the camera on a crane overhead, the microphone boom on a skiff to one side, Fleming and Hal Rosson on a skiff to the other. A couple of uniformed nurses stood on the sectional deck of the *We're Here* in case of an accident. At a signal from Fleming the storm began.

"And what a storm!" columnist Robbin Coons observed.

Huge paddles churn up a frothy sea, clouds of spray fly with a roar from a towering wooden reservoir, and a huge funnel batters Tracy's head with wind. The waves rise higher, higher, engulfing him, knocking him about as he yells his dialogue. Rescuers are John Carradine—just up from the flu—Dave Thursby, and Jack Stirling, all of whom get nearly as drenched as Tracy. And they do the scene three times. Before the last take Tracy, submerged in his art if ever an actor was, catches me leering on the sidelines and jeers, "You like to try it? If you've got to laugh, you might stay out of my line of vision!" But another wave breaks over him before I can explain it wasn't laughter but an expression I always wear when wondering whether Metro is trying to drown Tracy.

The six-page scene took three long days to shoot, the exchange between Tracy and Freddie Bartholomew playing primarily in close-ups. Screen-writer John Lee Mahin, who was present during much of the shoot, was puzzled early on by Fleming's distant staging of the scenes with Bartholomew. "I said, 'Geez, this is a beautiful kid, Vic. It seems to me you're not getting the close-ups of this kid.' He said, 'Wait till we need 'em. Wait till they'll have some effect.' I said, 'Well, when will that be?' He said, 'When he starts crying and breaking. That's when we'll go in to see him.' And this tough bastard starts to move in on him. He was right."

In an ever-rising state of panic, Harvey crawls out onto the splintered mast of the *We're Here.* "You're all right, aren't you? You aren't hurt, are you

Manuel?" And Long Jack, floating alongside Manuel, calls out to the captain. "The drift is tightenin' it! You got to cut loose, Disko—or it'll take him in half!" And Harvey, scrambling into a dory, glances around at the somber men on deck and then back at Manuel.

"No!" he gulps.

"We ain't cuttin' loose," Disko returns, "unless it's gonna help you free Manuel!"

And Manuel calls out, "You cut him away, Disko! You hear me?"

Resigned, the captain says, "Get me an ax," knowing that cutting the line is a task that only he can do.

"No!" pleads Harvey. "Captain Disko! No!"

With Freddie now within inches of Tracy's face, Fleming managed the most intimate of exchanges against the commotion of Barrymore's futile attempts at rescue, the ax's blows registering ominously on the soundtrack, Tracy bobbing and wincing in pain, striving mightily to convince the boy that he's really okay. "We have good times together, eh, little fish? We laugh, we sing, so you smile now. Come on, little fish . . ."

"Long Jack can fix it. You'll be all right, won't you Manuel?"

"Manuel, he be watching you. You be best fisherman ever."

And as the ax severed the line, the apparatus pulled Tracy down into the water and out of sight, Freddie clawing at the surface, the men restraining him, the cold finality of the moment weighing on both him and the audience.

Freddie Bartholomew managed the scene with tremendous restraint, on the verge of tears as the terror grips him yet never out of control, never permitting himself to completely let go. Tracy understood that it was Freddie's scene more fully than it was his own, and he played it as would an expert straight man, feeding the lines the boy could respond to, giving him the spotlight even as Fleming insistently cut to Manuel. In the end, it's the audience's empathy with Harvey, and not Manuel's brave exit, that so powerfully puts the scene across.

"Well, I got away with it," Tracy said after it was all over. "Want to know why? Because of Freddie, because of that kid's performance, because he sold it 98%. The kid had to believe in Manuel, or Manuel wasn't worth a quarter. The way he would look at me, believe every word I said, made me believe in it myself. I've never said this before, and I'll never say it again. Freddie Bartholomew's acting is so fine and so simple and so true that it's way over people's heads. It'll only be by thinking back two or three years from now that they'll realize how great it was."

One day on the lot a few weeks later, Tracy breezed into his dressing room and told Yvonne Beaudry they could see a runoff of the finished picture, which had taken five long months to shoot. Inside a studio projection room, they watched Manuel regenerate the pampered Harvey and then go to his watery grave. "When we emerged from the dark room into bright sunlight," Beaudry remembered, "I was ashamed that my eyes were filled with tears. To my astonishment, Tracy's eyes also were moist and red and he quickly hid them behind sunglasses."

CHAPTER 13

The New Rage

With the completion of his scenes for Victor Fleming, Tracy went into his next picture without a break. As he remembered it, "they hauled me out of the water on a Saturday afternoon when we finished *Captains Courageous.* Monday morning, I was standing in the middle of the street of a shell-torn village on the back lot, and Woody Van Dyke was ordering Harry Albiez, his prop man, to outfit me to the last cartridge."

The film version of a pacifist best seller, *They Gave Him a Gun* was initially to have been directed by Fleming, who saw it as "a great anti-war document." Then, when *Captains Courageous* ran seriously over schedule, Tracy was instrumental in getting Van Dyke to do it instead. He liked the speed at which Van Dyke worked and the fact that he wasn't fussy like Borzage or Lang. (Having just finished with Manuel, Tracy unconsciously lapsed into his quasi-Portuguese dialect during an early take and Van Dyke printed it anyway.) Replacing Jean Harlow as nurse Rose Duffy was Gladys George, a stage and screen veteran whose nomination for Best Actress (for Paramount's *Valiant Is the Word for Carrie*) paralleled Tracy's own for Best Actor.

Around the time of the Academy Awards banquet, Tracy was shooting battleground scenes in Chatsworth, a short drive from his Encino ranch on the same five hundred acres where exteriors for *The Good Earth* had been filmed. The winners, announced with considerable hubbub on the night of March 4, 1937, surprised practically no one, in part because they had been accurately handicapped in the trades as well as in the *Los Angeles Times,* giving the Best Actor nod to Paul Muni and Best Actress to Luise Rainer for her performance as Anna Held in M-G-M's *The Great Ziegfeld.* With Metro claiming the most employees among the academy's voting membership of approximately eight hundred, it was widely presumed that Rainer would win the award, as Norma Shearer, nominated for *Romeo and Juliet,* already had one. "Critics," according to the *Hollywood Citizen News,* "generally were of the opinion that Spencer Tracy as the priest in *San Francisco* ran Muni the closest race and that had he been placed in the [new] category of Supporting Actor he might have won that hands down."

Van Dyke finished *They Gave Him a Gun* in twenty-four days, remarkable given the logistics of the shoot. Tracy completed his scenes on March 20 and spent most of the following week lolling on the *Carrie B* waiting for the inevitable punch list of retakes that followed every Van Dyke production. He was back at work on the twenty-ninth when Susie had her tonsils and adenoids out at Good Samaritan Hospital. Then, granted a six-week leave of absence, he prepared to enter the hospital himself, placing a natural gift for morbidity on full display as he hopelessly garbled the doctor's prognosis and convinced himself he had cancer.

"I haven't been telling people because I wanted to wait until it was over," he confided to Howard Sharpe, who had just completed a multipart biography of him for *Photoplay,* "but I'm going into a hospital tomorrow and I've got a fifty-fifty chance of coming out of it. Except in a hearse. And if I do come out, I may never be able to speak again."

What doctors had actually told him was that there was a fifty-fifty chance his vocal cords would be damaged as a result of the surgery. Overall, they assured him, the operation was "not serious" and the only threat to his life would be in the unlikely event the gland was malignant. All the same, he spent the morning of April 6 finalizing his will and concluding morosely that he couldn't afford to die. "They take everything, one way or another," he told Sharpe. "I don't know what Louise and the kids would do."

He went to Confession, then entered the hospital with only a hardcover novel to keep him company. ("Hope [I] come back to finish this nice book," he wrote that night in his datebook.) His sole visitor the next morning was Jean Harlow, who told him she'd dropped around "for a game of handball." The surgery took all of thirty minutes, and Tracy seemed slightly disappointed the gland wasn't cancerous. Howard Strickling's office put out the news that Tracy had simply had his tonsils out, but someone from the Associated Press reached Dr. Clarence Toland, who actually performed the operation, and most AP members accurately reported the surgery was to correct "a chronic thyroid ailment."

While Tracy was in the hospital, *They Gave Him a Gun* was sneaked in

Huntington Park. Harry Rapf had eliminated all the antiwar lines, save one, and that one line got such a terrific ovation at the preview that Eddie Mannix ordered all the others restored. No one seemed particularly happy with the picture, and Maurice Rapf, the producer's son and one of three credited writers on the script, remembered hearing somewhere that Tracy had refused to play Fred Willis as a scoundrel because, according to Rapf, he was certain audiences would no longer "accept him as a heel." Writing in his datebook, Tracy himself thought the picture "bad" and the character of Willis nothing more than a "nice dumb guy." In other words, a mugg.

Predictably, the reception accorded *They Gave Him a Gun* didn't engage him nearly as much as that for *Captains Courageous,* which had its gala premiere at L.A.'s Carthay Circle on the night of May 14, 1937. Where *Gun* was essentially a programmer—albeit with some high-powered talent attached—*Captains Courageous* was a two-a-day roadshow attraction, a genuine event in the world of film. Unfortunately, the press preview at Grauman's Chinese a few weeks earlier had taken some of the gleam off the film's official opening, and a lot of top names passed on the privilege of paying five dollars apiece to see it again. Even with invites and comps worked in, the 1,500-seat theater was only half full, something of an embarrassment for M-G-M's Strickling, who also had to contend with several hundred union pickets.

Tracy, however, seemed oddly relieved by the forced intimacy of the evening, and although the reaction at the press preview had been overwhelmingly positive, he was still unsure as to how his work would be received by the general public. All he could see in his own performance were the tricks of the characterization—the makeup, the curly hair, the dime store accent. (At Grauman's, a man had patted him on the head and said, "All you needed was a derby hat.") Two lines of Portuguese had to be dubbed by another actor, and those lines grated every time he heard them. "This is Freddie's night," he told the radio audience in all sincerity, "and that's how it should be."

But the audience could see that night what Tracy could not: a glowing portrayal of all that was good and profound in a simple man of the sea. The mechanics of the performance mattered not nearly so much as its heart, and Louella Parsons reported bursts of applause from the likes of Clark Gable, Carole Lombard, Marlene Dietrich, and Douglas Fairbanks, Jr. Columnist Harrison Carroll, having passed on the press preview, marveled at the film's power to move such a jaded crowd: "Of all the stiff-shirted gentlemen and the décolleté ladies in the audience, I doubt if there was a single one who did not weep with Freddie Bartholomew over the death of Spencer Tracy, the story's lovable Manuel. The relationship of these two has been made into a masterpiece of screen sentiment."

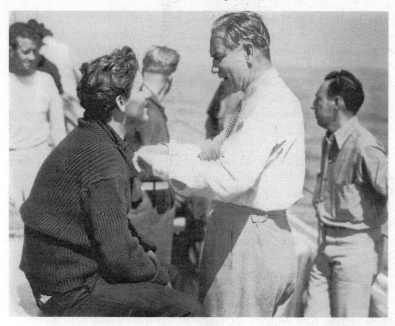

Tracy gave Victor Fleming full credit for the success of *Captains Courageous*.
(SUSIE TRACY)

Audiences, perhaps aware the picture wasn't another *Mutiny on the Bounty,* took their time embracing it. In Los Angeles, it started building after a dismal first few days, posting a second-week gross considerably better than the first. In New York, it followed *The Good Earth* into the elegant little Astor, Loew's premiere house for roadshow attractions, and did well without ever quite reaching capacity business. Pushing the film with characteristic candor, Tracy talked to any number of journalists, both foreign and domestic. He told Philip K. Scheuer he thought his performance "hammy" but was nevertheless convinced it was a great picture.

"The man to be thanked because *Captains Courageous* turned out as well as it did is the director, Victor Fleming. You'll never know what he went through—six months, mostly on a process stage with only three sections of boat to work with, the stinking smell of fish, Freddie Bartholomew limited to four hours of work a day—and Fleming himself sick as a dog half the time." To Gladys Hall he added: "He must have done a magnificent job, because it was the first picture of mine I ever saw where I sat and forgot all about myself, lost track that that was me up there."

Ida Zeitlin thought she caught something of Manuel's glow in a story Carrie Tracy told her about the family's move to New York in 1927. Carrie was lonely for her friends in Milwaukee, and asked her husband if he wasn't as well. "Well, no, Mother, I can't say that I am," John Tracy replied. "I just walk down Fifth Avenue and look at those wonderful buildings and stop in at that beautiful cathedral, and—well, what is there to be lonesome about?" And Zeitlin was reminded of Manuel bent over his vielle and telling Harvey about the songs his father wrote: "Songs about the sun and the sea, songs about the clouds, big songs about the wind and the storms, and little songs too about the tip of my mother's nose. Oh, my father, he feel beautiful inside!"

The release of *Captains Courageous* brought another wave of fan mail, and with it came offers of boats and ship models and long, rambling letters from Snug Harbor, the New York–based home for retired seamen. One envelope contained an invitation to cross the Atlantic in a thirty-four-foot ketch with the builder-owner, "age 62 and sound as a dollar."* Another, from an ex-army flyer, invited him to fly a low-wing monoplane across the ocean. "The publicity value of your presence," the writer concluded, "would repay me for the slight risk involved." A federal prisoner in Leavenworth offered to take him on a hunt for pirate treasure in the Caribbean if only Tracy could secure his release. Gold Star mothers wrote, having seen him in *They Gave Him a Gun,* and mail was still coming from his having played a priest, much of it now from Europe and Asia.

"I know that in my own case it never came so forcibly till now that pictures and the people in them carry a heavy responsibility," he said. "That wasn't the fact where the theatre was concerned. People weren't particularly swayed by a show or an actor or actress. At least not to the extent that their personal lives were affected. But pictures evidently go deeper."

Outwardly, the Tracy marriage was as solid as ever, and Spence credited Louise's forbearance, as he always did, for making it so. "She doesn't nag, you see. She respects my individuality, asks nothing," he explained one day during a joint interview. "If I say suddenly in the afternoon that I'm going to Ensenada for a few days, she doesn't ever ask why. She doesn't say, 'How long will you be gone? What're you going to do down there? Can't you take me with you?' She just smiles and tells me she hopes I'll have a good time."

"But it's a mutual freedom," Louise interjected. "He does the same. I never ask if I may do something; the choice is mine. The reason for most divorces is this business of husband and wife keeping tabs on each other. I

* "He saw you in the picture," said Gable sardonically. "He wants to get you out in the Atlantic alone."

don't wonder most of them go crazy. Anyway, if each really loves and trusts the other, what's the sense in prying about?"

It had been a year and a half since Tracy had taken a drink of anything stronger than tea. "No, not even a beer," he said.

Not even light wines. Nothing. And there's all the difference between night and day in the way I feel now. Everything is different. Me. Our home life. It just isn't the same at all, in any way. It's normal now. It's comfortable . . . I get a kick out of life such as I never had when I was on the merry-go-round. We take long drives in the evening, Louise and I. We sit home evenings and read and talk. We plan trips. The kids and I go swimming together. And riding. There's a flavor in doing all the so-called "little things." We have one or two couples in for dinner, the Walt Disneys, the Van Dykes, the Pat O'Briens.* That's social enough. We have our polo crowd, of course.

Despite such statements, Jane Feely could sense real tension when she came to visit over the month of June 1937. The ranch wasn't movie star fancy nor nearly as spacious as the rented house on Holmby. One entered the sizable living room directly off the front porch. There was no grand portico, no entrance hall. The sideboard was an old pine dresser, gleaming with brass and copper and Delft chinaware. The refectory table and chairs—there was no dining room—were hand-made and could seat ten in a pinch. The sofas were covered in cretonne, the overstuffed chair a splashy yellow. There were bookshelves, framed photos, a piano off to one corner. Down a long hall were the master bedrooms, in Spence's case severely plain in terms of decor. ("I never met anyone who so despises chi-chi," Dick Mook once commented, "and there is not one piece of furniture in the entire room that is not utilitarian.") Louise's room was almost as simple and, as with Spence's, done entirely in maple. Johnny's room, over in the new wing, was the nicest in the house, built for maximum exposure to the sun. Four-year-old Susie's room was nearly as devoid of frippery as her mother's, and the kitchen was done in tones of orange and red. The living space that got the most use was the screened-in porch out back, where most of the family's summer meals were taken. Out past the swimming pool was the bunkhouse where Jane stayed. Spence had originally thought he might live out there himself, but the central heating didn't extend that far, and the only source of warmth during winter was a small fireplace.

* When they entertained, which was rare, Louise always served the same thing—baked pork chop with a particular kind of baked apple. It was her signature dish.

Within days of Jane's arrival, Jean Harlow died unexpectedly of kidney disease at the age of twenty-six. Tracy was at the studio that day and was struck speechless by the news. Helen Gilmore, an editor with Bernarr Mac-Fadden's *Liberty* magazine, came upon him in the studio cafe. "I can't believe it," he said, staring out the Venetian blinds. He told of Harlow's visit to Good Samaritan just ahead of his surgery and how it turned out to be the same hospital in which she died. Earlier, in a piece for *Screenland,* Tracy had celebrated Harlow's spirit, relating, for instance, how she had given him a black eye shooting a scene for *Riffraff.* ("She meant to pull her punch, but overplayed her hand.") On *Libeled Lady* he considered himself the least of the four stars, referring to himself around the set as "Zeppo." Harlow, he said, "did something for me that no one else had ever done, moved me physically around to put my face further into the picture, saying, 'Get your mug in there, will you?'"

Louise had heard things about Harlow—her drinking, her affairs, and her rumored abortions—and had little to say when Spence brought the news. "He came home," said Jane,

> and I remember being in the room when he was telling Louise about it, and she said, "Well, you know, there are stories . . ." Something under her breath. And he said, "The HELL with those stories! Anytime I ever worked with her she arrived on time, she knew her lines, and she was ready to work. I don't care what she did or who she did it with—I don't believe any of it and I don't want to hear any of it! As far as I'm concerned, she was a co-worker that I had a great deal of respect for." Words to that effect. He did a tremendous defense of Jean Harlow and he said, "I understand it's a Christian Science funeral, but this is one I *will* go to."
>
> [Louise] would say, "I'm just not at home with those people." But she did go to Jean Harlow's funeral. "If you're going, I'll go with you." She came to a great deal more understanding of herself than she was ever given credit for, I think, and was able to live with herself so much more peacefully . . . I would see her being buffeted, ignored by so-called Hollywood inner circles . . . She was having to buy into stuff that she knew was really crass. Spencer knew it was crass, that it was really the seamy side of life . . . There was anger between those two people, [and] every so often it would erupt.

Louise had enrolled Johnny in a ballroom dancing class in the hope it would improve his coordination. The class met once a week, and the final session was a party attended by parents and guests. Louise took Jane, who danced with several of the boys, and afterward she took the kids for ice cream. It was late by the time they got back to the ranch, laughing and full of high spirits, and Spence was there pacing the floor. "Where the HELL have you been?" he demanded, his face purple with rage. "I've called every hospital, I've called the cops, I've called everybody! I thought you were going to be home by ten o'clock!"

"Why, we were . . . nothing . . . We just went out and had—"

"WHY in the HELL didn't you CALL?"

"Well," said Louise, "I would call, Spencer. I thought you'd be in bed."

"By God, you've got this girl here visiting who doesn't even belong to us, and this boy here. God knows you could have been banged up on the highway . . ."

Jane struggled to get away as quickly as possible.

God, he'd worked himself into a *state,* probably because he didn't have anything else to do. He was just furious. Even then, she didn't come back at him—"Well, why didn't you come with us?" She just calmly took it. So many times she just sort of took those tirades. Anything to keep peace. And anything not to lower herself. And that just made him madder, I think. There are always those kinds of problems in a marriage, but this one had to be lived so publicly . . . I think his self-esteem was very low. By the same token, I think Louise's was not. I think she was comfortable. She knew her limitations, but the thing I don't think she knew was how deeply hurt and vulnerable and wounded she was. I don't think she admitted those things.

The last time Jane had visited, the Loretta Young affair was heating up and Spence had been working for Frank Borzage. Now, four years later, she found him again working for Borzage, the same meticulous approach to coverage visibly wearing on him after working for such decisive and hard-charging men as Fleming and Van Dyke. The picture was *Big City,* a romance of modern-day New York in which Tracy had been paired with one of Metro's prestige properties, the German-born stage actress Luise Rainer. She had recently won the Academy Award for her role in *The Great Ziegfeld,* and her subsequent work in *The Good Earth* established her as one of the screen's top actresses. So far, however, she had failed to catch on with the public, and *Big City* was an obvious attempt to commonize her.

Putting Tracy opposite Luise Rainer ensured she had someone of equal weight to play against. She was, however, showing the signs of disenchantment that would end her movie career after three short years in California, and her attitudes didn't play well with her new costar, at least not at first. "I can remember his coming home one day in time for dinner," Jane said. "God, it was hot and he was just wilted. He said, 'I hauled that Viennese lump* up and down those stairs twenty times today! God!' I remember his saying something about talking to her about the work, Stanislavsky and the Group Theatre. He said to her, 'Why don't you and I go to New York and live in a garret?' "

Rainer, who didn't click with Borzage and thought the picture "pretty idiotic," kept mainly to herself. At the same time, Tracy was preoccupied with the fact that Weeze was in Good Samaritan for a biopsy, having noticed a lump on her breast. It was, as it turned out, benign, a simple cyst, but she would be in over the weekend, and Spence, relieved and fidgety, figured his costar was not so much a snob as a profoundly unhappy woman whose recent marriage to the New York–based playwright Clifford Odets was already on the rocks.

"I was married to a wonderful man, whom I dearly loved," Rainer said, "but it wasn't working, and, of course, it was a great heartache for me. While I was doing *Big City* with Spencer I had a friend-secretary, a woman, and he asked her, 'Does Miss Rainer like sailing?' And Hannah, my secretary, came to me and said, 'Mr. Spencer Tracy says do you like sailing?' I was pretty much down and out inside, so I said to her, 'I don't know. What kind of sailing?' Anyway, to make a long story short, he had a boat, I think in San Pedro, and we all spent the weekend together."

They powered out to Long Point, on the front side of Catalina, arriving around 2:30 on a Sunday morning. "He was terribly sweet and dear, but I think he was a bit shy of me, too, knowing also that I was perturbed at the time. He was sensitive to that and, moreover, I did not have the average Hollywood personality. I was more quiet—or whatever you may call it—but he was immensely kind and dear and comforting." It was hot and sunny that next day—no breeze—and they didn't get back to the yacht club until early evening. That night was the night Tracy made a note in his datebook: "18 months—1 year and a half—without a drink!!!"

After a rough first week, the mood on the set of *Big City* lightened, and when Borzage kept at a tense scene all morning and well past noontime, shooting it "up, down, and around," Tracy said to him pointedly: "How about LUNCH, Mr. Lang?" Borzage smiled wanly, ordered one final take, then dismissed the company, Tracy making off to the commissary with a visiting journalist. "It isn't worth it," he moaned, clearly beat from roiling the same emotional energy over and over. "None of this is. Oh, I have no kick coming. The money is fine and I like it out here. But making pictures

---

* Luise Rainer was German, but to deflect growing anti-German sentiment the studio said she was Viennese.

Tracy and Luise Rainer listen as director Frank Borzage explains a scene on the set of *Big City,* 1937. (SUSIE TRACY)

is a terrible tax on your health, and nothing is worth that." Watching his weight, Tracy ordered cottage cheese and matzos for lunch, then added lamb chops and ice cream when the waitress said, "Is that all you're going to have?"

By the time Sidney Skolsky watched a scene being made toward the end of production, he could truthfully report to his readers that Tracy and Luise Rainer were enjoying themselves. Rainer's technique—if one could call it that—was not unlike Tracy's own. "I never acted," she said. "I *felt* everything." And she eschewed makeup, as much, at least, as an actress at M-G-M would be allowed. Tracy told Elizabeth Yeaman he thought Helen Hayes the screen's finest actress, but quickly added that he also admired Sylvia Sidney, Beulah Bondi, and Rainer, who, with her big soulful eyes and her self-done hair, projected a waiflike quality unique among his leading ladies.

Indeed, whatever success *Big City* achieved as a film was due in large part to the brittle chemistry that developed between its two unlikely stars, both of whom, at least initially, would have preferred doing something else entirely. Said screenwriter Dore Schary, who had once shared the stage with Tracy as a minor actor in *The Last Mile,* "Those of us working on the film had a marvelous time—a happy time—but while the trade reviews were good, the picture simply didn't work. Perhaps Sam Goldwyn in his infinite wisdom was right when he said, 'A happy set means a lousy picture.' "

On June 26, 1937, a week after Louise's release from the hospital, she and the kids sailed for Hawaii. Spence was in the midst of *Big City,* working most days, and urged them to go on without him. In Hawaii, Louise took the children to see *Captains Courageous;* Johnny had already seen it, but this would be Susie's first time watching her dad on screen. The accent and the curly hair didn't fool her, and when it came time for him to slide away, Freddie calling after him, she was agape. "I just sat staring at the screen in disbelief," she said. "I was stunned, and Mother said, 'No, no, Daddy's fine. He's at home.' In retrospect, I think I was probably too young to see it, and I have trouble watching that scene to this day."

Tracy took a suite at the Beverly Wilshire for the balance of the shoot. They finished *Big City* late on the evening of July 27 and he left the hotel the following morning, spending his next few days aboard the *Carrie B.* He was struggling with the boat, anxious to keep it and yet increasingly unable to justify the expense for what were largely weekend getaways. He was bringing home $1,734.25 a week, but was still supporting his polo habit and a small stable of racehorses, the most prominent of which, April Lass, had finished in the money her very first start. Louise and the kids got back on August 7, and she and Spence went out to Riviera that same afternoon, playing five chukkers together, the first time either had been on a horse in over a month. The next day, Spence recorded his worst game ever, Walter Ruben, picture executive Ken Fitzpatrick, and Walt Disney all having played "horribly." His time on the boat had obviously taken its toll, and he made the decision that it had to go.

There was talk of reteaming Tracy and Freddie Bartholomew in Kipling's *Kim,* which had been in development a couple of years, but more immediate plans had him going into the next Joan Crawford picture, a shopgirl trifle called *Three Rooms in Heaven.* Tracy wasn't happy about the assignment—he disliked Crawford's work as an actress and knew the picture would do him no credit. Mook thought it simply the part's size that galled him, but for Tracy it was more basic than that: "If I'm any kind of actor, I can make a run-of-the-mill part come to life. I don't mind her part being fatter or larger than mine. I'd a lot rather people would leave a theater wishing they had seen more of me in the picture than have them go out feeling they had seen too much. The thing that upsets me about this picture is that that girl is such a *phony.* And it comes through in her portrayals."

He was being pressured to play another priest, something he vowed he

Aboard the *Carrie B,* circa 1937.
(SUSIE TRACY)

would never again do. He put in for vacation time, anxious to return to Honolulu with Louise, but was told not to go because the Crawford picture would be starting within days. When he suddenly got permission to take two weeks, it came as a surprise and he forgot about Hawaii altogether, impulsively making arrangements to go on a fishing trip to British Columbia instead. He left for Seattle, settling in for the journey with a newspaper and a stack of magazines.

At Puget Sound, Han Jamison, a local journalist and a genuine admirer who had just seen *Captains Courageous,* asked him why the shot of Manuel holding his nose as he was pulled underwater wasn't cut from the picture. "Why Manuel wasn't holding his nose," Tracy replied, pronouncing it Man-oo-el. "He was crossing himself and the camera just happened to catch his hand as it passed his nose." The answer seemed to satisfy his inquisitor, but it was yet another flaw in a performance that was, for Tracy, all too full of them, and for every sharp little point of imperfection, a stab of guilt, imperceptible at times but ever-present. He caught the boat on schedule, running on little, if any, sleep, and spent the morning of August 20 fishing off the coast of Canada. Then, later that same day, after exactly one year and eight months on the wagon, he took a drink—something, perhaps, as seemingly innocent as a single bottle of beer—and, as he later recorded in his datebook, "spoiled it all."

Flying from Seattle to San Francisco, where he lingered over a long weekend, Tracy returned to the Beverly Wilshire to indulge in his longest and most serious bender in three years. From Monday, August 23, the pages of his datebook told the story: "Binge!" he wrote for most days, noting finally on Friday, September 3, "Came home—ended siege." The next day he added: "At home sick—these are sad pages."

And then: "Back on wagon! This time for [a] real stretch—"

Since the release of *Fury,* Joe Mankiewicz had been producing the Joan Crawford pictures for M-G-M. ("You're the only one on the lot that knows what to do with her," Mayer had said to him.) The collaboration had so far yielded mixed results, including Crawford's only costume drama, *The Gorgeous Hussy.* The new story Mankiewicz had for her was an original by Katharine Brush, whose racy 1931 novel *Red Headed Woman* had been the basis of Jean Harlow's breakout film. Submitted by agent Harold Ober, "Marry for Money" was considered excellent material but doubtful for pictures "unless the heroine is whitewashed a little." Mankiewicz, who prided himself on "extracting the suds from soap opera" (as Crawford so eloquently put it), embraced it as a challenge of sorts and set to work on a script with playwright Lawrence Hazard.

Tracy was not an obvious choice for the millionaire shipping magnate who pursues Crawford's noble character, but the pairing was consistent with the strategy of putting him opposite Metro's biggest female attractions. Directing would again be Borzage, though the whole enterprise this time would be weighted toward the woman, with Tracy relegated to a supporting role. The result was a complete mismatch on the part of the two principals, their lack of screen chemistry exacerbated by a story in which Crawford's fiercely straight-arrow character eventually marries—but does not love—Tracy's. At thirty-two, Crawford was too old for the part of Jessie Cassidy, late of Hester Street, and, the carefully diffused lighting of George Folsey notwithstanding, looked it. Seemingly aware of all this, Borzage produced a remarkably static motion picture, long on dialogue and good looks, short on the kind of action that had come to distinguish Tracy's better work on the screen. The only real surprise about *Mannequin* was that its two stars got on as well as they did.

Tracy went back into the studio a little sheepishly, having effectively delayed the start of *Mannequin.* He saw Borzage and Joan Crawford and had a long talk with Eddie Mannix, who, he noted, was "wonderful" about it. Norma Shearer asked him to make a test for the role of King Louis XVI in *Marie Antoinette,* a flattering proposition that would mark his first time in period costume. He met with director Sidney Franklin and saw the tests of other actors vying for the part. Saturday was spent rehearsing with Crawford in the morning, Shearer in the afternoon. The test was shot at night the following Thursday after a full day's work. Tracy thought the result "no good" even though Shearer, much to his amazement, said that she liked it.

Mannequin finally got under way on September 14, and Tracy noted his weight at 176 1/4 in his datebook. He dug in again at the Beverly Wilshire and, at some point during the six weeks it took to shoot the picture, fell into an involvement with his costar, who had recently separated from actor Franchot Tone. Joan Crawford shared the signal quality of nearly all of Tracy's women—availability. The affair, which apparently generated little, if any, emotional heat, extended beyond the picture, but not by very much. Crawford contracted pneumonia during production—or so she said—and stubbornly reported to work with a 102-degree temperature until her doctor intervened. Getting her back into shape took a few days, and Dr. William Branch whisked her out to the Uplifters Club on the pretext of getting some fresh air into her. She sat in the car, its doors locked, and watched as Dr. Branch and Tracy played polo. In time, she was stick-and-balling a bit, and after the picture wrapped, she and Spence spent a day posing for stills on horseback.

In later years Crawford appeared to be of two minds about Tracy. In her autobiography, published during his lifetime, she said it was "inspiring" to play opposite him, and in a public statement several years after his death, she called him "one of the most beautiful men" she'd ever known. "Pure male with a mixture of small boy attitudes which made him beguiling beyond belief." Privately, though, she expressed real bitterness over *Mannequin,* contending that Tracy was so miscast "he made an absolute muddle out of my part, which wasn't all that great to begin with." She continued: "At first I felt honored working with Spence, and we even whooped it up a little bit off the set, but he turned out to be a real bastard. When he drank he was mean, and he drank all through production. He'd do cute things like step on my toes when we were doing a love scene—after he chewed on some garlic."

Tracy, of course, was completely dry during the making of the film and for a considerable time thereafter. (His datebook entry for October 4: "1 month on the wagon instead of 21 months! Jackass!") Crawford's anger was surely over the fact that it was Tracy who ended the dalliance and not Crawford herself. Her obsessive-compulsive behavior and slavish devotion to the business of being a movie star would quickly have grated on him, and when the brief sexual infatuation had faded, he would have lost no time in distancing himself. A few months later, he reportedly came off at her while rehearsing "Anna Christie" for the *Lux Radio Theatre.* "For crissake, Joan, can't you read the lines?" he erupted as she nervously fumbled with her script. "I thought you were supposed to be a pro."

Joan Crawford and Tracy in a candid moment on the set of *Mannequin* (1937).
(PATRICIA MAHON COLLECTION)

Tracy had been off radio since February, when Louis B. Mayer, under pressure from exhibitors, imposed a ban on broadcasting for all contract players. The practice of putting film stars on the air in tab versions of their latest pictures had been blamed for weak showings at the box office, and *The Good Earth* and *The Last of Mrs. Cheyney* became the first Metro releases with no radio exposure whatsoever. By summer the blanket restric-

Tracy disliked radio, but the money it paid made it difficult
to refuse. Here he prepares for a *Lux Radio Theatre* broadcast of "Arrowsmith" in October 1937. With him are Fay
Wray and host Cecil B. DeMille. (PATRICIA MAHON
COLLECTION)

tion appeared to be loosening, and Loew's gave its consent for the American
Tobacco Company to enter into agreements with six reigning M-G-M personalities, Robert Taylor, Myrna Loy, and Tracy among them, to appear on
programs sponsored by the company and produced by its agency, Lord &
Thomas. The studio retained the right of script approval, and American
Tobacco agreed to supply each artist's "smoking needs" with a carton a week
of Lucky Strike cigarettes.* Tracy didn't appear for American Tobacco during the run of the agreement, but was among the stable of stars—which
included virtually everyone other than Greta Garbo and Norma Shearer—
to appear on Metro's own weekly program, a frantic vaudeville of premium
names known collectively as *Good News of 1938*.

* Tracy began smoking Luckies in the navy, but was never a heavy smoker.

The show, a historic collaboration between M-G-M and the Maxwell House division of General Foods, originated from Hollywood's El Capitan theater every Thursday night (so as not to conflict with movie attendance on Fridays and Saturdays). Jeanette MacDonald, Allan Jones, Eleanor Powell, George Murphy, Judy Garland, Sophie Tucker, and Buddy Ebsen all crowded into the first broadcast on November 4, and Tracy, along with Joan Crawford, Robert Young, Mickey Rooney, and Ted Heeley, was part of the second installment on November 11. Having seen *Mannequin* at the studio only two days before ("Stinks!" he wrote in his datebook), he and Crawford now performed an episode from the picture, really just a teaser, thus discharging his contractual obligation to make such an appearance. The next time he emoted on *Good News,* he collected a fee of $3,500 for his trouble.

Tracy had just committed to making a picture called *Test Pilot* for Victor Fleming when, on November 20, 1937, Eddie Mannix's wife was killed in a bizarre automobile accident outside of Palm Springs. Bernice Mannix had gone to the desert with family friends and had gambled into the early morning hours at the Dunes, a popular nightspot run by a Detroit mobster named Al Wertheimer. Wertheimer was driving her back to the desert home of Joe Schenck, where she and a niece were staying, when he suddenly swerved to avoid a tow truck that had stopped for a stalled car on the highway. Slamming on the brakes, Wertheimer lost control of his coupe, which left the pavement and overturned, throwing its driver clear but crushing its thirty-seven-year-old passenger. Reached at home, Eddie Mannix was rushed by air to Banning, where the body had been taken. The couple had been married eighteen years.

Tracy saw Mannix the next afternoon and was an active pallbearer at the High Mass celebrated in Beverly Hills the following morning (as were Harry Rapf, Clark Gable, Woody Van Dyke, and Hunt Stromberg). He went straight from Good Shepherd to Riviera, where he played furiously and lost to a six-goal champion. That evening, he sat with Mannix, Howard Strickling, and others at the former's modest two-bedroom house on Linden Drive. The following morning, Spence and Louise left to accompany Mannix, his niece Alice, and Strickling on the train back to Boston, where Bernice would be laid to rest. "I remember seeing Uncle Eddie and Tracy going back for hot fudge sundaes, I guess to keep Tracy away from the booze," Alice said. "They ate a lot of hot fudge sundaes between L.A. and Boston."

Eddie Mannix couldn't have children, so Bernice had adopted her nieces and nephews and loved having them around. They all crowded into their grandmother's house at Somerville, where Margaret Fitzmaurice had presided over the first Catholic family to move into town. She had nine children, made her own soap, and saw that their three-story house—and all the kids—were spotless. Tracy was immediately taken with her, her quiet dignity and the fact that she made wonderful marble cake without a recipe.

The first afternoon, rubbing his hands together, Tracy said, "Grandma, what kind of ice cream would you like?"

"Oh, I think strawberry," she said after a moment.

And so Tracy put on his hat and coat and walked down the long driveway, past a clutch of onlookers, ignoring them completely, and hied himself up the hill to a little store where he could buy a pint of strawberry ice cream. Then he took her by the hand, led her into the kitchen, and sat for the next hour, just the two of them, eating the ice cream and talking. The next day, following the funeral, he repeated the exercise, and when it came time for him and Louise to leave, he took her face in his hands and kissed her gently on both cheeks. "You're the most beautiful woman I've ever met," he said softly.

As they drove away, Grandma Fitzmaurice was glowing. "What a nice man," she said to her granddaughter Jean. "Who is he?"

Even if Eddie Mannix's own mother-in-law didn't know who Spencer Tracy was, millions of moviegoers did. Just a week before he left for Boston, Tracy sat for another talk with Ed Sullivan, whose dispatch the following day carried the headline NEW RAGE IS SPENCER TRACY. Sullivan wrote: "Voting contests that are being conducted throughout the country to determine the ranking cinema heroes and heroines reveal that American girls are switching from Robert Taylor and Tyrone Power, or at least the type they represent, to the more stalwart type of hero suggested by Spencer Tracy. Every poll shows that Tracy is gaining by leaps and bounds, and theater managers say that the bulk of his votes are coming from girls and women who have become a trifle wearied of gentler heroes and want their romance raw, rough, and resolute."

The New Rage and his wife arrived in Manhattan intent on seeing a few shows and ducking the press as much as possible. They paused briefly to pay their respects to Eddie Mannix's own family in Fort Lee, where his brother owned a bar and staged cockfights. On Broadway they saw *Room Service, Golden Boy, Hurray for What!* (the new Ed Wynn show), and George M. Cohan in *I'd Rather Be Right.* They had a nice visit with George M. after the show, and were introduced to the former governor and presidential candidate Al Smith. Spence had to get back to Los Angeles for the start of the new Fleming picture, but Louise lingered an extra week, primarily to do some Christmas shopping and see some old friends. When she returned on

December 8, Spence had the news that Dr. Dennis had confirmed a hernia and that he was in for another operation after the first of the year. On the nineteenth he played his last game of polo for some time to come. ("Suffered terribly," he wrote in his book.) Three days after that, he was fitted with a truss.

Test Pilot wasn't a picture that either Tracy or Gable wanted to make. In Tracy's case it collided with his plans to take his family to Europe, but he decided to do it once the studio offered to sweeten his deal. As reported by the *Los Angeles Times,* Nicholas Schenck bestowed a "starring contract" worth $6,000 a week—a bit of an exaggeration in that Tracy's billing clause remained the same as before and the rate of compensation was only $4,000 a week. Still, it was a substantial bump from the $1,750 he had been getting, and he approached *Test Pilot,* at least at first, with a good deal of enthusiasm. In addition to Gable, he'd be appearing again with Myrna Loy and Lionel Barrymore, and Fleming, after the experience of working with him on *Captains Courageous,* had become just about Tracy's favorite director. ("The most attractive man I ever met in all my life," he told an interviewer.)

The source material, a manuscript titled *Wings of Tomorrow,* was by Frank "Spig" Wead, a former test pilot for the U.S. Navy who turned to writing after a freak accident left him confined to a wheelchair. A Wead story had been the basis of *Hell Divers* for M-G-M, and *Ceiling Zero,* based upon Wead's book and play of the same title, had been a hit the previous season for Warner Bros. A studio reader thought *Wings of Tomorrow* had "everything that *Ceiling Zero* had as a play and a lot more besides . . . The characters are excellent, the dialogue fine, the whole thing top-notch." It was, the report concluded, "suitable for Spencer Tracy."

The reason Gable said he resisted the picture was that he didn't understand "what the story was getting at," a complaint echoed by Myrna Loy. As the movie took shape, it was Fleming's enthusiasm that held the project together. Gable's reticence may also have come from the shifting balance between his character, Lane, the test pilot, and Tracy's, the no-nonsense mechanic, and the unthinkable possibility that Tracy could somehow end up with the girl. Originally, the property had been assigned to Lucian Hubbard, whose production of *Wings* won the first Academy Award for Best Picture. Hubbard put Bertram Millhauser on the script, but when he left to rejoin Paramount in the spring of 1937, the property passed to Bud Lighton, who worked out a whole new version of the story with John Lee Mahin. Fleming, one of Hollywood's more prominent amateur pilots, became the obvious choice to direct. In the months following, the screenplay passed from Mahin to Vincent Lawrence, then Waldemar Young, and then to Wead himself.

Filming commenced on December 7, coincidentally the same day the results of the poll Ed Sullivan had mentioned were announced by the Chicago Tribune-News Syndicate. Conducted by fifty-five metropolitan newspapers, the survey of more than 20 million was to determine the "King" and "Queen" of Hollywood for the year 1937. On that day, Sullivan officially proclaimed Clark Gable and Myrna Loy the winners. Gable, with 22,017 reader votes, outdistanced Robert Taylor, Tyrone Power, William Powell, Nelson Eddy, and Tracy, who came in sixth with 11,253 votes. Similarly, Loy outpolled Loretta Young, Jeanette MacDonald, Barbara Stanwyck, Sonja Henie, and Shirley Temple to take her title.

Gable, seemingly unaware of the promotion, "smelled a publicity stunt" when a delegation appeared on the set. "Anyway, they gave Myrna and me big plush crowns about a foot high, and they wanted to take pictures of us in them. I had visions of these big ears sticking out from under that crown. I backed away. So what did Tracy do? He used that as his cue to try every conceivable way to get that crown on me."

The following morning, Tracy had the entire crew lined up as Gable walked onto the stage. At Tracy's cue, the electricians and grips broke into a chorus: "Here comes the bee-yootiful king! All hail! All hail!" Gable, whom Tracy normally called "Moose," took the ribbing good-naturedly enough, then he joined in with more of the same when Loy appeared moments later. Tracy laid it on so thick that Gable and Loy approached a joint appearance on *Good News* with a considerable amount of dread. "That broadcast tonight will be a photographers' clambake," Tracy said. "And you two are going to look very comical when those newspaper photographers start telling you to wear the crown over your right ear and then your left ear . . ." Loy came close to canceling out altogether before she learned they wouldn't be required to pose in the crowns, as neither she nor Gable wanted Tracy to get his hands on those pictures.

"After our would-be coronation," Loy said, "Spence would hail Clark as 'Your Majesty'; Clark would call Spence a Wisconsin ham, and Spence would counter with, 'What about *Parnell?*' " (Ironically, *Parnell*, the story of the great Irish nationalist leader, had originally been purchased for Tracy but got earmarked for Gable in a textbook example of bad casting.) "From start to finish of [*Test Pilot*] we had laughs," Gable said. "Ribbed each other constantly. It reached the point where it took us two hours to do one certain scene that should have taken 20 minutes. All because we started kidding about how we would probably ham it up, until we got such a cockeyed slant on the scene we couldn't get halfway through it before one of us would laugh in the other's face. The day [Tracy] was doing his death scene, I accused him of taking all day to die. 'Gable,' he said, 'I'm just getting even for all the time you took making those love scenes.' "

Since Gable and Tracy rarely socialized off the set, it was widely assumed they didn't like each other and that their supposed friendship was a sham, an invention of Howard Strickling's publicity machine. By most accounts, though, the two men genuinely enjoyed each other's company, and it was only by necessity their relationship was professional in nature and not as personal as it might otherwise have been. Gable's drinking habits were widely known, and shortly after Tracy began working on the Culver City lot, the two men went off for lunch one day and disappeared. The studio, Tracy later told a coworker, sent people out looking for them, but nobody could find them, and they were gone two or three days. "I don't know where the hell we were," he said.

After he swore off alcohol in December 1935, Tracy kept a respectful distance, joking and lunching with Gable* but resisting the after-hours invitations and the entreaties to go on hunting and fishing trips. Tracy had no stomach for hunting—as a kid he had killed a bird and never forgave himself—and the boozy world Gable inhabited with such aplomb would very quickly have proven lethal to the equilibrium Tracy struggled to maintain. "If you went out to Gable's place," said publicist Eddie Lawrence, "everything was king-size—all the glasses. You were drunk with one glass." As Joe Mankiewicz put it, "You couldn't be around Clark without drinking."

Much of *Test Pilot* was shot on location at a variety of airfields in and around Los Angeles. San Diego's Lindbergh Field stood in for Mineola, Alhambra for Wichita. The film's opening scenes were made at Burbank's Union Air Terminal, where John Tracy was introduced to Myrna Loy. ("What picture do you remember her in?" his father prompted. "*Whipsaw!*" responded Johnny.) Despite one Oscar nomination and the prospect of another, Loy thought Tracy needier than when she last worked with him. He seemed unsure of his performance opposite Gable and disinclined to accept Fleming's assurances.

Gable had no pretensions when it came to his acting, and his admiration of Tracy's singular gifts was boundless. "I always try to be my best with Spence the first take, and let that be the print," he once told John Lee Mahin, "because if I start fooling around he'll kill me." Gable's makeup

---

* Tracy and Gable always shared the same table in the M-G-M commissary. "It was called the Directors' Table," said Howard Strickling. "Gable and Pidgeon and Bob Taylor, Tracy, and Cedric Gibbons, and all the writers. It was a big table, because there were 30 or 40 of them. They had this dice box, and low man paid for the lunch. If you had a three on the dice, it might cost you $35 or $40. Again, you might go along and eat for nothing for three weeks."

man, Stan Campbell, could remember a sequence that Tracy, riding in the back seat of a car, dominated while Gable and Loy held the foreground. "Any other star but Clark would have had them cut that shot," Campbell said, "but Clark was never jealous of his fellow players. When the film was screened, he said, 'Look at that guy Tracy, sitting there doing nothing and stealing our scene.' He thought it was wonderful that Spence showed up so well."

If Fleming's attentions toward Gable left Tracy feeling isolated, he must have felt even more so after an incident at Riverside's March Field drove a wedge between them. After spending a crisp January morning shooting exteriors, the principals were invited to have lunch with some of the officers, who wanted to fly Gable, Fleming, and Tracy over to Catalina in one of the B-17 bombers being used in the picture. Myrna Loy, who wasn't part of the conversation, overheard Tracy decline with thanks. "I noticed that the fliers seemed to understand what he was about, but Gable and Fleming started in on him, ragging him for not going. You know how men are. They made all sorts of demeaning cracks while Spence just sat there. It infuriated me, but not having heard the buildup I kept my mouth shut."

The minute the others left the table, Tracy leaped up from his seat, grabbed Loy by the arm, and walked her across the field to where a car was waiting to take them back to their hotel. "What's the matter?" she asked. "What's going on here?" He fumed silently for a time, then blurted it out: "Well, goddamn it, you know what would happen when I went with them. When they get off that plane, the first thing they'll do is head for a bar. You know I can't do that." Then it dawned on her: he was afraid of falling off the wagon.

Said Loy, "Gable and Fleming didn't understand this; I mean they refused to understand and had simply kept ragging him. Rather than risk a relapse, Spence had sat there in front of all those men and taken it. 'You know I can't do that,' he repeated in the car to Riverside, trembling with anger. I tried to comfort him: 'Yes, darling, I know you can't do that, I know. Calm down, now. Quiet down.' He was so mad I resolved then and there not to let him out of my sight."

She suggested an early dinner at the eccentric Mission Inn, hoping to keep him "out of harm's way" by eating before the others got back. "We were finishing a very glum dinner when the prodigals returned. 'Look at 'em!' Spence growled. 'Didn't I tell you?' They had indeed gone to a bar and got clobbered. 'All right,' I said. 'What are you going to do now?' He answered ominously, '*Well*, I don't know.' As we passed their table, Gable and Fleming were being relentlessly buoyant. I stopped to blast them, but Spence, after a very curt nod, bolted. When I ran after him, he had vanished."

Loy got her friend Shirley Hughes and combed the downtown bars, but they couldn't find him anywhere. The next morning, Tracy didn't show for work, and everyone suddenly assumed the worst.

> We were stuck there on location unable to shoot without him while calls buzzed between March Field and M-G-M. "My God," Victor moaned to Benny Thau, "we've got a situation on our hands!" I thought, "Yeah, you sure have, and you damn well deserve to have one, too." A few minutes before noon, Spence strolled nonchalantly onto the set, bid everyone a jaunty good morning, and went to work. When Gable and Fleming started threateningly toward him, I headed them off, took them aside, and gave 'em hell: "Haven't you clowns done enough? How dare you do a thing like that? You know he has to be careful. Where are your brains?" I really laid them out while Spence worked smugly on.

At the core of *Test Pilot* was Tracy's mother hen relationship with Gable, a quality Fleming sought to emphasize in his notes, a level of camaraderie and affection between men normally reserved for stories of war and dire

On location for *Test Pilot* with Myrna Loy and Clark Gable, 1937.
(PATRICIA MAHON COLLECTION)

sacrifice. That Tracy managed a kind of primal jealousy between Gunner and Loy's character, Ann, is a testament to their on-screen chemistry and the way the two men were balanced under Fleming's knowing direction. Where Loy has Gable's attention, his interest in all things sexual, Tracy has his heart, and the perilous work they do together bonds them in a way that no woman ever could. Tracy understood the equation, had worked it through to an extent that Gable, perhaps, had not. That he saw their inter-action for what it was is clear from a comment he made in the fall of 1957, while attending a screening at the home of actress Laraine Day. The picture was *Bombers B-52,* and as it started, one of the massive old B-17s used in the earlier movie rolled into view. "That plane was used in the picture *Test Pilot,*" he said aloud, "in which Myrna Loy and I were both in love with Clark Gable."

Gable, as it turned out, was living at the Beverly Wilshire while making the picture, so over the course of production Tracy spent a lot of time with Joe Mankiewicz. The urbane, pipe-smoking producer didn't drink, which made his house at the beach a safe haven as well as a handy place to flop. "We saw each other several times a week," Mankiewicz said. "I got to know him very well. And I got to know Louise very well. It was very strange; we went dancing, we went to the theatre, we'd have dinner, we'd laugh a lot. Go to the fights with Spence."

It was while Tracy was staying with him that Mankiewicz got a glimpse of the preparation that went into a Tracy performance. "I would come home at night and pass his bedroom door and he'd be working. He'd be working extremely hard . . . [H]e'd come to the set the next day and say to the continuity girl, 'What are we shooting today, kid?' and she'd [think], 'Oh my God, he doesn't know his lines.' But in fact he'd worked all night long. He was fully prepared." It was, perhaps, the legacy of the boy magi-cian, the instinct that compelled him to hide all the work, to keep the secrets to himself, leaving the impression that it all came out of thin air, effortless and magical, a thing of mystery and wonder.

Part of Tracy's calculation for *Test Pilot* was the game of one-upmanship he and Gable liked to play. "I came home and Spence was in the guest room," said Mankiewicz.

I heard the sound of cracking nuts. Now I opened his door and he was sitting there and he was cracking walnuts. I said, "What's that all about?" He says, "I'm just thinking up a little something here." . . . And I went to bed. Well, when the film came out, appar-ently what happened was that he'd suggested to Victor Fleming, "Look, Vic, while this is going on . . . give me something to do with my hands at least. I mean, I got a bowl of nuts or something that I can crack while this scene is being played." Well, Fleming thought that was a marvelous idea. The prop man came up with a bowl of walnuts, and to everybody's surprise Spence cracked these walnuts in between lines from Gable to Loy and Loy to Gable . . . The soundtrack was completely laced with cracking walnuts, and you had to cut to Spence repeatedly in order to justify this sound.* Now that's not an instinctive bit; that's a man who takes his work very seriously.

Joe was also fond of Louise, enjoyed being with her. "Louise was a very attractive woman. Lovely dark hair, clear complexion, soft eyes. We went dancing, and I could always make her laugh. Very literate. Intelligent. Spence never said anything the least derogatory about her, never any of those asides that let you know he was trapped."

A dozen times Joe was on the verge of asking his friend "what the hell went wrong" between the two of them. "But fortunately, and unfortunately, I'd done enough work in psychiatry to know, to figure it out for myself what it was." Tracy spent Christmas morning with the kids, the afternoon with Louise at Santa Anita, then returned home to the beach in the evening. Johnny's deafness, Louise's forbearance were things he could no longer face on a daily basis. He beat an emotional retreat, born of a need to function, a need to survive.

"He didn't leave Louise," Mankiewicz said. "He left the scene of his guilt."

Just after the first of the new year, Louise returned to Honolulu, intent on spending the entire month of January away from home. Spence was working most days, plagued by headaches and the insomnia that had always afflicted him, fueled as it was by the countless cups of tea and coffee he consumed as part of his daily ritual. Crawling out of the black hole of depression was impossible in the middle of the night, when his thoughts ran wild and he endured the torment of his sins. Desperate for sleep, he arrived on the set more worn out than ever, cranky and nervous and sometimes at wit's end. Someone suggested a massage, and he found a rubdown eased the pain in his head and helped him to relax. He took to noting the sleep he got each

* Another bit of business worked out between Tracy and Fleming was Gunner's practice of sticking a wad of chewing gum on the surface of Gable's plane before a flight. A good luck ritual, it's an ominous sign when he neglects it on the altitude run that ends his life.

night in his book: 3:30 a.m. to 6:50 a.m. without a massage, 12:30 a.m. to 7:00 a.m. with one.

He met Joseph P. Kennedy one night at dinner with Mannix and M-G-M's Billy Grady and took note of the fact that the current chair of the U.S. Maritime Commission was soon to become America's ambassador to the Court of St. James's. *Mannequin* opened in New York on January 20, 1938, and, much to its costar's astonishment, was a hit despite some decidedly mixed notices. Production on *Test Pilot* ground on into February, a seemingly endless picture to make.

On February 2, to celebrate Gable's thirty-seventh birthday, a corner of Stage 12 was done up coronation style, and Tracy had Gable's stand-in wheel in a huge cake topped with a candy crown. "I wear this Irish costume, King Gable, to remind you of *Parnell*," the man announced. "Always remember it, Kingey, because the theater owners will never forget it." Eddie Mannix came down to the set and placed the crown on Gable's head as Tracy egged him on. Then Judy Garland sang a specially written song on the subject of the King's worst film ever. Gable sought his revenge a few days later when he had the hot fudge sundae that always appeared at the finish of Tracy's lunch made with a perfectly formed scoop of mashed potatoes. Tracy dug into the thing and devoured it down to the last spoonful without ever changing expression.

Tracy always credited his first Academy Award nomination to an extraordinary run of pictures, going as he did from stark drama to screwball comedy in the space of five months. He talked about the "sudden break" of both *Fury* and *San Francisco* and how two in a row had been "something to shout about" when *Libeled Lady* came along and took him in an entirely different direction. "This business of achieving dramatic effect on the stage or screen is principally a matter of contrast," he said at the time. "A thing is dramatic only when it is presented in contrast with something else . . ."

The awards were going through a metamorphosis, and where there were scarcely seven hundred academy members selecting the winners for 1936, an agreement with the Screen Actors Guild placed the nomination process in the hands of the guild's senior members for the year 1937. The winners, in fact, would be selected by both the senior and junior memberships of SAG, as well as the member bodies of the Directors and Writers guilds, a total of some fifteen thousand workers. The nominations were announced on the night of February 6, 1938, and although Tracy thought he had a weaker overall résumé for the year—*They Gave Him a Gun, Big City,* and *Mannequin* flanking *Captains Courageous*—he was again included among the nominees, as were Charles Boyer (for *Conquest*), Fredric March (*A Star Is Born*), Robert Montgomery (*Night Must Fall*), and Paul Muni (*The Life of Emile Zola*).

With the awards now sanctioned by the guilds, Tracy seemed only slightly more at ease with the accolade, even as he conspired to avoid the March 3 banquet at the Biltmore Bowl. With *Test Pilot* due to wrap in a week, he was granted a three-week suspension to have his hernia operation, thus ensuring he would be in the hospital the night of the dinner. "He couldn't handle open approbation," Joe Mankiewicz said, "and he couldn't handle being rejected. He was embarrassed when people told him he was a good actor, but he was terrified by the idea of people not telling each other he was a good actor."

When Tracy entered Good Samaritan on Monday, February 21, there wasn't any widespread speculation he would win the Oscar, Muni again being the odds-on favorite with Montgomery a close second. However, due to heavy rains and flooding, the ceremony was postponed a week, somewhat endangering his plans to be completely unavailable. Then an infection set in, lengthening his stay in the hospital an equal number of days, and he was still safely laid up when Louise came to visit on the afternoon of March 10.

"I kept feeling that I had to get home, that I should be there in case," she remembered. "He said, 'No, don't go.' Until finally his mother called and said, 'You'll have to come home right away. They say he's going to get it.' And I was still at the hospital!" Caught off guard, Louise had to wear what she had on hand, a full black dress, very sheer, embroidered with pink flowers. "I'll never forget trying to dress. Poor Mother Tracy was frantic: 'You'll be late!' " (Her lateness was chronic; Spence always referred to her as "the late Mrs. Tracy.") Publicist Otto Winkler collected her in a studio car, and as they inched down Grand Avenue toward the red-carpeted entrance to the Bowl, crowds of spectators strained for a look. Louise was seated with L. B. Mayer's party, as were Robert Morley, the Sidney Franklins, the Hunt Strombergs, Bernie Hyman and his wife, the Weingartens, the Van Dykes, and Mervyn LeRoy. Norma Shearer, in a long-sleeved gown of shimmering white sequins, brought her mother.

In most ways, it was a typical academy event. It started far past the hour set, and, as hosted by radio comedian Bob Burns, ran so late that someone suggested it should first have been previewed in Glendale. The crowd of 1,400—well over the room's stated capacity—was packed in to the point of immobility. The new spirit of cooperation with the Guilds was evident in the prominence on the program of Robert Montgomery, the president of SAG, King Vidor, president of the Directors Guild, and Charles Brackett, vice president of the Writers Guild. James Francis Crow of the *Hollywood Citizen News* hailed it as "an Academy renaissance," considering the precar-

The awarding of the Oscar for *Captains Courageous,* March 10, 1938. Left to right: Louis B. Mayer, Luise Rainer, Louise Tracy, and director Frank Capra. (HERALD EXAMINER COLLECTION, LOS ANGELES PUBLIC LIBRARY)

ious condition the organization had been in just twelve months earlier. "[S]ome," Crow reported, "thought it would not survive."

Presenters, including Cecil B. DeMille, Douglas Fairbanks, Irving Berlin, and W. C. Fields, had handed out a total of twenty-two statuettes, including another to Luise Rainer, when it came time to reveal the winner for Best Actor. Tracy's name was announced, and the room exploded at the news of a genuinely popular win. Mayer escorted Louise to the podium, and academy president Frank Capra handed the Oscar to him. "It's a great privilege," said Mayer, "to be a stand-in for so great an artist and, great as he is as an artist, he's still a greater man. I think the right one to receive this is his fine wife, Mrs. Tracy." Mayer turned to Louise and handed her the award, and she stepped to the microphone. "Thank you for Spencer," she said, "and for Johnny, and for Susie, and for me."

The line had been Spence's idea in those last frantic moments at the hospital. ("If you have to go up, why don't you say this?") And like the hat he always wore cocked over his left eye, it was a sly tribute to his mentor

Cohan, whose famous curtain speech from the days of the Four Cohans was always, "My mother thanks you, my father thanks you, my sister thanks you, and I thank you."

Crow, of the *Citizen News,* called it the "most gracious" moment of the evening, and when Louise later phoned Spence at the hospital, after appearing before newsreel cameras and repeating the line, he wept.

CHAPTER 14

Enough to Shine Even Through Me

When Dore Schary began work on the script of *Boys Town* in December 1937, it was at the behest of John Considine, who had landed at M-G-M after his brief tenure at Fox. Considine, a lifelong Catholic, was struggling with the story of Father Edward J. Flanagan and his home for orphan boys, a project that seemed a natural for Spencer Tracy. Metro's story editor, Kate Corbaley, had been looking for another "priest role" for Tracy since the release of *San Francisco,* and, in the case of *Boys Town,* parts could be arranged for both Freddie Bartholomew and Mickey Rooney.

Or so they thought. Considine had just pulled the plug on an unfinished screenplay by Bradbury Foote, having previously nixed treatments from Eleanore Griffin and the writing team of Walter Wise and Hugo Butler. Griffin, in fact, had traveled to Nebraska to meet the Reverend Flanagan, and her twenty-six-page story formed the basis of everything to come. All Considine knew of Boys Town, at least initially, was the material contained in a magazine article titled "The Boy Who Shot His Father," and, at first, Flanagan feared he would make another orphanage picture "after the pattern of *Oliver Twist.*" Said Schary: "After reading what had been written and studying the history of Father Flanagan's unique institution, I told Considine that the error holding up the project was casting Freddie Bartholomew in an atmosphere where he clearly didn't belong. My suggestion was to do away with the character completely and concentrate on the relationship between Tracy as Father Flanagan and Rooney as the rough, unmanageable new recruit into Boys Town."

Within days, the author of *Ladies in Distress* found himself aboard a train bound for Omaha. Being an Orthodox Jew, Schary had never before entered a priest's home, and he wasn't sure how to behave when Flanagan came ambling down the stairs. "I expected robes or something, but he came down in a coat and tie and said, 'How are you doing?' I said, 'Very cold.' He said, 'A little scotch will take care of that.' We had a couple of drinks and I fell in love with him. He was a darling fellow."

Flanagan was tall, bespectacled, spoke with a slight brogue. "He didn't look a bit like Tracy, but he had Tracy's charm, his smile and twinkle." The priest told his visitor that he had specifically asked Considine to send him a Jew: "I kept saying to M-G-M, 'Don't send me any Catholics. Why don't you get hold of a young Jewish kid? He'll know what I'm talking about.' "

"Now what would make you say a thing like that?" asked Schary.

"How do you think I got into this business? How do you think this place was built? Because a Jewish man understood what I was doing and gave me money."

Schary had brought the outline of a new story, and Flanagan was pleased with what he saw. Over the next few days, story elements "flowed quickly and surely," and a new treatment was on Considine's desk by Christmas. Tracy, however, resisted all efforts to get him on board. ("I'm just a straight man," he complained to Louise after reading the thing.) In January Dore Schary returned to Boys Town in the company of J. Walter Ruben, who was now assigned to direct the picture. Even with Jack Ruben attached—he had directed *Riffraff*—Tracy balked, unwilling to play another guy "with a collar turned backwards."

As the pressure on the actor built, Yvonne Beaudry became increasingly conscious of his moodiness, his unpredictable funks. "Some days he sat grimly alone, his broad shoulders hunched, his face stony. Then, I hated to approach him with matters requiring his attention: letters and checks to sign, appointments to keep, telegrams and flowers to send . . . In some ways, Tracy reminded me of my father—a look in his eyes, a mocking expression on his ruddy face, which lit right up when he grinned. I responded to him with respect and a little awe. He was a lot bigger than I as well as older, though I deemed myself a buffer between him and the encroaching world."

In the end, he was persuaded to take the part of Father Flanagan by Eddie Mannix. "He did it really because of Mr. Mannix," Louise affirmed. "[Mannix] wanted to do that picture, and he wanted him to do it. [Spence] said [to me], 'I just can't turn it down.' " When the news reached Boys Town, Father Flanagan responded with a flattering letter to Tracy, obviously calculated to seal the deal: "Your name is written in gold in the heart of every homeless boy in Boys Town because of the anticipated picture you are going to make for us, and every boy here, and all of our alumni, are talking about you, thinking about you, and praying for you every day."

A few days later, on February 10, 1938, Benny Thau notified the studio accounting office that Spencer Tracy was to be classified henceforth as a star.

A shrewd hand at the art of publicity, Father Flanagan knew the value of the Boys Town story—to Hollywood and to Boys Town itself. He accepted a paltry $5,000 fee for the film rights with the understanding that a successful motion picture could be worth hundreds of thousands of dollars to the institution, perhaps even millions. On February 18, he arrived at Culver City in the company of Morris E. Jacobs, founding partner of Bozell & Jacobs. (It was Jacobs who came up with the famous image of one boy carrying another and the caption, "He ain't heavy, Father, he's m' brother.") The two men laid out an ambitious promotional plan that involved joining the reach and resources of Metro-Goldwyn-Mayer with publicity and media contacts forged by Flanagan and his organization over a span of twenty years. What they proposed was a major branding campaign for both Flanagan and Boys Town that would "win space in abundance in such magazines as *Life, Time, Newsweek,* and newspapers throughout the United States."

Over lunch on that rainy Friday afternoon, Tracy met Father Flanagan for the first time. Clad in his leather flying jacket for *Test Pilot,* his face streaked with makeup, Tracy struggled to make conversation with the first living person he had ever been asked to play. "All actors," he told the priest, "do everything possible to live their part—to be the very image of the person they are portraying. But few actors, Father, have the opportunity of being confronted by that person. That makes the going even rougher, for as I play this part I will be thinking not only of you but of what you will think of me . . . I'm so anxious to do a good job as Father Flanagan that it worries me, keeps me awake nights."

What Father Flanagan saw in Tracy was a consummate actor already at work: "As he talked, I could feel his eyes upon me, studying my every little mannerism: the way I sat in the chair, the way I talked, the way I pushed the hair back from my forehead. I knew he was studying me—the man he was going to become—as searchingly as I studied him. I almost knew what was running through his mind." Photos were made of Flanagan with Tracy, with Mickey Rooney (who asked for his autograph), with actor Lewis Stone, a personal favorite. Jack Ruben suggested that Andrew Cain, one of the boys at Flanagan's home, be considered for the role of Pee Wee, the mascot character in Dore Schary's treatment, and Morris Jacobs thought it would make for good publicity to send the boy out to California for a test.

While still in the hospital, Tracy received a letter from Joe Kennedy. The newly installed ambassador congratulated him on his win as Best Actor and advised him that every time Kennedy himself won a prize he made someone give him a trip. He went on to suggest that Tracy should, therefore, make Metro give him a trip abroad. And though Spence wasn't enthused about the idea, Louise thought it would "do him good" and worked to make it happen. Dr. Toland approved a leisurely cruise aboard the Panama Pacific liner *Virginia* with Dr. Dennis along to keep an eye on the patient. Louise, juggling her own set of responsibilities, would meet the ship in New York on April 11 and, after a five-day layover, sail with Spence for Genoa, the first planned stop on a three-week European holiday.

Never having learned to relax, Tracy dreaded a six-week absence from the studio. ("He's the restless type," Clark Gable said of him. "Maybe it's the Irish in him. The only time he's contented to be where he is is when he's working.") He fretted about the huge London crowds that reputedly met stars visiting from the States. (Louise asked him what he'd do if he were Robert Taylor "and really had something to worry about.") He also heard he would be expected to wear white tie and tails at formal functions. ("They go in for that a lot over there, don't they?") Once he was resigned to the trip, he visited Bill Powell in the hospital, where the forty-five-year-old actor was himself recovering from surgery.

Earlier in the month, Powell had discovered bleeding and was diagnosed with rectal cancer—the exact same disease that had taken the life of John Tracy at the age of fifty-four. Surgeons recommended complete removal of the rectum, but that meant Powell would have to evacuate into a bag for the rest of his life, something he said he just couldn't abide. Instead, he chose the option of a "temporary" colostomy and a program of radiation. With the lower colon bypassed, the cancer was removed, but it would be six months before Powell would know if it was gone for good. He was, Tracy noted, "pretty blue and sick" that particular afternoon.

Tracy had a morbid fear of disease—cancer in particular—and the talk with Powell obviously stuck with him. The trip through the canal began pleasantly enough, but then he developed a mysterious itch (" . . . but good!" he wrote in his book). It worsened, and he spent his thirty-eighth birthday in agony, convinced that he, too, had rectal cancer. He could remember how his father had wasted away under the disease, the terrible sight of such a powerful and energetic man in death: "I looked at what was left—just practically nothing. I couldn't find that big, proud, Irish son-of-a-gun in the remains. And right then and there I made plans. Anything like that ever happened to me, I'd check out . . . I'm scared. It's a thing there's no prevention for. There's nothing you can do. We're helpless. Sitting ducks. If it hits, it hits. And when that's the way your father goes—or your mother—it's only natural to live with the specter of it. Or try."

Denny had a look at him and told him no, he didn't think so, but that he'd arrange for treatments when they reached port. The passengers were respectful, kept their distance. "Of course, I was sick . . . I still walked with a cane . . . but they didn't speak to me or ask for autographs. When we arrived in New York, though, boy!" At the Twenty-first Street pier Tracy was surrounded by longshoremen who wanted autographs and mobbed by a star-struck crowd of women, one of whom wanted to kiss him and was seen pleading with a cop for permission to do so. When they arrived at the Sherry-Netherland, Denny located an oncologist and Tracy had his first x-ray treatment—the same sort of radiation therapy his father endured and that Bill Powell undoubtedly had in his future. No relief. "Rectal trouble terrible," he wrote on the twelfth. "Itch awful," he added the next day.

They didn't see any shows—he couldn't sit long enough to enjoy one. *Test Pilot* opened at the Capitol Theatre, and the end of Lent contributed to a fabulous gate of nearly $60,000 in the first week alone. Critics generally thought the picture well done, albeit overlong, and most commented on the brevity of Tracy's part. At the hotel he sat for a couple of interviews, calmly sipping from a glass of ginger ale, giving no indication of the turmoil within.

The Tracys went their separate ways in New York, Spence roaming the city like a wounded tiger, his posture and gait warning strangers away. Selena Royle "saw a figure coming down the street, all hunched over and with a hat over to one side in that way of his, and I knew it had to be Spence . . . so I went up to him and threw my arms around him and said, 'Well, you always said you wanted to be as good as Lionel Barrymore, and now you are . . . and better.' "

The daily treatments continued, and all he wished by now was to be home again. On Saturday, April 16, the UP reported a "mild relapse" that caused him to cancel reservations on the Italian liner *Rex*. "Tracy will sail Wednesday with his wife for a three weeks' vacation," the dispatch continued, but he no longer cared about making the trip. "More treatment," he glumly noted that day. "And more" the following, Easter Sunday. If he went to Mass at St. Patrick's, as he always tried to do, he made no mention of it. Prayer, desperate and all-consuming, may finally have had an effect, though, for on Tuesday, April 19, the itch was suddenly gone, and there was, after three weeks of constant torture, genuine and blessed relief.

He found himself at the Lambs that night, but the atmosphere was depressing, most of his old pals having decamped for Hollywood. He dined with actor Wallace Ford—who was playing *Of Mice and Men* at the Music Box—and the two engaged in a "friendly" dispute over a check for $5.60. Sometime that night, with all the dread of the last month having drained from him completely, he took a drink after seven months and two weeks of sobriety.

Actor David Wayne, new to Broadway, happened onto the scene in the club's fabled taproom: "The huge supply of liquor that was stacked behind the bar he swept off and hurled to the floor and about the room. It looked as if a hurricane had struck. I know, because I walked into the place a few hours after the destruction began. It was awesome! Some two days later he was still on his feet amidst the ruins of the club, and there was nothing anyone could do about it. The by-laws at that time forbade the expulsion of any member as long as he remained on his feet."

According to Wayne, the studio had an ambulance standing by so that when Tracy "finally collapsed" he could be lifted aboard and driven to a waiting plane. Six long days passed before the siege came to an end. Attempts to contact Louise were unsuccessful; first she was "in" and then, when advised as to what the club was calling about, she was "out." As someone party to the event observed: "What she should not see, she would not see."

Billy "Square Deal" Grady, the former Broadway agent who described himself as the studio's "eyes and ears" in New York, secured two plane tickets west, but after nearly a week of steady drinking, Tracy was in no shape to be seated alongside civilians. Grady quietly turned in the tickets, and M-G-M chartered a private plane out of Newark at a cost of $3,000. In Los Angeles, Tracy managed to slip away and went missing for six days. At no time did he attempt to contact Louise, nor Carroll, and there were no sightings at any of his usual haunts. "No one was able to find him," said Dore Schary, "until it occurred to somebody to look in the polo stables he had. And they found him there asleep—and quite under the weather."

He was hospitalized, and the consulting physician on the case told him and Louise that if he continued to drink as he had that season, in five years he would be dead.

"Unfortunately, Spencer Tracy is still very much under the weather," John Considine delicately advised Father Flanagan in a letter on April 27, when Tracy was in fact missing and nowhere to be found. "He was all ready to sail for Europe but at the last minute decided that it would be better for him to come back to his home and try and recuperate from the effects of the serious surgical operation he underwent a month or so ago. I shall let you hear from me again as soon as I get some definite information about his condition."

On May 3, with Tracy in the hospital, Considine sent the Reverend Flanagan a copy of Dore Schary's latest version of the screenplay, which combined early material from Eleanore Griffin with Schary's own progressive drafts, designed to make Flanagan's character less a straight man and more the idealistic young priest who willed his boys' home into being. Where reality intervened, Schary had a melodramatic equivalent to make the same point: the gradual dawning on "Father Eddie" that serving the needs of homeless boys would prevent them from growing into homeless men became a tense monologue from a condemned prisoner on the night of his execution. The mysterious source of the original seed money for the home—presumed by many to be Omaha attorney Henry Monsky— became a benevolent pawnbroker, standing shoulder to shoulder with the priest throughout the film.

Flanagan responded by inviting Considine, screenwriter John Meehan, director Norman Taurog—Jack Ruben having fallen ill—and Tracy to Omaha for a conference over the script, but Tracy, eager to make the fiasco of the New York trip up to Louise, elected instead to take her on a quick cruise to Hawaii, vowing to return in time for the start of *Boys Town* on June 2. Their two weeks in Honolulu came off without incident; on their way home he was able to note in his book: "One month sober— Wonderful!!!" With the script unfinished, the picture didn't actually start until the sixth, new pages coming daily from Meehan and Jack Mintz, a writer and gag man brought onto the picture by Taurog.

Tracy had previously appeared in two pictures with Mickey Rooney, but there was no interaction between the two of them on *Riffraff* and very little on *Captains Courageous*. Since finishing the latter, Rooney had appeared in nine features, two in the newly inaugurated Andy Hardy series with Lewis Stone and Fay Holden. On *Boys Town,* the seventeen-year-old Rooney would share over-the-title billing with Tracy, a remarkable rise in prominence since joining M-G-M (at $150 a week) in August 1934. "Mickey Rooney," said Joe Mankiewicz, "was a pretty cocky little fellow . . . When Tracy and Rooney met on the set of *Boys Town,* Rooney started playing games . . . While Spencer was talking, Rooney would sort of play with his handkerchief in his pocket, or adjust his tie, or the stale sort of scene-stealing bits, and Tracy turned to him the very first day and said, 'I understand you claim to be the world's greatest scene stealer. Let me tell you something, you little snot. The moment I catch you trying to louse up a scene I'm in, I'll send you to Purgatory. You'll wish you'd never been born, because I can do it.' And he made Rooney believe that."

After a week shooting the early scenes between Father Flanagan and the incorrigible Whitey Marsh, Rooney went off to complete *Love Finds Andy Hardy* and Tracy moved on to the founding of Flanagan's first home for boys in 1917, solid, largely factual material that paired him with actors Leslie Fenton and Henry Hull. With his weight down to 170, Tracy was able to play two slow chukkers of polo on June 8, his first in nearly seven months. It was like being back at the beginning again, having to nerve himself into taking the field, the adrenaline high all but forgotten, the fear almost insurmountable. "I darn near died," he said, recalling the occasion. "I can't enjoy the game anymore. It's a worry now. I get to thinking, 'Maybe nothing will happen, but I might take a spill. Then the picture stops. And people get thrown out of work.' "

On June 22 unit manager Joe Cooke wired Boys Town from Salt Lake City:

ARRIVE OMAHA THURSDAY MORNING. COMPANY WILL ARRIVE SATURDAY. WOULD RATHER YOU NOT MENTION ARRIVAL SO AS TO KEEP CROWDS AWAY.

Of course the company of fifty-eight was the biggest, by far, ever to hit Nebraska. When they arrived early in the evening of the twenty-fifth, several thousand jammed Omaha's Union Station to catch glimpses of Tracy and particularly Mickey Rooney, who had become just about the hottest thing in pictures. Henry Hull was along, as were actors Gene Reynolds, Frank Thomas, Bobs Watson (and his mother), Jimmy Butler, Sidney Miller, Donald Haines, and Tommy Noonan. All others—director Taurog, his first and second assistants, the script girl, two sound engineers, first and second cameramen and assistant, second-unit cameraman and assistant, wardrobe man, makeup man, cashier, two prop men, three grips, a stills man, a welfare worker, five electricians, a camera car driver, writers Meehan and Mintz, associate producer O. O. "Bunny" Dull and a secretary, and a publicity trailer unit headed by Frank Whitbeck (with cameraman, assistant cameraman, and grip)—were able to pass unnoticed.

Tracy, accompanied by Carroll and his stand-in, Jerry Schumacher, was welcomed by Father Flanagan and Omaha mayor Dan Butler, who presented both him and Mickey Rooney with floral keys to the city. The formalities over, Spence gamely made his way to a waiting cab, enduring another mob scene at the Fontenelle Hotel. "The lobby was crammed with people who claimed to be relatives of Mickey Rooney," reported the *Lincoln Sunday Journal and Star,* "or to have gone to school with Spencer Tracy."

Taurog spent all day Sunday scouting locations on the Boys Town campus. Monday morning, the first shots were made just after nine, a shrill whistle signaling quiet, gold foil reflectors augmenting a battery of booster lamps in the already sweltering heat. Tracy, sunburned from Hawaii, needed only a little lotion to take the shine off, a little graying at the temples his only makeup. Mintz, in Dubonnet shirt and white jacket, pipe in hand, studied each scene from the sidelines, looking for bits of business to inject, as Taurog, in helmet and brown pants, sat motionless next to the camera. By noon the temperature had hit 105 degrees and only dipped below 100 after nightfall.

Directing his first film under a new M-G-M contract, Taurog proved equal to his reputation as a skilled handler of children. Still, all the young principals in *Boys Town* were professional actors, and nothing a director could say would match the primal impact of playing opposite a man of Tracy's gifts, looking into his eyes and establishing a connection.

"He was artless," said Gene Reynolds, who played the handicapped Tony Ponessa in the picture. "You never caught him acting. He was very facile. He would take in what you gave him, process it, and give it back." Sidney Miller, the bookish Mo Kahn, thought Tracy the best listener in the world: "When I did a scene in *Boys Town,* I swear those eyes bore into mine." Tracy, he recalled, was once asked by the cameraman to cheat his look to Miller's right ear. "He refused. He wouldn't look away from my eyes. If they wanted his full face, they were going to have to bring the camera around."

Most prominent among the kids was seven-year-old Bobs Watson, who played the diminutive Pee Wee. "In one of the first scenes," he remembered,

> I come in and ask for candy, and they establish that I get it. In the next scene when I come in for candy, he gives me some and asks, "Have you brushed your teeth?" I hadn't brushed my teeth and I lie about it and say, "I lost my toothbrush." "Lost it? Well, we're going to have to do something about this" and he makes a big deal about it, which plays on my guilt. So I start to put the candy back. Just before we shoot the scene, Norman Taurog, the director, said, "Bobby, now when you're putting the candy back, don't look at it. Reach in your pocket, take it out, and look Uncle Spencer right in the eyes." And I'll never forget those eyes.

Watson's great talent was his ability to cry like no other child in pictures, and Taurog never had to resort to the usual tricks—stories of dead dogs, dying grandparents, and the like. "I can't explain it," he once said, "but when tears were needed, I cried, and they were honest and real. In *Boys Town,* when Mickey Rooney left, it really broke my heart. I used to see Rooney and Spencer Tracy in a very idealized way." Tracy, he remembered, was fatherly and warm. "Often, after a scene, he'd reach over and hug me and take me on his lap. I felt like a little puppy. I would follow along and stand close, hoping he'd call me over, and often he would. He'd say, 'How're you doing?' and put his arm around me."

Tracy and Rooney never really warmed to one another, despite press feeds to the contrary. "During lunch," said one *Boys Town* alumnus, "Tracy comes in and then they serve him his food, and Mickey used to agitate him. They had this long table, so Mickey comes in [and sits] across from him and [takes] off his shoes and socks and put[s] them right up in front of the plate. Oh, Tracy, he was burning a hole through it." Frank Whitbeck once confided to a friend that his principal role on the *Boys Town* location, other than to shoot a one-reel featurette called *City of Little Men,* was to keep "Tracy off the booze and Mickey Rooney off the girls." At a dinner one night, Whitbeck froze when he saw a waiter pouring wine into Tracy's glass, but Tracy, just a few weeks sober, never touched it.

The filming attracted huge crowds of spectators—as many as five thousand a day—and Father Flanagan had to spend most of the money he was paid by M-G-M on repairs to the property. Tracy, who disliked location work under the best of circumstances, ducked under an umbrella whenever he wasn't needed, Schumacher bringing him water and the makeup man running cubes of ice across his forehead. "The crew had a great time," said Gene Reynolds. "The women of Omaha just rolled for them. Any kind of connection with Hollywood, I guess. Even the prop boys were getting laid."

The company worked eleven straight days in Omaha, finishing on the afternoon of July 7, 1938. Tracy slipped out of town on a Union Pacific Streamliner the next morning at two, riding up front with the engineer and having himself a grand time. Back at Culver City, the cast and crew of *Boys Town* settled in for another four weeks of interiors.

Between shots, Tracy went about the business of breaking in a new secretary, having lost Yvonne Beaudry to an auto accident. With a sprained back and a pronounced limp, Yvonne went home to New England after finding him a replacement, a red-headed Irish girl in her mid-twenties named Peggy Gough. Unlike Beaudry, Peggy had no ambitions to be a journalist or a world traveler and was an experienced secretary. She wasn't terribly busy, especially when her boss was out of town, so she was assigned to help Johnny by typing the stencils for a weekly newspaper he had started publishing.

At the age of eleven, Johnny took up pencil and paper and declared he was going to draw a comic strip, slipping his earliest efforts under his mother's door. "Certainly the 'drawings' were the worst I ever had seen," she said. "We were in hysterics—behind his back. It was his first effort of any kind to do anything, to make something, entirely by himself, and no first efforts, I am sure, ever have met with greater acclaim. And we had to admit that every few days brought marked improvement."

One day he asked how Walt Disney got Mickey Mouse into the paper, and his mother had to explain, somewhat carefully, how Walt Disney had been an adult when he broke into print, and that Johnny might well be able to do so once he had grown into adulthood himself. That, however, wasn't the sort of answer he wanted to hear, and he decided he would start his own newspaper to hasten the process. What he wanted, it turned out, was extra copies of his drawings to send his grandmother and others, and Louise told him that when he got his paper together they would find a way of getting it printed. It took a year and a half and a lot of help from his private tutor to get out the first issue, a weekly he called *The News.* Soon its production took the place of what had come to pass for an education.

"The schooling was insufficient," Johnny later wrote. "It seems to me I spent too much time on the newspaper and fooling around . . . I didn't have the vocabulary to study and think. A dictionary was quite handy all the time, but I didn't use it much. [My tutor] didn't understand the needs of a deaf child. Of course, obviously too, I was lazy and not curious intellectually. I was thinking of the newspaper, every issue of which I was very anxious to send out, and of 'Jack Smith,' a comic strip which I had just created to be drawn for the paper."

They bought him a secondhand duplicating machine and some stencils. Most of the "news" in the *News* concerned the Tracys—new movies, polo triumphs, comings and goings. The cover of the first issue carried a drawing of Mickey Mouse, courtesy of Walt Disney. It said: "Good luck to Johnny Tracy!"

Boys Town finished on August 6, 1938, and had its first sneak in Inglewood on the fourteenth. Tracy was unimpressed. "Carroll," he said to his brother as they left the theater, "that's the worst picture I ever saw." There were, however, laughs, applause, and tears, as Dore Schary remembered it, and at the conclusion the audience cheered.

There had been some discussion of having the world premiere in Washington—Flanagan had at one time been sold on the idea—but then came rumblings from within Omaha, the mother city, and the insult of being bypassed. "Washington—no!" the Most Reverend James H. Ryan, bishop of Omaha, thundered. "It would not do Boys Town a particle of good to have the premiere there. If it has to be away from Omaha, make it at least New York." Father Flanagan lobbied Frank Whitbeck: "In reality Omaha gave us our first start and gave us our first building—and paid for

Tracy at his Encino ranch with daughter Susie and son John, circa 1938.
(HERALD EXAMINER COLLECTION, LOS ANGELES PUBLIC LIBRARY)

it—and it is now our chance to pay back our debt to Omaha by having the premiere here." The matter was pretty much in the hands of the distribution people, but Frank Whitbeck had a word with Al Lichtman, a Loew's vice president, who in turn took the matter up with H. J. Shumow, manager of the Omaha exchange.

Father Flanagan and Bishop Ryan were invited to California, where they were feted at a studio luncheon. L. B. Mayer posed for pictures between the two men, Tracy with his arm around Flanagan's shoulder and Rooney, on his best behavior, talking animatedly with the bishop. Next came the season opener of *Good News,* with Tracy and Rooney performing punchy little scenes from the movie, followed by Mayer's introduction to the nationwide listening audience of the real Father Flanagan.

After the broadcast, the studio contingent motored crosstown to Westwood for the official press preview, an event that went better than anyone could have hoped. "There was applause several times as the picture progressed," Gus McCarthy of the *Motion Picture Herald* wrote. "Generally, however, the spectators watched and listened silently, but they almost tore up the seats at the finish."

As *Daily Variety* reported, "Pure sentiment, the decent, courageous, unselfish impulses of men and boys, time after time was applauded as no picture in years has been approved. This spontaneous outburst is the

The launching of *Boys Town* on the M-G-M lot. Left to right: Mickey Rooney, Bishop James H. Ryan, Louis B. Mayer, the Reverend Edward J. Flanagan, and Tracy. (PATRICIA MAHON COLLECTION)

keynote to the showmanship the offering represents, and to the kind of showmanship which may sell *Boys Town* for one of the season's smash money makers." Tracy, said the *Hollywood Reporter,* "gives a brilliant, restrained performance that should put him in direct line for a second Academy Award. Even when he is not seen on the screen, his guiding presence is felt every moment." No one seemed to differentiate between the honest, understated footage of Father Flanagan's early struggles and the overheated melodrama that highjacked the picture once Mickey Rooney made his appearance. *Boys Town* packed a sentimental wallop, and every review that came out of the showing was an unqualified rave.

On Sunday, September 4, Tracy, Rooney, Flanagan, Ryan, and actress Maureen O'Sullivan left for Nebraska and the world premiere of the picture. When their train arrived in Omaha on the sixth, it was met by an estimated twenty thousand people, and the crowd swelled to more than thirty thousand for the premiere the next evening. One hundred and ten policemen and another forty firemen struggled to maintain control as the crush filled Douglas Street along two city blocks and spilled over onto side streets, threatening to snap the steel wire barriers strung for the event. Fans lined the rooftops and leaned out of office windows. Tracy, taking in the spectacle, said, "This thing makes a Hollywood premiere look like a dying hog."

Inside the Omaha Theatre, all 2,500 seats were filled as a procession of local dignitaries welcomed the filmmakers. O'Sullivan made a brief appearance, and the Boys Town a cappella choir sang. Father Flanagan spoke of the good he hoped the movie would accomplish, and the showing began with the roar of the M-G-M lion. As in Westwood, applause punctuated much of the film, particularly when Omaha landmarks were recognized or mentioned. At the fadeout, Father Flanagan was asked to escort Tracy and Mickey Rooney to the stage, where Tracy stood with his arm around Rooney as he had in the picture. After saying, "Words fail me for the first time," Rooney predicted another Oscar for his costar. Tracy's first words in the hushed auditorium were inaudible, as if stifled by emotion. Then he was heard to say: "You thanked us for coming here. We should get on our knees to you." He proceeded to return Rooney's compliment, telling the crowd that Rooney was destined to become "one of the great actors of his day."

Still neither an admirer of the script nor of his own performance, Tracy chose his next words carefully. "I do not like to stand here stripped clean of Father Flanagan," he said, adding that if the picture was great, it was because "the great goodness and sweetness and beauty of the soul of this man shines even through me to you."

During his days at Fox, when Tracy misbehaved it generally hit the papers. His tangles with the police made the wire services, and his relationship with Loretta Young was about as public as one could get. His hospitalization in 1934 was explained as a polo accident, but other episodes were reported with a fair degree of accuracy. Had he torn up the Lambs Club while working at Fox, word likely would have gotten out; the Lambs membership was too far-ranging and included press agents and columnists. Fox management lacked the wherewithal—and likely the willingness—to stifle unflattering ink. In the Fox model, theaters and real estate were the assets, not the contract players Winnie Sheehan hired by the dozens. And, like most other studios, Fox didn't build stars because Fox—Sheehan and Wurtzel in particular—didn't know how. With no investment to protect, a second-tier player like Spencer Tracy could make a drunken scene in Yuma, and the police and the press were free to say whatever they wanted. That all stopped when Tracy joined M-G-M.

The joint philosophy of Louis B. Mayer and Irving Thalberg was that the stars on the payroll were hard-dollar assets in the same sense that equipment and real estate were assets—more so in the case of Metro because the Loew's theater circuit was considerably smaller than those of Fox and Paramount. Mayer was fond of likening talent to precious stones: "If you have a diamond or a ruby, you take care of it, you put it in a safe, you clean it and polish it." It was the only business, he once said, where the assets walked out the gate every night. After Thalberg's untimely death, the stars weren't nurtured quite as creatively as before, but the men Mayer and Thalberg had put into place shared their values and attitudes, and principal among them was Howard Strickling.

The quintessential company man, Strickling had been a publicist for the old Metro organization before the merger that created Metro-Goldwyn. He left because he expected to get fired anyway, and Mayer found him working in Paris for Rex Ingram. Persuaded to join the newly assembled company, Strickling set about building the largest and most efficient publicity machine the industry would ever know. "Early on," he said, "I learned that people need help, and the secret of my job was learning how to help them. Help them and they help you. That's what M-G-M was all about, and it was particularly true for the actors—most of them were insecure and overly sensitive and self-centered, so you had to convince them you had their best interests at heart."

Strickling controlled access to the world's greatest assemblage of contract talent, and when he and his staff "helped" a particular journalist or outlet, their "help" was expected in return. When something potentially damaging occurred, Strickling started working the phones. In cases where an incident occurred out of town, a representative was often dispatched. Strickling was close to Billy Wilkerson and had staff allocated to all principal branches of the media—newspapers, fan magazines, radio, the trades. Many of his senior people also had responsibility for three or four stars apiece, and some of them lived in constant terror of what one of their charges might say to the press. Mickey Rooney was irrepressible, a raging pint-sized package of hormones on a breakneck ride to Number One. Tracy needed more protection than supervision; he was plainspoken when talking to journalists, brutally frank with pals like Mook. "Ask Tracy an honest question," said a columnist for the *Washington Star,* "and you are likely to get the most honest answer you ever heard."

At first he was under watch, his reputation at Fox having preceded him. "We actors are like the children of very wealthy parents who keep a very close watch on us, have guards and spies set over us," he observed not long after coming to Metro. "The studio is the mama and papa of the actor. The whole world, the press, the public are the guards and spies. We can't really be ourselves much of the time." Eddie Mannix and Billy Grady were his confidants, more or less responsible for keeping an eye on him. After New York and the Lambs Club, he was placed on a shorter leash, someone from the studio being omnipresent whenever he found himself out among the public. "It was a world unto itself," Maureen O'Sullivan said, "and I would think that if M-G-M had a fault, they over-protected us. If there was bad publicity or something coming up, you took it up with Howard Strickling. Life was taken care of, and this spoiled us."

Strickling had people who handled the distribution of photographs, others who coordinated special events—premieres, banquets, important visitors. Unit men responsible for individual pictures worked for Strickling, as did the people who arranged transportation and answered fan mail. "In Howard's book," said Ann Straus, one of his longtime employees, "M-G-M girls didn't drink, they didn't smoke, they didn't even have babies. But he was a hard taskmaster. He wanted perfection, and he got it." There were limits to Strickling's reach, and his stuttering betrayed the constant pressure he was under—"It made it difficult to take dictation from him," said Eddie Mannix's secretary, June Caldwell—but he was on call twenty-four hours a day, seven days a week, and there was no aspect to the business of being a movie star that escaped his oversight.

It was not in Howard Strickling's interest to make Tracy available to the press in October 1938. Just before *Boys Town* had its world premiere, Tracy learned he had been assigned a picture titled *A New York Cinderella* and he wasn't at all happy about it. The story and script were designed to showcase an actress who had just six pictures to her credit, the most notorious of which was a Czechoslovakian feature in which she appeared nude and simulated orgasm. It was the sort of thing he thought he was finally past, and the problem ate at him as he trained eastward in the company of Bishop Ryan and Father Flanagan.

Hedy Lamarr was L. B. Mayer's project, a dark, radiant beauty the old man first encountered in London. She was Hedwig Kiesler at the time, on the run from a bad marriage and a featured player in a handful of European movies. Like Luise Rainer, Kiesler had been with Max Reinhardt, who reportedly called her "the most beautiful woman in Europe." Unlike Rainer, Kiesler was genuinely Viennese at a time when such a distinction was becoming increasingly important. Brought to this country, she was renamed "Lamarr" after the 1920s beauty queen Barbara La Marr, with Mayer taking personal charge of her career. He loaned her to producer Walter Wanger for her American debut in a stylish independent called *Algiers*. Tracy had seen the film, liked Charles Boyer's work and thought the girl photogenic but had no interest in propping her up, particularly in a picture as vapid as *New York Cinderella* promised to be.

"I have often wondered," Flanagan wrote Tracy on November 1, "how you came out with the making of that picture concerning which you sent the telegram to Mr. Mannix from the train. I hope that you did not have to make that picture, but there is so little that we hear at Boys Town that I am perfectly in the dark as to what picture you are making now." By the time Tracy received the letter, he had already started the movie—a "stinker," he noted in his datebook—and had seen it shut down after only a few days' work.

The director, Josef von Sternberg, had been engaged to give Lamarr the same glistening treatment he had given Marlene Dietrich a decade earlier. (*Algiers,* in fact, looked like a Sternberg picture, due in large part to the work of cinematographer James Wong Howe.) On the first day of filming, Sternberg attempted his first take at 10:20 in the morning, and wasn't satisfied until 4:30 in the afternoon. Lamarr photographed well, but she had no energy and precious little personality. The story had her chasing Tracy's character, a selfless doctor, but the material, in Sternberg's judgment, was "silly." He tried fixing the script but found he could do nothing with it. "Each detail of this film, on which I worked not more than a week, was predetermined by a dozen others," he wrote in his autobiography. "Other directors were better fitted to participate in this kind of nonsense, although this may well be beyond the ability of anyone."

The atmosphere on Sternberg's set was tense. "He wouldn't stand for any noise on the set," said actress Laraine Day, who was playing a minor part in the picture, "and if you wanted to talk to him, you had to write your name on a blackboard and then he would deign to talk to you if he wanted to." Tracy notched six months on the wagon, loafed, and played tennis—a new passion for which he was taking lessons. They started up again on November 14 with Frank Borzage directing, then again pulled the plug at the end of the same day. A week later, after further rewrites, they started the picture yet a third time with the title *I Take This Woman.* Soon, it was being referred to around town as *I Re-Take This Woman.*

Borzage was as friendly and easygoing as Sternberg was aloof. ("There's no mistaking the easing of tension since Borzage took over the picture," a visitor observed.) Disgusted with the script by Jim McGuinness, who, unsuited to women's pictures, had turned in a lifeless assemblage of clichés, Tracy indulged in a brief flirtation with Hedy Lamarr, who, according to Billy Grady, was the subject of a one-night stand. Tracy was living at the Beverly Hills Hotel, prompting rumors of another separation. In addition to his usual habit of moving out for a picture, his wing of the house was under renovation, adding a bathroom and a dressing area. The rumors, he told Harrison Carroll, were "never more untrue."

Indeed, he was back at home by mid-December, despite the fact that the picture was still very much in production. An exhibitors' poll released on the twenty-third named him fifth in a list of the biggest moneymaking

Spence and Louise at one of the infrequent premieres they
attended as a couple. (SUSIE TRACY)

stars of the year, placing him ahead of such luminaries as Robert Taylor,
Tyrone Power, Gary Cooper, Bing Crosby, and Errol Flynn. Christmas was
with family, Aunt Emma Brown visiting from Freeport, Carrie, Carroll and
Dorothy, Weeze and the kids.

"*I Take This Woman,* starring Hedy Lamarr and Spencer Tracy, has been
shooting for 60 days and nobody has been able to think of an ending for it,"
Sheilah Graham reported in her column of December 26. "The great problem is whether or not to bring Hedy and Spencer together at the end. Oh,
please let them have each other. I'm so tired of finales where the heroine

goes off into a dark fadeout, wistfully followed by the eyes of the hero . . ." The seemingly interminable picture finished—to no one's particular satisfaction—on January 19, 1939. A week later, Tracy was advised by Eddie Mannix that it had been "shelved indefinitely."

"Just imagine," Tracy said. "Hedy had to chase me all during the picture—and I had to run away! Imagine Hedy having to chase any man and not get him! Not only didn't it make sense, but it made Hedy unglamourous. Well, anyway, Metro can't say I didn't warn them. I told them at the start the picture was no good, and for once I was right."

After observing three days of *Boys Town* being filmed in Omaha, Tracy's uncle Andrew got the idea to have a print of the completed film sent to Williamsville, in upstate New York, where Spencer's eighty-three-year-old aunt, Sister Mary Perpetua, was living. Having taken her vows in 1875, the nun had never seen a moving picture, and Andrew thought Spencer's playing a priest would be a terrific introduction to his work as an actor. Frank Whitbeck promised to arrange a showing, and everyone at the convent was invited to attend. Sister remembered Spencer all right—not as an actor but as a truck driver who came through Buffalo during the brief time he had been on the payroll at Sterling Truck. "A bum!" she'd erupt when his name came up. Pressed, she'd tell how she and another nun had been to downtown Buffalo and had seen his name on a marquee. "Humph! He never called me up, never wrote to me, never invited me out!" They couldn't seem to make her understand that he wasn't physically present at the theater, so her half-sister, Jenny Feely, went to Williamsville to be with her for the showing.

"She was in a wheelchair," Jenny's daughter, Jane, said of the nun, "and they wheeled her in to see the movie of her nephew as Father Flanagan. All the nuns were there and they thought it was great, it was wonderful, and they congratulated her afterwards. 'Wasn't that wonderful?' they'd say. 'Yes,' she'd say, 'Father Flanagan, he was a good man. He had an orphanage, you know.' Because she had run an orphanage. Mama said she wasn't really sure that she connected Spencer with Father Flanagan."

Boys Town drew fresh attention to Tracy's work as a priest, coming as it did some two years after his turn as Father Tim in *San Francisco,* as no one had stepped up and attempted another modern priest in the interim.* The reviews of the New York dailies weren't quite as laudatory as the ones that

---

* Pat O'Brien's performance as Father Jerry Connolly, a character clearly patterned after Father Tim, didn't come until the release of Warners' *Angels With Dirty Faces* in November 1938.

had come out of the press preview, Frank Nugent, for one, pointing out the "artificial plot leverage" that came to the rescue once the screenwriters realized they had made Whitey Marsh "too tough a nut to crack" in the natural development of the story. "The highway accident involving Pee Wee, his little chum; the bank robbery and kidnaping; the flood of tears in the last reel, strike a too-familiar discord. It manages, in spite of the embarrassing sentimentality of its closing scenes, to be a consistently interesting and frequently touching motion picture."

Tracy's performance was universally praised, and several prominent critics predicted another Oscar win. When Edwin Schallert of the *Los Angeles Times* omitted his name from his annual list of proposed nominees, the volume of Schallert's mail swelled in protest. (One letter objecting to the snub was signed by thirty-six students from Santa Monica Junior College.) "The omission is duly recognized," Schallert assured his readers in a follow-up, "and certainly Spencer Tracy merits a place in the nominations for both his performances in *Test Pilot* and *Boys Town.* And from a practical standpoint, Mr. Tracy could win the Academy statuette again this year if the voters in the organization are so minded. In fact, Mr. Tracy's qualifications as an actor would entitle him to win the award almost every year."

Boys Town was a big commercial success, taking in over $4 million in worldwide billings. As Schallert discovered, there was broad popular support for Tracy's Best Actor nomination, and when the announcement came down on the night of February 5, 1939, nobody was surprised other than perhaps Tracy himself. The nominations, made by Class A members of the Screen Actors Guild, put James Cagney up for his work in *Angels With Dirty Faces*—a terrific performance—as well as Charles Boyer (*Algiers*), Robert Donat (*The Citadel*), and Leslie Howard (*Pygmalion*). M-G-M came away with four productions, including *Boys Town,* in the Best Picture category. Norman Taurog was nominated for Best Director, John Meehan and Dore Schary for Best Screenplay, Schary and Eleanore Griffin for Best Original Story. In all, *Boys Town* took five nominations.

Tracy thought himself merely competent in the role of Father Flanagan, and talk of another honor frankly made him uncomfortable. "It isn't that I think it is disrespectful or sacrilegious to play a priest," he hedged, "but I think a role of this kind demands more than is in one's power to give. Long after I'm forgotten, Father Flanagan will go down in history as one of the great humanitarians of the century." Privately, he feared people would confuse the man with the actor and vote for the priest and his good deeds, not for a performance that was, by his own reckoning, pretty routine. He was relieved when Cagney was thought to have a big lead in the early balloting, then less so when *Variety* reported the "general belief" the winner would be either Cagney or himself.

"Only an actor like Mr. Tracy and an
actor like young Mickey Rooney, or
someone equally good, could possibly
carry a story without any love interest for
more than ninety minutes and make you
like it," wrote William Boehnel of the
New York World-Telegram.
(SUSIE TRACY)

The festivities at the Biltmore didn't begin until eleven o'clock on the
night of February 23, and the awards for acting weren't announced until
well past midnight. Bette Davis' win for *Jezebel* had been expected, but
Tracy's win over Cagney and the others was considered an upset. When
Tracy, in black tie, stepped up to the trophy-laden center table and began to
speak, Louise could see he was embarrassed. "I could tell by the tone of his
voice," she said. "He wasn't himself at all." Handed the Oscar by Sir Cedric
Hardwicke, he took a long moment to collect his thoughts. "I honestly do
not feel that I can accept this award," he said, his eyes cast downward. "I do
not deserve it. I can accept it only as it was meant to be for a great man—
Father Flanagan, whose goodness and greatness must have been enough to
shine even through me."

Sensing the sincerity of his words, the crowd responded with "thunderous" applause. "I was all primed," said Clark Gable, "to suggest that maybe
they had counted the ballots for the year before by mistake. But he stopped
me cold before I ever started." Tracy dutifully beamed for the flash photographers, a cigarette in one hand, his statuette in the other. Heading for the

Greeting Bette Davis at the Academy Awards dinner. Davis collected the Best Actress statuette for *Jezebel*. (AUTHOR'S COLLECTION)

door, he came alongside screenwriter Laurence Stallings. "I didn't see *Boys Town*," Stallings told him. "I don't know whether you deserved the award for that or not, but you certainly deserve it for the performance you just gave."

Tracy responded to Father Flanagan's wire of congratulations:

> THE CREDIT IS DUE YOU AND I AM GLAD WE GOT IT FOR
> THE SAKE OF BOYS TOWN.

He also wired Bobs Watson, whose trademark crying jags nearly stole the show: HALF OF THE STATUE BELONGS TO YOU. Two days later, on the night of February 27, Father Flanagan's assistant brought a box to him. Inside was Tracy's *Boys Town* Oscar, an added plate bearing the inscription:

> TO FATHER FLANAGAN
> WHOSE GREAT HUMAN QUALITIES, KINDLY SIMPLICITY AND INSPIRING
> COURAGE WERE STRONG ENOUGH TO SHINE THROUGH MY HUMBLE EFFORTS.
> SPENCER TRACY

In the four years since Spencer Tracy and Fox Film Corporation parted company, both had gone through extraordinary changes. Where Tracy was scarcely a blip on the box office barometer in 1935, a critics' darling and little more, he was now fifth-ranked among all American film stars and had two Academy Awards to his credit. Similarly, where Fox had been limping along under the fitful leadership of Winfield Sheehan, Darryl F. Zanuck was now in charge of production, having taken over in the wake of a deal that merged 20th Century Pictures with Fox Film to create 20th Century-Fox. Under him, Fox became a writers' studio—the polar opposite of M-G-M, where the writers worked in service of the stars. Screenplays at Fox were developed with little regard for who on the lot could play them, and when no one on the payroll proved suitable, Zanuck had no qualms about going outside and borrowing the people he needed.

When M-G-M, in effect, took over Tracy's contract—moneywise it was a lateral move—Fox reserved the right to make one additional picture within a year's time at a rate of $3,000 a week. It was almost a corporate face-saving device, something thrown in as an afterthought, and when Zanuck was apprised of their "gentlemen's agreement" in March 1936, he expressed no interest whatsoever in taking advantage of it. Ironically, he was then in the early stages of developing a picture about Welsh journalist Henry Morton Stanley's 1871 expedition in search of the Scottish missionary David Livingstone, the project that would ultimately bring Tracy back to the studio.

According to screenwriter Philip Dunne, Zanuck's early attempts at a scenario were completely lacking in suspense and, from a historical perspective, "pure eyewash." Failing to break the back of the story didn't diminish Zanuck's faith in the idea, however. In June 1937 he sent a thirteen-member crew, headed by second-unit specialist Otto Brower, to Africa to shoot authentic backgrounds and wildlife. Having previously been on safari himself, Zanuck gave Brower a list of locations—Lake Nakura for flamingo shots, Arusha for the Zanzibar sequence, Serengeti for various animals—and Mrs. Martin (Osa) Johnson as technical adviser. Included in the Brower company were three doubles, one calculated to match Tyrone Power, whom Zanuck envisioned for the lead. Over a period of four months Brower and his crew made nine camp moves across Kenya, Tanganyika, and Uganda, exposing nearly a hundred thousand feet of film.

Prior to Brower's departure, Zanuck had made *Stanley and Livingstone* part of the studio's 1937–38 program, lining it up alongside *Alexander's Ragtime Band* and *In Old Chicago* as his top pictures of the year. While Brower was away, Sam Hellman, Ernest Pascal, and Edwin Harvey Blum attempted screenplays. Zanuck thought Hellman's dialogue weak: "Not dramatized enough—punch into personal story—too narrative." By the end of the year, the project had been tabled. When Dunne and his writing partner, Julien Josephson, were assigned in the spring of 1938, they read all that had come before and tried to get out of it. Zanuck, in the meantime, had told the story to director Henry King, and it was King who suggested a complete reversal of Stanley's motivation.

"Forget the silly business of the missionary befriending the boy from the work house," Dunne wrote in his memoir. "The new Stanley has never even heard of Livingstone. He's a hard-boiled city news reporter whose only ambition is to bust the Tweed ring in New York, but he's browbeaten by his equally hard-boiled publisher, Bennett, into undertaking the search for Livingstone as a great publicity stunt for the newspaper . . . Kicking and screaming, as it were, Stanley—no longer handsome Tyrone Power but now rough Spencer Tracy—goes unwillingly to Africa."

Tracy, who knew Zanuck from his polo days and *Looking for Trouble*, took time to meet with him while awaiting the start of *A New York Cinderella*. Expecting to do *Northwest Passage* in the spring, Tracy wasn't enthused about a second consecutive adventure subject nor the prospect of spending half a year on location. A loose loan-out agreement existed between M-G-M and Fox as a result of the latter having loaned Tyrone Power to Metro for *Marie Antoinette*. In return, Zanuck expected Myrna Loy for *The Rains Came* and Tracy for *Stanley and Livingstone*.* King had come aboard as director, and by November 26, 1938, Tracy was officially set for the film.

The script was finalized on January 18, 1939, and the picture, budgeted at $1,338,000, began shooting on February 2 at the Fox Hills studio Tracy had once considered home. Now merely a guest, he found himself assigned skater Sonja Henie's dressing room, an insistent blue-and-white affair with lace trimmings and gewgaws throughout. He told columnist Harrison Carroll he was afraid to turn around for fear of knocking something over.

They were three weeks into production when the academy dinner took place, and both Tracy and Walter Brennan came away with awards. (Brennan was Best Supporting Actor for his work in *Kentucky*, his second win in three years.) The following morning, both men were applauded by several hundred extras when they stepped onto the set. Although the shoot went smoothly enough, Tracy fretted over the line "Dr. Livingstone, I presume?"

* Officially, Tracy's participation in *Stanley and Livingstone* was entirely separate from the deal for Power and was apparently based on Tracy's personal conviction that he did indeed owe Fox another picture.

and argued against its inclusion in the script. A perennial punch line—the quote may even have been apocryphal—he could think of it only in the context of a joke and was convinced that audiences would laugh.

"He came to me one day," recalled King,

> and said, "You don't mean to tell me that you're going to do that old chestnut about Dr. Livingstone, I presume?" And I said, "We have to do it. We couldn't do the picture without it." He said, "I can't say it, I can't say it." Well, this worried him to death, but he had neglected to think [about it] . . . I said, "Spence, did you ever stop to think that this man has had that fever, that swamp fever, just a few days before this? You've carried him through all this, and now when he comes into Dr. Livingstone's place he can hardly walk. And he sees this man. He says, 'Doctor . . . Livingstone . . .' " Spence says, "I could kill you, I could murder you. You played the scene for me and I didn't have sense enough to think about it."

When the time came, Tracy got the line out, but it took several takes, he said, because he couldn't say it without laughing.* He bet Zanuck's associate producer, Kenneth Macgowan, the preview audience would laugh as well, and—to take the curse off—told the old joke about the drunk who wanders into a bar to whoever visited the set. Having weathered the making of *Marie Gallante,* King was understandably wary of Tracy. "*In vino veritas,*" he would later say. "Get someone drunk and you find out what they really are like. They're either sweet and lovable or ugly and hateful. Spencer was an ugly drunk." Tracy, however, was good-natured and cooperative on *Stanley and Livingstone,* and when King had to stop a scene between Tracy and Cedric Hardwicke because of airplane noise outside, Tracy ran his tongue up the side of his mouth and casually remarked, "Over at M-G-M we have *soundproof* stages."

He later said:

> I'm slowly improving. I don't go through the agony I did when I was making four or five pictures a year. Boy, it's awfully hard to be good four times a year. Nowadays, I'm making three. And I take time out to try to get laughs on the set. If an airplane flies overhead

---

* There was no panting in the take that was used, just the weary realization on Stanley's part that after nine months on the African continent his quest has finally paid off. "Dr. Livingstone," he says with growing certainty as the figure approaches, adding the "I presume" as an afterthought.

and action has to stop till the sound dies away, I don't go higher than a kite. I take things more calmly now. But—I haven't reached the ultimate in calmness yet. The sitting, waiting, still gets me. It's the only thing that gives me a hankering for the stage. I'd like to go back—not to stay, but once every two or three years—just to get a performance out of my system in one evening.

However much trouble the "I presume" line gave him, Tracy's most impressive moment in the film came with his impassioned address before the Society of British Geographers, a speech totaling nearly four hundred words. King wanted to capture the scene in a single take, Stanley barely suppressing his rage at the society's skeptical membership. "Dr. Livingstone is out there!" he insists, building to a crescendo. "He is old and he is sick and he needs your help to carry on the great work he has undertaken—the work that is indicated, however inadequately, upon those maps. Reject those maps, withhold your aid, and you destroy him. Reject those maps and you close Africa for a generation to come. Reject those maps, gentlemen, and you break faith with the greatest geographer and one of the greatest men of our times!"

Covered by two cameras, the stirring speech was unlike anything Tracy had yet attempted, three and a half minutes of uninterrupted screen time, flawlessly delivered, a virtuoso turn in a film that was otherwise more stoic than exciting. Gladys Hall, present on the set and expecting an interview, thought he "might really tuck in his chin this time, beetle his eyebrows and go 'Harrummph!' and give me the business," but instead he went over, ever conscious of downplaying the work he always put into the job of acting, plopped down in a chair beside her, and said, "Ever hear the one about the drunk . . . ?"

Toward the end of production, Hedy Lamarr, newly married to Fox writer-producer Gene Markey, visited the set, hailing him as "Spennzer" and standing in for actress Nancy Kelly for a shot where Stanley is standing on the deck of an East Indian steamship and looking down at the character of Eve Kingsley. Only the week earlier, Tracy had told Sheilah Graham that Lamarr was "in a spot" with the shelving of *I Take This Woman*. "Do you realize," he said, "it will be six months at least before the public sees Hedy in a picture? That makes a year off the screen for an actress who has made only one picture. Her next picture must be good—and don't think Hedy doesn't know it."

He did a Lux broadcast the night of March 27, then boarded a train for Sun Valley, Idaho, to shoot the Wyoming Territory sequence that opens the picture. He worked all day on the twenty-ninth, leaving for home at 11:00 p.m. and arriving back in Los Angeles on the morning of March 31. He had time for tennis with Louise and a swim in the pool before reporting back to the Fox lot. He celebrated his birthday the following week with tennis, seven periods of polo, and dinner at home with Louise and the kids. He was thirty-nine years old and, as he told his family and friends, he was beginning to feel it.

CHAPTER 15

A Buoyant Effect on the Audience

Tracy saw *Stanley and Livingstone* in a studio projection room on April 11, 1939, and thought it only fair. "Might be entertaining, not great," he wrote in his book. "Predict fair bus[iness], fair reviews. Just so-so." He left the next day for another try at the European vacation that had gone so disastrously awry the previous year. Frank Whitbeck accompanied him as far as Omaha, where a meeting had been scheduled with Father Flanagan and Bishop Ryan to discuss the possibility of a sequel to *Boys Town*.

Tracy wasn't keen on the idea, but he felt a profound sense of responsibility toward Father Flanagan and the young citizenry that had embraced him so fervently. The studio cleared a profit of more than $2 million on the picture, yet the institution itself had seen only $5,000 in rights money. Also, the tidal wave of donations Flanagan expected after the film's release failed to materialize, and contributions, in fact, dropped sharply, supporters assuming that Boys Town was suddenly flush with cash. Perversely, the only thing the movie succeeded in boosting was the number of applicants for admission, most of whom had to be turned away. "Next time I come to Hollywood," Flanagan told the *New York Times,* "I'm going to get myself an agent."

Tracy arrived in New York on April 16 and spent the week playing tennis, taking long walks around the city, and seeing shows. As always, he delighted in the big musicals—the Noël Coward revue *Set to Music,* Olsen

(PATRICIA MAHON COLLECTION)

and Johnson's *Hellzapoppin'*, Jimmy Durante and Ethel Merman in *Stars in Your Eyes*. He dined one night with Helen Hayes and Charles MacArthur, another with Beatrice Lillie. Louise arrived on the twenty-first, and they sailed for England the same day.

The weather was beautiful, the seas calm. They reached Cherbourg on the morning of the twenty-sixth, Southampton later that afternoon. Tracy had heard the British crowds were fierce, but he was completely unprepared for the near riot that greeted him as the boat train pulled into Waterloo Station. The place was mobbed, mostly by fur-clad women eager to get a glimpse of the star of *Boys Town*. "The crowd that charged him on the platform must have been at least a thousand strong and at times looked nasty," the British film critic Caroline Lejeune reported. "It was a case of get out or get under." A porter and six women were trampled in the melee; Arturo Toscanini, famed conductor of the NBC Symphony Orchestra, was swept off his feet and flung against a baggage truck.

The railway police closed in around the Tracys, and since they couldn't slip them down the milk chute as they had Robert Taylor, they drew all the near-side blinds on the train and then moved them through the off-side doors into an empty down-train, which they then ran back along the tracks to the last wayside station. Police told the throng, "Your hero has left," but the women milled for hours, bouquets and orchids in hand, meeting all the trains as they arrived. "The crowd was still whooping and waiting at Waterloo," Lejeune's dispatch concluded, "when Mr. and Mrs. Tracy, rather white about the gills and a good deal shaken, slipped out unseen at Vauxhall onto a bare platform under the cold April stars."

They shook up the staff at Claridge's by rising at six the next morning, strolling the empty streets of London, Spence toting his 16mm movie camera, returning in time for a nine o'clock breakfast. They saw the changing of the guard, then took off for Windsor Castle. "What am I doing in London?" he said in answer to a reporter's question. "Nothing. Just let London look after me. I have been trying to get here for two years. It was hardly worthwhile coming for such a short time, but I was determined to make this trip." The studio arranged a formal news conference—his first ever—and he fielded questions while sipping a glass of Vichy. What did he think of London? What struck him most about it? "I've got to think fast," he said. "People will try and make me pronounce on politics. Those questions have to be answered guardedly." No, he said, he'd never had a proposal in the post. "An Anti-Nazi League in Hollywood? No, that's something I've never heard of."

He was asked about his newest picture. "I haven't seen a finished version of *Stanley and Livingstone*," he lied. "I don't know—maybe it's all right. You could take that subject fifty ways. I am sure that when I say 'Dr. Livingstone, I presume' it'll be one almighty laugh in every hall." He said his next picture would be *Northwest Passage* with Wallace Beery and Robert Taylor, and then probably *The Yearling*. "I think that's one of the finest books I've ever read. I'm hoping we'll get round to it this summer."

It rained almost every day. They saw Joe Kennedy, played tennis with his daughters Pat and Eunice, lunched with the Kennedy family. ("All the Kennedys," Tracy once said, "remind me of my father.") In Paris he discovered Maxim's, with its crocks of thick yellow cream, and spent an evening in the company of actor Jean Gabin, the stocky Parisian "Everyman" whose career had, in many ways, paralleled his own. Gabin, he said, wanted him to remain in Paris and make a picture. "I will tell you what we do," Gabin said. "We will make one picture here and then we will forget all about movies and go fishing—for a year." Tracy suggested that Gabin come to Hollywood and make a picture there. "I can hardly talk French," the actor responded. "How could I learn to talk English?"

Tracy enjoyed every minute of his time in France. In London the autograph hunters pursued him on bicycles. In Paris he was never once asked for his signature. "You'd go in a shop to buy something and order it delivered to your hotel. Invariably with the delivery would come a note from the shopgirl who waited on you to this effect: 'I did not wish to embarrass you by telling you how much I enjoyed your last picture, so I am expressing that enjoyment in this note.' " They sailed from Le Havre on May 5, arrived at Southampton that evening, and left for home at midnight, affording Spence a brief look at Ireland, which, as far as he was concerned, made the entire trip worthwhile.

"We arrived in the morning at Cobb, and the sun was shining and there was Ireland before us. I've never experienced so deep a thrill. I could feel it in the pit of my stomach. This is where my grandparents had come from— this was my real homeland and the sensation was almost overpowering in its intensity. I was up on the bridge with Paddy, the old Irish pilot, and I guess he knew what was going on in my heart, because he smiled at me. 'God bless you, lad,' he said, 'the door latch is always out.' Some day, I'm going to Ireland and I'm going to take Pat O'Brien with me. What a time Pat would have over there."

The return trip was nasty in comparison to the going—fog, rain, and rough seas, and the ship pitched furiously. Tracy was planning to meet up with Lincoln Cromwell in New York, as he was anxious for the young man to take his second year of internship in Europe. He was offering, in fact, to pay travel expenses for Cromwell and his new wife to make an investigatory trip over the summer. Upon docking, however, he was advised that his mother had suffered a stroke in Los Angeles, and he and Louise left for Chicago within hours. They were relieved to find Carrie doing "pretty well" in California and that her doctors expected her to make a complete recovery.

In Los Angeles he sat for a long interview with Ed Sullivan and seemed genuinely altered by the experience of visiting Europe. It appeared that everyone he encountered in England and France had seen *Boys Town,* and that the picture struck an undeniable chord with every segment of the audience.

After nearly a decade in Hollywood, Tracy had come to regard the broad canvas of the screen as a public trust, a place where the great social issues of the day could be defined and portrayed and where the spiritual values of hope and goodwill could be reinforced. The best characters, he said, gave voice to the ideals of the common man and sent people home "feeling that there was dignity to life and to living, and some point to muddling along." He couldn't help but note that after five years of indifferent pictures at Fox—virtually none of which had a transformative effect on an audience—he had risen to the very pinnacle of stardom on a core group of productions at Metro-Goldwyn-Mayer—*Fury, San Francisco, Captains Courageous,* and *Boys Town.* "I'll tell you what I'd love to play: *Grapes of Wrath.* That is a story that has tremendous social significance to it. It's big, important. It has guts. I wish that Darryl Zanuck could borrow me from Metro and Jim Cagney from Warners for that one. I promise you that we'd play the hell out of it, or at least die in the attempt."

He went on to tell Sullivan that he thought Robert Morley's rangy performance in *Oscar Wilde* "great"—it was the one Broadway play he had permitted himself—but he found the material itself repulsive, dealing as it did with the historic trial for pederasty ("gross indecency") that led to Wilde's undoing. "I left the theater feeling ashamed to have seen such a play. I felt sort of unclean, because to a normal person the topic is almost obscene. The play itself obscured the performance. After all, experienced actors shouldn't have to prove they can give great performances. That should be taken for granted. The most important thing is for the play itself to have a buoyant effect on the audience."

While Tracy refused to take the Academy Award seriously as a symbol of artistic merit, it did bolster his standing within the industry and underscore his growing popularity with the moviegoing public. Progressively more space was being devoted to him in newspapers—particularly by the syndicated columnists—and the yearly number of articles in the fan magazines had more than quadrupled since 1935. He naturally withdrew from such heightened interest, preferring to talk with Dick Mook and Gladys Hall and Ed Sullivan and, sometimes, to Louella Parsons, who always invoked their Freeport connections. (Parsons was born in Freeport in 1881 but had moved to Dixon, thirty miles south, by the time of Tracy's birth in 1900.) Journalists were always hanging around the sets at Metro, but they were all carefully supervised and prohibited from talking to the stars without an okay from Howard Strickling.

Tracy did talk to journalists when he traveled, particularly in New York, where he figured he might one day return to the stage. "I had wires from Sam Behrman and Guthrie McClintic last season asking me if I were available for a play," he told William Boehnel of the *World-Telegram,* "but when

I replied that I thought I might be able to arrange it I never heard from them again. Maybe I'd better stick to Hollywood." The more he worked with "some of the big directors," he told his pal Mook, the more he realized what "really fine things" could be done in pictures. "I still hope to do more plays on the stage, but I'm still not big enough in pictures to dictate the terms of my contract. And the mounting quality of pictures compensates for not being able to do worthwhile stage plays—if I were lucky enough to find them."

Emboldened by Tracy's public comments, Theresa Helburn of the Theatre Guild approached him in the spring of 1939 with the idea of his starring in a revival of Bernard Shaw's *The Devil's Disciple*. He couldn't argue with the quality of the material, and the play hadn't been seen on Broadway since 1923, when a young Basil Sydney played the rebel Dudgeon. There was a whole generation of playgoers who had never seen it, Helburn argued, and another that had probably forgotten it. "And it occurred to me that now that Shaw has at last yielded to the movies [with Gabriel Pascal's production of *Pygmalion*], this one will be bound to come along soon and perhaps you and Metro might have ideas about it similar to mine."

Louise thought it would be good for him to get out of Hollywood and the deadening routine of making movies, if only for a short while. "The motion picture business is a very demanding one in some ways," she said.

> Very. And it was very difficult [to adjust to it] . . . [Spence] was going to come out [to Hollywood] anyhow—the money and everything else was interesting—but I think he felt that this was something he could do in the daytime and then [he] would be free . . . Of course, that was not true. His nights were taken: he read scripts and then he studied for the next day. And although he didn't do much studying, he thought a great deal about it. He even worked over weekends . . . He took it very, very seriously, and . . . he thought about so many little things. People say he's so natural, [that] he just gets up and talks. He used to laugh about people saying things like that. If they but knew the time you take to just give that little bit, that particular line you throw away, its own thing. It wasn't anything you just got up and did—that natural thing—and he did a great deal of that at night.

Tracy thought he might make a quick trip to New York to meet with Theresa Helburn, but then the decision was made to go ahead with *Northwest Passage*—despite the fact there was only half a script—and by July 4 he was in McCall, Idaho, for the start of production. It wasn't a picture he particularly wanted to make anymore, and although he kicked about going, the whole project had been designed around him and there was no getting out of it. His location work so far had been limited to Riverside, Catalina, La Jolla—day trips. *Boys Town* meant twelve days in Nebraska, but apart from the heat they weren't exactly roughing it. *Northwest Passage* would be an altogether different experience—six weeks on the banks of Payette Lake, a hundred miles north of Boise near the Oregon border. It would be an unusually physical shoot with a lot of river work, a lot of stunt work, a lot of people.

Tracy's character was a colonial frontiersman and Indian fighter, a man as lean and rugged as the times and the terrain could make him. Yet he had ballooned to 189 pounds—the heaviest he had ever been—and hardly looked the part. He vowed that he would lose ten pounds in time for the picture, but as far as Louise could tell, the day he left for location he had lost just two of them. "Don't worry," he told her. "The food is going to be terrible, and between that and the heat and the ticks and getting up at five-thirty in order to start shooting at seven, I'll be thin enough when we reach the trek back from St. Francis. And there won't be a drug store or a sundae anywhere within miles." When she saw him off at the station, she noticed a large box of chocolates tucked under the coat he had draped over one arm. "Just a little present mother gave me," he said airily.

To make the trip he recruited Pat Elsey, his trainer and masseur, to come with him and help get him into shape. Elsey would be in addition to his stand-in, Jerry Schumacher, and his new dresser, Larry Keethe. Louise would come to visit at some point during the ordeal, and although the studio would have a doctor on site, he persuaded Howard Dennis to be there for at least the first week. Director King Vidor, while amused at the posse Tracy gathered, had to admit the picture depended on him, and were he to fall ill or somehow injure himself, the entire mechanism would grind to a halt. "He was well taken care of," Vidor said. "I guess in the long run it was more important that he remain well than anyone else."

Tracy, who had been attached to the film for nearly two years, thought Kenneth Roberts' best-selling novel a great read but was increasingly dubious about filming the entire story, which could rival the anticipated running time of *Gone With the Wind*. Book I of Roberts' novel covered Major Robert Rogers' daring incursion deep into enemy territory during the French and Indian War, culminating in his raid on the Abenaki Indian village of St. Francis, where the village and fully a quarter of its population were destroyed. Book II—the second half—followed Rogers' later years, his life as a profligate, his descent into alcoholism and financial ruin. It was the same trajectory Tracy observed in the play *Oscar Wilde,* and he feared that Rogers' fate would obscure his performance, as Wilde's downfall, in his judgment, had obscured Morley's. "I'll play him up to the point where he has achieved his objective," Tracy declared, "but I'll be darned if I'll play him when he becomes a drunkard. Audiences won't want to see him in that stage of his life."

Roberts' 709-page book was published in June 1937 and was already in its eighth printing when M-G-M bought the picture rights in September of that year, planning to make *Northwest Passage* its first feature in the radiant new Technicolor process. Woody Van Dyke was the first director assigned to the film, and it was Van Dyke who spent two weeks scouting locations in British Columbia. Tracy was the studio's "immediate choice" to play Major Rogers; the sunburn he got in Hawaii in May 1938 had been requested specifically for the purpose of making Technicolor costume tests. Van Dyke fell away from the project over delays and a scheduling conflict, and King Vidor, whose direction of *The Citadel* the previous year had brought him an Academy Award nomination, was selected to replace him. Vidor brought Laurence Stallings, one of his favorite writers, to the project, and the two men quickly figured out a way to incorporate both halves of Roberts' novel into a single coherent screenplay. "Hunt Stromberg, the producer, didn't go for it," Vidor remembered, "so he had a writer named Talbot Jennings come in and begin work."

Vidor memoed Eddie Mannix: "As yet there is no complete story line upon which Mr. Stromberg and I have agreed . . . The trek to St. Francis and the return within the next few days will be in good shape . . . But I want to go on record here that I am definitely against starting the production without a full script, so that we know where we are going." Jennings began revising Stallings' screenplay while Vidor made preparations to leave for McCall under protest. "At this time," he said, "I had to bring the production up to the location because the water level of the lake where we were shooting was going down. We had to start filming right away. When I was leaving, Stromberg told me, 'By the time you finish the first part of the picture, I'll have the second part sent up.'"

The company had taken over a huge summer resort camp on the shore of the lake, and some four hundred actors and technicians—including Tracy, Robert Young, Walter Brennan, Nat Pendleton, and Isabel Jewell—were housed there. A tent city for the 450 Indians used in the film stood three miles north of the main camp. A special train from Los Angeles brought twelve carloads of props and three additional carloads of uniforms and costumes. There were seventy-five rough-looking characters—mostly stunt personnel—imported from Hollywood to play the principal men under Rogers' command. Another 175 were recruited from among the local lumberjacks and miners. French frontiersmen and oarsmen were also hired locally, and many did double duty as the day's work required. The Idaho

National Guard supplied the 225 British soldiers needed to man Fort Ticonderoga; in all, it was said the company employed over fifteen thousand extras and bit players.

Tiny McCall, population several hundred, was overwhelmed by the hordes seeking employment on the film. "There were quite a few unsavory characters joining the gold rush," Vidor's assistant director, Harrold Weinberger, recalled, "including a half dozen or so whores up from Boise and other points south or north, and a troupe of professional gamblers . . . The hookers were occupying half the rooms in the small and only hotel in town. I saw them all many times about town. They weren't bad at all to look at. They were prospering. I was told their rates ran from $10 to $25 a trip. Pretty good for the 1939 economy . . . The hotel management must have gotten some kind of cut considering all the towels and linens that were required."

Tracy managed to endear himself to actor Robert Young during their first morning on location. "We were in this renovated camp which had been unused for about 20 years," Young said, "so you can imagine what kind of shape it was in . . . So they stuck up a service tent and the caterer brought the tables and chairs and the stove and everything else in there. Well, we went to breakfast, or whatever the hell the first meal was that we had there, and Spence stood up, threw the plate clear across the tent." They had been served powdered eggs. "Oh, it was awful. He went right to the unit manager [and] said, 'When you correct the situation, I'll be back. I'll be on the set. Otherwise, don't bother me. Don't even talk to me.' Well, you don't think the telephone wires didn't get hot the next day. I don't know how the hell they produced it that quickly, but the next day there was a new unit manager. It was the most incredible transformation you ever saw. Overnight, there was a complete transformation; we had the most divine food . . . I watched him and I thought to myself, man that's great. That's power."

Filming began with Rogers' address to his men, crudely mapping their route on a surface of rock. One of the men graphically describes the atrocities of the Abenaki warriors against their fellow Rangers, then Rogers goes on to suggest fates of a similar sort for the settlers on the border farms—the survivors of whom now comprise much of his force. ("If it was over quick, they were lucky.") Grimly determined, they say nothing, all eyes fixed on their leader. "Now, if there's any man here who doesn't want to follow me against these Indians, he can step out now and nothing will be said at home." And, of course, no one does.

Tracy held Rogers taut during the scene, letting the words and the images grip the audience with the harshness of their clarity. Maintaining Rogers' intensity during the balance of the film while avoiding a one-note performance would be a cruelly taxing job. The first two weeks on location involved some of the heaviest physical labor of the entire shoot, particularly an arduous sequence in which the Rangers drag their whaleboats over a steep hill to elude the French. "I said, 'Well, just include me out,' " Walter Brennan, who was making his third picture alongside Tracy, remembered. "They said, 'Why?' And I said, 'Rogers' Rangers only lugged those boats over the hill once. We lugged them over ten times and they were real boats.' Boy, that was a strenuous job . . ."

Tracy was no happier than Brennan, and there were exchanges between King Vidor and Hunt Stromberg about the possibility of bringing the entire company home. "Young, Brennan and I wore out our Rogers' uniforms in two days," Tracy said. "Pine branches, boulders, underbrush, swamp, mud, river rocks and things . . ." Robert Young, playing the fictional Langdon Towne, could remember having to strip outside his cabin each night—as did all cast members—and throw his clothes onto a sheet to more clearly see the ticks crawl off. "We weren't wearing buckskin, we were wearing suede, or something like that, to approximate buckskin. We grew our beards. We weren't allowed to wash our clothes, and we went through mud and slime and . . . oh, unbelievable. It kept getting worse, and then we'd hang those things out at night and they would turn sour. If you got on the downwind side you couldn't stand it; you'd faint. [It would] make you throw up, it was so bad."

Even with Pat Elsey on hand, Tracy had to be bullied into the routine of a daily rubdown and dry clothes. "He becomes so thoroughly the character that he is portraying that he forgets to take the sort of precautions which he needs as a star," Elsey said at the time. "He depends on me to take those precautions for him." King Vidor thought Tracy a bit of a pill, even as, in Vidor's estimate, he made up for it. "As long as somebody's giving you a marvelous performance, you just don't worry about the little things." Tracy, he said, wasn't difficult to handle or direct, but he did have his days.

He kept threatening that he was going home from location. I tried and tried to think up something to do. Finally, I told my assistant director to go over to Boise, find a good-looking woman and put her on salary secretly, buy her some nice-looking clothes, and employ her to just come and sit and watch the shooting. You know, as a tourist. And so we did this. It gave Spencer someone to play up to, you know? To perform for. He'd go over and talk to her between takes. But one day, after about four days of this, she came over to me and said, "It's a nice easy job, Mr. Vidor, a pleasant job. But do I have to ride around in his automobile and listen to his problems?"

Well, we told her she'd have to handle that herself. But that's all she was employed to do—just be there, sit and watch like a tourist. And it *worked!* All of a sudden, he stopped talking about rushing home.

Stromberg, in Culver City, was sending new pages up nearly every day, convinced that Talbot Jennings was investing his scenes with "more strength and emotional warmth" than Stallings had managed. Tracy hated shooting with revised dialogue, which reminded him of the old days in stock where part of the job was forgetting old material while absorbing the new. On July 20 he cabled Eddie Mannix:

SERIOUS CHANGES IN DIALOGUE JUST BEFORE SHOOT-
ING ARE BAD ENOUGH IN THE STUDIO, BUT HERE THEY
ARE IMPOSSIBLE ON TOP OF PHYSICAL HANDICAPS.
SOME DECISION MUST BE MADE AS TO WHAT WE ARE
GOING TO SHOOT. I HAVE STUDIED AND BELIEVE IN
NEW JENNINGS SCRIPT AND THOUGHT WE WERE GOING
TO SHOOT IT. I ALSO UNDERSTAND VIDOR'S POSITION IN
WANTING TO COMBINE [THE] TWO, BUT I CANNOT
ASSUME RESPONSIBILITY FOR PERFORMANCE WHEN THIS
IS DONE ON THE SET.

Stromberg promptly made the decision to send Talbot Jennings to Payette Lake. Vidor and his crew were shooting the burning of St. Francis, an extraordinarily brutal sequence for its time, involving the same controlled-burn techniques pioneered for *Gone With the Wind.* Exposed negative was flown nightly to Los Angeles, where it was processed at Technicolor's Hollywood plant and sent on to the studio. Stromberg would see the rushes and then have them sent to Payette via Boise where Vidor and his crew would have them screened in what was once a gambling hall.* It took twelve days to complete the sequence, and by the time the final takes were made, the copper tubing that fed the flames with gasoline had literally melted away. The remains of the ten-acre village were doused with 150 gallons of kerosene, and the heat from the blaze was so intense it could be felt against the granite cliffs on the opposite side of the Payette River.

Tracy grew increasingly irritable as production wore on, anxious to finish and intolerant of anything that might cause a delay. "He had an expression," Vidor remembered. "I think it was 'Happy days!' which meant they just were not worrying about the film, not worrying about anything. There

* In addition to cinematographer Sid Wagner's regular crew, a complete Technicolor crew of sixteen headed by William V. Skall was part of the company.

On location near McCall, Idaho, with director King Vidor, 1939.
(AUTHOR'S COLLECTION)

is always a big group in a company like that; they have hours and hours to sit around and play cards and yak without having the responsibility of making the film. That always seemed to annoy him and he'd say, 'Happy days, happy days!' They were just making a lark out of the whole thing."

Tracy's big speech in the picture comes when Rogers and his men reach Fort Wentworth and discover it abandoned. Running up ahead of them, Rogers takes in its weathered boards, the brush sprouting in its central yard, the utter emptiness of the place where they were to have had their first real food in weeks, and as his men approach excitedly, he leans up against a collapsed section of gate and breaks into tears. It was part of Vidor's plan to signal a crack in Rogers' heroic facade, a hint of the trouble to come in the second half of the story. Tracy, said Vidor, fought him bitterly: "At the end of the picture he breaks down for a minute when the British are not there to meet him at the fort. Well, Spencer didn't want to cry. I persuaded him, though, and he did it, and I think he liked the results. But he didn't want to, not at all. He said, 'A strong man would never cry.' "

Pulling himself together, Rogers rallies his demoralized men. ("Now the first thing we have to do is get this fort in shape—for Amherst and his men when they get here with the food.") And when they balk he launches into what was dubbed his "Moses speech" by King Vidor: "Moses went without the slightest taste of food for 40 days! He didn't have any good cooked roots. No, not a thing. He didn't have a single bite, did he Towne?" The first take was spoiled when the bulky Technicolor camera ran out of film, the second when Tracy stumbled over a word in a Bible passage. Vidor called for a third take, and Tracy did the entire three-minute-and-thirty-five-second speech flawlessly, his character teetering on the brink of madness, a shrewd amalgam of desperation and hope. When he finished there was dead silence. Vidor called "Cut!" and the crew erupted in a burst of applause.

More than any other bit in the picture, it was this one scene that caused Vidor to regard Tracy as just about the best actor with whom he ever worked. "Everything that Spence did," he said, "came over with tremendous conviction." Stromberg wired Vidor:

AGREE WITH YOU THAT SPENCER'S MOSES SCENE IS GREAT, JUST SCREENED IT WITH TALBOT AND WE WERE VERY ENTHUSIASTIC.

Vidor suggested that Stromberg communicate his enthusiasm directly to Tracy, and Stromberg did so, wiring:

HAVE SCREENED RUSHES FROM TWO TO THREE TIMES EACH DAY THEY ARRIVE WITH ONE SCREENING DEVOTED EXCLUSIVELY TO SIZING UP YOUR PERFORMANCE AND TO SAY THAT I AM ENTHUSED AND ABSOLUTELY POSITIVE THAT WE ARE HEADED FOR A WONDERFUL ACHIEVEMENT IS PUTTING IT CONSERVATIVELY.

The company finished at Payette Lake on August 14 after forty-two days in the wilderness, and resumed work eight days later in the relative comfort of M-G-M's Lot 3. Tracy had time for a few days at home, swimming and playing tennis, but there was no polo, and after two months away from the fields, he was anxious and sore and unable to sleep. He had played fairly regularly up until the death of Captain C.T.I. "Pat" Roark on February 21.

Roark, forty-three, was a nine-goal player, Irish-born and mourned on four continents. It was the first fatal accident among the game's high-goal players, a very public reminder of how easily even a world-class player could lean forward and put a shot across the front of his horse and get the stick momentarily caught in its legs. Roark's horse stumbled while up against a team of international cup players, threw him heavily to the ground, then rolled over and crushed him. Spence had played that morning at Alhambra's Midwick Country Club, and he and Louise were among the horrified crowd of five thousand when the accident occurred later that same day. Roark lingered for two days without regaining consciousness, then died from his injuries following brain surgery.

Tracy took Pat Roark's death hard. "I think he blamed himself for it," said David Caldwell, who was fourteen at the time and whose parents, Orville and Audrey Caldwell, were among the Tracys' closest friends. Had Roark played opposite Tracy that morning at Midwick? Could the six periods Tracy noted in his datebook have left Roark unduly fatigued? Off his game opposite the hard-riding cavaliers of Hurlingham? Had his horse been part of the morning action? (Tracy noted in his book that he had tried three different ponies that day.) The answers are all lost to time, and the field itself has long since been given over to development. Years later, in 1972, when Jane Ardmore asked Louise why Spence had given up the game, she said it was after the death of Captain Pat Roark, "a close friend."

He took to stick-and-balling at home with Johnny every morning, riding through the alfalfa behind the house, but grew increasingly anxious about it. He bought a life insurance policy—he was already covered for health and accident through Lloyd's of London—but when he had dinner with a friend on the night of March 18, he was so "nervous [he] did not want to come home" and instead spent the night in a guest house. On the twenty-sixth—Passion Sunday—he went to Mass but ran late in the rain and missed lunch with the kids. That evening he visited the Flemings—Vic had assumed direction of *Gone With the Wind*—and stayed until midnight. "[I] thought I was nervous," he observed in his book, "until I saw Victor. Bad shape."

He managed seven chukkers of polo on his birthday and played in a charity game on Easter Sunday, but otherwise he didn't go back again until May 19, after returning from his trip to Europe. He threw himself into tennis but wasn't very good at it—Louise routinely beat him—and it didn't counter his weight gains as effectively nor wear him out as thoroughly.*

---

* "He had a very good eye with quick movements," Louise said. "Could have played a good game of tennis if he had started early enough. But he never cared about doing anything like that. The theatre, yes. You gave your best, but he played games for fun. He never cared who won."

Having Pat Elsey on location at Payette Lake helped get him through the picture, but massage could only treat the symptoms of the tension that was continually building inside of him. ("Spencer always had the motor running," said Frank Tracy, "even as a kid.") And being sixteen months sober meant he could no longer use booze as a release. "I was sorry to see him sell his boat," Clark Gable remarked. "He used to work off excess steam on that. He's a guy who needs something to help him work off excess steam."

"It would be wonderful," Tracy had told an interviewer that previous year, "if I could drop my worrying when I leave the set—not carry that home with me, not keep on agonizing after hours about whether a role is good or whether I'm giving it everything it could have. I don't force my worries on other people as a rule, but I cannot escape them myself. That's the penalty for working so hard at my job. I can't get to sleep at night for the nerves jumping. And then I wake up in the middle of the night, thinking of something I should have done or ought to do."

Louise said:

I saw that he was getting more and more nervous. I wanted very much for him, regardless of what it was, to just insist that he have six months or, if he had to, a year [off]—not just sometimes [when] he would have six months [off] but he would never know [when]. There might be three pictures come up, and he was always in the midst of something. If [we] could just leave and we could go someplace . . . I can remember we talked about [going] down in the West Indies, one of those places, and I felt that if he could just do that, just get away and really forget. [That if] he knew he wasn't going to do a picture for, you know, a year maybe . . . and he did try to think about [it].

Tracy had just a week off between the finish of *I Take This Woman* and the start of *Stanley and Livingstone,* and his subsequent five-week vacation was more hurried than relaxing. He was idle seven weeks before the start of *Northwest Passage,* but there was tremendous uncertainty surrounding that project and endless rewrites. Seven weeks into production, only half the projected film was complete, and he was looking at a comparable period of time to finish the other half. Then they were talking of putting him directly into another picture or attempting to salvage the decidedly worthless Hedy Lamarr vehicle for yet a third time. On August 10, 1939, as the exterior scenes at Crown Point were being filmed, Tracy wired Leo Morrison instructing him, as per Louise's suggestion, to arrange a six-month leave of absence or, barring that, to get him out of his M-G-M contract altogether.

He was in the studio tank matching river shots—the famed "human chain" sequence—when Frank Whitbeck advised him that word of his telegram had reached Eddie Mannix. He spent the next morning—August 24—in the tank again, then went home in the afternoon with a bad head cold. In a state of terrible fatigue he wrote Mannix directly:

Frank told me that you seemed upset because of my wire to Leo Morrison which, I understand, reached you secondhanded. I was just as much upset at feeling I had to wire Morrison, but you must realize that the stress of the moment and general conditions, coming together as they did, and the fact that I seemed out of touch with anyone at the studio may have had something to do with it. Anyway, I am sorry it happened because, whatever the problem, I certainly have no desire to hurt you.

The problem seems to be the culmination of many things, and it seems to me that the only thing to do is to get away for an indefinite period upon the completion of this picture. If I were ill physically, that would be the only thing I could do, and, as I certainly am mentally, it seems the only alternative which holds some hope. That may not solve it, but the fact remains that the problem is there and, at the moment, I am at a total loss as to just how to work it out.

At the outset, please believe that in no sense is there any quarrel with the studio or with anything they have done in my regard. I hope I appreciate that without Metro and the help I received here Heaven only knows where I would be now. Whatever arises out of this, I sincerely hope it will never be considered anything but a situation which must be worked out with complete good feeling between the studio and myself.

I am fully cognizant and appreciate to the utmost that the pictures I am given are the best pictures that the studio has to offer, and the parts, the best that any actor could hope for. It is just that I hope to prolong my value to the studio; to protect my health, both mental and physical, and to preserve whatever it is that I have as long as I can for my family.

I once promised Mr. Mayer and you, too, I think, that if the time ever came when I felt I should stop, I would tell you. It seemed to me that the time has come. Louise has gone through trying periods with me, and is going through probably the most trying now, and feels as I do.

I feel that perhaps, in the future, if an arrangement could be made whereby I could do a picture, then have a definite vacation period, the mental stress I subject myself to, or inflict upon myself, during the making of a picture would be lessened with the knowledge that, when I finished, I might relax. <u>I say might</u>.

I realize your great problems in regard to production, and I want to be fair. That is why I want you to know immediately how I feel, and I also would like to have the matter settled as I probably have eight more weeks of hard work on this picture, and I would like to do it with as much peace of mind as possible.

You may not be in sympathy with some of the foregoing, and you may even think it self-indulgence—I hope that it is not. Some of us have strange problems—all of us different ones—and no one rule can be set to govern any, or all, of us. At any rate, what I have said here has been written after many sleepless nights of thought, and it is honest. After all, I have little to gain by all this except, I hope, some peace of mind.

Tracy was still in bed on the twenty-eighth, running a fever of 102 degrees, when Mannix and the M-G-M legal department started grappling with the question of how to respond. An oral statement of the company's attitude was recommended unless there was a definite refusal on Tracy's part to render services at the start of his next picture. Nobody wanted to antagonize him while *Northwest Passage* was still in production, and so the studio interiors and the film's early scenes in the village of Portsmouth were made in an atmosphere of affable silence. "He was very intuitive," Robert Young said of Tracy, "and whatever he did, he just always came out right. [Vidor] never talked to him. I mean, what's the point in talking to him? Tracy, sort of, almost unconsciously, knew more about how that scene should be played than the director did."

Vidor finished the first half of the picture on September 15, 1939, and the cast was retained on salary while Stromberg and Talbot Jennings polished the second half of the script. The standoff that Mannix had feared would come with the completion of *Northwest Passage* never took place. Tracy's constant fretting over expenses—John's care and education, Louise and Susie, Carroll, their mother, his aunt Mame's medical bills, his aunt Jenny and her daughter—would only intensify were his income suddenly to cease. ("He worked so hard and had such a big tow line," as his cousin Jane put it.) He'd never be able to relax, and if he did take six months off, he could never be sure they'd still want him when he came back. "I couldn't do that," he finally said to Louise. "I couldn't stay away like that and wonder. I couldn't. I just couldn't do it."

One of the steadying mechanisms in Tracy's life was a weekly dinner with a few pals to talk shop and swap stories. It started with actor Frank

McHugh's wife, whose stepfather was a minister in West Hartford, Connecticut. They were trying to raise money for a Sunday school program, and someone got the idea of sending a blank autograph book out to Frank, who was at Warner Bros. with Pat O'Brien and Jimmy Cagney. "Now Frank NEVER asked anybody for autographs," said Mrs. McHugh, the actress Dorothy Spencer, "but he said, 'Well, for Katherine [Dorothy's mother] I'll do it.' " Four loose pages from the book were dispatched, with the request that Frank sign one and have the other three signed by O'Brien, Cagney, and Spencer Tracy.

"Spence was at M-G-M," Frank McHugh recalled, "and I did not know his home address or phone. So I sent a letter and the blank page to him [at the studio] and asked him to sign. He did, and enclosed a letter in the return [envelope] to the effect that he thought it was rather sad that old friends, living in the same town, had to communicate by mail, and suggested that the four of us get together for dinner. In the meantime, Jim and Spence had dinner together and talked it over and decided that the four of us should get together regularly and talk and dine. That is: Spence, Jim, Pat, and myself. Which we did."

The meetings began in February 1939. O'Brien drank scotch, but McHugh was on the wagon and Cagney didn't drink at all, save for an occasional glass of wine. They'd go out for dinner and end up at the Trocadero for ice cream and cookies. Actor Lynne Overman was the first added member, McHugh having known him since 1926. Dry and insinuative, Overman was, in McHugh's words, "one of the wisest, wittiest, and gentlest companions" he'd ever known. "He had a keen sense of good taste for [the] excellent but simple things of life. Food and drink seemed to be his hobby. You could also add ladies." Frank Morgan and Ralph Bellamy later completed the core group, and it became a Wednesday night tradition, the various members dropping in and out as their work schedules permitted. Their wives, who never joined in, called it "the Boys' Club."

According to Cagney, it was columnist Sidney Skolsky who hung the name "Irish Mafia" on the group, although Morgan was German, Bellamy was English, and Allen Jenkins, who joined in occasionally, was of early American stock. "There was no thought of it having anything to do with our Irishness," Cagney said. "But Skolsky, of course, had to make a big thing of it and call it the Irish Mafia. Such nonsense. We happened to be people who liked each other and that is all."

Stromberg continued to wrestle with *Northwest Passage* into November 1939. Originally the plan had been to film the entire book and release it with an intermission, as David Selznick intended to do with *Gone With the*

The core of the group that came to be known—erroneously—as the Irish Mafia. Left to right: James Cagney, Frank McHugh, Pat O'Brien, and Tracy. (PATRICIA MAHON COLLECTION)

Wind. When King Vidor wrapped the first half, however, it was over two hours in length and had cost more than $2.5 million—extraordinary for its time. And, unlike *GWTW,* the picture had, for all practical purposes, an all-male cast and virtually none of what was politely referred to at the time as "feminine interest." At a negative cost of $4 million, *Northwest Passage* would surpass *Ben-Hur* as the most expensive picture in M-G-M's fifteen-year history. In November it was prudently decided to finish the picture with a new ending and release it as *Northwest Passage* (*Book I—Rogers' Rangers*) with the intention of filming Book II as a separate feature once Book I had proven itself commercially.

"I did the entire picture in three months of work," Vidor recounted,

and at the end of that time I still had not received the second part of the script. I called the studio and they said, "Come back." So I loaded up the trains with all of our stuff and we came back. When I saw the producer he said, "Keep the actors on salary. We'll have it in another week." They were sitting right where I had left them three months before. They were probably still working on the same line of dialogue. After another week no progress had been made, so the head of the studio said, "Take these people off salary." I went to New York and started to work on something else. After I got to

New York they called me up. Jack Conway had written a different ending to the story. We didn't have jet travel then, so I said, "Okay, let Conway shoot the tag," and left it at that.

Tracy was happy to be done with the picture and hoped the issue of Book II would never come up again. "When a truly historical character is the hero of a bestselling novel, then you are really up against it," he said wearily. "Everyone who reads the novel has his own picture of the physical and mental characteristics of a man like Rogers. The actor can read everything available on the character, pick out his more human or understandable traits, and go from there, discarding the unessentials. But he is likely to disappoint a lot of people . . . I have tried to get Rogers' mental attitude, his psychology. I don't know whether I have succeeded; I can only hope."

While he was on location with *Northwest Passage,* enthusiasm at Fox was building for *Stanley and Livingstone.* On July 11 associate producer Kenneth Macgowan wired him at McCall:

THE PREVIEW WAS REALLY EXTRAORDINARY. WHEN WE GOT TO THE THEATER IN INGLEWOOD WE WERE DISMAYED TO FIND THAT ABOUT THREE-FOURTHS OF THE AUDIENCE RANGED FROM BABES IN ARMS AND FIVE YEAR OLDS TO HIGH SCHOOL BOYS AND GIRLS. THE AVERAGE AGE COULDN'T HAVE BEEN OVER FIFTEEN. TO OUR SURPRISE AND DELIGHT THEY WENT FOR THE PICTURE HOOK LINE AND SINKER. EVERY REACTION WAS SPLENDID.

By the time the press preview took place at the end of the month, Zanuck was talking up the idea of a sequel covering Stanley's later life and career in politics, a notion predicated on the availability of Tracy, an increasingly unlikely proposition. Zanuck never got the flippant tone he sought to achieve for Stanley, and the *Reporter* thought the picture "almost severely scholarly in its approach." It was, nevertheless, a big and appealing film, idealistic in its posture and grand in its scope, the African footage giving it the texture, in parts, of a documentary. That it lacked dramatic punch was more a failing of the screenplay than of the cast or the director, but it also lacked the kind of hokum that often distinguished a Hollywood biography, at least up to the end, where Stanley (hardly the salvationist the movie suggests) returns to Africa to the strains of "Onward Christian Soldiers."

Contrary to Tracy's early assessment, *Variety* predicted "socko biz" for *Stanley and Livingstone* and turned out to be right. Strong billboard and snipe support from the studio—and some unseasonably rainy weather—helped fill the New York Roxy, where Tracy's name meant considerably more than it had in the old days. The picture sustained a three-week stand, then went out as the first big Fox release of the new season. With *I Take This Woman* on the shelf and *Northwest Passage* still in production, it stood to be Tracy's only release for the year 1939. "Wrong <u>again</u>!" he wrote in amending his earlier prognostication. "<u>Big hit</u>."

Until *Stanley and Livingstone,* Tracy had been off screen for nearly a year—since *Boys Town*—an almost intolerable length of time for a major star. Yet his absence hadn't affected his standing with either exhibitors or the public. "Comes the revolution!" wrote Edwin Schallert in anticipation of the year-end exhibitor polls.

This year, if any, there will be the biggest shake-up ever in the stars that rule the motion picture box office. Four years the top-notcher in most polls, Shirley Temple, will probably register in about third place. Clark Gable, runner-up to the child star, may hit shakily around fifth or sixth. The winners will list about as follows: Spencer Tracy, Bette Davis, Shirley Temple, Sonja Henie, Clark Gable, Tyrone Power, Deanna Durbin, Mickey Rooney, Errol Flynn, and Charles Boyer and Irene Dunne as a team. The order may not be exactly correct, but those are the ones likely to be supreme and all the charges and counter-charges against this writer may be duly filed around the end of the year when listings are more or less officially proclaimed.

Schallert's predictions were largely accurate. Tracy placed third behind Rooney and Power in the Quigley poll of moneymaking stars, but firmly ahead of Gable, who came in fourth. Shirley Temple's standing had fallen due to advancing age—she was eleven—and Gable's one release of the season had been the atypical *Idiot's Delight.* (He was otherwise offscreen making *Gone With the Wind* for Selznick.) In October, *Fortune* published the results of a survey by Elmo Roper that asked two questions of the moviegoing public: Who is your favorite movie actor? and Who is your favorite movie actress? To the second question, 4.6 percent of all respondents answered Bette Davis, followed by Myrna Loy, Jeanette MacDonald, Irene Dunne, and Norma Shearer in descending order. (Temple, who ranked first in 1937, placed sixth.) To the first question, Clark Gable, Tyrone Power, Wallace Beery, and Lionel Barrymore placed second through fifth, respec-

Tracy photographed at his Encino
ranch, January 2, 1941.
(AUTHOR'S COLLECTION)

tively. In first place, named by 5.6 percent of all respondents, was Spencer Tracy.

Buoyed, perhaps, by the milestone, Tracy began looking at boats again, casually at first, and then with a certain urgency, given that he could, at last, permit himself a modicum of luxury. Off days were spent at the ranch playing tennis with Louise, lunching on the patio and sometimes meeting friends for tea. He saw Cagney, O'Brien, and the others on Wednesday nights, and celebrated nineteen months of sobriety on the first day of

December. He had a wonderful Christmas that year, playing polo at Riviera on the twenty-fourth and visiting the newly married Gables, who had settled in Encino, later that same evening. On Christmas Day he went to Mass as usual, then spent the balance of the day loafing at home. Dinner was with the children, Louise, his mother, Carroll and Dorothy. "Beautiful weather," he wrote in his book. "Much to be thankful for."

CHAPTER 16

Someone's Idea of Reality

The triumph of *Boys Town* enabled John Considine to get approval for a project he had long wanted to do, a biography of Thomas Edison split into two movies—one his boyhood, the other his years at Menlo Park. To play the Great Man, Considine had at his disposal the nation's top male stars—Mickey Rooney and Spencer Tracy. He assigned Dore Schary, who had shared an Academy Award with Eleanore Griffin for his work on *Boys Town,* to develop both pictures in collaboration with Hugo Butler.

As subsequently rewritten by Talbot Jennings and Bradbury Foote, the screenplay for *Edison, the Man,* bore no greater resemblance to Edison's life than *Boys Town* had to Father Flanagan's, but it afforded Tracy the kind of inspirational role he was now actively seeking, and he embraced it with rare ebullience. On October 24, 1939, he and Howard Strickling boarded a train for Chicago at the invitation of Henry Ford, who had been Edison's neighbor at Fort Myers and who had reconstructed Edison's original laboratory complex on the grounds of his Ford Museum in Dearborn, Michigan. From there the men traveled to New York and West Orange, where they spent the day with Edison's widow and his son Charles, now assistant secretary of the navy.

Tracy was particularly cheered by nine reels of film provided by General Electric, pictures made in the twenties of Edison reenacting experiments, relaxing at his estate in Florida, being interviewed before a radio microphone by E. W. Rice, Jr., the late president of General Electric. Hearing Edison's voice as an old man was of less use to Tracy than seeing his walk, his smile, his expressions when conversing with others. Tracy was taller by a couple of inches, but in overall appearance remarkably similar to the man shown in photographs from the 1870s. "We will make these changes," Jack Dawn, the head of the M-G-M makeup department, decided. "Tracy's hair will be parted on the right instead of the left and will be combed downward across the head instead of upward. We will make his eyebrows a little more bushy and his forehead slightly larger. There's practically nothing to it."

Dawn's conception of Edison at age eighty-two was similarly spare; the first test was shot on November 20, and Tracy, when he saw the results, thought them "pretty good." After the nerves and privations of the previous year, he was embarking on a job he genuinely found enjoyable, and his mood around the studio as well as at home was uncharacteristically buoyant and relaxed. With Louise resting in Santa Barbara, he had the kids to himself. He swam, lunched on the patio, played tennis with John, and dined with his mother.

It couldn't last.

On Friday, November 24, he made the forty-minute drive to the studio for lunch, a habit he picked up when he wasn't working to keep abreast of developments. "If I were to believe everything I read about myself and the roles I'm supposed to be lined up for," he said, "I'd go crazy. Not only does M-G-M buy about twelve stories a year for me—if you're to believe what you read—but all the other studios have options on my services too. This may sound flattering, but to me it's just confusing."

He learned that day that *Edison* had been postponed in favor of yet another version of *I Take This Woman,* and his mood blackened accordingly. Bernie Hyman, the original producer, had thrown out the first sixty pages of Charlie MacArthur's original story and turned it, in the words of MacArthur's longtime collaborator, Ben Hecht, "from a civilized comedy into a Darkest-Metro soap opera." Tracy was glad when the picture was shelved. "It was so bad," he told Gable, "we had to make retakes before we could even put it on the shelf. And when we put it on the shelf, we had to promise the other pictures there that it was only for one night."

He officially got the word the following Monday, and spent the entire day in conference with the new producer, Larry Weingarten. No one was deluded as to the artistic merits of the film, but Metro had close to $1 million tied up in it thus far, and the goal was to get the thing into releasable shape. There was also Mayer's championing of the project, Lamarr being for him the equivalent of Goldwyn's Anna Sten, a personal obsession whose appeal was always somewhat lost on the public. Lamarr's first M-G-M

On the set of *I Take This Woman* with Louise and Susie.
(AUTHOR'S COLLECTION)

release, *Lady of the Tropics,* had flopped at the box office. "They didn't want me to make *I Take This Woman,*" the Old Man told the actress defiantly. "Well, *now* we will make it."

Whole sequences would be salvaged from the earlier version, while enough new material would be shot to substantially reshape the story. Tracy returned to the studio on December 1 to fight with Eddie Mannix over the requirement that he make the new scenes, but it was a losing battle considering there was no possible way to remove him from the picture without completely reshooting it from scratch. The only consolation was that the new material would be directed by Woody Van Dyke, who was sure to finish the thing as quickly and cheaply as possible. ("There's nothing wrong with it that $200,000 or $300,000 can't fix," Van Dyke had reportedly said.) Tracy returned to Encino, where a nervous stomach plagued him all weekend. Filming resumed on Monday, December 4. "Worse than ever," he wrote in his book.

Van Dyke was in rare form. "[Y]ou did one rehearsal, you shot it, and you printed it," said Laraine Day, who had been with the picture all along. "That was it. There was no fooling around with anything. You just knew your lines. You could blow your lines, you could change them all over, and he wouldn't change printing it. As long as you hit your marks, Woody Van Dyke would say 'Print it' and he would finish the picture in 23 days."

Weingarten, who had already done a picture with "One-Take Woody," knew his routine all too well. "Now Mr. Van Dyke was an alcoholic," he once explained to a roomful of film students, "but he was right there all the time. But you could set your watch the moment he left the studio. At five o'clock he was out the door and went for the alcohol. And we used to run out of sets. We'd have five for the day, and the art department would call screaming, 'He's going to be through!' What are they going to shoot next? And if another set wasn't ready, out he went."

As Tracy announced to Sheilah Graham when she walked on the set one day, "This is where I came in—a year ago!"

He saw a rough cut of *Northwest Passage* on September 22 and, despite all the misgivings, thought it a "great adventure." Stromberg still had a lot of tinkering to do, and Tracy would spend a total of thirty-two days on retakes. The prospect of a second film grew remote when Germany's invasion of Poland closed off much of the European market. Even so, the studio had a backlog of other pictures in the queue for him—one after another— and as he looped the last strands of dialogue in early January 1940, he put Leo Morrison to work seeking a substantially greater amount of time off between pictures. As part of the ensuing negotiation process, he was obliged to endure a three-hour session with L. B. Mayer—an experience he would happily have dispensed with had there been a way to get around it.

Tracy's relationship with Mayer had always been cordial but distant, and he was anxious to keep it that way. He never allowed his judgment to be superseded by Mayer, and Eddie Mannix once told him that Mayer didn't like him because he knew that Tracy was "onto him." Any dealings he had with the studio, he once said, were through Mannix or Benny Thau, the soft-spoken Austrian who handled contractual matters, or very occasionally through Nicholas Schenck, Mayer's boss, who made the big decisions regarding the talent on the lot. Tracy's deal permitted him six consecutive weeks of vacation in the first, third, fifth, and seventh years of the agreement, and eight consecutive weeks in the second, fourth, and sixth. But it never quite worked out that way, and so far in the current year he had been permitted just four consecutive weeks.

The studio, for its part, was unwilling to sacrifice any measure of flexibility without building incentives into the deal that would serve to keep Tracy sober and available whenever he was supposed to be working. On January 9, 1940, Tracy met with Thau, who agreed to three consecutive months of vacation if he would do *Edison, the Man*, and *The Yearling* first. That plan lasted only long enough to get him on board for another picture with Clark Gable, and soon he found himself committed to three in a row: *Edison, Boom Town,* and *The Yearling*. On February 21 Thau and Mannix agreed to four weeks off between *Edison* and *Boom Town*, and as much as four weeks off between *Boom Town* and *The Yearling* (which would be another location shoot, tougher to accommodate). After *The Yearling*, Tracy was to have four consecutive months with pay. Through Leo Morrison, Thau offered a $25,000 bonus, returnable only were Tracy unable (or unwilling) to appear in *Boom Town*. Further, should he "take sick" after *Boom Town* and not do *The Yearling*, he would get only three months' vacation, not the four he would otherwise have.

Comfortable enough with the accommodation and girded for the work ahead, Tracy began *Edison, the Man* on January 15. With the concurrence of director Clarence Brown, he chose to play Edison as the beneficiary of divine guidance, a man doing God's work for the benefit of mankind. "He was a very prayerful guy, you know, in his own way," journalist Adela Rogers St. Johns pointed out. "I don't think it was a church way particularly, but he said to me—I'm remembering the wonderful little talks we had when we were both working at Metro—'You know, God showed Edison how to light up cities.' He got very excited about the people he was playing and the characters he did."

Edison's son asked that his father not be made to seem "too perfect" in the picture—cigars, he noted, had been substituted for chewing tobacco— and he suggested some leavening traits for the character, a certain tactlessness and, at times, downright rudeness that Tracy was able to incorporate into his performance. Everyone, from Henry Ford on down, commented on Tracy's striking resemblance to the old man. For his part, Tracy found the picture a joy to make, and he was uncommonly accessible when journalists visited the set. One day, Gladys Hall pulled a "quickie" questionnaire on him, testing his patience:

> *What was the first job at which you earned money? And what did you buy with it?*
> "Selling newspapers in Milwaukee. A ham sandwich."

> *What was the outstanding incident of your childhood?*
> "When I tipped the ice box over on my brother."

> *When do you want to retire from the screen? And what would you do then? That is, do you have any special plans for the future?*

"Tonight. That answers the first half of your question. I have no
   special plans for the future. I only want to sleep and eat, eat and
   sleep. That answers the second half."

Have you any special fears?
"Yes. I'm afraid of Garbo. Put that down."

*Have you ever been so discouraged that you contemplated abandoning
your career? If so, when?*
"Yes. About fifteen minutes ago. Just after the last scene."

What do you consider the most useless sport or pastime?
"Staying awake."

What is your favorite book?
"Steinbeck's *Red Pony.*"

Your favorite flower?
"A rose . . . aw, I don't know. Put down anything. What the hell's
   the difference?"

Sheilah Graham came upon him one day as he was handing a one-
hundred-dollar check to Woody Van Dyke. "It's a bet I had," he explained.
"I bet Woody that *I Take This Woman* would never be released." Quickly
changing the subject, he mentioned *The Yearling* and Billy Grady's nationwide search for a boy to play Jody. "Whoever he is," said Tracy, "he's a star
already. The part is so surefire that the boy should be put under contract for
five years right away—without waiting for the picture to be completed.
Three or four years ago, Mickey Rooney would have been fine for the part,
but I can't see him cuddling a fawn now . . . not unless Fawn was the name
of a girl."

The studio pulled a sneak preview of *Northwest Passage* in New Rochelle
(five hundred cards, Tracy noted) but was unable to get the picture into theaters until February 1940, as the demand for prints of *Gone With the Wind*
was taxing the capacity of Technicolor's processing plant. After seeing it,
author Kenneth Roberts discharged his agent, but the preview notice in
Daily Variety was wildly favorable, describing it as "the kind of stuff male
audiences look for but seldom find. Very little romance. A few flashes only
of a few women. No lovemaking. No dalliance. No man-woman emotional
problems. Tough, hard stuff in the morning of America, during the French-

Indian War, when frontiersmen now known as patriots had to be about their bloody chores in settling the right of sovereignty over a continent."

When Metro finally did release the picture ("as one would release a wounded duck," Roberts suggested) it was warmly welcomed by both the public and the critics, some of whom considered it worthy of a place alongside Selznick's masterpiece as one of the signal achievements of the talking screen. The world premiere in Boise predated its New York opening by several weeks, and anticipation began to build as a national ad campaign revved an otherwise lethargic market. *Northwest Passage* opened big at the Capitol Theatre, where it remained through Holy Week, eventually posting worldwide rentals in excess of $3 million. Coming hard on the humiliation of *I Take This Woman*—which was a critical as well as commercial disaster—it was good news for Tracy, who hadn't had a hit for his home studio in eighteen months.

With *Edison* in the can, he drove to Palm Springs for a long weekend at La Quinta and was introduced by Tim Whelan to Greta Garbo. "It would be a pleasure, Mr. Tracy, to play in one of your pictures sometime," Garbo said to him. "And I would be delighted to play even a butler in one of your films, Miss Garbo," he responded. Garbo had been contemplating a biography of Marie Curie, the Polish scientist and discoverer of radium, for a couple of years, and Tracy's participation would ease the concerns of Eve Curie, youngest daughter of the title character, who feared the casting of Garbo as her mother would overshadow the equally important work of her father, Pierre. But with *Boom Town* looming, it would take the unlikely postponement of *The Yearling* to make it happen.

Tracy spent his fortieth birthday golfing with Eddie Mannix and producer-director Victor Saville, newly arrived from England. Three days later he started *Boom Town,* a big, brawling tale of Texas wildcatters originally purchased for Gable, Tracy, and Myrna Loy in the heady days following the release of *Test Pilot.* Tracy had no objection to doing the picture, and despite the tensions between them on *Test Pilot,* he and Gable maintained a genuine affection for one another. "They spent half their time, each one trying to understand the other," Adela Rogers St. Johns said. "Gable looked at Tracy as the greatest actor in the world. He would stand at the edge of the set and watch him in utter admiration of the acting ability . . . Tracy adored Gable, as everybody did. He would say, 'Can't act, doesn't care, and everybody loves him better than any actor that was ever born.' "

When Gable attended the Atlanta premiere of *Gone With the Wind,* Tracy shot off a congratulatory wire:

"GONE WITH THE WIND" MAY BE THIS YEAR'S GREATEST
PICTURE BUT I STILL REMEMBER "PARNELL."

The principal screenwriter on *Boom Town* was John Lee Mahin, who had as his source a novelette from *Cosmopolitan* magazine called "A Lady Comes to Burkburnett." With Myrna Loy unavailable for the part of the lady, producer Sam Zimbalist took the extraordinary step of borrowing Claudette Colbert from Paramount, thus reuniting the two Academy Award–winning stars of *It Happened One Night*. Hedy Lamarr campaigned for the fourth role, a seductress who didn't appear until the top of the third act, and the picture suddenly took on a size that made it one of the most anticipated of the season. Early on, the Metro sales team decided to showcase *Boom Town* as a solo attraction at premium prices, the rationale being its stellar cast made it "like four pictures in one."

For Tracy, it wasn't a particularly difficult shoot. Many of the exteriors were done in process, and the only real location work was a two-day stretch at the Taft oilfields near Bakersfield. Wardrobe, contractually the responsibility of the actor on a modern-dress picture, became a matter of swapping out clothes with genuine laborers. "Larry Keethe, our wardrobe man, thought I was crazy when we bought a bunch of new work clothes and went down to a building project around here, looking for a couple of workmen about my size. We traded the new outfits for those a couple of guys were wearing. They thought I was crazy, too. But you can't look like a worker in the oil fields, walking into a picture in brand-new dungarees. They must be baggy and faded from sweat and dirt and many washings."

Tracy amused himself bantering with Gable, who usually gave as good as he got. When the King stalked onto the set during an early rehearsal, he delivered his first line but went up on the second. "Can you imagine that?" Tracy moaned with an exaggerated sigh. "The guy's memory is down to *one* line now!"

Later, Gable took a shot at Tracy while chatting with Harry Evans of *Family Circle* magazine. "Say," he said, pretending not to notice his costar was within earshot, "did you hear that Tracy is going to do *Ninotchka* on the air with Rosalind Russell?" Evans, playing along, said that he had heard such a rumor but doubted his ears.

"Well," said Gable, hoisting his left eyebrow quizzically, "that should be a new experience for radio listeners. That Russell is smart, you know. Let him try to underplay her, and you know what will happen? He'll drop his voice a little, and she'll drop hers. He'll take his next speech a little softer, she'll whisper a little lower. He'll mutter his next line, and she'll murmur. The listeners will be twisting the knobs off their dials trying to hear what's going on. And suddenly they'll hear nothing, not a sound." He paused a moment to observe Tracy. "And that," he concluded, "will be the first time on record that two radio performers will have voluntarily gone off the air!"

Claudette Colbert thought the back-and-forth between Gable and

Tracy "better than a circus" but acknowledged that Tracy's technique—
what Louise called "that natural thing"—took some getting used to. "Here's
how it goes," she said of her heaviest scene opposite him.

> I've tried to commit suicide, and I'm half hysterical and trying to
> explain my action to Spencer. After weeping and carrying on and
> just about knocking myself out, with him just standing there, I
> declare that he can never understand. "You could never know what
> it means to love anyone so much!" I scream. And after I stop on this
> high melodramatic note, he nods that big head of his a few times,
> sticks his chin out, looks up and away, and murmurs, "Yeah, yeah.
> I wouldn't know about that." And steals the whole scene! Not a per-
> son in the audience will remember what *I* said. The way that man
> underplays everybody keeps the audience listening for *him* to
> speak.

Production was moving along beautifully when, on April 25, Gable was
injured in the staging of a fight. Toward the end of the picture, Square John
tries to knock some sense into Big John, who has gone off with the exotic
Karen Vanmeer. ("In between the rough stuff," said Tracy, "I had to sit
around while the King played love scenes with Hedy Lamarr.") Tracy later
described the mishap to his friend Stewart Granger:

> One evening we tried to finish off a fight sequence, but there was
> one shot left over for the following morning, Gable taking a punch
> on the chin from me, off camera. I told them that I'd be god-
> damned if I was going to get up at the crack of dawn just to stand
> off camera and have my fist pass in front of Gable's chin and told
> them to get someone else. They got a fighter, a real boxer. They
> stood him next to the camera and told him to throw a punch as
> Gable approached, but to "pull" it an inch away from Gable's chin.
> Did he understand? Sure. Did he need a rehearsal? Hell, no. Okay.
> Camera, action, and the boxer let one go, forgot to pull it, and
> knocked Gable down. There was a stunned silence as Gable lay on
> the floor spitting out teeth. The boxer looked in horror at the
> movies' most valuable human being whom he'd just disfigured. He
> took off out of the studio, out of L.A., and some think out of the
> country. He was never seen again. Gable accused me of fixing the
> whole thing. I just told him he needed a new set of teeth anyway.

Gable famously wore dentures; he would occasionally pull them out to
shock people, particularly women who seemed just a tad too admiring. The

blow damaged his upper plate and split his lip, which required four stitches. Tracy had nine days off, time he passed swimming, playing tennis, and doing a retake in old-age makeup for *Edison, the Man*. On May 1 he marked two full years on the wagon, and the following day tipped the scales at 192 1/2 pounds—his heaviest ever.

He thought *Edison* a "good little picture—not great" but didn't think it stood much of a chance commercially. So when plans were finalized for the world premiere in Orange, New Jersey, he made the unusual decision to go east to support it. The schedule on *Boom Town* was arranged to create a seven-day window in which he wouldn't be needed, and on May 12 he and Louise left on the Super Chief in the company of Howard Strickling and his wife.

The *Edison* premiere, the centerpiece of a three-day celebration, was spread over six theaters and was practically a replay of the *Boys Town* event in Omaha. A crowd of twenty thousand movie-mad fans flooded the Oranges, forcing Tracy to creep into the gala ball at the local armory through a back door. The crowd on the outside began to chant "We want Tracy! We want Tracy!" And with the mob pounding on the walls and hanging from the windows, Tracy became aware that he had lost his collar button—either to a fan or to the commotion itself—and was having a tough time holding his neckpiece together. Most of the four thousand dancers on the floor of the ballroom joined in a hunt for the button before photos could be taken with the Edisons, Governor A. Harry Moore, and other distinguished guests. When the crowd outside refused to disperse, it was arranged for Tracy and his leading lady, actress Rita Johnson, to wave to the throng through an upper window, an appearance that triggered fifteen minutes of wild cheering.

There was scarcely time to see anything in New York, but Spence and Louise caught a performance of *There Shall Be No Light*—with Lunt and Fontanne—on their last night in town. Back in California, Tracy settled into the final days of production on *Boom Town* while giving interviews in support of *Edison*. Significantly, he talked to author-educator John Erskine, who challenged him on notions of art and artifice and "whether the ideas of experience furnished by our pictures are complete and true; whether the ideals are high enough or important enough for adults." Impressed by the amount of process work being employed on *Boom Town*, Erskine asked whether it was good to accept "the doctrine that accuracy of information was the same as truth to life." In other words, was realism achieved in any meaningful sense by photographing actual places for backgrounds?

"Of course not," said Tracy. "That sort of thing gives us authentic information about a place, but realism, as I understand it, must be contributed by the actor, not by the camera." Asked if he thought the drive for such "historical accuracy" was the result of showing audiences too many news-reels and travelogues, he said, "Of course. It's a good thing too—in its place. We all like to see places as they really are or were. But a play is something else." He thought a moment. "I'd go even farther. The portrayal of a charac-ter is not only separate from the background, or scenery. It may also be, to a certain extent, separate from the most notable accomplishments of the character. In portraying Edison, for example, it wasn't enough to tell the audience what they already knew: that Edison invented his light bulb. Even when he wasn't accomplishing anything, in the intervals between achieve-ments, he must have been recognizable as a great man. I kept asking myself, 'What was he like when he wasn't inventing?' "

"That's all very well for great men," Erskine said, "but what about the lesser folk?"

"The same for them," Tracy replied. "In *Grapes of Wrath*, for example, the characters are terms in a social and economic problem, but they are also human beings, and they would be individuals even if the problem didn't exist."

"But how can a character be portrayed as 'great' aside from what he does?"

"Well, sometimes a man is great because of what he refuses to do, and sometimes the character of a famous man is revealed in small things which his fame overshadows. In the Edison film, for instance, the inventor's courage and persistence count for more than his success. To build up the real Edison, we tried to suggest those little ways of friendship, those instincts of loyalty and justice, which made the men in his laboratory devoted to him, and I had to indicate his qualities in his manner, in so far as I could, even when I was saying or doing nothing in particular."

"Even so," said Erskine, "how true to history were you? Did you give the real Edison?"

"My *idea* of Edison."

"Then the portrait isn't realistic?"

"Realism," said Tracy, "is always someone's idea of reality. It gets the name of 'real' when the audience agrees it is true. If I can't convince the audience, then the portrait won't seem real, no matter how true it is."

The day he finished *Boom Town*, Tracy left by rail for Chicago and his first visit in eighteen years to the campus of Ripon College. Professor H. P. Boody had sought his return as early as 1927, and regularly thereafter. In 1936 there was talk of awarding Tracy an honorary degree, and in 1939 a movement to bring the premiere of *Northwest Passage* to Ripon drew the support of Wisconsin governor Julius Heil. On November 6, longtime

Ripon president Silas Evans wrote Tracy at M-G-M, advising him the trustees wished to confer upon him "a form of doctor's degree" appropriate to his achievements and trusting that he would "consider it an honor" to receive such a degree. Responding by wire, Tracy assured Dr. Evans that he would indeed appreciate the honor and could come after completion of the Edison picture "in about eight weeks" or, if he preferred, during commencement. "I shall arrange to be there if I have to fly and can stay only a day."

There followed a flurry of proposals and counterproposals, first regarding *Northwest Passage,* later *Edison, the Man,* and the possibility that Tracy could stop at Ripon on his way home from New Jersey. *Boom Town,* now ten days behind schedule, intervened, and so the plan was shifted to commencement on June 10, 1940, with *Edison* having its Wisconsin premiere at the five-hundred-seat Campus Theatre. As Frank Whitbeck went on ahead to supervise arrangements, Tracy, accompanied by Carroll, boarded a train east for Chicago.

In Milwaukee they stopped at the University Club, where they caught up with Gene Sullivan, a prominent attorney and Carroll's brother-in-law. Nibbling Milwaukee rye bread, Tracy met the press, nervously running his hands through his graying hair and talking excitedly of Louise's racehorse, Holsworthy. ("Twelve starts and win or place every time!") He revealed to the group that he had given up polo and was amused to know that Gus Christy was still at the Athletic Club. "What'll you have to drink, boys? Come on, don't be bashful!" Then, glancing out a window toward Lake Michigan, "Some fog, eh? I didn't recall Milwaukee was so damn foggy, but I'm glad to be back."

Somebody asked whether he might return to Broadway. Reflectively, he said, "I don't think so . . . Every time I see my friend [George Jean] Nathan, he tries to lure me back to the stage, saying he'll find a great play for me. But I guess not. I've never lost interest in the stage though. I get to New York to see the plays . . . The stage is still the best place for training an actor, don't forget that. Any youngster who wants a Hollywood career should go there by way of New York or some other stage—playing in stock, what there is left of it. Don't go to Hollywood to begin. What chance is there out there? They've got no facilities for training actors."

He and Whitbeck made the two-hour drive to Ripon the next morning, and at noon he became the honored guest of the school's seventy-fourth graduating class. Having donned cap and gown, Tracy was escorted to Ingram Hall, where he posed for pictures with Silas Evans, Professor Boody, J. Clark Graham, and a number of former classmates, including J. Harold Bumby, Tracy's former teammate and the man who witnessed his audition before Franklin Sargent in 1922. After a commencement address

from Dr. Gordon Laing, dean emeritus of the University of Chicago, everyone moved outside to accommodate a crowd estimated at 2,500 for the
actual ceremony. Professor Boody spoke first: "Today marks for me the
close of 25 years of teaching at Ripon College, and I consider it a most
happy coincidence that on this anniversary I am permitted to present one
of my former students for an honorary degree—one whose friendship and
loyalty have been more precious to me than rubies, and whose rise to
the top of his profession I have watched with ever-increasing pride and
admiration."

Boody presented Dean Graham, under whose guidance Tracy's first
public performances were given. "Spencer Tracy, the world knows you as
many people, for in your time you have played many parts. But Ripon College knows you in another role—that of the eager youth who spoke his lines
impromptu to the cues of life. That youth we remember with affection,
both for himself and the great promise that he displayed even then . . . The
task of the actor, as Shakespeare remarked, is, and ever has been, to hold the
mirror up to nature to interpret the deepest passions of the human soul,
and thereby cleanse it through pity and terror in the classic Aristotelian
sense. To that distinguished company you indubitably belong." Silas Evans
spoke of Tracy's sincerity and intelligence, his mastery of his art. "Your acting has not only been highly entertaining," he said, "it has been thoroughly
educational, and on behalf of the board of trustees of the college, it gives me
great pleasure to present the degree of Doctor of Dramatic Art, with all the
privileges and duties appertaining thereto."

Tracy moved to the microphone. "There are some things I intended to
say," he said in a voice choked with emotion. "I wanted to thank Dean Graham and Professor Boody in particular for the great confidence they displayed in me and for their help. And if through my work I have done some
small justice to their confidence, I am happy indeed. There are some other
things I wanted to say about Ripon, but it seems that when you get to them
you don't say them. Perhaps it's better this way . . . I had intended saying
something to the graduating class. Please bear with me, because when you
come back, you'll feel this too. I'd like you to accept from me a 'God bless
you all and give you strength to carry on.' "

The ovation that greeted his remarks continued as the procession
slowly made its way to the president's home for a luncheon that included
Mayor Carl Zeidler of Milwaukee. He was then whisked back to West Hall,
his old campus home, where he was presented with a small golden gavel in
commemoration of his time as leader of Alpha Phi Omega. Following a
reception at the home of Professor Boody, he was driven out to the Green
Lake home of Harold Bumby, now a successful industrialist whose various
enterprises included a major interest in Speed Queen. A sitdown dinner for

Accepting an honorary doctorate at Ripon College, June 10, 1940. Left to right: Silas Evans, college president, Tracy, Professors H. Phillips Boody and J. Clark Graham. (PATRICIA MAHON COLLECTION)

fifty was staged at the Bumby household, where the guests included Lorraine Foat Holmes, who hadn't seen him in several years. He looked heavier, she observed, and grayer, but was still very much the Spence she always knew.

Tracy said, "This day will live with me as the greatest so far in this part of my life." Walter Monfried, long the *Milwaukee Journal* theater and music critic, would also remember it, but for a somewhat different reason. At the end of commencement exercises, Monfried made his way to a telephone and called the *Journal.* "I have the Tracy story," he said. "Do you want to take it now?"

"Hell, no!" his city editor replied. "Italy has just gone to war against France and England—Tracy can wait 'til tomorrow!"

With its top-heavy assortment of players, *Boom Town* opened in New York over the Labor Day weekend and handily played to more people than any single attraction since *Gone With the Wind.* Tracy made a quick visit east, ostensibly to support the picture but in reality to meet with Franklin

Delano Roosevelt, who received him in the Oval Office on September 16, 1940.

The president, who was in a close race for a third term against Wendell Willkie, thanked Tracy for his help in shoring up support within the film industry. Pat O'Brien had just been elected chairman of the "Hollywood for Roosevelt" committee, and although Tracy generally disapproved of actors giving off their political preferences, he agreed to lend his name to the cause, as had Myrna Loy, Thomas Mitchell, Alice Faye, Betty Grable, Douglas Fairbanks, Jr., Humphrey Bogart, and Jimmy Cagney. Robert Montgomery was O'Brien's counterpart on the Republican side, and his constituents included Walt Disney, Fred Astaire, Lionel Barrymore, Gary Cooper, Jack Warner, Bing Crosby, Irene Dunne, and Louis B. Mayer.

While in Washington, Tracy fielded the usual questions at an afternoon "press party" arranged by the studio. Asked again if he ever thought of going back to the stage, he replied, "Another picture like *I Take This Woman* and I might have to in order to eat." He said that any play that came along for him would likely have to wait a couple of years. His next picture, he told the group, would probably be *Tortilla Flat,* followed by *The Yearling.* What he didn't say—doubtless because he didn't want to answer the questions that would inevitably follow—was that he would be starting the *Boys Town* sequel in the space of a few weeks.

The studio was pressuring him to do *Dr. Ephraim McDowell,* the story of the pioneering American surgeon, and had already put novelist and biographer Gene Fowler to work on a script. Tracy didn't like the story and didn't much care to do another period picture, nor, for that matter, another biography. He had a tense meeting with Eddie Mannix on October 17, followed by a session on the twenty-first with Mannix, Benny Thau, and Neil McCarthy. It was the opening salvo in negotiations over a new contract, and Tracy went through the motions of doing costume and makeup tests while a sometimes heated discussion ensued.

At first, Father Flanagan was dubious about a second picture. Given the drop in contributions after the first picture appeared, he worried a second could sink the entire enterprise. Broadway's Gene Buck, a close friend and the president of ASCAP, advised him privately on the matter of a sequel: "I think you got a rotten deal, which I deplore and which I believe eventually will straighten itself out . . . Please do not, for any consideration at the moment, without first thinking it through, lend your name or your institution to any second edition." Eventually the studio pledged to build a dormitory with some of the earnings from the film, and a check for $35,000 was cut in June 1939.

The formal contract for a second Boys Town film was signed in February 1940 and called for a cash payment of $100,000. John Considine promised "completely a new story" that would follow the lives of some of the boys as they "step out of Father Flanagan's Boys Town into the world, and will portray the continued interest of Father Flanagan in the life of his wards even after they leave Boys Town." Considine, who was accompanied to Omaha by screenwriter Jim McGuinness, promised the new picture would be made on "quite an elaborate scale" and that "a great deal of the filming" would take place in Nebraska. In the middle of a building campaign, Father Flanagan heralded the signing of the new deal: "The large debt of our Home will be reduced by the amount to be paid us, and we will be given another opportunity to present to the world the humanitarian and character-building work that is being done in Boys Town."

Tracy said nothing when presented the script, provisionally titled *Boys Town Sequel,* and Louise, who thought the original "stuffy," saw no point in trying to talk him out of it. The film went into production in Culver City on November 4, 1940, and Considine's assurances to the contrary, there would be no location work for either of its two stars. As it progressed, it was as if the movie was made under a complete publicity blackout. There were no on-set visits, no interviews given, no advance ballyhoo approaching the scale of the first production. Louise was gone much of the time, Johnny having returned, at age sixteen, to the Wright Oral School in New York City, and Tracy seemed more focused on preparations for his next picture than on the work at hand.

Tracy's first conference on *Dr. Jekyll and Mr. Hyde* took place on November 8, 1940, when he met with Eddie Mannix, producer Victor Saville, and Vic Fleming, who was set to direct the picture. Saville's original idea had been to star Robert Donat, who was to have made the film at the former Alexander Korda studios at Denham. Donat was said to be "enthusiastic" and, moving forward, M-G-M acquired the rights to Robert Louis Stevenson's original story from Paramount, where previous versions had been made in 1920 and 1931. The war intervened, and Saville settled in California while Donat chose to remain in England.

In New York, Howard Dietz was incredulous; Metro didn't make horror pictures, and certainly not with their top stars. *Jekyll and Hyde* was different, in that it had always been an important stage vehicle—notably for Richard Mansfield—and the two Paramount versions had featured John Barrymore and Fredric March, respectively. When Donat's participation became impractical in the spring of 1940, Saville naturally thought of Tracy as the studio's only credible candidate for the title role. Tracy resisted the part at first, unsure of how he'd handle it, and relented only after Fleming got involved and proposed to do something new and daring with the idea.

Frank McHugh could remember a night at one of the regular Boys' Club dinners when Tracy said he was considering the picture and asked the others if they thought he should do it. Lynne Overman spoke up and advised against it.

"Why?" asked Tracy.

"You would not be good in it," he said quietly.

Tracy, a bit of indignation now creeping into his voice, asked, "Why would I not be 'good in it'?"

"Nobody," said Overman, "ever is."

John Lee Mahin, Fleming's frequent collaborator, had been on the project since April, working under Saville's direct supervision and sticking closely to the 1931 screenplay by Percy Heath and Samuel Hoffenstein. Tracy, as it turned out, had an entirely different conception of the character, one that was intensely personal and, to him, painfully obvious. "I will never forget," said Adela Rogers St. Johns, "the time that he explained to me that . . . there was supposed to be some magic, evil drink that Dr. Jekyll invents that turns [him] into Mr. Hyde. And this is a magic formula. And Spence said, 'Nothing but liquor. That's all. He's just trying to show you that you can be Dr. Jekyll, and if you drink enough booze you end up in the gutter as Mr. Hyde. That's all there is to it—it's just booze.' And I said, 'Well, *you* ought to know.' And he said, 'I *do* know. That's why I'm telling you!' "

Tracy elaborated:

I had always been fascinated by the story and saw it as a story of the two sides of a man. I felt Jekyll was a very respectable doctor—a fine member of society. He had proposed to a lovely girl and was about to marry her. But there was another side to the man. Every once in a while, Jekyll would go on a trip. Disappear. And either because of drink or dope or who-knows-what, he would become— or should I say turn into?—Mr. Hyde. Then in a town or neighborhood where he was totally unknown, he would perform incredible acts of cruelty and vulgarity. The emotional side of Jekyll was obviously extremely disturbed. The girl, as his fiancée, is a proper lady. But as his fantasy whore, the girl matched his Mr. Hyde. She would be capable of the lowest behavior. The two girls would be played by the same actress; the two men would be me.

Tracy had the idea of doing the transformations from Jekyll to Hyde entirely without makeup, as he remembered Barrymore having done them in 1920: "The change was not essentially physical. It went deeper than that. It was his soul that turned black. As a matter of fact, Mr. Hyde would have been better able to carry out his diabolical crimes had he been handsome, suave, polished. Not only that, but a handsome Mr. Hyde would have been more believable and the contrast between his appearance and personality more interesting."

On December 16, he dined with Saville, Fleming, and Mahin, and they ran the silent *Jekyll and Hyde*. Barrymore, they discovered, did the transformation in one shot but, once established as having changed to Mr. Hyde, relied on makeup to put across the effect. The look was in some respects subtle and in other ways outlandish, with putty fingers extending the hands and a phony chin accentuating the actor's scarecrow frame. The results inconclusive, the men decided to make a test to see if a strictly cerebral version of the story was even possible. Meanwhile, with Mahin's completed script in the bank, Saville turned to journalist and playwright John L. Balderston, whose name had been associated with some of Hollywood's most prominent horror pictures, including *Dracula* and *Frankenstein*. Balderston reviewed Mahin's work and began framing the problem by setting forth the dual nature of man and Plato's metaphor of the soul as a charioteer driving two horses—the good horse and the bad horse.

On December 23, Tracy, who had just finished with the *Boys Town* sequel, shot a test of the initial transformation scene as written by Mahin. The following day, Christmas Eve, he screened the test and sadly pronounced it "no good." Said Mahin, "They made tests without makeup, but he couldn't bring it off, he couldn't contort his face enough." Fleming thought they'd have another go after the first of the year, but Tracy's enthusiasm for the part evaporated. Convinced he could never pull the thing off and would simply make a fool of himself, he started maneuvering to get out of the commitment. Fleming kept him on board, certain they were onto something extraordinary, but Tracy remained unhappy for the balance of the project.

During his time as director of *Gone With the Wind*, Fleming had been the object of a campaign by David Selznick to interest him in a new contract player, the Swedish import Ingrid Bergman. Selznick made sure that Fleming saw *Intermezzo*, Bergman's American film debut, and that he subsequently considered her for a role in his first picture to follow *GWTW*, which *Jekyll and Hyde* would likely be. Bergman, twenty-four, was already at work at M-G-M in a picture called *Rage in Heaven*, and on December 18 she shot a test for *Jekyll and Hyde* with actor Edward Ashley as Dr. Jekyll. Bergman was apparently tested for the part of Beatrix, Jekyll's fiancée and traditionally the ingenue part in the play. She was, however, "fed up" playing nice girls, and when she saw the test, her instincts told her the better role would be that of Ivy the barmaid—Miriam Hopkins in the 1931 version—and she put in for that part instead. As Saville remembered it,

"Ingrid came to Fleming and me and suggested the roles should be reversed and she should play the prostitute. The idea was immediately appealing. The obvious photogenic purity of Bergman would react to the evil part of the good Dr. Jekyll."

By late January, Bergman was set for Ivy but the part of Beatrix was yet to be cast. In fact, much of the supporting cast was still in question, except for Donald Crisp and the English actor-director Peter Godfrey. Tracy, Fleming, and Saville had broken the characters of Jekyll and Hyde into numbered variations and were making—and remaking—tests of each. Tracy's Jekyll makeup was generally okay, but the Hyde makeup was still to be tested. The Jekyll wardrobe was ready for fittings, but the Hyde wardrobe was at a standstill until Tracy, Fleming, and Saville could agree on the amount of padding for each of the four changes in the script—which was being rewritten.

On the matter of the transformations, it seemed as if every department on the lot had been mobilized to come up with a solution. The Cartoon Department would have a preliminary test by the end of the month, and cinematographer Paul Vogel was trying various methods suggested by tint and lab specialist John Nickolaus. Olindo Ceccarini, an authority on color photography as well as sound, had pretty much exhausted the possibilities of blue light, while Jack Dawn's makeup department was preparing a test of hand transformations. Nobody had yet undertaken to watch Rouben Mamoulian's 1931 version, in which the initial transformation was accomplished with a filtering method keyed to colored makeup. Apparently no one wanted to be influenced by—or accused of merely copying—a version that was not simply well regarded but had actually won an Academy Award for Fredric March.

Increasingly nervous and unhappy, Tracy dreaded the start of the picture and was unable to get to sleep most nights until two or three in the morning. On January 28 he took Johnny to the studio to see "the Jekyll & Hydes of old" and to watch all of the tests he had made. "Pred[ict] Jekyll & Hyde will be bad," he wrote in his book later that night. "Picture & I will get panned by critics. This will be big bust." Louise dragged him off to La Quinta for a long weekend—he had given her a new Lincoln Model 57 coupe for Christmas—and they spent their days on the tennis court. ("Weeze won the championship," he noted.) They drove home, stopping at Pomona on a Sunday night to see a preview of *Men of Boys Town*.* "Too saccharine," he concluded. "Dull and unbelievable. Will not do as well as original."

---

* Tracy's title, for which he was awarded fifty dollars.

Fleming had *Jekyll and Hyde* laid out so as to shoot all the Jekyll script first, then all the Hyde script, and then the transitions from Jekyll to Hyde and vice versa. Still lacking final decisions on Hyde and the transformation scenes, he was nevertheless able to begin filming on the morning of Tuesday, February 4, 1941. Tracy, in a miserable mood, commemorated the occasion in his book: "Start of Jekyll & Hyde, what may well be the worst picture ever made. It will get panned, I will get panned—It will flop!"

Since both Fleming and Tracy wanted a closed set for the Hyde passages, it was thought best to get the press in and out early while Tracy was still in the guise of Dr. Jekyll. Cast at the last minute as Beatrix was M-G-M contract player Lana Turner, whose previous output for the studio had been limited to B-picture romances and musicals. Given Bergman's earlier roles and Selznick's stewardship, it was assumed that Turner would be playing Ivy, not Bergman, so there was an element of surprise in revealing Turner to the world as the virginal daughter of Sir Charles Emery.

Fleming spent four days shooting the ornate dinner party at which Jekyll first expounds his theories of good and evil, Beatrix demurely seated to his left. The table was designed to accommodate twenty guests and was divided into three sections so that one section could slide away to enable intimate shots of the other two. On the third day of coverage, director George Cukor brought W. Somerset Maugham to the set. With Tracy in his soup-and-fish, Cukor explained to the eminent British author that he was in the process of remaking *Dr. Jekyll and Mr. Hyde*. When Tracy had finished playing the scene for the umpteenth time, Maugham turned to his host and asked, "Which one is he now?"

Maugham, perhaps, had heard there wasn't going to be any "ape makeup" in this version of the story. "We're going to try to make Hyde a believable man," Tracy told John Chapman, syndicated correspondent for the *New York Daily News*. "When the picture was first proposed I even suggested that Hyde never be pictured, except maybe the back of his ear or something like that, but it didn't work out. But he'll be a recognizable human being." Visitors found that Tracy wasn't as interested in discussing Turner as he was her luminous costar. "The Hyde part isn't believable when you come right down to it. But if the audiences are convinced, I think it will be because of Ingrid Bergman. There is an actress! I don't throw the word 'great' around—just use it on Helen Hayes and a couple of others—and I think Miss Bergman is great. She'll make Hyde. It's like *Captains Courageous*. Here I was with an accent picked up from all parts of the world, and I wasn't believable. But there was Freddie Bartholomew looking at me wide-eyed and believing—so the audience did, too."

Eager and passionate, Bergman loved the role of Ivy and worked hard at it. "Ingrid," said Victor Saville, "came to my office most mornings to per-

Tracy saw Ingrid Bergman as the key to putting his Mr. Hyde across on screen. She campaigned for the role of Ivy and worked hard on her accent. (SUSIE TRACY)

fect her accent—we decided on the very posh upper-Tooting style—'Ouw, yereversonice, aren't yer.'"

Tracy's fascination with the actress soon extended to their off hours as well, and with Bergman's husband in Rochester studying medicine, she had a lot of free time on her hands. The two first dined together on March 21, fittingly after all the Jekyll scenes had been completed and Tracy was now working exclusively as Hyde. He had taken a room at the Beverly Wilshire and was spending most weekends sailing with Jimmy Cagney. They dined again the following week, and again the week after. They celebrated his forty-first birthday on the set of the picture, with Myrna Loy and Mickey Rooney stopping by for cake. Louise took him to dinner that night at Ciro's (with the Disneys) and then left the following day for New York to check up on Johnny.

With Louise out of town, Tracy began dining with Bergman almost every night and continued to do so after the picture finished on April 12. Bergman, for her part, thought Tracy "wonderful" as a leading man and recorded as much in her diary. "I watched her relationship with Spencer on *Dr. Jekyll and Mr. Hyde*," said John Houseman, a vice president for Selznick with responsibility for bringing Bergman along as an actress. "But that's not uncommon in this business."

Fleming, whose work on the film was careful and studied, may have stirred the pot by investing the picture with a strong undercurrent of sexual tension, boldly Freudian in its exploration of the unconscious mind. The intensity of the scenes between Ivy and Hyde, their imagery and sadism, became the film's most daring break with the versions of the past. ("So this is what has destroyed the world from the beginning, this poison, but it is a pleasant thing," says Hyde.) With Bergman, Tracy was alternately solicitous and petty, conscious of giving her everything she needed as an actress, yet terrifically uncomfortable with the material and Fleming's approach to it.

By agreeing to play Hyde with makeup, Tracy surrendered his actor's instinct to Fleming's conception of the role, and it was never a satisfactory fit. Still, he managed Jekyll without the ramrod stiffness of Fredric March nor the matinee posings of John Barrymore. What he brought to the part was a profound normality that could be distorted and amplified as Hyde took control; the connection between the two sides of the character had never been as blatant. When first in the grip of his dark side, Jekyll examines himself in the mirror as a medical doctor might examine a patient. At once astonished and yet altogether fascinated, he says, "Can this be evil, then?" and bursts into a nervous laugh.

Taut and unblinking, Hyde takes unrestrained glee in the languid terror of Bergman's Ivy, all breathless and slow as if snared in a trap from which she can't possibly escape. The design of the makeup wasn't as outlandish as for previous incarnations, more an exaggeration of Tracy's own familiar features, in keeping with the notion that it was Jekyll's soul that turned black. The most obvious embellishment was a grotesque set of false teeth. Said Victor Saville, "We had to make six sets of teeth as the fangs fully developed— booming voice of Tracy from the stage, 'Bring on the choppers!' "

What Fleming and Mahin ultimately produced was a deft exercise in sadomasochism, something very different from the exploration Tracy had first imagined, a sort of tour of the psyche of an addict, the emotional need, the physical intolerance, the divide between the security of home and the debauchery of the street, the shame and self-loathing that withered the spirit, the mortal sin that, in the judgment of the church, killed the soul. Finding the intersection between actor and character—characters, in this instance, for he took to referring to himself as "we" around the set—was an abnormally draining process, fluid and imprecise and inordinately dependent upon Fleming's oblique direction. "It isn't often," said Tracy, "that an actor is actually emotionally upset by a role. Mr. Hyde is one of the few I have played that took everything out of me."

The transformation scenes remained a problem, and as of April 7 they were yet to shoot the first time Jekyll takes the "dope" (as Saville, in a nod to Tracy's concept, always referred to Jekyll's mysterious potion). The final days were in some ways the toughest, as Hyde's zeal begins to leave him, and all that is left is an unconstrained fury, bottled lightning in a corroded shell of a man. Tracy spent his days on the set barely speaking to others, his only respite his evenings alone with Bergman. It rained constantly during the course of the shoot, and his mood could not have been lifted by the release of *Men of Boys Town,* which came just days before the finish of the picture.

Katherine Brown, Selznick's story editor, came west with Bergman's two-and-a-half-year-old daughter, Pia, and Spence had all three to the ranch for a weekend. One night they went to King Vidor's place for dinner and then, as Tracy later noted, "ditched the guests." Their time together was rapidly drawing to a close: Bergman was preparing to do *Anna Christie* in Santa Barbara under John Houseman's direction, while Tracy would be going east for the start of *The Yearling.* On his last day in town, a Monday, they played tennis in the morning, were apart in the afternoon, but together again for dinner, the tenth such occasion in the space of two weeks. The following day, Tracy boarded the Super Chief for Chicago, expecting to be gone for at least eight weeks.

In mid-February Tracy lunched with Nicholas Schenck, the diminutive "general" of the Loew's empire, and accepted the terms of a new deal that would expressly limit the number of pictures he could be required to make in a given year. The seven-year contract, which paid $5,000 a week, held the studio to three Tracy pictures in the first, third, fifth, and seventh years of the agreement, and just two in the second, fourth, and sixth. In addition, Tracy would be permitted, under certain conditions, to return to the legitimate stage in each of the even years of the pact. His billing, which in the past had always been "first featured," was now for the first time spelled out as "that of star or as that of a co-star with one or more other co-stars." The new agreement, which was signed on April 15, 1941, retroactively took effect with the start of *Jekyll and Hyde.**

The Yearling, Marjorie Kinnan Rawlings' tale of a boy's life in inland Florida, was an immediate sensation when it was published by Scribner in March 1938. Sixty thousand copies were sold in the first month alone. M-G-M snapped up the picture rights for $30,000, and by September all the particulars were in place: Tracy would play Penny Baxter under Victor Fleming's direction, with Gene Reynolds taking the role of Penny's son,

---

* Contrary to legend, Tracy's M-G-M contract never called for top billing.

Jody. John Lee Mahin, who fell in love with the book and urged the studio to buy it, was at first to write the screenplay, but then Mahin clashed with producer Sidney Franklin, who said Mahin "didn't realize the sensitivity of it" and had him put off the project.

Franklin, who was producing the film version of Paul Osborn's Broadway success *On Borrowed Time,* induced the playwright, who was new to screenwriting, to tackle *The Yearling.* Osborn, as it turned out, was an inspired choice, sensitive and knowing, and his script, completed in July 1940, was a masterful job. Second-unit work began the following January, as a full Technicolor crew, battling bugs and humidity, struggled to get shots on film that matched the fanciful compositions of California-based sketch artists.* By the time Tracy arrived on May 2 at Ocala, where the company had leased a farm, some members of the dispirited crew had been on site nearly four months. Tracy and Fleming were worn out as well; having just finished *Jekyll and Hyde,* neither man had as much as a week's vacation before nature mandated the start of *The Yearling.*

Tempers were short from the beginning. The principal problem was the yearling itself. Since most deer are born within a narrow May–June window and grow quickly, the studio's animal handler, a former elephant trainer named George Emerson, conspired to have a small fleet of does timed to give birth in successive weeks so that Fleming and company would always have a newborn available. Breeding began in October 1940; Emerson presided over a small zoo on Lot 4 and gathered a veritable menagerie of trained animals for use in the film. When it came time for shooting to begin, they were all loaded into a pair of rail cars especially designed for the movement of livestock and transported to the central Florida location.

In the two years since the film's announcement, fifteen-year-old Gene Reynolds had grown too old to play Jody, and a hectic search was launched to find a replacement. Billy Grady hit nine cities in twelve days and shot tests of maybe thirty kids. It was, however, the first boy on his first stop in Atlanta who bore the most uncanny resemblance to the author's conception of what Jody should look like, and twelve-year-old Gene Eckman was ultimately given the part. Imported to Culver City for training, Eckman was enrolled at the studio schoolhouse with instructions to spend as much time as possible with the deer being raised by Emerson on Lot 4. The boy was allowed to read the script but told not to memorize the dialogue. Josephine Dillon, Clark Gable's first wife, was given the task of coaching him and moderating his thick Georgia accent.

---

* Fleming had been so impressed with the continuity sketches of William Cameron Menzies on *Gone With the Wind* that he had key sequences for *Dr. Jekyll and Mr. Hyde* designed in the same manner. For *The Yearling,* he had the entire screenplay sketched in advance.

"We will not be able to take tests of clothes with Spencer Tracy and the boy until this coming Monday," Sidney Franklin advised his brother Chet, who was directing the second-unit work in Florida, "which is unfortunate, but there is nothing we can do about it. He has been playing Mr. Hyde to such an extent that we're afraid to put him with the boy for fear he would tear him to pieces. It seems to be affecting his disposition, so we have to leave the poor guy alone until he gets out of character which we hope will be Monday."

Fleming made some tests, simple process shots on a treadmill in which Tracy and Eckman were seen ambling down a forest pathway. Said Eckman, "I remember Victor Fleming told me, 'Gene, stop looking at Spencer Tracy like a star. He's your father.' It was one of the first scenes I made with Tracy and he was very nice. I remember he sat down at that point to help me get over this awe of him . . . We worked it out so that we could carry on a conversation and I wouldn't feel so out of place."

Though author Rawlings had sent him a warmly inscribed copy of *The Yearling* when he was first confirmed for the role, Tracy was physically wrong for the part of Penny Baxter and he knew it. In the book, Penny is described as having "grown to maturity no bigger than a boy. His feet were small, his shoulders narrow, his ribs and hips joined together in a continuous fragile framework." Tracy, on the other hand, was broad and solid and weighed nearly two hundred pounds. Publicist Eddie Lawrence was assigned to accompany him to Ocala, and Lawrence caught up with him just as he was emerging from a projection room after running the tests. "Spence," Lawrence began, "what a pleasure to do this journey with you—" Tracy cast a burning eye in Lawrence's direction and, in a voice dripping with disgust, said, "Looks like I ATE the boy!" and stalked off.

Casting for the part of Ma Baxter was contentious, Fleming being dead set against the popular favorite, British stage and film actress Flora Robson, who had the long, plain look the story demanded. "Fleming was violently pro-Nazi," said Anne Revere, the New York–born actress who was instead given the part. "This was '41, we hadn't entered the war . . . and he was violently opposed to the English and anyone who was interfering with the boys over there. So he wouldn't have her, he was against all English." Revere had played a one-day bit as an aggrieved mother in *Men of Boys Town* and gained Tracy's endorsement. Fleming initially told her she had the "wrong bony structure" for the role but tested her anyway. "When they put Spence in the part," she said, "they tried to make him look small by getting everything else very big . . . They took me and duped me up; they put great platform shoes and a big bosom on me, and tried to make me look very large."

For Tracy, the experience was a replay of *Northwest Passage,* but in a climate not nearly as agreeable, the palmetto and scrub holding in the heat like a damp blanket. "He is, with the possible exception of Mr. Fleming, the hardest-working man on the 79,000-acre lot," Sidney Whipple observed during a visit to the set for the *New York World-Telegram.* "He routs himself out of bed at 6 o'clock in the morning and thereafter is in the field. He worries and frets and deprecates his own talent. He rehearses his lines and practices for constant improvement in his action. He squats in the sun-baked cornfield for interminable conferences with director Fleming. He completely submerges himself in the character. When he disappears after a 12- or 14-hour workday, it is either to engage in further conferences with Mr. Fleming over the script and tomorrow's shooting or, more rarely, to engage in a little fishing in nearby Lake George. This is his only recreation."

Fleming, even with the deliberate pace of production, wasn't getting what he wanted. "I was only on the set twice," Marjorie Kinnan Rawlings said in a letter to a friend,

and I could tell Fleming wasn't satisfied with Anne Revere or the boy. He was very nervous, taking sleeping tablets, etc., and felt he could handle things much better on the Hollywood sets. The wind registered on the sound track, not sounding like wind at all, etc. The boy, Gene Eckman, in looks and personality seemed quite all right, but the sound man had me listen in, and it was true, as he complained, that the boy was not enunciating and his lines were not registering. Tracy was bored and morose, Anne Revere is not Ma Baxter as I visualize her, but had a fine pioneer look and I thought she was all right, but she didn't seem too "put out" emotionally in the one scene I saw her do.

"I will be the first to say I was not ready for it," Anne Revere acknowledged. "I hadn't had enough experience in pictures. But I was not the cause of the debacle. First, they couldn't *understand* the kid. And Spence would laugh and say, 'Well, I'm only a hundred pounds overweight.' The whole thing started to look absurd! So finally they packed it up and took it home."

Tracy commandeered a new Cadillac the production manager had purchased and, hiring a driver, proposed that he and Eddie Lawrence ride over to Jacksonville to catch a train. When they got to Jacksonville, Tracy told Lawrence he liked riding in the car and was in no hurry to get home. "You know, Eddie, American Airlines goes through St. Louis—we'll go to St. Louis." When Lawrence said that he was going to call the studio, Tracy said grandly, "Oh, forget the studio!"

Said Lawrence, "He loved to needle you—a lot. So finally, going through Georgia, I saw this old fashioned praline factory, and they had big bags of pralines hanging down. And I knew Spence, so I gave the boy six

With Gene Eckman and Anne Revere in one of the few stills to emerge from the Florida location of *The Yearling*. (ACADEMY OF MOTION PICTURE ARTS AND SCIENCES)

bucks (or whatever it was) and I said, 'You take Mr. Tracy over—' and in the meantime I called the studio. They said, 'Good God, where is Spencer?' Because this was after [it was known that he had] periodic problems . . . I told 'em, 'Look, I'll keep in touch with you. There's nothing else I can do. Tracy's fine—he hasn't had a drink.' "

From Atlanta they moved on to Nashville, where they put up for the night at the Hermitage and, with M-G-M's pull, got the Presidential Suite.

And then the next morning Tracy said, "Look, we'll go to Chicago." I said, "All right, Spencer, we'll go to Chicago." So we went up through all that wonderful country . . . [and] we got to the Blackstone Hotel. And they scared me to death. The guy who took the bags said, "Oh, Mr. Tracy, I'm the one who bought you the booze, remember?" Oh boy, here we go, here we go, here we go. But we didn't. I had the most wonderful four days with Spencer. He was warm, he was friendly, we walked a lot, went to the lake . . . Helen Hayes was in town, and he called her and we had dinner at the Ambassador East, and I remember she kind of laid him out. He was talking about, oh, he wanted to go back into theatre. And she said, "Spencer. Sunday matinees, you know. And night shows? I don't think you'd care for that." But it was a pleasant time until finally Spence said, "I guess we'd better get home."

Tracy objected when Lawrence said that he would get him a compartment and take a roomette for himself. "No, no, no," he said. "A compartment to sit up in, and a compartment to lie down in, and I want you to have a compartment. Three compartments." As soon as they boarded the train, Lawrence, remembering his first encounter with his charge on the set of *Riffraff*, sought out the porter. "Look," he said. "This compartment? You never, never knock on the door, never, never bother the occupant. Don't even make up the beds." That night on the Chief they ordered steaks, and Tracy, who marked three years of sobriety on May 1, made the only reference Lawrence ever heard to his alcoholism. "Eddie," he said glumly, "I'd love to have a glass of beer. But you know if I have one beer I'm gone."

Back at the studio, there was a hot session over the fate of *The Yearling*. "How can I," Fleming reportedly asked, "make a picture whose essence is that people love each other, when no one in the cast loves anyone or loves being down there or loves making the picture?" The next day, Eddie Mannix floated the possibility of King Vidor taking over as director, and Tracy, who was friendly with Vidor but not particularly close, made no objection to the idea.

Tracy made another test with Gene Eckman on May 27, and Eckman, he acknowledged, was "better" than before. However, according to Sidney Franklin, the studio was "more or less turning against the boy and the mother" and the problem of quickly recasting the roles became the film's undoing. In June, Tracy appeared in tests with actresses Frances Farmer and Ruth Hussey, both as possible replacements in the part of Ma Baxter, but the animals were growing and the time for returning to Florida had passed. *The Yearling*, for reasons of weather and landscape as well as wildlife, had to be filmed in the spring. The decision to postpone it was made on June 13, 1941. The studio's total investment at the time was estimated at $500,000.

Dr. Jekyll and Mr. Hyde had its first sneak before a paying audience on June 18, but Tracy simply noted the event in his datebook with a question mark. One thing was certain: the scenes in which Jekyll turned into Hyde didn't work and would have to be redone. Editor Harold Kress recalled that when he was first assigned the film he asked, "What about his changes?" They had

Tracy resisted playing Mr. Hyde with makeup and regretted doing so for the rest of his life. (SUSIE TRACY)

hired, he discovered, some thirty animators to put close-ups of Tracy on cells because someone had sold Victor Saville on the idea. "Well," said cinematographer Joe Ruttenberg, "there were many tests made . . . thousands of dollars spent on making experiments with certain chemicals that certain lights would change, and it didn't work out at all."

On July 14 Tracy returned to the studio to confer on the effects for *Jekyll and Hyde.* With the press preview only a week away, the changes would have to be made quickly. "We dissolved," said Ruttenberg of the ultimate—and most obvious—solution. "We sat him down, tied his shoulders and put his head in one of those old fashioned still photographer's gadgets to keep his head steady, and we kept grinding one or two frames at a time as the make up was being changed . . . It took hours . . . same position . . . It was like doing an animated film, you know." Tracy, said Ruttenberg, patiently submitted to the tedious process of filming all three of the on-camera transformation scenes over the course of two long days. "He was very uncomfortable and very cooperative. He realized how much trouble it was."

Tracy saw Ingrid Bergman the night he finished with the new transformation shots, unconvinced they would make any difference and still fretting over his performance. The trade showing took place in Los Angeles on July 21, and the early returns were a lot more positive than he expected. *Daily Variety* faulted the film's length, suggesting that Fleming held his scenes "beyond their fullest realization" but nevertheless pronounced the picture exceptional in every respect. The *Reporter* called it a "master screen work" and praised the "magnificent" performances of both Tracy and Bergman. "Tracy wisely chooses to play Hyde with the smallest application of makeup, and his face, though radically altered with the assistance of Jack Dawn's creations, is no longer a visage designed to haunt little children. Tracy's interpretation reaches deeper into the characterization, and his playing makes it more memorable for not being merely another protean feat. His Jekyll and Hyde is the top portrayal of a top actor's career."

Tracy was in San Francisco with Bergman when *Dr. Jekyll and Mr. Hyde* had its world premiere at New York's Astor Theatre on Tuesday, August 12, 1941. The following day, he saw the notices in the metropolitan dailies and carefully listed the good versus the bad in his book. "Worst panning for an actor ever received?" he wrote. "The horrible notices of 'Mr. Hyde.' He! he! All bad for [the] picture business [in] New York." To be sure, the reviews were generally slams, and Tracy took the brunt of them, Bergman and even Turner coming off considerably better. Ted Strauss, in the *Times,* said that Tracy's portrait of Hyde was "not so much evil incarnate as it is the ham rampant."

Archer Winston in the *Post* chimed in by calling the role a "ham's holiday," and Cecelia Ager reported laughter at the Monday press screening in *P.M.* "They laugh," she said. "It's funny, watching Mr. Tracy's sweet, strong face with the iron jaw that yet flexes with emotion take on the look of Frankenstein's Karloff, Teddy Roosevelt, Victor MacLaglen, and finally Gargantua the Great, in orderly progression. (It's just as funny when he does it backwards)." A scene of Hyde spitting grape seeds drew razzberries, and humorist Harry Hershfield, seated near Lee Mortimer of the *Mirror,* was heard to remark that he didn't know Abbott and Costello had been "suddenly substituted for Spencer Tracy." A few fell to the other side: Howard Barnes, Eileen Creelman, and Norton Mockridge all thought him superb, but the overall consensus was that Tracy's Hyde was over the top, and it became a shame that would never leave him.

Fortunately for Metro-Goldwyn-Mayer, the public didn't care what the critics thought, and the picture opened strong, the first Tracy picture to play the upscale Astor since *Captains Courageous.* Nicholas Schenck wired the ranch:

WE ARE DOING THE BIGGEST BUSINESS OF ANY FILM THAT EVER PLAYED THE ASTOR. THIS INCLUDES "GONE WITH THE WIND," "PYGMALION" AND "GOODBYE MR. CHIPS." ALSO TODAY'S BUSINESS WHICH TOOK PLACE AFTER THE NOTICES IS BIGGER THAN YESTERDAYS WHICH WAS IN ADVANCE OF THE NOTICES PROVING

THAT WE ARE A SUCCESS . . . THE PEOPLE THAT WE
HAVE QUERIED COMING OUT OF THE THEATRE UNI-
FORMLY SAY THE PICTURE AND YOUR PERFORMANCE ARE
EXCELLENT.

Rain and cooler weather made the film strictly SRO at most performances, and it held to its remarkable pace in its second and third weeks as
well. The studio, however, knew it had to do something about the laughs
the picture drew, and Tracy's datebook entry for August 15 reads as follows:
"Studio cutting 'Jekyll & Hyde'—but not en[ough]!" He was still holed up
at the studio on the eighteenth ("Hyde-ing" as he put it) and the editing
wasn't completed until the night of the twenty-first, the improvements still
nevertheless in time for the critical Labor Day weekend, the traditional start
of the new season.

Dr. Jekyll and Mr. Hyde went on to broader critical acclaim elsewhere
and worldwide billings in excess of $2 million. Tracy, however, could never
reconcile the film's success with the critical roundhousing he endured in
New York. Perversely, he took to quoting the Abbott and Costello line
whenever the subject of the film came up, erroneously attributing it to
Cecelia Ager.

Dick Mook told him that he didn't seem himself at all, that since winning the Oscars he was only preoccupied with topping his own performances. Tracy didn't agree with that, but he took a moment to formulate a
response.

"It wasn't the awards," he said finally. "Naturally I was flattered, but
when I stop to think of some of the others who've received the awards, I
don't take them too seriously. Perhaps I *do* worry over my work, but it isn't
for fear I won't get another award. It's because I'm bothered about the poor
parts I'm getting . . . I guess maybe I'm near the end of my rope. I've been
in pictures almost twelve years now, and I'm not a juvenile anymore. Well,
it was fun while it lasted and neither the stage, nor pictures, nor Hollywood
owes me a thing. In fact, they've all been mighty good to me."

CHAPTER 17

Woman of the Year

I'm afraid you're going to have trouble finding anything to photograph," Louise Tracy told the photographer accompanying Dick Mook. "You see, we wanted a house that would be a home—a place that would be comfortable to live in rather than one that would look well in pictures but which would be depressingly formal. As a matter of fact, we have hardly any really good pieces."

There was the little tilt-top table that had belonged to Louise's great-grandmother, as had the chairs on either side of it. And there was the sideboard—the old pine dresser with the new matching top—but everything else was contemporary maple, some pieces, like the dining set, built to order, while others came directly from the showroom floor. All serviceable, comfortable, but hardly showplace rare or extravagant by the standards of even small-town America. Louise wondered why any magazine would want to take pictures, much less publish them, but Mook was an old friend and had drawn an assignment for yet another intimate look at Spencer Tracy and his family.

The ranch itself made for better photo ops, and the same magazine, *Screenland*, had run a pictorial spread a few months earlier, all exterior shots made by an M-G-M photographer showing Spence and the kids out among the animals, pitching hay, working the fields, drinking from the garden hose, and nuzzling the dogs. The headline was "Tracy Takes It Easy," but

A rare day together on the ranch, as captured by a studio photographer, 1939.
(SUSIE TRACY)

what it showed was an increasingly rare event, a day spent at home where
Spence was indeed at rest, his wife and kids enjoying the air, the sun, the
dust kicked up by the horses and the cars, the notion that this was as far
away from the studio as one could get and still earn the extraordinary living
he had come to expect from his position as a genuine star of the movies.

Tracy wasn't there the day Mook showed up; he was shooting *Edison,
the Man,* and so Louise gamely showed Dick around, poking into Spence's
modest room, where the desk was piled high with scripts and mail and random scraps of paper, notes he had written himself and stuffed in his pockets. Two wastebaskets had come from an old lady who made them both
herself—one pictured Stanley, the other Livingstone, and both arrived

accompanied by a bill for sixteen dollars. A globe sat to one side, to the other a bookcase that held a model of the *Carrie B* (which Mook always referred to as "Tracy's Folly"). The other rooms were similarly plain, though homey and obviously lived in. There were no formal areas nor guest rooms, nothing set aside for company or otherwise off limits to the kids and the dogs.

They strolled out back, past the pool and the tennis court and the one-time bunkhouse, to where the horses were kept, White Sox, Johnnie, four or five racehorses, none on the level of Man o' War nor ready even for Santa Anita but all right for the lesser tracks. "At least we think they are," Louise said. She pointed out a small horse, a yearling, which they had entered in a breeder's sale. "What a shame to sell her," Mook, the Tennessee horseman, remarked. "No," Louise said. "We've had our fun with her while she was growing up. Racehorses are an expensive proposition. We'd better get our money out of her if we can. We'll probably sell the other racers, too, when we can, and only keep the polo ponies."

It was a crisp, windy day, and with the kids in school and Spence off making a picture, the place seemed quiet and empty and Louise somewhat subdued, as if she had everything she could possibly ask of life except happiness and a sense of purpose beyond John and the job of being Mrs. Spencer Tracy—a role that qualified her, in the opinion of many, as a candidate for sainthood. At the age of forty-three she was no longer playing competitive polo, no longer in the swim of things at Riviera. Her friend Audrey Caldwell once allowed as how Louise should never have given up the stage, but it had been nearly twelve years since that abbreviated season at Lima, where she had last appeared before an audience as leading woman in a company of actors.

"That's all there is—there isn't any more," she said to Mook, wryly echoing Ethel Barrymore's famous curtain line. "Are we going to see you again soon, or are you going to go on ignoring us?"

If Louise knew of Spence's relationship with Ingrid Bergman, she never let on. If anything, she made it easier for him by absenting herself from the Encino ranch, either with trips to Arizona or Palm Springs, or her frequent visits to New York, where Johnny was once again a student at the Wright Oral School. Spence was on the wagon, working constantly, home, at times, for tennis and swimming, occasionally for dinner out or a movie in the company of friends. They attended the premiere of Disney's *Fantasia* at the Carthay Circle and caught up with *Citizen Kane* some four months after its release. On a day-to-day basis they were leading separate lives—purposely, it would seem, for when Louise was in residence, Spence usually was not, and when he was around, Louise often was elsewhere, leaving the children in his care and the care of the help—Miss Lystad, Susie's Norwegian nurse; Margaret, the family cook; Hughie, who took care of the horses and lived out back of the property. Spence's presence at the dinner table became something of an event, and Susie would later remember his palming quarters ("What's that behind your ear?") as the last vestige of his childhood magic act.

"I could see a change over the years," said Chuck Sligh, whose business occasionally brought him to Los Angeles.

When I first went to California in '34 or '35 I stayed at their house . . . they certainly seemed very happy and everything was fine. And [then] I was at the ranch maybe twice. The first time I went, I remember specifically because Louise said, "Spence isn't going to be here because he's making a movie and he has to get in for makeup and everything very early in the morning. It's a lot easier for him to stay at the hotel and be there in the morning instead of driving way into there from here. So why don't you just take his room and stay there?" So I did. And I looked in the closet and there were, oh, four or five or six suits . . . but the next time I went out there and stayed in Spence's room, I opened the closet door and there was practically nothing.

Tracy was also distancing himself from his brother Carroll, whom he blamed for getting him into "deep trouble" with the Internal Revenue Service. At one point, as he later told it, he was sure he was going to jail, and a man from the IRS actually appeared at the studio to audit his records.

"I keep seeing the name Feely," the man said. "Jenny Feely, Aberdeen, South Dakota. Who is that?"

"That's my aunt."

"I see regular payments . . ."

"Yes, that's right. You can ask her. I send checks to her."

"And she lives on Washington Street in Aberdeen?"

"Yes, sir."

"Well," said the man, "I know Jenny Feely who lives on Washington Street in Aberdeen, South Dakota. My name is Walter Higginbottom, and I was born and brought up two blocks up the street from her." He closed the file lying in front of him on the table. "That's all right, Mr. Tracy."

Spence's cousin Frank was out over the summer of 1940, and the tension between the two brothers was palpable. "It was a period," said Frank, of two or three months—two or three *months*—that he and Carroll did not speak. He didn't even look at him. He'd sit by the pool (and the kids were in Hawaii with Louise, or somewhere) and he'd talk to me and he wouldn't even LOOK at Carroll. Carroll usually picked me up at the hotel and drove me out there. We'd sit around for a couple of hours, have lunch, and [Spence would] never talk to him. Never even look at him. He wasn't even there . . . surely there must have been some business points they had to discuss, or SOMETHING . . . Carroll never opened his mouth. That went on for a couple of months. And then when the ice finally broke, it just barely broke. It was like "pass the salt" or something. Matter of fact, most of the time I was out there, they didn't speak.

One night Spence and Frank were driving to the studio to see a picture. It was just the two of them, and Spence began to ruminate on the matter of his big brother. "I don't know what the hell to do with Carroll," he said. "Christ, he's been out here seven years and he still doesn't do anything. I pay him $250 a week . . . he's always on the golf course, when I want him I can't find him, or when I want him he's doing something for [somebody else] . . . the guy's all screwed up . . . I don't know what the hell to do with him. But he's my brother. I love the big lug. What am I going to do?" He spoke, Frank said, in a tone of almost complete disgust. "If it weren't for me getting him out here in California," Spence said, "he'd still be selling malted milk in Milwaukee for Sam Thompson."

Where Carroll was an almost constant source of frustration for his younger brother, Peggy Gough, Tracy's secretary, was a godsend. A graduate of UCLA, she handled the job with quiet efficiency, sorting the mail, taking dictation, helping her boss cope with the weird business of being a movie star. Working out of his combination office–dressing room on the second floor of an apartment building on M-G-M's Lot 1, she diplomatically fielded appeals for money and what Tracy called "oddments"—buttons from his jackets, locks of hair, contest prizes and the like. She ordered stills from his movies, answered fan mail, made luncheon and dinner reservations, sent out photos, turned down party invitations, delivered messages, and kept the number at the house in Encino a closely guarded secret.

Pleas for autographs were the most common, and they came in all sorts of forms. People would see him leave his car and poke hastily scrawled scraps of paper through the windows. One went so far as to scratch a name and address into the paint of his new Lincoln, which he then had to have refinished. Before going to work for Tracy, Peggy never knew how many requests a public figure could get—hundreds a month, not to mention appeals from legitimate charities, which also numbered in the hundreds.

"He is a very charitable person," she said at the time. "In fact, many of his friends call him a sucker, but he just laughs it off. You've no idea how much can be given away right inside the studio itself—not a day passes that some extra or old-time actor doesn't come up with a hard luck story, and the only ones he refuses are the ones he knows are downright fakes who make a business of it, and, unfortunately, there are a good many of them."*

There was also the matter of the fan club, a job of care and feeding for which he was profoundly unsuited. One of the earliest rackets in the movie business, clubs had been known to charge fans as much as $2.50 a year to officially admire a preening film idol and another fifty cents for a lithographed picture of same. The money went into the pockets of organizers or, in some cases, the star himself. After a vogue that lasted well into the twenties, such organizations fell into disrepute, and some studios—such as Fox—forbade them altogether. It was radio that fueled a new wave of them in the mid-thirties, and soon men like Howard Strickling saw the value in building and maintaining mailing lists so that when the sales organization had trouble selling its block into a place like Kokomo, the local fan clubs could be rallied into action. The membership of Jean Harlow's fan club reportedly topped fifteen thousand at the time of her death.

In Tracy's case, a club took shape after *Captains Courageous* but fell apart with the illness of its president, a woman known simply as Miss Barclay. When a club member wrote in, Peggy explained the situation and the woman wrote back, offering to form another on Tracy's behalf. Mrs. Frances Rasinen of Detroit had previously run a club for singer-actor Johnnie "Scat" Davis and came well recommended for the job. With annual dues set at fifty cents, she built up a membership in short order, Tracy agreeing to sign a five-by-seven photo to each new member. The inaugural issue of the club's quarterly newsletter, *The Tracy Topper*, was published in October 1940, but Mrs. Rasinen proved to be high maintenance, and in the club's prime Peggy was responding to two or three letters a week, juggling dozens of names and addresses and trying as best she could to keep everyone happy.

There was time to talk over the summer of 1940, and cousin Frank asked Spence about acting. "I said, 'Did you ever think about doing anything else?' He said, 'Well, my Dad wanted me to go into business with him, and I was only interested in medicine. I'd have liked to be a doctor, but I knew I could never make it academically. Maybe I was bright enough, but I didn't have any kind of dedication. I had no motivation at all. You know,

---

* Tracy was a big tipper, a practice Louise thought terrible. "You think these people make a lot of money," he lectured. "They don't. It's only a few of us who do it; other people don't. I can do it and like to do it, so don't talk to me about it."

school was abhorrent.' " And then he told Frank what he had told Pat O'Brien, that one of the things he had really thought about was being a priest, but, as with medicine, he never thought he could "get through the Latin and all that stuff."

Frank struggled to control his look of surprise. "What?" he said.

"I don't go to church as much as I should," Spence continued. "I get to Mass fairly regularly, but I could be a lot better. This kind of life, sometimes you're traveling, sometimes you're working. Sunday's just another Tuesday or Wednesday. I don't practice the religion the way I should. I often thought about the priesthood. I went to St. Rose's for those years. Nuns. Every year. They drill that religion into you. I've got it in my head. I know what's right and wrong, I know what's sinful. I know. It bothers me. I've got a conscience."

David Caldwell, Audrey and Orville's fifteen-year-old son, felt quite close to the Tracys. "I never had the impression of Spence as a movie star," he said. "He was always very friendly and seemed to be interested in asking about things I was doing. And Louise certainly kept in pretty close touch. She even got me to help John very often with his studies." David was at the ranch one day, passing through the succession of rooms that included Spence's, when he noticed the Oscar for *Captains Courageous* sitting on the bookcase.

"There was always a great deal weighing on him, I must say . . . I said, 'Oh, that's what this looks like.' And he said something which was close to these words: 'There are qualities that make a man a good actor but don't necessarily make him a good man.' I was just very shocked at that statement. It was in a calm voice from him . . . but it had a lot of meaning behind it."

The idea for *Woman of the Year* came from director Garson Kanin, who conceived it as a vehicle for an actress he had designs on marrying. Kanin, twenty-eight, had been with RKO three years, having spun a year's apprenticeship with Samuel Goldwyn into a chance to direct a picture for producer Robert Sisk. A specialist in snappy comedies, Kanin was rushing to complete *Tom, Dick and Harry,* his seventh movie for the studio, when he described his concept to screenwriter Ring Lardner, Jr. Kanin's principal character was modeled on columnist Dorothy Thompson, who was, according to *Time* magazine, one of the two most influential women in the nation. (The other was Eleanor Roosevelt.) His notion was to portray a courtship between the outspoken political pundit and a hardheaded sportswriter—the *Post's* Jimmy Cannon in Kanin's mind—who worked on the same paper. "[T]hey clash in print about something; meet; clash in person; both wrong, both right—not bad!"

"Gar," Lardner said, "had decided he needed a writer conversant with the New York newspaper world to work on the script, and Paul [Jarrico, who wrote *Tom, Dick and Harry*] had volunteered me. To further complicate matters, Gar had just been drafted into the Army, so we talked out a story line in the couple of days before he went off to training camp, leaving his share of the project to his brother Mike." Michael Kanin was no more established in the profession than Lardner, having written only a few programmers at RKO.

It was an unlikely arrangement, two out-of-work screenwriters with only a logline of an idea, but through Garson Kanin they had access to one of Hollywood's hottest properties, the newly rejuvenescent Katharine Hepburn, whose shrewd co-opting of the rights to *The Philadelphia Story* had brought her one of the biggest hits of the season. Kanin had been linked romantically to the thirty-four-year-old actress ever since it came out that he and she had been the only witnesses to the midnight wedding of Laurence Olivier and Vivien Leigh. Within days, Kanin and Hepburn were denying marriage rumors of their own.

Ring Lardner and Michael Kanin began working out the story from the sportswriter's perspective, which Lardner then wrote up in the form of a first-person narrative for submission to Hepburn. "Garson," said Lardner, "probably sent it to her; he was the one who knew her personally. And she responded very well to it. And then we got up this plan of her taking it herself to Louis B. Mayer and talking to him about it."

It was a sweet position for Katharine Hepburn, who had come to prominence in the early thirties but whose later pictures weren't calculated to sustain a brand image. She won the Academy Award for *Morning Glory*, her third movie, and her version of *Little Women* was an astounding commercial hit. Yet she played character parts and oddballs, and where it once had seemed that audiences couldn't get enough of her, by 1938 she was part of Harry Brandt's infamous ad in the *Hollywood Reporter* in which the president of the Independent Theatre Owners Association labeled her, along with Mae West, Joan Crawford, and Marlene Dietrich, "box office poison."

"They made a mistake with me at RKO and renewed my contract," Hepburn later said. "They shouldn't have done that. I was washed up. If I had gone on making pictures that year I would have been not only washed up, but enshrouded and buried. So I bought out my contract."

She left the movies and returned to the stage, where Philip Barry and his *Philadelphia Story* awaited her. Sensing the quality of Barry's play and its profound commercial potential, she paid $30,000 for the film rights, then passed those rights to Howard Hughes—with whom she had been linked romantically—with the understanding that any deal he made for them would include the proviso that she play the self-centered Tracy Lord, a part that Barry had written with her in mind. It was, of course, the property that had value at the time, not Hepburn, whose participation would otherwise have been a shaky proposition.

Under Joe Mankiewicz's careful supervision—he had the entire stage production recorded and then clocked for laughs—*The Philadelphia Story* was a startling success. Hepburn walked away with an Oscar nomination as well as new currency with the moviegoing public. Said Mankiewicz, "Having had a very good time and a very successful time with Kate on *Philadelphia Story,* in her typical fashion she brought me a screenplay. An untitled screenplay, unauthored as far as the title page was concerned, because she wouldn't tell me who wrote it. She said, 'Read this.' I read it." Mankiewicz thought it "absolutely marvelous" but wasn't empowered to make a deal. "And she hadn't said what she wanted for it, and I said, 'Kate, I have nothing to do with that. That's up to the higher levels of L. B. Mayer, but I would love to do it.' "

Since *Philadelphia Story* had generated more than $3 million in worldwide billings for M-G-M, Mayer was only too happy to consider the new eighty-nine-page property, which carried the gold-plated title *The New Philadelphia Story.* Mankiewicz had already passed the material to Kenneth MacKenna, Metro's West Coast story editor, and MacKenna, in turn, had handed it over to Sam Katz, one of the rare members of the executive team who actually read the things given him. Having built enthusiasm all around, Hepburn caught a Stratoliner for the coast and took a bungalow at the Beverly Hills Hotel. A meeting was scheduled between her, Mankiewicz, Mayer, and Benny Thau for the next morning. "I was terrified," she said. "Mr. Mayer is a charming man, and I was afraid he'd talk me into promising something I had no intention of doing. He began by saying a lot of nice things to me—still not knowing who wrote the story or how much I'd ask. And I said a lot of nice things to him—the usual preliminaries to hitting each other over the head."

Once she had them snared, Hepburn outlined her terms: $40,000 for the story and another $60,000 for the shooting script. She asked $100,000 for herself as star (the same fee she had commanded for *Philadelphia Story*), $10,000 commission on the deal, and an extra $1,000 "for telephone calls and things." The entire package—Hepburn, original story, screenplay— was valued at $211,000, and she stuck to her guns, rejecting an initial offer from Sam Katz of $175,000 "for the whole business." Mike Kanin remembered that he and his partner were astonished: "We would have been lucky to get $10,000 for the script under our own names. As it was she got

$100,000 plus agent's fee of ten percent—for herself. I couldn't say it was all a big conspiracy against Metro, but we were quite breathless with the speed of it. We had nine days in which to finish the script. We holed up, and with the aid of a lot of Benzedrine managed to do it." It instantly became the costliest original ever purchased for the screen; it was only after the deal had been set that Hepburn revealed its authors as two novice screenwriters whose earnings had previously amounted to no more than $200 a week.*

With two-thirds of the screenplay drafted, Hepburn took it to George Stevens, who had directed one of her better films at RKO, *Alice Adams*. "My great buddy George Cukor had to be offered things first," she said, "but he didn't know a baseball game from a swimming match, so I thought this picture had to be directed by a very male man, and that's George Stevens."

With a deal at Columbia, Stevens thought Hepburn was bringing him something that could be made there.

Kate called on me and gave me this script to read. I said, "Kate, this is the only time in my life that I've read a motion picture script that I think is ready to go." [A script] that was excellent in every way. She said, "Well, why don't we make it?" I said, "What about the last part?" She said, "Well, the boys are working on it." And it didn't seem very difficult to finish it. I said, "That's a good idea. Bring it over to Columbia and we'll make it." She said, "I can't." I said, "Why?" She said, "Because I promised it to Louis B. Mayer. I thought you'd leave here and make a deal at Metro." I said, "Things are so pleasant for me I really shouldn't do it." So I don't know what happened, but I agreed to go to Metro and make the picture. And we hadn't had the last act written.

According to Lardner, the script was written initially with Clark Gable in mind. ("Because of M-G-M we thought Gable was more likely.") Hepburn, however, saw an opening when the postponement of *The Yearling* gave her a shot at Spencer Tracy. She had asked for him when making the deal for *Philadelphia Story*—Gable and Tracy both—and both, she was told, had turned the picture down. "I knew he was a brilliant actor," she wrote of Tracy. "And he represented just the sort of American male of that era. That's why I was anxious to have him do it." She had first laid eyes on

---

* Having taken part in the reorganization of the Screen Writers Guild in 1937, Ring Lardner, Jr., had been branded a radical by M-G-M East Coast story editor William Fadiman. Hepburn's keeping the authorship of the untitled treatment a secret was partly a negotiation tactic, partly to keep Lardner's name from scotching the deal.

him at the Harris Theatre during a performance of *The Last Mile* ("a remarkable show") and had been captivated by him ever since *Captains Courageous,* a performance she described as "shattering."

"I don't think Spencer had any idea who I was. I don't think he was that much of a movie fan." Actually, they already had appeared together in other media, so Tracy was certainly well aware of her. In 1933 they shared a two-page pictorial spread ("*Screenland*'s Double Honor Page"), Tracy posed with Colleen Moore, Hepburn opposite with Douglas Fairbanks, Jr. In 1938 Walt Disney put them on screen together in *Mother Goose Goes Hollywood,* a seven-minute cartoon which had Tracy fishing Freddie Bartholomew from the ocean while Hepburn, all jaw and cheekbones, circled them with an outboard motor, dressed as Bo-Peep and looking for her sheep.

Tracy was on vacation when Joe Mankiewicz put the idea to him. Based on what little he had seen of Hepburn, he didn't think it would work. She could play screwball, as she had opposite Cary Grant, and she could play earnest parts like Terry Randall in *Stage Door,* but *Woman of the Year*—Joe's title—was the sort of comedy at which Carole Lombard and Rosalind Russell excelled. Hepburn, he had heard, was difficult and wore pants all the time. (He thought she was a lesbian, Hepburn would later note with some amusement.) David O. Selznick, who was responsible for bringing her to RKO in 1932, spoke of a "curious kind of masculine drive" that was off-putting to a lot of men. "I never felt she was really unattractive. I think she just appeals to certain people." It was only after Tracy had been persuaded to see *The Philadelphia Story*—Hepburn's first true glamour girl part—that all his reservations fell away and he agreed to the assignment.

Tracy returned to the studio on a hot and humid August day, still smarting from the *Jekyll and Hyde* notices and eager to see the picture cut as drastically as possible. He and Mankiewicz were exiting the Thalberg Building—which Joe had dubbed the Iron Lung, the air-conditioned administration building where "paralytic minds were at work"—when they encountered Hepburn on her way in. "I have no idea where she might have been going," said Mankiewicz. "She stopped as we stopped. I said, 'Well, it's certainly high time you two knew each other.' " Hepburn was in slacks, wearing no makeup, her angular architecture—which caused one detractor to remark, "Throw a hat at her and wherever it hits it will hang"—on full display. Her eyes were a pale, nearly colorless blue-gray, her skin drawn tightly across her freckled face. She affected an illusion of height, which gave her a psychological advantage over a lot of men, not simply her costars. "Spencer was five-eleven, I was five seven and a half," she said. "I wore very high heels." She always disputed what Joe Mankiewicz remembered her as saying as they stood on the landing that led to the guard's gate and the lot beyond: "I might be a little tall for you, Mr. Tracy."

"I wouldn't have been dumb enough to say what I [supposedly] said to him," she asserted decades later—and she had a point, given how badly she wanted Tracy to be in the picture. According to Hepburn, there was instead an awkward silence. "I couldn't think of anything to say, so I said, 'Sorry I've got these high heels on. When we do the movie, I'll be careful about what I wear.'"

It wasn't quite the wholesale emasculation Mankiewicz recalled, but it had much the same effect. "And Spencer's just sort of eyeing her. He did that, and she didn't know at the time that he was going to pay her back. But I spoke up and said, 'Don't worry, Kate. He'll cut you down to size.' And she smiled and walked on. And we walked on." Said Hepburn, "I think he thought I was awful. And he said [to Joe], 'She has dirty fingernails. Her hands are dirty. And she's bossy.' That was his impression of me. Not that I was too tall. I think he just found me rather unattractive and disappointing. And thought: 'My God, what am I stuck with?'"

They proceeded, said Mankiewicz, to study each other's pictures, and Stevens' first rushes betrayed a softening in Hepburn's normally strident delivery, while Tracy seemed to be upping his energy level a notch. "There they were," said Mankiewicz, "imitating each other." At first Hepburn fretted she would be "too sweet" in the part. "Katie," said Stevens, "you get out there and be as sweet as you can be. You'll still be plenty nasty." Then she objected to Stevens' introductory image of her, a generous sampling of leg from Tracy's perspective, the first genuine cheesecake shot of her career. "It's not like crossing your legs in front of a man," Stevens argued, painfully aware of her lack of credentials as a movie sexpot. "You don't know your leg is showing. But he sees it. And the audience sees it. And everybody remembers it and forgives you when you are *not* being feminine."

Hepburn was not an instinctive actor. She questioned everything, debated everything, would happily have rehearsed the same scene all day if she could. The director's guidance—the director's discipline—was essential to her delivering her best work. Tracy was just the opposite. He talked very little about the character he was playing, did his scenes, and rarely, if ever, relied on the director. Where Hepburn was constantly leaping into the void, Tracy was watching, observing, taking in what she and the other members of the cast were doing. "Acting to me," he once said to Sylvia Sidney, "is always reacting."

"We never rehearsed together," Hepburn said. "He hated to do more than one take. I never cared how many takes I did. That was curious. But Spencer's peak concentration was the first take. And it was usually the best." She could remember an early scene in the back room of Pinkie Peters' tavern—modeled on Bleeck's, the famous newsmen's hangout underneath the *Herald Tribune* building in New York—where Sam and Tess are getting to know one another. "Spencer had the most extraordinary technique. I mean, he was so natural you thought he'd blown. And I was hoping he'd like me. So I was struggling to be very easy and very with it, and I knocked over a glass of water. And I saw him take his handkerchief out of the pocket and start to dry it up. So I took the table napkin and dried a little bit off, and then disappeared under the table to dry the rest of it. I thought: The old son of a gun. I'll show him. I'm not really as silly as I look. So we went right on playing the scene."

Tracy and Hepburn got to know each other in much the same way, having dinner one night ten days into production. The conversation came around to *Dr. Jekyll and Mr. Hyde,* which Hepburn had made a point of seeing.

"Very interesting," she said.

"Oh no—no—nothing—rotten," he said. "I just can't do that sort of thing. It's like constructing a dummy and then trying to breathe life into it. I like to be the dummy myself, and then make people—force people—to believe that I'm whatever I want them to believe. Inside out—instead of outside in. No makeup."

She studied his face. "His ears stuck out. And he had old lion's eyes. And he had a wonderful head of hair. And a sort of ruddy skin, really like mine. I mean, he was not as freckled as I am, but he was ruddy. And . . . [a] nice mouth." Both were at loose ends in terms of relationships. Ring Lardner knew that Gar Kanin was "kind of in love" with Hepburn and remembered her once asking whether she should marry him. "I think he probably realized it was a very unlikely thing with Kate. Although, as I said, she did say to me, 'What do you think?' I don't think she ever took it too seriously or that she was in love with him." And Tracy had been to San Francisco with Ingrid Bergman not long before the start of the film, but now Bergman was off in New York with her husband and daughter.

There was a surprising amount they had in common. Both had thought about careers in medicine, and both had influential fathers who didn't take the theatre seriously as a vocation. As kids, both loved movies—westerns in particular—and both staged amateur performances for the neighbors. Hepburn displayed real talent as an actor at Bryn Mawr, just as Tracy had at Ripon. Both got their professional starts in stock, and both came to Hollywood expecting to go back to Broadway. Hepburn did, disastrously in *The Lake,* spectacularly in *The Philadelphia Story.* Tracy, of course, never had. The Theatre Guild still wanted him for *The Devil's Disciple*—and there was talk of Eugene O'Neill's new play, *The Iceman Cometh*—but Metro complicated things by insisting on first refusal and the right to put in money. Similarly, Hepburn was aiming to do *Saint Joan* for the Guild and wanted Orson Welles to direct. Within days, Philip K.

Katharine Hepburn's attraction to him was immediate and intense. Director George Stevens takes note. (PATRICIA MAHON COLLECTION)

Scheuer's column in the *Times* carried an item: "Katharine Hepburn, a lady who wastes no time, has apparently communicated her enthusiasm for the stage to Spencer Tracy . . . Now he says he may appear in a play with Katie."

They settled into a comfortable pattern of working with one another, Hepburn considering every possible nuance of a given scene while Tracy gently heckled her from the sidelines. "I think he was so steady," she said, "and I was so volatile, that we exasperated each other. And we challenged each other, and that was the fun of it." When John Chapman visited the set on September 12, Hepburn was at a rostrum rehearsing a speech, while Tracy was sitting out in the audience, haw-hawing loudly and doing his best to throw her off. "We are told that this is the big new friendly feud. Spence and Miss H. had never worked together before, and each at first was a little in awe of the other; but now they are in the happy Hollywood state of amiable insult. 'We will now pause,' announces Tracy, 'while Miss Hepburn rewrites the script.' "

George Stevens, meanwhile, was demonstrating a bit of wordless business, Tracy's character having happened onto the speaker's platform, unsure of where he was and unable to get off. Tracy, Hepburn soon decided, was modeling his performance on the deadpan mannerisms of their esteemed director.

"I never met a man I knew as quick as I knew Spence," Stevens commented.

> And he felt the same about me. So he'd come in a little early, and he'd come over in my little office and sit down and we'd talk, or I'd go in his dressing room. And all of a sudden I hear a knock on the door, and the door opens and it's Katharine. She says, "What are you two conspiring about?" "Well," he says, "you know, Kate, I like guidance on things . . . And this man is our director, and I'd like to get some guidance from him. And I asked him a question: How can I be such a damn fool to get into a picture with a woman producer and *her* director? How can I be such a dumb bastard as that, Katharine? And you know what he tells me? He says, Well, Spencer, I can't understand it. That sounds pretty stupid to me. How can you do it? Can you give me a good reason? he says. No I can't." It took me a long time to get the answer: He wanted to make a picture with Kate Hepburn.

In *Woman of the Year,* Sam Craig and Tess Harding start out as rivals, sparring with each other in their respective columns. The publisher of the paper calls them in to make peace, and Sam is startled by the cool, determined beauty of his adversary. Out of earshot, he asks her to a game at Yankee Stadium—her first—and patiently explains the ins and outs of baseball. She reciprocates, and he walks into a postbroadcast cocktail party in which none of the distinguished guests appears to speak English. Awkward and uncomfortable, Sam makes the best of it, then slips out the door. The next day, she asks him to drive her to the airport, and he finds himself onstage as she's delivering an address before a hall full of women. Their snatches of time together don't add up to much, and Sam can't tell what she's up to. As they reach LaGuardia, his dissatisfaction, as the script put it, "oozes out of every pore."

"What's the matter, Sam?"

"Nothing," he says.

"Sure?"

"Well, I dunno. I can't quite figure you out. What are you trying to prove? Why am I here?"

And when she catches her breath and says, "I thought you might want to kiss me good-bye," Tracy calmly takes it in, processes it, then turns himself away from the camera, ostensibly to glance down the terminal corridor, but also to make sure the most significant kiss of his entire career takes place completely out of sight of the audience. The camera moves in, Hepburn in profile as he draws her toward him, her lips apart, the moment of contact perfectly obscured by the brim of his cocked hat. It is brief but heartfelt, passionate and completely unencumbered by concerns of lighting, position, focus. It's the back of his head, her chin, the muffled soundtrack, their eyes laser-locked on each other as he releases her. It's as real as any kiss in the history of the medium, the look of astonishment on her face, the deadly serious look on his, screen acting at its finest . . . if it was acting.

"Mike Kanin and I were frequent visitors to the set," said Ring Lardner, "and what we saw happening there was the final blessing on the venture. When you write a love story, you hope that the actors will make it seem convincing, but you scarcely expect them to actually fall for each other. A familiar sight on a movie set comes when the director calls 'Cut!' and the two lovers withdraw abruptly from a tight embrace, briskly heading off in separate directions as if to emphasize the nothing-personal aspect of their physical contact. Kate and Spence wanted to be together off camera as well as on."

With Johnny attending school in Manhattan and Susie, now nine, still at Brentwood, there was little to occupy Louise beyond the running of the house. It was a gilded but solitary existence, broken only by her occasional visits with Audrey Caldwell, the former actress from Australia who was her closest friend and only true confidante. Spence was living at the Beverly Hills Hotel, making the picture, home Sundays and holidays. Carroll Tracy slipped quietly into the role of liaison between husband and wife, scheduling their times together as one might arrange meetings and conferences. With so much time on her hands, Louise began writing a book about her struggle to rear, educate, and mainstream a boy who was profoundly deaf, its purpose to give "a *complete* account of one family's experiences with a deaf child, to the end that other deaf children may prosper." The title she gave the book was *The Story of John*.

Louise Treadwell Tracy was a skilled and facile writer, and her words flowed with the same candor that distinguished her infrequent talks with the press. With her background in journalism, she was incapable of portraying an event inaccurately, nor could she temper her opinions in the name of diplomacy. She could avoid a subject altogether—Spence's infidelities, for example, even though the Loretta Young affair was a matter of public record—but once she chose to tackle something—public school administrators, clueless doctors, antique attitudes on the part of the public, and baseless misconceptions—she did so with a sharpness and conviction that were startling. "Unless I write as fully, as clearly and as honestly as I am capable of doing," she said, "my purpose has no hope of accomplishment."

And so she began her book with these words: "He was sleeping late that afternoon, too late. He probably would not want to go asleep again that night until long after he should. I would waken him. I went out onto the porch where he slept, and as I went, I called 'Johnny, Johnny, time to wake up.' He did not move."

Woman of the Year took almost nine weeks to shoot, finishing on Saturday, October 25, 1941. Louise was vacationing in Arizona, but if Spence was involved with Katharine Hepburn he didn't note anything about it in his datebook. He was still seeing Ingrid Bergman—had dined with her on the sixteenth—and it was about this time that Bergman's husband, Petter Lindstrom, prevented his wife from returning with Tracy to San Francisco to discuss "future roles." When Louise did get back from Phoenix, Spence drove her down to Balboa, and they spent the day looking at houses and boats. That evening they dined at Carroll's, where a frail Mother Tracy celebrated her sixty-sixth birthday.

Louise was in Palm Springs when *Woman of the Year* had its first preview on November 14. In the movie Tess and Sam are wed at a perfunctory ceremony, but the marriage veers spectacularly off course when she asks him what he'd think about having a child. He thinks, of course, that she is pregnant, only to discover that she's adopted a Greek orphan. "Two weeks ago they made me chairman of the Greek Refugee Committee and I accepted without thinking much about it. And then while you were away they held a meeting and some idiot suggested that I should take the first one."

The boy is already lost in the whirlwind of Tess' life, and Sam takes pity on him when there's no one to babysit on the night Tess is to be named America's Outstanding Woman of the Year over a nationwide radio hookup.

"Well," she says dismissively, "Chris will be all right, Sam. He's old enough and, besides, we'll be home before midnight."

"He can do a lot of crying in four hours," Sam shoots back.

Tracy's "business," Stevens observed, "is always behind his eyes. Whatever Spence does behind his eyes—if he thinks the audience should turn to his character, something takes place behind his eyes. You hear it in the sound of his voice. You see it in the direct look in his eyes. You know he's on and he's the man to be heard . . . It's just as authoritative as if he rapped on the table with a gavel."

Tess goes on to the banquet alone, and Sam, having made his stand, calmly returns the boy to the orphanage, where other children speak his language and he won't be trapped in an empty apartment. Sam completes the paperwork while the broadcast is on in the background, and when Tess returns to the apartment, her plaque under her arm and the press in tow, he is nowhere to be found.

Hepburn, during the writing of the script, suggested the climactic sequence the preview audience saw that night: Tess covers an upcoming prizefight for the missing Sam, while Sam can be found, in a game attempt at meeting his estranged spouse halfway, studying French and Spanish at Mademoiselle Sylvia's, a language parlor that Sam's friend Pinkie takes for a bordello. When he learns he's picked a washed-up fighter named Dunlap in the column Tess has so obligingly ghosted, Sam sprints from the building in a panic. ("Who did it? Who wrote that tripe?") At the fight, Tess materializes directly behind him and fesses up to the writing of the column. "We didn't know where you were. It had to be written." And then she tells him she hasn't been a woman or a wife or anything to him.

SAM
(with heavy skepticism)
And now you know just how to go about it?

TESS
(enthusiastically)
Yes, Sam . . . we'll move out of the
apartment, get a little house out of town
somewhere. I'll make it a real home, honest.
I'll learn how to take care of it . . . and you.

SAM
And you'll cook, sew, and order the
groceries? Drive me to the station every
morning?

TESS
(exultant now in the picture)
Yes, Sam—!

SAM
You're not making sense.

It was, said Ring Lardner, "one of those kind of it's-all-starting-over-again endings." The picture got over at preview, but only to a point. "And there was a lot of confusion," Hepburn admitted, "and a lot of slight—shall we say—unpleasantness. Anyway, they shot my end. And the minute my end came up at the preview, the interest dropped dead. So Mayer came to me and said, 'It was a wonderful preview.' And I said, 'Mr. Mayer, it was a great preview up to such and such, and then, at the end, which I'm totally responsible for, [it] laid an egg.' And he said, 'How much to fix it?' And I said, 'About two hundred thousand dollars.' And he said, 'Go ahead.' So I rushed back, and everyone was, you know, suggesting ends, ends, ends."

George Stevens had returned to Columbia, and it was Joe Mankiewicz who figured out what the picture needed. "Philip Barry wrote the definitive play about Kate," he said.

> About Kate. For Kate. *Philadelphia Story.* In which [there was] a woman so superb, so elevated in class, so intelligent, so accomplished, so everything, that she antagonized every woman in the audience, because this is superwoman. Philip Barry wrote the play in which she got her comeuppance, and the audience loved a comeuppance, loved her for taking it, and this was the start of Kate's second career. That formula, that needed element, in what was otherwise a woman so perfect that she could not be tolerated by the mass female audience . . .
>
> I called John Lee Mahin, who was a very good writer, and he and I and George Stevens, the director, sat down and I said, "Look, what I think this needs is what Phil Barry discovered . . ." and I devised this new ending in which she tries to make breakfast. This was a retake. And it was the equivalent of her being taken apart in *Philadelphia Story.*

Tracy was present at the November 14 preview but wasn't quite sure what to make of the audience's reaction. "Good, I think," he wrote in his book, a question mark accompanying the comment. Lardner, who wasn't there, thought the ending "too feminist" for Mayer and the studio brass. "The executives at M-G-M, including Joe Mankiewicz, supported by George Stevens, felt that the woman character, having been so strong throughout, should be somehow subjugated and tamed, in effect."

Hepburn, who had been in on the development process almost from the beginning, wasn't happy with the new ending and wasn't shy about saying so. "Mayer was away," John Lee Mahin remembered, "and Sam Katz was in charge of the studio. Hepburn came into Sam's office; *wham,* she threw what I had written on the desk and said, 'That's the biggest bunch of crap I've ever read!' Sam was bewildered; he was looking at Stevens. Tracy was stuck on her, but he knew this ending was for him and not for her, so he was sitting there and he wasn't saying a word. Finally, Sam said, 'George, what do you think?' George didn't even answer. 'Sam,' he just said, 'why don't you put [up] that apartment on Stage 3, we'll shoot it in the morning.' And Sam said, 'Oh, that's fine, that's fine.' "

Stevens, whose career began with two-reel comedies, envisioned a sequence devoid of dialogue, Tess managing her kitchen duties with clattering incompetence, Sam looking on with scarcely a grimace, toast shooting skyward, the coffee boiling over, an innertube of a waffle threatening ominously to burst. "Now *there*," commented Tracy, "is a real meaty hunk of business. I *look*." Hepburn was similarly bewildered: "I've never done anything like this in my life. Honestly, George, I don't know a thing about gag comedy." Stevens remained adamant, promising his two leads the revised sequence would never be shown if it wasn't any good. "The first ending we shot was wrong," he told them. "Why? Because it didn't put over the idea we were shooting for. Kate *talked* about being a good wife. Audiences don't want talk. They want action. In this new finish, Kate doesn't talk. She *acts* like a good wife as nearly as she can. She tries to cook. To the point of being ridiculous. But she's trying."

The new material took eleven days to shoot, Stevens, formerly a gag man for Laurel and Hardy, having worked out an array of mechanical gags that were, he declared, "foolproof." He gave Hepburn what he called "W. C. Fields business"—trying to button her dress, struggling to keep her straps from slipping, juggling the various kitchen gadgets. But what really made the scene work, Mankiewicz said, were "the kind of looks, or non-looks, of Tracy. The other directors would have had Tracy react. Instead of which, George had Tracy play it the way George would, gives this quiet look, that Indian impassivity, while Kate made a ninny of herself making toast. That's George."

To make the retakes for *Woman of the Year,* Tracy broke off from shooting *Tortilla Flat,* his first picture for Victor Fleming since the *Yearling* debacle. Tracy's relationship with the book's author, John Steinbeck, dated from a late-night encounter at Chasen's in the early summer of 1939, when Steinbeck was reeling from the uproar created by the publication, just two months earlier, of *The Grapes of Wrath.* The men talked until 2:30, comparing notes on the odd burden of fame and parting with the hope they would soon work together.

That fall, as Tracy was preparing to play Thomas Edison, he and Fleming approached Steinbeck with the notion of filming *The Red Pony* at M-G-M, an idea to which the author, now flush with royalty money, was decidedly cool. Steinbeck was suspicious of Hollywood in general and Metro in particular, having just seen the first screen adaptation of one of his books, *Of Mice and Men,* spectacularly filmed by director Lewis Milestone at the tiny Culver City studio of Hal Roach. "There was great unity," he wrote, "because only one man touched it, and that was Milestone." That sort of unity, he argued, was impossible at the producer-dominated mechanism that was M-G-M.

A subject far closer to Steinbeck's heart was a six-week collecting trip to the Gulf of California he was planning with marine biologist Ed Ricketts. He described their plans to Tracy one night over dinner, saying they planned to write a book to pay for the trip and invited him along.* Having just started *I Take This Woman* for the third time, Tracy was in the mood for a long break and volunteered to secure a boat for the expedition. Three days later, he drove Steinbeck, his wife Carol, and Louise to San Pedro to see the *We're Here,* which looked to be ideal. Then the owner wanted too much money and the deal collapsed. "I look on you with peculiar and strong affection," Steinbeck wrote Tracy, "which must be the result of some profound recognition. I hope it will remain like that. Meanwhile, think about joining us at Guaymas."

Louise was all for it, but Spence, as it turned out, could manage only four weeks between the finish of *Edison, the Man,* and the start of *Boom Town* and had to settle for a short trip to Phoenix instead. In September 1940 Steinbeck had Tracy to the house he had built at the Biddle Ranch, Los Gatos, where he was preparing the narration for a documentary that had been shot in Mexico over the spring. Codirected by Herbert Klein and Alexander Hammid, *The Forgotten Village* told the story of a cholera outbreak in the rural village of Santiago and the clash that takes place between the healing traditions of the village elders and modern medical science. Steinbeck asked Tracy if he would narrate the completed film and was delighted when he said that he would. "He has a great heart," Steinbeck wrote his friend, actor Max Wagner. "I knew he would want to do it."

Tracy had just started *Jekyll and Hyde* when he saw a rough cut of *The Forgotten Village* in a screening room at M-G-M. He professed to like the film but was guarded and, Steinbeck thought, "a little afraid" of Herbert Klein's direction. Steinbeck came down to Los Angeles, but by the time he arrived, Klein was ill and in the hospital and Tracy had been told he couldn't do the narration, suggesting to him that the studio had played along just long enough to get *Jekyll and Hyde* under way. Steinbeck blamed Eddie Mannix for the double cross and briefly plotted revenge, intending to "blast" Metro's forthcoming production of *Tortilla Flat* and wondering in a letter to his agent if they couldn't make trouble over the similarities between *The Red Pony* and *The Yearling,* which extended to the name of the boys (which in

---

* The book that resulted from Steinbeck's excursion was *Sea of Cortez.*

both cases was Jody). "If we don't want money we might easily get a court order," Steinbeck suggested. "And I want to plague them as much as I can."

The flap over *Forgotten Village* was allowed to die down—Burgess Meredith replaced Tracy as the film's narrator—and an olive branch was extended in the form of an offer to adapt *Tortilla Flat* to the screen. "I had a letter yesterday from your charming bosses asking whether I would like to collaborate on *Tortilla Flat,* in which, it was said, you were to be," Steinbeck wrote Tracy in mid-June. "I replied that I would like to very much if I could be happy doing it—my happiness requiring control of the script, a lot of money, and the right to work somewhere but Hollywood."

Steinbeck couldn't see how anything more than a series of blackouts could be made from his tales of idyllic poverty in the hills above the California coast. He had already seen one failed attempt at dramatization—a Broadway play that lasted all of five performances—and doubted anything better could come from a film version. When he sold the screen rights to Paramount in 1935 he needed the money, and he wasn't kidding when he offered Metro, which acquired the rights in 1940, $10,000 to simply take it off the market. Producer Sam Zimbalist put John Lee Mahin on the script, and the two men were in Monterey, soaking up the local atmosphere, when they encountered Steinbeck at a local bar where the fishermen and soldiers drank.

"What are you doing to my story?" the author demanded.

"We've butched it up plenty," came the reply.

What they had done, other than to remove a lot of the sex, petty theft, and drunkenness of the book, was to change the ending, focusing on the "poison of possessions" and letting Steinbeck's romantic hero, Danny, live only to have him married off—another form of death among the paisanos of the novel. Much to everyone's surprise, Steinbeck asked to see the script and actually liked it, telling Mahin that he'd made the story "a hell of a lot more fun" by taking all the "drama and message" out of it. Over a midnight session at Chasen's, Steinbeck told Tracy much the same thing and blessed the making of the film, at least to the extent that he could approve of anything Metro did with his material.

Steinbeck's conniving Pilon was not unlike Manuel in that the role required both makeup and an accent (not to mention singing), but Tracy never resisted the assignment as he had *Captains Courageous* and had, in fact, been linked to the project for more than a year. The accent seemed to flow naturally from the script's Runyonesque dialogue, suggesting the mixed blood of the paisanos and the notion they spoke both English and Spanish in an equally unique manner. His skin was darkened as it had been for Manuel, but his hair was left uncurled, hidden as it was under a battered hat with a white poppy poked carelessly into its band.

Victor Fleming exuded an unquestionable authority—Tracy always addressed him as "Mr. Fleming" in front of the cast and crew—and the decorum on the set was exemplary. The shoot was confined almost entirely to indoor sets, the largest, on M-G-M's Stage 3, being a fanciful exterior designed by Paul Groesse, weedy yards and rickety fences and a dirt road leading off to a panoramic view of Monterey and the ocean beyond.

In a rare stab at ethnic fidelity, Zimbalist tried borrowing Rita Hayworth to play Dolores Engracia "Sweets" Ramirez and then, failing that, dropped Hedy Lamarr into the part about the same time John Garfield was secured on loan from Warner Bros. for the role of Danny. Once Lamarr was set for the picture, Tracy conspired to stash his ever-present box of chocolates—which usually occupied the third drawer of his dressing room desk—in her dressing room instead, figuring that casual visits to a frequent costar would not be nearly as scrutinized as trips to his own on-set trailer, where his weight was carefully monitored and he endured a constant razzing from the crew over his addiction to sweets.

"I can see," said John Erskine, "that the kind of truth which only the actor can convey is something the audience will recognize out of their experience. But, to secure this effect of convincing reality, should pictures give us any particular kind of story or character which we don't get now?"

Tracy thought a moment. "I doubt it," he said finally. "We get all kinds of characters, don't we? The only restriction is in what we are permitted to say about them."

"But that's the same thing as not being allowed to portray them."

"Not quite the same thing. If all types of characters are already permissible on the screen, we shall gradually win the privilege of understanding them."

"You're not interested, then, in people of any particular economic group?"

He looked surprised. "Why should I be? I am interested in people. They may be in one group today and in another tomorrow."

Still, Erskine thought Tracy was interested, more than he realized, in characters rising "from a lower to a higher condition" and that, from talking to him, he would always prefer people who could survive their successes and "bear their weight of human sorrows." He was also sure that although Tracy was more interested in interpreting people than in putting over any social or economic theories, his interpretations suggested a politically liberal point of view, something that was implicit in the generosity of his own spirit.

"But," said Erskine, "the films which we seem to demand cannot possibly cover the whole range of a mature person's experience. Our pictures must be growing toward a real presentation of life, but only a small part of our life is presented."

Tracy agreed. "I like to believe the audience will gradually accept more and demand more; then the screen will give it to them. That's the tendency now, don't you think?"

"You speak of the audience," said Erskine, "and I admit that theirs is the controlling influence, but why shouldn't screen actors of the first rank demand something too? In other arts—architecture, sculpture, painting—the great artists set the pace for the public."

"In those other arts," Tracy replied, "the leaders can wait for the public to catch up. But the actor must speak to his public immediately during the performance. However, there is no reason why we shouldn't exercise more leadership than we do. I believe there is a gradual pressure in that direction. But I think it should be leadership in artistic ideals, rather than in political or economic or social theories, since pictures are the art of the people and should give a real portrait of them rather than of the individual artist."

"Shouldn't a film give more than a portrait of individual characters in themselves? Shouldn't we be able to see from a number of individual screen characters something that we'd all recognize as a true account of life, the general principles of it, the inevitable relations of cause and consequence?"

"And you don't think the screen gives those principles?"

"I don't. Do you?"

"I wouldn't say the screen is entirely false to life, but I agree that it sometimes dodges the deeper principles, sometimes soft-pedals what you call cause and effect."

"To that extent," asked Erskine, "aren't pictures selling out the audiences?"

"Maybe the audience isn't fooled," Tracy replied. "Perhaps they are willing to accept a certain amount of nonsense, as they accept a dramatic convention, in exchange for something else which they really enjoy."

"But great dramatists don't feed the world nonsense. If audiences habitually find their entertainment in stories that aren't true, they'll lose the ability to find pleasure in stories which are. Shan't we end up after much picture-seeing by believing that the homes of the rich in America are as the pictures portray them, and that the poor almost never occur, and the middle class, unless it is comical, never exists? That's the picture our screen asks us to recognize as true, isn't it?"

Tracy laughed. "You're a little hard on us, but you and I don't disagree. I hope pictures will tell the whole truth of life while I'm still on the screen."

CHAPTER 18

I've Found the Woman I Want

Katharine Houghton Hepburn came from the kind of family that Spencer Tracy, in another life, might have wished for himself. Her paternal grandfather was an Episcopalian minister in Hanover County, Virginia, her grandmother a Powell, the family having lost a three-thousand-acre plantation during the Civil War despite having freed their slaves decades earlier. The Reverend Sewell Stavely Hepburn was known for his dramatic flair at the pulpit, a strain of talent that may have passed to his eldest granddaughter. Her father, Thomas Norval Hepburn, was similarly gifted in oratory and, like Tracy, honed his skills in college. A born healer, Dr. Hepburn was reputed to have been Connecticut's first urologist. In 1910 he became secretary of the Connecticut Social Hygiene Association, capping a crusade against venereal disease initiated by his wife, the former Katharine Martha Houghton.

Mrs. Hepburn was descended from money and position yet always held the less privileged in her sympathies and spent her life fighting for the vote, broad access to birth control and family planning services, and the right of free expression in all its permutations. She was a graduate of Bryn Mawr, where she took a master's degree in 1900. Four years later she married Tom Hepburn, who was then in his final year of medical school. Not wanting to practice in a big city, Tom took her to Hartford, where he became an intern and later a resident at the hospital.

Her activism dated from a 1908 talk she attended on the struggle to gain voting rights for women, and was further galvanized by the great English suffragist Emmeline Pankhurst, who came to Hartford the following year and was a guest in the Hepburn home. After Mrs. Pankhurst's visit, she formed local and statewide organizations to press for the right to vote and lauded the subsequent ratification of the Nineteenth Amendment for raising the legal status of women from "children, idiots, and criminals" to "self-respecting adults." Her interest in legalized birth control dated from 1921, when she became a familiar figure around the state capital, urging repeal of a restrictive 1869 law, declaring, with typical directness, that a woman "ought to have some say in the number of children she has." She became a close friend of the pioneering social activist Margaret Sanger, and if she ever feared ostracism for her and her husband's activities, she never said so, and she encouraged an unconventional spirit in each of her six children.

Kathy, the second eldest, was born in May 1907. She was a well-balanced child, quick-witted and creative, with the intensity of her mother, the good looks of her father, and the boundless energy of both. She grew into a spirited competitor, mastering golf, tennis, and swimming, and learned early on to go after whatever she wanted, which, as she grew into puberty, included men who interested or otherwise attracted her. It became family lore, later recounted in her autobiography, that she pursued the poet H. Phelps Putnam with such fervor that her father took Putnam aside and, likening his daughter to "a young bull about to charge," threatened to shoot him if he laid hands on her. She posed nude for the camera while still a student at Bryn Mawr, married at twenty-one, and went determinedly her own way at twenty-five, having taken Ludlow Ogden Smith as her husband and then cast him aside when he was no longer of value in her drive to become a star. "Kate," said George Stevens, "didn't absolutely have to have a husband as most women do. She could get things done without turning her problem over to a man to succeed with or fail with."

In love with herself (as she readily admitted), Hepburn took a succession of beaux, graduating to some of the most accomplished and best-known men in America. "I've never discovered any evidence whatsoever that she was a lesbian," said her niece, actress-playwright Katharine Houghton. "She had many more affairs with men than people know about, always rich and/or powerful men that could benefit her career in some way. I do think she really loved Spencer as much as she was capable of loving anyone besides herself. But for her the great aphrodisiac was POWER, not sex, and I believe if she were asked, she would concur."

Agent Leland Hayward and industrialist Howard Hughes were two of her more serious involvements, but she generally seemed to approach the opposite sex as if roaming the aisles of a fancy toy store, initially delighting in the gyrations of a clever mechanism, then tearing it apart to see how it worked. "Leland and Howard were both sweet and fun," she said, "but I cared more about me than I cared about *them*." Hayward memorably described her on his deathbed as "The best. God, yes." And Hughes stayed in touch long after he had disappeared from public sight.

Press reports not long after Hepburn's arrival in Los Angeles had her marrying actor Joel McCrea, and John Ford became a particular favorite in the mid-thirties, when he directed her in *Mary of Scotland*. Although linked superficially to Garson Kanin at the time she met Tracy, she was living for the summer with sculptor Robert McKnight, whom she had known since the age of fifteen. "Why in the world don't I marry him?" she wondered. "I know him . . . I like him . . . we both like tennis." She was attracted to strong, decisive men with outsize personalities, ofttimes married, frequently alcoholic. "I always liked bad eggs, *always,* always—and always attracted them. I had a lot of energy and looked as if I was (and I *was*) hard to get— wasn't mad about the male sex—perfectly independent, never had any intention of getting married, wanted to paddle my own canoe, didn't want anyone to pay my way."

There was something mystical about the Tracy name. One of her first memories of New York was sitting on a tenement balcony watching the Tracy tugboats go by. Then later came the role of Tracy Lord in *The Philadelphia Story.* There can be no doubt that she targeted Spencer Tracy as the project that became *Woman of the Year* took shape, but it's unlikely that falling for him was part of the plan. It happened so fast that it took her by surprise, and it must have been Tracy's initial reticence combined with his willingness to play along—albeit on his own terms—that girded her resolve. "We started our first picture together and I knew right away that I found him irresistible. Just exactly that, irresistible."

Tracy, of course, was at the top of his game, outdistancing even Clark Gable as an attraction at the American box office.* There was no longer any chasing, as there had been for Loretta Young, and women routinely tumbled for a man of his stature. Joe Mankiewicz could remember the sight of one script girl nudging another as they observed Tracy in casual conversation with a third. "He'd have them off their feet like THAT!" Mankiewicz said, snapping his fingers for emphasis. Gable once observed a similar scene in the company of unit publicist Emily Torchia. "You know," he said in mock indignation, "Spence can outdo me with these girls!"

"He did have quite a line of conquests," Claire Trevor acknowledged.

---

* Gable, however, was considerably more popular internationally.

"Women loved him. He was a *very* attractive man." Tracy knew where to go to avoid being seen by the press, especially when he was with somebody well known, and when he was spotted alone with, for example, Ingrid Bergman, it was never at a popular nightspot like Ciro's and was, therefore, never reported. "To me," said Sheilah Graham, "it was something you didn't print. Because I had been warned very severely never to print stories of married producers and directors who had extra-marital affairs with girls . . . My boss John Wheeler [founder of the North American Newspaper Alliance] said, 'Never write about the romances of married men.' And I stuck to that quite scrupulously."

In 1940 Tracy was seen publicly with Olivia de Havilland on at least two occasions, a fact that got reported in the columns precisely because it wasn't presumed to be an affair. The actress' official date, it was explained, was Tim Durant, a buddy of Tracy's from the Uplifters Club who had suddenly taken ill. The two men had grown increasingly close in the late 1930s and Durant, for a while, assumed Carroll's duties as a traveling companion following the IRS debacle of 1939. "He was not only a great artist," Durant said of Tracy, "but a fine friend. We had much in common and many good times together . . . We stopped off in New York on the way to England, where a crowd of fifty spent all night outside Claridge's Hotel to await the chance of seeing Spencer the next morning."

A tall, good-looking guy who was generally regarded as one of the best-dressed men in Hollywood, Thomas W. "Tim" Durant was a stockbroker in the mid-1920s when he met and married Adelaide Brevoort Close, the eldest daughter of famed cereal heiress Marjorie Merriweather Post. When they divorced, Durant, an unrepentant womanizer, was awarded their place on Bedford Drive, a main house and two guest houses on several acres of prime Beverly Hills real estate. He rented out the main house for a tidy sum and took up residency in the larger of the two guest houses, a secluded bachelor pad tastefully furnished in early American. Entered off an alleyway, the other guest house—presumably a servants' quarters—was often borrowed by friends for trysts. Tracy stayed there when he couldn't bear the drive to Encino, and Durant once told actor-producer Norman Lloyd the Tracy-Hepburn affair was conducted in that house.

Durant worked for Charlie Chaplin, officially as a writer but more specifically as a personal assistant, and he brought Tracy into Chaplin's circle, where he frequently served as a fourth for tennis. He was also well connected socially and introduced Tracy to, among others, Harry Crocker, of the San Francisco banking family, and Betsey Cushing Roosevelt, the president's erstwhile daughter-in-law, with whom the two men stayed when visiting East Hampton. Durant was likely Tracy's closest confidant in the early days of the Hepburn relationship, and although she was certain and unwavering in her attraction to him, he was likely dubious of anything more than a quick and memorable liaison. "I think that you imagined I was a lesbian," Hepburn wrote in an epistolary chapter years after his death. "But not for long. Did you."

In him she saw a man as solid and admirable as her own father, warm and witty and full of unexpected observations. "They were the only two men in her life who really challenged her," Katharine Houghton commented, "and she felt comforted by the boundaries they set for her. My grandfather was a more classically handsome man than Spencer, but they both exuded a vigorous and not-to-be-messed-with male energy." The balance Tracy brought to her life was oddly liberating in that she could be as bossy and as much a pain in the ass as she pleased, and she knew that when she had gone too far, when she had provoked and jabbered and carried on past all reasonable tolerance, he would simply say, as no man had said to her before, "Kate, shut up!" It was an accommodation he taught her, one she had always sought from others but had never before given herself.

Hepburn was like Louise in that they were both athletic, both actresses of some attainment, both plainspoken in a world where directness didn't always count as a virtue. But where Hepburn could be confrontational, Louise was not, and where Kate saw a man in need of love and maintenance, Louise saw a job she was no longer able to do. What remained of the marriage was trust, friendship, and a sense of shared experience that was well-nigh unbreakable, but it was no longer a thing that was sustainable or mutually nourishing. Spence had outlets—his career, women, his small circle of friends. Louise had Johnny, Susie, her book, and her horses. She had the world-famous Tracy name, but it wasn't nearly enough for a woman of her drive and intellect.

The relationship with Katharine Hepburn contributed to a time of almost unprecedented turmoil for Spencer Tracy; not since 1933–34 had his life been so completely shaken by a sequence of events. He was already deeply involved with Hepburn—more than he had been with any woman since Loretta Young—when he made his only network appearance with Ingrid Bergman on the *Lux Radio Theatre*. Kate and he were doing retakes for *Woman of the Year*, and she was plainly jealous of the fact that he was seeing Bergman again, even in a strictly professional capacity. ("Kate never felt she was beautiful enough for him," said Katharine Houghton.) Spence wasn't himself that night, and Bergman later characterized the broadcast as a fiasco, noting that Tracy read his part "as though he was appearing at gunpoint." Kay Brown went so far as to advise Bergman that she shouldn't do radio anymore, and Selznick, who thought Bergman lost a lot of her appeal over the air, agreed.*

Filming concluded in a miasma of shock after the Japanese attack on Pearl Harbor. Tracy summarized events in his datebook: "Air raid warnings L.A. Enemy planes sighted over San Francisco. Japs gain big advantage: Bombed Manilla, captured Wake Island, Guam Island." On Monday, December 8, President Roosevelt went before a joint session of Congress to call for a declaration of war against Japan. Three days later Adolf Hitler furiously declared war on the United States. Kate, committed to the new Philip Barry play, returned east to spend the holidays in Connecticut with her family, leaving Spence in California with Vic Fleming and the cast of *Tortilla Flat.* Johnny arrived home from school on the nineteenth, and Christmas was spent at the ranch with Carroll and Dorothy and Mother Tracy, rain falling late into the day.

He marked three years and eight months of sobriety as the new year began. The first days of 1942 were filled with work and news of war. He had a rare day off on January 6—Fleming was ill—and spent it playing tennis at the ranch with Louise. The next day he attended a bachelor luncheon thrown by L. B. Mayer for Mickey Rooney, who, at the age of twenty-one, was marrying starlet Ava Gardner. Ribald advice was offered the bridegroom by the likes of Clark Gable and Robert Taylor, then Tracy struck a more ominous note when he told the story of the sink and the marbles: "You'll never have a year like your first year. Every time you make love to her then, you put a marble in the sink. After that, every time you make love to her, you take a marble out. But Mickey, you know what? You'll never empty the sink."

Tortilla Flat was behind schedule, the rushes listless and uninspired. Tracy was looking forward to being free of it when, on January 11, he formally accepted the chairmanship of the Motion Picture Committee for Celebration of the President's Birthday, an event that kicked off the yearly door-to-door fund drive of the National Foundation for Infantile Paralysis— commonly known as the March of Dimes. Without mentioning his own son's battle with poliomyelitis, he posed for photos with Bette Davis, enlisting her help for a national radio appeal and the traditional birthday ball to

---

* Tracy subsequently canceled an appearance on CBS' *Silver Theater* and, with one minor exception, never again appeared on a commercial radio broadcast. "I think the reason he isn't on the radio more is because it makes him so nervous," Peggy Gough commented at the time.

be held in Washington at the end of the month. "We of America may well be thankful that we may pause amid this world conflict to hear the pleas of these little sufferers," Tracy said in a statement for the cameras. "We are their only hope."

His work for the foundation was interrupted less than a week later when, on a windy Friday night, Carole Lombard disappeared in the air over southern Nevada. She and Clark Gable had married in March 1939—as soon as his divorce from Ria Gable became final—and for the first time in his life Gable married for something other than the furtherance of his career. "They're suited to each other," Tracy said approvingly at the time of their first anniversary. "They're two regular people. And from where I sit, it looks like love."

And indeed it did—in spite of Gable's continued philandering. The couple bought and refurbished Raoul Walsh's Encino spread, a two-story Connecticut farmhouse on twenty acres of land about five minutes from the Tracy ranch. They all golfed together, Carole gamely lugging her own clubs, Eddie Mannix usually completing the foursome, and socialized occasionally—holiday parties and the like. Lombard was genuinely solicitous of Spence, sensitive to his predicament amid the free-flowing scotch of the Gable household. "Carole Lombard was a very big star in her own right," said Adela Rogers St. Johns, "much loved by Hollywood. But everybody who went to the rambling white house overlooking the San Fernando Valley knew it was Clark's house. Carole had created and maintained it to suit him. It was the most joyous house I was ever in."

Tracy liked Lombard, liked her sense of humor and her ability to make Gable laugh. It was as if her appeal stood completely apart from the fact that she was also a world-class beauty, a gifted comedienne, and a fine dramatic actress. She made the ideal home for her husband, doing what he did, liking what he liked. Lombard had been east selling U.S. Series E Savings Bonds—now widely being referred to as war bonds—and had reportedly raised $2.5 million in her home state of Indiana when, eager to return west to her husband and a new picture, she muscled her way onto a TWA Skysleeper bound for Burbank, accompanied by her mother and M-G-M publicist Otto Winkler. After an unscheduled refueling stop in Las Vegas, the plane took off in clear skies on the last—and reputedly easiest—leg of an eighteen-hour trip that had begun in Indianapolis at four in the morning. All authorities had to go on were eyewitness accounts of an explosion and flames along the steep eastern face of Mt. Potosi, thirty-two miles southwest of the airport. Gable, who was awaiting his wife's arrival at home, was removed to Las Vegas on a chartered flight, where he was dissuaded from making the arduous climb to the crash site by Eddie Mannix and publicist Ralph Wheelwright, both of whom went in his stead. He holed up at the new El Rancho Vegas resort on Highway 91, and it was there he learned there had been no survivors.

Tracy worked most of Saturday at the studio—"pretty upset," as Peggy Gough recalled—then left for Nevada at five that afternoon. He drove six straight hours, arriving in Vegas at eleven that night. Gable was composed but hadn't slept, hollow-eyed with grief. Tracy sat with him, Howard Strickling, and the others, said little, remained at hand. The charred bodies were recovered from the wreckage, wrapped in army blankets, and taken down the mountain by horseback. Tracy remained at the hotel with Gable until 8:30 the next evening, then returned to Los Angeles, where he was due back on the set of *Tortilla Flat*. The funeral, in Glendale on the afternoon of the twenty-first, was private and strictly limited to immediate family and friends. Gable, hidden from view in an alcove reserved for the family, said nothing during the course of the service, which consisted of a few readings and a simple affirmation of faith. It was over in ten minutes. "Clark, beyond consolation, would talk only to Fieldsie, Carole's great friend and manager, Madalynne Fields," said Myrna Loy, one of the very few marquee names invited to attend. "He wouldn't talk to anyone else, no matter who it was."

Spence was there with Louise, but his mind was focused elsewhere—on his mother, who had suffered another stroke that day and was, as he noted in his book, "very low." He worked only until noon the following day, a Thursday, then went to be at Carrie's side. She appeared to recognize Carroll and him, smiled at them faintly and clasped hands. Apparently she did not speak, although according to family lore she said to Spencer, "Take care of Carroll." The next day, January 23, 1942, she had yet another stroke and died very quietly at the age of sixty-six. She did not, according to Spence's entry in his datebook, seem to suffer.

The next day, Spence, Carroll, Louise, and Dorothy accompanied Carrie Tracy on her final trip home, fourteen years after her husband had been laid to rest in Freeport's Calvary Cemetery. The train was met at Dixon by a hearse from the Eichmeier & Becker funeral home, while Spence and Carroll and their wives were collected by their sad-eyed uncle Andrew and driven into town. The scene at the Hotel Freeport was chaotic—news of the great star's impending arrival had been published in the *Journal Standard*—and the lobby was packed with the morbid and the merely curious. "People were clustered around him, probably bodyguards, and they were trying to whisk him through," recalled Marie Barcellona, the hotel's longtime desk clerk. "But he was very gracious—he took time out to stop and talk to someone he apparently knew or someone that knew his mother. He looked much more youthful and thinner in person."

The townspeople remembered the gentle, white-haired woman who occasionally came to Freeport to visit her sister, a chauffeur-driven limousine carrying them through the streets of town with a stately grace. Some longtime residents could think back to the days when she was still Carrie Brown of Stephenson Street, Ed Brown's younger daughter and one of the most beautiful women in a hundred-mile radius. Spence had time to venture out, as if avoiding the pending business at hand, and he paid a call on Elmer Love, who was briefly a classmate of his at the Union School on South Chicago Avenue. "He was just as common as he could be," said Josephine Love, Elmer's widow, "and had such a wonderful personality. You wouldn't think he was a big famous star. He talked about his old school chums. 'Whatever happened to so and so?' he would ask. He and Elmer had quite a conversation. He laughed when he told Elmer that his wife was a little jealous of his leading lady, Katharine Hepburn."

A simple funeral took place on the afternoon of January 26. Carrie had embraced Christian Science in her later years, but her sister Emma was active in the First Presbyterian Church and had the pastor, a Dr. Odiorne, officiate. It wasn't as emotional an occasion as the funeral for John Tracy had been, Carrie having lived into her mid-sixties, but Spence wept all the same and kept pretty much to himself. The ground at the cemetery was frozen solid, and Carrie couldn't be buried in the Tracy plot alongside John until after the spring thaw. They left for Chicago the next morning in a heavy fog and were back in California on the twenty-ninth.

The filming of *Tortilla Flat* dragged on endlessly, and the picture was still in production when *Woman of the Year* opened at the Radio City Music Hall on February 5. After a mid-December sneak in which the new ending had played flawlessly, the studio got behind the picture in a big way. Metro budgeted $2.5 million annually in display advertising, dividing it among general circulation magazines, farm magazines (which accounted for eight million rural subscribers), the various fan magazines, and 145 newspapers reaching a combined circulation of 31 million readers. Immediately after "The Hepburn Story," a serialized biography, appeared in five consecutive issues of the *Saturday Evening Post*, M-G-M ran a full-page ad in the magazine for *Woman of the Year*. Two-column teasers followed in 118 key city newspapers: "SPENCER TRACY is crazy about KATHARINE HEPBURN—but she's too busy!" A cartoon pictured her surrounded by photographers, with Tracy knocked to the ground in the stampede to get to her. "She's the WOMAN OF THE YEAR!"

The lines around the Music Hall, despite some nasty weather, reflected the enormous popularity of *The Philadelphia Story* when it played the same theater in December 1940. (At that point, it had been seven years since Hepburn had last filled the place with *Little Women*.) Tracy's personal drawing power had long been established, having built steadily since 1936 and been demonstrated most recently with the crowds that flooded the Astor to see *Dr. Jekyll and Mr. Hyde.* The combination of the two names was seemingly all the people needed to drive *Woman of the Year* to a first week's total of $99,000—which was essentially capacity business for the 5,945-seat venue.

"They call the new Music Hall offering *Woman of the Year,*" William Boehnel wrote in the *World-Telegram,* "but I think a far better name for it would be *Film of the Year,* for seldom have I seen a more freshly written, gayer, wiser, more beautifully acted and directed entertainment than this one. To begin with, it has Katharine Hepburn and Spencer Tracy in the leading roles. This in itself would be enough to make any film memorable. But when you get Hepburn and Tracy turning in brilliant performances to boot, you've got something to cheer about." Bosley Crowther said practically the same thing, adding that *Woman of the Year* made him feel "like tossing his old hat into the air and weaving a joyous snake dance over the typewriter keys" for the first time in months. Propelled by exceptionally strong notices in all the New York dailies, *Woman of the Year* built to an even better $102,000 in its second week. It stayed a total of six weeks, equaling the unprecedented run of *The Philadelphia Story,* an astonishing feat for a picture that had neither a book nor a play for its foundation. As it made its way across the country—it reached Los Angeles in April—*Woman of the Year* showed its strength in the biggest cities, amassing a domestic gross of $1,937,000. When Tracy reached New York on February 16, Hepburn was reveling in the film's success and eager for another pairing of the new Tracy-Hepburn team.

But first there was the matter of *Without Love,* the Philip Barry play to follow *The Philadelphia Story.* As with the latter, Barry wrote it with Hepburn in mind, and she owned a 25 percent interest in it—same as the playwright. As part of the arrangement, she agreed to play the part of Jamie Coe Rowan for $1,000 a week, enabling the Theatre Guild to fulfill a promise to its subscribers that a Hepburn play would be part of its 1941–42 season. The *New York Times* carried a formal announcement on January 19, and performances were set to begin in New Haven on February 26, 1942. Yet nothing seemed terribly certain as Tracy hit town. The play itself was an awkward fusion of romance and diplomacy, a set of implausible plot turns animated by a curiously unappealing mix of characters. Left unspoken was the most basic of the show's flaws: an utter lack of chemistry between its star actress and her staid leading man, actor-playwright Elliott Nugent.

Hepburn had little time to devote to Tracy. Being what she described as a "one track Charlie," she poured all her energies into the hopeless task of making the play work. They saw each other when they could, generally late at night, but it wouldn't do for him to be haunting rehearsals and he scrupulously stayed away. He saw shows: Maurice Evans' *Macbeth*, Cheryl Crawford's revival of *Porgy and Bess*. On the nineteenth he fulfilled a commitment to Garson Kanin, now with the Division of Information in Washington, to record the narration for a one-reel subject titled *Ring of Steel*. ("I am the American soldier . . . the ring of steel around democracy.") Then, with little else to do in New York City, he asked his seventeen-year-old son to spend the weekend with him at the River House, a swank art deco club and apartment complex at the eastern terminus of Fifty-second Street. There were squash and tennis courts, a swimming pool, a floating dock for pleasure craft. The weather was beautiful, but Johnny was reticent about staying alone with his father and all they managed to do was play a lot of tennis. "The boy had told me he wanted to talk to me," Tracy said to Matie Winston, principal of the Wright Oral School, "but then he withheld any closeness of communication. Why?"

Johnny had been home for the holidays, but his father hadn't been around much. The children were reared Episcopalians, so there hadn't been the critical bonding that Spence had enjoyed with his own father. And whenever Tracy saw his son, Louise was always there as if to act as interpreter. At school Johnny was one of fifteen boarders, and, for almost the first time in his life, he began reading on his own, using a dictionary to expand his vocabulary and focus his mind. Miss Winston tried explaining, tactfully, that maybe Johnny's reticence came from a desire to have more regular interaction with his dad, a greater sense of companionship and exchange. Louise wasn't writing as regularly as before and Spence hardly ever wrote at all—even postcards. The boy rightly felt abandoned, and then there was his father's habit of bringing his hand to his mouth when he spoke, which made the reading of his lips impossible.

"He can't see your lips!" Louise would scold, and he would say, "Oh, yes, yes . . . ," and then two minutes later he'd be doing it again. "He went through life with his hand over his mouth," Louise said. "It was one of his firmest habits, and he couldn't break it. He tried very hard." At an age when a young man naturally yearns for the company of his father, a very basic disconnect separated Johnny and his dad, and the boy sometimes got to see more of his father on screen than in person. "John was always a little overwhelmed by his father," his mother said. "[Spence] expected a great deal of him, and John always felt he was not up [to it], I think . . . Their conversations were always like 'talking times.' He would [sometimes] get down to something that was serious, but they never really discussed things as men might."

And so Tracy continued to ask, "Why won't the boy talk to me?" but he could never fully grasp the reasons. He spent the rest of the day glumly knocking about the city. That night, he and a ravenous Kate managed a late supper at Sherman Billingsley's Stork Club, where they sat for a time with Lieutenant Jimmy Stewart and actress Phyllis Brooks. In an AP wirephoto that circulated the next day, Tracy could be seen to the right of Stewart and Brooks, a worn and quizzical look on his face and a tall drink in front of him. Kate was nowhere to be seen, and within a couple of days, neither was he. "Weather beautiful," he wrote in the last entry to be found in his pocket diary. "Another perfect day."

The next two weeks passed in something of a blur. Studio records show that he spent four days in the exclusive Harkness Pavilion of Columbia-Presbyterian Hospital, admitted under the fanciful name of Bernhardt (as in Sarah) and accompanied by Hepburn, who took her own private room nearby. Broadway columnist Dorothy Kilgallen caught wind of the arrangement and, completely unhindered by Howard Strickling's legendary control of the West Coast media, printed the first public intimation of the Tracy-Hepburn relationship in her column of March 13, 1942. Howard Dietz, Metro's New York–based director of advertising and publicity, made little secret of his dislike for Tracy and considered him to be Culver City's problem when he wasn't in town on official business. "Tracy," said Dietz, "had the mistaken idea that a movie star can have the freedom of the city and the right to put it into practice. He had no idea how to handle people, and he drank at an unpredictable rhythm."

Kate had never before witnessed Tracy under the influence of alcohol and had no idea of the depths to which his binges could take him. She stayed with him as long as she possibly could, but when she left town with the company of *Without Love,* there was nothing to prevent him from falling back onto the sauce. *Tortilla Flat* had been put before a preview audience in Los Angeles, and he was needed back in California for retakes. He had remained friends with Myrna Loy, and although they hadn't worked together since *Test Pilot,* the studio occasionally presumed upon that, thinking that she could somehow handle him when he gave them extraordinary trouble.

"We both happened to be in New York," Loy remembered,

when Benny Thau called from Hollywood: "Myrna, we're waiting to start Tracy's picture, and he's there on a bender, holed up at the River House with his male nurse. See what you can do?" I called; Spence asked, "Where are you?" and I told him. I shouldn't have. He was at the door of my St. Regis suite in no time. Days of drinking had left him belligerent. He made his usual play for me, bringing his fist down with such emphatic frustration at one point that he smashed a glass-topped coffee table. Then he turned defensive. "You don't have to worry about me anymore," he said like a sulky child. "I've found the woman I want." As he outlined the virtues of Katharine Hepburn, I was relieved, but also a bit disappointed. As selfish as it sounds, I liked having a man like Spence in the background wanting me. It's rather nice when nothing's required in return.

Without Love had its first performance in Princeton on March 4, 1942, and the reaction was nowhere near what they had hoped it would be. Tracy didn't go but attempted a boozy call to eighty-six-year-old Sister Mary Perpetua instead, possibly to tell her that in the wake of his mother's death he was taking steps to amend his birth certificate and that his middle name would soon, at long last, reflect his baptismal name, Bonaventure, in place of Bernard. His datebook entry for March 6 read, "Back on wagon" but then those words were crossed out.

"Apparently they just couldn't handle him in the New York office," said Eddie Lawrence, who came to town on unrelated business and was pressed into service. "They were *exhausted*. So I went over to the hotel. They greeted me like a long lost friend. And they were just bringing him out. They were cutting him down, a little bit of brandy or whatever they do. I was hungry—I hadn't eaten anything—and I said, 'Spencer, I'm going to eat something.' So we talked. There were two doctors there, and I think they were giving him some form of medication, because the stomach obviously [couldn't hold anything]."*

On March 11, while Hepburn was playing a week's stand in Baltimore, Tracy was placed on a United Airlines flight to Los Angeles in the care of a doctor. In California, he continued to drink, and there were discussions at the studio over the proper course of action. Thau, Eddie Mannix, and Joe Cohn conceded that Tracy was "in no condition to do retakes," but a staff lawyer advised that formal notice be served "to protect our position." Tracy's failure to report for work meant that all payments by the studio could cease and that his time absent could be counted against the eighteen weeks' vacation to which he was entitled under the terms of his contract. Thau advised Leo Morrison of the need to serve formal notice but expressed concern over "Tracy's reaction to this notice, particularly in his present state." Morrison phoned Carroll, and the two men agreed that Morrison would collect the notice at the studio mail room, thereby effecting delivery, but would not show it to his client.

Tracy later told Stewart Granger that Vic Fleming, waiting to make

---

* Treatment for alcoholism was often based on aversion therapies, where the consumption of liquor was accompanied by a powerful emetic. (Some so-called liquor cures even involved the use of leeches.)

retakes on *Tortilla Flat,* was the only one left who seemed to care at all about him.

I'd been picked up by the police and thrown into the drunk tank; I was filthy, unshaven, and ill. Vic found out where I was, squared the press, the police, and the studio, and took me home. He had a Filipino servant and, giving him instructions to bathe, shave, and put me to bed, went to get his doctor. After being given a thorough examination, I was lying there like death when Vic came in with a case of Scotch. He put it down beside my bed and went to the door. Turning back he said, "Spence, I've just talked to the doctor. He tells me one more bash like that and you'll be dead. I want you to do me a favor. Drink that whole case of Scotch. It's the last time you'll see me, Spence. I'm through." And he went out and left me alone.

Tracy declared himself back on the wagon after nineteen days adrift. Eight days later, on March 23, he reported back to the set of *Tortilla Flat,* where he dutifully appeared for Fleming in five days of retakes. Finally free of a film he had grown to loathe, he left town again, bound for New York with every intention of spending his forty-second birthday in the company of Katharine Hepburn. Fueled by coffee and little else, he arrived in Manhattan on March 30, the same day it was announced that *Without Love* would continue to tour. With the show stuck in Philadelphia, Tracy, as he recorded in his book, suffered a monumental attack of the "jitters." Fearful that he would again take to the bottle, he left the same day for home, and instead spent his birthday—Easter Sunday—with Louise, Johnny, and Susie in Palm Springs.

Kate, meanwhile, was fighting a losing battle to keep *Without Love* afloat. The play had been altered considerably since Princeton, bringing the platonic relationship between Hepburn and Nugent into sharper focus while scuttling large chunks of the war plot. "Kate," said actress Audrey Christie, who was playing a supporting role in the production, "was miserable throughout the tour. Elliott Nugent was drinking because he was aware of his inadequacy, and she hated that. But she concealed her feelings beautifully and was always considerate to Elliott. She used to drive her car out into the country in various places and scream to get her frustrations out, decades before anyone thought of primal-scream therapy."

Tracy left for New York again on April 16, this time in the company of Tim Durant. *Keeper of the Flame* had been announced as the next Tracy-Hepburn picture, and Kate was now publicly advancing the idea of Spence replacing Elliott Nugent when *Without Love* ultimately reached Broadway.

Observing his forty-second birthday in the company of his family. Note the tall glass of milk to his right. (SUSIE TRACY)

Tracy went to Boston to confer with Jimmy Cagney—they were working up bits for a Hollywood Victory Caravan—as Kate took the play to her hometown of Hartford for two completely sold-out performances. She was welcomed extravagantly—seven curtain calls—but her mania for privacy was on full display, and despite a heartfelt curtain speech in which she spoke warmly of family and old friends, station porters, and even taxi drivers, she would see absolutely no one.

The show moved on to Cleveland, then to Pittsburgh, where Tracy was spotted in the opening night audience, furtively slouched in a rear seat. He told Karl Krug, drama critic for the *Sun-Telegraph,* that he had been in Washington and "just stopped off to see the show." He denied that he was going to replace Elliott Nugent but said that he thought Barry's play could "form the basis" of a good movie. His presence strengthened the suspicions of Kaspar Monahan, critic for the rival *Pittsburgh Press,* to whom he said much the same thing: "Mr. Tracy said he was going to leave immediately after the performance. But I noted at final curtain that he was not in too great a hurry to get out of town or to neglect to run backstage and congratulate Miss Hepburn."

Tracy was, in fact, on his way to Baltimore for a general checkup at Johns Hopkins, the same distinguished institution where Tom Hepburn had studied medicine and met his future wife. Tracy had never before crossed the continent to see a doctor, much less take a battery of tests, but Kate had arranged the visit in the aftermath of his most recent bender. On the afternoon of May 12, he sat apologetically across from clinician Louis V. Hamman, having just given his name to a clueless admissions nurse as "Mr. Clark Gable." He said he was sure there was nothing physically wrong with him, that he was just neurotic, and that it was not right for him to be wasting the doctor's time.

"His symptoms," Dr. Hamman said in his notes,

> are of rather long standing, ten years at least. He is introspective and says he suffers from vague fear, fear of what he does not know. He adds that part of it, he supposes, is fear of disease. Five years ago he was advised to have the thyroid out. Either doctors told him or in some way he found out that occasionally an enlarged thyroid is carcinoma, and he at once decided that it would turn out to be cancer. He goes on to explain that there has been great solicitude on his part about his heart. When he gets nervous or excited, his heart races, throbs and pounds and skips beats. He insists there is something wrong with his heart, but his doctor says over and over again that there is nothing wrong. He sleeps poorly. Goes to bed early, wakes and reads a while, goes to sleep again and then wakes about five or six in the morning and gets up. He has been doing this for a long time. He now enjoys the early morning hours, likes to be out of doors or preparing for his work by reading plays, and so on.

Tracy went on to give a brief résumé of his schooling, his time at Ripon, and his early days on the stage.

> He loves acting, puts his whole heart into it, and gives it all his energy and ability. He has never learned to play, cares only to fish and cannot do that for long. He will start off on a vacation intending to spend a month, and after three or four days will go back to Hollywood. Therefore, he has worked not only intensively but more or less continuously. As soon as he finishes one play he is off on another. He realizes that this makes a heavy demand upon his nervous energy because he puts a great deal of energy into every-

thing he does, and I think he knows he pays for this in the symptoms that he has. About ten years ago, he started out on periodic alcoholic bouts. Up to that time he had drank very little. After a play he would begin to celebrate, and would keep it up for a week or ten days. These periods of drinking would come about every eight months. Six years ago, he decided that things could not go on that way, and for two years he did not drink anything. Then he fell and had another bout of drinking. After that he went for four years without drinking, and then was off on another bout some three months ago. He says the last bout was utter folly. He decided that, not having had any alcohol for four years, he could handle it, but found that it was impossible for him to do so.

The patient summarized his unremarkable medical and family histories, his height and weight (fudging the latter by about ten pounds), and said he usually smoked ten cigarettes a day. "The patient is a well-nourished man, stockily built and of robust, vigorous appearance," Dr. Hamman concluded. "He is a very engaging person, and in telling his symptoms often laughs at himself."

Tracy spent the next three days getting a pretty thorough going-over. Teeth and eyes were checked, hearing, glands, sinuses, organs, respiration were all found to be normal. A blood analysis fixed his cholesterol level at 168, well within acceptable range, and a routine test for syphilis came back negative. X-rays showed his heart and aorta to be of normal size and shape and his lungs to be clear. A sleep observation under the supervision of Dr. Samuel Crowe, founder of the school's division of otolaryngology, took place on the night of May 14, when Tracy was given a single Nembutal tablet, a dosage mirroring words he had written for the first time in his datebook the previous year: "one pill." He was coming to rely on barbiturates to quiet a mind that was constantly turning, but all that Dr. Crowe could suggest was to reduce alcohol and tobacco consumption to a minimum. The patient was discharged on the fifteenth with the finding "no organic disease diagnosed."

The following morning, he made the five-hour drive back to Pittsburgh, where Kate was giving her final matinee and evening performances of *Without Love*. Hepburn commemorated the occasion by engaging in a wrestling match with a photographer for the *Bulletin-Index* who snapped her without permission as she arrived backstage. The camera was smashed and the man suffered a few scratches before the two were separated by a cop who had heard the scuffle. The engagement closed with nearly $40,000 in the till—an excellent week—and Tracy drove her on to Cincinnati, the next stop on the company's seemingly endless tour of the provinces, then went on to Chicago, where he met up with Carroll for the return trip to Los Angeles.

Keeper of the Flame was the work of the Australian-born poet and novelist I.A.R. Wylie, a story specifically designed for the screen and submitted to Metro-Goldwyn-Mayer just weeks ahead of the Japanese attack on Pearl Harbor. Set for serialization in the *American Magazine,* it told the story of ace war correspondent Steve O'Malley and his assignment to write the biography of a New England governor and self-styled patriot named Robert Forrest. Forrest's death inspires a wave of mourning befitting a beloved national figure, but unlike *Citizen Kane,* another film of the time with a similar setup, the author keeps the subject of O'Malley's inquiry completely offstage, following instead the journalist's interactions with local townspeople and the young widow as he uncovers the secret life of an American fascist.

The model for Forrest became a matter of some discussion when the book was published by Random House in the spring of 1942. Speculation ranged from William Randolph Hearst and Henry Ford to Franklin Delano Roosevelt. Wylie herself would never say, and all director George Cukor would allow was that "[w]e made this picture during a period of undercover Fascism in this country . . . Certain things were in the air but hadn't come out into the open. I suppose, to draw attention to them, we exaggerated."

The property was for Tracy from the very beginning, and he was announced for the role in December 1941. *Keeper of the Flame* didn't take on urgency, however, until Hepburn committed to playing Christine Forrest in April 1942. Aglow from her twin triumphs in *The Philadelphia Story* and *Woman of the Year,* she was instrumental in getting Cukor assigned to the picture and in arranging a test for Audrey Christie in the part of Jane Harding, O'Malley's colleague and sounding board.

"I'm most anxious to start the new film," she told the *Cleveland Plain Dealer,* deftly taking ownership of the project. "The script has been written by Donald Ogden Stewart, who did the excellent screen treatment of *Philadelphia Story,* and George Cukor will again direct me . . . I want to repeat *Woman of the Year,* both as a picture and as a box office hit, for I really think it was an excellent film."

Without Love closed in Buffalo on May 30, and Hepburn promptly headed west, where June 2 had been set for the start date. She most likely read Stewart's screenplay, developed under the supervision of producer Victor Saville, on her way out to California. The role of Christine, she said, fascinated her. "She is a woman, strong, resolute, placed in a tragic position in life. Thinking back, I am surprised to find that I have never played a mature woman. I have played girls, girls, girls—all sorts of girls, shy, whimsical, flamboyant, tempestuous—everything but mature human beings."

Having previously consumed the novel, Hepburn found much to dislike about the script and the changes that had been made. Stewart had based his conception of O'Malley on the knowledge that Tracy would be playing the part, contending that in the novel the character came off as an "impotent eunuch who plays sad love scenes." Hepburn, it seemed, wanted a film as true to Wylie's original as humanly possible. As Stewart complained in a letter to his wife, the journalist Ella Winter, "I created an intelligent character with action as his keynote . . . Is it not interesting that Miss H., not an active character in the story, is Goddamned if there will be an active male in the same story?"

Kate originally had thought that she would stay away from the development of the script, knowing that she was considered a troublemaker on the M-G-M lot. ("I thought, 'Express your opinion when asked, but don't go over everybody and don't try to be too helpful. Just keep your place and be an actor.' ") But it was difficult for her to be on the outside of things, if not completely impossible, and all she really managed to do was to be critical without being helpful, excited by the subject matter but no longer by the character she was being asked to play.

Stewart, who had won an Oscar for his work on *Philadelphia Story,* thought Wylie's book "exciting screen material" and saw his primary job as making sure the picture "accurately reflected the 1943 background."* Hepburn, Stewart told his wife, was not so much interested in the script as she was in control and had gone over the heads of both Saville and Cukor in taking her demands directly to the studio brass. In the book, Christine ensures her husband's death when she chooses not to warn him that a bridge is out. Under the Production Code, a character who commits murder must be punished. But was passively allowing someone's accidental death to occur the same as a willful act of murder? When the screenplay was first submitted to the Breen office, Saville purposely held back the ending, in which both Steve and Christine decide, in effect, to "print the legend" now that Forrest himself is safely dead. But the administrators of the Code could sense the direction in which the movie was headed: "We assume . . . that in order to comply with the provisions of the Code, you will either clear Christine of any suspicion of murder or else will punish her. Otherwise, we could not approve the finished picture."

---

* Stewart, who had been president of the Hollywood Anti-Nazi League, also appreciated the political message of the film and thought his work on it could be, in the words of his wife, "a contribution to this war against Hitler."

A significant change that occurred on Hepburn's watch was the compounding of her character's guilt. Where before Christine had merely failed to warn her husband of the danger he faced, she now became responsible for disabling the bridge as well. Nearly all of Christine's scenes were rewritten, but there came a point when the beleaguered Saville felt he had to push back:

> A full conference was called in the executive producer's office and all were present: Hepburn, Tracy, Cukor, Stewart, and myself. Katie was the first to speak, which she did with great passion and at length. She told us the story as she would like to see it. When she had finished, we looked at Tracy, who passed, as did Cukor and Stewart, and all eyes turned to me. I guess I must have been a little edgy as, just before going into the meeting, I had heard on the radio of the disastrous defeat of the British army by Rommel and the probability that Egypt would fall. In that frame of mind, my reaction was quite without compromise. "Katie has told us a very good story, but that's not the story I want to tell, and if you prefer to use hers I suggest you get yourselves another boy." Dead silence, broken only by Tracy getting up. "That's it, boys. Let's go to work." And they all left the room.

Other than the original start date of production, Tracy recorded nothing in his datebook during the month of June 1942. He and Kath—the name he had taken to calling her in private—attended John Barrymore's funeral on the second but otherwise kept a low profile. Louise, surely aware that something was up, wrote Matie Winston late in the month, saying that she thought she needed to do something—find a job, go back to the stage, get busy and contribute something to the war effort. Johnny and Susie were home for the summer, but there was the matter of Susie's schooling to resolve, for gas rationing had made the commute to Brentwood impractical. Miss Winston, who once told Louise she thought she looked like Greer Garson, encouraged her to "[t]ake another flier while you are still so young and pretty. Send Susie to me. Hearing children work in beautifully here."

Tracy never spoke of *Keeper of the Flame,* never said what he liked about it or what he didn't. It was a good part for him in a picture that had something important to say, but he didn't involve himself in the writing process the way Kate felt compelled to do. His part was solid, as tailored for him as any part he had ever played. The actor most at risk on the picture was Hepburn herself, and no one was likely to watch out for her the way that she was used to watching out for herself. Another incomplete script was submitted to the PCA in early July, and again Joseph I. Breen warned that "if it is to be indicated that Christine is guilty of her husband's murder, she will have to be punished if the picture is to conform to the requirements of the Production Code."

Still committed to a picture in which he passionately believed, Don Stewart found himself excluded from the story conferences Saville was now having almost daily. "I shall not resign," he vowed, "as long as there is a chance to save the 'message' (not my face). Is it not humiliating that all the discussion now takes place without my being allowed to participate . . . ?" He returned to his farm in the Adirondacks after completing the screenplay, and when filming began on July 14, Christine was guilty of murder in the first degree. Hepburn was tense—resigned, seemingly, to the failings of the script as she saw them, satisfied, perhaps, that it was at least a strong part for Tracy and that the story mirrored the antifascist sentiments of her mother. The battle for control had considerably dimmed her enthusiasm for the project, and it was starting to look less and less likely the film could end on the romantic note that both she and the studio seemed to require.

After a few days of filming, change pages began appearing that would establish Christine's innocence. Don Stewart's final contribution to the picture was a "tag" ending wired from New York on September 1 that had O'Malley kissing her and then jumping aboard a train, the camera holding on Christine's face as it pulled away. Hepburn had played roughly a third of the picture believing her character to be guilty. Now she was faced with playing the rest of it knowing her innocence. She was short with people on the set, quiet and typically unresponsive to the demands of publicity.

Tracy felt comfortable twitting her, something no one else would have dared to do. "Emily," he grandly told Emily Torchia on the first day of production, "you know, this is an *open* set." His own sets were usually closed, but he went out of his way to be welcoming, Kate generally ignoring his attempts at baiting her. "The only person he was hard on," Torchia remembered, "was the script girl, who had to worry about continuity. Mr. Tracy never wore makeup when I knew him, and he had his hair combed just once a day—in the morning. Now, of course, all day long he ran his hands through it, and his hair would never match from one shot to the next. The script girl would be beside herself. Once he said to a script girl, 'Think you're going to survive?' "

George Cukor had directed Hepburn in five pictures, beginning with her first, *A Bill of Divorcement,* and always knew precisely what she needed. Tracy, on the other hand, took some getting used to because his command of the character was so extraordinarily complete. "Kate says I was always giving *her* hundreds of suggestions," Cukor said in 1971, "but none to Spence. Well, Spence was the kind of actor about whom you thought, 'I've got a lot of things I could say to you, but I don't say them because you *know*,' and the next day everything I'd thought of telling him would be there in the rushes. Also, I was never sure whether Spence was really listening when I talked to him. He was one of those naturally original actors who did it but never let you see him doing it."

The supporting cast was exceptionally good and included Richard Whorf as the dead man's conniving secretary, Forrest Tucker, Frank Craven, Horace McNally, Percy Kilbride, Donald Meek, Howard Da Silva, and eleven-year-old Darryl Hickman as Jeb Rickards, a young acolyte who blames himself for the accidental death of his idol. Hickman was working on two other pictures simultaneously and could appreciate Tracy's impatience with Cukor and Hepburn as they worked their way through a page of dialogue. "Before they shot take one," he said, "Cukor and Hepburn would talk and talk and talk about the scene, about the characters, whatever, and Tracy would stand there, first on one foot and then the other, and finally, after about twenty minutes, Tracy would say, almost under his breath, 'Let's get on with it, Kate.' And when Tracy said, 'Let's get on with it, Kate,' we shot the scene." And then, much as Joe Mankiewicz had observed on *Woman of the Year,* Tracy and Hepburn would seem to compete and undercut one another. "In the intimate scenes, Tracy would go low and Hepburn would go lower. The sound man would have to yell, 'Cut! I'm not picking them up!' "

As the film progressed, Tracy's relationship with Hickman's tormented boy became more complex and shaded than the one with Hepburn's Christine, the unintended consequence of a character written more as a cipher than as a grieving wife with a terrible secret to keep. ("I think," Cukor said, "she finally carried a slightly phony part because her humanity asserted itself, and the humor.") Jeb's scene on a dark hillside, an emotion-charged exchange full of beats and transitions in which he decides that he can trust O'Malley, was, as Hickman later put it, "the most difficult scene I played as a child actor." He credited its success to Cukor, who walked him through it change by change, and to Tracy, "who was so 'with you' as an actor that you could feel his energy. He was very still and very quiet and very unspoken, but he was with you psychically in a way that I have never felt from another actor. He *listened* to you with such intensity that he literally drew you into himself. It isn't that he *did* very much; in fact, he did almost nothing. But he created a connection that was so intense that you couldn't pull yourself away from him."

Director George Cukor makes Darryl Hickman's close-ups for *Keeper of the Flame.*
"Tracy never budged," Hickman recalled. "He was there with me every step of the
way." (DARRYL HICKMAN)

Hickman knew nothing of craft, but he came to see his time with Tracy
and Cukor as the beginning of a process of learning that culminated in a
successful career as a teacher of acting.

The only thing Tracy said to me directly, at some point during the
shooting of that scene, was, "I think if you took more time there,
you'd make a better transition." I didn't know what the word
"transition" meant, but I got the sense of what he was talking

about. He never, ever said anything to me, but I could feel his respect and that meant a lot. He would sit there when I did my closeups, and—I swear, we shot my closeups for a day—Tracy never walked away from that apple box he was sitting on. Most big-time stars would get up and go to their dressing room, then they'd come back and maybe they'd feed you your lines from beside the camera or maybe they wouldn't. Tracy never budged. He was there with me every step of the way. And he gave me the same performance when he was beside the camera that he gave me in front of the camera. And that wasn't the way most of those big-time movie stars did it.

Kate would appear on the set on days she wasn't needed, sometimes to confer with Cukor, invariably to sit near the camera and watch Tracy as he worked. The pace of production was glacial, and the picture took as long to make as *Tortilla Flat*—nearly eleven weeks. As it dragged on, Hepburn's partners at the Theatre Guild grew increasingly worried that she would be unable to rejoin *Without Love* as originally planned. The Guild's business manager, Warren Munsell, began wiring in July, looking for a commitment to open the play in Columbus on September 17. Before long, it became apparent that Hepburn was ducking them. "What are you up to that you keep changing your phone number?" Theresa Helburn, Langner's codirector at the Guild, wired on August 9. "I will guard your secret if you will send it to me. How is the picture going and how are things relative to our September dates?"

Now that she was on more intimate terms with him, Kate could plainly see the stress Spence put himself under during the course of a film and the psychological toll his insomnia was taking. When he wasn't fretting about the picture, his part, and what he was doing with it, it was his life and the way he was living it. "He felt the miseries that he'd brought on people were avoidable," she said, "and that if he hadn't existed the world would have been better off." Unworthy of God's forgiveness, he could see only darkness before him, eternal punishment by fire, the literal interpretation of hell as preached to believers. Overwhelmed by a sensitivity to everything around him—the emotions of others, the stir of the wind—his heart beat furiously and occasionally it would skip, a chilling, ever-present reminder in the depth of the night that he could be taken at any moment.

He hated himself at times like these, hated his inability to live up to his own moral and professional standards, to be the good man he aspired to be, the man his audience believed him to be. Worse, he was unable to express these thoughts and feelings to anyone other than himself, for, as with Louise, Kate wasn't Catholic—wasn't anything, for that matter—and he knew that whatever he had to say, should he say it, would be taken, however politely and sympathetically, as nonsense. He would appear on the set every morning looking red-eyed and haggard, and he would speak to nobody. He'd disappear into his dressing room and not emerge until it was time for the first shot to be blocked. Everyone assumed he was hungover, but he wasn't drinking anything stronger than tea at the time. He was just desperate for sleep, and his fatigue threatened the concentration he needed to do his best work.

As the wires from New York grew more insistent, Hepburn brokered the sale of *Without Love* to M-G-M for $260,000, a figure she hoped would satisfy all the parties involved so that she could put forth what she really wanted, which was to get out of doing the play in New York altogether. The studio was talking more pictures for the two of them, and Tracy had gotten her interested in Paul Osborn's script for *Madame Curie,* which he had originally hoped to do with Garbo. The thought of Hepburn as the great Polish scientist struck everyone as odd, and Hedda Hopper reminded her readers that Irene Dunne had been the original choice for the role. Regardless, she was desperate to stay in California, desperate to stay with Spence and to help him get a handle on this curse that seemed to drain him of all life. Sleep had never been a problem for her; she retired early, slept soundly, often rose before dawn. If he could just set his mind to it, he could do that as well, and if it meant staying at M-G-M a while longer and making a few more pictures, then that was what she wanted and what she needed to do.

Another wire from Terry Helburn on September 1 considerably upped the pressure:

> I MUST ADVISE YOU THAT SHOULD WE OPEN MORE THAN TWO WEEKS AFTER OUR AGREED DATE OF OCTOBER FIFTH WE WILL OWE A WEEKS SALARY TO MOST OF THE CAST FOR WHICH WE WILL HAVE TO HOLD METRO RESPONSI- BLE SINCE YOUR CONTRACT WITH THEM EXPIRES OCTO- BER FIRST AND BEGINS WITH US OCTOBER FIFTH.

While Tracy spent the Labor Day weekend with his family in Encino, Hepburn took pen in hand and began drafting a letter to Helburn, her partner Lawrence Langner, and Phil Barry, the gifted playwright whose work was at the center of it all. "I want to talk to you very seriously about the play," she wrote. "I do not think you should have me do it. There are many reasons for my coming to this conclusion and I wish you would read them and think about them seriously." She went on to warn that she would not stay with the show past her contracted time, which meant that they could play New York for a maximum of twelve weeks.* She was not good in the part, she added, and she could not play well with Elliott Nugent. ("We are just unfortunate together.") She said that she thought the play needed considerable work— new work, not revision—and that it was almost impossible to act in such a thing without conviction. "I am sunk to feel this way—but I have right along—and in a way I feel that I have done my part in it. I have played on the road to good business—made back the investment—helped settle the movie rights. You have certainly not lost anything by having me in it . . ."

The letter was lucid, reasoned, and made a solid case against dragging her back to Broadway for what was sure to be a drubbing. She thought about it, slept on it, then realized they would be hell-bent on bringing it in regardless. In Spence's absence, Hepburn redrafted the letter and added a strictly emotional appeal: "Finally—for personal reasons—it will crucify me to be tied up in N.Y. for four months. I shall be frantic and miserable and I beg you not to force me to do it. In these times life is entirely uncertain, and for the sake of the extra money you may make with me in it, you may be ruining me. Please, as my friends, think these points over seriously . . . I have done the best I can do—please let me out of it—"

Postmarked September 7, 1942, the letter reached the Fifty-second Street offices of the Theatre Guild on the twelfth. Barry was "thunderstruck" when he read it, and Helburn and Langner set about the task of drafting a measured reply. While they sympathized deeply with the "emotional disturbance" she seemed to be in, there were duties and obligations that could not be overlooked. Barry's career as a dramatist had to be considered, as did the Guild's continuing position as an institution of the American theatre. They put the best possible spin on *Without Love,* insisting that audiences liked Hepburn better in it than they had in *Philadelphia Story.* "The fact that you are in pain when you are playing with Elliott is merely because you see Spencer in it, but the audience doesn't, and everybody thinks that you and Elliott make a good team in it. You did yourself until you got feeling strongly about Spencer in it, and you are surely too good a trouper to let a purely personal point of view stand in the way of an objective success . . ."

After every conceivable argument had been committed to paper, they decided it would be wisest to talk it over with Kate in person. Helburn sent a telegram on the thirteenth: "YOUR LETTER OF COURSE A SHOCK TO US ALL . . ." and said that she would see her in Hollywood that coming Wednesday. The meeting was a hurried affair, and Hepburn's hasty exit

---

* Hepburn's commitment to the play was actually for sixteen weeks. Allowing for a two-week tryout period, she could have been required to play a maximum of fourteen weeks on Broadway, not twelve.

left their talk unfinished. Helburn thought she had an agreement from Kate to take the play into New York as long as their Detroit opening was postponed until October 26 and that Hepburn would cover a week's worth of cast salaries out of the extra money she would be getting from Metro for her additional time on the picture. Back in New York, Helburn announced to the press that *Without Love* would arrive on Broadway in November.

They finished *Keeper of the Flame* on September 22, with a do-over on a key scene set for the following week. Actress Pauline Lord was revered on the New York stage, where she had starred in O'Neill's *Anna Christie* and *Strange Interlude,* but she was almost completely unknown to movie audiences, having appeared in just two pictures. Her role as the vindictive Mrs. Forrest promised fireworks in the company of Tracy and Hepburn, but she was nervous and fidgety, overwhelmed by the mechanics of moviemaking, and Cukor had to nurse her along. The scene didn't work well, and Saville, in collaboration with playwright Leon Gordon, drafted a set of retakes in which the part of Mrs. Forrest would be taken by Margaret Wycherly, an equally prominent—and considerably more seasoned—actress of both stage and screen. Wycherly's revised scene, which made her character more crazy than evil, took three days to shoot. The film was readied for preview as Saville and Gordon busied themselves with still more emendations, and after putting it all before an audience it was decided that Christine would have to be guilty of murder after all. Soon, the men had forty-five pages of new material to shoot.

It was now October 6, and Hepburn was due in the East for rehearsals on the twelfth. New scenes requiring her participation, including her death at the hands of her husband's former secretary, were dated as late as October 10. Tracy finished with his scenes on the seventeenth—Kate was long gone by then—and left within days for a new round of tests at Johns Hopkins, his principal complaint being "insomnia and general nervousness with vague feelings of fear."

He met briefly with President Roosevelt on the twenty-ninth for a conference regarding a possible trip to England but was nowhere to be seen when the very public funeral of George M. Cohan took place at St. Patrick's Cathedral on November 7. At Johns Hopkins, a physical exam, as before, showed him to be in good health and completely normal. His first night of monitored sleep displayed a familiar pattern: asleep four hours, then awake thirty minutes, asleep for another hour, then awake ninety minutes. He got a total of six and a half hours with the aid of Nembutal, an hour less the following night. He remained at the hospital a total of four days and was discharged, it was noted, "with his condition improved."

New York saw the opening of *Without Love* while Tracy was at Johns Hopkins, and Tracy hired a car to return to Manhattan on the afternoon of

November 12. The play and Kate were, in her words, "roasted," but the public disagreed with the critics, came, and evidently liked it well enough to send their friends. Tracy remained close at hand, marking ten months of sobriety on December 15, 1942. The city was under a blackout order, and the darkness after nightfall was the darkness of a country lane. No theater marquees could be lit, no restaurants could be lighted from the street, and it was possible to walk past Radio City Music Hall and not know it.

Another conference with Roosevelt, this time in the company of Robert Emmet Sherwood, overseas director of the Office of War Information, confirmed that Tracy would soon leave for Great Britain to convey Christmas greetings to American and British soldiers. The plan lost momentum, though, as the president began preparations for a secret conference with Winston Churchill at Casablanca. Kate was dutifully serving her time on the stage of the St. James Theatre when Spence left for Chicago on the eighteenth, arriving back home in Los Angeles on the evening of December 21. Christmas, as usual, was at the ranch, where he and his brother Carroll observed their first Yuletide together since the passing of their mother.

Tracy spent the next four consecutive days in Encino, his longest uninterrupted stretch of time there in more than a year.

CHAPTER 19

Not the Guy They See Up There on the Screen

Within days of receiving Matie Winston's letter, the one that urged her to "take another flier," Louise Tracy was presented with the opportunity she craved. "I've always had to have a project," she later said. "Never occurred to me that it might be a big business." Louise had met somebody who was part of a group of older people who were hard of hearing. "They met every so often, played cards and complained," she said. "I felt that I wanted to get more deeply interested. I wondered what was going on and what could be done . . . I met once with them, but I didn't know enough."

Through the group she learned of a workshop at the University of Southern California for social workers, teachers, and parents of the hard of hearing. She took Johnny, now eighteen and home from school, and met Dr. Boris Markovin, who was the director of a reading clinic at USC. "He just asked, asked, asked questions," she said of Dr. Markovin. "He want[ed] to know everything about everything.'

"He said, 'Mrs. Tracy, why don't you *do* something for the deaf?'

"I said, 'What could I do?'

" 'Well, of course you [could] do something. Didn't you ever think of anything you'd like to do?'

"Then I said, 'I guess if there was anything that I would like to do, it would be to have a little nursery school where children and their mothers could learn together.'

" 'Do it!' he said."

Dr. Markovin asked her to give a talk at the workshop banquet. When Louise wondered what she'd say, he told her just to tell them what she had told him. "You tell them this story," he said, and she said that she would try.

Putting aside *The Story of John,* Louise worked up a speech and read it to Spence, who was preparing to start *Keeper of the Flame.* He thought it was great. "It was just about John and the difficulty of being deaf," she said. "I know I was scared stiff." She talked about coping with her son's deafness, her struggle to find help, her realization that a deaf child could be taught. State schools for the deaf didn't admit children until the age of six; who was supposed to teach them before six? "Maybe a dozen of us had heard about this program and Dr. Markovin had rounded them up. [We] had our punch and talked about the possibility of doing something. These were mostly mothers of young children. That was quite a step forward because somebody had to take the lead, and Dr. Markovin kept pushing me. He said, 'Can't we all meet someplace? Can't we meet at your house?' I said, 'Well, I'll set a date . . .' "

The meeting took place on July 18, 1942, when fifty mothers crowded into the modest Tracy ranch house on White Oak. Louise called the meeting to order and introduced a speaker from the California Society of Crippled Children, who told the mothers that it was up to the parents of a handicapped child to see that things were done for him or her. Most parents, he said, wanted to pass their cares on to somebody else. An organization of parents could accomplish more than a single person. A Mrs. Richard Simon of San Francisco sent a plan for the formation of such an organization, its goals centering on prevention, education, rehabilitation, and employment. A roundtable discussion touched on matters of doctor education, audiometer tests for schoolchildren, and a lessening of the dependence on private schools, "because each school believes the way they teach is the right way."

A motion was made for Louise to take the chairmanship.

I finally got my wits about me and I said I didn't know what I could do. They were looking at me. "The only thing I have is a correspondence course from the Wright Oral School. If we can form kind of a group and start meeting together, maybe we can do something." So we started, and our first meeting was at the Biltmore Hotel. They let us have [a meeting room] for five dollars. It was just at the beginning of the war; transportation was going to be difficult. I think we started to meet every two weeks . . . Dr. Markovin popped up again and said, "Why don't you go down to the [university]?" He was head of a reading clinic and he said, "We have a little back porch." It was really makeshift. We had one meeting there, and then Dr. Markovin said we could go in the office there, which had been a living room, at a certain time of day.

We had to look for a teacher. She was very nice and smart, but she had no idea about talking to parents. She gave lists of books they could read, but they wanted something that you could do right now. After about four meetings, I said, "Well, this is pretty bad." In the meantime, I must have been looking around. I had heard of the parent-teacher leaders—there were about 14 of them—engaged by the Department of Education. They got this program going and met on a Saturday . . . I never envisioned having children coming to the clinic. It was simply to pool our experiences, [but] they brought these children along with them. It was an all-day meeting. Each mother was given one child—not her own—to observe so they could look objectively, and the teacher gave them a thing to look for. The teacher got all the mothers together and talked to them about child development, and she asked them what they had observed.

There were just twelve mothers to start—thirteen counting Louise—and still attendance lagged. "We hung on by a thread," she said. In September Dr. Rufus von Kleinschmid, the president of USC, offered the use of a two-story cottage at 924 West Thirty-seventh Street. The first meeting of the Mothers of Deaf and Hard-of-Hearing Children took place at the newly acquired "Mothers' Clinic" on October 17, 1942. A course on child guidance was announced, and Mrs. Florence Browne offered to give whatever spare time she had to the testing of children for hearing disorders. Louise reported that two checks had been received: one for five dollars and the other for $1,000. She asked that members donate as much furniture as possible so that the money could be spent on equipment, and she called upon each mother to give at least one day a month to act as "hostess."

The call went out for volunteers to paint floors, and officer elections were held. "We got some furniture . . . we got some carpeting . . . we did some painting." Once they had a telephone and some letterhead, Louise felt emboldened enough to hire a secretary. When she settled on a candidate, she told the woman it wasn't much of a job "but someday it might be." As they all worked toward an official opening, she hung a shingle over the door of the plain mustard-yellow house at the edge of the campus. It read

JOHN TRACY CLINIC

. . .

In the year following the rousing reception for *Woman of the Year,* there was only *Tortilla Flat* to keep the Tracy name in front of some 80 million domestic moviegoers, and even the kindest of critics greeted that picture with muted enthusiasm. He was announced for a film with Wallace Beery, an immigration epic for King Vidor, and a Byron Morgan story called *By the People.* Betty Rogers let it be known that he was her personal choice to play her late husband in Warners' planned biography of Will Rogers—a prospect Tracy privately found horrifying—and Fox was anxious to borrow him to play A. J. Cronin's gentle priest in *Keys of the Kingdom. The Yearling* remained a possibility, and he at one point shot a test with Roddy McDowall replacing the rapidly growing Gene Eckman as Jody, but all the studios, not just M-G-M, were being pressured to increase their war content in the months immediately following Pearl Harbor, and an outdoor fable set in the 1870s would now have to wait for peacetime.

Tracy rejoined Hepburn in New York, where he was once again reported as taking a "rest cure" at a local hospital. When *Keeper of the Flame* opened there in February 1943, Kate was just finishing her run in *Without Love* and glad to be rid of it. The play had been profitable, but it was far from playing to capacity business and a credit to no one. *Keeper* continued a bleak streak for Hepburn, a good picture that could have been great without the meddling of Victor Saville and Leon Gordon and the rigid dictates of the Breen office. The notices were mixed, most offering up praise for Spence, indifference for Kate. ("Miss Hepburn is Hepburn," the advance review in *Variety* noted, "with the usual mannerisms and studied delivery of lines.") That her artificiality stemmed, in part, from her confusion over her character's innocence or guilt at any given moment in the story was lost on everyone, save Tracy, Cukor, and, of course, Hepburn herself. All that she would allow, somewhat disingenuously, was that she was proud of Metro for not turning it into a "routine garden-variety love story."

Donald Ogden Stewart, seemingly indifferent to the damage done to the third act of his screenplay, proclaimed *Keeper of the Flame* one of Hollywood's "most important productions," hailing an industry "which is now grown up and has begun to mature politically, with a full consciousness of present-day problems." Stewart's good-natured reception of the picture may have been due in part to Kate's diligent fence mending, having belatedly come to the realization that the screenwriter had left Culver City hating her. She wrote him a desperate letter of explanation, expressing both affection and admiration and recounting how she had successfully seen *Woman of the Year* through the scripting process "[b]ut only after horrible scenes with everyone and his brother in all the conferences and everyone

Tracy and Hepburn in *Keeper of the Flame* (1943). (SUSIE TRACY)

loathing me even though they used the stuff and would have been badly off without it." She admitted that on *Keeper of the Flame* she was "as wrong as wrong" and supremely sorry for it.

"I was guilty as far as you were concerned of the great crime of that lot—lack of enthusiasm and excitement. May I add to this that for the first time in my life I am humbly—sweetly—desperately in love—was then, and frantically trying to understand this feeling and to become a woman rather than a working automaton which I have been for years—<u>Don</u>—try to understand and to forgive me—"

In later years Don Stewart embraced a story that had Louis B. Mayer witnessing the film for the first time at the Radio City Music Hall and storming out in a fury when he realized what the picture was really about. "I can't vouch for it," he said cheerfully, "but I'd be very happy if it were true." Ironically, *Keeper of the Flame* managed to better the Music Hall's first-week figures for *Woman of the Year,* confirming the box-office potency of the Tracy-Hepburn combination. A weak draw in rural playoffs, the picture nevertheless managed to outgross its predecessor, and work on the next Tracy-Hepburn collaboration began immediately.

Tracy, in the meantime, went into a wartime ghost story titled *A Guy Named Joe*. Producer Everett Riskin, the elder brother of screenwriter Robert Riskin, had been responsible for a number of Columbia's upper-tier productions, including *Theodora Goes Wild, The Awful Truth,* and, most recently, *Here Comes Mr. Jordan,* a hit picture with a similar premise. It was Riskin's notion to pair Tracy with Irene Dunne, his star from *Theodora* and *Awful Truth,* and it was at his behest that Dunne, one of the industry's most prominent freelancers, was brought to Metro-Goldwyn-Mayer on a two-picture deal.

Tracy and Dunne knew each other casually—they were godparents to Pat O'Brien's adopted son, Terry—but they had never before worked together. For her part, Dunne said that she admired Tracy's work and was looking forward to the assignment. Tracy, who by now was rarely talking to the press, said nothing. Filming began on February 15 with Victor Fleming directing a screenplay by Dalton Trumbo. It was the fifth picture together for Tracy and Fleming—sixth counting the aborted *Yearling*—and the two men were typically chummy while Dunne, who had never before worked at M-G-M, sat quietly off to one side, knitting as the crew bustled around her. She was now forty-four years of age—old by Hollywood standards—and would soon slip into character parts. Fleming, she recalled, was not well, and nobody seemed terribly happy. It didn't help that he scheduled an angry exchange between Dunne and Tracy as the very first scene to be shot. "It was winter," she said, "it was dark and raining and the whole set was gloomy."

Tracy's relationship with Hepburn was common knowledge, and Dunne began work on *A Guy Named Joe* convinced he had wanted Kate for the picture, not her. Having started taking Dexedrine—in part to counter the dopey effects of the Nembutal he was now routinely gulping at bedtime—Tracy's mood on the set was uncharacteristically buoyant. Dunne plainly thought him obnoxious: "The first few days, Spence was VERY difficult, testing me out. He badgered the director, Vic Fleming, and behaved badly until I told him to settle down."

Tracy's inclination to joke about his age put her on the defensive, given she was seventeen months his senior and acutely conscious of it. When he went up—blew a line—he said, "I guess I'm just getting too old. I might as well play character parts and stop kidding myself." Similarly, Dalton Trumbo could remember watching some early rushes in the company of Fleming, Everett Riskin, and Eddie Mannix: "As the star appeared on the screen with his leading lady, a voice rumbled back from the darkness of the front row: 'Look at that pair of overage destroyers!' It was, of course, the incomparable Tracy in a moment of discontent."

Dunne was also thrown by Tracy's refusal to rehearse. "I don't particu-

larly like to rehearse a lot," she said, "but I don't like not rehearsing at all."
Fleming wasn't terribly sympathetic, making it difficult for her to get her
bearings. "We had trouble understanding each other," she said of Tracy.
"He was my hero. Then, when we started working, he got the idea that I
thought he wasn't a hero anymore. Which was not true. But he had this big
mental thing, and there was even talk of taking me off the film. That's one
thing I'll always say about L. B. Mayer. I knew they were going to be looking at some film, and I made up my mind I was going to be my *best*—my
best, my best, my *very* best. So they came out of the projection room and
Mayer said, 'If we're going to replace anybody, let's replace Tracy.' Which
they never would have done, of course. But I'll always remember that. And
we ironed everything out, Tracy and I."

Said Emily Torchia, "Victor Fleming was always boss on the set and
Tracy was macho. It didn't take a week before both of them were bringing
tea for Irene and waiting on her. She's a perfect example of the soft-spoken
woman who turns men on more than sexpots." Dunne would later recall
the picture as her "most difficult," not simply because of Tracy, but also
because of the almost constant shifts in personnel. "I enjoyed working with
Tracy," she said in retrospect, "but physically we had a lot of problems like
changing hairdressers and different makeup people. Cameramen. We had
to change cameramen. All those things tend to make the thing not run
smoothly."

At first glance Fleming was as unlike Tracy as any man could be. Tall
and spare with nervous gray eyes, he was, Eddie Lawrence remembered, a
great cook, a real gourmet with fifty or sixty different recipes for bouilla-
baisse alone. "He'd taken a walking trip around the Mediterranean and up
through France and every place he got a recipe." Yet Fleming said at the
time that he thought Tracy probably the only guy in the world who really
understood him. "We're alike: bursting with emotions we can't express;
depressed all the time because we feel we could have done our work better.
When we were making *A Guy Named Joe* we had many differences of opinion, Spence and I. Many times he came into the office here, mad as the
devil about something. He'd just sit on that divan over there and we'd trem-
ble at each other for five minutes without saying a word. Then he'd get up
and walk out, and we'd both feel better."

Actor Van Johnson joined the company in early March, playing Ted
Randall, the young airman who becomes Irene Dunne's love interest in the
wake of Tracy's death. At twenty-six, Johnson found himself cast in the
awkward role of swain to a woman old enough to be his mother. It took
Fleming's sensitive but no-nonsense direction to put their relationship
across in a way that wasn't jarring—nor even particularly noticeable—to
the audience. "I finished the first take," Johnson remembered, "and Mr.

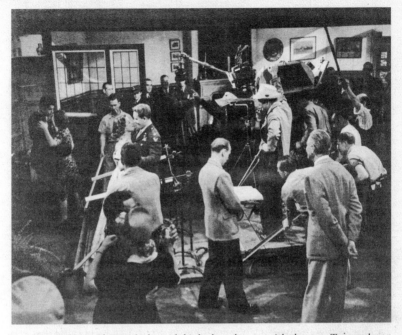

Director Victor Fleming (right, with his back to the camera) looks on as Tracy and Irene Dunne dance to the strains of "Wonderful One" for *A Guy Named Joe.* Note the makeshift corral that keeps the two stars in focus. (SUSIE TRACY)

Fleming said, 'Print that.' I looked to Tracy for approval. He said, 'Is that the way you're going to play it?' Well, I shriveled. He was joking, of course."

Tracy recalled that Johnson had once asked for his autograph outside Romanoff's in Beverly Hills, and he was naturally disposed to taking younger actors under his wing. "He liked young actors," said Barry Nelson, who was playing a featured role in the picture, "and he tried to help them— not so much in telling you how to read anything, but he certainly was a role model. He came on always perfectly prepared—long speeches, whatever. You would think he'd been out carousing all night or something, and he had that way about him on the set as if nothing mattered too much, but you knew that he'd worked very hard the night before. He was not only letter perfect but interpretation prefect."

Production moved at Fleming's usual deliberate pace until the night of March 31, 1943, when Van Johnson was critically injured while driving a group of friends to the studio to run off a print of *Keeper of the Flame.* Broadsided at the intersection of Venice and Clarington, just a block north of the main gate, he was thrown from the car and ended up with his head

braced by the curb. "My face was wet," he said, "and I thought it was raining, but it was blood . . . My nose was up against my eyes, and my scalp had
come unstuck. They lifted it up like a flap and poured in handfuls of sulfa."

At the hospital Johnson overheard a doctor say, "He'll never work in
pictures again, even if he does live." Down three quarts of blood, he was
only able to survive, it was theorized, because regular donations at the Red
Cross had conditioned his system. Reportedly, Tracy was the first person
from the studio permitted to see him. "Van Johnson is so sick from that
automobile accident," Sheilah Graham reported in her column of April 7,
"that his doctors are afraid to operate."

Fleming shut down the picture because Johnson, playing a young
recruit under Tracy's ghostly tutelage, was in almost every scene. As discussions centered on whom they'd get to replace him, Tracy went to Irene
Dunne and urged a show of solidarity. "I was in the Hollywood Presbyterian Hospital, all packed in ice, and the eye was closed, and they put a plate
in my head," said Johnson, "and that was when Irene Dunne and Spencer
Tracy went to Mr. Mayer and said, 'Let us wait for Van.' That gave me a
goal, it gave me sunlight at the end of the tunnel, because everybody said,
'He won't photograph . . .' " Eddie Lawrence remembered the gesture as a
measure of the regard Tracy had for a young actor who considered him a
mentor. "Now that was really something to do," he said, "because that was
a [matter] of time commitments. And Spence went down there to see Van
practically every day until Van came back. They stopped the picture
because of Spence. For Van Johnson, they wouldn't stop the picture.
Spencer had to put his weight in there because they wouldn't have done it
otherwise."

They resumed filming with a double on April 13, but there was only so
much work they could do without showing the young flier's face or hearing
his voice. Within a week, *A Guy Named Joe* was shut down indefinitely.

The official opening of John Tracy Clinic took place on the evening of February 1, 1943. After introductions at Norris Hall on the USC campus, the
nearly three hundred attendees were invited to tour the old clapboard house
on West Thirty-seventh, where classes on child psychology were ongoing
and where a new series of Saturday morning talks would focus on the formation and development of the elementary sounds of speech. A correspondence course, based on a long-discontinued one from the Wright Oral
School, was in its early stages of development, and a nursery school observation group had just been added. On prominent display was the clinic's
first publication, *Suggestions to the Parents of Deaf and Hard-of-Hearing
Children* by Louise Treadwell Tracy. At the open house, Doris Jackson, who

would soon fill the role of secretary to Mrs. Tracy, observed the founder's husband keeping very much to himself and doing his best to go unnoticed amid the festivities of the open house. "I can remember Mr. Tracy—him rubbing his hand down the woodwork saying, 'This is nice . . .' "

At first, said Louise, Spence seemed pleased she had decided to name the clinic after John; then, after thinking about it, he didn't think it was such a good idea after all.

He felt it was a great mistake to have called it that, because the impression became so firmly ingrained with people that this was the Tracys'—they were paying for everything, and then they thought Metro-Goldwyn-Mayer was paying for it. The things were just absurd. We needed money. We couldn't have taken care of the whole thing even had we wanted to. It was too much money, and also we felt it was not ourselves, it was too big a thing, that if it were as worthwhile as we thought, and as necessary, everybody should have a hand in it, because then it was everybody's and it would be much bigger. This was not a little family thing at all.

Contributions for the first year came to $1,440, while expenses ran close to $5,000. "Mr. Disney was one of the first contributors we had. I remember he gave us a hundred dollars. Before we were organized or incorporated or anything, I signed a little letter. I had my nerve, but then they didn't have all the restrictions they have now. So I just wrote a little letter and we had it printed and I got a list of names from one of those people who furnish names. It was a silly list of five-thousand people, and a lot of people were on that list who couldn't give ten cents. We sent it out, and out of the five-thousand, we had maybe sixty contributors. Not too many, but one of them was Mr. Disney, who I was sure would."

At its inception, John Tracy Clinic was the first institution of its kind that was entirely free, and the only one that was exclusively for the parents of deaf and hearing-impaired children. It was a model destined to cost money; the Wright Oral School had charged one hundred dollars for its correspondence course alone and couldn't come close to breaking even. When they had stretched their meager resources as far as they could, Louise went to Spence: "He thought about it, and we talked about it a little, and he said, 'How much do you figure it would cost for a year? Would ten-thousand dollars be enough?' I said, 'My heavens, yes, that would be wonderful.' So he gave us the ten thousand and he said, 'We'll try it and see what happens.' And he really, for the first three years, with very minor exceptions—these nickels and dimes that we got from a few people—he furnished all of the money."

In March the clinic began offering tests for mothers coping with the emotional and psychological stress of parenting a child with special needs. All manner of kids were being brought to the clinic—not just the hearing impaired—and although testing wasn't mandatory, Louise found that all the mothers seemed to want it. All had experienced the same basic stages of denial, anger, and grief, and all benefited from the kind of emotional support they could only get from one another. Louise drew on her own experiences in shaping the program, arranging for the help and services she wished that she'd had when her own little boy was not yet six and she was constantly being advised to wait until he was older—precious learning years being lost forever. She was also intimately aware of the damage the birth of a handicapped child could inflict on a marriage and that while it was too late for her and Spence, other marriages could be addressed and saved with the psychological counseling they never had for themselves.

Louise went to Howard Strickling at M-G-M and asked how they could get publicity. He said there was no problem, that he would make some phone calls, and articles appeared in the *Los Angeles Times,* the Hearst papers, and May Mann's syndicated "Going Hollywood" column. Mann described a woman who typically came to work in a simple blue suit and hat to match, a ring of linked platinum horseshoes—studded with diamonds and rubies, a gift from Spence—on the small finger of her right hand, her simple white gold wedding band on her left, down on her knees scrubbing the floors before the kids came in. "The children must not sit on dirty floors," she told the clinic's new executive secretary. "You can run a typewriter. I can't. But I know how to scrub and clean."

News of the clinic spread quickly; inquiries poured in. In July the clinic initiated its first summer session, an intensive six-week course for mothers and children set up by Mary New of the Lexington School for the Deaf. Miss New came from New York without salary—only the barest of expenses were paid—and presided over a program designed specifically for parents and children who came from out of state and couldn't otherwise participate. Sixty-two years later, Carol Lee Wales, who attended the last two weeks of that first summer session, could still vividly recall the old frame building and the playground, and the tutor helping her with her speech during individual sessions upstairs. "She would put my hand on her cheek or throat to feel the sounds, and we blew on feathers or tissue to see the breath sounds."

Spence was preparing to write another $10,000 check when he told Louise it was time to formalize the arrangement. "If I'm going to give all this money," he said, "we've got to set something up. You have to incorporate or else I can't take it off on the income tax." To get it all together, Louise instinctively turned to her polo buddies, the closest and most enduring cir-

John Tracy Clinic's first summer session, July–August 1943. Carol Lee Wales is the child whose painting Louise is admiring. (CAROL LEE BARNES)

cle of friends she had. She called Neil McCarthy, the millionaire sportsman and attorney whose racing silks were represented at all the major tracks, and asked him what to do about incorporating. "It's very simple," he said. "I'll do it for you. I'll be your secretary." Then he said, "You know, you have to have some people to incorporate." She called Walt Disney, whom she had first met "riding and playing out on the dirt field. He played with all the women. He was a beginner, you see, and he just loved it for the fun. Both he and Roy Disney played. So I called him and asked if he would go on the board, maybe be the vice-president. 'Sure,' he said. So we had him and Mr. McCarthy and then Mrs. Caldwell, Mrs. Orville Caldwell, one of my very best friends."

Tracy filled his time away from *A Guy Named Joe* recording broadcasts for Armed Forces Radio and visiting hospitals up and down the California coast, shaking hands, signing autographs, posing for pictures. Occasionally he showed up at the Hollywood Canteen, where he was known to sing "Pistol Packin' Mama" to the soldiers, a song he would eventually teach to Gary Cooper. Kate was in and out of town, keeping in touch by phone, permit-

At the Hollywood Canteen.
(PATRICIA MAHON COLLECTION)

ting Spence to cover her airfare when she went to New York to visit her mother, who was ill, and her train fare when she returned. In May the studio announced that Tracy would star in *They Were Expendable* for producer Sidney Franklin, an unlikely occurrence with *Joe* hanging fire for the foreseeable future. On the twenty-fifth of that month, with Van Johnson still decidedly on the mend, Irene Dunne went on with her second picture for Metro, *The White Cliffs of Dover*, an earnest tearjerker inspired by Alice Duer Miller's famous poem.

The meetings of the so-called Boys' Club had become less frequent, though no less important to its individual members, who shifted from time to time. "When Spence was off the sauce, he was kind of a sour guy," James Cagney recalled. "He would shun company, so I would have dinner with him alone. I think he was a very sad man. I made no demands on him. It was just small talk mostly." The experience of public dining soured considerably for the group after Tracy's 1942 binge, when retakes for *Tortilla Flat* had been held up several weeks. "It was never announced where we would have dinner," Frank McHugh remembered. "It was a guarded secret. However, we could never elude 'Square Deal' [Billy] Grady. He would invariably show up and sit at another table alone. Keeping an eye on Spence, no doubt, [while he was working]."

Whenever they wanted privacy, the boys would meet at the home of one of the members. "All the wives," said Dorothy McHugh, "were perfectly willing to arrange it and disappear, but whoever you had for a cook, it got to be this terrible rivalry. You know, who had the best dinner. Somebody would come home and say, 'You should get that pie at the Cagneys! The best I ever tasted!' " When it came Spence's turn, the group assembled at Kate's rented house in Beverly Hills, "and she would be there with Ethel Barrymore and people like that. But, of course, the wives never went! She would maybe not have it be the Boys' Club night, but would invite them to a dinner party."

Van Johnson's recovery was speedier than anyone expected, and work on *A Guy Named Joe* resumed in early July 1943. He still suffered from frequent headaches and fatigue and was left with facial scars that required heavy makeup and careful lighting to hide, but the effect was remarkably subtle, and the rushes betrayed no hint of the trauma he had been through. Irene Dunne was in a tougher spot, because Johnson's return put her in the unenviable position of having to shoot two pictures simultaneously, portraying Dorinda the seasoned pilot on some days, the misty-eyed Susan Dunn on others. "I've always lived the characters I played," she said, "and to be these two entirely different women at the same time was unbearable."

Tracy's Pete Sandidge* was one of his richest creations, a cocky hotdogger of a pilot who lent himself to endless colorations, unseen and unheard as he was by the earthly members of the cast. "He brought the art of reacting to a new height," Barry Nelson observed. "I would get to see the dailies, and what I didn't learn sitting on the set . . . because it's very hard to see the expressions . . . you could see them in the close-ups and two-shots in the dailies. You saw how much he had added in his thought process of what that character was thinking when someone else was speaking . . . He was always right on the button; there was never a wasted movement, a wasted thought, never an extraneous one, great economy in his playing."

In Sandidge, Louise could see Spence as he was at home, the sparkle in his eyes, the puckish Irish humor, the natural intensity of a man always up on his game. "I have seldom lost myself in a picture when he was on," she once commented. "I was always watching him." However, in *A Guy Named Joe* she could immerse herself, revel in it, forget, for a change, that it was a

---

* It's worth noting that there was no character named Joe in *A Guy Named Joe*. The title came from a famous remark by General Claire Chennault of the Flying Tigers: "Boys, when I'm at the stick, I'm just a guy named Joe."

movie. "You can just see him as he was," she said of it. "It was just so real. He had some of the same funny expressions. There were so many things he did . . . I liked him very much in *A Guy Named Joe*."

Production was closed down once again in mid-August so that background plates could be made by a second unit in Florida. The Hollywood Victory Committee took the hiatus as an opportunity to propose a tour of the Pacific for Tracy that would take him to Hawaii, Canton, Fiji, New Caledonia, Brisbane, and Samoa beginning September 20 and continuing through the end of October. Tentatively agreeing to the plan, he was plainly dubious of making high-profile appearances where performances might be expected of him. "What can I do?" he said to Adela Rogers St. Johns. "I'm no good. I'm just an actor. I have to have a part and a play and everything, and how can you do that? I can't talk well myself. I'm not the guy they see up there on the screen at all. I'm just a very ordinary man and probably not nearly as sure of things as they are. I can't sing or dance or tell stories. Send someone who can make 'em laugh, somebody who has something to offer."

He was back on the set of *Joe* following Labor Day, his plans for the Pacific tour now conflicting with Fleming's schedule and the studio's need to keep him available for retakes once his vacation kicked in. Leo Morrison was in the process of negotiating a new contract when someone noticed it contained no provision for retakes during his vacation periods, which started at six weeks and could extend to twelve weeks if he did two consecutive pictures or twenty-four weeks if he elected to do a play. *A Guy Named Joe* wrapped on September 20, 1943, with considerable miniature work yet to be shot, meaning it would likely be a month before the film could be previewed and any fixes identified. In lieu of the Pacific tour, Tracy agreed to go north into Alaska to visit some newly established bases, taking with him a small troupe of performers that included Marilyn Maxwell, Nancy Barnes, and comedian Johnny Bond.

Kate was in the first days of filming *Dragon Seed* when he left, a growing anxiety over the mere act of flying taking hold of him as he arrived in Seattle. It had been many years since he had seen Lois and Kenny Edgers, now a dentist with a thriving practice, and with the weather fogging in plane traffic, he seized the opportunity to meet them for dinner. Walking into Spence's suite at the Olympic Hotel, Kenny could see that he was on the phone with Louise. "Here's Kenny now," Spence said to her, "and you should see him. He has hardly any gray hair!" Tracy, of course, had begun to gray early. He had just been informed that the Alaskan base had no accommodations for the women in his troupe and that the weather was unsatisfactory. As they waited it out, the pressure mounted for a decision on his part.

Taking advantage of their proximity to Victoria, Tracy phoned Lincoln

Cromwell, now also in private practice and with a young family. "Spence told me to get right on over there," Cromwell recalled. "There was no saying no to the man, so I just closed my office and took the afternoon ferry across the Sound. Evidently, he needed me for moral support." Tracy told Cromwell that his troupe was in a "state of rebellion" and many wanted to turn back. According to him, the actors and showgirls were afraid of flying and of entering a war zone, which Alaska technically was, and that he was having little success in reassuring them. "I was all for Spence, but after a day the truth of the situation became clear to me. He, himself, was the source of the fear and dissension circulating through the group."

Tracy was plainly terrified of flying any farther, and the final omen had come the day before, when a waitress in the hotel coffee shop told him that she had also served Wiley Post just before he left on his fateful flight to Alaska with Will Rogers. "On a conscious level, Spencer appeared unaware that he was the author of the rapidly spreading 'rebellion' in his troupe. However, he finally acceded to the consensus and, after three days, they all returned by plane to Los Angeles."

Kenny Edgers had a call from Spence at 4:30 one morning, asking him to come down to the Olympic and help him decide what to do.

He said he had been "directed" for so long that he'd lost the ability to make decisions. In these small hours, among other things, he said he envied me the necessity of making "either-or" choices. Either people made his decisions for him, or it was a matter of choosing some tangible item (car, clothing, etc.) and he could have anything he wanted. He had five Cadillacs and the planning of acquiring anything had lost its kick. So he worried about his public image. After he returned to Hollywood, he phoned me several times to inquire if Seattle papers had unfavorable publicity. No mention had been made and his days of agony were unnecessary.*

Tracy told Lincoln Cromwell the younger man obviously "needed a vacation" and insisted on his accompanying them on the flight back. For the next two weeks Cromwell saw him daily, staying with him in his two-bedroom suite at the Beverly Hills Hotel, where Tracy had left him upon their arrival in L.A.

---

* Well, not quite. Hedda Hopper, aware of his cozy relationship with Louella Parsons, reported on Tracy's aborted trip at the top of her October 27 column: "What happened to the Alaska Trip? What caused him to change his mind? The boys up there are starving for entertainment and they've been waiting to welcome him for many months." It was just the sort of humiliating publicity he feared.

He went on up the hill to see Katharine Hepburn. Later that evening, he sent a limousine down to bring me up to her house ... I knew that he and Mrs. Tracy had been living apart since my first year at McGill. At the party Spencer gave for me between my first and second years of medical school, Louise Tracy was conspicuous by her absence. I recall that I spent most of that evening sitting across the table talking with Katharine Hepburn, while Spencer tromped back and forth in front of the window, looking down at Hollywood below. He was still preoccupied with his aborted Alaska excursion. Miss Hepburn had grown up in a medical family ... and she was interested in—and conversant with—a variety of medical topics. We had a long, spirited discussion about biology, medicine, and philosophy with Spencer participating little, if at all.

During the days, Spence went to work at the studio, and I drove around Los Angeles, renewing old friendships. He made his car available for my use, even requesting the Rationing Board to make more gas available for me. I repaid him by running some of his errands. One of these was to return a heavy parka he had borrowed from Jimmy Roosevelt to wear in Alaska. Spencer was a dedicated Democrat, with friends high up in the Roosevelt administration. In the evenings, we would go out to a restaurant to eat or have food sent up from the hotel. Spence did no cooking there. While still at medical school, I had been cautioned by Dr. Dennis to avoid alcohol—both the subject and the substance— when with Spencer. During this period, however, we usually had a couple of drinks before dinner, and Spence never over-indulged. At no time I was with him did he conduct himself as anything but a gentleman.

Kate was no more a drinker than Louise, but where Louise's tactic was sheer avoidance, Hepburn would give him a drink and then challenge him to handle it. Like most Americans of the time, she considered the abuse of alcohol a failure of the will, though not necessarily the moral failing that temperance crusaders and prohibitionists contended. There's every indication, in fact, that she never especially wanted Tracy to quit drinking altogether. He maddened her, grieved her at times, but never bored her. "You have to say, 'What do you expect of life?' I've known several men who drank too much and they were all extremely interesting." To their friend Bill Self she was blunter still: "All of my men have been drunks."

It was like a badge of honor, a pattern she had no interest in breaking. "I don't think anything destroyed Spencer," she said, "except the fact that he had produced a son that was very severely handicapped and he felt responsible for it. And he was absolutely unable to face it . . . I never interfered in a stupid way. And I never tried to moralize about the evils of drink. And if I interfered in a clever way, why, it wouldn't be interfering, would it? Well, I'd just try to change the atmosphere. But a drinker is going to stop on his own. I think you can very seldom influence anyone to stop."

And so with Kate Hepburn at his side, Tracy began a period in which he tried moderating his drinking rather than stopping it entirely, a shaky proposition when, as Audrey Caldwell once observed, all he needed was "a dessert with rum in it" to set him off.

Joe Mankiewicz believed Tracy and Hepburn well matched because "if you were going to be in an intimate relationship with Spence it had to be one where essentially you took care of him, waited on him, cleaned up after him. Spence was in your care. On good psychological grounds the alcoholic is in that infantile position. He renders himself helpless, which is a state of infancy and which is the most powerful position that the human being is ever in. He has to be taken care of as an infant. He has to be wiped and dried and fed and dressed and cleaned as an infant. And Kate, I think, wanted to do that."

Tracy never touched booze around Louise and the kids, and neither Johnny nor Susie could remember ever having seen him with a drink in his hand. One evening he drove Lincoln Cromwell out to the ranch for dinner. "We spent the night there, and I remember, after Spence had gone to bed, the long conversation Louise and I had concerning her feelings about Spencer and their marriage. Finally, she asked my advice: Should she divorce him? While I could certainly see her side of the situation, my basic loyalty was to Spencer and I felt that if he had wanted a divorce, he would have asked for it. I replied to her that since most things seemed to be going smoothly between them, without a lot of emotional strain, I could not see what a divorce would accomplish. In short, I advised her to do nothing."

In October Tracy was asked to appear at a rally of twelve thousand War Chest volunteers in Colorado, headlining a three-hour bill of entertainment that included opera star Mona Paulee, the eighty-piece symphonic band from Buckley Field, a soldier chorus of sixty voices, and the stars of the WACavilcade, a national touring company of thirty. Studio publicist Hal Elias was assigned to go with him.

Prior to going I had never met him, and Howard Strickling, who was head of publicity, called me into his office one day and he [said], "I want you to meet Spencer Tracy." So Tracy knew that I was to accompany him to Denver—that was where the war bond drive was supposed to take place. And he said, "Hal, I want one thing understood." He said it very sternly. "Nobody is going to tell me when and how much to drink."

He was very self-conscious of his heavy-drinking reputation. And I said, "Spence, I'm not making this trip to be a guardian and tell you when and what to drink. I'm merely there to protect the publicity interests of M-G-M and YOUR interests." That settled it. Now we arrived in Denver, and we retired to a beautiful suite of rooms. I'll never forget—there was a dining room table in the middle of the room, and it was loaded with liquor of every description. They knew it was Spencer Tracy, and they knew he was a heavy drinker. So he looked at it and said, "Hal, give all these bottles to the motorcycle escort who brought us over here." And Spencer Tracy didn't take one drink during the entire trip.

Tracy returned to M-G-M to make added scenes for *A Guy Named Joe,* which, like *Keeper of the Flame,* had run afoul of the Production Code. The War Department had never been enthusiastic about the picture and only grudgingly provided cooperation after two major revisions in the screenplay. ("The presence of hovering ghosts of deceased pilots, and the unreal, fantastic, and slightly schizophrenic character of the scenario hardly combine to produce a sensible war time film diet," the chief of the Information Branch complained.) The picture's ending, as written by Dalton Trumbo and staged by Fleming, had Irene Dunne's character crashing after the bombing of an enemy ammunition dump, thereby reuniting her with Tracy's Pete Sandidge at the fade-out. The PCA's Joe Breen objected to the ending on the presumption that Dorinda's commandeering of the bomber—intended for the Van Johnson character—constituted a willful act of suicide, which was, under the Code, never to be "justified, or glorified, or used specifically to defeat the ends of justice." Everett Riskin's office had new scenes ready on November 4, and Irene Dunne and her husband were flown in from Mexico City for the reopening of production. With the mandated fixes and some revised miniature work, *A Guy Named Joe* finally finished on December 4, 1943, after 107 days before the cameras. Tracy started his next picture the following morning.

The Seventh Cross was the story of seven escapees from a German concentration camp in 1936. It was written by Anna Seghers, a Communist refugee who had made her way to Mexico in the opening days of World War II and obviously knew of what she wrote. The commandant swears he will return all the escaped men and display their bodies on crudely fashioned crosses in the prison yard as a lesson to the others. It is the one who ultimately escapes to freedom, George Heisler, who leaves the seventh cross empty.

When published in 1942 by Little, Brown, Seghers' book was an immediate best seller, moving more than three hundred thousand copies in the space of twelve days. Pandro S. Berman, the producer responsible for most of Kate's pictures at RKO, got Metro to buy the rights and subsequently sent the draft script, by first-time scenarist Helen Deutsch, to M-G-M contract director Fred Zinnemann for his "opinion." Zinnemann had graduated to B-level features after serving an apprenticeship in the studio's short subject department. He already knew the book well and thought it would make a very good movie. His participation, it turned out, was contingent upon Tracy's approval.

Zinnemann approached the project with characteristic zeal, marking up his copy of the novel and storyboarding the entire movie with his own thumbnail sketches. On his heavily annotated copy of Deutsch's October 22 script he wrote, "This is about the dignity of human beings." He ran a number of Tracy's M-G-M pictures and decided to model Tracy's performance on his work in *Fury.* He did a good deal of character analysis and wanted Tracy to see *The Informer.* He also thought Tracy needed to lose weight for the role. Since the entire picture was set in Germany, standing sets on Lot 2 had to be modified, and the supporting cast became a colorful collection of refugees and character people headed by the husband-wife team of Hume Cronyn and Jessica Tandy.

Cronyn, making only his third film, bonded instantly with Zinnemann, who was bullied by a headstrong cinematographer in the person of Karl Freund. "His lighting took hours," Cronyn remembered. "Walking onto the set, threading one's way through the light stands, was like entering a bamboo thicket, and some lamp or other would inevitably get nudged and have to be refocused." Tracy had worked with Freund before and knew him to be punctilious and overbearing, but Zinnemann was completely thrown by him. "Freund was anything but a friend," said Zinnemann. "He was loud, slow, and obstreperous; working with him was like pulling out teeth, one by one." Within days the picture was behind schedule.

"Zinnemann was first chosen as director for *The Seventh Cross,*" said Katharine Hepburn, "and Spencer did not know him [other than he'd] done some picture in Germany, and I cannot remember the name of it.* Very distinguished, so Spencer said, Okay, he would take [him]. After a

---

* Zinnemann had codirected, with Curt Siodmak, Edgar G. Ulmer, and Robert Siodmak, *People on Sunday* (1930), a well-regarded and widely seen German feature that was also one of Billy Wilder's earliest writing credits.

week, Metro wanted to yank Freddie Zinnemann off that picture. They were not satisfied with what he was doing, and Spencer said, 'My friends, if you yank him, I'm joining him. You can make up your minds to that. You should not have suggested him in the first place. Now you have to give him the chance.' "

Backing down, Berman, who was also overseeing the production of *Dragon Seed,* peopled the stage with surrogates, including Helen Deutsch (who was, said Zinnemann, "possessive about changing a dot or a comma") and his longtime assistant, Jane Loring. "I felt it was very important to get across the fact that just because you were a German it didn't mean automatically that you were a monster," Zinnemann said, "which at the time many people thought was the case—naturally enough, in view of what was going on. The film was a study of the people Tracy met when he was running for his life, people who were forced by his presence to get off the fence, one way or the other; either they helped him or they didn't help him. Some took great personal risks; others, who were old friends, turned their backs and wouldn't have anything to do with him."

Morale was low, and Tracy's dark moods were sharpened by the drinks he now permitted himself at the end of each workday. Hume Cronyn thought him "a lovely man" who had a "rough tongue" on occasion, particularly after having imbibed a few. Seated one evening in Tracy's dressing room, drink in hand, Cronyn shot to his feet when Hepburn, whom he had never before met, walked in. "Spence was feeling morose," said Cronyn, "and made no effort to move or introduce us. Perhaps he assumed we knew one another. I introduced myself. We shook hands and she said, 'I hope I'm not interrupting anything—please sit down.' She was tall, slim, beautiful, and very direct, and her look was as firm as her handshake. I was aware that she was appraising Tracy and conscious of his mood."

Hepburn turned to him and said cheerfully, "How are you doing, old man?"

"On my ass."

"Problems?"

But he was drinking and didn't bother to answer. She continued, "I think I'll get myself a drink."

Cronyn got up again. "Can I get it for you?" he said.

"She told you to sit down!" Tracy snapped, as though Cronyn were hard of hearing. Cronyn sat down, and presently Kate joined them.

"Spence seemed withdrawn into sullen reverie. I wondered what was wrong; he'd been talkative enough before Miss Hepburn arrived, despite the irritation he expressed over the time it was taking to light our scenes. Miss Hepburn talked to me, ignoring Spence's silence. She asked me about the film and what I was playing; she knew the script well. She was charming. At one point she produced a cigarette and I got up to light it for her. That did it."

Tracy exploded: "Why don't you two find a bed somewhere and get it over with?"

"I stood there, frozen, until the match burned my fingers," said Cronyn. "Miss Hepburn just smiled."

Tracy waved him down. "Sit down, for Christ's sake! You keep bouncing around like corn in a popper!"

Cronyn finished his drink and got out as quickly as possible; there was something about Kate's presence that addled Tracy, as if she were revealing a dark secret about the two of them she had no business exposing. It wasn't jealousy, Hepburn insisted: "No. No, he'd had a few."

Joe Mankiewicz, who knew both men intimately, agreed, though not quite for the same reason. "Hume had done two things that were irritating Spence. Jumping up from that seat when she came in and jumping up now. 'Let me do it for you.' Because it's obviously 'good manners,' because Kate Hepburn, in my life, in my world, is perfectly capable of fixing her own friggin' drink if the drinks are there. If it's troublesome to get, well . . . And getting up as she comes into the room! Again, at our age and our status in the business, we don't do that. But if you're Hume . . . 'and I got up to light her cigarette!' " He laughed. "Knowing Spence, he's picked the three spots where his temper is going boom, boom, boom!"

There may have been yet another reason for Tracy's irascibility. Ingrid Bergman had been back on the M-G-M lot shooting Patrick Hamilton's Victorian thriller *Gaslight,* and one day she was photographed on the set of *A Guy Named Joe* talking with Tracy and Irene Dunne. As soothing as Kate's presence could be, it could also be disruptive, for she had fallen deeply in love with a man who could never tell her that he loved her.* "I have no idea how Spence felt about me," she wrote in her memoir. "I can only say I think that if he hadn't liked me he wouldn't have hung around." But now it was Kate who was hanging around, and she was going through a period where she was obsessed with him. Hairstylist Helen Hunt once told Katharine Houghton of a time when Hepburn staked out the grounds of the Beverly Hills Hotel with a loaded shotgun, certain that Tracy was fooling around on her—presumably with Bergman. "Kate," said Houghton, "was fiercely jealous of Bergman."

Sexually, Tracy and Hepburn were simpatico—so much so that Kate confided to their friend Eugene Kennedy that she had once asked a doctor

---

* "I think Spencer was afraid of emotion beyond a certain point," Mankiewicz said, "and even devotion beyond a certain point. I think he distrusted himself because he was afraid of what might happen if he took a drink."

Ingrid Bergman, in costume for *Gaslight,*
visits the set of *A Guy Named Joe.*
(PATRICIA MAHON COLLECTION)

if Spence could get injections to "lower his libido." Emotionally, they were
on different planes, and she was very possibly crowding him at a time when
he felt particularly vulnerable to bad publicity. He laid out Sheilah Graham
one day over a "veiled allusion in the column regarding his private life" and
he was rapidly adopting Kate's policy of never talking to the press, ever.

Tracy's irritability became the stuff of legend during the making of *The
Seventh Cross,* in part because there were an unusual number of observers on
the set. "I never tried missing a scene when Tracy was playing," Hume
Cronyn said. "His method seemed to be as simple as it is difficult to
achieve. He appeared to do nothing. He listened, he felt, he said the words
without forcing anything. There were no extraneous movements. Whatever
was provoked in him emotionally was seen in his eyes." Said Zinnemann,
"When a signal from the M-G-M grapevine said that he was about to do an
important scene, all the young hopeful contract players would sneak on the
stage and, lost in awe and fascination, would watch him from protective
darkness."

The Seventh Cross was unusual for a Tracy picture in that he played the first thirty minutes with no dialogue. On the run, the guards and their dogs after him, the SS keeping watch, George Heisler is a hunted man, desperate and worn. To achieve the effect, he submitted to a Prussian haircut and a gray-toned makeup job accentuated by the fact that he had dropped eight pounds in as many weeks. When a writer from *Time* magazine dropped by the set in January 1944, Tracy described himself as "a box of chocolates broadened out into a character actor" and explained the drop by noting that the war had curtailed his normal supply of sweets. By the time Signe Hasso, the Swedish actress, arrived to play the last act as Tracy's love interest, he was tense and withdrawn at times but had settled into a more comfortable frame of mind, helped, perhaps, by the fact that Karl Freund had fallen ill and had been replaced for a spell with Robert Surtees.

"To work with Tracy was the easiest thing in the world," Hasso later wrote. "We rehearsed once and that was it. I remember the director, Fred Zinnemann (it was his first big picture) got a bit nervous about only one rehearsal, but Tracy said, 'I know my lines. Signe knows hers. Let's have a cup of tea while they set the lights. And you too, Fred. You need a cup of tea.' Fred wasn't so sure that he needed any tea, but, of course, off he went for a tea session, where no work was discussed. We talked about life in general, and Fred grew more and more nervous. However, when the scene was lit and the camera ready to shoot, we did it in one take. And Fred was again happy."

When Frederick Othman, Hollywood correspondent for the United Press, visited the set, Tracy was in a pretty good mood, noting dryly that this was the first time in years that a man and wife—meaning the Cronyns—had played a man and wife on the screen and just as well, too. He then charged Jessica Tandy, making her American film debut, with walking into a scene just to take her husband's paycheck away from him. This, he suggested, set a bad precedent, even as Tandy herself blushed and denied the whole thing. Only once she was out of earshot did he allow that Tandy was "one of the finest actresses ever to get into the movie business."

Relaxing in his dirt-caked pants, his torn sweater and greasy leather jacket, he went on to discuss work in general, saying that although a film actor made a lot of money, he usually earned every cent in the loss of many of the joys that other people took as a matter of course. Sunshine, for instance. "I think, probably, that the only man who can be happy all the time under contract to a movie studio is a dumb one, the really dumb one who signs up to act for five years and who does exactly that, without a care or a worry about the sort of thing that is handed him. There are some people like that in pictures, and I think they are the only ones who have licked the problem of being happy, though in Hollywood."

A Guy Named Joe was released during the filming of *The Seventh Cross*, having drawn rave reviews in press previews arranged hastily to get the film onto the market as M-G-M's Christmas attraction. Van Johnson's callow performance sounded a sour note to only a few of the New York critics, who overall lauded the film for its deft management of a difficult subject and decried only the Breen-induced ending that caused it, in the words of one reviewer, to "virtually explode" in her face. The trade notice in the *Hollywood Reporter* diplomatically suggested that the finale would satisfy the majority of audiences, "although there can be debates about who should get the girl." Bosley Crowther, less forgiving, condemned "a finish that is as foolish as anything we've seen—and which thoroughly negates the film's philosophy, which is against heroic stunts and one-man shows."

Whatever the picture's failings, both Tracy and Dunne were praised elaborately, the *Reporter* noting how Tracy's abilities "permit him to make more out of a simple 'gosh' than many actors achieve from a Shakespearean soliloquy." Its arrival triggered a powerful rush at the box office, leading to seven strong weeks at the Capitol Theatre at a time when the public's demand for "demilitarized" fare was growing. With total billings of $5,363,000, *A Guy Named Joe* surpassed even *San Francisco* to become Tracy's highest-grossing film ever. In early January, with a new contract almost ready to sign, Tracy told columnist Harrison Carroll he was refusing all assignments for at least three or four months because he wanted to visit camps and bases instead. "I worked on *A Guy Named Joe* for eleven straight months," he said, "and you can't go on tour with retakes, extra scenes, and work hanging over your head. When I visit camps next time, I want to feel I don't have to hurry back."

He backed that statement with a formal letter to Benny Thau, advising the studio, in effect, that at the completion of *The Seventh Cross* he would be leaving for an indefinite period. A few days later, Eddie Mannix took him aside and agreed that after he finished the picture he would be permitted "a certain number of weeks" to go abroad and entertain the troops and that upon his return he would have a four-week vacation before having to start another film. The new contract, which took effect on February 26, 1944, guaranteed him six weeks' vacation at the completion of each picture and paid $5,277.52 a week or, given the agreed-upon limitation of five productions in any two-year period, approximately $110,000 a picture—good money for a major star, but by no means top dollar.* It should be noted, however, that Tracy averaged little more than one picture a year during this period, so his actual compensation worked out to roughly $250,000 a film. It was a moot point anyway, as a presidential anti-inflation order signed in

* By way of comparison, Claudette Colbert's deal with Paramount called for $150,000 a picture.

1942 limited the nation's heavy earners to an annual income of $25,000 after taxes.

As it turned out, Mannix's generous assurances of time off were conditional, for he and the rest of management were eager to have Tracy play Lieutenant Colonel Jimmy Doolittle in *Thirty Seconds Over Tokyo,* the story of the famed 1942 raid over Japan that had been turned into a best-selling book by Captain Ted Lawson and the Hearst Syndicate's Bob Considine. Tracy had repeatedly rejected the role, which had him presiding over briefings and little else. "Anybody could go on and do that," he complained to Louise. "It's silly. Why should I do it?"

Producer Sam Zimbalist settled on Paramount's Brian Donlevy to play Doolittle instead, but Donlevy lacked Tracy's power at the box office and the studio had an investment of nearly $3 million to protect. In November 1943 an item was fed to Louella Parsons assuring her readers that Tracy would indeed be playing the Doolittle role. "Spence is a smart boy," Parsons commented, "even though the part doesn't have as much footage as Captain Ted Lawson's (the role Van Johnson will play)." He was still resisting the assignment in February 1944 when filming began on M-G-M's massive Stage 15, where a section of flight deck from the U.S.S. *Hornet* had been fabricated to hold an actual B-25 Mitchell bomber on loan from the army.

The Seventh Cross finished on March 8, with Tracy agreeing to just four weeks off in lieu of the six to which he was now entitled. On April 9 he would start *Thirty Seconds Over Tokyo*—a three-week job—and do whatever retakes were required for *Seventh Cross.* Then he would have eight consecutive weeks to tour as he pleased.

CHAPTER 20

The Big Drunk

The debacle of the Alaskan tour weighed heavily on Tracy for months afterward. Scores of movie figures were now in uniform, and many of the ones who weren't—Bob Hope, Cagney, Bing Crosby, virtually all the women—gave tirelessly to the job of morale on the home front as well as overseas. Metro alone had Melvyn Douglas, Robert Taylor, Jimmy Stewart, Van Heflin, Richard Ney, and Robert Montgomery on active duty, with Mickey Rooney and Red Skelton soon to follow. Tracy's pal Gable had enlisted with the U.S. Army Air Forces and flown combat missions in Europe. All Tracy had to show for the war effort were his hospital visits, a little radio work, and a few high-profile appearances for war bonds and the like. More than ever, his neuroses were dictating his actions, and only the scotch he permitted himself seemed to bring him relief.

Kate spent the 1943 Christmas season in Los Angeles—her first away from her family—and thought the experience "horrible." The studios all quit work at noon on the twenty-fourth, then everyone proceeded to get drunk. The weather was hot and it didn't seem like Christmas at all. Spence gave her some old after-dinner coffee cups, an antique silver bell, a fireplace set—poker and tongs—and ten crisp new fifty-dollar bills. When *Time,* in its review of *A Guy Named Joe,* said he was, as usual, "extremely competent," she and Spence spent an entire evening looking through a dictionary, Tracy maintaining the words always applied to him—capable, competent, etc.—just meant he knew enough "not to fall down." And, for as much as she could say to the contrary, he insisted there was a world of difference between "extremely competent" and "brilliant."

Hepburn was on a campaign to film Eugene O'Neill's *Mourning Becomes Electra* with herself as Lavinia and Greta Garbo as her murderous mother. Spence, in the meantime, had arranged to visit navy bases on the Wisconsin shore of Lake Michigan as the first step toward greater involvement with the Hollywood Victory Committee. With four days of retakes on *The Seventh Cross* now behind him, he and Carroll set out for Chicago on May 13, first to visit the Great Lakes Naval Training Center, where he himself had trained in the waning months of the last war, and then on to Manitowoc to see the shipbuilding yards and talk with the officers and crew of the newly launched submarine U.S.S. *Icefish* (for which he was named mascot). In Milwaukee he saw Buck Herzog of the *Sentinel* (who described him as "bronzed from his first vacation from film chores in many months") and said he planned to go on to New York for a round of visits to government hospitals.

In Freeport the boys visited their uncle Andrew and aunt Emma, and relatives drove in from nearby. Ann Willits, the nine-year-old granddaughter of the late Frank J. Tracy, could recall Spence telling her about Susie, who was close in age, and asking if she knew how to play hopscotch. "I did, but I said, 'No.' And much to the frustration of Aunt Mame [Andrew's wife], who had lunch ready, he showed me how to play. I remember asking my mom and dad on the way home how he just happened to have chalk in his pocket."

Emma Brown, a classic maiden lady who favored black clothing and wore dresses until they were threadbare, was in her seventies but still owned the family feed business on Galena Avenue. "Aunt Mum" would typically meet her nephews at the Hotel Freeport, where Spence, in particular, would hole up and rarely leave. "They were the closest three people you ever saw," said Bertha Calhoun, "Aunt Mum and Carroll and Spencer."

Whether Tracy made it to New York or not is unclear, for his drinking was growing steadily worse. M-G-M studio records show he was "ill" a total of sixteen days on *The Seventh Cross,* and Fay Kanin, Michael Kanin's wife and later writing partner, got a glimpse of such illness firsthand: "I remember having to meet Spencer for lunch at one of the fancy Beverly Hills restaurants—I don't remember which one—and he had been drinking. *Boy,* had he been drinking . . . we had a perfectly good time, though."

Herzog recalled that Tracy was imbibing freely in Milwaukee, Carroll hovering protectively, and his drinking likely continued in Chicago after Carroll returned to California. Actress Edith Luckett, who toured with Tracy in *The Baby Cyclone,* had settled in Chicago after marrying Dr. Loyal

Davis, a prominent neurosurgeon, in 1929. Tracy generally saw the Davises when he was in town for any length of time, and according to Luckett's daughter Nancy, he stayed at the family's East Lake Shore Drive apartment so often that he "practically became a member of the family."

Katie Treat, widow of Earl Treat, the founder of the Chicago chapter of Alcoholics Anonymous, remembered a call placed to her husband by Edith Davis sometime in the mid-1940s. "Lucky" (as she was known to her friends) told Earl

> that she had a friend that she had been on the stage [with] . . . He was in great trouble at the Blackstone [Hotel], but she was going to move him up to their house . . . Would Earl come to their house and talk to this man? So Earl galloped down there and Nancy opened the door . . . and it was Spencer Tracy who was in trouble. And he *really* was. He would go to the Blackstone and hole in there and just drink himself to death. And they'd go and get him and take him home. So Earl kept track of him and every time Spencer came to town he'd call Earl and they'd have lunch or dinner together and Earl would [talk to him]. Spencer didn't stop drinking—he kept right on—so finally he said to Earl, "How would you like to go to Hollywood?" Earl said he had never really thought of going to Hollywood. Spencer said, "I'll move your family out there, I'll give you a house and a car and all the servants you need if you'll dance attendance on me and keep me sober." And Earl said, "I'll tell you something: If I accepted that, *I'd* be drunk in a week!"

The concept of alcoholism as a disease didn't originate with Alcoholics Anonymous, but A.A. certainly popularized the notion. Embracing it helped build the organization by persuading potential members they were truly "powerless over alcohol," the first step in an ongoing journey to sobriety. But making alcoholism a disease negated the idea of personal responsibility and the sense of guilt it engendered. Tracy could never accept the idea that he wasn't personally responsible for his drunken lapses, for he could never fully justify the self-loathing he carried deep within himself. Kate, moreover, dismissed out of hand the idea of Spence going to Alcoholics Anonymous. Tracy, she pointed out, was "the biggest star in the world" and were he to join A.A. he wouldn't be anonymous for very long. "There are certain people who JUST CAN'T go to places like that. Spencer was a really curious, enormously complicated, very oversensitive human being with an enormous problem [that there was] no way out of."

Loyal Davis' son Richard knew that Tracy and his father were "very, very close" and that Tracy spent time in Chicago hospitalized under his father's care. "There was a very private floor at Passavant [Memorial Hospital]—the top floor—and I remember he was there maybe six weeks getting dried out. Loyal and Edith kept that very quiet." This was likely around the time of Tracy's Midwestern tour, for there are few gaps in the time line that would accommodate such an extended period of treatment.* Moreover, Richard Davis, on leave from the army, attended the Democratic National Convention in the company of his parents and Mayor and Mrs. Edward J. Kelly in mid-July 1944, and Tracy, he recalled, was there with them. Franklin Roosevelt was nominated for a fourth term, but the party found itself split over a Supreme Court decision invalidating whites-only primaries in Texas and the South.

"The big issue," said Davis, "was black voting rights, and Spencer Tracy just went bananas about this. He could not understand why there were all these ridiculous rules about blacks voting in the South, and he didn't waste any time telling Mayor Kelly. I can't say that my father [who was an arch conservative] disagreed with Spencer Tracy. I don't think he said anything. He respected Spencer Tracy's viewpoint."

Hepburn had been east herself, due back at the studio June 1 to begin work on the film version of *Without Love*. Tracy likely returned to Los Angeles the following month but was not seen publicly until August 12, when he recorded an episode of *Command Performance* for Armed Forces Radio. Back at the studio, he spent five days shooting a two-reeler in support of the Seventh Victory Loan for Canada called *Tomorrow, John Jones*. Played entirely in pantomime, the film was designed to be shown throughout the British Dominion during the October drive, carrying either a French or English narration track as appropriate. He would later receive a special citation for his work in the film from the Canadian Motion Picture War Services Committee, as would L. B. Mayer and all the others involved in its making.

The Seventh Cross was released on September 1, 1944, and became the best-reviewed picture Tracy had made since *Woman of the Year*—something of a surprise to its recalcitrant star. "This picture is going to be an *artistic* success," he had groused to Rosalind Shaffer of the Baltimore *Sun* while waiting for a scene to be set up one morning on the grounds of the Riviera Country Club. "It will get one good review from one critic and not make any money."

In fact, it received high praise from all corners, starting in London where it was described in a studio teletype as "a box office smash that was

---

* It is unlikely, however, that Tracy was hospitalized for a period of six weeks. In August 1944 Jack Lait of *Variety*, subbing for Walter Winchell, reported that Tracy had spent "two weeks in a Chicago hospital, incognito," and this is probably closer to the truth.

accorded the best press in many war-weary months." It hit New York in late September, arriving at the Capitol after ten weeks of David O. Selznick's home front extravaganza *Since You Went Away*. Zinnemann's careful compositions (flawlessly executed by the dreaded Freund) and his placing of prominent European figures such as Helene Weigel and Helene Thimig in minor roles—bit parts really—gave the film an unusual texture for an M-G-M production. Taut and suspenseful, it was crowned by Tracy's spare and often wordless performance, a startling departure from the likes of *Tortilla Flat* and *A Guy Named Joe*. And if it wasn't quite the crowd-pleaser *Joe* had been, it did restore a certain luster to the Tracy brand.

On September 14 Tracy began a USO tour of Hawaii, visiting the wounded at thirteen army and navy hospitals in his usual low-key manner, refusing all press interviews and relenting only when Major Maurice Evans of the army's Entertainment Section dispatched a man to his suite at the Royal Hawaiian. Tracy, the man observed, was traveling with two snugly strapped brown suitcases, at least one of which was filled with liquor. He offered the obviously terrified young private, dripping in ill-fitting khaki, a long pull from what tasted like a bottle of bonded bourbon.

"I recall the liquor dribbling down my chin," Dan Alexander wrote. "Eventually, he removed the bottle, saying, 'Don't talk yet. Have another drink.' I did and now started feeling more relaxed. When I finished this second, Mr. Tracy asked if I smoked and bid me have a cigarette when I said yes. As I puffed, I became aware that he was scrutinizing me—and then, as if satisfied, he said, 'Now start your interview.' Which I did, handily, and then easily shared my notes with the waiting media."

Tracy made the rounds without fanfare, walking in unannounced and introducing himself individually to the men. He signed hundreds of short-snorters, pictures, and scraps of paper, and accepted scores of messages for delivery back home to relatives and sweethearts. In one ward, he saw Joe Breen's son Tommy, who had lost a leg in a raid on Saipan. In another, he struck up a conversation with a Midwestern boy who hailed, he discovered, from Ipswich. ("My God, Ipswich!" he erupted. "That's where my Uncle Frank Tracy lived . . .") Routinely, he started the day at 5:00 a.m. and continued until nightfall, taking just an hour out for lunch and a swim. On nine of his twelve days there, he also appeared at GI theaters showing *A Guy Named Joe* and *Thirty Seconds Over Tokyo*.

He arrived back in the States on the twenty-sixth, relieved to know that he didn't need a formal routine to do his bit for the troops. "You don't have to get up and do a song and dance," he said. "They just want to talk to you and know someone is thinking of them." He told Louella Parsons that he wanted to go back, and he started looking for a play he could do in the camps. "I actually think," said Adela Rogers St. Johns, "that he believed they would take one look at him and say, 'Is that Spencer Tracy? What a sell. Tell him to go away and send Betty Grable.' "

Katharine Hepburn regarded the film version of *Without Love* as a chance not only to fix the failings of the Barry play, which were manifest, but also to—at long last—do it with the proper leading man. Its sale to M-G-M had made news in 1942, but the selling price, as it turned out, wasn't nearly as unique as it seemed. That same season, Warners paid $250,000 for Irving Berlin's *This Is the Army,* Fox an estimated $300,000 for *The Eve of St. Mark.* Screenwriter Nunnally Johnson was heard to explain: "All the film companies got together and agreed not to pay less than $250,000 for any play."

At first the property was assigned to Leon Gordon, whom Hepburn may have blamed in part for her troubles on *Keeper of the Flame.* Gordon, newly elevated to the rank of full producer, brought in playwright Samson Raphaelson, Ernst Lubitsch's frequent collaborator, to do the script. In all, Gordon and Raphaelson spent six months working on the picture, the tension between them evident in the condescending tone Gordon assumed in his notes. Few problems seemed to get resolved, and the ending was satisfactory to no one.

Gordon put the material aside, and the project stalled until March 1944, when Hepburn was able to get the material reassigned to the studio's veteran comedy specialist, Larry Weingarten. Just prior to going east at the completion of *Dragon Seed,* she participated in at least one story conference in which Michael Arlen and Howard Emmett Rogers were given sections of the Raphaelson screenplay to review and revise. Within weeks, Weingarten had decided to start fresh with Donald Ogden Stewart, who was the obvious choice and who had a draft screenplay for Hepburn to see when she returned to California on June 16.

A problem with the original play was its topicality; *Without Love* was dated within two years of its first performance. Under Stewart, only the core of the loveless marriage was retained, Pat, the political economist, becoming a natural scientist working on an improved oxygen mask. In the revised character of Jamie, Hepburn may have been projecting some of her own feelings toward Tracy in making her the daughter of a famed research scientist whose interest in Pat is aroused by his own experimental work. "I often felt that she was submerging herself to him," her youngest brother, Dr. Robert Hepburn, said of Tracy. "I think, too, that Spencer was a sort of younger edition of her father in her mind. I think she admired his ruggedness."

When Tracy returned to Los Angeles and the Beverly Hills Hotel on September 28, Hepburn was already settled in a house on nearby Beverly

Grove and anxious to get *Without Love* before the cameras. "We actually are going to begin shooting next week," she reported to Terry Helburn in a letter. "I feel as though I'd already made the darned thing four times." The supporting cast, she went on, had been settled with Keenan Wynn, Lucille Ball ("she made a very good test"), Patricia Morison, Emily Perkins (her secretary and onetime dresser, appearing under the stage name of Massey), and Carl Esmond. The director, Harold Bucquet, was a veteran of Metro's Dr. Kildare pictures and had, like Fred Zinnemann, made his bones in the short-subject department. Bucquet had replaced the tubercular Jack Conway on *Dragon Seed,* and Hepburn, in the midst of a grueling five-month shoot, took a liking to him. Soft-spoken and English by birth, Bucquet was inclined to stay out of the way, and one principal cast member, when later asked, could scarcely recall him.

"As always," said Larry Weingarten, "Kate was into everything . . . People always said to me, 'She's trying to do everything.' And my reply was, 'The thing I'm afraid of, and you should be afraid of, is that she *can* do everything.' Producer, director, cameraman! That's what she was! Her idea of everything was always better than you could have ever envisioned." Actress-singer Morison, as a seventeen-year-old drama student, had witnessed the filming of Hepburn's New York screen test in 1932, but she didn't formally meet the actress until her first day on the picture. Casually clad in white linen pants and matching shirt, Kate was obviously running the show, head-to-head with the director and the cameraman while Tracy retreated to the relative calm of his dressing room. Morison knew Tracy from a formal dinner party a few years earlier when, attending stag, he had graciously offered to drive her home.

"I remember we stopped at the top of Mulholland Drive—not for anything romantic, but because the view was so beautiful. He didn't make a pass, which was unusual in those days. It was very refreshing." Tracy, she recalled, was always cordial and charming to her on the set of *Without Love,* his relationship with Hepburn an open secret. "I think in the business it was common knowledge. I knew it." Tracy was less cordial to the director, whom he seemed to regard as inept in matters of staging, and Hepburn went so far as to consult with George Stevens for a scene built entirely on physical comedy.

Sleeplessness had brought Tracy to the ragged edge of sanity, and neither booze nor medication could quell the demons within him. He tossed and heaved, his mind a tornado of shame and worry. "I didn't believe that he did it," Kate said years later, "and I lay on the floor of his room one night and watched him and he could not get to sleep . . . he twisted and he turned and it took him an hour and a half to quiet down at all." On October 29 she sat on the set, the script serving as a desk, and wrote a long letter to Ellen Barry, Phil's wife, telling them how appalled they'd be at the changes and eliminations made for the film and remembering with pleasure a month that she and her sister Peg had spent with the Barrys at their winter home on Florida's eastern shore. "When we finish the picture & the retakes & everything which will be around the first of February—Spence is going to take a year away from the studio—He is a wreck & cannot sleep & is feeling as though he might go mad—I have been trying to describe Hobe Sound to him—for it seems to me the perfect place for him to go . . . He thought he might go and take a quick look—between the end of shooting & the beginning of retakes & then if it seemed to be the spot he would go back for several months—"

Weather slowed an already troubled shoot, delaying location work during one of the wettest Novembers on record. Tracy was "ill" the last half of the month, eventually forcing a complete shutdown. "There were times they had to cancel a day's shooting," Patricia Morison remembered. "I didn't know why, but I understand now it was because he had been drinking. Which everybody knew was a problem except me. I didn't know why I suddenly had three days off. 'Well,' I thought, 'I don't have to get up at four anymore.' "

Tracy hated the character of Pat Jamieson and what Don Stewart had done to it under Hepburn's constant yammering. According to Larry Weingarten, he resisted the role "until the last day of shooting." Tracy "took sick" on *Without Love,* Weingarten believed, because his loathing of the part was "so violent." Hepburn had never before worked with him when he was hitting the bottle, and she assumed the burden of bringing him back. "Mayer was a practical man," she said,

> and I just used to call up and say, "Look, I need a little help here, and I'm going to move him out of the Beverly Hills Hotel and up into my house." It was very difficult to do that because, I thought, if any tragedy occurred, to have him in my house might be wildly difficult. But it had to be done, because I couldn't leave him in the hotel. Because he was so noisy that the hotel said, "Get him out." Carroll was a weak man, [and] I think that Louise just deliberately . . . did . . . not . . . know . . . [so] if I felt he was in trouble, I'd move into the hotel or else I'd move him into my house. But I was always afraid that something would happen and there would be a scandal that would embarrass Louise. It wouldn't have embarrassed me so much, but I really wanted her to be protected.

Nine working days were lost, but there wasn't a hint of trouble outside the gated walls of M-G-M. "We didn't publicize him," said June Dunham,

Howard Strickling's longtime secretary. "At times, he'd be in the room with Hepburn for three days while she sobered him up. But those things never got to the press." When Tracy returned on November 27, the tension on the set was fierce and it would only grow worse. A pervasive sense of doom settled over the company, so certain was almost everyone involved that the picture would be awful. "What goes on with Spencer Tracy?" Hedda Hopper wondered in her column of December 4. "He has become a verifiable matinee idol, wants to see rushes, and hasn't been nice to Lucille Ball on the set of *Without Love.* Could it be because he and Katharine Hepburn are no longer speaking?" By the thirteenth, conditions had deteriorated to the point where Keenan Wynn was reported to have taken a poke at assistant director Earl McAvoy.

The level of violence between Tracy and Hepburn is largely a matter of conjecture. "Mind you, I don't frighten easily," Kate once said, "but when he became . . . you know, he had a violent temper. At times, at times." In response to a question from A. Scott Berg, one of her biographers, she acknowledged that Tracy had once hit her. "She proceeded," wrote Berg, "to describe a fiendish night at the Beverly Hills Hotel. While Kate was trying to put Tracy to bed, he smacked the back of his hand across her face. She said he was so drunk she believed he neither knew that he'd done it nor that he'd remember."

Critic and author Martin Gottfried remembered Hepburn once telling him that Tracy used to "knock me around" when he drank too much. "When I expressed surprise, saying, 'I'd've thought that once would have been enough for someone like you,' she replied, 'Why? I could hit him back, couldn't I?' " Screenwriter Millard Kaufman and his wife Lori heard an even more startling revelation, as both were close to Signe Hasso. Once Hasso recalled to them a night when Hepburn phoned and asked if she could come over to stay. "Apparently," said Kaufman, "Tracy had beaten hell out of her."

Such reports didn't surprise Katharine Houghton, who was loath to regard her aunt Kat as anyone's victim, particularly Tracy's.

> She once told me that Spencer could stop drinking at will for months or even years at a time. Maybe this is what gave her the idea that alcohol was not an addiction. Maybe this is what gave her the idea that she could wrest the drink away from him with force. If he gave her a good whack on such an occasion, it's my suspicion that she asked for it. She was not a frail person. Anyone who's seen her in a film in which she exposes her impressive strong arms and broad shoulders, could imagine that she was a formidable physical adversary.

Christmas 1944.
(SUSIE TRACY)

For her part, Hepburn was conciliatory, even if she and Tracy stopped speaking for a time: "I don't think he'd ever hurt anyone. He'd be incapable of hurting anyone. Not physically violent with people at all." Then, considering the general question of Tracy's alleged rampages whenever he was truly in his cups: "Well, I think if you're drunk enough and you do something like that, is that the same? I mean, 'tisn't the same to me. If Spencer was sober he would never have touched anyone. But, I mean, if you're drunk and fight, it depends on how old you are and how much do they stop you when you say, 'Get outta here.' I don't think that means anything except that you're drunk."

Without Love officially finished on December 27, 1944, but neither Tracy nor Hepburn could leave town as yet. Samson Raphaelson was already at work on changes to Don Stewart's September 29 draft of the screenplay, and Dorothy Kingsley was preparing a set of retakes for Lucille Ball. Tracy himself did one day of retakes after the first of the year, but then was left idle for three weeks—two of which he evidently spent hammered. He had plans to attend the January 20 inauguration in Washington with Louise, as well as an invitation to afternoon coffee with the president and Mrs. Roosevelt the day before. But further work on the picture kept him in Hollywood until well past the historic event, and he must have been bitterly disappointed. It wasn't, in fact, until February 1 that he was finally cleared for travel, determined, as Kate wrote the Barrys, to take off the entire year. On the strength of *A Guy Named Joe, The Seventh Cross,* and *Thirty Seconds Over Tokyo,* however, the annual Quigley poll of exhibitors had confirmed him as M-G-M's top moneymaking star of the year 1944, and the most the studio would allow was the six-week vacation guaranteed under the terms of his contract.

In New York it was Hepburn's strategy to get Tracy into a play, since his deal with Metro allowed for one. In February 1944 he had made a tentative return to the stage in narrating Aaron Copland's *Lincoln Portrait* for two performances with the L.A. Philharmonic. Plainly, however, he was terrified at the prospect of going back to the theatre after an absence of fifteen years. When the Playwrights' Company offered him a comedy (likely S. N. Behrman's *Jacobowsky and the Colonel*), he replied, "It is delightful and amusing, but, I am afraid, not for me." He then shut off all further discussion by making a seemingly impossible request: "Please send me something by Bob Sherwood."

Kate tried letting the matter lie, busying herself with her own plans to appear for the Guild in a production of Shakespeare's *As You Like It.* Short term, everything from Tracy's perspective looked bleak, and he filled his days with morose thoughts and the dark certainties of an Irish temperament.

In the legend that grew up around Tracy and Hepburn, one of the most durable of images is that of Kate going bar to bar, after the fashion of a Gilded Age temperance song, looking for Spence. It was a notion she dismissed as "stupid" and made up: "In the first place I wouldn't do it because that would be too public for *him,* and in the second place I wouldn't do it because it would be too public for me, too. My friend, my driver then, who worked for me for forty-three years, was Charles Newhill. He used to go out publicly when Spencer was drinking [and] walking around New York City. Charles would be with him, [so] unless I were dumb, I would know he was out drinking." Newhill, a sturdy Italian, was a former boxer who could handle Tracy and at the same time protect him from himself and the public at large. "[Spencer] wasn't out all that much," she added. "He'd start it and go out, but then when he began to get really seriously into it he wouldn't go out. And I certainly wouldn't let him go out. I'd see to it that he couldn't go out . . . I was not able to solve his problems, but I was able to help him by seeing that he didn't fall down the stairs, you know, or break his goddamn neck or just be miserable."

Containing Tracy's impulses and abetting them were two different things entirely and would have elicited, in Joe Mankiewicz's estimation, two very different sets of responses. "Kate," he said in 1992,

has a whole new characterization that she's maintaining for herself—part Constance Collier, part Mrs. Siddons, and part some very elegant lady of affairs. There must be no touch of Marilyn Monroe–type life or Hollywood-type life. So when Kate says, "When Spencer asked for a drink, oh yeah, I gave him a drink," well, put yourself [in her position]. This isn't the first time we've been together. The whole thing of going to bed together . . . we're sort of tied together now. I'm Spence and I feel I've got to have a drink. It isn't like saying, "I'll have a scotch and soda." That saying "I want a drink" is an important mark . . .

He says, "I want a drink." Now she says, "Of course, Spence," and gets it for him. *She removes him of guilt.* She removes a certain amount of guilt, and that does not please Spence. That irritates him, because in a way she's shoving booze on him. Once you get into a twisted emotion, you've got to be able to trace the emotion and stay with it. And when she says, "I'll give you the drink," does that make him happy? Spence, if he wanted a drink, part of having a drink is knowing that he's doing something wrong and he can't help doing it. So whenever I hear the woman say, "No sir, I gave him these drinks"—that's horseshit. "I'm being a big woman now. I'm changing my character; I'm going back after the fact to change my characterization." Because if she *really* did that, it wouldn't have played. It just wouldn't have made sense. Because if she said, "I'll get you a drink," he probably would have exploded with anger: "Stay the fuck out of my life!" You know—*that* life. "The last thing I want is two years from now to think of you giving me drinks! Making me hate you!"

Oh no, that's really too easy . . . Once you start thinking that way about Spence, it was his guilt. But don't forget also he would have a kind of proprietary sense about that guilt. I've known several like that—alcoholics. My brother was one, but not like that. The kind Spence was . . . they're gone. And they not only accept the guilt, they *need* the guilt to see them through this thing. Spence locked in a hotel room, going to the bathroom in his pants . . . every disgusting thing he did to himself. "I am beating myself up." You know? This is what my father used to do. Jack Barrymore was a different kind of drunk. Spence was a black Irish drunk.

It was at Hepburn's four-story brownstone in the Turtle Bay section of Manhattan—where Tracy, according to her, was essentially under house arrest—that some of their worst moments took place. Whether giving him a drink or wresting one from his hand, her actions—or the words that accompanied them—could easily have provoked him to the point of reflexive violence and, possibly, something even worse. For in 1991 Hepburn recounted a time when Tracy, she said, tried to choke her. She described fending off the attack by pushing him into the closet that housed the ladder to the roof—a considerable feat of strength and choreography when he outweighed her by sixty or seventy pounds.

Katharine Houghton, when apprised of the story, didn't buy it, contending that "anyone who knew the house" would find such a scene absurd.

> Some sort of fight may well have occurred during which he tried to choke her, but the idea that she imprisoned a crazed Spencer Tracy in a very small closet is improbable for at least two reasons: First of all, despite her strength, I doubt she could have forced his bulk into that closet. And second, I doubt that she would have put a drunken man whom she loved into such danger. His only way out of that closet would have been to climb to the roof, and she certainly wouldn't have wanted to take the chance that he would fall from the roof. Over the years, Kate recounted various incidents that were complete fabrications—good stories, yes, but untrue . . . In all these fabrications, she cast herself in a good or heroic light . . . If Spencer had really wanted to strangle her, I'm sure he could have succeeded without much difficulty.

Still, given the events that ensued in the months that followed their time together in New York, it's clear something deeply disturbing happened between them, that Tracy had felt so out of control he never wanted to put himself in such a position again. For if the fight was over his drinking, as it most likely was, both parties could well have been enraged to the point of physical violence. "Assuming they had a fierce fight," Houghton continued, "what would really interest me is *why* they had a fight, and why Kate chose that particular fight to embroider into a tale. Was it because she felt guilt concerning her part in it? In the family we were all witness, from time to time, to her being maddeningly self-righteous and bossy, no doubt with good intentions, but still way out of line. With Spencer she may well have been guilty on occasion of what he rightly would have considered egregious behavior."

Was Hepburn's own culpability something she could never fully acknowledge? Did the fracas continue? Or was Tracy immediately docile, suddenly aware of what might have happened? Nobody knows; of the two people with direct knowledge of that night, only one ever spoke of it, and only briefly, off mike, as in the shared whisper of a confidence. "I don't know how he got so loaded, but he really did," said Bob Hepburn, who was in New York awaiting the commissioning of the navy hospital ship U.S.S. *Repose.* "I had to call the hospital—Presbyterian—and they came down and fetched him and dried him out somehow." Tracy's "rumored" arrival at Harkness Pavilion was reported by Walter Winchell on February 28, and on March 10 the studio quietly extended his vacation without pay for another six weeks.

Without Love moved into the Music Hall on March 22, 1945, and, despite pallid reviews, had the biggest Lenten opening in the theater's twelve-year history. Accompanied by Radio City's annual "Glory of Easter" pageant, the picture played to $17,000 on the first day alone and sold a record 92,138 tickets over the four-day holiday weekend. Tracy attended Easter Mass at St. Patrick's Cathedral, quietly and without fanfare, and was afterward photographed walking along Fifth Avenue, the first time he had been observed in public in more than a month. The next day he was seen lunching with Sherwood, who had just returned from service in the Pacific as a representative of the Navy Department.

"Are you ever going to write another play?" Tracy asked him. It had been five years since *There Shall Be No Night,* the playwright's Pulitzer Prize–winning account of the Russian invasion of Finland.

"I'm thinking about one," Sherwood replied, "and if it develops along the lines I contemplate, I'd surely like to have you in it."

When columnist Earl Wilson saw him on April 4, Tracy was already talking of the new Sherwood play as if it were a done deal. "I've got to go back to Hollywood and knock off an epic," he said, "then I'm coming back to Broadway to see if I can still act." He was drinking sarsaparilla from a demitasse cup, sober but weary on the eve of his forty-fifth birthday. "It's your goddamn movie name that causes you trouble," he went on. "You make so much money, your economic problem ceases to exist. No options to worry about. The dough rolls in. You forget how to act because you don't have to act anymore. I heard of a guy who had a 15-year contract at M-G-M. If I had a 15-year contract, I could think of nothing but to get a .45 and blow my brains out. To think of coming in that gate at M-G-M or, for that matter, any gate for 15 years! A Broadway show would give me a chance to see if I can still act. I used to be able to act. Broadway doesn't care about your goddamn movie name."

He was back in Los Angeles when FDR died in Warm Springs, Georgia, on April 12. His wire to Sherwood the next day, praising the playwright's radio address, urged him to get on with the play they had discussed—a call to postwar America to take on the greatest possible share of world leadership. "Whoever might be called upon to express your thoughts from a stage or screen would be highly honored, but that is really unimportant. It is only important that you write them and that they are imparted so the greatest number of people may know them."

Seen lunching with Louise at Romanoff's, Tracy told Louella Parsons he would make another picture before going into the Sherwood play so as to free up as much time as possible. "I would be off the screen for over a year if I waited until fall," he reasoned. "That's why I came home from New York." Having, however, passed on *They Were Expendable,* his talks with the studio weren't particularly productive. They squabbled over money, Tracy objecting to the inference he was worth only $110,000 a picture. The new deal, after a year's leave of absence, would limit the studio to two pictures a year, with his guarantee capped at $220,000 per annum. At one point, Leo Morrison let drop the fact that his client had authorized him to terminate his contract, a prospect no one on the executive side found attractive.

Kate returned to California with plans to do a picture, *Green Dolphin Street,* and make a Pacific tour as Spence had done. They had scant time together; he was committed to a six-week tour of Europe for the OWI and left for New York within days of her arrival. But once there, something happened and plans for the tour were aborted. Whether it was canceled, scarcely a week before VE Day, or whether it was Tracy who, once again, bailed on the trip at the last possible moment, nobody seems to know. Garson Kanin remembered Tracy once telling him that President Roosevelt had wanted him to deliver a top-secret message to "someone, somewhere" and that Tracy laid the trip's subsequent cancellation to the president's sudden death. "The thing I couldn't understand," Tracy said to Kanin, "was why me of all people. But, of course, I said nothing and agreed to do as I was told, that's all." Waiting at the River Club for the trip to get under way, Tracy, in Kanin's words, "fell ill."

Howard Dietz had assigned the judicious Milton Weiss to look after M-G-M's No. 1 star, and Weiss, in Dietz's opinion, had his hands full. "I'm at the Sherry-Netherland," Weiss advised Dietz over the phone one afternoon, "and the big man is drinking vodka martinis and smashing the glasses against the mirror back of the bar. He says you should be looking after him, not me, and he won't stop drinking until you show him that you care. You'd better come up here."

With Dietz's appearance, Tracy turned belligerent: "You were too stuck up to come and meet me yourself. Well, let's see if you can do better than Milton. Milton has it all over you as a diplomat. You think you're too high class to give aid and comfort to an actor. You've had shows on Broadway and you go for actors like Fred Astaire, Clifton Webb, and dancers. It makes you a high-class press agent. Furthermore, you look like me. Well, I won't go back to California unless you come with me."

Dietz managed to whisper instructions to Weiss, whose subsequent departure Tracy didn't seem to notice.

I got Tracy up to his suite on the seventh floor and worked on him. I finally got him to agree to go back to California. "But only if you come too," he said. We took a limousine to LaGuardia, and the three of us, Tracy, Weiss, and I boarded the plane. Tracy's consciousness was sketchy, so I left him in the hands of Milton, who gave instructions to the pilot to go west after I had climbed out. The plane took gracefully to the air, and I sank into a gratefully relieved sigh and headed for home and bed. The phone rang at midnight. It's your guess who was on the wire. "You thought you were rid of me," the voice said. "Well, I'll meet you in the bar at the Sherry-Netherland at nine o'clock. You'd better relieve Milton, he needs some sleep." Tracy was calling from Chicago.

Without Hepburn to contain him, Tracy ran amok in New York for the better part of a week, sometimes in the company of Charles Newhill, who was devoted to him, sometimes not. Agent Harold Rose's abiding image of him came from this period, when a cab rolled up to the Sherry-Netherland and Tracy came tumbling out of the back seat in the company of an obvious prostitute. Whitey Hendry, M-G-M's chief of police, was dispatched to New York, and it was Hendry and a few elite members of his studio constabulary who arranged for Tracy, fighting mad and struggling wildly against a set of camisole restraints, to be admitted to Doctors Hospital in the early morning hours of May 11, 1945.

CHAPTER 21

The Rugged Path

When Tracy was moved the following day, it was to a private room on a restricted floor where, under the name of Charles Newhill, there would be little chance of a Winchell or a Kilgallen catching wind of it. There he began the grueling process of cold-turkey detox, restrained, restless, hallucinating at all hours. Fed a liquid diet of milk, eggs, and fruit juice, he was given daily injections of thiamine chloride and turned every two hours like a premium side of beef.

He strained at the jacket, talking loudly and incoherently and tossing about furiously. He was incontinent, obstreperous, and when they removed the arm restraints, he struck out at the nurses. He thought he saw strange men hiding in the corners of the room and comely young women seated at the side of his bed. Sodium Luminal was administered at eight-hour intervals to promote sleep, and the patient alternated spells of confused drowsiness with fitful, often violent periods of rest.

By the morning of the thirteenth he was quieter, less restive, and said that he had been on a "big drunk" and was having terrible nightmares. He would cry uncontrollably for minutes on end, begging for cigarettes and then talking expansively of getting better. The doctor visited one afternoon and ordered his restraints removed. At once he started smoking and talking cheerfully of California. By the first of the week he was bathed, shaved, and welcoming visitors. "Very pleasant and friendly," the chart read. There were quiet conversations with the evening nurses, but still there were prolonged episodes of weeping. When plagued by intervals of restlessness and loud moaning, he was ordered off caffeinated beverages—coffee and Coca-Cola—and his sleeping briefly improved. Soon, though, he was fearful and restless again, and the medications no longer seemed to be working. He fell into a pattern of asking to be sedated just so he could get a little sleep, but then he was rarely out for more than two or three hours at a stretch.

Discharged on May 19, Tracy was still unable to sleep very much, but he was finally free of the symptoms of alcoholism. He made his way back to Los Angeles, where Kate was waiting for him and where her own Pacific tour was subsequently canceled because of "ill health." The events of the preceding three months had badly shaken them both, and now Tracy would be entering a period of unprecedented sobriety.

Producer Arthur Hopkins, who directed both Tracy and Hepburn in their Broadway debuts, had monitored the situation and kept in close touch with Kate in California. "Spence," he wrote her,

> is finding his way out . . . Spence, in his meditations, will learn discrimination. He will recognize the enemy and reject him. This is not a struggle, for struggle gives the adversary strength. It is not Will Power or Resolution. It is realization of God's presence and God's desire to strengthen us and make us useful to Him. You too, Kate, in strengthening Spence, strengthen yourself. Faith increases as you draw upon it. It is the accumulation of that [which] vanishes when not drawn upon.
>
> Above all, Spence must learn that a sense of shame is vanity and is an affront to God . . . when we pray, it is God who is praying with us. He wants us to understand and be free. Spence is learning this, and you and I with him.

By 1945 Robert Emmet Sherwood was widely regarded as the dean of American dramatists, a man whose death was likened by Maxwell Anderson to "the removal of a major planet from a solar system." The author of such varied fare as *The Road to Rome, Waterloo Bridge, Idiot's Delight,* and *Abe Lincoln in Illinois,* Sherwood had enjoyed a string of critical and commercial hits stretching back to the 1920s. At the time he proposed to write a play for Spencer Tracy, he held three Pulitzers for drama—one for each of his previous three plays. In the uncertain business of the American commercial theater in the days immediately following the Second World War, there was nothing more prestigious—nor closer to a sure thing—than a new play from the redoubtable R.E.S.

Tracy, of course, had attracted plenty of feelers from Broadway, most notably from Kate's friends at the Theatre Guild, who took his interest in *The Devil's Disciple* as a firm commitment and eagerly announced it to the press in August 1941. Paul Osborn put up an original on the basis of Tracy's praise for *Madame Curie,* and Oscar Serlin reportedly offered Metro "a terrific amount of money" to lend Tracy for his production of *The Moon Is Down,* which combined the talents of John Steinbeck and director Chet Erskine. By late 1943 the Guild's Lawrence Langner was sweetening the pitch by suggesting plays that would accommodate both Tracy and Hepburn, Eugene O'Neill's *Strange Interlude* and *Marco Millions* being his top choices. So convinced was Langner that Tracy and O'Neill would make a powerhouse combination, he tried arranging for Tracy to travel to Contra Costa, rationing notwithstanding, to meet the famously reclusive playwright. At the time, however, Tao House was in the grip of a flu epidemic and hospitable to no one.

In a subsequent letter to Langner, O'Neill thought *The Great God Brown* "a good bet" for Tracy but warned against *Strange Interlude* ("Nina's play—always has been") and *Marco Millions,* which he wasn't keen on seeing revived. "My best bet for Tracy would be *Lazarus Laughed,*" O'Neill wrote. "Now give heed to this and re-read it carefully in the light of what that play has to say today. 'Die exultantly that life may live,' etc. 'There is no death' (spiritually) etc. Also think of the light thrown on different facets of the psychology of dictators in Tiberius and Caligula. Hitler doing his little dance of triumph after the fall of France is very like my Caligula."

Though Tracy was genuinely thrilled with the substance of O'Neill's letter, he read *Lazarus,* with its masked chorus and its Greek pretensions, and frankly admitted he did not understand it. Kate didn't either, wasn't much on *Strange Interlude,* and didn't know *Marco Millions* at all. When queried, Langner said that even he couldn't fathom *Lazarus,* which, tellingly, had never had a New York production. "I have read it ten times," Langner said. "I think you have to be a Roman Catholic to really understand it. Maybe if Spencer and Gene got together they could work something out of it, especially as he seems to be willing to rewrite and might clarify for Spencer. I will drop Gene a line and find out whether he would like to talk about it to Spencer." O'Neill was ill, though, and by the time his precarious health improved, Tracy was committed to Sherwood and his new play and there wasn't much point in discussing the matter any further.

The gangling Sherwood was a founding partner of the Playwrights' Company, a producing organization specifically established to stage the works of its five principals, who, besides Sherwood, were Maxwell Anderson, Elmer Rice, S. N. Behrman, and the late Sidney Howard. After making his report to the navy, Sherwood set about developing his new play with characteristic discipline, producing two acts and fifteen scenes in little more than a month. As was the custom, Sherwood circulated the playscript among his colleagues at the company and was ready by the end of June to bring it west, where Tracy was nursing a torn leg muscle. "Madeline and I hope to arrive Beverly Hills about July 1st," he cabled on June 22, "and will then show you the manuscript and talk about it as planned."

Bearing the title *Out of Hell,* Sherwood's play followed the pattern of his two previous works, an earnest protagonist nobly chucking it all for the greater good of society, plunging himself into politics or, in this case, war, and suffering, in the end, a martyr's fate. Delayed in his travel plans, Sherwood airmailed a copy to Tracy on the twenty-eighth, dispatching another to actor Montgomery Clift (who he hoped would play opposite Tracy) the next day. Tracy read the play at once, reportedly within hours, and both he and Kate signaled their enthusiasm. "I felt he had things to say," Tracy said of Sherwood, "things well worth saying that you can't say in a picture."

In New York the playwright spoke with J. Robert Rubin, M-G-M's vice president and general counsel, and the terms for Tracy's services seemed satisfactory. When he finally reached Los Angeles, Sherwood and his wife put up at Kate's rented house on Tower Road, where there followed a series of convivial discussions. "You may be making a mistake with me," Tracy felt compelled to warn him. "I could be good in this thing, all right. But then, who knows? I could fall off and maybe not show up." At six feet eight inches, Sherwood towered over his prospective star, his rugged face set off by a neatly trimmed mustache. "Spencer, all I want for myself," he replied with a characteristic pause in the middle of his statement, "is to see this play played once by you."

He nearly got his wish.

In their early discussions, both men expressed a preference for Garson Kanin as director, even though Kanin's experience in directing for the stage was minimal. In London the army captain happily accepted the assignment, wondering only if Sherwood had the organizational pull to get him sprung from the military. Sherwood, working through both President Truman and his army chief of staff, General George C. Marshall, assured him that he did.

A letter of agreement dated July 13, 1945, committed Tracy to rehearsals beginning around Labor Day and an out-of-town opening "on or about" September 28. In exchange for playing Morey Vinion, Sherwood's quixotic hero, he was to receive 15 percent of the gross weekly box office receipts. A provision giving him the option of investing in the show on a dollar-for-dollar basis was added to the contract, but it seemed unlikely that Tracy would buy in.

Sherwood's sojourn in Beverly Hills sparked the first of a seemingly endless string of rewrites. Nobody was lacking for suggestions—not Tracy, not Kanin, certainly not Hepburn, nor Kanin's wife of three years, actress-playwright Ruth Gordon. According to Madeline Sherwood, her husband had already done "considerable revision" by July 26 and had sent new copies to his associates at the Playwrights' Company. There was another round of fixes almost immediately, giving the play, among other things, its perma-nent title—*The Rugged Path.*

Hepburn, who was convinced now more than ever that the best thing for Tracy would be, as their friend Constance Collier put it, to "find release from celluloid fetters," declared she was going to see him through this thing and passed on the chance to play Isabel Bradley in George Cukor's pro-posed filming of *The Razor's Edge.* Tracy tried dissuading her from turning the picture down, saying that he really only needed her for the last week of rehearsals and maybe the week of the actual opening, but to no avail. She had, by this point, convinced herself that she was absolutely essential to Spence's well-being, both personal and professional, and that he was inca-pable of managing the task without her.

When he heard the wartime limits on gasoline had been lifted, Tracy decided to motor east with Carroll, leaving Kate in California to further contemplate her decision. The men had so much tire trouble the first two hundred miles, they reconsidered, turned around, and set off again via rail, Hepburn, this time, accompanying them.

The train was booked solid and it was no secret who was on board. (Lawrence Tibbett, the acclaimed baritone of the Metropolitan Opera, was also a passenger.) At Freeport the boys visited with family—their uncle Andrew, aunt Mum, Jennie's daughter Jane, who was working at the USO in Savanna, and Kathleen and Henry Willits, who came over from Dubuque. They took a private dining room in the nearby village of Cedarville and had an elaborate family dinner, Spence talking freely of the work ahead. "I don't know whether this is going to work or not," he con-fided. "In the first place, I don't know if I've got the voice for it. I haven't been on the stage for years and years and I don't know if I'll make it. But I feel I want to try it." The woman who ran the kitchen had brought a couple of teenage girls in to help with the serving. "This little girl was just shak-ing," Jane Feely recalled. "The movie star! She was passing the plates around, and Uncle Andrew said, 'This is Mary Lou Whatever.' And she said, 'How do you do . . . Do you know Van Johnson?' Oh, Spencer loved that. He said, 'Yes, I do. What's your name? I'll get you an autographed pic-ture of Van Johnson. Carroll, see to it.' "

In New York he had an escape clause inserted into his contract, giving him an out during the first three weeks of performances and another during the New York run of the play. He had, he explained, full confidence in Sherwood's work; it was the lead actor who gave him pause. Could he still manage the sustained concentration he'd need to carry a play? Could he achieve the same level of purity he had learned to put forth on film? "Once," Kate remembered, "I asked Spencer some such foolish question like, 'How did you like my play acting?' and he stared at me for a moment and said, 'That's the strangest remark I ever heard. What is play acting? Do you mean the tricks some people pull on stage? If that's supposed to be acting, I don't like it.' "

Rehearsals for *The Rugged Path* commenced on the stage of the Barrymore Theatre on September 3, 1945. Johnny, in the hospital, had a telegram from his father the next day:

EVERYTHING WENT WELL EXCEPT I AM SCARED.

In Morey Vinion, Sherwood had fashioned a character as fitted to Tracy as a second skin—a career journalist, outwardly happy yet inwardly brooding and dissatisfied in his role as the "embattled liberal" in an otherwise conservative newspaper. "He's never been really happy," his wife admits. "Well—not since the first few months, and I sometimes wonder about how he <u>really</u> felt even then. When he got down to work in Europe, he began to take everything to heart as though he were personally involved, instead of just being an American reporter."

She asks him: "Do you want to get out of here, Morey?" And he tells her no, he doesn't, that he just wants to "stay put" for a change. "I want to have my own home in my own country. I told you I wanted my own home, and I meant it." Actress Martha Sleeper played Morey's frustrated wife, married to a man "incurably restless by nature," a "damned good newspaperman," which meant, as his father-in-law told him, "you'll be a damned poor husband."

MOREY
Oh, we got along all right, Harriet, despite
all reports to the contrary.

HARRIET
Yes, we've got along. Because we've both had
good manners.

"One of the banes of the existence of any playwright or director," said Garson Kanin, is the actor, especially the star, who doesn't really know his part. They sort of know it. In the Broadway theatre, I think it's more common for a player to know his part. In films [it's], "Oh, I'll take a shot at it." But Spencer was absolutely meticulous about learning his part, and learning it way ahead of time, and learning it so accurately. I used to kid him sometimes; I'd say, "Spencer, you even learn the typographical errors." He learned it absolutely exactly as written. Of course, after 15 years his theatre machine was a bit rusty and he was aware of that, but it didn't take him long—three or four days—and he was absolutely in there like a stage actor who had acted every night on the stage for 15 years.

Nearly three weeks into rehearsals, Tracy's contract with the Playwrights' Company remained unsigned. He now wanted, it seemed, a 25 percent stake in the show but was unwilling to put in any of his own money, M-G-M's Rubin having advised him that an investment on his part would likely put him in "an unfavorable tax position." Victor Samrock, the company's business manager, took up the matter with Carroll Tracy one morn-

Conferring with Captain Garson Kanin and playwright Robert Emmet Sherwood during preparations for *The Rugged Path*, 1945. (PATRICIA MAHON COLLECTION)

ing, saying they were in no position to grant a 25 percent share of the profits without a commensurate investment in the show. Tracy was, moreover, being offered the exact same terms accorded the Lunts and Katharine Cornell and Helen Hayes. Carroll said how sorry he was that the matter had not been settled in California and he assured Samrock that everything would be all right "in time." Later that afternoon, after conferring with his brother, Carroll again sat opposite Samrock and said, "Well, if you can't agree to Spencer's request, then you better get somebody else."

Tracy was ready to bolt, his confidence undermined by the fractious rehearsal process that comes with any new, untried work. Samrock tried laughing the thing off, repeating the gist of their earlier discussion and ticking off the costs associated with a production on the grand scale of *The Rugged Path*. "Carroll was quite friendly about it all," Samrock recalled, "and finally suggested, 'Well, I think I'll go up to Rubin's office and have him call John Wharton [co-director and general counsel for the Playwrights' Company] and maybe the two of them can settle it.' "

If the role of Morey cut too close at times, Tracy's discomfort—his projection of temperament—came out in his dealings with Samrock and Wharton, where Carroll could serve as both mouthpiece and whipping boy. In rehearsals Kanin found him "imaginative, resourceful, malleable"—a revelation. What he achieved was a clarity of interpretation that stretched beyond the intelligence, personality, and stamina he typically brought to a role. "His whole approach," said Darryl Hickman, "was to externalize as little as possible."

Driven by an abhorrence of artifice and a natural terror of monotony, Tracy was constantly distilling the character to its essential elements, his stage effects coming wholly from within, all clean, sharp lines, lucid and completely free of the tricks "some people pull on stage." When a scene required him to emerge from the ocean after five days of being shipwrecked, he told Kanin he would not wear an appliance designed to simulate a growth of beard.

"It'll look ridiculous," Kanin argued. "It'll bother the audience."

"No, it won't," countered Tracy.

"Why won't it?"

"Because I'll *act* unshaven."

The company was large, the production unwieldy, the script unready and better suited to the conventions of the screen. The first public performance of *The Rugged Path* was set to take place in Providence on the night of September 28, 1945. Recalling his abrupt dismissal from the Albee Players in 1928, Tracy relished a triumphant return to the city. "The play was sold out all three nights," he said, still harboring a grudge against the Albee

stock's old general manager, Foster Lardner, "and I've always hoped the bastard tried to get in and couldn't get a ticket."* Kate, who was in constant
attendance throughout rehearsals, appeared on the arm of Arthur Hopkins.
The Metropolitan was a big auditorium, plain and thoroughly unsuited to
the demands of live drama. Tracy filled all three thousand seats, and at
intermission it seemed as if all three thousand patrons wanted a close look
at Hepburn, who had placed herself on display in the front row. "I felt,"
said John Wharton, who observed the procession, "that it was not calculated to increase interest in the soul-searching of the character Tracy was
portraying. But this was minor. What was major was the inexplicable aura
of failure that began to settle over the play. Except for the one scene where
the men abandoned ship, the aura increased."

It was nearly 11:15 when Tracy took his curtain line. "I'm not worried
about you fellers," he told his ragtag band of guerrilla fighters as they faced
certain death in a Philippine jungle. "I wouldn't trade you for the best they
had at Valley Forge or Gettysburg or the Normandy beach-heads. You may
not have much to fight with, but you know what you've got to fight for.
That gives you dignity. And if the rest of the world—all the people back
home who see the war only as a lot of little arrows on little maps—if they
don't realize what you've fought for, and don't achieve it, then I say God
damn them—God damn them—God damn them to all Eternity."

"Spencer was superb," said S. N. Behrman, "a marvelously sustained
performance, very quiet, intensively felt. By that time Bob's reputation had
reached a pitch approaching infallibility. In the intermission a well-known
lady expressed her disappointment: 'Sherwood builds up a crisis for the
hero which he solves by giving him a job on a destroyer where he fries eggs.'
I left the theater with Arthur Hopkins, a meditative man. He said: 'No
playwright should be given as much power as Bob has been given. It dis-
tracts him from his true vocation—writing plays.' "

The *Variety* notice lauded the play's missionary intent while bemoaning
the sight lines and the wretched acoustics of the hall, factors that doubtless
informed the audience's tepid response. There was also the vague feeling
among the out-of-towners that they had seen it all before—trademark Sherwood with a coating of Hollywood star power. "Sherwood," said Wharton,
"knew something was amiss; he never fooled himself. But this time he
couldn't find the way to fix it. Tracy became worried; there was talk of closing out of town. Indeed, Miss Hepburn, whom I had known for years,
made a comment one day which astonished me. She said, 'John, I think it
will take a lot of courage to open in New York, and Spencer hasn't got that
kind of courage.' "

* He needn't have bothered; Lardner died in 1934.

"Desperate changes" were made between Rhode Island and Washington, D.C., where *The Rugged Path* was set to open a two-week stand at the National Theatre on Monday, October 1. Rehearsals grew tense as Tracy wrestled with all the new material, and when Kanin one day said to him, "We'll iron this out tomorrow, Spence, okay?" Tracy reportedly threw back, "If I'm still here tomorrow!" as he stalked out of the theater. The fact that he hadn't yet signed his Equity contract put the whole enterprise on a precarious footing, and Samrock, for one, was certain that disaster would accompany the Washington opening.

The first-night audience was studded with big names, including Justice and Mrs. Felix Frankfurter, Senator and Mrs. Arthur Vandenberg, and General and Mrs. Alexander D. Surles, yet it was Kate's appearance, hair upswept, in a long red evening wrap, that set the most necks craning. She attended with her friend Laura Harding, the American Express heiress, and when the curtain went up, she could plainly see that Spence was nervous. "Now he was never nervous," she said. "Never nervous. And the thing hadn't been going too well, and I thought, 'Oh dear, is he going to sort of . . . take that road?' And Laura Harding said to me, 'Is he nervous?' And, of course, I said, 'Oh, no, of course he's not nervous.' But he finally overcame it. But when you are aware that the material that you're playing is not of great interest to an audience, it's tough sometimes to keep from being nervous."

All the reservations Tracy had about his own capabilities—voice, technique, mastering an ever-changing part—proved to be completely without merit. Kate, in a letter to M-G-M makeup artist Emil Levigne, described his performance as brilliant: "[H]e really delivers the goods—easy, funny & moving—& I think the audience is positively bewildered by his naturalness—& he can be heard in the very last row—I know this because my usual spot is standing in the back . . ." Irene Selznick, escorted that evening by *New York Post* publisher George Backer, did not expect to see Tracy in the Sherwoods' suite after the opening, but she took the absence of Garson Kanin as an ominous sign. "Curiously," she wrote, "there seemed to be a party going on; several of Bob's friends, Washington celebrities of that period, were on hand—all very interesting, except that nothing constructive was happening. The play had problems, but not anything that couldn't be solved, and I thought it had a great chance." She watched as Anderson, Rice, and designer Jo Mielziner waited to confer—"twiddling their thumbs"—and Sherwood, all aglow, drifted into a spirited rendition of "Red, Red Robin"—a sure sign that nothing substantive would get discussed that evening.

Tracy fell ill with grippe in Washington, alternately dripping with sweat and then trembling with chills, knowing the first performance he missed, however sick he might legitimately be, would be laid to booze. Loading up on sulfa drugs, he struggled to the theater eight times a week, vomiting in the wings and, in Kate's words, looking back on his life at Metro "as a paradise which he didn't appreciate."

The show limped into Boston, where the Hub critics laid it out extravagantly. Louise trained up from New York and was dismayed by what she saw. "It didn't amount to anything," she said. "He didn't want to stay there. He always said, 'Should I get out of it?' It wasn't up to what he had hoped, and he just wanted to get back." Kate, of course, was in Boston as well, and it was her constant bucking up that kept him with the show, even when it was apparent that Sherwood wouldn't be able to fix the play's most fundamental faults. At the hotel, the author and his partners spent four hours trying to talk Tracy out of quitting; Sam Zolotow reported in the *New York Times* that he would be leaving the show on October 27, causing the vigorous advance sale in New York to come to a dead halt. Through Carroll, Tracy told Victor Samrock that he would stay with the play only if he could give a two-week notice at any time during its Broadway run, and Samrock, desperate to get the show into New York at any cost, had little choice but to agree. On October 22, his stamina gone, Tracy wired Samrock:

TWO WEEKS CONTRACT SATISFACTORY. OPENING NEW YORK NOVEMBER 10TH.

After nearly four months of back-and-forth, he had finally signed his Equity contract.

On the morning the show moved into New York, Garson Kanin came across Hepburn scrubbing the bathroom floor in the star dressing room. He wrote: "In the ten days prior to the New York opening all the important working relationships had deteriorated. Spencer was tense and unbending, could not, or would not take direction, which amounted to the same thing." With a *Life* magazine cover story pending that would focus national attention on the show, Tracy approached the New York opening as if preparing to face a firing squad. "I was a basket case," he remembered. *"A basket case!"*

Kate had taken him to see Laurette Taylor's gut-wrenching performance in *The Glass Menagerie* and he had come away regarding Taylor, whom he had never met, as "the greatest actor I ever saw and the greatest this country ever produced." (As Hepburn said, "She and Spencer had a tremendous amount in common, because they never drove a part—they just let it happen.") The day of November 10, his stomach in knots, Tracy left for the theater resentful of Kanin, Samrock, Sherwood, and the whole fraternity of critics who were doubtless planning to flay him alive. "When I came into my dressing room to get ready to go on, there was a little carnation stuck with a black pin and a little note written on tissue paper that said, 'Dear Mr. Tracy: I have always been a great fan of yours. Welcome home. Laurette Taylor.' She had stopped on her way to the theater and left it. So I said, 'Boys, if the lights go out now I still win. Fuck it.' I was relaxed that night, opening night."

Kate had been hovering, hoping he could concentrate. "It touched him so," she said of Taylor's thoughtful gesture. "He was so thrilled, because he had wild admiration for her, and he just put it in his button hole. When he came on, I thought, 'Ooh. Well. Never saw that [carnation]. I wonder who sent that?' But it certainly made him feel absolutely *there*." With the company thoroughly demoralized, Kanin thought the performance promising: "Spencer rose to the occasion and gave an overwhelmingly magnetic performance, but somewhere, about halfway through, the dramatic line failed to sustain. The play lost the audience and disintegrated."

"No newspaper man could ask for a better model than Mr. Tracy," averred Lewis Nichols of the *Times*. "Leisurely and assured, he is one of the most likable members of the fourth estate and whatever estate it is to which actors belong. His Morey Vinion is an honest man, an able editor, and a quizzical cynic; the performance is indeed fine. But Morey Vinion is almost the only cleanly-written part." Of the play itself, Nichols lamented its lack of power, Sherwood having abandoned the role of prophet and "forceful advocate" for that of historian, permitting the flashback structure to drain it of all passion. "To get the bleak news over immediately: Robert E. Sherwood's first play in five years has not been written with his best pencil."

The story was the same all over town. The *Herald Tribune*: "Robert E. Sherwood has mistaken a stage for a podium. The Playwrights' Company's offering emerges as a series of animated editorials rather than a challenging play." *P.M.*: "It is most palpably not a good play . . . It is not even at this moment in time a very provocative commentary on the issues confronting the world . . . Tracy's acting is likable, natural, and not unconvincing." *Time*: "One trouble with *The Rugged Path* is that it is not dynamic enough to avoid seeming emotionally dated." The *Sun*: "The new play is lacking in dramatic progression. It is more message than it is good theatre . . . Tracy . . . gives a solid, tender, biting performance." Andrew Tracy, writing his son Frank in China, summarized the reviews by reporting that the play seemed out of its time. "It's what they call, in the movie business, a turkey," he carefully explained.

Unlike Louise, who considered the gradual evolution of a character one of the great creative pleasures of the stage, Tracy, after fifteen years of working solely before the lens of a camera, could no longer welcome the audience into the process. Used to settling a performance and then moving on to the next shot or the next scene, he was effectively done with Morey Vinion by the end of the first week. "I couldn't say the same goddamn lines over and over and over again every night," he later groused to a friend. "I'd forgotten how boring that could be, how deathly boring that was. I wasn't creating anything. At least every day is a new day for me in films. Every day is new and when I get through with this film I'll go right into another one, and that's new. But this thing—every day, every day, over and over again."

There settled over the company a sort of grand acquiescence, as if everyone knew that it was Tracy who was keeping the play open and yet resenting him all the same. Anxious to keep their star satisfied and prove to him that he was indeed doing well, Victor Samrock had a number of standing room stubs added to the nightly till in order to bring the show to straight capacity business. The producers also bought several box seats to show a clean sheet on the statement. Tracy, in turn, kept to himself, arriving on matinee days at 2:46 for a 2:45 curtain and rarely speaking to the other members of the cast. Somewhere toward the end of the first week, he granted an interview to Eugene Kinkead of the *New Yorker*. "I can't say I'm enjoying myself," he said. "I'm gratified at my personal reception by the critics; I'm sorry they didn't like the play. I've looked up the record of plays that have been panned, plays with so-called stars in them, and I've never seen an instance of a serious play holding up under the kind of reviews we've had. Still, you find standees at all performances. I'm amazed. Our audiences give us hearty, healthy applause. I'm frankly a little confused."

He went on:

Metro wants me to come back. My next picture will be either *Sea of Grass* by Conrad Richter or *Cass Timberlane*—probably the former. I don't know what to do. I'm terribly upset. Sherwood to me really has great integrity, and I know the fabulous figures he's been offered to write pictures. It's a little discouraging. I think there's some of the finest writing in the play I've ever seen. I was amazed to find he was not treated with more respect by one or two of the critics. I've never known integrity like his. It's damned, damned unfortunate. Anyway, I'll stay with it until my boy John, who is flying from California soon, has seen it. He wants to see me act. I'd like to come back in another play, and in another play by Robert Sherwood.

Kinkead's piece ran in the "Talk of the Town" section of the magazine's issue of November 24, and the swell of organizational outrage was instantaneous. Tracy's statements, however well intentioned, brought an immediate decline in advance sales. Sherwood also considered it "one of the very worst blows of all" in their struggle to sell the movie rights. "This, of course, was followed by numerous newspaper items indicating that Tracy might leave at any moment, and the show was marked with the stamp of doom."

There were a few cast replacements—actors leaving for more promising jobs—and the gate started to slide as Christmas approached. Capacity at the Plymouth was $26,268 a week, but in the play's second month the average hovered at around $20,000, dipping some weeks to below $19,000. Playing to empty seats, Tracy feared his stature in Hollywood might suffer and let it be known that he was thinking of leaving the show on January 5. Sherwood, pleading poverty, had taken a job with Sam Goldwyn writing the screenplay for a home-front picture called *Glory for Me,** and from California he appealed to Tracy to allow the play one hundred performances, which would take it into the week ending February 9, 1946. "We are still the biggest legitimate gross in town," he stressed, "and will undoubtedly remain so through these bad two weeks then back to capacity."

Tracy said that he might reconsider his closing date, a statement that, like the previous one, got reported in the *New York Times.* Reacting to the damage such uncertainty did to the advance sale, both Samrock and Sherwood pleaded again for a definite decision. "I understand your problems," Sherwood told Tracy in a day letter, "and know that despite them you have given a magnificent performance in my play. But you must also understand, Spencer, that neither I nor the rest of the Playwrights' Company could get away with the obvious lie that we would close the play January fifth for any reason other than the fact that you are leaving it. This is not an attempt to trap you into extending the run. It is simply the situation in which all of us are placed."

Tracy took his heaviest blast in the press on December 23 when John Chapman of the *Daily News* bitterly assailed him under the headline HOLLYWOOD GO HOME: "The sooner Spencer Tracy goes back [to Hollywood], the better—and he should stay there." When the studio put out word that Tracy's return to Los Angeles was "imminent" and that he was wanted to play the role of President Truman in *The Beginning or the End,* Bob Considine's topical story of the atomic bomb, Victor Samrock seized control of the situation. On December 27 he notified the cast that *The Rugged Path* would close on January 19, 1946, completing an engagement of ten weeks, if not the one hundred performances for which Sherwood had so vigorously lobbied. The same day, the wire services carried the news that Tracy, solely on the strength of *Without Love,* had retained his position as

* Released as *The Best Years of Our Lives* (1946).

With Robert Keith onstage in *The Rugged Path*.
(AUTHOR'S COLLECTION)

one of the top five stars in America in the annual *Motion Picture Herald* poll of box office leaders.

The closing announcement triggered a recap in the January 2 issue of *Variety*, where Tracy's departure, the paper said, would not only mean "plenty of red for the Playwrights' Co., but a loss of employment by supporting actors." The star's desire not to continue, the item went on, was responsible for the fold. "It cost $75,000 to produce *Path* and the loss at this time is placed at more than $40,000. Show is costly to operate and virtually no profit was earned out of town. Grosses at the Plymouth have been exceptional, and it was figured *Path* could play well into the spring." The paper laid the blame squarely at Tracy's feet, suggesting the show had depended on the star's "whims" from the start.

No mention was made of Sherwood's negative reviews, which would have doomed the play with most any other star, nor Tracy's positive reviews, which were practically unanimous. *Variety* published on a Wednesday, and

Carroll called Victor Samrock the same day to say that Spence was in "quite an uproar" about it. "Am seeing the great man tonight," Samrock promptly advised Sherwood in a letter, "but now that the play has announced its closing, I am not worried about Spencer's innermost feelings, nor will I try to assuage his soul-searching doubts. On second thought, I will do these things if he promises to buy the moving picture rights for Metro."

Howard Dietz called editor Abel Green and arranged for *Variety* mugg Arthur Bronson to meet Tracy in his suite at the Waldorf Astoria and hear his side of the story. "I take the theatre seriously," Tracy told Bronson. "My record is good in it. The people I worked for—Herman Shumlin, the late George M. Cohan, and Sam Harris—they would have vouched for me." He denied that he was "running out" on the play and said the show was closing "for a simple, old-fashioned reason—it wasn't doing business." He pointed out that five other actors had already left and that Sherwood himself was out working in California. It had, in fact, been Sherwood who insisted on bringing the play into New York when it wasn't yet in shape. "If I had left," he said, "the play wouldn't have come in." Truthfully, he told Bronson that it was the producers who gave him—and the other actors—notice, and not the other way around. He then suggested to Bronson that he had never threatened to quit—a baldfaced lie.

Samrock was disappointed that there was no spike in business when the closing notice went up. He estimated the week of January 7 at $18,500 and felt the following week would be a little better. "I frankly thought the announcement would increase business," he said to Sherwood in a letter,

> but even so, I constantly have to catch myself up by realizing that $18,000 and $19,000 is still a lot of business in any country for any play. I would like to add that the lack of increase in business has hurt Mr. Tracy's pride (if he has any left). He has been constantly asking me to have you make a statement that the company is closing the play because of lack of business, and I have constantly been pointing out to him that while the play is not selling out, it is still doing good business, which shows that he is a draw, and I see no reason for making any statement at this stage of the game because it would only serve to create animosities.

Garson Kanin had gone off to direct his own play, *Born Yesterday*, and actor Efrem Zimbalist, Jr., who replaced Rex Williams in the part of Gil Hartnick, one of Vinion's colleagues on the paper, marveled at the spectacle of Tracy giving the actors notes after every performance. "Despite his notable achievements, he aroused little respect from our cast by insisting that all the actors maintain an artificially high pitch and level of performance," Zimbalist wrote in his autobiography. "When he slipped in comfortably underneath everybody else, the audience would say, 'He's so natural!' His notes comprised a list of those whose energy level was dropping (almost to normal). We all knew what his game was but were helpless to do anything about it."

When the last performance took place on the night of January 19, Samrock reported to Sherwood that the cast felt miserable "because the full impact of what can happen conveyed itself to them only after the last performance. It was sad and a little more than depressing." A letter of thanks over Sherwood's signature was distributed to the cast: "As a kind of final curtain on my relationship with Spencer, I must tell you that all his talk the last few days was, 'Where did I go wrong?' The only other note worth mentioning is that he fully promised me, without any prodding on my part, that he was returning to Hollywood and would proceed with all that was in him to sell the moving picture rights of *The Rugged Path*."

On January 24, Sherwood addressed both Samrock and press representative William Fields in acknowledging what both men had gone through in the interests of the play and their friendships with him. "I appreciate it very deeply, and I bitterly regret the initial mistake that I made when I first put my faith, and the fruits of long labors, in one who had proved, over and over again, that he possesses the morals and scruples and integrity and human decency of a louse. This, unfortunately, has not been merely one of those irritating experiences that one can laugh off and quickly forget. There certainly was an ugly kind of poison which spread to all of us and it is no easy task to get rid of it. I know we will get rid of it but, speaking for myself, it will not be forgotten."

CHAPTER 22

State of the Union

T he first meeting of the newly installed board of John Tracy Clinic took place on the evening of November 18, 1943. A new demonstration nursery was several weeks into its thirty-six-week session and hot lunches were being prepared daily by a rotation of volunteer mothers. Spence was fighting off a cold, eager to get the last shots for *A Guy Named Joe* in the can, but Walt Disney, otherwise immersed in the production of war propaganda at his Burbank studio, was interested in seeing firsthand how the clinic worked. It was when Louise was showing him around a few days later that they came upon the kids during nap time.

"Don't they have cots?" he asked.

"No," Louise told him. "They just sleep on mats on the floor."

The next day there were cots and, at Christmas time, a truckload of gifts—puppets and toys, all Disney-licensed, that could be used in teaching.

The service report at the February 1944 meeting was a succession of modest statistics: thirty-one children in the summer course, eight in nursery school, four in a weekly afternoon class. One hundred and seven families were enrolled in the correspondence course, twenty-five mothers were taking adult classes in child psychology and speech, some four hundred other families were assisted in some way via the mails. Granted its federal tax exemption status on June 19, 1944, the clinic had three full-time instructors. In February 1945 the original cottage was extended in the front, creating an annex and an entrance hall that displayed a map of the world on which colored pins marked all the places to which copies of the free correspondence course had been sent.

Collier's devoted three pages to the clinic in its issue of July 14:

> Little wonder the parents flock to this unique clinic with their handicapped offspring. They have heard how Mrs. Spencer Tracy, wife of the movie star, helped her born-deaf son, John, "to hear"— to find his normal place in everyday life through heightened observation, lip reading, and speech. John Tracy, now twenty, acts as natural and rugged as if he had been born with hearing. He drives his own station wagon through traffic, is a talented cartoonist, and plays tennis and polo. His training was no miracle. It was the result of long, patient years of faithful, sympathetic experimenting and persistence on the part of his mother. In gratitude, Mrs. Tracy now devotes her zeal and experience to developing this progressive clinic, in her son's name, for other deaf children all over the country.

Pictures surrounding the text showed Louise serving lunch to a trio of curly-haired moppets; Miss Hattie Harrell, formerly of the Rochester School for the Deaf, holding a boy's hand to her cheek as headphones amplify her voice; other instructors in group exercises as parents look on; and a lineup of giggling children arrayed along the rustic front porch of the clinic, some three, some four, one four and a half. Throughout, Louise preached the gospel of "normalcy," the importance of treating the child as if he or she could hear. "He must be talked to and played with and must be shown that he is loved and wanted." Though the annual cost of a family's participation in the demonstration nursery program had been set at $950, Louise was able, by simplifying the sense-training material, to get the cost of the correspondence course down to fifty-five dollars. "Today there is a long waiting list of parents eager for the home training instruction of the Tracy Clinic," the article concluded. "But they will have to wait until further facilities are available. Funds are urgently needed for more space, personnel, and material."

The *Collier's* piece brought a flood of new inquiries but no comparable flow of donations, and when Spence made the financial concessions for his return to the stage, the ever-increasing needs of the clinic could not have been far from his thoughts. In October, as the first troubled performances of *The Rugged Path* were taking place, John Tracy Clinic was granted the use of a second building on the SC campus, a small house next door to the original where two additional tutors could be located. That same month, a parents' auxiliary was formed and Louise began taking on speaking engagements, spending long hours away from the ranch. The drive from Encino took nearly an hour, and with John now a full-time student at Pasadena Junior College, Susie was left largely to her own devices.

The Tracy property was surrounded by the alfalfa fields of the Ador Dairy Farm, and during the war an army camp was directly across the street. Susie was never bored at the ranch; there was always something to do and she never felt she was stuck there. She rode her chestnut mare, Missy, to Encino Elementary, and Hughie would be waiting for her every day after school. At home, Margaret Hunt, the Tracys' cook-housekeeper, would have crackers and peanut butter and cold milk waiting. The closest businesses were on Ventura Boulevard, half a mile away, and Susie occasionally would go to a drugstore on Ventura to look through the movie magazines.

"She was a very happy, self-sufficient sort of child," her mother said. "I remember thinking, 'Well, I don't need to worry about you.'" People sometimes assumed that Susie was neglected by her parents, given Louise's relentless focus on her brother, but Susie could never remember feeling that way. When John was home, she'd go to his room and watch him get out his paper. Occasionally he'd take her and a friend to the movies. "Susie was a good lip reader," Louise commented. "She once said, 'I can lip read . . . ,' and I just looked at her. I said something without voice, and she told me exactly what I had said. She had watched him. John could always understand her, too. Susie always looked right at him when she talked."

John had gone through a flirtation with hearing devices in the early forties, first the stationary Phipps-Unit, with which he could hear "pretty well," then a Western Electric portable that enabled him to discern "low tones" from people up to five feet away. "Pretty soon, however, I got tired of the hearing aid. I didn't care much to wear it. I thought it drove me crazy. It puzzled and annoyed me. It made me feel nervous and impatient. Soon, I got in the habit of not wearing it anymore." The unit was so bulky it took a vest to hold it in place, and the battery alone was the size of a beer can. In April 1943 one of the Phipps-Units came home with John for a short while. "I could hear with it all right, but all I could distinguish was the lowness and highness of sounds . . . I tried my best to be patient when Mother insisted that I work with it. I just sat down and listened, that's all. I followed Mother with sounds she made through a microphone. It seemed very difficult to me."

He went on to work three days a week in a Beverly Hills studio, but after the summer of 1943 he stopped using amplification altogether. "Hearing sounds drives me nuts," he said, "and that's the truth. I cannot stand words. I like things when they are quiet and when they make me feel patient. Sounds annoy me. I *should* hear some to make better speech, but I feel it is too late to get into the habit of hearing speech or sounds. After all, I am happy and more comfortable the way things are—quiet."

In April 1946 Helen Keller visited John Tracy Clinic in the company of her secretary, Polly Thomson. "Encourage your child's desire to speak," she urged the mothers on duty that morning. Asked whether blindness or deafness was the greater handicap, Keller, without hesitation, replied that being deaf was the greater handicap because the blind "had more contact with their fellow man."

Tracy's return to M-G-M was as likely motivated by money as disappointment in Sherwood's play. There was general agreement among the critics in Washington, Boston, and New York that *The Rugged Path* was a personal triumph, albeit a qualified one. Yet the day after it opened on Broadway, Tracy advised Benny Thau that he wished to report back to the studio in ninety days, a condition of the leave-of-absence granted by Metro-Goldwyn-Mayer. Despite the business the show was doing, appearing in it cost him well in excess of $150,000, and the most he could afford to give the Playwrights' Company for something less than a masterpiece was three months. And even that, as it turned out, was too much. When he reported back to Culver City on February 4, 1946, he was immediately placed back on salary, even though the picture they had waiting for him couldn't start until Kate had finished with a thriller called *Undercurrent,* which was then only three weeks into production.

Their next picture together, *The Sea of Grass,* had been in the pipeline since 1937, the year Conrad Richter's lyrical tale of the changing Southwest was published by Knopf. The studio had it covered in galleys, the reader describing it as "the BEST story in its genre that I know of; it is beautiful, moving, dramatic, quick and subtle in turn, and has some of the most astounding characterizations to be found in any of the modern novels; acting it will be a privilege, directing and producing it a labor of love."

Bud Lighton took an early interest, and the picture was earmarked for Tracy and Myrna Loy in the days immediately following the completion of *Test Pilot.* "Its Western setting and pioneer flavor, similar to my own background, promised the kind of role I'd always wanted to play," Loy wrote. "They kept postponing it, however, and when they finally announced a starting date without informing me, I called Benny Thau and raised hell: 'What happened? Who's playing it?' When he said, 'Spence is doing it with Hepburn,' I realized what had happened. 'Oh, well,' I said, 'that figures.' I was mad as hell at Spence, at everyone."

Pan Berman inherited the project, Lighton having moved to Fox, and an early script by Vincent Lawrence and Earl Paramore was turned over to

Marguerite Roberts, who had done some uncredited work on *Undercurrent*. As usual, Kate involved herself in the writing process, and while Roberts found Tracy "marvelous to work with," she disliked Hepburn's intrusions: "I had worked with Hepburn on another picture, *Dragon Seed*. She frankly wasn't one of my favorite people. I admire her, and think she's a very interesting person, but she's a snob." Roberts chafed at the film's message, that the "nesters" settling the land would only ruin it when the rains failed to come and their crops dried up. "The Tracy character affected respect for the natural state of things, the undisturbed grass. He opposed the sodbusters, who wanted land. I had the Hepburn character note that his love for the natural state coincided with his becoming a millionaire off that very state. In other words, was his attachment mystical or opportunistic? [Director Elia] Kazan would have none of my viewpoint, only Tracy's."

Kazan learned of Richter's book while directing his first feature, *A Tree Grows in Brooklyn,* under Lighton's supervision at Fox. In New York, where he made his name staging *The Skin of Our Teeth,* Kazan had directed *Dunnigan's Daughter* for the Theatre Guild and made an immediate impression on Lawrence Langner, who in turn commended him to Tracy and Hepburn. Assured a $2.5 million budget and an all-star cast, Kazan had visions of creating an epic American western after the fashion of John Ford. "It is," he told the *New York Times,* "a fascinating and unusual love story with a psychological tinge." The *Times* went on to report that the studio considered *The Sea of Grass* its most imposing "physical" production of the year, allocating nearly five months to production, while shooting some forty thousand feet of background footage and second-unit work on the plains of western Nebraska.

Tracy was carried a full sixteen weeks before starting the picture on May 27, 1946. He filled the time getting his affairs in order, having earned substantially less in 1945 than in any year since the mid-thirties. Carroll had proven useless as a business manager, and when Peggy Gough went to Belgium with the American Red Cross, Tracy turned his affairs over to her replacement, a tall, raven-haired paralegal named Dorothy Griffith. "Miss G.," as she soon came to be known around the studio, had come to him through Frank Whitbeck, the salty West Coast promotions guru who had informally advised him for years. "Spencer was very bad at negotiating contracts or pictures to go in or stay out of," said Robert M. W. Vogel, who managed the studio's international operations, "and Whitbeck befriended him and was more or less his representative."

Although he considered investments from time to time, Tracy hadn't actually put money into anything other than annuities. He could never fully comprehend or justify the vast sums he was paid, and while he was openhanded about luxuries, he seemed most comfortable at the prospect of giving it all away. "I think I'm a pretty good businessman," he once said, "but I haven't got any consuming ambition to possess a lot of money. I'm one of those who believes that you can only sleep in one bed at a time, ride one horse, eat one meal, wear one suit of clothes."

His attitude toward wealth made him an easy touch, and a complete stranger with a compelling story could easily walk away with fifty or a hundred dollars, often over Carroll's strenuous objections. Once, Carroll remembered a petitioner who claimed he had worked for their late father in Milwaukee. He made some phone calls, asked some questions, became convinced the man was a phony, and told his brother as much. "Well, maybe there's just a chance he did," Spence said. "And if there's any chance, I want to give him something for Dad's sake."

This was a man, Miss G. decided, who needed protecting. Early in her tenure, she and her new boss worked out a way of deflecting the endless appeals that came his way, the clinic having come to take up much of what might otherwise have gone elsewhere. "I think it's possible," she said, "that every charitable organization, at some time or another, approached him for support."

Invariably an episode would begin with a call from Larry Keethe, Tracy's ubiquitous wardrobe man, who would say, "The boss wants to see you." On the set, Tracy would introduce her to a fund-raiser who had made it onto the lot, sometimes at his own invitation, sometimes at the invitation of a colleague or friend, and who had settled into one of the red leather lounges that lined his portable dressing room.

Mr. Tracy would say, "Miss G., how much money do we have in the till?" This meant honestly and for sure, "What's left in our charitable fund?" Often I would start with a tentative, "You could possibly manage a few thousand . . ." He would ask, "Have we got five Gs?" or "Have we got ten Gs?" and, learning that we did, he would say, "Let's write it." I would return to my office with the full particulars and write the check and return it for his signature.

On the other hand, if he wasn't about to contribute, he would say, "Miss Giannini, how much money do we have in the till?" This meant, "I don't think I want to go along with this one," and indicated that we play the scene. "Your charitable budget for the year is committed," I'd reply, and this was usually accompanied by a tightening of the face of our audience of one. Then I would brightly offer my suggestion: "However, we could postpone the new altar you promised the Sisters of—" And this line would be interrupted by quiet outrage on the part of Mr. Tracy. "Miss Giannini," he'd say, "are you suggesting that I renege on my promise to those wonderful nuns? Those dedicated women who spend their lives praying for good in this world?" And the fundraiser would suddenly look upon me with equal disapproval, as if I had suddenly assumed the head of Medusa. "Very well," I'd say. "That's the only suggestion I have, and Mr. Evans has been very firm about your commitments for the rest of the year." (Ross Evans was our tax man.) Then Mr. Tracy would reach for a cigarette, my cue to leave and tell the assistant director to call him for a shot. I'd depart, and a few moments later the assistant would say, "We're ready when you are, Mr. Tracy." His Nibs would warmly shake the hand of his guest, regretting ruefully that he couldn't help out "this time" and the fundraiser would leave knowing that Spencer Tracy was a fine man indeed and wondering how it was that he was stuck with such a horrible woman on his staff as Miss Giannini.

Where Miss Griffith occasionally did get into trouble was when she was pleading someone's case for a couple of lines in a Tracy picture.

He was rather like a school for young actors on the Metro lot. Inasmuch as I kept them at bay, I also knew something about them, their small credits and abilities. I didn't always try to help, but I did have my favorites, those I thought showed potential. An approach to Spencer Tracy was not easy. He always walked to the set, but never alone. Larry Keethe accompanied him or, sometimes, I walked with him and discussed business affairs. One did not accost a star of his magnitude, so the only way to try it was through me. If I thought someone capable, I would very often ask Mr. Tracy to give him a thought. One word from him to the director was all that was necessary. This aggravated him . . . superficially.

I frequently had to listen to a lengthy and well-played scene attesting to my incompetence. "Miss Griffith, what do I pay you for? You are paid to handle these demands without annoying me. I have all these problems . . . all these demands upon me . . . And you . . . What do you do? You come to me with every indigent actor on the lot . . ." Knowing very well I wouldn't bother him with anyone who wasn't a genuinely viable possibility.

I would take my leave with a "Very well, but he has—" whatever I thought he had, and more often than not, before the day ended, I would receive a call from Larry Keethe to come to the set. Mr. Tracy would have a few matters he wished attended to, and quite often it would end with, "Tell your newest protégé to see the assistant." Which meant he had been unable to resist reaching out a hand to an aspiring actor or actress who deserved a chance.

As the start date for *The Sea of Grass* approached, Tracy's indifference to the project became more pronounced. He had returned to M-G-M a heavier and older version of his former self, and where Louella Parsons could insist in her column that he had become "very handsome since his hair started turning gray," all he could see in the mirror was a character man who, at forty-five years of age, looked a good ten years older. Having briefly met Tracy the previous year, Elia Kazan was anxious about "the lard around his middle." Seeing the picture as a dust-blown backcountry story, he imagined its characters as lean and leathery, as wedded to the land as the cattle they grazed. His heart sank when he joined Tracy on Lot 4 to inspect two overfed geldings and choose one for him to ride in the picture: "He had not lost weight, he did not look like a Remington, he was not tight-waisted like the wranglers or even like Bud Lighton. Spencer looked . . . like the horses."

Kazan knew he'd been sandbagged when he was asked to approve sketches for costumes that had already been fitted. Berman liked them, he was told, and there was a considerable move on to get the film into production. Hepburn alone had some twenty changes. "Looks to me," said Kazan, "that every time she goes in to take a piss, she'll come bouncing out of the can in a snazzy new outfit." Designer Walter Plunkett, who had been dressing her since *Christopher Strong,* patiently explained: "She loves Spence, he's the love of her life, and she wants him to think that on any given day she's prettier than any other girl in the world."

"I thought you meant in the movie," Kazan said.

"The movie!" Plunkett erupted. "I'm talking about real life. Them! Is what matters!"

Soon Tracy had Kazan laughing at stories of how they did things at Metro, the attitudes of the producers in charge, the workings of the clattering assembly line that ground out the product. "At lunch," Tracy related, "Mervyn LeRoy was raving about a book he'd bought. 'It's got everything,' he said. 'Surprise, great characters, an important theme, fine writing! But,' he said, 'I think we can lick it.' Honest. That's what he said!" And Kazan, spiritually, threw in the towel. "We both laughed and we were buddies, he and I, I his admirer, he my star, and I had no fight left in me. Friendship had defeated me."

Undercurrent finished in early May, and Hepburn made a quick trip east to see her parents. Tracy stationed himself in Phoenix, where he occasionally went to paint for "occupational therapy"—dark, brooding desert landscapes, abstract to the point of being more about color and mood than representation, "just putting paint on cardboard," as Louise characterized it, but producing, over the space of a few years, several paintings that were, in her judgment, "very unusual and very good." Fanny Brice had gotten him started, sensing "a nervous time" and sending over a whole outfit—paint, oil, brushes, palette. Though he dismissed what he did as "daubing," he was downright jovial by the time he got down to work on *The Sea of Grass,* explaining to Earl Wilson that he was just a supporting player in the picture and that Kate was the true star. "You want to come out and watch Her Highness? It'll be very educational."

On the set, Wilson observed Hepburn in slacks, a towel around her head, congenial at first, less so as she realized he wasn't going to leave. ("Oh, are you still here?" she said after a costume change. "I thought we'd be able to avoid you.") Tracy knew the press irritated her, and it amused him when he could get people like Wilson to linger. "I did a scene that will revolutionize the industry," he began dryly, encouraging the columnist to stick around. "I walked over to a wagon and put a basket in it, and then I walked down the road. I did that whole gigantic scene without forgetting one thing. Of course, I didn't have any lines. You do a scene like that 15 times and you get silly. Now you know why actors go nuts." He went on to say that was why he wanted to get out of the movies entirely and go back to the stage.

Kazan was fond of multiple takes but made a calculated decision not to try and direct Tracy very much, knowing he would likely alienate his two stars without substantially improving the picture. "Tracy was great in take one," he said, "okay in take two. About take four he began to go down, and by take six he was not very good. After take seven he just wouldn't do any more. He'd say, 'What do you want?' "

Kazan, observed actor Melvyn Douglas, seemed to want "bursts of energy and an undertone of malevolence" he simply couldn't get from Tracy. "Spence projected a heavy, relaxed authority. He was wonderfully skillful but, finally, did not do what the director requested." Giving up on him, Kazan found Hepburn more accepting, and his one great achievement on *The Sea of Grass* was the unusually restrained performance he managed to coax from her. "Spence and Hepburn were lovers, and she was very protective of him," said Kazan. "She'd watch him shoot and say, 'Isn't Spence wonderful?' And I'd think, 'He's only giving a tenth of what he's got.' In one scene, he was supposed to come in from the open plains where it was snowing and he'd take a little water, throw it on his face, and make an entrance. His shoes looked like they had just been shined. I never could get him to stretch himself."

With director Elia Kazan, who, for myriad reasons, found *The Sea of Grass* a frustrating experience. (AUTHOR'S COLLECTION)

When Tracy told Earl Wilson he wanted to get out of movies altogether and go back to the stage, he wasn't just saying it for effect. Kate had committed to *As You Like It* for the Theatre Guild on the understanding that Tracy would also do something in the fall. In May, just as *The Sea of Grass* was getting under way, the Guild's Lawrence Langner came west, where the decision was made to go ahead with the sets and the costumes. "Now Kate," Langner urged, "don't sell yourself into slavery for another five years when you can be supporting me and Spencer by working for us in Shakespeare. As soon as Spencer quits, I am going to set the two of you up in a wonderful company which will go to London and will be known as the 'Old Trics'—the 'Old Trics' would be much better than the 'Old Vics.'"

Laurence Olivier had brought the Old Vic to New York with a company that included Margaret Leighton, Ralph Richardson, and Miles Malleson, and Langner proposed a similar setup for Tracy and Hepburn. "Everyone here is talking about Laurence Olivier," Langner said in a letter to Tracy on June 6, "and the reason isn't because he gives any one special performance (except in the case of Oedipus), but because they are seeing him in four different parts, playing old men, middle-aged men, etc. No trick to any good actor, but the public has gone wild with enthusiasm. Please consider very seriously a proposition that—when your contract is up—you and Kate, with the Guild, form a repertory company in which you would play in four or five masterpieces and set the country on fire by bringing back some of the real old-time theatre." Among the titles Langner proposed were *Dodsworth*, *The Devil's Disciple,* and O'Neill's *Desire Under the Elms*. "Hope you will discuss this with Kate before she commits herself to another five with M-G-M. The Theatre Guild is willing, as part of this proposition, to form an independent pictures corporation to make one outstanding picture each year in which you and Kate appear and in which, in addition to receiving your salary, you would also both have a share on a capital gains basis, so that you would only be paying 25% tax to the government."

Tracy mulled the proposition over, talked with Leo Morrison, and proposed to M-G-M that he go to a straight $110,000 per picture, drawing no salary between films as he was currently doing. An interoffice memo summarized his reasoning:

> He stated that he does not want to feel under obligation to the studio, which he would be if he continued to accept compensation when he is not working. He also feels that he does not want to be placed in the position that he had been two or three times in the past when a question has arisen as to whether or not he will do a picture and Mr. Mannix has called his attention to the fact that he has been on salary. He stated that the studio will not be able to get five pictures every two years and, as a matter of fact, will get only three or four at the most. He is perfectly willing to be paid on the basis of the pictures he does, even though it will mean less compensation to him than under the present agreement.

M-G-M always resisted per-picture agreements, nurturing instead a dependency on the narcotic of a weekly paycheck. Benny Thau countered with an offer to cancel paragraph 26 of Tracy's contract, which would mean that, were the agreement to be terminated, Tracy would not be obligated to repay any monies that he had received in excess of $110,000 per picture. The matter was allowed to lie dormant, and Tracy did not respond to Langner until July, when he apologized for not answering sooner and said that he was expecting to come east so they could "have a chat" around September 1. "The picture has been going very well," he added. "Kazan lives up to your recommendation." A week later, Guild records show he turned down *Damien* by Samoan playwright John Kneubuhl on the grounds that he "did not want to play another priest."

What happened next is unclear, but in proposing to go east and work in partnership with Hepburn on the New York stage, Tracy was changing the dynamic of his twenty-three-year marriage to an unprecedented degree. Tina Gopadze Smith, Dorothy Griffith's daughter, remembered her mother's account of a conference in Louis B. Mayer's office, sometime in the latter forties, in which Louise and, most probably, Spence participated (since it was Miss G.'s job to take down everything that got said). Was Mayer urging a reconciliation, as he so often did when the domestic lives of his players threatened the tranquillity and well-being of the studio? Or was he engineering a quiet separation, perhaps even a divorce, since one of the parties involved was Katharine Hepburn, one of his favorite people, proof positive, he once told his daughter Irene, that one could have "talent without temperament"?

The Tracy-Hepburn combination was a powerful draw at the box office, and it was generally known and acknowledged that Kate had played an important role in keeping Spence on an even keel. Louise, as the innocent party, would have to consent to a divorce under California law and agree to either adultery or extreme cruelty as specific grounds, thus risking adverse publicity that could affect Tracy's standing with the public. Did Mayer offer the use of his personal attorney? Help with a monetary settlement? Money, perhaps, for the ongoing maintenance and expansion of the clinic? No record now exists of that meeting, and Tina Smith could only remember, by her mother's account, what Louise said in shutting down the discussion: "I will be Mrs. Spencer Tracy *until the day I die*."

Was the clinic a factor in Louise's gravitational pull? Was it possible that, through the funding he provided, Spence had at last been given a way to respond to the deafness of their son that wasn't born of guilt and self-recrimination, something that was so thoroughly redemptive that it was to be preserved and fostered at any cost? Never a strong proponent of marriage, Kate was philosophical, if not completely aware of what was happening. "I can't live with Spence," she told their friend Bill Self, "and he *won't* live with Louise."

When *The Sea of Grass* wrapped on August 6, 1946, Tracy made a surprise announcement to Edwin Schallert of the *Los Angeles Times*. "I think we should appear in a film about two years hence," he said of the Tracy-Hepburn team,

and then I should play the father of Miss Hepburn. I can't stay young and act romantic heroes forever. Actually, a critic in the east who praised very highly our work in various pictures together also indicated that he hoped the matching of our personalities would not be carried to the point where audiences might ever weary of us.

Therefore, I believe that it is safer that we should rest on laurels gained, rather than try for new ones, and that probably *Sea of Grass,* which I believe will be a very great picture, should be the final one for a time. It has been a pleasure to work in various pictures with Miss Hepburn. Her honesty in her acting is a remarkable thing. She is the tops.

According to Schallert's report, which was picked up by the wire services and carried nationally, Hepburn had agreed to a new term contract with Metro-Goldwyn-Mayer "which still permits her to return to the stage." Langner had advised so strongly against such a commitment that either Tracy, or money, or both were likely factors in her decision. Certainly the quality of the material wasn't a major consideration; since *Woman of the Year* Hepburn had appeared in one troubled M-G-M production after another, and her next, *A Love Story,* in which she was to play Clara Schumann, would be yet another missed opportunity. When the contract was formally signed on September 15, 1946, it specified a term of three years at $4,792.33 a week, a bump in compensation of more than $1,200 a week from what she was paid for *The Sea of Grass.*

On August 29 Tracy responded to a note from Langner by saying that it seemed "impossible" to find out "anything definite regarding my plans for the full year" but that he was keeping at it and would know something shortly. Kate was going east for the month of September, and Tracy was due to start a six-week vacation himself, after which he was committed to *Cass Timberlane.* He was back in Los Angeles in time for a clinic board meeting on October 1—his seventh in the space of three years.

In August Louise had unveiled plans for a $500,000 fund-raising campaign to cover the cost of a new building to "meet the needs of the constantly expanding program." The clinic also obtained the services of a full-time psychologist, Mrs. Alathena Smith, in order to offer psychological counseling, group therapy, and psychological testing for children—a big step in rounding out the program. Another meeting on the eighteenth further clarified the future included a wealth of new programs, extended outreach on an international level, and ongoing refinement of the JTC correspondence course. It was more than one man could ever hope to support, and fourteen new members were added to the board. It was time to bring the public, the community at large, into the grand scheme of what John Tracy Clinic was to become.

Spence took off for Arizona as Kate began filming *Love Story** at M-G-M, but was back before long and present on the lot for much of its

* Released as *Song of Love* (1947).

production. "He would come on the set every morning," recalled Paul Henreid, Hepburn's costar on the picture, "say hello, and then, with a half-smile, ask me, 'Is she behaving herself?' Without smiling, I'd say, 'Oh yes, Spence. She's being marvelous.'

" 'Good, good.' He would turn to Hepburn. 'Now Kate, have you learned your lines?' Rather demurely, she'd say, 'Yes, dear.' He'd go on: 'Now don't forget. Say the lines loud and clear. Don't grin and make faces—just say the words.' And, grinning at him like a child, she'd say, 'Yes, Spence, I will.' "

Observing all this, Clarence Brown, who was directing the picture, once asked her, "Why the hell don't you find a guy you can marry and raise a family? Otherwise, one of these days when you're older you'll be all alone."

"Yes," she replied, "and I'll look back at all the fun I had."

With the exception of a trailer for the American Cancer Society, Spencer Tracy was entirely offscreen for the year 1946 and his popularity with the public plummeted. End-of-year surveys placed him well out of the top ten, the *Motion Picture Herald* having fixed him at number twenty-two, behind Van Johnson, Bob Hope, Humphrey Bogart, Margaret O'Brien, Roy Rogers, and Cornel Wilde, among others. (Bing Crosby again came in first.) It was as if the results underscored the precarious situation in which Tracy and a number of his contemporaries now found themselves, slipping in the marketplace as newer, younger personalities moved up. Gable placed thirteenth, Bette Davis fifteenth, Claudette Colbert nineteenth in a tie with Gene Tierney. Mickey Rooney, who had equaled Crosby's achievement by placing first for three consecutive years, failed to make the list at all.

M-G-M's new year was awash in Technicolor and all-star casts, the few genuine vehicles on the schedule relegated to B-picture status, the studio settling into a new epoch as the leader in glossy musicals and little else. As a nod to the tastes of prewar audiences, there was still Andy Hardy, still Wallace Beery, still Lionel Barrymore and Robert Montgomery, Ann Sothern and Myrna Loy, but their appearances were fewer, their aging audiences now staying home more with the radio and, in a few cases, the TV set, leaving the neighborhood theaters to changing tastes and kids who wondered what the big deal was over someone like Gable. *The Sea of Grass* was tossed in with the other black-and-white features, a major attraction but not the event it might once have been. Set to open at Radio City Music Hall, its initial success was virtually assured, given the receptions accorded the three previous Tracy-Hepburn collaborations. The big question was whether

Middle America would embrace a western so insistently artificial at a time when even Roy Rogers shot his pictures out of doors.

"I find my feeling for Spencer Tracy and Katharine Hepburn is a mixture of personal respect and professional regret," Shirley O'Hara wrote for the *New Republic*.

> I've admired them for years, and would still rather watch them than any other team on the screen, but in *The Sea of Grass* it seems wasteful to let two such good, attractive actors wander through a lavish production like thoroughbred somnambulists. Hepburn of the beautiful bones is more polished than ever; Tracy, though he is no longer a priest—here he is a colonel and what the press has called a Cattle Baron—is still playing Father Tracy and is getting more pensive and solemn and good every day. I think back to when he was just Spencer Tracy and an exciting actor, though I minded his always wearing a gray felt hat, and those days are like a noisy picnic remembered in church. His playing has always been on the quiet side, but now that former underacting seems like a wild romp in the sun. And yet I'm sure there is still fire and magnetism behind his strength. It must be some mistaken actor's mold he has made for himself (or his reputation), and the story chosen because of it, and the awed direction, that give his performance a static quality.

In Los Angeles, Louise and Jane Feely (in town for a job interview) went to a sneak at Spence's behest. "It was one of those performances that was not all great on his part," Jane recounted. "Louise said to me, 'This is her picture.' I said, 'Sure is.' When we came home, the phone rang. She said, 'Uh oh, there he is. That's Spencer.' On the phone she was a good hour. She had to answer all the questions—Which scene? What scene? What did you think? She was in the other room and I kept hearing her say, 'Well, it was her picture, Spencer. You let her have it. It was HER picture.' When she got off the telephone, I said, 'Was he not so happy with it?' She said, 'Well, it's his own fault. She walked off with scenes.'"

Remarkably, *The Sea of Grass* did more than $3 million domestically and another $1.5 million in foreign billings, making it the most popular, commercially, of all the Tracy-Hepburn features. It now remained for Tracy to see if he had the same kind of commercial appeal without Hepburn, given that he hadn't made a film without her since 1944. Starkly subtitled "A Novel of Husbands and Wives," *Cass Timberlane*, with its Book-of-the-Month Club cachet, its serialization in *Cosmopolitan*, and its rumored advance that ran well into six figures, seemed the perfect vehicle for an aging, albeit reluctant, matinee idol of Tracy's stature, its sedate, flute-playing judge a meaty counterpoint to any one of a dozen of the industry's livelier young actresses, a "half-tamed hawk of a girl, twenty-three or -four," in author Sinclair Lewis' words, "not tall, smiling, lively of eye . . ."

Metro paid $150,000 for the picture rights, Tracy involving himself in the development process to an unusual degree. As early as December 1946 he could be spotted in Superior Court alongside director George Sidney, dark glasses in place, observing a divorce action and drinking in the procedural atmosphere of the place. Treatments were commissioned from Sonya Levien and the novelist John O'Hara, who, according to producer Arthur Hornblow, Jr., wanted to "show Sinclair Lewis how the story should really have been written." O'Hara produced a series of "character portraits" and managed to collaborate with Levien on a draft that was, said Hornblow, "such an unsuccessful screenplay (unsuccessful in terms of the way we all felt about it) that we couldn't even produce it." When Tracy returned from New York and the debacle of *The Rugged Path,* playwright Sidney Kingsley was at work on a script that ultimately "stank" in the collective opinion of Tracy, Hepburn, and Elia Kazan.

Before the completion of *Sea of Grass,* Donald Ogden Stewart was summoned to the coast, where he and his wife, Ella Winter, established themselves on a corner of Salka Viertel's Santa Monica property, happily gardening in the Mediterranean climate and dining most Sundays at Kate's rented place on Beverly Grove Drive. Stewart thought the job "one of the most interesting and difficult" of his Hollywood career, since Cass, as portrayed in the novel, wasn't a very good part. "He falls in love with Jinny, a lively and mad younger girl from 'the wrong side of the tracks' and marries her against the opposition of his upper-class neighbors on the exclusive Heights. O.K. so far, but not particularly original. And for the rest of the novel, Cass sits around with what in show business we call 'egg on his face' while Jinny takes over." Stewart considered the problem and came up with a subplot, the kind of social content usually present in a Lewis book but somehow missing in the case of *Cass Timberlane.* "Cass was a judge, born into and surrounded by the upper class of his home town. Supposing *that* problem were to enter the picture? Supposing a judge had to fight for his judicial integrity and his self-respect against a danger of which he was only dimly aware—his affection for and belief in his best friends."

Stewart's work went a long way toward strengthening the character of Cass, but at the cost of leaving the character of Jinny underdeveloped, a point hit home in December when David Selznick refused the loan of Jennifer Jones for the role. Without Jones, Hornblow was at a loss over whom to cast in the part, having tested "virtually every young actress at the studio." He told the *New York Times* he was prepared to delay the picture until the proper woman could be found, and soon Sonya Levien was back at work on the screenplay, charged with punching up the character of Jinny. When Stewart got wind that much of his material had been cut in favor of Levien's new scenes, he was understandably miffed at being left out of the loop, communicating his upset to Hornblow through his wife, Ella. Filming began on March 29 with Lana Turner—George Sidney's idea—in the part of Jinny and nobody particularly happy with the script or the way the various drafts had been stitched together like a patchwork quilt.

Production limped along for nearly two weeks, at which point agent Harold Hecht advised Stewart that Tracy was "evidently upset about [the] present script." Two days later, Hecht informed his client that a letter from Arthur Hornblow was en route to him, asking that he return to California. "Tracy wants [you] to know that he feels all of it is [of] vital importance to him for you to do this and will regard it as [a] mark of your friendship for him." In his letter, producer Hornblow explained that despite the fact that both he and Tracy liked Stewart's script, it became clear after his departure for New York that "no likely actress for Jinny wanted any part of it."

"Tracy," said Ella Winter, "had refused to make a Judge-Meets-Girl picture with Lana Turner, and his refusal had been accepted as final by [the] producer and studio." Getting back to the "Wargate matter"—the ethical dilemma that confronts Judge Timberlane as his marriage is crumbling—was no easy thing, as about a quarter of the picture had already been shot. Filming resumed with a greater sense of mission, if not necessarily the wherewithal to accomplish it, and Stewart's changes, such as they were, came in the form of retakes about halfway through the course of production. "In the book," said George Sidney, "the judge is supposed to be 41 but he acts 65. We've tried to straighten that out. The story is really about two people who haven't sat down and thought out what their marriage means to them. Each has a different idea about it. The judge wants honesty, integrity, a marriage on his own terms. The girl wants freedom. She wants to go to New York, maybe to a cocktail party in the Waldorf Towers, all the things a small town girl dreams about."

The son of an M-G-M executive, Sidney, thirty, had been around the studio all of his adult life, initially as a director of *Our Gang* comedies. "I'd played polo with Spence and he called me 'Kid.' He came to my office for the first conference, full of his usual doubts, and asked, 'Kid, can you handle me?' Getting the fix on a character was agony for him . . . But once we started, and he had found the motivation, he was marvelous."

As with the previous picture, Tracy was surrounded by a cast of seasoned character people, among them Mary Astor, Albert Dekker, Margaret Lindsay, Rose Hobart, John Litel, Mona Barrie, Josephine Hutchinson, and John Alexander (who was known to both stage and screen audiences as the boisterous Teddy Brewster of *Arsenic and Old Lace*). From a publicity stand-point, the most fuss was made over Selena Royle, who had signed a term contract with M-G-M in 1943. Tracy had created a stir by coming onto the set of her first picture on the lot, *Mrs. Parkington*, and telling Sidney Skol-sky she was "one of the few people, when I was in stock, who thought I might someday amount to something on the stage." Apart from running into him at the studio, however, or into Louise at a premiere, Selena never saw either of them. Not knowing their situation at home, she was plainly bewildered by their seeming aloofness.

"I had pushed their baby's perambulator along the streets of Brooklyn while we both were playing there," she said. "We had worked together for months at a time, year after year. I had dined with them, they with me. We had shared a small amount of success together, and we always had been there to console when the going got tough for any one of us . . . I was never asked to their house, nor was my presence in Hollywood acknowledged in any way."

Selena was in *Thirty Seconds Over Tokyo*, playing Phyllis Thaxter's mother in the final minutes of the picture, and she was considered part of the M-G-M stock company when she was selected to play Louise Wargate in *Cass Timberlane*. It wasn't a big part, and she wasn't even sure at first if Spence knew she was in it.

"A huge cast of actors and extras were sitting around during one of the customary long waits while electricians work on the lights. Suddenly there occurred one of those complete silences which inexplicably descends on a large group of people . . . out of which Spence's voice boomed over a micro-phone, 'This is all your fault, Selena. If it hadn't been for you, I'd be driving a truck in Milwaukee and happy.'

"I replied that he might have been driving a truck, but he wouldn't have been happy."

Just four days into the run of *The Rugged Path*, another hotly anticipated show made its New York debut. *State of the Union* was the first new play in three years from the team of Howard Lindsay and Russel Crouse, and only the second to follow *Life With Father*, the phenomenal Broadway stage hit that was still playing to capacity houses six years into its run. A sharp topi-cal satire, *State of the Union* followed the presidential aspirations of one Grant Matthews, an idealistic and self-made industrialist who proves too wayward a candidate ever to win an election. Caught between a wife, a mis-tress, and a perceived duty to the nation, Matthews ultimately decides the price of public office is too great to suit his iconoclastic nature. As a com-mentary on the public mind-set of postwar America, it was everything *The*

Rugged Path was not—slick, funny, popular with both critics and the public, and the winner of the 1945–46 Pulitzer Prize for drama. If Tracy ever peered around the corner from the stage entrance of the Plymouth Theatre and envied his friend Ralph Bellamy the jackpot he had so decidedly hit with the part of Matthews, he never let on, other than to openly covet the movie role when the rights were sold to Paramount in May 1946.

The playwrights were powerful enough to insert casting approval into their contract with the studio, and when first Gary Cooper, then Ray Milland proved out of reach, the property passed to Liberty Films, Inc., and the most ideal of all American directors to tackle the subject—the inestimable Frank Capra. Tracy campaigned for the part, and within a month of Capra's involvement he was considered a lock, even as Liberty continued to dicker with M-G-M. "I'm getting old," Tracy explained laconically, "and I've never done a picture with Capra." Predictably, the sticking point became the price Metro would exact for the loan of one of its most valuable stars. As when Clark Gable was borrowed by Selznick for *Gone With the Wind,* the studio demanded the distribution rights to the picture in addition to a fee of $175,000. For its part, Paramount contributed the play and the services of Claudette Colbert. The net result from Tracy's standpoint was the best role, the best material, and the best director he had had in years.

At first it was thought *Cass Timberlane* would be delayed in favor of *State of the Union,* but with Tracy on board, Capra undertook a complete rewrite of the script to strengthen the character of Matthews, who would no longer vacillate under the competing influences of the play's supporting characters. The final shape of the picture owed as much to circumstance as design, Tracy's own involvement, however ideal, being the direct result of the playwrights' inability to deliver Gary Cooper and Paramount's subsequent willingness to surrender the property. The secondary part of the wisecracking columnist Spike McManus, first assigned Robert Walker, went to Van Johnson when Walker fell ill, Johnson, Angela Lansbury, and Lewis Stone all being M-G-M contract players. Shooting commenced on September 29, 1947, so the film could be in theaters well before the Republican and Democratic conventions of 1948—a contractual stipulation as well as a commercial imperative. The only non-M-G-M personnel in the cast would be Adolphe Menjou and the aforementioned Colbert, who would be appearing opposite Tracy for the first time since *Boom Town.*

Tracy ordered six new suits for the picture—three predictably gray, three blue. ("Spence owns plenty of suits," Larry Keethe observed, "but you can take my word there's not one suit among them that isn't blue, gray, or brown.") The first days of production were given over to introductory scenes with Kay Thorndyke, the conniving daughter of old Sam Thorndyke, a dying newspaper baron, and McManus, their star employee.

Tracy joined the shoot on October 8, playing the first of several intimate scenes with twenty-one-year-old Angela Lansbury, an awkward circumstance given the nature of the role and Lansbury's extreme youth. "We had a very tricky scene to play in which I was his mistress," she remembered. "Spence understood that I was a very young woman who had been cast in this role of a woman probably fifteen years older than I was. And he instinctively knew my sense of not quite knowing how to play this scene with him, which was in fact almost a love scene. And he was extraordinarily sensitive to that fact and helped in every possible way he could to make me feel at ease and not have any sense of embarrassment."

The quality of his cast was such that Capra effortlessly pulled ahead of schedule and was ready for Claudette Colbert a full week before her scheduled October 17 start date. The early call wasn't a problem for Colbert, forty-four, but working after five o'clock was, the actress being so famously fastidious over the way she was photographed that she refused to show the right side of her face to the lens and reputedly knew more about staging and lighting than some of her cameramen. She had a brief confrontation with Capra in his office ("My doctor says I get too tired—") and walked out on the picture when the director who guided her to her only Academy Award–winning performance refused to be limited to a seven-hour workday. "Oh my God!" blurted Sam Briskin, one of Capra's partners. "Everybody's on *salary*! Could cost us a fortune—"

Capra's boldness came in part from the fact that he was several days ahead of schedule, but the replacement of Claudette Colbert with a star of equal magnitude was essential to keeping the picture on track. Briskin called L. B. Mayer, Eddie Mannix (who, according to Capra, cheered the decision), then Tracy himself, whose first reaction was to laugh. When the project first landed at M-G-M and Tracy was officially confirmed as its star, there was widespread speculation that Kate Hepburn would join the cast, since Colbert was presumed to have been left behind at Paramount. She was reported to have just arrived on the coast—this was March 18—to do a Screen Guild broadcast and prepare for Metro's adaptation of the John P. Marquand novel *B.F.'s Daughter*, which was to be produced by Edwin Knopf.

Then something happened. In May, Hepburn garnered a lot of attention when she appeared at a rally for *New Republic* editor Henry Wallace at Los Angeles' Gilmore Stadium. Wallace, the former vice president and future Progressive Party candidate for president, had been denied use of the Hollywood Bowl. At Gilmore, a venue arranged on short notice, he drew a crowd of 28,000, among them Charlie Chaplin and his wife Oona, Edward G. Robinson, and Hedy Lamarr. Hepburn, dressed in a sweeping scarlet gown, struck out at the Thomas-Rankin committee investigating Hollywood in Congress and all but stole the show with fiery talk decrying an atmosphere of official intimidation toward the movie industry and the arts in general. "The artist since the beginning of time has always expressed the aspirations and dreams of his people," she thundered. "Silence the artist and you have silenced the most articulate voice the people have." She went on to denounce President Truman, Attorney General Tom Clark, and State Senator Jack B. Tenney, among others, as responsible for a "plot" to foist "thought control" on the "liberal and progressive people of America."

"I was backstage because I had some involvement in the meeting," Ring Lardner said, "and she seemed nervous just about speaking in public on politics, rather than nervous about endorsing Wallace . . . But she went ahead and made a very good speech." Hepburn created such an indelible impression that the afternoon Hearst paper described a "scarlet robe, and it was plenty scarlet," reflecting "in red" the "yogi's [Wallace's] philosophy." George Stevens, who later positioned her politically as a "liberal New England conservative," suggested her appearance that day was not so much out of support for Wallace or in service of Communist or socialist sympathies but simply because "she got mad when they wouldn't let him use the Hollywood Bowl." Hepburn herself always said that she was speaking against censorship, not particularly for Wallace, and that it was "the speech that almost ran me out of the business." Nobody could remember exactly what Wallace said during his half-hour address, but the Progressive Citizens of America later claimed to have distributed more than three million copies of Hepburn's talk, which was titled, aptly enough, "Thought Control."

Unofficially branded as "pink," Kate didn't work at all that summer, and when Metro announced that she and Tracy would be teamed for another picture, Hedda Hopper took care to print a reader's suggestion: "I hope Spencer Tracy and Katharine Hepburn won't be starred for the fifth time in *Before the Sun Goes Down.* Hepburn couldn't stand being called 'box-office poison' twice." It was then reported that Hepburn "had a real peeve on" because M-G-M gave the lead in *B.F.'s Daughter* to Barbara Stanwyck (who was presumably safer, politically, because she was known to be a Republican). Hepburn had, in fact, been idle nine months—people were reportedly throwing things at screens showing *Song of Love*—when Capra made the admittedly heated decision to let Colbert go her own way.

"What the hell happened?" asked Tracy as he took the director's call. "Goddamn you, I'm going to report you to the Actors Guild." Then he laughed: "You told that Frankie Froggie Colbert to go to hell, did you?"

Capra asked if he knew any actresses, any "friends" who weren't working, and, as calculated as the question now seems, claimed to have absolutely no one in mind when Tracy responded, "The *Madam!* I've been rehearsing my part with her, she's taking Colbert's role, at home here."

Capra's response: "My God, do you think she'd do it?" And Tracy's reply: "I don't know. She's kind of nutty that way, about people being in trouble. She's 'theatre' you know."

Hepburn took the phone and, according to Capra, said, "Sure! What the hell? When do we start?" She then, as she later remembered it, called Colbert herself. "Claudette I knew," she said, "and I called Claudette and I said, 'You know, they're just going to dump you and take me, because here I am and they're paying me. And I don't care what hours I work, and I think you're wrong to say you have to quit.' And she said, 'Please, just do the part, because I . . .' That's how it happened." Capra was amazed: "No contract, no talk of agents, money, billing—nothing. She worked day and night, all through the weekend, with the costume designer, Irene . . . I don't know anybody in the business who wouldn't have held us over a barrel for money—and we would have paid anything to save the picture."

Colbert's exit took place on a Friday, and Kate stepped into the role of Mary Matthews the following Monday, thus ending Spence's moratorium on further Tracy-Hepburn pictures little more than a year after he first proclaimed it. The irony of Hepburn's portrayal of the spurned wife with two children could not have been lost on those in the know, Lansbury's Kay zeroing in on Grant in much the same way Hepburn had targeted Tracy. "We all knew," Lansbury said, "but nobody ever said anything. In those days it wasn't discussed. They were totally hand-in-glove, totally comfortable and unself-conscious about their relationship. She wasn't the sort of woman that many men would be attracted to—the snugly, cuddly woman in the movies at that time. And yet because of her enormous affection and love for Spencer, she had the ability to subjugate this almost manly quality she had at times and become this wonderfully warm, irresistible woman."

The first scene between Tracy and Hepburn was one in which the estranged couple must share a bedroom in Menjou's "boarding house for political has-beens." Lansbury has deliberately left her glasses on the nightstand. Mary finds them and starts transferring bedding to the floor, Grant protesting her apparent decision to sleep there until she crawls into the bed and leaves the boards to him. Dissolve to the two of them in semidarkness, Mary peering down at her estranged husband from atop the mattress, Grant pensively puffing a cigarette below. She wonders if she has lost him for good, asks him if he wants a divorce. He scratches the back of his neck thoughtfully, winces at the directness of the question.

"The world thinks I'm a very successful man—rich, influential, happy," he says. "You know better, don't you Mary? You know that I'm neither happy nor successful . . . not as a man, a husband, or a father. You wanna know something else? I'm *glad* I'm down here on the floor. That's where I belong . . ."

Tracy was energized, engaged on *State of the Union,* tearing into the part of Matthews with renewed vigor and imagination. Similarly, Hepburn brought a deft balance of humor and pathos to the role of Mary, taking up the slack even as Capra, beset by business worries, grew distracted and oddly unsure of himself. "When Tracy and his 'bag of bones' played a scene," said Capra, "cameras, lights, microphones, and written scripts ceased to exist. And the director did just what the crews and other actors did—sit, watch, and marvel." Angela Lansbury saw it as a spiritual melding of two supremely talented people: "Their personalities as well as their talents were orchestrated so marvelously. I began to think of them as one person, really; I suppose most people did."

Scarcely a week into Hepburn's tenure on the picture, the hearings of the House Committee on Un-American Activities got under way in Washington with windy testimony from Jack Warner, L. B. Mayer, and the Russian-born novelist Ayn Rand. There followed a host of "friendly" film industry witnesses, the first of which, director Sam Wood, fingered Hepburn as having appeared at a recent meeting—apparently referring to the event at Gilmore Stadium—at which "Hollywood Communists" had raised $87,000. The next day, Adolphe Menjou, the first of the big-name actors to take the stand, seconded much of what Wood had said, stopping short of directly accusing specific people of being Communists, but noting that many "acted" like Communists, among them John Cromwell, Paul Robeson, Edward G. Robinson, Paul Henreid, and Alexander Knox.

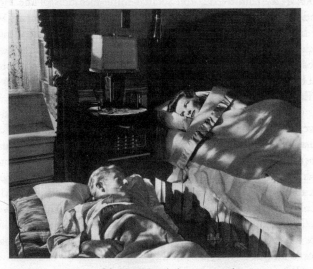

State of the Union (1948). (SUSIE TRACY)

Tracy disapproved—as did Gable—of marquee names muddling around in politics ("Remember, it was an actor who shot Lincoln"), but Hepburn had no such qualms and promptly aligned herself with the Committee for the First Amendment, an ad hoc organization of Hollywood heavyweights that included Humphrey Bogart, Henry Fonda, Eddie Cantor, Myrna Loy, Gregory Peck, Kirk Douglas, Rita Hayworth, and director William Wyler. The cornerstone of their collective effort to combat the grandstanding of Chairman J. Parnell Thomas and the eight members of his committee (which included Congressman Richard M. Nixon) was a broadside that characterized the investigation as an attempt to "smear" the industry and called the hearings "morally wrong" because "any investigation into the political beliefs of the individual is contrary to the basic principles of our democracy; any attempt to curb freedom of expression and to set arbitrary standards of Americanism is in itself disloyal to both the spirit and the letter of our Constitution."

Menjou, who had been cast as the hard-boiled Conover, Capra's Washington kingmaker in *State of the Union,* was affiliated with the Motion Picture Alliance for the Preservation of American Ideals, a rival group of virulent anti-Communists and right-wingers that counted John Wayne, George Murphy, Walt Disney, Ward Bond, and director Leo McCarey among its more outspoken members. The dapper old character actor, who had first worked with Hepburn in 1933's *Morning Glory,* was regarded as something akin to a ticking time bomb on the Capra set. "Scratch do-gooders like Hepburn," he was once heard to say, "and they'll yell *Pravda*!" To which Tracy countered: "You scratch some members of the Hepburn clan and you're liable to get an assful of buckshot." Tracy tolerated Menjou largely by ignoring him, while Kate found him merely ridiculous. The atmosphere on the stage was tense but cordial, everyone seemingly committed to bringing in the picture on time and, if possible, under budget.

"Bob Thomas worked for the AP and he always did good stories on the stars," Emily Torchia recalled.

Not gush, but he never went after them either. On *State of the Union,* Bob started to interview Adolphe Menjou and I thought, "Isn't that nice?" because usually, you know, they just want the stars. And I didn't hover, I walked away. The next day there was a terrible headline. Menjou had said something terrible about Miss Hepburn. You know, it was an awful time politically with McCarthy, and Menjou attacked her terribly. Oh, I almost lost my job. Mr. Strickling said, "How could you? How could you have walked away?"

"I can't face them," I said.

"Well, you have to," he said, and he walked me down to the set. Miss Hepburn and Mr. Tracy, they were both so quick to say, "Emily had nothing to do with it." And in that situation, Mr. Tracy never raised his voice.

Cass Timberlane opened at the Music Hall on November 6 and was a big hit with the matinee trade, the Armistice Day upsurge carrying it to an outstanding first week total of $145,000. *Variety* took its commercial appeal for granted, declaring Lana Turner's itchy performance as Jinny Marshland "the surprise of the picture" and noting that Tracy was made to "look wooden by comparison." Turner overshadowed Tracy in most of the reviews, turning the pulpy material into something of a breakout. Enthusiasm for her work in the picture drove domestic billings to nearly $4 million, making *Cass Timberlane* only marginally less successful than *Thirty Seconds Over Tokyo,* a remarkable circumstance given the film's listless pace and its unconscionable length.

The West Coast opening came amid an unusual amount of fanfare. The Kappa Kappa Gamma Alumnae Association sponsored a benefit premiere at Grauman's Egyptian Theatre for John Tracy Clinic that included a short film explaining the clinic's mission.

Listening Eyes was principally the work of Walt Disney, who funded the short for $12,000 and contributed its director, Larry Lansburgh. To control costs, students at the USC School of Cinema crewed and helped with sets, and the color stock was donated by Ansco. "He has been very much interested in our Clinic because he has known John since he was a little fellow and was on our original Board of Directors," Louise said of Disney, "and yet it took him five years to get around to 'allowing' that maybe he could make a picture about us."

Work began in June 1946, with Louise playing herself, advising the young mother of a deaf baby girl that her child isn't ready yet for nursery school and that, besides, there is only room for twenty children in the program. However, Louise continues, "We have room for *you* now, Mrs. Henry."

The storyline closely paralleled Louise's own experience as a parent, the baby sleeping late, the mother trying to rouse her in her crib and then taking her to the doctor for an examination. Spence, of course, spoke the narration, and when he laments that the young Mrs. Henry will never hear her daughter say "Mother," it mirrors his own comment from some twenty-two years earlier when he first learned that he himself was the parent of a deaf child.

Modest but professional, *Listening Eyes* did an exceptional job of explaining the clinic and its role in the lives of families with deaf and hearing-impaired children, and in the end Mrs. Henry "experiences a moment never to be forgotten" when, for the first time, little Betsy Henry does indeed form the word "Mother."

The crowd at the Egyptian that night was composed mostly of industry types, Lana Turner on the arm of her future husband, millionaire socialite Henry J. "Bob" Topping, Jr., Louella Parsons holding court in the lobby, a generous representation of Metro brass and contract players, many fascinated at the prospect of seeing the Tracy family together onstage and hearing from a woman who had been out of the Hollywood swim for so long there were some people who assumed she was dead.

"Mr. Tracy never talked about his family," said Emily Torchia, who handled publicity for the event. "It was very hard for him to talk about John. I'll never forget that night. He got up and made the most moving speech, how proud he was of John, how proud he was of Louise's work. It was the hardest thing for him to do, and he did it. It was a beautiful speech. Everyone was there, and there wasn't a dry eye. I've never, never forgotten it. It was one of the most impressive moments of my career."

CHAPTER 23

Adam's Rib

When they finished *State of the Union* on December 6, 1947, both Tracy and Hepburn were eager to return east, Kate to see her family and caucus with Helburn and Langner, Spence to pursue a production of Eugene O'Neill's *A Touch of the Poet,* also for the Theatre Guild. Working with O'Neill had been a long-held ambition, Tracy having initially been paired with the ailing playwright in 1943 when only revivals were on the table. Subsequently, O'Neill gave the Guild permission to stage *The Iceman Cometh,* the first new play of his to hit Broadway in twelve years, with *A Moon for the Misbegotten* and *A Touch of the Poet* to follow. Tracy had served notice on M-G-M in May, while deep in the midst of *Cass Timberlane,* that he intended to take a twelve-week leave of absence at the end of the year to do the play. Coupled with the six-week vacation due him upon the completion of every picture he made for the studio, he would have a total of eighteen weeks to rehearse and perform the show, with perhaps more time to be negotiated if all went exceptionally well.

Iceman was not the critical nor commercial success everyone had hoped it would be, and when *Moon for the Misbegotten* encountered casting and censorship problems on the road, O'Neill asked that it be withdrawn until his health improved and that *Touch of the Poet* be similarly postponed. Capra held his cast in Los Angeles over Christmas as he supervised the editing of *State of the Union* and determined if any retakes would be necessary, an unusually lengthy process due to the timeliness of the material. (He had a newspaperman on retainer—Bill Henry of the *L.A. Times*—whose sole job it was to inject contemporary political references into the dialogue and make sure nothing in the script was suddenly rendered obsolete by national or world events.) Growing more impatient by the day, Tracy was granted the start of his vacation on December 29, with the possibility that he could still be recalled at the end of six weeks, pursuant to the terms of his contract.

Still holding out hope the O'Neill play would somehow free up, he went off to Arizona to paint and ponder his future as an actor, as he would be turning fifty just as his current contract would be coming up for renewal. Langner offered another play, a consolation that lacked a woman's part large enough for Kate, but Tracy already had mastered the self-loathing Melody, contradictory and full of bluster, and was as fixated on *Poet* as he had been on nothing else since *Rugged Path*. "He read that play to me several times," Hepburn remembered. "O'Neill didn't like stars. And he never did ask him to do it. Which, I think, is a great pity, because I think Spencer understood that character." Langner remained convinced that if he could just arrange a meeting between Tracy and O'Neill, all doubts about the rightness of the package would be swept away.

In Culver City, Capra was hoping to preview *State of the Union* the first week in February, which would enable him to serve notice for retakes just short of the February 8 cutoff date. Dubbing stretched on, however, and the initial preview got pushed back a week, prompting Sam Briskin to ask Tracy, through Leo Morrison, for a week's extension on the deadline— something Tracy proved unwilling to grant. Lighting a fire under Capra, he said Liberty would have to pay him a daily retainer to go beyond the con- tractual notification period, knowing the company had come in some $450,000 under budget. Capra, as it turned out, didn't need him after all, and on February 9, 1948, Eddie Knopf spoke to Tracy in Palm Springs and asked him to travel to London to see Robert Morley in Morley's and Noel Langley's hit play *Edward, My Son,* and, while there, to make some back- ground shots for the picture version, which Knopf said he expected to start by the end of March.

Tracy, unhappy to be assigned a part so resolutely British, said at first that he would go to England but not make any location shots without being paid for them. Eddie Mannix, concerned he might be angling to break his contract, gave orders that Tracy was not to be required under any circumstances to make the shots, completely sidestepping the issue of whether or not he should have been given the picture to begin with.

Tapped for Arnold Holt, a ruthless, class-obsessed businessman who alternately charms and throttles his way from shopkeeper to peer of the realm, Tracy was seemingly the only star on the M-G-M roster who could reasonably be expected to handle the role—despite his refusal to attempt an accent. Having paid $160,000 for the screen rights, the studio could ill afford to lose him. Knopf engaged Donald Ogden Stewart to write the screenplay, and it was Stewart who suggested making the character Canadian, which solved the accent problem without making Tracy any happier. George Cukor's assignment as director was a further attempt at mollification.

On February 18, Tracy dutifully set out for New York in the company of Knopf, his wife Mildred, and Cukor, but then said that he would not see the play for fear he'd be unduly influenced by Morley's lusty performance. He thought Morley a wonderful actor, witty and florid, but as unlike him-self as any actor could be. Playing a part that Morley had specifically writ-ten to be played by Morley would be little short of ridiculous, and playing it straight would naturally rob it of its leavening strokes of finish and humor. Moreover, the part called to mind Tracy's only other attempt at a British character, Dr. Henry Jekyll, and the derision it engendered. "I know Spence so well," Louella Parsons commented, "and he thinks he's going [to England] now, but will he actually go when the time comes? He's not much on traveling too far from the home base."

Louella, of course, was right. Spence joined Kate in New York on February 22 and declared he was staying put, leaving Cukor and the Knopfs to travel on without him. There was still some hope that he could meet Eugene O'Neill and loosen up *Touch of the Poet* for a fall production, but the playwright had been hospitalized with a shoulder fracture and, although he was receiving visitors, he deflected a meeting with Tracy. Privately, O'Neill told Lawrence Langner, "I don't believe I could live through a production."

Suddenly concerned he had produced no income in the new year, Tracy had Leo Morrison advise M-G-M that he would report back to the studio on April 1 and ask that his salary for the rest of the year be prorated accord-ingly. He was back in Los Angeles by March 21, when he met with Cukor and Don Stewart to begin work on the script. Metro was planning a wide opening for *State of the Union,* promising "red hot, up-to-the-minute enter-tainment" so timely that it would be hitting hundreds of screens simultane-ously, one of "the greatest mass bookings in America's top theaters that has ever been undertaken in the history of our business." Indeed, the film had its world premiere in Washington on April 7, 1948, Capra seated alongside Harry S. Truman, who was mulling a run for the office he had ascended to with the death of Franklin Roosevelt.

"President Truman, according to those who watched closely—as presi-dential reactions always get watched—has a habit, much like a small boy watching a chase sequence, of lifting himself slightly from his seat when what he sees on the screen excites and interests him," said Charles All-dredge, the assistant secretary of the interior. "That's how he reacted to the story of a good man presidential candidate who almost lost himself and finally won out over himself and the bosses by appealing frankly to the people." Truman requested a print for the presidential yacht, then ordered yet another showing at the White House, after which he announced at a capital dinner: "There will be a Democrat in the White House in 1949, and you're looking at him!"

Emboldened, Capra hit the promotional trail, knowing that neither Tracy nor Hepburn could be counted upon to give the picture much in the way of support. Yet, when the film opened at Radio City on April 22, it was the two principal stars who garnered the lion's share of the press, Bosley Crowther finding Tracy "a much more attractive-looking candidate than anyone who has yet declared" and Kate giving "every assurance of making the most stylish First Lady we've had in years." Warmly greeted in nearly all critical corners, the movie performed well at the box office, though not quite up to expectations and nowhere near the record run of *I Remember Mama,* which had just preceded it at the Music Hall.

With topicality as its primary selling point, *State of the Union* played off quickly, posting domestic rentals in the range of $3.5 million—not bad, but lower than for *Cass Timberlane,* which demonstrated much greater appeal among women and had the added help of a best-selling book as its basis. It disappeared by the end of the year, never to be reissued nor widely shown on television.

Decades later, when Ronald Reagan exceeded his allotted time at a New Hampshire debate, the moderator ordered his microphone cut off. "I paid for this microphone!" Reagan famously stormed in protest. So obscure by then was *State of the Union* that practically no one recognized it as one of Tracy's lines from the picture.

In terms of publicity, Spencer Tracy generally did less to promote his movies than any star since Garbo—initially to cover his drinking, later because Kate herself had such an aversion to the press. (Her father disapproved of personal publicity of any kind, or anything else, for that matter, that smacked of "showing off.") Gradually, Howard Strickling tightened access to the point where he was not talking to journalists at all. "They used to say, 'He's a prick and he doesn't want to see anybody,' " Tracy explained. "They were partly right."

The only promotional efforts he made over the spring of 1948 were in support of John Tracy Clinic, which had officially been in operation now for five years. He broke his radio embargo to appear on Louella Parsons' ABC broadcast and made himself available for photos when Sophie Tucker turned over a $1,000 check to the clinic's building fund. The premiere of *Cass Timberlane* netted another $10,000 for the fund, and it soon got so he was better known around the lot for the clinic than for the pictures he was making.

"If somebody approached him," said June Caldwell, Eddie Mannix's secretary, "and had a problem with a child in the family, or if anyone needed help from the clinic, he was very sympathetic to that and he would make arrangements . . . I know of incidences [where people who] were working around the studio went down to the set and waited until he got a chance to talk to them, and he'd say, 'Certainly,' and he would give them a name and he would be helpful."

With the expansion of the clinic's board to eighteen members it was no longer practical to hold meetings at the ranch. When meetings shifted to the Biltmore downtown, Tracy started looking for a graceful exit. "We'd have a dinner meeting," Louise said. "One of the things that bothered him was that everybody had to pay for their own dinner. He thought that was absurd. He wouldn't come to one and not pay for the whole dinner. He invited them and he said, 'This is on me.' He couldn't see anybody else paying money for something that he would be involved in. I said, 'They're paying for their own.' He said, 'I know, but they shouldn't have to do that.'"

Alathena Smith, the clinic's staff psychologist, first came upon him one day by chance. He and John had pulled up in front of the main cottage in John's station wagon, and it was the young man driving that first caught her notice, not his famous parent. "I was very attracted to him," she said of John. "I observed his limping and I knew before he rounded the station wagon that this was a well-raised young man, taught to be polite." Instantly, she could sense the gulf between father and son, the inability of John to communicate with his dad on anything more than a superficial level. "The agony in his father's eyes [tore] my heart to pieces . . . to see a man not able to express feelings, deep feelings that you can't express . . . [They were only] on the cottage property for a moment, and all I can tell you is my antennae picked up agony, and the special kind of agony that I associate with not being able to get across and express yourself openly with warmth. I'd seen it before, knew about it . . . I think this was the trouble—the inability to communicate feelings [on the part of] both of them."

In May, word went around town that Dick Mook had died of a stroke in Memphis at the age of fifty-three. Five days later, Father Flanagan suffered a fatal heart attack while in Europe on a tour of Austria and Germany. Tracy was hit hard by the sudden death of a man so closely aligned with him in the public mind, furiously pacing the floor and craving a drink as at no other time in the three years since his last. "I watched my father walk the floor and bite his lips until they bled to keep from drinking," he had told his cousin Jane, "and I *know* what he went through." And now, alone with his aunt Jenny, he paced and he chewed, he paced and he chewed. "I'm not going to be like my father," he said with his voice cracking, tears welling in his eyes, blood trickling down his chin. "I'm not. I'm going to lick it!"

A wire went out to Patrick Norton, Monsignor Flanagan's assistant, who was in the process of returning to Boys Town the body of its founder:

THERE IS NOT MUCH I CAN SAY, OTHER THAN TO EXTEND MY DEEP DEEP SYMPATHY TO THE BOYS IN THEIR GREAT LOSS. THE MEMORY OF A MAN AS GREAT AS HE WAS WILL HELP SUSTAIN THEM IN THEIR SORROW FOR HE WAS TRULY A FINE A[ND] GOOD MAN.

Mercifully, Tracy was set to leave town again within a few days. M-G-M had revived a plan to make pictures at the former Amalgamated Studios, Borehamwood, under a new Anglo-U.S. films agreement that would enable American producers to use unremittable sterling for quota-qualifying productions.* For *Edward, My Son,* the scheme meant that Tracy would be surrounded by an all-British cast, headed by the Scottish-born actress Deborah Kerr. Of the Americans involved, there would be only himself, Knopf, Cukor, and Donald Ogden Stewart. He and Kerr left for London aboard the H.M.S. *Queen Mary* on May 22, Howard Strickling and his wife Gail accompanying them at Tracy's request.

"I've come to work," he told a dockside reporter upon his arrival, dispensing with the usual how-nice-it-is-to-be-here routine. "My new picture, *Edward, My Son,* should take ten or twelve weeks to make. If they get it over in eight weeks, I'll be glad. The idea is to get in and get out fast. There should be no hanging around." Asked the dreaded question about acting and his approach to it, he creased his brow, brick-red from the sun, and ran his tongue along his teeth, jutting his lower lip out in an expression of near pain. "You should know all about acting," he replied. "Britain has that side of the business sewn up. In America we have no actors to touch Olivier, Richardson, and Donat. Olivier is way out in front of anything we can pro-

---

* The agreement between the Motion Picture Association of America and the British government, which went into effect June 14, 1948, limited remittances to the United States to $17 million a year, plus an amount equal to the earnings of all British product released in the United States. The excess revenues, as much as $15 million annually, could be used in Britain for the production of American films with British personnel. In the ensuing two years, more than $10 million in frozen sterling was expended on film production and story acquisitions by five major American studios, M-G-M included.

duce. That is the tragedy of Hollywood. We are out of touch with the theatre and we have no real actors now. Our young boys lack theatre training."

He dismissed his alleged naturalness as an "instinct for the stage" and said that he had never really had to struggle to get on. "If you really want to know, it is just that I try no tricks. No profile. No 'great lover' act. I could never get by with things like that. I just project myself as I am—plain, trying to be honest. I am a guy who likes reading and an old man's game of tennis. I leave the frills to the youngsters."

Metro had poured £1 million into capital improvements at Elstree (as the studios were now known), making it the largest and most modern production facility in all of Great Britain. Portions were still under construction when Tracy arrived on the scene, and war-era Romney huts still dotted the property. Accepting his fate with a kind of grand resignation, he commenced filming there on June 9, the lone American in a cast of classically trained actors that included Ian Hunter, Mervyn Johns, Felix Aylmer, Ernest Jay, and, from the play's West End production, Leureen MacGrath. The pretense of the character's being Canadian instead of English fooled no one, and the changing of his name from "Holt" to "Boult" (to avoid confusion with Sir Herbert Holt, the onetime chairman of the Royal Bank of Canada) did nothing to bolster Tracy's own perceived legitimacy in the role. "If he sometimes appeared grumpy," said Deborah Kerr, "it was because he was not altogether happy about himself as Boult."

Unable to match Morley for dexterity and accent, Tracy delivered a performance so intense that he rendered the character, in George Cukor's words, a "cold-blooded monster" who cloaked a string of petty crimes in an obsessive concern for the well-being of his wastrel son, the unseen but ever-present Edward of the play's title. "It's rather disconcerting to me to find how easily I play a heel," Tracy remarked to Cukor. "I'm a better actor than I thought I was. When I was doing Father Flanagan, that was acting. This is not acting."

Hepburn arrived on June 10, registering at Claridge's and generally keeping a low profile. There was a vogue for extended takes, spurred by word of Alfred Hitchcock's use of nine- and ten-minute takes in his recent production of *Rope*. They were, however, making excellent time—three or four days ahead on a particularly tight schedule—and had some forty minutes in the can by the end of the third week. "It is very largely Spencer," Cukor acknowledged in a letter to a friend. "He is such an accomplished actor, works with such ease and surety, that we are able to do long, long scenes—five pages, in fact, which not only makes for speed in shooting but for fluency and flow in the scenes."

"The long takes didn't trouble him at all," said Freddie Young, the cinematographer on *Edward, My Son*. "If he couldn't remember his lines he'd just rub his nose and say something that seemed to make sense. He never dried up." Deborah Kerr recalled him as unfailingly helpful, and her Grand Guignol descent into drunkenness and old age brought her an Academy Award nomination. "George, do you mind if I tell her something?" Tracy asked one day as they were in the middle of a scene. Kerr was done up as a woman of sixty, gingerly sipping a drink. "You know, darling," he said gently, "when you're an alcoholic, you don't sip, you just throw the whole thing down." As Kerr later remarked: "Being young and not alcoholic, I didn't know that."

The pace of European production being considerably slower than in Hollywood, Cukor found himself adopting Tracy's way of working, trying fewer angles and making fewer takes. Exteriors shot at The Mall, Hammersmith, went so smoothly the company was in and out before most residents had a chance to notice. If Kate had come to London simply to provide moral support, she was doubtless relieved to be on hand when *Under Capricorn* began shooting on another stage on July 19. Starring opposite Joseph Cotten and Michael Wilding in Hitchcock's Technicolor production was Ingrid Bergman, who was promptly photographed alongside Tracy, smiling broadly, only months from her historic meeting with Roberto Rossellini.

They completed *Edward, My Son,* on July 30, 1948, but waited until after the Bank Holiday to have the wrap party in the studio's cafeteria, where the company presented Tracy with an autographed cricket bat (so amused he was by the terrible importance attached to the test match) and the studio sports club contributed a ball and a cap adorned with the club badge. Kate was "thrilled" with what she had seen of the picture but worried it might be "too long to keep the terrific punch going."

Tracy returned stateside on the *Queen Mary,* the Stricklings again accompanying him. Hepburn followed on the S.S. *New Amsterdam,* where she found herself quartered next to Paul Muni and his wife. The weather was dismal, communication between the two ships spotty at best. (She learned Clark Gable and Charles Boyer were aboard the *Queen* but complained that reception was so poor she "couldn't get any real dirt.") When the ship docked at the port of New York on August 12, photographers snapped an illustrious cluster of arriving passengers—Gable, Tracy, and a beaming Boyer—all, of course, under Strickling's watchful supervision.

Tracy was at the River Club into September, Hepburn alternately in Hartford and nearby on Forty-ninth Street. Metro had a new production chief in Dore Schary, the onetime actor and screenwriter who was being talked up around town as the "new" Thalberg—a dangerous appellation. Schary had played a minor part in *The Last Mile* and seemed a bit fixated on Tracy. Their first meeting in Schary's new suite of offices took on the tone of an amateur theatrical as Tracy, rubbing his hands in a dry wash, assumed the groveling posture of Uriah Heep. "I don't know if you remember me," he said in his very best Roland Young. "My name is Tracy . . . Well sir, you may remember that I was in a play with you called *The Last Mile* . . . Well, believe me, Mr. Schary, you can ask anyone in that play—I told all of them—just keep your eye on that young fella who plays the reporter—one day he's going to be head of M-G-M." Then, dropping the character, he added: "And so you are—you son of a bitch." Tracy told Schary he had no gripes, no complaints, that he was on the wagon and that he felt pretty good. "Just send me the stuff you want me to do. If I like it, I'll do it. If not, I'll tell you to get another player."

Schary's first production for M-G-M was to be William Faulkner's *Intruder in the Dust,* and it had already been announced that Tracy would play lawyer John Gavin Stevens with Claude Jarman, Jr., the eventual Jody of *The Yearling,* as his nephew. Within a month *Intruder* had been supplanted by *Robinson Crusoe,* a story that had been in and out of the columns for at least three years. Tracy disliked the prospect of traveling to Jamaica, where the exteriors were to be shot, and began making noises once again of wanting out of his M-G-M contract. In New York, Lawrence Langner pressed for word on *Touch of the Poet* and suggested to Kate that she arrange for *Captains Courageous* to be shown in Salem so that O'Neill and his wife Carlotta could see it.

By the first of the year, Tracy was set to do a different picture for Schary, the somewhat true story of how an itinerant newspaperman working for the American government partnered with a convicted smuggler to get much-needed rubber out of the Jap-infested territories of Southeast Asia. Called *Operation Malaya,* it had been set for Schary to do at RKO, where he had planned to star Robert Mitchum and Merle Oberon. When Howard Hughes, more interested in the growing Communist threat than wartime Axis enemies, pulled the plug on it, Schary arranged to have the material, which included a full screenplay by novelist Frank Fenton, brought to M-G-M. As his inaugural project for the studio, *Operation Malaya* was fast-tracked on the production schedule, a start date aggressively set for mid-February 1949. Tracy had just read Fenton's script, filled with the florid dialogue typical of Fenton's B-picture output, when he learned, over dinner at Romanoff's, that Victor Fleming had died suddenly at the age of fifty-nine.

Tracy had not seen much of Fleming in the four years that had passed since the completion of *A Guy Named Joe,* the last of their five pictures together. In the interim, Vic had directed just two additional films—Clark Gable's ill-fated return to the screen, *Adventure,* and a top-heavy version of the Maxwell Anderson play *Joan of Lorraine,* for which he had partnered with Ingrid Bergman and producer Walter Wanger. The epic film had recently had its New York and Hollywood premieres to very mixed reviews, and Fleming was reported to have been "exhausted" after the nearly two-year ordeal of getting it made. ("Vic Fleming wore himself out on that picture," Bergman later wrote. "He was here, there, and everywhere.") Fleming was vacationing in Arizona with his wife and two daughters when he began complaining of chest pains at the Beaver Creek Guest Ranch, about twenty miles east of Cottonwood. He died en route to the hospital.

"Mike Romanoff," remembered Susie Tracy, "was the one who told my father that Fleming had died. He came over to the table and very quietly said, 'Did you know about . . .' My dad was utterly stunned. He really couldn't say anything for a couple of minutes. Finally he said, 'Go ahead with your meal, but you'll have to excuse me. I can't stay.' And it was clear that he was very upset about it." Tracy attended the Fleming services on January 10, 1949, at St. Alban's Episcopal Church, as did Jimmy Stewart, John Wayne, L. B. Mayer, Van Johnson, Ingrid Bergman, and a number of others.

With the deaths of Dick Mook, Father Flanagan, and now Fleming coming within such a short span of time, Tracy found himself drawn closer to Gable, who was, as they both approached fifty, a touchstone to earlier and happier times. Schary's arrival had given the studio an atmosphere of uncertainty, for Mayer, Mannix, and Thau were no longer the triumvirate in charge of production, and all the producers on the lot had, for the first time since the heyday of Irving Thalberg, been consolidated under one man. Gable had come onto the set of *State of the Union* to be photographed with his old friend and costar, the two men grayer and heavier than they had been only a few years earlier but letting fly with the same good-natured insults. Not long after the Fleming funeral, at which Gable was a pallbearer, Tracy returned the favor by walking onto the set of *Any Number Can Play*.

"He and Gable went into Gable's dressing room," Darryl Hickman remembered, "and they *laughed*—I never heard two men carry on like Gable and Tracy carried on. They had a great relationship. They laughed and told old stories, and everything just shut down for about an hour while Gable and Tracy sat in that dressing room, and it *shook* with them having a ball. It was just a delight to sit there and listen to them do it."

Soon after, Gable ambled onto the stage where *Operation Malaya* was shooting, planted himself in a comfortable chair, and greeted the unlikely sight of Tracy, in white linen suit and Panama hat, gingerly making his way through a stand of jungle growth with a tremendous peal of laughter. "That's all right," shouted Tracy. "This time, *I* get the girl." Gable returned: "That's just because I'm not in the picture!" Later, when Tracy wandered

With Clark Gable during the filming of Gable's picture *Homecoming*, 1947.
(PATRICIA MAHON COLLECTION)

onto the set of Gable's next film, the King showed him a framed clipping from a Shanghai newspaper naming *Parnell* the best picture of the year. "Looky here Spence," he said, "and admit defeat." Underneath the yellowing review were scrawled the words "50 million Chinese can't be wrong." Tracy scornfully studied the display, then handed it back. "Well, King, now I know where you belong . . . in China."

Collegial and sweet-tempered, Dore Schary was sincere in his desire to raise the tone and profitability of the M-G-M program, taking personal responsibility for an announced slate of sixty-seven features for the 1949–50 season. Heading the list, *Operation Malaya* had the advantage of a short schedule and, given its cast and pretensions, the relatively modest budget of $1.3 million. Tracy took the role of Carny Carnahan, submitting to a prison buzz cut that had the effect of aging him ten years. Jimmy Stewart, playing the newsman, would share the screen with Tracy for the first time since *The Murder Man,* when he was, as he once remarked, "all hands and feet and didn't seem to know what to do with either." Sydney Greenstreet, John Hodiak, Lionel Barrymore, Gilbert Roland, and Valentina Cortese, borrowed from Fox, rounded out the principal cast.

A genuine potboiler, turgid and obvious, *Operation Malaya* was difficult to take seriously, and Tracy and Stewart played their parts as if they were making a "Road" picture rather than an exotic adventure yarn. "This normally would be a Gable-Tracy picture," Tracy told a visiting columnist who was somehow able to get on the set, "but Gable isn't available, so I am playing his part." Added Stewart: "Yeah, and I'm playing Tracy." Questioned about his next picture, Tracy said it was called *Love Is Legal.* "Naturally, I am playing MY part in a Katharine Hepburn picture."

Moments later, as if on cue, Hepburn came sauntering onto the set in a white flannel pantsuit, George Cukor at her side. "We want to talk to you," she said, ignoring the fact that director Richard Thorpe and the assembled cast and crew were ready to make a scene. "Well, fine," said Tracy, gesturing grandly toward the bustling set, "we'll call off all this."

Love Is Legal, of course, became known as *Adam's Rib,* possibly the best of all the Tracy-Hepburn pictures and certainly one of the sharpest romantic comedies ever to come out of Hollywood. Significantly, the idea, and the script that evolved from it, owed nothing to the development process that put producers in charge and rendered writers as interchangeable as transcription typists. Ruth Gordon and Garson Kanin had authored exactly one original screenplay, an uncommonly intelligent backstage drama called *A Double Life.* Written entirely on spec, it went on to earn Academy Award nominations for the Kanins and for George Cukor—who directed the film on loan to Universal—and a late win for Ronald Colman as Best Actor. Kanin described motoring through Connecticut on a dreary winter afternoon when he asked his wife to tell him "something interesting about Connecticut." She responded with the story of two couples who had divorced and intermarried after a week's vacation together in England. One couple was actor Raymond Massey and his wife, the actress Adrianne Allen. The other was William Dwight Witney and his wife Dorothy, both of whom, as it turned out, were successful New Haven attorneys.

"Can you see it as a movie?" Kanin asked excitedly.

"Not really," said Gordon. "Unbelievable. Too pat. Like life."

"What about just the first half then? Two lawyers. Married. And they get onto opposite sides of a case."

They began spinning the idea, and the obviousness of the casting hit them both like a bolt of lightning. "Kate and Spence!" they erupted in unison.

The screenplay, tentatively titled *Man and Wife,* came together with remarkable speed, and a first draft was back from the steno bureau on November 10. Following consultations with both Tracy and Hepburn—Kate in particular—a revised 152-page version was submitted to Dore Schary via Hepburn and the William Morris Agency on January 27, 1949. Three days later, a deal was closed for $175,000, which included the authors' services should any rewrites be necessary.

"It was the first time in thirty years the studio had ever seen a screenplay that was ready to shoot immediately, without changes," said Larry Weingarten, who was assigned to produce the picture with Cukor directing. So when Kate appeared with Cukor on the set of *Operation Malaya* and said to Spence, "We want to talk to you," it was not simply a social call she had in mind but an impromptu script conference.

Man and Wife grew expressly from the Kanins' intimate knowledge of the Tracy-Hepburn relationship, but putting that relationship on screen in all its tones and colorations was risky business, given how fiercely private the two people in question were. "Their on-camera relationship reflected both the easy intimacy they shared in the off-camera relationship and much of my own marriage to Ruth," said Kanin, who came west with his wife. "They were easy to write for."

That Cukor was assigned the project made perfect sense, as he too had observed Spence and Kate at close range over a number of years. Moreover, as an actress, Ruth Gordon had been directed by Cukor and knew his strengths. Their collective experience on *A Double Life* had been pleasant and rewarding. With Weingarten producing and, in effect, shielding the company from front-office interference, the package proved the perfect incubator for a well-crafted movie.* "The Kanins would do certain scenes," said Cukor, "and we would go to my house and read them and hear how they sounded aloud, then go to the studio where I would stage them kind of roughly with a camera and see how they worked."

The shooting final was dated February 24, 1949, with a start date set for late May. Tracy finished with *Operation Malaya* on March 24, and began his

---

* The change of title—the Kanins' original *Man and Wife* being deemed "dangerously indiscreet"—was the only executive mandate that stuck.

customary six-week vacation on April 4. Knowing the caliber of material he had to work with, Cukor lit into preparations and arranged to shoot the setup—an attempted domestic homicide—during two weeks of gritty location work in New York City. Performing these early scenes would be a quartet of young Broadway stage actors, all of whom would be playing their first substantial parts on screen—Tom Ewell, David Wayne, Jean Hagen, and, in the role of the earnest Doris Attinger, the rattlebrained defendant who pulls a Frankie-and-Johnny on her philandering husband, singer-actress Judy Holliday. Gar Kanin had brought Holliday to prominence in his play *Born Yesterday* (where she replaced, out of town, the show's original star, Jean Arthur) and was on a campaign to have her re-create the role of Billie Dawn in the film version. Columbia studio head Harry Cohn had already rejected the idea—even the making of a screen test—so it became Kate's idea to make *Love Is Legal* the test Cohn denied her by custom-tailoring the role of Doris to Holliday's very considerable talents.

When Tracy returned to Culver City on May 16, Hepburn was attempting to persuade Cole Porter to write something original for Kip Lurie, David Wayne's wisecracking songwriter, to sing to her character in the picture. (Kanin had written one, which everyone agreed was lousy.) Porter, at first, declined, maintaining the song's intended target, Madeline Bonner, had a name he could neither abide nor rhyme. Later, he agreed so long as the name of the character was changed from Madeline to Amanda.* ("Some of the things Kate goes in and demands!" marveled Cukor. "The Cole Porter song, for instance. Not the crappy sort of star demands. She always wanted something for the show.") The name of Tracy's character was similarly changed from Ned to Adam, and soon after the start of production the picture became officially known as *Adam's Rib*.

Filming began on May 31, 1949, Tracy and Hepburn settling into their roles with an effortless grace, their ad-libs, their intimacies and parries those of genuine lovers, not actors or movie stars, their scenes together a deft embodiment of what Kenneth Tynan called "a whole tradition of American sophistication," Tracy, the "placid, sensible panda," Hepburn, the "gracious, deadpan albatross," replacing "the crude comedy of flirtation" with the subtler, warmer comedy of marriage as practiced not by ingenues but by seasoned artists well into their forties. The home movie horsing around on the Kanins' Connecticut farm, the droll courtroom flirtations, the off-screen kiss (by now a trademark of the Tracy-Hepburn combination), the wordless looks.

---

* As it turned out, "Farewell, Amanda" was a trunk item, and Porter's insistence on the change of name was simply to facilitate its use.

Cole Porter plays "Farewell, Amanda," as Tracy and Hepburn listen on the set of
Adam's Rib, 1949. (SUSIE TRACY)

"It was human," said Cukor. "Comedy isn't really any good, isn't really
funny, without that. First you've got to be funny, and then, to elevate the
comedy, you've got to be human."

AMANDA

You were making some noises in the night.

ADAM

(immersed in his paper)
I always do. Don't I? At least you always say
I always do. How do I know?

AMANDA

(without looking up)
You do, but not this kind.

ADAM

What kind?

AMANDA

Can't remember exactly, naturally, but sort
of like ooooo-eehah! ooooo-eegah.
(She emits a series of strange groans and
grunts and whistles and wheezes.)
Like that, sort of.

ADAM

You don't say.

AMANDA

Yes.

ADAM

Fascinating.

AMANDA

(She looks at him.)
What?

ADAM

I say I sound fascinating.

AMANDA

(her lovely smile shining)
You'll do.

"I think," said Katharine Houghton,

that the film represents a fairly accurate dynamic—for one aspect
of their relationship, anyway. The banter and the flirtation seem
very genuine. I don't know that Spencer ever slapped her on the
rump or pointed a licorice pistol at her as he does in the film, but
the essence of the Bonner relationship seems right on. Yet Kate,
especially in the early years of their relationship, was never confident that she was good enough or beautiful enough to keep
Spencer's interest. Who knows why she felt that way, but she often
agonized over that. Amanda is more confident than Kate of her
spouse. I doubt that Kanin or Gordon ever suspected the depth of
Kate's insecurity, or maybe they simply chose not to address it. One
could say that the Bonners represent Tracy and Hepburn at their
best with each other. They certainly seem to be comfortable playing

Sharing an intimate moment in *Adam's Rib*. (SUSIE TRACY)

those roles, and I doubt that they would seem so comfortable if it weren't natural to them. Perhaps one could say that the Bonners were a couple they would have liked the world to think they were.

As Hepburn told Kenneth Tynan in 1952: "Spence and I have an agreement when we're working. If we fluff a line, we won't stop. In *Adam's Rib*, there was a scene with us dressing to go out, and I had to put on a hat and say, 'How do I look?' and he was supposed to say something good and flattering. What happened was, he stepped back and said: 'You look like Grandma Moses!' I stamped my foot and sort of yelped—but they printed it."

The youthful supporting cast brought out the paternal instincts of the veteran filmmakers—Cukor, the Kanins, Tracy and Hepburn. "In the course of the shooting of *Adam's Rib*," Kanin wrote, "Kate and Spencer involved everyone necessary in our master plan: the costume designer, Orry-Kelly; the hairdressers; the make-up people; the cameraman Joe Ruttenberg; the supporting players; everyone and everything was aimed toward Judy's making a hit." When it came time for Holliday's big scene, Amanda's jailhouse interview of the would-be murderess, Hepburn asked that Cukor set it up so that it showcased Judy, she in profile, framing the left edge of the shot, Eve March, her secretary, to the right, the whole thing played in one continuous five-minute take. "She was wonderful with Judy Holliday," said Tom Ewell. "She worked like a dog to throw the emphasis on her with extra lines and closeups. No other star ever did that."

The cast's crisp ensemble playing gave the film a tart, noirish edge
suited more to the stark independent productions of the time and not the
ultra-glossy tradition of Metro-Goldwyn-Mayer. One day on the set, Tracy
gave Cukor a mock scolding: "Damn it, George, why did you hire all these
young actors from New York? They're acting us old timers right off the picture!" The casting, though, was as much Hepburn's doing as Cukor's, as she
could take credit not only for Holliday's presence in the picture, but also
Tom Ewell's, Eve March's, and Marvin Kaplan's. "Hepburn called me personally in New York," Ewell recalled, "and said, 'Look, if you do this film,
I'll do everything I can to be your press agent.' She kept her promise."
Kaplan's soft-edged Brooklyn drone caught Hepburn's attention at a performance of L.A.'s Circle Players, and she referred him to George Cukor for
an interview. ("Katharine Hepburn's your agent," Cukor told him.) Freshly
graduated from USC, Kaplan made his film debut as the court reporter in
the picture.

David Wayne, on leave from Broadway's *Mister Roberts,* thought Tracy
"the greatest motion picture actor that ever was" and observed his work on
the set "in a kind of wonderment." Tracy's technique, Wayne decided, was
indiscernible: "I tried to measure why he was so right in the part each day. I
never knew him to not know every word of the script. I never knew him to
not be exactly right in every word and move the director suggested, but in

George Cukor directing *Adam's Rib.* Note the dubious look on Tracy's face.
(SUSIE TRACY)

addition to that he brought a mental aggrandizement to the scene that had not been hinted at by the authors."

The company spent two solid weeks on the courtroom set on which the Bonners' battle of wits takes place, the principal cast, excepting Wayne, gathered together under Cukor's watchful eye. Tracy was in his element, comfortable, in full command of the character and not particularly interested in the few things Cukor had to say to him. "Sometimes he would just say, 'Yes, George,'" as Marvin Kaplan remembered it. "I don't think he liked to be directed. But at the end of the day, when everyone else was tired, Hepburn could wrap her legs, her whole body, around this pole in the courtroom and watch and absorb like a sponge exactly what Mr. Cukor wanted her to do in the next day's shooting." Tracy would watch quietly, a mildly skeptical look on his face. "I don't think he was one for working out a lot of stuff," Hepburn said. "I think he knew it, then he *was* it."

On the day actress Hope Emerson—six feet two and 240 pounds—was to hoist him into the air (in support of Amanda's contention that "woman can be quite the equal of man in any and all fields"), Tracy was particularly boisterous, recalling the specialty acts and the tumblers he had seen in vaudeville as a kid.

"Hope Emerson was a very sweet woman who was not half as strong as she looked," said Kaplan. "Tracy was attached by wires, so he could sit in the air and it would look like she was holding him." Emerson was posed grasping Tracy's left foot, her enormous right hand supporting his rump like a bicycle seat. "He said such terrible things to her during the take— 'Watch it! Watch it! What are you doing down there?' The woman started to blush and then she put her hand down, and there he was left hanging in the middle of the air with no support whatsoever."

Edward, My Son had its New York opening during the making of *Adam's Rib*, and Tracy, as he had feared, took a drubbing from critics familiar with the wit and precision of Robert Morley's performance (which had just closed on Broadway). Bosley Crowther lamented the play had been "drained of its most trenchant poison" in its transfer to the screen, the "plainly un-British Spencer Tracy" acting the principal role. "Apart from the hopeless miscasting of Mr. Tracy," the *New Yorker* added, "the picture is fortunate in its acting." Morley himself thought the criticism unfair in that Tracy had been slammed for playing it too straight. "I'm not sure there was much alternative," the actor said in his autobiography. "When some years later I did it myself on television in the States, it was not very successful. It was much easier to play on the stage with scenery than it was to act in the more realistic settings which are necessary on the screen. A great deal of its initial success depended, too, on my speaking direct to the audience, and this device loses its spontaneity when attempted in the cinema."

Edward, My Son performed acceptably in New York, but with overhead loaded into its already inflated cost, the film became Tracy's biggest money-loser at M-G-M, and his first since *Northwest Passage.* His star was plainly fading, his future well and firmly fixed on a return to the stage. With the kids now grown and the clinic no longer dependent solely on his support for its survival, he seemed more comfortable with the natural arc of an actor's career, the inevitable easing into mature roles, the passing of the commercial mantle to a younger generation. Upon his arrival in England, fully aware that he was being led to the slaughter, he had noted that he had made "nearly 40 films" since 1930. (The number was actually forty-five.) "No matter what anyone says, I have been bad in about 30 of them. The fault has been my own."

Then he smiled, stuck out his jaw as if inviting somebody to take a poke at it, and strolled off, seemingly comfortable, at least for the moment, in his own skin.

CHAPTER 24

Father of the Bride

I had been acting in Hollywood since 1944," said William Self.

Soon after I got out here, I entered the Motion Picture Tennis Tournament, which was an annual event in those days, and I won it. All of a sudden, people knew in a vague way that there was a fellow named Bill Self who was an actor—or said he was—and a tennis player. Tim Durant called me up one day and said, "Would you like to play tennis with Charlie Chaplin?" I said, "Of course I would." So we started doing that. And then one day Tim called and said, "We're going to play across the street from Charlie's at Irene Selznick's tennis court with some mystery guests." I said, "Okay." I didn't have a car in those days, so Tim had to pick me up. We went to Irene Selznick's, and on the court hitting some balls were Spencer Tracy and Katharine Hepburn, Alfred De Liagre, Jr., the Broadway producer, and Oscar Hammerstein II. Not bad company.

I was introduced and we played some mixed doubles. Tim was a pretty good player. I was by far the best player and, therefore, everyone wanted me as a partner. Tracy was the worst player; he was not too bad at hitting the ball, but he was the worst at moving. So Tracy and I became partners. Later in the day, when we all sat around after we played, Hepburn was very aggressive: "So you're an actor. What have you done?" And then: "How can we help you?" Spencer was more laid back—I suppose he couldn't have cared less about meeting another actor—but Hepburn kind of went to bat for me, and almost immediately at M-G-M she got me something.* That group continued, I would say, for at least three or four months. I'd see all these people two or three times a week, and got to know them very well. At some point, Spence got very interested in me as someone who could play tennis with John. John, with all of his handicaps, was a pretty good player. Even with his bad leg, he moved remarkably well. So I started going to the ranch they had on White Oak Avenue to play tennis with John. And I played with Susie, and I played with Mrs. Tracy, who wasn't a bad player.

When *Malaya* started in February 1949, Bill Self had a bit as one of Sydney Greenstreet's henchmen. Later that spring, Self was cast as Klausner, the jury foreman, in *Adam's Rib*, giving him a box seat for the filming of the courtroom scenes. "The affection between Tracy and Hepburn was rather obvious," he said.

He would touch her, or they'd laugh about an inside joke of some kind. Stuff like that. It was all great for me, because they would reminisce a little bit about their early careers. I think that if you were around them, as I was day after day after day, it was evident that they cared for each other a great deal. And then people began to tell me things. Tim Durant would tell me what he knew about them, and so forth. I didn't know, when I was twenty-something years old, whether they were lovers or not, but I knew they cared a great deal about each other.

Then one day Hepburn talked to me about Spence—this was fairly early—and she said, "You know, Bill, Spence and I can't live together. We *are* together, but we can't live together." She was concerned about what I would think about Louise and the children, I guess. I think Spence was a little concerned about my seeing him one day, and then on the next day I was seeing Louise and John and Susie, and he wanted to be sure our stories were straight. We cooked up something so that if I did say that I had seen him, it was always that we had played some tennis at the Beverly Hills Hotel. Actually, I played tennis at the Beverly Hills Hotel with Kate. I never played there with Spence that I remember, but that was the cover story . . . Spence absolutely felt that Louise didn't know.

* This was likely *Homecoming* (1948).

On the tennis court, circa 1944.
(PATRICIA MAHON COLLECTION)

Kate played along, aware that Spence had a real need to believe that Louise didn't know, but she realized, of course, that Louise couldn't possibly have been so clueless. "She'd have had to have been so dense, which she wasn't. Smart woman. Unsensitive. What shall I say? I think she had no sense of magic, she had no sense of the enormous complication of an Irish drunk."

Chuck Sligh could remember a brief exchange with Louise while visiting Los Angeles in the early fifties. The kids were out on their own, and she was alone at the ranch in Encino.

Louise would round the three up so that we could all be together. This one time she called each of the children and Spence. Then she took me down to Chasen's and each of the others came in their own car, so we had five people and four cars. We had a nice dinner, friendly. Spence was, of course, always fun to listen to. Finally, somebody said, "Well, I guess we've got to be going." And each of them went out and got in their own car and went. Louise and I drove back to the house, and on the way out I said, "Louise, how come you and Spence are still married? I'm surprised you haven't divorced him. I know he's a Catholic, but—"

She said, "Well, he is a Catholic . . . and I thought at first this would all just . . . blow over . . . but it didn't . . . Now . . . I think it would be sort of silly after all this time to divorce him." And that was the end of *that* conversation.

In April 1949 Kate was finally ready to do *As You Like It* for the Theatre Guild, and it became a source of some tension between her and Tracy. For most of the time she had known him, she had made it her business to be where he was, to do what he wanted. "He couldn't have left me," she said. "I was too adorable—and sensible. I loved him and made a life for him that was irresistible to him. Otherwise, I think he would have wandered off."

Eight years into the relationship, with her Metro contract having lapsed and her only work being pictures in which she was costarred with Tracy, she needed to get away, to go back to the stage, to stretch herself and try something different. Over the summer of 1949 she worked with actress Constance Collier, whose roles had included Juliet and Portia and Lady Macbeth and who had excited her interest in Shakespeare after years of prodding on the part of Lawrence Langner.

Retakes for *Adam's Rib* finished the last week of August 1949. Hepburn staged the company wrap party and then headed east to Connecticut. Tracy followed shortly thereafter, installing himself at New York's Pierre Hotel. He was back in New York in October, beset by stomach troubles and headed for Boston, where he checked into Peter Bent Brigham Hospital for "the works."

As Kate could never be a part of the Tracy family, neither could Spence ever fit in with the Hepburns. "I think," said Kate, "he was embarrassed with Mother and Dad because he was married and because it had gone on so long. I didn't blame him, in a way." Still, she never really left home, went back most weekends when she was in New York. "And when I went back there, I didn't go to *my* atmosphere; I went to *their* atmosphere—of which I was a part."

Tracy always portrayed Kate's family as if they were Old Man Vanderhof's clan from *You Can't Take It With You*—strident, self-righteous, a little nuts around the edges. He loved twitting her about her "sacrosanct goddamn family" (as Katharine Houghton so aptly put it), throwing asides into master takes with the hope of sending her up. Shooting *State of the Union* on the set of a Detroit hotel room, his character was attempting to get a haircut when actor Frank Austin burst in through a side door, a pamphlet-wielding crackpot claiming to represent the eight hundred members of the League for the Abolition of Taxation. "The government should earn its own money like the rest of us!" he declared as Van Johnson hustled him from the room, "Abolish taxation!" Tracy, with an impish grin on his face, said to Hepburn. "Looks a little like your brother Dick," to which she laughed and then, almost as an afterthought, kicked him sharply in the leg.*

In five days of tests and x-rays at Brigham, nothing proved conclusive. On Saturday, October 22, Tracy made the two-hour drive to Old Saybrook, where the Hepburn family's summer estate, Fenwick, stood on three acres fronting Long Island Sound at the mouth of the Connecticut River. Katharine Houghton (née Grant, daughter of Kate's younger sister, Marion), age four, was there with her parents and older brother.

"I remember him standing in the large tile foyer," she said.

All of my family were assembled: grandparents, aunts, uncles, cousins. And, of course, Kate. I still have a vision of him standing there turning his hat in his hands and being quite nervous. I guess he must have come a little before lunch, and an autumn storm was brewing. At the dining table my older brother asked him to recite "Casey at the Bat" because we'd been told by my Aunt Katy that Spencer could do that very well. My grandfather, who was generally very suspicious of any of Kate's beaux, wasn't particularly enthusiastic about the performance. Spencer, after all, was a married man. My grandfather didn't know what he was about, what he was up to. The storm got worse and worse during lunch, and the little sailboats moored near the big breakwater south of the house were beginning to pull their moorings. Kate was watching them, as was everyone else in the family, but I don't think Spencer was. All of a sudden, Kate got up and said in a loud voice, "Everybody drop your pants and follow me!" So everyone, except the young kids, leapt up and took off their shoes and pants and tore out to the beach. The little boats were about to crash into our jetty. Spencer didn't move. He just sat there and said, "This whole family is nuts."

I don't remember his ever visiting the house again. I do, however, remember my Aunt Kate mentioning something about other visits on various occasions in the late seventies or early eighties. Driving back to New York City on I-95 she'd say, "You see that

---

* Richard Houghton Hepburn (1911–2000) was a free spirit, the self-styled playwright of the family, sporadically produced. "Dick was no more eccentric than the rest of them," Katharine Houghton said, "but he was closest to Kate in age and had been to Hollywood several times, unlike the rest of them. She had complex issues with Dick."

A dual portrait, apparently penned during the making of *State of the Union.* The inscription, in Tracy's barely legible hand, reads: "To the old one with love from THE PRESIDENT." (ACADEMY OF MOTION PICTURE ARTS AND SCIENCES)

Howard Johnson's?" I'd say, "Yes." She'd say, "Spencer used to stay there when I would come east to see Mother and Dad at Fenwick."

Tracy returned that same evening to Boston, where his test results pointed to an ulcer and not the malignancy he had feared. He met with Seymour Gray, a gastroenterologist and associate professor at the Harvard School of Medicine, who saw before him a "tortured soul" who had "an enormous guilt complex about his mute [*sic*] son, which he interpreted as a punishment from God for his sins."

Tracy went back to New York, where rehearsals for *As You Like It* were under way, and after a couple of days with little to do, flew home to Los Angeles, where Dr. Dennis affirmed all of Dr. Gray's findings. Nausea overtook him, and he spent nearly two weeks without an appetite. He met with Benny Thau at the studio, confirming a tentative start date for his next picture, but it wasn't until he went out to the ranch for dinner on November 9 that he began to feel better.

As You Like It opened in New Haven on December 8 before a capacity audience that included Dr. and Mrs. Hepburn and the playwright and novelist Thornton Wilder. Any doubts about Kate's fitness for the role of Rosalind were dispelled by a spirited, if not particularly commanding performance, and she was accorded seven curtain calls. Moving on to Boston, the show settled in at the Colonial Theatre, where Spence came to see her at Christmas, another sell-out engagement just prior to a limited Broadway run. *Adam's Rib* had already been put into release, its New York opening set for the twenty-fifth at the Capitol. Rain and threatening weather brought huge crowds. Bolstered by strong notices and all the advance press accorded *As You Like It,* the picture stayed a total of twenty-four days before pushing out into the boroughs, where it faded quickly—more quickly than anyone expected.

"All the Katharine Hepburn–Spencer Tracy pictures I made were just mediocre successes," Larry Weingarten lamented toward the end of his life. "When they got out of the big cities the fellows just didn't understand them and the women—they didn't go, it was too sophisticated for them." There was also the scattered picketing of theaters from Kate's presumed support of Henry Wallace and the Progressives.

Ironically, word-of-mouth benefited *Adam's Rib* more than any of the previous Tracy-Hepburn pairings, and it ended up being the most profitable of all their pictures after *Keeper of the Flame.* Spence's aunt Jenny, now living near her daughter in Renton, Washington, caught the buzz firsthand when she saw a doctor for stomach complaints—the family nerves that afflicted them all. "Mrs. Feely," the doctor told her, "you should get out and do things. Go to a movie, get your mind off your worries. I saw the most wonderful movie last night—you should see it. I've laughed all day long. The name of it is *Adam's Rib.*"

Jenny, a steely tone suddenly entering her voice: "No . . . I haven't seen it yet, but I suppose that I'll go."

"It's Spencer Tracy and Katharine Hepburn," the man continued, not knowing when to let up. "It's a riot—you really should see it."

"I don't think you'd laugh so much," she snapped back, "if it was *your* nephew making a fool of himself!"

"That was hard for her to take," her daughter Jane commented. "Oh, dear God. Katharine. Katharine Hepburn. 'The hussy.' It was always the woman [never the man]. Oh, heavens no. You *know* that he was dragged by his neck into that unholy alliance by this woman of no principles whatsoever. And my mother was not that kind—she was a very bright woman, an intellectual Catholic, very well informed. But on certain subjects like that, [the instinct of] the mother and her cub took over. It was never on your family's side; there was no fault there. That double standard—the lace curtains. Appearances must be kept up."

Andrew Tracy was the only member of the family to have actually met Kate Hepburn during one of his infrequent visits to California. "I don't think this Katharine Hepburn is such a big deal," he said, clearly and instantly taken with her. "She stuck her paw out and said, 'Hello, Uncle Andrew.' That was enough for me."

The situation with Louise was worrisome, the tension thick between Spence and his brother Carroll. Andrew's son Frank could remember his father describing his nephew's dressing room on the M-G-M lot, a living room and a bedroom alongside Gable's on the second floor of the building. "Sometimes Spence came in and went in his bedroom, laid down and took a nap. I remember Dorothy would be complaining about his treatment of Carroll, that Carroll would come home all shaky and white and pale, practically in tears and ready for a rubber room. And, meanwhile, Spence was back up there in his dressing room sound asleep, oblivious to the hellacious behavior that had caused this poor man to come apart."

Malaya went into distribution six weeks after *Adam's Rib*. A pulpy melodrama that held little sway with city audiences, it played off well in the sticks, its modest cost a considerable factor in its commercial success. Tracy returned to L.A. on January 6, 1950, and was present on the sixteenth when Louise's father, Allienne Treadwell, died in San Diego at the age of eighty-one. Spence had met the old man, a practicing lawyer who came up to Encino once in a while for dinner and to borrow money. Louise was bitter when she was young, but she had long since made her peace with him. "You have to forgive," she said. "Everybody does. You have to believe everybody does the best they can under the circumstances."

The father was, in the opinion of Alathena Smith, at the root of Louise's coolness. She was, as Dr. Smith put it, a "blood-red bleeding heart locked into a blue block of ice," for she had been hurt by a man before Spence. "Don't blame this on deafness," she warned Jane Ardmore, who was planning a book on Louise and the clinic. "She adored her father and her father left her mother." The memory of loss, the aversion to pain, held Louise at an emotional distance from even those closest to her. She got around it by giving herself to the work of the clinic and to young parents who reminded her of Spence and herself when they were confused and scared and unsure of what to do. "She shows it in the kindness in her letters," said Dr. Smith in 1972. "She'll spend 45 minutes on a paragraph to help some mother . . . She puts no limits on the help that I give to parents."

Louise was still invisible to much of the film colony, a solitary figure at her husband's previews, sometimes with John but just as often completely alone. "Occasionally we sat near her at some of the Tracy-Hepburn previews," said screenwriter Lenore Coffee, "and she had the air of an interested member of the audience; of course, no one knew her by sight." In the November 1949 issue of *Modern Screen,* Louise was featured in an article by Hedda Hopper, who made no secret of her dislike for Katharine Hepburn. Its title: "Hollywood's Forgotten Wives."

Hepburn, meanwhile, was slowly tightening her grip on Tracy, moving him away from Leo Morrison and into the hands of Bert Allenberg, who was now managing her own affairs at the William Morris Agency. Morrison was stunned when the process began, first by the appointment of Ross

Evans as Tracy's interim representative in August 1949, then by the formal request for a letter of termination at the end of the calendar year. Once payment in full had been acknowledged for all outstanding claims, Tracy gave his agent of twenty years a bonus "in appreciation of past services" even as he continued to duck his calls.

Kate also disliked Spence's ongoing residency at the Beverly Hills Hotel, where managing partner Hernando Courtright allowed him to live rent-free in exchange for being seen regularly in the Polo Lounge, where he sat quietly sipping tea in the late afternoon and signing autographs for the guests. He hated being put on display and had to be goaded by his secretary into doing it, but the simplicity of hotel life suited him. ("I've always liked to live in small places," he once said, "because I live a small life.") The arrangement horrified Hepburn, who began looking around for quarters where he could be content and cared for, and yet shielded from the public.

If, as Tracy sometimes said, acting was reacting, then no role could possibly have afforded him a better showcase than that of Stanley T. Banks, the hapless hero of *Father of the Bride*. The book was by Edward Streeter, a New York banking executive who, in a former life, had been a war correspondent and travel writer. Streeter's infrequent works, starting with 1919's *Dere Mabel*, distinguished him as a chronicler of the put-upon everyman, a wryly observant Boswell of human nature. When *Father* made the rounds in manuscript form, it was snapped up by the Book-of-the-Month Club, then by Metro-Goldwyn-Mayer, which paid $100,000 for the film rights. As soon as word of the purchase got out, comedian Jack Benny cornered Dore Schary at a party and said that he wanted to play Banks. According to Pan Berman, who had responsibility for the project, Schary said, "Great, marvelous, we'd love to have you, you've got it." And then he dropped his fait accompli in Berman's lap.

" 'Dore,' I said, 'Jack Benny is a wonderful personality, but he simply won't do. I know we don't even have to ask [Vincente] Minnelli, but if you want to . . .' " Minnelli had directed *Madame Bovary* under Berman's supervision and liked the idea of following it with a comedy.

> We did test Jack Benny and he made a valiant effort, but it was terrible because it wasn't for him. I went in and told Dore, "It's hopeless." Dore said, "I don't agree with you. I think it's great." I remained steadfast. "Well, who are you going to get?" he asked. I said Spencer. "You'll never get Spencer to do it." "I'll get him." "Well, then, you'll have to call Jack and tell him we're not going to use him." "*I've* got to call Jack? He's been a dear friend for years. We

dine in each other's homes once a month. We're all part of a gang together. Why should I have to call? If I had talked to him to begin with, I would have told him no in the first place." So I did. Jack didn't talk to me for ten years after that.

Tracy, said Berman, took about a week to make up his mind. Schary recalled a more complicated and angst-ridden process, which played itself out over a period of months and followed a pattern he came to regard as typical: "First there would be reservations about the original material, followed by a crashing refusal; then a quiet talk with suggestions of how it could be fashioned to suit Spence. This heart-to-heart would be followed by a wave of enthusiasm, later dispelled when the first script was born. With doubts returned, another conference had to be called, suggestions of how to change and improve the script would be on the agenda, and finally we would have Tracy's approval."

Assigned the screenplay was the husband-wife team of Frances Goodrich and Albert Hackett, both of whom thought the book "darling." Goodrich, moreover, had been courted by Ed Streeter as a young actress. "It's nice to think of my brainchild sitting in your lap like Charlie McCarthy while you put ideas in his head," Streeter commented in a letter to Goodrich.

Tracy's vacillations brought other potential candidates to the fore, and Streeter claimed to have heard unfounded reports "ranging from Harpo Marx to Paul Robeson." Fredric March and Walter Pidgeon were candidates, and even Charles Laughton got mentioned at one particularly grim point. "Spencer Tracy is the one I wanted," Streeter insisted, "but I heard that he was having contract trouble. March is obviously out, Laughton is my idea of nobody, and as for Benny I would nominate Abbott and Costello. Better than that, I would nominate myself."

Tracy was confirmed for *Father of the Bride* just as *Adam's Rib* went before the cameras. Kate arranged a dinner at which Minnelli made his pitch. "With you," the director told him, "this picture could be a little classic of comedy. Without you, it's nothing." Tracy, recalled Minnelli, was delighted. "He'd heard other people were being tested for the part, and he thought we weren't interested in him. All he'd wanted was to be wanted. Once Spencer accepted, the rest of the cast fell into place. It took no great imagination to cast beautiful young Elizabeth Taylor as the bride. Joan Bennett, with the same coloring as Elizabeth, seemed a logical choice to play the mother."

By then, the script had gone through two complete iterations and was headed for a third. After an initial bout of anxieties, the Hacketts did a sterling job with Streeter's simple yet universal tale, the withering of Mr. Banks translating neatly into three acts of progressive poverty and befuddlement. His plans go awry, and his desperation is evident when he offers his daughter $1,500 in cash to elope. (She thinks he is kidding.) He eventually falls completely from his family's notice, underfoot as the wedding planner, the caterer, and the florist take over. In the end he slogs wearily upstairs, the forgotten man who has to pay for it all, an image eventually adapted for the film's opening sequence in which Banks, his house strewn with the detritus of a chaotic reception, massages an aching foot as he empties confetti and rice from his shoe. "I would like to say a few words about weddings . . . ," he begins.

Tracy's immersion in the role permitted him to inhabit a character as cartoonish as Banks and deliver a fully dimensional human being. In a scene around the family dinner table, Stanley first learns that his daughter is "in love" with somebody named Buckley and that she intends to get married. Alternately skeptical, peevish, combative, and shell-shocked, Tracy managed the beats with a musical precision, never leaning into the role but simply allowing it to happen. "Who is this Buckley anyway? And what's his last name? I hope it's better than his first one. Where the devil does he come from? And who does he think is going to support him? If he thinks I am he's got another thing coming . . ."

He was, said Minnelli, an inspiration: "His instincts were infallible. He knew how to throw the unimportant things away, and he knew how to create the illusion of throwing the important things away too, so that they were inscribed on your mind. His way of speaking made you feel you'd stumbled on a great truth. You saw real life reflected in his face . . . and also strength."

In choosing to let Tracy set the pace of the film, Minnelli took advantage of his inner stillness, a steadiness about his eyes and head that suggested simplicity while masking a furious turning of wheels. "There wasn't a better man at comedy. He wasn't a mugger, at least not in scenes with other actors. The facial contortions came when he was alone and unobserved." Minnelli liked to point out a scene in which Banks mediates a reconciliation between his daughter and her fiancé and then finds himself stranded as they rush into each other's arms. "The father is left standing there, the unwanted third man, trying to figure out a way to gracefully exit . . . Spencer's reading was the essence of comedy, because it was achingly true. And he knew how well he'd done it, for no one had greater reason to feel secure about his ability than Spencer."

Actor Don Taylor, playing the unexceptional Buckley Dunstan, hadn't yet met Tracy when called upon to play his first important scene, the business of Kay Banks (Elizabeth Taylor) having slammed a car door on his hand. "We talked; we did the scene," said Taylor.

"Who is this Buckley anyway?" Tracy, Joan Bennett, and Elizabeth Taylor in *Father of the Bride* (1950). (SUSIE TRACY)

And Minnelli said, "Well, I think I'll have to print that." (Meaning, "Very good!") But ol' Spence said [growling], "No-o-o-o-o, Vincente, no, that's no good!" And he turned to me and he said, "I'm Spencer Tracy." I said, "I'm Don Taylor." Nobody had introduced us. Of course, I was mesmerized by him in every facet—as an actor, as a human being, and, you know, as a fellow man. He said, "C'mon!" and the two of us walked around the stage. We walked around twice, and we rehearsed the scene, ad-libbed a little bit, put it together, and came back, and Tracy said, "NOW we'll shoot it." And we shot it, and Minnelli said, "Cut! Print!"

Tracy hadn't seen much of Joan Bennett since the completion of *Me and My Gal,* and her presence on the set clearly delighted him. They were like old lovers, sharing confidences and irreverent memories and occasionally even finishing each other's sentences. "He was not quite as jovial as he used to be," Bennett later remarked, "but he was still the good natured, wonderful actor that he'd always been."

Each morning, Tracy would breeze past his secretary's office ("Top o' the mornin' Miss G.!") and mount the stairs to his permanent dressing room, where Larry Keethe would be awaiting him. Even a modern-dress

With Elizabeth Taylor on the set of *Father of the Bride*.
(SUSIE TRACY)

picture required close attention to wardrobe, and it was Keethe's job to know what tie, what suit, what shirt was necessary for any given scene, down to the smallest detail. Interiors of the Banks home had been assembled on M-G-M's Stage 26, where Tracy was always punctual for his nine o'clock call.

Bennett noticed how accommodating Tracy could be to his fellow performers, a trait that had not always distinguished him in the past. "If they wanted to rehearse, much as he disliked doing it, he would go ahead and rehearse with these people, these other actors, so that they could be secure in what they were doing." Elizabeth Taylor, who had been at M-G-M since 1943, regarded the opportunity to work with him as a master's class in the art of film acting: "Even at eighteen I learned so much by just watching Spence . . . it was his sense of stillness, his ability to use economy of movement, vocal economy. It seemed almost effortless. It seemed as if he wasn't doing anything, and yet he was doing everything. It came so subtly out of his eyes. Every muscle in his face."

Tracy, in turn, seemed to regard the boisterous Taylor as he might a second daughter, addressing her as Kitten (as he did in the film) and allowing her to call him Pops. "In between takes, he would be Spence . . . I mean we would really horse around. He'd chase me, rough me up. I'd tease him. But the minute the camera started, except once—I'd been naughty. I'd really been horsing around on the set, chasing him on a bicycle. And it was my closeup, and it was not a very intense moment, but a serious moment between father and daughter. The camera was on his back, and he played the whole scene with his eyes crossed, seeing how great my powers of concentration were. I could have killed him, but I didn't bust up." To his aunt Jenny he wrote: "We have been going along pretty smoothly on *Father of the Bride*—think it will be a nice, harmless movie."

Tracy's case of nerves persisted throughout the making of *Father of the Bride,* and though he merely seemed "more subdued" to Joan Bennett, he was convinced by the end of production that he had stomach cancer. Hepburn was in New York, where she was playing *As You Like It,* and he made plans to join her there, traveling to Boston for more tests at Brigham Hospital and another consultation with Dr. Gray. One day he surprised Bill Self by asking him to come along.

"Initially we were going to drive," Self recalled,

and he wanted me to help him drive to New York, which was kind of a legitimate reason. The plan was that I would pack and meet him at Chasen's for dinner. He had all the maps and was prepared for it. We were going to have dinner at Chasen's and then we were going to drive to Palm Springs and spend the first night in Palm Springs, then take off for New York. So I arrived at Chasen's with my bag. (He even made me go out and buy a hat, because I didn't have a hat. He said, "You can't be in New York without a hat." So he gave me some money and I went out and bought a hat.) I arrived at Chasen's and told the valet to put my bag in Mr. Tracy's car. I went in and Spence was sitting there. I don't remember if anyone was with him or not; there might have been Carroll.

He said, "Where you going?" I said, "I'm going to New York." He said, "Oh, that's interesting. I'm going to New York, but not tonight." I said, "Oh? You're not going tonight?" He said, "Well, I was going to drive to New York, but I'm not going to drive. I'm going to take the train." I said, "Well, fine. What's that mean to me?" He said, "You're going with me. I have your ticket."

Everybody says it would have been a disaster [to drive], and I have no doubt they were right. So we had dinner. I came home, caught [my wife] Peggy by surprise, and the next day we left on the train. The trip eastward was uneventful; we got along okay. The only eventful thing was that Fred Astaire and his wife were on the train, and that was the first time I ever met Fred and his wife. I didn't remind Fred of that meeting until many, many years later. Nothing came of it, but Spence was not anxious to team up with them . . . While on the train, I said to him, "Why am I with you?" He said, "Because if somebody isn't with me, people come up to me and talk to me. If I'm talking to somebody that I know, people don't usually come up." He said, "That's particularly true at dinner."

I never felt as close to Tracy as I felt to Hepburn. With me, Hepburn was very open. She'd say anything. She was just terrific. Tracy was much more reserved. I was careful not to talk about little things. He hated little conversations. "Small talk." I would have to choose my subjects carefully. He'd rather sit there silently. He once said to me about the New York trip, "You know the real reason I asked you to go to New York? You don't talk to me. I hate casual conversation. You and I don't talk about those kinds of things." I loved to talk about his career, because I didn't know that much about his career and I was a young actor. I wanted to know more about: How do you do it? And he did talk to me about his career, told me lots of stories about when he got going . . .

We got to New York. Spence went to his hotel, and I went to mine. Hepburn had borrowed a Rolls-Royce from somebody. The Rolls-Royce would drop her at the theater and then it would drop Spence and me at a different theater. I remember going to see Sir Cedric Hardwicke in *Caesar and Cleopatra*. Spence always sat in the back row; he would enter the theater late, and he would leave the theater the moment the curtain came down. We dashed backstage to say hello to Sir Cedric Hardwicke, which was kind of interesting to me.

Often, Tracy and Self would walk the theater district after a performance, Kate's show running later than most. "He told me all these stories about his drinking buddies and what he did and what he shouldn't have done. We were walking in the Broadway area, and we passed a theater

"Three Guys from Milwaukee" was the original caption for this M-G-M publicity photo. From left: Bill Self, Wisconsin state tennis champion; Tracy; and Frank Parker, U.S. national tennis champion. (WILLIAM SELF)

where he said, 'This is where John Barrymore played *Hamlet.*'" It was the old Harris Theatre, now a Forty-second Street grind house, where Tracy himself had played Killer Mears in *The Last Mile.*

I said, "Did you ever work with Barrymore?" He said, "No." And I, being facetious, said, "You would have made a great pair—a couple of drinkers like you." How stupid can you be? He stopped and said, "What do you mean by that?" I said, "Well, Spence, you know you're always kidding about the amount of drinking you did . . ." He said, "I don't *kid* about my drinking."

One evening we went back to Hepburn's theater and picked her up—or she picked us up if she had the car—and we went to the Pierre. We talked for hours. It was a terrific evening, because I was hearing two giants tell their stories. They talked about George M. Cohan . . . We talked until two or three in the morning. Earlier, Spence had said, "Call me at eight o'clock and we'll do something. Sightsee or something." I said, "Great." Then we talked much later than I expected. Spence said, "You take Katie back to her home." So I went with her, and I did that, and then the car dropped me off. The next morning at eight o'clock I thought, Well I can't call Spence at eight o'clock; we were up till four. I'll wait a little while. Nine o'clock I called, and he said, "Where the hell have you been??"

I said, "Well, Spence, I thought we were all up so late that I would hesitate to call you at eight o'clock." And he said, "Well, Bill, people who get along with me do what they say they're going to do." And he hangs up.

I had no money; he had been paying the bills. A few minutes later, Katie called and said, "What happened?" And I said, "Well, Kate, I was reluctant to call—you know how late we were up and I was concerned about calling him." She said, "Well, he's upset. Let him alone. I'll fix it up. Don't call him, don't bother him. Just stay put."

So I would say two or three days go by and I don't hear a word from him. She called me and said, "I'm working on it." I'm wandering around New York. I have no business there, no money, no nothing. I knew they were going to pay the bills. I wasn't worried about that. I just didn't know what to do. And then she called and said, "You're going home tomorrow, and you leave at such-and-such a time from Penn Station (or whatever it was) and don't be late." I said, "I'm not going to be late. Not after this."

So I met him at the station, and he was cool. Very awkward. My sole purpose for being there was to please him, and here I was and he wouldn't even talk to me. So we got on the train and we had to change in Chicago, and he warmed up. That was when he told me that he thought he had stomach cancer, told me about his doctor in Boston. And he excused himself for being so touchy, I guess by virtue of having this on his mind. So we got friendly enough. We got to Chicago, and we were met by the M-G-M representative, limousine and all that, and he had booked a suite for us at the Blackstone Hotel. When we got to the suite there was liquor in the room. He said, "I could get this guy fired for that."

They cleared the room of liquor, and Spence said that he was going to take a nap. He said, "You want the car?" I said, "Well, I went to the University of Chicago, and if I had the car I would go out there to my fraternity house and say hello to some of the guys. I would enjoy doing that." He said, "Go ahead, take the car. We'll leave here at such-and-such a time." I said, "Great." So I took the car, and I went out there and I bummed around. I was back well ahead of when I was supposed to be back, and I opened the door, and there was Spence sitting in a chair facing the door saying, "Where in the hell have you been??"

I said, "You know where I've been. I went out to the University of Chicago." He said, "Bill, I couldn't sleep. I can't go out for a walk. You know that. I'm stuck in this room. You've got the car." And he bawls hell out of me. Much to my surprise, I took him off. I said, "Mr. Tracy, you are too tough for me. When we get back, I never want to see you again. I don't want anything to do with you." I was amazed with myself for saying that because I thought, "I'm ruining my career. I'll never work at M-G-M again." He was *shocked*. He was shocked, and I was trembling, I was so angry. I don't mind being accused of something if I'm wrong, but I was so right. And on top of the other thing, which I was trying to do the best I could. This was totally uncalled for, and so we just gathered our belongings and went to the station and got on the train.

And then he came around and literally apologized to me. He said, "Bill, this whole cancer thing scared me and I've been very tight and I'm sorry." I said, "Well, that's fine. I just hope I haven't done anything wrong," and he said, "No, you haven't done anything wrong." In fact, when we got back to Los Angeles, the first thing he did was to take me to Palm Springs with his family, down to the Racket Club to play some tennis and make amends, I guess. It's the only time in my life I've ever been to the Racket Club. So everything seemed to be smoothed over. I never totally trusted him again, though. I just realized that I was dealing with a guy who could be pretty tricky.

Tracy observed his fiftieth birthday on April 5, 1950. Already assembled and previewed, *Father of the Bride* garnered 149 cards rating it outstanding or excellent and another 47 judging it to be "very good." The audience at the Bay Theatre in Pacific Palisades was split evenly between males and females in the eighteen-to-forty-five age group, and both Berman and Schary were instantly convinced they had a big hit on their hands. Schary, in fact, already had the Hacketts sketching out notes for a sequel.

"I know you will realize with what horror we went into such a venture," Frances Goodrich apologetically said in a letter to Ed Streeter. "But the studio felt so encouraged, after the very first days of shooting, that they wanted to be prepared . . . We feel like orphans on this one, sailing on uncharted seas . . . it is really terrifying. But we go on with our fingers crossed. We are doing, as you probably know, Kay's first baby. Are you puking already? Don't sue us."

As You Like It closed on June 3, the colorful production having received better overall notices than Hepburn herself, even as her infrequently seen legs were widely—and favorably—remarked upon. ("She has the greatest set of legs I ever saw on a woman," Tim Durant once said.) "They thought I was O.K.," Hepburn said in her autobiography. "Sort of half carps and half praise. Looking back on my notices which I did not read at the time, I have the impression that I was irritating to the critics. They liked me in *The Philadelphia Story,* but in Shakespeare—well—it was sort of 'she has a nerve to be doing this.' Well I don't know . . . At least I enjoyed it."

She was back in California when *Father of the Bride* was released nationally on the sixteenth. Already in the midst of a six-week engagement at the Radio City Music Hall, the film surpassed any of Tracy's previous features, bringing in more than $6 million in worldwide rentals and showing a profit of nearly $3 million on a cost of $1.2 million. From New York, where he had witnessed an advance screening on May 2, Edward Streeter wrote Tracy: "No one who ever sees the picture will be a more severe critic than I was last night in view of the fact that you were portraying ME. All I can say is that you have given me much to live up to, although it is more or less wasted in one sense of the word as I have no more daughters to marry off."

Tracy replied:

It is utterly impossible for me to express to you the pleasure your letter has given me. The fact that I admired your book so much has a great deal to do with this, plus, I suppose, the fact that this is the first time an author of a book in which I was part of the so-called movie version has ever written me except to warn me that it might be in my best interests to avoid him. Sinclair Lewis, whom I knew well enough to call "Red," has not spoken to me since the "version" of *Cass Timberlane,* and Kenneth Roberts, whose *Northwest Passage* I thought we did a pretty fair job [on], I understand has gone so far as to threaten bodily harm if I so much as entered the state of Maine. Since I had heard that you did not particularly like the script, I was doubly pleased to get your favorable reaction. Had I known this, I should certainly have called upon you last week when I was in New York, and now that I know you are not armed, I shall do so on my next visit.

The picture's notices were wildly favorable, coming as they did just six months after a similar embrace for *Adam's Rib.* (As *Variety* noted, "It's the second strong comedy in a row for Spencer Tracy, doing the title role, and he socks it.") Terms like "glamour-packed," "rich in comic invention," and "charming and refreshing" littered the reviews. Bosley Crowther used the first paragraph of his notice in the *Times* to heap praise on the book and then went on to say the movie was "equally wonderful . . . Mr. Tracy conducts himself with precisely the air of self-importance that a bride's father likes to think he has, coupled with the mingled indignation and frustration that he is sure to acquire. Further, he has a capacity to show that warmth and tenderness toward his own which flavors with universal poignance the irony of the joke on him. As a father, torn by jealousy, devotion, pride, and righteous wrath, Mr. Tracy is tops."

The pressure to do a sequel only increased with the film's commercial success, but given that Tracy's only experience with sequels had been the execrable *Men of Boys Town,* he resisted the idea. "Tracy didn't want to do the second picture," Pan Berman remembered. "What actor wants to do it again? I hated the sequel. I didn't want to do it, but knew money. You know the sequel isn't going to do as well." According to Minnelli, it was Hepburn who stepped in once again, perhaps as a favor, as Berman believed, for either Benny Thau or L. B. Mayer. "In her practical way, she convinced Spencer that he owed it to the studio to do the film. Movies were a business, after all, and the first picture had been such a huge success that this one couldn't fail either."

A draft screenplay was completed in April, but Tracy held out until plans for *Father's Little Dividend* collided with Minnelli's next project, an elaborate musical based on the works of George and Ira Gershwin titled *An American in Paris.* Tracy went east on September 2, joining Kate as she began rehearsals for the national touring company of *As You Like It,* declaring he would take the rest of the month off before starting the new picture. On the thirteenth he received a telegram from Pan Berman confirming an official start date of October 9. "Am very happy," Berman wrote, "because neither you nor I are getting any younger so we'd better get it made." When Hepburn opened in Hershey, Pennsylvania, on September 22, Tracy was back in Los Angeles. He wired:

> YOU MAY FORGET ALL THEM THINGS I LEARNED YOU ABOUT UNDERPLAYING BUT PLEASE REMEMBER THE REST. THE NEXT VOICE YOU HEAR I HOPE WILL BE MINE.

He signed the communiqué "Ever – Old Pot," a likely reference to all the coffee he guzzled.*

---

* Another frequent signature he used was T.O.T., which probably stood for "Tired Old Tracy." He rarely, if ever, signed his correct name with close friends. To the Kanins he was "Old Tom." To George Cukor he was always "Corse Payton," the flamboyant Brooklyn matinee idol known for billing himself as "America's Best Bad Actor."

According to Buck Herzog of the *Sentinel,* Tracy turned up in Milwaukee about a week later, completely unnoticed and making the rounds with Gene Sullivan. It was at the height of widespread rumors that Tracy and Hepburn were "more than just good friends," and both were fuming over a splashy article by Richard Gehman in the high-end arts and fashion journal *Flair* that helped fuel such talk. Profiling Hepburn, Gehman essentially outed the relationship, suggesting their devotion to each other was an established fact: "They are together whenever professional commitments permit: Tracy turned up in Boston when *As You Like It* was there, and in 1945 when he was playing in Robert E. Sherwood's *The Rugged Path,* Hepburn followed him about and, on one occasion, reportedly scrubbed the floor of his dressing room. They have often been seen riding in Hepburn's black Lincoln convertible (Connecticut license KH-6), but they have never furnished column material by appearing in a public place."

Since, in support of *As You Like It,* Hepburn had cooperated with Gehman, albeit minimally, Tracy may well have blamed her for the humiliation Louise no doubt suffered. Said Herzog: "We started the evening at the Club Madrid and wound up in the wee hours of the morning. He left the following day for Hollywood, followed by gossip column reports that his whirlwind courtship with Miss Hepburn, whom he had followed on tour, ended in a spat."

Joan Bennett remembered a phrase Tracy had picked up from Kate: "Bore, bore, bore . . ." She heard it at the start of *Father's Little Dividend,* but once he got into it, he actually seemed to be enjoying himself, racing through the picture in twenty-one days, seven days under schedule. "I went out to George [Cukor]'s for my first party to say goodbye to Viv[ien Leigh] and Larry [Olivier]—and Spence was there," Constance Collier wrote in a letter to Hepburn, hoping, perhaps, to mend the rift. "In all the time I have known him—I have <u>never</u> seen him look so well—really wonderful—very brown and thinner and he was so funny and charming."

At one point, Tracy became concerned that one of the twin babies playing his grandson in the picture was either hard of hearing or completely deaf. "I don't think anything was wrong," said Don Taylor, "but he was VERY concerned about it—I know that—and he called his wife." Louise came to the set, and Spence, in light of the *Flair* article, was uncommonly solicitous, posing for pictures with her and talking up her work with the clinic. "They were very sweet to each other," Taylor said. "She came on and he said, 'Hello! Hi! How are you?' They were dear. He introduced the mother, and his wife talked to the children."

With sets recycled from the first film, Minnelli was able to wrap the picture $150,000 under budget. "These last three comedies have entirely changed my viewpoint," Tracy told a visitor. "Where before I doted on doing dramatic roles, I have never been as happy as I am now. In these uncertain times I think the public wants escapist pictures and I hope I'll get my share of them."

There was never, however, an overabundance of comedies during Dore Schary's reign at M-G-M. Tracy was bolstered in his quest for escapist fare only by the knowledge that the Kanins were at work for him on another original. Carrying the title *Pat and Mike,* the story concerned a woman whose controlling husband has little time for their marriage. When Pat Ford tells off the wife of an important client, Joe blows up and tells her that she couldn't earn a penny on her own. Pat impulsively decides to turn athlete under the guidance of a local golf pro and quickly becomes the sensation of the Hot Springs Open. She attracts the attention of one Mike Cavanaugh, a destitute promoter, and goes on to phenomenal success in tennis and baseball under his shrewd management. It is Mike who tries injecting sex into sports by matching women against men, an idea that culminates in a big charity game between Pat's girls and the Giants. The girls, of course, win, and Pat comes to realize that it is Mike she truly loves.

Where *Adam's Rib* had come together quickly, all the pieces falling smoothly into place, *Pat and Mike* proved a much tougher job. Though conceived expressly for Tracy and Hepburn, the initial reader's report was not encouraging: "A not too successful attempt to pound a clever but slight and difficult idea into comedy form. It has lots of laughs, but despite the unquestioned ability and experience of the writers, it doesn't have quite the flair to put this sort of thing across. Many of the gags are pointless and familiar, as are the trick camera effects. And the galaxy of famous sports and political figures involved certainly deserve a better showcase."

Pat and Mike was still under development when Tracy finished with *Father's Little Dividend,* and the Hacketts said he proposed a plot for yet another sequel, this one taking him and Elizabeth Taylor on a European cruise. Joan Bennett, however, didn't remember it that way: "When they asked him to make another [sequel] to *Father of the Bride,* he said no, he didn't want to be playing Judge Hardy."

All this left him free for something a little closer to Schary's heart, a gritty courtroom drama called *The People Against O'Hara.* Anything but escapist fare, it began as an outline called *Johnny O'Hara's Life* by Eleazar Lipsky, a novelist and assistant district attorney who was attached for four years to the homicide bureau of New York County. The author of *Kiss of Death,* Lipsky proposed a robbery-murder scenario, detailing in documentary fashion the events flowing from an ordinary criminal act. "We will see not only the machinery of justice turning, but also the steps taken by the defense to anticipate the prosecution. The cat-and-mouse play between the two should develop simultaneously." Offered initially on an option basis, Lipsky subsequently submitted a 366-page manuscript, which became the novel on which the picture was officially based. Molding Lipsky's story into a star turn for someone of Tracy's magnitude took nearly a year.

The "contract trouble" Edward Streeter alluded to was typically over vacation and rest periods and the number of pictures Tracy could be required to make in a given year. In August 1949 a new interim agreement was signed that limited him to just two pictures a year and allowed thirteen consecutive weeks of vacation. Late in 1950 the William Morris Agency undertook a further modification of the deal, extending his rest periods to a minimum of six weeks between films and boosting his compensation to $150,000 a picture, or $5,769.23 a week on a fifty-two-week guarantee.

By doubling production, Schary had cut overhead costs per picture in half. He shortened production schedules—*Woman of the Year* took fifty-nine days to shoot while *Father of the Bride* took just twenty-eight days—and cut the average number of writers on a project from 7.3 (under the old Thalberg model) to 1.2—a dramatic reduction. He also began to root out the deadwood, bringing in younger directors who weren't mired in the old Metro ways and were used to working at a faster clip.

One of those men was John Sturges, a former editor who, at the age of thirty-nine, was younger than many directors on the lot by at least a decade. In little more than a year, Sturges had completed four films for M-G-M, including *The Magnificent Yankee*—which had so impressed Tracy that he recorded a voice-over for the film's trailer. Sturges, however, still needed Tracy's approval to direct him in *The People Against O'Hara.* "It was traditional," he said, "if you met anybody, you, your agent, and that person, if he was a star, had to meet at Romanoff's. And we did. And talked about the picture we were going to do. Very brief conversation. 'Look forward to it,' he said. 'Look forward to it,' I said. Both left. That's all there was to it."

Sturges later recalled that he and Bert Allenberg, Tracy's new agent at William Morris, were sipping martinis that day, while Allenberg's client was calmly drinking a cup of coffee. "Five years later we were talking about alcoholism, and I asked [Spence] how long it had taken him to get over the urge to drink. He reminded me of that moment at Romanoff's and said, 'You know, at that time I hadn't had a drink for five years, but I wanted that martini and I looked at it with as much longing as the day I quit.' So that's what the man lived with."

Tracy began his sixteenth year at M-G-M with a new agent, a new contract, and a new picture in *Father's Little Dividend* that was previewing even better than the original. "Audience chortled and howled throughout,"

Schary was advised by Larry Weingarten in a wire. "Ending played very well. Looks like this one will pay the rent."

Tracy was preparing to go east for a Red Cross broadcast and location work on *The People Against O'Hara* when it was announced that he had received an Academy Award nomination for his work in *Father of the Bride*—his first Oscar nomination since *Boys Town* a dozen years earlier.

CHAPTER 25

Rough Patch

Louise took Johnny and Susie to Europe over the summer of 1950, the last time she would likely have them together for an extended length of time. Johnny, twenty-six, was a student at Chouinard Art Institute, and Susie, who turned eighteen on the voyage over, had been accepted for the fall semester at the University of Arizona, Tucson. They toured France, Italy, Switzerland, and England, then returned home aboard the *Queen Elizabeth,* docking in New York on August 21.

Spence kept in touch by wire, postcard, the occasional phone call, and was there to meet the kids when they arrived back in Los Angeles by plane, their mother following by rail. "Well, it's great to see you back!" he beamed, and on the drive home he peppered them with questions: "How was it? Tell me about it! Did you enjoy Claridge's in London?" (He once told Stewart Granger he'd like to spend the rest of his life at Claridge's, the service and comfort were so outstanding.) True to their tag-team existence, Spence was off to New York the moment Louise hit town, pausing only for dinner with her at Chasen's.

Louise's profile was looming ever larger, her work with the clinic increasingly in the news. The *Los Angeles Times* named her a Woman of the Year on the last day of 1950, one of eleven civic leaders so honored for works as diverse as managing the city's philharmonic orchestra, serving on Stanford's board of regents, and swimming the English Channel. When the

Academy Awards were handed out in March 1951, it was she who attended with Johnny and Susie and Susie's friend Donna Bullard in tow. (José Ferrer beat out Spence for the Best Actor Oscar, which didn't seem to upset anyone very much.) The West Coast premiere of *Father's Little Dividend* was held to benefit the clinic's building fund, with Esther Williams, Cyd Charisse, Janet Leigh, Nancy Olson, Diana Lynn, and Maureen O'Hara serving as the welcoming committee. *Listening Eyes* was again shown, George Murphy acted as master of ceremonies, and singer Eileen Christy sang two songs. Christy and Murphy then led the audience in singing "Happy Birthday" to Tracy, who was, in Johnny's words, "very surprised to find out they knew it was his birthday."

Northwestern University awarded Louise an honorary doctorate in June, which prompted her husband to begin referring to his wife as "Dr. Tracy." He began worrying that his presence at certain events could have the effect of overshadowing Louise and her work, and he made sure he was out of town when the groundbreaking for the clinic's new building took place on July 28, 1951. He observed a groundbreaking of his own when George Cukor began work on a pair of cottages at the lower end of his Beverly Hills estate, one to serve as a secluded residence for one of the world's best-known actors. Settling on a place to live was no simple matter for Spence, and there was a brief period of time when he enlisted Bill Self's help while Kate was away on tour.

"I kind of scouted the town at one time," Self recalled, "trying to find a place for him, and reported back on a couple of places I thought were possibilities. He hated them all. He looked at me like I was an idiot. He calls up and says, 'That's a motel! You want to put me in a motel?' [Then] he was looking for a house, and he considered, believe it or not, Peggy and me *and* our child moving in with him. I guess semi-caretaker to him in a way, you know? We actually talked about that a little bit, and Kate and I talked about that a little bit, but it was always looked upon as being totally impractical. I felt it would destroy our relationship."

By the time Cukor came to the rescue, Tracy was living, in Kate's words, in "a terrible little apartment on South Beverly Drive down an alley off the actual drive. Trying to make it attractive was really not possible. In desperation we had Erik Bolin—French furniture maker—make some wooden valances for the curtains."

Tracy was a restless traveler when Kate was out of town—New York and back again, Chicago when he took the train, Freeport, Milwaukee once in a great while. Constance Collier was never sure where he was. "Did Spence come?" she asked when Hepburn was playing *As You Like It* in San Francisco. "I called twice but could not get him, so I suppose he went." And later: "I don't know if Spencer is here. I haven't seen him at all." He would slip in and out of town on a moment's notice. "I'd go out to the ranch to play tennis with Johnny," Bill Self remembered, "and Spencer would be there. And I didn't even know that he was in town. I'd say, 'What are you doing here? I thought you were in New York.' He'd say, 'No, I didn't go' or 'I came back last night' or something like that, but he would be there, and I think Louise liked that."

If there was one constant in Tracy's life at the time, it was Sunday Mass wherever he happened to be. "There was a time in my life in the late forties and early fifties when I went to Mass almost every Sunday at Good Shepherd in Beverly Hills," said Darryl Hickman. "Tracy was always there and sat by himself. Even though he was such a famous, recognizable film star, none of the parishioners ever approached him, including me. I had acted with him in two films when I was growing up, but I did what everybody else did—pretend I didn't know him, or even know who he was. We didn't dare intrude on such a 'private' public man. He would often be there before I arrived, a solitary figure standing in front of the church before Mass. Being so unapproachable, I wondered why he didn't go right in. Like so many other things about Tracy, I could never figure that out."

When Tracy went east for the Red Cross, it was to do *Father of the Bride* over the radio for the Theatre Guild. Larry Keethe accompanied him, and President and Mrs. Truman attended the broadcast in Washington with their daughter Margaret. Supreme Court Justice William O. Douglas, who first met Tracy in New York in the 1920s, had come to resemble him to such an extent that he was frequently taken for him in crowds. "By prearrangement, I waited for him at the rear exit," Douglas recounted in his autobiography. "Many people surged into the dimly lit alley, and taking me for him, asked, 'Mr. Tracy, will you give us your autograph?' I obliged, and several dozen took the forgeries home. Most of the crowd had gone when Spencer appeared, and my account of the episode made him chuckle as we sipped a nightcap in a secluded spot."

When Tracy arrived in New York to shoot exteriors for *The People Against O'Hara,* he found the entire troupe laid up with the flu. He had time for Mass at St. Patrick's, a walk in Central Park, shopping for shoes at Abercrombie and Fitch. The producer of NBC's *The Big Show,* a weekly all-star extravaganza, asked him to do a guest shot, and he agreed to go by the theater to "listen to it and see how they do it" but emphasized that he didn't think he wanted to appear. "Radio is the bane of my life," he groaned to Frank Tracy, who was in New York at the time and managed to meet up with him. "I can't handle it. I can't stand in front of that goddamn stick and *emote.* I can't do that. No good at it."

On March 6, he and Kate—who had just concluded her tour in Rochester—saw Claude Rains in *Darkness at Noon* and were spotted by one of Dorothy Kilgallen's informants. He was in Chicago on the tenth, headed back to Hollywood, when he drove down to Freeport to visit his aunt Mum in the hospital, where she had just undergone surgery for breast cancer. He saw his uncle Andrew and aunt Mame and was back in Chicago that same evening.

He still saw his friends at the Boys' Club but not with the frequency that he once had. Cagney was spending more time at Martha's Vineyard, Pat O'Brien was working nightclubs, and Frank McHugh was planning a return to New York City, where he could find work in the theater and on television. With Hepburn determinedly sustaining their relationship, Tracy had gradually become part of her social circle, uncomfortable with old friends who knew him from when he was still out and around with Louise. "When he came [to the Boys' Club dinners], which was rarely, he would not really join in," said actor Jimmy Lydon, who was invited into the group sometime in the mid-1940s. "He'd have a couple of knocks and he would just kind of sit and enjoy listening to everybody else."

In place of Joe Mankiewicz, Frank Borzage, Walt Disney, and Vic Fleming, Tracy was now spending his time with George Cukor, Constance Collier, Irene Selznick, and the Kanins. "I've never been able to see the Spence I knew so well participating in that group," Mankiewicz said of the shift.

> I used to go to the fights with him. He lived the life of a sports-writer, a sort of New York sportswriter—really tough. He liked going to the fights. He liked reading. We used to spend evenings together, reading. It was an extremely close relationship, so close that Spence was my eldest son's godfather, but after Kate enfolded him I saw nothing of him. He used to keep sending the same doll to Chris, his godson, when the boy was well into the age of puberty. Everything just stopped between us and I didn't see Spence at all. I think I got a phone call when I hit the jackpot—I got four Academy Awards or something*—and Kate called and said how pleased they were but Spence never got on the phone.

So it came as something of a surprise when Tracy learned that Pat O'Brien was having trouble finding work. Having finished off a seven-year contract at RKO, Pat found there was no work in features for a whole class of actor that populated films in the 1930s and '40s—when the major studios were routinely making forty to fifty pictures a season. Averages had dropped

---

* Mankiewicz won three Academy Awards (if you count Best Picture) for *All About Eve* (1950).

in the years following the war, and budgets had tightened. "During several discussions at dinner of the Boys' Club," said Frank McHugh, "it was concluded that the picture business, as we knew it, was on the wane." Major names like George Raft, Edward G. Robinson, Mickey Rooney, and Don Ameche were working in independent productions or, more frequently, on television, where the schedules were brutal and the money light. Pat sustained an average of two pictures a year, even into the fifties, but had three households to maintain and couldn't quite figure it all out. "I was confronted with a strange situation I did not think could ever happen to me," he wrote. "I suddenly could not get my foot inside a studio gate. I could not figure out what happened. Whatever it was, I was now unable to get a job in pictures."

Tracy's muscle at the studio, meanwhile, had never been greater. With the enormous success of *Father of the Bride,* he was once again polling as one of the nation's top stars, and *Father's Little Dividend,* thanks to promotional tie-ins with Sunbeam Bread, Libby's Baby Foods, Lux Soap, FTD, Lane Bryant, and others, was drawing on a par with the first picture in places like Buffalo, New Haven, Kansas City, and Los Angeles. He went to bat for his boyhood pal, landing Pat—whom he still called "Bill"—a featured part in *The People Against O'Hara* at $4,375 a week on an eight-week guarantee. "Spence had to put on a wild, desperate fight to secure the role for me," O'Brien said, "even threatening to walk out unless I was signed."

The two men lunched at the studio just five days after the deal was set, a pair of graying veterans in a picture full of youthful faces—Diana Lynn, William Campbell, James Arness, Richard Anderson. And when Tracy arrived in Manhattan for location work, Pat was there waiting for him, laid up with the flu like everyone else. "He wanted me to go out with him, but I just couldn't raise my head. A little later, when he had gone out, I learned that the director and producer and some of the other players were also sick with the flu and that Spence had taken over the job of filming the background shots down at the fish market."

Production resumed in Culver City on March 19. Tracy's character, Jim Curtayne, was written as a recovering alcoholic whose drinking had derailed a successful career as a criminal defense attorney. It was a grim and uncomfortable job for a man of his particular history, and where Pat was his usual gregarious self, taking the younger actors under his wing and proffering nonstop advice and encouragement, Tracy kept to himself, insular in a way he had not been on either of his two previous pictures. That he was trying to quit smoking at the time made him edgier still, and the other members of the cast were told to extinguish their cigarettes whenever he came onto the stage.

"Anytime I saw him he was all business," said James Arness, who had come to M-G-M to be in Dore Schary's *Battleground* and was playing the young defendant, the title character in the picture. "No kidding around or having fun—anything like that. He would, as a matter of fact, be offstage most of the time . . . They would call him and he'd come in and any kind of light conversation going on came to a screeching halt."

John Sturges made a practice of rehearsing every scene, a departure from the old Metro routine where even run-throughs were a sometime thing. "The thing I remember most about Spence," he said, "is the pleasure I had watching a scene played for the first time come alive by this man." Sturges, as Arness remembered it, would have the chairs arrayed in a semi-circle. "Mr. Tracy would be in the middle of this semicircle and the director would sit facing us. He would come onstage, walk up, 'good morning' briefly, and then we'd sit down and read through the scene, rehearse, and then get up and go onto whatever set it was and do it on its feet." Tracy was, as far as Arness could tell, devoid of any technique. "It wasn't an actor—this was a real guy in a real courtroom and you were on the stand."

As *The People Against O'Hara* worked its way toward completion, Katharine Hepburn left New York for London and the start of a new picture. Her world had been shaken by the death of her beloved mother just two weeks prior to her departure, and she had scarcely had a month's rest since concluding her tour for the Theatre Guild. It had been four years since she had made a film apart from Tracy, and her unpopularity at the box office rivaled the days when she had been forced to buy herself out of her RKO contract. Producer Sam Spiegel induced her to play Rose in *The African Queen* at a fraction of her usual fee with the promise of a percentage of the profits—a shrewd bargain considering the film's eventual popularity. Sweetening the deal was the prospect of working opposite Humphrey Bogart under the direction of John Huston. Both Tracy and Constance Collier feared for her health, but after pondering the offer she wouldn't be dissuaded.

Collier accompanied her to London, where the two took over a suite at Claridge's, and Tracy made plans to follow—at least as far as Europe—as soon as *O'Hara* had been completed. Spiegel was holding the company together in fits and starts while Huston polished the script, and Hepburn wondered if there would be enough money to cover even the cost of their room. When Tracy did leave for New York on April 27, it was in the company of Benny Thau, who would be making the trip with him. Together, they caught Pat O'Brien's opening as MC at the Plaza Hotel, then sailed for Naples on May 5 aboard the S.S. *Independence*. Obligingly, Tracy posed for press photos, perched on a rail on the ship's top deck and by the interior window of his stateroom, at age fifty-one a distinguished elder statesman of the American motion picture industry.

In Rome he met up with Kate and found the city "unbelievable" in its power and majesty. On the eighteenth, he was received in an audience with Pope Pius XII, an event he described as "truly the culmination of [a] life-long anticipation." His Holiness, he recounted, "received me at the same time he received 50 young crewmen from the U.S.S. plane carrier, the *Coral Sea*. It was a wonderful experience to be present when he talked with these young men and listened with such interest and sympathy to their adventures and problems. He commented sadly to me on their youth." The Holy Father, he concluded, was "wonderful" and blessed a rosary he had brought for his cousin Jane.

Hepburn left to start work on *The African Queen* on May 20. Tracy flew by Pan Am to Paris on the twenty-fourth—a terrifying experience when three of the plane's four engines quit in midflight. Although he had said he would spend an entire month on the French Riviera, he lingered just two days before moving on to England. In London he checked in at Claridge's and asked to be left "very much alone." A few hours later, dressed in a flannel suit and navy tie, he ambled down the stairs and greeted a reporter from the *Daily Mirror,* seemingly grateful for the company and practically pushing the man into a waiting armchair. "I'm just a white-haired, middle-aged movie star," he groused, shoving his lower lip out in a characteristic pose. "Who the hell cares about a guy like me?"

He took Constance Collier to see *Caesar and Cleopatra,* walked the town a bit with Benny Thau, and wired that he was shipping back a Fiat station wagon he had purchased for Susie. Kate, said Collier, was in the Congo writing "horrifying" letters and having "an awfully tough time I think, even she admits it, and it is hard to get her to admit anything like that."

By return mail Constance advised her that Spence would be cabling her "and said I might tell you that M-G-M have a picture by Gar Kanin called 'Mike and something' for you and he, so that is thrilling and a lovely thing to look forward too [*sic*]. So hurry up with that stunt, darling, and get back home." Spence, she added, was "longing for a letter from you saying things are a bit better. He is so desperately worried about you, but I know you and I think in spite of the terrible hardships you will find a way of getting a kick out of the place."

With Tracy in London, Hepburn naturally gravitated to John Huston for companionship. Huston remembered "the many nights I sat with Katie on the top deck of the paddle boat and watched the eyes of the hippos in the water all around us, every eye seemed to be staring in our direction. And we talked. We talked about anything and everything. But there was never an idea of romance—Spencer Tracy was the only man in Katie's life."

Tracy, however, resented her absence and may well have been in the midst of a midlife crisis. He seemed unsettled, unhappy, acutely conscious of his age and weight. One night in London he dined with Bill and Edie Goetz—she being the elder daughter of Louis B. Mayer—and the actress Joan Fontaine, whom he had never before met. He was withdrawn, Fontaine remembered, and not particularly good company. Later, he called her at her hotel and asked her to have dinner with him the following evening. She replied that out of respect to Kate—whom she knew slightly—she could not consider seeing him alone. He made a lame attempt at recovery, explaining that while he and Hepburn were "terribly good friends," they had a "completely platonic" arrangement.

"That's what they all say!" the actress responded, refusing to buy any of it. She left for Sweden within days, only to be greeted upon her arrival by another call from Tracy pressing her once again to see him when she returned to England. "I'm afraid not," she returned, shutting him down as forcefully as she could. "Not only is there Kate to consider, but you *are* a married man."

"I can get a divorce whenever I want to," came his reply. "But my wife and Kate like things just as they are."

Katharine Houghton believed that Tracy and her aunt were indeed going through a "rough patch" at the time, based on "inklings I got from scraps of things" that were said. "Losing himself in a beautiful woman was a bit like losing himself in drink, it seems to me, and he would go a long way to catching his prey, like telling Fontaine that he and Kate were just friends." Hepburn, meanwhile, asked Phyllis Wilbourn, Collier's secretary, to deliver a food parcel and some flowers to Tracy's room at Claridge's with a card signed "Lutie" (one of his many pet names for her).

"I think Spence's ulcer has been a little tiresome," Collier fretted in a subsequent letter.

He has been having a doctor all the time and staying in bed a lot. It's so silly of him to worry around with English doctors, they don't know anything and it would be much better if he flew back and went straight to Boston for a few days to check up with the doctors who understand his case. We drove down to spend the day with Viv and Larry. Spence was absolutely charming, though I think he had a little pain. We left in the afternoon. I do think he behaved too beautifully. Larry and the men were drinking all around him and yelling and very gay and Spence never wavered with his ginger beer, or whatever he was drinking. It must have been very difficult.

I think he has seen a good deal of Viv and Larry and they try to make him stay up late and it is very hard to resist that. Oh dear, how I wish you were here with him, I think he would stay in London and enjoy it. He loves the country so and it looks so wonderful. I lunched with him the other day at Claridge's . . . Darling, if you get a chance, persuade them to come home. Do do it. Spence is hanging around here, wondering whether to wait for you and if you only get back a little sooner, he will wait, I am sure, but it is very lonely for him without you though he is longing to see you.

Tracy did indeed leave town just a couple of days later, catching the *Queen Mary* and enduring one of the roughest crossings in the ship's fabled history. The men were back in L.A. by June 20, Tracy, specifically, to discuss a picture Dore Schary desperately wanted him to make, a costume drama of the Pilgrims' voyage to America, an unfathomable imperative with the deadly title *The Plymouth Adventure.* Schary had somehow become enamored of the story on the basis of a novel by Ernest Gebler, which had been purchased from galleys. Its acquisition was heralded in the *Hollywood Reporter* as "one of the biggest story buys in months," even as Schary himself acknowledged that films about the *Mayflower* were invariably jinxed. Envisioned as a Technicolor extravaganza, the production head wanted the picture top-lined by several major stars, and his quest for a rock-solid Captain Christopher Jones inevitably led him to Tracy.

"Dore Schary was sort of like a rabbinical student who feels badly about having become a mountebank," said veteran costume designer Lucinda Ballard, who was newly married at the time to Howard Dietz. "He was so moralistic and always wanting to do something about God or the pilgrims, which people don't want to see, and it really was one of the things that wrecked him in the end."

There was, in fact, a general feeling of disgruntlement among the old hands on the M-G-M lot, for Schary was a writer, not an administrator, and his bent for moralizing was milking all the sex and showmanship from the M-G-M brand. For a western called *Lone Star,* Schary had cut an unscripted shot of Ava Gardner strolling happily down a street, singing to herself, after an evening of obvious lovemaking with Clark Gable, maintaining the image was neither funny nor in good taste. Director Vincent Sherman could remember Tracy's rueful comment upon hearing the story over lunch one day. "Since Schary took over," he said, "there's no fucking in M-G-M pictures."

L. B. Mayer hated Schary's taste in material and, at the age of sixty-six, could feel himself being pushed aside by the younger man and his patron, Nicholas Schenck, whose relationship with Mayer had deteriorated to the point where the two men were no longer speaking. Thau, a Mayer partisan whose coolness toward Schary never wavered, had doubtless seen Mayer's ultimatum coming and conspired to be out of the country when the inevitable rupture took place. As he and Tracy departed for New York, Mayer was rumored to be part of a syndicate looking to buy a controlling interest in Warner Bros. for $25 million.

Reports of Mayer's resignation were circulating anew as Thau and Tracy quietly knocked about London. The announcement came on June 22, 1951, when the old man issued a statement through a spokesman saying that he was quitting the company that bore his name but not the industry he had helped establish. "I am going to remain in motion picture production, God willing. I am going to be more active than at any time during the last 15 years," Mayer was quoted as saying.

A formal farewell followed on the twenty-fifth. ("Naturally, I regret severing the ties and relationships that have been built up over the years . . .") Both Thau and Mannix took Tracy to dinner at Romanoff's to assure him that all was well within the company. Tracy had an afternoon appointment with Mayer on the twenty-seventh to say good-bye, and was on hand when Mayer officially left, treading a red carpet laid at the door of the Thalberg Building, the assembled executives and secretaries applauding as he made his exit.

There was a time when it seemed that Dore Schary's story department functioned largely for the purpose of generating material for Spencer Tracy. In 1950 alone, no fewer than seven properties were supposedly allocated to Tracy and his schedule, when only two could actually be made. *Yankees in Texas* dealt with the relocation of a Connecticut aviation plant to Texas during the war; *People in Love* was an original from Karl Tunberg and Leonard Spiegelgass; *Angels in the Outfield,* a comedy about a ball team so bad that only a miracle could save it.

Tracy resisted *When in Rome,* another comedy, because it had him playing a crook posing as a priest. *Jealousy* was one of those multipart affairs in vogue at the time, three stories of the green-eyed monster from three different perspectives, a different actress for each. He turned down *Amigo,* from a screenplay by Jo Swerling and Sy Bartlett, on the excuse that nobody could follow the late Wallace Beery as Pancho Villa. The flow continued into 1951 with greater success: *Plymouth Adventure* was always part of the mix, a bad idea that seemingly refused to go away, but January also brought the purchase of Ruth Gordon's autobiographical play *Years Ago,* for which Tracy was set to play her father (a role taken on Broadway by Fredric March). And several months later, *Pat and Mike* was formally added to the M-G-M schedule, intended, as always, to be another vehicle for Tracy and Hepburn.

Originally set as the second of Tracy's two pictures for the year 1952, *Pat and Mike* got moved up on the schedule when the script for *Plymouth*

Adventure ran afoul of its star. Then William Wellman, the original director, opted out. Schary offered the project to Mervyn LeRoy, who could tell it was a stiff without even bothering to read it. "Look," he said, "I've been waiting my whole life to see Spencer Tracy with a gun and a turkey in his hands." After nearly a year's worth of research, outlines, and notes on the part of screenwriter Helen Deutsch, Clarence Brown agreed to direct the thing, though he said that he wouldn't be available until November 1.

Schary, who had hoped to get the film under way sometime over the summer of 1951, apologized for unnecessarily bringing Tracy home from Europe and offered to send him back at the company's expense—officially for conferences with the Kanins, unofficially to be with Kate, who had just arrived back in London from Africa and was looking at several weeks of interiors before finishing *The African Queen*. *The People Against O'Hara* was previewed on the night of July 20, and Tracy was off the next morning for New York, pulling into town in the midst of a seasonal heat wave.

While in Europe, Tracy spent the company's money lavishly, covering most meals and car expenses to the tune of nearly $7,000—only about 30 percent of which could legitimately be charged to the continuity of *Pat and Mike*. He shopped for the family, did some interviews, went to Mass at Notre Dame. Kate came over from London on August 4 and they saw a Toulouse-Lautrec exhibition together, dining at the Coq D'Hardi that evening and kicking the story around with its authors. "I keep remembering seeing her in Paris with Spencer," said Lauren Bacall, who was there over the Bank Holiday with her husband Humphrey Bogart and John Huston. "She was wearing a dress. Spencer refused to take her out unless she wore a dress. She wore one of the two dresses that she owned and she was glowing, brimming over with joy."

Garson Kanin found the inspiration for *Pat and Mike* while watching a tennis lesson given Hepburn one day by four-time Wimbledon champion Bill Tilden. "She plays tennis like an actress," Kanin observed, "with a great sense of form and style." Her part of a "lady athlete" evolved quickly, followed a short time later by an amalgam of all the Lindy sports promoters he had ever known—the Tracy side of the equation. But while the title characters sprang forth fully formed, the plotting of the thing gave the authors fits. They darkened the husband's character, put Mike at the center of a scheme to throw a game, and had him falling desperately in love with Pat halfway through the story. No good; the relationships were all wrong.

Hepburn's input was sharp and detailed; Tracy's was more tempered and generalized. The material, Kate remembered, was "very intimately discussed between us all, which I think was an enormous help to everyone concerned. It was very 'ensemble' in spirit. And things we didn't like, or which irritated one, or you didn't understand, you were able to state it, which one doesn't always get an opportunity to do in this business. It was not just friendship, but an artistic collaboration." In the space of a few hours, they began to move the story toward the form it would eventually take.

Kate had to fly back to London on the sixth, leaving Tracy to a city shimmering with neon and light rain. It was a place he could only truly enjoy at sunrise and sunset, when he could go out in public and was less likely to be recognized. He and Ruth discussed *Years Ago*—she was writing the screenplay—and one night he was coaxed out of his room and his daily routine for a walk along the Champs-Élysées, a stroll that ended abruptly with a ringside table at the Lido. He appeared to be enjoying himself, a Coke conspicuously at hand, when a band of American acrobats pulled him up onto the stage and proceeded to make him part of a human pyramid. He was furious, reducing the check to confetti and threatening the manager with a bill from the William Morris Agency. Flash photos had been taken, and all he could think about was the impression they would make. ("Boy! That's *all* I need. Nightclub hi-jinks pictures plastered all over. They'll think Tracy's on the ol' heimerdeimer again.") Gar Kanin had the help of the M-G-M press department in confiscating them, and Tracy later claimed to have destroyed them all, although at least one print managed to survive. When Kate came to town again the following weekend, she refused to believe any part of the story until shown the evidence.

Tracy and the Kanins dined at Maxim's one night toward the end of his stay, and the party of five included actress Gene Tierney, who was in the process of divorcing her husband of ten years, the French-born fashion designer Oleg Cassini. Tracy seemed uncommonly interested in the green-eyed beauty, who had been in pictures since 1940 and spoke French like a native. Having made a film on the Argentine pampas that previous winter, Tierney said something to the effect that she was eager to work again in the comfort of an American studio.

Tracy rose to the bait with the subject of *Plymouth Adventure:* "He asked me if I were interested in doing the role [of Dorothy Bradford]," Tierney said, "and that led to the commitment." Two nights later, Tracy and the Kanins were back again, this time with Tierney alone completing a foursome.

"*Pat and Mike* with George Cukor was an agony to me," Katharine Hepburn admitted. "He kept saying, 'Sink the putt, Kate.' Well, the putt was thirty feet on a sloping green. 'Sink it. Sink it.' And Babe Didrikson was in that picture, and she finally taught me how to sink that putt. When I sank that putt, I really just jumped up and down for joy. But George never real-

Tracy unwillingly joined a band of American acrobats onstage at
the Lido in Paris. He later claimed to have destroyed all the photographic evidence, but this shot survived. (SUSIE TRACY)

ized how difficult anything was. At all. He was the funniest director in the
world to have direct that picture."

Cukor was, of course, on the show because he had directed all the previous films the Kanins had written—three so far. He knew nothing of
sports, had no interest in such matters, but thought of such a deficiency as
a positive. "Too many pictures dealing with golf have been approached
from the expert's point of view," he reasoned. "Nine hundred and sixty-five
out of 1,000 moviegoers don't know anything about the fine points of the
game either. Therefore, if I can stage a golf match in a way that will interest
me, then I'm pretty sure it will also look good to those 965."

The screenplay revision of October 5 recast Pat as a basketball coach at Southern Tech, engaged to Alan Fletcher, who also works at the school. She enters a golf tournament, but her confidence in herself is undermined by Alan's presence in the gallery. Mike sees her, gives her his card, and the script begins to crackle. Accompanied by the Kanins, Hepburn arrived in Los Angeles on October 10 so that talks with Cukor could begin. "Spencer," she said, "never used to join those conferences we had, George and Garson Kanin and Ruth Gordon—who wrote the scripts. We'd meet on the weekends, and Spencer would make a general comment on what he'd heard. During the reading of *Pat and Mike,* Spencer sat in a corner of the room when we had a reading of the script one night at George's house."

Tracy had already absorbed the words—which were not always easy to say in Mike's particular brand of "left-handed English"—and the character had been rolling around his mind since those conferences in Paris. Gradually, he had worked out a manner of speaking, a way of seeing things that brought the character to life, a minor-league sporting man "far more real and complex" than the person the screenwriters had imagined. "Spencer," said Cukor, "put his glasses on—we thought he would simply read the words—but suddenly he had departed and instead there appeared in his place this crude prizefighting manager of *Pat and Mike.* There was no sign of the Spencer Tracy we'd just seen there a minute before."

In time, Pat Pemberton became a widow, engaged to Collier Weld at a college in Gross Point, but Tracy's character remained essentially as he read it that first night, so vivid was the personality he brought to the role. As plans went forth for the picture, the seventh Tracy-Hepburn teaming in the space of a decade, Walter Winchell led his column of November 6 with a calamitous item: "M-G-M is sitting on an atomic bomb—trying to keep Katharine Hepburn's Greatest Romance *sotto voce.* Both stars are tired of Keeping It Quiet."

No one at the studio mentioned it, and if Louise saw it, she didn't say anything over dinner at Chasen's or during tennis with Bill Self and the kids. Spence drove up the coast to "paint the sea," contemplative as the start date for the picture grew near. Kate had committed to playing *The Millionairess* in England, her mother having "worshipped" every word the late George Bernard Shaw ever wrote. The engagement would require her to leave as soon as the picture for Metro had wrapped, and she would be overseas for much of the new year while Spence remained stuck in California with Schary and *Plymouth Adventure.* It didn't make for a happy time, and when the tests for *Pat and Mike* came back, the studio decided that Kate looked too thin and postponed the film three weeks while she fattened herself up. Spence, conversely, was too heavy and began popping a Dexedrine

Tracy and Hepburn with Ruth Gordon and Garson Kanin, screenwriters of *Pat and Mike*. (JUDY SAMELSON COLLECTION)

each morning to control his appetite. The goal was to lose twelve pounds by the start of production, bringing him to a trimmer 190.

With the picture temporarily on hold, Tracy turned his attentions to his new home on the Cukor property, which had been completed and would soon be ready for occupancy. Cukor seemed truly excited at the prospect of having such an illustrious tenant and involved Tracy and Hepburn in all the stages of design and construction. The plan had been to carve two homesites from a service yard at the very bottom of the director's somewhat kidney-shaped parcel, which was bordered on the west by Doheny Drive and on its southern end by St. Ives, a narrow and winding roadway that became almost impassable at times of heavy rain. He commissioned architect John Wolfe to design the two simple structures—the floor plan of the Tracy cottage forming an extended H, the master bed- and dressing room separated from the rest of the house by a recessed entryway and an outdoor patio—and had the plans sent for Spencer's perusal to the Arizona Inn, promising, in an accompanying letter, to drain the malarial swamps "to satisfy a certain touring actress" and assuring him that the sun regularly hit the property "once a week."

The living room was done in planks of wormy chestnut, an accent of used brick, painted a creamy white, framing a small fireplace. There was a pegged hardwood floor, cut on the bias, with French doors leading out onto the patio. Kate took charge of decorating the place, having purchased an old horsehair rocker—a naked frame, really—on Olvera Street and gotten it upholstered as a first step. An oak gateleg table, a basket base lamp, a desk fashioned from the valances of the apartment on Beverly. The colors were all subdued, the look warm and comfortable; it was a terrific contrast to the chichi of the main house. She saw to air conditioning, the fitting of the kitchen, shutters, towels, carpeting, draperies, a new vacuum cleaner, and had a corner cupboard and two pickled pear tables shipped out from the East.

Spence had been a renter for so long he had virtually nothing apart from his books and his things out at the ranch—and most of those would have to remain where they were. Kate finished with the furnishing of the cottage at 9191 St. Ives on December 12 and promptly left for New York and Connecticut to spend Christmas with her family. Tracy took occupancy six days later—on December 18, 1951.

They began shooting *Pat and Mike* on January 2, 1952, Ruth and Gar having, by then, returned east, where they could confer with Cukor via mail and by wire. The pressures on Hepburn were extraordinary, not just in the early golfing scenes, where she had to be even better than she was in real life (which was pretty good), but in the tennis scenes, where she would be partnered with stars like Don Budge and Frank Parker and pitted against Wimbledon sensation Gertrude "Gussie" Moran. Parker, who started in the days when men still played in flannel trousers, doubled as Kate's tennis coach, teaching her tournament form for the failed match against Gorgeous Gussie, when Collier's mere presence in the stands is enough to cause Pat to fumble the match.

The early material didn't involve Tracy at all, and his character didn't make his appearance until the second reel—long after the picture had been established in the audience's collective mind as Hepburn's. But where in the past she might already have started to grate on the crowd, her aloofness and self-assurance putting them on edge, she showed a winning vulnerability in *Pat and Mike* that was unlike anything else in her catalog. It comes as no surprise when she declines to throw a tournament at Mike's not-so-subtle suggestion. ("You see her face? A real honest face. The only disgustin' thing about her.") And she's plainly chagrined when she falters in the final moments of her match with Babe Didrikson Zaharias.

Tracy played with the cadences of the dialogue, the words having been arranged as they might form in the mind of a person like Conovan, ill educated but streetwise, a man within whom both wisdom and larceny collided in a jumble of syntax. "You see what happened anyway if youda been willing to happen on purpose you coulda been walking outta here with a nice bundle, with a bushel basket like I said? It just goes to show."

And when he admires Pat's retreating form in his Broadway vernacular, telling his diminutive associate, "Not much meat on her, but what's there is *cherce*," he not only reveals the early depth of his feelings for her but delivers one of the most warmly remembered lines in the history of the movies.

"Gar had written a line," said Larry Weingarten, "in which Spencer said of Kate, 'She's pretty well stacked.' I said, 'Do you know the meaning of this word? Kate is not well stacked. She has a small bust.' I pressured him, Cukor pressured him, and he came up with another line, 'There ain't much meat on her, but what there is is cherce!' It got the biggest laugh in the picture."

Kanin himself remembered writing the line as "choice" and that it was Tracy who insisted on delivering it as "*cherce*." Cukor, he said, made two takes, Tracy stubbornly sticking to the same reading for both. Mindful that Tracy "just flattened out" after the third or fourth take, Cukor obviously chose not to push it. "You've got to know that in directing . . . when to shut up, when to press."

For his part, Tracy liked to recall what George M. Cohan once told him: "Whatever you do, kid, always serve it with a little dressing." And so he took a perfectly serviceable line and, by filtering it through the prism of character, made it genuinely memorable. It was, as Bill Self learned, a process of refinement that never let up when he was shooting a picture. "Spence would say to everybody, 'Oh, I didn't sleep last night. I don't know what scene we're doing. Can I see the pages for a minute?' All nonsense, according to Hepburn. He was up all night running his lines. I know in the few little scenes I was in with him, or any scene where I was on the set when they shot it, God help you if you blew a line or missed your mark. He was very intolerant of other actors not being totally professional."

The sparring between Tracy and Hepburn lacked the sharp edges of *Adam's Rib,* Cukor achieving a gentleness and a lightness of tone that made the comedy seem effortless. The reason it worked, the director maintained, was that none of them took themselves very seriously. "We batted ideas around like tennis balls, we all *felt* the lines and situations without any kind of ghastly solemnity. If we all laughed, a line went in." And, as with Judy Holliday on their previous picture together, both took a paternal interest in Aldo Ray, the ex-navy frogman whom Cukor had starred alongside Holliday in *The Marrying Kind* and who was now playing Mike's dim-witted prizefighter, Davie Hucko.

It is in Mike's relationship with Hucko—"heavyweight champion of the world . . . in a couple of years"—that the true nature of his character emerges: small-time operator, disciplinarian, hustler, and patron to numerous hangers-on. When he comes down on Davie, he does so by demanding the answers to the Three Questions:

"Who made you, Hucko?"

"You, Mike."

"Who owns the biggest piece of you?"

"You, Mike."

"And what'll happen if I drop you?"

"I go right down the drain."

"And?"

"And stay there."

Pat signs a contract with Mike and his mysterious partners and is immediately put into training: no martinis, Mike tells her, no smoking, no late hours, no men "in any manner, shape, or form."

"What's to prevent me from smoking when you're not around?" she asks.

"When am I not around?"

"You don't expect to be watching me every minute . . . out of every . . . twenty-four hours . . . out of every day . . . do you?"

"If I have to, sure."

"Not sure I'll like that."

"Not askin' you to like it. But you'll see pretty soon I'll trust ya. Because you'll trust me. Because what's good for you is good for me and you for me, see? We're the same, we're equal, we're partners, see? Five-oh, five-oh."

Despite all this enforced intimacy, there is little to suggest the budding romance between Pat and Mike other than the care on his part, the glances on her part, the underlying attraction between the two actors playing the roles, the times again when their eyes locked, even when there was nothing more than a kiss on the cheek ("for luck") to suggest Pat's growing affection for her rough-hewn manager.

"I remember there was a scene in which Spencer massaged Kate's leg," George Cukor said. "No sex implied, but it was very sexy. You sensed the empathy between these two." Kate was stressed throughout the filming, being coached as she was in golf, tennis, baseball (the latter by Pinkie Woods, star pitcher of the Hollywood Stars, for scenes that were ultimately cut from the film), basketball, boxing, and judo (for a shot in which she clobbers two of Mike's "investors"). She was pushing herself—fear of mediocrity, fear of being only half good—and was battling to keep her weight up. It fell to Cukor to keep the production—as well as the strained relationship between his two stars—on an even keel. "George was like a big brother to Kate and Spence," Aldo Ray observed. "He was mother hen, nurturing them, holding them together."

With all the exteriors called for in the script, *Pat and Mike* was plagued by rain delays and ran over schedule. The company moved to Ojai in mid-February, finishing up there on the twenty-first. Hepburn was worn out, unsure of how the film would piece together, and had only a few weeks before she was due to leave for England and the start of rehearsals for *The*

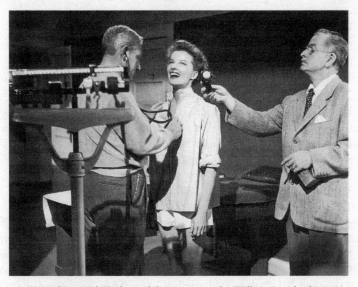

Tracy clowns with Hepburn while cinematographer William Daniels takes a reading. (AUTHOR'S COLLECTION)

Millionairess. When she left California, it was for Connecticut and Fenwick, and she would not return until summer at the earliest. Once again, she was putting a continent between the two of them, driving herself in a way that was extraordinary even for her. Tracy approached the filming of *Plymouth Adventure* with a renewed sense of dread, not only for the quality of the material he was playing, but for the time he would be trapped in Los Angeles when all he longed for was to be in London with Kate.

Gene Tierney wasn't a lock, at least initially, for the female lead in *Plymouth Adventure.* Schary resisted casting someone who wasn't an M-G-M contract player, and originally the talk had been of June Allyson doing the part. The film was populated with a number of British actors, Leo Genn and Barry Jones most prominent among them. With Hepburn gone, Tracy became almost unbearable to be around, sulky and petulant. When actress Dawn Addams, relatively new to Metro, was awarded the secondary role of Priscilla Mullins, the obligatory love interest and future wife of John Alden, Tracy could scarcely contain himself.

"I was having dinner with Spence at Chasen's," Bill Self remembered,

> and Clark Gable came in and sat down for just a talk. Spence said, "What do you know about an actress named Dawn Addams?"

Gable said, "I don't know anything about her much. She's a young contract player."

"She's playing Priscilla. She looks like she's made the voyage before."

"I don't know anything about her."

"Well, she's sleeping with someone. I have to tell you, this girl would not be in this movie if she wasn't sleeping with somebody."

Gable left, and a few minutes later Benny Thau came in. Spence called him over to the table. Thau sat down and Spence said, "How's everything?"

"Fine," he said, and at that point in waltzed his date for the evening. Thau said, "Oh, do you know Dawn Addams?"

Costume tests were made early in March, and Tracy's captain's outfit, with its knee-high boots, its braided coat, and its wide belt buckled tightly up around his belly, gave him a gnomelike appearance, rendering him shorter and rounder than he had ever before appeared on the screen, a sort of malevolent Mr. Pickwick of the high seas. Then he allowed them to darken his hair, which made him feel doubly ridiculous.

As the film's start date approached, Gene Tierney, to placate Tracy, was borrowed from 20th Century-Fox for a role that could have been played by almost anyone. Mollified, he permitted Dawn Addams to remain in the cast but drew the line at Peter Lawford, who had been set for the part of Gilbert Winslow, the affable scribe whose diary of the voyage forms the basis of a narration. "Lawford," said Frank Tracy, "was never prepared and was kind of an airhead, I understand. And Spence did, literally, tell him, 'Get the hell out of here!' "

Ten days prior to the start of filming, Lawford was shunted to the lead in a romantic comedy called *You for Me* and the role of Winslow was filled by John Dehner, a radio commentator and sometime actor who had recently completed a part in Metro's *Scaramouche*. Filming began on March 24, 1952, on M-G-M's Joppa Square, a grouping of exterior sets on Lot 2 that stood in for medieval Europe in scores of pictures and incorporated the Prussian castle used in *Conquest* (1937).

Since all the important action took place aboard the *Mayflower,* director Brown made the pricy decision to shoot the entire picture in sequence, keeping the whereabouts of the individual passengers and crew members straight and ensuring that the movements of the facsimile vessels matched the miniature work, which was extensive and taking place concurrent to the filming of the live action sequences. (The ship's principal model was one-eighth the size of the one on Stage 30 and crewed by a set of mechanical dolls.) Some five months of second-unit footage had been shot off Honduras by Arnold Gillespie's crew, covering all possible weather conditions and times of day for background plates.

"Spence got me a part in *Plymouth Adventure*," said Bill Self.

I had nothing to do in it; Clarence Brown hated me, I'm sure, because he didn't know what to do with me. I made five pictures with Spence, and in three of them I actually had a little something to do. In this one, I had nothing to do. One day, John was coming over to have lunch, and Spence came to me and said would I take John to lunch? I said, "I'd be happy to, but, you know, I'm in the first scene after lunch, doing nothing, but I'm in it." And he said, "There's not going to be a scene after lunch." I said, "Oh?' And he said, 'Yes. I have sent for Dore Schary. I'm getting out of this picture." Now, most people would not "send" for the head of the studio, so I said, "What's the matter?" He said, "Oh, I look like an idiot in this costume, they should have gotten Errol Flynn to begin with, it's a boring story, I regret that I'm doing it, and I'm going to tell Schary I'm out. Take John to lunch. Don't worry about the time you get back. I guarantee they won't need you." I said, "Fine." So I went to lunch. I have no idea what happened at that meeting, but when I came back everybody had been ready to shoot the scene, so Spence was back in the movie. But the thing that impressed me and I remembered was that he didn't go see Dore Schary, Dore Schary came to the set to see him.

Miss G., pregnant with her second child, had retired, leaving Tracy with a new secretary. For one of the few times in his career, he seemed to be having trouble breaking character between takes, and he was as irascible as Captain Jones over the fifty-seven days needed to shoot the film. He took an immediate dislike to actor Lloyd Bridges, who, as Coppin, the master's mate, was the captain's henchman and the most prominent member of the ship's crew. "I don't know why he hated me," Bridges said years later, shaking his head. Bill Self could recall Tracy referring to Bridges dismissively as "that *radio* actor," as if someone who worked in radio was the lowest form of life. "Tries to do too much with his voice" was all Tracy would offer by way of explanation.

"Oh," said Reggie Callow, who was first assistant director on the show,

he moaned and groaned all through the picture . . . When we went on the deck it was raining, and the actors had to stand with the water coming down. Tracy would say, "I'm an old, old man; I can't do all these things." So we had to baby him. He wasn't an old man;

he was in his fifties then, but he always kept saying what an old man he was. If you gave him a ten o'clock call, and you didn't get to him until about 10:10, he'd raise hell. He'd say, "Why am I called in at ten and it's now ten after ten?" So I had a great idea: I said give him an eleven o'clock call, and if at ten-thirty we realized we weren't going to get to him on time, I'd say, "Mr. Brown, would you mind skipping the next setup and set up Tracy?" So at eleven Tracy would walk in; he was always ready. I'd say, "Spencer, we're ready for you." And he'd say, "Oh boy, you're the greatest." After he did the first shot, he wouldn't mind sitting in his dressing room for the rest of the day without being called. But he had to get that first shot on time.

Predictably, Tracy picked up a cold, which didn't improve his disposition. The tension between Schary and the actor he professed to admire above all others only seemed to mount during the filming of *Plymouth Adventure,* and it came to a head on May 7, when an item in Mike Connolly's column in the *Hollywood Reporter* suggested "some fur" would fly over an interview Schary had given Lloyd Shearer for *Theatre Arts* magazine "in which Shearer writes: 'The old Mayer group of stellar personalities—Gable, Garson, Astaire, Pidgeon, Tracy—is just about washed up with today's predominantly young movie-goers, and Schary must find replacements.'" Schary heard from "three or four sources" that Tracy was "steaming" after having seen the item in Connolly's "Rambling Reporter" and he quickly drafted a letter denying that he ever said such a thing.

"To have this nuisance take place at any time is a lamentable experience for me," he wrote, "but I wanted to write to you and tell you, firstly, that it should not concern you as an artist; and, secondly, that it must not concern you in terms of annoyance at me. In these awful days of tension and quick tempers and strained relationships, I must ask you as a friend and as a man of good will to dismiss directing your anger against me and the studio, because you must know, if you think about it, Spence, that such an attitude does not in any way reflect our thinking about you. I have told you before—and I'll tell you again—I love you."

Having just passed his fifty-second birthday—and with his repeated lamentations about being "an old, old man"—it may have been important for Tracy to prove himself with a younger woman. Kate was in London, Louise busy with the completion of the new building. The Kanins were in New York, Cukor was in Europe, Carroll and Dorothy on a cruise. Gene Tierney, at thirty-one, was becoming increasingly aware of her wild mood swings, a symptom she would eventually come to recognize as manic depression. She was seeing actor Kirk Douglas, and in his autobiography,

Douglas described an endearingly quirky young woman who had a lovely overbite and insisted on his entering through a window when he came to see her at night. ("Maybe it was an aphrodisiac. I didn't question it.") Douglas made the mistake of telling her that he didn't want to get married—a sentiment he innocently thought they shared—and it seems it was around this time that Tierney chose to involve herself with Tracy. Apart from being one of the world's most beautiful women, she was a bright gal and a lively companion. "When my mood was high, I seemed normal, even buoyant," she said. "I felt smarter. I had secrets. I saw things no one else could see. I could see evil in a toothbrush. I could see God in a light bulb."

The intensity of the relationship—at least from Tracy's perspective—was evident when Tierney informed Kirk Douglas that she would be marrying her costar while production of *Plymouth Adventure* was still under way. "This all happened so quickly, I didn't believe it," Douglas wrote. "She showed me a saccharine letter that he had written, telling her that he wanted to arrange things so that they could go off together. 'Gene, I don't believe it,' I said. 'First, Spencer's married. He'll never get divorced. Second, he has a very intense relationship with Katharine Hepburn, and he'll never give it up.' " Douglas, of course, couldn't have known Tracy's state of mind, nor Tierney's exact motivation in telling him they would be wed. "I made the mistake of being blunt about not wanting to get married, and here was another man writing a flattering letter telling her what she wanted to hear."

All the while, Tracy was in touch with Hepburn by cable, advising her of plans to sail for England in June, possibly with the Kanins, possibly alone. The Clarence Browns and L. B. Mayer had taken him to dinner, and Old Man Mayer, he reported, was "absolutely insane" about the new house on St. Ives. When Kate sent reviews of her tour of the provinces, Spence wired back that they were wonderful, as were the initial notices for *Pat and Mike.* Tierney was committed to a second film for Metro, a Clark Gable picture to be shot in England, and since he was set to meet Kate in London as soon as he was cleared for travel, Tracy told Hedda Hopper he intended to heckle Gable from the sidelines as he played his romantic scenes with Tierney. Hopper commented: "Spence, who's been making love to Gene in his picture, thinks the King needs some lessons," pointedly adding that he would also be on hand for Hepburn's London opening in *The Millionairess.*

Tracy patched over his differences with Dore Schary and finished the movie, Brown boasting that they were able to make the entire movie on M-G-M's Culver City lot, save just one scene of the landing of the first settlers, which was done on a beach near Oxnard. "I never heard him tell anyone in the cast what to do . . . I never saw him tell anybody anything," Reggie Callow said of the director. "I don't know how the hell he ever made the picture."

CHAPTER 26

At Loose Ends

There is a fragment of black-and-white footage which constitutes the only filmed statement Spencer Tracy ever made on the subject of the clinic that bears his son's name. He stands at a microphone, eyes downcast, a hand tugging nervously at his bow tie. Behind him are seated Dr. Rufus von Kleinschmid, Los Angeles mayor Fletcher Bowron, and Goodwin Knight, lieutenant governor of the state of California. "This is certainly one occasion," he begins hesitantly, "where I may truthfully say that as hard as I try, I can find no reason, no excuse to bring motion picture acting into this particular occasion. Because there is no motion picture actor, living or dead, absent or present, who had anything to do with the building of this clinic. It was built through the inspiration of John, I suppose, in the beginning, by his mother, and by her—" And at that point the film runs out.

It was Saturday, May 3, 1952, and the clinic's new $250,000 complex at 806 West Adams was in the process of being dedicated. A crowd of 250 jammed the new auditorium—really a multipurpose room—and more clustered at the doorways, straining to get a look. Louise, her hands calmly folded in front of her, said the clinic was "as much a movement as it is a place, and wherever you find parents gathered together and helping their children, you find John Tracy Clinic." Then Spence, who had always determinedly remained in the background, was dragged into the meeting and spoke, as the *Los Angeles Times* reported, about a hundred words. According to the paper, the statement he begins in the film continued as follows: "—board of directors, and all of the others who have worked for it, the mothers and fathers of the children and all of the others who have helped." He was loath to acknowledge the money he had personally given over the course of the previous decade, even though the clinic would not have survived its first five years without his support. "I didn't do anything much," he once told his cousin Jane. "I gave them a few bucks to get started."

The building drive, when initiated in 1946, expanded the clinic's reach and established a broader fund-raising network than Louise had ever thought possible. In 1950, she was able to announce the purchase of one and a half acres of land near the USC campus after a substantial bequest from the estate of William Melvin Davey. And while the clinic was no longer dependent upon Spence's M-G-M income for its survival, he still gave $20,000 to $30,000 a year, a measure of redemption for which he was truly grateful. "This method of getting deaf children mainstreamed and educated early is really something new that Louise is doing," he said proudly, "and it is remarkable. It is ground-breaking."

He was in the midst of *Plymouth Adventure* and needed a reminder as to why he sometimes did the things he did on screen. Could he have gone freelance? Undoubtedly. Could he have exercised greater control over the pictures he made? Absolutely. But could he have managed the guaranteed

At the dedication of John Tracy Clinic's new Adams Boulevard complex with longtime wardrobe man Larry Keethe and daughter Susie Tracy. (SUSIE TRACY)

income that made his support of the clinic possible? Not quite so likely—at least not so that he could see. Metro paid him an annual salary of $300,000. To make that kind of money as an independent, he'd have to make two or three pictures a year—more than he was currently averaging—and when he laid off, there would be nothing at all coming in. Further, he really didn't know what he could ask on the open market and tended to devalue his own worth in comparison to others.

"Katharine Hepburn's best-kept secret will join her in London soon." It was Dorothy Kilgallen's lead item on June 5, 1952, and, of course, Kilgallen was correct as far as Tracy's intent was concerned. He had a date to fly east with Clarence Brown on the eighteenth and was sure of making a June 20 sailing of the S.S. *America* (on which Larry Weingarten had also booked passage). He declared on his passport application he would be gone four months, visiting England, France, Italy, and Sweden "for the combined purpose of business and pleasure" and told Louella Parsons he intended to rent a car and tour the continent. By the time he actually did set sail, however, he was on the *Queen Elizabeth,* not the *America,* it was July 1, not June 20, and his plan was to stay for no more than a month. On the ship were Walt Disney and his family, and Lewis W. Douglas and his wife Peg. Tracy, in a jocular mood, joined the Disneys one night for drinks. "Dad was kidding him about some woman who was chasing him all over the ship," Diane Disney, who was eighteen at the time, remembered. "At one point, he turned to me and started telling me about Susie and all the things she was doing. He was obviously very proud of her."

Tracy and the Douglases had met in England, where he was making *Edward, My Son,* and Lew was U.S. ambassador to the Court of St. James's. Since leaving the post in 1950, Douglas, an avid sportsman, had served as chairman of the Mutual Life Insurance Company. Douglas told the *Herald Tribune* he would do some trout fishing along the Test River near Southampton and see a number of old friends, including Prime Minister Winston Churchill. Tracy added that he and the Douglases "might visit Norway together."

In London Kate was a hit in *The Millionairess*—more so than anyone expected—and all Tracy and Weingarten could manage was standing room. Gene Tierney was in town, making Clarence Brown's picture with Gable, but Tracy spent a good deal more time with the actress' mother, Belle, than with Tierney herself. "My mother thought he was the most tormented man she had ever met," Tierney wrote of Tracy in her autobiography. "They had lengthy conversations about religion. She had returned to her Christian Science beliefs and could talk about them in an almost mystical way . . . A few times he asked me to lunch or dinner. He was relieved that my mother came along. These dates were perfectly respectable, but Tracy was watching the door in case Katharine Hepburn came in."

He was also stirring up picture material, having become enthused with Nobel laureate Pär Lagerkvist's novel *Barabbas,* the story of the thief spared crucifixion instead of Christ. The character's struggle to understand the nature of Jesus, his skepticism and his yearning to believe, held special resonance for Tracy, and he sent Dore Schary a script derived from the book, eager for his reaction. Schary came back almost immediately, saying he believed the script fell "far short" of a successful project for American audiences. "Believe it excessively brutal and in many instances highly censorable," Schary cabled. "Further feel that it is confusing in some aspects and that the final point will be remote to audiences at large." Bert Allenberg of the William Morris office communicated Tracy's desire to do it as an independent venture, and Schary offered to arrange a meeting with Nick Schenck to discuss the matter.*

Tracy also went to bat for Garson Kanin, who had written a comedy-drama called *A Flight to the Islands.* Based on a story by Elizabeth Enright, it offered a part for Tracy that was not unlike Stanley Banks, a put-upon family man escaping for a day to another town, another life. He gets a job, rents a room, applies for piano lessons, meets a girl and learns her story. Schary was enthusiastic at first, but then gave the script to Larry Weingarten, who didn't care for it at all, and to John Houseman, who said that he wasn't interested in doing it either. Deciding it wasn't material that could easily be dramatized, the production chief resisted an outright purchase, agreeing instead to an option deal which took months to settle.

Schary had just announced a slate of eighty-three features either completed, shooting, or in development, fifty-three of which were to be finished by January 1, 1954. It was an absurd number of films given the economic realities of the day, and he seemed overwhelmed by the sheer volume of product. "Unable to understand reply sent me [by] Schary ten days ago," Tracy wired Kanin in New York. "Stated all cleared, however confusion, slowness, and unawareness. You should understand by now plans indefinite. May slip from tightrope here any moment."

He did indeed slip from the tightrope in early August—not into the bottle, as Kanin may have feared, but into retirement . . . or at least a declaration of it. The announcement came in Stockholm, where Tracy had gone

---

* It is unclear whether Tracy sent Schary a translated copy of Alf Sjöberg's screenplay for a Swedish-language film of the same title, or Lagerkvist's own two-act play based on the book.

to see Alf Sjöberg's film of *Barabbas,* a work he described as "thrilling." Resigned to Schary's "absolute turndown" of an American version, Tracy told a man with the UP he planned to give up the movie business altogether. "When I have fulfilled my contract duties to Metro-Goldwyn-Mayer within some three years," he said, "I don't think there is anything else left for me than quit the screen."

The news, of course, went around the world, though nobody at M-G-M took it seriously. Then Kate had an attack of laryngitis that threatened to take her out of *The Millionairess,* and doctors advised her not to speak at all except when onstage at the New Theatre. Taking it all as a sign of exhaustion, Tracy was thinking of coming home when he received a telegram from the Kanins asking him to call their friend June Dally-Watkins at the Cumberland Hotel.

The business with Gene Tierney hadn't gone well, and Hepburn was so depleted it took everything she had just to get through the play each night. Spence, Kanin observed, was "[s]ort of at loose ends" and had "had a bad time in Paris" (presumably with Tierney, although he didn't say as much). When he told the Kanins on a call from London that he "needed a friend," Ruth shouted into the receiver, "Well, you've got two!" and they began making plans to join him in France toward the end of September.

Dally-Watkins happened along in the interim, a charming, self-assured Australian whom Gar and Ruth had met in Los Angeles through the Aussie costume designer Orry-Kelly. As a top fashion model, she had founded her country's first schools of deportment and was on a tour of the schools and modeling agencies of Western Europe. "At the appointed time," she recalled, "I saw him descend the hotel's marble staircase, glance at me and look away as if to seek out another face. It was obvious he had not been given a recognizable description, so I introduced myself and he seemed surprised. No wonder! Over afternoon tea he told me that Garson and Ruth had played a joke on him, saying I was an older actress from Australia and thought I would make a good mother for Debbie Reynolds' character in his next movie."

In London, June found Tracy solitary and "introspective," more interested in knowing about her than in talking about himself. "Spencer showed a romantic interest in me, and there was a spark between us that culminated in a kiss." She responded to his dry humor, the way he'd put things, and had no awareness of his relationship with Katharine Hepburn. "I was," she said, "twenty-five and stupid—well, let's say unworldly—and I was a single girl, traveling alone." They went to the ballet at Covent Garden, where he took her backstage to meet prima ballerina Margot Fonteyn. He didn't want to wait in Europe for the Kanins, though, and returned to New York before they had time to sail. ("Remaining here longer impossible," he wired.) June was scheduled to go on to Paris but promised to see him again when she returned to California.

While *Pat and Mike* had garnered excellent reviews, it was *The African Queen* that put Katharine Hepburn back in the public eye in a big way. Both she and Bogart drew Academy Award nominations for their roles in the picture, and Bogart subsequently won the Oscar for his work as Charlie Allnut after shrewdly and tirelessly campaigning for it. With Hepburn bringing *The Millionairess* to Broadway for a limited run, *Time* began preparations for a cover story on the forty-five-year-old actress and put researchers on the job in Connecticut, Los Angeles, and New York City. Kate's father, as always, refused to talk, as did the Kanins, but there were plenty of other witnesses willing to say their piece—stand-ins, crew members, journalists, and press agents among them. Cary Grant cooperated to the point of telling a couple of anecdotes, as did Howard Hawks, Joe Mankiewicz, George Stevens, and Eddie Knopf. George Cukor was circumspect, speaking only in generalities, and nobody would admit that she was in a long-term relationship with her frequent costar, Spencer Tracy.

Nobody, that is, except one.

Humphrey Bogart, according to *Time* staff writer Jim Murray, confirmed a romance did indeed exist, that he had seen Tracy and Hepburn together, and that Hepburn was "unaccustomedly subdued and effeminate" in Tracy's presence. And, he added, she didn't hog the conversational limelight on such occasions, a real departure for her.

"Ordinarily," Bogart said, "she talks a blue streak. We listened for the first couple of days when she hit Africa and then began asking ourselves, 'How affected can you be in the middle of Africa?' She used to say that everything was 'divine.' The goddamn stinking natives were divine. 'Oh, what a divine native!' she'd say. 'Oh, what a divine pile of manure!' You had to ask yourself, 'Is this really the dame or is this something left over from *Woman of the Year?*"

Tracy had remained in touch with Bogart over the years, but the two men weren't terribly close until *The African Queen,* through Hepburn, brought them together. Likely, as with Gable, it was Bogart's love of scotch that forced Tracy to hold him at a distance, but gradually Spence had developed the discipline to confront booze and stare it down, and his sobriety was no longer considered so precarious. Kate put them together—tentatively at first—and they found they enjoyed each other's company enormously, even as, socially, they were completely different animals. "Bogart and Tracy had a special rapport," said writer Peter Viertel, "based on their mutual admiration and strikingly devoid of professional jealousy."

Romanoff's was common ground for them both, but for entirely different reasons. There was nothing secluded about the hexagonal dining
room—even the entrance off the bar required a descent down a short flight
of steps that ensured all in the room had a chance to take notice—but
where Bogart used it as a showcase, a home away from home, a place to
hold forth, Tracy frequented the room because it was familiar ground and
no one was likely to bother him. The proprietor himself usually managed
the seating chart, a Lithuanian émigré and sometime actor who posed as
Prince Michael Dimitri Alexandrovich Obolensky-Romanoff, nephew to
the late czar of Russia, a harmless fiction that somehow suited a community
full of poseurs and phonies. "It's the parts, not the acting," Bogart told the
AP's James Bacon one day over lunch, commenting on his recent Oscar
win. "If it were acting, Spencer Tracy would win it every year."

"He was innately a marvelous actor," Lauren Bacall said of Tracy,

and also a hugely intelligent one. He and Bogie used to compare
notes on some of the actors who called themselves actors and what
they did during a scene. I remember they were discussing this one
actor standing in a scene. The actor would put his left hand on his
tie, and his right hand in his pocket. After a while he'd shift gears
and put his left hand in his pocket and his right hand on his tie.
Very funny stuff. They took no prisoners, those two men, because
they had real talent and they had respect for their craft, and the
people who called themselves stars, half of them were jokes.
Because of the studio system, some of them were in an exalted position they never should have been in. The talent did not require
that. It was great to be in their company, I must say. I just loved it.

The magazine, which hit the stands just prior to Labor Day, was largely
laudatory and mentioned only that Hepburn and Tracy were "fast friends."
Kate closed in London on September 20 and immediately returned to the
United States for minor surgery. She was in and out of Hartford in three
days, Tracy at hand the entire time. Emily Perkins, from her place in Maine,
urged a complete rest: "You and Spence should go to Ireland for three
months' quiet, go collecting shells by the seaside away from telephones and
so forth." George Cukor thought it "goddamn silly" for Kate to drive herself
so hard, closing one night, flying out the next day, then starting New York
rehearsals for *The Millionairess* practically without stop. "She's been arranging things on such a tight schedule for herself for the last three years or so,
driving herself to such a pace that I'm afraid of what will happen to her."

By September 29, Tracy was back at the Pierre Hotel, attempting calls
to the Kanins and June Dally-Watkins in Paris with no apparent success.

"Has she run off [with] handsome stranger?" he asked Gar and Ruth via cable. "Cruel after sweet letters. When coming here? Lonesome and discouraged and now broke." He also pressed for news of Gene Tierney, who had grown somewhat close to Ruth in the interim. "I was surprised," said Bill Self, "because once in a while Carroll and Spence would talk about some other affair that he was having or thinking of having while he was very involved with Hepburn. And I always—naively, I suppose—thought Spence had his affairs while he was married, before Hepburn, but when Hepburn came into his life, that was the woman of his life. And, apparently, that wasn't true."

Constance Collier reported Hepburn as resting, ready to start in again on *The Millionairess* and make the play as great a success on Broadway as it had been in England. "I can't tell you what we went through in London," Collier confided in a letter to George Cukor. "Kate was really ill, on the verge of a nervous breakdown. I think it is delayed shock. She has never let down since the death of her mother, and with the strain of the part and everything else, I think it piled up and really upset her terribly." Years later, Hepburn wrote of her mother's death and of the repression of grief that had by then become something of a tradition in the family.* "I stood—my mother—dead—my darling mother—the only mother I'll ever have—gone. I took her hand—still warm—unclasped her fingers from the sheet she had pulled up—and I kissed her and went down to Dad. No goodbyes. Just gone."

The Millionairess opened at the Shubert Theatre on October 17, 1952, but where the show had been widely acclaimed in London and the provinces, the reception of the New York critics was lukewarm at best. Kate's boisterous performance was sometimes unintelligible, even as she drew praise for the physical stamina she displayed in the part. ("Miss Hepburn can be understood clearly," Brooks Atkinson countered. "Perhaps that's the trouble.") Business was fine—they were sold out for the entire ten weeks of the run—and its star was reported as being in "fine spirits and good health."

Gar Kanin wrote Tracy at the end of the same month, saying that Gene Tierney's mother had called him but offering nothing more. Tracy took this as a bad sign and cabled back: NO REPORT GT GUESS BAD FOR OLD TOM. Concurrently, an item appeared in Kilgallen's column to the effect that Tracy was "facing a decision that could make front page news. If so, it will startle the public—but not show business." A few weeks after that, Walter Winchell compounded the news by suggesting that "Katharine Hepburn's long-time heart" would seek a "special dispensation" to marry.

---

* As her early stand-in, Adelaide Doyle, recalled, "She was very close to her family and she called her mother all the time—maybe every day."

Curiously, it was around this time that Tracy sent Louise and Susie, who were in New York on a brief holiday, backstage to see "Kath" after a performance of *The Millionairess.* Susie had already met Hepburn on the set of *Adam's Rib,* but Louise had seen her only on screen, never in person, and how Spence imagined it going is anyone's guess. Susie was completely unaware of the relationship between Hepburn and her father—they were simply coworkers as far as she knew—but Louise would remember the strained cordiality of the encounter and the attention Hepburn lavished on her twenty-year-old daughter.

That Kate was caught off guard is almost a certainty, but why did Louise do it? Did she fix her adversary with a knowing glare? Did she insert a little dig into her greeting or her reaction to the performance? Did she gain any satisfaction from having the upper hand for once? Had the column items somehow emanated from Hepburn's camp? And was suddenly putting his wife and daughter on display Spence's way of answering them? Or, in choosing to go, was Louise answering them herself? "Don't ever leave me," Spence had said to her, and she assured him that she never would.

Kanin finally wrote Tracy on December 1, saying it was about time to accept the fact that it was "good-bye Charlie" with respect to Gene Tierney. She had recently been in the papers, photographed on the arm of Prince Aly Khan, the notorious playboy and estranged husband of actress Rita Hayworth. Gar asked Ruth to call Tierney at her hotel and see if she could find out exactly what was going on, but Gordon had already had a "great big girl-talk" on the subject, and it seemed that Tierney had been deeply stuck on another man—the implication being that it was Kirk Douglas—and that his alleged treatment of her was what drove her back into the "maelstrom of Paris highlife." Tracy, in a handwritten Christmas letter to Gordon, complained she was "difficult to get information" from ("like you just refuse any word of talks with G.T.") but then acknowledged having received a "nice letter from her—sort of the 'kiss off' " that appeared to end the matter once and for all.

Plymouth Adventure was released on November 28, 1952, a Thanksgiving turkey that inspired more respect than praise, more lip service than business. While Clarence Brown readily admitted it was "not my best, not by any means," Dore Schary was relentlessly optimistic about the picture, advising Tracy by cable of how well it was doing in preview ("cards wonderful, reaction good") and how well Tracy's performance had been received ("You are simply great and everybody says so.") The press preview on October 20 had been polite, dignified, like the opening of a museum exhibit. The notices carefully embalmed the picture, Bosley Crowther labeling it "a thoroughly respectful and respectable adjunct to the schoolroom histories," while Otis Guernsey, in the *Herald Tribune,* called it "the kind of film in which the characters cannot help being self-conscious of destiny."

Most reviewers noted the truly spectacular storm sequence at the movie's core but reserved comment on the pallid on-screen romance between Tracy and the doomed Gene Tierney. Business was weak from the outset, with its first-day gross comparable to that of *The Magnificent Yankee,* a modestly filmed play that boasted Louis Calhern and Ann Harding as its nominal stars. It went on to lose $1.8 million on total billings of just over $3 million—a disastrous showing.

Near the end of his life, Schary contemplated what exactly happened with the picture. "It sank!" he said after thinking a moment. "*Plymouth Adventure* had some wonderful things. The voyage. Clarence Brown did some great things. But we made terrible mistakes in the casting. I thought some of the people were good. I thought Tracy did well, Gene Tierney was nice, Leo Genn was properly stolid, but Van Johnson was a thorough error, just terrible. It just never worked. Maybe because pictures where they wear long knickers and those big collars can't be made real. They can't come to life. I wanted that picture very badly; I fought for it. But it was a loss."

When Ruth Gordon began dabbling in autobiography, the results came in the form of articles in *Forum* and the *Atlantic Monthly.* In 1944 she collected her experiences as a hopelessly stage-struck young girl living on the outskirts of Boston into a play called *Journey to a Star.* Two years later, a substantially revised version titled *Years Ago* opened at the Mansfield Theatre in New York with Fredric March as Clinton Jones, Florence Eldridge as his wife Annie, and Patricia Kirkland as the playwright's own younger self, Ruth Gordon Jones. The play was a modest hit, lasting 206 performances, and March walked off with the Tony that season for Best Actor. Just prior to its closing in May 1947, M-G-M was erroneously reported as having agreed to pay $425,000 to bring *Years Ago* to the screen, an astounding sum for the time. Much later, the price was fixed at a more realistic $75,000, and Metro acquired the rights with the understanding that Spencer Tracy was to star in it.

The screenplay was drafted over the summer of 1951, then put on ice as *Pat and Mike* and *Plymouth Adventure* took precedence. By the fall of 1952, the picture was moving toward production with Debbie Reynolds in the part of Ruth, an idea that had followed the property since its purchase. Tracy was happy to do the picture, but was against the casting of Reynolds, and over the space of sixteen months did everything he could to scuttle it. The first salvo came in the form of a letter from Garson Kanin to George

Cukor in August 1951. Tracy, Kanin advised, was "not at all convinced" that Reynolds was the best possible choice, worried, perhaps, that the picture would be burdened with "the usual sweetening of songs, dances, and funny sayings" (as some early coverage had threatened). Gar urged open minds, as Ruth's dream was to see Tracy in the part of Clinton Jones and she didn't much care who played herself. The name of Wanda Hendrix was briefly floated, then it came down in Sheilah Graham's column that Reynolds was out because she was "too old" for the part—she was twenty at the time—and that the role would likely go to Margaret O'Brien.

Cukor, however, wasn't willing to give up on Debbie Reynolds quite so easily and shot a test of her in September 1952. "I'm keeping my fingers crossed," he wrote Ruth, "I think we've got our girl." But then he soured when he saw the footage and wondered if she was "exceptional enough." Her strength was in her averageness, he said, and she had never before played a straight—that is, nonmusical—part. He suggested tricking her up a bit to give her a little character but lamented how very little of the "odd fish" there was about her. Tracy liked Reynolds, thought her clever enough but felt very much the same as Cukor. And neither of the Kanins thought much of the test, Ruth not minding it so much as Gar, who judged it a lot of "superficial nonsense." Walter Plunkett was hard at work on Reynolds' clothes, but the casting of the part still wasn't settled when, on November 18, Tracy wired Kanin at St. Moritz:

MEETING S[C]HARY NOTHING RESOLVED. LOOKING GIRLS. AFRAID WORD WILL BE GO AHEAD PRESENT SETUP. UNBELIEVABLE LACK HELP BY PRODUCER. ONLY COURSE WOULD BE REFUSAL DO PICTURE WHICH OF COURSE WILL NOT DO.

With the start date fast approaching and no one else on the horizon, Tracy and Cukor went jointly to actress Jean Simmons, who was under contract to Howard Hughes and had recently starred for M-G-M in *Young Bess*. Simmons knew Tracy casually, as he occasionally came to the house to play poker with her husband, actor Stewart Granger. "He had the most wonderful sense of humor," she said. "Wicked Irishman, you know—with a twinkle. I don't know how other people felt about him; I just adored him."

She leaped at the part and the opportunity of working with both Tracy and Cukor. Dore Schary, who had resisted the change from Debbie Reynolds, acknowledged that Simmons was more interesting, more ambiguous in her gifts, more likely, in terms of her looks, to grow into the woman who was to become Ruth Gordon. As Ruth herself wired on the twenty-seventh:

MAD ABOUT JEAN SIMMONS. SHE WILL BE ABSOLUTELY
GREAT.

With Simmons set, they turned to the matter of casting the mother, a part nearly as vexing as that of Ruth. Early on, the Kanins had mentioned the possibility of doing the picture to Helen Hayes, who seemed "extremely interested" and dubious as well. "But would Spencer want me in the picture?" she asked. "He usually prefers younger girls." They later talked of Shirley Booth, but Booth was in rehearsals for *Time of the Cuckoo* and unavailable. Tracy liked Dorothy McGuire, but the studio thought the $75,000 she asked excessive. Her agent, Kurt Frings, suggested Teresa Wright, whose salary was more in line with what Metro was willing to pay. Cukor said he liked Wright well enough but thought her a bit on the dreary side. Maureen Stapleton and Jane Wyman were mentioned, as was Uta Hagen (whom Garson Kanin considered "one stunning actress"). In the end they settled on Wright, Cukor having decided she didn't have to be dreary: "I think she can have some edge and get the comedy out of the part. At least we'll see."

Particular care was given the design of the sets, which were as true to the original rooms of the Jones house as humanly possible, given the demands of the camera crew and the staging of the action. Cukor and Ruth Gordon made a trip to the Wollaston neighborhood where she grew up, and where there were still neighbors who remembered her. They ended up, he noted proudly, with six volumes of reference—snapshots, interiors of Mellin's Food Company (where Ruth's father worked), dressing rooms, hotel interiors, etc. "There was," said Teresa Wright, "a lot of talk about the preciousness of the research."

Filming was set to begin on December 15, 1952. There was concern over the title—*Years Ago* implying a nostalgic riff for the elderly—and the Kanins suggested *Fame and Fortune* as a substitute. With the sets already standing and the film comprised mostly of interiors, Cukor insisted on two weeks of rehearsal, after which he proposed to shoot the entire picture in just three weeks.* It was, as Jean Simmons later noted, "most unusual" but the ideal way of getting such an intimate production up on its feet. Mastering the American accent was the most difficult part of the job for the London-born actress, and she worked with a coach over the entire course of production. "There was a wonderful woman," said Cukor, "who was a most distinguished voice production teacher, Gertrude Fogler, and Jean is a very talented and accomplished actress, and within a week she sounded exactly like an American girl of that period and of that class and did it very subtly."

---

* The official schedule was twenty-four days.

After six days of rehearsal, Tracy wrote Garson Kanin in Paris: "We are going along well with the work. The girl 'Ruth' is, I venture to say, just about the greatest talent these old misty rum-soaked eyes have seen! 'Pipe' and very short haircut—characterization for Clinton—hair short for 'youth,' so they told me, since mother is played by Shirley Temple.* Otherwise, same old fellow as in *Plymouth Advent[ure]*, which is playing to the worst business since they took the hay out of the balcony."

June Dally-Watkins, meanwhile, was back in Los Angeles after her grand tour of Europe, gathering marriage proposals as she went and expressing "pretty deep stuff" (Kanin's words) on the subject of Spencer Tracy. In Rome, however, she had become involved with actor Gregory Peck, who was much closer to her own age, and who invited her to accompany him to Paris, a proposal she fearfully and foolishly—as she later acknowledged—declined. By the time she got back to California, she was homesick and eager to return to Sydney. Tracy had a car and driver meet her at the airport.

"He had also organized my hotel accommodation and began to turn up his efforts to seduce me: 'Why stay at the hotel? Move in with me while you're in town.' Maybe Spencer would have cherished me, but I wasn't about to take the risk of finding out. By now I knew of his relationship with Katharine Hepburn and was curious as to why she never appeared or attended any of the social gatherings that I went to with Spencer."

Hepburn, of course, was still in New York, finishing up her run in *The Millionairess*. Tracy took June to the Bogarts' annual Christmas party on the twenty-fourth, and to Cukor's another night for dinner. "After I rejected Spencer's advances, he continued to treat me well and respect me. He even arranged for one of his cars to be at my disposal. It was the first time I had driven an automatic car, and it came with a remote control to open his garage door. I'd go around the block to his house again and again to test the remote control, such was its novelty value." Benny Thau invited her to the M-G-M lot and suggested the establishment of a personal development school for the studio's starlets. Arthur Loew was smitten as well and mounted a campaign to keep her in Hollywood. Kate arrived back in California at just about the time Dally-Watkins left for home, but she didn't stay for long.

"One time I was playing a scene," Jean Simmons recalled. "I was having a bit of trouble, and she sort of put her head around the corner. I heard him say, 'Get out of here!' I thought, 'My God, you can't talk to Kate Hepburn like that!' But I knew she was there, and I think that's why I was getting nervous."

---

* Teresa Wright's early movie roles were as a young girl, even though she was in her twenties. Born in 1918, Wright was thirty-four years old when she played Annie Jones.

The actual filming of *Fame and Fortune* got under way in January 1953. Tracy had lost weight and was in a far more agreeable frame of mind than for *Plymouth Adventure,* where his moodiness and his baiting of Dore Schary had been the talk of the studio. "He didn't seem intense at all," said Jean Simmons. "It just seemed like rolling off him, easy. Obviously, he'd be up half the night—working, working, working, and then would come on totally prepared. He would say to me, 'Listen, kid, just know your lines and get on with it.' No silliness or temperament—anything like that. Just get on with it."

Cukor was skilled at creating a comfortable work environment—a necessity when shooting in tight spaces—but had the annoying habit of telling actors how to say their lines. Simmons had never met Ruth Gordon, so she looked to him for the proper cadence of speech. "I had to rely totally on George Cukor, who was so funny because he would get up and play my character—and it was oh so much better than I could possibly do . . . George would say, 'This is how you do it.' And then he would go up to Spence—and they were great friends—and start to do it and Spencer would just walk away. He'd say, 'Shut up, George!' "

Clinton works himself into a state over money, the cost of food, the perpetual poverty he sees for himself. "I live on hash and stew and Louisiana cat meat, for all I know, and I got a taste for oysters and curry the way they used to fix 'em in Bombay." When he discovers a thirty-five-cent theater magazine in his daughter's room, he is apoplectic. "Thirty-five cents! Did you get stung thirty-five cents for this thing?" Cukor was struck by Simmons' response to the force of Tracy's fury: "Talk about people who can be scary. Spence could be scary. He and Jean Simmons adored each other, but when we rehearsed the scene his anger was so real that she started giggling. 'I know I'm old and not much good,' Spence said, 'but does this broad have to laugh in my face?' 'No, keep it in, Jean,' I said. 'When you're absolutely terrified you piss yourself with a kind of laughter. It's real." Said Simmons of Tracy: "I was fortunate enough to have known him before I worked with him, and he was oh such a help to me because when you saw him work, it didn't seem like acting at all. He just *was.* He was the most truthful actor I ever worked with."

When Ruth rebels at her father's dictum that she become a physical culture teacher, she sits her parents down and proceeds to assault them with recitation and song. "He loved and respected Jean Simmons," said Cukor,

who gave a wonderful performance, and there was a scene when she wanted to be an actress and she stood on the steps in their house [and sang] and she was starting things off rather badly. And Spencer looked at her and he did something very funny: for no reason at all, he looked at the mother as though she had talked this girl into doing something. But then he looked at her with this eloquent face of his and his face changed color. And I said, "That was lovely." He said, "Well, I remember when I told my father that I wanted to be an actor and he looked at me, this skinny kid with big ears, and he said, 'Oh that poor little son of a bitch; he's going to go through an awful lot.' "

As Tracy told it, it wasn't the disappointment his father felt at his son's not coveting a career in business, but rather concern the boy seemed to have so few of the essential gifts of an actor. "In the play it is so interesting," said Cukor, "that both Ruth and her mother are scared to tell the father about her ambitions because they think he would object on purely conventional grounds, that she would become 'fast,' etc. They under-rate him. He has none of those conventional scruples, he's just concerned that she be spared the disappointment and heartache in undertaking something for which she has no obvious qualifications." Tracy also recounted how hurt he was when he told his girl of his ambitions. "She all but laughed at him," Cukor related, "and it almost killed him when he overheard her making some cracks to her girlfriend. He must have been completely unlike her idea of what an actor should be, nothing like the leading man of the Milwaukee Stock Company—Bert Lytell, or a real matinee idol type."

As Clinton speaks of his own wretched childhood, his mother's suicide and workhouse conditions, he punctuates the scene with the building of a sandwich—slicing the bread, spearing the meat, retrieving the ketchup from the pantry, chewing and talking, chewing and talking. Actor Richard Burton had read the speech and was observing on the set that day. "He was devastating," Burton emphasized. "Devastating."

Tracy made it so eloquent, said Cukor. "He was funny and he had the authority to switch from comedy to rather serious [material] and did it wonderfully." And in the end, after promising to stake Ruth to a spell in New York, he loses his job and can no longer count on the bonus that was to have, in part, funded the trip. She can't go, he tells her, but her determination is fierce, and he listens with a growing sense of admiration and pride. ("He never acted listening," Simmons commented, "which is what a lot of actors do—they 'act' listening.") It awakens in him a realization that maybe she does have what it takes "if it's gumption that it takes to be an actress." He removes his cherished spyglass from the mantel, wraps it carefully in newspaper, and presents it to her as the most precious of commodities—a chance to do what she knows that she must.

In the hands of a lesser actor, Clinton Jones would have been a one-note performance, all bluster and broad takes, but in Tracy's care he became an amalgam of all the fathers of the world who want something more for their children than what they had for themselves—an education, a place to live, good food on the table, and a chance to do the work they love best. "When he sold that spyglass," Jean Simmons said, "it broke my heart."

Cukor completed *Fame and Fortune* a few days over schedule. Larry Weingarten thought it too long and was talking eliminations before they had even finished. Garson Kanin, meanwhile, was in Europe with his wife, urging Tracy to join them and plying him with news of available women. ("Do you know Evelyn Keyes? Ruth and I think her a charming girl . . .") While the deal for *Flight to the Islands* had been finalized, the script was "pretty stinkin' " (Tracy's words), and he was told that if he wanted to do it—since he owed the studio a second picture in the first year of his new three-year contract—he and Gottfried Reinhardt, who was set to direct the picture, would have to go to Paris to meet with Kanin and see if it could be whipped into shape.

Tracy wanted the trip "like he wanted a hole in his head" but he also wanted to clear his schedule for an outside picture and had few other immediate options—a "lousy" book called *Jefferson Sellick* and a story titled "Bad Time at Honda." Hepburn was in New York, catching the new shows with her *Millionairess* costar, actor-dancer Robert Helpmann, but her relationship with Tracy was at its nadir—her chronic absences having taken their toll—and she left for Jamaica with Irene Selznick before he arrived in town on February 23. Tracy and Reinhardt set sail aboard the *Queen Mary* on the twenty-fifth, arriving in Cherbourg on March 2. They dined with the Kanins the following night and connected with George Cukor on the evening of the sixth.

The topic of conversation wasn't so much *Flight to the Islands* as *Fame and Fortune,* which had been previewed to mixed results. Length was a problem—easily correctable in Larry Weingarten's estimation—but so was some of the throwaway dialogue Tracy permitted himself in the early reels. "I knew this would be a disturbing element," Weingarten reminded Cukor, "and, of course, there is no way to cure it. Audiences insist on hearing every word and understanding it, otherwise they are annoyed and the very thing you strive for is lost." Weingarten wanted to make some cuts that Cukor was resisting, but the quality of Tracy's performance was never in question. "The comedy, of course, played brilliantly, and Spence's scene at the table— where he speaks of his childhood—was applauded."

There was a lot of tweaking of the sound, and the picture had to be redubbed because Sidney Franklin thought Jean Simmons' voice "irritating if she uses the higher register." At Weingarten's urging, the sound department leveled out everyone's dialogue to the extent of distorting the performances, and Cukor and the producer clashed bitterly over it. Finally,

Dore Schary allowed the whole movie to be remixed after diplomatically permitting the two men to agree on the balancing of certain scenes. In addition, there was trouble over the title—practically no one liked *Fame and Fortune*—and somebody suggested *Father and the Actress* in a wan attempt to tie the film to the *Father of the Bride* franchise.

A preview at the Fox Theatre in Inglewood played better, with men and women liking it equally and 105 of 160 cards rating it very good or better. It had, Cukor observed, a curious effect on an audience: "At first they think they're seeing a 'homey' sentimental comedy. They dote on Spence, laugh at his jokes. Then they're taken aback by the strength of his feelings and his occasional bursts of violence. They're gradually forced to the realization that he isn't quite the old peach they'd first taken him for. But when the picture is over, the audience feels that they've met an extraordinary human being."

When Tracy docked at New York on March 26, 1953, he didn't return directly to the studio, as originally anticipated, but instead boarded a plane for Cuba, where he was to meet for the first time with Ernest Hemingway, whose novella *The Old Man and the Sea* was to be the first outside picture allowed him under his new deal with Metro. *Life* had published the story in a single installment in its September 1, 1952, issue, an event in American literature that moved more than five million copies in the space of two days. Scribner followed with its hardcover publication, selling out on an initial print run of fifty thousand copies.

Hemingway's agent, Leland Hayward, was bombarded with calls from Hollywood—Bogart, Tracy, Jimmy Stewart. Alexander Korda phoned from London. Hayward referred them all to Alfred Rice, the author's lawyer, convinced it could never be filmed without destroying the honesty and simplicity of the original. It wasn't until Hayward connected the material to the popular stage readings of *Don Juan in Hell* and *John Brown's Body*—in which the actors worked in evening clothes—that he saw the performance of *The Old Man and the Sea* as a genuine possibility. He called Tracy, who was smarting from the tepid reception of *Plymouth Adventure* and squabbles over the fate of *Fame and Fortune,* and put the idea to him. The following day he wrote Hemingway: "Of all Hollywood people, the one that comes the closest to me in quality, in personality and voice, in personal dignity and ability, is Spencer Tracy."

Tracy thought it "a tremendous idea" and said, "What about the motion picture rights? Why can't we do this lecture idea, and after that do it as a motion picture?" Hayward detailed the problems he saw in filming the thing, of preserving the integrity of it. Said Tracy, "Let's make the picture absolutely as simply and honestly as we can—make it actually in Cuba—

make it silent—and I will commentate the whole motion picture." Hayward thought it a wonderful idea and told Tracy that if he wanted to do it, he would come on as producer—assuming they could make a deal with Hemingway.

Just after the first of the year, when Tracy was deep in the shooting of *Fame and Fortune,* Hayward came west, meeting with Bert Allenberg and, later, with Tracy himself. A fundamental misunderstanding arose: Tracy assumed that he would be playing the Old Man as well as speaking the voice-over. Hayward, on the other hand, assumed they would use another actor, maybe a Cuban, in the part. He wrote Hemingway at Finca Vigia, fearful the prospect of seeing Tracy in the role would "destroy the appeal of the venture" for him. "I can only tell you that he looks great—is as enthusiastic as a human being can be about doing anything—and is one of the biggest and most important stars in the motion picture business. He understands all the hardship he may have to undergo to make it—has no star-like ideas or theories—and in my own mind I feel he would probably be very believable as the Old Man—providing we could make him lean and hungry looking."

By February 1953 Hayward was talking widescreen and Cinerama and whether shooting the picture in Ansco Color would be preferable to Eastman. Eddie Mannix told them they were crazy not to make it in 3-D, and Fred Zinnemann, now a hot commodity with *High Noon* and *Member of the Wedding* to his credit, expressed a keen interest in directing it. The deal, as outlined by Hayward, called for a ten-year license on the rights for a price of $150,000, plus an additional $100,000 to be paid Hemingway for his services as screenwriter. Tracy would receive $150,000 as star of the picture, and Hayward $50,000 as producer. All three would split the net profits on an equal basis, with the film reverting to Hemingway at the end of the license period. The partners were looking at filming it in September and October, when, according to Hemingway, the weather would be at its "loveliest" (provided there were no hurricanes) and when both Tracy and Zinnemann would be available.

Hemingway urged Tracy to come to Cuba so they could "talk things over" and so that Tracy could see some of the old fishermen "before they die so that he will know things that cannot but be helpful to him when he takes it on the road." With *Flight to the Islands* set to start on June 4, Tracy traveled to Havana on April 3, a turbulent and unnerving flight that abruptly terminated when a typewriter fell from overhead storage, injuring a passenger and smashing into Tracy's leg. The plane made an emergency landing at Miami for x-rays, which showed that while the leg was swollen there were no breaks. The flight resumed at 4:00 p.m. "Rough to Havana," Tracy wrote in his datebook. "Ernest Hem[ingway] worth it."

Havana was sunny and hot. They visited Cojímar (the "Old Man's town"), did some fishing and swimming, and talked business with Hayward on the last day. Tracy reiterated what he had said before—that he was committed to filming the book and nothing more. "Hemingway," he said, "was afraid of having the book cluttered up with a commercial love story." On Easter, Hemingway inscribed for Tracy a copy of *The Old Man and the Sea*, "To Spencer Tracy from his friend Ernest Hemingway." He added: "Looking forward to the long fight we'll win together." He wrote to Alfred Rice, "We are in a big fight from now on in and can make a terrific killing if we make a great picture. But there won't be any great picture nor nothing unless Tracy and I carry the ball most of the time. He knows it and I know it. Everybody is going to have to work like hell and we are going to have to do the miracle stuff." In his summary to Leland Hayward, Hemingway said: "Had a very good and practical time with Spencer. We understand each other and get along fine. I feel like I'd known him about 150 years."

Tracy was back in New York only a few days when Louise reached him—very late at night—with word that their son John had eloped with a neighbor girl named Nadine Carr. The news didn't come as a complete surprise, as John had already come out with plans to be married, having raised the subject over dinner with his father as early as December 1951. "Din. John—Valley—John's Wedding!" Tracy wrote incredulously in his datebook. A few days later: "Din. Valley—John's Marriage Plans!" Neither he nor Louise was happy; the bride-elect was seventeen, a junior at Van Nuys High School, and scarcely mature enough for marriage. Neither, for that matter, was Johnny, who, at age twenty-eight, reflected the sheltered nature of his upbringing. "He believes that he lives in a world of peace and dignity and quiet, of gentleness and kindliness and smiling faces," his father once said of him. "Well, he is going to continue to believe that, so far as it is in my power." And Johnny did, naive as to the ways of the world, sunny and worry-free and as willful, at times, as a petulant six-year-old. "I think people thought, 'Well, for goodness' sake, let him do things himself!' " Louise mused in 1972. "I think I probably at times did much more for him than I should have. I went out of my way. He had so many troubles when he was little. He had such a difficult time that you just felt you had to [help] in any way, and while I don't think doing things for him . . . really did any good, sometimes it's all you know to do."

Spence's views were similarly conflicted, informed as they were by his own deep feelings of responsibility. "I only saw him and his son once," said Seymour Gray. "And his reaction—he sort of laughed, he was laughing at himself. He said, 'Oh my God.' He looked at the sky and all that. [I said,] 'What's the matter with you? This is a handsome, well-adjusted boy. What difference does it make?' He said, 'You don't understand. It's *my* fault. I did it.' Yeah. That set him, made the drinking even worse, because he had tremendous guilt related to this boy."

John's first view of Nadine was on horseback, and they were soon playing foot polo on Sundays, recruiting Nadine's half-sister, Eveline, and a neighbor boy, Don Elderson, to create a foursome. On December 20, 1951, the bride's family went ahead with a prenuptial compliment at the Carr home, twenty guests celebrating the prospect of a June wedding. Louise was aghast, unable to prevent her adult son from marrying, Joe Carr and his family seemingly happy to facilitate their daughter's entry into a rich movie star's family, even though she was underage and had yet to finish her schooling. When June came and went, Louise hoped the matter had blown over.

"I went to Las Vegas with them," Susie Tracy recounted.

> They asked me to go and I thought, "Well, I would rather be with them than to be here when they call to say what they've done." Because I knew that my mother was going to be upset, to say the least. So I thought I'd better be there. I went also because I wanted to be sure that everything went the way it should. And that I thought I should be there in order to send them off . . . I think she was pushing for it, because he went back and forth about it—"Shall I, shall I not?" John's friend Jim Marsters, who had been with him at Wright Oral School, tried to talk him out of it, and our cousin George Payson said the whole idea was "ludicrous at best." I felt they should have at least waited until she graduated—April to June isn't so very long—but, you know, we were kids. We didn't know what we were doing . . .
>
> Nadine called [my mother], I remember that, and then she put me on the phone. Thanks a lot. I mean, my mother was not happy from the very beginning. I don't know what I said to her. She wanted to know why I didn't stop it, and why I ended up going with them. Later, I wondered if they would have gone through with it had I told them I wasn't coming . . . Then they were married legitimately—legally—at the church the following day. We drove to Las Vegas, came back, and then they were married again the next afternoon. We were crossing the parking lot, going into the Episcopal church in Encino, and that was when my uncle Carroll made the classic line: "Well, Suze, never a dull moment in this outfit!"

John's father wasn't any happier than his mother, but what he had to say on the matter was never set down anywhere. His notes in his datebook abruptly stopped a few days before his son's wedding, but his agita-

tion was on full display in an April 13 telegram he sent from New York to
Ruth Gordon:

> STILL HERE. LEG NEEDS WATCHING. SHOULD FLY COAST
> FAST. FROM CUKOR TODAY WORST NEW TITLE: FATHER
> AND THE ACTRESS. THIS, RUTH, I PROMISE [I WILL]
> FIGHT WITH LIFE'S BLOOD. THAT MAY BE THE LAST PIC-
> TURE I EVER MAKE THERE, BUT IT WILL GO OUT
> [UNDER] THAT TITLE AND BAD DUBBING GEORGE
> DESCRIBES OVER L[ARRY] W[EINGARTEN]'S DEAD AND
> MY TORN BODY.

Gottfried Reinhardt returned from Paris infinitely more enthused
about *Flight to the Islands* than when he had left, Kanin practically having
written a whole new script. But Tracy had always been the one pushing it,
and most of the work and money put into it had been at his behest. It was
difficult stuff, a drama of the mind, an excursion from within, and breaking
the back of the story, figuring out how it could be done in filmic terms, was
no easy matter. Tracy's faith in Kanin, his ability to somehow do the impossible, was boundless, and he told Reinhardt on his last day in Paris that the
only thing that really worried him was that Reinhardt wasn't as enthusiastic
about the thing as he was.

When Reinhardt handed him the revised screenplay in New York, he
was 100 percent certain that Tracy was bound to love it. And then it was
Reinhardt who was dumbfounded when Tracy said after reading it, "This is
not for me." Said Reinhardt: "I first thought that he was joking, but then I
realized that I was to witness this strange mind pulling the final switch on
me. His actual objections were, incidentally, of a very minor nature . . .
What shocked me most, however, was that he suddenly seemed concerned
about Dore's reaction. He kept saying, 'I think Dore will be disappointed.'
And 'after all, Dore's suggestions have been more or less disregarded.' "

Back at the studio, both Schary and Mannix dismissed Tracy's behavior
as typical of his preproduction jitters. "I remembered Spence's original attitude toward this project when we were still on our way over," Reinhardt
said in a letter to Kanin. "I could not rid myself of the impression that what
he uttered in Paris was mostly lip service and that he never really wanted to
make this picture, at least not now." Schary thought the script much better
than it had been, but he still had serious doubts about the "clarity of the
theme." Charles Schnee, the line producer on the project, liked it very
much. Mannix, too, thought it much improved, while Kenneth
MacKenna, the studio's story editor, expressed disappointment. All had

considerable doubts about the commercial potential of a film so intimate, so lacking in romance, spectacle, excitement. When Tracy delivered the death blow over lunch with Schary, he spoke "purely as an actor," presumably with serious doubts about carrying so much of the load. After nearly a year's work, the plug was unceremoniously pulled on *Flight to the Islands* just six weeks before it was set to go before the cameras. Tracy never addressed Kanin directly on the subject, and Kanin never let on that he knew from Reinhardt exactly what had happened.

Besides, Kanin had other projects before Tracy: an idea for a picture based on Benjamin Franklin's years in France, to be written in collaboration with either Thornton Wilder or Bob Sherwood. Then another for him and Kate, to be made in Europe and known, at various times, as *Cat and Mouse* and *It Takes a Thief.* Kanin wrote the opening, which George Cukor described to Gavin Lambert:

> You were on a European train and you saw a lady in black sitting in one corner of a compartment, all alone. The camera moved very slowly up close to this lady—and it was Spence dressed as a widow. Then you discovered he was the head of a currency-smuggling gang based in Zurich. Spence was going to appear throughout the picture in different disguises. People in the State Department knew this chicanery was going on, and they got the best T-man from the Treasury—and it was Kate. She had this ruthless drive and purpose, and she was going to track him down and bring him to justice, like whoever-it-is pursues Valjean in *Les Misérables.* Then halfway through the picture she realizes she's stuck on him.

Tracy, Cukor suggested, may simply have felt that he and Hepburn were "getting too old" to do that sort of a film, but he just as likely was in no mood to make another picture with her, and neither, it would seem, was she in any hurry to do another with him. It appears she knew of his affair with Gene Tierney—Katharine Houghton believed so—and may well have been aware of the Kanins' role—particularly Gar's—in abetting it. Tracy, moreover, was wild at the prospect of doing *The Old Man and the Sea*— Pulitzer and, as it would turn out, Nobel Prize–winning material—and nothing else could be nearly so attractive. He acknowledged to Leland Hayward he was "perfectly willing" to make a comparatively "bum" movie in order to get sprung from M-G-M to make *Old Man,* but instead he made a handshake agreement with Eddie Mannix, promising, in effect, to make two pictures for the studio during the second year of his contract, bringing them current with three pictures for the first two years of the deal. Metro, in turn, would distribute the Hemingway subject but would otherwise have no direct participation in the project. And so, one by one, the stories Kanin proposed for Tracy all faded away.

Tracy began a sixteen-week vacation on June 16, traveling to New York to meet up with the Hemingways, who were preparing to sail for Europe, and to undergo what had become his annual checkup routine at Peter Bent Brigham Hospital in Boston. He considered doing *The High and the Mighty,* an original story for the screen about a seemingly doomed airliner for Duke Wayne's production company, Wayne-Fellows, but was put off by the knowledge that Bill Wellman would be directing the picture. "It's a real, honest story, just full of enthusiasm," Wellman said. "And Tracy read it and thought it was lousy, wouldn't do it." Reluctantly, Wayne ended up playing the role of the pilot himself and the picture became one of the outstanding commercial hits of 1954. It also garnered six Academy Award nominations, including one for Wellman as Best Director.

Tracy, it seemed, wasn't much interested in doing anything other than *The Old Man and the Sea,* and due to Hemingway's travel schedule—which pretty much obliterated the rest of the year—that wasn't going to be possible anytime in the immediate future. Kanin, who with Ruth was spending the summer on the French Riviera, implored him to come join them at Cap Ferrat: "I am absolutely convinced that you would love it here, and that the climate and atmosphere would be highly beneficial. Good food and pasteurized milk abounds, and what you would love most of all would be the peace of it."

On August 1, Tracy compliantly notified Metro that he was going to Europe, first to Cannes to see the Kanins, then on to Paris and London. Ten days later, with Tracy already in France, Louella Parsons phoned Eddie Mannix to check the persistent rumor that M-G-M was buying out Tracy's contract. "Far from it," Mannix told her, confirming instead that Metro would be releasing *Old Man* as Tracy's picture to follow *The Actress* (as *Fame and Fortune* had come to be titled). Parsons, however, was aware of Tracy's growing disgruntlement with the studio and went on to report that he and M-G-M would be ending their "long and happy association of over 18 years" after he completed the two remaining pictures on his contract. Hedda Hopper, apparently noting the Parsons item, mentioned *Bad Day at Honda* as a story purchase for Tracy, naming Sam Zimbalist as producer and George Sidney as director. "Looks like Spence's co-starring days with Katharine Hepburn are over," she wrote with obvious satisfaction.

The Kanins were waiting when Tracy stepped off the boat at Cannes, and they all drove back together to Cap Ferrat. Tracy fell in love with the place immediately, and they were all splashing around in the Mediterranean before noon. "It's no more than what we deserve," he said contentedly, settling in for a stay of indeterminate length. Home was Les Rochers, the villa that Paris Singer, an heir to the Singer sewing machine fortune, had built for dancer Isadora Duncan. The food gave him trouble at first—his ulcer was acting up—but the next morning he was up early and off to Mass. "He didn't speak one word of French," Kanin commented, "but, still, he went to church that morning and came back quite happy."

Tracy mailed an oversized picture postcard of the historic village to Louise in California. "This is it," he wrote. "Old Florentine, brought piece by piece. Fabulous swim Mediterranean outside door. Good trip. Present fighting pylorics, etc., but have hopes for this. Swim, long walk yesterday."

He seemed to be having such a marvelous time that Gar gingerly raised the possibility of his ending the "shocking routine" of too much coffee, Dexedrine, and sleeping pills at night. He wasn't defensive, as Kanin might have feared, and promised to make a real stab at cleaning himself up. They talked about *Flight to the Islands* and *Cat and Mouse,* and then Tracy noticed a little rash on his side. Gar and Ruth tried telling him that it was nothing, but a doctor promptly diagnosed it as shingles (*zona* in French). As the doctor began treating the condition, his patient "suddenly got worried" about an operation that Kate had undergone. Spence hadn't known about it but apparently found out after the AP picked up on the news and the *New York Times* printed it. By then, France was paralyzed by a general strike, almost all of the nation's two million public workers having walked off their jobs, and it was impossible to phone or telegraph. With Tracy increasingly anxious, the inflammation plaguing him stubbornly refused to clear up. Finally and reluctantly, the Kanins drove him to Nice, where they put him on a plane bound for London. He kept promising to come right back, but they somehow knew that he wouldn't.

Kate, whose surgery had been for skin cancers, flew to be with him in England, and it was there that they enjoyed a reunion, having had only minimal contact with one another since the completion of *Pat and Mike.* However good it was for Tracy and Hepburn, who were still in London together a month later, Kanin lamented the event as an opportunity lost.

"It was very, very sad," he wrote. "The main reason for the sadness was that if only everything hadn't gone wrong, that place would have proved a godsend to Spence. I think he would have piled up years of health, and I know that he would have wanted to stay quite a long time."

CHAPTER 27

A Granite-like Wedge of a Man

"T hat film . . . got more critical acclaim from the critics than any film I ever made in all the years," said Larry Weingarten, reflecting upon the curious commercial fate of *The Actress*, "and we didn't make enough to pay for the ushers in the theater . . . I like to think that that very week this picture was produced, color came into full bloom and CinemaScope. And we were black and white on a little screen."

The industry was indeed awash with new technologies: widescreen, 3-D, stereophonic sound, and a whole host of new color processes, all employed with the intent of providing audiences with an entertainment experience they couldn't get from television, where old movies were quickly becoming a programming staple. Dore Schary refused to be part of the panic, assuring a conference of exhibitors that "television will start to worry about us" if new pictures were good enough. "I have a hunch . . . people will ultimately accept television as something they can use when they choose to. I don't believe that singing commercials, quiz shows, and 20-year-old potboilers will ever take the place of movies and other healthy diversions."

It was an admirable stance in the spring of 1952, but by the following summer all bets were off, and even 3-D was no longer the grind house novelty it had been just a few months earlier. *The Actress* drew solid trade notices, *Variety* praising its "excellent word-of-mouth values," and the film

opened well at New York's Trans-Lux 60th Street, a former newsreel emporium usually given over to British fare like *The Holly and the Ivy* and *Tight
Little Island.* The bigger Broadway theaters were showcasing the bigger
M-G-M releases—*Mogambo, Torch Song, Lili, Julius Caesar.* Tracy's performance was warmly received, Bosley Crowther declaring it worthy of yet
another Academy Award. "For the vitality that Mr. Tracy puts into this role
of a poor but earnest father who is confused because his little girl is determined to become an actress is worth a bottle of vitamin pills. The sense that
he gives of a good man, harassed with making ends meet and with all the
other vague frustrations to which the domesticated male is heir, yapping
about his difficulties but bearing his burdens honorably, is such as to give
other humans the spirit and humor to bear their own."

The Actress left the Trans-Lux after a respectable eight-week engagement, scarcely noticed amid the hoopla accompanying a record run for *The
Robe,* which offered Jean Simmons in color and widescreen at the nearby

As Clinton Jones, flanked by Jean Simmons and Teresa
Wright in *The Actress,* the film version of Ruth Gordon's
autobiographical play *Years Ago.* (SUSIE TRACY)

Roxy. Left to fend for itself in an increasingly hostile market, the picture ended up posting a loss of nearly $1 million—a horrendous showing for a star of Tracy's caliber. Weingarten felt the film lacked a happy ending and had wanted to "frame" the story with the successful Ruth in a wraparound, an idea Cukor opposed.

"Failure," said Dore Schary, "is a more common occurrence than success, and most times, the reasons for failure are apparent—so you swallow and go on to the next effort. But *The Actress* was beautifully played, written, and directed, and was one of those failures that depress you. It's like pitching a no-hitter but losing one to zero."

Tracy arrived back in New York aboard the *Queen Elizabeth* on September 29, 1953, Hepburn following by air the next day. M-G-M had agreed to count *The Old Man and the Sea* as one of the pictures on Tracy's contract, loaning him, in effect, to himself for a straight payment of $150,000. Production was set to begin in February 1954, provided Tracy could complete another picture for Metro in the interim. He had, however, rejected a screenplay for *Bad Day at Honda,* forcing a complete rewrite. And *Digby,* a sort of *Flight to the Islands* set in Scotland, wouldn't be ready for production until the completion of *Old Man.* When 20th Century-Fox put in for him in October 1953, Tracy's schedule was not only clear but, for once, he was eager to work.

In August, as Tracy was ailing in the south of France, Darryl Zanuck was spinning story ideas. At hand was a draft screenplay, a new version of *House of Strangers* set in the old west. At Sol Siegel's behest, Richard Murphy had taken Philip Yordan's screenplay for the earlier picture, which had been directed by Joe Mankiewicz, and transposed it with such fidelity that Zanuck feared they had "adhered too closely to some of the elements that made the original picture a box office disappointment even though it was a fine picture."

A downbeat tale of family feuds and hatreds, its principal motivations were money and lust, things that, in Zanuck's estimation, always produced "a sort of sickening feeling in the pit of the stomach." To take the curse off it all, he proposed a racial divide: three older sons against a younger brother by a different mother—an Indian. "The boys are now only half brothers. Joe [the youngest] is only half-caste. Matt [the father] is the squaw man . . . I can see only Spencer Tracy as Matt. With contact lenses, Jeffrey Hunter would make a wonderful Joe. He is young and he has guts and he has high cheekbones. The other three brothers should be on the Irish side like Tracy."

The deal for *Broken Lance* was set in mid-November, bringing Metro

$250,000 for ten weeks. Astonished at the price, Tracy exacted $40,000 of the amount as a donation for the clinic. He then lay low in Los Angeles, speaking with Cukor mostly by telephone and scarcely communicating at all with the Kanins, who, by then, were situated in England. He was back in New York with Hepburn when the loan to Fox was announced to the press, the two of them spotted as they crept into a performance of *Teahouse of the August Moon.* Kate had committed to filming *The Millionairess* in England with Preston Sturges adapting and directing. It would put her in London at just about the time Zanuck's western was set to begin, but with the Hemingway picture now delayed a year—until Tracy had finished out his M-G-M contract—they would likely have the summer together in Europe.

By Christmas, Tracy was in Palm Springs, polishing his riding skills and doing his best to drop some weight. Responding to a chatty New Year's letter from the Kanins, he wired:

STARTED NEW YEAR RIGHT. WHOOPING COUGH. NOW DESERT TRY TO LEARN WHICH END HORSE TAKE MY PLACE. AS CUKOR QUOTE OLE WESTERN STAR ON TRAIL TO BARN UNQUOTE.

He was back in Los Angeles when Emily Torchia made a seemingly impossible bid for his attendance at the Golden Globes dinner, where he was a likely win as Best Actor for *The Actress.*

"Of course I'm not going," he said gruffly.

"It's *very* important," she pleaded.

"I know. Howard Strickling told you to come down here and ask me." He thought a moment. "Okay, I'll go. IF you get yourself a date. And you get me a date . . . with Grace Kelly."

He knew Clark Gable had been squiring the twenty-four-year-old actress around London. Having been nominated herself as Best Supporting Actress for *Mogambo,* Kelly was a good sport about it and went, though she declined Tracy's invitation to go out for a drink afterward.* "But he got so much pleasure out of teasing Clark Gable," said Torchia. " 'I had a date with Grace Kelly!' "

That previous August, Tracy and Gable had reconnected in Paris, having not seen each other in nearly a year. They did the town, Tracy uncaring, for once, at the prospect of being seen in public. There was great cama-

---

* News photos of the two seated together at Santa Monica's Club Del Mar, where the event took place, were enough to prompt the following item in Dorothy Kilgallen's column: "Lovely Grace Kelly's newest admirer is a Hollywood star who has been Katharine Hepburn's close pal for years."

Tracy escorted Grace Kelly to the Golden Globes dinner in
Santa Monica, 1954, but the actress declined an invitation to
drinks afterward. (AUTHOR'S COLLECTION)

raderie between them, and Gable had already made the decision not to resign with Metro, his well-known antipathy for Dore Schary being only one
of the reasons. ("As far as M-G-M is concerned," said Clarence Brown,
"Dore Schary was the beginning of the end.") The studio had offered Gable
a new two-year contract but refused his demand for a percentage of the
profits on his future pictures, something virtually all top-tier freelancers
were getting. He resented never having gotten a piece of *Gone With the
Wind,* which had grossed nearly $100 million, and was mad at the studio's
refusal to give him a 16mm print of the picture.

"He was disgusted, upset, and angry," said Howard Strickling, "and he
wanted no part of M-G-M ever again." Gable's final day on the lot, when
he posed for a few stills and cleaned out the remaining items in his dressing
room (one of which was a framed *Parnell* poster), came on March 2, 1954.
When he drove through the back gate for the last time, having firmly
declined the offer of a farewell party, Tracy was on location near the Arizona
border town of Nogales, making his first scenes for *Broken Lance.*

Zanuck had committed to the picture in a big way, giving it an all-star
cast, a $2 million budget, and the full CinemaScope treatment. Originally
paired opposite Tracy on a seven-week guarantee was Dolores Del Rio,

returning to the American screen after an absence of twelve years. Richard Widmark was cast as the eldest of the Devereaux sons, Hugh O'Brien and Earl Holliman his younger brothers. And filling the roles of the young lovers in the film were Fox contract players Robert Wagner and Jean Peters. Wagner, in particular, was gaining in popularity, having appeared in a string of increasingly prominent pictures, the latest of which, Henry Hathaway's $3 million production of *Prince Valiant,* was set for an April release.

"He saw me in a picture I did called *Beneath the 12-Mile Reef,*" Wagner recalled, "and said, 'This kid would be great.'" Tracy wanted him for the role of Joe, the half-breed son of Matt and Señora Devereaux originally envisioned by Zanuck as going to Jeffrey Hunter. Wagner shook Tracy's hand at the Golden Globes, thanking him for the boost and telling him how much he was looking forward to being in the picture.

"Well, I am too, son," Tracy said.

"The first time I ever saw him," Wagner continued,

> was at Riviera, where he got hurt once playing polo. I was just a kid, and he got hit with the ball or something. I remember he was on the grass and all these guys were out there, and then he got up and got back on the horse and I thought, "Wow, is that great!"
>
> I had a resistance to my being in the movies from my father, you know. He didn't want me to go into the movie business. So when Spence saw me in this movie and asked me to be in *Broken Lance* with him, it was great because he put his arm around me and he said, "You can really go someplace." And I was one of a hundred and fifty good-looking young guys with a lot of hair in Hollywood.

As a boy, Wagner had lived at the Bel Air Country Club, where he occasionally caddied for Clark Gable. "He was always a terrific guy. I told him I got a job with Spence: 'Jesus, can you imagine? I am going to do a movie with Spencer Tracy.' He said to me, 'Grab a prop and keep moving, kid.'"

Counting unbilled bits, Wagner had appeared in twelve motion pictures by the time of *Broken Lance* and thought he knew something of screen acting.

> The first scene I had with Spence, we were on location in Arizona and we had to ride up into this sequence. I don't remember what the dialogue was, but he said something like, "Were they here? Where did they go?" This guy says, "They went down that way." And Spence says, "Did you hear that?" And I say, "Yeah, they went that way I guess."

He said, "What? What was that? Can you bring it up a little next time so I can hear the cue?" And we ride back the next time and I bring it up a little. [Afterward,] I said, "Jesus, I'm sorry. I didn't think there were very many people who could underplay you."

He said, "Come here." And he'd get that sort of face. "Come here!" He had this portable dressing room, and [we went inside and he] shut the door and sat down. He said, "Do you really think you could underplay me? Do you *really* think you could? Because you could *never* underplay me. That is not the point. What are you thinking about that for? Why would you be thinking that you could underplay me? Why don't you think about playing the scene and being honest in it and bringing something of yourself to it and taking all this other stuff out of the way? Why don't you think about *that* instead of being a smartass son of a bitch and trying to underplay me?"

I could see he was really starting to get hot. I said, "Yes sir, Mr. Tracy. You are absolutely right, and thank you very much." He said, "Kid, get out of here!" But the fact that he took the time to do that was a big thing.

Directing *Broken Lance* was Edward Dmytryk, a former cutter who had graduated from formula product at Paramount to the first wave of film noir at RKO. Known as one of the Hollywood Ten, Dmytryk had rebuilt his career after a stretch in prison (and a controversial appearance before the House Un-American Activities Committee) with a series of pictures for producer Stanley Kramer, the last of which, *The Caine Mutiny,* was still awaiting release. For *Broken Lance,* Dmytryk peopled the Santa Cruz Valley with a cast and crew numbering 130 individuals, along with forty steers and twelve unusually spirited horses.

Tracy and Dmytryk got on famously, in part because the director recognized the level of effort his fifty-three-year-old star was putting into his work. "He'd agonize over everything. He was searching for the character's key." Finding himself in a character was never easy for Tracy, and a long drive at the end of a workday gave him time to ponder the seemingly endless problem of inhabiting another man's skin. For accommodations, Tracy chose to alternate between the Arizona Inn in Tucson, seventy miles from where the *Broken Lance* company was based, and Pantano Ranch, Lew Douglas' 100,000-acre spread some thirty miles north at Sonoita.

Dmytryk knew that Tracy had played polo but wasn't aware that it had been a number of years since he had last been on a horse. Tracy noted that

Clark Gable refused to ride on camera and that Gary Cooper had to be hoisted into the saddle and would only ride at a slow walk.* "Spence did everything but say flatly that he didn't want to ride, and I refused to take any hints. So, when the time came, he rode, and he rode extremely well— all of which added to the authenticity of the scenes."

Settling in, Tracy briefly turned his attentions to Jean Peters—who was being wooed by Howard Hughes—and persuaded her to dine with him. Otherwise, he took his meals at the Douglas ranch or back in Tucson, where he attended Mass and frequently ate alone. Dolores Del Rio, her visa having been held up in Washington "pending investigation of her political affiliations," was replaced by Katy Jurado, another Mexican actress, nineteen years her junior and in the international spotlight for a flashy supporting role in *High Noon.* Jurado arrived in Nogales on March 9 and stayed for the remainder of the location schedule, taking on a dour character part in lieu of the smoldering seductresses she frequently played in her native country.

Tracy's death scene, shot on the last day out, went contrary to the calamitous symphony of thunder and horse's hooves that Zanuck had once conceived, Matt quietly slipping off the saddle, having died without anyone even knowing it. "He got so pissed off," remembered Hugh O'Brien, "because, not mentioning any names, a couple of people blew their lines. He said, 'Take a close-up of me lying here, goddamn it, then shoot around it, because I'm not going to lie here in the hot sun for another two hours!' "

Location work wrapped on the thirteenth, and Tracy, fueled by a gigantic thermos of coffee, drove all night to get back to L.A., hitting town just after noon and dining at the ranch in Encino that same evening. The "St. Ives Roy Rogers" seemed fine, Cukor dutifully reported in a letter to Hepburn, adding they'd had some "ecstatic notes" from Zanuck with regard to the rushes. Though Tracy had dropped five pounds during his time in Arizona, he had little hope of keeping it off.

Metro was talking *Highland Fling* (the aforementioned *Digby*) as his next picture, and Tracy drove out to Culver City to confer with Larry Weingarten and director Ronald Neame. Neame's droll comedy *The Million Pound Note* (*Man with a Million* in the United States) had garnered considerable attention for its use of Gregory Peck in what otherwise would have been an art house attraction. Tracy met the Englishman for lunch at Romanoff's, where he gave him a small sampling of his disenchantment with the studio.

"I found him down-to-earth, personable, and honest," Neame said.

---

* Cooper's trouble was due to a bad back.

"He gave me a warning, though. 'M-G-M is a tricky studio. It's a dangerous machine. The executives think nothing of mowing people down. The person who'll help you deal with them is Kate Hepburn. She's in London, and I'll ask her to speak with you.' Once back home, I met with her at Claridge's. She is a brutally frank, incredibly articulate, and vehement lady. She spoke against the studio system generally, and M-G-M specifically. Her advice on how to survive amongst their hierarchy was simply, 'Stay away from them!' "

Production on *Broken Lance* resumed at Fox Hills on March 19, 1954, and Tracy expressed satisfaction at having gotten through the riding scenes with a minimum of fuss. "At first I had been diffident at working with Tracy," Dmytryk said,

> but as the film progressed, I found he was very receptive to changes of inference or emphasis. Once only he resisted a suggestion of mine, and in doing so exhibited what was one of his greatest talents. In studying a scene we were to do in a couple of days, I found one long speech that was rather stiffly written. I had reworked it until I felt it was more playable. "Look, Eddie," Tracy said, "I've already learned the words. Why don't you let me try them the way they are? If you don't like it, I'll look at your rewrite." I agreed, and later we shot the scene. He hadn't changed a word in the original speech, but he broke it up and played with it in such a way that it seemed the most natural scene in the world.

Dmytryk likened Tracy's handling of dialogue to the phrasing of an accomplished jazz singer, taking a "leaden line" and making it shine like gold. "The odd thing was that he felt it was nothing special—that it was just something that every actor owed his art."

Richard Widmark had declined to sign a new contract with Fox, and Zanuck retaliated by assigning him to *Broken Lance,* where he was accorded fourth billing after Tracy, Wagner, and Jean Peters.

> I told Tracy I was trying to get out of the movie, but it had nothing to do with him. I told him, "You're the greatest actor, and I've admired you since I was a babe in arms." He understood completely. Strangely enough, a few weeks later, we were shooting a scene and I had nothing to do—just stand around. It was Spence's scene; he was doing all the talking. I happened to be standing in the wrong place or something, and he looked up and said, "Who the fuck do you think is the star of this picture?" I said, "Oh, Spence,

come on." Then he got embarrassed. That's the other side of Tracy. He could be very petty and egomaniacal.

Tracy was impressed when he learned that Sol Siegel, the line producer on *Broken Lance,* was the same man who had fired Eddie Dmytryk from Paramount in 1940. That it was the same Sol Siegel who wanted him for a picture at Fox thirteen years later gave Dmytryk a measure of "personal vindication" that made the offer of *Broken Lance* irresistible. So when the AP's Bob Thomas visited the set, Tracy puckishly appropriated the story, suitably embellished, and claimed for the first time that he himself had been fired from Fox in 1935. There was nobody to contradict him—Thomas didn't know any better, both Winnie Sheehan and Sidney Kent were dead, and Zanuck hadn't yet arrived on the scene when Tracy made the move to Metro.

"But one thing pleased me about the whole affair," Tracy said to Thomas. "At eight o'clock that night, my agent took me over to M-G-M to have a talk with Louis B. Mayer. At nine o'clock I was signed to a contract, and I've been there ever since."

The column ran nationally, suggesting that Zanuck could have had Tracy in his stable of stars all along had his predecessors only behaved more judiciously. Perhaps more to the point were reports that Tracy would be leaving M-G-M at the end of his current contract.

"Will I sign again? I don't know. At first I didn't think I would because I didn't think they wanted me. Nobody said anything about staying. I think that's why a lot of actors leave. But we have started having talks, and something may come of it. I still have three pictures to make for them. After that, who knows?"

When Tracy left for New York and London on April 24, it was to meet up with Kate and prepare for the filming of *Highland Fling,* which was set to go at the end of June. Based on the book *Digby* by David Walker, the script was by Angus McPhail, whose *Whiskey Galore* was one of the comic gems to emerge from Michael Balcon's Ealing Studios. The settling of arrangements to shoot the film in Scotland coincided with the cancellation of *The Millionairess,* which, despite Hepburn's participation and a "brilliant" screenplay from Preston Sturges, collapsed under its own weight.

She was back in New York when Tracy's TWA flight touched down at Idlewild, and they met for an intimate dinner the next night at the Pierre. A pinched nerve—an old neck injury—was troubling him, and he needed three fillings in his teeth replaced. They dined with Laura Harding, Constance Collier, the Douglases (who were passing through town), the Leland Haywards, Irene Selznick. Tracy filled the time between meals and doctor appointments watching the Army-McCarthy hearings on TV.

In London they met up with the Kanins, the Don Stewarts, George Cukor (whose M-G-M contract would soon be up), the Douglases (again), Bobby Helpmann, and Michael Benthall. Tracy's guests drank freely around him; one night with the Stewarts, he noted Guinness Stout and Ale in his book with some big question marks following the entry. Two nights later, in the same company, he drew a picture of a bottle of Dubonnet on the page. Once with Kate, Helpmann, and Benthall, the party collectively killed a quart of scotch, though if Tracy personally had any, he didn't make a note of it. Sleeping was difficult—one night he managed barely an hour—and he upped his intake of Seconal capsules to as many as four a night.

He stayed at Claridge's, Hepburn around the corner at the Connaught. They made no show of their time together but neither could they count on Howard Strickling's stifling of the press as they had in California. Their behavior patterns were largely dictated by Hepburn's management of the circumstances. "She once told us that she and Tracy had never spent the night together under the same roof," remembered Sandy Sturges, who was in town with her husband Preston and their young son. Kate maintained it was Tracy's tossing and turning that was, at least in part, responsible: "I think Spencer found life very difficult and I found him very fascinating. So he couldn't sleep. Well, I don't want to sleep in a bed with someone who can't sleep."

Eddie Dmytryk, who was in London making a picture for producer David Lewis, observed their routine:

> On our first evening, Tracy, Hepburn, Ambassador Douglas (whom I had met in Arizona), and I had dinner at an excellent Italian restaurant in Soho. We dined well and stayed late, then walked back to the Claridge, where Spence and I were staying. On arriving at the hotel, Douglas excused himself, and Spence went up to his room while I took Miss Hepburn around to the tradesman's entrance at the rear of the building.* We took the freight elevator up to Tracy's floor (the operator knew her well) and joined Spence in his suite. There Katy made coffee for him and we chatted until it

---

* Claridge's had requested that Hepburn not wear trousers in the "public rooms" of the hotel, which, of course, included the lobby. Hepburn's solution, rather than to wear a dress when visiting Tracy, was instead to come up in the service elevator. Management at the Connaught imposed no such restriction.

was time for her to say good night. Again, I escorted her to the freight elevator, through the rear entrance, and a block or so down the street to the Connaught, where she was staying.

On May 30, Tracy went to Mass and took a long walk through London on his own. Sometime during the course of the day, he discovered that *The People*, a Sunday tabloid with a circulation in excess of five million, had devoted half a page to an article with the following headline: "For 12 years they've kept Hollywood's gossips at bay—Now LOGAN GOURLAY reveals the secret romance of Spencer and Katie."

Veiled references to the relationship from American columnists—Sheilah Graham, Winchell, Kilgallen in particular—stretched back to *Woman of the Year*, but never before had a mass-circulation publication so blatantly fingered them.

For more than 12 years they have succeeded in remaining "just friends, that's all, just friends" though it may not always look that way [Gourlay wrote]. Indeed, there are all the signs of the usual Hollywood affair. They have popped up together in several of the world's capitals. At the moment they are here in London, not entirely by coincidence. In 1952, when she was appearing in *The Millionairess* on the London stage, he flew over from America. Each night he had a box reserved at the theatre. Each night he sent her a bouquet. While Hepburn was filming *The African Queen* here, Tracy turned up conveniently for a holiday. Yet this is the first time the newspaper spotlight has been turned on their relationship. How have they kept out of the headlines all this time? One answer is—discretion.

Gourlay went on to skirt the onerous English libel laws by branding the relationship "a genuine platonic friendship" while letting the tone and substance of the article speak for themselves. There were a few howlers—Gourlay had Hepburn entering into three separate marriages, the second with Howard Hughes—but most of the observational details were accurate.

Throughout the years they have remained reticent, shunning publicity. When I met him last year in Hollywood, all he would say was: "Yes, I know Katie very well." She has always restricted herself publicly to saying that "Spencer is one of my closest friends." (On less public occasions she calls him "Spence.") The other night on one of their few public appearances together in London during their current visit, I saw them leaving one of the Mayfair clubs. She had to be helped into the car, probably because she was wearing an evening gown instead of her usual slacks. Tracy managed to do it in a gallant—but brotherly—way, although he is suffering from a twisted arm nerve at the moment. It's fortunate that Hepburn is around to solace him—in a purely sisterly way, of course.

Tracy dined alone at Claridge's that night, downing three bottles of Guinness and tossing four Seconals in after them. "[F]or din[ner] Claridge's—Helpmann!! and Hepburn!!" he noted the next evening. "No grog." On June 3 he learned from Bert Allenberg that *Highland Fling* had been called off. Dore Schary followed up with a phone call, saying only that the picture was off "for this year" and that he would like to start *Bad Day at Honda*—retitled *Bad Day at Black Rock*—on July 15. In its thirtieth year as a production entity, Metro-Goldwyn-Mayer was reducing its feature film output by 40 percent. "Years ago, every picture made money," Eddie Mannix explained. "Today every picture is a big gamble—but if you hit the jackpot you make a lot more."

Tracy lingered in England, not only because Hepburn had committed to a film in Italy—*Time of the Cuckoo* for director David Lean—but because his cousin Jane was in Ireland visiting family and would soon be making her way to England. Jane's mother, Spence's aunt Jenny, had always maintained that she married her late husband because he said that he'd take her to Ireland. But then, of course, he never did.

"I was to go to London when I finished in Ireland," Jane said,

because I had a cousin who lived there. I also had a very dear friend from Seattle who was working for the Air Force and lived in London, so I had two places to go where I wouldn't be a burden or have to be put up by him. First we went in as a group, May and Donald [my cousins] and I, to have dinner at Claridge's with him. Then I went to stay with my friend Phyllis for two or three days, and then Phyllis and I had dinner with him, and there was this young man whose name I can't remember who was sort of the liaison for the studio. (He was the person who chauffeured him around.) [Spencer] asked for ice cream for dessert. Everybody else had a drink, but, of course, he didn't. He said, "I own the third floor of Claridge's and they don't have any chocolate ice cream."

I sensed how much he was annoyed or didn't want people that he didn't know coming up and tapping him on the shoulder. He couldn't understand why this obsession. I think the idea of celebrity just appalled him. The fact that he *was* one bothered him. It didn't amount to much in the long run because, I think, he was beginning, maybe a little bit at that time, to understand himself. Why he was there and, you know, what his life was about. I remember I thought at the time that he seemed as if he had worked so hard, and yet he didn't feel that he had accomplished a great deal. I think that having a little bit of power over what he did was also something he wanted desperately. He knew I did a fair amount of reading and he said, "If you read anything let me know. We"—he would always say "we"—"need some ideas, we need some scripts, we need some writing that is decent." He was telling us about *Bad Day.* He told us about the train that comes into this barren little town. And the man who gets off. We all said, "And then what happens?" And he said, "See the picture!" That was the one he was about to do.

And then, when Phyllis went home, we had another visit, and this man left so that he and I could have a private visit. We talked about my mother and about what a great gift this had been for me and for her and about little quirks about people in Ireland and my own family and how much we had meant to one another over the years. He said he envied me my Irish experience. He couldn't get over the little things that I told him had happened there. The smile would just stay on his face, and he would just laugh and laugh of the various personalities and the people and the reception I got. I said to him, "Someday I may need you." And he said, "If you do, you just call." And he knew what I meant. We said goodbye, and that was that until the next year.

There was never any recognition of the fact that there was a Katharine Hepburn or that he was living away from home. It certainly was known, but I think my mother just simply did not accept it, and, of course, I didn't either. I often wonder why in the world I didn't think of it at the time, but my friend did. Phyllis knew it. She said, "Well, everybody knows." And, of course, I said, "Yeah, well, so she's here. Don't ask me to introduce you!"

On July 1, Tracy rode with Kate to Southampton and boarded the *Queen Mary.* On the crossing with him were Benny Thau, Jimmy and Gloria Stewart, and the evangelist Billy Graham. The voyage was smooth, the weather warm and sunny. In New York he caught a TWA sleeper for Los Angeles, arriving back in the midst of a record heat wave.

Temperature fluctuations had come to bother him terribly, as did weather variations of almost any sort. He was now fifty-four years old—the age at which his father had died—and he was convinced he would not live much longer. Fixating on the Hemingway project, the words "Old Man" struck him as an apt label, and he used it constantly. He was, Leland Hayward said, "counting the weeks" until he could begin work on the picture.

There were now two screenwriters working on the project independently: in Europe, Hemingway had chosen Peter Viertel, John Huston's frequent collaborator, while Hayward had selected Paul Osborn, an idea Tracy hailed as "brilliant." They were still planning to shoot the film over the spring and summer of 1955, but now Hayward had two other major pictures to make: *Mister Roberts,* during which he was contending with director Josh Logan's nervous breakdown, and *The Spirit of St. Louis,* the story of Charles Lindbergh's history-making flight across the Atlantic.

The basis for *Bad Day at Black Rock* was a 1947 magazine story by Howard Breslin titled "Bad Time at Honda." When actor-writer Don McGuire brought it to M-G-M in 1953, it was with the idea that he would adapt it to the screen. McGuire had been working in tandem with director Joseph Pevney at Universal-International, his best-known writing credit being the bizarrely fascinating Frank Sinatra vehicle *Meet Danny Wilson.* He took a crack at a screenplay, reportedly on spec, and though Dore Schary didn't care for McGuire's take on the material, the story appealed to the moralist in him.

Schary paid off McGuire, acquiring the underlying rights, and assigned the project to screenwriter Millard Kaufman, whose *Take the High Ground* was one of the production chief's personal productions for the 1953–54 season. It didn't seem like obvious screen material for Spencer Tracy, its hero being about thirty-five and a former platoon leader, but Schary almost immediately saw Tracy in the role of John J. Macreedy, a "granite-like wedge of a man" who had about him an air of "monumental dependability, self-confidence, and quiet humor." As Schary's daughter Jill wrote in 1963: "Daddy loves all stories about disastrous problems that are overcome. One of the major characters must be A Decent Human Being. To Daddy, the Decent Human Being looks like Spencer Tracy."

"Dore," said Millard Kaufman, "liked the idea of the persecution of the Japanese-Americans in World War II because he was a bit enraged by it, and so was I. So he asked me if I wanted to do it and I said, 'Yes,' and he gave me this thing."

Once Kaufman began moving in the right direction, Schary re-teamed him with his *High Ground* director, Richard Brooks, and made the producer his newly appointed editorial executive, Charles Schnee. Early on came the matter of the title: John Wayne had just come out with a picture called *Hondo,* and they feared that calling their film *Bad Day at Honda* would confuse filmgoers into thinking they had already seen it. Kaufman's first incomplete draft of the screenplay was titled *Bad Day at Parma,* a title that pleased no one. Then Kaufman, while location scouting in Arizona, came upon a post office and gas station collectively known as Black Rock. "So I called Schary and said, 'Why don't we call it Black Rock? And do it in California?'"

The first full version of *Bad Day at Black Rock* was ready for review by the middle of September. In a story conference, Schary suggested opening with a narration and dictated other economies in storytelling. "Let's give him a bad arm," he said of Macreedy. "Nobody can resist playing a cripple." He wanted the porter in the opening shot to offer to help Macreedy with his suitcase, so that Macreedy could insist on carrying it himself.

"You can't really write a screenplay for an actor," Kaufman observed, "because actors don't even have the average of, say, a ballplayer who is a good hitter. If you hit the ball once at three times at bat, you are worth a fortune. An actor will interpret something and decide he wants to do it once in twenty times if he's a star—that is, a guy in demand. So, no, I wasn't figuring on Tracy, and anyway . . . I wasn't really interested in him. I thought he was too old. [The character] was a platoon leader. I was an old platoon leader in the Marine Corps and I was twenty-five. Most of the kids in my outfit were not old enough to vote."

Kaufman and Brooks, himself a novelist and screenwriter, went back to the director's office to begin work on a revision. "We were only into it about ten minutes," Kaufman remembered,

when Brooks, who was in a slow burn for either being assigned to this or because he said he totally disapproved of it and didn't like the scene, or whatever the reason, suddenly picked up the phone and dialed. I heard him say, "Spence, this is Richard. Mill and I are working on this thing, but don't expect anything much because it's a piece of shit." So he hung up and I said, "What are you doing??" And before he could answer, the phone rings and it's Schary. He says, "Get up to my office immediately."

Tracy had just called and told him that the director said that what we are working on for him—and him alone—is "a piece of shit." So we go up to Dore's office, and attending the meeting along with Schary and Herman Hoffman, who is Dore's assistant, is Brooks, myself, and Charlie Schnee . . . And Charlie, when he realizes from Dore what has happened, challenges his director, who is twice his size, to step outside. He wants to hit him. Spencer comes in and Dore says, "Look, let me tell you the story." And he starts in on some really dumb idea. He was trying his best, and I found out later that all this encouragement was because they had a play-or-pay deal with Tracy. So they were doing anything to keep him. [Tracy] was really very much a presence, and he was listening . . . Dore spins the story, making it up as he goes along, and it is rather silly and infantile—not infantile, adolescent. It was kind of a modern western theme, and I thought, "Oh boy, we are really in trouble." And we were. Very calmly, Spencer said, "There are people who"—and this is a paraphrase, I never wrote it down—"consider me possibly the best actor in America. So why are you giving me this shit?" And he walked out.

Now Dore, as I say, did not do a very smart thing, but he had to do something. Later he did something that was very, very astute and that was this: When I finished the screenplay, he sent a messenger with the thing to Spencer with a note saying, "We have Alan Ladd to play the part. However, this was written for you and we thought you might like to take a look at it." In about two hours, Spencer called back and said, "Get rid of Alan Ladd. I want to do it." So we got him back.

Kaufman's revision, carrying the alternate title *Day of Reckoning,* was dated November 4, 1953. "We simplified it and gave it the core," Schary said. "I felt always, too, that in the original there was something lacking in the man's point of view. I felt there was no real reason in the screenplay why this man did particularly what he did. He just came into the town. There seemed to be no reason for him beyond making this gesture [of delivering a medal to the Japanese-born father of a soldier in his platoon]. I felt that there had to be a deeper psychological root which perhaps would pay off for us. So then I had the notion—it was my idea—to make him crippled in one arm, so that he came to this town with a sense of no longer being able to function, hating what happened to him."

The script went to New York, where Nicholas Schenck took it to be another of Schary's pricey morality tales—a dated story of antique prejudices—and said he didn't think Schary should do it. Within days, an item in the *Hollywood Reporter* indicated that the film was being put off "indefinitely."

"The quarrel," said Schary, "was healed finally by Mr. Schenck saying he'd let me make the picture. He wouldn't oppose it. The whole argument took place during the time when I was having this whole series of problems about my attitudes toward the job, and I certainly said—and I felt it very strongly—that if I had to fight to make this picture, there was no point in staying around."

In January 1954 Tracy agreed to do the film after *Highland Fling* but was never completely on board. "I think his opinion may have been colored by some people at the studio who felt it would be a very unsuccessful picture," Schary suggested.* "We then spoke again [in April] and he said, 'What do you really think will happen with this picture?' I said, 'Spence, this is not a twelve-million-dollar picture. But if it's successful, if we do it well and it comes off, it's the kind of picture that will receive perhaps the penetration of *Crossfire*† and, if you're good in it, I think your chances for recognition are wonderful in it.' Well, he didn't know. So he left very undecided that day. There were some things about the script that bothered and disturbed him . . . In the beginning he was not enthusiastic."

Tracy was in London when Kaufman's final draft, eliminating the opening narration, was okayed for production. It would be a couple of weeks before he learned that *Highland Fling* had been canceled and that *Bad Day* had been moved up to a July 15 start date with Vincente Minnelli directing. To Schary's mind, Minnelli had the advantage of having made two pictures with Tracy. He was, however, just coming off the demanding musical fantasy *Brigadoon* and was reluctant to take it. John Sturges signed on with scarcely a month's notice and quickly saw the opportunities in marrying the sweep of widescreen with the desolate stretch of wreckage known as Black Rock.

"The people at Metro didn't really have any faith in CinemaScope or the concept of widescreen," Sturges said.

> They were enamored of 3-D, which to me was the passing fancy—not widescreen, which was obviously the picture of the future. So then word came back from New York: "Make one in widescreen. They're doing business." So I rushed up and said, "Now with the orders from New York, let me make one." They said, "You don't want to make this one—there's nobody in it." I said, "What's that got to do with it?" Well, to them, if you had widescreen, that meant thousands of extras, thousands of togas, amphitheaters with Christians being mauled by lions, and so on. They said, "What are you going to do with all that space?" I said, "Well, the idea of a man, Tracy, in a black suit standing against this empty space. Doesn't that tell you something? Isn't that better the bigger the screen?"

Sturges envisioned a panorama of complete isolation, a place where a handful of people could hold a grim secret between them. He had, said J. J.

---

* Kate later admitted that she, too, never cared much for *Black Rock*.
† One of Schary's signal achievements at RKO, *Crossfire* (1947) was based on Richard Brooks' 1945 novel *The Brick Foxhole*.

Cohn, "an idea that it ought to be done on location. Dore turned to me and said, 'What do you think, Joe?' I said, 'Well, I think we can do it on lot number three, but I don't think it would be too much of a difference to shoot on location. Why not let John Sturges go and pick a location, then we'll figure the cost.' So John Sturges went out and, I think, [selected] Lone Pine, if I remember rightly."

It was indeed Lone Pine, some two hundred miles due north of Los Angeles, where *Greed, Gunga Din, High Sierra,* and countless B-westerns had been filmed and where every angle offered a fresh expanse of the rugged Owens Valley. They found a spur on an old Southern Pacific easement that could, with care, support the modern streamliner that delivers Macreedy to Black Rock and sent a crew up to build a cluster of wind-worn buildings, a task that took all of eleven days.

According to Schary, Tracy appeared in his office one day toward the start of production. "Kid, you can get yourself a new boy," he said. "I'm not going to do the movie." This came as no surprise to Schary, who had grown used to Tracy's vacillations. Mannix was in talks with Bert Allenberg and the William Morris office over a new three-year term for Tracy, and Schary may have interpreted this particular maneuver as a negotiating tactic. Tracy had, however, been up all night convincing himself he wasn't up to the job—that he hadn't prepared enough, that he wasn't going to be good enough—for, as his datebook shows, he was awake until 5 a.m. and only able to sleep with the aid of four and three-quarters Seconal capsules.

"Okay," said Schary.

Tracy, he recalled, seemed surprised. "You mean it's okay? Really?"

"Sure. I was supposed to make only twenty or twenty-two pictures this year. It won't make a fuss if I lose one." Schary then advised his recalcitrant star that Nick Schenck might well insist on suing him to recover the costs incurred in the run-up to the picture—sets and cast in particular—and estimated the total at $480,000.

Tracy backed off, but not before eliciting a promise from Schary that he would make the dusty trip north to visit the set. The following week, John Sturges had his first and only conference with Tracy regarding the picture: "I anticipated various approaches to 'Why can't we do this in the studio?' and, sure enough, they occurred. I talked him out of them. He said, 'Well, you don't want [the heat] to affect the acting, do you?' I said, 'Spence, you're not going to tell me you can't act in hot weather.' And he laughed and he said, 'I guess I'll forget the rest of my speech.' He wanted to build the set on the back lot."

Tracy went shopping for clothes at Rothschild's, where he purchased a plain gray suit to wear in the picture. "He hardly had it altered," said Millard Kaufman, "because he wanted it to look like [it belonged on] a guy that just got out of the Army. And it did. It didn't really fit him the way that Gregory Peck, for example, would have had a suit fit." Sturges recalled him discussing the clothes: "He said, 'I figure [Macreedy's] from the east, he'll wear a hat, okay?' And I said, 'Sure, you can use [it] in the sun, the shadows, you know—for looks.' He said, 'Don't think I won't.' And [he] showed up in that and it looked great."

On the morning of Sunday, July 18, 1954, Tracy set out for the western edge of Death Valley, where the temperature was one hundred degrees and a room awaited him at the Frontier Motel. John Sturges had assembled a stellar cast in the brief time allotted him. The role of Reno Smith, Macreedy's nemesis in the picture, was filled by Robert Ryan, a human counterpart to the weathered surroundings of Black Rock. M-G-M contract player Anne Francis would be Liz Wirth, the solitary girl in the cast, John Ericson her timid, ineffectual brother Pete. Dean Jagger, Walter Brennan, Ernest Borgnine, and Lee Marvin filled out the roles of the principal townspeople, the sixty-year-old Brennan making his fourth appearance in a picture with Tracy.

"My first scene was after I had supposedly knocked [Tracy] off the road," Borgnine remembered.

> The first scene we did together was when he comes back to town after that. My line was, "Well, if it's not Macreedy, the world's champion road hog." I had been asked by Walter Brennan, "I understand you're a fairly good country actor. I'd like to see your scene." Everybody was watching. As Tracy came out of the car and started to cross, I forgot every line I had. All I could see were these two Academy Awards coming at me. And then my first line popped into my head. We did our scene, and then he walked through the door. The director said, "Cut! Print!" Walter Brennan went by and said, "Good enough." And Tracy came back out: "Kid, you did all right. I like working with you. You look a man right in the eye."

At night, the company would adjourn to Lone Pine, where the daytime temperature was 112 degrees and there was little to do after dark. Tracy would open his room for snacks and cocktails, keeping strictly to soft drinks for himself. "It seemed like a form of torture almost," Anne Francis remarked. "He would invite all the actors up to his suite at the end of the day for cocktails, and he'd sit there and drink his 7-Up while everybody else was having cocktails."

Hepburn was shooting *Time of the Cuckoo* in Venice, and there was a cable or a letter from her every day or two. Walter Brennan, whose politics were every bit as conservative as Adolphe Menjou's, made the mistake of

commenting one night on Kate's supposedly leftist views, the memory of
her appearance for Wallace still trailing her after seven years of innuendo.
"He said that Katie didn't have 'good judgment' or common sense," Anne
Francis remembered, "and that topped it for Tracy—he went icy cold." The
following day, Sturges found the two men weren't speaking.

Tracy's scenes with Robert Ryan were a highpoint for the people on
location, Ryan conforming, in Millard Kaufman's words, to "D. H.
Lawrence's disturbing observation of the American hero as 'cold, hard-eyed,
isolate and a killer.' The characterization applied equally well to Ryan's
American heavy." A taut confrontation between the two men was staged as
if an idle conversation between two Midwestern schoolboys, Tracy seated
on a bench, his eyes downcast, Ryan casually standing before him, hands
folded in front, squinting into the sun and speaking with the softness of a
chaplain. ("Komoko. Sure, I remember him. Japanese farmer. Never had a
chance . . .")

"We never rehearsed," said Ernest Borgnine. "If [Tracy] rehearsed, I
never saw it. They just said, 'Let's shoot it.' On *Bad Day*, when Tracy is sitting on the bench and Robert Ryan is talking to him, Tracy has his head
down. And I'm there thinking, 'Nobody's going to be looking at him.' And
on screen you couldn't take your eyes off him. And Bob Ryan was doing
everything but loosen his pants."

John Ericson recalled,

I was sitting on the porch there—you know, the one in the opening
shot. They were down by the gas station . . . The whole crew was
around there, and they were down there for quite a while. I got
tired of sitting up there in the sun, and so I said to whoever I was
with, "I'm going to go and see what they're doing." Because I could
hear them talking away, and I thought they must be having a discussion about the scene . . . So I started ambling down the road,
and I got halfway down, shuffling in the gravel and all, and then I
stopped. "Oh, my God—that's the scene they're doing!" It sounded
like they were having a conversation, and everybody was just standing around, taking notes or watching to see what's going to be next.
So I tiptoed on up there, and there was Tracy doing his close-up
with Robert Ryan off camera. And I thought to myself, "My God,
he makes those words sound like they're coming out of his mouth."
They weren't written, you know? He's really thinking before he
answers. When he opens his mouth, he reacts to what he's heard.

After the scene, Tracy flopped into a chair next to Millard Kaufman.
"Ryan is bristling with a kind of cerebral muscle, you know, and he's a

tough guy. And Spencer sits down next to me and says, 'Does Ryan scare you?' At first, I didn't know what he was talking about, and then I realized he was talking about the scene that he had just finished. So I said, 'No, I've known Bob Ryan for years. He's a fine man. No, he doesn't scare me.' And Tracy said, 'Well, he scares the hell out of me.' "

Much to Tracy's satisfaction, Dore Schary did indeed make his promised appearance on the hottest day of the shoot, when the location temperature climbed to 114 degrees. "Dore, you got a great script here," Tracy told him that day. "However, the critics are going to love it, but nobody's going to go see it." And then, echoing Nick Schenck's concerns, he added, "It's out of its time."

Tracy made the five-hour trip home that evening, driving out to the valley on Saturday to discuss John's plans for a divorce after fifteen months of marriage.

The release of *Broken Lance* came on July 29, 1954, when the picture opened its New York engagement at the Roxy Theatre. Tracy had seen it twice, once

Tracy and Robert Ryan play a tense exchange for *Bad Day at Black Rock*. Director John Sturges, in sunglasses and white cap, is seated next to the camera. (PATRICIA MAHON COLLECTION)

by himself, again with Louise and the kids. (Weeze thought the picture good and said it would do excellent business; Spence judged his own performance more harshly and thought he had overacted in spots.) The trade notices were wonderful, *Variety* proclaiming "a grownup CinemaScope, a process that has lived up to the pioneer *The Robe.*"

Presented in four-track magnetic sound, *Broken Lance* promised audiences the kind of visual and aural thrills they now seemed to demand in pictures, and it came close to matching the success of *The Robe* in its initial engagements. The family dynamics and Tracy's commanding performance as the hard-bitten Devereaux also seemed to resonate across generational and cultural lines.

"I thought I put my old man in *Broken Lance,*" screenwriter Richard Murphy commented, "and my son says, 'Goddamn, there's dad.' So I guess the father's universal. I went to Japan later on, and have a very dear friend over there, whom I met when I was shooting *Three Stripes in the Sun,* and the guy said to me, 'I saw *Broken Lance*—it's exactly like my father!' Tracy didn't look very Japanese, but I can see what the guy meant."

When work on *Black Rock* resumed in Culver City on August 9, Tracy was at work on a painting of Mount Whitney he had started on location. The heat had been a considerable distraction, and in Culver City temperatures were twenty-five degrees cooler. The pressure that always accompanied the start of a film had dissipated; Sturges was working ahead of schedule, printing a lot of initial takes, supremely confident in the script, the actors, and the footage he had. "We shot almost no film at all—no negative, that is, because you shoot negative and then you print part of it— I think something like 86,000 negative [feet] for the whole picture. Only a handful of scenes were ever take two. Scene after scene after scene after scene was take one."

After the implicit threat of violence colors the whole tone of the film, it finally erupts in the town diner, where Coley Trimble (Borgnine) crowds Macreedy to the point of no escape. Tracy, anxious about the scene, went to Sturges and Millard Kaufman.

"He was rather apologetic," Kaufman remembered,

> and he said, "I need a double for this." John said, "Why?" And he said, "Well, if I hit somebody, I don't think I'd be able to stop." Now that could mean one of two things: It meant that he was so involved in a fictional character that it became natural or realistic to him to such an extent that he would get carried away by it. It could also have meant that he simply didn't want to do it, which happens quite often with actors who are bright enough to give you another excuse for it. And he certainly was that. I don't know what it was.

On location near Lone Pine for *Bad Day at Black Rock*. Left to right: Robert Ryan, Tracy, and studio head Dore Schary. (AUTHOR'S COLLECTION)

All I know is that he did not want to hit anybody, so we got a double—and if you notice in the picture, all the close stuff with Coley, Ernie Borgnine, is over Spencer's shoulder and you don't see his face because it wasn't him.

"I wondered," said Borgnine,

how the hell a man with one arm was going to fight me, and I'm a big husky guy. I went to John Sturges. "What do you have in mind?" [he said.] "Judo," I said. And Sturges said, "Okay, do it." So we got the stunt guy and worked out the scene.* I figured I'd have somebody else double me, but Sturges wanted me to do it. Jesus Christ, what have I started? Well, I got ready and they put this piece of rubber in my hand full of blood. And we got started. I take the first blow, and his knee comes up and into my face and misses me by a quarter inch. I hit my face with the sponge and dropped it

---

* According to Millard Kaufman, the Breen office restricted the use of karate chops "because it wasn't fighting heroically. Dore said, 'What the hell? The guy's got one arm.' And so they let it get by."

and the blood spurted out. And Spence was standing there watching and said, "Jesus Christ, they killed him!" Then I went through the [screen] door. In rehearsal, the door flew open. But for the take, they had closed the door, and locked it, and I can still see the screws flying out the door when I went through it. I picked up myself, and the take was fine. And then I went to find the son of a bitch that had locked the door. Well, no one would own up to it. Years later, I visited John Sturges in Cuernavaca, when he's shooting *The Magnificent Seven,* and he owned up to it. It was Sturges that had locked the door.

Sturges said,

We were interested in [*Black Rock*] as a film, and what could be called the "message" in the film, to us, gave it the dimension of reality in the characters. It fleshed them out, it made them meaningful, gave them points of view. You can't play scenes at a surface level. That's Spence's great trick in acting. Well, it's not a trick; he has great ability in acting. He wasn't playing on top. He was playing what was underneath.

He told me his method. It's most interesting. I think it accounts for the substance in Spence's work, certainly not just the talent of his ability on the screen. He would take the script, he told me, take it out to the desert, read it aloud, the whole script, not just his part, to evaluate not only the picture, [but] his relationship to it. And, perhaps most important of all from Spence's standpoint, he said, was where he should come on and where he should lay back. You can't hit all the time. You can't overwhelm all the time. And Spence would lay away until those moments when he felt he should come on. And the nicest compliment I ever got as a director was when he said, "You know where those are too." He said, "I can tell." Then he would do that again—read it aloud. The only thing Spence ever suggested in a script were cuts of himself, so that he wasn't on too much. Then he said that he prepared in a way that just kind of had to be a secret. He said, "It's mechanical." He'd memorize the lines, then he wouldn't look at them for five days. So that when he looked at people, he was hanging onto them as if he was listening to them for the first time—because, in fact, he *was.* He wasn't that sure what they were going to say.

"He listened," said Millard Kaufman, "with every fiber of his entire body. It was almost to say he was leaning toward you to pick up every word.

And then he knew a great deal about film. He knew what would work and he knew apparently what would not. I remember on more than one occasion we'd do a scene and the setup would be finished and John would say, 'Thank you. Cut. Let's go over here.' And Spencer wouldn't budge. He'd just stand there with his finger on his nose, the way he always does, and frown, and John would look over there and say, 'Let's do it once more.' So, he was not a passive actor. He knew what was going on every minute of the time."

John Ericson's big scene with Tracy came at the top of the third act, when Macreedy knows that Smith and his men are going to kill him. Doc Velie (Brennan) has come over to Macreedy's side, but there's not much he can do without help.

"Tracy said to me, 'What are the ideas in your head about this scene?'" Ericson recalled. "And I told him . . . He said, 'All very good. You've got seven or eight things right there, but you've got to take the most important one—the one that works for you—and that's the only hat you hang on the hat tree. That's all, and you play *that*. Otherwise, it gets so cluttered up the audience is going to have a problem figuring out what's going on. Because you've got seven different things going. The other six things can be underneath the surface, but you don't let those out. You just have this one thing you hang your hat on.' That was a wonderful piece of advice."

When action was called, Tracy was positioned at the hotel registration desk, Brennan behind and a little to the left of him, Ericson on the other side of the desk in his nominal position as the clerk on duty. "Nobody's helping him," said Ericson,

and he's talking to me, trying to get me to say what happened. And I won't say anything. He finally takes a bottle of booze and sets it on the counter in front of me and says, "It's going to take a lot of whiskey to wash out your guts." And I reach down to grab the bottle and take a swig. Sturges, I remember, had said, "John, now reach for the bottle." So I look at the bottle and the scene's not working.

It's not working, and it's getting to be quitting time for Mr. Tracy. (He quit at four o'clock every day. He was there bright and early, but he quit at four.) Finally, Tracy said to Sturges, "This scene isn't working." And I said, "Yes, it's not working. I'm very uncomfortable in this scene."

So Tracy says, "I'll tell you what: Let's call it a day. We'll go at this in the morning."

I said, "Great. Thank you."

Sturges says, "Okay, quittin' time!"

Next morning we come in, and we were getting ready for the

scene again. Tracy comes out. "You know what's wrong with the scene?" he says, and he looks at me. He looks at Walter Brennan. He looks at Sturges. And he's waiting for somebody to respond. And we're all afraid to respond because we're thinking this genius here is really going to show us up, you know?

He said: "The problem is, when John goes for that whiskey bottle, we break eye contact. Can't he just grab the bottle without breaking eye contact?"

I said, "I sure as hell can."

Sturges said, "Okay, roll 'em." So we did it, and that's how the scene is.

The climactic face-off between Macreedy and Reno Smith takes place in the desert, Smith armed with a hunting rifle, Macreedy only his wits and his one good arm. Taking cover behind his jeep, Macreedy improvises a Molotov cocktail with an empty soda bottle and the gas in the vehicle's tank. In order for the incendiary to have any value, the audience must know that Macreedy would be carrying matches.

"I had in the script," said Millard Kaufman, "that Macreedy was a smoker. So to show a kind of determination (if you could call it that; anyway, it was theatrical) I had him at one point light a cigarette by taking a book of matches out of his pocket and, with one hand, flipping into a horseshoe shape a single match, [which he] rubs against the striking surface, and then he puts the flame to the cigarette. And Spencer calls and says, 'Look, I'm an old man with arthritis. Why don't I have a Zippo, which everybody in the army had? I still got a few of them.' I said, 'Fine.' "

Freed from a bit of business better suited to Lon Chaney in his prime, Tracy ignited the device with a common cigarette lighter and sent Ryan's stunt double to a sizzling death. The last scene in the picture becomes a reversal of the first, the train pulling into Black Rock, Macreedy leaving the younger Komoko's medal with the remaining townspeople as a way of giving them "something to build on."

"What's the excitement?" the conductor asks as Macreedy climbs aboard. "What happened?"

"A shooting," Macreedy says.

"Thought it was something. First time this streamliner's stopped here in four years."

"Second time," Macreedy corrects as he disappears into the car.

Tracy left for Europe on August 30, stopping off in Manhattan to see New York Giants manager Leo Durocher and his wife, the actress Laraine Day.

Troubled by the pinched nerve in his neck, he spent the month of September following a regimen of traction and heat treatments while attending the playoffs and the first two games of the World Series.

"We were just going into the winning streak that clinched the pennant," Durocher remembered, "and I was able to keep him with us for the next two weeks by convincing him that I needed his advice. 'How could you leave me now?' I'd say every time he pleaded that they were waiting for him in Europe. 'I can't possibly win without your help.' I kept him in New York while we were winning the first two games of the World Series and was aghast when he suggested that I would have to go the rest of the way without him."

Tracy boarded the *Andrea Doria* on October 2 and was at sea when he got the news that the Giants had prevailed over Cleveland to win the world championship.

The voyage was smooth at first, the weather warm and clear, and he was able to limit his drug intake to a couple of Demerols. The water got considerably rougher the fourth day out, and he gobbled five Seconals on top of the pain medication, upsetting his stomach and keeping him confined to quarters for much of the following day. That evening, he laid off the barbiturates altogether and took some wine with his dinner. The next day he tried mixing a couple of Seconals with brandy to predictable results.

In 1977 King Vidor remembered back to a doctor he met aboard the steamer on its next crossing to Naples: "He'd been on the trip before, with Spencer, and he's had to stay up each night talking with him, drinking with him. When Spencer got off at Genoa, he wouldn't get off . . . he came right back on the same boat. So this doctor took another trip to rest up from Spence keeping him up at night the trip before!"

Tracy consulted a doctor who prescribed the spa cure at Montecatini Terme. He spent the next three weeks at the historic Tuscan baths, making day trips to Piza, Civitella, and Florence, seeing Michelangelo's *David* and unfinished *Pietà* and losing himself in Will Durant's book *The Renaissance*. Kate arrived on October 25, and they spent their days driving through the mountains and hill towns, picnicking on the beach, touring the countryside. By November 1, his use of Seconal was down to three capsules a night and he was sleeping more soundly. When he left for Rome on the eighth, he was completely drug-free for the first time in years.

From his rejuvenative Italian sojourn, Tracy returned to a world of aggravation in California. While in Montecatini, he had spoken with Louise by phone and learned that his estranged daughter-in-law, the one Johnny had announced his intention of divorcing, was in fact pregnant.

"Perfect!" he said.

Nobody was happy about it, least of all John. "I was there when Nadine told John that she was pregnant," recalled Susie Tracy. "He just looked at her and said nothing. And then he turned and went back to his room. I think he was stunned."

Louise had been house hunting, the State Highway Commission having routed the new Ventura Freeway through the property on White Oak. She hated the thought of moving after nearly twenty years on the ranch, even though Spence thought it time: "He had said for several years, 'It's a wonderful place, but it is not practical. Susie is growing . . . nobody is going to come out here to see her. It's no good either from the standpoint of friends for John—everybody is over on the other side.' They didn't want to move, but he said it would be much better for the children. And then he said also the Clinic was quite a trek for me."

Tracy was sure that *Bad Day at Black Rock* would be a disaster—a commercial long shot and a stinker to boot. Schary ran it for him just days after production closed, and an opening reminiscent of *High Noon* got the film off to a listless start. "Bad picture?" Tracy wrote in his datebook. "Nothing— mediocre. Grade B."

Nothing the studio was offering promised to be any better. John Houseman wanted to pair Tracy and Montgomery Clift in a union drama called *Bannon*. Another picture, a western called *Jeremy Rodock,* had script and casting problems. The far more interesting action was coming from other studios. At Paramount, he had committed to *The Mountain,* based on a novel he had tried to option himself. William Wyler had proposed *The Desperate Hours* opposite Humphrey Bogart, and though Tracy wasn't keen on the story, he took six weeks to say no, laying the blame to billing problems. Sol Siegel was offering *The Captain's Table,* a broad comedy based on the novel by England's Richard Gordon. And there was, of course, *The Old Man and the Sea,* for which Hemingway had agreed to yet another postponement.

Under the circumstances, it was hard for Tracy to get excited over another term at Metro. The studio was offering three pictures, nonexclusive, at $150,000 each, while Tracy's freelance rate, first with *Broken Lance,* then with *The Mountain,* had been firmly established at $250,000. Moreover, Dore Schary was in trouble, losing ground with Schenck and unhappy with the way the industry in general was going. On December 28, 1954, Tracy met with Eddie Mannix at the studio and tentatively okayed the new three-year deal, Mannix agreeing to route all outside picture money through the studio so that it could count toward Tracy's company pension. On January 7, 1955, Bert Allenberg followed up with a letter to Mannix outlining the contemplated deal, granting Metro preemptive rights but otherwise agreeing to loan Tracy's services to other producers and studios when he requested it. Exempted were *The Captain's Table, The Mountain,* and *The Old Man and the Sea,* all three of which were to be completed by the fall or winter of 1956. "I understand that you have not yet made it as a firm offer," Allenberg wrote Mannix, "and that you will let me hear from you at such point."

Although they were essentially the same age, Bert Allenberg was a stark contrast to the man he represented, tall and natty, a charming bankerlike figure where his impish partner Abe Lastfogel was more avuncular, a down-home type who grew up on New York's East Side. Both had deep roots in the industry, Allenberg from his longtime partnership with the famously nurturing Phil Berg, Lastfogel from the early years of William Morris, which he joined as an office boy at the age of fourteen.

Bert Allenberg understood the care and feeding of a man as insecure as Spencer Tracy, while at the same time maintaining absolute credibility with men like Mannix, Thau, and Dore Schary. All had genuine affection for Tracy—Mannix and Schary in particular—and all had come to understand, each in his own way, the demons that sometimes possessed him. In the peculiar business they were in, men like Tracy, who could capture and retain for decades the fascination of a worldwide audience, were rare indeed, like the precious gems of which Mayer used to speak. There were, in fact, only a few leading men who shared the pantheon with Tracy—Gable, Bogart, Gary Cooper, Cary Grant, Jimmy Stewart. Cagney, maybe. Fred Astaire, if you counted musicals. And of them all, only Tracy was still part of the dwindling roster that had at one time boasted "more stars than there are in Heaven."

Bad Day at Black Rock, its opening moments fixed by Herman Hoffman, had its first public showing at Loew's 72nd Street Theatre in New York on December 8, 1954. Tracy, who was in town but did not attend, was told afterward the picture "held the audience spellbound," a claim backed by the trade reviews, which were unanimous in their praise. He remained dubious until New Year's Day, when calls came from Sam Goldwyn, Danny Kaye, Leland Hayward, and others. Incredulous, he wrote in his datebook: "Black Rock good???"

He conferred with Schary, Thau, and producer Sam Zimbalist on January 12 and tentatively okayed *Jeremy Rodock* with the understanding that the female lead was to be offered to Grace Kelly, who, with the December release of *The Country Girl,* was suddenly Hollywood's hottest actress. Tacitly agreeing to do the picture, Kelly asked to see a script. Two days later, Thau called and said she was stalling. "BET TURN DOWN," Tracy wrote in his book.

The situation became clearer over the following week: Kelly, an

M-G-M contract player, had, with the exception of *Mogambo,* made her most notable films on loan-out—to Stanley Kramer for *High Noon,* to Alfred Hitchcock for *Dial M for Murder* and *Rear Window,* to Paramount for *The Country Girl.* Now George Stevens wanted her for *Giant,* and she was using *Jeremy Rodock* as a bargaining chip. Tracy was infuriated. "Wishes reserve decision," he wrote in his datebook. "I wish replace fast. Studio inclined give her way. 'I.E.' loanout to Stevens' Giant after ours. Her announcement reading script stupid because other girls asked if turndown—which obvious is—or wedge for Giant. Hell with Kelly. Get someone. ??? Bergman??? Call from Allenberg—told him facts of life re: his handling of business."

Disgusted, Tracy doped himself extravagantly—ten Seconals—and boarded a flight to New York for his annual physical, this time at Harkness under the supervision of Dr. Dana Winslow Atchley. Kate, meanwhile, had committed to a six-month tour of Australia with Bobby Helpmann and the Old Vic, a company of twenty-eight players performing *Measure for Measure, Taming of the Shrew,* and *The Merchant of Venice* under the direction of Michael Benthall.

Tracy arrived in Manhattan in time to see the opening of *Black Rock* on February 1, an event only in the sense that he didn't expect it to do well at all. M-G-M's big picture of the moment was a reissue of *Camille,* and Broadway in general was in the grip of near-zero temperatures. The film performed nicely in its opening stanza at the Rivoli, bolstered, no doubt, by exceptional notices—novelist John O'Hara called it "one of the finest motion pictures ever made"—and Tracy's concurrent appearance on the cover of *Life* magazine. ("A Great Star Ages Gracefully" was the title of the accompanying article.) It all faded quickly, though, the weather crippling practically every attraction apart from *The Country Girl, Cinerama Holiday,* and Garbo's 1936 classic, which inspired long lines and set house records at the Normandy. *Bad Day at Black Rock* was gone by the time Tracy returned to Los Angeles on the twenty-seventh.

As predicted, Grace Kelly declined *Jeremy Rodock,* citing a poor script, and Tracy began wondering if he was making the right choice. The story was by Jack Schaefer, the author of *Shane,* but it was only a short story, and somehow it resisted the efforts of screenwriter Michael Blankfort to give it a plot. Director Robert Wise met Tracy for the first time at a conference in early March.

"He was practically selling me on the picture," Wise remembered, "he was so enthusiastic." They talked about locations. "We had the idea of getting high up in the mountain scene and hav[ing] lovely green meadows, lakes, and mountains all around as the setting for it. We thought that would be a good change in the background for a western. Tracy called me the next day and asked, 'Bob, do you think we're really right about that? Do you think it's going to be good for me?' He was getting all kinds of second thoughts about it, so I found myself having to buck up his enthusiasm for it."

Thau and Schary expressed concerns that Tracy did not "feel committed to Rodock." Tracy's worries weren't assuaged when Grace Kelly went public on the suspension Metro had handed her, confirming she had declined the picture after reading the script. "I'm not trying to be difficult or temperamental," she told the *Los Angeles Times*. "I just don't feel I'm right for the part in *Jeremy Rodock*."

By the middle of March, Zimbalist had Blankfort working on a complete revision of the screenplay, and Tracy agreed to a three-month extension that would free him to travel to Europe. In New York he dined with Mannix and Howard Strickling, met Constance Collier for tea, and spent forty-five minutes on the phone to Kate in London. He flew over on the eighteenth, slept soundly the first night, then fell back into his Seconal habit, popping as many as seven capsules a night.

Hepburn was, of course, deep into rehearsals for her upcoming tour of Australia but found time for dinner most nights, and they occasionally could be seen walking together in Hyde Park. On the twenty-fourth he had two rodent ulcers removed from his face, aggravating the fear of cancer he had long held within him. The procedures were described to him as routine, and the medication caused him to sleep nearly six hours the following night. But then late the next evening, in his suite at Claridge's, he fell off the wagon, scribbling in his datebook: "1 AM," the drawing of a bottle, and the words "Here we go."

Between March 27 and April 8, 1955, he was confined to his suite at Claridge's under a doctor's care and attended by a pair of nurses. He took his last drink on April 2 ("FINI," he wrote in his datebook) and spent the rest of the week "recuperating." He passed his fifty-fifth birthday with a cake but otherwise saw no one other than Kate. "Poor Spence must necessarily be alone a good deal," Constance Collier mused to Hepburn in a letter, "though I suppose you have your evenings together, you can't be working at night." The Kanins, stopping at the hotel while Ruth was appearing in *The Matchmaker*, attempted "endless abortive and unsuccessful telephone calls" but could make no contact. When he left for home on the ninth, Tracy did so without contacting them, and nearly two months would pass before Gar could manage a letter.

Back at the studio, Tracy ran *On the Waterfront* and became enthused at the idea of Eva Marie Saint for *Jeremy Rodock*. ("Wonderful," he wrote in his book.) Wise and Zimbalist were equally high on the idea, but Saint turned the part down within a matter of days. ("Par for the course," said Tracy.) They tested Constance Collier's latest protégée, Marjorie Steele, the wife of A&P heir Huntington Hartford, but the test was weak and Steele had little experience. By the time David Selznick turned it down on behalf of Jennifer Jones, pointing out how similar the role of Rodock was to that of Devereaux in *Broken Lance,* Tracy was having serious qualms about doing the picture.

"I talked to Spence," Collier wrote Hepburn on the sixteenth. "He is very unhappy and feels your leaving him for so long and doesn't seem to understand why you do it—but he calmed down—and I think will come on [to New York]. He is to call me tomorrow and we will make arrangements. You must keep him happy until you go and the time will not seem so long.* I hope everything will be alright over there and you will get things straightened out. Don't let anything delay your return if Spence come[s] on."

The growths removed from his face in London, Tracy learned, were malignant, and it was recommended that another spot on his face be tested. The biopsy was set for April 25 in Los Angeles, which turned out to be a bad day all around. He awoke with stomach cramps and a mild temperature and was attempting to sleep them off when he got the news that Constance Collier had died suddenly of a heart attack at the age of seventy-seven. She had been like a second mother to Hepburn, a personal as well as a professional mentor, and it fell to Spence to phone Kate in London and break the news. A week later, he motored to San Francisco in a driving rain to meet her as she prepared to leave for Sydney on Qantas. He had Carroll with him, and the two of them attended Mass together at Old St. Mary's.

The day Hepburn departed, he learned he had yet another malignancy and that surgery would be necessary. He was up at 3:00 a.m., on the road at 5:30, back home again by two in the afternoon. He dined alone that night and needed the help of six Seconals to get to sleep. The surgery took place at St. Vincent's Hospital on the morning of May 12, 1955. The doctor had to go in deeper than he expected, and while all basal cell eruptions were removed, it was feared there would be scarring that could delay the start of the picture. The matter of casting the girl had become a dispiriting problem; nobody seemed to want the part. Schary may have thought it had something to do with the title, for he changed it to *Tribute to a Bad Man,*

---

* Hepburn once told David Lean she was "almost certain" that if she and Tracy had married, it wouldn't have lasted. "She was saying that it's almost impossible to hope that anyone, husband or wife, can understand what it's like when this creative thing takes hold and they find themselves suddenly pushed aside into fourth or fifth place."

one he had a particular liking for, having previously hung it on one of John Houseman's pictures.*

After both Eva Marie Saint and Jennifer Jones turned it down, the studio put forth a Greek girl named Irene Papas, who had made what Benny Thau termed an "exciting test." Papas was in Rome, but could be in California on a few days' notice, having been put under contract with virtually no vetting of any kind. Sam Zimbalist talked of putting a new writer on the screenplay, but then nothing happened, and when Tracy asked to see the test of the new girl, he was told they were going to shoot one specifically for *Tribute*.

Nothing seemed to be going right. When the stitches from the surgery came out, the scar was nastier than expected, a sort of upside-down Y on the left side of his face. Despite repeated fittings, his wardrobe for the picture was too tight. The script still needed work—more than they seemed to think—and on the twenty-third he told off Zimbalist. ("Moron!!!" he wrote in his datebook.) The following day he was shown the new test of "the Greek" and thought it horrible. "Zimbalist—Wise BLOW UP," he recorded that day. "Girl simply awful. Schary & I agree, others no. Schary suggests Dorothy McGuire." When Tracy finally met Papas, an austere woman with jet-black hair and bushy eyebrows, he could scarcely contain himself. "Boy or girl???" he wrote in his book. "The Greek it is," he conceded. "[V]ote of Schary, Wise, Zimbalist against me (Dorothy McGuire)."

The casting of Papas brought *Tribute to a Bad Man* still closer to *Broken Lance*—Papas essentially repeating the Katy Jurado role—and whatever enthusiasm Tracy retained for the project quickly boiled away. In a conciliatory gesture, the studio took out a full-page ad in the trades, formally congratulating him for having been named Best Actor at the Cannes Film Festival (for *Bad Day at Black Rock*) and "Outstanding Western Star" (for *Broken Lance*) at the Silver Spur Awards in Reno. "Wear your 'Silver Spurs' in health and happiness in your new picture *Tribute to a Bad Man*," the copy chirped, but if Tracy was in any way mollified, it didn't show. The day after the ad appeared, he had a blowdown with Larry Keethe when his pants still wouldn't fit—after five tries—and Keethe, after nearly twenty years on the job with Tracy, tendered his resignation.

Shooting began at Montrose, Colorado, on June 1, with Irene Papas and actor Robert Francis (*The Caine Mutiny*) filming scenes for which Tracy was not required. Tracy departed for location that same day, arriving with Carroll early the next evening. According to Tracy's datebook, Wise was "shocked" at the scar on his face and ordered camera tests to see if it

* The release title was *The Bad and the Beautiful* (1952).

would show. The following morning they all drove up to the Rodock Ranch. "Wonderful set built upon mesa [at] 8700 ft. elevation—surrounded 14,000 or [so] over Rocky Mts.—snowcovered peaks." The weather was beautiful and clear, and the company, bedeviled by bad weather, got in a full day's work for a change.

Tracy had been set to start shooting on the sixth, but with all the weather delays, Wise thought he might not actually be needed for another week. He spoke by phone with Schary and decided to go back to L.A. to have the scar examined by his doctor. With Wise's blessing, Tracy left Montrose on the morning of the fifth, took the short route through Cedar City, and was in Las Vegas by 7:30 p.m. Wise called him in Los Angeles the next day to tell him that the tests made of the scar had come out okay.

Privately, Tracy asked Bert Allenberg to explore the possibility of starting the picture in Culver City and leaving the location work until last, but the studio just as privately nixed the idea, as none of the interior sets had yet been constructed. He was up at 3:30 on the morning of the tenth to place a call to Australia. "[T]alked Old One," he noted in his book. "Wonderful connection. Dear Old One."

Kate thought *Tribute* "a story with no merit whatsoever." At her suggestion, Tracy met with Benny Thau and asked that the film be postponed. Thau said it couldn't be done, then Allenberg pointed out that Tracy was supposed to start *The Mountain* for Paramount on August 1. "Allenberg gibberish threat of 'suit by Paramount' etc. etc.," Tracy wrote. "What hogwash—lies, deceit, sickened by it all." Then Howard Strickling called to advise him that there was a "plot" afoot to have Strickling go back with him to Colorado.

There was no word from the studio after that, and on June 13 there were discussions between Floyd Hendrickson and George Cohen as to how best to serve notice on Tracy that he was liable for damages if he failed to report for work. "[M-G-M counsel Saul Rittenberg] and GC both feel that we are in a better position to give oral notice to Bert Allenberg rather than formal written notice," Hendrickson wrote, "because in this way we are simply advising what is going to happen and, therefore, doesn't sound legal or like an ultimatum but still has legal effect."

That evening, Tracy boarded a United Airlines flight for Denver, arriving back in Montrose on the morning of the fourteenth. The weather was bad—Wise got only one scene in the can—and Tracy wasn't called for work at all. The next day was sunny and clear, and Tracy shot his first scene for the picture, Rodock's entrance to the ranch. The company finished the day with a barn interior. "[G]ood day's work," Tracy wrote. "Bob Wise agrees with foregoing." That evening, assistant director Arvid Griffin barbecued steaks and tomatoes for everyone on an outdoor grill.

"We arranged our shooting up at the ranch," said Wise,

in a way that [Tracy] could come up for only an hour or two the first couple of days to get acclimated because it was much higher than the town we were staying in. After that, I still took it very easy—just two or three hours a day. He was being a little irascible with both Bob Francis and Irene Papas, but I attributed that to the altitude. He kept complaining about shortness of breath and suggesting that we move the location to a lower altitude. Finally, about the fifth day, he had a bit of action where he had to bend over and pick up a horse's hoof and examine it. When he came up, he kind of gasped and said, "Bob, you better get someone else to replace me. The only way I can finish this film is if you can scrub this location and we go down to a lower place." I just about had it up to my eyeballs by that time. I said, "Okay, Spencer, we go down the hill and talk to the studio." I called Sam Zimbalist, who knew of the problems I was having, and told him I couldn't continue with Tracy. An hour later he called me back and said that Tracy was out of the picture.

Tracy tersely recorded the events of the day in his datebook: "Wise and Griff[in] talk to Strickling—all feel cannot go on in altitude . . . [C]all to studio. Replaced."

Said Wise: "I went over to see him. I was so angry at this man because of the mess he caused, but he was so emotional about it." Tracy, he recalled, was almost in tears. "It's the end of my career," he told the director. "I'm finished. I'll never make another picture." Wise, at first, could muster little sympathy for a man who had given him such fits. Like everyone else, Wise thought Tracy had conspired to make *The Mountain* during the time it would have taken to rebuild the sets at a lower elevation. "After one hour of this, as mad as I was, I was also feeling sympathy and sorrow for him. Tracy always came on the screen like the Rock of Gibraltar, yet he was actually the reverse of his screen image."

That night, Tracy made a one-word entry in his datebook: "Gin!" He caught an 11:00 p.m. flight out of Grand Junction, arriving back in Los Angeles at three in the morning. Tom Pryor of the *New York Times* got hold of the story and ran it as an eight-inch item on the twenty-first:

This morning the studio publicity department said Mr. Tracy had experienced difficulties working in a high altitude. Montrose, on the western slope of the Rocky Mountains, is 5,820 feet above sea level. Later, a studio executive acknowledged that the altitude was not the only cause of Mr. Tracy's return. "Spencer is very exacting about everything he does," the executive said, "and he is unhappy about several things. The studio has to determine if it wants to give in to him on some points." Metro executives are meeting with the actor's agent, Bert Allenberg of the William Morris agency, and it is expected that a decision about Mr. Tracy's continuance will be made within forty-eight hours.

Had Eddie Mannix been on hand, had Kate been there, had Tracy had the kind of gentle handling and reassurance he always needed at the start of a picture, the outcome might have been different. Mannix, however, was recovering from a heart attack, Hepburn was eight thousand miles away with her own set of responsibilities, and Dore Schary could never justify to the New York office the moving of an outdoor set while a company of 110 sat idle on location.

There was a time, back in the heyday of the studio, when such a move might have been possible, particularly for a star of Tracy's magnitude. But 1955 wasn't 1940, M-G-M no longer dominated the world entertainment landscape, and the economics of picture making had irrevocably changed. The men who had come up in the time of Mayer and Thalberg, of block booking and studio-owned theater chains, were having to reorient their thinking to the new realities of the marketplace, where flickering black-and-white pictures on a home TV set generally trumped the big screen as long as those flickering pictures were free.

Dore Schary was troubled in later years by the widely held presumption that Tracy had been fired from M-G-M. "That's crazy. That's crap. Total crap," he erupted when asked about it in 1978. "A stupid story. A ridiculous, stupid story." Tracy had completed three of the four pictures required of him under his contract, and the contract was up as of August 1, 1955. "I would *never* have fired Spencer Tracy," Schary insisted. Might he simply have been at the end of his rope? "I would never have been at the end of my rope with Spence. He was always worried whether a picture was good for him, whether he wanted to do it. Back and forth. But that is not true . . . Just . . . not . . . true. And I would know *that*."

Schary thought that maybe Robert Wise was part of the problem, that he had no real knowledge of the culture at M-G-M. Years of coddling on the part of the studio had created a dependency that Wise couldn't possibly understand. "He just got scared," Schary said of Tracy. "He began to get short of breath. A guy like Tracy needed a *father* [in a director]. He needed someone around to kind of look after him. And I don't think Wise gave him that. I think another director might have solved that problem, pulled him through the picture. But Spence was by then pretty well convinced that he was very sick."

On June 25, 1955, Tracy made the following entry in his datebook: "Finished at Metro! June 18 last salary day. Phone by Allenberg to Thau. Eddie M. away!!! The end of 20 years. Feel I did my best for last pic."

Eddie Mannix was stunned when he returned to the studio and was briefed on what had taken place in his absence. "Well," he demanded, "why the hell didn't you take it down to three thousand feet and do the picture?"

CHAPTER 28

The Mountain

Tracy's removal from *Tribute to a Bad Man* eliminated any conflicts with Paramount and the anticipated August 1955 start of *The Mountain*. He focused on family matters: his month-old grandson, Joseph Spencer, John's thirty-first birthday, Susie's twenty-third birthday, Louise's hunt for a new house.

"I bet I looked at 150 houses," Louise said. "I looked at every house in Beverly Hills that came on the market. I got so discouraged; there was always something wrong." The house she finally settled upon was a gated two-acre estate on Tower Road—three bedrooms, four baths, a vast lawn sloping down to the pool. "It was so quiet and lots of birds and trees," she said. "I felt it would be the closest thing to the country. That was the big point. Then it had a lot of little points. It had a three-car garage. We had this beautiful piece of furniture, my great-grandmother's secretary, and we had to have nine-and-a-half-foot ceilings to get this thing in. The ceilings were very high . . . It was a beautiful house."

There were, of course, calls to and from Australia and meetings with Leland Hayward. In from New York, Herman Shumlin tried persuading Tracy to join the cast of *Inherit the Wind* for four weeks, long enough to give the play's star, Paul Muni, a rest. Then Tracy had a courtesy call from Benny Thau, the last official interaction he was to have with M-G-M. Eddie Mannix had held up his pension payout—a sum amounting to $221,000 and change—until he had extracted an oral agreement from Bert Allenberg that Tracy would "sometime" do another picture for Metro at $150,000. ("No one but Mannix wants it," Allenberg told his client, but since Tracy was technically one film shy of his contractual commitment, he was advised to go ahead and accept the provision.) Now, after much talk of shelving *Tribute to a Bad Man*—and turndowns from both Clark Gable and Gregory Peck—Thau wanted Tracy to know that Jimmy Cagney had agreed to do the picture after Nicholas Schenck had called him at Martha's Vineyard and put it on a personal basis, asking him to "jump in" for his old friend. Said Cagney, "I was about as interested in working as I was in flying, which means a considerable level below zero, but after much gab, I agreed. I specified that I would need at least two or three weeks between jobs, and then I would come out and do it." Tracy's reaction to the news: "Who cares?"

In Australia, Hepburn had drawn unwanted attention of her own from a celebrity-starved press. "Is there a romance in Katharine Hepburn's life?" asked the *Sydney Sun*. "We will say that there is. It's Spencer Tracy. He loves theatre, watched all the rehearsals at the Old Vic Company, and flew back to New York in the plane with Katharine." Hepburn did her best to deflect such items, consenting to a joint news conference with Bobby Helpmann where she batted back questions she considered too personal. "I saw a report where Spencer was said to have flown from London to see my rehearsals," she said. "That's not true because there was no one at the rehearsals. But, yes, Spencer was in London at the time. He joked that they wouldn't let him in. 'I was too lowbrow,' he said."

The scrutiny followed her to Brisbane, where the Old Vic Company opened at His Majesty's Theatre on July 18. "Katharine Hepburn's first waking thought today was to put a call through to Spencer Tracy," the *Brisbane Telegraph* reported. "Spencer Tracy, though 10,000 miles away, was the only person who would get a word from Miss Hepburn this morning. It is understood that the Old Vic star phones him daily. A Sydney message says it is rumored that Spencer Tracy may take a brief holiday at Surfer Paradise during the Old Vic three-week season in Brisbane. For the whole morning, Miss Hepburn remained in her room at the city hotel, surrounded by the knick-knacks she insists on carrying around the world. These include three portraits of Spencer Tracy." Sheilah Graham picked up on all the Queensland crosstalk and ran a slightly more oblique item in her *New York Mirror* column: "Katharine Hepburn, now in Australia, is spending something like 100 dollars a day in phone bills to her long-time love . . . that's love."

Hepburn was also working her way through the loss of Constance Collier, her almost daily phone calls, her wires and letters. "We miss Constance so much," Theresa Helburn wrote her, "I realize what her loss must mean to you. You have really lost two mothers in a comparatively short time. But at least you had two wonderful ones."

There was more to discuss than strictly personal matters. Through Bert Allenberg, Kate was negotiating with Hal Wallis to play Lizzie Curry in Paramount's adaptation of *The Rainmaker.* Wallis wanted to pay $135,000, but Hepburn was holding out for $150,000 and director approval. (Wallis would not agree to a deferred deal, similar to the one Hepburn made for *The African Queen,* in which she would accept half her normal fee up front in exchange for a cut of the profits.) She would talk with Tracy by phone, then Tracy would relay her messages to Allenberg.

"Spence told me today about his talk with you and your approval of the financial terms and your strong feeling about the director," Allenberg wrote her on July 15, "hence, I will attempt to make the deal on the basis of you having full director approval."

In London the year before, Jane Feely had said: "Someday I may need you." And now she did. In a call from Seattle, she relayed the news that her eighty-one-year-old mother, Spence's beloved aunt Jenny, was in the hospital, gravely ill with cancer of the esophagus. She asked that he come to Renton, and instantly word came back that he would.

"Practically the next day, the arrangements were made," Jane said.

He was going to come by himself, which was unusual. I had not thought to say, "You come, too, Carroll." And I think that hurt Carroll's feelings. Carroll, of course, was the one that you always talked to in order to get in touch with Spence . . . A broken hip was what put [my mother] in the hospital, and then they did the exploratory things, checked and found out that she had the can-cer . . . One of the nurses said, "We have a patient down there in room twenty-three, and she thinks that she's related to Spencer Tracy." They were kind of watching her, you know? And so the next day he arrived, and that nurse was flabbergasted.

They had a couple of good visits in the hospital. My mother had a tremendous sense of humor. When she first saw him, she said to him, deadpan, "Have you got work?" I think he liked talking with her, maybe more than he did with his own mother, because his mother was a very sad person; she mourned the loss of her husband until she died. I think also that he was a little afraid of her, and he certainly didn't want to offend her in any way.

When the subject turned to Carroll, he echoed the words he had once spoken to Frank Tracy: "Carroll . . . I don't know what to do about Carroll. Carroll should have gone back to Wakashan, had his own life, his own success . . ."

"He was a great success as a husband!" Jenny Tracy interjected. Spence's face, Jane recalled, was stricken at the remark.

They went on to talk about family and about the old days, and she did not ever, either in my hearing or when they had a private talk, talk about [the fact that] she knew she was dying. I'm certain she did [know], but, in our family, nobody told anybody that anyone was sick or dying. I think it took an awful lot more out of him than I had any idea that it did. I didn't realize how stressful it was for him to get on a plane by himself, come over here into a strange area.

I had dinner with him at the Olympic Hotel—we didn't go into the dining room, we had dinner in a suite—and we had a good visit about Ireland, and how fun it had been. We talked, because I was thinking, "What am I going to do?" He said, "You don't worry. You need a cushion, and here is the beginning of it." And he left a check for two or three thousand dollars. "Don't have any worries about taking care of her. Do whatever you have to do."

I went to the airport with him when he left. We stopped to have a cup of coffee at the counter. It was amazing—nobody approached him. Everything was just fine until a waitress came with his cup of coffee. As she was pouring the coffee, she was staring at him and she poured the coffee all over the counter. "Oh!" He was able to laugh over that one. When we talked afterward about Mama, he said, "You know, she does not demand attention—she *commands* it. All I can think of with her sitting in that bed is Ethel Barrymore." There were so many things about her that were dramatic enough, I think, to appeal to him.

Jenny's time in the hospital was brief—six weeks—and Spencer underwrote it. When she died, word came through Carroll that the funeral expenses were to be covered, too.

The Mountain, at first glance, would have seemed an unlikely vehicle for Spencer Tracy. The work of the prolific Russian-born novelist and historian Henri Troyat, it told the story of a retired mountain guide pressed back into service when an airliner crashes in the French Alps. Based on an actual event, the 122-page novel was first published in the United States in 1953. Tracy read a review of the book in England; subsequently, he gave it to Eddie Dmytryk. "It's a simple story," he later said, "full of honest suspense and character, a Cain and Abel tale of two brothers on a mission to a wrecked airplane in the Alps. They fight the elements, themselves, and each other. It depicts the contrast of good and evil. An emotional back-breaker, believe me."

He tried getting Metro to buy the rights, only to learn that Paramount had snapped them up for the bargain price of $10,000. Within a couple of months, Tracy had made a deal with Don Hartman, Paramount's production chief, to star in the picture as soon as he was free of his M-G-M contract. Alpine weather conditions dictated a start in late August or early September, when the snow level would be at seven thousand feet and the daytime temperature at Luzern would be a very tolerable sixty-five degrees. Dmytryk signed on in May while Tracy and Sam Zimbalist were locking horns over *Tribute to a Bad Man*. The irony was lost on no one that Tracy gained his release from that picture on the basis of altitude, only to step into a part that would put him at elevations considerably higher than the six thousand feet he found so debilitating at Montrose.

Tackling the script was the Oscar-nominated screenwriter Ranald MacDougall, whose previous job for Paramount had been the listless Humphrey Bogart comedy *We're No Angels*. Agreeing with Tracy that the story was essentially "Cain and Abel on a mountain," MacDougall deliberately simplified the two brothers—the older one embarking on one last climb to rescue survivors, the younger intent more on looting the crash site than on checking it for signs of life. The result became a treatise on the nature of human greed, a sort of snowbound *Treasure of the Sierra Madre*.

Having carefully balanced the story between the two competing characters, MacDougall clashed with Dmytryk over the casting of twenty-five-year-old Robert Wagner as brother to the fifty-five-year-old Tracy. "To me, as a primal contest between simple good and simple evil, it called for an equality of forces involved," MacDougall said. "Wagner seemed to me to be a born loser in a contest with Tracy. I am not questioning the ability of Wagner as an actor by this, merely stating my approach to the subject. I had written the part with Charlton Heston in mind.* As an antagonist for Tracy, it seemed to me the outcome of the contest would be in doubt with a stronger man. With Wagner, I felt that the younger man would emerge as being petulant rather than powerfully evil. Also, of course, the mountain

---

* Heston was thirty-one at the time. In the book, Isaiah Vaudagne, the elder brother, is fifty-two, while Marcellin is "barely thirty." In MacDougall's screenplay the brothers were renamed Zachary and Chris Teller, their ages unspecified.

climbing contest of man against nature did not play as well as it might have with a stronger pair."

Dmytryk explained his rationale: "Spence had had a good relationship with Robert Wagner during the shooting of *Broken Lance;* he also had a very realistic attitude regarding his own box office appeal. He felt that Wagner might attract the younger and larger audience and suggested we try to borrow him from 20th. I agreed with his analysis (as it turned out, we were both somewhat in error) and 20th was willing, so R.J. was set."

As an added gesture of both fondness and respect, Tracy spoke to Paramount and arranged for the billing clause of his contract to be modified, permitting Wagner's name to be placed above the title, the first time the younger actor had been accorded equal billing with a star of Tracy's stature.

"It was extraordinary," said Wagner, "and it made a big difference in my career because it took me out of being homogenized with all these other people. He made very sure that I had a dressing room at Paramount and that I was on dressing room row with all of them, so I was there with Bing Crosby, Bob Hope, Dean Martin, Jerry Lewis, Spencer Tracy, Bill Holden, me. He did that for me. I said to him, 'Jesus, Spence, thank you so much.' He said, 'That's okay, I wanted you to have it.' He was sure that I had the same thing."

However much he initially wanted to do the film, Tracy began to tense up as the start of production grew near. He fretted over individual lines of dialogue, disapproved of the supporting cast assembled by Dmytryk— Claire Trevor, William Demarest, Barbara Darrow, Richard Arlen.

The prospect of a long plane trip filled him with dread, for the actor who hated location work above all others had somehow committed himself to the ultimate location picture. "I can't do it," he finally said to Dmytryk. "It's just not the part for me. How about Gable? I think he's free, and he'd be perfect. Or Robert Young?" Dmytryk was gently reassuring but at a point decided that Tracy needed—and wanted—a firm hand. "When he stalled again, I simply said the car and driver would be calling to take him to the airport at a certain time, and I would expect to see him there. That was it. He showed up."

To calm Tracy's nerves on the flight that took them to Europe, R. J. Wagner presented him with a St. Bernard medal, Bernard being the patron saint of mountaineers. "He wore it on a chain around his neck throughout the trip and never once took it off." They paused for a few days in Paris, putting up at the Raphael and taking in the nightlife. Bert Allenberg saw Tracy there and dutifully reported back to Hepburn that he was looking and feeling fine: "He was leaving the next morning for Chamonix and seemed to be in excellent spirits." Dmytryk bought a convertible, planning to have the car shipped back to the States.

"The three of us drove together from Paris to Geneva," Wagner recalled, "then up to Chamonix and the French Alps to get acclimated. That was the first time ever that there had been a company up there shooting." Their arrival at Chamonix preceded the start of production by a couple of weeks, time to acclimate and train with Charles Balmat, a prominent Alpine guide whose ancestor, Jacques Balmat, was said to have been the first to climb Mont Blanc in 1792.

"Mr. Tracy is very unhappy with his accommodations," production manager Harry Caplan advised his office in Los Angeles, the Hotel Les Alpes being something less than the Sun Valley resort Tracy had evidently envisioned. "We offered to rent (he proposed it) a chateau so that he could have more privacy. However, before looking at some chateaus, I took A. C. Lyles [Dmytryk's assistant producer] to the Le Savoy Hotel and Lyles agreed with me that he (Tracy) and all the Paramount staff might be better off there . . . Tracy is one of those artistic people who is a complainer. The room is filthy, the rugs, beds are dirty, and the food (being pension plan) has no variety or selection to it."

Caplan had started out in the thirties as prop man to the Marx Brothers and W. C. Fields, so he was used to difficult talent. It fell principally to Eddie Dmytryk to nurse Tracy along while the company was on location. "Our unit is definitely being run by Mr. Tracy," Caplan reported a couple of days later.

> Eddie kowtows to his every wish. As a result, it is hard to get organized. We found Tracy a chalet (apartment) but now he doesn't want it. I added some rugs to his room [and] am employing an English-speaking chamber maid, and we are painting the doors and closets in his room . . . Tracy has been complaining because the coffee isn't here. He complains and criticizes at the drop of a hat. This location is very difficult and trying and this added problem does not make it any easier for us. He is very evasive about okaying wardrobe and Eddie sides with him. The reason I wired for new shirts is because he says these we brought are too small. [Assistant director] Bill [McGarry] has brought him three other types to no avail . . . I have a feeling Mr. Tracy is not going to do the things that Mr. Dmytryk said he would. He walked over about one mile of mountain today and gave up, returning to the hotel. He hasn't as yet gone to the top of the Teleferique.

The advantage of locating the shoot on the Aiguille du Midi in the Mont Blanc massif of the French Alps was the Téléphérique de l'Aiguille du Midi, the historic aerial tramway that climbs the north face of the mountain, depositing its passengers near the top of the 12,800-foot summit. In terms of facilitating the transport of both equipment and personnel, it was unmatched anywhere in Europe and effectively made location work for *The Mountain* feasible. Tracy's distrust of the thing was obvious, and he had plenty of time to formulate disaster scenarios as he haggled with Caplan and struggled for rest.

"Maybe," suggested Robert Wagner, "he was just giving them trouble . . . I was below him in the hotel, and I could hear him pacing around because he had a very difficult time sleeping." Hepburn, particularly, knew how rough the location was going to be on him and arranged for Margaret Shipway, David Lean's script supervisor on *Time of the Cuckoo,* to serve as Tracy's secretary, a soothing presence over the course of the shoot. In her tweed skirts and cashmere sweater sets, Shipway had a civilizing effect on the crew, always "smiling and friendly and interested" in whatever was going on, serving the same approximate role as the young woman from Boise who was hired to sit calmly and demurely alongside Tracy on the set of *Northwest Passage.*

"Just a short line to let you know we started shooting today," Maggie wrote Hepburn on the morning of August 29. "Weather is doubtful but the crew are all happy and keen. Have settled in this hotel now—they've painted Mr. Tracy's bedroom—and apart from the dreadful smell of new paint he's more comfortable . . . Mr. Tracy's sense of humor is wonderful— we laugh and laugh. I think he's a marvelous person. He talks about you all the time."

Shooting began with the making of stereo plates, POV shots, and long shots of the doubles in action. There was bad light all morning and hail by noon, causing the company to quit after lunch. Dmytryk found himself moving scenes around to take advantage of whatever light he could get, frustrating Harry Caplan's attempts at creating a rudimentary schedule. Maggie Shipway worried that Tracy wasn't eating very much and that the noise from a nightclub opposite the hotel was keeping him awake nights.

R. J. Wagner was as unnerved by the extreme elevations as Tracy and just as wary of the new single-cable Téléphérique. "I didn't want to get on that thing too many times, and we had to shoot up there. As a matter of fact, *I* had to shoot there. It wasn't Spence, but Spence said he'd go with me. I was very hesitant about it always. Eddie Dmytryk was up there with the crew, and I had to come around and get up into this thing, and [Spence] said, 'Come on. I'll go with you.' And it got halfway up, and it went off the cable!" The car had, in fact, lurched to a stop with such force that it swung up and hit the cable, shattering the glass. As it rocked back and forth, R.J. felt Tracy's arm around him. "I thought we were falling . . . and boom! It stopped, and we looked out the window and we were hanging [by the protective iron covering that served as the wheel housing] in the middle of this cable."

At a sheer drop of eleven thousand feet, it was as heart-stopping a sight as either man had ever beheld. "Those damn things are scary enough when all is going well," Dmytryk said, "but to be caught in one of those claustrophobic cubicles, swinging in the void . . ." Frank Westmore, the unit makeup man, was among the crew members observing the scene: "From our viewpoint on the Aiguille du Midi, we could see the little car below us, swinging wildly from side-to-side and bouncing frighteningly against a now-slack cable."

There was nothing the crew could do other than keep their eyes on the tiny figures gripping the safety bars inside the car. "So we wait," said Wagner, "and they sent an open work car down. I thought, 'Jesus Christ, we're going to have to get out of this thing and get in there?' And then go up because it came from up above?' I mean, it was very, very frightening. So they come down and they leave and then they back the thing down again. I think, 'Jesus, it's going back down.' And, indeed, no, they put it back [on the cable], and it would go back up." The car took what seemed like an eternity to make its way up to the platform.

"When it ground its way into the station," Westmore said, "Tracy staggered out looking twenty years older than he had that morning." The irony of the incident was that once everyone had safely reached the summit, there was nothing to do but sit around and wait for a break in the light. Finally, they made a couple of shots for the trailer showing the crew sitting it out on the rocks. Then Tracy had to ride back down the mountain in the very same car that had balked carrying him up. "He went up there for me," Wagner said of Tracy, "that is all I know. He was with me. He went up there because he knew that I was really frightened. I think it was after that experience, that next couple of days, that he got into drinking a little bit."

There was no grand tumble, at least not on location, but rather a controlled leavening that put everyone on edge. The night of the Téléphérique incident, Wagner found Tracy in the hotel bar, where he was "completely drunk—gone! It was startling, because he had become an entirely different person."

Tracy was given to quicksilver twists of temperament that alcohol only served to exacerbate. "Strangely, he was very talkative and friendly, actually charming," said Frank Westmore, "telling all sorts of fascinating Hollywood stories, even as his head sagged lower and lower on his chest. He ordered another round of drinks." It looked as if he would be in for an early night when he abruptly snapped to and hurled a brandy snifter at the face of the bartender.

"As I remember," said Wagner, "the bartender made some kind of remark. And out of that remark Spence took exception and picked up his glass. It came out of nowhere, just out of nowhere. Flash anger." Wagner stuck his right hand out to deflect the glass and reflexively closed his hand in on it, shattering it in his palm and driving the shards deep into his middle fingers.

"Tracy was oblivious to everything by then," Westmore said, "and didn't even know that he was being wrestled from his chair by members of his crew and hustled up to his room. I helped our company doctor as he stitched and bandaged Bob's hand, meanwhile pondering the practical consideration of how I would mask the gashes for the remainder of the film." Westmore was able to cover the injury with a combination of collodion and makeup, neatly concealing the stitches. "A contrite Tracy watched the procedure, barely remembering what had happened the night before."

Fortunately, the light improved and Tracy and Wagner were able to begin working together. They and the crew were usually roped together in groups of four, lest someone disappear into a hidden ravine, and they wore crampon spikes to keep from slipping. The members of the company came to dread the rending sounds of the avalanches, which they could hear more often than see. "I was very, very frightened of the mountains and the crevices," Wagner admitted. "We were on a piece up there and saw an avalanche, and it was at least a mile away, and we backed up when we saw that thing break. And I remember in the book they referred to the sound as 'the tearing of silk.' And it was that."

At the end of a full workday, Tracy was too tired to create much trouble. "Conditions are a little better," Caplan, obviously relieved, reported to the studio. "Tracy has settled down a little. He is a natural born crabber. I had it out with him and we seem to be friends. He is going to work Sunday (tomorrow) as a favor to Bill [McGarry] and myself. The last two days of shooting we have done a lot of work but [neither] I nor Bill can quite understand the way Eddie is shooting . . . He is very evasive. He is transferring a lot of work to the studio on account of Tracy. This means we will have a lot of plates and need many rock sets."

Lloyd Shearer, the West Coast correspondent for *Parade,* observed Tracy in the hotel bar, impassively sipping milk and absorbing a lecture from Harry Mines, the unit publicist. "We have a still photographer," Mines was heard to complain, "and his job is to take pictures. You won't let him, and I think that's pretty uncooperative."

Tracy had a long and well-deserved reputation for coming off at photographers who got in his line of sight, clicked while a scene was in progress, or otherwise got on his nerves. Pat Elsey could remember kneading the tension from his shoulders after an ill-timed candid was snapped on the set of *Northwest Passage.* Bill Self once saw a studio photographer come up and

On location for *The Mountain*, 1956.
(ROBERT WAGNER)

take his picture while the two men were deep in conversation. "Spence turned to him and said, 'You're going to click yourself right out of the business.' Well, at that point, the guy faded away."

Tracy ran a hand across the weathered face he once likened to an outhouse door and fixed Mines with a withering stare. "Did you mention the word 'job'?" he demanded, allowing the word to hang in the air.

Well, I've got a "job" too. I've got a job to act in this picture, and I mean to do it as well as I can. I'm not going to let anyone interfere with that. I get up at 5:30 every morning, and we've got to hike up the mountain. It's 10, 12, 13 thousand feet up. How many times have you been up, Harry? Once? Well, the air's pretty thin up there, and after you trudge for two hours, it's a little hard to breathe. I stand in the snow with a pack on my back and I try to give the scene everything I've got. I'm concentrating on the lines and the mood and the take, and then in the middle I suddenly hear camera shutters clicking. I'm sorry, but it breaks my concentration. I know that stills have to be taken, but let's shoot 'em a little distance away."

Then Tracy, according to Shearer, got to his feet, smiled good-naturedly, and said, "Don't make me a heavy. Let's go in and eat." The next day, he spent two hours posing in the snow, giving the photographer his complete cooperation.

As unpopular as he was with Mines and Harry Caplan, Tracy was well regarded among the rank and file, having seen that the crew was made more comfortable after they were stuck at the Hotel Les Alpes. "You know Spence," Wagner said. "Everybody loved him. He was wonderful and very funny and had a terrific edge on his humor." When R.J. complained one day that Dmytryk was working him too hard—a measure of the location's difficulty and the relative thinness of its air—Tracy handed him a stern look. "Young man," he said as if back playing Father Flanagan, "you ought to get down on your knees every night and thank God you work in the most overpaid business in the world."

There were constant delays getting equipment and personnel to location by foot and by jeep. Days were often overcast and no film could be exposed, while at other times it rained and snowed. Takes were ruined by mike shadow. Mercifully, one take was all that was usually necessary when all the elements cooperated. There was no coverage, and certain shots intended to be made on location—particularly close-ups—were deferred to the studio.

Much of the tension dissolved with the completion of the mountain sequences, and the company began working close to the hotel on the introductory scenes for Wagner's character of Chris. ("You there—boy!") A few miles from Chamonix was the town of La Tour, where the village scenes were shot, and where Claire Trevor and E. G. Marshall joined the company. Trevor would recall how Tracy adored R. J. Wagner—whom he called "Bobby"—and how Wagner loved him. Marshall would remember the relish with which Tracy read aloud a letter from Hepburn, who was in Melbourne at the time. "Only parts," Marshall qualified. "We should all have such a correspondent."

Location work on *The Mountain* ended with a retake, as the weather prevented further shooting at the village. After lunch, the B Unit went to the first Téléphérique station to shoot plates, and the ordeal was at last at an end. There was a party that night and a presentation to the guides who had made the whole expedition possible.

"It was quite a wingding," Eddie Dmytryk recalled, "and, naturally, many toasts had to be drunk with the excellent local wines. Just as naturally, Tracy had to drink them." Said Wagner:

> It was the end of the location and everyone was rather relaxed. And he started off by stopping and having a beer, then a little piece of cheese, and everyone was all very happy . . . When we left [Chamonix], it was Claire Trevor, [her husband] Milton [Bren], myself. We were all in a van coming down the hill, and I remember Spence took his hat off and he went, "Whooow!" and flung it right out into the Alps. We got down to Paris, and it didn't take much for him . . . Spence was very nervous about flying . . . I think he was very anxious, and when we got on the plane he had a few belts on the plane. We landed in New York and got on another plane to come to L.A., and he was out of control.

The flight was to be met at LAX by Louise and Susie, but Carroll headed them off, gravely whispering something in Louise's ear. "It was the first inkling I ever had that he had a drinking problem," Susie remembered. "On the way home, my mother explained it a bit, saying it was something he'd had to battle all his life."*

Where he went, whom he was with, is uncertain to this day. "Carroll came and got him," said Wagner, "and they took him away." Tracy's datebook entry for the twenty-eighth carries a picture of a jug and the notation "Home TWA 11 PM <u>drove.</u>" The final two days of September show identical words: "out" and "orchestra." ("He wasn't belligerent," said Wagner. "He said, 'We'll get the band and we'll get together.' ")

"For the next six days," wrote Eddie Dmytryk, "I received daily progress reports: This quiet, very private man was on the town, and in spades. I shot what few scenes I could without him, then closed down. On day seven, he was in the hospital with a bleeding ulcer. I planned to restart production a

---

*When Susie was in high school, her best friend tried telling her that her father had a drinking problem. "Oh, he doesn't drink," Susie insisted. "He orders ginger ale or 7-Up whenever we have dinner with him."

week from that day, and in a week he showed up, ready to work. For a few days he had a bottle of milk constantly at hand. Then it was back to Cokes again and what Warren G. Harding called 'normalcy.' "

Somewhat chastened after ten days of "illness," Tracy became a model employee, welcoming visitors to the set—Cary Grant, Pearl Bailey, Jesse Lasky, Donald O'Connor—and cooperating with the press to the extent of handwriting the answers to eighteen questions submitted him by Jack Hirshberg of the studio's publicity department. On what basis do you select your roles? one question asked. "Don't just want to make movies at this stage of the game," he replied. "I'm an old bastard. Hard to please." Do you ever want to direct? "No. Lack patience to deal with actors." Teet Carle, who had worked with Tracy as a publicist at M-G-M, was now publicity director at Paramount: "[Tracy] prompted the tops in good fellowship reunions when I met him in the studio café. I was his 'old buddy' whom he had missed. Maybe he, at long last, was sleeping better."

At the beginning of production, Tracy had notified Bill McGarry and Harry Caplan that he was accustomed to taking a ninety-minute lunch (although it was not mentioned in his contract). At the studio he fell into the habit of returning to the set thirty to forty-five minutes later than expected, setting off another round of internal hand-wringing. On the set he was reflective, telling Lloyd Shearer he was going to "take it easy" after *The Old Man and the Sea*.

> Now, don't get me wrong. I'm not retiring. The only time an actor really retires is when they don't want him anymore. I don't think that's true in my case, although maybe it is. But I don't see any point in making run-of-the-mill pictures. People can get as much of that stuff as they want on television. I'm not money hungry, and what I'd like to do is make maybe one picture a year or even less. But I want the picture to be memorable, something substantial and worthwhile. When I get out of my Thunderbird these days, my back hurts. And it's not because of the driver's seat. It's because I'm not a kid anymore. And if I'm going to do a picture, I want the story to be solid and meaningful and entertaining. When the public walks out of the theater where a picture of mine's been playing, I want to feel that the people have gotten their money's worth.

He was working interiors the day his uncle Andrew died in Freeport at the age of seventy-two. It wasn't unexpected; Andrew Tracy, in his forty-second year at the bank, had endured a trumped-up embezzlement investigation that left his spirit broken. Spence had sent Carroll to Freeport for

moral support, and Carroll had brought Gene Sullivan down from Milwaukee. Results of a lie detector test were inconclusive, and a grand jury refused
to indict him.

"So the whole thing evaporated," said Andrew's son Frank.

And after that he was never any good healthwise. His mental attitude was very sour. A couple of times I met with him in Chicago at
the Blackstone when Spence was going through. And Spence
would say, "Jesus, your dad is in terrible shape." I'd say, "Yeah, he
is." He'd say, "That goddamn bank. That's all he's got in his head.
No wonder he couldn't get by a lie detector—the goddamn bank
was like his wife. Could accept no criticism, wouldn't sign that
non-indictment thing . . . it was loyalty." I said, "That's the way he
is, Spence. That's the way he is. He's straight as an arrow. He'll
accept no criticism of his character or his actions." And Spence
said, "Well, it's gonna kill him." Spence was very good to him, very
concerned. He used to call up from California: "How's he doing
today?" And when he died, he called and said, "I can't make it.
We're finishing up *The Mountain*. This picture's a stinker, and I
want to get it in back of me. I hate it. I've been buried in the thing
for so long. I think in two weeks we can wrap it up here, and I'm
going to stay with it."

Tracy's loathing of a picture was, for once, well founded. By purposely
reducing the Teller brothers to "simple good and simple evil," Ranald Mac-
Dougall had robbed them of all shading. *The Mountain* was ill written, miscast, awkwardly staged—and almost everyone, at least secretly, seemed to
know it. "Oh, God, that was a terrible picture!" Claire Trevor exclaimed in
1983. "It goes on forever and it's bad. Spencer Tracy plays the older brother
of Robert Wagner who was then a beanpole, he was so skinny. He looked
like he was twelve years old, and Spence had already gotten heavy and old-
looking. It was ludicrous." Eddie Dmytryk admitted that he never should
have done the picture: "[Tracy] was playing Bob Wagner's older brother but
looked like Bob's grandfather. We poured him on the plane but he continued drinking back here. It was an awful situation. I realized I had become
his keeper."

Tracy tried mightily in individual scenes, and occasionally he prevailed
on a crowded soundstage when all eyes were upon him. Dmytryk described
a scene toward the end of the picture in which Zachary recounts the climb
and the rescue of the lone survivor, an Indian girl, and casts himself in a
harsh light, insisting the hero of the day was his younger brother, killed in
the process. "It is a long scene, running five to six minutes, interrupted only

In 1943, Andrew B. Tracy visited his famous nephew on the set of *A Guy Named Joe.* (PATRICIA MAHON COLLECTION)

by one short question from E. G. Marshall near the beginning. I shot Tracy's close-up first, as was frequently my custom, to ensure that this shot, in which most of this scene would be played, had all the freshness and spontaneity possible. As usual, Spence nailed it in the first take. At the finish, most of the crew was crying. I said, 'Cut,' and looked over at E.G. [Marshall]. Tears were streaming down his face. 'I wish all the method actors could watch this man work—just once!' he said."

Kate's Old Vic tour ended in Perth on November 11, and she quietly returned to town via American Airlines on the sixteenth. That night Tracy noted in his book: "Din[ner] with Old Rat [with food] from Chasen's."

Filming finally concluded with scenes inside the wreckage of the plane on the nineteenth, and again he dined alone with Kate, as he had every night since her return. When she flew back to New York on the morning of the twentieth, she called from the airport, and again that evening from Hartford. In a few days she was off to London, where she would be making a picture with Bob Hope. In the nine eventful months just ended, Spence had seen Old One exactly four days.*

In the aftermath of her mother's death, Jane Feely came to California for an extended visit, and she met the Tracys at Chasen's one night for din-

---

* Tracy liked to tease Kath about her age, pointing out that he had given her joy in her "latter days." The name "Ratty" was a term of affection they tossed between themselves, though never in public. "Old One" and "Old Rat" were generally applied in the third person.

With Edward Dmytryk.
(PATRICIA MAHON COLLECTION)

ner. Spence had brought two Christmas presents for her, one of which was
a Madonna of hammered brass he had found for her in Chamonix.

It was a beautiful thing, and then a little carving of the Last Supper,
one of those tiny, tiny things that he had picked up over there. And
we had a nice visit. He said that he was cooking for himself, and it
was obvious, of course, that he wasn't at home—he had eaten
wieners for the whole last week. And there was this feeling that he
was lonely, that he was standing apart from the rest of them at the
table. I detected a little sadness there, but thought: "It is none of
your business. Stay out of it." It was hard to be very, very loyal to
Louise and to think as much of her as I did, and also think as much
of him as I did . . . That dinner was kind of strained. It was—oh,
you know, they talked back and forth about family matters and
what everybody was doing, what John was doing, but there were
two different people, two different households. It was as if he was
living in one country, and she in another.

On December 24, Tracy attended the Bogarts' annual Yuletide party,
where he noticed singer Rosemary Clooney peering out a picture window, a
study in holiday sadness. They'd met, but she knew him mostly from the
movies.

"What's the matter?" he asked, staring out the window alongside her.

"I don't know," she said, her husband, José Ferrer, dancing with Betty Bacall just a few feet away. "I've never been to a party on Christmas Eve. I guess I'm just homesick."

His voice was strong, but he was not unkind.

"Get used to it," he said.

Nineteen fifty-six would at last be the year of *The Old Man and the Sea.* Fred Zinnemann had signed on as director after two years of hesitation—John Ford, Vittorio De Sica, David Lean, and John Sturges were discussed in the interim—and Peter Viertel had produced a screenplay in collaboration with Ernest Hemingway that Tracy, for one, thought "great." Leland Hayward had made a distribution deal with Warner Bros. that called for full financing and, after the picture returned twice its negative cost, 50 percent of the gross. In December Tracy recorded a scratch track narration so that he could "come to grips with the characterization" and show that he could carry the descriptive voice-over in Viertel's script as well as the thoughts and words of Santiago, the Old Man.

"I had a good feeling about the way he approached the characterization of the Old Man," Zinnemann said in a letter to Hemingway. "As to the descriptive part, I think that it will have to be read like poetry; like a ballad, with an underlying rhythm to it. Spencer tended to read these descriptive parts a bit too objectively, rather like a report. I think that when we do the final narration, it should give the impression of rising out of a musical mood, created by one softly strumming guitar."

As the new year began, Hemingway defined their two principal problems: finding a boy to play Manolo and getting Tracy in "some sort of shape," as he now weighed, stripped, 215 pounds. For the job he recommended a man named George Brown, an old friend and his own personal trainer, who could, he said, make Tracy "look as much like a Cojimar fisherman as possible" in the space of six weeks. When Tracy advised Zinnemann he would be going to Europe for a couple of months "to be near Katharine Hepburn," it was arranged for Brown to meet him in Cuba around March 1, affording them six weeks of uninterrupted work. Tracy, however, did not go to Europe, despite word from Kate that she and Bob Hope were hopelessly mismatched and that the picture was, for all intents and purposes, a stiff. He remained in town, fielding offers from Columbia and Fox, loafing, watching way too much TV, and subsisting primarily on weenies and frozen dinners.

He saw *The Mountain* for the first time on February 17 and pronounced himself "disappointed" with the picture. "Mountain is failure—think must be ending," he wrote in his datebook. "Wrong—always thought wrong. Phony. Should go back get brother. Or at least look at mountain at end. ??? Critics will pan. Some lukewarm. Very <u>moderate business.</u> Retakes for 3 days would fix."

John had left Nadine and Joey, taking a room on Tower Road and once again joining the family dinners. Louise always had a lot to talk about; she was traveling regularly, had plans to add a new two-story wing to the clinic, and was in line for an honorary doctorate from MacMurray College, her fourth. "Clinic, clinic, clinic," Spence would say, throwing the kids an exasperated look. They would usually have hamburgers when he came to dinner, sometimes chicken and maybe a vegetable (if Louise could force one down him). "Quiet, Susie," she'd say to her daughter, "and let Father talk about himself."

The Academy Award nominations were announced on the eighteenth, and once again both Tracy and Hepburn were up for top honors—Spence for *Bad Day at Black Rock,* Kate for *Time of the Cuckoo* (released in the United States as *Summertime*). Tracy was so unimpressed he didn't even mention the nominations in his datebook. Both he and Kate would be in New York when the awards went off, neither paying the slightest attention. He left Los Angeles on March 6, already a week late, and did not begin training in New York until the twenty-first.

Zinnemann, meanwhile, was in Cuba fuming, contending that Tracy had let his partners down by not commencing his program of training until three weeks later than promised. The picture's direct cost was estimated at $1,904,000 (plus $264,280 in overhead), based on the idea of doing everything straight, without process or traveling mattes, except for the action of the jumping fish. This accounted for sixty days of shooting in Cuba, seven days at the studio, and one day in New York. For interiors, a studio had been reopened in Havana that hadn't been used in five years.

From New York, George Brown reported that Tracy, his diet supervised by Hepburn, was losing weight at a "very satisfactory" pace. He was not, however, submitting to a physical training routine designed to tone the muscles used in the work of fishing. According to Zinnemann, Hepburn didn't want Tracy submitting to Brown's workouts, and Tracy would be in much better shape "if George were allowed to do his work."

When he left for Miami on March 26, Tracy's weight still wasn't where it needed to be and the scheduled start of production was scarcely two weeks away. Certain he was in for flack from both Zinnemann and Hemingway, he had two drinks aboard the plane to Miami, two more on the jump to Cuba. At Havana, he and Brown were met by Zinnemann and assistant director Don Page. They were taken to the Hotel Nacional, where

Tracy insisted on ordering himself a Dubonnet cocktail. "He proceeded to have several," said Page. When he arrived for dinner that evening at Finca Vigia, he was clutching two bottles of Dubonnet, one of which he had already opened. Hepburn's flight got in at 8:30, and when told that Tracy was with the Hemingways, she phoned the Finca and then asked to be taken there. "Loaded," Tracy recorded in his book. "Home bed 1 AM."

Tracy and Hepburn (and her friend Laura Harding) were to share a fully staffed seaside estate at Tarara, about ten miles outside of Havana. Nothing was said about his condition the next morning, and he swore off the booze then and there. ("NO DRINKS IN MORNING OR THERE-AFTER!!!!!!!") He submitted to a beach workout with Brown, saw Zinnemann at his house, and was told how happy the director was to have him. What he referred to as the "1st Court Martial by Hayward and Zinnemann" didn't come until the following afternoon. Told how much he "had them frightened," given the money involved, Tracy promptly offered to withdraw from *The Old Man and the Sea.* "Zinnemann said if I left <u>he would,</u>" Tracy afterward noted. "I said I would think it over!"

The second court-martial, which occurred on the thirty-first, took on the tone of an intervention when Hemingway joined in. "You're a rummy!" the author said accusingly. "What the hell! Admit it!" He went on to dare him to get out the Bible and swear to the ten years of sobriety he claimed. "[Again] I offered to withdraw," Tracy recorded, "but said I would have to stay if they sued. They would."

The company quickly divided into armed camps—Page and Zinnemann on one side, Tracy and Hepburn on the other. Kate, as always, was fiercely protective of Spence, ever vigilant in matters of abuse or perceived disrespect, and could strike with the ferocity of a rattlesnake. Among the production team, she was awarded the code name "George Arliss" after the long-faced British character actor with the prominent cheek bones. Hemingway, who couldn't abide a man who could not hold his liquor, found it impossible to utter the name of the star of his film and took to tartly referring to him simply as "the artist."

Tracy's deal called for a rate of $5,769.24 a week for twenty-six weeks beginning April 15, 1956, the official start of the picture. Hemingway left that same day for the Cabo Blanco Fishing Club in Peru, intent on photographing the film's marlin sequences. Once on salary, Tracy could be given calls, and Don Page asked him to go to Cojimar where they would shoot all the beach scenes and get together with the technical adviser, a Cuban fisherman who would get him acquainted with handling the oars and the lines.

"Whose idea is that?" Tracy asked, and he was told by Page that it was Zinnemann's and his own.

"He said he didn't know whether he would do it then or wait until we started shooting on Monday the 23rd," Page recounted in a memo. "At that time, the Old Man's boat will be tied up as we will be using it." Clearly agitated, Tracy then raised the subject of his first night in Cuba and the matter of his drinking. He said "all Hollywood knew about it" and that Page must have done a lot of talking. "I straightened him out, and told him that if he felt I was a stool pigeon I would just as soon get off the picture right now. He feels no one in the company likes him and <u>he</u> doesn't like anyone connected with us. As for his promise to lose weight, it seems to me that he is as heavy now as he has always been, and I recall Mr. Zinnemann stating to Mr. Hayward that if Tracy did not lose the necessary weight that he would not start the picture with Mr. Tracy, as he would be laughed right out of the theater."

For the part of Manolo, Zinnemann settled on eleven-year-old Felipe Pazos, Jr., the brown-eyed son of a prominent Cuban economist. Tracy appeared for a wardrobe test with the boy on April 21, and Hayward wired his enthusiastic approval of the results from his offices in Burbank. Actually getting some film exposed, however minor the footage, seemed somehow to relieve all the tensions of the previous month.

"Tracy is behaving fairly well these days," Zinnemann related in a note to Hemingway. "He went out with us in a pretty rough sea. It didn't seem to bother him too much. He is going again Wednesday morning . . . George Arliss is getting ready to leave. She is going to do a picture with Burt Lancaster, as you know. It is going to be a gruesome twosome. Pity the poor director."

Back from a trip, Jack Warner viewed the wardrobe test on May 1 and added his own vote of confidence:

I THINK TRACY LOOKED EXCELLENT AND I VISUALIZE
HIM AS BEING OUR OLD MAN OF THE SEA. HE JUST
STEPS RIGHT OUT OF THE BOOK AND THE BOY IS A TEN
STRIKE.

Filming officially began on May 4, when Tracy's call was for 4:45 a.m. in order to make "dawn shots" of the Old Man returning home. Progress was slow, as most of Zinnemann's shots were dependent upon the time of day, limiting Tracy's working hours almost exclusively to mornings. Don Page, himself an actor (known professionally as Don Alverado), loathed Tracy, and since it was Page's job to give Tracy his calls, every official interaction took on an air of belligerence.

Tracy again had a dawn shot—rowing at sunrise—on the morning of May 10 and was dismissed for the day at 11:30. Page gave him an afternoon call for the following day, with work to continue after dinner with night

Filming in Cuba with novelist Ernest Hemingway.
(AUTHOR'S COLLECTION)

exteriors featuring the boy. Tracy, he said, informed him that he would show for the afternoon but would not work that night and that Page could inform both Hayward and Zinnemann. Tracy's pocket diary for the day carries the words: "Opinion wrong shooting. Blow-up with Leland."

What Tracy had noticed was that Felipe Pazos had been given a 4:45 call for that next morning, and that Zinnemann and Page expected him to work an eighteen-hour stretch—something that would never have been required of a youngster on an American set. Tracy refused to make the night shots simply so the boy would not have to work. He noted in his book that he was ready to leave for location the following afternoon when a call came from Hayward: "Day lost because alleged refusal work to-nite, etc. <u>False.</u>"

The company was shut down, and the next morning a letter from Hayward was hand-delivered to Tracy's house at Tarara: "We notify you that your default in your contract has forced us to stop production and shut down, and we will hold you responsible."

Bert Allenberg had attorney Lawrence Beilinson call Hayward, and an appointment was set for the following day, a Sunday. Hayward came to talk, saying that he was in a bad spot, liable for the production to Jack Warner—who thought Zinnemann was moving too slowly—and that Don

Page had been forced on him by the studio. (Page was the ex-husband of Ann Warner and the father of Jack Warner's step-daughter, actress Joy Page.) Having cleared the air, Tracy agreed to continue with the picture but said he thought it doubtful that Zinnemann would stick with it.

A wire went out to Steve Trilling, Warner's executive assistant, in Burbank:

BYGONES ARE BYGONES COOPERATION COMPLETE PRO-
DUCTION RESUMED INFORM ALL CONCERNED HAYWARD
TRACY ZINNEMAN

Beginning May 17 they planned to shoot all the land scenes, which would take a month, followed by four weeks at sea with Tracy. The crew would be cut for two weeks of second-unit work, then Zinnemann would go to New York to shoot a sequence at Yankee Stadium. The project would wrap with two weeks of process work in Burbank. Zinnemann, who saw the story as "the triumph of man's spirit over enormous physical power," was discouraged when Hemingway failed to land a thousand-pound black marlin off Peru. The company was forced to substitute a mechanical version so big and cumbersome it took two flat cars to get it by rail to Florida. "Hemingway hated it at first sight," said Zinnemann, "and christened it 'the condomatic fish.' When it was put in the Gulf Stream near Havana it sank without a trace and was never seen again."

Zinnemann grew disenchanted with the choice of Felipe Pazos, and there was talk of replacing him. On the seventeenth Tracy worked with a second boy, shooting duplicate scenes, before it was decided to stick with Pazos. Hemingway, when he returned from Peru, declared that he, too, was unhappy with the boy, describing him as "a cross between a tadpole and Anita Loos." In a letter to his friend Gianfranco Ivancich, Hemingway seemed resigned to the situation: "As you know, there was some difficulty with the artist, but they say that is all straightened and we have a docile artist now, but to me in the stills I saw last night he still looked very fat for a fisherman and the boy looks very tiny. There is nothing that a rubber fish cannot fix. In later stills he looks much better and he is such a good actor he can probably surmount most things."

Work moved to the Old Man's shack and, according to Tracy's diary, Zinnemann demanded the replacement of the boy. A call was put into Hayward, and the producer arrived in Havana on June 4. Though Tracy had managed to drop seventeen pounds, Zinnemann still considered him too heavy to play the role, and Pazos' size only served to emphasize his girth.

"Tracy was most certainly a problem," Zinnemann said. "He was not doing his job. Everybody, except Leland Hayward, was a problem, including myself. There were a lot of egos on that movie." Hayward lined up with Zinnemann and Hemingway in calling for the boy's replacement. Zinnemann became convinced that Tracy was out to sabotage the picture: "He seemed malevolent and hostile. The crew hated him and he hated them back. Day after day, there was the sense that no progress was being made on the picture."

Anonymous squibs began to appear in the press: "Spencer Tracy's newest all-day buddy is Cuban dictator Batista. They play golf together every morning. Batista's caddies also carry machine guns around the course." And: "Spencer Tracy and another gent had one of the bloodiest fist fights in Havana's history. Ernest Hemingway had to be restrained several times from massacring Tracy all over Cuba."

In 1992 Zinnemann recalled a second drinking episode "which interrupted shooting for several days." A thirdhand reference to Tracy and Hemingway having broken up a bar is unconfirmed in any of the memos or wires preserved in the Jack Warner, Leland Hayward, Fred Zinnemann, Ernest Hemingway, or Warner Bros. collections, and Peter Viertel, in his 1992 memoir *Dangerous Friends,* includes no such story. Zinnemann only remembered that Hemingway once threatened to go looking for Tracy with a shotgun "but that was just one of those silly gestures of his."

Hayward clashed with Zinnemann over the director's insistence on doing as few process shots as possible and scolded him for making three shots of Tracy that could easily have been done on the Warner lot in Burbank. Zinnemann decided to make the long shots on the ocean with Tracy's double, saving close-ups for the process stage. In exchange for the time off, Tracy agreed to give the company four additional weeks. Then Hayward, channeling Warner, told Zinnemann that he had to start the second-unit work in Cojimar no later than July 25 "or else."

When Tracy visited the set to say good-bye on June 13, Zinnemann asked him to stay until Hayward arrived for a "showdown." On the sixteenth, Tracy had a call from Hemingway "apologizing for madness, etc." That same day, Zinnemann received a cable from Jack Warner:

SAW DAILIES INTERIOR CUBAN CAFE CANNOT UNDER-
STAND WHY YOU DID NOT SHOOT INDIVIDUAL OF TRACY
WHEN YOU WERE THERE AND LIGHTED FOR IT . . . YOU
ARE SHOOTING TOO MANY SUPERFLUOUS TAKES AND
SCENES . . .

Specifically, Warner was objecting to a flashback shot over Tracy's shoulder (to cover his age) even though its composition was clearly indicated in the script. Said Zinnemann: "Shooting most of the movie in the studio tank seemed to be the only way out; unfortunately, I could not see how this could be done . . . Suddenly the story seemed pointless. It made little sense to proceed with a robot pretending to be a fish in a studio tank pretending to be the gulf stream with an actor pretending to be a fisherman." His withdrawal from the picture was reported in Louella Parsons' column of June 23, 1956.

"The argument had nothing to do with Spence," Leland Hayward told Parsons via telephone from Havana. "He finished his scenes in time and begged Zinnemann to remain. The trouble was strictly between Zinnemann and myself over locations—of all things. Fred wanted to remain in Cuba, and I felt it wasn't practical to stay any longer. Warners agreed."

Tracy, who spoke to Parsons as well, said he never had any argument with Zinnemann and that they were good friends. The following day, he flew back to New York, where he sequestered himself in a suite at the Pierre and slept on and off for hours at a stretch.

"Did not take any calls from <u>Gar</u>!!!" he wrote in his book.

When Tracy arrived back in Los Angeles, Hepburn, for once, was already there, finishing off her first week of filming *The Rainmaker*. Spence had dinner on Tower Road that first night back—it was John's thirty-second birthday—but otherwise spent the week with Kate. He had been absent from St. Ives for three months and seemed to enjoy burrowing in, seeing no one in particular and basking in some near-perfect weather. There was talk of resuming *Old Man and the Sea* in the waters off Nassau, but he thought Hayward too eager to get going again and opposed such a move. He backed the more cautious approach of the picture's new director, John Sturges, who wanted time with the script and favored closing the film down until fall or even the spring of 1957. Under protest, Hayward eventually agreed to the delay.

After nearly a decade of hotel living, Tracy's move to 9191 St. Ives effectively put an end to any hopes of reconciliation between him and Louise. In earlier days, he could still come to the ranch for meals and the occasional game of tennis with John, and he still had a room there where he could lie down on Sunday afternoons and take a nap. ("Do an *el foldo*," as he put it.) After 1951, though, the house on White Oak was no longer his legal address, and when Louise chose the house on Tower in 1955, she did so with the wrenching knowledge that it had only three bedrooms—one for her, one for Susie, and one, should he ever need it, for John. According to Eddie Dmytryk's wife, the actress Jean Porter, it was about this same time that Louise told Spence that he could have a divorce if that was what he wanted.

"One time at Romanoff's—this is after we had heard that Mrs. Tracy was willing to get a divorce—I said, 'Why don't you and Katie get married?' He said, 'Too late. I've asked her. She said, 'No, I don't want to do it now. It doesn't matter. We've lived this long with things this way.' I think she enjoys her independence. We're together all the time anyway. So I'm not pushing her. And she's not pushing me.' "

St. Ives seemed the perfect home for him, simple and spare. "I don't own one damned thing I'd miss for more than five minutes if I lost it or it were swiped," he once said to Garson Kanin. "I like to check in and check out." For years he didn't spend much time there, and Cukor, who never could tell whether he was in residence or not, took to referring to him as "my elusive tenant" in his notes to Kate. ("My elusive tenant turns up at his little home from time to time, unexpected and unannounced. Before I know it, he's gone again . . .") He never really settled in until he came to regard the location as a permanent base, as he had the Beverly Hills Hotel for so many years.

"He knew the way from the Beverly Hills Hotel down Beverly Drive into Beverly Hills to Romanoff's," said Kate,

and he knew the way to go to Chasen's . . . George built him a charming house and Spencer rented it, but his sense of direction . . . he didn't know where he was. Well, what to do, what to do? Being a simple fellow and a sensible man, he thought, "Well, I'll go down Doheny to Sunset, and I'll go back Sunset to the Beverly Hills Hotel. And then I'll go from there." Well, everything was fine until one night he and his brother Carroll decided that they'd go to Chasen's. So Spencer got into the car to drive it. He backed out of the garage, he turned onto Doheny, got to Sunset and turned right, and Carroll thought, "What the hell is he doing?" But he shut up, and Spencer continued until he got to the Beverly Hills Hotel. He turned left, he went down Beverly Drive, he got to Santa Monica, he turned left, he got to Beverly Boulevard, and he turned right, and he went down Beverly Boulevard and he got to Chasen's. It was there on the corner, and they drove into the parking lot.

But before he got out of the car, Carroll said to him, "Spencer, you could have gone out your driveway, straight down Doheny, across Santa Monica, still down Doheny, across the beginning of Melrose, and you would have arrived at Chasen's in two minutes instead of ten." Spencer was thrilled. He said, "Is that really true?" Carroll said, "Yes, it's true, Spencer. You live right up there on <u>that</u> hill." When I heard that story for the first time I said, "It's amazing he ever found Dr. Livingstone, isn't it?"

A rare snapshot of Tracy and Hepburn at a private function, circa 1956.
(JUDY SAMELSON COLLECTION)

Tracy enjoyed a measure of contentment at St. Ives. Gone were the half-hearted days of womanizing he had known in the early 1950s. After five years of life on the run, Hepburn had once again returned to make "a life for him that was irresistible" so that he would not, as she put it, wander off.

"I think he thought Kate very attractive," Joe Mankiewicz said,

and Kate somebody he could talk to. Not only that, but [some-body] he could listen to. But most of these [other] women couldn't amuse him. Kate had anecdotes, Kate came in with gossip, Kate was like marrying *The Hollywood Reporter,* except she knew everything from all sources. And one thing Spence was very, very curious about [was] gossip. He loved to hear stories about people. Well. Would you like to have Ingrid Bergman come in and tell you stories about people? Or would you like to have Joan Bennett tell you about people? But KATE, who had the entire mirage of English society and French society and Riviera society and Florida society, plus the theatre society! Constance Collier, up and down, coming in with gossip. This was kind of a jackpot of entertainment for Spence. And, in a way, a kind of tribute to him. Laying all this at his feet. Oh, this was a tremendous jackpot that Spence hit. What he liked in terms of entertainment, liked more than anything else in the world, was gossip about people—who's doing what to whom. Kate never went out after it, but my God it came to her. Cukor! Cukor was the Generalissimo of gossip! Both homosexual and heterosexual. And here he sat in the middle of this place, and all these busy bees gathering this honey for him! This information. [A] constant, never-ending source of information, gossip, and amusement for him. He didn't have to go out, sit through a whole night of conversation before he got to bed with a woman. This was wonderful, because Louise wasn't about to tell him who was doing what to whom. Louise wanted to keep him comfortable and happy, give him books to read.

By 1956 the break with Louise was so complete that Spence wasn't even on hand for her sixtieth birthday. In the days leading up to the event, he made two attempts to leave for New York—one by air, one by rail—and canceled both times. He finally got away on July 24, taking a TWA sleeper flight to Idlewild and spending the next three days at the office of his dentist, Dr. Carl Bastian. He went to Mass at St. Patrick's, dined with Bert Allenberg and Benny Thau, spent the night of Weeze's birthday attending a performance of *My Fair Lady* with the Allenbergs and Frank Sinatra. ("You made the little wop cry!" he rather sweetly told Rex Harrison afterward.) The following evening he dined solo with Sinatra and, as he noted in his datebook, the "grape."

"Well," said Sinatra, "we lifted a few, in New York particularly. You know, Jesus, at four o'clock in the morning, five o'clock . . . and I was doing six shows a day at the Paramount [in between showings of *Johnny Concho*] and had to look fairly well—not like I was dying at 132 pounds. He said, 'Oh the hell with it. We'll have another one and you'll be there on time and you'll be great.' I said, 'Thanks a lot.' "

Tracy had known Sinatra since the day in 1945 when the singer walked up and introduced himself on the M-G-M lot. "I was in a sailor suit doing a dance picture with [Gene] Kelly, and he thought I was in the Navy . . . He said, 'Where are you stationed?' And I said, 'Right here.' And, of course, I teased him for about five minutes. And then he said, 'Oh, you're the guy with the swooning and all that stuff.' And I said, 'I guess so.' And we became fast friends after that. Immediately."

The break with Louise had never been clean, never final, never the sort of thing where the parties could heal and move on. It was an open wound for them both, something neither of them could face or acknowledge. "In a way," said Seymour Gray, "he did love her. He felt responsible to her. There was the time he had this fight with Hepburn in front of me about this coat that he bought [Louise]. Hepburn was furious. 'Why didn't you buy me one?' He said, 'Because you don't need one. And you've got enough money to buy your own.' I think he admired her and had enormous respect for her . . . And I don't think Spencer wanted a divorce."

And yet he ran from Louise on the occasion of her sixtieth birthday, and he hated himself for it. Two weeks later he emerged from another self-induced stupor at the Pierre and placed himself under the care of Dr. Richard Stock, a prominent cardiologist at Columbia-Presbyterian Hospital. On August 18, 1956, Carroll Tracy quietly settled the hotel bill for $2,700, and he and Kate, who had just finished work on *The Rainmaker*, took him home to California.

CHAPTER 29

The Last Hurrah

Doubtless the conversation between Tracy and Frank Sinatra touched on the condition of their mutual friend, Humphrey Bogart. In February 1956 Bogart had undergone surgery for esophageal cancer, and both men were tracking his progress. Early in July, having just returned from Cuba, Tracy and Hepburn visited the Bogarts' Holmby Hills estate. "Bogie post-operative seems very ill," Tracy wrote in his datebook. "Weighs 120 lbs." There was no improvement in August and, after a Labor Day visit, Tracy mused, "Poor Bogie—6 mos??" The arrival of his namesake, Tracy Stewart Granger, on September 10 cheered him considerably, and he postponed a drive to Las Vegas to visit Jean and the baby.

As *The Mountain* neared its September release date, Tracy's attitude toward the film hardened and, as with *Bad Day at Black Rock,* he became convinced it would be a flop, a "disaster." His bleak outlook may have been influenced somewhat by an ill-advised attempt on the part of Paramount to recover the money the studio figured his eleven days of "illness" had cost the company. Bert Allenberg initially agreed they were entitled to perhaps $50,000, yet Tracy had finished his role in the picture in the twelve weeks allotted under the terms of his contract, and cast insurance had already paid $11,000 toward the alleged loss.

In the end, studio head Y. Frank Freeman felt they were unlikely to recover anything more without incurring the expense (and unwanted publicity) of a lawsuit, and the money was ultimately rolled into the negative cost, which came to $2,119,000. *Variety* handed the film a pan, judging Tracy's performance as "no more than adequate" and rightly placing much of the blame for the picture's failure on Ranald MacDougall's script and the uneven direction of Eddie Dmytryk. The *Reporter*, on the other hand, thought it wonderful, a reaction that clearly left its top-billed star flummoxed. All the trade notices agreed the film's best moments took place on the mountainside, where the dialogue was held to a minimum and the process plates were used to good effect as the Teller brothers make their ascent to the summit.

"Tracy was an actor, not a mountain climber," Dmytryk wrote,

yet no one, in my opinion, ever made mountain climbing more real, more harrowing, or more perilous than he did. In one scene, while supposedly standing on an inch-wide ledge (I used inserts made with his climbing double to establish this) he reaches for a crack, finds it filled with ice, carefully takes out his ice ax and chips it away, replaces his ax in his belt, and finally, after a breathless pause, makes the short leap necessary to reach the next handhold. Throughout the scene, shot in close-up, he was standing on the bottom of an upturned apple box, perhaps eight inches off the ground, but you would have sworn it was a matter of life and death on Everest. That's acting. In the final film I let the scene run without a cut, except for a couple of foot inserts—it must have lasted a full four minutes. Only an actor of Tracy's caliber could have sustained a scene of this kind for so long.

The New York opening put Tracy on edge, and the day it took place he recorded a "big temper blow up with Kate." To cool down, he took a drive up the coast in his new Lincoln convertible, returning in time for dinner on Tower Road.* The notices weren't terrible, he found, but neither were they laudatory. He listed them carefully in his book, noting where the film had been panned but where his own performance had been well received. The *Times*, the *Post*, *Saturday Review*, and *Newsweek* were all counted as bad; the *Herald Tribune*, the *News*, the *New Yorker*, and *Time* good—at least so far as his personal notices were concerned. Herbert Kupferberg of

* The tension between Tracy and Hepburn may have been exacerbated by the appearance of an article in the October issue of *Inside Story* titled "That Tracy-Hepburn Affair." Pictures of Spence and Kate were balanced with shots of him with Louise. The text alleged "monumental scenes in the Tracy household" and went further than any previous publication in suggesting a long-standing sexual relationship.

the *Herald Tribune* found Tracy's work as Zachary Teller "intensely moving," while Bosley Crowther described an actor who had allowed his rugged old guide to waver between "a vague sort of peasant valor" and gawking stupidity. "It is hard to determine how to take him, except as a first-class mountain goat."

After eight years of exile in foreign locales, an unbowed Katharine Hepburn began work on *The Rainmaker* with the same "no press" policy that had made her such a headache for the publicity people at M-G-M. "We made inquiries with interviewers," said Teet Carle, "and found that not one had any need (or desire) to do stories on her. I went on the set to tell her we would protect her and keep away media folks."

It's possible that Hepburn got wind of such widespread apathy, for in August 1956, having just retrieved Tracy from his latest New York misadventure, she sat for a formal one-on-one with Edwin Schallert, the drama editor of the *Los Angeles Times.* Schallert was conscious of how rare an occasion this was and said as much in the lede of his write-up. The paper played the story up big, giving it a prominent page-one placement and accompanying it with a generous head shot gamely peering out at the reader, eyes flashing, teeth shining, collar upturned, at forty-nine the "queen of the international stars" (as the caption would have it). The talk focused on the new movie, in which she had been paired with Burt Lancaster, but ranged over a number of topics, her travels, her likes and dislikes, and her by now legendary pictures with Spencer Tracy.

"It is regrettable," she lamented, "that no one has been able to find a comedy, such as we formerly did, which would be suitable for us." Within days, Fox production chief Buddy Adler was on the phone to Abe Lastfogel with just such a comedy, a modest hit on Broadway titled *The Desk Set.*

Adler had picked up the rights as part of an investment strategy that gave Fox an ownership stake in several plays, the final price in each case calibrated to the length of the play's New York run. In the role of the spinsterish Bunny Watson, head of the research department of a major TV network, the show had starred Shirley Booth, a masterful comedienne who was never much of a draw in the movies (despite having collected an Academy Award for her work in *Come Back, Little Sheba*). As with *Time of the Cuckoo,* Booth ceded a role she had created onstage to Hepburn, the crucial change of Bunny ending up with computer consultant Richard Sumner (instead of her boss) having already been effected in a draft screenplay. Adler had originally given the property to writer-producer Charles Brackett, who lasted scarcely three weeks on the assignment. ("It's not my cup of tea," Brackett fretted, "and every time I rewrite a scene it gets worse.") Eventually, *Desk Set* was settled on the husband-wife team of Henry and Phoebe Ephron.

The initial offer from Fox was $250,000 for the Tracy-Hepburn combo, plus a 10 percent split of the gross after the film had earned double its negative cost in rentals. Kate didn't like the up-front money, and there was friction between her and Bert Allenberg when she said as much directly to the studio. Fox upped the ante to $350,000 and 30 percent of the profits, which, profits being what they were in Hollywood, didn't sound all that much better. Eager to meet a projected start date of November 1, Adler finally approved an offer of $400,000—$250,000 for Tracy and $150,000 for Hepburn—and 50 percent of the net profits. Tracy saw the first seventy-five pages of the Ephrons' revised screenplay on October 2 and thought them only "fair." Lastfogel finalized the contracts on October 22, the team splitting 10 percent of the gross after $4,400,500 and 20 percent after $4,750,000—an extraordinary deal for their first picture away from M-G-M.

Tracy's dismay at the first seventy-five pages resulted in an all-day script conference between Hepburn and the Ephrons, Kate clad in her familiar white slacks and matching shirt. "That morning, she and Spence had read the script aloud and had marked where changes in his role, his lines, his activity, could improve the script," recounted Henry Ephron. "By the end of the day we were on a friendly, warm basis, wildly enthusiastic when we got the script past a sticky spot and violently depressed when we didn't."

The second day they were joined by Walter Lang, the veteran Fox director who had been assigned the picture, and whose previous films for the studio had been the top-drawer musicals *The King and I, There's No Business Like Show Business,* and *Call Me Madame.* The Ephrons considered Lang an ally—he had filmed their sly 1950 satire *The Jackpot*—and figured it would be "three against one" if they ever came to loggerheads with their leading lady. Someone had the idea to do a crucial scene—Sumner's interrogation of Bunny by way of a personality test—on location, and Adler went for it. ("Shoot in New York, start at Fifty-seventh and Madison, outside the IBM building, and take them west on Fifty-seventh Street to Sixth Avenue where they would lunch at one of those outdoor Jewish delicatessens.") Hepburn and Henry Ephron made a quick trip east to scout locations for the sequence.

Bogart, meanwhile, was fading rapidly. Tracy endured the gut-wrenching business of a visit on November 16 and found him frail and depleted. Pulling up a chair at the foot of the bed, he began to tell jokes, his coffee nearby, kidding around with his old friend as he always did. "He was great with Bogie when Bogie was sick," said Lauren Bacall. "Katie used to say, 'He was tortured before he went to your house, put on a great act when he was there, and was tortured when he left.' " That night, Tracy made a rueful note in his datebook: "Poor Bogie. Not long—2 months?"

In the following days, his mood sank—there was trouble with his new Lincoln, trouble with *The Mountain,* trouble with the revised script of *Desk Set.* On Sunday, the *L.A. Times* ran a piece by movie columnist Philip K. Scheuer titled "TV Offers a Second Look at So-Called Film Classics." Leading the article was a case in point—Tracy's own version of *Dr. Jekyll and Mr. Hyde.*

"For one thing," Scheuer wrote, "Tracy's portrayal (and movie) undoubtedly had its merits, though I was hard put to discover many of them when the film was first released in 1941 and I would hardly call it a masterpiece today. It was, I felt, inferior to the Jekyll-Hyde of Fredric March in 1932 and even to that of John Barrymore as far back as 1920, and I would have confided as much to everybody within earshot, if anybody had been there to listen."

To Henry Ephron, the reaction was obvious and easy to imagine. "I could see the whole scene: Spencer reads the L.A. *Times,* gets violently angry, and then reads the script in no mood to read a script. Soooo, it was no surprise to me when Kate showed up Monday morning and said, 'Spencer wants out. How about Fred Astaire?' " Ephron called Buddy Adler, who not only wasn't interested in Fred Astaire, but didn't even want Hepburn if Tracy wasn't part of the package. He went back to Kate and asked for a group meeting as soon as possible: "I'm sure that if all three of us talk to him, we'll get him back in the picture."

The meeting the next morning was little more than a rally, a rousing pep talk orchestrated along the lines of what the Hacketts—Albert and Frances—had recommended when Ephron called them for advice. "Phoebe, Walter, and I said, in as many ways as we could, 'You're a great actor. No one else can play the part. Without you the picture is nothing.' Within an hour he said, 'Okay, kids. I'm not trying to get votes. Just pay me my money when the picture is over.' Strangely, Hepburn seemed a little sad. She wanted him in the picture, but she also wanted him to be strong and not so susceptible to flattery."

Shooting was set to begin Christmas week in Manhattan, the location work timed to the seasonal look of the city. Told by his friend Denny to take off twenty-five pounds, Tracy committed to dropping thirteen pounds in twenty-four days, putting him at 198 for the formal start of production on January 14. With Bogart's condition worsening, Tracy feared he would be caught out of town when the end came.

"Call from Betty Bogart to call [their business manager] Morgan Maree!" he wrote in his book on December 14. "Talk of Memorial Service for Bogie! Deliver eulogy?!? WOW! Could be any day—could be 3 mos? To see Bogie (seemed same??) Betty discuss[es] his death."

Reluctantly, Tracy left by rail for New York on the twenty-first, choosing the Hotel Westbury in lieu of the Pierre, the scene of his last bender. On Christmas Eve he dined alone at the Westbury but met Garson Kanin afterward for coffee. On Christmas Day he attended eight o'clock Mass at St. Vincent's Cathedral—Kate was in Connecticut—and ate dinner in front of the TV set at the hotel.

A publicity gimmick had Hepburn screening the young New York actresses tentatively selected for *Desk Set,* some of whom would go on to California for testing. Blond Dina Merrill had trained at the American Academy; Kate and Fox casting director Billy Gordon had seen her on television with Phil Silvers. Sue Randall, likewise trained at the academy, had her own fifteen-minute soap opera, *Valiant Lady,* on CBS. Ash blond Merry Anders had once been under contract at Fox, while Diane Jergens was something of a TV and movie veteran, a recurring role on *The Bob Cummings Show* having been her most prominent credit.

Tracy was taking part in the interviews at Fox's Fifty-sixth Street offices when a call from the coast advised them both that there wasn't going to be any location work after all. "It would make the picture too expensive," Ephron later explained, "and by some crazy rule of thumb they had, no Tracy-Hepburn picture should cost over $2 million."* As Tracy noted in his book, the savings to the company could amount to as much as $200,000. "Forget New York," he told Ephron. "We don't have to walk down Sixth Avenue to do a scene. We're getting four hundred thousand for this picture, Kate and I, and if we can't play a scene in front of a black backdrop and get all the laughs there are, we're stealing your money."

They left New York under the cover of darkness, eluding, in particular, the Kanins. "Does the Westbury know that you have left?" Gar inquired in a note a week later. "They seem to be taking messages ad infinitum." Back on the coast, they phoned and then again visited the Bogarts—first on January 4, the last time together on the evening of the twelfth.

"When anyone is desperately ill," said Kate, "you get a feeling, 'Oh, dear, it's going to be soon,' which struck me. So Spencer and I went to the house, and [Bogart] was sitting in a chair in his bedroom—sitting in a wheelchair—and then we got up to go so as not to exhaust him. And I kissed him goodbye, walked over to the door, and Spencer walked over and patted his shoulder and said, 'We're on our way.' And Bogie reached up with his hand and patted Spencer's hand, looked at him, and said 'Goodbye, Spence.' " The way he said it that night had special resonance, and they

* Without the location work, *Desk Set* was budgeted at $1,997,470.

could both tell that he meant it. "When we were downstairs, Spence looked at me and said, 'Bogie's going to die.'"

"Very weak—semi-conscious," was the way Tracy recorded the patient's condition in his book that night. He spent the thirteenth—a Sunday—on "the hill" (as he referred to the house on Tower Road) dining with Louise, John, Susie. A call came the next morning from Betty Bacall—Bogart, she told him, had died at 3:00 a.m. Work on *Desk Set* was to begin within hours.

"I originally wanted him to deliver the eulogy," Bacall remembered. "He called me up immediately and said, 'I'd never get through it.' It was just too emotional." He told her he could have done it for someone he wasn't as close to, but not Bogie, dear Bogie. "I remember when he delivered the eulogy at Walter Huston's memorial. He was brilliant, but shaky."

The mood on the set was somber as Tracy played his first scenes in the reference library of the Federal Broadcasting Company, initially with Dina Merrill, Joan Blondell, and Sue Randall, soon with Hepburn, who marches in with a box from Bonwit Teller under her arm.

"My name is Richard Sumner," he says pleasantly, emerging from her office.

"Well, numerologically that's very good," she smiles, taking the advantage and offering her hand. "There are thirteen letters in your name."

"You calculate rapidly."

"Up to thirteen anyway."

The verbal jousting in Sumner's introduction to Bunny Watson followed the familiar Tracy-Hepburn pattern. "They did all their own blocking and rehearsing before they came on the set," said Dina Merrill. "They knew exactly what they were going to do. All the director did was tell them where the camera was and work the other actors into the scene."

There were no calls on the fourth day of production, as Tracy and Hepburn were freed to attend the memorial service at All Saints Episcopal Church. Tracy arrived, according to the *Los Angeles Times*, "grief deep-etched in his broad face." Hepburn, the paper reported, was already there. "Katie," said Bacall, "managed to get into the church before anyone else did, and she was sitting there when they came in." As the service began at 12:30 p.m., John Huston reading the eulogy, a minute of silence was observed on the nearby Fox lot, where together Bogart and Tracy had made their first feature, *Up the River,* twenty-seven years earlier.

It was Walter Lang's idea to stage the questionnaire scene—the one originally set to be done on location—on the roof of the network's building some forty flights above Midtown, Sumner brown-bagging their lunches, pigeons everywhere, the spectacular New York skyline serving as backdrop. Sumner sets out coffee, sandwiches, takes out a notepad and a pen.

"Often, when we meet a person for the first time," he begins, checking his notes, "some physical characteristic strikes us. Now, what is the first thing you notice in a person?"

"Whether the person is male or female," Bunny replies.

Stifling a grin, he makes a note. "Now this is a little mathematical problem . . . ," he continues, catching himself and picking a cup up off the table. "Celery or olives?" he offers.

She peers inside. "Four olives, three pieces of celery."

Withdrawing the cup, he glances inside. "Right," he says.

"Uh-huh."

"That doesn't happen to be the question."

"Oh."

He reads: "A train started out at Grand Central with seventeen passengers aboard and a crew of nine. At 125th Street, four got off and nine got on. At White Plains, three got off and one got on. At Chappaqua, nine got off and four got on. And at each successive stop thereafter, nobody got off and nobody got on until the train reached its next to the last stop, where five people got off and one got on. Then it reached the terminal."

"Oh, that's easy," she smiles. "Eleven passengers and a crew of nine."

"That's not the question."

"Oh, sorry."

"How many people got off at Chappaqua?"

"Nine."

He stops short of biting into his sandwich. "That's correct," he says.

"Yes, I know."

A bemused look comes over his face. "Would you mind telling me how you arrived at that?"

"Spooky, isn't it?" she says, shivering in the cold. "Do you notice that there are also nine letters in Chappaqua?"

Hepburn later characterized the eight-minute sequence as "a remarkable example of comedy acting between two people who really, more or less, knew what they were doing." Fiercely proud of the work she and Spence were doing together, she scolded him when he branded a scene lousy ("You don't know what you're talking about—the director knows what he's doing") and demanded the full attention of the cast and crew when the two of them were at work.

"Kate saw me reading a magazine one day on the set," Dina Merrill recalled, "and she came over. She said, 'Dina, what are you reading?' I said, 'Oh, just an article in this magazine.' She said, 'I don't want you ever to do that again. You're a beginner here. You should watch Spence and me.' Yes, ma'am! That was the last time I brought a paper or a magazine or anything to the set—and she was right."

Tracy, who was averaging just three hours of sleep a night, was "dead tired" and irritable, certain *Desk Set* would be another clunk of a picture. "Lang is <u>nice</u> man," he wrote on the sixteenth day of production, "but <u>child-ish</u> director. Ephron—producer—<u>dumb.</u> Bad pic[ture]. K. bad. Me bad."

Owing to Tracy's presence, Hepburn monitored every aspect of life on the set, even to the point of bringing props in from her own home. "She was a mother hen," Merrill said, "worrying if he had a cold, or might catch one. It was like he was her child." Her constant hovering irritated him, and he seized on every possible opportunity to put her in her place. "Shut your mouth," he'd tell her. "Go back where you belong in vaudeville and keep out of here." Dina Merrill found him "just as sweet as he could be" but full of hell: "He gave it to her pretty good; one day she came on the set with her hair pinned up in a horrible bun—she always looked like an old shoe anyway—and he was giving an interview. He stopped what he was saying, gestured at her and said, 'And that, gentlemen, is our star!'"

Henry Ephron, fascinated by the obvious bond between them, haunted the set like a stagestruck teenager. "Tracy, we discovered, was incurably a mischievous kid. Once, when Hepburn left to go on the set, leaving me and Tracy together, he whispered, 'She's never forgiven me for Bergman.' He said it affectionately . . . She must have loved him terribly. Phoebe once asked Kate what it was about Spencer that fascinated Kate. She said, 'I'm like a little fly that buzzes around him all the time, and every once in a while he gives me a good swat.'"

When the AP's Bob Thomas visited the set, he congratulated Hepburn on her Academy Award nomination for *The Rainmaker* and asked if she'd be attending the ceremonies. "Of course not," she replied. "I didn't even go when I won the Oscar for *Morning Glory*." Tracy furled his brow as if trying to recall a past life. "Let's see," he said. "That was back in 1902, wasn't it?"

"Yes," she returned, "and you won in 1901 and 1906."

"These awards," he said, waving off the subject, "don't mean a damn thing. They may add some dough to a picture's gross, but they don't do anything for actors. The big names out here aren't actors anyway. They're personalities. I know of only one great actor and he's coming out here soon. Guy named Laurence Olivier." Thomas thought Hepburn had a good shot at the Oscar, but Tracy disagreed. "Naw, I don't think so. Bergman will get it." Ignoring the obvious jab, Hepburn went on to praise the Mexican comedian Cantinflas, who had made an international hit for himself in *Around the World in 80 Days*. "Such style! Such wit! He is simply sensational." And he was not, she was quick to add, nominated for anything.

When Walter Lang called them to the set, Hepburn slipped out of the white slacks she was wearing and back into Bunny Watson's prim business suit. The set, an almost exact copy of the Broadway original, was crowded with the steel-gray console, whirring processing cabinets, and flashing display screen of Emmarac, the enormous job-killing computer Sumner has installed on the main floor of the library. Scene completed, she changed back into her slacks and blouse and greeted Cary Grant and Deborah Kerr, visiting from an adjacent stage where Leo McCarey was shooting *An Affair to Remember.* They launched into a spirited discussion of Kate's decision to do *The Merchant of Venice* at the American Shakespeare Festival in Stratford. ("It's better to try something difficult and flop," she said, "than to play it safe all the time.") When Lang again wanted them, Hepburn had to be bodily dragged away by Tracy, who added a small kick for good measure.

On the thirty-third day of production, they played their longest scene in the film together—eight pages of material in which Bunny and Sumner dine on fried chicken in Bunny's apartment. Gig Young, playing her boss and longtime boyfriend, comes in on the exchange and finds both of them in bathrobes, Sumner having gotten drenched in a cloudburst. Then Joan Blondell arrives, adding a note of farce to the sequence and giving Tracy an audience for an improvisational exit, a Skeltonesque turn as a drunk that left the atmosphere giddy.

"2 days scheduled—done by 2:30—Katie wonderful," he noted proudly in his book. They finished interior work on the picture two days later, the final shot featuring the trademark Tracy-Hepburn kiss, Kate with her back to the camera, Spence drawing her to him in perfect symmetry with their first screen embrace sixteen years earlier. It would be, Tracy had said, their last picture together. "Who is going to hire us after this?" he asked, acutely conscious of his age, his white hair, the ever-deepening lines in his face. "He felt he was too old for the part," Lang remembered, "and he was; but Katie wanted him and I wanted him. We all wanted him, so he did it."

Included in the principal cast and crew of *Desk Set* were three notorious drinkers—Tracy, Gig Young, and cinematographer Leon Shamroy. "Shammie" was by far the most practiced, a brusque, cigar-chomping raconteur who played the horses prodigiously. "It was obvious that Katie really had kind of a schoolgirl crush on Shamroy," said Henry Ephron, "and Phoebe said, 'Katie, what do you see in Shammie?' She said, 'He's a rascal.'" On their last night of shooting they were on the Fox lot's New York street, where Bunny and Sumner catch a ride with a coworker and his quarrelsome family. Staged in a driving rain, the scene took from midnight to 5:30 in the morning to complete. "Shammie had a bottle of whiskey. Spence said, 'Goodbye, everyone!' grabbed the empty bottle of whiskey, and said, 'See you in June!' and took off."

Desk Set closed four days under schedule and $131,800 under budget. Buddy Adler was so pleased he phoned Fox president Spyros Skouras from

With Jesse L. Lasky during the making of *Desk Set*.
(BETTY LASKY)

the projection room. ("Good news was so scarce around the studio those years," commented Henry Ephron.) When a preview was set for Pasadena, Ephron called Hepburn and extended an invitation. "Thank you," she responded, "but we never go to previews." Tracy took the phone: "Henry, would you send a script to my son John? Send it to the Tracy Clinic. His mother will take him to the preview, and if he's read the script beforehand, he'll have no trouble following the picture."

After the preview, Louise, who could be excused for detesting the movie, came over to the Ephrons in the lobby. "It's wonderful," she said graciously. "We're going to call Spencer as soon as we get home."

Work on *The Old Man and the Sea* had resumed on July 2, 1956, but the Nassau expedition was, by and large, a failure. They got some long shots of the boat with the fish lashed alongside, they got some backgrounds for Tracy, some sunrises and sunsets, and some usable shots of shark fins racing through the water. There were, however, no live sharks to be photographed—at least none that would respond to direction or appear in numbers large enough to make an impression on screen. The artificial fish, they found, was completely unphotogenic, and it was subjected to repainting after some tests were made. Carefully posed, the fish would be convincing enough dead, but as a living thing it was pretty much hopeless. Nassau was a costly location, even_without Tracy's participation, and production was suspended again on July 28, John Sturges wanting to rethink every aspect of what had been done so far. Soon he found himself at odds with Ernest Hemingway's mania for realism.

"They got mixed up with reality and film," he later said.

The fact that the story takes place in the Gulf Stream off Cuba doesn't mean that that's the right place to shoot it. It isn't. The Gulf Stream goes at 12 miles an hour and it's rough. They took a very realistic approach to the film. And if you're going to do that, then I don't think Spencer Tracy was a good choice. He's an actor of obvious skills and emotional power and all the things that make him such a great actor. But he's certainly not a starving Cuban fisherman. I think if you attack the picture that way, you're in trouble. The plans they had to get the shark, the plans to get the fish, got all scrambled up and 50 sets of people came up with 50 sets of solutions and the first thing they knew was that they'd spent $3,000,000. Why I took it on I'll never really know. I knew Tracy well. The idea intrigued me, to play it as an exercise in imagination and emotion. A theatrical approach. Now if anyone objected to that, the hell with them—they weren't going to like the film. This approach I found interesting and I felt I could profit by the mistakes they'd already made.

At Warner Bros., Leland Hayward had Zinnemann's footage cut together. In early July he and Tracy ran the material—opening with the Old Man coming into the harbor and continuing through to his leaving at dawn—and thought it all quite beautiful, some of it breathtakingly so. They talked of where the narration should go and how it might conflict with the scripted lines of spoken dialogue. They decided it would be almost impossible to mix the two on shore, and Hayward suggested that the voice-over carry the story until the Old Man found himself alone out at sea. "He didn't remember when he first began to talk aloud when he was by himself," the narrator would say. "If the others heard me they would think I was crazy," the Old Man would then say aloud, "but since I am not, I do not care." Whether Tracy could take both roles—that of the narrator as well as that of the Old Man—was still undecided.

Tracy deflected other offers, eager to be done with the marathon project. He saw Sturges and cinematographer James Wong Howe off for Hawaii on June 9, 1957, and followed on the fifteenth accompanied by John, Larry Keethe, and a new secretary, Jeri Tyler, whose job it would be to keep John entertained. The Kona Inn was a beautiful place with a large pool, and John and Jeri spent their days swimming, sunning, shopping, and practicing tennis. Kona had been selected because there was no current or tide to speak of, the color of the water was right, and it was possible to shoot very close to shore. It was, in other words, a quiet location that could, above all else, be controlled. A rented camera barge called the *Julie B.* was outfitted as a floating soundstage, with recording equipment, a dressing room for Tracy, a makeup room, a commissary, and film refrigeration facilities. It also boasted a twenty-foot camera boom and a crane for raising and lowering the diving bell used for underwater filming.

"Although we had powerful generators and scores of reflectors," Howe later wrote, "we used them as little as possible for the simple reason that the movement on the Old Man's boat on even the slightest swell would reveal their presence as a fixed source of light. Instead we used only the sun as our natural source of light. An important reason for this was the desire to give the audience the intense feeling of heat from the glare on the water—the intense exhausting heat the Old Man of the story was getting. And without the use of artificial balanced light, it was necessary we keep changing the position of the camera barge to maintain the proper light source angle."

Lighting became such a severe problem that filming took more time than anticipated. Tracy's double, Harold Kruger, typically worked a ten-

Shooting *The Old Man and the Sea* in Hawaii. Cinematographer James Wong Howe is behind the camera. (AUTHOR'S COLLECTION)

hour day, while Tracy himself appeared in just two, three, or four setups. "This picture is becoming my life's work," he groused to a visiting reporter from the Associated Press. "The book is a masterpiece and should make a great picture. I believe in it. You'd have to believe in it to stay with it after all the troubles we've had. By now there isn't a chance to make back all the money we will spend, so we're concentrating on making something worthwhile."

He was on his best behavior, but Hemingway, for one, could not be placated. His Old Man still weighed 210 pounds, a fact Hayward confirmed in a phone conversation. "Tracy can make money playing fat men now," the author thundered in a subsequent letter, "or he can always get by in those toad-and-grasshopper comedies with Miss Hepburn, but he is a complete and terrible liability to the picture and has been since he presented himself out of condition in 1956." Hemingway was also unhappy that Hayward had asked Paul Osborn to go over Peter Viertel's latest draft of the screenplay to "make the dialogue more playable."

A half day's work on June 26 completed the water exteriors, and Tracy was able to leave for L.A. via Honolulu several days ahead of schedule. It was 110 degrees in Burbank the day he walked onto Warners' Stage 7, where a tank held a million gallons of water tinted with candy dye and Jimmy Howe was struggling to duplicate the single-source lighting he had achieved at Kona. Sturges spoke to Tracy "very frankly" and told him that he was still too fat, yet Sturges and Hayward both had to acknowledge that Tracy's ulcer made it "damned hard" for him to diet as he should. Hayward assured Hemingway they were photographing their star "very, very carefully" and that while they were both fully aware of the problem, no one else would be. Work got under way again on July 5, with Tracy expecting to be another two months on the picture.

There were camera problems that first day—"par for the course," as Tracy said—and they got exactly one shot in the can. The following Monday was given over to process work, and the ultraviolet lights needed for Arthur Widmer's new blue screen effects were so strong (2,300 kilowatts) that Tracy was suffering from eye burn—an injury akin to welder's flash—by the end of the second day. The doctor gave him drops and ordered him to work only half days in front of the UV lights, a restriction that hobbled the company still further and made the matching shots more difficult.

Felipe Pazos, now twelve, was brought to California for interiors and had to be photographed just as carefully as Tracy to keep from jolting the audience with a year's growth. "This time we are going to rehearse with him carefully," Hayward assured a dubious Hemingway, "and try to treat him with some kindness and understanding which he never had before." Tracy played the film's first dialogue scenes with young Pazos, still not sure how the narration would work in around it. Reshot by Sturges were Zinnemann's scenes at the terraza, where the boy buys the Old Man a beer after eighty-four days without a fish, and a lengthy exchange in the Old Man's shack, where Santiago talks hopefully of the work ahead. ("Tomorrow is the eighty-fifth day. Eighty-five is a lucky number.") Paul Osborn always felt the core of the picture was the relationship between the Old Man and the boy, and now their love for each other was finally coming across. "He is very appealing and very touching," Hayward said of Pazos. "The fact that he is little and has that serious face has been greatly utilized by John Sturges, and he comes out of it like a little boy who is trying very hard to be a grown up and like a man. Sturges has done an extraordinary job with him."

They finished with the boy on August 6, leaving the balance of the work to be done on the process stage and in the tank. Howe created the glare of the tropical sun with a blazing bank of photo floods that pulled sixty thousand watts of electricity when fully illuminated. Bob Thomas visited the set to do a piece on why the film had taken so long and found Tracy in his dressing room.

"Maybe Zinnemann couldn't stand to see my face every morning," Tracy suggested. "I don't know. Anyway, he finally quit." The company, he said, burned through $3 million in Cuba, yet the Cuban footage would comprise only 20 percent of the movie. By then Jack Warner figured he was in too deeply to scrap the thing and approved another $2 million to get it completed. "Luckily," said Tracy, "they had an actor who was stupid. I put off other pictures to remain available for this one. I've got *Ten North Frederick* to do at Fox and *The Last Hurrah* at Columbia, and I didn't know if they would wait for me. Fortunately, both schedules have been pushed back . . . Yeah, I really wanted to do *The Old Man and the Sea*. But if I had known what trouble it was going to be, I never would have agreed to it. This is for the birds."

It was when floating alone in the tank on Stage 7 that Tracy's value to the troubled company became most forcefully apparent, for he had nothing other than the Old Man's words and his wits as an actor to carry the picture. The quiet routine at sea, the flying fish, the man-o'-war hovering overhead . . . and then comes the first tentative tugs at the line. "Never have I had such a strong fish," he speaks wearily, "or one that acted so strangely . . . Maybe he's too wise to jump. He could ruin me with a jump . . . or one quick rush . . . Maybe he has been hooked many times before and he knows this is how he must make his fight." And then the resolve that comes when, rising to the night sky, the line clutched powerfully in his hands, he pulls at it with all the strength that is in him. "Fish,"

he declares, his jaw set for battle, "I love you and I respect you very much—
but I will *kill* you before this day ends!"

As Hayward wrote Hemingway, "The difference in Tracy's performance
is amazing. Freddie kind of played him like he was a senile old man totter-
ing around barely able to walk or stand up. Sturges has directed him obviously like he is an old man but still with great virility and great strength still
in him. Obviously unless he did have these qualities it would be impossible
for him to go through the ordeal that he had to. Spencer is deeply moving
in the picture and very believable."

By August 9 they had roughly two weeks of work left to do, yet they
still had not resolved the problem of narration. Knowing Tracy did not feel
that he could play the part, say the dialogue, and do the voice-over as well,
Hayward had actor Joseph Cotten record a scratch track that could be used
for cutting purposes. He then proposed that Hemingway himself do the
narration—a job Hemingway said that he "could not and would not do."
On August 30, Tracy marked his fifty-first and final day on the film, bringing an end, nine days behind schedule, to a project that had been foremost
in his mind for nearly five years. The following day he shaved off the beard
he had grown for the role and rewarded himself with a TV dinner.

As his father was making the final shots for *The Old Man and the Sea,* John
Tracy was on the witness stand in Los Angeles Superior Court, giving testimony in the divorce action he had brought against his estranged wife,
charging her with mental cruelty and seeking custody of their child. Nadine
Tracy testified that John had treated her as a servant and that he had
repulsed her after the birth of their son. "If I put my arm around him he
would say, 'Let me alone.' " She told the court that on the day they separated, she took the baby with her on a shopping trip and returned to find
that John had cleared out. A custody agreement had already been arrived at,
leaving only the financial issues to be resolved when they met in court on
August 28.

On the stand, Johnny's excellent lipreading skills failed him and he
struggled to make himself understood. Louise volunteered her services,
relaying questions in a way he could easily read and "interpreting" the
answers he gave. He told the court that he had never been employed but
that he hoped to become an artist. He said that his income came primarily
from a trust left by his maternal grandfather, and that during the marriage
his father had made him an allowance of seventy-five dollars and then later
one hundred dollars a month. He indicated that he would not oppose
Nadine's being granted the divorce on her cross complaint, and the judge

directed him to pay seventy-five-dollars' monthly alimony and one hundred dollars in child support, less than half the $472 Nadine had sought. Spence took the family to dinner at Romanoff's that evening, noting ruefully in his book that John had dropped ten pounds over the course of the ordeal.

Kate, meanwhile, was in Stratford, fulfilling the commitment to the American Shakespeare Festival she had originally made for the 1956 season. Under Jack Landau's direction, her fiery Portia, first seen on the Old Vic's Australian tour, was a sensation—eloquent and graceful and enthusiastically received by most of the morning papers. When Spence promised to come back for *Much Ado About Nothing,* she was giddy with excitement.

"She spoke of him openly," the festival's artistic director, John Houseman, remembered, "and always with a mingling of loyalty, tenderness, and admiration. We all shared this admiration and hoped that he would presently appear among us. Several times that summer, Kate joyfully announced his imminent arrival, then reported that he had been detained or prevented. Finally, during *Much Ado,* the great day came when Kate, with a young girl's enthusiasm, proclaimed that this time Spencer was really coming. His plane ticket was bought and all the arrangements were made. On the evening of his arrival—carefully chosen as an *Othello* day—she drove off alone, in a state of high excitement that she made no attempt to conceal, to [Idlewild] Airport to meet him."

Tracy's datebook shows that he made an attempt to talk to John on September 13. ("Out of it," he recorded, "no luck . . . ") He boarded an American Airlines flight for New York the next morning, arriving on the East Coast at five o'clock. His entry for the day includes a word that suggests the scene Kate must have encountered upon her arrival: "Load." He was bundled off to the Sherry-Netherland, where the room, he noted, was air-cooled. His entry for the next day, September 15, contains just three words: "missed Stratford" and then again the word "load." Humiliated, Hepburn told the company that Tracy had missed his flight.

"He never did appear," said Houseman.

Officially, Tracy was in New York on the first leg of a publicity tour that was to take him to Europe in advance of *The Old Man and the Sea.* The Kanins, who were to accompany him to Montecatini, found it impossible to book space on the S.S. *Independence* but promised to follow in a few days aboard the *Île-de-France.* Tracy himself noted three continuous days of drinking at the Sherry-Netherland, having placed himself in Dr. Stock's expert care. He slept most of September 18 and 19 and until noon on the twentieth. Rous-

ing himself, he spoke to Louise by phone and had calls from Hayward and
Bert Allenberg. He dined with Kate at the hotel that evening, took all three
meals in her company the next day, and was well enough for a drive on the
twenty-second.

Warners' New York office finally caught up with him on the twenty-
fifth. Tracy told them he had the Asiatic flu and would not be meeting with
the press at all. He thought he might still go to Europe and was looking at
cars for the trip as late as the twenty-eighth. At 2:30 the following morning
he abruptly decided he wanted to go back to California. Kate made the
flight on two hours' notice and was there on St. Ives with him that night to
serve dinner.

As *The Old Man and the Sea* inched toward completion, Tracy faced a log-
jam of properties vying for his attention. The most promising of these,
however, went away within days.

Hecht-Hill-Lancaster had acquired the rights to the two Terence Rattigan one-acts known collectively as *Separate Tables,* and the offer had been
made for Laurence Olivier to direct and star in the picture. Olivier and
Vivien Leigh traveled to Los Angeles to finalize the deal. Spence, of course,
had known Vivien since 1940, when he presented her with the Oscar for
Gone With the Wind. Later, he helped Larry master his Midwestern accent
when Olivier was preparing for the part of the tragic Hurstwood in William
Wyler's production of *Carrie.* The two men were subsequently photographed together on the set of *Father's Little Dividend,* but their paths seldom crossed. "I have often thought we both sensed an affinity in our fates,"
Olivier wrote, "as people well might who felt that their lives are a bewildering mixture of incredibly good and incredibly bad fortune." It was over dinner at George Cukor's that Olivier was seized with the notion of adding
Tracy to the cast as the hard-drinking writer John Malcolm. He put the idea
to Tracy as a sort of fait accompli.

"Won't Burt Lancaster want the part?" Tracy asked.

"No," Olivier assured him. "He's agreed that you do it."

What Olivier didn't tell Tracy was that he had put the request forth in
the form of an ultimatum and that the reaction of the "Young Duke" was
sharper than anyone expected. "We had a party to celebrate," Tracy remembered, "and then the Oliviers flew home. When he arrived, a call was waiting from Hollywood. Lancaster had decided he wanted the role. 'Either
Tracy does it or you can't have us,' Larry said. But Lancaster was determined. Larry rang me that night. 'Well, old cock,' he said, 'we've all been
fired.' I said, 'That'll teach you to ask for me.' "

Far more resilient as a pending project was *Ten North Frederick,* from

With Laurence Olivier on the set of *Carrie* (1952).
(PATRICIA MAHON COLLECTION)

the best-selling novel by John O'Hara. Tracy was first sent the book in February 1956, with Fox saying they'd buy it if he would agree to do it. As with *The Power and the Glory*, O'Hara began the novel with a corpse and then unfolded the story of Joe Chapin in flashback. Trapped in a sterile marriage, Joe falls in love with a younger woman named Kate. Hemmed in by social convention, he decides that he must remain with his wife. "The practice of love had gone out of their life together; they continued to live in the same house, eat their meals together, expose themselves to the intimacies of living together; and Edith could count on Joe to pay the bills . . . There was nothing, certainly in the public prints or in the public view that could be inferred to be proof or hint of a change in their relationship . . . they behaved toward each other with the same precise politeness they had observed all their lives." Meanwhile, unable to marry Kate, Joe Chapin methodically drinks himself to death.

"WOW!" Tracy wrote in his book. "Not for me!"

Nothing more was said about *Ten North Frederick* until Buddy Adler showed such an unbridled enthusiasm for *Desk Set*. He called Tracy one day in March 1957 and expressed hope that something could be worked out for the O'Hara story, which was being developed by Charles Brackett and writer-director Philip Dunne. Where Tracy saw a character and a plotline that hit far too close to home, Dunne saw one of the greatest of all modern novels: "It is the story of the first citizen of a representative American city, of his wife, his son and daughter, and of his brief political career. Above all, it is the story of the girl who brings him happiness too late. It is a touching story, both realistic and intensely dramatic."

Tracy relented, and in April a deal was struck for the same money and percentages as for *Desk Set*. He briefly tried getting out of the commitment in June, pro forma, but the real trouble over *Ten North Frederick* didn't start until Adler began pushing a protégée, actress-model Suzy Parker, for the role of Kate. Tracy didn't think Parker could act, and there followed a flurry of tests—Dina Merrill, Marjorie Steele, Inger Stevens. According to Merrill, Adler "had the hots" for Suzy Parker, and in the end no one else would do for the part. Tracy told Allenberg to get him out of the picture, and there was a momentary threat from Fox of a lawsuit.

Adler backed off, convinced he had an even stronger use for Tracy—as Professor Unrat opposite Marilyn Monroe in a modern remake of *The Blue Angel*. There was no director yet attached, but the plan was to do the film that summer in Europe. Tracy was intrigued enough to have a look at the 1930 original with Emil Jannings and Marlene Dietrich. "Fabulous pic[ture] & part," he wrote in his book. "O.K. if right <u>director.</u>" By the time the deal was made, however, *Desk Set* had proven a failure, reporting domestic rentals of just $1.7 million. The best Adler could do was a straight salary of $200,000. The deal was still hanging fire on October 29 when Louis B. Mayer died of leukemia and Irene Selznick asked Tracy to read the eulogy.

Kate described the chaotic funeral at Wilshire Boulevard Temple as "something out of the black" with Spence "almost having a fit" while Irene was "lost in the search for simplicity." Two thousand mourners gathered under the temple's great vaulted ceiling as another three thousand onlookers crowded outside. From high in the organ gallery Jeanette MacDonald sang "Ah, Sweet Mystery of Life." Seated below was a veritable Who's Who of Mayer's M-G-M family—Robert Taylor, Eleanor Powell, Fred Astaire, Jimmy Stewart, Red Skelton, Van Johnson, Howard Strickling, Clarence Brown, Billie Burke, Jimmy Durante. Great masses of flowers surrounded a casket draped with red and white roses. Tracy spoke of a "shining epoch" that seemed to pass with Mayer's death, an epoch of which he clearly felt a part. "There were giants in those days," he said firmly, "and there are giants in these days—but rarely. Louis B. Mayer was a giant. The merchandise he handled was intangible—something that met the primary human need for entertainment. He knew how to take people out of the everyday world and into a dream world. Even those long associated with him marveled at where he found his insight. He did not find it; he earned it by knowing people."

The deal for *The Blue Angel* was okayed just after the first of the year, but with stipulations: that Monroe would be the costar, that Tracy would receive first billing, that Adler would personally produce the picture, and that it would be made in color. The drop in price was to be covered with a percentage of the gross after breakeven. Within a week there was "Monroe trouble" and Tracy, by now having heard all the horror stories, told Allenberg he wanted out. Word was passed to Fox's Lew Schreiber, who felt the studio would probably work out a deal with the actress and then come back. "No soap!" was Tracy's response.

Hepburn, who thought *Ten North Frederick* "a big bore," was instrumental in bringing Tracy's next picture to fruition. Jack Ford had set up a deal at Columbia to make Edwin O'Connor's *The Last Hurrah* and wanted Tracy to play the part of O'Connor's engaging old Irish pol, Frank Skeffington. The story was a natural fit for both men, the passing of an era in American politics in which showmanship and patronage won the hearts and votes of the immigrant poor and the New England bluebloods were the perennial enemies of the people. After a brief flirtation with Jimmy Cagney, Ford set his sights on Tracy for the role and refused to give up.

Kate knew there had been "not too much interest" between the two since Tracy had been unable—or, in Ford's mind, unwilling—to do *The Plough and the Stars* in 1936. When Leland Hayward, at Eddie Mannix's urging, wanted Ford to direct *The Old Man and the Sea,* he put the idea forth to Tracy, knowing there would be serious reservations. Tracy wired:

BRILLIANT DIRECTOR OF YOUR CHOICE. ONLY FEAR: QUESTION HE WILL SHOOT SCRIPT IF NOT PAPA YOU ME.

Tracy was sent O'Connor's novel in February 1956, and he devoured it in two days. "Great but <u>NO!!</u>" he wrote in his book. "John Ford?? Told Allenberg no 'Hurrah.' " In September Columbia came back with an offer that was promptly rejected by Abe Lastfogel: $125,000 plus 25 percent of the profits. Being "Irish and smart," Ford applied to Hepburn for help. One night at her place—the "aviary" on what was once the John Barrymore estate—Allenberg complained that involving her was "unethical" of Ford, a statement that elicited from Tracy a "sharp reminder to him of the facts of life." The next afternoon Hepburn arranged the first substantive talk between Tracy and Ford in some twenty years.

"Kate 'Agent' with Ford for Hurrah," Tracy wrote. "Met with him. Deal now possible." Columbia's Harry Cohn made the same offer as before, then raised it, under pressure from Ford, to $175,000 and 10 percent of the gross after breakeven. Tracy again said no, and four days later Allenberg appeared on the set of *Desk Set* with word that Ford "wanted a deal" but was still working to bring Cohn around. Subsequently Ford told Hepburn that he would not make the picture without Tracy.

The back-and-forth continued into March 1957, when Tracy made the decision to keep his schedule open for *The Old Man and the Sea*. Kate notified Ford—who wanted to start May 1—and Ford, not wishing to wait any longer, said in a fit of pique that he would move ahead with Orson Welles in the role. "End of Hurrah!!" Tracy wrote. Eight days later, "Pappy" was once again on the phone to Hepburn; Columbia had upped the offer to $200,000 but said they wanted to start June 1. "Par!" Tracy responded. "NO!" The deal wasn't settled until May, when the producers agreed to push the start of production back to January 1958. Tracy went off to Hawaii to do *Old Man and the Sea*, and Ford lined up a picture in London to fill the time.

The Last Hurrah was not without controversy, the character of Skeffington having been modeled on Boston's legendary mayor (and onetime Massachusetts governor) James Michael Curley. As the story goes, an enterprising newspaper editor sent the eighty-one-year-old Curley a set of galleys with the hope that Curley would file a review of the O'Connor book. Curley took little more than a fleeting glance at the galleys before returning them to the paper with a terse one-line notice: "The matter is in the hands of my attorneys."

His outrage was short-lived. O'Connor painted Skeffington with obvious affection, saving the sharp edges for the rogues, bigots, and hypocrites who opposed him on the battlefield of public approbation. In a time and place where Irish political operatives did what they felt they had to do for the advancement of their people, Curley was a hero to the men and women of South Boston, a fierce and colorful advocate for the disenfranchised. In time, he began referring to himself as "Skeffington" and was heard to have said on at least one occasion, "I like best the scene where I die." Despite the apparent change in Curley's attitude toward the book, Columbia took the precaution of paying the former mayor, governor, and convicted felon $25,000 in exchange for his signature on a release shielding the corporation from any legal action that might otherwise result from the production and exhibition of the movie.

After striving for more than a year to get Tracy committed, Ford set about creating the most comfortable of working environments. The script, written by Ford's frequent collaborator Frank Nugent, was such a faithful job of adaptation that it was scarcely mentioned in the few meetings between Tracy and Ford that led up to production. Surrounding Tracy in the film would be, as Ford put it, his "ex-pals and ex-playmates"—Jimmy Gleason, Wallace Ford, Frank McHugh, and, making his first major studio appearance in six years, Pat O'Brien. Ford filled out the cast with a sterling collection of character people, Basil Rathbone, Donald Crisp, Edward Brophy, John Carradine, and Jane Darwell among them. Jeffrey Hunter was borrowed from Fox to play Adam Caulfield, the pipe-smoking sportswriter invited to follow one last campaign by his uncle Frank, and the cast was completed with such vintage names as Ricardo Cortez, Basil Ruysdael, Edmund Lowe, Anna Lee, Ruth Clifford, Hank Mann, Tom Neal, Mae Marsh, and Julius Tannen.

A wardrobe fitting on February 13 gave Ford an opportunity to stress the importance of Tracy's performance in the film. This was a big picture, Ford emphasized, with a budget of $2.5 million and an aggressive thirty-five-day schedule. Tracy would have a wonderful line of support, but in the end it would be up to him—and him alone—to carry the picture. Tracy spent the next few days at home, studying the script, honing his characterization. From the book he knew Skeffington as a vigorous seventy-two-year-old, a man of thoroughgoing cynicism who nevertheless made himself the most accessible of public figures, comfortable in the knowledge that all successful political activity harbored an element of quid pro quo.

"I'd like to say that I have a theory about acting," Tracy had said at the time of *The Mountain.* "But I don't. It's just that I was born a sentimental Irishman, and I play the parts the way they react on me." The way the part of Skeffington reacted on him was a constant source of delight to John Ford. He was, Ford later said, a "wonderful guy" with whom to work. "When I say Spencer Tracy is the best actor we ever had, I'm giving you something of my philosophy of acting. The best is most natural. Scenery never gets chewed in my pictures. I prefer actors who can just be."

Filming began on February 24, 1958. Returning to Gower Gulch for the first time since *Man's Castle,* Tracy marveled at the span of time. "John Ford—after 28 years—!" he wrote in his datebook. The first scene that morning had Skeffington descending the staircase of the mayoral mansion, the usual crowd of supplicants gathered outside the gate. Pausing on the landing before a portrait of his late wife, he gently removes the single rose at its base, as he has done every day since her death, and replaces it with a fresh one. He then pauses to gaze up at her, warmed by her memory. The moment is as brief as it is heartfelt, and it energizes him for the day ahead.

Tracy resisted *The Last Hurrah* because of John Ford's involvement, but the experience was a pleasant surprise for both men.
(SUSIE TRACY)

"Well, Winslow," he says, resuming his descent, "is the lark on the wing this morning?"

Surrounded in this initial scene by Gleason, Brophy, O'Brien, others, Tracy's natural charm and authority took hold, and he was at once the wily politician of O'Connor's famed novel. Regarding the stack of wires on his desk—the result of his announcement that he will run for reelection—he says wryly, "We should be getting a kickback from Western Union." To which one of his henchmen responds, "I spoke to them about it last year—negative."

Though envisioned by Ford as a character study, much of *The Last Hurrah* was played as broad comedy, the humor rooted in the reality of the Irish-American experience. When Skeffington storms the restricted battlements of the Plymouth Club, he does so with a Jewish ward healer in tow. When a prominent banker blocks a slum clearance project, Skeffington appoints the man's wastrel son to the post of fire commissioner and then uses the resulting photographs as blackmail.

When it came time to shoot Knocko Minihan's wake, Ford told a visitor it was probably the "most hilarious episode" in the entire story. "The wake is as obsolete as a dinosaur today," Tracy explained, "but in the old days among the Boston Irish they were practical and often enjoyable affairs. They allowed neighbors and friends of the deceased to get together as a kind of relief from the grimness." There was also, added Jimmy Gleason, a serious side to the mayor's presence at such an event. "In those days in Boston, an elected official was a tribal chieftain as well, the tribe, of course, being the Irish. So it was incumbent upon the elected official to attend those affairs, it was he who took care of the financial burden of the widow."

Thirty days into production, Tracy wearily commemorated his birthday. "58 years old," he said in his book, "and feel 90." He dined that evening with Louise and the kids, Kate typically making herself scarce. On April 7, work shifted to the Columbia Ranch in Burbank, where Ford began shooting exteriors.

Tracy plainly had fun making the picture, and the fireworks many anticipated between him and Pappy Ford never came. "[T]hey were both, shall we say, gentlemen of very strong habits," Hepburn said, "and Spencer liked to take a nap in the afternoon. He could get up early and go to work, but just absolutely would wilt. So [John], instead of making a problem of this, used to say, 'God, I'm exhausted. You know, I think we've done a full day's work and I don't know why the hell you don't go home.' And there were two enormously talented people sort of stalking around like prize bulls in the ring, having a deep understanding of each others' wickednesses. It always used to entertain me."

Night work on the ranch captured the events that follow Skeffington's defeat at the hands of a telegenic Republican, the wooing of the electorate having evolved from hand-to-hand engagement to the sterility of the electronic age. The old line's frustration with this turn of events is seen in the great pumpkin face of Ditto Boland, Skeffington's loyal lieutenant, who is not quite so button-down as the others. Ed Brophy, making his final appearance in a feature picture, pulled out all the stops that night, racing up to his boss' limousine and throwing his overcoat and his prized homburg to the sidewalk, stomping on them as he sputtered threats of physical violence. "I'm on my way over to that McCluskey's headquarters! I'm gonna step right up and poke him in the eye! I'm gonna tell him to his face—"

As they rehearsed the scene, Tracy calming him and telling him to get ahold of himself, retrieving the hat (his "hamburger") from the pavement and carefully pressing it back into shape, Ford eyed the plate glass storefront adjacent to campaign headquarters and decided to have Brophy let fly with a brick once Tracy's car had cleared the shot. The sixty-two-year-old actor had just one chance of hitting the window dead square, and in the end it broke clean, the shattering of one generation's traditions in service of another's.

The rest of the night was spent setting up and staging a midnight victory parade for the opposing candidate, Skeffington making his way home on foot, a solitary figure in the foreground, the clamor and fire of a newer— if not necessarily better—administration fading off into the distance. It was a particularly long and complicated tracking shot, requiring the services of eight assistant directors and hundreds of extras, two hundred lighted torches, lapel pins as big as silver dollars. They didn't finish until 5:00 a.m., but the resulting shot became one of the most prized in the Ford catalog.

The Last Hurrah didn't finish in thirty-five days—Tracy never thought it would—but it did come in $200,000 under budget. Ford printed so many first takes that the final shooting ratio was just six to one—almost unheard of on a major feature. Tracy completed his final scene—Skeffington casting his vote on election day—at 4:10 p.m. on April 24, 1958. "Happy picture!" he wrote in his book. "Ford great!"

Just prior to finishing up *The Last Hurrah,* Tracy had a call from John Sturges: Ernest Hemingway had run *The Old Man and the Sea* and said that he liked it very, very much. Tracy was astonished; he himself wasn't happy with the picture. Since shooting had wrapped at the end of August, he had been locked in an ongoing battle with Hayward over the handling of the soundtrack. Tracy's preference had always been to play the Old Man silent and speak his words in voice-over, the same approximate technique that had been dubbed "Narratage" for *The Power and the Glory.* But nobody liked the idea of a $5 million silent movie, and he dutifully made a preliminary narration track for editing purposes, a dubbing job that took three days. In October, the film cut, he went back and did the final voice-over, which involved his speaking the narrative as well as the words and thoughts of Santiago, the latter in the voice of the Old Man. It was a technique that worked, despite all the hand-wringing that led up to it, and by the middle of November, Hayward could report to Hemingway that the picture was entirely finished "with the exception of a couple of minor inserts."

On January 9 they had taken it to Riverside, where the reaction of a near-capacity house—which had come to see *A Farewell to Arms*—was so good the studio people were a little surprised. "Worth all the agony everyone went through—I think," Louise reported in a letter to a friend. "Whether it is worth the ulcer Spence wound up with is a question. But it is a fine, fine picture." Even Tracy thought the reaction good. " 'Old Man' seemed to go well," he wrote in his book the next day. "Think excellent, true pic. Should get good reviews. Business??? <u>Very dubious.</u>" He made some minor suggestions—things to cut—but when he ran the picture again in March, he found that not one of his changes had been made and his mood soured again. "[N]o suggestions followed—<u>stinks!</u>—will get panned."

According to Hayward, Hemingway said the picture had "a wonderful emotional quality and is very grateful and pleased with the transference of his material to the screen. He thought Tracy was great (in light of his quarrels with him this is quite a compliment) . . . the photography was excellent . . . the handling of the fishing and the mechanical fish very good. Had some minor dislikes . . . [B]ut all in all he was terribly high on the picture and very pleased with it."

For a second preview in May, Tracy wanted Betty Bogart to see it. "I went to the preview with Carroll Tracy," she recalled, "and he was waiting for me at his house afterwards for the full report. Things like that meant something to him." Her reaction was so positive it threw him, and he thought for a moment that he might be overreacting. "Is it great???" he wondered. A few days later he phoned Sturges about the changes he wanted. He was unhappy with the ending, the titles, and the scene toward the end with the tourists, which he thought out of tone with the rest of the sequence. Two days later, he had his answer: Warners refused to make any of the changes he wanted. That day he suffered the "worst ulcer pains yet" and the upset continued into the evening hours, when he irritably dined at Romanoff's with the Durochers, the Wagners (Bob and Natalie), and Betty Bogart (with whom he gratuitously picked a fight). He was chronically tired, unhappy, ill, and uninterested in work.

When Tom Pryor of the *New York Times* visited the set of *The Last Hurrah,* it was, in part, to check a report that Tracy was looking upon the picture as his own professional swan song. "Well," said Tracy, "twenty-eight years is a long time. I started with John Ford and it has been suggested that since he is directing this film it might be an appropriate time for me to call it quits. You know, the beginning and the end with Mr. Ford." Asked who had made such a suggestion, Tracy took on a sardonic smile.

"I have heard the suggestion," he replied. "In fact, I have been told that the people have voted for it."

CHAPTER 30

Our Greatest Actor

If Spencer Tracy considered retirement in the spring of 1958, he could be excused a certain pessimism. His first two films away from M-G-M had been commercial failures; even the potent Tracy-Hepburn combination was no longer considered box office magic. *The Old Man and the Sea* could never break even, no matter how much the public got behind it. And the grind of filmmaking wore on him as it always had.

"Spence," said John Sturges, "could have been cast as the leader of the Irish revolutionary group very easily. He was a rebel, and he tolerated—but unwillingly—certain requirements of civilization. Also, he had within him this dynamo of jittery nervous energy, and you can't carry that around all the time, find ways to express it. You have to wait a while. In a movie, scenes are lit, you have to ride in a car to work, and so on. And I'm sure they chopped away a bit at Spence. He said they did, anyhow."

He watched his finances carefully; a balance sheet as of May 31 showed assets—cash, stocks, insurance, the house on Tower Road—amounting to $692,000. Expenses were primarily allowances—$2,500 a month to Louise, a like amount divided among others. When Andrew Tracy died in 1955, he took over the support of his widow, Mame. And, of course, there was always Carroll, who had to be provided for even when there was nothing coming in. Charitable contributions—primarily the clinic—amounted to

$30,000 or more a year, and gifts accounted for another $10,000 or so. His own expenses were meager in comparison—generally no more than $1,000 a month.

Hepburn was touring *Much Ado About Nothing* during the early days of *The Last Hurrah,* but she kept in close touch by phone. The *Much Ado* company's stage manager, Bernie Gersten, made the jumps between cities with her, and he would help with the luggage and whatnot at each successive hotel. Gersten reported that the first thing she did after checking in was to make two long-distance phone calls to announce her safe arrival: one to Spencer Tracy in California and one to her father in Hartford, Connecticut. When Hepburn returned from New York on March 10, she brought with her a container of Irish stew. "Dear Katy," Tracy wrote in his book.

They were by now a familiar sight, as comfortable and inseparable as a pair of old shoes. Some nights they could be observed quietly browsing the Pickwick bookstore on Hollywood Boulevard. On studio lots, shielded from the public, they were less circumspect, Tracy playing the role of the alpha dog to Kate's humble and adoring mate. "She was meek and motherly," said Sheilah Graham,

> and you knew she lived only to please the man she treated as lord and master. He knew the extent of her devotion and played on it to the end. He seemed to delight in bawling her out—no one knew how it was in private. Once she stopped to tie her shoelace and he shouted, "What's the matter, Kate?"
>
> "Well, I—"
>
> "Hurry up, goddamn it."
>
> She left the lace untied and ran . . . At the beach home of their friends [the Erskines] he would sprawl in an armchair like Professor Higgins with Eliza Doolittle and command, "Put another log on the fire, Kate." And she would jump to attention and say, "Yes*sir,*" like a junior officer to the captain, and get the wood while he watched . . . She would take anything from Spencer because she admired him so much. She was his slave, and he used his power over her. But he also knew he needed her.

"I think he was *utterly* dependent upon her," said actress Betsy Drake, adding that there was a part of Tracy that could be cruel. "Whatever she did, she was vulnerable to him." Yet Drake's abiding memory of the two of them was at the "wonderful ritual" of the Sunday screenings at Irene Selznick's house on Summit Drive, Spence telling his familiar stories, Kate hanging on his every word. "She was *abject,*" said Sally Erskine. "Abject. It was really lovely to see them together, because she just glowed when they were together. She would sit at his feet, and if he just patted her on the head she reacted as if he had given her the Taj Mahal. Just a marvelous sight. I thought he showed love, I really did. In his face, his attitude. I [just] don't think he ever said anything."

When Hepburn went off to Greece in May 1958, it was in advance of Tracy's own planned arrival in Italy, where he would again visit the works of Michelangelo and the sites associated with the life of the great artist. During the course of *Last Hurrah,* Tracy and Jack Ford had talked of filming the life of *Il Divino,* and Tracy thought some time in Florence and Rome and particularly Carrara would serve as inspiration. As soon as Kate was gone, though, he seemed to lose his focus, loafing at home and occasionally driving out to the beach.

"Spence was down with us Saturday and Sunday," Chet Erskine reported in a letter to Kate on May 27, "and, the weather being beautiful, we had a marvelous time. The sea was calm but cold, as usual, and the swimming grand. Spence went in with me, and afterward we toasted in the sun and gossiped in our customary manner. He read parts of your letter concerning the wonders of Greece and we pondered the possibility of bringing the Acropolis over here and setting it up in the hills behind our houses where we could enjoy it without the inconvenience of travel . . ."

Eddie Lawrence, who also owned a house at Malibu, remembered Tracy from this period: "He would come up every once in a while. I really think he was lonesome."

Tracy's favorite thing in the world was to drive up the coast, the top down on his Thunderbird, the wind blowing through his hair. Occasionally he'd take Sally Erskine with him, driving as far as they could and then stopping for lunch. She never saw him take a drink, but he would talk about it. "He would say, 'Oh, Sally, I used to be in the gutter.' He told me the most horrible things about himself. I was somebody new to confess to, perhaps— I don't know what it was, perhaps younger."

Tracy's spirits were buoyed somewhat by the trade reviews for *The Old Man and the Sea,* which were extraordinary by any standard. Jack Moffitt, weighing in for the *Hollywood Reporter,* called it "a beautiful piece of visual poetry" and averred that Tracy's work as the Old Man was "so intimate and revealing of universal human experience that, to me, it almost transcended acting and became reality." *Variety* went further, labeling the picture a screen classic: "One of Tracy's remarkable achievements, adroitly guided by Sturges, is almost a negative one, but actually the most important. Despite that he is on the screen fully three-quarters of the picture, much of it by himself, his presence does not become oppressive. He has no one to play off of, no other actor by whose presence he can achieve contrast or relief. Within the limitations of the role he can only strive for minute shadings. He does this to create one of the screen's memorable roles."

In June the movie was screened at the Venice Film Festival and Expo 58 in Brussels, and it was requested for fests in Brazil and Canada. Tracy was still in town on June 12 when Kate called from Rome to say that she would be returning to New York in a few days. He wired the Kanins in Paris to expect him after a "short stay" in Manhattan, but he was still in California when Hepburn touched down at Idlewild. She was back in L.A. on the seventeenth, back preparing his dinner, back snuggling at his side for TV, back being all that she could be for him. There would be no trip to Europe, though he would continue to think and talk about it well into the fall.

When Stanley Kramer started working in the property department at Fox, moving furniture on and off sets, the year was 1933 and Spencer Tracy was one of the twelve name attractions on the company payroll. It's conceivable Kramer worked on one of Tracy's early pictures, but the divide between the grips on the swing crew and the on-camera talent was considerable, and the two men never crossed paths.

Both jumped from Fox to M-G-M, Tracy as a featured player on the studio's fabled talent roster, Kramer as a researcher for the costume department. After a few weeks Kramer was transferred to Editorial, where he apprenticed and eventually became a cutter's assistant. ("The pay was low, the glory was small, but it was a good place to learn how to put a movie together.") Through an uncle who happened to be a talent agent, Kramer found work writing for radio—guest shots for *The Chase & Sanborn Hour* and Rudy Vallee, episodes of *Big Town* starring Edward G. Robinson. He sold a spec script to Republic and eventually joined Irving Briskin's B-picture unit at Columbia.

In 1940, at the age of twenty-seven, Kramer was hired as casting director, story editor, and general factotum by Albert Lewin, the producer who had at one time been his boss at M-G-M. It was Kramer's doing that a relatively unknown Glenn Ford played the juvenile lead opposite Margaret Sullavan in Lewin's first United Artists release, *So Ends Our Night.* On their second picture together, *The Moon and Sixpence,* Kramer was elevated to the position of associate producer. The film, lacking marketable stars, wasn't a success, and Kramer was working for producer Val Lewton when he was drafted in 1943.

He spent the rest of the war in the Signal Corps, working out of the former Paramount studio complex on Long Island. Energetic and resourceful,

Stanley Kramer returned to Hollywood at a time when independent production was remaking a landscape once dominated by the major studios. Setting out to do what Lewin and his partner David Loew had done on a smaller scale, Kramer optioned two of Ring Lardner's better-known works, *The Big Town* and *Champion,* and went looking for a deal.

Big Town, retitled *So This Is New York,* was set up at Enterprise, but the film flopped commercially. Rebuffed by the banks, Kramer sought private capital for *Champion* and eventually secured it from a retired garment manufacturer living in Florida. Guaranteed with lettuce money from central California, *Champion* turned out to be a huge success. It made a star of Kirk Douglas and set Kramer on his way. There followed a series of productions, all financed with money from "drygoods manufacturers, wildcat oil operators, and all sorts of people."

A graduate of New York University, Kramer had a taste for class material—often plays that had proven themselves on Broadway. As a producer he amassed one of the industry's most impressive postwar résumés: *Home of the Brave, The Men, Cyrano de Bergerac, Death of a Salesman, High Noon, The Member of the Wedding, The 5,000 Fingers of Dr. T, The Wild One, The Caine Mutiny.* He put Marlon Brando onscreen before anyone else, hired Eddie Dmytryk straight out of prison, filmed original screenplays by Carl Foreman, Michael Blankfort, Edward Anhalt, and Dr. Seuss.

In 1955 Kramer began directing and, after a shaky start, landed a six-picture deal with United Artists. His first film under the new contract, *The Defiant Ones,* was finished and awaiting release when he approached Tracy about playing a role he had rejected on two previous occasions—that of Henry Drummond in Jerome Lawrence and Robert E. Lee's enduring stage hit, *Inherit the Wind.* Herman Shumlin had been the first to come calling, thinking he could get Tracy for old times' sake and the promise of a limited run. Tracy, of course, had other commitments, and Shumlin got a similar turndown from Fredric March, who was vacationing in Europe with his wife, the actress Florence Eldridge. Later that same year, Burt Lancaster's partner, Harold Hecht, optioned the play and offered to set the deal up anywhere—M-G-M, Paramount, Fox, Columbia, Universal—if only Tracy would play the lead. Again, the timing wasn't right.

Tracy went on to do *The Old Man and the Sea* and forgot all about *Inherit the Wind* until Kramer nabbed the rights for $200,000 and a percentage of the gross. Like Hecht, Kramer had Tracy in mind from the outset, but first he went to March—whom he knew from *Death of a Salesman*—and got his commitment to play Brady, the Gilded Age orator modeled on William Jennings Bryan. The people at UA were wary of the material—based on the storied Tennessee trial over the teaching of evolution in the public schools—and feared a backlash from Christian fundamentalists. "You're going to have enough trouble with the subject matter," one UA executive warned Kramer. "Why take on Tracy? How can you take a chance?" Kramer consulted with March, who said simply, "He's a great actor. Let's go."

Kramer had been nursing a fascination with Tracy since his days at M-G-M, where, as a lowly cutter's assistant, he had once introduced himself to his idol. "Everyone identified with Tracy from the time he started, when he was a redheaded tough guy—drunk, breaking the windows of cafes and being picked up by the police. Even in those early days nobody could really explain why it was that up against Mr. Movies—Clark Gable— everybody always wanted Tracy to get the girl. He was stocky and he underplayed it. He was kind of the good guy, full of sacrifice, the clichéd character. But, by gosh, he gave it so much more, and somehow you never wanted to see him go. Then, as his stature grew and he became the premiere character actor of his day, he had what a lot of fellows just dream about."

Bert Allenberg drove a hard bargain. Sensing Kramer's resolve, he held firm to a fee of $250,000. Tracy hadn't had a hit since *Bad Day at Black Rock,* hadn't made the top ten since *Father's Little Dividend,* but he was still widely regarded as the gold standard among American film actors, the best Hollywood had to offer. "Kramer said that he wanted to direct it," Tracy later recalled, "but that if I'd rather have another director he'd try to get whoever I wanted—Gar Kanin or whoever. But I'd seen the job Kramer did on *The Defiant Ones* and I told him that was good enough for me."

The deal was settled just as *The Old Man and the Sea* and *The Last Hurrah* would again be putting Tracy's drawing power to the test. *Old Man* came first, with a gala world premiere on October 7, 1958, to benefit the March of Dimes. Kate braved the crowds at New York's Criterion Theatre, something she was ordinarily loath to do, trying her best to distract from advance press clouded with news of the picture's troubles and its $5.5 million price tag. The notices were mixed, the critics admiring the filmmakers' guts more than their results, but there were still some who applied the word "masterpiece" to the picture and none at all who mentioned the matter of Tracy's weight. The first week's take was surprisingly good—$32,000 for fourteen showings—and the picture continued to draw well into November. The pattern repeated itself in key cities around the country, intense interest in the first two or three weeks, then a precipitous dropoff that was both startling and ominous.

Columbia moved *The Last Hurrah* into the Roxy on the twenty-second, timing its appearance to the midterm elections, and the picture went over big despite heavy rains that, according to *Variety,* clipped as much as $20,000 off the first week's gate. Metro's *Cat on a Hot Tin Roof* was the town's big winner in the comparably sized Music Hall, but *Hurrah,* helped by strong notices, held firm in its second week, bettering its first by some $15,000. It continued into its third and fourth weeks, falling off in much the same manner as *Old Man and the Sea.* In the end, neither film was a success, *The Last Hurrah* posting a loss of $1.8 million.

As both films were playing themselves out, their star was at Harkness Pavilion, where he had gone for a checkup, some forced dieting, and the removal of a basal cell eruption on his nose. He spent nearly two weeks at the exclusive facility, enduring a battery of tests and a series of cardiograms that showed, much to his dismay, no trouble at all. All the dieting, he decided, was at the expense of his ulcer, and he was still only three pounds to the better. "Out!" he wrote at the end of thirteen days, and he promptly fled to the Gotham Hotel.

Tracy was back in Los Angeles on November 25 when Bert Allenberg suffered a cerebral hemorrhage at the home of client Danny Kaye. Allenberg lingered two days at Cedars of Lebanon and died without regaining consciousness. Tracy was an active pallbearer at Sinai Temple on the twenty-eighth, as were Joel McCrea, Edward G. Robinson, Stewart Granger, Benny Thau, Leo Durocher, and Frank Capra.

It had been a lousy year, rife with disappointment, and being named Best Actor by the National Board of Review did little to bolster his spirits. He considered the Old Man far and away the toughest part he'd ever played and resented all the press about the tank and the phony marlin and such. ("Unless you can arrange for someone to deliver a live 3,000-pound marlin to you once a day for the sharks to chew up, how are you going to do the story?") He also thought parts of *The Last Hurrah* overcooked—particularly Minihan's wake and the death scene in which the cardinal comes to call.

"You liked all that schmaltz," he said accusingly when his cousin Jane told him she loved the film. "Yes, I did," she insisted. "That's where we were all from." And then there was that line she thought so marvelous: "We're not all descended from kings, you know."

He saw Ethel Barrymore, who was twenty-one years his senior, and said gloomily, "Ethel, I'm getting old."

"Yes," she said, "just like Jack and Lionel and me . . ."

When Tracy hit his blue moods, Hepburn redoubled her efforts to look after him. Dina Merrill recalled a day in March 1959 when she saw Hepburn standing in line at the airport. "I said, 'Kate, where are you going?'

" 'Well,' she said, 'Spencer is going to make *The Devil at 4 O'Clock* in Martinique, and I'm going down to find him a house to live in.'

"As if nobody else could do that!" Merrill exclaimed. "She wasn't even in the picture!"

The Devil at 4 O'Clock promised to be yet another rough shoot, the sort of location picture Tracy hated to do. It was the last deal Bert Allenberg had set up for him, and he stuck with it despite learning, just after the first of the year, that producer Fred Kohlmar had no script, no director, and a projected start date of April 15. It was, Tracy told Abe Lastfogel, impossible, and he was no less dubious when he learned the West End's Peter Glenville would likely direct the film. He finally saw forty-two pages of script on January 21 and thought them terrible. He sent Lastfogel back to Columbia's Sam Briskin and asked that production be postponed until an entirely new script could be developed. A subsequent meeting with Glenville revealed the new writer to be Bridget Boland, the woman who had written *The Prisoner,* the first of only two movies Glenville had ever directed. "Start June 1???" Tracy wrote in his book. "<u>I doubt!!</u>"

He was also reviewing the draft screenplay for *Inherit the Wind* and cabling his comments to Stanley Kramer, who was in Australia filming *On the Beach.* A hit, *The Defiant Ones* had garnered nine Academy Award nominations, adding considerable luster to the other projects on Kramer's schedule. Unwilling to sacrifice *Wind* for something as ephemeral as *Devil at 4 O'Clock,* Tracy had Columbia agree to a stop clause that guaranteed his release no later than September 1, 1959.

Once again, he found himself an unwilling participant in the annual Oscar race. *The Old Man and the Sea* had made a number of ten-best lists, and it was widely assumed that Tracy would be nominated for either the Hemingway picture or *Last Hurrah.* Of the four other nominees, handicappers assumed Tony Curtis and Sidney Poitier, both with nominations for *The Defiant Ones,* would cancel each other out, leaving the field to Tracy, Paul Newman (for *Cat on a Hot Tin Roof*), and David Niven (who had taken the part Olivier was to have played in *Separate Tables*). The *Los Angeles Times'* Philip K. Scheuer declared his preference for *Old Man and the Sea,* noting that, as virtually its only actor, Tracy should get the major credit for sustaining it. "What would it have been without him?" Yet, when fingering the "probable" winner, Scheuer went with Niven. The ceremony took place April 7 at the Pantages Theatre in Hollywood. Tracy watched it on television and later pronounced the event "a new low" in entertainment. As predicted, David Niven took the award for Best Actor.

In May Hepburn traveled to London to make *Suddenly, Last Summer,* for Sam Spiegel and Joe Mankiewicz. Based on Tennessee Williams' play of the same title, the picture, which joined her for the first time with Elizabeth Taylor and Montgomery Clift, promised to be one of the year's major

releases. Tracy stayed behind, immobilized by Kohlmar's frantic prepara-
tions for *Devil at 4 O'Clock*. In June he attended George Burns' triumphant
opening at the Sahara Hotel in Las Vegas, then mourned the death of Ethel
Barrymore with a rosary at Good Shepherd. In July he was reported by both
Sheilah Graham and Hedda Hopper as visiting the set of *Suddenly, Last
Summer* and taking part in a London charity event called *Night of 100 Stars*.
When pressed by British reporters about how much he earned and how old
he was—two matters with which Fleet Street always seemed unnaturally
obsessed—he said: "I earn $300,000 every Friday. And I am 78 years old."

He was back in Los Angeles for Natalie Wood's twenty-first birthday
and the party thrown in her honor by Frank Sinatra at Romanoff's. There
was talk of a picture with Sophia Loren, as Garson Kanin had written a
script to be shot in Italy titled *Big Deal*. Over the phone, Tracy approved
Kanin's idea and the arrangements. Two days later, Abe Lastfogel called to
say that the deal was not yet set. According to Tracy's book, Kanin, who had
not directed a movie since 1941, wanted $100,000 in cash, another
$100,000 deferred, and 50 percent of the profits. "Now!" Tracy wrote in dis-
gust. "Shenanigans!"

"The young actors who are coming along are interesting," Tracy told
William Weber Johnson of *Time* magazine.

> They know so much about acting, how it should be done, and they
> are perfectly willing to tell you about it. I guess I've never really
> known about acting, how it should be done. And I remember
> George M. Cohan, who taught me more than anyone else ever has
> about the theatre—he and Jack Barrymore were probably the great-
> est we've ever had—I remember him telling me the same thing,
> that he really didn't know how it was done, that you just do it. I
> guess maybe when I was a young punk in the theatre and people
> came backstage to say that I'd done a terrific job, I was the same
> way. And I was probably intolerant; I probably looked at older peo-
> ple and thought, "Why you old, fat slob, why don't you quit?"

And then he gave his own ample girth a friendly pat.
George Cukor commented: "I've never had a really gifted, magical
actor go into long explanations and long theories and long intellectualizing
about the acting process . . . Tracy used to tell you, 'Well, I certainly
learned those lines, spoke those eight pages down to every *if, and,* and *but*.
I knew every word.' That's all he would tell you. Now there was a great deal

else that went on with him, but he wasn't telling it to you. That would have taken the magic out of it somehow, to have chewed it all over beforehand."

Cukor perceived a certain musicality to the way Tracy approached his work, a quality of speaking that came from the time when he first went on the stage in the early 1920s. Indeed, he could remember the way the young Katharine Hepburn struck him when he watched the screen test she had made for RKO, a scene from the Philip Barry play *Holiday:* "[T]hat was a period when there was a sort of slightly affected, almost singing way of speaking. There was a rhythm in the lines, and she spoke it that way. And it was a sort of rather grand life. They were all very swell. And Philip Barry had his own note as a writer, and she almost sang that note. As a matter of fact, years later she did another play of Phil Barry's, and . . . Tracy said, 'Yes, I thought all you people sang it so nicely, all of you.' "

Eddie Dmytryk picked up on it when he likened Tracy's phrasings to those of a great jazz singer. And it was while on location for *The Mountain* that he heard Tracy say something akin to it himself. "Our company was resting between setups on a path above the glacier. Somehow or other, a young, English-speaking hiker got through our lines and approached Tracy, who usually avoided people. The young man was interested in the theatre. Before Tracy could escape, he was asked that dreadful question, 'Mr. Tracy, what is the secret of great acting?' Spence fixed him with a fishy eye. 'Read the lyrics, kid,' he said. 'Read the lyrics.' But how many could read the lyrics like Spencer Tracy?"

Humphrey Bogart knew it was an illusion, that the wheels were always turning, but that Tracy never showed the mechanism at work. "He covers up," Bogart said. "He never overacts or is hammy. He makes you believe he is what he is playing." Laraine Day saw a hint of it in *The Last Hurrah,* the precision with which Tracy tackled a scene. "Well, for example, an actor is normally trained never to turn his back on an audience, unless it's for some deliberate purpose . . . Tracy is talking [to Jeffrey Hunter] and he's going to walk to a window over there. So he walks away from the camera and stoops and picks up a pin for absolutely no reason, sets it on the table, and continues on. And I will bet you that no one in that theater will remember he ever did that. But watch his performances: they are filled with everyday things like that. Finding a little thing here, a little thing there and getting rid of it, but you're never aware that he's done it." Said James Cagney, who loved watching him: "I'm easy to imitate, but you never saw anyone imitate Spence Tracy. You can't mimic reserve and control very well."

Tracy's best performances were orchestrated in movements, as in a symphonic score. He touched on this when he told John Sturges he would go over a script, read it aloud, and determine "where he should come on and where he should lay back." There was no impact in hitting all the time, no advantage in constantly trying to overwhelm an audience. To do it well required the right material, and only occasionally did he get it. *Fury* was such a script, as were *The Show-Off, The Power and the Glory,* and, curiously, *Northwest Passage.* He never thought he had achieved it with *Jekyll and Hyde,* couldn't feel it with *Edison* or *Cass Timberlane.* The best pictures with Kate had it—*Woman of the Year, Adam's Rib, Pat and Mike. Father of the Bride* had it; *The Actress,* certainly. And, of course, *Bad Day at Black Rock,* though you couldn't have convinced him of that at the time.

"Spencer Tracy is the kind of actor I like to watch," Marlon Brando told Truman Capote in a 1957 *New Yorker* profile. "The way he holds back, *holds* back—then darts in to make his point, darts back. Tracy, Muni, Cary Grant. They know what they're doing. You can learn something from them."

Despite the quality of Frank Nugent's screenplay, there was no real chance for Tracy to open up in *The Last Hurrah,* no darting in and darting back. Ford had surrounded him with such a broadly drawn cast of characters that he went through much of the film serving as straight man to actors like Gleason, Brophy, Wally Ford, Frank McHugh.

Inherit the Wind would be an entirely different proposition, however, a shrewd dramatization of one of the century's most colorful trials, a story pulsing with the natural ebb and flow of controversy. In taking on the role of Henry Drummond, Tracy would be assuming the mantle of one of Kramer's boyhood heroes, the crusading criminal defense attorney Clarence Darrow. It was Darrow's courtroom battle with Bryan, spurred by the determination of the American Civil Liberties Union to challenge a Tennessee law forbidding the teaching of evolution in the schools, that defined both men in the public imagination: Darrow, the passionate Chicago progressive, squaring off against Bryan, the bumptious Bible-thumper. They were images—cartoons almost—that proved irresistible to Lawrence and Lee, radio dramatists with a keen understanding of religious intolerance and the underpinnings of commerce at the heart of most great debates. The play opened on Broadway in the spring of 1955 and was an immediate sensation, bagging Tony awards for Paul Muni as Drummond and Ed Begley as Bryan's counterpart, Matthew Harrison Brady. The show ran for two years, more than eight hundred performances, then went out on the road with Melvyn Douglas in the Drummond role and Begley continuing as Brady.

In opening it up, Kramer turned to Nedrick Young and Harold Jacob Smith, the screenwriting team behind *The Defiant Ones.* Young and Smith went back to the original transcripts of the trial, studying the way the playwrights had given majesty to the words and ideas originally spoken in court. A full year of development went into the screenplay, which they were still trying to "improve and sharpen" as Kramer established a production office on the moribund lot at Universal City.

"*Inherit the Wind,*" said Kramer, "became more and more topical as it spun around inside my head . . . The picture had so many basic things in it in which I believe. Darrow telling [H. L.] Mencken that the trouble with William Jennings Bryan was that he looked for God too high up and too far away, that there is more power in a single child's imagination than in all the shouted amens and hosannas in church. These were things that hit home with me and excited my imagination. I thought I could reach a mass audience with the ideas embodied in that picture."

Rehearsals for the principal members of the cast began on October 12, 1959, Kramer intent on staging the film in lengthy takes, giving his two stars the freedom to go at each other without fear of interruption. The supporting cast was comprised of Gene Kelly, Florence Eldridge, Dick York (as Cates, the high school biology teacher at the center of the storm), Donna Anderson, Elliott Reid, and Harry Morgan. The first two days of shooting were given over to nighttime scenes in the empty courtroom, York and Anderson establishing their relationship, he the heretic schoolteacher, she the earnest preacher's daughter. Kelly entered the scene as the Mencken-esque reporter Hornbeck, chomping an apple and lending a big-city perspective to the backward antics of the rural South.

Tracy and March took their places on the third day of production, the set now crowded with extras—reporters, photographers, jurymen, farmers, wives, kids, policemen. While March was anticipating considerable time in the makeup chair—skullcap, hairpiece, greasepaint, body padding—Tracy, as usual, required nothing other than a light dusting of powder.* A genuine reporter, Thomas McDonald of the *New York Times,* was on hand to witness the filming of their preliminaries, Kramer intent on starting in the courtroom proper and continuing in sequence until all the court interiors had been completed. "The actors' first exchange before the cameras was the opening courtroom sequence in which Mr. March asked permission to remove their coats because of the heat. Mr. Tracy then took off his coat and sarcastically explained that the colorful suspenders he was wearing were purchased in Mr. March's hometown in Nebraska. When Mr. Kramer finally said, 'cut,' the courtroom, full of extras and the crew, broke into spontaneous applause, an unusual occurrence on a Hollywood set."

Kramer told McDonald that he considered *Inherit the Wind* the third point in a three-pronged attempt to provide "provocative" film fare. "In *The Defiant Ones* we dealt with the problem of race. *On the Beach,* which will be

---

* The schedules show that March had a 7:00 a.m. makeup call, while Tracy was given a 9:00 a.m. call.

On the set of *Inherit the Wind*. Left to right: Gene Kelly, Donna Anderson, Dick York, director Stanley Kramer, and Tracy. (PATRICIA MAHON COLLECTION)

released in December, concerns the big question, the Bomb. And now I'm dealing with what I consider the third major problem today, freedom of speech and, more important, freedom of thought. From the standpoint of box office, I think people want thought-provoking material on the movie screen—something they can't get on their home screen."

Said one crew member proudly, "It takes us as long to get one shot as it takes one of those TV outfits to make a whole show." Indeed, *Inherit the Wind* was the only theatrical motion picture shooting on the Universal lot, the rest of the plant having been given over to Revue, the television arm of MCA, the talent agency that now owned the 480-acre facility. Conscious of the big-screen values his picture needed, Kramer kept a camera crane and two operators available at all times, a source of some amusement to Tracy.

"We were rehearsing and practicing some camera moves on a boom, which gives you a chance for another movement," Kramer recalled, "and Spence said, 'Why years ago I could remember at M-G-M, why Eddie Mannix came down on the set and he took the boom away from guys like you . . . They took it away, they locked it up in a room. They wouldn't let you get near it.' He said, 'Here we are moving all over the place like a frightened barracuda.' I got the message, which was: Let's shoot this picture and let's not start moving all over the place."

Donna Anderson, relatively new to films, remembered Kramer's mobile camera as a challenge Tracy chose to ignore. "When the shot was on me, I was doing waltzes around people because he wanted the camera to be working in. If I was saying something, I had to justify moving this way and then moving that way so he could have the fluidity in this little space with the camera. Well, when it came time for Spencer Tracy, he just said, 'The camera will find me.' "

Drummond's admonition to Rachael and Cates in the now empty Hillsboro courtroom, Hornbeck off to one side, the townspeople's taunts still ringing in their ears, was Tracy's first opportunity to come on, to take command of the film, the camera slowly circling him in one continuous three-minute take.

"I know what Bert is going through," he tells the minister's daughter. "It's the loneliest feeling in the world. It's like walking down an empty street, listening to your own footsteps." And then to Cates, a harder edge to his words: "But all you have to do is to knock on any door and say, 'If you'll let me in I'll live the way you want me to live and I'll think the way you want me to think,' and all the blinds will go up and all the doors will open and you'll never be lonely, ever again. Now it's up to you, Cates. You just say the word and we'll change the plea— That is, of course, if you honestly believe that the law is right and you're wrong. Now if that's the case, just tell me and I'll pack my bag and go back to Chicago where it's a nice cool hundred in the shade."

The business, the body language, the passion behind the eyes. There was no polish to Tracy's Drummond, nothing mannered in his ragged delivery. Tracy, said Kramer, "reduced everything to a fine powder of simplicity, and that takes hard work, it takes a lot of hard work. 'Improvisation,' he always said, 'is perspiration.' There's so much advance work to do so you can recognize something good if you saw it."

There can be little doubt the performance took a lot out of him, and he didn't seem well during the course of the shoot. Said Kramer,

> I had been warned that he could be a bit irascible at times and kick up his heels if things got a little tight or if they weren't going so well . . . He was doing a scene, about the third or fourth day we were shooting, and he mumbled a line, which is a stock-in-trade, really. He'd throw away a line or put an emphasis somewhere. He'll play with it and tinker with it and put it here and put it there and finally get it the way he wants it, and that's one of the reasons he's so wonderful and so natural.

And I cut the scene and said, "Spence, I know what you're

doing with that line," but I said, "We just didn't understand it at all. It didn't come through at all." So there was a long pause, and when I tell you a long pause I mean a pause—you could have driven a train right through this pause—and he looked at me and he kind of clenched his teeth. He was overdoing it purposely a little bit. He looked at me and said, "Mr. Kramer"—just about in that tempo, but he never calls me Mr. Kramer. He said, "You know, it has taken me just about thirty years to learn how to read a line in that fashion. Now you want something out of *Have Gun, Will Travel* evidently. If that's what we're dealing with, just say so."

There wasn't any answer because I never did think of the snapper. He did it 14 different ways, and he was just setting the stage properly. Anyway, for some reason after that, and I choose to believe that it was because the material was right and we had a rapport and he felt I was doing my job and God knows he was doing his, he went along just fine. The cooperation and the driving intensity to do the job was beyond anything I'd ever experienced.

"Everyone on the set was sort of petrified when Tracy came about," remembered actor Jimmy Boyd, who at age twenty was chosen to play Howard, one of Cates' biology students. "Once he was on the set, everyone shut up." Reared in the South, Boyd himself wasn't familiar with Tracy or his work. He was a semiregular on *Bachelor Father,* a Revue TV series shooting two stages over, and always seemed to be in transit between the two jobs. "He just smiled," Boyd said of Tracy. "He heard that I was quite a swinger around town. Spencer would motion me over to sit with him. Then he'd ask, 'What blonde were you with last night?' It wasn't that he was so serious, he just thought it was kind of funny."

The give-and-take between Tracy and March seemed to energize them both, and the long scenes they played were done without cuts. "I had about 250 extras as spectators on the set," Kramer said, "and because of the camera movement I wasn't able to do what we usually do, which is snip part of them every day so that when you do a closeup or whatever, but we were moving in circles and I needed them there. As a result, for some 35 days these 250 people sat there and watched these fellows go at each other, and they started to applaud at the end of each scene alternately. Both of them came alive under the influence of the applause."

March's character was, by definition, the more theatrical of the two, a man used to filling whole arenas in the days before amplification. ("I seen him once," Meeker, the bailiff, tells Cates. "At a Chautauqua meeting in Chattanooga. The tent poles shook!") The courtroom makes a puny theater for a figure of such size, playing to the crowd as he does with grand gestures and thundering oratory. Drummond, the old warrior, lies back, permitting the bombastic Brady to do the heavy lifting of the buffoon. It made for a bantering relationship between the two actors, each of whom had obvious affection for the other.

"Better stand up," Tracy advised columnist Joe Hyams as March approached. "Here comes the Doctor Doctor. Freddie has two doctorates. He just got his second from his alma mater, Elmira."

"Tracy's got a doctorate, too," March shot back, taking a seat for himself. "Got his right after *Captains Courageous*. They wanted to take it away from him after he did *Jekyll and Hyde*."

Hyams observed Tracy taking Gene Kelly aside to warn him that March had been cracking walnuts during what was supposed to have been Kelly's close-up. March, in turn, urged Tracy to tell Hyams when he was going to retire. "When you've seen this picture all put together," Tracy retorted, "you will have seen me in my prime. I cracked Brazil nuts all through your scenes."

There was, to be sure, a considerable amount of fly-catching, March with his food, his sweating, his belches and grimaces. "He wouldn't put down the fucking fan," Tracy later said of his colleague's performance. Yet he allowed, "It was a lot of fun. I love Freddie. We got along beautifully, wonderfully."

Donna Anderson, who was studying with a coach, tried talking to Tracy about acting but could never get much out of him. "He was very nice to me," she said. "I would ask him about acting, and he would say, 'There's nothing I can teach you. You either are an actor, or you're not. And you are.' Then he'd change the subject with a wave of the hand."

Gene Kelly, who hadn't played many straight parts, was plainly uncomfortable in the role of Hornbeck but had taken the job with the hope that he might learn something from working on a picture with two old masters like March and Tracy.

"I could understand and see what Fred was doing," he later said.

He was like Olivier. A wonderful technician. You could *see* the characterization taking shape—the cogs and wheels beginning to turn. If you studied his methods closely, it was all there, like an open book. But with Spence it was just the reverse. He'd play a scene with you, and you'd think nothing much was happening. Then, when you saw the rushes, there it all was—pouring out of his face. He was quite amazing. The embodiment of the art that conceals art. It was impossible to learn anything from Spence, because everything he did came deep down from some inner part of himself which, to an outsider anxious to learn, was totally inaccessible. All you could do was watch the magic and be amazed.

The script afforded Tracy many passages of eloquence, but the film's most memorable moments come when Drummond calls Brady to the stand as an authority on the Bible. Their scalding exchange is rooted in fact, as Darrow had done the same thing with Bryan in 1925. Kramer shot these exchanges in four- and five-minute takes, completing the entire sequence in the space of a few days.

"We had quite a system worked out whereby we started at nine, worked until twelve, had a two-hour lunch, and we quit at five. Both of these fellows would eat lunch and lie down for a while, and if we were due back at two, at a quarter of two they were both saying, 'Well, are you ready? We're here. We're here.' And, boy, they'd be ready to go, and we'd quit at five, and, you know, that in six hours as against an eight-hour day we really did a tremendous amount. It was a 180-page script which we did in 41 days, and that's pretty fast shooting."

Donna Anderson could recall how amazed people were that Kramer was shooting the picture "like it was on stage. I didn't go in that often [when I wasn't needed], but I went to that one long shot. It was an incredible thing to see those two guys work."

> BRADY
> Your Honor, I am willing to sit here and
> endure Mr. Drummond's sneering and his
> disrespect. For he is pleading the case of the
> prosecution by his contempt for all that
> is holy.

> DRUMMOND
> I object, I object, I object.

> BRADY
> On what grounds? Is it possible that
> something is holy to the celebrated agnostic?

> DRUMMOND
> Yes! The individual human mind. In a
> child's power to master the multiplication
> table there is more sanctity than in all your
> shouted "Amens!" "Holy, Holies!" and

"Hosannas!" An idea is a greater monument
than a cathedral. And the advance of man's
knowledge is a greater miracle than all the
sticks turned to snakes or the parting of
waters! But now are we to forgo all this
progress because Mr. Brady now frightens us
with a fable?

"They'd go through these long, long scenes together," said Jimmy Boyd. "Sometimes the camera rolled for five minutes, and Spencer wouldn't forget a word." Elliott Reid, who had a box seat for the Brady-Drummond confrontation, marveled at the experience: "Tracy was so *good*. And to sit there, *that close* to the performance . . . I thought he was wonderful, just wonderful. And I watched it live all those weeks. I had chills once in a while watching him because, well, first of all, the material had so much to do with what we believed, and what seemed to be the intelligent view of this world. And because he had such power, Tracy. Just in the way he moved toward the witness. There was power without being overstated, without being hammed up. He was so real, he was so true . . . He was as perfectly cast in that part as anybody I can imagine."

The speed at which they worked became a matter of some pride to Tracy, who wasn't shy about pointing it out. "Tracy was very funny," Kramer said.

We were doing these seven- and eight-page scenes at a clip. When the production manager would come on the set, Tracy, for some reason, would quiet everybody down. He'd ask for complete quiet and then he'd turn to the production manager, who was Clem Beauchamp, and say, "Well? Say something! Say something!" And Beauchamp would say, "What do you mean, Spence? What are you getting at?" He'd say, "What am I getting at? Over on the next stage they're shooting television shows. You know how many pages they did yesterday? Seven pages. You know how many we did yesterday? Eight-and-a-half! Now put that in your pipe. What are we? Fifteen pages ahead?" And Beauchamp would say, "We're right on schedule. That's all." "Right on schedule? How can we be on schedule? We did eight-and-a-half pages yesterday. I haven't done eight-and-a-half pages since 1935!"

Tracy completed *Inherit the Wind* on Friday, December 18, and spent Christmas with the family—Carroll and Dorothy, Louise, the kids. He and Larry Keethe caught a red-eye to New York the following week, Tracy enclosing himself in a suite at the Waldorf Towers and briefly tumbling off the wagon. There was talk in the columns of him and Clark Gable reteaming for the film version of Irwin Shaw's *Two Weeks in Another Town,* but the only firm commitment on his calendar was *The Devil at 4 O'Clock.* His blood pressure was high—over 200—and a tooth that had been giving him trouble was found to be cracked. He rested a few days, went out for a long walk finally on January 7. "Flowers for Kathy," he noted in his datebook.

Lauren Bacall was starring at the Lyceum Theatre in *Goodbye, Charlie,* and Tracy and Hepburn made one of their infrequent forays into the Broadway theater district to see her. "At one performance I knew someone special was out front," she remembered, "but I didn't know who—from the rumbling backstage, it must be someone important. I was afraid to think it might be Spence and Kate—they would never come together, and he'd never come at all, I didn't expect that. But when the curtain came down, into my dressing room walked Katie—adorable, warm, loving—full of compliments. And then the door opened again and in he walked. I threw my arms around him—he'd actually come to the theater and sat out front through the whole play. It moved me beyond words."

Most of Tracy's meals were taken at Hepburn's home on Forty-ninth Street. Dinner sometimes included the Kanins, Bobby Helpmann, Larry Olivier on a couple of occasions. About this time, actor Larry Kert was renting the top floor apartment in Stephen Sondheim's house just to the east. One afternoon, he later told a friend, he was looking out the window, over the back garden, when he saw Kate doing the same thing from her window next door. "And then," he recounted, "I saw a pair of hands on her shoulders. The next thing I knew, Spencer Tracy was behind her, gazing out over Katharine Hepburn. It was like a dream, I thought I was in a movie."

A writers' strike was looming on the coast, threatening to disrupt Columbia's plans to put *The Devil at 4 O'Clock* into production. Tracy stayed east, noting "heart flutters" that gave him cold sweats and kept him to his bed. Three cardiograms showed nothing—all normal—and he was told the flutters "mean nothing." Louise was traveling on the East Coast—Washington, Pensacola—and they talked almost daily. Abe Lastfogel called to say that Frank Capra was interested in directing *Big Deal* with Tracy and Sophia Loren and asked if he could be home by Monday. The next day Tracy left by rail, stopping at the Blackstone in Chicago and arriving back in L.A. on February 8, 1960.

The picture foremost in Tracy's mind that spring wasn't the movie for Fred Kohlmar, nor even his proposed pairing with Sophia Loren, but rather a project that had been gathering momentum for three years. It originally came to him by way of Philip Langner, the son of Theatre Guild founder Lawrence Langner and his wife, Armina Marshall. Langner had been scouting properties when over the transom came a teleplay destined for the noted CBS anthology series, *Studio One*. Titled "A Child Is Waiting," it tackled the difficult subject of institutionalized care for the mentally retarded. Langner saw in it a possible adaptation for the stage and bought the theatrical rights from the show's twenty-eight-year-old dramatist, Abby Mann. Within months, Mann had another, even more ambitious play for television, and Langner "immediately got more interested in that."

Mann's new play told the story of Dan Haywood, a humble jurist from "the backwoods of Maine" recruited to help preside over the military tribunals of the political and industrial leadership of Nazi Germany—the judges, lawyers, financiers, and businessmen who enabled the Third Reich to function. "It struck me as fantastic," Mann said, "that perhaps the most significant trial in all history had never been treated artistically and little journalistically. Casual research unearthed an even more startling fact. Of the ninety-nine men sentenced to prison terms in the second of the Nuremberg trials, not one was still serving his sentence."

Though Abby Mann had written "Judgment at Nuremberg" for television, from the outset he envisioned only one actor in the role of Judge Haywood—Spencer Tracy. Langner, through his parents, knew Katharine Hepburn and knew they could get the play to Tracy through her. "Kate," Langner recalled, "was out at the Shakespeare festival in Stratford, which my father had started. She and Alfred Drake were starring out there, so Abby and I drove out to Stratford, where they had a guest house on the festival grounds where they put up the stars. We knocked on the front door, and Kate came to the door. There we were with our script. I said, 'Oh, Kate, you look so wonderful. You've got a terrific sunburn . . .' She said, 'That's not a sunburn! Those are *spots!*' You can imagine my mortification; I turned a deep crimson."

Hepburn did indeed get the script to Tracy, who liked what he saw so much that he said he would do it if they could line up a director and some financing. Mann spent nearly two years refining the play, writing in the interim for *Matinee Theatre, The United States Steel Hour, Studio One,* and, ultimately, *Playhouse 90,* which dramatized his story "Portrait of a Murderer" in 1958. Tracy subsequently put Stanley Kramer onto "Judgment at Nuremberg," though Kramer was still in Australia shooting *On the Beach* when *Playhouse 90* produced the play in April 1959, Claude Rains taking the role of Judge Haywood. "It is his tremendous responsibility," Kramer later said of the character, "to decide whether [the four judges on trial in the story] merely carried out the law, as written by the Nazis, or were guilty of crimes against humanity."

Kramer's deal for the rights to the teleplay—$150,000 plus another $50,000 for Mann's work as screenwriter—was finalized in January 1960. Tracy okayed the deal to star in the picture on February 16 for the same money as for *Inherit the Wind*—$250,000 against a percentage of the gross. With *Nuremberg* in the offing, he was relieved when Columbia pulled the plug on *Devil at 4 O'Clock,* citing a pending SAG strike for which Tracy had already signaled his support. It was just as well; *Devil* was to have been Tracy's fourth film in a Roman collar, a whiskey priest tending the children afflicted with leprosy on a small volcanic island. With the cancellation, the film lost Peter Glenville, Bridget Boland, whose work on the script hadn't yet been completed, and costar Sidney Poitier. There was still a chance *Big Deal* would come to fruition, but an attempt by Capra to set the picture up at United Artists collapsed over money, as neither Tracy nor Loren were considered bankable.

In May Kate left for Stratford for another season with the Shakespeare festival, and Tracy followed her east in the company of Abe Lastfogel. Alone in New York, he immediately started drinking again, a bout with the bottle that lasted three days. Following a day of recuperation, he checked into the Waldorf and was well enough to go to Mass at St. Patrick's Cathedral. Kramer called, confirming that Laurence Olivier had been set for the role of Ernst Janning, the principal defendant in *Judgment at Nuremberg.* Delighted with the news, Tracy effectively blew off a dinner with Lastfogel and Gar Kanin, who was desperately trying to keep *Big Deal* in play. An agreement with Universal-International was brewing, but again the money was insufficient, and Tracy, in effect, told them both to forget it. He drove out to see Kate at Stratford, putting up at a nearby motel.

In Stratford, Hepburn was asked by *Newsweek* if there could be such a thing as an American—as distinct from a British—style of playing Shakespeare. "I don't know," she mused. "You'd have to take our greatest actor—who is he? Spencer Tracy, I imagine, and contrast him with their greatest—Larry [Olivier] or Gielgud. There's something about the great American actor that's like a clipper ship in action, a sort of heart's directness. Spencer has it. He could do Shylock, or Lear, or Macbeth. We could do Macbeth together." The thought, of course, horrified Tracy, who had little interest in Shakespeare and refused to stretch himself with the verse roles Kate was so doggedly tackling. "It was the thing she didn't admire about Spencer," Bill Self said, "and she told me this more than once: 'You know, he has never reached his potential as an actor.' She's off doing Shakespeare, Spence is sitting by the pool. She often would say, 'Spence has never reached his potential, but it's his fault.' Maybe he knew his limitations better than she did."

Dutifully, Tracy returned for Kate's opening in *Twelfth Night* on June 4, 1960, then he left her to the festival for the remainder of the summer, content to spend his time dieting and loafing back in California. There was talk of reviving *Devil at 4 O'Clock* with yet another script and Frank Sinatra joining the cast, but there was still no director and no firm commitment on Tracy's part. Yet Fred Kohlmar, who harbored fond memories of *Boys Town*, seemed obsessed with the idea of Tracy in the role of the bad-tempered Father Doonan and pursued him with a fervor that was, to some, baffling. By the end of June, Mervyn LeRoy had signed on as director, but Sinatra still hadn't formally committed. He was, however, anxious to make a picture with Tracy and was offered $600,000 to take the role of a convict temporarily consigned to a labor crew at Father Doonan's South Seas hospital. Once he did commit, Sinatra did everything possible to accord Tracy the respect he was due, ceding first billing when, in reality, he was by far the bigger draw.

"When we did that film," Sinatra remembered,

Mervyn LeRoy said to me, "We have a little problem with your desires and Spencer's desires." And I said, "Well, like what?" He said, "Well, you know, he likes to come in very early in the morning and he doesn't want to work beyond four o'clock in the afternoon, and you want to come in later and work till six or seven o'clock." . . . I said, "Well, what are we going to do about the problem?" He said, "I don't know, but . . . you're friends and he doesn't want to talk to you about it. He doesn't want to, you know, upset the apple cart, so to speak." And I said, "Well, I'll talk to him about it." So I did. I went up to his house and we sat and had a cup of tea, and we talked about it. And I said, "Now we have a problem here." "Oh," he said, "naw, it's no problem, Kid." He said, "It's going to be all right." I said, "You know why?" I said, "Because what time do you want to start? Three o'clock in the morning? Four in the morning? I'll be there." He said, "No, no." He said, "Now that's going too far." He said, "Well, you know, I just don't want to work late in the afternoon." And I said, "Well, you're not going to be able to in this picture because of the lighting problem. In the mountainous areas where we'll be shooting in Maui, we lose all the light at two o'clock, three o'clock in the afternoon." He said, "No kidding?" I said, "That's true. You're not going to work beyond three o'clock." He said, "Well, we can start anytime you want." I said, "We won't get any work done. We'll have to start early." So we did start shooting at seven or seven-thirty in the morning. So we got a full day's work in.

An advance crew was working over the tiny town of Lahaina, the ancient capital of Hawaii, when Tracy received word from his brother Carroll that Emma Brown, their venerable aunt Mum, had died in Freeport at the age of ninety. Famously parsimonious, Emma Brown had sent cash gifts to her nephews every Christmas—as if Spence needed the money. "She could send them a certain amount each year to help keep her taxes down," Bertha Calhoun recalled. "They sent her fur coats and televisions, all kind of things she wouldn't buy for herself . . . Any big thing in the house that you would consider a convenience—she wouldn't buy that, so that's what they'd give her for Christmas." Spence said he wouldn't come back for the funeral, that it would be a mob scene if he did. "When they buried Emma there were people there at the funeral hiding behind the tombstones because they thought Carroll was Spencer. It was terrible."

Upon Carroll's return to Los Angeles, Tracy withdrew from *The Devil at 4 O'Clock,* citing a conflict with the scheduled start of *Judgment at Nuremberg.* In a statement, Columbia's Sam Briskin said the studio considered the Hawaiian location work "too hazardous" to assure the completion of Tracy's scenes by December 16, the absolute drop-dead date for Tracy's release to Stanley Kramer. In the meantime, Kramer was flogging the release of *Inherit the Wind,* which had its world premiere as a two-a-day attraction at London's Astoria Theatre on July 7, 1960.

The early notices were superb, the trades rhapsodizing over every element of the picture—Kramer's direction, Ernest Laszlo's evocative black-and-white photography, Ernest Gold's exquisitely restrained musical score, the stark vocals of Leslie Uggams. "Tracy has the lines, the ringing phrases and sentences, purposely homely at times, the insistence of mind over matter, the shafts of irony by which Bryan and the proponents of ignorance were routed," James Powers wrote in the *Hollywood Reporter.* "He delivers them, and a deep humanity, by enormous conviction and force of intelligence." *Variety* called Kramer's pairing of Tracy and March "a stroke of casting genius. They go at each other on the thespic plane as one might imagine Dempsey and Louis would have had time and circumstance brought them to the same ring. Both men are spellbinders in the most laudatory sense of the word. If they aren't two contenders in the next Academy sweepstakes, then Oscar should be put in escrow for another year."

Curiously, the British public didn't flock to the theater to see the heralded clash of the titans, and Kramer would later talk of forlornly standing in front of the Leicester Square cinema "with reviews I could have written myself" and watching as "no one came." The American premiere was set for July 21 in Dayton, Tennessee—the site of the original courtroom battle—with several members of the original jury commemorating the thirty-fifth anniversary of the trial. Kramer's New York press representative, Meyer Beck, got in touch with John T. Scopes, the Louisiana geologist who, in 1925, was the man on trial for the teaching of evolution, and persuaded him to help promote the film, following a "carefully scheduled itinerary" that culminated in Scopes' return to the town H. L. Mencken once famously dubbed "the buckle on the Bible belt."

The mayor, who proclaimed a Scopes Trial Day, called the resulting crowd the second-largest in Dayton's history. Scopes noted little change in the place—the Butler Act was still on the books and teachers were still required to sign a pledge that they wouldn't teach evolution—and he said that he was certain the verdict would be the same were the trial to be repeated. "I enjoyed the movie," Scopes later wrote in a memoir. "Of course, it altered the facts of the real trial. I was never jailed and I hadn't met my future wife until years later in Venezuela. I didn't mind such small liberties. They had to invent a romance for the balcony set. Also, Matthew Harrison Brady, the Bryanlike character, died nearer the close of the trial than Bryan had. What was important, though, the film captured the emotions in the battle of words between Bryan and Darrow . . ."

The $2.2 million movie generated little heat in its initial openings, despite some of the strongest reviews of Tracy's career. A boycott active within 17,000 American Legion posts was likely a factor, as actor-screenwriter Nedrick Young had pleaded the Fifth when asked to testify before the House Committee on Un-American Activities in 1953. (Under the pseudonym of Nathan E. Douglas, Young had collected an Academy Award for his work on *The Defiant Ones*.) Kramer fired back at National Commander Martin B. McKneally, characterizing the Legion's announced stand against "a renewed invasion of American filmdom by Soviet-indoctrinated artists" as "reprehensible" and "as totally un-American as anything I can imagine." His principled stand did nothing to win him—or *Inherit the Wind*—many friends in the heartland, where UA's flawed release strategy had, unfortunately, placed the picture ahead of its New York and Los Angeles openings.

As originally scheduled, *The Devil at 4 O'Clock* would have prevented Tracy from actively promoting the picture, which, surprisingly, he told Kramer he would do. Then Sinatra, alarmed at Tracy's withdrawal, went to work on him, as Tracy was, in effect, the only reason Sinatra was doing the picture. Kramer pushed off the start date of *Nuremberg*, hoping to free up Tracy for a round of promotional appearances, and Tracy left for Hawaii two days later.

Kate, who thought Liam O'Brien's screenplay a bore and wasn't overly fond of Sinatra, went under protest, having finished at Stratford only a week earlier. Actor Kerwin Matthews, cast as a young priest sent to the island to take over for Father Doonan, could vividly remember the malevolent glint in her eye: "The first day on location on Maui—standing exactly where the first pilgrims landed on a Hawaiian island—I met the Hepburn thing. I had a present for her—a book to read, *Hawaii,* which would explain so much about the islands. I gave it to her. She walked out on a pier and threw the book in the ocean, saying, 'Who wants to know anything about this awful place?' Because she was always next to Spence, no one had a chance to talk to him. No one got a chance to know him, even though I tried constantly." Hepburn, said Mervyn LeRoy, kept a wary eye on Tracy at all times. "She never interfered with us in any way, and never tried to offer any suggestions. She just watched Spence."

Actor Gregoire Aslan, who had worked with such heavyweights as Alec Guinness, Orson Welles, and John Huston in a career spanning two decades, was nonplussed at the prospect of making a picture with Tracy. He recalled that he was visiting his sister and her family in London when he caught *Inherit the Wind* at the Astoria. "Well," he said, "I thought it was near perfect. And I came back shaking and saying to my brother-in-law, 'I have just witnessed the greatest performance, and I wonder if I'm not going to act with the greatest actor in the world?' I was terribly moved. I try to be the character myself when I'm playing something, and when I play with him I have not an answer but I get the answer from the Catholic priest he's playing. So it's not a surprise it's just so easy." Kerwin Matthews concurred: "Our working together was magic—he was always patting me on the shoulder at the end of each take. We could have been good friends; [he could have been a] 'father figure' to me, as was Lee J. Cobb."

A highlight of the four-week trip was the celebration of Mervyn LeRoy's sixtieth birthday on October 15. More than seventy people attended the party, which was organized by LeRoy's wife Kitty and held at Kula Lodge, 3,200 feet up the slopes of Maui's Haleakala volcano. Smoked black wattle steaks were served, and Sinatra sang the lyrics to four songs written expressly for the occasion by Sammy Cahn.

"When it came Tracy's turn to give his talk," publicist Bob Yager remembered,

> he got up there and he said that he wanted to welcome Mervyn LeRoy into the Sixty Club. LeRoy was sixty years old, and Spencer is sixty years old, and he said he has welcomed James Cagney, he has welcomed Pat O'Brien into the club, and that soon he would be welcoming his very dear friend Clark Gable into the

club . . . And then he looked toward Sinatra and he got that Irish pixie look and I knew immediately something was going to come out. He said, "And Frank, I would like to welcome you to the Sixty Club, but, unfortunately, I can't. It is not enough to LOOK sixty, you have to BE sixty to get into this club." Well, it wrapped up the whole evening. There was a tremendous roar, and Frank laughed the loudest . . .

Sinatra got itchy as filming progressed; occasionally he would refuse to do a close-up or make an additional take, and on one such occasion, apologized to the cast and crew by cooking a spaghetti dinner.

"The problem," said Jean-Pierre Aumont, "was that Sinatra would only work in the afternoon. In the morning he hired a private plane and hopped from island to island trying to convince the startled inhabitants to vote for Kennedy in the next presidential election. Around two o'clock he returned, exhausted, at the precise moment when Tracy was retiring for the day to his rooms. How, in these conditions, the scenes between Tracy and Sinatra were shot is a mystery to me."

Sinatra's shifting moods were well known within the industry. According to his longtime valet-aide George Jacobs, the singer developed a serious fixation on Kate when he saw her in the see-through tank suit she wore during her sunrise swims in the ocean. One night toward the end of the shoot, Jacobs was called upon to cook dinner for Tracy and Hepburn as Sinatra's guests for the evening. "It could be that Mr. S was feeling particularly horny and frustrated, because he was extra edgy that night. When I served the spaghetti marinara, which I had made a million times for him, he tasted it, started raving that it wasn't *al dente,* and picked up the bowl and threw the pasta all over me and my white jacket. This was the only time he had ever abused me, but once was enough. Tracy and Hepburn were so appalled that they left immediately, while Sinatra cleared the table by smashing all the dishes."

When the company returned to Los Angeles, another eight weeks of shooting remained—far more than anyone, particularly Sinatra, had anticipated. Tracy's promotional plans for *Inherit the Wind* got scuttled, and the film had to make its New York and L.A. debuts with just Kramer and the UA promotions team in support.

In Manhattan, it opened to solid business at the Astor and the Trans-Lux on Eighty-fifth Street, but neither venue was at capacity, despite another round of exceptional notices. (Bosley Crowther called it "one of the most brilliant and engrossing displays of acting ever witnessed on the screen.") Said Kramer, "[I]n many of the first run houses, in order to get the terms we wanted, which I think was, let's say, above average, I had to run sneak previews in order to show theater managers how an audience would react to these fellows going at it, and the audience reaction was so marvelous, in a matter of seconds so much better than any other picture I've ever been associated with. I mean by an audience reaction that upon eight or ten occasions breaking into a wild applause during the film."

Yet the film failed everywhere—a bitter disappointment. "It was a double disappointment because United Artists had said, 'Look, we don't want you to make this film. You're making it with two old men—Tracy and March—nobody wants to see them. You'll never get a woman in the theater. You'll never get any feminine audience whatever.'" By the time the picture had its Hollywood opening at Grauman's Chinese, the industry had written it off as a flop.

The cornerstone of Tracy's anticipated campaign on Kramer's behalf was an interview with a feature writer for *Look* named Bill Davidson. Tracy didn't know Davidson, hadn't seen his work, and only agreed to sit for him at Kramer's request. According to Joe Hyams, Davidson was "a good reporter," but when *Inherit the Wind* failed to generate any heat at the box office, it looked as if the magazine would kill the story, holding Davidson's material in abeyance until another picture came along.

Others made their way to the supposedly closed set of *Devil at 4 O'Clock*—Jack Bradford of the *Hollywood Reporter,* Murray Schumach of the *New York Times,* Neil Rau of the *Los Angeles Examiner,* Lee Belser of the *Mirror.* To Schumach, Tracy denied the occasional rumor that he intended to direct: "I have thought about directing. I don't know enough about directing. I could never stand some of the things I have seen directors put up with from actors. I would kill the actors. Not to mention some of those beautiful actresses." To Rau he explained the volcanic lava on the set was really Hollywood snow—shredded plastic—sprayed gray to look like ash. To Belser he mourned the deaths of Whitey Hendry and Clark Gable.

Gable's death at the age of fifty-nine came as a terrific shock, as King had just finished a picture with Marilyn Monroe and was expecting a child by his fifth wife, the former actress Kay Williams. To UPI's Vernon Scott, Gable had acknowledged that he was transitioning to character parts but said he wasn't so sure he could do it with the success that Tracy had enjoyed. "Tracy is that rare exception," he said. "He completed the transition beautifully. Spencer can play anything he wants except young men. I hope I can do the same thing."

On November 6, 1960, two days after finishing the Monroe picture, Gable suffered a heart attack. He was hospitalized and seemed to be recovering when he was killed by a second thrombosis on the evening of November 16. The funeral three days later was a simple affair, mirroring the rites for Carole Lombard eighteen years earlier. Tracy, who served as a pallbearer, arrived alone, sunglasses shielding his gaze from reporters and fans, his white hair glistening in the morning sun. "I've known a lot of wonderful people in this business," he said. "They're just about all gone now."

With John F. Kennedy's narrow victory on November 8, 1960, Sinatra lost what little interest he retained in *The Devil at 4 O'Clock* and the gulf between him and Tracy widened. "By the end of *Devil at 4 O'Clock*," said Kerwin Matthews, "Tracy was barely tolerating Frank."

With actor Robert Taylor at the funeral of Clark Gable, November 19, 1960. (AUTHOR'S COLLECTION)

"He'll call Frank Sinatra 'The Other Fellow,' " Bob Yager said at the time. "He'll come on the stage and say, 'Where's the Other Fellow? Where's the star of this picture?' He'll be needling Sinatra, and he'll keep saying, 'I know I'm not the star of this picture. Sinatra is the star. After all, my last picture wasn't a success, and they've got Sinatra in this picture to insure its success.' " When not in front of the camera, Sinatra was on the phone arranging entertainment for Kennedy's inaugural ball. Since he was always referred to as "Mr. S" around the set, Tracy began referring to himself in the third person as "Mr. T."

Well over $1 million had been spent on sets—a record for a Columbia picture. The figure included $500,000 for Hawaii alone. ("We built," said Mervyn LeRoy, "a lovely set there—an entire village, complete with a street, a church, and even a jail.") It reportedly cost another $500,000 to create a miniature of the island on a farm outside of Fallbrook. They spent $150,000 to build a hospital on the back lot at Fox, $100,000 to replicate the lush Maui vegetation on Columbia's Stage 8. Given the money riding on the picture—more than $5 million—Tracy plainly regarded Sinatra's behavior as unprofessional.

Stanley Kramer, eager to start *Judgment at Nuremberg*, was monitoring the situation: "I called him one morning and said, 'How're things going?' He says, 'Well!' Just like that, but I can't use the language he used. 'I've been in this business ONLY thirty years. Just thirty years, that's all, and you know what I'm doing? I'm playing scenes with a double. How do you do that? Now tell me, am I a goddamn fool or am I a goddamn fool?' He just told them [the double] reads Sinatra's lines better than Sinatra does. Sinatra had said, 'Hot or cold, I'm leaving on Thursday.' And Spence said, 'I don't know what's going on. I just don't know what's going on.' He's really funny about it; burned up too."

With Sinatra's departure, Tracy was left to finish the picture by himself. When Pete Martin of the *Saturday Evening Post* came calling, he was shooting actor Bernie Hamilton's death scene and unhappy the interview had been scheduled for such a crucial day. "This is the boy's big chance," Tracy said of Hamilton. "I remember these scenes. I used to play them. Now he plays it in my arms, you know, he dies, and if he's good as he is . . . this kid's going to steal this picture. So we want to do it well, you know, as well as we can."

They quickly got onto the subject of Martin's recent appearance on David Suskind's show, a panel discussion that included the aforementioned Bill Davidson. Martin said of Davidson, "He kind of came through in his true colors the other night—a sneering son of a bitch . . . You're in for a surprise, Spencer, I think."

"Going to be a blast, eh?"

"Well, he may be nice to you, but . . ."

"I don't think so . . . He can say I used to get drunk. He could bring up some of these old things—I couldn't care less. I don't think he'll let himself in for libel . . . He seemed such a nice guy and I think, you know, he liked me. Yet remember he said he doesn't like any actor."

Tracy was in and out of the dressing room all morning, Martin getting his questions in between setups. A range of subjects got touched upon, though none very deeply. The talk was liveliest when Tracy spoke of *Judgment at Nuremberg*. "I'll tell you *Nuremberg* is the best script I've ever read," he said.

Inherit the Wind I thought was a great script. I've made two or three pictures in my time that I thought were good: *Captains Courageous, Inherit the Wind.* Why, [if it was] just a job, I couldn't function that way—without thinking, without thought. That I'd come here in the morning like a mechanical toy. Jesus Christ, I don't do that! I don't look at every script. I know sometimes scripts are bad. I don't think this [one] is any great shakes . . . I'm getting more choosy. *The Old Man and the Sea,* even though it was not a great financial success, when you do things like that and *Inherit the Wind, Nuremberg*—you know, it's hard to turn around and put on the sheriff's suit again. But they don't come. Fortunately, I don't have to work. I don't have all the money in the world. If I live too long I'd have to worry. My family would have to worry if I lived too long, but I don't like to figure that way.

He told Martin that Olivier had dropped out of *Judgment at Nurem-berg,* tied up as he was in New York with *Becket.** In replacing him, Kramer had gone to Burt Lancaster, whom Abby Mann thought all wrong for the part, but who was just about the screen's hottest star. "I admire Kramer," Tracy said. "I don't know how the hell he gets the money to put on these shows."

"He says, 'The way I get these people is I don't take the money myself.' "

"That's right," Tracy said. "He's telling the truth, because I had the percentage and I get the figures and you'd be amazed to know what Stanley Kramer takes out of a picture."

With Lancaster's addition to the cast, Tracy's percentage was adjusted to make room for Lancaster's. "Joe Hyams came in here," Tracy told Martin,

and said he talked to Lancaster. Then Stanley called me up to tell me that Dick Widmark was going to do the picture, which pleased me mightily. You know he's paying Lancaster a tremendous amount of money—much more than he's paying me or anybody else. And a big percentage. I said, "I think I should tell you, Stanley, that Lancaster told Joe Hyams he would have done the picture for nothing. I think it's always nice to know these things. He also said that there would have to be a little rewriting done." And I said, "I would like to know if Lancaster is going to rewrite the script or if Abby Mann is going to rewrite it. Because if Lancaster's going to rewrite it, I might have to read it over a little more carefully." That's when he said, "Geez, you've got a needle that long and you're stick-ing it in. Go ahead, turn it around." I said, "Well, I'm just telling you Kid, you could have gotten him for nothing apparently. Also, Burt says he's playing a 'bit.' He's playing the part Larry Olivier was going to play."

"How much does he get?" Martin asked. "A quarter of a million?"

"Well, I'm not going to quote this . . ."

"I'll see him myself. I'll find out."

"How much did you say?"

"A quarter of a million? A picture?"

"Oh, come now."

"You mean a lot more than that?"

---

* Actress Joan Plowright, whom Olivier was soon to marry, was also in New York, appearing at the Lyceum in *A Taste of Honey.*

"Twice that. Twice that. And against ten percent of the gross. The Other Fellow gets twice *that!* Or seven-fifty or something."

"I did Lancaster when he was working for Mark Hellinger and wasn't even doing anything."

"Now he gets half a million," Tracy said. "I shouldn't tell you—don't tell him. I only know that because . . ."

Tracy was called for more of Bernie Hamilton's death scene, a quick reaction shot, a couple of lines called up to where Sinatra should have been standing. "Frank wasn't there. A fellow came down and said to me, 'That's the best scene you've ever played in your entire career.' And I was looking at a stick. So I said, 'Well maybe I should have played the whole thing to a stick.' " When he returned to his dressing room, the shot in the can, Tracy had scarcely been gone ten minutes.

"Well, that didn't take long, Spence," Martin said.

"Well," said Tracy, deadpan, "I'm awful good . . . No, the truth is they shoot it once with me and they figure, well, we can't get any better from the son of a bitch. It's like trying a suit on me. You know it's only so far you can go."

CHAPTER 31

The Value of a Single Human Being

Frank Tracy sat in his Florida apartment and contemplated the spectacle of Dorothy and Louise Tracy. "Dorothy and Louise were two very different kinds of people," he said. "Dorothy and Louise, my God. Nothing wrong with Dorothy morally or whatever, but she was a chatterbox. Never stopped talking. Drive you right out of your mind. My dad used to say, 'For Chrissake, is she coming over here? God, as soon as she hits the door, that's it.' Never had anything to say. Nothing was ever amusing, informative, nothing. Carroll would just sit there and smile."

In particular, Frank recalled a time when Carroll and Dorothy Tracy were visiting Freeport. "I was home for a weekend or something, and I remember sitting in the living room talking about Spence and Louise. My mother or father said, 'Well, they never got divorced. That's a plus.' And Dorothy said, 'Well, of course not. She's not going to give up being Mrs. Spencer Tracy. She's never going to give that up.' They seemed very . . . the word isn't bitter . . . critical maybe. I was very surprised."

Dorothy's perception of Louise and her use of the name was more widespread than Frank could have imagined. Many in Spence's circle felt the same way, though Kate herself never said a word. "Being Mrs. Spencer Tracy publicly was more important than being the wife of Spencer Tracy," George Cukor said of her, but it was simplistic to assume that Louise somehow needed to bask in the glow of her husband's celebrity. "She was certainly a saint," Jane Feely said, "but in the very best sense of being a saint. She was a true servant of God and a true carrier of the cross, but in a very human way, which is what a saint is. She grew and grew and grew, that woman . . . Especially as she grew in stature with the Clinic, she became a person of whom *she* could be very proud, and of whom Spencer was very proud. Whatever she may have felt, whether she knew or she didn't know, she knew who she was. Maybe better than he knew who he was. And I think he envied that. She had found herself in that."

Louise was now sixty-four, as white-haired as her husband and no longer able to manage an enterprise that had grown beyond her wildest dreams in size and complexity. "I am trailing the Clinic by many lengths," she wrote her friend Mary Kennedy Taylor in 1958. "I would be, even if I had plenty of time. It has grown too big and too involved for my simple mind. Thank goodness we have a good administration and staff—over 30 of us now." The original building was expanded in 1956 with a two-story wing and basement, increasing the overall floor space on the new campus to some thirteen thousand square feet. By 1960, families in fifty-six countries were enrolled in the clinic's yearlong correspondence course, the newest translations being in Croatian and Serbian.

"She would say, 'I am so tired,' " Jane remembered. "She was over-whelmed with how big the institution had become. I think she felt inade-quate to it because she hadn't had a formal education. She had had to not only establish and work on this clinic, she had to educate herself in this field and she had become an expert, but it had taken a lot out of her. A lot more than I think anyone, maybe even she, realized."

In 1954 Dr. Edgar L. Lowell was recruited from Harvard to assume the role of administrator, freeing Louise from the day-to-day responsibilities of management. As director in charge, she still oversaw the clinic's core services—consultations, hearing tests, parent classes, the demonstration nursery school, the correspondence course, and the summer sessions—while Dr. Lowell started research and teacher-training programs. From everything he had heard, Edgar Lowell was surprised to find that Spencer Tracy was as interested in the clinic's business as he apparently was.

"I was always very gratified," he said,

that he read my reports. I'm a great one for writing things out. Numerable times Mrs. Tracy would say, "Mr. Tracy would like to know what did you mean by that?" I said, "Well, at least I know someone is reading my report." I remember one time when he was in France making *The Mountain* we had a series of delayed conver-sations because he would call one night and I would get the message the next time I saw her . . . [W]hen we had the first big league ball game in Los Angeles, a benefit for the Tracy Clinic at Wrigley Field, Baltimore and Chicago played the first big league game. Mr. Tracy showed up, but he showed up about the second inning, when everyone was looking straight ahead, and left about the eighth inning so there wasn't a big spotlight on him in their box that would detract from her.

There were the tentative overtures Spence would make to become more involved with the clinic, but Louise held him at a careful distance, the clinic being the one distinct thing in their lives that she could genuinely call her own. "He felt it did absorb my life," she said,

and it did. Once you got into it, it was so big and it was so demanding . . . [T]wo or three times he said, I think sincerely, "Could I learn enough about that clinic that I could go out and talk some about it?" He said that many times. "Could I?" he said. "I would like to do that." "Well," I said, "you have to really work, you have to have learned an awful lot—much more, you know. A lot of work goes into it. You don't know why, you don't understand this and that. You really have to study . . . [T]hey ask you questions and you can't get up before people and not really know." "No," he said, "I suppose not, but you know, I'd like to do that." [He] could never get down to all the little things about the details.

In the end, Tracy's participation was limited to the funding he could so readily provide. "They used to call him and tell him how much it was," Dr. Lowell said, "and he would write the check for that amount."

In December 1960 writer-director George Seaton and a group of supporters gave a recognition dinner in Louise's honor at the Beverly Hilton Hotel. Y. Frank Freeman, the retired president and chairman of Paramount Pictures, served as chair of the sponsoring committee, which was comprised of a number of civic and business leaders, Mr. and Mrs. Justin Dart, Dr. and Mrs. Norman Topping, Leonard Firestone, Jimmy and Gloria Stewart, and Walt Disney among them. Close to one thousand guests jammed the hotel's International Ballroom to hear keynote speaker Billy Graham, and thousands more watched the event, hosted by Robert Young, on TV. Dr. Graham gave a generic forty-minute talk on the challenges of communication, gearing his remarks to a largely Republican crowd still smarting from the narrow defeat of Richard Nixon at the polls.

When it came time for Louise to speak, her wavy hair dyed a silvery blond, she talked of the original twelve mothers at the clinic, how they made curtains and re-covered furniture while their husbands plastered the walls. "The first person I would like to mention," she said, "is my husband. Without his interest, without his support, moral as well as financial, there would never have been a clinic." Tracy, of course, was nowhere to be seen on the dais. "I assumed that he would be up on the front table," said Dr. Lowell. "He had a table in the very back." Louise gave an impassioned talk, her voice quivering at times, and was accorded a five-minute standing ovation at its conclusion. "I have never been so moved by anything in my life," she said. Over the course of the evening she kept an eye out for Spence, who was pacing, ducking in and out of the ballroom. "Sometimes he would go to the back and you could see him in a little cubby hole there. He was embarrassed. He always said, 'It's your show.' "

As the clinic's namesake, John Tracy was present that night, beaming out over the room even as he faced yet another challenge in a life overwhelmed by them. Having been fitted with thick glasses at the age of seven, he was diagnosed in 1940 with retinitis pigmentosa, a narrowing of the field of vision that can end in complete blindness. Apart from early problems with night vision, John functioned fairly well, driving his own car and attending classes, first at Pasadena, later at UCLA and Chouinard Art Institute. In 1952 he was hired briefly as an assistant art director when Bill Self began producing *The Schlitz Playhouse of Stars*. "I had an art director, Serge Krizman, and he needed some help. I said, 'I'd like you to try John, because he's a good artist.' After a couple of weeks, Serge came to me and said, 'Bill, he's not a help, he's a hindrance. He's a good enough artist, but I can't communicate with him. It's very embarrassing.' So I had to let John go. It was very hard to help John."

In 1957 Walt Disney found John a job at the studio, where he was eventually put in charge of the cell library. "He did a lot of things," said Ruthie Thompson. "He started out in the art props. He was such a nice guy. He said, 'God put me on this earth for a purpose. I just hope I've fulfilled it.' " John left Disney when his eyesight got so bad that he could no longer drive. At the age of thirty-six he began to learn sign language. "He decided that after his eye trouble began to become pronounced," said his mother. "He said, 'I think maybe I would like to take some lessons.' In the early days we were never exposed to it."

The Devil at 4 O'Clock finished on December 29, 1960—two weeks over the guaranty period specified in Tracy's contract. The William Morris office contended he was owed another $50,000 by Columbia Pictures, but the studio disputed the charge, pointing out that he had been sick five days on the picture. Production never stopped, however, and Tracy had worked to get rid of Sinatra, who finished two weeks ahead of schedule. After a call from Abe Lastfogel, Columbia coughed up $25,000, agreed to another $15,000, but disputed the final $10,000. "Par for the course!" said Tracy.

Stanley Kramer, meanwhile, was readying *Judgment at Nuremberg* for the cameras, affording Tracy a minimal six-week break between pictures. "There was so much distribution objection at United Artists to this down-beat, uncommercial subject," Kramer said, "that the only way to get it made was with an all-star cast." An old hand at candy-coating difficult material, Kramer loaded the first film he ever directed, *Not as a Stranger,* with six major names. For *Judgment* he loyally insisted on Tracy's casting as Dan Haywood, even as United Artists pressured him to use Jimmy Stewart instead. "Tracy's no lodestone," one of the UA executives declared. "I remember listening to the conversation," said Abby Mann, "and Kramer was upset. He said, 'What do you mean he's no lodestone?' He just wouldn't desert a friend."

Kramer soothed the management at UA with the casting of Burt Lancaster, who, with the release of *Elmer Gantry,* was in line for an Oscar nomination. Artistically, he justified the move with the reasoning that Lancaster was not the "obvious choice" for the part. "His character was guilty and he was aware of it—that gave him a hook and I think he grabbed it." The Austrian actor Maximilian Schell was retained from the TV production, and Kramer filled out the cast with Richard Widmark, Montgomery Clift, Judy Garland, and Marlene Dietrich.

Dietrich's character provided a compelling counterpoint to the Germans on trial. "We thought there should be a woman, or a romance," said Abby Mann,

> and, at the time, Stanley said to me, "I'd like to use Paul Newman and his wife [Joanne Woodward] in the film." He said, "Supposing [Haywood] has a daughter, and the daughter has an affair with Newman?" I tried it, but it didn't seem to work. Then [in Berlin] I met a woman who was the widow of a general. She was talking to me about herself, and she was saying, "My husband was a soldier. I didn't want him to be hanged, but to be shot. I wanted a soldier's death for my husband, and I hated the Americans for not permitting it." She said, "I'm writing a book about it," but I could sense that she would never finish the book because she didn't want to tell how much Germans were really involved with what happened. So I came back, and I met with Stanley in a Chinese restaurant. He said, "How's the Newman part coming?" "Well," I said, "you know . . ."

And I told him about this woman. I said, "I wonder whether Dietrich might do this?" He said, "That's a good idea!" That was the major difference between the TV version and the film. And I must say Marlene was wonderful.

Clift agreed to do the film for expenses, as Kramer needed the name value but couldn't afford the actor's usual salary. "Since it's only a single scene and can be filmed in one day," Clift told the *New York Times,* "I strongly disapproved of taking an astronomical salary. But in the business I felt it was more practical to do it for nothing rather than reduce my price or refuse a role I wanted to play."

Garland was the last major figure added to the cast, having not appeared in a movie since *A Star Is Born* in 1955. Her part, like Clift's, was that of a prosecution witness, but she could ill afford to play the role for free. Her deal was for a flat $35,000; Kramer made the surprising announcement in New York, garnering considerable publicity for the picture.

"We call these 'pace-setting performances,' " Kramer said. "Their function is not unlike those of the runner who sets the pace in a key race for the man who is out to set a record. These are speaking roles that last up to seven minutes on the screen. They have an explosive quality—that is, a beginning, a middle, and an end—and are pertinent to the main theme. Unlike cameos, they don't simply drop an actor in front of some scenery for the value of his name on the marquee; they utilize his talents in more than one scene and in a developing type of characterization."

Kramer followed up with a full-page ad in the *Times,* committing to a December 14 premiere at Kongresshalle in Berlin, the scene of the first public screening of *Inherit the Wind.* Immediately following the premiere, *Judgment at Nuremberg* would open in the major European capitals and in reserved seat engagements in six U.S. cities, including New York, Chicago, and Los Angeles. The failure of *The Diary of Anne Frank* as a roadshow attraction didn't faze him, and he pointed instead to the record advance that had greeted the benefit openings of Otto Preminger's *Exodus.* "It's our intent to go hard ticket, but I wouldn't want to book 45 theaters now." The setting of a target date (*der Tag*) would serve as a "tremendous psychological drive" for everyone connected with the picture.

The first reading for the cast was held on February 15, 1961, four long tables forming a square on Revue's Stage 28, where the film's dark-paneled courtroom interior had been erected. Originally, Kramer had wanted to shoot the film in the actual courtroom in which the trials had taken place. "We couldn't," he said, "because it's still in use today. So we took measurements and carefully re-created it on the soundstage in Hollywood, although we finally had to scale down some of the dimensions for the involved camera movements. A courtroom . . . is a very static set. The attorneys had to be separate and distinct from the defendants and witnesses, by law. So the film becomes a ping-pong game unless you try to move the camera, which I tried—not always successfully—to do."

The read-through was scheduled for 9:00 a.m. but was late in starting because Maximilian Schell had yet to arrive. One of several holdovers from the original *Playhouse 90* production, Schell had prepared for the movie version by reading the entire forty-volume record of the Nuremberg trials.

"Eventually," said Marshall Schlom, Kramer's new script supervisor,

Max Schell arrived—he had gone to Western Costume for a fitting or something. When he came in, he didn't have a script. He said, "I left it in my car." I had a bunch of scripts, so I helped everybody out. Lancaster came in and sat down and put his glasses on and set his script in front of him. Widmark put his glasses on and had his script in front of him. Judy wasn't there, Monty Clift wasn't there, but Bill Shatner was there, all of the defendants, Werner Klemperer and the others, they were all there. There were probably fifteen or twenty in all. Spencer came in with his script; he put his glasses on and he opened his script. The rest of them just left it there, but he opened his script as if he wanted to check something. At that point, Stanley introduced everybody; some of the people knew each other, of course. Everybody was very respectful of Tracy, and it was all very formal. Stanley kept it that way. There was some kind of aura, a feeling we were a step above normal films, that we were doing a film that Stanley felt just had to be made.

Tracy's part in the film, at least the portions in the courtroom, was fragmented. His part went all the way through, but for a period of time it was just "Would you speak up?" and then six pages later he would have an interjection, and that's the way it was in the script. So he did the same thing with this reading—he would follow for a while and then he'd remember, "Oh, I think I have a cue coming up," and he'd look at his script again. Widmark had memorized his whole part—he never opened his script. Lancaster was a gentleman, very eloquent. He sat with the script open in front of him and did it very carefully. Everybody had their own way of doing this reading, but I remember Spencer vividly because he just didn't have much to do. His major scenes were with Marlene Dietrich; in the courtroom he only had this one speech where he read the verdict.

So Tracy was sort of like a fox that was hiding in the bushes. He played everything very low key. My first impression of him was:

Gee, you're sitting here with Spencer Tracy—you have to be impressed. But he didn't seem to be this typical big-time actor who needed to be "on" all the time. He didn't need to impress anybody. And that spilled over into the production, because we eventually had to get everybody into the witness box. They all had to tell their stories, they all had to have their day in court. They all had their turn being in the spotlight, and Tracy was always sitting in the background. By the time we got to Tracy's work, which was basically the decision, all of the big stars had already had their turns. And he was lying there waiting . . .

In Abby Mann's mind, the power of the screenplay depended on an actor of Tracy's authority in the part of Judge Haywood. "Tracy was the embodiment of America in a way. You think, 'Well, this is an ordinary guy.' But like a lot of guys like him, he's not ordinary." It was as if a lifetime of careful refinement had prepared him for the role, the summation of an entire career. "*Time* magazine said that in *Inherit the Wind* I acted less and less," Tracy said to Joe Hyams. "Isn't that the goal? Ethel Barrymore once told me when I asked her about acting, 'The idea is to be yourself,' and George M. Cohan said the same thing, 'to act less.' I finally narrowed it down to where when I begin a part, I say to myself, 'This is Spencer Tracy as a judge' or 'This is Spencer Tracy as a priest or as a lawyer,' and let it go at that."

That said, he bristled at the inference that he was just playing himself. "Who the hell do you want me to play?" he would thunder. "Humphrey Bogart??" And then: "An actor's personality is, naturally, a part of his performance. Alright, so you like mine. Big deal. Thanks."

Chester Erskine went on to explain that "what he really meant was, 'This judge is Spencer Tracy' or 'This priest is Spencer Tracy' or 'This lawyer is Spencer Tracy.' He had learned how to bridge the gap between the real and unreal, the objective and the subjective. He did not act, he *was*." Tracy, he continued, belonged to a school of art "which believed in selection—not how *much* the actor could do in any given scene, but how *little* he had to do to make the point, the constant refinement and editing of a performance until it had reached its minimum to make the maximum, the difference between those two margins being the audience's own emotional participation." As John Ford once said of Tracy: "I think he could play anything that he believed in."

Following a week of rehearsal, getting the company on its feet, Kramer began shooting *Judgment at Nuremberg* on Wednesday, February 22— Washington's Birthday. Working in sequence, he completed Scenes 24 through 26 and part of 27, the first scenes to take place in the courtroom at the Palace of Justice.

"The Tribunal will arraign the defendants," Tracy said, delivering his first lines. "The microphone will now be placed in front of the defendant Emil Hahn." His other lines that day were equally dry, and work broke off just ahead of Dick Widmark's opening statement, a scene that would involve some ambitious camerawork. Impassioned and letter-perfect, Widmark's speech the next day was covered with a 360-degree pan of the camera that took in the entirety of the courtroom and its spectator mix.

"Everyone in the crew had to carry the cables and equipment around in a circle for that," Kramer explained. "It's the funniest thing in the world to see happen on the set. Out of the dullness of the situation I circled him in order to pick up Tracy and the judges in the shot without simply cutting. It was just something I worked out—where Widmark's lines would occur in relation to who is seen in the background. We rehearsed a long time for that—to photograph people just at the right Widmark line."

Throughout the tedium of the technical rehearsals, Tracy remained in place, patient and compliant. "All you can do," he said of the inherently static nature of the action, "is play it. The big difficulty in this picture is in Mr. Kramer's lap as a director."

Widmark's scene was followed by Maximilian Schell's equally impassioned opening statement for the defense. Testimony began with Widmark's examination of actor John Wengraf, playing Ernst Janning's former law professor. "When we started to shoot," said Marshall Schlom, "Tracy would come in and do the off-stage shots as well. When he was off stage, he would say, 'Come sit next to me.' And then he would say, 'Nudge me when I'm supposed to say something' because every five or six pages he had to say something like, 'Objection sustained.' "

Marlene Dietrich was on hand from the beginning, observing on the stage and distributing cookies and danishes to cast and crew members, some of whom had worked with her when she made *Destry Rides Again* on the Universal lot in 1939. She had no substantive scenes in the courtroom; it is, rather, Mrs. Bertholt's former house in Nuremberg that Haywood is assigned as a residence during the course of the trial. He comes upon her for the first time in the kitchen, where she is retrieving some of her belongings.

At age fifty-nine Dietrich was playing an athletic woman in her forties. "She was nice," said Widmark, "but she used to drive Tracy crazy. He didn't use makeup and she had to fix up to the nines. He'd go nutty waiting to do their scenes together." Hepburn, with her father, was touring the Middle East—Egypt, Lebanon, Syria, Jordan—leaving Tracy to pass the time with Dietrich between shots. "She was very respectful," said Marshall Schlom.

"She liked being the star attraction normally, but with Tracy there she knew her place . . . She was a good cook, apparently, and she loved to be friendly and shmooze and laugh and be joyful. Around Tracy, though, she was much more sedate, quieter, letting him have the stage." Dietrich would later describe Tracy in her autobiography as "the only really admirable actor with whom I worked."

Tracy began talking of retirement again, saying another picture would be anticlimactic after *Judgment at Nuremberg.* He turned down Otto Preminger, who wanted him for *Advise and Consent,* and was also said to have been Harper Lee's choice for Atticus Finch in *To Kill a Mockingbird.* Bob Yager remembered a telling remark that Tracy made to photographer Phil Stern, who was shooting *The Devil at 4 O'Clock* in Hawaii for Globe Photo. Stern had taken some pictures of Tracy—portraits—and when he showed him the prints he said, "I think they're very, very good character shots of you." Tracy examined the images impassively. "When you get to my age," he said, "it is hard to say when a picture is a wonderful character study or when it's just a picture of an old man."

As expected, he drew another Oscar nomination for *Inherit the Wind,* even as Fredric March, another two-time winner, was shut out of the running. Tracy was clearly pained by the omission, even as he sought to distance himself from the proceedings. "I have to admit to you—Freddy—that I am wondering a bit if maybe the votes were tabulated in Cook County . . . ," he wrote in acknowledging his costar's gracious wire of congratulations. "But I thank you—a good Democrat—for giving me the benefit of the doubt—and how I miss you in the daily entanglements of Stanley Kramer's camera moves."

To press such as Pete Martin or Joe Hyams, Tracy rarely missed an opportunity to alienate the voting membership of the academy. "I care about a great many things," he told Martin, "but I sure as hell don't give a fiddler's damn about the Academy Awards, and I was honest from the beginning. I never did. When I was winning it, and when I was nominated a great many times."

Nor did he buy Martin's suggestion that a nomination somehow brought paying customers to see an otherwise underperforming film. "I was nominated for *Old Man and the Sea,*" he said, "which grossed fifteen dollars, seven of which they found in the aisle. I was nominated for *Bad Day at Black Rock,* which was not a success at the box office. It has nothing whatever to do with it. Maybe the awards, but the actors nominate. And the actors nominate if they think you give a good performance. What the hell has the picture got to do with it? Nothing. Not a goddamn thing."

Tracy in his rented home on the George
Cukor estate. The chair was an old horsehair
rocker that Hepburn had reupholstered.
(HEARST COLLECTION, UNIVERSITY OF
SOUTHERN CALIFORNIA)

Nevertheless, Columbia pulled *The Devil at 4 O'Clock* from its scheduled summer release, spotting it instead for the fall, presumably in the belief
that by now any Tracy performance, regardless of the material behind it,
merited a nomination.

Montgomery Clift paced the floor of his room at the Hotel Bel-Air, struggling for words. "I can't really answer you honestly," he said. "I was offered
$300,000 for another role. That would have been the highest per diem ever
paid. But what I did, I don't consider it—what's the word? I knew it yesterday . . . altruistic. It's not altruistic on my part. People milk pictures, and I
felt for this role which was to be shot in four days . . . Why did I do it? I
really don't know."

He was speaking to a writer for the *Los Angeles Times* who had asked him
why he had chosen to make *Judgment at Nuremberg* for nothing. "Maybe
you can tell me," Clift said to the man. "You look brighter." The *Times'*
Don Alpert suggested that perhaps he just wanted to. "I feel so embarrassed," the actor responded. "I really feel embarrassed. Nobody understands that. I wanted to play it. Deeply. As in D-E-E-P-P-P-L-L-L-L-Y. But

you see, that's so far from the conscience of people here. They think it has to be for publicity or something."

Clift was still embarrassed when he arrived on the Revue lot, sporting a "very bad haircut" because he believed the awkward man he was to play, Petersen, would have gotten a special haircut before testifying against war criminals.

"Monty Clift came in at nine o'clock," Marshall Schlom recalled,

and there was a hush on the set. What a troubled man he was. And all of us knew that. He was very nice, but you could tell he was frail. He was a shell of what he used to be. He came in and Stanley shook his hand—there were warm welcomes—and he sat him down in the witness box. Monty had a thermos, which we all figured was coffee. We started to do some lighting, and Stanley was talking to him, and then Stanley walked away. Clift opened up the thermos and poured . . . and it wasn't dark liquid. It was liquor; it was a sidecar (which I found out later). He poured this into the lid of the thermos, and he held it for a second and looked at it. And then he felt three hundred pairs of eyes on him. He looked up and he looked around at all of us watching him, and he said, "Fellows, I'm sorry. I need this." It tore our hearts out.

Clift's scene was the testimony of a man sterilized by the Nazis because he was deemed "mentally incompetent." Widmark's examination concerned the events leading up to the procedure, including a 1933 attack on the family. "Some S.A. men broke into our house," Clift recounted. "They broke the windows and doors. They called us traitors and tried to attack my father." Widmark delved into the examination that stemmed from Petersen's later application for a driver's license, Kramer's camera circling Clift to show the entirety of the courtroom, the faces of the listeners—Tracy, Widmark, Schell, Lancaster.

"They asked me, 'When was Adolf Hitler and Dr. Goebbels born?' "

"What was your reply?"

"I told them I didn't know, and I didn't care either."

His uncertain response to the laughter in the room is to smile weakly, his wide childlike eyes darting to all sides.

"Montgomery Clift was at a very, very low point in his life at this time," Widmark said. "He was drinking a lot. I think he was on dope. And after twelve o'clock you couldn't use Monty . . . he'd have to go home, he was out of it. But I remember, especially one morning, I was the lawyer interviewing Monty and he couldn't make it, he couldn't remember, he couldn't put

On the set of *Judgment at Nuremberg*. Left to right: Richard Widmark, Tracy, Montgomery Clift, and Burt Lancaster. (PATRICIA MAHON COLLECTION)

two and two together, and he was just a total mess. And Tracy just said, 'Talk to me. Play it to me, Monty. Just look at me and play it to me.' You know, he was like a pop, you know, real, sweet, nice pop. And Monty kind of . . . 'Okay.' And he played it to Spence and it came out great." Said Kramer: "Spencer was the greatest reactor in the business. Monty did play to him, and the words poured out of his mouth—the results were shattering."*

There was trouble in Schell's cross-examination, when his character, Rolfe, asks Petersen a simple question the Health Court always asked: Form a sentence from the words "hare," "hunter," "field." Petersen's grappling with the question prompts a meltdown, one of the most difficult scenes in the entire picture.

"This happened on a Thursday," Marshall Schlom remembered.

---

* Despite his early work with the Group Theatre, Montgomery Clift did not consider himself a Method actor. His technique, in fact, was remarkably similar to Tracy's, although Clift was not the quick study that Tracy happened to be. Described by Lee Strasberg as the "perfect Method actor" because he came by it naturally, Tracy thought Stanislavsky's emotional or "sense memory" technique, when misapplied, encouraged overacting—the doing of more than was necessary. Method actors, he felt, sometimes obscured the meaning of the text in the crafting of a performance. "If I remember correctly," said Chester Erskine, "he said, 'They don't let it breathe.' "

Friday, we went to dailies, and Stanley wasn't happy with them. He invited Monty to come in and look at them, and he agreed that it wasn't what it should be. I got a call on Saturday morning from Monty Clift. He said, "Monday, I'm going to do my part over again. Can you give me an exact copy of what I said? I want to do the same words, and I want to know exactly what I said. Can you furnish me that on paper?" I said, "Okay." So I made a hasty call to the cutter and said that I needed to come in and transcribe exactly what was on film. Monty said, "Would you send it to my hotel?" I did what he asked for, and I sent it to him by courier . . . and Monday morning he came back in and he re-did it and it was a different performance.

Carefully, Clift adjusted his dialogue, scratching out Mann's fussy stage directions and reconfiguring his lines to make them more disjointed—not complete sentences but rather bursts of painful memory, irrationally arranged. "He was bound and determined to do a better job," said Schlom, "and he was so emotional. He was a real basket case. I think nothing Stanley or maybe even Tracy could have said to him would have calmed him down. Fidgeting, fidgeting, forever fidgeting. I was rather new to movies at the time, especially big-time movies, and I was nervous for him too."

It was torturous to watch Clift as he worked his way through the scene that day, but all the anguish ultimately proved to be worth it. "It was marvelous," said Widmark.

Judy Garland brought her own circuslike atmosphere to the set, arriving early and drawing applause from the cast and crew. "I wanted Julie Harris for the part," Kramer remembered. "I was about to start dealing for Julie when I opened the newspaper that night. There was an item in it about Judy Garland. I even forget the item. But I said to myself, 'Stanley, what's the matter with you? Judy Garland is the actress you want. She knows the suffering I want.'"

Garland was cast as Irene Hoffman, a woman who was sent to prison for having an affair with a sixty-five-year-old man who was Jewish, a part played on television by the Czechoslovakian actress Marketa Kimbrell. Garland reportedly worked weeks with a coach to perfect a slight German accent, and her tearful testimony was as gut-wrenching as Clift's. When she completed her five-minute scene, there was again applause.

"It's a cliché come true," wrote columnist Sidney Skolsky. "I never believed it before, always smiled when I heard about it. Now I was seeing it with my own eyes. Everybody—Tracy, Lancaster, Widmark, Schell,

Kramer, the extras, applauded. When I say everybody, I'm including me."
Said Richard Widmark: "It meant a lot to her. It was therapy and it gave her
great confidence."

"Wasn't that a performance!" Tracy marveled. "I don't object to playing
stooge to Judy. She's a great actress, eh? You know, in all the years Judy and
I have been together at M-G-M we never did a movie together. I guess Judy
was eleven or twelve when I first arrived at Metro." Mickey Rooney made
his way onto the set, prompting a frenzy of activity with photographers
from as far away as West Germany, where there was intense interest in the
film and its subject matter. "Mickey knew Stanley," said Marshall Schlom,
"but he had to come in to say hello to Tracy and Judy, and the three of them
hugged each other. The photographers went crazy, and it almost brought
tears to your eyes. In context, it was just wonderful."

It is Rolfe's badgering of the witness that prompts Janning, the most
prominent of the defendants, to break his self-imposed silence. ("Are you
going to do this again?") Said Lancaster, "I am almost a symbol of the
dilemma in Germany during the Nazi period. I am the man of good intention who did things of which he did not approve. I am a man who once had
a reputation for integrity and honesty; a concern for the law. But I am cynical about this trial. I doubt the ability of the judges. I am a man who has,
in a sense, retreated into another world. At the same time I must not be a
man in a cataleptic state. I must become involved in the trial."

Tracy, who never ceased chiding Lancaster over his billing and his compensation, had become so fixated on Lancaster's appearance in the picture
that his scenes on the stand were the only ones he specifically noted in his
datebook. "Lancaster, who was a wonderful actor and a wonderful man,
was miscast," said Abby Mann. "Olivier wanted to do it originally, and
Stanley and I went to talk to him about it. He had a very interesting grasp
of it. But he was courting his soon-to-be wife, and he didn't want to play an
older guy. At least that was part of what he said. As a matter of fact, a lot of
people liked Burt in it, but I didn't, and neither did Stanley eventually."

Tracy's twitting of Lancaster may also have had something to do with
the fact that Lancaster had been nominated for an Academy Award for his
work in *Elmer Gantry*—and that he was the odds-on favorite to win. (The
other nominees for Best Actor were Trevor Howard for *Sons and Lovers,* Jack
Lemmon for *The Apartment,* and Olivier for *The Entertainer.*) When Lancaster, in fact, did win the award on the night of April 17, he thanked even
"those who voted against me" and was careful to bring the statuette onto the
set at Universal City the next morning so that he could show it to Tracy. A
week later, Tracy committed to playing General William T. Sherman in *How
the West Was Won,* an all-star western to be directed, in part, by John Ford.

As the various cast members completed their big scenes, attention fell naturally to Tracy as he prepared to deliver the verdict of the tribunal. Diet-rich was often with him in photographs taken on the set, sleek in black slacks and top, welcoming his visitors, Supreme Court Justice William O. Douglas among them. "We laughed a lot together since his sense of humor was like mine," Dietrich said. On the night they filmed a walk through the rubble of Nuremberg, standing sets on the back lot dressed to suggest bol-stered landmarks still erect after the ravages of war, she brought apple strudel for the crew and could be observed huddling with Tracy as they sipped hot chocolate. "You're really not my type," he'd tell her. "You're Con-tinental; I'm just an old fart." (They were, in reality, a mere twenty months apart in age.) "Spencer Tracy was a very lonely man," Dietrich concluded, "or so he seemed to me."

The morning of the verdict began like most others, the courtroom packed with extras and the principal cast members (Dietrich, this time, included). The core of the scene had timed out at six minutes, the rest—the entry of the judges, the passing of the sentences, the dissenting opinion of Judge Ives (Ray Teal)—brought it to approximately nine minutes, uncom-fortably close to the capacity of a single film magazine. "During rehearsals," said Kramer, "Spence commented on the length of the speech and won-dered if there were some way in which he could do it all the way through. We thought about it and finally came up with the solution that worked."

Following the film's completion, Kramer, with a publicist's zeal, gave the length of the speech as thirteen minutes and fourteen seconds and claimed that he had used two cameras to capture it—one starting at the beginning, the other starting at the seven-minute mark. Marshall Schlom remembered it differently: "Stanley had asked me to get the verdict, type it, capital letters, triple-spaced. He had told me, 'I'm going to take your typed verdict, I'm going to put it in a folder, and I'm going to tell him just to read it.' I was standing there when he went up to Tracy and said, 'Spencer, here's your folder. You can bring it in with you. Just open it up, and all you have to do is read it. Marshall has typed it out, it's in capital letters, it's triple-spaced. You shouldn't have any problems with it.' Tracy said, 'Okay.' He had no intention of doing that, not one. But we had no inkling of that."

Tracy entered with the folder in hand, sat, opened it, and, without looking down, began to speak:

> The trial conducted before this Tribunal began over eight months ago. The record of evidence is more than 10,000 pages long and final arguments of counsel have been concluded. Simple murders and atrocities do not constitute the gravamen of the charges in this indictment. Rather, the charge is that of conscious participa-tion . . . in a nationwide government-organized system of cruelty

and injustice in violation of every moral and legal principle known to all civilized nations . . .

As he spoke of the evidence, how it supported the charges against the defendants and how the "real complaining party" at the bar was civilization, Kramer's camera trucked slowly to the right, catching the back of Lancaster's head in the prisoners' dock.

Men who sat in black robes in judgment of other men. Men who took part in the enactment of laws and decrees the purpose of which was the extermination of human beings. Men who, in executive positions, actively participated in the enforcement of these laws—illegal under even German law.

He spoke of Janning as a tragic figure. "We believe he loathed the evil he did." Yet compassion for "the present torture of his soul" should not "beget forgetfulness of the torture and the death of millions by the government of which he was part." He spoke also of how the trial had shown that "under a national crisis" ordinary and even "able and extraordinary men" could delude themselves into the commission of crimes "so vast and heinous that they beggar the imagination."

Marshall Schlom recalled looking over at Kramer and seeing that he was "getting a little itchy" as the scene progressed. "I think he was a bit worried that maybe Tracy wasn't going to finish before the camera ran out of film." Tracy continued, his voice at times betraying the emotional weight of the words he was saying.

No one who has sat through the trial can ever forget them. Men sterilized because of political belief . . . A mockery made of friendship and faith . . . The murder of children . . . How easily it can happen . . . There are those in our own country, too, who today speak of the protection of country, of survival. A decision must be made in the life of every nation at the very moment when the grasp of the enemy is at its throat. Then it seems that the only way to survive is to use the means of the enemy, to rest survival upon what is expedient, to look the other way . . . Only the answer to that is: *Survival as what?* A country isn't a rock . . . it's not an extension of one's self—it's what it stands for. It's what it stands for when standing for something is the most difficult . . .

Before the people of the world . . . let it now be noted . . . that here in our decision, this is what we stand for: Justice . . . Truth . . . and the value of a single human being.

Facing the four defendants in the dock, he then proceeded to pass life sentences on Emil Hahn, on Friedrich Hoffstetter, on Werner Lammpe, and, finally, and with difficulty, on Ernst Janning.

"Tracy didn't read it," said Marshall Schlom. "Tracy had memorized this whole thing, which was ten minutes long. It was one reel of raw stock going through the camera. He did the wider shot first, take one, which was a print, and then we did his close-up, and take one, and it was a print. And he was just as sly as a fox, because now *he* had his day in court. He had trumped all the other suits, and it was wonderful to see because he didn't make anything out of it. But he was lying in wait, he was gonna get everybody. Of course, each one of these people on the stand had done their part, and, sporadically, there had been some applause. But when it got to Tracy, everybody—the entire crew and cast and two hundred extras—were sitting and watching this and when he did take one, letter perfect, without reading it, the applause was thunderous."

When Kramer felt he had everything he needed—well before noontime—he wrapped the company for the day. "Let's all go to lunch," he said, "and then we can go home." It was at that point that Burt Lancaster approached Tracy. "How did you do that so easily?" he asked.

Tracy took the question in stride. "You practice for thirty-five years," he said quietly.

When *Judgment at Nuremberg* finished in California on May 4, 1961, Kramer still had a week's worth of location work to do in Germany. Tracy wasn't happy about going. ("He urgently didn't want to do that," said Philip Langner.) Then Kate said that she would go along, and the plan suddenly became more feasible. Tracy flew to New York on May 7—"loaded," he later wrote in his book—and was met at the airport by Hepburn, who, according to Dorothy Kilgallen, "almost conked a cameraman when he focused his lens at the reunion." In town, she registered him at the Plaza Hotel, a curious event witnessed, coincidentally, by their friend Bill Self.

"I was with a friend of mine," Self recalled, "and I said to my friend, 'If Kate's here, chances are Spence is here.' So we went around to the back of the Plaza where the elevator is, and I saw Spence over in the corner with his collar up and his hat pulled down, standing in the shadows." Their eyes met, but Self, who hadn't seen Tracy in years, kept his distance. "My friend said, 'Oh, there's Spencer Tracy. Go say hello to him.' I said, 'I wouldn't go near him with a ten-foot pole.' He said, 'You're kidding. I thought you knew him.' I said, 'I *do* know him, but he's hiding, and I'm not going to reveal his hiding place.' I wouldn't go near him . . . I never said a word to him, never acknowledged him or anything."

Tracy boarded a Lufthansa flight to Frankfurt on the evening of May 9, arriving in Germany the next morning, again, as he noted in his book, "loaded." The five-hour drive to Nuremberg was followed by a day's rest, after which he and Kramer and his crew got to work, capturing street scenes and generally opening the picture up as much as possible. On the sixteenth the company moved to Berlin, where a press conference took place. Additional exteriors finished the picture on May 20, exactly on schedule. The same day, Tracy received Roderick Mann, film columnist for the *Sunday Express,* in his suite at the Berlin Hilton. Sipping coffee, he told Mann that he had just been reading a piece on Gary Cooper, who had died of cancer the previous week: Was he really an actor? Or just a personality?

"What a bore those arguments have become," he moaned. "I thought Cooper was great. I hardly knew him, but I always admired him. What could he have done better in a film like *High Noon*? Played it with a broken arm or an accent? Cooper used to be very proud because John Barrymore once said of him: 'He never makes a wrong move on the screen.' The truth is Cooper hardly ever made *any* move. He didn't have to, he was so good . . . I remember Garson Kanin, the playwright, once asking me what I thought was the most important thing about acting. 'Learning the blasted lines,' I said. Another time someone asked me what was the first thing I looked for in a script. 'Days off,' I said."

He finished his coffee and carefully put the cup down on the table. "I never watch my old movies on TV," he continued. "Or any old movies, come to that. Too many of my friends are dead. I don't want to be reminded. How can I watch an old Bogart film? Bogie was a friend of mine. I saw a lot of him before he died. I can't watch him now; I switch the set off. In Hollywood, where you're dead you're very dead. Sometimes you're even dead before you're dead. They're always happy to give you a boost on the way. Like that special Academy Award for Gary Cooper. Until they did that nobody even knew he was ill. Why couldn't they have left him alone? Bogie, Gable . . . now Cooper. All my contemporaries are going. Who knows? Maybe it'll be my turn to bat next."

With *Judgment at Nuremberg* out of the way, Tracy and Hepburn returned to Frankfurt, where they spent two days driving along the Rhine and taking in the countryside. From there they traveled to Paris, an eight-hour trip, stopping once again at the Raphael and meeting up with the Kanins for dinner. The next two weeks were idyllic—rising early, walking the city, eating elaborately. A toothache put an end to it all on June 10, complicating Tracy's last days in the city with dental appointments. They boarded the *Queen Elizabeth* in Cherbourg on the fifteenth, taking adjoining staterooms for a five-day voyage that was foggy and unusually rough. (When advised, upon arrival, of the proximity of his frequent costar, Tracy feigned surprise: "If she's on the ship I wouldn't know it.") In New York he was trapped by autograph seekers at Fiftieth and Park Avenue, had dinner with Abe Lastfogel, went to Mass at St. Patrick's Cathedral, and bought a new Lincoln Continental to take back to Louise. He tooled out of Manhattan on the morning of the twenty-ninth, passing through Pennsylvania, Ohio, and Missouri, stopping at motels along the way.

The black car with the creamy interior was completely unexpected, though Tracy often impulsively bought things for his wife. ("Weeze, I thought you'd like that.") Usually he gave her jewelry; occasionally paintings. "He said once, 'Let's go over and look at these pictures' in some man's house," she remembered. "We went over and he had some very nice things. There was this darling little Grandma Moses and he said, 'Wouldn't you like this?' Well, he got it right there." He once bought her a Paul Clemens oil in much the same manner. "He would pop up with things."

Tracy was still making his way across the country when Abby Mann viewed a rough cut of *Judgment at Nuremberg*. A letter was awaiting him when he returned to St. Ives: "Every writer ought to have the experience of having Spencer Tracy do his lines. There is nothing in the world quite like it. You are, in a way, the Chekhov among actors. Your work is honest, clean, simple, and enormously meaningful."

Gratified, Tracy responded via his favorite mode of communication, a telegram:

AFTER FINISHING NUREMBERG THE HARD WAY DRIVING ACROSS THE COUNTRY I FOUND YOUR OVERWHELMING MESSAGE. ALL I CAN SAY AFTER READING IT IS IF THE LIGHTS GO NOW I STILL WIN. PLEASE DO NOT FORGET IT WAS A GREAT PRIVILEGE TO SAY THOSE WORDS.

With the general euphoria that attended the completion of *Judgment at Nuremberg*, it was easy to forget that *The Devil at 4 O'Clock* was still in production. The effects work—primarily the volcanic eruption at the film's conclusion—took months to complete. (The island miniature alone took four months to build.) Then in July, just as Tracy was arriving back in Los Angeles, a camera crew was hastily dispatched to Hilo to shoot the eruption of Kilauea on the Big Island of Hawaii. (An extra crew had been stationed at Kilauea during the film's location work on Maui, but nothing had happened.) Minus its final pieces, the picture was previewed on July 13, where

354 out of 385 cards rated it either good or excellent. Emboldened by a second, equally successful preview in Pasadena, Columbia set a budget of $1,700,000 for global advertising and promotion, prompted, in part, by the record business being done by *The Guns of Navarone.* Cosponsoring with Squibb, the studio committed to a month of ABC's *Evening Report*—a buy alone valued at $100,000—and set mid-October openings for the picture at New York's Criterion Theatre and the Stanley Warner in Beverly Hills. At a negative cost of $5,721,786, *The Devil at 4 O'Clock* was the most expensive picture Columbia had ever made.

Hepburn, meanwhile, had committed to one of the most demanding roles she would ever tackle, that of the drug-addled Mary Tyrone in Ely Landau's production of *A Long Day's Journey into Night.* Director Sidney Lumet wanted Tracy to play Mary's husband James, a role modeled on the author's own father, but Tracy resisted the suggestion, even when Kate thought that he might be talked into it.

"Look," Tracy said to Lumet, "Kate's the lunatic, she's the one who goes off and appears at Stratford in Shakespeare—*Much Ado,* all that stuff. I don't believe in that nonsense—I'm a movie actor. She's always doing these things for no money! Here you are with twenty-five thousand each for *Long Day's Journey*—crazy! I read it last night, and it's the best play I ever read. I promise you this: If you offered me this part for five-hundred thousand and somebody else offered me another part for five-hundred thousand, I'd take this!"

Kate exclaimed, "There he goes! No! It's not going to work!" and the three proceeded to have what Lumet later remembered as "a charming breakfast."

While Hepburn went off to make the film in New York, Tracy remained in Los Angeles, watching television and weighing offers he had little interest in accepting. He had agreed to play Pontius Pilate in George Stevens' much-delayed version of Fulton Oursler's best-selling novel, *The Greatest Story Ever Told,* but it was an all-star affair, a "cut rate deal" as he described it. There was also talk of him doing *The Leopard* in Sicily for Luchino Visconti, but the choice had been somewhat forced on Visconti by Fox, which had specified one of four American box office stars as a condition of financing the film. (Gregory Peck, Anthony Quinn, and Burt Lancaster were the others.) Although he agreed to read the script, Tracy balked at spending five months on location or submitting to an interview with the director, and Lancaster wound up playing the part of the autocratic Prince Salina. Tracy was, in fact, settling into a pattern where he would work only for certain directors—Ford, Stevens, Stanley Kramer—and otherwise considered himself retired. That he was soon to be seen in two of the biggest films of the year scarcely seemed to matter, and he and Kate spent much of the remainder of the year apart.

The Devil at 4 O'Clock, though generally received as the superficial product it was, turned out to be Tracy's biggest commercial success since *Father of the Bride,* with gross receipts amounting to $4,555,000. As an element of commerce, however, it lost more money than *Inherit the Wind* and *Plymouth Adventure* combined. Tracy made no comment on the fate of the picture, and his relationship with Sinatra seemed to survive the ordeal. *Judgment at Nuremberg* was the greater concern, and Kramer held firm to his plan for a December premiere in Berlin, despite an increasingly tense political climate that in August saw the closing of the border between East and West Berlin and the construction of a wall to prevent defections to the West.

"I wanted Spencer to go to Berlin for the world premiere," Kramer recalled, "and Kate didn't want him to go. I said, 'How can you tell him not to go? The trip wouldn't hurt him, and you said you'd go with him.' She replied, 'It seems such a stupid thing to do. What do you want to flaunt him in front of the Germans for?' I said, 'I'm not flaunting him. Willy Brandt's invited us. Let's go.' She was reluctant, but finally she agreed." Kramer had not seen Tracy and Hepburn together much—she was mainly out of town when *Inherit the Wind* and *Judgment at Nuremberg* were made. "As soon as [they arrived in Berlin,] she got him set up in his place with all the pill bottles and everything, and all the prescriptions, and then took off his shoes and put on his slippers, and put his robe around his shoulders. She was like a nursemaid, really."

More than three hundred newsmen from twenty-six countries had traveled to the partitioned city to cover the event, some 120 columnists and political commentators alone having been flown in via charter from New York. Tracy, as the film's principal star, was closely questioned by reporters at a press conference. Did he believe every word he said in the script? "Yes." Why did he take a role like this at this stage of his career? "Money." (*"Gelt!"* an interpreter shouted in German.) To most questions he answered simply yes or no. Finally one journalist, apparently irked, asked, "Do you always answer just yes or no?"

"No!" he shot back.

Even with Tracy, Montgomery Clift, Maximilian Schell, Richard Widmark, and Judy Garland in attendance, the premiere was pretty much a bust. Tracy grew ill and left the Kongresshalle—just seven hundred yards from the Berlin wall—shortly after the film began. (A UA representative later explained it as a "flareup of an old kidney ailment.") Most of the Germans attending the champagne dinner afterward were poker-faced, some thinking the film badly timed given the country's division.

"There was a buffet for fifteen-hundred people," Kramer recalled, "and only two-hundred showed. I had been raised to know that the perfect trib-

At the Berlin premiere of *Judgment at Nuremberg*. Left to right: Tracy, Montgomery Clift, Judy Garland, and Stanley Kramer. (AUTHOR'S COLLECTION)

ute at the end of a film was like at the end of Lincoln's Gettysburg Address—total silence. We had total silence, but I knew it wasn't a perfect tribute. The press was very divided, some saying that all the Germans should see the film if they aspired to be a cosmopolitan city in Berlin again, others saying it's just raking over old coals for what?"

Many felt the film too long, but Friedrich Luft, a German theater critic, found it a "fair and human statement" of the problems of responsibility and guilt for war crimes. "I think people in Germany will accept it." Conversely, Wolfgang Will, who reviewed the picture for the West Berlin tabloid *BZ,* thought it went much too easy on the Nazis. "This is a fable of Nuremberg, a downright counterfeit," he wrote. "Much worse things happened at those trials than what was portrayed." According to a report in the *Los Angeles Times,* four German papers praised the film, one condemned it, and a sixth was noncommittal.

Tracy and Hepburn departed for Paris via chauffeured limousine, only to be denied access to the Autobahn that crossed East Germany because Tracy lacked a visa. The car detoured back to East Berlin, a distance of thirty-eight miles, to comply with the requirement, and they weren't finally ensconced at the Raphael until well past dark. Continuing on to Le Havre, Tracy boarded the liner *United States* for New York, leaving Hepburn to catch a flight to London.

In Los Angeles, the West Coast premiere of *Judgment at Nuremberg* was a benefit for John Tracy Clinic, with George Cukor, Walt Disney, Burt Lancaster, Ronald Reagan, Dinah Shore, and Robert Young listed among the twenty-five members of the ticket sales committee. With seats selling for twenty-five and fifty dollars each and former Vice President Richard Nixon heading the guest list, the sold-out event raised $50,000 for the clinic. Louise, escorted by John, hosted a champagne reception in the theater's lobby after the film and spoke briefly of the clinic's work: "It is a place where parents of deaf babies and young children may come for encouragement and guidance to help their children."

The trade reviews, which appeared in October, were admiring and respectful, even as the film's length and top-heavy casting—for which Abby Mann later took some of the blame—were called into question. As the *Variety* review stated from the top: "The reservations one may entertain with regard to Stanley Kramer's *Judgment at Nuremberg* must be tempered with appreciation of the film's intrinsic value as a work of historical significance and timeless philosophical merit. With the most painful pages of modern history as its bitter basis, Abby Mann's intelligent, thought-provoking screenplay is a grim reminder of man's responsibility to denounce grave evils of which he is aware. The lesson is carefully, tastefully, and upliftingly told via Kramer's large-scale production."

Internationally, the film was playing in thirty-six cities by Christmas of 1961. However, with its initial U.S. engagements limited to New York, Los Angeles, and Miami Beach, most Americans learned of the movie through the national magazines, many of which gave Kramer and the picture full marks for intent and delivery. Henry Luce's *Time* (which in 1939 had named Hitler "Man of the Year") was an exception, accusing Kramer of cynically timing the release of his movie to coincide with the reading of the verdict against Adolf Eichmann. In *Show,* Arthur Schlesinger, Jr., pondered the extent to which movies could serve as a medium for the intelligent discussion of complicated problems and pronounced the film brilliant but confused. "It has the raw force of an eloquent pamphlet without clear direction or logical conclusion."

Unfortunately, one of the film's key showcases, with more than seven million readers, was in the pages of *Look,* where Tracy's 1960 interview with Bill Davidson, killed after the failed release of *Inherit the Wind,* was raised from the dead and reslotted for the magazine's January 30 issue.

"I had a friend—I went to Marquette with him—named Jerry Zimmermann," Frank Tracy said.

[H]e was an associate editor at *Look.* Well, he did a lot of traveling. And, [since] he and his wife were from Milwaukee, they used to get back and forth. Whenever he came through town he'd call me; we'd have lunch or dinner, a drink, or something. He came through one day about 1960 or so, and he said, "Do you know Bill Davidson?" I said, "No, I never heard of him. Who is he?" He said, "He works for *Look*. He's a full-time, part-time kind of guy, but he's on the payroll. I see him from time to time. We share information on stories we're doing and so on. He told me he's doing a piece for *Look* on Spencer Tracy." I said, "Oh yeah?" Nodded. "It's going to be a Spencer Tracy–Katharine Hepburn story." I said, "Ohhh." He said, "I've not seen it, but he's talked to me about it. The Tracy family ain't gonna like this." I said, "Would it do any good—should I talk to him?" He said, "Oh Christ, no, don't talk to him. He's a bastard. He'd be all over you, he'll never let go of you. He'd follow you to your grave. He has a technique of making something serious or horrible . . . he develops things that way. Everything he's ever written is written in that vein. He's a real son of a bitch. You want to stay away from him. But I just thought I'd let you know that this is coming. It ain't gonna be good. I think it's a series. Brace yourself. This is going to be a firecracker." So I called Carroll. They knew about it, they knew something was in the works. I got the impression that Carroll didn't understand that it was going to involve Hepburn, because he kind of said, "Ohhh." Something like that.

"In 1960," recalled Eddie Lawrence, "I was back [in New York] and I went up to see Katharine, you know, just as a courtesy to see her, and she was really quite disturbed. Tracy was going to do a cover story for *Look,* and Katharine said, 'I just feel worried that they're going to use the story about Spencer and me.' I said, 'Look, if [editorial director] Dan Mich, as you tell me, has agreed that Spence has rights to look at the story, you don't have a thing to worry about. He's not going to break it. It's unusual in the first place that *Look* would ever let you see the story.' "

Bill Davidson and *Look* had parted company over the writer's outside assignments and his practice of inflating expense reports. By the fall of 1960, his name was gone from the masthead as a contributing editor and he was working at *McCall's.* Warned by Pete Martin that Davidson was "a sneering son of a bitch," Tracy sailed for England with Hepburn just after Christmas 1961, the ship carrying Noël Coward, Victor Mature, and Sir Ralph Richardson and his wife among its 122 first-class passengers. When *Look* hit the stands a month later, readers were surprised by the relentlessly negative tone of the piece.

"At 61," the profile began, "Spencer Tracy is ornery, cantankerous, sometimes overbearing, sometimes thoughtless. He is a rebel, a loner, a man of mystery who occasionally disappears for weeks at a time. Little of his behavior has been reported in newspapers. Yet he has been the object of nationwide hunts by his studios. During his appearance in more than a hundred plays and films, he has led an unorthodox private life, has staged violent revolts against his producers and directors, and wrecked studio sets."

Davidson went on to sketch Tracy's early life, largely drawing the details from clipping files and studio-compiled bios. Tracy's discovery of John's deafness was misportrayed, and most of the revelatory statements in the piece were attributed to conveniently anonymous sources. One "friend" explained how Tracy's drive to help his son "overcome his handicap" increased his natural tendency to escape his problems and contributed to his "roistering" in Hollywood. "John's deafness also helped bring Spence and Louise together," the friend continued, "but, paradoxically enough, it set up a situation that drove them apart and led him to seek the companionship of Katharine Hepburn."

John Tracy subscribed to *Look,* but Louise saw the article first. "John doesn't need to see this," she said to Susie, and the rest of the week was spent deflecting questions of how the issue could have gone astray. (Susie herself chose not to read it.) Eddie Lawrence was surprised at how Dan Mich had apparently reneged on his pledge to let Tracy see the article, perhaps having forgotten their original bargain in the two years it took to get the piece into print. "Of course," he said, "you can never trust 'em anyhow."

Davidson later claimed that Tracy had talked openly of his relationship with Hepburn during their 1960 interview (speaking of her as "Kate, my Kate"), but publicist Pat Newcomb, who Davidson said was present at the meeting, had absolutely no memory of such an exchange. (Newcomb met Tracy through R. J. Wagner and Natalie Wood but said that Tracy never spoke of Hepburn in front of her, either privately or in an interview.) Joe Hyams saw a more basic distinction: "We were local reporters [unlike Davidson] and, of course, we knew that Rock Hudson was gay and things like that, but we'd have never written about it. He was a national reporter; maybe that's why he did it. For us, that would have been a betrayal. We could have lost all our contacts. So it never occurred to me to write about Tracy and Hepburn."

On a more positive note, Tracy received his eighth Academy Award nomination for *Judgment at Nuremberg* but ended up losing to Maximilian Schell, who, in his acceptance speech, praised the picture, its director, and the other members of the cast, "especially that grand old man, Spencer Tracy." Tracy called him and said, "You son of a bitch! I don't mind you winning the award, but calling me the grand old man, as if I'm some sort of ancient monument, is just too much!"

   The film itself was wildly successful as a two-a-day roadshow attraction, playing sellout houses for months in New York and Los Angeles and drawing heavily in cities like Washington and Toronto. As was frequently the case with highbrow entertainment, though, the film never caught on in general release, where its extreme length limited the number of showings a theater could manage. Produced on a budget of $3,170,000, *Judgment at Nuremberg* recorded a domestic gross of approximately $4 million and extended a near-perfect record of losses for Stanley Kramer at United Artists.

CHAPTER 32

Something a Little Less Serious

I'm tired of controversy," said Stanley Kramer in October 1960. "After I finish my next picture, *Judgment at Nuremberg,* I'm making the biggest comedy in the history of the business—*Something a Little Less Serious.* It's a long Keystone Kops comedy. Somebody said to me, 'You should do something a little less serious,' and so we used that as the title."

The original title of the story had been *So Many Thieves,* and it was the brainchild of a transplanted Missourian named William Arthur Rose. Having settled in England at the end of the war, Rose became the journeyman screenwriter who in 1952 conceived a comedic gem about an antique auto race called *Genevieve*—an original script that won him the first of four Academy Award nominations. He went on to write a string of British classics: *The Maggie, Touch and Go, The Ladykillers, The Man in the Sky,* and *The Smallest Show on Earth,* four of which were for Michael Balcon's Ealing Studios. It was, in fact, one of Rose's stories that formed the basis of the very last of the great Ealing comedies, *Davy.*

Bill Rose loathed the idea of working in Hollywood, but with Ealing's demise in 1957, he found himself adrift and scrambling for work. After a long dry spell, he traveled to California to make the rounds in April 1960, meeting Kramer for the first time in his office on the Revue lot. Rose, as Kramer later remembered it, pitched *So Many Thieves* along with four other story ideas, verbally developing the property as a "giant comedy" with an all-star cast of comedians, a "monster chase story, heavily larded with visual humor, and spun off against a background of time pressure in which, literally, every minute of screen time represented exactly two minutes of elapsed time in terms of the story's progress."

When it came time to put the story down on paper, however, Rose found himself blocked, and his agent at William Morris, Mike Zimring, urged him to simply write it out in the form of a letter. Zimring charged Kramer $20,000 for the resulting document, and another $330,000 for the original screenplay. Rose retreated to his home on the Isle of Jersey to begin work on the script, and Kramer caught up with him only briefly that summer—once in London, again at Cannes.

Rose had a mania for structure. Collaborating with his British-born wife Tania, the first few months of work were spent developing a proper character mix and puzzling out the mechanics of the thing. "For weeks and weeks and weeks," recalled Tania Rose, "there were these eighteen feet of cardboard lying across our living room floor, marked out as if for some outsize game of snakes and ladders. There was a large white square outlined in blue with blue arrows leading out of it every which way which had simply COLLOQUY written in the middle. And then there was a bit of a grind while Bill got out the dialogue."

The Roses turned in their first draft, carrying the title *Something a Little Less Serious,* just as *Judgment at Nuremberg* was being readied for release. But the massive 297-page script lacked an ending. "We tell ourselves that if there are to be a hundred comedians involved in this business we shall have a thousand suggestions for our pay-off to contend with before this last page is ever shot, and that a lot of them are likely to be better than any of our own devising. And if not, then we tell ourselves that, having got this far in little more than a year, we aren't really likely to need more than another year to get a last page which really will be The End."

In December 1961 Kramer and his attorney, Samuel S. Zagon, got Arthur Krim to agree to accept *Something a Little Less Serious* as one of the pictures due under Kramer's contract with United Artists. A budget of $5 million was approved, along with the casting of Ethel Merman, Sid Caesar, Mickey Rooney, Buddy Hackett, and Spencer Tracy. Wrote Kramer:

> From the onset, we were all agreed that to make it as overpowering an assault of the risibilities as possible, casting should concentrate on the top comedians of the world—all of whom would play straight parts, not their usual characterizations—to heighten the comedic effects of the script itself. That's where the trouble started. Nightclub and television commitments usually are arranged long in advance . . . It became apparent after the first three telephone

calls that the only way in which we would get all these people together for the minimum of three months in which each would work, would be to shoot in the summer, when they were free of television commitments and could, hopefully, juggle their nightclub dates . . . Happily, everyone we approached was tremendously interested. Not in the parts we had in mind. There was a considerable amount of horse-trading before we finally arrived at a completed cast.

In spite of his obvious affection for Kramer, Tracy wasn't convinced he belonged in such company and was frankly wary of the entire affair. If the whole point of the movie was a mass assemblage of great comedians, then just where exactly did he fit in? He had, of course, played comedy but never the kind of low comedy that Rose was envisioning. Kramer, however, was convinced a cast of some fifty comics needed the rock-solid core that only Tracy could provide. As he worked to complete his principal cast with Milton Berle, Dick Shawn, Phil Silvers, Jonathan Winters, and Terry-Thomas, the title was changed to *It's a Mad, Mad, Mad, Mad World* to more adequately reflect the overwhelming size and ambitions of the picture. Still, the lack of an ending bothered Tracy, and he was afraid the whole top-heavy enterprise could turn into one impossibly long shaggy dog story. In May 1962, as Kramer was shooting stunt car footage outside of Palm Springs, Tracy busied himself recording a narration track for *How the West Was Won.**

"The script and the casting were completed almost simultaneously," Kramer recounted. "Bill Rose had come over from England to spend some six months with us and with the actors, as they were hired, delving into characterizations and fighting off the inevitable suggestions for padding of this or that part."

The 305-page shooting script was divided into two volumes—one for dialogue, the other for business. First-unit work began on June 1, 1962, with Sid Caesar and Edie Adams trapped in the basement of a hardware store. The individual comedians—Caesar and Milton Berle in particular—were asking for changes, which kept Rose, a notoriously slow writer, grinding out pages just ahead of production.

---

* Tracy had withdrawn from *How the West Was Won* when the shooting of the Ford sequence conflicted with location work on *Judgment at Nuremberg*. His continued involvement with the film was due principally to Bing Crosby having earmarked his cut of the picture—reportedly 10 percent of the world gross—for the building of a new wing at St. John's Hospital in Santa Monica. (Crosby's company had produced the record album on which the film was based.) Irene Dunne, who headed the hospital's auxiliary committee, was instrumental in assembling the all-star cast.

"I am eager and needful for the revisions," Kramer prodded in a memo to Rose on June 14. "I am in complete agreement with all of them as we have discussed and I would particularly need a chance to read the conclusion for Tracy. He is my danger point at this moment and I feel that I must hold him."

A month later, with first-unit work having shifted to the desert, the matter of an ending was still to be settled:

> Tracy has never appeared in Palm Springs [to observe the filming and greet the cast] and I have never attempted to force the issue just for my own peace of mind. He has wanted out of the picture several times but finally agreed to go ahead. In regard to the end scene, when you edit it, I would urge that you give some consideration to the most basic, corny idea of all—some big statement on the subject of greed, human beings, and morals. The more I think of the finale the more I believe that the framework you have is correct but it needs a classic statement sandwiched in too for denouement to wrap up the whole sorry plight of these mad people.

Kramer knew his credibility was on the line, for he had never before directed a comedy and had produced only one—the completely forgotten *So This Is New York.* He likened the first few days of production in the desert to something out of *Alice in Wonderland:* "It became a three-day staring contest. I stared at them, waiting for them to start being funny, to display the precision timing and comedy knowledgeability for which they were justly famed. And they were waiting for me to start telling them what to do."

In the end Tracy agreed to go ahead with the film, even as Louise—who thought it "too much, too strenuous"—advised against it. ("He wasn't well," she explained.) The deal was for $250,000—far more than what anyone else in the picture was getting—and in lieu of his usual percentage, Tracy would be paid another $150,000 at breakeven. As an added incentive—and a sop, perhaps, to Louise—Kramer's production company agreed, as a signing bonus, to make a $5,000 donation to the clinic.

Tracy's first day on the film was July 27, 1962, when he made some police station exteriors in the port city of Long Beach. The real work began August 1 on a private estate at Portuguese Bend, near Rancho Palos Verdes, where several acres had been dressed to suggest a municipal park in the fictional city of Santa Rosita.

"We didn't know how sick Spencer Tracy was," Buddy Hackett later said, "but he came in late the first day. We had broken for lunch when he came in. Now we're sitting around after lunch, talking like comics do, and

Spencer Tracy says, 'Well, are we going to get started?' And Phil [Silvers], who had never known him, said, 'Spence, you've never worked with guys like these. They're all richer than you are.' " The boys, Silvers explained, had waited for him a good while, and now they figured that *he* could wait a little. "So we all went out, did the first shot, then [the next day] we found out he was ill. Even though he was ill, he'd show up on days he didn't have a call.* I'd sit down at his feet and he'd ask questions about how we started."

"The comedians," said Marshall Schlom, "treated him as if he were God. When he came on the set, it was: 'Do you want a glass of water?' They *valued* his being there, and maybe that all paid off for Stanley. The only [other] one who got that kind of respect was Buster Keaton. When Buster worked, the comedians were toast. They fell apart." Sid Caesar, the quietest of the principal comics, was also the most awestruck: "Seeing [Tracy] made me flash back to Loew's Proctor Theatre in Yonkers when I saw him on the big screen in *Captains Courageous* with Freddie Bartholomew. Tracy kept to himself during most of the shooting. Every morning he would say, 'Hello, Mr. Caesar,' but we hardly ever spoke."

On location, Tracy seemed to favor the women, particularly Edie Adams and Dorothy Provine. To Adams, who hadn't done much movie work, he offered words of encouragement. To the twenty-seven-year-old Provine he seemed very much like her own father, and he would sit with her at lunch. "Everyone knew that he was not very well," she said. "He'd say, 'What time is your call tomorrow?' I'd say, 'Six o'clock.' He'd say, 'Oh, well, we'll change that.' So then he'd change his own call to later."

The fact that Tracy looked old and diminished on camera wasn't helped by his refusal to wear makeup. He was aided in his early scenes by the trademark hat he wore cocked over one eye, a show of bravado on even the toughest of days. He often arrived late and left early, laid low by bladder troubles, his own chronic sleeplessness, and the continuing loss of his friends and contemporaries. "We got to the set one day," Caesar recalled, "and heard that Marilyn Monroe had died. Tracy was real broken up about that. He turned to me and said, 'You think they would have stopped shooting for a minute out of respect.† A star dies and the studio doesn't stop for a

---

* This impression was likely created because Tracy was officially "on hold" whenever a stunt double was working as Captain Culpepper. Tracy had two doubles for *Mad World*—one for driving, the other for strenuous activities like running and climbing. "We had rubber masks molded on plaster casts of actors' faces for the stunt men to wear," said Carey Loftin, who was Kramer's stunt coordinator on the show. "When John Hudkins, who doubled for Spencer Tracy, walked in wearing his mask, Tracy said, 'My God! Who's that?' "

† This was probably the day of Monroe's funeral, August 8, as production records show that Tracy didn't work August 5, the day of Monroe's death, which was, incidentally, a Sunday.

minute. Clark Gable brought so much money into M-G-M and no one stopped when he died. There was no respect.' "

He got winded easily during the chase scenes through the back alleys of Long Beach, and the shots were mostly of his double, Tracy only breaking into a run for a few feet at a time. "During the filming of *Mad World* with all the comedians," said Kramer, "I think that Spencer Tracy was in poorer health than I could remember: he had bad color and no stamina whatsoever. But then, even though this lack of energy showed, I think he had his best time ever during the making of a film."

Off camera Tracy sat watching the comedians work, clearly fascinated at how they differed from actors. "The people whose memories have lived are entertainers, not actors," he once observed. "Bert Williams, Al Jolson, Jack Benny. They're entertainers and they're allowed their wonderful instincts without any cages or anybody telling them, 'No, stop there.' Now some of them, of course, go way over and have to be held down. But great artists like Benny and Williams and Jolson—Gee, I want to tell you, when I watch a fellow like Bob Hope do a monologue, or Benny, the timing is something to behold." Said Buddy Hackett: "He just loved watchin' the guys."

Kramer was under terrific pressure to bring the picture in on budget, and it took all his considerable skills as a producer to bring the thing off at all, let alone well. Despite the controls he had in place, the stunt-flying

Two old masters: Tracy briefly shared the screen with Buster Keaton in *It's a Mad, Mad, Mad, Mad World.* (SUSIE TRACY)

sequences nearly wrecked him. "It had been budgeted at $6.3 million," Marshall Schlom remembered,

> but Paul Mantz was draining the budget with overages. His deal was that he and Frank Tallman, the two partners in Tallmantz Aviation, were budgeted at $1 million, [but] Stanley was so frustrated with Mantz he was ready to choke him. Paul drained him.
>
> There was this flying unit which Paul and Frank were doing, and they were supposed to supply stunt flying and process plates and points of view, things like that, but they found a gravy train in Stanley. There was a unit manager assigned to this unit, Austin Jewell, an old-time unit manager from M-G-M, but he was ineffectual . . . No wonder Stanley was running out of money. The flying stuff was supposed to take a couple of weeks, and it was taking a couple of months . . . Mantz kept piling on the bills, the accountant would pay them. Two-thirds through the picture, no money. Stanley went to United Artists to get the extra money, and UA wouldn't give it to him. UA said they would scrap the picture.

Kramer's patron at UA had always been Max Youngstein, the onetime partner and vice president of the company who had backed Kramer when he first said that he wanted to direct. But Youngstein had retired after the Berlin premiere of *Judgment at Nuremberg,* and the remaining management at UA seemed to regard *Mad World* as another surefire money loser, outsized and unfunny. Kramer eventually had to raise outside capital to complete the picture, even putting in some of his own. Meanwhile, he was struggling to finish with Sid Caesar by Labor Day, when Caesar was due to begin rehearsals in New York for *Little Me.* By the time they retreated to the studio in early November, the pressure was off. "They had to get rid of the comics because they all had other dates," Tracy explained at the time. "They let me go to the end. The hell with me."

Tracy's principal scenes took place in Culpepper's office, which had been constructed on Revue's Stage 29. The cast had been winnowed down to just Tracy and his police station colleagues: Alan Carney, William Demarest, Charles McGraw, Zasu Pitts, Madlyn Rhue, Ken Peters, and Harry Lauter. Concurrently, a second unit was assembling the slapstick finale in which the cast finds itself trapped on the collapsing fire escape of an abandoned high-rise, a sequence accomplished with composite elements and the integration of miniatures.

For Tracy, whose comedy had always grown from character, Culpepper, like all the characters in *Mad World,* was pretty much a cipher, as one-dimensional as a cartoon. Rose gave him a bit of a backstory, saddling him with an unhappy marriage, a whining daughter, and a pending retirement that looked anything but cushy. It wasn't much for him to go on, and with nine days of work ahead of him, Tracy made use of a device he had never before needed in his long career—an "idiot board" (as John Barrymore used to call it). "We'd have to set up a cue card here and there—not word for word, but just reminders of little things," said Marshall Schlom. "And he asked for it."

Whatever real playing Tracy did in the picture was confined to these Greek chorus scenes, mostly opposite Bill Demarest, who had been with him as far back as *The Murder Man* and was an old hand at playing cops. It's Culpepper's fifteen-year obsession with the Smiler Grogan case that animates him, the buried loot he's sure is right there under their noses. Cracking the case should be reflected in the size of his pension, Culpepper argues, his pliable face a spectrum of emotions. ("Now come on, Aloysius, get in there and pitch a little for me, will ya? Now you know, you know Al, I got it coming . . . .") It was a tough part, tougher than it looked, and the scenes on Stage 29 didn't go as smoothly as they might have at an earlier time, when he wasn't as drained of energy and stamina. "When you get to my age," he told a visiting newsman, "you want to do a picture that's about something—*Judgment at Nuremberg, Inherit the Wind.* I don't know what the hell this picture's about. But I like to play comedy. It's hard to explain. There's a lot more joy connected with it. This picture has been an experience."

Did he have any regrets? "No," he said, his thoughts turning to the clinic. "I have a project in life, and the acting money has provided for the project to a great extent. So when I cool at least I will have done that. I didn't do anything about it; Mrs. Tracy did. But the movie money helped when it was needed. But I don't like to talk about it. It was a little thing started with one little house and now it's all over the world."

Tracy had finished his scenes for *It's a Mad, Mad, Mad, Mad World* and was looping dialogue for Kramer the day Kate's father, Dr. Thomas Hepburn, died at the family home in West Hartford at the age of eighty-two. His death was not unexpected; he had been in failing health for nearly a year, enduring gallbladder and prostate surgeries and growing progressively weaker. Kate remembered that he seemed to be "just quietly leaving" this world: "He smiled—he looked at us and he just slowly stopped breathing. His chin fell. He closed his eyes—he was gone—just gone. [My brother] Bob and I sat there. Such a remarkable man Dad had been. So strong. So definite. So tough and funny."

Tracy remained in California but stayed in close touch by phone and by wire. Katharine Houghton, then a sophomore at Sarah Lawrence College, remembered taking the train home and going with her parents to the house on Bloomfield Avenue where Dr. Hepburn was "lying in our version of a wake and my step-grandmother, who was Italian, was making a great holler and fuss appropriate to her tradition." Although the family was observing its tradition of deeply suppressed grief, it was clear to Katharine that the loss of her grandfather had left her eldest aunt devastated.

> Although I have no specific memories of Kate's grieving process at the time, from things she said to me over the years, I know that this death was the most poignant in her life to date . . . Not only did she have an unusually profound father-daughter relationship with her dad, brimming with mutual love and respect and, to a certain extent, a shared viewpoint on life, but his presence gave her a powerful position in the family and (in her mind) in the world at large. I've no doubt she focused more completely on Spencer after Hep's death because he was now her only lifeline to herself . . . Tears, public moaning and groaning about death was never the Hepburn way, but that doesn't mean her grief was any less poignant.

Long Day's Journey into Night would be the last audiences would see of Katharine Hepburn for five years. Once the house on Bloomfield was cleaned up and vacated—it was donated to Hartford University—she flew west to California to be with Spence, and that year—atypically—they spent Christmas together in Palm Springs, "enjoying the rain."

For the first time in memory, both Tracy and Hepburn saw a clear horizon—no commitments of any kind. (He was forced to pull out of *The Greatest Story Ever Told* when it looked as if production in Utah would conflict with the filming of *Mad World*.)* Kate settled back into what she referred to as "Jack Barrymore's birdcage," the sparsely furnished aviary on Tower Grove where a stained-glass image of actress Dolores Costello dominated the living room. She did some minimal press to support *Long Day's Journey*—even welcoming Hedda Hopper into her home—but was typi-

---

* The films, as it turned out, did not overlap, but Tracy, who disliked the idea of playing the man who ordered Christ's crucifixion, passed on *Greatest Story* anyway. ("Do you think George Stevens is really that good a friend of mine?" he mused to Kate.) At a party in early November, Stevens reportedly asked Bill Demarest, "Are you friendly with Spencer Tracy?" And when Demarest said, "Sure, I love the guy," Stevens moved on without a word. Hedda Hopper caught wind of the story and, ever ready to stir up trouble, called Stevens' office to ask if Tracy would perhaps be starring in Stevens' next picture, only to be told rather curtly that Stevens didn't expect to be finished with *Greatest Story* "for at least six months" and that he hadn't even thought of another.

cally dismissive of a ninth Oscar nomination, which would, in fact, come in March.

The Academy Awards ceremony on April 8 brought David Lean to town, his *Lawrence of Arabia* having received ten nominations. Lean dined one evening with Tracy and Hepburn, neither of whom he had seen since the casting of *The Bridge on the River Kwai*, when he and producer Sam Spiegel had come to Kate's New York home to try to persuade Tracy to take the part of Colonel Nicholson.

"Spencer, who read a great deal, had read the book *Bridge Over the River Kwai* and said, 'I can't do that part,' " Hepburn remembered. "And the first evening, he wouldn't say yes. Then they said, 'Can we come to dinner tomorrow night?' And I said, 'Fine, come on.' So they came the next night, and he said, 'You can't. It isn't right. You should have Alec Guinness play that part. He's the only person whose personality is really suited to it.* I'm not English.' " In declining the picture, perhaps Tracy was remembering his discomfort over *Edward, My Son*.

Lean was pleased to find Hepburn "greatly calmed and more tolerant" than she was during the making of *Summertime*. "Kate," he wrote, "amazed me by saying she thought that monogamy and marriage as we know it is all wrong. (This is a reaction to all the guilt she used to carry around about her love affair with Spence.) As we agreed, if society suddenly changed and it was alright to have free love we wouldn't all be dancing into any more beds than we do at the present. Even less perhaps . . . Kate says she finds it damned difficult to live in the same house as a man. Not, I presume, that she doesn't spend a lot of nights up with Spence . . . She makes me laugh like mad because she's part schoolgirl, part very logical man, and part straight as they come woman."

There was some talk of work—*Seven Days in May*, briefly, playing the president, and an offer from Dino De Laurentiis to do Abraham in a film based on the Holy Bible. Louise didn't think he should work at all. "He should have quit after *Mad World*. That took a great deal out of him." Kate also knew the strain of a role on him, the toll that it took: "It was so hard for him to get to sleep. He was a real artist inside, that's where he did his work, preparing for a role, you couldn't see it, just as you couldn't see it in his acting."

He had begun seeing a psychiatrist, Dr. Karl Von Hagen, who was chairman of the Department of Neurology at the USC School of Medicine. Tracy and Dr. Von Hagen would sit together. Kate would retire to another room, but she could never hear an exchange of voices. She wanted to take

---

* At the time Lean thought Guinness wrong for the part because he lacked the "size" they needed.

him away for the summer, and Dr. Von Hagen thought the best prospect was a rental near Chester and Sally Erskine at Malibu.

It was at Traucas Beach that Tracy received a letter—accompanied by a script—from John Ford. "I would appreciate it very much if you would read this script, *Cheyenne Autumn,*" Ford wrote. "This, of course, is the first draft . . . overlong . . . overwritten, but that's the way I prefer the first draft."

The proposal was to play Carl Schurz, the "first great liberal of our country, Secretary of the Interior, and the man who finally settled the Indian question. He tells the story in narration and finally comes in at the finish in person. This would entail about a week's work on your part. This is not a charity job as Abe Lastfogel will tell you, but a firm, legitimate offer." The picture was being produced by Bernard Smith, who had managed the filming of *How the West Was Won* and envisioned another all-star epic, one entirely under the direction of Jack Ford. Tracy could see no reason not to do the picture, given the minimal amount of work involved, and signaled Lastfogel to go ahead and make the deal.

Hepburn described that summer in Malibu as "a very quiet time," the first time in twenty-two years that she and Spence had actually lived together. By all accounts, he seemed relaxed, though frail, down to 180 pounds, a weathered shadow of his former self. They had completed two months together in the house on Broad Beach Road when, one Sunday, Tracy began having trouble breathing. Kate managed to get him out to the car; then, certain it was a heart attack, she called for help from the nearby Zuma Beach fire station. When the men arrived, they found him "ashen gray and his breathing extremely labored" as Hepburn, seated next to him, held his hand and soothed him as best she could. "Be calm and just relax . . . Everything is going to be all right." As the rescue team began administering oxygen, Sally Erskine summoned a doctor from a nearby house, who gave Tracy an injection. To cover the awkward circumstances, Kate told the authorities they were about to go on a picnic. "This is a hell of a way to spend a picnic," Tracy commented as he began feeling better.

A private ambulance arrived, followed by Tracy's personal physician of the moment, Dr. Karl Lewis. The patient was able to walk to the ambulance—he refused to lie down—and, accompanied by his brother Carroll, was delivered to St. Vincent's Hospital at approximately 2:30 p.m. Early that evening Dr. Lewis announced that he had suffered "a little congestion of the lungs" and developed shortness of breath. "He is recovering, improving, and feeling fine." Later, Louise, who left the hospital shortly before midnight, told reporters, "He is doing as well as can be expected. He seems to be coming along very nicely. We hope he will be able to come home in two or three days." In the news reports, it was invariably

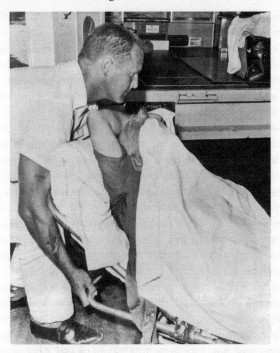

Shielding himself from news photographers as he is wheeled
into St. Vincent's Hospital. (AUTHOR'S COLLECTION)

noted that Louise Tracy and her husband had been "estranged for many years." The *Los Angeles Times* added the seemingly gratuitous information that Katharine Hepburn was "a divorcee."

Letters came from all over the world, and wires arrived from friends and professional acquaintances as diverse as Betty Bacall, Lew Douglas and his family, Earl Kramer (Stanley being in Europe), and Buddy Hackett. Judy Garland sent flowers, George Cukor a scold:

SEE WHAT HAPPENS WHEN YOU EXPOSE YOURSELF TO
THAT FRESH SEA AIR? COME BACK TO THE DANK SMOG
OF ST IVES AND YOULL BE OKAY FOREVER

From his hospital bed, Tracy dictated replies, Hepburn faithfully taking them down in longhand. By July 23—two days after the attack—he was reported as feeling fine, sitting up and eating well. Dr. Lewis told the press that Tracy was suffering from pulmonary edema, the inability of the heart to pump effectively, thus causing an accumulation of fluid in the lungs. A spokesman for St. Vincent's added that he would remain in the hospital for "a few days while they are making tests." When he did finally leave, Carroll at his side, Tracy had been hospitalized for twelve days. Telling the nurses he was "feeling fine," he was driven home to St. Ives, where Kate had effectively taken up residence. A new phone line had been installed for her personal use, leaving the original to serve as Spence's direct line to Louise.

"I have been thinking about Spencer," Tim Durant wrote Kate, "and the possibility of getting him to start riding again. Let's face it, at our age it is the mildest but most complete of all forms of exercise. Every muscle is in use but the horse does the hard work. You can choose your own gait and one has the therapy of a massage with the esthetics of being out of doors. I have a very quiet horse which he could start on. He used to be a good rider, and I sincerely feel if he took it up again it would be a great thing for him as it has for me. The ranch has complete privacy and is easily accessible."

But Tracy's blood pressure was now dangerously high, aggravated by anxiety, and the notion of putting him on a horse—even a "very quiet" one—was unthinkable. He was, in fact, back in the hospital "just to have some tests made" by the end of the month, and he remained there through the middle of September. "Katharine Hepburn could have her choice of several important Broadway plays," Dorothy Kilgallen told her readers, "but she's turning down all New York offers to stay near ailing Spencer Tracy in Hollywood. Her devotion to him for more than two decades has been absolutely selfless."*

While Tracy was in the hospital, he confessed to Kate that when he got out he wanted a snappy little sports car. "But then he said, 'It wouldn't do, would it—with the white hair and everything?' And I said 'Shoot, if it's what you want, get it.' So he ordered it and it was delivered to the hospital the day he got out and we went down together and there it was at the curb." It was a dark blue Jaguar XK-E two-door convertible, one of the sexiest (and most powerful) production cars on the road. "All the nurses were leaning out of the windows, watching us. So he got behind the wheel and I got in beside him and he tried to start the motor and it wouldn't start. And it *wouldn't* start. So I jumped out, opened the hood, took a bobby pin out of my hair, and in two minutes flat I had it fixed. All the nurses started applauding. I took a bow. And we drove off in a blaze of glory."

Hepburn was by now in full control of Tracy's care, coordinating his medications, fixing his meals, maintaining his house, scheduling his guests. Her cooking was famously poor, and Frank Sinatra remembered being served a steak that "looked like it had been jumped on by 14 soccer players"

---

* Earl Wilson printed a similar item a couple of days later.

when he came to visit. "However, in the middle of dinner the three of us are seated and having dinner, the lights went out. And I said to Shanty [his nickname for Tracy], 'Where's the fuse box?' 'No, no, no,' he said. 'No, no, no. She does all that kind of work. Kate—fix the lights.' Sure enough, sure enough, she said, 'Yes, Spensuh!' And she got a screwdriver and a pair of pliers, and I swore that she was going to electrocute herself, but she knew exactly what to do."

With Kate effectively making St. Ives her base in California (leaving Phyllis Wilbourn to occupy the birdcage), Tracy added a codicil to his 1961 will, bequeathing the contents of the house—furniture, fixtures, paintings—to his brother Carroll, who could in turn pass on to Hepburn everything that either belonged to her or that she wished to keep. She honored the simplicity of his home, the spare comfort designed into it, and did virtually nothing to alter it other than to move some clothes and a few personal effects into the spare bedroom. Close at hand at all times were oxygen (in case of another edema attack) and morphine (in the event of "cardiac distress").

With Tracy in such delicate shape, the world premiere of *It's a Mad, Mad, Mad, Mad World* nearly passed unnoticed within the little household. As with *Judgment at Nuremberg,* Kramer flew in members of the world entertainment press, taking over the Beverly Hilton and working a packed schedule of conferences, tours, and fetes. The press preview was set for November 3, 1963, at the new Cinerama Dome in Hollywood, followed by the invitational Mad World Ball with a number of cast members in attendance. The official world premiere took place four days later as a benefit for the Women's Guild of Cedars-Sinai Hospital. Louise went and, as usual, called Spence the minute she was home. "He had been doing very serious things," she later said. "I thought it was awful." Kate subsequently saw the movie herself and pronounced it "funny as hell." Tracy, as far as anyone knows, never watched it.

The early trade notices were wonderful, predicting big things at the box office, while the secular press was more divided, the reactions ranging from "wild and hilarious" (Bosley Crowther) to "appalled by nearly everything I saw and heard" (Philip K. Scheuer). Being, in some respects, the godfather of the picture, Crowther was one of the few major critics to comment at length on Tracy's crucial role in the comic mechanism Kramer and Rose had so painstakingly devised.

"[I]t isn't that Mr. Tracy is funny," he wrote,

so much as it is that he is cynical and sardonic about this wholesale display of human greed and is able to move from this position into ultimate command of the hoard when the parties converge upon it and he is there to take it away. In this respect, Mr. Tracy seems the guardian of a sane morality in this wild and extravagant exposition of clumsiness and cupidity. While the mad seekers are tearing toward the money in their various ways—in automobiles that race each other in breathtaking sweeps on hairpin turns in the wide-open California desert, in airplanes that wobble overhead—Mr. Tracy sits there in wise compliance, the dignity of the law. And then, by a ruse I dare not tell you, he shows how treacherous his morality is.

Audiences kept the L.A. and New York reserved-seat engagements at capacity, while Kramer whittled away at the picture, stung by widespread comment that it was just too long, too loud, too much. When the murder of President John F. Kennedy occurred on November 22, attendance slumped badly at theaters across the nation as Americans remained glued to their TV screens. A rebound of sorts took place over the long Thanksgiving Day weekend and, thanks to advance sales, the film was back to smash business by the end of the month.

Tracy found himself top-billed in the biggest, most talked-about picture in the world, Kramer's elaborate $400,000 press junket having paid off in a tsunami of ink. He was now, however, just 160 pounds, completely unphotographable, and in the aftermath of the Kennedy assassination, the Morris office notified Warner Bros.—Ford already being on location in Utah—that he couldn't possibly do *Cheyenne Autumn,* that his doctor didn't feel he was up to it. When the withdrawal was made public at the end of the year, it was with the news that Edward G. Robinson, who had himself suffered a serious heart attack the previous year, would step in as his replacement.

Into the new year, Tracy was plagued with bouts of dizziness and depression. At times his blood pressure surged into stage-two hypertension, and Hepburn feared that he would suffer a stroke. His potassium and blood sugar levels were too high; Kate continued to manage his diet, feeding him peas, carrots, fruits, eggs, melba toast, and iron supplements and lecturing him on the merits of a positive attitude. To bolster his spirits, she bought him a puppy—part police dog, part coyote—he named Lobo.

Stanley Kramer and Abby Mann came to dinner on February 4 to discuss *Ship of Fools,* for which Mann had drafted a screenplay. Kramer pitched Hepburn for the part of Mary Treadwell, but Kate said that she wouldn't do the film—any film—without Spence. ("I think," said Mann, "one of the reasons Stanley wanted Hepburn was to get Tracy.") The day Hepburn called Mann to tell him what she thought of *Ship of Fools,* Abe Lastfogel and

Phil Kellogg (the head of William Morris' Motion Picture Department) stopped by to talk with Tracy about making another picture, this one with Steve McQueen.

The Cincinnati Kid was based on the breakout novel of the same title by Richard Jessup, a writer more familiar to the readers of genre paperbacks than hardcover fiction. Jessup had modeled his book on Walter Tevis' *The Hustler,* substituting cards for pool. Producer Martin Ransohoff wanted Tracy for the role of the old master, Lancey Hodges, who, in the game of stud poker, was known simply as The Man. After reading the book, Tracy expressed an interest if Ransohoff, best known for his TV work, could land McQueen, who was inclined to commit only if Tracy was. The tentative casting was announced in March 1964 with an October start date, giving Tracy time to regain some of the weight he had lost. The screenplay was assigned to Paddy Chayefsky, the man responsible for scripting Ransohoff's most recent production, *The Americanization of Emily.*

Hepburn resumed her morning tennis workouts at the Beverly Hills Hotel, even as Tracy continued to lose weight. After a bout of stomach trouble in May he was down to 158 pounds, fully clothed, and she began wondering if he could even be insured for a picture. Yet he seemed in good spirits and felt well enough to drive over to Columbia, where Kramer was shooting *Ship of Fools* with Vivien Leigh, Simone Signoret, and José Ferrer. He had a good time, stayed until 3:30, but was photographed on the set looking painfully thin and pale, coffee cup in hand, seated alongside actress Elizabeth Ashley. The next day, papers carried the picture nationwide, labeling the shot as his "first public appearance in a year."

Kramer said to him: "I have your name on a director's chair next to mine. Why don't you go through the picture with us?" He went back a couple of more times that week, then fell into a routine of going in just once a week, specifically to have lunch with the director. "He'd come in a half hour or an hour early," remembered Marshall Schlom, "just to hang out, and since he knew me from *Judgment* and *Mad World,* he'd come over and sit next to me. He'd want to know everything that had been going on, any gossip. He'd watch them shoot, then Stanley would call lunch and they'd go off together."

Production on *Ship of Fools* was slowed by Lee Marvin's alcoholism and Vivien Leigh's harrowing mood swings, which necessitated electroshock treatments. Kramer was happy to have Tracy on the set to talk to visiting journalists, somewhat taking the heat off the picture's troubled cast. When assistant director John Veitch shouted "First team!" one morning, signaling the stand-ins to step out of the scene so the stars could take their places, Tracy, after the manner of an old fire horse, rose from his chair as if to answer the call.

"Yeah, I've dropped 35 pounds," he told the AP's Bob Thomas, down-playing his various bouts of illness. "Now I can't understand how I was able to pack all that weight around. How did I get rid of it? Just by cutting down on the chow. And I get some exercise every day. I've got a dog, and we go for long walks in the country." He played along with the notion that he was studying Kramer's technique as a director, but nobody took him very seriously. "Stanley's as good or better than any director I've worked with. And I've worked with some of the great ones. I learned a lot watching Stanley work these last few weeks. The main thing it takes to be a director is patience. And I just don't have the patience. I may never direct a picture." He cast an appreciative glance toward twenty-four-year-old Elizabeth Ashley. "I really come down here to look at the girls."

One day he was sitting with Marshall Schlom when an unfamiliar man approached with a dog-eared roll of paper. "Mr. Tracy," the man began, offering him the roll, "I'm from M-G-M . . ." Tracy accepted the sheet and began uncurling an oversized print of a photograph so wide that Marshall had to take one edge in his right hand as Tracy held the other in his left. Before them was a group picture of the Metro star roster, sixty-five world-famous faces gathered for Louis B. Mayer's birthday in 1943. There, seated front and center, was the old man, flanked by Kate on one side, Greer Garson on the other. Tracy himself was in the second row, directly behind the studio boss, clad still in the leather flight jacket he wore in *A Guy Named Joe*, Wallace Beery was to his right, Walter Pidgeon his left, the entire M-G-M galaxy (sans Gable) surrounding them.

"The studio is coming up on its fortieth anniversary . . . ," the man began, but Tracy seemed transfixed, taking in the images of Red Skelton, Hedy Lamarr, Van Johnson, Irene Dunne, Lewis Stone, Lucille Ball, June Allyson, Lionel Barrymore, Jimmy Stewart, Marilyn Maxwell, Mickey Rooney, Margaret Sullavan, Robert Benchley, Donna Reed, Esther Williams, Bill Powell, dozens of others. "We'd like to restage this photograph, with everyone sitting exactly where they were twenty years ago, and leaving the chairs empty for those who have passed away."

By this time, Tracy was ignoring the man completely, lost in thought and a cascade of memories. Finally, leaning in toward Marshall, an impish grin crept over his face. After a moment he began to point with his free hand. "Her," he said warmly, indicating one of the actresses in the front row. "Her," he added, pointing to another. "Her . . . ," he continued. "And her . . ."

By August, Martin Ransohoff had a director in Sam Peckinpah. "I thought that *The Cincinnati Kid* had the feel of a western," Ransohoff said, "and felt that Sam would give that kind of feel to it. I was interested in doing a gun-fight with a deck of cards; *The Cincinnati Kid* was almost a romantic west-ern." Paddy Chayefsky couldn't see it that way, having written it more as a character study. On August 3, Ransohoff and Peckinpah came to see Tracy, admitting they had no script. Alternatives to Chayefsky were discussed—Ring Lardner, Dalton Trumbo. As Hepburn noted, Tracy was "not too impressed" with Ransohoff, and two days later, while taking a phone call from the producer's secretary, he said the hell with it. Ransohoff managed to reengage him over the search for a girl to play Christian, and Tracy was persuaded to drive to the studio one day to watch a test made of Sharon Tate, a young actress Ransohoff had under personal contract. He had, how-ever, lost so much weight that Joe Cohn, one of the very few of the old guard still left on the Metro lot, didn't even recognize him.

To write the new screenplay, Ransohoff hired Ring Lardner, who had spent the previous fifteen years blacklisted as one of the Hollywood Ten. It was Ransohoff's idea that Lardner accompany him to a meeting with Tracy and Hepburn, thinking, apparently, that the cowriter of *Woman of the Year* would somehow forge a stronger bond with *The Cincinnati Kid*. At St. Ives, Kate answered the door and received Lardner warmly.

"Spence was in his dressing gown," Lardner remembered. "He looked pretty bad." At some point, struggling to make conversation, Ransohoff told Tracy that Joe Levine was making a picture about Jean Harlow. Tracy didn't have much to say about Harlow, so Ransohoff added that Carroll Baker—"the titless wonder"—was going to play her. "At the phrase 'the tit-less wonder' I noticed Tracy, who was sitting very still, his eyes went to Kate to see her reaction to this phrase. And she didn't show any at all, but there was the faintest smile on Tracy's face, because [of] how she would react, with her particular figure, to this crude bastard talking about 'the titless wonder.' "

The meeting likely had the opposite effect of what Ransohoff had intended, for when the new script came in, Tracy read it and then, in Kate's words, "complained of bellyache." The next day Phyllis read the script and had the same reaction—she also complained of a bellyache. In a subsequent meeting with Lastfogel and Kellogg, it was agreed to view anything else from Ransohoff "only at arm's length."

There was, besides, a much more promising project in the offing, as producer Walter Wanger had optioned Louis Auchincloss' new novel, *The Rector of Justin,* and proposed to turn it into a film for Tracy and Hepburn with George Cukor directing. On September 25, Wanger and Cukor came to lunch, and they all parted company thinking they had a firm commit-ment. Then Cukor found the tone of Wanger's follow-up "disquieting" in that Metro *seemed* very excited about it and that Wanger *hoped* to sign contracts. "To me," Cukor said, "it sounds alarmingly like so many of the messages I'm getting these days, 'Don't call us we'll call you.' "

By late October, Peckinpah had replaced Ransohoff as Tracy's day-to-day connection with *The Cincinnati Kid,* dropping off a revised script on the twenty-ninth and confiding that he didn't much like Ransohoff either. Hepburn thought the script more like the book, but the troublesome part of Lancey "still about [the] same." Phil Kellogg, hyping the indisputable fact that the script was indeed better, urged Tracy to do the picture, as did Ransohoff and Peckinpah, and, at least momentarily, Tracy said that he would. He was, however, undecided again after they left and "appalled" at their pushing him.

"It is very hard to know," Kate wrote. "Spence said that he got very tired going to Kramer studio. He puzzles me—he wants the associations but the WORK? Phyllis finished & Carroll & thought script better but part not—I told Spence I personally would not do it—too mediocre a part—could say as they have just said that McQueen would play* it then he ST can withdraw—the other parts are really better than his & it's just not good enough."

In consultation with Lastfogel and Kellogg, it was decided to warn Ransohoff that Tracy would "probably not do" the picture but that he would still read further revisions of the script. Ransohoff responded by saying that he couldn't wait any longer and would be forced to look for somebody else. Tracy said okay—the answer was no. Hepburn's notation the next day was that Metro would not wait twelve hours for Tracy to read a new ending to the script, so the picture was off. "Spence very thrown by apparent slam to his position—the part was very poor & I feel it was correct to turn it down. It may affect Rector of Justyn [*sic*]. Peckinpah called to say how sorry he was & how nice two people we were. I hope we were right—I think he would have been miserable doing a bad part."

At Kate's suggestion, Walter Wanger signed playwright Sam Taylor to adapt *The Rector of Justin,* but the whole project felt shaky. Wanger told Cukor the studio was mad at Tracy over *The Cincinnati Kid,* but Cukor thought Wanger was just "being used." Steve McQueen wrote Tracy on November 18, expressing regret they wouldn't be involved together on the picture. "I was looking forward very, very much to working with you." Tracy responded on the twentieth, saying that he, too, was sorry it didn't work out. "I had felt from the book that it could develop into a very interesting part and a wonderful situation between them, but somehow the old man never came to life for me, and when you're my age, you just cannot

---

* Steve McQueen's contract gave him the option of withdrawing from the film were Tracy unable—or unwilling—to do it.

play someone you don't comprehend. I think you are very wise to go ahead, for while it's not the book, it's a damn good part."

His health by now was a constant worry—to Kate, to Louise, to his close friends and family, and to the various doctors who attended him. There were days when Hepburn took his temperature hourly, and he was regularly bedeviled by bellyaches, constipation, colds and fevers, and the edema that occasionally returned, creating a drowning sensation that induced very real and sustained panic. One night over the telephone, while talking to Louise, he suffered an attack of some sort—probably breathlessness—and Louise, thinking him alone, jumped in the car and made the twelve-minute drive to St. Ives unannounced. She found him better, calmer, by the time she arrived, but the invisible wall that divided his two households had been, for the first time, intolerably breached.

"Don't EVER do this again!" he scolded, concerned as much for Louise's own protection as he was for Kate's. Visibly shaken when she returned to Tower Road, she described to Susie what had just transpired. "I don't know if Kate was in the other room, or hiding in a closet, or if she was even there at the moment," Susie said, "but obviously he wanted to make sure that [my mother] never came uninvited again."

By any measure, Tracy was a high-maintenance patient, and the office of his then regular doctor, William Paul Thompson, was downtown at Good Samaritan Hospital, a good thirty-minute drive from the house on St. Ives. In August 1964 Dr. Thompson put Tracy onto a former student of his, Dr. Mitchel Covel, a cardiologist who was on the clinical faculty of the UCLA School of Medicine. Dr. Covel began seeing him on a near-weekly basis, sometimes in his office on the Westwood campus, just as often at his home above Sunset, where the slightest upset could prompt an anxiety attack.

"There was always some reason," Dr. Covel said.

He or Kate would call. Kate was his Chief Administrative Assistant; she looked after him very well. She was sensitive to his complaints and needs and his anxieties ... He would have some minor illness—colds, sore throats, diarrhea ... In January of 1965 I did a complete evaluation of him, physical examination and tests. My diagnosis then was hypertensive cardiovascular disease. Heart disease due to high blood pressure, with past congestive failure ... At that time, too, diabetes appeared. It had been diagnosed before, [but] he hadn't been on diabetes medication ... He had a well-established diagnosis of heart disease and diabetes, and he was treated for both with medications.

A late snapshot of Louise and Spencer Tracy, taken at the house on Tower Road in August 1964. (SUSIE TRACY)

The patient's weight stabilized, but he was still twenty pounds lighter than he had been for *It's a Mad, Mad, Mad, Mad World,* and he had, by general consensus, looked terrible in that. With Kramer's mammoth comedy having marked its one-year anniversary, on its way to domestic rentals of $19 million in its first four years of release, the only work Tracy could manage was the narration of *The Ripon College Story,* a half-hour promotional film he did as "a very special friend" of the school.

Early in 1965, producer Alan Pakula and director Robert Mulligan, the team behind *To Kill a Mockingbird* and *Love with the Proper Stranger,* submitted a draft screenplay combining John Cheever's episodic novels *The Wapshot Chronicle* and *The Wapshot Scandal* into a single picture, hoping to interest Tracy and Hepburn in playing the two principal characters, Leander and Honora. Invited to St. Ives, Mulligan was immediately struck by Tracy's appearance—older, smaller, and frailer than he expected. "But the familiar grin was there. His voice was strong and his handshake firm. As we were introduced, his eyes fixed directly on yours and remained there for what seemed a long moment. Alan and I said later, it wasn't so much Tracy looking at you but looking into you—and allowing you to do the same to him."

In discussing the script, Hepburn thought her part underwritten, and there was "challenging Yankee flint" behind every remark she made.

Tracy seemed amused by all this—and then interrupted her. It was done softly, with a smile. He called her "Kathy." He told her he was sure that we got the point, because she had been "emphatic" as usual. She smiled, turned to us, and said that as a peace offering she'd make some tea. Tracy then gave his notes. It was a completely different experience. His questions and remarks were all carefully thought out and non-combative. They were specific, focused on character—on how Leander served the story in certain scenes and on how he related to other characters. He was interested in emotional detail. His copy was marked with tabs, and he suggested moments from the novel. Would we consider including them in the next draft? We agreed to do that. It was a wonderful demonstration of a real actor at the work of breaking down a script.

The Wapshot project never came to fruition, nor did a proposed series of six one-hour specials titled *The Red, White & Blue* that would have marked Tracy's network television debut. With no other prospects for work, he and Hepburn settled into a period of quiet domesticity. Kate painted and wrote, while Tracy read a great deal—everything from Pope John's *Journal of a Soul* to the murder mysteries he would then send on to Louise. ("He would go through half a dozen in a week," Louise said. "He had a standing order with the bookstore.") Lunches were sometimes with friends, dinners were often quiet affairs served on trays in front of the TV set. "We led a tiny little life," Kate wrote in her autobiography. "But it was very satisfactory. I felt very necessary to [him] and I really did enjoy that immensely. At a time when most ladies of my age were falling apart because they were no longer desirable—either personally or career-wise—I was wanted every hour of the day and night."

She had to get away sometimes—to the beach, for tennis, shopping. On May 7, Tracy called Dr. Covel after stuffing himself with five hot dogs. "His diet was terrible most of the time until Kate took over. Five hot dogs! I don't know whether he was compulsive or *im*pulsive . . . [He had] indigestion. He thought he was having heart problems, or a heart attack. It was just—dog-itis! Hotdogitis." The patient's blood sugar was also intolerably high. "He had a blood sugar of 200 when normally it shouldn't be above 110. Part of the reason was that he was drinking Cokes all the time, and they're full of sugar. My advice to him then, among other things, was to switch to Diet-Rite Cola and Dad's Low-Cal Root Beer."

On June 23, he found Tracy upset by the death of David Selznick, who had suffered a heart attack at the age of sixty-three. "I just had to go over to him and talk to him," said Dr. Covel, "and calm him down." Abdominal cramps were frequent, as were urinary tract infections. In late August 1965 Tracy was admitted to Good Samaritan for tests and observation and the possibility of routine prostate surgery.

He underwent a prostatectomy on September 4, a Saturday, and for the next ten days his condition was generally regarded as good. Louise visited regularly, as did Kate, their comings and goings carefully monitored by Carroll, who staked out a place in the lobby to ensure no awkward encounters took place.

On the morning of September 14 Tracy was groggy, then semiconscious; by three in the afternoon his skin was mottled, his breathing a series of rapid, labored respirations. He went into shock, then turned blue as his kidneys began to fail. Dr. Covel explained the resulting condition, lactic acidosis, as "an electrolytic chemical disorder, when the chemicals in the body get out of whack because the kidneys aren't operating."

Tracy was put on a breathing machine, fed, medicated, and sustained intravenously. By late the following day, September 15, 1965, he was comatose and not expected to survive the night.

CHAPTER 33

A Lion in a Cage

We needed prayers," Louise wrote, "and although I am sure a magnificent team of doctors helped, I believe it was the prayers of many people that brought him through. He was just all but gone Wednesday night when suddenly there was a little, just a <u>little</u>, turn upward."

There had been a question as to whether they were going to do peritoneal dialysis—an early form of the procedure done through the abdominal cavity—but the improvement, which Dr. Covel characterized as "a kind of miracle," prompted them to hold off. Tracy was responsive on the seventeenth—"out of danger," as the papers reported—and continued to improve steadily until they stopped the intravenous fluids and took him off the respirator on the morning of the twentieth. Visiting times were carefully—and strictly—coordinated to allow for Louise's comings and goings. "When Louise would come," said Dr. Covel, "Kate would disappear. Kate was there most of the time, as I recall." One day, as Louise was visiting, the phone rang and she reflexively picked it up. "Kate?" said Garson Kanin, calling from New York.

"He hated to be sick," Louise said. "While he wanted us to come and see him, we'd get there and he'd say, 'Well, you might as well go home now.' It disturbed him to be so ill. He hated it." During the crisis, John remembered his mother as calm, quiet, matter-of-fact. "I bumped into her going into the hospital one day," said Virginia Thielman, who oversaw the corre-

spondence course at the clinic, "and I'm sure it was a very difficult time . . .
You felt a poignancy and a sadness but always with dignity . . . Mrs. Tracy
would not wear her heart on her sleeve." Spence would show them cards
and telegrams when they came, and on their last visit, just prior to his
release on September 28, the doctors lined up so that Louise, John, and
Susie could "shake hands in gratitude for their efforts to save his life."

Tracy went home with medications for his diabetes, his heart, and kidneys, "practically normal" (as Louise put it) but very weak. Dr. Covel, who
lived five minutes away, saw him most days, early in the morning or late in
the evening. "He was the kind of guy," the doctor said, "who almost needed
constant medical care—either in the form of real illnesses, crises, or support
and reassurance. That was one of the reasons we got along so well, I guess,
because I understood. Other physicians who were less patient—well, he
wouldn't tolerate them."

In October Tracy developed a rash that covered much of his lower body,
an unpleasant side effect of one of the medicines he was taking. Frank Tracy
visited on Halloween and was startled by his appearance: "If I hadn't known
it was Spence who was coming through the door, I might not have recognized him. The change was shocking—almost eerie. He looked terrible, all
shriveled up, weak. He was pale and half-shaved; he had missed under his
chin, around his throat, leaving them grizzled white . . . I shook hands with
him and thought, 'Why, he's a little old *coot!*' "

The current issue of *Motion Picture* carried the cover story "Spencer
Tracy's Fight for Life!," but it was mainly a rehash of the old triangle business that had also graced recent issues of *Confidential, Modern Screen,* and
Inside Story. All showcased the same news agency shot of a distraught Louise
behind the wheel of her car, intermingled with stills of Spence and Kate
from their various films together. Hepburn wasn't there when Frank came
to visit, and the subject never turned to her, however obliquely.

He said, "Jesus, Frank, I never realized. I got letters from nuns in
Australia praying for me, from priests in England I never knew." He
was crying. He said, "I didn't—" I said, "For chrissakes, Spence,
you're a big star! You're all over the world and have been for thirty
years! They all saw you and admired you." [From] some grade
school in Australia the nun wrote and the kids all signed it. All praying for him. He couldn't believe it. He said, "I heard from all my old
friends—telegrams, letters, cards. The only guy I didn't hear from,
the son of a bitch, was Cagney." He and Cagney got into some sort
of a fight . . . I know Pat O'Brien tried to get them together on several occasions. (A couple of times he almost made it. They were
going to have dinner, both of them were going to be in New York,

or something, and Pat got it all set up, and one guy called up and said, "I can't make it. I've got to do something else . . . ") Spence said, "That son of a bitch wouldn't even wish me to get well."*

There was now a further narrowing of his world, a result of both ill health and acquiescence. Kate became his full-time physician, the one who slept in the room at the other end of the hall, the one at the other end of the buzzer he always kept at the side of his bed. "She was one of the best doctors he ever had," said Dr. Covel. "And when they were together, happily, I think, he didn't feel he had the need for [the alcohol, the barbiturates, and the amphetamines] . . . They were just devoted to one another. Just violently interested in each other's welfare. They worshiped one another."

Katharine Houghton saw it from a more pragmatic angle: "Once he was sort of an invalid, Kate no longer had to worry about his dalliances. They had their 'quiet little life' as she called it, and she and he thrived on the stability of their routine."

There were chest pains, which had to be checked to make sure they weren't something new. They usually turned out to be muscular, but then there were also the colds and rashes, malaise and nausea. "And, of course, they were all major problems for him. Somebody who was a little more stable wouldn't have called a doctor. [To him] these were major things, major episodes." On December 8 his heart was skipping beats, an old problem that had persisted for decades.

"I talked to him at length at home and it became apparent that much of the agitation was because Kate and I were urging him to take exercise. And he got upset about that. And the skipped beats were because he got upset about us advising him to get off his fanny and do something instead of sitting in that wonderful chair he had. And then the skipped beats made him even less inclined to get out of his chair. It was a vicious cycle."

---

* Frank was under the impression the falling out had something to do with *Tribute to a Bad Man,* but, if it did, neither man ever mentioned it. Cagney disputed Garson Kanin's assertion that he and Tracy lost touch because it was he who stopped calling. "Bullshit," Cagney said in an exchange with his biographer, John McCabe. "I had hardly ever called him because he was almost never at the number I was given, and so it became a kind of ritual between us that he would call *me.* At any hour of day or night . . . As for my calling him less and less, again bullshit. *He* started to call *me* less and less, I always assumed for reasons of health. Pat said that he began to get fewer calls too, and there was no one closer to Spence than Pat. And as to Kanin's implying that Spence and I were at loggerheads because Spence was liberal and I became a Republican, *triple* bullshit. Spence always respected other people's moral and political commitments even if they were a hundred and eighty degrees different from his—as long as those commitments were honestly held, as mine certainly were. Spence was not only a great actor, he was a great *heart,* and a great heart does not turn away from old friends because they are different from you."

Among those who found their way to St. Ives in the days following Hepburn's occupancy were some of the Catholic priests who wrote to Tracy, men who, in many cases, came of age at a time when he was redefining the public face of the church in *San Francisco* and the *Boys Town* pictures. While Kate had no personal interest in religious dogma of any sort, she readily indulged the spiritual needs Spence so clearly had without ever really understanding just how deeply held they were. One such priest who made the trek up Doheny was Eugene Kennedy, a professor of psychology at Loyola University, Chicago, who had written in the days following the news of Tracy's brush with death. Father Kennedy found himself struck by the few distinctive accents that softened the room in which Tracy spent so much of his time—the stormy Vlaminck seascape above the desk, the stuffed goose suspended in full flight, the bowls of freshly cut flowers. He found his host clad in tan slacks and a dark blue cardigan, clutching a ball for Lobo.

"Your letter touched me very much," Tracy told him as they entered his bedroom, stark in its simplicity. "To hear from priests and nuns who were praying for me . . ." His eyes glistened as he reached for a wooden Madonna he had found in Chamonix. "This is something I truly love," he said, barely above a whisper. "It's so simple . . ." Dinner was ready—roasted stuffed chicken as prepared by Ida Gheczy of George Cukor's staff—but there was still a minute or two to talk without Kate overhearing. "You know," Tracy continued, "I thought about being a priest once; I guess every Catholic kid does, or did anyway. I don't know how they feel with all these changes taking place. Now Pope John XXIII, he was my kind of Pope. But with this Vatican II, I'm not sure that priests believe in sin anymore or still hear confessions." He paused a moment, then caught the priest's eyes.

"You still know how to?" he asked.

In the lean times that followed the dissolution of Ealing, William Rose tinkered with the idea of a play, a farce concerning a white family in South Africa whose only daughter appears one day with a black man she is intent upon marrying. By 1958 Rose had the story fully developed for the stage. In 1959 and again in 1961, he tried without success to interest various people, including Stanley Kramer, in filming it. At the time, Kramer naturally thought of Sidney Poitier, who was soon to star in Kramer's *Pressure Point*— a picture he was producing but not directing—but both he and Rose were in the midst of preparing *It's a Mad, Mad, Mad, Mad World,* and there wasn't any time—or creative energy—left to expend on the development of another comedy. The idea did, however, stick in Kramer's mind, and one day on the set of *Mad World* he mentioned it to Tracy.

"The substance of that conversation was, 'I don't know whether I will ever do it, but Rose has a hell of an idea, a hell of a part for you.' And I said, 'I think what would be terribly interesting—I don't know whether she is interested, but co-starring you and Katharine Hepburn in starring roles as a vehicle . . .' The role I described to Mr. Tracy was a successful, liberal man who was a father, head of a family, very well off, substantial, married to a modern woman, liberal. All I can recall is the liberal aspect of the gentleman in question in the story." Kramer, apart from work, saw Tracy a few times a year. At some point Tracy asked, "What happened to it?"

Mad, Mad World completed Kramer's commitment to United Artists, and in August 1962 he signed a three-picture deal with Columbia that was to commence with *Ship of Fools*. Kramer's second film was to have been *Andersonville,* an ambitious blending of MacKinlay Kantor's Pulitzer Prize–winning novel and the 1959 Broadway play *The Andersonville Trial*. He worked nearly two years on a screenplay, first with Millard Kaufman, later with Abby Mann, but the commercial failure of *Ship of Fools* soured his relationship with the studio. "When they budgeted it—and we started to build sets down in Georgia—it was too much money for them. But they had a commitment to me and they said, 'We'll go for any picture up to $3 million to get rid of your commitment, to pay you off.' "

At the time, Bill Rose was in California, completing work on *The Flim Flam Man,* a one-off for producer Lawrence Turman and 20th Century-Fox. When told that *Andersonville* was about to be abandoned, Rose pressed Kramer to do one of his original stories.

I pointed out that I had profited enormously by my standards from our previous association, and that a film I had written the previous year called *The Russians Are Coming, The Russians Are Coming* was also prospering, and that I was in a position to be of service to him and would like to be. Stanley, I recall, said that the difficulty was in finding a story. I assured him I had a hundred stories and urged him to stop thinking in terms of a story and to start thinking in terms of what I call "marquee value." I recall saying specifically, "Who are the actors with whom you most like to work?" Stanley reflected and mentioned first Spencer Tracy as being the man for whom he had the most respect and affection in the business, but he pointed out that Mr. Tracy had been unwell and had not worked professionally since our first venture, *It's a Mad, Mad, Mad, Mad World.* He said it would be marvelous to have a story which would suit the talents of both Spencer Tracy and Miss Katharine Hepburn. I assured him that such a story would not be difficult to write, and asked what other actors he most enjoyed working with. He then said that his association with Sidney Poitier had been a particularly happy one and that he had great admiration for him. At that point, I said with some enthusiasm that if he got a pretty girl to play the part of Mr. Tracy's and Miss Hepburn's daughter he had the entire cast for the racial prejudice comedy which I had been trying to sell him for several years. Stanley was almost totally unimpressed.

Kramer, however, mentioned the idea of combining Tracy, Hepburn, and Poitier in a picture to Mike Frankovich, who was in charge of production at Columbia. "He took the ball," Kramer said, "and discussed it at New York and we had a carte blanche on the material." He then spoke to Tracy: "I decided to go ahead with that idea of Rose's that I talked to you a long time about. He's very enthusiastic about it and I don't feel I can make the picture without you."

Tracy said, "I'm in."

"I want Kate to do that other part," Kramer added. He spoke to Hepburn later that same day.

I said that I thought it was possible that the woman's role was as good or better than the role I was asking Tracy to play. Her response to that was, "Well, it doesn't have to be if he's going to do it and if the role is at all reasonable, you know, I'd be interested in certainly doing it." I mentioned to them at the time that I hoped to speak to Sidney Poitier sometime directly after that, and that I was hopeful I could get him to play the part because I don't know who else I would want for it, and his part might not be as large as theirs in the film, so it bothered me as to whether or not he would take it. But I said I would certainly, on my own background with him, approach him on the strongest possible level.

This was, Kramer emphasized, before they had a script—it was just an idea and a package. "I told Mr. Tracy and Miss Hepburn we were trying to make a comedy of miscegenation." Shortly thereafter, Kramer flew to New York and met Sidney Poitier at the Russian Tea Room. Poitier was enthusiastic about the idea of handling it as a comedy. "He, at the time, agreed that he thought it would be an adventure, and he told me that I had carte blanche to go ahead and feel he would be part of the project."

It was only then that Kramer got back in touch with Bill Rose. "Stanley, who was in California, called me in the Channel Islands in Jersey and said, 'I must have been out of my mind.' I asked why and he said, 'That story. I want it.' I said, 'Which story?' He said, 'The race comedy.' He said that he had spoken to Tracy and to Miss Hepburn and to Poitier and that all three had reacted with great excitement and enthusiasm and that he had had time to think about the project and that he was determined to do it. He asked if I had been serious in my proposal, and I said that I had been."

On July 5, 1966, Columbia formally agreed that Spencer Tracy, Katharine Hepburn, Sidney Poitier, and Samantha Eggar were preapproved for the project. Rose would receive $50,000 for his original story and another $150,000 for the screenplay (plus 7.5 percent of the profits). "My suggestions," said Kramer, "encompassed a Negro maid who was involved in the story, the priest, but Mr. Rose had the fire for this story. He had the last scene written in the story, which he could recite almost verbatim as it finally appeared on the film up to and inclusive of the line, 'Screw all the bigots. The thing for you to do is get married.' He worked all the ideas backwards from that, really, because that was the theme of it, the importance of it."

The development of the script took place during nighttime walks and meetings held in the drugstore at the Beverly Wilshire Hotel. "One of the things to which we devoted a good deal of time during those discussions," said Rose,

> was the question of the professional status of any of the central characters, and I recall specifically advancing the notion that the tone of the entire production was going to be very firmly set by the personality of Miss Hepburn. I asked that whereas Mr. Tracy was perfectly believable and acceptable in roles which ranged from a high court judge to an impoverished Cuban fisherman, that Miss Hepburn appeared to me to have distinct limitations and, for want of a better American word, an excess of class. Thus, it seemed to me it would make no sense if she played, say, the wife of a cop on the beat whose daughter became involved with a Negro cab driver. We discussed various possibilities for the character that Mr. Tracy was ultimately to portray, bearing in mind that he had to be a character of such class or status that it would be wholly credible for a personality of Miss Hepburn's obvious status and class to have married. We considered among other possibilities that Tracy might be a United States senator or that he might be the head of a large engineering firm.

Tracy had reached a point in his life where offers had slowed to a trickle, primarily on the perception around town that he was either retired or too sick to work. Hepburn's absence from the marketplace only reinforced such notions, and so it came as a surprise in mid-July when he attended a wedding reception for Frank Sinatra and Mia Farrow. Kate had gone ahead with

George Cukor, the bride's godfather, and Tracy drove separately, pulling up at Edie and Bill Goetz's house in his familiar old Thunderbird, the first time anyone had seen him in months. "He had no thought of going," Cukor said, "but was appreciative of the invitation. Then he thought he might go, and he vacillated back and forth. Finally, he did attend the reception, and stayed only a little while, but of course he was the hit of the affair. He always enjoyed himself once he arrived somewhere . . . but he just hated to *go*."

The appearance established to the Hollywood elite that he wasn't dead quite yet and indirectly prompted an offer from producer William Dozier to make a cameo appearance on the hit TV series *Batman*. Dozier tried appealing to Tracy's sense of fun, suggesting that he must have grandchildren who would get "a big boot" out of his appearing on the show. In his reply, Tracy acknowledged that it would indeed be fun "but not for my first 'live' time on TV. I expect to be vastly overpaid for that."*

Subsequently, Bill Self brought a more substantial proposal, the idea of building an entire series around a character Tracy would play. "I was now president of Fox Television," he said,

> and I ran into Cukor on the lot, who was doing something. He said, "Bill, have you seen Spence and Kate lately?" I said, "No, I haven't. It's my fault. I've been busy." He said, "You know, he's very fond of you and he knows how well you've done. He watches some of your shows. You really ought to give him a call." I said, "Well, I certainly will." So, remembering some of my past experiences, I called Kate. And I said, "You know, I'd love to come see Spencer, but I never know where I stand with Spence. I'm cautious to call him up." "Oh," she says, "call him up. He'd really love to see you." I said, "What do you think he'd say if I offered him a job?" She laughed. And she said, "Go ahead."
>
> So, anyway, I went up to see them . . . and he couldn't have been nicer. And she couldn't have been nicer. We reminisced and told some stories, and I said, "Spence, I'm going to suggest something to you and I hope you're not offended." He said, "Go ahead." I said, "Well, I have a series I'm planning called *Bracken's World*. It takes place on a movie lot, we have our own police department, our own fire department, our own schools, chorus kids and all that kind of stuff. Bracken is the lead, and if you would consider it, I could structure every script so that your scenes were very confined."

---

* Tracy later told an interviewer that he remembered Maggie Sullavan's supposed response when offered a Hardy Family picture: "I'll do one when it is titled *Death Comes to Andy Hardy*." Said Tracy: "And I'll do a *Batman* when it's called, 'Death Comes to Batman.'"

I knew he wasn't well. "Most of the time, when you see Bracken, you see him in his office. People come to him. Or if you want to vary it a little bit, you come to a projection room. But it's not a series where you'd have to do a lot of physical things. And you play the head of the studio." He said, "Well, that's kind of appealing. What are you going to pay me?" I said, "Spence, I'm not going to discuss with you what I'm going to pay you. I know you're with the William Morris Agency and Abe Lastfogel." He said, "No, no. Come on Bill, we've known each other a long time. What are you going to pay me?"

So I said, "Well, I didn't come here prepared to discuss business with you. I have no idea." "Well," he said, "you must have some idea." I said, "Well, I know what television in general can afford to pay. I will ad-lib to you a formula, in that I will pay you $10,000 a day for every day you work, with a minimum of maybe two days a week that you get paid no matter what. If you work three days, you get $30,000. If you work two days you get $20,000. I just know that we can afford that; whether it's fair or not, I don't know." So he says, "Well, that doesn't sound too bad." He looked at Kate and said, "What do you think?" and she said that didn't sound too bad. So, anyway, we had that conversation. He said, "I'll let you know. Let me think about it." Kate walked me to the door, and she said, "Bill, Spence needs it, but I want to warn you—he may not be up to it. We're praying that he can get through the new picture." She said, "I wouldn't count on it."

Anyway, I took all this information back to NBC, and Herb Schlosser, who was head of West Coast at that time, said, "What's he look like?" I said, "I beg your pardon? What do you mean? What's he look like? He looks like Spencer Tracy." He said, "Well, is he too old?" I said, "You got to be kidding. This is the biggest Academy Award winner that would ever be on your network. You ought to thank your stars that he's even considering it." And he said, "I'd like to meet him." I said, "Well, let me see what I can do." So I called Spence and said, "Herb Schlosser, the head of West Coast, blah, blah, blah, wants to meet you." Spence says, "Why does he want to meet me?" I said, "Well, you know, he wants to be sure I'm not lying to him about the possibility of your doing it. And he'd like to report to his boss in New York that he actually met with you about it." He said, "He just wants to see if I'm too old or something?" I said, "Of course not." So we set up a meeting.

Schlosser was one hour late to the meeting up at Spencer's house. And they were fuming. I was embarrassed. So the doorbell finally rang, and Kate goes to the door and opens it and says, "Are you Mr. Schlosser?" He says, "Yes." She said, "You're very rude." He said, "Well, I apologize." That's the way the meeting started. So, at the end of the meeting, Schlosser left, and he and I walked out to the street. He said, "Well, he looks fine." So, I went back in and Spence was showing all this interest. I went back to my office, and then I got a phone call from Abe Lastfogel. He said, "Bill, what the hell are you doing? I've known you twenty years. You know you shouldn't talk to Spence about money." I said, "I know that. *He* doesn't know it." And I went through the whole thing about what happened. He said, "Well, look. We're not going to work for that kind of money. If Spence does a television series, and he likes your idea, he's going to have to have ownership, he's going to have to have residuals, he's going to have to have some controls, et cetera and so forth." I said, "Fine. If he really goes forward, we'll sit down and talk about all of those things. At the moment, I'm not sure he's really going to do it."

Once Tracy committed to the new picture, which quickly picked up the title *Guess Who's Coming to Dinner,* Stanley Kramer got into the habit of stopping by St. Ives whenever there was news to report. "The anticipation of going to work again was one of the things which bolstered him up a great deal," Kramer said, "and one of the reasons why I was anxious that he be kept apprised of as much as I knew at the time, because we did not have a script per se." At first, Kramer left the exact plot of the film murky, positioning it to Columbia management as a "social comedy" while cobbling together all the elements of the package, principal among them assurances that the film would go forward should ill health force Tracy to drop out.

On September 21, Kramer outlined the specifics of the deal in a memo to Columbia's Gordon Stulberg: Tracy would receive $200,000—$50,000 at the end of photography, $75,000 one year later, and the balance a year after that. Also $150,000 deferred from profits. Hepburn would get $150,000 and a small percentage of Kramer's own share of the profits.

Hepburn will be in the third position behind Tracy and Poitier, but I have agreed to talk to Poitier about letting her split the two men just for balance . . . No compensation shall accrue either to Spencer or to Katie until they have either completed rendition of their services in the picture . . . Katie will be covered by cast insurance and will have to take a cast physical. Spencer will not be covered by any insurance. It is understood that if Spencer is unable to finish the rendition of his services because of his physical condition or his failure or refusal to perform, neither he nor Katie will be entitled to any compensation unless the picture is released containing the results and proceeds of his services. In other words, if he should finish 75% of his services and then is unable to continue for health reasons, they would not be entitled to any compensation unless the picture is not re-shot and they appear in the roles for which they are employed in the picture and it is released . . . Katie would have the option to play the female role if Spencer's part were recast and re-shot.

Four days later, Kramer announced the project by way of a press conference held in the studio dining room. Tracy, looking dapper in a blue blazer and gray slacks, was in the best of moods, relaxed and agreeable. How did he feel about going back to work? "I feel great about this one," he said. "I keep reading about actors who have turned down 30 or 35 scripts. I've turned down a couple and they've been made . . . It was just as well I turned them down. But I knew Stanley would come up with something eventually." What was it like filming with Miss Hepburn? "Gee whiz, I can't remember. What's it been? Ten years? *Desk Set* was the last one. No. We worked well together. We didn't mind cutting one another off now and then." He said he rarely saw motion pictures any more, and that "mostly I just stay home and read books." When pressed, he mentioned enjoying several recent war novels and Bernard Malamud's *The Fixer*.

The news got excellent play in the domestic press, and the accompanying photos showed Tracy looking better than he had in years, robust and smiling. In October, Bill Rose sent 102 pages consisting of "part dialogue, part discussion, and part treatment" that would form the basis of the screenplay. He returned to California in December and completed a first draft in early January 1967. As was his habit of forty years, Tracy gave Rose's script to Louise for her reaction, and she, in turn, passed it along to Johnny and Susie. Nobody liked it—particularly Louise. ("I had to say I didn't. I couldn't say that I did.") Spence and Louise had always been on opposite sides of the political spectrum, and as the kids had been reared in their mother's church, so had they also come to subscribe to her political beliefs. "He was a Democrat," said Susie, "surrounded by Republicans."

Weeze didn't much care for the subject matter, nor did she like Rose's comedic treatment of it. Yet it was material both Spence and Kate felt strongly about; Tracy, in fact, had personally broken the color line at Romanoff's in 1954 when he brought Willie Mays to dinner. ("Well, a gasp went up when a black man walked into the room," said Laraine Day, who was married to Leo Durocher at the time. "Tracy just cut that right off and put him down at the table and pretty soon then everybody was eating again, after they got over the initial shock.")

"We were all very taken aback that he was going to do a picture like that," Susie remembered. "He came up to the house on Tower Road, and we walked around the motor court, all of us . . . He wanted to do it; I think he was a little testy that we weren't more for it. My mother said, 'Would you want Susie to marry a black man?' 'Oh,' he said, 'I wouldn't care if Susie said she wanted to marry a fuzzy-wuzzy.' I think he was just annoyed that we didn't [like it] and that was the tack he took. He just sort of bristled at the whole thing." Louise advised against doing the picture. "However," she qualified, "if you must work, you won't find an easier one, excepting for that long speech [at the end]."

With filming set to begin in March, only the role of the daughter was left to be filled. Kramer had decided that he didn't need a big name in the part and was on the verge of giving it to Hepburn's twenty-one-year-old niece, Katharine Houghton. In May 1964, when Houghton was still an undergraduate, Kate had sent over some pictures when Kramer was casting *Ship of Fools.* The following year, while passing through New York, Kramer caught Houghton in Garson Kanin's staging of *A Very Rich Woman* at the Belasco. "She had a small part," he remembered, "but she impressed me." About the same time Carl Reiner read her for a part in *Enter Laughing.* "We had a wonderful time together," Houghton recalled. "He was very funny about saying I was a good little actress but not a good Jew." It was Reiner who reminded Kramer that Houghton was Hepburn's niece.

In the fall of 1966, Kramer was bound for New York to see "many young actresses" when Hepburn told him, "You must see my niece." Said Kramer: "I went, I saw her, and I was completely intrigued." In California he asked Hepburn if she thought young Kathy was up to the role. "We discussed my trepidation that if it were not played very carefully it might be thought to be very silly, could go overboard very easily, but we wanted to maintain this attitude of almost never-never land despite everything." Houghton, who turned down a role on TV's *Peyton Place* to remain available for the film, met Kramer in New York for a formal audition. "I asked him what he wanted me to read and he said, 'Start at the beginning and read all the parts.' So I did. I was particularly good as Poitier."

Actress Karen Sharpe, who had recently become Stanley Kramer's third wife, recalled that the choice came down to Mariette Hartley, who, at twenty-six, was in the proper age range, and Katharine Houghton. "I said, 'What does she look like? And can she act?' He said, 'Well, she looks a little bit like Kate.' I said, 'Take her. Use her.' He said, 'Why?' I said, 'Because she's her *niece.* It's great for the film; it's great publicity. Why not do it? She's got Kate and Spence, and she's got *you.* You're the director—*do it.*' "

Houghton was set for the film in late January 1967. According to Abe Lastfogel, her aunt reviewed and approved her deal, which included options on four additional pictures. "She's a bloody lucky girl," Hepburn said, "to be starting with Spence."

The screenplay had been finalized and Kramer's production manager, Ivan Volkman, was working out the shooting schedule when Tracy suffered another attack of pulmonary edema on the morning of February 19. "He'd been pretty well controlled with his heart medications and his diet," Dr. Covel said, "[but] he'd been off his diet, had been taking an extra amount of salt, which helps to precipitate heart failure. You take an overload of salt. Part of the treatment of heart failure is to restrict the salt and get rid of the extra salt in the body with diuretics. He'd go off his diet and eat something he liked . . . He awakened with shortness of breath . . . took some coffee and went back to bed and was again short of breath. He called his house-keeper for oxygen. She was unable to start it and he panicked and became severely short of breath. The rescue squad was called, and I was called . . . He was treated with morphine intravenously, and by twelve noon he was back to normal."

The episode made the papers on the twenty-first, prompting Tracy to call the doctor, worried he was putting Kramer and the studio at too great a risk. "I went over to the house to see him. He was fine . . . I thought he could work if it could be properly controlled." At first Kramer assumed Tracy to be uninsurable. Then two insurance doctors consulted with Dr. Covel and it looked as if he could be insured, but at the astronomical premium of $71,000. (By comparison, the cast insurance premium for *Mad World*, covering thirteen artists, including Tracy, was $193,820.) With insurance and neither Tracy nor Hepburn accepting compensation until their scenes had been completed, Frankovich and Stulberg were willing to take the risk.

Then came the matter of billing. Tracy would, of course, be billed first above the title, but for the first time in their nine pictures together, Hepburn's name would not be next to his—Sidney Poitier's would. Graciously, the younger man had ceded first position to Tracy but held firm to second billing, despite Kramer's having spoken with him, at Kate's insistence, about letting her split the two men "just for balance." Aside from being Hollywood's only black leading man, Poitier was also Hollywood's only black movie star. Arguably, he was a bigger draw at the box office than either Tracy or Hepburn. Kate, however, thought it only appropriate, given their history, that she and Spence be billed side by side and was likely nursing a grudge the day the forty-year-old actor was brought to the birdcage for an initial meeting.

"When I arrived at her door and that door opened, she looked at me and didn't say a word and didn't crack a smile," Poitier recalled. "But that was her M.O. After the longest while she said, 'Hello, Mr. Poitier,' and I said, 'Hello, Miss Hepburn,' and the conversation began. I could tell I was being sized up every time I spoke, every response I made. I could imagine a plus and a minus column, notations in her mind. That's how big a step this was for her, at least to my mind.* After that first meeting, Stanley took me to Tracy's house [off] Doheny Drive for a little dinner party with the two of them and some other guests. This time Miss Hepburn was much more natural and at ease, but it was still obvious that I was under close observation by both of them."

Poitier wasn't a man with a chip on his shoulder, but he was sensitive to whites who may never have encountered blacks who were doctors, teachers, lawyers . . . or actors. "I must say I haven't known any colored person particularly well," Hepburn freely admitted at the time. "I've never had one as a friend. But I can't see any difference and I'm sure there isn't any difference. It's all a question of a man is a man is a man." Bill Rose's script was as much about the generational divide in families as it was about race, all the parents in the story having presumably been born between 1900 and 1910, when the racial equation in America was vastly different. Poitier gave them the benefit of the doubt: "I looked at them as ordinary, decent folks. And in fact they turned out to be that—and a hell of a lot more. But they were anxious early on, for good reason, and they simply had to find out about me."

It was, Poitier said, some evening.

When the delicious meal was over and the after-drinks had been served, Miss Hepburn encouraged Mr. Tracy to entertain us with some of the classic stories he had a reputation for spinning. They were delightful stories, beautifully told, but more arresting than the stories was Miss Hepburn's reaction to them. Although she must have heard them dozens of times, she listened to each one with wide-eyed fascination, as if she were hearing it for the first time. It was heart-warming to see how much affection flowed between that man and that woman. He treated her with an offhand appreciation, but at the same time he obviously loved her. "Oh, Katie, just shut up and let me tell the story," was one of the ways he showed her who was boss. And I got the impression that was the way she liked it.

---

* In all fairness, Hepburn would likely have "sized up" any prospective costar she didn't already know personally. "I think Kate always gave her co-stars the once-over inspection," said Katharine Houghton. "I know she did with Nick Nolte because I saw it."

Preproduction on *Guess Who's Coming to Dinner* began on March 6, 1967, when Kramer began making process plates and shooting car runthroughs at San Francisco International Airport. Sidney Poitier and Katharine Houghton, dressed to work, flew in the following morning to film exteriors at the airport and on the sidewalk outside the art gallery owned in the movie by Hepburn's character, Christina Drayton. When, at the end of a long day, Houghton got to her room at the St. Francis Hotel, there was a message to call Kate.

"The film's going to be canceled," Hepburn told her niece. Spooked by the news of Tracy's most recent edema attack, the insurance company had backed away, declining, in effect, to shoulder the risk of Tracy's illness or death at any price. Working the phones—and unwilling to settle for another actor in the role of Matt Drayton—Kramer struck an eleventh-hour bargain with Frankovich and Stulberg, agreeing to defer his own $300,000 salary until the successful completion of Tracy's scenes. "My head was on the chopping block," he said. "Spencer was shot to pieces by all those years of drinking. If he died, I'd be ruined."

Rehearsals began the following Monday on Columbia's Stage 9, where the entire ground floor of the Draytons' French Colonial home—entry hall, living room, study, sewing room, dining room, pantry, kitchen—had been erected. Designed by Robert Clatworthy, the set included a terrace and garden area, and a panorama of the city below. A conference table and ten chairs had been set up on the terrace, with floor heaters scattered about and six stage dressing rooms off to one side. Kramer got the cast on their feet the next day, working through the early scenes involving Houghton, Poitier, Hepburn, and actress Isobel Sanford as the family's longtime housekeeper, Tillie. Tracy wasn't required that day, and it was then that Kramer outlined his plan for getting the picture made.

"His idea," said Marshall Schlom, "was that we would shoot up to about four or four-thirty, light for the next morning, and then, because of Tracy's health, bring Tracy in at ten o'clock, do all of his work, and then he'd go home and then I would play Tracy offstage. Stanley pitched this at the reading, and they all said, 'Absolutely.' I said, 'I'm not an actor, but I will study his delivery and I'll try and do it as best I can.' Poitier was great. He put his arm around me and said, 'I have faith in you.'"

Tracy appeared the next morning for a makeup test, as the Caucasians in the cast had to wear a dark base to narrow the contrast, for photographic purposes, between their skin tones and those of the African American actors. He then joined Kate on the set to rehearse his first scenes in the picture, the ones in which Matt hears for the first time of Joey and John's plans to be wed. It would, in some ways, be the most intense three days of rehearsal Tracy had ever endured for a picture, taking his character up to the point where he comes out against the marriage. "In the rehearsals," Kramer said, "I drained Kate and Spencer. I made them simply give out every single idea, every concept they could. Once I came to shooting, I'd exhausted all the avenues and that was going to be the best I could do."

"We had some tensions on the picture," Kramer acknowledged.

I was irritated by [Kate's] fear over her so-called "ugly neck"—she wore scarves and high collars, and "played low." Many times she would come in a room and kneel, or sit down at once, so people wouldn't be aware of her neck. During rehearsal, Tracy would be sitting there; suddenly she'd come in and she'd kneel. He'd say, "What the hell are you doin' kneeling?" And she'd say, very grandly, "Spencer, I just thought it would be appropriate," and he'd mock her highfalutin' accent, saying, "*Spensah!* Christ, you talk like you've got a feather up your ass all the time! Get out of there, will yah?" And she'd start to say, "I just thought that—" and he'd snap out, "Just do what the director guy tells you, will ya?" and she'd reply, humbly, "All right." She'd take anything from him. She'd take nothing from anybody else, from him everything.

Filming began on March 20 with Joey and John's arrival at the house and continued chronologically for the balance of the week. Tracy remained sequestered in his home on St. Ives, studying the script and conserving his energy. At night he would enjoy the single Danish beer he permitted himself—"I'm having my one beer," he would say—and eat supper with Kate and Katharine (whom he called Kath or sometimes "the kid").

"My aunt had no desire to be a wife," Houghton remarked. "That was something almost repellent to her. But I think the role of helpmate and companion and 'significant other' (or whatever you want to call it) was something she took great pride in. She was very proud of Spencer. She *adored* him. And she also thought that he was a consummate artist. If she hadn't felt he was a consummate artist she wouldn't have been interested in him. It far outweighed any of his other peccadilloes . . . She always felt that he was a better actor than she was, and she liked that. It comforted her to feel that she was in the presence of somebody who was superior to her."

Tracy's work on the picture began with a ten o'clock call on Monday, March 27. Matt enters the house through a side door and encounters Tillie, who, arms waving, tells him, "All hell's done broke loose now!" In Rose's script, Drayton bolts through the living room, banging his knee on a table and noisily knocking over some bric-a-brac on his way to the terrace. Tracy eschewed the cheap slapstick for subtler business, playing the scene as a concerned father, slightly befuddled when told an unfamiliar doctor is on the premises. ("The key to Spencer is that he plays with humor always," said Hepburn. "He sees the ludicrous side to everything.") He finished at 11:30 and left for the day, leaving the reaction shots and close-ups of the other actors to be played with Marshall Schlom.

The next day was a different story. Invigorated by the work, Tracy stayed until three, completing the first part of the lengthy scene in which Matt meets John Wade Prentice for the first time. The next day he remained until 4:15, and the day after that until 4:50. Nine days into filming, Sidney Poitier had a critical scene to play with just Tracy and Hepburn in Matt's study, where Prentice tells Joey's parents there will be no marriage unless they unequivocally approve of the union.

"I had all the words," Poitier said. "Very well written scene too. And came time, and I'm thoroughly rehearsed. I knew everything I wanted to do. I was prepared to do my shadings, had little nuances here and there, was ready I thought. The quiet came on the set, as usually it does just before they roll. They rolled the camera, and I'm ready to start the scene and I started the scene. And suddenly into my mind came the realization that I am working in concert with these two people. I went up. I couldn't remember a word. I blew every line for at least 45 minutes. I couldn't—I couldn't work. I was awestruck, actually. Simple as that."

Hepburn said:

[H]e had played quite a few scenes with me first, which didn't discombobulate him at all. He just was Sidney Poitier, a good actor. But when he first met Spencer, Spencer was sitting in the foreground . . . I was standing back . . . and Poitier comes in from the side to ask Spencer for his daughter's hand in marriage. And Poitier came in and looked at Spence and couldn't think of a word. Not a word. Just blank. So, Kramer said, "Well, let's try it again." And the same thing happened. He got about one line out and dried. So this was a rather serious situation. Kramer said, "Well, let's do it tomorrow morning." [The next morning] I said to Spencer, "I'm on my way. What time are you going to leave?" And he said, "I don't know what time I'm going to leave. I may not go at all." I said, "What the hell do you mean, you may not go at all? It's Poitier's big scene." And he said, "Yes, that's what I mean. I think he might be happier without those two old owls staring at him."

So he didn't go—I went. I thought, "Well, he's just wrong." But I thought, "Well, he's pretty sensitive," on my way down. So I went to my dressing room, and I wrote a note to Stanley Kramer and sent it over to him on the set. I didn't appear. I said, "I'm here

Tracy began work on *Guess Who's Coming to Dinner* in high spirits.
(SUSIE TRACY)

in case you want me." And he had someone rush back and say, "Please stay where you are."

With the picture under way, Hepburn did her best to manage the working environment at the studio as thoroughly as she controlled the living environment at home. "She wanted us all to learn how to play tennis at the Beverly Hills Hotel," Leah Bernstein, Earl Kramer's secretary, remembered. Nothing and nobody escaped her attention, and she weighed in on matters of wardrobe, lighting, and camera angles, as well as the fine art of washing one's own hair. She called it "keeping the set alive so everyone won't go to sleep," but she also admitted to a long-held ambition to direct a picture. "She and I had a strange relationship," Kramer reflected, "because I loved Tracy, and I think he loved me, and, in a way, I felt for a while that Kate and I were rivals. Isn't that a peculiar way to feel? Of course, we weren't. But he'd keep saying to Kate, 'Don't bug him, don't bother him. Jeez, he's worked it out, for Christ's sake.'"

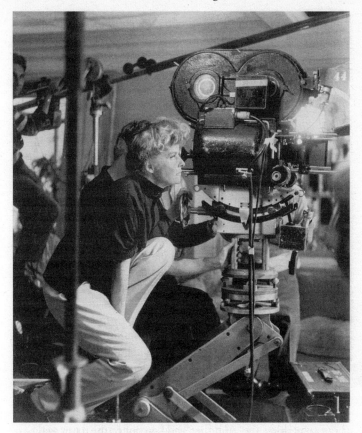

Little escaped Kate's notice. She was a constant presence on the set when
Tracy was working. (SUSIE TRACY)

Tracy worked a full day on his sixty-seventh birthday, playing his first
scene with veteran actor Cecil Kellaway, who, at seventy-three, was having
trouble mastering his lines. Tracy and Hepburn assured him it was "just one
of those days" and stayed with him as Kramer made multiple takes, literally
piecing his performance together line by line. That evening was like any
other, dinner in the living room at St. Ives, Tracy in his horsehair chair,
Kath to his right on the couch. "Your job is to entertain Spencer every time
I go out of the room," her aunt had told her, and Tracy, it seemed, was only
too eager to engage her.

"Kath," he said to her one evening, "you studied philosophy?"

"Yes."

"Now, if your aunt comes back in the room, change the subject."

"Okay."

"What do you think happens when you die?"

Houghton recalled:

This was a conversation that had no end, a metaphysical conversation, but I didn't have my aunt's attitude that it was not something intelligent people talked about. She would be happy to talk about sex or vivisection or anything you wanted to talk about, but you couldn't talk about anything to do with life after death. Spencer would say, "She thinks that when you die you just rot in the ground." So he wouldn't talk about it in front of her. There were a few priests that he was friendly with, and I know he talked with them about metaphysics, so I was sort of a poor substitute for a priest when they weren't around.

I said, "Well, I can tell you what I *don't* think happens." He said, "What?" And I said, "I don't think you go to Hell or Heaven." He said, "You don't think I'm going to pay for my sins in Hell?" I said, "No." He said, "What do you think is going to happen to me?" I said, "I think that your spirit will live on and that all kinds of wonderful and mysterious things will happen to you."

What he was really thinking when he would ask me these questions, I don't know. But he did say to me, "I'm going to pay for my sins. I've not been a good person, and I'm going to pay for it." I would say, "I think you *have* paid for it. I think you pay for your sins on this earth, in this life. I don't think it's going to happen after you die." He'd say, "Shhh—here she comes." So then we'd talk about something else. And then she'd go out of the room again.

I'd say, "Come on, Spencer. You've been a wonderfully positive influence in this world on millions of people whom you don't even know. You can't just discount that." And he would say, "I haven't done anything worthwhile except for the John Tracy Clinic." So all the peccadilloes, the other women, the fights, the binges— whatever it was that was going through his mind as his litany of sins—haunted him.

Production moved ahead fitfully, Tracy channeling all the energy he could muster into his time before the camera, brightening and then fading again like a manually powered lightbulb. "I think," said Marshall Schlom, "he was embarrassed that it got down to this, that his career ended up with his not being able to act the way he normally would act. We were all pulling for him, obviously, [but] in *Judgment at Nuremberg* he was a vital man. He wasn't vital on *Guess Who's Coming to Dinner* at all. We supported him, and we felt badly for him. And it was as if he was thinking, 'Okay, you're sensitive and I'm letting you down.' I think he was that kind of a man, that he had that kind of integrity. I personally felt very badly because I had to stand there and say his words for him. And I know how he must have been embarrassed about that."

By the middle of April, Tracy's energy was flagging, and Kramer reverted to his original plan. Each day Tracy would arrive on the stage at ten o'clock, made up and ready to work, and the filming of the master shot would generally be the first order of business. Kramer would move in for Tracy's close-ups, the few over-the-shoulder shots that were deemed necessary, and then he would leave for home when the company broke for lunch.

"Kramer tried to work him as little as possible," said Katharine Houghton, "and when he did work, almost always only his shots were done. He was always letter perfect, and sometimes improvised some amusing dialogue. It was a big thing every time he did a scene and it got in the can." More acutely aware than anyone of what was riding on the picture, Tracy took to calling out to Sam Leavitt, Kramer's director of photography, "Did you get any of it, Sam?"

Between shots he would sit calmly drinking from an ever-present glass of milk, an ice cube bobbing on its surface. ("Milkman, milkman!" he would call. "If I couldn't have my one glass of beer at night, I'd really be through.") Jack Hamilton, a senior editor from *Look,* came to the set and was surprised by Kate's almost conspiratorial welcome, due in part to the presence of actor Roddy McDowall, who was serving as photographer for the magazine. "I know what you fellows are after," she told them. "I'll try to give you something interesting." Later, Hamilton was plopped down next to Tracy, and eventually Hepburn marched off. "Do you notice she's the same with everybody—how she always tries to help people?" Tracy mused, regarding her affectionately. "She helps little Kathy, she helps Cecil Kellaway in his long dialogue, she helps me, she helps you . . ."

George Glass, Kramer's associate producer, began allowing selected journalists to visit what was otherwise considered a closed set. UPI's Vernon Scott observed a scene being made and spent a moment with Tracy and Hepburn between shots. "He is the best actor I've ever seen or worked with," Kate said in a familiar refrain. "I'm still learning things from Spence."

"She doesn't know what she's talking about," Tracy grumbled, clearly pained at such hyperbole.

"Oh, yes I do. He can focus on a line or an expression thoroughly. His mind seems absorbed totally by what he's doing. I've never seen anything like it. I try, but it's not the same."

Rehearsing a scene for *Guess Who's Coming to Dinner*. Left to right: Sidney Poitier, Tracy, Katharine Houghton, Katharine Hepburn, and Stanley Kramer. (PATRICIA MAHON COLLECTION)

Columnist Dorothy Manners came the following week and had her moments with Tracy completely apart from Hepburn. "This is absolutely my last picture," he said flatly. "I've had it and I feel my fans have had it. From now on I hope to spend my time catching up on the places I've wanted to go, the books I've wanted to read, the people I want to know better." Manners wondered if the state of his health had something to do with his determination to retire. "No, I feel well. I'm just too old to go on. I don't talk about my birthdays. I had one right on this picture, but no one came around with a cake. I would have thrown it right in his kisser."

The most lengthy interview Tracy gave on the set of *Guess Who's Coming to Dinner* was to journalist Roy Newquist, who was compiling material for what was to become a book on the making of the film. Tracy talked of his early days in the theater, Kate seated at his side, urging him on. ("Well, tell him how you got the job with George M. Cohan—that's a good story.") He sounded tired, displaying none of the vigor he showed on camera. "I miss M-G-M," he said at one point, "but all the people I really knew there are gone. Scattered or dead. There's hardly anyone I know there, now. I'm the last of the tribe."

One figure from his M-G-M days, now in his mid-thirties, was sneaked onto the set one day by a friend of his, a studio plumber, "literally through the back door." He found Tracy sitting alone.

"Uncle Spencer?" he said, walking up to him.

Tracy's eyes shot up, regarding him warily.

"I'm Bobs Watson. I played Pee Wee in *Boys Town.*"

"Oh my God! Bobby!" Suddenly he was full of life. "Bobby, how are you? What are you doing?" Watson had been working as an actor, taking occasional roles on television.

"I'm going into the ministry," he said.

Tracy froze a moment, a bit shocked, and then he said with a smile, "That's just fine . . . That's marvelous! I'm happy for you. I'm really proud of you."

"And I wanted to tell you that though I know it was a role, the way you were as Father Flanagan—the warmth and loving and caring I felt—was a major influence on my decision to enter the ministry."

When Bobs Watson recalled the encounter in 1991, he had been a Methodist minister for twenty-two years. "I could tell that he was very moved, that it made a profound impact on him." Had he gone through channels, Watson would never have gotten on the set, as Hepburn routinely discouraged guests. "I was going to go visit him," Jean Simmons said, "and I was told that it was better not to because he was not well. I should have insisted, and I regret that I didn't." A. C. Lyles, who was based nearby at Paramount, called and Kramer asked that he delay his visit. "Please wait until we call you," he said.

Hepburn was busy crafting her own performance while seeing to Tracy's health and well-being, knowing he could suffer a serious setback at any time, delaying the picture or shutting it down entirely. "She was under more pressure than anybody," said Katharine Houghton. "To see the love of your life fading before your eyes—she was *extremely* tense through the whole picture."

As bossy and insufferable as she could be under normal circumstances, Kate grew even more controlling as the film progressed, desperate to see Tracy through what would likely be his final role. "One night—it was a Saturday night—I said I was going to go out with friends," Houghton remembered.

She absolutely hit the ceiling. I can understand she might be worried that I'd get in a car accident or something, but it was also an extraordinary way to behave to a younger woman who was in her twenties. If I had been in my teens, I could see her saying, "Who is it?" and "Where are you going?" But she also knew me well enough by now to know that I was not a drinker or high-liver. I certainly wasn't going to jeopardize my work. I was very, very disciplined. So she blew the whole thing up into a great brouhaha that then became *Spencer* was angry with me. Phyllis Wilbourn called and said, "Your aunt is very upset with you. And not only that—Mr. Tracy is very upset with you." That really bothered me, because I didn't want him to be angry with me.

Before I went out with my friends, I stopped at the house and she came to the kitchen door. I said, "I want to speak to Spencer." She said, "You can't. He's in bed." As if I'd killed him. I said, "Well, I'm going into the bedroom." So I walked into the bedroom, and there he was in bed with his pajamas on. I was very upset, and I sat down by his bed and I said to him, "Spencer, I don't want you to be angry with me. I'm sorry that I caused all of this trouble, but I'm just going out with my friends. We're going to dinner at one of their homes in Pacific Palisades. They're very nice people, and they don't misbehave. They don't do drugs." (I didn't say "drink" because I didn't want to offend him.) "I'll be back early . . . " He said to me, "Don't worry about it, Little Kath. Your aunt is just a big fuss."

He knew her game, but I think she also *had* gotten him upset. I think she had gotten him into a kind of *How dare she?* frame of mind. Then Kate lit into me later: "Spencer thinks you're the most ungrateful person in the world. Here I have done all of this for you and you're so ungrateful." Her way of talking to me was one of the reasons I left Hollywood soon after the film was over. It did not impress me as the right way to behave. If she was doing that to me, I have to assume that she did it to other people, and maybe, to a certain extent, she was manipulative with him too.* After that, he seemed to forget about it, but she hung onto it. And she told me persistently, and other people too, that Spencer didn't like me. And I don't believe that was true. I don't know that he had any wild feelings about me one way or the other. There was never any unpleasantness between us. He was always very good to me, always very protective of me.

The element of the film that concerned Tracy the most was the climactic speech he had to make to the assembled members of the Drayton and Prentice families. With stage directions, it took up nearly five single-spaced pages in the script. He brooded over it, practicing the scene around the house. One

* Houghton recalled her mother's warning when she left for Los Angeles: "Watch out for Kate—she'll knock you down so that she can pick you up."

evening, when Katharine Houghton was sitting with him at St. Ives, he turned to her and started to tell her something. "The moment I walked into this house this afternoon, Miss Binks said to me, 'Well, all hell's done broke loose now.' I asked her, naturally enough, to what she referred, and she said, 'You'll see.' And I did. After some preliminary guessing games, at which I was never very good, it was explained to me by my daughter that she intended to get married . . ." At first Houghton thought he was talking about Susie, and then it dawned on her that he was speaking to her in character.

Kramer knew he couldn't possibly shoot Matt's statement in one continuous take. "But," he said,

> it was the summation of everything he felt. What everybody else felt. What they should feel. Et cetera, et cetera. "And don't interrupt me!" That sort of thing. So it had to be made to *feel* like one. My own experience as an editor helped some, because I broke it into five sections, so that he only had to do one page per day. Maybe one day was one-and-a-quarter pages and the next day was three-quarters, depending upon where it ended. But it always ended on a turn and an exit, so that it could be picked up on the next day. Or on a close-up, so it could drop back to a [wider] shot the next day. And it was all plotted out, rehearsed, reviewed with him how he would do it. And he was such a consummate artist that it [just felt] as one.

Kramer scheduled a private rehearsal—only the two of them and Marshall Schlom—for Saturday, May 6. There would then be a full rehearsal with the cast on Monday morning. Then the actual filming of the scene would begin, five days in all.

Tracy worked as usual on May 4, then was caught short of breath while Kate was still at the studio. "He was sitting in a chair hyperventilating," Dr. Covel remembered. "Over-breathing out of anxiety." He had no call for Friday, and Hepburn thought it best to forgo the Saturday rehearsal Kramer had scheduled. The rehearsal for Monday had to be scratched as well, and Kramer was forced to substitute a San Francisco bar scene with Poitier and Houghton for Tuesday's scheduled work on the summation.

In a letter to a journalist, George Glass described the on-the-set situation as "tenser than tense." There was a terrific sense of relief when Tracy reappeared on Wednesday morning and work on the sequence could finally begin. The company was now five days behind schedule, but Kramer could see no way of picking up speed without exacerbating Tracy's latent anxieties and risking the completion of the picture. The actors took their positions, and, after some preliminaries, Tracy began his oration:

MATT

I have a few things to say and you just might
think they're important. This has been a very
strange day—I don't think that's putting it
too strongly. I might even say it's been an
extraordinary day . . .

The first day's work was completed at 11:45 and Tracy went home to nap
as he did on Thursday and Friday, working for the week a total of six hours
and ten minutes. On Monday it took another two hours for Tracy to work
up to the point where, on Tuesday, the fifth day, he could make one of the
most affecting speeches of his life. His call, as usual, was for ten o'clock, but
Kramer, in concert with Bill Rose, had eliminated the last scene in the
script, where the families gather at the airport to see John and Joey off to
Geneva. This would be it—the end of the picture—and it couldn't be done
in the space of two hours. Tracy, for the last time on *Guess Who's Coming to
Dinner,* would work a full day.

Told by Mrs. Prentice, in a previous scene, that he has forgotten it all,
forgotten what true passion is, Matt has remained out in the night air, pondering what she has said, what Christina has said, what John and Joey have
said, and attempting to square it all with his own values and beliefs. Rose's
screenplay called for Matt to show fierce intensity, to shake his head, to register uncertainty, doubt, anxiety.

Now he stands staring vacantly up into the
night at where, when he was a boy, Heaven
was said to be. His glance moves slowly but
with the speed of light from star to star as he
recalls exactly what it was like to love
Christina as he first loved Christina. And it's
true: he <u>had</u> forgotten, and he knows it. He
stands there, and his expression now reveals
a kind of astonished wonder. He seems
stunned. Quietly, but aloud:

MATT

I'll be a son of a bitch . . .

Tracy had dispensed with the tics and grimaces called for in the text,
giving the audience a clean slate on which to overlay the character's
thoughts and transitions. Now he would give voice to his convictions and
pay tribute to the woman who had made herself an indispensable part of his

life for more than a quarter century. "And here I came to visit that particular day," said Karen Kramer. "Kate came up to me: 'You must be very quiet—Spence is working.' I said, 'Kate, I've been in the business many years. I'm not going to speak, so don't worry about it.' 'All right,' she said, 'but you've got to be quiet to stay. This is a very important part of the picture.' She was being a director. Spencer would just look and roll his eyes."

Seated next to Roy Glenn, Sr., a veteran of previous films with Sidney Poitier and the *Amos 'n Andy* TV series, Tracy began:

MATT

Now Mr. Prentice, clearly a most reasonable
man, says that he has no wish to offend me
and wants to know if I'm some kind of *nut*.
And Mrs. Prentice says, like her husband,
I'm a burnt-out old shell of a man who can't
even *remember* what it's like to love a woman
the way her son loves my daughter . . .

There were breaks throughout the day, during which Tracy rested. "Our reaction shots were done without him, at least mine were," said Katharine Houghton. "I vividly remember pretending like mad that I was watching and listening to him." Kramer plotted Tracy's movements around the room as if choreographing a dance number, the goal being to position Hepburn in the shot at significant moments, Spence, appropriately enough, in the foreground, Kate, eyes glistening, in the soft focus of the background.

Tracy continued when filming resumed:

And strange as it seems, that's the first
statement anybody's made to me all day on
which I'm prepared to take issue. Because I
think you're wrong. You're as wrong as you
can be. I admit that I hadn't considered it.
Hadn't even thought about it. But I know
exactly what he feels for her, and there is
nothing—absolutely nothing—that your
son feels for my daughter . . . that I didn't
feel for Christina. Old? Yes. Burnt out?
Certainly. But I can tell you the memories
are still there—clear . . . intact . . .
indestructible. And they'll still be there if I
live to be a hundred and ten. Where John
made his mistake, I think, was attaching so

> much importance to what her mother and I
> might think. Because in the last analysis it
> doesn't matter a damn what we think. The
> only thing that matters is what they feel, and
> how *much* they feel . . . for each other. And
> if it's *half* of what we felt . . . that's
> everything.

The catch in his voice was as genuine as anything he ever displayed on the screen, and, by all accounts, Kate's tears were just as real. "It was a superb, moving, and flawless performance," wrote Charles Champlin, the columnist and film critic for the *Los Angeles Times,* who had been allowed on the set to watch, "and when at last Stanley Kramer, gently enough, said, 'Cut,' there was a burst of applause."

Kramer captured reaction shots of them both, Kate, her lips quivering, Spence, smiling warmly, contentedly, back at her, and then the company broke for lunch. The afternoon was a long one, more resolution, a benediction of sorts for the two lovers soon to be off on their new life together. "Every person on that sound stage that afternoon became engrossed with Spencer Tracy's character as that remarkable actor did his job," Sidney Poitier wrote. "With unbelievable skill and finesse he dotted his i's and flicked his commas, and hit his periods, and touched down lightly on his conjunctions on his way to making magic. We, his fellow actors in the scene, began falling under his spell until he had succeeded in converting all of us, one by one, into a single, captivated audience."

At the conclusion of the scene, Christina marches forward and gives her husband a firm shake of the hand, a wry, congratulatory gesture for finally coming to his senses, another Tracy-Hepburn fade-out based on restraint and good sense, as any other actress on the screen would have tearfully thrown her arms around him and bawled like a baby. "They didn't need to embrace," Kramer later explained. "They never did embrace. They needed only to have the foundation of something that was very special. That's what you look for in your life all the time. They had it. Whether they had it in real life and in their performance is almost beside the point. They had it."

"They must have been very relieved when that scene was finished," Katharine Houghton said. "It was the end of the film, most likely Tracy's last film, and maybe even his last days. Everyone on the set knew he was ill, but I'm not sure they knew *how* ill. Kate knew. Kramer knew. I knew—just exactly what was at stake. After Spencer's monologue the atmosphere on set was very emotional, but not entirely celebratory because one couldn't help but think ahead and dread what was soon to come."

At the end of the day, Tracy put his arm around Kramer: "You know,

Kiddo, if I die on the way home tonight, you are all right. You can release the picture because my scenes are finished, and you don't need me for these last three days."

The pressure was off. He had done it.

The cast came together again on May 19, Tracy and Hepburn making the scenes that would surround a little self-standing vignette in which the Draytons go out for ice cream and Matt backs into the souped-up jalopy of a belligerent black kid. Scene 73 showed their return to the house. Tracy was required to mount the stairs, turn, and deliver a furious tirade to Hepburn, then continue up the staircase to the second floor. Kramer wanted to see if Tracy could manage the entire scene in one continuous take, but it was soon apparent that he lacked the breath for it. "After one step," said Marshall Schlom, "he was huffing and puffing."

Dorothy Gopadze—the venerated Miss G. of Tracy's M-G-M days—had been waiting for a good time to bring her fourteen-year-old daughter to the studio. "He didn't know we were on the set," said Tina Gopadze. "He was so ill . . . Miss Hepburn sent word over to us: 'Don't let him see you.' "

It was a grueling morning. Finally, Kramer broke up the scene, parceling it so that Tracy could deliver his lines in a medium shot without any climbing. "He came off and he was shaking," said Tina.

> And then he looked at Mom and his eyes got wider and wider, and he started tearing up. He said, "Well! Funny thing your being here!" She said, "This is my daughter Tina." He looked at me and said, "*You're* the reason I lost Miss G.!" We all sat down on that set overlooking San Francisco, and it was with Mr. Poitier and Katharine Houghton and Miss Hepburn and Mr. Tracy. He and Mom talked a little bit. In the meantime, Miss Hepburn turned to me and said, "Don't ever drink. Don't ever smoke. You have to have a wonderful exemplary attitude. Do you play sports?" I said, "Yes, I do. I play tennis." She said, "Good. Don't end up like your mother by drinking and smoking. Your mother's a wonderful person, but *you* must never do these things." Mr. Tracy didn't say anything, but he kept glancing over at me . . . They were done shooting for the day, and he wasn't feeling well.

On Saturday he again suffered shortness of breath. ("There are all kinds of scripts for these episodes, either real or anxiety or heart failure," Dr. Covel commented. "You can't be certain.") It was good for him to have Sunday to rest up.

On Monday, May 22, Tracy and Hepburn began the ice cream sequence on Columbia's Stage 8 using the process plates made in San Francisco. "I rehearsed the ice cream eating scene with [Alexandra Hay]," Kate said, "because she had never done anything. I didn't want her to blow when she was suddenly playing with Spencer. People got terrified, because they had this curious feeling that they were into something that was far different from just actor to actor. It was deep, exciting. And their minds went."

Later came the most basic of all process shots—a driving scene in a breakaway car. In the script, Matt is still boiling from an angry encounter at the drive-in.

> MATT
> What the hell is it today? Less than twelve
> percent of the people in this city are colored
> people, and I can't even have a dish of Oregon
> Boysenberry Sherbert without running into one!

"I remember we shot the scene several times," said Marshall Schlom, "and as many times as he wanted to, he purposely mispronounced the name—for fun, of course. I think the flavor's name had a ring to it that he loved, and he had a ball rolling the syllables around in his mouth . . . I remember sitting at dailies watching the scene several times, and I detected an ever-so-slight mispronunciation each time." The version Kramer chose to use had Matt angrily pounding the steering wheel and substituting "Boozenberry" for "Boysenberry." The next day, the two scenes with Hay were completed without incident.

On Wednesday, May 24, D'Urville Martin, as Frankie, the kid with the roadster, played his scene with Tracy, again on the process stage. "I rehearsed quite a bit with Stanley Kramer," Martin recalled.

> In his trailer, in his office . . . [Then] I rehearsed with Spencer Tracy. We rehearsed over and over and over. This little scene! And finally Kramer said to me, "You're not going to do it like that, are you?" I said, "No, I'm waiting to do it for the cameras." He said, "Okay, let's roll the cameras." Then he told me, "Look, for the first take, I want you to be really vicious, mean, cold, selfish." And I was!
>   Tracy reacted to the way that I did it. His face turned red, and he came back so *real,* so angry and violent, that it scared me. I thought maybe he was going to have a heart attack . . . In between takes, Katharine would go over to him, straighten his tie, tuck in his shirt. She was always doing that kind of thing to him between takes—brushing his hair—and he was always saying, "Awwww,

(SUSIE TRACY)

shucks!" You know, like a big kid in a Jackie Cooper movie. He'd say, "Leave me alone!" But he wouldn't mean it.

One thing they did for me that I noticed they did for everybody on that set. [Martin had requested—and received—permission to observe on the set and was there every day.] No matter how big or how small, they treated everybody on that set as if they were the star. They made *me* feel that I was the greatest actor in the world. I mean, between takes they would compliment me and tell me how fantastic I was. The two of them . . . I noticed the patience that they had with all the other actors, like Cecil Kellaway. He only had a few lines in one scene, and they must have made about thirty takes just to get those few lines out right. They always encouraged him, and they were always patient, and they were always sort of festive, and they made him feel good. They made *everybody* feel as if they were the greatest thing since the wheel.

On Tracy's final day on the picture, he was in at ten and finished at ten minutes to twelve.

"How much will it cost to have it repaired?" he asked the kid with the roadster.

"Well look at it!" Martin shouted. "Thirty or forty bucks it'll cost! Did you see it? Stupid old man! You oughtn't be allowed out! You ought to be put away someplace—in a home or something!"

"Here!" Tracy returned savagely, stuffing a crumpled bill into Martin's hand. "There's fifty bucks! Don't bother to have the thing fixed—buy a new one!!"

When Stanley Kramer called, "Cut!" and then "Print!," Ivan Volkman, Kramer's production manager, stepped onto the set and addressed the crew. "Ladies and gentlemen," he announced, "that was Mr. Tracy's last shot." The applause was instantaneous, vigorous. Tracy and Kramer met at the camera and embraced, the crew's applause sweeping over them in waves. No one could have mistaken the weight of the moment. A career that had stretched nearly half a century—from the dusty wings of the long-demolished Palace Theatre in White Plains to the golden heyday of Metro-Goldwyn-Mayer, from Boys Town and San Francisco to Black Rock and Nuremberg—had drawn to a close. Tracy shook hands with Sam Leavitt, waved to Marshall Schlom, and slowly made his way to the stage door. At the doorway, he stopped, the applause still rumbling, waved, and then turned and exited.

When the door closed behind him and the clapping died down, Kramer said, "That's the last time you'll ever see Spencer Tracy on film." And Kate, who, during the shot, had been crouching to one side of the camera, lit into him, a white-hot flash of anger. "[T]hat made me wild," she said. "I thought that was a silly thing to say. And I said to Stanley, 'Why? You know?' And poor Stanley was very upset. I attacked him."

That morning Hepburn had handed Marshall Schlom an envelope. He pocketed it, didn't open it until they had finished work for the day. Inside were a check for one hundred dollars and a handwritten note:

> *Dear Marshall*
>
> > *With thanks and thanks and more thanks—for doing my duties—please get something you want— you deserve it—*
> >
> > > *With affectionate gratitude from us both—*
> > > *ST and KH*

That evening a party for the cast and crew was held on Stage 8. "The party, accordingly, had a valedictory tone," Charles Champlin wrote, "and there were lumps in the throat and tears which the good food and drink couldn't set aside." Hepburn explained Tracy's absence by saying, "He gets too sentimental at things like this." Kramer was uncharacteristically emotional, at one point on the verge of tears: "Have you ever seen an era end? Tracy was originally a legit actor, but he has become the greatest 'movie actor.' When I go out, I'd like to go out like he did."

Kate addressed the crowd, paying tribute to Kramer and to the people behind the scenes. "You are the people who make an actor able to act," she told them. "I don't know how many of you realize that. But I shall be everlastingly grateful to you. I know that your help made a helluva lot of difference to Spence."

Tracy, meanwhile, was home working the phone, elated, relieved, and a little surprised by it all. "Finished!" he cried as Garson Kanin came on the line. "Do you believe it? *I* don't. I was betting against myself all the way. I owe me a fortune. I may welch. But *finished.* Are you impressed?"

"No," Gar replied. "What impressed me was you *starting.*"

"I get it," he said. "Everybody's down at the party. Both Kathies—everybody."

"Why not you?"

"Hell, no. Too emotional. This is it. The Big Wrap-Up. I've retired."

"You should have gone to the party."

"I thought I might, but then right after the last shot today, Stanley said, 'That's the one!' and I knew it was over and we shook hands and he started to cry and so did I, and I figured the hell with it and came home. I think I've got about five beers in me! But did you hear me, Jasper? I finished the picture!"

"He was very pleased," said Louise. "He was very funny [when he came around] the next day. We were all sitting around talking about finishing it, and he said, 'I told Stanley if I died tomorrow he had the picture. He had enough.' He didn't think there would be any retakes. He said, 'He's got the whole thing.' He said, 'I didn't think I would make it.' He pulled out a wad of bills and he said, 'There. I've gotten my first payment.' He gave us all a nice fat bill. 'There,' he said. He was very tired."

And so he settled back into his cloistered existence in the cottage on St. Ives, still tossing and turning and struggling to sleep. "No bunk—no makeup—no over-interest in clothes—only a few rather pathetic personal treasures," Kate would later write. "His Carrara marble Madonna made for him and given to him by the carvers at Carrara—a book signed, given to him by Bob Kennedy—a little silver orchestra given to him by Stanley Kramer—'May your music play on and on'—an old tweed coat—a comfortable pair of shoes—an old hat given to him by Jack Ford—his chair—his car—his few dear friends. He was like a lion in a cage. You gave him meat, he ate the meat. You gave him water, he drank the water and then he walked up and down, up and down in the cage of life, looking out, and in those eyes you saw the jungle—the freedom—the fear—the affection—unblinking, unguarded."

On May 27, Dr. Covel found him "depressed and very anxious" because of recurrent episodes of shortness of breath. "He was very anxious about that: Why was this happening?" He was better over Memorial Day, seemed to be regaining some strength. At the behest of a news magazine, he was asked to confirm his retirement. "Well," he hedged, "there was a fellow named Eddie Leonard on the stage and he made 471 curtain speeches announcing his retirement. Sarah Bernhardt made 178 curtain speeches announcing her retirement. I always announce my retirement—until the next picture comes along."

He was anxious and short of breath again on June 6, and there was a mounting sense of dread about him, as the attacks were coming with greater frequency. He was "all right and stable" by the eighth, but the doctor was concerned: "I went to see him, and I was thinking of taking him to the hospital . . . He didn't want to go." The doctor's note in his file that day: "We'll wait."

He visited Tower Road again on the morning of the ninth, driving himself in his old T-bird, the top down, his ever-present sunglasses giving him a jaunty look he rarely affected on screen. "He would wear—even on the warmest days—a shirt, a sweater, and a jacket," Susie said, "and I wondered if that was to make him look a little heavier." He seemed fine, stayed for about an hour. Susie told him a friend in Australia had written a script and asked if he would read it when he had some time. "Oh, sure," he said. "Give it to me now." Bill Self was reading it, she told him, and she would have to get it back. "Well, when he's done with it," her father said.

They all walked outside, stood at the car and chatted. Louise kissed him on the cheek, and he told her that he would call her later. Louise, John, and Susie took in an unlikely double feature that night: *The Dirty Dozen*—action John could easily follow—and *Georgy Girl*. The second phone in Louise's bedroom—the hot line between the hill and St. Ives—rang when they got home, the familiar signal—two rings and then silence. "Sometimes he would carry on long, long conversations," Louise said. "Other times it would be just 'How is everybody?' and 'How is everything?' and 'Well, all right, talk to you later.' " On that night he said: "I'll talk to you tomorrow, Weezie."

He went to sleep, and when Kate thought him settled, she crept out of the room as she always did and down the long hall to her own bedroom at the opposite end of the house. He had the buzzer right next to his bed if he wanted anything, and she always took the bell with her if she went anywhere inside, its cord "two miles long." He didn't ring, but about three o'clock she heard him shuffling down the hall toward the kitchen. They always kept the kettle at a very low boil, and he would get up in the middle of the night and brew himself a cup of tea. When she heard that he had reached the kitchen, she got up, put on her slippers, and started for the door.

"Just as I was about to give it a push, there was the sound of a cup smashing to the floor—then clump—a loud clump." He had arrested; his heart had stopped beating. "Just stopped—BANG! The box broke. The container had just become too small for all that—what would you call it?— all that wild stuff whirling around inside. Peace at last."

She crouched down and took him up in her arms. "No life—no pulse—dead." His eyes were closed, the tea spilled all over him. "Dear, dear friend—gone. Oh, lucky one. That's the way to exit. Just out the door and—gone."

She called Phyllis Wilbourn up at the old Barrymore place. "Spence's dead."

"I'll come . . ."

She called Ida and Willie, who lived in the cottage next door, and they helped her get him onto a rug, and then the three of them dragged him the length of the house and managed to get him back into bed. She drew up the covers and then lit some candles. "He looked so happy to be done with living, which for all his accomplishments had been a frightful burden to him."

Dr. Covel was the first to arrive. He found Kate in a state of shock, unsure of what to do next. "Call the family? Call Stanley Kramer? Move out—no—yes—then call. Phyllis came. We moved all my stuff—clothes, personal stuff—out into my car. Then I thought—God—God—Kath— what are you doing—you've lived with the man for almost thirty years. This is your home. Isn't it? These walls—this roof—this spot on the earth." Calmly, deliberately, she unloaded the car—clothing, personal effects, paintings off the walls—and carried everything back into the house.

And then she awaited the arrival of Louise Tracy.

When the phone rang on Tower Road, Susie Tracy glanced at the clock: 3:50 a.m. She reached for the extension, but her mother, in her own room, had already picked up. Susie heard Dr. Covel's voice: "Hello? Louise?" And she heard her mother say, "Oh no—" She placed the handset back in its cradle and got out of bed. When she reached her mother's room, Louise was sitting on the edge of the bed in a kind of a daze. "Father's gone," she said. "We'll have to wake John."

By 4:30 they had gotten themselves together and left for St. Ives, Susie piloting her mother's black Lincoln, the one her father had driven across country, all three of them crammed together in the front seat. When they arrived at the house, the gate was open and Susie pulled right in. Kate emerged from inside to meet them, putting her arm around Susie, who, in turn, automatically put her arm around Kate.

Susie thought back to a phone conversation she had with her father in which he had said that the Kramers were expecting a baby. They had decided, he told her, to name it Spencer if it was a boy, Katharine if it turned out to be a girl. There was a pause, as if he needed a reaction. "That's wonderful, Daddy. I think that's fine." There seemed to be so much unsaid, hanging there in the air. "He was acknowledging that I knew about Kate," she later said, "and that he knew I knew. I was so pleased . . . I felt it was the beginning of a new relationship for us. I was an adult, and he was opening a door."

Carroll, distraught and unshaven, was already there, as was Dorothy, and George Cukor was lingering in the background. Louise, Susie, and John made their way to the bedroom, the candles still flickering in the predawn darkness. He had said that he was going to have his hair cut short, but they hadn't yet seen it. And then Susie glanced to one side and saw all the medications lined up on the desk, two rows—at least a dozen prescriptions, probably more. Dr. Covel came in and said quietly to Louise, "Would you like me to give you something?"

When Susie emerged from the room, Kate was waiting for her. "Susie," she said, giving her the car keys, "would you take my car off the road and park it up the hill?" Susie found Hepburn's black Chrysler across the street and drove it up around the curve on St. Ives to where it could not be seen from the house. Then she returned and they again found themselves standing in the hallway, groping for words.

"We were good pals," Hepburn finally said to her.

Kate had called Howard Strickling, and they all had to wait as he drove into town from his ranch in Chino, some fifty miles to the east. She mouthed a few comforting words to John, who was stoic, stunned as they all were. Later, she approached him in the living room and offered him breakfast. Nobody else seemed particularly hungry, but John was gratefully addressing a meal of eggs, toast, and coffee when Strickling arrived. The press would have to be notified, inquiries would have to be managed. Louise accepted a cup of coffee, went back down the hall again to be with Spence. "Well," Hepburn later acknowledged, putting her own distinctive spin on the situation, "she was in a peculiar spot—no doubt about that. She could never bear to admit failure. Now he was dead. And he would never come back. She had dreamed—hoped—imagined that he would. This strange woman—me—had obviously been with him when he died."

Carroll had called Cunningham & O'Connor, a mortuary scarcely two blocks from where the Academy of Motion Picture Arts and Sciences had its headquarters. What suit to give them? Hepburn had gathered together some old clothes—gray slacks, a brown tweed jacket.

"But he was my husband," Louise protested. "I should pick out the—"

"Oh Louise," said Kate, "what difference does it make?"

Once they had gone—first the doctor, then Cukor, then Strickling, who had made all the appropriate calls, Dorothy stepped up to Phyllis and presumed to ask for the keys. "What did you say, Dorothy? The keys to this house—our house?" Dorothy was silenced by Phyllis' indignation, the stark reality of the situation having left her, for one of the few times in her adult life, completely and utterly wordless.

The next thing Susie knew, they were driving to the mortuary with Ross Evans at the wheel. Louise and she waited in the car while Carroll and Evans picked out a mahogany casket, the cost of which, along with the undertaking, would run nearly $3,000. "Well," said Louise, who was dreading an out-of-state speaking tour, "I guess I don't have to go on that trip now."

At Forest Lawn, the iconic cemetery where Clark Gable, Carole Lombard, Jean Harlow, and Irving Thalberg were interred, Louise was drawn to a private garden outside the Freedom Mausoleum, near where the ashes of Walt Disney had been placed the previous year. Gently, Ross Evans steered her away, knowing the neighborhood to be a little too pricey for the means of the Tracy estate. Around the corner they found another spot, walled in brick and gated, shown on the plot map as the Little Garden of Divine Guidance, roughly half the cost of the other location—$19,262 with bench and endowment.

The news media had the story by six that morning, and reporters began working the phones. "Some idiot called me at seven o'clock in the morning," Jean Simmons remembered, "and said, 'What is your reaction on Spencer Tracy's death?' And I just hung up. I thought: 'How awful can people be?'" Lauren Bacall was on a flight to Boston when her husband, actor Jason Robards, overheard the news from a passenger in a nearby seat. She had been one of the people he and Kate had called the week they finished the picture. Karen and Stanley Kramer were in Las Vegas when Stanley heard the news from his son, Larry. Eddie Dmytryk had spoken to Tracy just the previous week. "I'm not feeling up to par," Tracy had confided.

The news was all over the radio by midmorning, and calls began to come into the house on Tower Road, where the housekeeper fended off strangers and deflected nosy inquiries from the press. Strickling had fed his contacts the story that Tracy had been alone at the time of his death, that he had, in fact, died in his sleep. His body was discovered at six in the morning by Ida Gheczy, who first summoned Dr. Covel, then Carroll Tracy, the actor's brother. Arriving shortly thereafter was Mrs. Tracy, who lived nearby, accompanied by their son and daughter. Katharine Hepburn, Mr. Tracy's longtime friend and costar, appeared with director George Cukor, who for years had rented the hillside house to the two-time Academy Award winner.

Stanley Kramer told the *Los Angeles Times* that he "worshiped" Mr. Tracy. "I'm glad for his sake that he could make the picture. It was better than sitting at home. That wasn't his way." The *New York Times* described him as "one of the last screen titans of a generation, a star whose name alone spelled money at the box office." Bob Thomas, in his AP dispatch, wrote: "The death of Tracy erases from the Hollywood scene a performer whom most other actors considered the best in American film history." James Powers, in the *Hollywood Reporter,* characterized him as "a man of pure metal in a tinsel community." The *Freeport Journal Standard* remembered that, as a boy, Tracy had spent his summers in Freeport and that both his parents were buried there.

In Evergreen Park, outside of Chicago, where he was appearing with his wife in *Holiday for Lovers,* Pat O'Brien told the *Milwaukee Journal* he was "in a state of shock all day" after getting the news. "We were friends for 50 years," he reminisced. "We were at Marquette High together, we enlisted in the Navy together in World War I, and we were roommates in New York when we were attending the American Academy of Dramatic Arts. The only time we weren't together was college. Spence went to Ripon and got interested in dramatics there. He played a little baseball. I went to Marquette and was Red Dunn's substitute on the football team."

Obituaries appeared worldwide. The *Times* of London saw Tracy as "[t]ough, honest, and indomitable, a man of sober authority and rugged good sense" who became "a symbol on the screen of all those qualities which represented the pioneering spirit of America." The *Daily Telegraph* appropriated Maximilian Schell's "grand old man" appellation, while *News of the World* reported that he had outlived most of his contemporaries. "Bogart, Clark Gable, Gary Cooper are all dead," Tracy was quoted as saying. "Jimmy Cagney has taken his millions off to retire and I'm alone. It gets lonely."

And in Moscow, the Soviet director Sergei Gerasimov, writing in the government newspaper *Izvestia,* eulogized him as one of the great artists of the modern cinema. "By remaining true to himself, Spencer Tracy opened for many persons the best traits of his people . . . Soviet audiences came to love him for his manly sincerity, his just, kind, and somewhat sad view on the intricate world around him."

CHAPTER 34

A Humble Man

The last time she saw him was in profile. He was laid out in an open casket for the Rosary on Sunday night. His strong Irish face had diminished with the years, the thick brown hair of his youth now white and closely cropped. Both Susie and Louise remarked on how much better he looked than he had the previous morning. Had the mortician touched him up? Given him the coating of base he had tried to avoid his entire professional life? The scene seemed surreal, formal, quiet, and airless, not at all like Knocko Minihan's wake, where he might have been more at home, Jimmy Gleason greeting the guests, Ed Brophy, Frank McHugh, and Wally Ford mingling among them, keeping the liquor flowing and passing the hat for the widow. There were a lot of flowers on display, bushels of them, and Dorothy went around checking the tags. On some of the arrangements the tags had been removed, and she found later that these were the tributes Katharine Hepburn had sent. Earlier, Kate had come to the vigil and she had placed a little painting of flowers under his feet.

The priest led the mourners in prayer for the soul of the departed, candles flanking the casket, a gold crucifix on display. After the service he approached Louise and Susie and said that they could either take the cross with them or have it placed in the coffin. Louise deferred to her daughter, who thought for a moment and then said that she thought it would be nice if it went into the box with him. Kate returned later that night, after the vigil had ended, and wanted to place "a few little tokens" in the casket. Dorothy had ordered the lid closed, and they apologized; Kate told them it really didn't matter, that she would just stay for a minute. "I would have liked to have seen his face once more—but what was the difference— yesterday—today—tomorrow . . . He was gone—Dad was gone—Mother was gone."

A requiem mass was celebrated on Monday, June 12, at the Immaculate Heart of Mary Catholic Church in the East Hollywood section of Los Angeles, a decidedly working-class area of town chosen for its proximity to the cemetery. Serving as active pallbearers were George Cukor, Stanley Kramer, Bill Self, Frank Sinatra, Jimmy Stewart, John Ford, Garson Kanin, and Abe Lastfogel. Numbered among the honorary pallbearers were Edward G. Robinson, Lew Douglas, Robert Taylor, Larry Weingarten, Benny Thau, Tim Durant, R. J. Wagner, Loyal Davis, Chester Erskine, Harold Bumby, Chuck Sligh, Jack Benny, George Burns, Mike Romanoff, and Senator George Murphy. Howard Strickling, in striped pants and dark vest, escorted Louise, who appeared somewhat lost in a fog of grief. Msgr. John O'Donnell, who had served as a technical adviser on *Boys Town,* offered a simple forty-five-minute mass in which he praised the deceased as "a humble man who kept removed from the limelight." The some five hundred attendees included Gregory Peck, Leo G. Carroll, Laraine Day, Dave Chasen, Billy Grady, Robert Mitchum, and Walter Winchell. Another 250 onlookers were gathered outside.

A private graveside ceremony followed, though most of the thirty-five cars that joined the procession to Glendale were uninvited. At Forest Lawn, Strickling saw a TV truck parked on the roadway in front of the Freedom Mausoleum and directed cemetery officials to have it removed. "Nobody gets out of the car," he declared. "We're not moving until they leave!" Appropriately, the marble tablet eventually affixed to the brick wall enclosing the garden plot bore no individual names, dates, or epitaphs. It simply read TRACY.

More accolades appeared in the weeks that followed. *Newsweek* coupled its Tracy obituary with one for Dorothy Parker, who had died in a New York hotel room three days earlier. Acting? "I don't like anything about it," Tracy was quoted as saying. "But I did very well by it. I learned the trade well. It's never been very demanding. It doesn't require much brainwork. Acting is not the noblest profession in the world, but there are things lower than acting—not many, mind you, but politicians give you something to look down on from time to time."

Senator Robert F. Kennedy had a statement inserted into the *Congressional Record.* Bosley Crowther lamented Tracy's passing as breaking "one more strong and vibrant cable in the slowly crumbling bridge between

Tracy's casket is carried into the church. Active pallbearers included
James Stewart and Frank Sinatra. (PATRICIA MAHON COLLECTION)

motion pictures of this generation and the great ones of the past." Stanley
Kramer shut himself up in a room and, on an impossibly tight deadline,
wrote a remembrance for *Life* that appeared under the title "He Could
Wither You with a Glance." It began:

> I can't explain why I was never able to say to him what I wanted to
> say: that he was a great actor. Everyone else said it a thousand times
> over, but I never managed it. Once I told him I loved him. That
> came quite easily, and he believed me and was emotional about it.
> But I was afraid to say "Spencer, you're a great actor." He'd only say:
> "Now what the hell kind of thing is that to come out with?" He
> wanted to know it; he needed to know it. But he didn't want you to
> *say* it—just *think* it. And maybe that was one of the reasons he was
> a great actor. He thought and listened better than anyone in the
> history of motion pictures. A silent close-up reaction of Spencer
> Tracy said it all.

In the days following his death, Kate busied herself acknowledging the
cards and wires she had received from friends and acquaintances and
prominent strangers, all in her own hand, often on Spence's notepaper. To

A stricken Louise Tracy is escorted from the church by Howard Strickling.
(PATRICIA MAHON COLLECTION)

Justice William O. Douglas she wrote of how she was always trying to hold
him up as a fine example of a walker, "[b]ut I must say it didn't have much
effect." To Joan Blondell: "What can one say—He was such a delicious +
remarkable man + actor—I was lucky to be around him for so long." To
Anne Pearce Kramer: "He was really a unique creature, Spencer + I was
lucky to be the one—So I try to think of that + I am glad he did not have a
humiliating half alive time—just stopped." To Jack Hamilton: "So there is
silence where once a delicious Irish wit sparkled my days with laughter and
tears—It seems incredible doesn't it—I did not realize about death—the
end—the absolute end—This roadblock will never be removed. Now we
will see how much character I really have."

Dorothy Gopadze wrote of her gratitude when her daughter was permitted to visit the set of *Guess Who's Coming to Dinner.* "Do you remember
A Guy Named Joe? I'd like to think of Mr. Tracy prowling around Heaven
right this minute, telling the Archangel Gabriel he expects him to be better
organized."

From London, Vivien Leigh wired, "DEAREST GIRL MY WHOLE
HEART IS WITH YOU." And then a week later: "I am blinded with sorrow for you . . ." Three weeks after writing that note, Leigh herself was dead
of tuberculosis at the age of fifty-three.

From San Francisco, Joe Cohn wrote of the "wholehearted devotion,
care, and companionship" that Kate had given Spence. "Because of this you
made his life a <u>much</u> richer one—far too many people are so unfortunate
they never encounter this in their entire lives. I hope the realization of this
and the awareness that you were <u>never</u> found wanting when he needed you

will in some measure ease the loss of a truly magnificent person and a rare rare companion."

She responded: "Your letter was so touching and I am so grateful to you for making me feel happy about myself—I just really loved Spence—he—well I said to him just the other day—You know my friend—you just get to me—And he did—I was lucky—And he just wasn't a bore was he—such a unique slant—so funny—He was so pleased to get your wire at the beginning of the picture—And he did a fine job—& finished it—But I think Joe—he was tired out—he'd led quite a life—And his heart just stopped—He was getting a cup of tea in the kitchen at 3 AM as he often did—& I was just coming through the door to help him—when—& it was the end—no struggle—no terror—just end."

The estate was valued at $1,049,675, of which $226,526 was in cash, the rest in assets. The house on Tower Road was appraised at $200,000, but Tracy's personal effects and property were worth just $1,880. Carroll inherited almost everything in the house on St. Ives, along with Spence's 1958 and 1961 Thunderbirds. Once all claims and expenses had been paid, the final valuation of the estate was $664,147. Louise claimed half pursuant to the terms of the will and half by virtue of her community property interest. A trust for John and Susie was established in March 1968, and for the period 1968–70 it received a total of $46,000 from the estate. John benefited separately from a trust established by his maternal grandfather, Allienne Treadwell, which included shares in the family newspaper business.

Carroll Tracy felt lost without his brother, who had been his employer and benefactor since 1933. He and Dorothy settled into a much quieter life in their apartment on Spalding Drive, and it was there that he suffered an even greater blow when his wife died on Christmas morning, 1967.

"It was a terrible shock," he wrote Kate. "Went to mass Xmas eve came home after stopping for dinner. Had a pleasant evening. Said the angina pains were bad but would not call a doctor. Next morning I walked in [the] room and it was all over. I knew she had not been feeling well for some time. She was so tired and had lost interest in so many things. All the doctors said nothing could have been done. She would never tell me when she felt bad."

Carroll vacated the apartment and told Bertha Calhoun in a letter that he would never go home again. He lived in a hotel for as long as he could, but within a year of Dorothy's death he was in a rest home in Santa Monica. Louise worked diligently to have him in a good place—and under some Medicare—but there was a huge bill to be paid, and she struggled under the weight of it all.

John Tracy Clinic was closed the morning of Spencer Tracy's funeral, but it reopened to get on with the work at hand. Louise, however, was absent for several months, adjusting to the loss she had endured and answering by hand the mountain of cards and letters and donations that flowed in. When she returned, the clinic launched a $3 million growth campaign, starting with a $100,000 gift from the Disney Foundation. In its twenty-fifth year, John Tracy Clinic's work was spread across ninety-four countries in fifteen languages. In 1972, at the age of seventy-five, Louise agreed to a series of interviews with freelance journalist Jane Ardmore, who had the notion of ghosting an autobiography. Louise saw it as a chance to tell the clinic's story, but Ardmore knew there would have to be a lot about Spence in the book for it to find a wide audience. Howard Strickling pushed the idea, but in the end Louise put two restrictions on the project that sealed its fate. Indulging her writer's pride of long ago, she would not take a byline on a book authored by somebody else. And she would not, under any circumstances, discuss her husband's relationship with Katharine Hepburn.

Later that year, she was the guest of honor on an episode of Ralph Edwards' *This Is Your Life,* welcoming Pat O'Brien, Walter Pidgeon, Dr. Lowell, and some of the families who had come back to Los Angeles to celebrate the clinic's thirtieth anniversary. As she approached eighty, Louise grew more forgetful, and in 1974 she resigned from the board of the clinic, promising they had not yet seen the last of her. She still came in from time to time, whenever Susie could drive her, and she still spoke at graduations and special occasions. By the summer of 1977, when she was asked to give a talk in the auditorium, Susie was dubious and thought seriously of calling it off. "But as long as she was talking about the clinic," Susie said, "she was usually okay."

Susie drove her that day, not sure what was going to happen. Once her mother was in front of the group, however, a reflex kicked in, and the things that she had said so many times before—giving hope and encouragement to young families that had been wounded as hers had once been—came tumbling out. It was as if she had been asked to work the old magic one final time, just as Spence had done on the set of *Guess Who's Coming to Dinner* a decade earlier. Susie returned her to Tower Road, and by September Louise was under twenty-four-hour nursing care, her mind clouded by arteriosclerosis and at least one stroke.

She died in 1983 at the age of eighty-seven.

Stanley Kramer saw a rough cut of *Guess Who's Coming to Dinner* within days of its completion and knew he had everything he needed by June 1.

Editor Robert C. Jones had begun work on the picture with the first dailies, following Tracy's performance with an eye toward vigor as well as nuance. The early scenes of befuddlement weren't hindered by Tracy's occasional lapses of energy. "But," said Jones, "in the last twenty minutes, he had to take control of that entire group." Assembled at first for performance alone, the summation scene suffered whenever Tracy showed fatigue.

"He would run out of gas. I'd have to cut away to someone I wouldn't normally cut to [in order to] change takes on Tracy. I was going through and looking for the best takes I could find on each line—and in some cases using lines from over his shoulder and putting them into his mouth. Actors tend to be more relaxed if they're offstage, so I'd steal those lines, too . . . There would be, sometimes, wide discrepancies; he couldn't complete a sentence, couldn't think of the words . . . We also treated his voice in mixing to give it more energy."

Jones and Kramer grappled as well with a tremor Hepburn had developed, which, at times, caused her head to bobble, particularly during close-ups. Kramer would minimize the problem by discreetly calling for another take, but Jones still had to be on the lookout for it when assembling a sequence. Editing scenes that contained both Tracy and Hepburn became especially tricky, bolstering Tracy's energy level while diminishing any involuntary movements on the part of Kate. "We tried to hide it as much as possible," Jones said.

Guess Who's Coming to Dinner was scored at the Goldwyn studios over the week of September 18, 1967. Previews had demonstrated a profound impact on audiences, but Kramer knew that he was in for rough sledding, given his reputation for issues-oriented moviemaking. A true believer in film as an agent of social change, Stanley Kramer could come off as needlessly pompous in interviews where he alternately disparaged the "message" angle while embracing the notion that a truly important film had to be about something of size and weight. Pauline Kael declared open season on him in her 1965 essay "The Intentions of Stanley Kramer," a withering review of *Ship of Fools* prefaced by a snarky career overview. That Kael misunderstood Kramer's work as a producer didn't seem to matter, and her views gained traction with a generation of critics eager to tear down the shrines of their elders. Branded as hopelessly old school, Kramer was seen as simplistic and naive, a throwback to the sedate fifties when he was first making his mark.

For his part, Sidney Poitier knew that Kramer and Rose had pushed the major studio envelope as far as it would go. He had previously explored interracial romance in *A Patch of Blue,* but that film was art house fare compared to *Guess Who's Coming to Dinner,* which would have to win broad favor with the moviegoing public to justify its cost.

"How possible was it then, in 1967, to make a film like that in America? It was close to impossible," Poitier said in 2006. Early on there was criticism that he was too perfect to be realistic, that the filmmakers, in their zeal to make the dilemma about race and nothing else, had robbed him of human frailties and, in the minds of some, his blackness. Poitier, however, had to be an equal and balancing force to Tracy, to push back in a way that would have been impossible had he been a mechanic or a short-order cook. Could the average black man identify with the character of John Wade Prentice? Or was the identification, as Kramer contended, more generational than racial?

"Who says it's a story only about the black man?" Kramer demanded. "It's about young and old viewpoints, and in this case the bone of contention happens to be the acceptance of interracial marriage. But this film says that the new generation won't live like the last generation simply because that's the way it's supposed to be. Life has moved on."

Ideally, the film would appeal to older viewers as the ninth and final teaming of Spencer Tracy and Katharine Hepburn. To younger audiences, the presence of Sidney Poitier and the theme of interracial marriage would be the drawing cards, Poitier having appeared in two recent hits, *To Sir, With Love* (released June 14) and *In the Heat of the Night* (released August 2). Hepburn, eager for audiences to see Tracy's last performance, agreed to a press conference in late October, a side-by-side with her niece at the New York restaurant 21. Acknowledging she had regularly avoided the press in the past, she said brightly, "I'm getting nicer in my old age. Most people become grumpy." In tan slacks and a black turtleneck sweater, she cut a striking figure, her finely chiseled features belying even her official age of fifty-seven. In good form, she told a female reporter that her clothes were a mess and a male reporter that he was talking a lot of Freudian rot. When the subject turned to Tracy, however, her manner changed abruptly.

"I think Spencer and Laurette Taylor were the best actors I've ever seen," she said. "They were both Irish and both had problems in their lives, but they were so direct. They had concentration." As she got deeper into the subject of Tracy, her remarks veered toward intimacy and grew poignant. As an actor, she said, he was as simple and unadorned as "a baked potato." In contrast, she described herself as "a dessert, with lots of whipped cream." He had no mannerisms, she added. "He never got in his own way. I still do." She listened to a question about Tracy and then answered carefully and with some feeling: "I think Spencer always thought that acting was a rather silly way for a man to make a living. He felt he should have been a doctor or something. We both came from backgrounds totally removed from acting. But he was of such an emotional balance, you know, that he had to be an artist."

George Cukor saw *Guess Who's Coming to Dinner* at an advance screening in November and couldn't stop raving about it. "I think the film itself is one of the finest I've ever seen: human, dignified, passionate," he told Roger Ebert of the *Chicago Sun-Times*. "I believe Katharine feels the same way, and that's why she's allowing herself to be interviewed to promote it, something she almost never does. In a sense, she's doing it as an act of gratitude to Kramer, who cast Tracy in the picture even though his life was no longer insurable. It was a tremendous risk, and we must be grateful to Kramer for taking it."

Noël Coward wired Kate the moment he saw it:

HOW WONDERFUL THAT DEAR SPENCE'S LAST PERFOR-
MANCE COULD BE ONE OF THE FINEST HE HAS EVER
GIVEN WHICH IS SAYING A GREAT DEAL.

Her response: "What a wonderful, lovely looking, sensitive creature I've spent so much of my life with. I know that I am lucky—he kept me hopping and I never had time to think about myself. So—on again, alone . . ."

The trade notices were unabashedly ecstatic, *Variety* predicting "torrid b.o. response throughout a long-legged theatrical release." And while the opinions of the press were divided along predictable lines, the older generation praising the film extravagantly, the younger despising almost everything about it, Tracy's performance was singled out for praise in nearly every instance. "He and Miss Hepburn glisten with style," Robert Kotlowitz wrote in *Harper's Magazine*. "They are crusty, tough, intelligent, and sentimental, the essence of Yankeeness. Without even holding hands, they manage to suggest that they have had a bracing physical life together. Their intimacy crackles on the screen, and it is their exchanges—snapping and barking and laughing at each other—that give the film its only reality."

Tracy, Brendan Gill wrote in the *New Yorker*, gave "a faultless and, under the circumstances, heart-breaking performance . . . [B]eing aware that it was the last picture he would ever make, he turned his role into a stunning compendium of the actor's art; it was as if he were saying over our heads to generations of actors not yet born, 'Here is how to seem to listen,' 'Here is how to dominate a scene by walking away from it.' Moreover, the very words he spoke were written for him deliberately as 'last words.' " And, added Joe Morgenstern, "when Tracy gives his blessings to the lovers in a noble speech that was written as a melodrama's climax and may now serve as an artist's epitaph, when he says his say about youth and yearning and whether an old, white-haired man is necessarily a burned-out shell who can no longer remember the passion with which he has loved a woman, then everything wrong with the film is right and we can see, through our tears, that the hero we worshiped was just what we always knew he was, an authentically heroic man."

Even a skeptic as hidebound as Andrew Sarris fell under the spell of the film's final minutes, Mrs. Prentice's accusation that Drayton had forgotten true passion still ringing in his ears. "As Tracy repeats the charge to himself, Kramer shifts deliberately to a profile shot of Tracy on the left foreground of the screen and Hepburn, her eyes brimming with tears, on the right background looking at Tracy, and Tracy says no I have not forgotten, and he says it very slowly, and the two shot is sustained by a ghostly immortality, recording the rapturous rapport between a being now dead and a being still alive, but a moment of life and love passing into the darkness of death everlasting, and anyone in the audience remaining dry-eyed through this evocation of gallantry and emotional loyalty has my deepest sympathy."

One who did remain dry-eyed through that evocation of gallantry and emotional loyalty was Louise Tracy, who was given a private screening in a projection room at Columbia Pictures. With her were John and Susie, Carroll and Dorothy, her sister Eleanor, others from the extended family. Susie found her father's summation "very difficult" to watch and was concerned for her mother, but Louise remained quiet and impassive throughout. "I liked him very much," Louise said years later of her husband's final performance. "I didn't like the picture. He shouldn't have done that picture."

Columbia's ad campaign was dominated by the full-figure images of Poitier and Houghton walking arm in arm, the catch line "A love story of today" clearly putting the emphasis on Poitier and the miscegenation theme. Tracy and Hepburn were shown in subordinate positions, almost as afterthoughts. Upon its release in December 1967, *Guess Who's Coming to Dinner* was an immediate sensation, breaking the all-time single-week records at both the Victoria and the boutique Beekman in New York City. The story was the same in Los Angeles, where it promptly broke the house record at the venerable Westwood Village. Kramer flogged the film exhaustively, eventually putting in appearances on college campuses to stir up discussion and prompt word of mouth, a goal ultimately crushed by the same generational disconnect the movie depicted. There were other hit films in the marketplace—*Wait Until Dark, Valley of the Dolls, Camelot,* the upstart *Graduate*—but none dimmed the broad appeal of Kramer's now-famous gamble. In two years domestic rentals would exceed $22 million, making it the most successful picture in Columbia's history.

The film's commercial fortunes were compounded by an astounding ten Academy Award nominations, including Best Actor, Best Actress, Best Director, and Best Picture. The Tracy family attended the Oscar ceremony on April 10, 1968, at Santa Monica Civic Auditorium, with Louise planning to go up to the podium were Spence actually to win, just as she had done exactly thirty years earlier for *Captains Courageous*. In the long runup to the major prizes that evening, they saw the film shut out in nearly every category, with only William Rose scoring a win for his original story and screenplay. Hepburn took the Oscar for Best Actress, a big surprise, clearing the way for the Best Actor statuette to go to Rod Steiger for *In the Heat of the Night*. Sidney Poitier, who had starred in three smash hits that year, wasn't nominated for any of them.

Kate chose to take her award—which George Cukor accepted on her behalf—as "a nice affectionate pat on the back for us both—very touching." Sometimes, though, she privately admitted that she was "disgusted" that Tracy didn't also win an Oscar.

"I think very often about Spence," Stanley Kramer reflected in a letter. "I guess, in recent years, I never really considered a project in which he didn't participate in my thoughts. I miss so much the feeling he always gave me of a confidence in me—and how my ego really swelled when he would tell somebody how he felt about me. I really did love him. I came to him—and he to me—so late. But I never wanted to make it easier for anyone to be as great as he always was. I guess he made it seem so easy—and it isn't, God knows."

A few days after Tracy's death, the phone rang on Tower Road. The housekeeper announced that Miss Hepburn was calling, and Louise decided to take it in the privacy of the downstairs den. "You know, Louise, you and I can be friends," Kate remembered saying. "You knew him at the beginning, I at the end—or we can just pretend that—I might be a help with the kids." John and Susie were now forty-two and thirty-four, respectively.

"Well, yes," Louise said, pausing for emphasis. The razor-sharp wit she had spent a lifetime suppressing now came to the fore. After twenty-six years she finally had her husband's lover in her crosshairs, and the temptation to pull the trigger was too great to resist. "But you see, I thought you were only a *rumor* . . ."

The shot hit its mark with deadly accuracy. "After nearly thirty years?" Hepburn raged in her autobiography. "A rumor? What could be the answer to that?" Louise later told Susie that Kate had said that she would like to get to know Johnny and Susie "as an extension of Spencer." Then she added, unnecessarily, "I play tennis."

"Well," Louise said, "I'll think about it."

She was coming up the stairs as Susie emerged from her room. "Well," Louise said, a hint of admiration creeping into her voice, "that took guts."

"It was," Hepburn later wrote, "a deep and fundamental wound—

deeply set—never to be budged. Almost thirty years Spence and I had known each other—through good and bad times. Some rumor. And by never admitting that I existed—she remained—the wife—and she sent out Christmas cards. Spencer—the guilty one. She—the sufferer. And I—well now, I was brought up in a very unconventional atmosphere. And I had not broken up their marriage. That happened long before I arrived on the scene."

Hepburn came to believe that she had taken the easy road, that she had declined to force the issue, to "straighten things out," as she put it. If there had been a divorce, "then everyone—and in this case, Susie and Johnny—would have been able to know their father with me. It would have been better. But it would have had to be pushed by Louise—the loser in the situation. Yet it would, I believe, have been ennobling to her. And supremely honest. And it would have made it easy for him to do—what would in this case have been the direct and simple thing for him to do. Then he could have had the best of both worlds. And if he had felt that it was her idea, his guilt would have been removed."

But, of course, it could never have been that simple. Tracy's guilt ran far deeper than Kate could ever imagine. And Louise's paralysis was rooted in her heritage, her Victorian upbringing and her inability to work through many of the same issues she saw as an impressionable young girl in the marriage of her father and mother. "Spencer's faith, along with unbreakable bonds of an emotional sort, is what kept him married to Louise," Eugene Kennedy said. "He felt as a Catholic that he had been married, and that he could not be, as it were, un-married. That is one of the reasons Kate and Spence felt that I understood them. I appreciated what it meant to be in love and to have an institution holding terrific sway over your choices."

Hepburn eventually got to know Susie, who, at the urging of her friend Susan Moon, went up and spoke to her one morning through the chain-link fence of the tennis courts at the Beverly Hills Hotel. Kate gave her a phone number, told her to call at any time. It wasn't until October 1969 that Susie had a reason to call. "It's Carroll," Kate said immediately, knowing without being told that Spence's older brother had died. In 1975 Susie published a short piece in the *Ladies' Home Journal,* an as-told-to with Jane Ardmore called "My Friend: Katharine Hepburn." If her mother ever saw the piece, she never mentioned it, and the relationship continued after Hepburn left the house on St. Ives in April 1979 and returned permanently to New York and Connecticut. "Kate," said Katharine Houghton, "was always thrilled when Susie called or visited."

In the latter months of 1967, Hepburn busied herself with the planning of a TV special that would document Tracy's life and work. Written by Chester Erskine, the show would be all-inclusive, inviting on-camera contributions from Louise, Carroll Tracy, Joe Mankiewicz, George Cukor, the full range of family, friends, and coworkers. She got M-G-M to throw in as the producing company, furnishing the film clips, and ABC to commit a two-hour time slot. But the whole thing hinged on Louise's cooperation, and ultimately, after reading the script, she declined to participate, failing to see clearly in Erskine and Hepburn's version the man she had known longer than any of them.

Soon Hepburn was back in the swim of making movies, traveling to France to make *The Lion in Winter.* Director Anthony Harvey found her "enormously vulnerable" and said that Tracy was practically never out of her mind. "She was mad about him in every way." It was Tracy, Katharine Houghton observed, who brought out a selflessness in her. "It fulfilled something deep in her nature. Spencer, in fact, may have been surprised to observe that it was he alone, his living, breathing presence, that enabled Kate, after her father's death, to carry high that standard which she so admired—'character!' When she lost Spence, the center of her life was destroyed. And I think every year that took her farther away from him caused her life to further unravel. Their relationship seemed to me to balance both of them—a yin and a yang."

Katharine Hepburn never saw *Guess Who's Coming to Dinner,* could never bear to. Katharine Houghton saw it only after she was asked to accept the David di Donatello Award for Best Foreign Actor on Tracy's behalf in August 1968. "That last speech of Tracy's was a killer," she said. "At the award ceremony they showed the film, and afterward I was supposed to go up and make an acceptance speech. I got up to the podium and burst into tears. I couldn't say anything except, 'Thank you.' Anna Magnani threw her arms around me and said something charming like, 'In Italy we respect tears, not words. You do not have to speak.' "

On the morning of the funeral, Kate and Phyllis Wilbourn arrived at the mortuary a little after eight, intent, she later admitted to Bill Self, on following the hearse to the church and then slipping inside. They found no one there, just the hearse, and they drove up into the driveway.

"Is anyone coming?" Kate asked.

"No."

"May we help?"

"Why not?"

So they helped lift Spence into his place in the vehicle, and they shut the door. Then the hearse pulled away, out onto Melrose Avenue and east toward the church. Kate and Phyllis jumped into Kate's dependable old Chrysler and followed along after it, a miniature procession on a six-mile

journey through rush-hour traffic, at once brazen and yet proudly anonymous. Through La Cienega Boulevard they crept, east along the upper border of Larchmont Village, then past the Desilu Studios complex that
abutted Paramount. What Hepburn was thinking is anyone's guess, but her
musings must at some point have touched on Louise and how Spence was
always at pains to protect her, to keep her safe from humiliation and the
scrutiny of the press. That Kate was now contemplating the crashing of his
funeral was something he would not have wanted, no matter how heartfelt,
how necessary, such a grand gesture might have been.

Passing under the Hollywood Freeway, she turned left onto Vermont,
past Los Angeles City College and on toward Santa Monica Boulevard.
There would be a crowd of onlookers at the church, as there was for all
celebrity funerals, photographers and TV cameramen shouldering their
16mm gear, eager to run off and get their footage processed and cut for the
six o'clock news. Just how unseen could she possibly be, slipping into the
back as if no one would know her? In a practical sense, they would all be on
the lookout for her, the reporters, the freelancers, the autograph hounds for
whom no event was too sacred to work. Left at Santa Monica, doubling
back now, the Immaculate Heart of Mary six blocks ahead on the left. Of
course she wouldn't go, couldn't go. She didn't want, as she later told Bill,
any "fuss."

As the church came into view, they could see the crowds, the people
arriving, the cops managing the traffic, the pallbearers, perhaps even Louise
and the family awaiting his return. "Goodbye, friend—here's where we
leave you . . ."

And with that she tapped the brake and watched as the hearse and its
precious cargo eased away.

The Biographies of Katharine Hepburn

No fewer than twenty-five books exist on the life and career of Katharine Hepburn, and all, to varying extents, touch on her decades-long relationship with Spencer Tracy. The first major Hepburn biography, Charles Higham's *Kate* (1975), drew its strength from the author's interviews with a number of Hepburn's friends and coworkers, including Laura Harding, Larry Weingarten, and George Stevens. In writing of the "deep, overpowering love" Hepburn felt for Tracy, Higham came closest to getting it right. Later attempts were less advantaged but made more prodigious use of archival resources. Anne Edwards' *A Remarkable Woman* (1985) was thicker than the Higham book but relied more on previous books and clippings than original research and is riddled with errors. According to Edwards, Tracy's affair with Loretta Young extended into 1938, and Louise Tracy was "president" of John Tracy Clinic until her death in 1983. Edwards' source notes sometimes lead nowhere, and the heft of her book is, in part, the result of padding.

Barbara Leaming appeared to do a better job of library work in her *Katharine Hepburn* (1995) but misread the correspondence in Bloomington's John Ford Collection and proclaimed "Pappy" Ford the true love of Hepburn's life. The Ford correspondence in the Hepburn Collection at the Academy of Motion Picture Arts and Sciences shows that while Ford nursed a lifelong crush on Kate, she reciprocated with a genuine but studied fondness—probably after a brief infatuation—and was in touch with Ford's wife and kids over the decades.

Leaming's biases extend to her lurid coverage of Tracy, whom she portrays, in the words of Larry Swindell, as "a brutal whoremongering drunkard with no redeeming qualities." Leaming makes the common mistake of regarding Bill Davidson's inventions as fact when she reports that Tracy disappeared into the Hotel St. George in Brooklyn "many times through the years," his only luggage "a case of Irish whiskey." On page 308, she describes Tracy as a mean drunk "who beat up a prostitute in a bordello called Lu's," another imaginary episode lifted from Davidson. She goes on to inform the reader that *Up the River* was made by RKO and that, upon its completion, Tracy was told by studio executives to learn "something about film technique" by observing Ford at work on *Seas Beneath*—a neat trick since Tracy was appearing onstage in *The Last Mile*—first in New York, then in Chicago—during the time *Seas Beneath* was in production. On page 401, Leaming goes Davidson one better when she states that Tracy "blamed his own visits to brothels and the venereal infections he contracted there" for Johnny's deafness. There is no source given for this allegation—and one would make no difference as such an occurrence would have been a medical impossibility.

After Spencer Tracy's death in 1967, it was established conclusively that the cause of John Tracy's deafness (and eventual blindness) was type 1 Usher syndrome, a recessive disorder inherited when both parents pass the same mutated gene to a child. Spencer and Louise Tracy were both carriers, and a roll of the genetic dice resulted in John's condition—a one-in-four chance. Susie Tracy, with the same parentage, was born without Usher syndrome, meaning she did not inherit the same changed gene from both parents. Needless to say, genetic disorders cannot be caused or transmitted by "venereal infections." While it is true that syphilis can mimic the symptoms of Usher syndrome—deafness and retinal damage—the syphilis bacterium can only be passed to a child via his or her mother. If the father alone is infected and the mother is not, the child cannot be infected.

None of Spencer Tracy's confidential medical histories makes any mention of venereal disease at any time in his life. Leaming's assertion that he blamed his own "venereal infections" (note the plural) for his son's deafness is pure conjecture, unsourced and unsupported by the facts. Even so, a 2003 monodrama called *Tea at Five* insistently perpetuates this myth when the playwright puts the following words into the mouth of Katharine Hepburn: "The boy. Johnny. You see, his son was conceived when Spence unknowingly had a venereal disease. Gonorrhea." Katharine Houghton, with considerable justification, characterized the play as "trash."

A. Scott Berg's *Kate Remembered* appeared within days of Hepburn's death in 2003 and provides the best summary overview of Hepburn's life and work, framed as it is in the form of a memoir of the author's friendship with the actress. There followed three more biographies, all part of a curious subgenre pandering to an audience that apparently wants to be told that practically everyone in Old Hollywood was secretly gay. *Katharine the Great* by Darwin Porter came first in 2004, followed by James Robert Parish's *Katharine Hepburn: The Untold Story* in 2005 and William J. Mann's *Kate: The Woman Who Was Hepburn* in 2006.

While the unsourced Porter book is impossible to take seriously and the Parish is merely insinuative, the Mann book offers fifty-six pages of notes and sources, which encouraged readers and reviewers alike to embrace its wildest assertions with a minimum of skepticism. Standing almost alone in their dissents were Richard Schickel ("In the end, the book is just gossip-mongering with high-end aspirations") and John Anderson of *Newsday,* who called it "a dishy, needy book" unworthy of its subject. "Mann's style— a slightly elevated version of the journalism-as-salespitch practiced by the likes of *Entertainment Weekly*—abets his smarmy search for facts to support his claims about (1) Hepburn's sexuality (she may have had lesbian affairs with, among others, longtime companion Laura Harding); (2) what gnarled complexes really lay behind the alliance with Spencer Tracy; and (3) how much of Hepburn's image was founded in fact. But Mann's desperation to prove such points—none of which is as critical to Hepburn's ultimate cultural importance as any one of a dozen film performances—makes the experience of *Kate* rather tiresome."

Rumors accusing the pants-wearing actress of lesbianism date to the early thirties and are as venerable as the oft-whispered suspicion that Mae West was really a transvestite. To put across his thesis, Mann at the outset seeks to establish that Tracy and Hepburn never lived together, that Hepburn surrounded herself with known lesbians (making the old guilt-by-association case), and that Garson Kanin's 1971 book *Tracy and Hepburn* was a conscious and well-meaning exercise in mythology. "After seventy years," the author states in a self-aggrandizing preface, "I thought it was finally time to tell the story outside the star's control."

In having at the legend, Mann not only seeks to show that Hepburn herself was bisexual, but that, in a sort of revisionist scorched-earth policy, almost everyone around her was equally ambiguous, including Spencer Tracy. To pull that off, he must establish that Tim Durant was gay—no easy task—and that Tracy himself had assignations that could, in some form, be documented. He lards his notes with claims of thoroughness, but in Tracy's case he doesn't start off well. He cites Selden West, Larry Swindell's 1969 Tracy biography, Bill Davidson's ubiquitous hatchet job, the Wisconsin Historical Society, U.S. Census records, Milwaukee city directories, and World War I draft registrations in documenting Tracy's early life and still manages to get most of it wrong. John Tracy, for instance, was never a truck driver, and the story of his going from tavern to tavern on the night of Spencer's birth is yet another fanciful invention from Davidson. He misses the Freeport connection entirely, has Tracy slipping into a soldier's uniform in 1917, training at Norfolk rather than Great Lakes, graduating from Northwestern in 1921, and entering Ripon at the same time as Kenny Edgers. Later, he confuses Encino with the house on Tower Road, repeatedly referring to the ranch in the flatlands of the San Fernando Valley as "The Hill."

While these might all seem like little things, they go to a pattern of inaccuracy that unfortunately seems to permeate the book. The author sets up John Tracy as an emotionally distant man who "drank hard" and, in the modern cliché, "withheld praise." He notes all the standard newspaper items, the Sunset Boulevard arrest and the Yuma episode with Hugh Tully, and lays the public exploitation of "little Johnnie [*sic*] Tracy's deafness" to the M-G-M publicity machine. All this, of course, leads up to speculation as to just what the nature of Tracy's torment really was. Mann insists the relationship between Tracy and Hepburn wasn't physical and—bizarrely—cites as proof the testimony of people who never knew Tracy or observed the relationship firsthand: Gavin Lambert, James Prideaux, members of George Cukor's inner circle, and the anonymous voices that populate all books of this ilk. Finally, on page 336, he gets around to his smoking gun, a "male madam" named Scotty Bowers (coyly referred to in the text simply as "Scotty").

Bowers is full of glib stories and revelations, all cheerfully unverifiable. He claims, for example, a "long, happy association" with Vivien Leigh and another, in a *Variety* interview, with Tyrone Power. Mann devotes considerable space to establishing Bowers' credibility. ("I've never known Scotty not to tell the truth," the late Gavin Lambert is quoted as saying.) He then allows Bowers to torpedo himself with the very first statement attributed to him. Bowers describes his initial encounter with Spencer Tracy as having taken place at Cukor's home soon after the end of the war: "That was the first time, but it went on for years. *Tracy would be drinking when I arrived. He'd get so loaded. He'd sit there drinking at the table from five o'clock in the afternoon until two in the morning,* when he'd fall onto the bed and ask me to join him . . . And in the morning he'd act like nothing happened. He'd just say thanks for staying over" (emphasis added).

What Bowers obviously didn't know when he made that statement is that Tracy was completely sober from the time he was discharged from Doctors Hospital in May 1945—nearly four months before the end of the war—until well into the fifties. And, of course, he was never the guzzler Bowers portrays him to be. Later, on page 383, Bowers reappears to again assert a relationship, reputedly showing up at St. Ives sometime in 1956 while Hepburn is in the kitchen washing dishes. Tracy is once again portrayed as drinking, while Hepburn is shrewish: "She'd tell him he was a fool just to sit there and drink. She could be very cutting to him. Then she'd walk off and leave us alone to have sex."

Here, as before, it should be noted that Tracy, except for his lapses in Cuba and New York City, records no drinking in his datebooks for 1956 and 1957. Moreover, his address book, a 1952 gift from Constance Collier that he used for the rest of his life, shows no entries for Scotty Bowers, the Richfield station he managed, nor anyone under any name or identification whatsoever who could possibly have functioned in the capacity Bowers claims for himself. Such a story, in fact, asks the reader to believe that Hepburn, so famously protective of Tracy she would not even allow cast members near him on the set of *The Devil at 4 O'Clock,* would freely walk away and leave him to the company of "Cukor's friend from the gas station" so that the two of them could "have sex."

These key scenes are embroidered with comments from a handful of minor figures who present themselves as having the real dope on Tracy and Hepburn. Press agent Richard Gully, who died in 2000, is quoted from a posthumous *Vanity Fair* profile as saying that Tracy was a bisexual who was "never sober" (thus establishing he had very little—if any—real knowledge of Tracy). "I don't think he functioned as a man," Gully added. "He and Katharine Hepburn had chemistry only on screen." In nearly six years of work on this book, I have not encountered one person who actually knew both Tracy and Hepburn who would endorse such a statement. In the same article, it should be noted, Gully fingered Giancana lieutenant Johnny Roselli as the true assassin of John F. Kennedy, claimed that Cary Grant had a "fleeting crush" on him, and spoke of Danny Kaye's "love affair" with Laurence Olivier as if he knew of it firsthand—although the allegation of such a relationship was thoroughly discredited in Terry Coleman's definitive biography of the actor.

Elliot Morgan, a member of George Cukor's circle of cronies and acolytes known as the "chief unit," is quoted as saying, "We knew Spencer wrestled with homosexuality." Morgan goes on to suggest that Tracy and Tim Durant were lovers. "We definitely thought there was something between them." Durant was a lot of things, but to the people who knew him well he was anything but homosexual. "Jesus Christ!" erupted actor Norman Lloyd, who met Durant in 1942 and considered him a dear friend. "Tim was the envy of every man in Hollywood for all the women he had." Durant's second wife, the author Mary Durant, patterned the serial womanizer Hoyt Bentley after him in her novel *Quartet in Farewell Time.* Later, his stepdaughter, Eleanor Cooney, wrote of him in her moving account of her mother's descent into Alzheimer's, *Death in Slow Motion.* Describing him as a "charming prick," Cooney doesn't portray Durant as gay at all. Her mother, she says, "laid him bare like a frog on the dissection tray" when she painted him as "part rogue, part hungry poet, and part matinee idol" in her 1963 book.

There is no hint of homosexual activity in the Tracy papers nor in anything I have seen or learned elsewhere during the course of researching this book. There is evidence to the contrary, particularly in the Ruth Gordon–Garson Kanin papers at the Library of Congress, where Tracy repeatedly plumbs for word of Gene Tierney and June Dally-Watkins; and, of course, in his 1941 and 1942 datebooks, where he notes his times with Ingrid Bergman.

A thorough criticism of *Kate: The Woman Who Was Hepburn* will have to wait until an authorized biographer is granted access to Hepburn's journals and the correspondence still retained by her estate. Nevertheless, the book inspired a backlash from Hepburn fans, relatives, and friends who often knew the players and the situations far better than the people assigned to review it. Postings on such sites as Amazon inspired a spirited debate, into which the book's editor frequently—and defensively—waded. From New Jersey, political consultant Sherry Sauerwine circulated a compelling point-by-point rebuttal to the book that runs fifty-eight single-spaced pages.

"I've read a lot of bios through the years," Sauerwine wrote by way of introduction, "and never encountered one wherein the writer was so determined to bend the reader (let alone the subject) to his will."

Stage Chronology

R.U.R.

By Karel Čapek. English version by Paul Selver and Nigel Playfair. (Frazee Theatre, January 1, 1923.) Management: Theatre Guild. Cast: Henry Travers, Mary Bonestell, William Devereux, Percy Waram, Kathlene MacDonell, Myrtland LaVarre, Marlyn Brown, Charles Esdale, Whitford Kane, Beatrice Moreland, John Rutherford, Spencer Tracy (First Robot), Richard Coolidge, Bernard Savage, Mary Hone, Charles Ellis. Staged by Philip Moeller. Also toured.

THE WOOD PLAYERS

(Palace Theatre, White Plains, N.Y., April 16, 1923.) Manager: Leonard Wood, Jr. Company: Louise Treadwell, Ernest Woodward, Delores Graves, Frederick Hargrave, Helene Niles, Alma Powell, Charles S. Greene, Fairfax Burgher, Thomas Hudson, Helen Edwards, Spencer Tracy, Valentine Winter, Edward Crandall. Director: Kendal Weston.

THE WOOD PLAYERS

(Empire Theatre, Fall River, Mass., June 13, 1923.) Manager: Leonard Wood, Jr. Company: Louise Treadwell, Thomas Williams, Delores Graves, George Simpson, Millie Beland, Jack W. Cowell, William Williams, Helen Edwards, Spencer Tracy. Director: Raymond Capp.

THE WOOD PLAYERS

(Fulton Opera House, Lancaster, Pa., July 2, 1923.) Manager: Leonard Wood, Jr. Company: Delores Graves, William Williams, Ernest Woodward, Ione Bright, Dorothy Hall, Thomas Williams, Borden Harriman, Louis Kracke, June Webster, Spencer Tracy, Helen Olcott. Director: Raymond Capp.

THE STUART WALKER STOCK COMPANY

(Cox Theatre, Cincinnati, September 10, 1923.) Manager: Stuart Walker. Company: Lucile Nikolas, Tom Powers, Clark Hoover, Judith Lowry, William H. Evarts, Edward Andreas, Norvin Gable, Agnes Horton, Spencer Tracy, Barnara Bridge, Aldrich Bowker, Ethel Downie, William Kirkland, Tom Springer, Genevieve Addleman, Charles Capehart, Boyd Agin, Wayne Huff, Regina Stanfiel. Director: Stuart Walker.

A ROYAL FANDANGO

By Zoë Akins. (Plymouth Theatre, November 12, 1923.) Management: Arthur Hopkins. Cast: Ethel Barrymore, Cyril Keightley, Jose Alessandro, Teddy Jones, Beverly Sitgreaves, Edward G. Robinson, Virginia Chauvenet, Charles Eaton, Lorna Volare, Harold Webster, Denise Corday, Walter Howe, Drake deKay, Aileen Poe, Frank Antiseri, Spencer Tracy (Holt). Staged by Arthur Hopkins. Twenty-four performances.

THE PROCTOR PLAYERS

(Proctor's Theatre, Elizabeth, N.J., December 3, 1923.) Company: Russell Hicks, Ruth Rickaby, Harry Huguenot, Olga Hanson, Charles W. Dingle, Spencer Tracy, Jessie Brink, Walter J. Winter, Joe Moran, William Gerold, Thelma Ritter, Marguerite Bishop, Joe Crehan, George Barbier, George Bylett, Harold Burnett. Director: A. J. Edwards.

THE PLAYHOUSE STOCK COMPANY

(The Playhouse Theatre, Winnipeg, January 14, 1924.) Company: Allyn Gillyn, Coates Gwynne, Jetta Geffen, Jeanette Connor, Del McDermid, Spencer Tracy, Harrison Hoy, Jay J. Mulrey, Tom Richards. Director: Kendal Weston.

THE LYCEUM STOCK COMPANY

(Lyceum Theatre, Pittsburgh, April 7, 1924.) Manager: William H. Wright. Company: Marguerite Fields, Matthew McHugh, Catherine McHugh, William Crookshank, Cliff Boyer, Spencer Tracy, Eugene G. Harper, Nellie Booth, Arthur Mack, Ernest Gantier. Director: John Ellis.

THE BROADWAY PLAYERS

(Powers Theatre, Grand Rapids, Mich., June 16, 1924.) Manager: William H. Wright. Company: Selena Royle, Kenneth Daigneau, William Laveau, Halliam Bosworth, Spencer Tracy, Arthur Kohl, Ramon Greenleaf, Herbert Treitel, John Ellis, Charlotte Wade Daniel, Elsie Keene, Elizabeth Allen. Director: John Ellis.

THE MONTAUK PLAYERS

(Montauk Theatre, Brooklyn, N.Y., September 22, 1924.) Manager: William H. Wright. Company: Selena Royle, Spencer Tracy, William Laveau, Georgia Backus, Halliam Bosworth, C. Porter Hall, Ramon Greenleaf, Herbert Treitel, John Ellis, Josephine Royle, Charlotte Wade Daniel. Director: John Ellis.

THE BROADWAY PLAYERS

(Powers Theatre, Grand Rapids, Mich., April 12, 1925.) Manager: William H. Wright. Company: Selena Royle, Spencer Tracy, William Laveau, Halliam Bosworth, Josephine Royle, Herbert Treitel, John Ellis, Charlotte Wade Daniel, Ernest Gantier. Director: John Ellis.

THE SHEEPMAN

By Charlotte B. Chorpenning. (Stamford Theatre, Stamford, Conn., October 9, 1925.) Management: Boothe, Gleason & Truex. Cast: Dodson Mitchell, Margaret Borough, Spencer Tracy (Jack Roberts), Emmett Shackelford, Thomas Findlay, James Seeley, Max Walzman, Paul Jacchia, Carleton Macy, Julius Seebach, A. O. Huhan, Charles F. Burns, Marshall Hale, Claude E. Archer. Staged by James Gleason. Tryouts only.

THE TRENT STOCK COMPANY

(Trent Theatre, Trenton, N.J., November 3, 1925.) Manager: Walter Reade. Company: Ethel Remey, Spencer Tracy, Louise Huntington. Director: Frank McCoy.

THE BROADWAY PLAYERS

(Regent Theatre, Grand Rapids, Mich., February 8, 1926.) Manager: William H. Wright. Company: Helen Joy, Spencer Tracy, William Laveau, Betty Hanna, Ann Constant, Halliam Bosworth, Herbert Treitel, John Ellis, Charlotte Wade Daniel. Director: John Ellis.

YELLOW

By Margaret Vernon. (National Theatre, September 21, 1926.) Management: George M. Cohan. Cast: Chester Morris, Selena Royle, Hale Hamilton, Shirley Warde, Spencer Tracy (Jimmy Wilkes), Marjorie Wood, Harry C. Bannister, Frank Kingdon, Jane Wheatley, Richard Freeman. Staged by John Meehan. 132 performances.

NED MCCOBB'S DAUGHTER

By Sidney Howard. (Princess Theatre, Chicago, February 20, 1927.) Management: John Cromwell. Cast: John Cromwell, Florence Johns, Spencer Tracy (George Callahan), Burke Clarke, Harriette MacGibbon, Elmer Cornell, Robert Wayne, Arthur Cole, Joseph Daly, Ranold Savery. Staged by John Cromwell.

Note: Tracy left the cast after six weeks.

THE WRIGHT PLAYERS

(Faurot Opera House, Lima, Ohio, April 17, 1927.) Manager: William H. Wright. Company: Spencer Tracy, Louise Treadwell, Porter Hall, Vincent Dennis, Geraldine Browning, David Livingstone, Joseph Demier, Isabelle Herbert, Anthony Blair, Kitty Cosgriff, Harry Horne. Director: Harry Horne.

THE BABY CYCLONE

By George M. Cohan. (Henry Miller's Theatre, September 12, 1927.) Management: George M. Cohan. Cast: Grant Mitchell, Natalie Moorhead, Spencer Tracy (Gene Hurley), Nan Sunderland, William Morris, Georgia Caine, Agnes Gildea, John T. Doyle, Joseph Allen, Charles F. McCarthy. Staged by Sam Forrest. 187 performances. Also toured.

STOCK AT THE OHIO THEATRE

(Ohio Theatre, Cleveland, June 24, 1928.) Leading man: Pierre Watkin.

Note: Tracy appeared in productions of *The Baby Cyclone, Broadway,* and *Lulu Belle.*

WHISPERING FRIENDS

By George M. Cohan. (Broad Theatre, Newark, N.J., August 21, 1928.) Management: George M. Cohan. Cast: Spencer Tracy (Joe Sanford), Georgia Caine, Walter Edwin, Gwenn Lowrey, Jack McKee, Kathleen Mulqueen. Staged by Sam Forrest. Tour only.

NIGHTSTICK

By John Wray, the Nugents, and Elaine Sterne Carrington. (Freeport Theatre, Freeport, Long Island, November 5, 1928.) Management: Russell Mack. Cast: Spencer Tracy (Tommy Glennon), Marjorie Crossland, James S. Barrett, Clara Palmer, Frances Horine, Victor Kilian, Donald Dillaway, Jerome Sheldon, Owen Martin, Frederick Strong, Harry Jenkins, Vera Trett, Loretta Puck, Emil Hirsch. Staged by Arthur Bouvier. Eight performances.

THE LESTER BRYANT STOCK COMPANY

(Auditorium Theater, Baltimore, December 24, 1928.) Manager: Lester Bryant. Company: Edna Hibbard, Spencer Tracy, Pat O'Brien, Martin Walfson, Frank McHugh, Philip Van Zandt, Alex Campbell, Harry Stafford. Director: Noel Travers.

CONFLICT

By Warren F. Lawrence. (Fulton Theatre, March 6, 1929.) Management: J. E. Horn (Spad Producing Co.). Cast: Spencer Tracy (Richard Banks), Edward Arnold, Frank McHugh, Peggy

Allenby, Dennie Moore, Charles Scott, Albert Van Dekker, Jack Mead, Mabel Allyn. Staged by Edward Clarke Lilley. Thirty-seven performances.

SALT WATER

By Dan Jarrett (uncredited: Jean Dalrymple). (Playhouse, Mamaroneck, N.Y., May 27, 1929.) Management: John Golden. Cast: Spencer Tracy (John Horner), Edythe Elliott, Una Merkel, George Spelvin, Claude Cooper, Robert Burton, William Edmunds, Alan Goode, James C. Lane, Harry Lawrence, Patricia O'Hearn. Staged by John Golden. Tryouts only.

Note: Tracy was fired after the play's Atlantic City engagement.

THE E. F. ALBEE PLAYERS

(Albee Theatre, Providence, R.I., June 24, 1929.) Manager: Foster Lardner. Company: Selena Royle, Spencer Tracy, John W. Moore, Walter Kenmore, William Harrison, Charles I. Schofield, Mal Arthur, Mal Kelly. Director: Charles I. Schofield.

NIGGER RICH (THE BIG SHOT)

By John McGowan. (Royale Theatre, September 20, 1929.) Management: Lee Shubert. Cast: Roderick Maybee, Spencer Tracy (Eddie Perkins), Don Beddoe, Adelaide Hibbard, Elvia Enders, Eric Dressler, John A. Butler, Helen Flint, Franklyn Fox, Richard Taber. Staged by the author. Eleven performances.

DREAD

By Owen Davis. (Belasco Theatre, Washington, D.C., October 20, 1929.) Management: Sam H. Harris. Cast: Spencer Tracy (Perry Crooker), Madge Evans, Miriam Doyle, Frank Shannon, George Meeker, Edwin Stanley, Marie Haynes, Helen Mack, Kathleen Comegys. Staged by the author. Tryouts only.

Note: The play closed after its Brooklyn engagement.

BLUE HEAVEN (VENEER)

By Hugh Stange. (Garrick Theatre, Chicago, December 22, 1929.) Management: Harry L. Cort, Charles H. Abramson. Cast: Joanna Roos, Spencer Tracy (Charlie Riggs), William Roselle, Betty Brown, John Kane, Harold Waldrige, Edith Shayne, Robert Sinclair. Staged by the author.

Note: Tracy replaced Henry Hull in the role of Charlie Riggs and played a week at the Forty-eighth Street Theatre in New York prior to Chicago.

THE LAST MILE

By John Wexley. (Sam H. Harris Theatre, February 13, 1930.) Management: Herman Shumlin. Cast: Spencer Tracy (John Mears), James Bell, Howard Phillips, Hale Norcross, Ernest Whitman, George Leach, Joseph Spurin-Calleia, Don Costello, Herbert Heywood, Orville Harris, Ralph Theadore, Richard Abbott, Henry O'Neill, Clarence Chase, Allen Jenkins, Albert West. Staged by Chester Erskine. 289 performances. Also Chicago.

Note: During Tracy's absence over the summer of 1930, the part of Mears was played first by Thomas Mitchell, later by Allen Jenkins.

THE RUGGED PATH

By Robert Emmet Sherwood. (Plymouth Theatre, November 10, 1945.) Management: The Playwrights' Company. Cast: Spencer Tracy (Morey Vinion), Martha Sleeper, Rex Williams, Clinton Sundberg, Lawrence Fletcher, Vito Christi, Kay Loring, Ernest Woodward, Emory Richardson, Gordon Nelson, Jan Sterling, Henry Lascoe, Ralph Cullinan, Nick Dennis, Theodore Leavitt, Paul Alberts, Sandy Campbell, Sam Sweet, Lynn Shubert, Howard Ferguson, William Sands, David Stone, Clay Clement, Edward Raquelo. Staged by Captain Garson Kanin. Eighty-one performances.

Film Chronology

TAXI TALKS (VITAPHONE VARIETIES)

Vitaphone Release #995–996. Producer: Murray Roth. Director: Arthur Hurley. Story: Frederick and Fannie Hatton. Photography: E. B. DuPar. Production and distribution: Vitaphone. Release date: June 1930. Running time: 14 minutes. Cast: Evelyn Knapp, Roger Pryor, Mayo Methot, Vernon Wallace, Katherine Alexander, Spencer Tracy (Joe).

THE HARD GUY (VITAPHONE VARIETIES)

Vitaphone Release #1036. Producer: Sam Sax. Director: Arthur Hurley. Story: Betty Ross. Adaptation: Burnet Hershey. Photography: E. B. DuPar. Production and distribution: Vitaphone. Release date: September 1930. Running time: 12 minutes. Cast: Spencer Tracy (Guy), Katherine Alexander, Valli Roberts, Arch Hendricks, Pat Kearney.

Note: Some sources suggest that Tracy appeared in a third Vitaphone subject. *The Strong Arm* was filmed in the latter half of March 1930, but there is no documentation in either the Warner Bros. Archive at USC or in Tracy's personal papers to suggest that he was in it. He never claimed to have appeared in a third Vitaphone subject at any point in his career.

UP THE RIVER

Director: John Ford. Staged by William Collier, Sr. Story: Maurine Watkins. Music and lyrics: Joseph McCarthy, James F. Hanley. Photography: Joseph August. Editor: Frank Hull. Production and distribution: Fox. Release date: October 12, 1930. Running time: 92 minutes. Cast: Spencer Tracy (St. Louis), Claire Luce, Warren Hymer, Humphrey Bogart, William Collier, Sr., Joan Lawes, George MacFarlane, Gaylord Pendleton, Sharon Lynn, Noel Francis, Goodie Montgomery, Robert E. O'Connor, Robert Burns, John Swor, Joe Brown, Morgan Wallace.

Note: Existing prints of the film run eighty-four minutes.

QUICK MILLIONS

Director: Rowland Brown. Screenplay: Rowland Brown, Courtenay Terrett. Additional dialogue: John Wray. Photography: Joseph August. Editor: Harold Schuster. Production and distribution: Fox. Release date: May 3, 1931. Running time: 69 minutes. Cast: Spencer Tracy (Daniel J. "Bugs" Raymond), Marguerite Churchill, John Wray, Warner Richmond, Sally Eilers, George Raft, Robert Burns, John Swor, Edgar Kennedy, Harry Myers, Dixie Lee.

SIX CYLINDER LOVE

Associate producer: John W. Considine, Jr. Director: Thornton Freeland. Based upon the play by William Anthony McGuire. Adaptation: William M. Conselman, Norman Houston. Photography: Ernest Palmer. Editor: J. Edwin Robbins. Production and distribution: Fox. Release date: May 10, 1931. Running time: 71 minutes. Cast: Spencer Tracy (William Donroy), Sidney Fox, Edward Everett Horton, Una Merkel, El Brendel, William Collier, Sr., Lorin Raker, Bert Roach, William Holden, Ruth Warren.

GOLDIE

Associate producer: A. L. Rockett. Director: Benjamin Stoloff. Based upon the film *A Girl in Every Port* (story: Howard Hawks; adaptation: James K. McGuinness; scenario: Seton I. Miller; titles: Malcolm Stuart Boylan). Adaptation and dialogue: Gene Towne, Paul Perez (uncredited: Howard J. Green). Photography: Ernest Palmer. Editor: Alex Troffey. Production and distribution: Fox. Release date: June 28, 1931. Running time: 59 minutes. Cast: Spencer Tracy (Bill), Warren Hymer, Jean Harlow, Jesse De Vorska, Lina Basquette, Eleanor Hunt, Maria Alba.

SHE WANTED A MILLIONAIRE

Associate producer: John W. Considine, Jr. Director: John G. Blystone. Dialogue director: William Collier, Sr. Story: Sonya Levien (uncredited: Winfield R. Sheehan). Continuity: Sonya Levien. Screenplay: William Anthony McGuire. Photography: John F. Seitz. Editor: Louis Loeffler. Production and distribution: Fox. Release date: February 21, 1932. Running time: 74 minutes. Cast: Joan Bennett, Spencer Tracy (William Kelley), Una Merkel, James Kirkwood, Dorothy Peterson, Douglas Cosgrove, Donald Dillaway, Tetsu Komai, Constantine Romanoff.

SKY DEVILS

Producer: Howard Hughes. Director: Edward Sutherland. Story: Joseph Moncure March, Edward Sutherland. Dialogue: Robert Benchley, Joseph Moncure March, James Starr, Carroll and Garrett Graham. Music: Alfred Newman. Photography: Gaetano Gaudio. Editor: Douglas Biggs. Production: The Caddo Company. Distribution: United Artists. Release date: March 12, 1932. Rereleased: 1939 (Astor Pictures Corporation), 1979 (Universal). Running time: 89 minutes. Cast: Spencer Tracy (Wilkie), William Boyd, George Cooper, Ann Dvorak, Billy Bevan, Yola D'Avril, Forrester Harvey, William B. Davidson, Jerry Miley.

DISORDERLY CONDUCT

Director: John W. Considine, Jr. Story and dialogue: William Anthony McGuire. Continuity: Del Andrews. Photography: Ray June. Editor: Frank Hull. Production and distribution: Fox. Release date: March 20, 1932. Running time: 82 minutes. Cast: Spencer Tracy (Dick Fay), Sally Eilers, El Brendel, Dickie Moore, Ralph Bellamy, Ralph Morgan, Allan Dinehart, Frank Conroy, Cornelius Keefe.

YOUNG AMERICA

Director: Frank Borzage. Based upon the play by John Frederick Ballard. (Suggested by Pearl Franklin's "Mrs. Doray" stories.) Screenplay: William Conselman (uncredited: Maurine Watkins). Photography: George Schneiderman. Editor: Margaret Clancy. Production and distribution: Fox. Release date: April 17, 1932. Running time: 70 minutes. Cast: Spencer Tracy (Jack Doray), Doris Kenyon, Ralph Bellamy, Tommy Conlon, Raymond Borzage, Beryl Mercer, Sarah Padden, Robert Homans, Dawn O'Day.

SOCIETY GIRL

Associate producer: A. L. Rockett. Director: Sidney Lanfield. Based upon the play by John Larkin, Jr., and Charles Beahan. Screenplay: Elmer Harris. Music: George Lipschultz. Photography: George Barnes. Editor: Margaret Clancy. Production and distribution: Fox. Release date: May 22, 1932. Running time: 74 minutes. Cast: James Dunn, Peggy Shannon, Spencer Tracy (Doc Briscoe), Bert Hanlon, Walter Byron, Marjorie Gateson.

THE PAINTED WOMAN
Director: John G. Blystone. Based upon the play *After the Rain,* by Alfred C. Kennedy. Screenplay: Guy Bolton, Leon Gordon. Music: George Lipschultz. Song: "Say You'll Be Good to Me" (music and lyrics: James F. Hanley). Photography: Ernest Palmer. Editor: Alex Troffey. Production and distribution: Fox. Release date: August 21, 1932. Running time: 73 minutes. Cast: Spencer Tracy (Bill), Peggy Shannon, William Boyd, Irving Pichel, Raul Roulien, Murray Kinnell, Laska Winter, Chris-Pin Martin, Paul Porcasi, Stanley Fields, Wade Boteler, Jack Kennedy.

ME AND MY GAL
Director: Raoul Walsh. Story: Philip Klein, Barry Conner. Screenplay: Arthur Kober (uncredited: Frank J. Dolan, Philip Dunne, Charles Vidor, Al Cohn). Music: George Lipschultz. Song: "Oleo the Gigolo" (music: James F. Hanley; lyrics: Val Burton). Photography: Arthur Miller. Editor: Jack Murray. Production and distribution: Fox. Release date: December 24, 1932. Running time: 79 minutes. Cast: Spencer Tracy (Danny Dolan), Joan Bennett, Marion Burns, George Walsh, J. Farrell MacDonald, Noel Madison, Henry B. Walthall, Bert Hanlon, Adrian Morris, George Chandler, Will Stanton.

FACE IN THE SKY
Associate producer: Miles Connolly. Director: Harry Lachman. Dialogue director: William Collier, Sr. Story: Miles Connolly. Screenplay: Humphrey Pearson. Music: Louis De Francesco. Song: "Parade of the Ads" (music: Val Burton, Will Jason, Arthur Lange; lyrics: Val Burton, Will Jason). Photography: Lee Garmes. Editor: Ralph Dietrich. Production and distribution: Fox. Release date: January 22, 1933. Running time: 77 minutes. Cast: Spencer Tracy (Joe Buck), Marian Nixon, Stuart Erwin, Sam Hardy, Lila Lee, Sarah Padden, Russell Simpson, Frank McGlynn, Jr., Billy Platt, Guy Usher.

20,000 YEARS IN SING SING
Executive producer: Hal B. Wallis. Associate producer: Robert Lord. Director: Michael Curtiz. Based upon the book by Lewis E. Lawes. Adaptation: Courtenay Terrett, Robert Lord. Screenplay: Wilson Mizner, Brown Holmes. Music: Bernard Kaun. Photography: Barney McGill. Editor: George Amy. Production: First National. Distribution: Warner Bros. Release date: February 1, 1933. Rereleased: 1956 (Dominant Pictures). Running time: 81 minutes. Cast: Spencer Tracy (Tommy Connors), Bette Davis, Arthur Byron, Lyle Talbot, Warren Hymer, Louis Calhern.

SHANGHAI MADNESS
Associate producer: A. L. Rockett. Director: John G. Blystone. Based upon the story by Frederick Hazlitt Brennan. Adaptation: Austin Parker, Gordon Wong Wellesley. Screenplay: Austin Parker (uncredited: Edward T. Lowe). Music: Louis De Francesco. Photography: Lee Garmes. Editor: Margaret Clancy, Alexander Troffey. Production and distribution: Fox. Release date: August 4, 1933. Running time: 68 minutes. Cast: Spencer Tracy (Lieutenant Patrick Jackson), Fay Wray, Ralph Morgan, Eugene Pallette, Herbert Mundin, Reginald Mason, Arthur Hoyt, Albert Conti, Maude Eburne, William von Brincken.

THE POWER AND THE GLORY
Producer: Jesse L. Lasky. Director: William K. Howard. Screenplay: Preston Sturges. Music: Louis De Francesco. Photography: James Wong Howe. Editor: Paul Weatherwax. Production and distribution: Fox. Release date: October 6, 1933. Running time: 77 minutes. Cast: Spencer Tracy (Tom Garner), Colleen Moore, Ralph Morgan, Helen Vinson, Clifford Jones, Henry Kolker, Sarah Padden, Billy O'Brien, Cullen Johnston, J. Ferrell McDonald, Robert Warwick.

THE MAD GAME

Producer: Sol M. Wurtzel. Director: Irving Cummings, John G. Blystone. Story: William Conselman. Screenplay: William Conselman, Henry Johnson. Music: Samuel Kaylin. Photography: Arthur Miller. Production and distribution: Fox. Release date: October 27, 1933. Running time: 78 minutes. Cast: Spencer Tracy (Edward Carson), Claire Trevor, Ralph Morgan, Howard Lally, J. Carroll Naish, John Miljan, Matt McHugh, Kathleen Burke, Mary Mason, Willard Robinson.

MAN'S CASTLE

Director: Frank Borzage. Based upon the play by Lawrence Hazard. Screenplay: Jo Swerling. Music: W. Franke Harling. Photography: Joseph August. Editor: Viola Lawrence. Production and distribution: Columbia. Release date: November 20, 1933. Rereleased: 1938, 1950. Running time: 75 minutes. Cast: Spencer Tracy (Bill), Loretta Young, Marjorie Rambeau, Glenda Farrell, Walter Connolly, Arthur Hohl, Dickie Moore, Helen Jerome Eddy.

THE SHOW-OFF

Producer: Lucien Hubbard. Director: Charles F. Riesner. Based upon the play by George Kelly. Screenplay: Herman J. Mankiewicz. Photography: James Wong Howe. Editor: William S. Gray. Production and distribution: Metro-Goldwyn-Mayer. Release date: March 9, 1934. Running time: 79 minutes. Cast: Spencer Tracy (J. Aubrey Piper), Madge Evans, Henry Wadsworth, Lois Wilson, Grant Mitchell, Clara Blandick, Alan Edwards, Claude Gillingwater.

LOOKING FOR TROUBLE

Producer: Darryl F. Zanuck. Associate producers: William Goetz, Raymond Griffith. Director: William Wellman. Story: J. R. Bren. Screenplay: Leonard Praskins, Elmer Harris. Music: Alfred Newman. Photography: James Van Trees. Editor: Hanson Fritch. Production: 20th Century. Distribution: United Artists. Release date: March 9, 1934. Running time: 77 minutes. Cast: Spencer Tracy (Joe Graham), Jack Oakie, Constance Cummings, Morgan Conway, Arline Judge, Paul Harvey, Judith Wood, Joseph Sauers, Robert Elliot, Paul Porcasi, Charles Lane.

BOTTOMS UP

Producer: B. G. DeSylva. Director: David Butler. Dance director: Harold Hecht. Story and screenplay: B. G. DeSylva, David Butler, Sid Silvers. Music: Constantine Bakaleinikoff. Songs: "Turn on the Moon," "I'm Throwing My Love Away," "Little Did I Dream" (music and lyrics: Harold Adamson, Burton Lane). Song: "Waitin' at the Gate for Katie" (music: Richard A. Whiting; lyrics: Gus Kahn). Song: "Is I in Love I Is" (music and lyrics: J. Russel Robinson). Photography: Arthur Miller. Editor: Irene Mora. Production and distribution: Fox. Release date: March 30, 1934. Rereleased: 1935 (20th Century-Fox). Running time: 84 minutes. Cast: Spencer Tracy (Smoothie King), Pat Paterson, John Boles, Sid Silvers, Herbert Mundin, Harry Green, Thelma Todd, Robert Emmet O'Connor, Del Henderson.

"NOW I'LL TELL" BY MRS. ARNOLD ROTHSTEIN

Producer: Winfield Sheehan. Director: Edwin Burke. Screenplay: Edwin Burke. Music: Arthur Lange. Song: "Fooling with the Other Woman's Man" (music and lyrics: Lew Brown, Harry Akst). Photography: Ernest Palmer. Editor: Harold Schuster. Production and distribution: Fox. Release date: May 11, 1934. Rereleased: 1935 (20th Century-Fox). Running time: 87 minutes. Cast: Spencer Tracy (Murray Golden), Helen Twelvetrees, Alice Faye, Robert Gleckler, Henry O'Neill, Hobart Cavanaugh, G. P. Huntley, Jr., Shirley Temple, Ronnie Cosbey, Ray Cooke, Frank Marlowe, Clarence Wilson, Barbara Weeks, Theodore Newton, Vince Barnett, Jim Donlan.

MARIE GALANTE

Producer: Winfield Sheehan (uncredited: Julian Johnson). Director: Henry King. Based upon the novel by Jacques Deval and its English-language translation (titled *That Girl*) by Lawrence S. Morris. Screenplay: Reginald Berkeley (uncredited: Dudley Nichols, William Drake, Courtenay Terrett, Sonya Levien, Samuel Hoffenstein, Seton I. Miller, Henry King, Robert Low, Jack Yellen, Marcel Silver, Edmund Hartman, Seymour Stern). Music: Arthur Lange. Song: "Song of a Dreamer" (music: Ray Gorney; lyrics: Don Hartman). Song: "Un Peu Beaucoup" (music: Arthur Lange; lyrics: Marcel Silver). Song: "Shim Shammy" (music and lyrics: Stepin Fetchit). Song: "Serves Me Right for Treating Him Wrong" (music and lyrics: Maurice Sigler, Al Goodhart, Al Hoffman). Song: "It's Home" (music: Jay Gorney; lyrics: Jack Yellen). Photography: John Seitz. Editor: Harold Schuster. Production and distribution: Fox. Release date: October 26, 1934. Rereleased: 1935 (20th Century-Fox). Running time: 88 minutes. Cast: Spencer Tracy (Dr. Crawbett), Ketti Gallian, Ned Sparks, Helen Morgan, Siegfried Rumann, Leslie Fenton, Arthur Byron, Jay C. Flippen, Stepin Fetchit, Robert Loraine, Frank Darien, Tito Coral.

IT'S A SMALL WORLD

Producer: Edward Butcher. Director: Irving Cummings. Based upon the story "Highway Robbery," by Albert Treynor. Screenplay: Sam Hellman, Gladys Lehman (uncredited: Albert Treynor, F. McGrew Willis). Music: Arthur Lange. Photography: Arthur Miller. Production and distribution: Fox. Release date: April 12, 1935. Running time: 71 minutes. Cast: Spencer Tracy (Bill Shevlin), Wendy Barrie, Raymond Walburn, Virginia Sale, Astrid Allwyn, Irving Bacon, Charles Sellon, Nick Foran, Belle Daube, Frank McGlynn, Sr., Frank McGlynn, Jr., Bill Gillis, Ed Brady, Harold Miner.

THE MURDER MAN

Producer: Harry Rapf. Director: Tim Whelan. Story: Tim Whelan, Guy Bolton. Screenplay: Tim Whelan, John C. Higgans (uncredited: Herman J. Mankiewicz). Music: Dr. William Axt. Photography: Lester White. Editor: James E. Newcom. Production and distribution: Metro-Goldwyn-Mayer. Release date: July 12, 1935. Running time: 70 minutes. Cast: Spencer Tracy (Steve Gray), Virginia Bruce, Lionel Atwill, Harvey Stephens, Robert Barrat, James Stewart, William Collier, Sr., Bobby Watson, William Demarest, John Sheehan, Lucien Littlefield, George Chandler, Fuzzy Knight, Louise Henry, Robert Warwick, Joe Irving, Ralph Bushman.

THE MURDER MAN TRAILER

Tracy appears in a brief exchange of dialogue with Virgina Bruce and director Tim Whelan.

DANTE'S INFERNO

Producer: Sol M. Wurtzel. Director: Harry Lachman. Screenplay: Philip Klein, Robert M. Yost (uncredited: Henry Johnson, Lou Breslow, Rose Frankin, Lester Cole). Music: Samuel Kaylin. Photography: Rudolph Maté. Editor: Al DeGaetano. Production: Fox. Distribution: 20th Century-Fox. Release date: August 23, 1935. Running time: 88 minutes. Cast: Spencer Tracy (Jim Carter), Claire Trevor, Henry B. Walthall, Alan Dinehart, Scott Beckett, Robert Gleckler, Rita Cansino, Gary Leon, Willard Robertson, Morgan Wallace.

WHIPSAW

Producer: Harry Rapf. Director: Sam Wood. Based upon the story "The Whipsaw," by James Edward Grant. Screenplay: Howard Emmett Rogers. Music: Dr. William Axt. Photography: James Wong Howe. Editor: Basil Wrangell. Production and distribution: Metro-Goldwyn-Mayer. Release date: December 18, 1935. Running time: 80 minutes. Cast: Myrna Loy, Spencer Tracy (Ross McBride), Harvey Stephens, William Harrigan, Clay Clement, Robert Gleckler,

Robert Warwick, Georges Renevant, Paul Stanton, Wade Boteler, Don Rowan, John Qualen, Irene Franklin, Lillian Leighton, J. Arthur Hughes, William Ingersoll, Charles Irwin.

RIFFRAFF

Producer: Irving Thalberg. Associate producer: David Lewis. Director: J. Walter Ruben. Story: Frances Marion. Screenplay: Frances Marion, H. W. Hanemann, Anita Loos (uncredited: John Lee Mahin, George S. Kaufman, Theodore Reeves, Carey Wilson). Music: Edward Ward. Photography: Ray June. Editor: Frank Sullivan. Production and distribution: Metro-Goldwyn-Mayer. Release date: January 3, 1936. Running time: 89 minutes. Cast: Jean Harlow, Spencer Tracy (Dutch Muller), Una Merkel, Joseph Calleia, Victor Kilian, Mickey Rooney, J. Farrell MacDonald, Roger Imhof, Juanita Quigley, Paul Hurst, Vince Barnett, Dorothy Appleby, Judith Wood, Arthur Houseman, Wade Boteler, Joe Phillips, William Newell, Al Hill, Helen Funt, Lillian Harmer, Bob Perry, George Givot, Helene Costello, Rafaelo Ottiano.

FURY

Producer: Joseph L. Mankiewicz. Director: Fritz Lang. Story: Norman Krasna. Screenplay: Bartlett Cormack, Fritz Lang. Music: Franz Waxman. Photography: Joseph Ruttenberg. Editor: Frank Sullivan. Production and distribution: Metro-Goldwyn-Mayer. Release date: June 5, 1936. Running time: 90 minutes. Cast: Sylvia Sidney, Spencer Tracy (Joe Wilson), Walter Abel, Bruce Cabot, Edward Ellis, Walter Brennan, Frank Albertson, George Walcott, Arthur Stone, Morgan Wallace, George Chandler, Roger Gray, Edwin Maxwell, Howard Hickman, Jonathan Hale, Leila Bennett, Esther Dale, Helen Flint.

SAN FRANCISCO

Producers: John Emerson, Bernard H. Hyman. Director: W. S. Van Dyke II. Operatic sequences: William von Wymetal. Montage sequences: John Hoffman. Story: Robert Hopkins. Screenplay: Anita Loos (uncredited: Herman J. Mankiewicz). Music: Edward Ward. Song: "San Francisco" (music and lyrics: Gus Kahn, Bronislau Kaper, Walter Jurmann). Song: "Would You" (music and lyrics: Nacio Herb Brown, Arthur Freed). Photography: Oliver T. Marsh. Editor: Tom Held. Production and distribution: Metro-Goldwyn-Mayer. Release date: June 26, 1936. Rereleased: 1938, 1948, 1955 (Metro-Goldwyn-Mayer). Running time: 115 minutes. Cast: Clark Gable, Jeanette MacDonald, Spencer Tracy (Father Tim Mullen), Jack Holt, Jessie Ralph, Ted Healy, Shirley Ross, Margaret Irving, Harold Huber, Edgar Kennedy, Al Shean, William Ricciardi, Kenneth Harlan, Roger Imhof, Charles Judells, Russell Simpson, Bert Roach, Warren Hymer.

LIBELED LADY

Producer: Lawrence Weingarten. Director: Jack Conway. Story: Wallace Sullivan. Screenplay: Maurine Watkins, Howard Emmett Rogers, George Oppenheimer. Music: Dr. William Axt. Song: "You" (music: Walter Donaldson; lyrics: Harold Adamson). Photography: Norbert Brodine. Editor: Frederick Y. Smith. Production and distribution: Metro-Goldwyn-Mayer. Release date: October 9, 1936. Running time: 98 minutes. Cast: Jean Harlow, William Powell, Myrna Loy, Spencer Tracy (William Haggerty), Walter Connolly, Charley Grapewin, Cora Witherspoon, E. E. Clive, Lauri Beatty, Otto Yamaoka, Charles Trowbridge, Spencer Charters, George Chandler, William Benedict, Hal K. Dawson, William Newell.

YE MERRY GENTLEMEN

Production and distribution: Metro-Goldwyn-Mayer. Release date: Christmas season, 1936. Cast: Clark Gable, Spencer Tracy, Robert Taylor, William Powell.

THEY GAVE HIM A GUN

Producer: Harry Rapf. Director: W. S. Van Dyke II. Based upon the novel by William Joyce Cowen. Screenplay: Cyril Hume, Richard Maibaum, Maurice Rapf. Song: "A Love Song of Long Ago" (music: Sigmund Romberg; lyrics: Gus Kahn). Montage effects: Slavko Vorkapich.

Photography: Harold Rosson. Editor: Ben Lewis. Production and distribution: Metro-Goldwyn-Mayer. Release date: May 7, 1937. Running time: 97 minutes. Cast: Spencer Tracy (Fred Willis), Gladys George, Franchot Tone, Edgar Dearing, Mary Lou Treen, Cliff Edwards, Charles Trowbridge.

CAPTAINS COURAGEOUS

Producer: Louis D. Lighton. Director: Victor Fleming (uncredited: Jack Conway). Based upon the novel by Rudyard Kipling. Screenplay: John Lee Mahin, Marc Connelly, Dale Van Every (uncredited: Harvey Gates, Tom Kilpatrick). Music: Franz Waxman. Songs: "Ooh, What a Terrible Man," "Don't Cry Little Fish" (music: Franz Waxman; lyrics: Gus Kahn). Photography: Harold Rosson. Editor: Elmo Veron. Production and distribution: Metro-Goldwyn-Mayer. Release date: June 25, 1937. Rereleased: 1946, 1962, 1973 (Metro-Goldwyn-Mayer). Running time: 118 minutes. Cast: Freddie Bartholomew, Spencer Tracy (Manuel), Lionel Barrymore, Melvyn Douglas, Charley Grapewin, Mickey Rooney, John Carradine, Oscar O'Shea, Jack LaRue, Walter Kingsford, Donald Briggs, Sam McDaniels, Billy Burrud.

BIG CITY

Producer: Norman Krasna. Director: Frank Borzage (uncredited: George B. Seitz). Story: Norman Krasna. Screenplay: Dore Schary, Hugo Butler (uncredited: Horace McCoy). Music: Dr. William Axt. Photography: Joseph Ruttenberg (uncredited: Clyde De Vinna). Editor: Frederick Y. Smith. Production and distribution: Metro-Goldwyn-Mayer. Release date: September 3, 1937. Running time: 80 minutes. Cast: Luise Rainer, Spencer Tracy (Joe Benton), Charley Grapewin, Janet Beecher, Eddie Quillan, Victor Varconi, Oscar O'Shea, Helen Troy, William Demarest, John Arledge, Irving Bacon, Guinn Williams, Regis Toomey, Edgar Dearing, Paul Harvey, Andrew J. Tombes, Clem Bevans, Grace Ford, Alice White. As themselves: Jack Dempsey, James J. Jeffries, Jimmy McLarnin, Maxie Rosenbloom, Jim Thorpe, Frank Wykoff, Jackie Fields, Man Mountain Dean, Gus Sonnenberg, George Godfrey, Joe Rivers, Cotton Warburton, Bull Montana, Snowy Baker, Taski Hagio.

MANNEQUIN

Producer: Joseph L. Mankiewicz. Director: Frank Borzage. Story: Katharine Brush. Screenplay: Lawrence Hazard. Music: Edward Ward. Song: "Always and Always" (music: Edward Ward; lyrics: Bob Wright, Chet Forrest). Photography: George Folsey. Editor: Frederick Y. Smith. Production and distribution: Metro-Goldwyn-Mayer. Release date: January 21, 1938. Running time: 95 minutes. Cast: Joan Crawford, Spencer Tracy (John L. Hennessey), Alan Curtis, Ralph Morgan, Mary Phillips, Oscar O'Shea, Elizabeth Risdon, Leo Gorcey.

HOLLYWOOD STEPS OUT

Tracy is caricatured in this one-reel Merrie Melodie, produced in color by Leon Schlesinger and released by the Vitaphone Corporation on April 2, 1938.

TEST PILOT

Producer: Louis D. Lighton. Director: Victor Fleming. Story: Frank Wead. Screenplay: Vincent Lawrence, Waldemar Young. Music: Franz Waxman. Photography: Ray June. Editor: Tom Held. Production and distribution: Metro-Goldwyn-Mayer. Release date: April 22, 1938. Running time: 120 minutes. Cast: Clark Gable, Myrna Loy, Spencer Tracy (Gunner), Lionel Barrymore, Samuel S. Hinds, Marjorie Main, Ted Pearson, Gloria Holden, Louis Jean Heydt, Virginia Grey, Priscilla Lawson, Claudia Coleman, Arthur Aylesworth.

ANOTHER ROMANCE OF CELLULOID

Producer: Frank Whitbeck. Production and distribution: Metro-Goldwyn-Mayer. Release date: April 1938. Running time: 10 minutes. Cast: Norma Shearer, W. S. Van Dyke, Lewis Stone, Mickey Rooney, Spencer Tracy, Myrna Loy, Clark Gable.
Note: Tracy is seen with Gable and Loy on the M-G-M lot.

HOLLYWOOD GOES TO TOWN (M-G-M MINIATURE)

Director: Herman Hoffman. Production and distribution: Metro-Goldwyn-Mayer. Release date: August 1938. Running time: 9 minutes.

Note: Tracy is one of the many stars seen arriving for the premiere of M-G-M's *Marie Antoinette* at the Carthay Circle Theatre in Los Angeles.

BOYS TOWN

Producer: John W. Considine, Jr. Associate producer: O. O. Dull. Director: Norman Taurog. Story: Dore Schary, Eleanore Griffin. Screenplay: John Meehan, Dore Schary (uncredited: Jack Mintz). Music: Edward Ward. Photography: Sidney Wagner. Editor: Elmo Veron. Production and distribution: Metro-Goldwyn-Mayer. Release date: September 9, 1938. Rereleased: 1957 (Metro-Goldwyn-Mayer). Running Time: 93 minutes. Cast: Spencer Tracy (Father Edward Flanagan), Mickey Rooney, Henry Hull, Leslie Fenton, Gene Reynolds, Edward Norris, Addison Richards, Minor Watson, Jonathan Hale, Bobs Watson, Martin Spellman, Mickey Rentschler, Frankie Thomas, Jimmy Butler, Sidney Miller, Robert Emmett Keane, Victor Kilian, Boys Town A Cappella Choir.

MOTHER GOOSE GOES HOLLYWOOD

Tracy is caricatured in this one-reel Silly Symphony, produced in color by Walt Disney and released by RKO-Radio Pictures on December 23, 1938.

FOR AULD LANG SYNE NO. 4

Will Rogers National Theatre Week, Major L. E. Thompson, Chairman. Production: 20th Century-Fox. Distribution: all major exchanges. Release date: April 29, 1939. Running time: 10 minutes. Cast: Raymond Massey, Spencer Tracy, Deanna Durbin, Robert Emmet Sherwood, Lowell Thomas.

Note: Tracy participates in this fourth annual appeal for the Will Rogers Memorial Hospital in Saranac Lake, New York.

HOLLYWOOD HOBBIES

Producer: Louis Lewyn. Director: George Sidney. Production and distribution: Metro-Goldwyn-Mayer. Release date: May 3, 1939. Running time: 10 minutes. Cast: Joyce Compton, Sally Payne, William Benedict.

Note: Tracy is briefly glimpsed as one of the many stars attending a celebrity baseball game at Gilmore Field in Los Angeles.

STANLEY AND LIVINGSTON

Producer: Darryl F. Zanuck. Associate producer: Kenneth Macgowan. Director: Henry King. (Safari episodes: Otto Brower.) Dialogue director: Lionel Bevans. Story: Hal Long, Sam Hellman. Screenplay: Philip Dunne, Julian Josephson. Music: Louis Silvers. Photography: George Barnes (Safari episodes: Sidney Wagner). Editor: Barbara McLean. Production and distribution: 20th Century-Fox. Release date: August 18, 1939. Rereleased: 1947 (20th Century-Fox). Running time: 101 minutes. Cast: Spencer Tracy (Henry M. Stanley), Nancy Kelly, Richard Greene, Walter Brennan, Charles Coburn, Sir Cedric Hardwicke, Henry Hull, Henry Travers, Miles Mander, David Torrence, Holmes Herbert, Montague Shaw, Brandon Hurst, Hassan Said, Paul Harvey, Russell Hicks, Frank Dae.

AFRICA SQUEAKS

Tracy is caricatured in this one-reel Looney Tune, produced by Leon Schlesinger and released by the Vitaphone Corporation on January 27, 1940.

I TAKE THIS WOMAN

Producers: Lawrence Weingarten, Bernard H. Hyman. Director: W. S. Van Dyke II (uncredited: Josef von Sternberg, Frank Borzage). Story: Charles MacArthur. Screenplay: James Kevin

McGuinness (uncredited: John Meehan, John McClain). Music: Bronislau Kaper, Arthur Guttmann. Photography: Harold Rosson. Editor: George Boemler. Production and distribution: Metro-Goldwyn-Mayer. Release date: February 2, 1940. Running time: 97 minutes. Cast: Spencer Tracy (Dr. Karl Decker), Hedy Lamarr, Verree Teasdale, Kent Taylor, Laraine Day, Mona Barrie, Jack Carson, Paul Cavanagh, Louis Calhern, Frances Drake, Marjorie Main, George E. Stone, Willie Best, Don Castle, Dalies Frantz, Reed Hadley.

NORTHWARD, HO! (M-G-M MINIATURE)
Director: Harry Loud. Screenplay: Herman Hoffman. Music: Daniele Amfitheatrof. Photography: Jackson Rose. Editor: Roy Brickner. Production and distribution: Metro-Goldwyn-Mayer. Release date: February 23, 1940. Running Time: 10 minutes.
Note: Tracy is seen in this promotional short about how the studio prepares to send a company on location, in this case for *Northwest Passage*.

NORTHWEST PASSAGE (BOOK I—ROGERS' RANGERS)
Producer: Hunt Stromberg. Director: King Vidor (uncredited: Norman Foster, Jack Conway). Based upon the novel by Kenneth Roberts. Screenplay: Laurence Stallings, Talbot Jennings. Music: Herbert Stothart. Photography: Sidney Wagner, William V. Skall (Technicolor). Editor: Conrad A. Nervig. Production and distribution: Metro-Goldwyn-Mayer. Release date: February 23, 1940. Rereleased: 1956 (Metro-Goldwyn-Mayer). Running time: 125 minutes. Cast: Spencer Tracy (Major Robert Rogers), Robert Young, Walter Brennan, Ruth Hussey, Nat Pendleton, Louis Hector, Robert Barrat, Lumsden Hare, Donald McBride, Isabel Jewell, Douglas Walton, Addison Richards, Hugh Sothern, Regis Toomey, Montagu Love, Lester Matthews, Truman Bradley.

EDISON, THE MAN
Producer: John W. Considine, Jr. Associate producer: Orville O. Dull. Director: Clarence Brown. Story: Dore Schary, Hugo Butler. Screenplay: Talbot Jennings, Bradbury Foote. Music: Herbert Stothart. Photography: Harold Rosson. Editor: Frederick Y. Smith. Production and distribution: Metro-Goldwyn-Mayer. Release date: May 10, 1940. Running time: 111 minutes. Cast: Spencer Tracy (Thomas A. Edison), Rita Johnson, Lynne Overman, Charles Coburn, Gene Lockhart, Henry Travers, Felix Bressart, Peter Godfrey, Guy D'Ennery, Byron Foulger, Milton Parsons, Arthur Aylesworth, Gene Reynolds, Addison Richards, Grant Mitchell, Paul Hurst, George Lessey, Jay Ward, Ann Gillis.
Note: Tracy is seen in a promotional announcement for this film at the end of *Young Tom Edison* (1940).

BOOM TOWN
Producer: Sam Zimbalist. Director: Jack Conway. Montage sequences: John Hoffman. Based upon the story "A Lady Comes to Burkburnett," by James Edward Grant. Screenplay: John Lee Mahin (uncredited: Lawrence Hazard). Music: Franz Waxman. Photography: Harold Rosson. Editor: Blanche Sewell. Production and Distribution: Metro-Goldwyn-Mayer. Release date: August 30, 1940. Rereleased: 1946, 1956 (Metro-Goldwyn-Mayer). Running time: 117 minutes. Cast: Clark Gable, Spencer Tracy (Square John Sand), Claudette Colbert, Hedy Lamarr, Frank Morgan, Lionel Atwill, Chill Wills, Marion Martin, Minna Gombell, Joe Yule, Horace Murphy, Roy Gordon, Richard Lane, Casey Johnson, Baby Quintanilla, George Lessey, Sara Haden, Frank Orth, Frank McGlynn, Sr., Curt Bois.

MEN OF BOYS TOWN
Producer: John W. Considine, Jr. Director: Norman Taurog. Screenplay: James K. McGuinness. Music: Herbert Stothart. Photography: Harold Rosson. Editor: Frederick Y. Smith. Production and distribution: Metro-Goldwyn-Mayer. Release date: April 11, 1941. Running time: 106 minutes. Cast: Spencer Tracy (Father Edward Flanagan), Mickey Rooney, Bobs Watson, Larry Nunn, Darryl Hickman, Henry O'Neill, Mary Nash, Lee J. Cobb, Sidney Miller, Addi-

son Richards, Lloyd Corrigan, Robert Emmett Keane, Arthur Hohl, Ben Weldon, Anne Revere.

DR. JEKYLL AND MR. HYDE

Producer: Victor Saville. Director: Victor Fleming. Montage sequences: Peter Ballbusch. Based upon the novella *The Strange Case of Dr. Jekyll and Mr. Hyde,* by Robert Louis Stevenson. Screenplay: John Lee Mahin (uncredited: John L. Balderston, Paul Osborn). Music: Franz Waxman. Photography: Joseph Ruttenberg. Editor: Harold F. Kress. Production and distribution: Metro-Goldwyn-Mayer. Release date: September 5, 1941. Rereleased: 1954 (Metro-Goldwyn-Mayer). Running time: 127 minutes. Cast: Spencer Tracy (Dr. Henry Jekyll/Mr. Hyde), Ingrid Bergman, Lana Turner, Donald Crisp, Ian Hunter, Barton MacLane, C. Aubrey Smith, Peter Godfrey, Sara Allgood, Frederic Worlock, William Tannen, Frances Robinson, Denis Green, Billy Bevan, Forrester Harvey, Lumsden Hare, Lawrence Grant, John Barclay.

WOMAN OF THE YEAR

Producer: Joseph L. Mankiewicz. Director: George Stevens. Screenplay: Ring Lardner, Jr., Michael Kanin (uncredited: Garson Kanin, John Lee Mahin). Music: Franz Waxman. Photography: Joseph Ruttenberg. Editor: Frank Sullivan. Production and distribution: Metro-Goldwyn-Mayer. Release date: February 13, 1942. Running time: 112 minutes. Cast: Spencer Tracy (Sam Craig), Katharine Hepburn, Fay Bainter, Reginald Owen, Minor Watson, William Bendix, Gladys Blake, Dan Tobin, Roscoe Karns, William Tannen, Ludwig Stossel, Sara Haden, Edith Evanson, George Kezas.

RING OF STEEL

Producer: Philip Martin, Jr. Director: Garson Kanin. Screenplay: Wallace Russell. Music: Morton Gould. Photography: Carl Pryer, Louis Tumola, Ray Foster. Editor: Robert Jahns. Narration: Spencer Tracy. Production: Office for Emergency Management, Film Unit. Distribution: Warner Bros. Release date: April 2, 1942. Running time: 9 minutes.

TORTILLA FLAT

Producer: Sam Zimbalist. Director: Victor Fleming. Based upon the novel by John Steinbeck. Screenplay: John Lee Mahin, Benjamin Glazer (uncredited: Paul Osborn). Music: Franz Waxman. Lyrics: Frank Loesser. Photography: Karl Freund. Editor: James E. Newcom. Production and distribution: Metro-Goldwyn-Mayer. Release date: May 22, 1942. Running time: 105 minutes. Cast: Spencer Tracy (Pilon), Hedy Lamarr, John Garfield, Frank Morgan, Akim Tamiroff, Sheldon Leonard, John Qualen, Donald Meek, Connie Gilchrist, Allen Jenkins, Henry O'Neill, Mercedes Ruffino, Nina Campana, Arthur Space, Betty Wells, Harry Burns.

KEEPER OF THE FLAME

Producer: Victor Saville. Associate producer: Leon Gordon. Director: George Cukor. Based upon the novel by I.A.R. Wylie. Screenplay: Donald Ogden Stewart (uncredited: Leon Gordon). Music: Bronislau Kaper. Photography: William Daniels. Editor: James E. Newcom. Production and distribution: Metro-Goldwyn-Mayer. Release date: February 5, 1943. Running time: 100 minutes. Cast: Spencer Tracy (Steven O'Malley), Katharine Hepburn, Richard Whorf, Margaret Wycherly, Forrest Tucker, Frank Craven, Horace McNally, Percy Kilbride, Audrey Christie, Darryl Hickman, Donald Meek, Howard Da Silva, William Newell.

U.S. WAR BONDS TRAILER

Release date: 1943. Cast: Spencer Tracy.

A GUY NAMED JOE

Producer: Everett Riskin. Director: Victor Fleming. Story: Chandler Sprague, David Boehm. Adaptation: Frederick Hazlitt Brennan. Screenplay: Dalton Trumbo. Music: Herbert

Stothart. Song: "I'll Get By"(music: Fred E. Ahlert; lyrics: Roy Turk). Song: "I'll See You in My Dreams" (music: Isham Jones; lyrics: Gus Kahn). Photography: George Folsey, Karl Freund. Editor: Frank Sullivan. Production and distribution: Metro-Goldwyn-Mayer. Release date: March 10, 1944. Rereleased: 1955 (Metro-Goldwyn-Mayer). Running time: 121 minutes. Cast: Spencer Tracy (Pete Sandidge), Irene Dunne, Van Johnson, Ward Bond, James Gleason, Lionel Barrymore, Barry Nelson, Esther Williams, Henry O'Neill, Don DeFore, Charles Smith, Addison Richards.

THE SEVENTH CROSS

Producer: Pandro S. Berman. Director: Fred Zinnemann. Based upon the novel by Anna Seghers (as translated by James A. Galston). Screenplay: Helen Deutsch. Music: Roy Webb. Photography: Karl Freund. Editor: Thomas Richards. Production and distribution: Metro-Goldwyn-Mayer. Release date: September 1, 1944. Running time: 113 minutes. Cast: Spencer Tracy (George Heisler), Signe Hasso, Hume Cronyn, Jessica Tandy, Agnes Moorehead, Herbert Rudley, Felix Bressart, Ray Collins, Alexander Granach, Katherine Locke, George Macready, Paul Guilfoyle, Steven Geray, Kurt Hatch, Kaaren Verne, Konstantin Shayne, George Suzanne, John Wengraf, George Zucco, Steven Muller, Eily Malyon.

HIS NEW WORLD

Director: Frank Whitbeck. Narration: Spencer Tracy. Production: Metro-Goldwyn-Mayer. Distribution: War Activities Committee—Motion Picture Industry. Release date: none determined. Running time: 10 minutes.

Note: Tracy narrated this short film designed to promote interest in the Army and Navy Air Corps Enlisted Reserves. The Dialogue Cutting Continuity in the Metro-Goldwyn-Mayer script collection at USC is dated September 14, 1944, but no record of release can be found.

TOMORROW, JOHN JONES!

Producer: Jerry Bresler. Director: Harry Beaumont. Screenplay: Carey Wilson. Music: Max Terr, Nathaniel Shilkret. Production: Metro-Goldwyn-Mayer (for the Canadian Motion Picture War Services Committee). Release date: October 23, 1944. Running time: 15 minutes. Cast: Spencer Tracy (Sergeant Major John Jones), Phyllis Thaxter, Fay Holden, Hank Daniels.

Note: *Tomorrow, John Jones!* was the official Seventh Victory Loan film for Canada.

THIRTY SECONDS OVER TOKYO

Producer: Sam Zimbalist. Director: Mervyn LeRoy. Based upon the book by Captain Ted W. Lawson and Robert Considine. Screenplay: Dalton Trumbo. Music: Herbert Stothart. Song: "I Love You" (music and lyrics: Art and Kay Fitch, Bert Lowe). Song: "Deep in the Heart of Texas" (music: Don Swander; lyrics: June Hershey). Photography: Harold Rosson, Robert Surtees. Editor: Frank Sullivan. Production and distribution: Metro-Goldwyn-Mayer. Release date: December 5, 1944. Rereleased: 1955 (Metro-Goldwyn-Mayer). Running time: 138 minutes. Cast: Van Johnson, Robert Walker, Tim Murdock, Don DeFore, Gordon McDonald, Phyllis Thaxter, Horace McNally, John R. Reilly, Robert Mitchum, Scott McKay, Donald Curtis, Louis Jean Heydt, William "Bill" Phillips, Douglas Cowan, Paul Langton, Leon Ames, Bill Williams, Robert Bice, Dr. Hsin Kung, Benson Fong, Ching Wah Lee, Alan Napier, Ann Shoemaker, Dorothy Ruth Morris, Jacqueline White, Selena Royle, Spencer Tracy (Lieutenant Colonel James H. Doolittle).

WITHOUT LOVE

Producer: Lawrence Weingarten. Director: Harold S. Bucquet. Based upon the play by Philip Barry. Screenplay: Donald Ogden Stewart (uncredited: Samson Raphaelson, Dorothy Kingsley). Music: Bronislau Kaper. Photography: Karl Freund. Editor: Frank Sullivan. Production and distribution: Metro-Goldwyn-Mayer. Release date: May 4, 1945. Running time: 111 minutes. Cast: Spencer Tracy (Pat Jamieson), Katharine Hepburn, Lucille Ball, Keenan Wynn,

Carl Esmond, Patricia Morison, Felix Bressart, Emily Massey, Gloria Grahame, George Davis, George Chandler, Clancy Cooper.

OUR VINES HAVE TENDER GRAPES TRAILER

Tracy plays an extended scene with actress Margaret O'Brien. Release date: September 1945.

NATIONAL CANCER WEEK TRAILER

Release date: April 21, 1946. Cast: Spencer Tracy.

THE SEA OF GRASS

Producer: Pandro S. Berman. Director: Elia Kazan. Based upon the novel by Conrad Richter. Screenplay: Marguerite Roberts, Vincent Lawrence (uncredited: E. E. Paramore, Jr.). Music: Herbert Stothart. Photography: Harry Stradling. Editor: Robert J. Kern. Production and distribution: Metro-Goldwyn-Mayer. Release date: April 25, 1947. Running time: 122 minutes. Cast: Spencer Tracy (Colonel Jim Brewton), Katharine Hepburn, Robert Walker, Melvyn Douglas, Phyllis Thaxter, Edgar Buchanan, Harry Carey, Ruth Nelson, William "Bill" Philips, Robert Armstrong, James Bell, Robert Barrat, Charles Trowbridge, Russell Hicks, Trevor Bardette, Morris Ankrum.

CASS TIMBERLANE

Producer: Arthur Hornblow, Jr. Director: George Sidney. Based upon the novel by Sinclair Lewis. Adaptation: Donald Ogden Stewart, Sonya Levien. Screenplay: Donald Ogden Stewart. Music: Roy Webb. Photography: Robert Planck. Editor: John Dunning. Production and distribution: Metro-Goldwyn-Mayer. Release Date: January 9, 1948. Running time: 119 minutes. Cast: Spencer Tracy (Cass Timberlane), Lana Turner, Zachary Scott, Tom Drake, Mary Astor, Albert Dekker, Margaret Lindsay, Rose Hobart, John Litel, Mona Barrie, Josephine Hutchinson, Selena Royle, Frank Wilcox, Richard Gaines, John Alexander, Cameron Mitchell, Howard Freeman, Jessie Grayson, Griff Barnett, Pat Clark.

LISTENING EYES

Director: Larry Lansburgh. Photography: Hal Albert, John Norwood (Ansco Color). Production: USC School of Cinema, Walt Disney Productions. Distribution: John Tracy Clinic. First public showing: January 19, 1948. Running time: 18 minutes. Cast: Louise Tracy, Alathena Smith. Narrator: Spencer Tracy.

STATE OF THE UNION

Producer-director: Frank Capra. Associate producer: Anthony Veiller. Based upon the play by Howard Lindsay and Russel Crouse. Screenplay: Anthony Veiller, Myles Connolly (uncredited: Frank Capra). Music: Victor Young. Photography: George J. Folsey. Editor: William Hornbeck. Production: Liberty Films. Distribution: Metro-Goldwyn-Mayer. Release date: April 30, 1948. Running time: 124 minutes. Cast: Spencer Tracy (Grant Matthews), Katharine Hepburn, Van Johnson, Angela Lansbury, Adolphe Menjou, Lewis Stone, Howard Smith, Charles Dingle, Maidel Turner, Raymond Walburn, Margaret Hamilton, Art Baker, Pierre Watkin, Florence Auer, Irving Bacon, Charles Lane, Patti Brady, George Nokes, Carl "Alfalfa" Switzer, Tom Fadden, Tom Pedi.

EDWARD, MY SON

Producer: Edwin H. Knopf. Director: George Cukor. Based upon the play by Robert Morley and Noel Langley. Screenplay: Donald Ogden Stewart (uncredited: Luther Davis). Music: John Woodridge. Photography: F. A. Young. Editor: Raymond Poulton. Production and distribution: Metro-Goldwyn-Mayer. Release date: June 10, 1949. Running time: 117 minutes. Cast: Spencer Tracy (Arnold Boult), Deborah Kerr, Ian Hunter, James Donald, Mervyn

Johns, Leureen MacGrath, Felix Aylmer, Walter Fitzgerald, Tilsa Page, Ernest Jay, Colin Gordon, Harriette Johns, Julian d'Albie, Clement McCallin.

ADAM'S RIB

Producer: Lawrence Weingarten. Director: George Cukor. Screenplay: Ruth Gordon, Garson Kanin. Music: Miklos Rozsa. Song: "Farewell, Amanda" (music and lyrics: Cole Porter). Photography: George Folsey. Editor: George Boemler. Production and distribution: Metro-Goldwyn-Mayer. Release date: November 18, 1949. Running time: 101 minutes. Cast: Spencer Tracy (Adam Bonner), Katharine Hepburn, Judy Holliday, Tom Ewell, David Wayne, Jean Hagen, Hope Emerson, Eve March, Clarence Kolb, Emerson Treacy, Polly Moran, Will Wright, Elizabeth Flournoy.

MALAYA

Producer: Edwin H. Knopf. Director: Richard Thorpe. Story: Manchester Boddy. Screenplay: Frank Fenton. Music: Bronislau Kaper. Photography: George Folsey. Editor: Ben Lewis. Production and distribution: Metro-Goldwyn-Mayer. Release date: January 6, 1950. Running time: 95 minutes. Cast: Spencer Tracy (Carnahan), James Stewart, Valentina Cortesa, Sydney Greenstreet, John Hodiak, Lionel Barrymore, Gilbert Roland, Roland Winters, Richard Loo, Ian MacDonald, Tom Helmore.

FATHER OF THE BRIDE

Producer: Pandro S. Berman. Director: Vincente Minnelli. Based upon the novel by Edward Streeter. Screenplay: Frances Goodrich, Albert Hackett. Music: Adolph Deutsch. Photography: John Alton. Editor: Ferris Webster. Production and distribution: Metro-Goldwyn-Mayer. Release date: June 16, 1950. Rereleased: 1962 (Metro-Goldwyn-Mayer). Running time: 93 minutes. Cast: Spencer Tracy (Stanley T. Banks), Joan Bennett, Elizabeth Taylor, Don Taylor, Billie Burke, Leo G. Carroll, Moroni Olsen, Melville Cooper, Taylor Holmes, Paul Harvey, Frank Orth, Rusty Tamblyn, Tom Irish, Marietta Canty.

FOR DEFENSE, FOR FREEDOM, FOR HUMANITY

Production: Metro-Goldwyn-Mayer. Release date: March 1951. Running time: 3 minutes. Tracy urges the audience to support the annual Red Cross Drive.

FATHER'S LITTLE DIVIDEND

Producer: Pandro S. Berman. Director: Vincente Minnelli. Based upon characters created by Edward Streeter. Screenplay: Frances Goodrich, Albert Hackett. Music: Albert Sendrey. Photography: John Alton. Editor: Ferris Webster. Production and distribution: Metro-Goldwyn-Mayer. Release date: April 4, 1951. Running time: 82 minutes. Cast: Spencer Tracy (Stanley T. Banks), Joan Bennett, Elizabeth Taylor, Don Taylor, Billie Burke, Moroni Olsen, Richard Rober, Marietta Canty, Rusty Tamblyn, Tom Irish, Hayden Roarke, Paul Harvey.

THE PEOPLE AGAINST O'HARA

Producer: William H. Wright. Director: John Sturges. Based upon the novel by Eleazar Lipsky. Screenplay: John Monks, Jr. Music: Carmen Dragon. Photography: John Alton. Editor: Gene Ruggiero. Production and distribution: Metro-Goldwyn-Mayer. Release date: September 7, 1951. Running time: 102 minutes. Cast: Spencer Tracy (James F. Curtayne), Pat O'Brien, Diana Lynn, John Hodiak, Eduardo Ciannelli, James Arness, Yvette Duguay, Jay C. Flippen, William Campell, Richard Anderson, Henry O'Neill, Arthur Shields, Louise Lorimer, Ann Doran, Emile Meyer, Regis Toomey, Katharine Warren.

PAT AND MIKE

Producer: Lawrence Weingarten. Director: George Cukor. Screenplay: Ruth Gordon, Garson Kanin. Music: David Raksin. Photography: William Daniels. Editor: George Boemler. Production and distribution: Metro-Goldwyn-Mayer. Release date: June 13, 1952. Running time:

95 minutes. Cast: Spencer Tracy (Mike Conovan), Katharine Hepburn, Aldo Ray, William Ching, Sammy White, George Mathews, Loring Smith, Phyllis Povah, Charles Buchinski, Frank Richards, Jim Backus, Chuck Connors, Joseph E. Bernard, Owen McGiveney, Lou Lubin, Carl Switzer, William Self. As themselves: Gussie Moran, Babe Didrikson Zaharias, Don Budge, Alice Marble, Frank Parker, Betty Hicks, Beverly Hanson, Helen Dettweiler.

PLYMOUTH ADVENTURE

Producer: Dore Schary. Director: Clarence Brown. Based upon the novel by Ernest Gabler. Screenplay: Helen Deutsch. Music: Miklos Rozsa. Photography: William Daniels (Technicolor). Editor: Robert J. Kern. Production and distribution: Metro-Goldwyn-Mayer. Release date: November 28, 1952. Running time: 105 minutes. Cast: Spencer Tracy (Captain Jones), Gene Tierney, Van Johnson, Leo Genn, Lloyd Bridges, Dawn Addams, Barry Jones, Noel Drayton, John Dehner, Tommy Ivo, Lowell Gilmore.

THE ACTRESS

Producer: Lawrence Weingarten. Director: George Cukor. Based upon the play *Years Ago* by Ruth Gordon. Screenplay: Ruth Gordon. Music: Bronislau Kaper. Photography: Harold Rosson. Editor: George Boemler. Production and distribution: Metro-Goldwyn-Mayer. Release date: September 25, 1953. Running time: 90 minutes. Cast: Spencer Tracy (Clinton Jones), Jean Simmons, Teresa Wright, Anthony Perkins, Ian Wolfe, Kay Williams, Mary Wickes, Norma Jean Nilsson, Dawn Bender.

TEXAS THEATERS' CRIPPLED CHILDREN FUND TRAILER

Director: Harry Loud. Narration: Spencer Tracy. Release date: 1953.

A VISIT WITH SPENCER TRACY

Production: Metro-Goldwyn-Mayer (for the Variety Clubs of New England in association with the Boston Red Sox). Release date: 1954. Running time: 3 minutes. Cast: Spencer Tracy. Tracy urges support of the "Jimmy Fund," established in Boston for the research of childhood cancers and the care of children with cancer.

BROKEN LANCE

Producer: Sol C. Siegel. Director: Edward Dmytryk. Story: Philip Yordan. Screenplay: Richard Murphy. Music: Leigh Harline. Photography: Joseph MacDonald (CinemaScope, DeLuxe Color). Editor: Dorothy Spencer. Production and distribution: 20th Century-Fox. Release date: July 29, 1954. Running time: 96 minutes. Cast: Spencer Tracy (Matt Devereaux), Robert Wagner, Jean Peters, Richard Widmark, Katy Jurado, Hugh O'Brian, Eduard Franz, Earl Holliman, E. G. Marshall, Carl Benton Reid, Philip Ober, Robert Burton.

BAD DAY AT BLACK ROCK

Producer: Dore Schary. Associate producer: Herman Hoffman. Director: John Sturges. Based upon the story "Bad Time at Honda," by Howard Breslin. Adaptation: Don McGuire. Screenplay: Millard Kaufman. Music: André Previn. Photography: William C. Mellor (CinemaScope, Eastman Color). Editor: Newell P. Kimlin. Production and distribution: Metro-Goldwyn-Mayer. Release date: January 7, 1955. Rereleased: 1962 (Metro-Goldwyn-Mayer). Running Time: 81 minutes. Cast: Spencer Tracy (John J. Macreedy), Robert Ryan, Anne Francis, Dean Jagger, Walter Brennan, John Ericson, Ernest Borgnine, Lee Marvin, Russell Collins, Walter Sande.

THE MOUNTAIN

Producer-director: Edward Dmytryk. Based upon the novel *La neige en deuil*, by Henri Troyat (English translation by Constantine Fitzgibbon). Screenplay: Ranald MacDougall. Music:

Daniele Amfitheatrof. Photography: Franz F. Planer (VistaVision, Technicolor). Editor: Frank Bracht. Production and distribution: Paramount. Release date: September 19, 1956. Running time: 104 minutes. Cast: Spencer Tracy (Zachary Teller), Robert Wagner, Claire Trevor, William Demarest, Barbara Darrow, Richard Arlen, E. G. Marshall, Anna Kashfi, Richard Garrick, Harry Townes, Stacy Harris, Yves Brainville.

DESK SET

Producer: Henry Ephron. Director: Walter Lang. Based upon the play by William Marchant. Screenplay: Phoebe Ephron, Henry Ephron. Music: Cyril J. Mockridge. Photography: Leon Shamroy (CinemaScope, De Luxe Color). Editor: Robert Simpson. Production and distribution: 20th Century-Fox. Release date: May 15, 1957. Running time: 102 minutes. Cast: Spencer Tracy (Richard Sumner), Katharine Hepburn, Gig Young, Joan Blondell, Dina Merrill, Sue Randall, Neva Patterson, Harry Ellerbe, Nicholas Joy, Diane Jergens, Merry Anders, Ida Moore, Rachel Stephens.

THE OLD MAN AND THE SEA

Producer: Leland Hayward. Director: John Sturges (uncredited: Fred Zinnemann). Based upon the novella by Ernest Hemingway. Screenplay: Peter Viertel (uncredited: Ernest Hemingway, Paul Osborn). Music: Dimitri Tiomkin. Photography: James Wong Howe. Additional photography: Floyd Crosby, Tom Tutwiler. Underwater photography: Lamar Boren (WarnerColor). Editor: Arthur P. Schmidt. Production and distribution: Warner Bros. Release date: October 11, 1958. Rereleased: 1961 (Warner Bros.). Running time: 86 minutes. Cast: Spencer Tracy (The Old Man), Felipe Pazos, Jr., Harry Bellaver.

THE LAST HURRAH

Producer-director: John Ford. Based upon the novel by Edwin O'Connor. Screenplay: Frank Nugent. Photography: Charles Lawton, Jr. Editor: Jack Murray. Production and distribution: Columbia. Release date: October 22, 1958. Running time: 122 minutes. Cast: Spencer Tracy (Frank Skeffington), Jeffrey Hunter, Dianne Foster, Pat O'Brien, Basil Rathbone, Donald Crisp, James Gleason, Edward Brophy, John Carradine, Willis Bouchey, Basil Ruysdael, Ricardo Cortez, Wallace Ford, Frank McHugh, Carleton Young, Frank Albertson, Bob Sweeney, William Leslie, Anna Lee, Ken Curtis, Jane Darwell, O. Z. Whitehead, Arthur Walsh.

INHERIT THE WIND

Producer-director: Stanley Kramer. Based upon the play by Jerome Lawrence and Robert E. Lee. Screenplay: Nathan E. Douglas [Nedrick Young], Harold Jacob Smith. Production design: Rudolph Sternad. Music: Ernest Gold. Songs: "(Give Me That) Old Time Religion," "Battle Hymn of the Republic." Vocals: Leslie Uggams. Photography: Ernest Laszlo. Editor: Frederick Knudtson. Production: Lomitas Productions, Inc. Distribution: United Artists. Release date: October 11, 1960. Running time: 126 minutes. Cast: Spencer Tracy (Henry Drummond), Fredric March, Gene Kelly, Florence Eldridge, Dick York, Donna Anderson, Harry Morgan, Elliott Reid, Philip Coolidge, Claude Akins, Paul Hartman, Jimmy Boyd, Noah Beery, Jr., Gordon Polk, Ray Teal, Norman Fell, Hope Summers, Renee Godfrey.

THE DEVIL AT 4 O'CLOCK

Producer: Fred Kohlmar. Director: Mervyn LeRoy. Based upon the novel by Max Catto. Screenplay: Liam O'Brian. Music: George Duning. Photography: Joseph Biroc (Eastman Color). Editor: Charles Nelson. Production and distribution: Columbia. Release date: October 18, 1961. Running Time: 127 minutes. Cast: Spencer Tracy (Father Matthew Doonan), Frank Sinatra, Kerwin Mathews, Jean-Pierre Aumont, Gregoire Aslan, Alexander Scourby, Barbara Luna, Cathy Lewis, Bernie Hamilton, Martin Brandt, Lou Merrill, Marcel Dalio, Tom Middleton, Ann Duggan, Louis Mercier, Michele Montau.

JUDGMENT AT NUREMBERG

Producer-director: Stanley Kramer. Associate producer: Philip Langner. Based upon the teleplay by Abby Mann. Screenplay: Abby Mann. Production design: Rudolph Sternad. Music: Ernest Gold. Song: "Lili Marleen" (music: Norbert Schultze; lyrics: Hans Leip). Song: "Liebeslied" (music: Ernest Gold; lyrics: Alfred Perry). Photography: Ernest Laszlo. Editor: Frederick Knudtson. Production: Roxlom Films, Inc. Distribution: United Artists. Release date: December 19, 1961 (roadshow); May 19, 1962 (general). Running time: 189 minutes. Cast: Spencer Tracy (Judge Dan Haywood), Burt Lancaster, Richard Widmark, Marlene Dietrich, Maximilian Schell, Judy Garland, Montgomery Clift, William Shatner, Werner Klemperer, Kenneth MacKenna, Torben Meyer, Joseph Bernard, Alan Baxter, Ed Binns, Virginia Christine, Otto Waldis, Karl Swenson, Martin Brandt, Ray Teal, John Wengraf, Ben Wright, Howard Caine, Olga Fabian, Paul Busch, Bernard Kates.

HOW THE WEST WAS WON

Producer: Bernard Smith. Directors: John Ford, George Marshall, Henry Hathaway. Screenplay: James R. Webb. Music: Alfred Newman, Ken Darby. Photography: William Daniels, Milton Krasner, Charles Lang, Jr., Joseph LaShelle (Cinerama, Metrocolor). Editor: Harold Kress. Production and distribution: Metro-Goldwyn-Mayer. Release date: November 1, 1962 (European premiere); February 20, 1963 (U.S. premiere). General release: 1964 (35mm). Rereleased: 1969 (70mm). Running time: 155 minutes. Cast: Carroll Baker, Lee J. Cobb, Henry Fonda, Carolyn Jones, Karl Malden, Gregory Peck, George Peppard, Robert Preston, Debbie Reynolds, James Stewart, Eli Wallach, John Wayne, Richard Widmark, Brigid Baalen, Walter Brennan, David Brian, Andy Devine, Raymond Massey, Agnes Moorehead, Harry Morgan, Thelma Ritter, Mickey Shaughnessy, Russ Tamblyn. Narrator: Spencer Tracy.

IT'S A MAD, MAD, MAD, MAD WORLD

Producer-director: Stanley Kramer. Screenplay: William Rose, Tania Rose. Production design: Rudolph Sternad. Music: Ernest Gold. Songs: "It's a Mad, Mad, Mad, Mad World," "Thirty-One Flavors," "You Satisfy My Soul" (music and lyrics: Ernest Gold, Mack David). Photography: Ernest Laszlo (Ultra Panavision, Technicolor). Editors: Frederick Knudtson, Robert C. Jones, Gene Fowler, Jr. Production: Casey Productions, Inc. Distribution: United Artists. Release date: November 7, 1963 (roadshow), July 25, 1964 (general). Rereleased: 1970 (United Artists). Running Time: 190 minutes (roadshow), 161 minutes (general). Cast: Spencer Tracy (Captain C. G. Culpepper), Milton Berle, Sid Caesar, Buddy Hackett, Ethel Merman, Mickey Rooney, Dick Shawn, Phil Silvers, Terry-Thomas, Jonathan Winters, Edie Adams, Dorothy Provine, Eddie "Rochester" Anderson, Jim Backus, Ben Blue, Joe E. Brown, Alan Carney, Chick Chandler, Barrie Chase, Lloyd Corrigan, William Demarest, Selma Diamond, Peter Falk, Andy Devine, Norman Fell, Paul Ford, Stan Freeberg, Louise Glenn, Leo Gorcey, Sterling Holloway, Marvin Kaplan, Edward Everett Horton, Buster Keaton, Don Knotts, Charles Lane, Mike Mazurki, Charles McGraw, Cliff Norton, Zasu Pitts, Carl Reiner, Madlyn Rhue, Roy Roberts, Arnold Stang, Nick Stewart, The Three Stooges, Sammee Tong, Jesse White, Jimmy Durante.

Note: While *It's a Mad, Mad, Mad, Mad World* was shot in Ultra Panavision, a 65mm anamorphic process, it was initially exhibited under the trade name Cinerama, a 35mm three-camera process. The film was not originally conceived as a Cinerama production but was rather embraced by Cinerama, which had been working to develop a single-lens, single-projector system for more than a year. A two-picture deal between Cinerama and United Artists (for *Mad World* and *The Greatest Story Ever Told*) was concluded in August 1962. In exchange for the promotional use of the Cinerama logo (and the cachet of opening the film in Cinerama venues with specially adjusted prints), UA paid Cinerama a licensing fee of $50,000.

THE RIPON COLLEGE STORY

Technical Advisers: Leonard W. Vaughn, Richard Kubik. Production: Rick Spalla Video Productions (16mm color). Distribution: Ripon College. Release date: 1965. Running time: 30 minutes. Cast: Jack Ankerson, Margaret Kuney. Narrators: Spencer Tracy, John Willis.

GUESS WHO'S COMING TO DINNER

Producer-director: Stanley Kramer. Associate producer: George Glass. Screenplay: William Rose. Production design: Robert Clatworthy. Music: Frank De Vol. Song: "Glory of Love" (music and lyrics: Billy Hill). Photography: Sam Leavitt (Technicolor). Editor: Robert C. Jones. Production and distribution: Columbia. Release date: December 11, 1967. Rereleased: 1972 (Columbia). Running time: 108 minutes. Cast: Spencer Tracy (Matt Drayton), Sidney Poitier, Katharine Hepburn, Katharine Houghton, Cecil Kellaway, Beah Richards, Roy E. Glenn, Sr., Isabel Sanford, Virginia Christine, Alexandra Hay, Barbara Randolph, D'Urville Martin, Tom Heaton, Grace Gaynor, Skip Martin, John Hudkins.

Notes and Sources

Frequently cited archives, collections, and libraries have been identified by the following abbreviations:

AADA   American Academy of Dramatic Arts, New York
  AFI   Louis B. Mayer Library, American Film Institute, Los Angeles
AMPAS   Margaret Herrick Library, Academy of Motion Picture Arts and Sciences, Los Angeles
   BT   Hall of History Collection, Boys Town, Nebraska
  DOS   Donald Ogden Stewart–Ella Winter Collection, Yale Collection of American Literature, Beinecke Rare Book and Manuscript Library
   EH   Ernest Hemingway Papers, John F. Kennedy Presidential Library, Boston
   ES   Edward Streeter Collection, Fales Library, New York University
  FOX   20th Century-Fox Collection, Theatre Arts Library, Special Collections, University of California, Los Angeles
 FXSC   20th Century-Fox Script Collection, Cinematics Arts Library, University of Southern California, Los Angeles
  JKA   Jane Kesner Ardmore Collection, Margaret Herrick Library, Academy of Motion Picture Arts and Sciences, Los Angeles
  JTC   John Tracy Clinic, Los Angeles
 KHLA   Katharine Hepburn Collection, Margaret Herrick Library, Academy of Motion Picture Arts and Sciences, Los Angeles
 KHNY   Katharine Hepburn Collection, The New York Public Library for the Performing Arts
  LOC   Library of Congress, Washington, D.C.
  MGM   Metro-Goldwyn-Mayer script collection at the Cinematics Arts Library, University of Southern California, Los Angeles

NYPL   Billy Rose Theatre Collection, The New York Public Library for the Performing Arts

PC   Playwrights' Company Collection, Wisconsin State Historical Society, Madison

RC   Ripon College Archives, Ripon, Wisconsin

SK   Stanley Kramer Papers. Department of Special Collections, Charles E. Young Research Library, University of California, Los Angeles

SLT   Spencer and Louise Tracy Collection, Los Angeles

SW   Selden West Collection, Los Angeles

TGC   Theatre Guild Correspondence, Yale Collection of American Literature, Beinecke Rare Book and Manuscript Library

TH   Top Hat Productions, New York

UCLA   Film and Television Archives, University of California, Los Angeles

USC   Cinematics Arts Library, University of Southern California, Los Angeles

WB   Warner Bros. Archives, University of Southern California, Los Angeles

CHAPTER I   GENERAL BUSINESS

3   The first time: Louise Tracy interview with Jane Kesner Ardmore, 6/27/72 (JKA). See also J. P. McEvoy, "Will They Get Wise to Him?" *This Week,* 5/24/42.

4   "delightfully cultured": Undated ad, *Daily Reporter* (SLT).

5   "If you saw him": Mrs. Spencer Tracy (guest columnist), "Walter Winchell," *Los Angeles Evening Herald and Express,* 7/31/39.

5   dead center of the stage: Jules Eckert Goodman, *The Man Who Came Back,* unpublished playscript, 1916 (NYPL).

6   Business improved: Details of the Wood Players in White Plains are from *Variety,* 4/19, 5/3, and 5/10/23; and *Billboard,* 6/9/23.

6   "The way he did it": McEvoy, "Will They Get Wise to Him?"

7   "Great Lover type": Walter Ramsey, "Life Story of a Real Guy," Part 2, *Modern Screen,* July 1934.

7   Gedney Farm Hotel: Details of the Palace Theatre and the Gedney Farm Hotel are from Reneda Hoffman, *It Happened in Old White Plains* (White Plains, N.Y.: Efficiency Printing Co., 1989); and Hoffman, *Yesterday in White Plains: A Picture History of a Vanished Era* (Tuckahoe, N.Y.: Little Art Graphics, 2003).

7   "Mother loved the theatre": Louise Tracy's history of the Treadwell family is from an interview with Jane Kesner Ardmore, 6/15/72 (JKA).

10   Campbell gave her work: Although Louise Treadwell's film appearances were unbilled, the Bebe Daniels comedies directed by Maurice Campbell during her time in California were *Two Weeks With Pay* (1921), *The March Hare* (1921), and *One Wild Week* (1921). The William deMille feature was likely *After the Show* (1921).

12   "My father": Ardmore, 6/15/72.

13   In Fall River: Details of the Wood Players in Fall River are from *Billboard,* 6/23 and 7/14/23; *New York Times,* 6/26/23; and *Variety,* 6/28 and 7/19/23.

14   "If you don't marry": Ramsey, "The Life Story of a Real Guy," Part 2.

15   "dispensation": The church required six instructions for the non-Catholic, and Louise took these in Milwaukee. John Tracy, who was upset by the requirement—thought they were being too hard on her—accompanied her.

15   "Mrs. Brown": McEvoy, "Will They Get Wise to Him?"

16   "Arthur Hopkins": Edward G. Robinson (with Leonard Spigelgass), *All My Yesterdays* (New York: Hawthorn Books, 1973), p. 72.

16   "He had one line": Ethel Barrymore, *Memories* (New York: Harper, 1955), p. 250.

17   "a rice pudding diet": S. R. Mook, "Checking Up on Tracy," *Screenland,* April 1942.

17   "old man": S. R. Mook, "He's Often Been Hungry," *Movie Mirror,* August 1932.

17   "The first week": S. R. Mook, "Spencer Tracy Talks About His Past," *Screen Book,* April 1936.

17   "I went up": Ardmore, 6/27/72 (JKA).

17   "Miss Treadwell": *Winnipeg Free Press,* 1/29/24.

18   "give him credit": *Variety,* 1/31/24.

19   "chairs on the stage": Spencer Tracy, unpublished interview with Pete Martin, December 1960 (USC).

20   "generous applause": *Grand Rapids Herald,* 6/17/24.

21   St. Mary's: Details of the birth of John Tracy are from birth certificate #8152, County of Milwaukee.

21   "afraid of him": Interview with Ardmore, undated (JKA).

21   "She is beautiful": *Grand Rapids Herald,* 6/24/24.

22   *Charley's Aunt:* The profitable and unprofitable plays of the 1924 season are identified in a letter from Mrs. L. S. Billman, manager of the Powers Theatre, to Clarence L. Dean, *Grand Rapids Herald,* 9/14/24.

22   "A lack": Selena Royle, unpublished autobiography, American Heritage Center, University of Wyoming, p. 50.

21   "fitting man": *Grand Rapids Herald,* 7/15/24.

24   "two minutes": Interview with Ardmore, undated.

CHAPTER 2   A BORN ACTOR

25   Merrill Park: My knowledge of Merrill Park comes primarily from John Gurda's excellent book *The West End* (Madison: University of Wisconsin Press, 1980). Gurda also did the research and copy for a Merrill Park poster published by the city's Discover Milwaukee project in 1983, which provides a concise historical overview of the neighborhood.

26   St. Paul Avenue: John Tracy's residential and work addresses are from Milwaukee City Directories, 1899–1926, and Milwaukee census records, 1900, 1910, and 1920.

26   John D. Tracy: Details of John D. Tracy's life are from Freeport census records, 1880; *Freeport Daily Democrat,* 1/30/1901; *Freeport Journal-Standard,* 2/11/18; and genealogical information provided by Jane Feely Desmond and Sister Ann Willitts, O.P.

26   "Galway": The name "Tracy" derives from the surname O'Treasant (from the Gaelic *treassach,* "embattled"). "O'Treasant" was established in Galway in the twelfth century. Variations include O'Trassy, O'Tressy, O'Trasey, Trassey, Tressy, Tracey, and Treacy. Although no one seems to know what John D. Tracy's middle initial stood for, it is known that his mother's maiden name was Donnelly, and it may well be that his full name was John Donnelly Tracy.

26   settled in Freeport: The best single reference on Freeport and its history is Mary X. Barrett, *History of Stephenson County* (Freeport, Ill.: County of Stephenson, 1970). Harriett Gustason's "Looking Back" columns for the *Freeport Journal-Standard,* which have been collected into a series of books by the Stephenson County Historical Society, are invaluable for preserving the recollections of Freeport's elder citizens. Leslie T. Fargher's manuscript *Life and Times in Freeport, Illinois* (1967) at the Freeport Public Library was also helpful.

27   Caleb Brown: The Browns of Freeport are documented in *Portrait and Biographical Album of Stephenson County, Ill.* (Chicago: Chapman Brothers, 1888); *Freeport Daily Journal,* 1/8/1887, 10/11/1897, and 5/18/1910; and various editions of the Freeport City Directory.

27   "I would sit": Jane Feely Desmond to Selden West, February 1992 (SW).

28   "In accordance": *Freeport Daily Journal,* 8/30/1894.

29   Carroll Edward Tracy: *Freeport Daily Democrat,* 6/15/1896; and the baptismal record at the Church of St. Mary, Freeport, Illinois.

29   Dr. O'Malley: Details of the birth of Spencer Tracy are from birth certificate #3714, County of Milwaukee, and the baptismal record at the St. Rose Congregation, Milwaukee.

29 "name him": Jane Feely Desmond to Selden West.

30 village of Bay View: My knowledge of Bay View comes principally from John Gurda, *Bay View, Wis.* (Madison: University of Wisconsin Press, 1979); and "Walking Tours of Bay View," a series of maps published by the Bay View Historical Society. Arthur J. Hickman's manuscript *Bay View as I Remember It* (1985) at the Bay View branch of the Milwaukee Public Library was particularly helpful, as was Erwin F. Zillman, *So You Will Know . . .* (Milwaukee: Erwin F. Zillman, 1966); and Melvin A. Graffenius, *A City Park for the South Side* (Milwaukee: Bay View Historical Society, 1990).

31 "He's a throwback": Walter Ramsey, "Life Story of a Real Guy," Part 1, *Modern Screen,* June 1934.

31 "He was in dresses": Peggy Hoyt Black, "That Tough Tracy Kid," *Picture Play,* February 1937.

32 kindergarten: According to archival records maintained by the Milwaukee Public School District, Spencer Bernard Tracy was registered for A.M. Kindergarten in June 1906. I am grateful to Montina Nelson of Trowbridge Elementary School of Discovery and Technology for checking this for me.

32 "signs of wanderlust": *Chicago Daily News,* 12/26/36.

32 "Being sentimentally Irish": Louis Sobol, "Voice of Broadway," undated (NYPL).

32 "Spencer's exploits": Kay Proctor, "Ex-Bad Boy," *Screen Guide,* April 1937.

34 "Uncle Andrew": Jane Feely Desmond to the author, via telephone, 2/19/04.

34 "He was terrible": Bertha Calhoun to the author, Freeport, 7/19/06.

35 "wild ideas": Ramsey, "Life Story of a Real Guy," Part 1. The Jesse James picture was likely G. M. (later "Broncho Billy") Anderson's *The James Boys in Missouri* (1908), a particularly appealing attraction since it had been banned in Chicago. The life of Christ may have been the French import *The Birth, the Life, and the Death of Christ* (1906). Each film ran approximately twenty minutes.

35 "bag full of candy": Frank Tracy to Selden West, 11/21 and 11/22/91 (SW).

35 "round him up": Harriett Gustason, "Looking Back," *Freeport Journal-Standard,* 7/14/84.

35 "all these things": Jane Feely Desmond to the author.

36 "tiny lad": Buck Herzog, "Older Brother Helped Him Over Rough Spots," *Milwaukee News-Sentinel,* 8/27/38.

36 "gone back": McEvoy, "Will They Get Wise to Him?"

36 "Spencer was always punished": Herzog, "Older Brother Helped Him Over Rough Spots."

36 "A tough kid": Black, "That Tough Tracy Kid."

37 St. John's Cathedral: Details of the third-grade curriculum at St. John's are from *Manual of the Course of Studies for the Catholic Schools of the Archdiocese of Milwaukee* (Milwaukee: Edward Keogh Press, 1903).

37 "He remembered this nun": Frank Tracy to Selden West.

37 "unlit taper": *Milwaukee News-Sentinel,* 8/27/38.

38 "Admission": "Jaunts with Jamie," *Milwaukee Sentinel,* 6/28/67. The oft-repeated story of Tracy having set fire to one of his childhood homes doesn't appear to be based in fact. It first appeared in a 1940 autobiography issued by the studio in which Tracy supposedly confessed to having "accidentally started a fire in our basement and the fire department had to be called." In his 1962 profile of Tracy for *Look,* Bill Davidson ran with the incident and reported the fire as coming "close to burning down the family home." By 1988 Davidson had decided that Tracy had deliberately started the fire after a furious argument with his father. Ten years after that, Christopher Andersen, in his book *An Affair to Remember,* added fresh details: "As flames shot out of the basement windows, fire trucks came roaring up the street. The entire neighborhood gathered outside on the street to watch the firemen battle the blaze for twenty minutes before finally bringing it under control. John was rigid with rage, but Carrie placed her hand

on the trembling boy's shoulder while she explained to the fire captain that Spencer had been experimenting with cigarettes in the basement."

In 1992 Selden West spent long hours with Captain Jeff Burke of the Milwaukee Fire Department, reading the huge handwritten ledgers of Milwaukee fire calls from 1908 through 1918. Although it's possible such an event took place prior to 1908, there was no record of a call to any of the Tracy addresses.

38   movie emporiums: My information on early Milwaukee movie theaters comes chiefly from Larry Widen and Judi Anderson, *Milwaukee Movie Palaces* (Milwaukee: Milwaukee County Historical Society, 1986). Individual issues of *Milwaukee Journal* were also consulted.

39   "the wrong kids": Jane Feely Desmond to Selden West.

39   "a good one": Kitty Callahan, "Spencer Tracy," *Family Circle*, 6/5/42.

40   "enacting scenes": Spencer Tracy, "Making Faces at Life" (Part I), *Milwaukee Journal*, 4/29/40.

40   "we have told people": "Flo" to Carrie Tracy, 1931 (SLT).

40   "scarcely tall enough": Carroll E. Tracy (with Fred Dudley), "The Kid Brother," manuscript, 1943 (AMPAS).

41   Sterling Motor Truck: John Tracy joined the Sternberg Motor Truck Company sometime in 1914. The name was changed to Sterling when, due to the war in Europe, it became difficult to sell trucks bearing a German name.

41   failed spectacularly: Spencer Tracy's grades for Wauwatosa High School were reported to Northwestern Military and Naval Academy on a form provided by the Academy in October 1919 (SW).

41   "enjoyed school": Tom Wright, "When Spencer Tracy was Seventeen," *Movies*, August 1941.

42   "badness": "Spencer Tracy," summary biography, 1937 (SLT).

42   "I remember Rockhurst": *Kansas City Star*, 2/29/48.

42   "I started": Richard T. English, "I'm a Mug[g] and Proud of It," *Hollywood*, September 1934.

42   "clearest recollections": Pat O'Brien (as told to S. R. Mook), "My Pal, Spencer Tracy," *Screen Book*, March 1939.

42   "iron men": A dollar was sometimes referred to as an "iron man."

43   "All of us Catholics": Pat O'Brien, *The Wind at My Back* (New York: Doubleday, 1964), p. 39.

43   "Spence and I": *Milwaukee Journal*, 6/11/67.

43   "I was itching": Spencer Tracy, "There Was a Guy . . . ," *Screen & Radio Weekly*, December 1937.

44   "Jackie" band: The term "Jackie" was widely used in the media during the Great War in lieu of the word "sailor." It was presumably derived from the British "jack-tar."

44   "The bands played": O'Brien, *The Wind at My Back*, p. 41.

44   "I was out of the house": Tracy, "The Kid Brother."

45   "Landsman for Electrician": Tracy's official military personnel record was destroyed in a fire at the National Personnel Records Center in July 1973. Details of his military service are drawn from health and enlistment records at the National Archives.

45   "The training": Wright, "When Spencer Tracy was Seventeen."

45   "polite specimens": Proctor, "Ex-Bad Boy."

46   "got into the Navy": Spencer Tracy, "Film War Too Real to Suit Private Tracy," *New York Daily Mirror*, 5/8/37.

46   "turned that city over": Wright, "When Spencer Tracy was Seventeen." Bill Davidson's 1988 Tracy biography *Tragic Idol* contains many obvious fabrications, including the memories of one Stanley Fischer, whom the author identifies as one of the men in Tracy's unit at Norfolk. Yet a search of the U.S. Navy muster rolls at the National Archives by Rebecca Livingston of the Naval/Maritime Team established there was

no one with that name stationed at either Great Lakes or Norfolk; both "Fisher" and "Fischer" were searched. (Courtesy of Tracey Johnstone.)

46   "He was a handful": Jane Feely Desmond to the author. According to an item in the *Aberdeen Daily News* of August 8, 1917, "Spencer Tracy of Kansas City, Mo., has arrived in the city for a three weeks' visit with his uncle and aunt, Mr. and Mrs. Patrick Feely. He will also spend some time in Ipswich with his uncle, Frank Tracy."

47   Davidson Hall: My knowledge of Northwestern Military and Naval Academy comes from Michael J. G. Gray-Fow, *Boys and Men* (Lake Geneva, Wis.: Northwestern Military and Naval Academy, 1988). Conversations with Robert B. Edgers and various years of the school catalog were also helpful.

47   "college question": H. H. Rogers, Spencer Bernard Tracy High School Credits, undated notes, circa 1920 (SW).

47   "Assuming that Spencer": John D. Tracy to Colonel Davidson, 2/2/20 (SW).

48   "During the summer": Lois and Kenneth Edgers, "The Spencer Tracy We Knew," unpublished manuscript, circa, 1968 (courtesy of Robert B. Edgers).

49   "something with my hands": *Milwaukee Journal,* undated clipping, 1936.

CHAPTER 3   A SISSY SORT OF THING

50   "I remember": H. P. Boody, "Spencer Tracy at Ripon," *The Forensic,* January 1936.

50   "most popular man": Lola Schultz Castner to Selden West, via telephone, 3/17/92 (SW).

51   "enjoyed the trips": Edgers, "The Spencer Tracy We Knew."

52   "a fellow in our house": Professor J. Clark Graham, as quoted in Donald Deschner, *The Films of Spencer Tracy* (New York: Citadel Press, 1968), p. 34.

53   "one of the strongest actors": *Ripon College Days,* 3/17/21 (RC).

53   trip herself up: *Milwaukee Journal,* 7/22/45. See also Clemens E. Lueck, undated manuscript (RC).

54   "proved himself": *Ripon College Days,* 6/23/21 (RC).

55   "My God": Ibid.

56   "fond of Spence": Lorraine Foat Holmes to Selden West, Wellesley, Mass., 6/20/92 (SW).

56   "more arguments": Sobol, "Voice of Broadway."

56   "The Dean": Carol Holmes Phillips to Selden West, 1/22/92 (SW).

58   "Of all the wonders": These lines, from *Julius Caesar,* Act II, Scene II, are reversed.

58   flunked Zoology: Spencer B. Tracy, Ripon College Student Record.

58   "The response": H. P. Boody, *Suggestions for the Actor* (Ripon, Wis.: Pi Kappa Delta, 1926), p. 21.

59   Bad weather: My account of the *Truth* tour is drawn from *Ripon College Days,* 12/26/21 and 1/10/22, and Selden West's interview with Lorraine Foat Holmes.

61   "I found": Spencer Tracy, "Professor Boody Pointed My Nose Toward the Stage," *The Forensic,* January 1936.

61   "His quiet manner": *Ripon Commonwealth,* 1/17/22.

61   "As a result": Deschner, *The Films of Spencer Tracy,* p. 35.

62   "There were two places": Curtis MacDougall, "Rambling Reminiscences," unpublished manuscript, February 1985 (SW) (courtesy of Priscilla Ruth MacDougall).

63   "home fires": *Ripon College Days,* 2/22/22 (RC).

65   "anything like a skit": Larry Swindell, *Spencer Tracy* (New York: World Publishing, 1969), p. 28. See also Roy Newquist, *A Special Kind of Magic* (Chicago: Rand McNally, 1967), p. 144.

66   "sensitive & masculine": Tracy's original evaluation sheet is at the American Academy of Dramatic Arts.

67   "His ability": *Ripon College Days,* 4/11/22 (RC).

68   Defects in speech: Details of the AADA curriculum are from the 39th Annual Cata-

logue of the American Academy of Dramatic Arts and the Empire Theatre Dramatic School, 1922–23 (AADA).

68 "quite the place": ST to Lorraine Foat, 6/2/22 (SW).

68 "very ambitious": *New Canaan Advertiser,* December 1969 (SW).

69 "pulling wires": O'Brien, "My Pal, Spencer Tracy."

69 "two steep shaky flights": O'Brien, *The Wind at My Back,* p. 55.

70 "Don't worry": Eleanor Cody Gould, *Charles Jehlinger in Rehearsal* (New York: American Academy of Dramatic Arts, 1958), pp. 1–10.

71 He wrote "good": The original evaluation sheet for Olive Lorraine Foat is at the American Academy of Dramatic Arts.

71 "Pat and I": Lloyd Shearer, "Spencer Tracy," *Parade,* 12/18/55.

72 "Dear God": Scott Eyman, "Interview with Pat O'Brien," *Films and Filming,* April 1982.

72 "couldn't afford": *Films and Filming,* March 1971.

72 "I didn't know": Spencer Tracy, "Making Faces at Life" (Part III), *Milwaukee Journal,* 5/1/40.

72 "Spence and I": Pat O'Brien, "Spencer Tracy As Is," *Screenland,* November 1951.

72 "hot stuff": *Chicago Tribune,* 11/14/37.

73 "I shall always be grateful": ST to Frances Fuller, 4/3/62 (AADA).

74 "soft spot": Sobol, "Voice of Broadway."

CHAPTER 4   THE BEST GODDAMNED ACTOR

76 "credit to dramatic stock": *Billboard,* 10/11/24.

76 "a hard critic": Ardmore, "Tracy," n.d. (JKA).

77 "My salary": Ramsey, "Life Story of a Real Guy," Part 2.

78 horrifying discovery: Louise Tracy always remembered that her son John was ten months old when she learned of his deafness, which would mean the discovery took place in April 1925. She also consistently remembered that she and her husband were planning to go out that night. In Grand Rapids, Spencer Tracy worked seven nights a week beginning April 12, 1925, so the event most likely occurred sometime between April 5, the day he began rehearsals for *The Nervous Wreck* (which was also his twenty-fifth birthday), and April 11, the last night he would have free.

78 "sleeping porch": Ardmore, "John," n.d. (JKA).

78 "awakening from a nightmare": Louise Treadwell Tracy, *The Story of John,* unpublished manuscript, circa 1941, p. 1 (SLT).

79 "gained in poise": *Grand Rapids Herald,* 4/13/25.

79 "hated the idea": A. D. Rathbone IV, "Out of Spencer Tracy's Yesterdays," *Photoplay,* October 1940.

79 "naughtiest thing": Emily Clagett Deming to Selden West, Grand Rapids, 3/21/93 (SW). See also *Grand Rapids Press,* 11/20/79.

80 "inconvenient indisposition": *Grand Rapids Herald,* 4/21/25.

80 "John hears": Tracy, *The Story of John,* p. 3.

81 "deaf and dumb": Ardmore, "John," n.d.

82 "I was in love": Larry Swindell to the author, Moraga, Calif., 6/28/05.

82 "Acting gave us": Swindell, *Spencer Tracy,* p. 45.

83 "out of the faint": Royle, unpublished autobiography, p. 51.

83 "no one I wanted to act with": Swindell, *Spencer Tracy,* p. 45.

83 Spence was involved with: When Selden West asked Emily Deming if Tracy had affairs with any of the other women in the company, she replied, "Well, the ingénue and he had a pretty good time together. Betty—she was the ingénue." Betty Hanna (1903–76) joined the Broadway Players on April 5, 1925, and remained with the company for the rest of the season. Later, when asked if Hanna had been an "item" with Tracy, Deming replied, "Rather briefly, as I remember it." Larry Swindell interviewed

Louise Tracy in 1968 and noticed that she would "freeze a bit" when Selena Royle's name was mentioned. However, in her unpublished autobiography, Royle was mystified as to why Louise was so cool to her when she arrived in Hollywood in 1944, something that likely would not have surprised her had she actually slept with Spencer Tracy.

84   "all the crazy things": Ardmore, "John," n.d.

84   "lost her interest": Ramsey, "Life Story of a Real Guy," Part 2.

84   "just broke down": Ardmore, "John," n.d. In *The Story of John,* Louise remembered that she told her husband of their son's deafness in July 1925. In "Life Story of a Real Guy," Spencer Tracy remembered it was on a Sunday. The earliest Sunday on which Tracy would not have had to give a performance would have been July 5, almost exactly three months from the time when Louise first learned of John's deafness.

84   "Words of encouragement": Tracy, *The Story of John,* p. 5.

84   "pin him down": Ardmore, "Tracy," n.d.

86   "That good-for-nothing!": McEvoy, "Will They Get Wise to Him?"

86   "gripping": *Stamford Advocate,* 10/10/25.

86   savvy notice: *Variety,* 10/14/25.

87   "exactness": *Trenton Times,* 11/10/25.

87   "evidence of a temper": Ethel Remey to Selden West, via telephone, 1/3/78 (SW).

87   "Fortunately for John": Tracy, *The Story of John,* p. 11.

87   "no kind of a life": Ardmore, "Tracy," n.d.

88   "last stand": Tracy, *The Story of John,* p. 12.

89   "nice young man": Louise Tracy to Jane Ardmore, 7/5/72 (JKA).

91   "a reprieve": *Chicago Tribune,* 11/14/37.

91   "best opportunity": Tracy, *The Story of John,* p. 33.

91   "purposes of prestige": *Variety,* 9/29/26.

91   "Lambs Club": ST to Pete Martin.

91   "direct his shows": John McCabe, *George M. Cohan: The Man Who Owned Broadway* (Garden City, N.Y.: Doubleday, 1973), p. 205.

91   "scared to death": ST to Pete Martin.

92   "During rehearsals": Royle, unpublished autobiography, p. 52. See also McCabe, *George M. Cohan:* "After giving an order or a change in direction," she remembered, "he would say, 'Gay-head, gay-head,' which meant, 'Go ahead, go ahead.' We never knew why he used that particular pronunciation."

92   Nat Goodwin: McCabe, *George M. Cohan,* p. 214.

93   "a wonderful night": Tracy to Ardmore, 7/5/72.

93   "nervous theatrical dynamite": *Variety,* 9/15/26.

94   "delighted the heart": *New York Journal,* 9/22/26.

94   "rang the doorbell": Tracy, *The Story of John,* p. 27.

95   "very disturbed": Ardmore, "John," n.d.

95   "like any father": Barry Norman, *The Hollywood Greats* (New York: Franklin Watts, 1980), p. 73.

96   "You see, Billy": Pat O'Brien to Ralph Story, "Spencer Tracy: An Unauthorized Biography" (Ronald Lyon Productions, 1975).

97   "very happy": ST to Chamberlain Brown, 2/28/27 (NYPL).

97   "Business is only fair": ST to Chamberlain Brown, 3/7/27 (NYPL).

98   "never believed in this": Ardmore, "Tracy," n.d.

98   third week's gross: Weekly figures for *Ned McCobb's Daughter* are from *Variety,* 2/23, 3/3, 3/18, and 4/13/27.

98   "Wright's proposition": ST to Chamberlain Brown, 3/14/27 (NYPL).

98   "One evening": Tracy, *The Story of John,* p. 42.

99   "to avoid thunder": *Lima Sunday News,* 5/15/27.

99   "How many bankers": *Lima News,* 4/12/27.

100   "Miss Louise Treadwell": *Lima News,* 4/25/27.

100   "threw me a line": Ardmore, "Tracy," n.d.

100   "Things are running along": ST to Chamberlain Brown, 5/14/27 (NYPL).

100   "specially written part": *New York Times,* 10/9/27.

101   "It is the lead": Chamberlain Brown to ST, 6/7/27 (NYPL).

101   "the big chance": ST to Chamberlain Brown, 6/10/27 (NYPL).

CHAPTER 5   DREAD

102   "I sent your wire": Chamberlain Brown to ST, 6/7/27 (NYPL).

103   "this clipping": ST to Chamberlain Brown, 7/1/27 (NYPL).

103   "terrible mess": ST to Chamberlain Brown, 9/19/27 (NYPL).

104   "cocked my head": ST to Pete Martin.

104   "Listening": "Cohan Was Original Good Listener," undated clipping (SLT).

104   "her latest letter": Tracy, *The Story of John,* p. 51 (SLT).

105   " 'feel' his lines": Spencer Tracy, "That Grand Guy Cohan," *Modern Screen,* December 1932.

105   "look like a bum": William F. French, "The Greatest Friendship in Hollywood," *Modern Movies,* February 1938.

107   Radio: Tracy also mentioned working in radio in a letter to a Miss Cochrane dated December 19, 1927. The only radio program sponsored by the Standard Oil Company of New York (SOCONY) during the run of *The Baby Cyclone* featured the close-harmony team of Gus Van and Joe Schenck, two seasoned vaudevillians who delivered "rapid-fire comedy and high-altitude records in the vocal scale" over WEAF and six stations of the National Broadcasting Company. Whether Tracy was indeed the show's folksy announcer, known simply as "Sam the Touring Man," is seemingly lost to memory, for the man behind the voice was never publicly identified.

107   "Florida!": Ardmore, "Tracy," n.d.

108   "a long time": Jane Feely Desmond to Selden West.

108   "up at your apartment": John E. Tracy to ST, 3/1/28 (SLT).

108   "He adored this son": Lorraine Foat Holmes to Selden West.

108   "Spence, at that time": Charles R. Sligh, Jr., to Selden West, Delray Beach, Florida, 11/23/91 (SW).

109   "a very separate part": Jane Feely Desmond to Selden West.

109   "I am desperate": John E. Tracy to ST and Carroll Tracy, 4/21/28 (SLT).

110   "He got sick": Garson Kanin, *Tracy and Hepburn* (New York: Viking Press, 1971), p. 146.

112   "Dry times or wet": O'Brien, *The Wind at My Back,* p. 122.

112   "Mother dear": ST to Carrie Tracy, n.d. (SLT).

113   "An unemployed actor": O'Brien, *The Wind at My Back,* p. 76.

114   "I didn't like my part": Clark Gable (as told to James Reid), "My Pal, Spencer Tracy," *Screen Life,* July 1940.

115   "The final impression": *New York Times,* 3/7/29.

115   "So there we all were": Jean Dalrymple Oral History, Columbia University, 1979.

115   "Next season": ST to Chamberlain Brown, n.d. (NYPL).

115   "we had played together": Royle, unpublished autobiography, p. 53.

116   "nothing stagy": *Providence Journal,* 6/25/29.

116   "Upstairs and down": Tracy, *The Story of John,* p. 59.

117   "The women": Newquist, *A Special Kind of Magic,* p. 145.

118   "You'll—never—have": The unpublished text of *Dread* is in the Copyright Office's Drama Deposits collection at the Library of Congress.

118   "spit fire": *Washington Post,* 10/21/29.

118   "going to Brooklyn": Kanin, *Tracy and Hepburn,* p. 41.

118   "parlance of the stage": *Brooklyn Standard Union,* 10/30/29.

119   "most enthusiastic": *New York Herald Tribune,* 5/26/40. Tracy told Broadway colum-
       nist Ed Sullivan the same thing.

119   "laugh about *Dread*": Tracy, *The Story of John,* p. 42.

119   "I don't remember": Jane Ardmore, "Mrs. Spencer Tracy's Own Story," *Ladies' Home
       Journal,* December 1972.

119   "Louise flamed": Mook, "Checking Up on Tracy."

120   "a pretty disconsolate guy": O'Brien, *The Wind at My Back,* p. 120.

CHAPTER 6   THE LAST MILE

123   "how it will feel": Robert Blake, "The Law Takes Its Toll," *American Mercury,* July
       1929.

123   "Blake's sketch": Wexley originally cut Blake's mother in for 5 percent of the author's
       royalties. Once the play hit big on Broadway, friends in Texas sent Mrs. Ella Blake to
       New York, where she demanded a bigger share. Eric Pinkler, Wexley's agent, arranged
       to raise her share to 20 percent when it became apparent that the entire first act was
       derived almost entirely from Blake's work. Subsequently she attended a performance
       and was introduced to the cast.

123   "It was one o'clock": *Dallas Morning News,* 4/13/41.

124   "A few of his performances": Chester Erskine, "Spencer Tracy: The Face of Integrity,"
       The Movie (UK), No. 7, 1980.

124   "so *violent*": Ardmore, "Tracy," n.d.

125   "The sixteen": Herman Shumlin, "Teamwork and 'The Last Mile,' " *New York World,*
       5/20/30.

125   "cooperative and disciplined": Chester Erskine, *Spencer Tracy: A Biographical and
       Interpretive Symposium,* treatment for a TV documentary, circa 1968, p. 15 (SLT).

126   "I cannot remember": Spencer Tracy, "Long Runs Wear," *New York Telegraph,* 4/6/30.

126   "rank melodrama": *Hartford Times,* 2/7/30.

127   "Some individuals": *New York Sun,* 3/31/30.

129   "No detail": *New York Daily News,* 2/14/30.

129   "Nothing this season": *New York American,* 2/14/30.

130   "I was supposed to": Newquist, *A Special Kind of Magic,* p. 146.

131   "say I was gone": Howard Teichmann, *Smart Alec* (New York: Morrow, 1976), p. 149.

131   "A prison play": *New York Evening Post,* 2/14/30.

131   "desperation and fury": *New York Telegram,* 2/14/30.

131   "taut, searing": *New York Times,* 2/14/30.

131   "grimly effective": *New York Sun,* 2/14/30.

131   "thrillingly savage": *New York World,* 2/14/30.

131   "the final seal": *Commonweal,* 4/9/30.

132   practically sold out: Weekly figures for *The Last Mile* are from *Variety,* 2/19, 2/26, 3/5,
       3/12, 3/26, and 5/28/30.

132   "Mr. Erskine's direction": *New York Times,* 2/17/30.

132   "enthralled by the terrible": *Life,* 3/7/30.

132   "Nobody ever said": Newquist, *A Special Kind of Magic,* p. 145.

133   "doesn't photograph well": McEvoy, "Will They Get Wise to Him?"

133   "What have I done": The first reel of *Taxi Talks* is preserved at the Library of Congress,
       but no audio is known to exist. A dialogue continuity for the film is in the Warner
       Bros. Archives at the University of Southern California.

134   "It was all strange": Kanin, *Tracy and Hepburn,* p. 47.

135   "I liked it": *Philadelphia Inquirer,* 9/16/73.

135   "I'd meet Spencer": John Ford and Katharine Hepburn to Dan Ford, n.d., John Ford
       Collection, Manuscripts Department, Lilly Library, Indiana University, Bloomington.

135   " 'I'd like to have him' ": Newquist, *A Special Kind of Magic,* p. 146.

136 "The producer": Elisabeth Goldbeck, "Some New Evidence About Spencer Tracy," *Movie Classic,* December 1932.

137 "AS SHOW MUST OPEN": Tracy's contract for *Up the River* is in the 20th Century-Fox collection at UCLA.

138 "Sheehan wanted": Peter Bogdanovich, *John Ford* (Berkeley: University of California Press, 1968), p. 52. *Variety* credited the idea of the two men breaking back into the prison to a Fox publicity man named Joe Shea.

139 "I'm in Hollywood": Frank Tracy to Selden West.

139 "That's all John needs": Tracy, *The Story of John,* p. 65.

139 "[Ford] called us to the studio": Claire Luce, unpublished autobiography (courtesy of Mrs. Jeanne Selvin) (SW).

140 "It was interesting": Joan L. Jacobsen to the author, via telephone, 5/1/07.

140 "some base color": Michael F. Blake to the author, via e-mail, 4/23/07.

141 a new contract: A letter dated August 16, 1930, advised Tracy that the studio intended to exercise a six-month option on his services commencing June 1, 1931, as allowed in his contract.

142 "must get home": Tracy, *The Story of John,* p. 66.

CHAPTER 7   QUICK MILLIONS

143 "Poor Tommy": Swindell, *Spencer Tracy,* p. 77.

143 "Well acted": *Variety,* 9/3/30.

143 "THOUGHT OF DEAR DAD": ST to Carrie Tracy, 8/31/30 (SLT).

144 "walking down Park": Charles R. Sligh, Jr., to Selden West (SW).

144 Gardner's offer: Jack Gardner to Sol M. Wurtzel, 9/1/30 (FOX).

144 "Forwarding you today": Sol M. Wurtzel to ST, 9/4/30 (FOX).

145 "magnificent and terrifying": Deschner, *The Films of Spencer Tracy,* p. 20.

145 "My Dear Mr. Wurtzel": ST to Sol M. Wurtzel, 9/12/30 (FOX).

145 "a pack of fools": Tracy, *The Story of John,* p. 69 (SLT).

146 "Sheehan refused to go": Bogdanovich, *John Ford,* p. 52.

146 "Can you imagine": *New York American,* 10/13/30.

147 "worst actor": Ramsey, "Life Story of a Real Guy," Part 2.

149 "William Fox": Details on the battle for control of Fox Film are from "The Case of William Fox," *Fortune,* May 1930; and various issues of *Variety.*

150 "The Sheehan influence": *Motion Picture Herald,* 7/28/45.

152 "The remarkable thing": S. N. Behrman, "You Can't Release Dante's Inferno in the Summertime," *New York Times Magazine,* 7/17/66.

152 "Terrett knew well": Philippe Garnier, *Honni Soit Qui Malibu* (Paris: Bernard Grasset, 1996), p. 123.

153 negative cost: The cost of *Quick Millions* is from the research library of Karl Thiede.

154 "Look at that man": Lewis Yablonsky, *George Raft* (New York: McGraw-Hill, 1974), p. 60.

156 "what a time I had": John Ford to Dan Ford, n.d., John Ford Collection.

157 "Mr. Tracy's performance": *New York Times,* 4/18/31.

157 brutally bad: The week's figures for *Quick Millions* are from *Variety,* 4/22 and 4/29/31.

158 flat rate: Details of the Hughes loan-out are from Tracy's Legal Department file (FOX).

158 Armory in Culver City: The shooting schedule for *Ground Hogs* is in the Jack Mintz Collection (AFI). Mintz was unit manager on the picture.

158 "take three steps": Ridgeway Callow Oral History with Rudy Behlmer, 1974 (AFI).

159 "It had always been there": Interview with Ardmore, 7/5/72.

159 "shy side": Ardmore, "Tracy," n.d.

160 "seen a few rushes": S. R. Mook, "Spencer Tracy as I Know Him," *Screen Book,* March 1938.

160   "drink the least little bit": Interview with Ardmore, 7/5/72.

161   "direct imitation": *Variety*, 6/30/31.

161   undeniable losers: *Quick Millions* posted a loss of just under $3,000 on worldwide
       rentals of $278,000. Figures for both *Quick Millions* and *Six Cylinder Love* are from
       the research library of Karl Thiede.

161   "most marvelous picture": Ruth Biery, "Worry! Who—Me? Say!" *Photoplay*, Decem-
       ber 1932.

163   twelve drafts: The writing of *She Wanted a Millionaire* is documented in the Fox script
       files at USC and UCLA.

163   "rather private person": Joan Bennett (and Lois Kibbee), *The Bennett Playbill* (New
       York: Holt, Rinehart & Winston, 1970), p. 216.

164   lose weight: *Variety*, 8/11/31.

165   "YOU HAVE LOST": Jane Feely Desmond to the author, via telephone, 2/23/04.

                   CHAPTER 8   THE POWER AND THE GLORY

169   "wild, attractive Irishman": Bennett, *The Bennett Playbill*, p. 209.

169   "Having an affair": Rumors of Tracy's involvement with Joan Bennett and John Con-
       sidine's jealousy are discussed by Ruth Biery in "Worry! Who—Me? Say!" although
       Biery says all this was going on while Tracy was still addressing the actress as "Miss Ben-
       nett." Bennett herself, in an interview with David Heeley and Joan Kramer in 1985,
       said, "I didn't know him socially at all, so I can't account for his behavior off the set."

170   "my dressing room": Doug Warren, *James Cagney: The Authorized Biography* (New
       York: St. Martin's Press, 1983), p. 132.

173   Sheehan's attorney: Details of Winfield Sheehan's illness are from *Variety*, 12/8/31,
       12/22/31, and 1/12/32.

173   *Sky Devils*: Details of the film's pre-release engagements are contained in a memo from
       Lincoln Quarberg to Hal Horne, 1/29/32 (AMPAS). The film did equally well in New
       York, where brisk business was reported at the 2,200-seat Rivoli.

174   "After the preview": S. R. Mook, "Tough to You," *Picture Play*, September 1932.

174   "go down to the brewery": Mook, "Spencer Tracy as I Know Him."

176   "ever since they can remember": *Silver Screen*, July 1932.

176   "telephone repairmen": O'Brien, *The Wind at My Back*, p. 156.

176   "six days off": Dan Thomas, "Movie Colony Glimpses and Inside Stuff," undated
       clipping (SLT).

176   "the picture that sold me": Mook, "Checking Up on Tracy."

176   "future B.O. strength": *Motion Picture Herald*, 4/2/32.

176   "domestic rentals": Worldwide rentals of $548,693 yielded a profit of $19,456 on *Dis-
       orderly Conduct*. According to the research library of Karl Thiede, the film's negative
       cost was $298,972.

177   "The last two parts": S. R. Mook, "Tracy Talks!" *Screenland*, January 1934.

177   "I could not but add up": Tracy, *The Story of John*, p. 123.

177   "I was so pleased": Interview with Ardmore, 6/27/72.

178   "I was disappointed": John Tracy, "My Complicated Life" (Part One), *Volta Review*,
       June 1946.

178   "a little more absurd": *Los Angeles Times*, 6/19/32.

178   "steadfast faith": S. R. Mook, "The Man Who's Had Everything," *Screenland*, October
       1943.

178   results of a survey: *Variety*, 8/23/32.

179   "If pressed": Mook, "Tough to You."

179   considerably richer: Details of Tracy's loan-out to Warner Bros. are from his Fox Legal
       Department file.

179   "going to a picture": Mook, "Spencer Tracy as I Know Him."

180   "every possibility": Lewis E. Lawes to Jack L. Warner, 8/12/32 (WB).

180   Warren Hymer: Hymer's behavior on the set of *20,000 Years in Sing Sing* is documented in the film's production file (WB). Tracy's handling of Hymer is described in S. R. Mook, "Every-Day Tracy," *Silver Screen,* January 1933.

180   "crazy about my performance": Whitney Stine, *"I'd Love to Kiss You . . .": Conversations with Bette Davis* (New York: Pocket Books, 1990), p. 129.

182   "only George Arliss": Stine, *"I'd Love to Kiss You,"* p. 131.

183   "joked his way through it": Joan Bennett to David Heeley and Joan Kramer, New York, 11/20/85 (TH).

183   "giving medals": Mook, "Spencer Tracy as I Know Him."

184   "an atrocity": *Variety,* 9/27/32.

184   "something about horses": Thomas, "Movie Colony Glimpses and Inside Stuff."

184   "He comes home": Mook, "Tough to You."

185   "people he liked": Spencer Tracy, "My Pal, Will Rogers," *Hollywood,* December 1935.

185   "first to the café": *New York Times,* 8/25/35.

187   "feel about nightlife": Mook, "Spencer Tracy as I Know Him."

188   all-time low: *Me and My Gal* finished its week at the Roxy with a pallid $22,000 and fared no better in general release. An exhibitor in Harrisburg, Illinois, called it a "rough and ready comedy-drama that has its moments, and at times seems to show promise of getting somewhere but never reaches there, and when it's over you have the feeling that it was just another little picture with detectives and bad bank robbers all mixed up with the wisecracks of Tracy and Bennett. We ran it on a Sunday and Monday and were sorry, as it drew very poor on these days" (*Motion Picture Herald,* 4/15/33). According to the research library of Karl Thiede, worldwide rentals totaled just $391,564. With a negative cost of $308,684, the film posted a loss of $82,550.

189   "very much makeup": *New York Sun,* 2/24/33.

190   "The manuscript crackled": Jesse L. Lasky (with Don Weldon), *I Blow My Own Horn* (Garden City, N.Y.: Doubleday, 1957), p. 246.

190   "predicate all our plans": *Variety,* 1/17/33.

191   "They sent me the script": Colleen Moore to the author, via telephone, 3/26/77.

192   "sex relationship": Sidney Kent to Winfield Sheehan, 3/7/33.

192   "The schedule calls": Preston Sturges to Solomon Sturges, 3/27/33, Preston Sturges Collection, Department of Special Collections, Charles E. Young Research Library, University of California Los Angeles.

194   "dialogue overlapped": S. R. Mook, "Master Mugg," *Screenland,* April 1933.

195–96 "This isn't a business": Philip Trent (Clifford Jones) to Selden West, via telephone, 9/29/93 (SW).

196   "I was 21 years old": Lincoln W. Cromwell, M.D., *Dear Spence: Letters to Spencer Tracy from His Medical Student,* unpublished manuscript, 1980, preface, p. 1 (SW).

197   "four to eight films a year": Mook, "Master Mugg."

197   "ogling the poinsettias": Tracy, "The Kid Brother."

197   "go out and get drunk": (Suspect Name Redacted), interview with victim's former driver, 6/27/34, FBI file 7-749 (SW).

197   "the best of my recollection": Colleen Moore to Selden West, 12/9/77 (SW).

197   "He just went on": Colleen Moore to Selden West, via telephone, 12/15/77 (SW).

198   "when the latter picture is released": *Hollywood Reporter,* 4/29/33.

198   "wandered off": Frank Tracy to Selden West (SW).

198   "what Carroll needs": Frank Tracy to Selden West, via telephone, February 1993 (SW).

199   "What are you dissatisfied about?": Tracy, "Making Faces at Life" (Part V).

199   "complement his realities": Fay Wray, *On the Other Hand* (New York: St. Martin's Press, 1989), p. 145.

200   "most daring": *Hollywood Reporter,* 6/19/33.

200   "frightened us": Ibid., 6/20/33.

201   "most in all the world": *Los Angeles Examiner,* 6/23/33.

201   Sheehan got $3,000: Details of Tracy's loan-out to Columbia are from his Fox Legal Department file.

        CHAPTER 9   THE AMOUNT OF MARRIAGE WE'VE EXPERIENCED

202   "The situation was not": Frederick Lewis, "Spencer Tracy Conquers Himself," *Liberty,* 10/9/1937.

203   "They had decided": Lorraine Foat Holmes to Selden West.

203   "Borzage had a way": James Bawden, "Loretta Young," *Films in Review,* November 1987.

203   "Irritable as a bear": Mook, "Tough to You."

204   "Her diction": Jane Feely Desmond to the author.

206   "Louise and I stood up": Carter Bruce, "I'm Glad I Married Before I Came to Hollywood," *Modern Screen,* October 1933.

206   "The papers forced us": S. R. Mook, "The Truth About the Tracy Separation," *Movie Mirror,* November 1933.

206   "I gave them a statement": Mook, "Tracy Talks!"

207   "very susceptible": *New York Times,* 3/30/95.

207   "Spencer and I": Jack Grant, "Get Your Heart Broken Early," *Movie Classic,* March 1934.

207   "Such fire": Bawden, "Loretta Young."

207   "Spencer asked me": Grant, "Get Your Heart Broken Early."

208   "The story was a trifle": Bawden, "Loretta Young."

208   "conscious of Loretta": Gladys Hall, "Spencer Tracy's Love Confession," *Movie Mirror,* March 1934.

208   "gorgeous person": Howard Sharpe, "The Adventurous Life of Spencer Tracy" (Part 3), *Photoplay,* April 1937.

208   "meant *Lee* Tracy": Joan Wester Anderson, *Forever Young* (Allen, Tex.: Thomas More Publishing, 2000), p. 70.

209   "grows in stature": *New York American,* 8/17/33.

209   "a more exacting role": *New York Daily Mirror,* 8/17/33.

209   "No more convincing performance": *New York Times,* 8/17/33.

210   "its first seven days": Figures for *The Power and the Glory* are from *Variety,* 8/22, 8/29, 9/5, and 9/12/33. "A very good picture, but a box office flop," reported an exhibitor in Elvins, Missouri. "Marvelous acting by Spencer Tracy. Too depressing and slow for the masses" (*Motion Picture Herald,* 11/11/33).

210   "going to the set": Jane Feely Desmond to the author.

210   "Her dining tete-a-tete": *Los Angeles Examiner,* 9/14/33.

211   "I've been in love": Grant, "Get Your Heart Broken Early."

211   Madge Evans admitted: Larry Swindell to the author.

212   "not a devout Catholic": Jane Feely Desmond to the author.

213   "I *hope* you're not": Jane Feely Desmond to Selden West (SW).

213   "What could I say": Leatrice Joy to Selden West, via telephone, September 1977 (SW).

213   "Securely held": *Los Angeles Examiner,* 9/22/33.

213   "anything of this sort": Sharpe, "The Adventurous Life of Spencer Tracy," Part 3.

215   "so cheesy": Claire Trevor to Selden West, New York City, 10/4/95 (SW).

215   "He liked the way": John Gallagher, "Claire Trevor," *Films in Review,* November 1983.

215   "run a story": S. R. Mook, "Tracy Fights Through," *Screenland,* May 1935.

215   "I'd known Louise and Spencer": Mook, "The Truth About the Tracy Separation."

215   "good time": Mook, "Spencer Tracy As I Know Him."

215   "There's nothing about it": Mook, "The Truth About the Tracy Separation."

217   "The talk": Jack Oakie, *Jack Oakie's Double Takes* (San Francisco: Strawberry Hill Press, 1980), p. 160.

217   "The studio believes": MPPDA memorandum, 6/6/33 (AMPAS).

218   "impossible to eliminate": Sam Briskin to Dr. James Wingate, 7/22/33 (AMPAS).

218   "a fine and tender picture": Dr. James Wingate to Harry Cohn, 10/13/33 (AMPAS).

218   "matter-of-fact sincerity": *Hollywood Reporter,* 10/11/33.

219   "enchanted with the romance": Wray, *On the Other Hand,* p. 230.

220   "off-set scenes": Undated clip, December 1933 (SLT).

220   "How could it?": Hall, "Spencer Tracy's Love Confession."

222   "The superintendent": Ramsey, "Life Story of a Real Guy," Part 2.

222   "doing arithmetic": Tracy, *The Story of John,* p. 112 (SLT).

223   "being deaf": Tracy, "My Complicated Life," Part 1.

223   "domestic rentals": According to the research library of Karl Thiede, domestic rentals for *Man's Castle* totaled $388,000 in its initial release.

223   "the name of Spencer Tracy": *Hollywood Reporter,* 1/23/34.

223   "put on the shelf": Ibid., 1/25/34.

224   The script: Mankiewicz also received credit for adapting the play at Paramount. That version was released in 1930 under the title *Men Are Like That.*

226   "still married to Louise": Ramsey, "Life Story of a Real Guy," Part 2.

227   "Pete Are Silverton": The full text of the extortion letter is contained in FBI file 7-749.

228   "I felt ashamed": Tracy, "My Complicated Life," Part 1.

229    $2,500 option: Details of the deal between Mrs. Carolyn Rothstein Behar and Fox Film Corporation are from the Fox Legal Department file on *Now I'll Tell* (FOX).

230   "Tracy does the impossible": *Hollywood Reporter,* 2/22/34. *The Trouble Shooter* (retitled *Looking for Trouble*) was released the same day as *The Show-Off.*

231   "capital performance": *New York Times,* 3/17/34.

231   "His appeal": *Evening Standard,* 6/4/34.

231   bargain price: Figures for *The Show-Off* are from *Variety,* 3/20 and 3/27/34; and the Edgar J. "Eddie" Mannix ledger at the Margaret Herrick Library (AMPAS).

232   "deposited in the room": William Bakewell, *Hollywood Be Thy Name* (Metuchen, N.J.: Scarecrow Press, 1991), p. 60. Wayne later told a business associate that Tracy, drunk and belligerent, had sucker punched him, and that he had reflexively—and unapologetically—knocked him out.

232   "Spence was a darling": Judy Lewis, *Uncommon Knowledge* (New York: Pocket Books, 1994), p. 17.

233   "Hollywood's too easy": *New York American,* 4/22/34.

233   filled the Roxy: Box office figures for *Now I'll Tell* are from *Variety,* 5/29, 6/5, and 6/12/34. According to data in the research library of Karl Thiede, domestic rentals just about equaled the film's negative cost of $308,200. Foreign rentals amounted to $167,900, roughly 30 percent of the worldwide total of $472,300. It was carried on the books at a loss of $45,290.

234   "I am sure the pressure": Anderson, *Forever Young,* p, 75.

CHAPTER 10   AND DOES LOVE LAST?

236   " 'aren't going to do that' ": Ardmore, "Tracy," n.d.

237   "Never have I seen women": Tracy, *The Story of John,* p. 151.

238   "No one asked any questions": Mook, "The Truth About the Tracy Separation."

239   "In most ways": Louise Treadwell Tracy, *The Broader Outlook,* unpublished playscript, circa 1934 (SLT).

241   "Tracy at the time was in bed": George Wasson to Jack J. Gain, 7/2/34 (FOX).

243   "Speaking of TRACY": *Los Angeles Examiner,* 7/5/34.

243   "mention of Loretta's name": Jack Grant, "Why Loretta Young Broke Up Her Romance," *Movie Mirror,* October 1934.

243   "not an experienced actor": Ted Perry and David Shepard, *Henry King, Director: from silents to 'scope* (Los Angeles: Directors Guild of America, 1995), p. 89.

244   "Here is where": Ted Perry, Henry King Oral History, unedited manuscript, Directors Guild of America.

244   "middle of the flight": Robert Nott, "The Kinks of Comedy," *Filmfax,* December–January 1994.

245   "I recommended": Neil McCarthy to Alfred Wright, 4/5/39 (FOX).

245   "most severe penalty": *Variety,* 9/11/34.

245   "mounted the horse": Tracy, "My Complicated Life," Part 1.

246   "Immersed as we were": Cromwell, *Dear Spence,* p. 38.

247   "The studio gumshoed": Lasky, *I Blow My Own Horn,* p. 247.

247   "Forget what's happened": Mook, "Tracy Fights Through."

248   "While discussing the contract": Jack J. Gain to Sidney R. Kent, 11/1/34 (FOX).

248   "Spence's naïveté": Mook, "Checking Up on Tracy."

249   "The drama aims": Outline, *Inferno,* by Philip Klein and Rose Franken, 6/22/34 (USC).

249   "He clouts the engineer": Eric Knight to Paul Rotha, 10/27/34, Paul Rotha Papers, Department of Special Collections, University of California, Los Angeles.

250   "prove to the unsuspecting public": Louise Treadwell Tracy, "The Women Take to Polo," *Polo,* June 1935.

250   "Our shots": *Abilene Morning News,* 11/23/34.

250   "Spencer Tracy reconciliation": *Los Angeles Evening Herald and Express,* 12/8/34.

251   "They gave him a lot of time": Claire Trevor to Selden West.

252   "I ran amuck": Gladys Hall, "Why My Wife and I Are Together Again," *Movie Mirror,* May 1935. Bill Davidson, in his 1988 biography of Tracy, quotes a late publicity man, one Jim Denton, as saying the actor showed up drunk one morning on the set of *Dante's Inferno* and chased director Harry Lachman around the stage. Winfield Sheehan, when summoned, supposedly ordered the soundstage locked with Tracy asleep inside it. Denton went on to assert that Tracy awoke at some point and trashed the set, causing approximately $100,000 in damage.

    Dante's Inferno was shot at Western Avenue, not Fox Hills, and Sol Wurtzel would have been summoned in such an instance, not Sheehan. Claire Trevor, who would have been present, recalled no such incident, and Ralph Bellamy, who, according to Davidson, "vividly" remembered it, makes no mention of it in his 1979 autobiography. Moreover, there is nothing about Tracy damaging a set in any of the trade papers, nor in his Fox legal file, where a penalty would doubtless have been documented had Tracy caused anywhere near that much damage.

    Davidson, incidentally, first reported such an incident in his 1962 profile of Tracy in *Look.* In that article the incident is said to have occurred in 1933, not 1935, and the alleged quotes are attributed to a "movie executive" who was a reporter at the time.

254   "finest actor": Mook, "Checking Up on Tracy."

254   "I am Spencer Tracy": *Los Angeles Examiner,* 3/5/33.

254   "ranch life": Hall, "Why My Wife and I Are Together Again."

254   "They fired me": *Hollywood Citizen News,* 4/14/52.

255   "Old pact": *Variety,* 11/13/34.

255   "successful in securing": Leo Morrison to ST, 4/10/35 (SLT).

255   "no question in my mind": Astrid Allwyn Fee to Selden West via telephone, 1/9/78 (SW).

255   "half loaded": Charles Higham, *Hollywood Cameramen* (Bloomington: Indiana University Press, 1970), p. 141.

256   "go off to Virginia": Frank Tracy to Selden West.

256   "drunk and resisting": *Los Angeles Times,* 3/12/35. See also *Los Angeles Examiner,* 3/12/35.

257   "so sadly lacking": *Hollywood Reporter,* 3/25/35.

257   "should rest before": *Los Angeles Examiner,* 4/1/35.

257   "wounding his vanity": Allvine, *The Greatest Fox of Them All,* p. 153.

CHAPTER 11   THAT DOUBLE JACKPOT

258   "Without stars": Irving G. Thalberg, undated draft memo to Nicholas Schenck (author's collection).

259   "We recognize": Memorandum of Agreement between Spencer Tracy and Metro-Goldwyn-Mayer, 4/2/35, Turner Entertainment/SW.

259   "by mutual consent": Cancellation Agreement between Spencer Tracy and Fox Film Corporation, 3/30/35 (SLT).

259   "very flattering offer": *Los Angeles Times,* 4/3/35.

260   "most valuable stars": *Los Angeles Examiner,* 3/12/44.

260   "pieces of property": Tracy, *The Story of John,* p. 161.

261   "a million dollars": *Los Angeles Examiner,* 5/16/35.

261   "first-rate yarn": *The Murder Man,* synopsis by Edward Hogan, 3/21/35 (MGM).

261   binge-drinking insomniac: In the original dialogue continuity by Tim Whelan and Guy Bolton, Steve Gray is "morose and drinks too much" but is not a binge drinker. The scene introducing Gray on the merry-go-round after a disappearance of several days first appears in a dialogue continuity by John C. Higgins dated May 22, 1935 (AMPAS).

263   "quiet, compelling conviction": *Daily Variety,* 7/6/35.

263   Loew's Capitol: Figures for *The Murder Man* are from *Variety,* 8/7/35. According to the Mannix ledger, the film cost $167,000 and returned a profit of $78,000 on total billings of $397,000.

263   "criminal reporter": *Variety,* 7/31/35.

263   "fairly exciting": *New York Telegraph,* 7/28/35.

264   "greedily accepted": *Screen and Radio Weekly,* 8/25/35.

264   final tally: According to the research library of Karl Thiede, domestic and foreign rentals for *Dante's Inferno* totaled $786,200. With a negative cost of $748,900, the film posted a loss of $269,900.

264   "went to pieces": Scott Eyman, *Print the Legend: The Life and Times of John Ford* (New York: Simon & Schuster, 1999), p. 149.

264   "sat around talking": Tracy, "My Pal, Will Rogers."

265   "my sense of humor": *Los Angeles Examiner,* 8/19/35.

265   "sorry you were sick": Judith Wood to Selden West, via telephone, 2/3/93 (SW).

265   "Tracy's gassed": David Stenn, *Bombshell: The Life and Death of Jean Harlow* (New York: Doubleday, 1993), p. 195.

265   "A press agent": Teet Carle, "Magnificent Katharine Hepburn: A Study in Magnetism," *Hollywood Studio Magazine,* August 1974.

266   "wiped me out": Eddie Lawrence to Selden West, Los Angeles, 8/6/93 (SW).

268   "had me scared": Charles Darnton, "Down With Romance!" *Screenland,* February 1937.

268   "contrasting me to Jean": Myrna Loy (with James Kotsilibas-Davis), *Being and Becoming* (New York: Knopf, 1987), p. 122.

269   "very much surprised": Tracy, "My Complicated Life," Part 1.

270   "I think every woman": Lyn Tornabene, *Long Live the King* (New York: Putnam, 1976), p. 193.

270   "I called him for it": Patrick McGilligan, *Film Crazy* (New York: St. Martin's Press, 2000), p. 247.

271   "Judy Garland": It is perhaps the existence of these innocent photographs that prompted Bill Davidson to include an assertion in his 1988 book *Tragic Idol* that Tracy dated Garland "who then was only fifteen." The information supposedly came from James Cagney and, significantly, was published only after Cagney's death. Joe Mankiewicz, who was seriously involved with Garland in the forties, characterized the story as "absolute bullshit," as did Garland's third husband, Sid Luft. Dependably, Christopher Andersen repeated the story, adding details. According to Andersen, the

relationship began in January 1937, when Garland was only fourteen: "Jimmy Cagney warned his friend the inevitable gossip could ruin his career. [But] Tracy continued to see Garland privately, and after their romance ended, they remained close . . ." In Andersen's account, Cagney's warning is of the career-ruining potential of the "inevitable gossip" rather than the effect an arrest for statutory rape could have had on Tracy's future. There is, of course, no evidence whatsoever that Tracy and Garland were involved at any time in their lives.

271   "Who said that?": Undated clipping (NYPL).

271   "He shouldn't have said that": Dottie Wellman to Selden West, via telephone, 7/12/95 (SW).

271   "a lot of fistfights": McGilligan, *Film Crazy,* p. 247.

271   "a little misunderstanding": *Los Angeles Examiner,* 12/4/35.

272   "We've been friends": *Los Angeles Times,* 12/4/35.

272   "The beaut": *Los Angeles Evening Herald and Express,* 12/5/35.

272   "I told my idea": Patrick McGilligan, ed., *Backstory* (Berkeley: University of California Press, 1986), p. 219.

272   "let you make this film": Kenneth L. Geist, *Pictures Will Talk* (New York: Scribners, 1978), pp. 76–77.

273   "dictate it": Gordon Gow, "Cocking a Snook," *Films and Filming,* November 1970.

273   "they killed my dog": Norman Krasna's original story, as dictated from memory by Joseph L. Mankiewicz, is in the M-G-M collection at USC, along with story conference notes and draft screenplays by Leonard Praskins and Bartlett Cormack.

273   "talked to Fritz": Joseph L. Mankiewicz to Selden West, Bedford, New York, 1/17/92 (SW).

273   "Sacco and Vanzetti": Newquist, *A Special Kind of Magic,* p. 145.

274   "Tracy . . . is a lawyer": Fritz Lang and Leonard Praskins, "Notes of Story Conference," 8/31/35 (MGM).

274   "walking along the street": Jeanette MacDonald, Oral History with Mr. and Mrs. Robert C. Franklin, Columbia University, June 1959.

275   six words: Gottfried Reinhardt, Oral History with Mr. and Mrs. Robert C. Franklin, Columbia University, 1959.

276   "soap opera": Anita Loos, *Kiss Hollywood Good-by* (New York: Viking, 1974), p. 129.

277   "a little dubious": Ardmore, "Tracy," n.d.

277   "an unhappy man": John McCabe to Katharine Hepburn, 3/14/86 (KHLA).

277   "I was seventeen": Kanin, *Tracy and Hepburn,* p. 24.

277   "awful scared": *New York Sun,* undated clipping (NYPL).

277   "I'm a Roman Catholic": Sharpe, "The Adventurous Life of Spencer Tracy," Part 3.

277   "didn't think I ought": "Spencer Tracy Learned a Lesson," *Picturegoer* (UK), 12/11/37.

278   "Here we were": Gable, "My Pal, Spencer Tracy."

278   "less self-conscious": Patrick McGilligan, *Tender Comrades* (New York: St. Martin's Press, 1997), p. 702.

278   "Lambs Club": Gable, "My Pal, Spencer Tracy."

278   "Gable is a <u>mess!</u>": Edward Baron Turk, *Hollywood Diva* (Berkeley: University of California Press, 1998), p. 181.

278   "all the stories": Joseph Newman to the author, via telephone, 11/25/03.

279   "I like Tracy": Turk, *Hollywood Diva,* p. 181.

280   "first day's work": Sam Katz to Fritz Lang, 4/22/36 (AFI).

280   "peanut addict": Gail Gardner witnessed this exchange and described it in her syndicated column of April 18, 1936.

280   "big ego": *Boston Globe,* 7/7/74.

281   "Lang . . . would have": Joseph L. Mankiewicz to David Heeley and Joan Kramer, New York, 1985 (TH).

282   "He gained a lot": Joseph Newman to the author.

282   "We were pretty serious": Gable, "My Pal, Spencer Tracy."

282   "Aces" Hatfield: Herman J. Mankiewicz's partial screenplay, dated January 9, 1935, is
       in the Turner/M-G-M Scripts Collection (AMPAS). Anita Loos' earliest draft of the
       screenplay, also incomplete, is dated April 23, 1935 (MGM).

283   "When Sylvia Sidney": Tracy, "Making Faces at Life," Part 4.

283   "Now figure Spence": Joseph L. Mankiewicz to Selden West.

283   "I can't stand this": Joseph Ruttenberg, American Film Institute Oral History with
       Bill Gleason, 1972 (AFI).

283   "In shooting": Joseph Ruttenberg, Southern Methodist University Oral History with
       Ronald L. Davis.

286   "The earthquake was flat": *Los Angeles Times,* 6/3/77.

286   "hell on everybody": Scott Eyman, "Joseph Ruttenberg," *Focus on Film,* spring 1976.

286   "we worked like slaves": *New York Herald Tribune,* 12/20/36.

286   "bad to much worse": Joseph L. Mankiewicz to Heeley and Kramer (TH).

287   "solitary salted peanut": The *Fury* screenplay, by Bartlett Cormack and Fritz Lang,
       including deleted scenes and the original ending, can be found in John Gassner and
       Dudley Nichols, eds., *20 Best Film Plays* (New York: Crown, 1943), pp. 521–82.

288   "A man gives a speech": Peter Bogdanovich, *Fritz Lang in America* (New York: Praeger,
       1969), pp. 27–28.

288   "I agree": Joseph L. Mankiewicz to Fritz Lang, 4/25/36 (AFI). It should be noted that
       almost everything Lang had to say with regard to the genesis and editing of *Fury* con-
       flicts with the archival record. "I had found a four-page story by Norman Krasna—I
       wanted to do that" (*The Real Tinsel,* p. 342). The Production Code file notes that
       Mankiewicz verbally outlined the story to Iselin Auster and Geoffrey Sherlock on
       August 21, 1935, and furnished a written treatment the next day. In separate inter-
       views both Krasna and Mankiewicz agreed that it was Mankiewicz, and not Lang,
       who remembered the story and committed it to paper when Krasna himself had
       forgotten it.
          "Mr. Mankiewicz came late to the project. It was I who chose the subject and
       worked on the script . . . During the course of shooting he became the producer"
       (*Focus on Film,* spring 1975). Notes from the first story conference between Lang and
       Leonard Praskins are dated August 31, 1935. Notes first showing Mankiewicz's partici-
       pation are dated September 3, 1935. When a full script (titled *The Mob*) was sent to the
       PCA for review on January 24, 1936, the cover letter clearly identified Mankiewicz as
       the producer. Filming began on February 20, 1936.

288   "test under fire": Joseph L. Mankiewicz to Heeley and Kramer.

288   "a first preview": Geist, *Pictures Will Talk,* p. 80.

288   "all very well": "Loew's Inc.," *Fortune,* August 1939.

288   "often been asked": Bogdanovich, *Fritz Lang in America,* pp. 29–30.

289   "Peter Lorre": Geist, *Pictures Will Talk,* p. 78. Lang also asserted that "because he
       drank like a fish" Tracy's contract with Metro provided "that if he had so much as a
       glass of beer they could throw him out." There was, of course, no such clause in Tracy's
       M-G-M contract, dated April 8, 1936, other than standard language regarding public
       behavior (the so-called morals clause) and the artist's inability to render services by
       reason of mental or physical incapacitation.

289   "I don't think Spence": Joseph L. Mankiewicz to Selden West.

289   "great document": Spencer Tracy, 1936 datebook (SLT).

289   "Fritz Lang": *New York Herald Tribune,* 12/20/36. Lang was born in Vienna, but made
       his early films in Germany.

                              CHAPTER 12   THE BEST YEAR

290   "The house": S. R. Mook, "Spencer Tracy's Home Life," *Screenland,* March 1940.

291   "consummate exhibition": *Daily Variety,* 5/19/36.

292   "It looked hopeless": *Honolulu Star-Bulletin,* 5/28/36.

292 "most courageous": *New York World-Telegram,* 6/6/36.

292 a "builder": *New York Enquirer,* 6/14/36.

292 The picture ran up: Figures for *Fury* are from *Variety,* 6/10, 6/17, and 6/24/36; and the Mannix ledger.

293 *The Plough and the Stars:* Director John Ford later blamed Irving Thalberg's death for the cancellation of Tracy's loan-out to RKO, but Thalberg was still alive when the reversal was made public in July 1936. There is some reason to believe that Ford held Tracy personally responsible for welshing on the commitment, which would have teamed him with actress Barbara Stanwyck and a predominantly Irish cast that included Una O'Connor, Erin O'Brien Moore, Bonita Granville, Mary Gordon, and five members of the Abbey Players (imported from Dublin). Once again, actor Preston Foster was substituted for Tracy, and the resulting film was not only less than Ford had hoped, but subsequently butchered by the studio. It would be more than twenty years before Ford and Tracy would again work together on a picture.

293 "What the movies need": *Los Angeles Evening Herald-Express,* 2/18/36.

294 "a truthful man": Charles Bickford, *Bulls, Balls, Bicycles & Actors* (New York: Paul S. Erikson, 1965), p. 227.

295 "peered frantically": *Hollywood Citizen News,* 6/25/36.

296 "most difficult role": *Variety,* 7/1/36.

297 "another brilliant portrayal": *New York Times,* 6/27/36.

297 "A year ago": Ed Sullivan, "The Best Bet of the Year," *Silver Screen,* September 1936.

297 "HAD WONDERFUL TRIP": ST to Sol Wurtzel, 6/26/36 (AMPAS).

298 "You'll never know": Ed Sullivan, "A Prediction that Came Doubly True," *Silver Screen,* April 1940.

299 "Walking on the set": *Hollywood Citizen News,* 7/2/36.

299 "He moped": Loy, *Being and Becoming,* p. 141.

299 "cashier's office": Darnton, "Down With Romance!"

299 "do his best": Sheilah Graham, *Confessions of a Hollywood Columnist* (New York: Morrow, 1969), p. 37.

300 " 'beginning to gain weight' ": Kitty Callahan, "Spencer Tracy," *Family Circle,* 6/5/42.

300 "an unrevealed script": *New York Times,* 7/3/36.

300 "Fought against it": Gladys Hall, "You Can't Put Spencer Tracy into Words," *Motion Picture,* November 1937.

301 "his first part": Ida Zeitlin, "Manuel the Lovable," *Modern Screen,* October 1937.

301 "every picture in town": Hall, "You Can't Put Spencer Tracy into Words."

301 "So what?": Harold Keene, "How Spencer Tracy's Love Survived Its Greatest Test," *Movie Mirror,* October 1937.

302 "Susie . . . was only four": Tracy, *The Story of John,* p. 176.

302 my hair curled: Newquist, *A Special Kind of Magic,* p. 149.

302 "fall on your ass": Bosley Crowther, notes, Eddie Mannix interview, May 1953, Bosley Crowther Collection, Brigham Young University.

302 the funeral: Michael Sragow, in his biography of Victor Fleming, incorrectly reports that Tracy fell off the wagon as a result of Thalberg's death. By evidence of his own datebooks, Tracy was completely dry before and during the filming of *Captains Courageous.*

Bill Davidson, in *Tragic Idol,* asserts more generally that Tracy went on a bender during the picture, in part to put across a lurid scene at the opening of his book. Davidson quotes M-G-M publicist (and later producer) Walter Seltzer, who worked briefly under publicity chief Howard Strickling. According to Seltzer's quote (as reported by Davidson), Tracy turned his rage on the furnishings in his sixth-floor suite at the Beverly Wilshire, heaving chairs against the walls and bringing his fists down on the surface of a small writing desk with such force that it was smashed in two. Lamps were shattered, mirrors broken, bottles flung at doors and windows. Management allegedly called Carroll, who was admitted to the locked room, then called Strickling's office at M-G-M when the commotion went unabated. When the door to the suite was unlocked with a passkey, studio security personnel accompanying Strickling and "half of the publicity department" supposedly witnessed the sight of Tracy wrestling his brother toward an open window with the obvious intent of adding him to the topography of Wilshire Boulevard.

When queried about the quote Davidson attributes to him, Seltzer responded: "That is inaccurate. I wasn't there and never witnessed such a thing. It might possibly have happened, but that's something Howard never would have talked about. I don't know where Bill got that; I knew Bill and we talked often, but that particular quote was a complete fabrication." Walter Seltzer to the author, via telephone, 4/16/08.

302   "practicing dialect": "Spencer Tracy's Learned a Lesson."

303   "Tracy was sore": Capt. J. M. Hersey, "The Log of the *We're Here,*" *Woman's Home Companion,* April 1937.

303   "full schedule": Mickey Rooney, *Life Is Too Short* (New York: Villard Books, 1991), p. 94.

304   "purposely set out": Victor Fleming, "Filming *Captains Courageous*—A Director's Own Story," *Captains Courageous* souvenir program, 1937.

305   "put on a clean shirt": *New York Times,* 12/13/36.

305   "educated Portuguese": Hall, "You Can't Put Spencer Tracy into Words."

306   "warm feelings": Freddie Bartholomew in *M-G-M: When the Lion Roars* (Part Two—"The Lion Reigns Supreme"), Turner Pictures/Point Blank Productions, 1992.

306   "Slick as a whistle": Spencer Tracy, "The Log of the *We're Here,*" *Picturegoer,* 12/11/37.

307   "There is a drawbridge": S. R. Mook, "For More Than Money," *Screenland,* May 1938.

307   "Stubby Kruger": Hersey, "The Log of the *We're Here.*"

308   "Anything for release": Yvonne Beaudry, "Tracy and Beaudry," *Silurian News,* May 1992.

309   "idealistic role": *Chicago Daily News,* 5/29/37.

309   "I think of you": ST to Lincoln Cromwell, 1/12/37.

310   "As everyone knows": *Oakland Tribune,* 1/31/37.

310   "well on my way": *Los Angeles Times,* 5/16/37.

310   "I'm alive today": Sharpe, "The Adventurous Life of Spencer Tracy," Part 3.

310   thyroid: A goiter is typically the result of low iodine in the diet, a condition the body attempts to correct by stimulating the production of hormones in the thyroid gland. In the days before iodine was routinely added to table salt, goiters were common in inland areas where the soil was often deficient in iodine. In the United States, Milwaukee was considered part of the "goiter belt."

311   "And what a storm!": *Abilene Reporter-News,* 3/14/37.

311   "a beautiful kid": McGilligan, *Backstory,* p. 252.

312   "got away with it": Zeitlin, "Manuel the Lovable."

313   "When we emerged": Beaudry, "Tracy and Beaudry."

CHAPTER 13   THE NEW RAGE

314   "they hauled me out": Spencer Tracy, "Film War Too Real to Suit 'Private' Tracy," *New York Daily Mirror,* 5/8/37. Tracy's datebook for 1937 shows that he completed *Captains Courageous* on Monday, February 15, and started *They Gave Him a Gun* the next day.

314   "anti-war document": *Los Angeles Times,* 5/16/37.

315   most employees: Walter Seltzer remembered a meeting of the sixty-member M-G-M publicity staff in 1939: "Our boss, Howard Strickling, announced that through the generosity of the studio, all of us as of now are members of the Academy; he had enrolled everyone and paid the initiation fee. There was general jubilation and thanks, then he proceeded to tell us how we were to vote." ("History of Hollywood Ups and Downs," Associated Press, 2/23/05.)

315 "Critics": *Hollywood Citizen News,* 3/5/37.

315 "haven't been telling": Howard Sharpe, "The Startling Story Behind Spencer Tracy's Illness," *Movie Mirror,* July 1937.

315 "game of handball": Helen Gilmore, "Spencer Tracy's Tribute to Jean Harlow," *Liberty,* spring 1972.

316 "accept him as a heel": Maurice Rapf to Selden West, 11/30/95 (SW).

316 "derby hat": Newquist, *A Special Kind of Magic,* p. 149.

316 "stiff-shirted gentlemen": *Los Angeles Evening Herald-Express,* 5/15/37.

317 "man to be thanked": *Los Angeles Times,* 5/16/37.

317 "magnificent job": Hall, "You Can't Put Spencer Tracy into Words."

318 "Fifth Avenue": Zeitlin, "Manuel the Lovable."

318 "publicity value": McEvoy, "Will They Get Wise to Him?"

318 "heavy responsibility": *Chicago Daily News,* 5/28/37.

318 "She doesn't nag": Hall, "You Can't Put Spencer Tracy into Words."

318 "He saw you": Ted Shane, "He Should Worry," *Liberty,* 12/15/45.

319 "despises chi-chi": Mook, "Spencer Tracy's Home Life."

320 "I can't believe it": Gilmore, "Spencer Tracy's Tribute to Jean Harlow."

320 "She meant to pull her punch": Darnton, "Down With Romance!"

320 "He came home": Jane Feely Desmond to Selden West.

322 "wonderful man": Luise Rainer to the author, via telephone, 12/30/03.

322 "It isn't worth it": *New York World-Telegram,* 4/16/38.

323 "I never acted": Marie Brenner, *Great Dames* (New York: Crown, 2000), p. 175.

324 "a marvelous time": Dore Schary, *Heyday* (Boston: Little, Brown, 1979), p. 88.

324 already seen it: The first time Johnny saw his father on-screen was in *Sky Devils.* "I remember him sitting there," Louise said. "Suddenly, the first time John saw him on the screen, he just sat there and said, 'Fa-ther.' " He saw *Captains Courageous* for the first time with his cousin Jane: "I cried and cried when he drowned, and John looked around and, even though he couldn't hear, he could see people looking at me, so he tapped me on the shoulder and said, 'Don't cry, don't cry. Father dived in the water, went under the boat, and came up on the other side.' "

324 "staring at the screen": Susie Tracy to the author, via telephone, 1/10/08.

324 the boat: Tracy sold the *Carrie B* to director Michael Curtiz for $12,000. The next time he saw the boat, it was dirty and renamed the *Do De Do.* Eventually ownership fell to actor Dick Powell.

324 "any kind of actor": Mook, "For More Than Money."

325 holding his nose: *Milwaukee Sentinel,* 6/28/67.

325 "spoiled it all": Spencer Tracy, 1937 datebook (SLT).

326 "whitewashed a little": Lucile Sullivan, "Marry for Money" coverage, 6/11/36 (MGM).

327 "Pure male": Joan Crawford, as quoted in the program for a Tracy Retrospective at Wesleyan College, 1973.

327 "an absolute muddle": Roy Newquist, *Conversations with Joan Crawford* (Secaucus, N.J.: Citadel, 1980), p. 81.

327 "For crissake": Bob Thomas, *Joan Crawford* (New York: Simon and Schuster, 1978), p. 125.

330 "hot fudge sundaes": Alice Mannix to the author, via telephone, 8/2/06.

331 "what kind of ice cream": Jean Wright to the author, via telephone, 9/21/06.

331 "Voting contests": *Chicago Tribune,* 11/14/37.

332 "most attractive": Hall, "You Can't Put Spencer Tracy into Words."

332 "The characters are excellent": Joe Richardson, "Wings of Tomorrow" coverage, 1/27/36 (MGM).

333 "King" and "Queen": The voting tallies are from the *Hollywood Citizen News,* 12/7/37.

333 "big plush crowns": Gable, "My Pal, Spencer Tracy."

333 "That broadcast tonight": *Hollywood Citizen News,* 12/11/37.

333 "our would-be coronation": Loy, *Being and Becoming,* p. 152.

333   "From start to finish": Gable, "My Pal, Spencer Tracy."

334   "went off for lunch": Marshall Schlom to the author, Brea, Calif., 8/14/06.

334   "be my best": John Lee Mahin to Lyn Tornabene, 10/17/73 (AMPAS).

334   "Directors' Table": Howard Strickling to Lyn Tornabene, 10/25/73 (AMPAS).

335   "Any other star": Jean Garceau (with Inez Cocke), *"Dear Mr. G——"* (Boston: Little, Brown, 1961), p. 76.

335   "I noticed that the fliers": Loy, *Being and Becoming*, pp. 152–54.

337   "That plane was used": Laraine Day, Southern Methodist University Oral History with Ronald L. Davis, 7/17/79.

337   "We saw each other": Joseph L. Mankiewicz to Selden West (SW).

337   "come home at night": Norman, *The Hollywood Greats*, p. 78.

337   "in the guest room": Joseph L. Mankiewicz to Heeley and Kramer.

338   "very attractive woman": Joseph L. Mankiewicz to Selden West, Bedford, New York, 10/3/91 (SW).

339   "I wear this Irish costume": *Hollywood Citizen News*, 2/4/38.

339   "achieving dramatic effect": *Los Angeles Examiner*, 11/3/36.

340   "open approbation": Norman, *The Hollywood Greats*, p. 77. Tracy told a version of the story to Garson Kanin that suggests purposeful avoidance of the banquet, claiming that Dr. Dennis had merely told him he had an "incipient hernia" and that the surgery was entirely elective. However, Tracy's 1937 datebook makes it clear that the diagnosis was conclusive. "Have definite hernia," he wrote on December 17, long before his Best Actor nomination for *Captains Courageous*. "Should be operated upon."

340   "I had to get home": Ardmore, "Tracy," n.d.

340   "an Academy renaissance": *Hollywood Citizen News*, 3/11/38.

341   "If you have to go up": Ardmore, "Tracy," n.d.

CHAPTER 14   ENOUGH TO SHINE EVEN THROUGH ME

343   "the pattern of *Oliver Twist*": Monsignor E. J. Flanagan, "The Story Behind Boys Town," *Photoplay*, November 1938.

343   "After reading": Schary, *Heyday*, p. 93.

344   "I expected robes": McGilligan, *Film Crazy*, p. 194.

344   "just a straight man": Ardmore, "Tracy," n.d.

344   "grimly alone": Beaudry, "Tracy and Beaudry."

345   "written in gold": Rev. E. J. Flanagan to ST, 2/4/38 (BT).

345   "win space": Rev. E. J. Flanagan to John Considine, Jr., 2/12/38 (BT).

345   "All actors": Rt. Rev. Edward J. Flanagan, "I Meet Myself in Spencer Tracy," *Liberty*, 10/8/38.

346   "do him good": *Variety*, 4/27/38.

346   "the restless type": Gable, "My Pal, Spencer Tracy."

346   discovered bleeding: Details of William Powell's 1938 battle with cancer are from an interview with the actor in *Time*, 5/10/63.

346   "pretty blue": Spencer Tracy, 1938 datebook (SLT).

347   "what was left": Kanin, *Tracy and Hepburn*, p. 146.

347   "I was sick": Franc Dillon, "Meet Father Tracy," *Picture Play*, December 1938.

347   "saw a figure coming": Swindell, *Spencer Tracy*, p. 152.

347   "Tracy will sail": *Los Angeles Times*, 4/17/38.

348   "huge supply of liquor": David Wayne to James Fisher, 12/14/92, as quoted in James Fisher, *Spencer Tracy: A Bio-Bibliography* (Westport, Conn.: Greenwood Press, 1994), p. 17.

348   "should not see": Swindell, *Spencer Tracy*, p. 153.

348   a private plane: Details of Tracy's evacuation from New York are in notes taken from Spencer Tracy's M-G-M personnel files by Selden West in 1992, Turner Entertainment/SW. The same day, according to Lambs Club records, Tracy was suspended

from the privileges of the club for violation of House Rule #13 "pending action by the Council." A violation of House Rule #13 was "conduct unbecoming a member" (NYPL).

348   "able to find him": Dore Schary in *M-G-M: When the Lion Roars* (Part Two—"The Lion Reigns Supreme").

348   "Unfortunately": John Considine, Jr., to Rev. E. J. Flanagan, 4/27/38 (BT).

349   "Mickey Rooney . . . was a pretty cocky": Joseph L. Mankiewicz to Heeley and Kramer.

350   "darn near died": James Reid, "Even Barrymore Calls Him the Best," *Motion Picture,* November 1938.

351   "He was artless": Gene Reynolds to the author, via telephone, 2/6/06.

351   "eyes bore into mine": Dickie Moore, *Twinkle, Twinkle Little Star* (New York: Harper & Row, 1984), p. 161.

351   "one of the first scenes": Tom and Jim Goldrup, *Growing Up on the Set* (Jefferson, N.C.: McFarland, 2002), p. 306.

351   "can't explain it": Moore, *Twinkle, Twinkle Little Star,* p. 73.

352   "During lunch": "The Story Behind the Movie: Alumni Remember *Boys Town,*" posted at boystownmovie.org.

352   "Tracy off the booze": Beth Day Romulo to Selden West, 10/17/92 (SW).

353   "schooling was insufficient": Tracy, "My Complicated Life," Part 1.

353   "that's the worst picture": Robbin Coons, "Plain Guy," *Screen Guide,* February 1948.

353   "Washington—no!": Rev. E. J. Flanagan to Frank Whitbeck, 8/12/38 (BT).

354   "There was applause": *Motion Picture Herald,* 9/10/38.

354   "Pure sentiment": *Daily Variety,* 9/2/38.

355   "brilliant, restrained performance": *Hollywood Reporter,* 9/2/38.

355   "dying hog": *Omaha Morning World-Herald,* 9/8/38.

355   "If you have a diamond": Howard Strickling to Lyn Tornabene, 10/25/73 (AMPAS).

357   "Early on": Gary Carey, *All the Stars in Heaven* (New York: Dutton, 1981), p. 108.

357   "an honest question": *Washington Star,* 9/17/40.

357   "like the children": Hall, "Spencer Tracy Speaks His Mind."

358   "world unto itself": Maureen O'Sullivan in *M-G-M: When the Lion Roars* (Part Two—"The Lion Reigns Supreme").

358   "In Howard's book": Ann Straus, Southern Methodist University Oral History with Ronald L. Davis.

358   "made it difficult": June Caldwell to the author, Culver City, Calif., 9/22/04.

358   "I have often wondered": Rev. E. J. Flanagan to ST, 11/1/38 (BT).

359   "Each detail of this film": Josef von Sternberg, *Fun in a Chinese Laundry* (New York: Macmillan, 1965), p. 277.

359   "He wouldn't stand": Laraine Day to Barbara Hall, Academy of Motion Picture Arts and Sciences Oral History, January–March 1997 (AMPAS).

359   "There's no mistaking": *Los Angeles Evening Herald-Express,* 11/26/38.

360   "*I Take This Woman*": *Dallas Morning News,* 12/27/38.

361   "Just imagine": *Dallas Morning News,* 3/8/39.

361   "Humph!": Frank Tracy to Selden West.

361   "in a wheelchair": Jane Feely Desmond to Selden West.

362   "highway accident": *New York Times,* 9/9/38.

362   "The omission": *Los Angeles Times,* 1/13/39.

362   "it is disrespectful": Dillon, "Meet Father Tracy."

363   "I could tell": Ardmore, "Tracy," n.d.

363   "I honestly do not feel": *Hollywood Citizen News,* 2/24/39. The story that the name on the Oscar, due to an engraving error, was "Dick" Tracy instead of "Spencer" is apparently untrue. The origin of the story is unknown.

363   "all primed": Gable, "My Pal, Spencer Tracy."

364   "I didn't see *Boys Town*": ST to Pete Martin.

366   "Not dramatized enough": Story conference notes, 6/16/37 (USC).

366   "Forget the silly business": Philip Dunne, *Take Two* (New York: McGraw-Hill, 1980), p. 58.

366   loose loan-out: In a letter dated 9/2/39, 20th Century-Fox agreed to compensate Loew's Incorporated $75,111.11 for the loan of Tracy (FOX).

367   "He came to me": King to Perry, Directors Guild Oral History.

367   "*In vino veritas*": Henry King, as quoted by Larry Swindell to the author. The old Irish equivalent: "Alcohol takes the varnish off anything."

367   "*soundproof* stages": *Los Angeles Evening Herald-Express,* 3/18/39.

367   "I'm slowly improving": Reid, "Even Barrymore Calls Him the Best."

368   "tuck in his chin": Hall, "You Can Only Defeat Yourself."

368   "Do you realize": *Dallas Morning News,* 3/8/39.

CHAPTER 15   A BUOYANT EFFECT ON THE AUDIENCE

370   "Next time I come": *New York Times,* 11/1/38.

372   "The crowd that charged": *New York Times,* 5/14/39.

372   "What am I doing in London?": Unidentified clipping, 4/27/39 (SLT).

372   "think fast": *Film Weekly,* 5/6/39.

372   "All the Kennedys": Kanin, *Tracy and Hepburn,* p.65.

374   "*Grapes of Wrath*": *Hollywood Citizen News,* 5/29/39.

374   "I had wires": *New York World-Telegram,* 4/16/38.

375   "hope to do more": Mook, "For More Than Money."

375   "And it occurred": Theresa Helburn to ST, 5/25/39 (TGC).

375   "motion picture business": Interview with Ardmore, 7/5/72.

376   "Don't worry": *Los Angeles Evening Herald and Express,* 7/31/39.

376   "well taken care of": Nancy Dowd and David Shepard, *King Vidor: A Directors Guild of America Oral History* (Metuchen, N.J.: Scarecrow Press, 1988), p. 180.

377   "I'll play him": Sullivan, "A Prediction That Came Doubly True."

377   "Hunt Stromberg": Dowd and Shepard, *King Vidor,* p. 182.

377   "no complete story line": King Vidor to Eddie Mannix, 5/17/39, as quoted in Rudy Behlmer, "To the Wilderness for *Northwest Passage,*" *American Cinematographer,* November 1987.

377   "At this time": Dowd and Shepard, *King Vidor,* p. 182.

378   "unsavory characters": Harrold A. Weinberger, unpublished autobiography, circa 1972 (USC).

378   "renovated camp": Leonard Maltin, "Conversations: Robert Young," *Leonard Maltin's Movie Crazy,* spring 2003.

379   "include me out": Walter Brennan, Oral History with Charles Higham, Columbia University, 8/11/71.

379   "Young, Brennan and I": Hall, "You Can Only Defeat Yourself."

379   "wearing buckskin": Maltin, "Conversations: Robert Young."

379   "He becomes so thoroughly": John R. Wolfenden, "Spencer Tracy as Seen by His Best Friends," *Australian Women's Weekly,* 1/6/40.

379   "marvelous performance": King Vidor to Selden West, Los Angeles, December 1977 (SW).

380   "SERIOUS CHANGES": ST to Eddie Mannix, 7/20/39, as quoted in "To the Wilderness for *Northwest Passage.*"

380   "He had an expression": King Vidor to Selden West.

382   "AGREE WITH YOU": Hunt Stromberg to King Vidor, 8/3/39, King Vidor Papers, Department of Special Collections, Charles E. Young Research Library, University of California, Los Angeles.

382   "HAVE SCREENED": Hunt Stromberg to ST, 8/4/39, King Vidor Papers.

383   "he blamed himself": David Caldwell to the author, via telephone, 11/4/06.

383 "a close friend": Interview with Ardmore, 8/1/72 (JKA).

383 he was so "nervous": Spencer Tracy, 1939 datebook (SLT).

383 "a very good eye": Ardmore, "Tracy," n.d. (JKA).

384 "motor running": Frank Tracy to Selden West (SW).

384 "I was sorry": Gable, "My Pal, Spencer Tracy."

384 "It would be wonderful": Reid, "Even Barrymore Calls Him the Best."

385 "you seemed upset": ST to Eddie Mannix, 8/24/39 (SLT).

386 "very intuitive": Maltin, "Conversations: Robert Young."

386 "big tow line": Jane Feely Desmond to the author, 2/23/04.

386 "I couldn't do that": Interview with Ardmore, 7/5/72.

387 "Frank NEVER asked": Dorothy McHugh to Selden West, Cos Cob, Conn., 1/31/92 (SW).

387 "Spence was at M-G-M": Frank McHugh to Ralph Bellamy, 7/5/77, Ralph Bellamy Papers, Wisconsin State Historical Society, Madison.

387 "There was no thought": James Cagney to Selden West, 2/11/78 (SW).

388 "I did the entire picture": Dowd and Shepard, *King Vidor,* p. 182.

389 "historical character": Grace Wilcox, "Injuns!" *Sunday Magazine, Detroit Free Press,* 2/4/40.

389 "THE PREVIEW": Kenneth Macgowan to ST, 7/11/39, Kenneth Macgowan Papers, Department of Special Collections, Charles E. Young Research Library, University of California, Los Angeles.

389 "severely scholarly": *Hollywood Reporter,* 8/1/39.

390 "Comes the revolution!": *Los Angeles Times,* 8/27/39.

390 survey by Elmo Roper: Full results of the survey can be found in *Fortune,* November 1939.

CHAPTER 16   SOMEONE'S IDEA OF REALITY

394 "make these changes": *Los Angeles Evening Herald and Express,* 10/27/39.

394 "believe everything": Flo Marshall, "Six Characters in Search of Spencer Tracy," *Movies,* November 1940.

394 "civilized comedy": Ben Hecht, *Charlie* (New York: Harper, 1957), p. 160.

395 "They didn't want me": Hedy Lamarr, *Ecstasy and Me* (New York: Bartholomew House, 1966), p. 71.

395 "did one rehearsal": Laraine Day to Barbara Hall.

396 "was an alcoholic": Lawrence Weingarten, American Film Institute Seminar with James Powers, 1/23/74 (AFI).

396 Tracy was "onto him": Bosley Crowther, notes, Spencer Tracy interview, 5/10/53, Bosley Crowther Collection, Brigham Young University.

397 "a very prayerful guy": Adela Rogers St. Johns to Ralph Story, *Spencer Tracy: An Unauthorized Biography.*

397 a "quickie" questionnaire: Hall, "You Can Only Defeat Yourself."

398 "a bet I had": *Dallas Morning News,* 1/25/40.

398 "the kind of stuff": *Daily Variety,* 2/8/40.

399 humiliation: While Tracy's personal reviews were good, *I Take This Woman* was variously described in the press as "lame and inept," a "pretty sorry affair," and an "amazing blend of tedium and trash." Stubbornly, the studio booked it into Radio City Music Hall—a real shocker for the industry, given the picture's almost legendary status—and the results were predictably disastrous. It did well enough in playoffs, however, to hold the overall loss to $325,000 on a final cost of nearly $1.3 million.

399 "They spent half their time": Adela Rogers St. Johns to Ralph Story, "Spencer Tracy."

399 "THIS YEAR'S GREATEST": Gable, "My Pal, Spencer Tracy."

400 "thought I was crazy when": Callahan, "Spencer Tracy."

400 "Can you imagine that?": Harry Evans, "Hollywood Diary," *Family Circle,* 8/23/40.

401   "One evening": Stewart Granger, *Sparks Fly Upward* (New York: Putnam, 1981), pp. 348–49.

402   "ideas of experience": John Erskine, "The Private Mind of Spencer Tracy," *Liberty*, 8/24/40.

404   "What'll you have": *Milwaukee Journal*, 6/10/40.

405   "Today marks": *The Ripon Alumnus*, June 1940.

407   "Roosevelt": Louise, a Republican, supported Willkie in the election.

407   "Another picture": *Washington D.C. News*, 9/13/40.

407   "you got a rotten deal": Gene Buck to Rev. E. J. Flanagan, 8/23/39 (BT).

407   "step out": *Boys Town Times*, 2/23/40.

408   "stuffy": Ardmore, "Tracy," n.d.

409   "You would not be good": Frank McHugh to Ralph Bellamy.

409   "never forget": Adela Rogers St. Johns to Ralph Story, "Spencer Tracy."

409   "always been fascinated": Katharine Hepburn, *Me* (New York: Knopf, 1991), p. 274.

409   "Barrymore": Richard Mansfield, who predated Tracy's theatergoing years, was also reputed to have accomplished the transformation sans makeup.

409   "the change": Unidentified clipping, January 1941 (SW).

410   "tests without makeup": J. D. Marshall, *Blueprint on Babylon* (Tempe, Ariz.: Phoenix House, 1978), p. 31.

411   "Ingrid came to Fleming": Roy Mosley, *Evergreen: Victor Saville in His Own Words* (Carbondale: Southern Illinois University Press, 2000), p. 146.

411   *Men of Boys Town*: A mechanical affair, the *Boys Town* sequel lacked the sincerity and emotional heart of the original. (Bobs Watson to director Norman Taurog: "Do you want halfway down tears or all the way down tears?") Father Flanagan went through the same promotional motions as for *Boys Town*, coming to California for another "tribute" luncheon, this one broadcast live over NBC, but privately he thought the film fell "far below" the standard of the original. When the picture opened sluggishly, Louise wrote Spence from New York: "Got quite a few of the papers with the <u>Boys Town</u> notices. Considine should go out and stay drunk after those."

412   "Which one": This famous anecdote has been repeated dozens of times, usually portraying Maugham as having watched a scene of Tracy as Mr. Hyde. Its earliest telling, however, is in "Hollywood's New Bogey Man" (*Hollywood*, July 1941), in which writer Tom De Vane places himself on the set of the dinner scene after four days of shooting. Tracy tells the story on himself, pinpointing it as having occurred the previous day. Garson Kanin later quotes him as telling it, considerably embellished, in *Remembering Mr. Maugham*, pp. 121–23.

412   "The Hyde part": *Chicago Tribune*, 2/22/41.

412   "Ingrid . . . came to my office": Mosley, *Evergreen: Victor Saville in His Own Words*, p. 146.

413   first dined together: Tracy's relationship with Ingrid Bergman is documented in his 1941 datebook (SLT).

413   "I watched her relationship": Laurence Leamer, *As Time Goes By* (New York: Harper and Row, 1986), p. 72.

414   "six sets of teeth": Mosley, *Evergreen: Victor Saville in His Own Words*, p. 146.

414   "emotionally upset": *Silver Screen*, August 1941.

415   "that of star": Contract between Loew's Incorporated and ST, 4/15/41, Turner Entertainment/SW.

417   "tests of clothes": Sidney Franklin to Chester Franklin, 3/28/41, as quoted in Sidney Franklin's unpublished memoir, *We Laughed and We Cried*, p. 365 (courtesy of Kevin Brownlow).

417   "I remember Victor Fleming": Eugene Eckman to the author, via telephone, 7/28/04.

417   "what a pleasure": Eddie Lawrence to Selden West.

417   "violently pro-Nazi": Anne Revere to Selden West, circa 1978 (SW).

418   "hardest-working man": *New York World-Telegram*, 5/17/41.

418   "on the set": Marjorie Kinnan Rawlings to Beatrice H. McNeill, 6/24/41, as quoted in Gordon E. Bigelow and Laura V. Monti, eds., *The Selected Letters of Marjorie Kinnan Rawlings* (Gainesville: University Press of Florida, 1983), pp. 204–05.

420   "How can I": Louis D. Lighton to Elia Kazan, as quoted in Elia Kazan, *Kazan: A Life* (New York: Knopf, 1988), p. 311.

421   "we dissolved": Joseph Ruttenberg, American Film Institute Oral History.

422   "master screen work": *Hollywood Reporter*, 7/22/41.

422   "They laugh": *P.M.*, 8/13/41.

422   Abbott and Costello: *New York Mirror*, 8/13/41. "I remember Spencer talking about those bad reviews," actress-playwright Katharine Houghton wrote in an e-mail. "They still rankled so many years later primarily because he hadn't wanted to wear the makeup and did so against his better judgment. He was mad mostly at himself for caving in."

422   "BIGGEST BUSINESS": Nicholas Schenck to ST, 8/13/41 (SLT).

423   "It wasn't the awards": Mook, "Checking Up on Tracy."

CHAPTER 17   WOMAN OF THE YEAR

424   "have trouble finding": Mook, "Spencer Tracy's Home Life."

427   "I could see a change": Charles R. Sligh, Jr., to Selden West.

427   "the name Feely": Jane Feely Desmond to Selden West.

428   "two or three months": Frank Tracy to Selden West.

428   Peggy Gough: The studio's fan mail department took care of mail for stars and contract players who didn't have secretaries of their own (or whose secretaries didn't handle fan mail). Generally speaking, fan letters weren't answered. Those requesting photos got a postcard listing the price of a picture (which, according to Peggy Gough, annoyed a good many people). Besides Tracy, the stars at M-G-M who had secretaries of their own to deal with fan mail were Robert Taylor, Robert Montgomery, Nelson Eddy, Jeanette MacDonald, Joan Crawford, and the Marx Brothers. See also: "Calling All Secretaries," *Modern Screen*, June 1940.

429   "very charitable": Peggy Gough to Mrs. Frances Rasinen, 11/11/40 (courtesy of Patricia Mahon).

429   " 'doing anything else' ": Frank Tracy to Selden West. In the book *Tragic Idol*, author Bill Davidson quotes Carroll Tracy as supposedly saying that one of John Tracy's "greatest hopes" was that one of his sons would become a priest. Both Jane Feely Desmond and Frank Tracy doubted the quote was genuine. "I can't imagine Carroll emoting that much about anything. Really," Frank told Selden West in 1991.

430   "impression of Spence": David Caldwell to the author.

431   "clash in print": Garson Kanin, *Tracy and Hepburn* (New York: Viking, 1972), p. 80.

431   "Gar . . . had decided": Ring Lardner, Jr., *I'd Hate Myself in the Morning* (Emeryville, Calif.: Thunder's Mouth Press, 2000), p. 91.

431   "Garson . . . probably sent it": Patrick McGilligan, ed., *Backstory 3* (Berkeley: University of California Press, 1997), p. 203.

431   "They made a mistake": *Dallas Morning News*, 10/6/41.

432   "a very good time": Joseph L. Mankiewicz to George Stevens, Jr., 11/3/82, *George Stevens: A Filmmaker's Journey* Collection, AMPAS.

432   "I was terrified": Lupton A. Wilkinson and J. Bryan III, "The Hepburn Story" (Part I), *Saturday Evening Post*, 11/29/41.

432   "We would have been lucky": Jim Murray, "Kate, the Untamed Shrew," draft *Time* cover story and interview transcripts, 1952, Time Magazine Morgue/SW. Although both Ring Lardner and Michael Kanin confirmed the $100,000 sale to Metro, the August 1, 1941 agreement transferring ownership of the property to Loew's Incorpo-

rated specified a payment of $40,000 for the rights to the story. The $100,000 figure was to include all work on the screenplay as well as the story rights. Garson Kanin later described working on the script with his brother, Lardner, and Hepburn in a suite at the Garden of Allah. Kanin was in uniform, on a short leave. Food and drink, he recalled, were sent over from Chasen's.

433   "George Cukor": Katharine Hepburn to George Stevens, Jr., 11/3/82, *George Stevens: A Filmmaker's Journey* Collection (AMPAS).

433   "Kate called on me": George Stevens to Charles Higham, circa 1974, Charles Higham Collection, USC.

433   "Gable was more likely": Doug McGrath, "Ring Lardner, Jr./Maurice Rapf," *On Writing*, August 1997.

433   "brilliant actor": Katharine Hepburn to David Heeley and Joan Kramer, New York, 9/5/85 (TH).

434   "I don't think Spencer": Katharine Hepburn to Heeley and Kramer.

434   lesbian: Hepburn, *Me,* p. 400.

434   "masculine drive": Murray, "Kate, the Untamed Shrew."

434   "She stopped": Joseph L. Mankiewicz to Heeley and Kramer, New York, 1985 (TH).

434   "Spencer was five-eleven": Katharine Hepburn to Heeley and Kramer. Although Hepburn claimed to be taller, her 1927 passport, issued when she was twenty years of age, gave her height as five feet six inches, and her niece, Katharine Houghton, believes this to be correct.

435   "dumb enough": Ibid.

435   "think of anything to say": Katharine Hepburn in *The Spencer Tracy Legacy,* WNET/MGM/UA Entertainment, 1986.

435   "eyeing her": Joseph L. Mankiewicz to Heeley and Kramer.

435   "I was awful": Katharine Hepburn to Heeley and Kramer.

435   "There they were": "The Hepburn Story," *Time,* 9/1/52.

435   "too sweet": *New York Times,* 2/21/43.

435   "crossing your legs": Harry Evans, "Hollywood Diary," *Family Circle,* 6/26/42.

435   "Acting to me": Gregory J. M. Catsgs, "Sylvia Sidney," *Filmfax,* November 1990.

435   "We never rehearsed": Katharine Hepburn to Heeley and Kramer.

436   "Very interesting": Hepburn, *Me,* p. 274.

436   "ears stuck out": Katharine Hepburn to Heeley and Kramer.

436   "very unlikely thing": McGrath, "Ring Lardner, Jr./Maurice Rapf."

437   "wastes no time": *Los Angeles Times,* 9/13/41.

437   "he was so steady": A. Scott Berg, *Kate Remembered,* p. 194.

437   "new friendly feud": *New York Daily News,* 9/13/41.

438   "I knew Spence": George Stevens to Charles Higham.

439   "Mike Kanin": Lardner, *I'd Hate Myself in the Morning,* p. 95.

439   "a *complete* account": Tracy, *The Story of John,* p. 117.

440   discuss "future roles": Leamer, *As Time Goes By,* p. 73.

440   Tracy's "business": George Stevens, unpublished interview with Pete Martin, December 1960 (USC).

441   "a lot of confusion": Katharine Hepburn to George Stevens, Jr.

442   "the definitive play": Joseph L. Mankiewicz to Heeley and Kramer.

442   "too feminist": McGilligan, *Backstory 3,* p. 204.

442   "Mayer was away": Ibid., p. 249.

443   "meaty hunk of business": Evans, "Hollywood Diary."

443   "the kind of looks": Joseph L. Mankiewicz to George Stevens, Jr.

444   "great unity": John Steinbeck to ST, 1/9/40 (SLT).

444   "peculiar and strong affection": John Steinbeck to ST, 1/9/40 (SLT).

444   "a great heart": Elaine Steinbeck and Robert Wallsten, eds., *Steinbeck: A Life in Letters* (New York, Viking Press, 1975), p. 216.

444   "a little afraid": Ibid., p. 224.

445   "don't want money": Ibid., p. 225.

445   "charming bosses": John Steinbeck to ST, 6/12/41 (SLT).

445   screen rights: Paramount purchased the rights to *Tortilla Flat* at the behest of writer-
       producer Benjamin "Barney" Glazer, but the project went nowhere after George Raft
       declined the role of Danny. Glazer subsequently acquired the rights from Paramount
       when he moved to Warner Bros. in 1938. Paul Muni, who expressed a keen interest
       in doing the film, asked Steinbeck to write the screenplay, an offer which met with
       much the same answer that Metro received a few years later. Glazer sold the rights to
       M-G-M for $65,000 in April 1940.

445   "butched it up": *New York Times,* 11/30/41.

445   "a lot more fun": Marshall, *Blueprint on Babylon,* p. 32.

446   "kind of truth": Erskine, "The Private Mind of Spencer Tracy."

       CHAPTER 18   I'VE FOUND THE WOMAN I WANT

449   Katharine Houghton Hepburn: For details on the history of the Hepburn family that
       differ from other published sources, I am grateful to Katharine Houghton.

449   "I've never discovered": Katharine Houghton to the author, via e-mail, 11/3/06.

450   "Leland and Howard": Myrna Blyth, "Kate Talks Straight," *Ladies' Home Journal,*
       October, 1991.

450   "The best": Brooke Hayward, *Haywire* (New York: Knopf, 1977), p. 317.

450   "Why in the world": Hepburn, *Me,* pp. 89–90.

450   "liked bad eggs": Ralph G. Martin, "Kate Hepburn: My Life and Loves," *Ladies' Home
       Journal,* August 1975.

450   "our first picture": Hepburn, *Me,* p. 395.

450   "off their feet": Joseph L. Mankiewicz to Selden West.

450   "outdo me": Emily Torchia to Selden West, via telephone, 8/2/93.

450   "line of conquests": Claire Trevor to Selden West (SW).

451   "something you didn't print": Sheilah Graham Oral History, Columbia University.

451   "a great artist": Tim Durant to Katharine Hepburn, 1967 (KHLA).

451   the Tracy-Hepburn affair: Norman Lloyd to the author, Studio City, 9/4/06.

452   "imagined I was a lesbian": Hepburn, *Me,* p. 400.

452   "the only two men": Katharine Houghton to the author, via e-mail, 5/7/08.

452   like Louise: It's interesting to note that both women played *The Man Who Came Back*
       in stock—Louise in 1923, Hepburn in 1930.

452   "appearing at gunpoint": Ingrid Bergman (with Alan Burgess), *Ingrid Bergman, My
       Story* (New York: Delacorte Press, 1980), p. 108.

453   "never have a year": Rooney, *Life Is Too Short,* p. 188.

453   "he isn't on the radio": Peggy Gough to Mrs. Frances Rasinen, 12/1/41 (courtesy of
       Patricia Mahon).

454   "We of America": *Los Angeles Examiner,* 1/12/42.

454   "suited to each other": Spencer Tracy (as told to James Reid), "My Pal, Clark Gable,"
       Screen Life, May 1940.

454   "a very big star": Adela Rogers St. Johns, *Love, Laughter and Tears* (Garden City, N.Y.:
       Doubleday, 1978), p. 329.

454   Mt. Potosi: Locals knew the mountain as Double Up Peak, after the Double Up Mine
       on its eastern face. In news accounts of the time, the crash scene was erroneously iden-
       tified as "Double or Nothing" or Table Mountain. One later account mysteriously
       placed the crash at Mt. Olcott.

455   "pretty upset": Peggy Gough to Mrs. Frances Rasinen, 3/23/42 (courtesy of Patricia
       Mahon).

455   "Clark, beyond consolation": Loy, *Being and Becoming,* p. 169.

455   "People were clustered": Harriett Gustason, "Looking Back," *Freeport Journal-Standard,* 6/23/84.

457   "just as common": Ibid.

457   capacity business: Figures for *Woman of the Year* are from *Variety,* 2/11 and 2/18/42; and the Mannix ledger.

457   "new Music Hall offering": *New York World-Telegram,* 2/6/42.

457   "tossing his old hat": *New York Times,* 2/6/42.

458   "The boy had told me": Matie E. Winston to Louise Tracy, circa June 1967 (SLT).

458   "He can't see your lips!": Ardmore, "John," n.d.

459   "mistaken idea": Howard Dietz, *Dancing in the Dark* (New York: Quadrangle, 1974), p. 280.

459   "Benny Thau called": Loy, *Being and Becoming,* p. 154.

460   Bonaventure: Milwaukee County Certificate of Birth No. 3714, corrected 8/24/42 "by order of State Board of Health."

460   "They were *exhausted* ": Eddie Lawrence to Selden West.

460   "no condition": F. L. Hendrickson, internal memo, 3/12/42, Turner Entertainment/SW.

461   "I'd been picked up": Granger, *Sparks Fly Upward,* p. 283.

461   "Kate . . . was miserable": Charles Higham, *Kate* (New York: Norton, 1975), p. 117.

462   "just stopped off": *Pittsburgh Sun-Telegraph,* 5/12/42.

462   "Mr. Tracy said he": *Pittsburgh Press,* 5/12/42.

463   "His symptoms": Johns Hopkins Hospital, History No. 260076, May 1942 (SW).

465   The property: The *New York Times* reported that M-G-M acquired the rights to the story from RKO for $50,000, but the studio script files at USC show the book was submitted for consideration by the Frank W. Vincent Agency.

465   Hepburn committed: As late as April 10, Hepburn was expected to appear in *Frenchman's Creek* at Paramount. The first mention of her doing *Keeper of the Flame* appeared in Edwin Schallert's column of April 18. Her twelve-page contract for the picture, calling for a fee of $100,000, was dated July 18, 1942.

465   "I'm most anxious": *Cleveland Plain Dealer,* 5/5/42.

465   "She is a woman": Dorothy Manners, "La Hepburn Chooses to Ignore Stage-or-Screen Enigma," n.d.

466   "impotent eunuch": Donald Ogden Stewart to Ella Winter, as quoted in Patrick McGilligan, *George Cukor: A Double Life* (New York: St. Martin's Press, 1991), p. 168.

467   "We assume": Joseph I. Breen to Louis B. Mayer, 5/2/42 (AMPAS).

467   "A full conference": Mosley, *Evergreen: Victor Saville in His Own Words,* pp. 156–57.

467   "another flier": Matie E. Winston to Louise Tracy, 7/5/42 (SLT).

468   "Christine is guilty": Joseph I. Breen to Louis B. Mayer, 7/7/42 (AMPAS).

468   change pages: The writing of *Keeper of the Flame* is documented in the M-G-M script files at USC and AMPAS.

468   "*open* set": Emily Torchia to Selden West.

469   "hundreds of suggestions": Gavin Lambert, *On Cukor* (New York: Putnam, 1972), p. 101.

469   "take one": Darryl Hickman to the author, via telephone, 11/21/05.

469   "she finally carried": Lambert, *On Cukor,* p. 172.

471   "What are you up to": Theresa Helburn to Katharine Hepburn, 8/9/42 (TGC).

471   Appear on the set: As Darryl Hickman said, "He was clearly not a happy man. He would come in in the morning and he would be so shut down. It was so strange. Personally he was that way, but when the camera rolled, whatever was there would open up and he would use it."

471   "He felt the miseries": Katharine Hepburn to Phil Donahue, *Donahue,* Transcript #3358, 12/13/91.

472   "I MUST ADVISE YOU": Theresa Helburn to Katharine Hepburn, 9/1/42 (TGC).

472   "I want to talk to you": Katharine Hepburn to Theresa Helburn, Lawrence Langner, and Philip Barry, 9/7/42, Philip Barry Papers, Georgetown University. A preliminary draft of this letter, minus the "for personal reasons" appeal, is preserved in the Katharine Hepburn collection at New York Public Library.

473   "you are in pain": Theresa Helburn, undated notes (TGC).

473   "A SHOCK": Theresa Helburn to Katharine Hepburn, 9/13/42 (TGC).

474   "insomnia": Johns Hopkins Hospital, History No. 260076, November 1942 (SW).

CHAPTER 19   NOT THE GUY THEY SEE UP THERE ON THE SCREEN

476   "have a project": Ardmore, "Clinic," 7/20/72 (JKA).

477   The meeting took place: Minutes of Mothers' Meeting, 7/18/42 (JTC). See also Louise Tracy to Neil S. McCarthy, 7/20/43 (JTC).

477   "got my wits": Ardmore, "Clinic."

478   The first meeting of the Mothers: Minutes, 10/17/42 (JTC). The $5 check came from a doctor at L.A.'s Orthopedic Hospital. The $1,000 check likely came from Louise herself.

479   "rest cure": *Lowell Sun*, 1/18/43.

479   "Miss Hepburn is Hepburn": *Variety*, 12/16/42.

479   "garden-variety love story": *New York Times*, 2/21/43.

479   "most important": *New York Times*, 2/21/43.

479   "horrible scenes": Katharine Hepburn to Donald Ogden Stewart, 12/15/42 (DOS).

480   "can't vouch": "Donald Ogden Stewart," *Focus on Film*, November–December 1970.

481   "It was winter": James Harvey, "Irene Dunne Remembers," *Film Comment*, January–February 1980.

481   Tracy's relationship: In 1971 Irene Dunne told Roddy McDowell that Tracy was difficult at the start of *A Guy Named Joe* "because he wanted Kate." McDowell repeated what she said to Selden West in a phone conversation on 2/23/97 (SW). Given her prior commitments, it is unlikely that Hepburn could have done the film; she was appearing on Broadway in *Without Love* when Dunne's casting was announced in December 1942.

481   "first few days": James Bawden, "A Visit with Irene Dunne," *American Classic Screen*, September–October 1977.

481   "too old": *Los Angeles Evening Herald and Express*, 3/13/43.

481   "As the star appeared": *New York Times*, 8/6/67.

481   "refusal to rehearse": Harvey, "Irene Dunne Remembers."

482   "always boss": *Los Angeles Times*, 3/16/73.

482   "enjoyed working": Ibid. Dunne told David Chierichetti she thought *A Guy Named Joe* was "one of the finest pictures I ever made."

482   "walking trip": Eddie Lawrence to Selden West.

482   "We're alike": "A Director Named Fleming," *The Lion's Roar*, January 1944.

482   "the first take": Van Johnson in *Spencer Tracy: Triumph and Turmoil*, Peter Jones Productions/A&E Network, 1999.

483   "liked young actors": Barry Nelson, Southern Methodist University Oral History with Ronald L. Davis.

484   "My face": Pete Martin, "Bobby-Sox Blitzer," *Saturday Evening Post*, 6/30/45.

484   "Hollywood Presbyterian": Van Johnson, undated interview clip for Turner Classic Movies.

485   "I can remember Mr. Tracy": Doris Chambers to Jane Ardmore, 7/10/72 (JKA).

485   "a great mistake": Ardmore, "Clinic."

486   "dirty floors": *Ogden Standard-Examiner*, 4/7/43.

486   "She would put my hand": Carol Lee Barnes to the author, via e-mail, 6/16/05.

486   "give all this money": Ardmore, "Clinic."

488   "off the sauce": Doug Warren (with James Cagney), *James Cagney: The Authorized Biography* (New York: St. Martin's Press, 1983), p. 132.

488   "never announced": Frank McHugh to Ralph Bellamy.

489   "All the wives": Dorothy McHugh to Selden West.

489   "lived the characters": David Chierichetti, "Irene Dunne Today," *Film Fan Monthly,* February 1971.

489   "art of reacting": Barry Nelson Oral History.

489   "seldom lost myself": Ardmore, "Tracy," n.d.

490   "I'm no good": Adela Rogers St. Johns, "Man of Conflict," *Photoplay,* February 1945.

490   "Here's Kenny": Edgers, "The Spencer Tracy We Knew."

491   "no saying no": Cromwell, *Dear Spence,* p. 298.

492   " 'What do you expect' ": Katharine Hepburn to Phil Donahue.

492   "All of my men": William Self to Selden West, Beverly Hills, 8/3/93 (SW).

492   "destroyed Spencer": Katharine Hepburn to Selden West, Fenwick, 10/18/91 (SW).

493   "dessert with rum": David Caldwell to the author.

493   "intimate relationship": Norman, *The Hollywood Greats,* p. 83.

493   "We spent the night": Cromwell, *Dear Spence,* p. 301.

493   "never met him": Hal Elias, Academy of Motion Picture Arts and Sciences Oral History (AMPAS).

494   "hovering ghosts": Edward L. Munson, Jr., as quoted in *American Film Institute Catalog: Feature Films 1941–1950,* Film Entries A–L, p. 967.

495   "lighting took hours": Hume Cronyn, *A Terrible Liar* (New York: William Morris, 1991), p. 168.

495   "Freund was anything": Fred Zinnemann, *An Autobiography* (New York: Scribner, 1992), p. 52.

495   "Zinnemann was first chosen": Katharine Hepburn to Heeley and Kramer.

495   "very important": Gabriel Miller, ed., *Fred Zinnemann Interviews* (Jackson: University Press of Mississippi, 2005), p. 58.

496   "feeling morose": Cronyn, *A Terrible Liar,* pp. 169–70.

497   "he'd had a few": Katharine Hepburn to Phil Donahue.

497   "done two things": Joseph L. Mankiewicz to Selden West.

497   "I have no idea": Hepburn, *Me,* p. 396.

497   "fiercely jealous": Katharine Houghton's memory of what stylist Helen Hunt told her during the making of *Guess Who's Coming to Dinner* is from a conversation with the author, New York City, 5/4/06.

497   "afraid of emotion": Norman, *The Hollywood Greats,* p. 89.

498   "lower his libido": Eugene Kennedy to the author, via e-mail, 6/29/07.

498   The original Sheilah Graham story, a discussion of the stars on the top-ten list of the *Motion Picture Herald,* ran in January 1943. "Spencer Tracy has already been mentioned as Number 10," Graham wrote. "He used to be higher on the list. Spencer is losing out because he is losing interest in his film career, putting private affairs in top place." The following month, Tracy berated Graham on the set of *A Guy Named Joe* for writing about his personal life. "No one is interested in that," he said. "There's so much else going on in life, who cares what I do on my own time? And even if they did, it's none of your business . . . Mind you, I'm not saying yes and I'm not saying no in regard to some of the things you implied. That's beside the point, which is that you shouldn't have mentioned my private life at all." Graham was so unnerved by the exchange that she devoted her entire column of February 24 to it.

498   "M-G-M grapevine": Zinnemann, *An Autobiography,* pp. 50–51.

499   "easiest thing": Signe Hasso to James Fisher, 7/29/93 (SW).

499   "happy all the time": *New York Morning Telegraph,* 1/21/44.

500   "virtually explode": *Spokane Spokesman-Review,* 5/7/44.

500   "there can be debates": *Hollywood Reporter,* 12/24/43.

500   "foolish": *New York Times,* 12/24/43.

500   total billings: According to the Mannix ledger, *A Guy Named Joe* cost $2,627,000 and
       returned a profit of $1,066,000.

500   "eleven straight months": *Los Angeles Evening Herald and Express,* 1/10/44.

500   "certain number of weeks": F. L. Hendrickson, internal memo, 2/5/44 (Turner Enter-
       tainment/SW).

501   "Anybody could go on": Ardmore, "Tracy."

501   "smart boy": *Los Angeles Examiner,* 11/20/43.

                    CHAPTER 20   THE BIG DRUNK

503   "bronzed from his first": *Milwaukee Sentinel,* 5/19/44.

503   "I did": Sister Ann Willits, OP, to the author, via e-mail, 8/11/05.

503   New York: M-G-M records show that Tracy returned to the studio at some point dur-
       ing his vacation period to do one additional day of retakes on *Thirty Minutes Over
       Tokyo,* but exactly when this occurred is unknown.

503   "closest three people": Bertha Calhoun to the author.

503   "having to meet Spencer": Fay Kanin to the author, Santa Monica, 1/9/07.

504   "member of the family": Nancy Reagan, *My Turn* (New York: Random House, 1989),
       p. 78.

504   "she had a friend": Katie Treat to Conrad Oakerwohl, 7/1/85, SobrietyTalks.com. Mrs.
       Treat remembered that Nancy Davis was in her early twenties at the time. Born Anne
       Frances Robbins on July 6, 1921, Davis (the future Mrs. Reagan) would have been
       twenty-two years old in May 1944.

504   "certain people": Katharine Hepburn to Selden West (SW).

505   "very private floor": Bob Colacello, *Ronnie and Nancy* (New York: Warner Books,
       2004), p. 182.

505   "*artistic* success": *Baltimore Sun,* 5/21/44.

505   "two weeks": *Port Arthur News,* 8/19/44.

506   "I recall the liquor": Dan Alexander to Katharine Hepburn, 9/29/91 (SW).

506   "song and dance": *Los Angeles Examiner,* 10/19/44.

506   "he believed": St. Johns, "Man of Conflict."

507   "All the film companies": *Time,* 6/14/43.

507   "submerging herself": Dr. Robert Hepburn in *Katharine Hepburn: On Her Own
       Terms,* CBS News Productions/A&E Network, 1995.

508   "begin shooting next week": Katharine Hepburn to Theresa Helburn, n.d. (TGC).

508   "As always": Higham, *Kate,* p. 126.

508   "we stopped": Patricia Morison to the author, via telephone, 7/17/04.

508   "I lay on the floor": Katharine Hepburn to Phil Donahue.

509   "finish the picture": Katharine Hepburn to Ellen Barry, n.d., Philip Barry Papers,
       Georgetown University.

509   "practical man": Katharine Hepburn to Selden West.

509   "didn't publicize him": June Dunham to the author, via telephone, 3/30/05.

510   "What goes on": *Chicago Daily News,* 12/4/44.

510   "I don't frighten": Katharine Hepburn to Selden West.

510   "fiendish night": A. Scott Berg, *Kate Remembered* (New York: Putnam, 2003), p. 212.

510   "expressed surprise": Martin Gottfried to Selden West, 5/25/99 (SW).

510   "beaten hell": Millard Kaufman to the author, Brentwood, 10/14/03.

510   "once told me": Katharine Houghton to the author, via e-mail, 7/28/08.

511   "he'd ever hurt anyone": Katharine Hepburn to Selden West.

512   "February 1": According to studio records, when Bucquet needed a shot of Pat enter-
       ing Jamie's home in Washington, D.C., it was Carroll who doubled for his brother.
       The shot was made on February 7, 1945; Tracy was already in New York.

512   "delightful and amusing": Playwrights' Company, unpublished write-up for Elliott

Norton, *Boston Post,* n.d., Playwrights' Company Collection, Wisconsin State Historical Society, Madison.

512   "first place": Katharine Hepburn to Selden West.

513   "new characterization": Joseph L. Mankiewicz to Selden West.

514   tried to choke her: Katharine Hepburn to Selden West.

514   "Some sort of fight": Katharine Houghton in an e-mail to the author, 12/4/09.

515   "got so loaded": Dr. Robert Hepburn to the author, via telephone, 4/11/05.

515   "write another play": Playwrights' Company, write-up for Elliot Norton.

515   "I've got to go back": Earl Wilson, *Hot Times* (Chicago: Contemporary Books, 1984), p. 41.

516   "called upon": ST to Robert Emmet Sherwood, 4/13/45, Robert Emmet Sherwood Papers, Houghton Library, Harvard University.

516   "off the screen": *Los Angeles Examiner,* 4/17/45.

516   Tracy objecting: Details of Leo Morrison's talks with the studio are from F. L. Hendrickson, internal memos, 4/18/45 and 4/28/45, Turner Entertainment/SW.

516   "I couldn't understand": Kanin, *Tracy and Hepburn,* p. 64.

516   "Sherry-Netherland": Dietz, *Dancing in the Dark,* pp. 280–81.

517   Agent Harold Rose's: Suzanne Antles to the author.

CHAPTER 21   THE RUGGED PATH

518   cold-turkey detox: Details of Tracy's stay are from Doctors Hospital Admission Record No. 61253, May 1945, Beth Israel Hospital/SW. In a telephone interview with Selden West on 2/7/96, actor Don Taylor repudiated Bill Davidson's embroidered account of Taylor's having seen Tracy at Doctors Hospital, calling it "melodramatic horse manure." Taylor heard that Tracy had been admitted in restraints but emphasized that he never personally witnessed such a scene.

519   "finding his way": Arthur Hopkins to Katharine Hepburn, 6/12/45 (KHNY).

520   "My best bet": Travis Bogard and Jackson R. Bryer, eds., *Selected Letters of Eugene O'Neill* (New Haven: Yale University Press, 1988), p. 548.

520   "ten times": Lawrence Langner to Katharine Hepburn, 3/20/44 (TGC).

521   "things to say": Eugene Kinkead, "The Rugged Path," *New Yorker,* 11/24/45.

521   "making a mistake": Kanin, *Tracy and Hepburn,* p. 96.

522   "going to work": Jane Feely Desmond to Selden West.

522   escape clause: Out of town Tracy could leave the play for any reason with a two-week notice. In New York he would be able to give notice if the gross dipped below $16,000 for any three consecutive weeks.

523   "foolish question": *New York Times,* 2/21/43.

523   "One of the banes": Garson Kanin to David Heeley and Joan Kramer, New York, 1985 (TH).

524   a 25 percent stake: Rubin may have suggested the cut Tracy was taking in his weekly income more than justified an equity stake in the production. At capacity, Tracy's 15 percent of the gross would have brought him roughly $3,900 a week, about $1,400 less per week than he would have made under the terms of his M-G-M contract. Later, when business slipped, he would have been earning closer to $3,000 a week, which put him on a par with Elliott Nugent, who was getting about the same for his turn in *Voice of the Turtle.* Frank Fay, by comparison, was making $2,500 to $3,000 a week in *Harvey,* a terrific hit, while Walter Abel was reportedly collecting $2,000 a week in *The Mermaids Singing,* a flop.

525   "quite friendly": Victor Samrock to Robert E. Sherwood, 9/17/45 (PC).

525   "imaginative, resourceful": Kanin, *Tracy and Hepburn,* p. 96.

525   "look ridiculous": Garson Kanin, *Together Again!* (Garden City, N.Y.: Doubleday, 1981), p. 89.

525   "sold out": ST to Pete Martin.

526   "not calculated": John F. Wharton, *Life Among the Playwrights* (New York: Quadrangle/New York Times, 1974), p. 137.

526   "Spencer was superb": S. N. Behrman, *People in a Diary: A Memoir* (Boston: Little, Brown, 1972), pp. 226–27.

526   "something was amiss": Wharton, *Life Among the Playwrights,* p. 137.

527   "iron this out": *Los Angeles Daily News,* 2/16/46.

527   "never nervous": Katharine Hepburn to Heeley and Kramer.

527   "delivers the goods": Katharine Hepburn to Emil Levigne, n.d. (courtesy of Judy Samelson).

527   "party going on": Irene Mayer Selznick, *A Private View* (New York: Knopf, 1983), p. 278.

528   "didn't amount": Ardmore, "Tracy," n.d.

528   "ten days": Kanin, *Tracy and Hepburn,* p. 97.

528   "basket case": ST to Pete Martin.

528   "She and Spencer": Katharine Hepburn to Charles Higham, circa 1975 (Charles Higham Collection, USC).

529   "It touched him": Katharine Hepburn to Heeley and Kramer.

529   "Spencer rose": Kanin, *Tracy and Hepburn,* p. 98.

529   "No newspaper man": *New York Times,* 11/12/45.

529   "mistaken a stage": The New York dailies all ran their reviews of *The Rugged Path* on 11/12/45. The *Time* notice appeared in its issue of 11/19/45.

529   Andrew Tracy: Frank Tracy to Selden West, 10/18/95 (SW).

529   "same goddamn lines": Edward Dmytryk, Southern Methodist University Oral History with Ronald L. Davis, 12/2/79.

531   "worst blows": Robert E. Sherwood to Victor Samrock, 1/11/46 (PC).

531   Poverty: Sherwood put $18,000 into *The Rugged Path,* a 25 percent stake in the production. In a statement to him dated April 30, 1946, the play showed losses and expenses of $87,476.66 and an operating profit on Broadway of $18,671.01. Sherwood's share of the loss amounted to $17,201.41; for his investment he received a refund of $798.59. See also Ed Sullivan's column of 11/25/55.

531   "legitimate gross": Robert E. Sherwood to ST, 12/12/45 (PC).

531   "your problems": Robert E. Sherwood to ST, 12/18/45 (PC).

532   top five stars: Bing Crosby headed the list again, as he had in 1944. Van Johnson appeared in second place, Greer Garson in third, and Betty Grable in fourth.

533   "the great man tonight": Victor Samrock to Robert E. Sherwood, 1/2/46 (PC).

533   "My record is good": *Variety,* 1/9/46.

533   "increase business": Victor Samrock to Robert E. Sherwood, 1/9/46 (PC).

533   "notable achievements": Efrem Zimbalist, Jr., *My Dinner of Herbs* (New York: Limelight Editions, 2003), p. 59.

534   "full impact": Victor Samrock to Robert E. Sherwood, 1/21/46 (PC).

534   "I appreciate it": Robert E. Sherwood to Victor Samrock and William Fields, 1/24/46 (PC).

CHAPTER 22   STATE OF THE UNION

537   "very happy": Interview with Ardmore, 7/5/72.

537   "I got tired": John Tracy, "My Complicated Life" (Part Two), *Volta Review,* July 1946.

538   "the BEST story": R. B. Wills, "The Sea of Grass" coverage, 9/18/36 (MGM).

538   "Its Western setting": Loy, *Being and Becoming,* p. 192.

539   "worked with Hepburn": McGilligan, *Tender Comrades,* p. 578.

539   "fascinating and unusual": *New York Times,* 4/21/46.

539   "bad at negotiating": Robert M.W. Vogel Oral History (AMPAS).

540 "pretty good businessman": Hall, "Spencer Tracy Faces Forty."

540 "just a chance": Zeitlin, "Manuel the Lovable."

540 "every charitable organization": Dorothy Gopadze, "Pardon My Pink Slip," unpublished manuscript, n.d. (courtesy of Tina Gopadze Smith).

542 "very handsome": *Middletown* (N.Y.) *Times Herald,* 2/21/47.

542 "not lost weight": Elia Kazan, *Kazan: A Life* (New York: Knopf, 1988), p. 309.

543 "watch Her Highness?": Wilson, *Hot Times,* p. 38.

543 "in take one": Jeff Young, *Kazan: The Master Discusses His Films* (New York: Newmarket Press, 1999), p. 31.

543 "bursts of energy": Melvyn Douglas and Tom Arthur, *See You at the Movies* (Lanham, Md.: University Press of America, 1986), p. 149.

543 "lovers": Young, *Kazan,* p. 31.

544 "don't sell yourself": Lawrence Langner to Katharine Hepburn, 5/18/46 (TGC).

544 "Everyone here is talking": Lawrence Langner to ST, 6/6/46 (TGC).

545 "under obligation": F. L. Hendrickson, internal memo, 6/25/46, Turner Entertainment/SW.

545 "going very well": ST to Lawrence Langner, 7/15/46 (TGC).

546 "Mrs. Spencer Tracy": Tina Gopadze Smith to the author, Milwaukee, 7/9/06.

546 "I can't live": William Self to the author, Los Angeles, 2/20/04.

546 "two years hence": *Los Angeles Times,* 8/11/46.

548 "come on the set": Paul Henreid, *Ladies Man* (New York: St. Martin's Press, 1984), p. 178.

549 "I find my feeling": *New Republic,* 3/17/47.

549 "not all great": Jane Feely Desmond to the author.

550 "unsuccessful screenplay": Arthur Hornblow, Jr., Columbia University Oral History, March 1959.

550 "falls in love": Donald Ogden Stewart, *By a Stroke of Luck* (New York: Paddington Press, 1975), p. 285.

551 "Tracy wants": Harold Hecht to Donald Ogden Stewart, 4/13/47 (DOS).

551 "Tracy . . . had refused": Ella Winter to Jessie Weingarten, n.d. (DOS).

551 "In the book": *New York Sun,* 9/10/47.

552 "their baby's perambulator": Royle, unpublished autobiography, p. 55.

553 "I'm getting old": Frank Capra, *The Name Above the Title* (New York: Macmillan, 1971), p. 388.

553 "plenty of suits": Larry Keethe, "I Call It Heart," *Photoplay,* September 1948.

554 "very tricky scene": Angela Lansbury to David Heeley and Joan Kramer, Los Angeles, 12/13/85 (TH).

555 "I was backstage": McGilligan, *Tender Comrades,* p. 413.

555 "she got mad": Murray, "Kate, the Untamed Shrew."

555 "the speech that almost": Newquist, *A Special Kind of Magic,* p. 66.

555 Hedda Hopper took care: *Los Angeles Times,* 9/1/47.

555 "had a real peeve on": *Los Angeles Evening Herald-Express,* 9/9/47. By December the studio was denying rumors that Hepburn's contract had been abrogated. "Don't be surprised," wrote Harrison Carroll, "if she comes out with a statement similar to the one made by Humphrey Bogart. She has already stated her views in an interview with a radio commentator a few days ago, in which she said she was not a communist sympathizer."

555 "What the hell happened?": Higham, *Kate,* p. 132.

556 "Claudette I knew": Katharine Hepburn to Heeley and Kramer.

556 "No contract": Higham, *Kate,* p. 133.

556 "We all knew": Al Weisel, "An Uncommon Woman," *Premiere,* September 2003.

557 " 'bag of bones' ": Capra, *The Name Above the Title,* p. 390.

557 "Their personalities": Swindell, *Spencer Tracy,* p. 208.

558 "Bob Thomas worked": Emily Torchia to Selden West (SW).
559 "surprise of the picture": *Variety*, 11/5/47.
560 "Mr. Tracy never talked": Emily Torchia to Selden West.

CHAPTER 23   ADAM'S RIB

562 "He read that play": Katharine Hepburn to Heeley and Kramer.
563 "live through": Arthur and Barbara Gelb, *O'Neill* (New York: Harper & Row, 1973), p. 885.
563 "red hot": *Variety*, 3/24/48.
563 "President Truman": *Variety*, 1/5/49.
564 "more attractive-looking": *New York Times*, 4/23/48.
564 " 'He's a prick' ": ST to Pete Martin.
565 "If somebody approached": June Caldwell to the author.
565 "dinner meeting": Ardmore, "Clinic."
565 "very attracted": Dr. Alathena Smith to Jane Ardmore, 7/26/72 (JKA).
566 "I watched my father": Jane Feely Desmond to the author.
566 "I'm not going to be": Frank Tracy to Selden West.
566 "NOT MUCH I CAN SAY": ST to Patrick Norton, 5/19/48 (BT).
566 "I've come to work": *Daily Express*, 5/28/48.
567 "appeared grumpy": Eric Braun, *Deborah Kerr* (New York: St. Martin's Press, 1978), p. 118.
567 "disconcerting to me": Richard Schickel, *The Men Who Made the Movies* (New York: Atheneum, 1975), p. 177.
567 "largely Spencer": George Cukor to Signe Hasso, 7/13/48 (AMPAS).
567 "long takes": Freddie Young, *Seventy Light Years* (London: Faber and Faber, 1999), p. 74.
568 "do you mind": Emanuel Levy, *George Cukor: Hollywood's Legendary Director and His Stars* (New York: Morrow, 1994), p. 171.
568 "thrilled": Katharine Hepburn to George Cukor, 8/10/48.
568 "real dirt": Ibid.
569 "remember me": Schary, *Heyday*, p. 180.
570 "wore himself out": Bergman, *Ingrid Bergman, My Story*, p. 181.
570 "Mike Romanoff": Susie Tracy to the author, Brentwood, 12/15/04.
570 "He and Gable": Darryl Hickman to the author.
570 "That's all right": *New York Daily News*, 7/9/49.
572 "all hands and feet": Sidney Fields, "Stewart Sticks to Movies," undated clipping (SW).
572 "This normally would be": Undated clipping (SW).
572 "Can you see it": Garson Kanin, "*Adam's Rib:* The Genesis," *Memories*, October–November 1989.
573 "first time in thirty years": Higham, *Kate*, p. 135. Technically, this could be correct, in that *Woman of the Year* was still unfinished when the studio bought it in July 1941.
573 "The Kanins would do": George Stevens, Jr., *Conversations with the Great Moviemakers of Hollywood's Golden Age* (New York: Knopf, 2006), p. 284.
574 "Some of the things Kate": Crowther, notes, Tracy interview.
574 "whole tradition": Kenneth Tynan, "Katharine Hepburn," *Everybody's Magazine*, 6/28/52.
575 "It was human": Lambert, *On Cukor*, p. 201.
576 "the film represents": Katharine Houghton in an e-mail to the author, 10/14/08.
577 "Spence and I": Tynan, "Katharine Hepburn."
577 "In the course of the shooting": Kanin, *Tracy and Hepburn*, pp. 157–58.

577   "She was wonderful": Charles Higham, *Celebrity Circus* (New York: Delacorte, 1979), p. 47.

578   "Damn it, George": David Wayne to Selden West, 9/21/93 (SW).

578   "in a kind of wonderment": Fisher, *Spencer Tracy: A Bio-Bibliography*, p. 47.

579   " 'Yes, George' ": Marvin Kaplan to the author, via telephone, 11/19/06.

579   "a lot of stuff": Katharine Hepburn to Heeley and Kramer.

579   "drained of its most": *New York Times*, 6/3/49.

579   "hopeless miscasting": *New Yorker*, 6/11/49.

579   "I did it myself": Robert Morley and Sewell Stokes, *A Reluctant Autobiography* (New York: Simon and Schuster, 1966), p. 207.

580   "nearly 40 films": *Daily Express*, 5/28/48.

                    CHAPTER 24   FATHER OF THE BRIDE

581   "acting in Hollywood": William Self to the author.

583   "so dense": Katharine Hepburn to Selden West.

583   "round the three up": Charles R. Sligh, Jr., to Selden West.

584   "couldn't have left me": Myrna Blyth, "Kate Talks Straight," *Ladies' Home Journal*, October 1991.

584   "the works": Tracy's stay at Peter Bent Brigham Hospital is documented in his 1949 pocket datebook (SLT).

585   "I remember him standing": Katharine Houghton to the author.

586   "tortured soul": Seymour Gray to Selden West, 2/14/92.

587   "mediocre successes": Lawrence Weingarten, AFI seminar.

587   "Mrs. Feely": Jane Feely Desmond to Selden West.

587   "such a big deal": Jane Feely Desmond to the author, via telephone, 3/29/04.

588   "Spence came in": Frank Tracy to Selden West (SW).

588   "blood-red bleeding heart": Dr. Alathena Smith to Jane Ardmore.

588   "we sat near her": Lenore Coffee, *Storyline* (London: Cassell, 1973), p. 118.

588   "live in small places": Kanin, *Tracy and Hepburn*, p. 13.

588   comedian Jack Benny: Pandro S. Berman, undated interview, Vincente Minnelli autobiography files (AMPAS).

590   "there would be reservations": Schary, *Heyday*, pp. 217–18.

590   "my brainchild": Edward Streeter to Frances Goodrich Hackett, 1/24/49 (ES).

590   "the one I wanted": Edward Streeter to Frances Goodrich Hackett, 7/18/49 (ES).

590   "little classic of comedy": Vincente Minnelli (with Hector Arce), *I Remember It Well* (Garden City, N.Y.: Doubleday, 1974), p. 218.

591   "We talked": Don Taylor to Selden West, via telephone, 2/7/96 (SW).

592   "not quite as jovial": Joan Bennett to David Heeley and Joan Kramer, New York, 11/20/85 (TH).

594   "Even at eighteen": Elizabeth Taylor to David Heeley and Joan Kramer, Los Angeles, 12/17/85 (TH).

594   "going to drive": William Self to the author.

597   "limousine": According to Edward Dmytryk, Tracy once asked Hepburn why she continued to work for M-G-M, a studio that was "far too patronizing" for her tastes. "It's worth it when you go through Chicago," she said.

598   assembled and previewed: Details of the initial preview for *Father of the Bride* are from the film's script file at USC.

598   "I know you will realize": Frances Goodrich Hackett to Edward Streeter, n.d. (ES).

599   "greatest set of legs": Norman Lloyd to the author.

599   "I was O.K.": Hepburn, *Me*, p. 267.

599   the film surpassed: Figures for *Father of the Bride* are from the Mannix ledger.

599   "No one": Edward Streeter to ST, 5/4/50 (SLT).

599   "utterly impossible": ST to Edward Streeter, 5/16/50 (ES).

600   "equally wonderful": *New York Times*, 5/19/50.

600   "Tracy didn't want": Berman, undated interview, Minnelli files.

600   "In her practical way": Minnelli, *I Remember It Well*, p. 238.

600   "Am very happy": Pandro S. Berman to ST, 9/13/50, Turner Entertainment/SW.

600   "YOU MAY FORGET": ST to Katharine Hepburn, undated telegram (KHLA).

601   outed the relationship: A 1948 profile in *Movieland* detailed "the most incredible sort
       of rumors" about Hepburn. "In Hartford, Connecticut, Miss Hepburn's home town,
       a typist who works for the Aetna Life Insurance Company told me, 'You know, of
       course, that she's been madly in love with Spencer Tracy for years. Everyone knows
       that. But Mrs. Tracy won't give him a divorce.' " But Richard Gehman's 1950 asser-
       tions weren't labeled as rumors.

601   "They are together": Richard Gehman, "Hepburn," *Flair*, December 1950.

601   "We started the evening": *Milwaukee Sentinel*, 6/12/67.

601   "my first party": Constance Collier to Katharine Hepburn, Monday (NYPL).

601   "anything was wrong": Don Taylor to Selden West.

601   "last three comedies": Arthur Frudenfeld, "Tracy Got Best Breaks on Walker Date at
       Cox." Unidentified clipping (NYPL).

602   "not too successful": W. Kendall Jones, "Pat and Mike" coverage, 3/4/50 (MGM).

602   "machinery of justice": Eleazar Lipsky, "Johnny O'Hara's Life," story outline, 5/13/49
       (MGM).

603   "It was traditional": John Sturges to David Heeley and Joan Kramer, Los Angeles,
       12/13/85 (TH).

603   "Five years later": Norman, *The Hollywood Greats*, p. 90.

604   "chortled and howled": Lawrence Weingarten to Dore Schary, 1/5/51, Turner Enter-
       tainment/SW.

CHAPTER 25   ROUGH PATCH

605   "great to see you": John Tracy to Selden West, via fax, n.d. (SW).

606   "I kind of scouted": William Self to the author.

606   "terrible little apartment": Hepburn, *Me*, p. 398.

606   "Did Spence come?": Constance Collier to Katharine Hepburn, Sunday (KHNY).

606   "I don't know": Constance Collier to Katharine Hepburn, 1/13/51 (KHNY).

607   "There was a time": Darryl Hickman to the author, via e-mail, 4/5/07.

607   "By prearrangement": William O. Douglas, *Go East, Young Man* (New York: Random
       House, 1974), p. 432.

607   "bane of my life": Frank Tracy to Selden West.

608   "When he came": Jimmy Lydon to the author, via telephone, 1/16/06.

608   "the Spence I knew": Norman, *The Hollywood Greats*, pp. 81–82.

609   "I was confronted": O'Brien, *The Wind at My Back*, p. 308.

609   "all business": James Arness to the author, via telephone, 2/14/04.

610   "The thing I remember": John Sturges to David Heeley and Joan Kramer, Los Ange-
       les, 12/13/85 (TH).

611   "truly the culmination": ST to Jenny Feely, Tuesday.

611   "received me": *Los Angeles Evening Herald and Express*, 7/8/51.

611   "I'm just a white-haired": *Daily Mirror* (London), 5/28/51.

611   "awfully tough time": Constance Collier to Theresa Helburn, 6/8/51 (TGC).

611   "M-G-M have a picture": Constance Collier to Katharine Hepburn, 5/29/51 (KHNY).

611   "many nights": John Huston, *An Open Book* (New York: Knopf, 1980), p. 202.

612   "terribly good friends": Joan Fontaine to Anne Edwards, as quoted in *A Remarkable
       Woman* (New York: Morrow, 1985), p. 279.

612   "rough patch": Katharine Houghton to the author, via e-mail, 11/4/06.

612   "Spence's ulcer": Constance Collier to Katharine Hepburn, 6/6/51 (KHNY).

613   "Dore Schary was sort of": Lucinda Ballard, Southern Methodist University Oral History with Ronald L. Davis.

613   "Since Schary took over": Vincent Sherman, *Studio Affairs* (Lexington: University Press of Kentucky, 1996), p. 227.

615   "I've been waiting": Mervyn LeRoy, Southern Methodist University Oral History with Ronald L. Davis, 5/16/77.

615   "seeing her in Paris": Lauren Bacall, *By Myself and Then Some* (New York: Harper Entertainment, 2005), p. 495.

615   "She plays tennis": Kanin, *Tracy and Hepburn*, p. 169.

615   "intimately discussed": John Kobal, *People Will Talk* (New York: Knopf, 1986), p. 338.

616   "*all* I need": Kanin, *Tracy and Hepburn*, p. 177.

616   "He asked me": *Los Angeles Times*, 4/6/52.

616   "an agony": Katharine Hepburn to Heeley and Kramer.

617   "Too many pictures": *New York Times*, 1/20/52.

618   "those conferences": Kobal, *People Will Talk*, p. 338.

618   "put his glasses on": Charles Higham and Joel Greenberg, *The Celluloid Muse* (London: Angus and Robertson, 1969), p. 64.

618   "atomic bomb": *The Daily Record* (Stroudsburg, Pa.), 11/6/51.

618   "paint the sea": Spencer Tracy, 1951 datebook (SLT).

618   *Millionairess*: Hepburn was reported to be reading the play in April 1941, when she was considering doing it on Broadway. In a 1975 interview she spoke of Shaw having wanted her to do a movie of it. "I read it aloud and thought the first act was good, the second act was worse, and the third act was absolutely hopeless. So I said no."

619   "touring actress": George Cukor to "Corse," 2/8/51 (AMPAS).

621   "written a line": Higham, *Kate*, p. 150. In early drafts, the exact line is "She is beautyfully stacked, that kid." In the draft of November 28, 1951, the word "stacked" was changed to "packed." The word "choice" does not appear as "*cherce*" in any draft of the script. It is still "choice" in actor Chuck Connors' copy of the script at USC, which contains changes to December 27.

621   "just flattened out": Robert Emmet Long, ed., *George Cukor: Interviews* (Jackson: University Press of Mississippi, 2001), p. 148.

621   "Spence would say": William Self to the author.

621   "batted ideas": Higham, *Kate*, p. 150.

622   "Spencer massaged": Ibid.

622   "a big brother": Levy, *George Cukor*, p. 206.

623   "dinner with Spence": William Self to the author.

624   "Lawford . . . was never": Frank Tracy to Selden West.

625   "got me a part": William Self to the author.

626   " 'old Mayer group' ": *Hollywood Reporter*, 5/7/52.

626   "this nuisance": Dore Schary to ST, 5/7/52, Dore Schary Papers, Wisconsin State Historical Society, Madison.

627   "When my mood was high": Gene Tierney (with Mickey Herskowitz), *Self-Portrait* (New York: Wyden Books, 1979), p. 173.

627   "happened so quickly": Kirk Douglas, *The Ragman's Son* (New York: Simon and Schuster, 1988), p. 170.

627   "making love": *Los Angeles Times*, 5/29/52.

CHAPTER 26   AT LOOSE ENDS

628   "one occasion": This film is archived at John Tracy Clinic. Coverage of the dedication was published in the *Los Angeles Times*, 5/4/52.

629   "do anything much": Jane Feely Desmond to the author.

630   "Dad was kidding": Diane Disney Miller to the author.

630   "My mother thought": Tierney, *Self-Portrait*, p. 173.

631   "excessively brutal": Dore Schary to ST, 7/18/52, Dore Schary Papers, Wisconsin State Historical Society, Madison.

631   "Unable to understand": ST to Garson Kanin, 7/30/52, Gordon-Kanin Papers/SW.

632   "thrilling": ST to Garson Kanin, 7/30/52, Gordon-Kanin Papers/SW.

632   "fulfilled my contract": *Albuquerque Tribune,* 8/6/52.

632   "at loose ends": Garson Kanin to George Cukor, 9/5/52, Gordon-Kanin Papers/SW.

632   "needed a friend": Garson Kanin to ST, 9/4/52, Gordon-Kanin Papers/SW.

632   "appointed time": June Dally-Watkins, *The Secrets Behind My Smile* (Cambelwell, Victoria, Australia: Viking, 2002), p. 99.

632   "twenty-five": June Dally-Watkins to the author, via telephone, 8/25/06.

632   "Remaining here": ST to Ruth Gordon and Garson Kanin, 9/9/52, Gordon-Kanin Papers/SW.

633   "subdued and effeminate": *Time* interview transcripts, 1952.

633   "Bogart and Tracy": Peter Viertel, *Dangerous Friends* (New York: Doubleday, 1992), p. 238.

634   "It's the parts": *Dallas Morning News,* 4/13/52.

634   "marvelous actor": Lauren Bacall to the author, via telephone, 2/10/06.

634   "You and Spence": Emily Perkins to Katharine Hepburn, 8/22/52 (KHLA).

634   "goddamn silly": George Cukor to Garson Kanin and Ruth Gordon, 9/11/52 (AMPAS).

635   "run off": ST to Garson Kanin, 10/1/52, Gordon-Kanin Papers/SW.

635   "I was surprised": William Self to the author.

635   "I can't tell you": Constance Collier to George Cukor, 10/13/52.

635   "I stood": Hepburn, *Me,* p. 48.

635   "understood clearly": *New York Times,* 10/18/52.

635   "fine spirits": George Cukor to Constance Collier, 10/23/52 (AMPAS).

635   "NO REPORT": ST to Garson Kanin, 11/1/52 (LOC).

635   "facing a decision": *Lowell Sun,* 10/31/52.

635   "special dispensation": *Charleston Daily Mail,* 11/26/52.

635   "very close": *Time* interview transcripts, 1952.

636   "Don't ever leave me": Ardmore, "Tracy," n.d. When later asked about this particular quote, Chuck Sligh replied, "I could easily imagine that he said that. I don't *know,* but I could imagine. He NEEDED her. You know, these daily telephone calls and so on. I think that all indicated a need for her help. Whether she was still his wife actually or not."

636   "good-bye Charlie": Garson Kanin to ST, 12/1/52, Gordon-Kanin Papers/SW.

636   "difficult to get information": ST to Ruth Gordon, n.d. (LOC).

636   "not my best": Scott Eyman, "Clarence Brown: Garbo and Beyond," *Velvet Light Trap,* spring 1978.

636   "cards wonderful": Dore Schary to ST, 7/23/52, Dore Schary Papers, Wisconsin State Historical Society, Madison.

636   "simply great": Dore Schary to ST, 7/31/52, Dore Schary Papers, Wisconsin State Historical Society, Madison.

636   "thoroughly respectful": *New York Times,* 11/14/52.

637   "the kind of film": *New York Herald Tribune,* 11/14/52.

637   total billings: The figures for *Plymouth Adventure* are from the Mannix ledger.

637   "It sank!": Dore Schary to Selden West, New York, 1/5/78 (SW).

638   "not at all convinced": Garson Kanin to George Cukor, 8/18/51, Gordon-Kanin Papers/SW.

638   shot a test: Reynolds' test was shot on the fly, sandwiched between rehearsals of the musical numbers for *I Love Melvin* (1953).

638   "exceptional enough": George Cukor to Ruth Gordon and Garson Kanin, 9/26/52 (LOC).

638   "superficial nonsense": Garson Kanin to George Cukor, 12/10/52 (AMPAS).

638   "MEETING": ST to Garson Kanin, 11/19/52, Gordon-Kanin Papers/SW.

638   "sense of humor": Jean Simmons to the author, via telephone, 1/10/05.

639   "MAD": Ruth Gordon to George Cukor, 11/27/52 (AMPAS).

639   "extremely interested": Garson Kanin to ST, 7/9/51, Gordon-Kanin Papers/SW.

639   "have some edge": George Cukor to Ruth Gordon, 10/10/52 (AMPAS).

639   "a lot of talk": Levy, *George Cukor,* p. 210.

639   "wonderful woman": George Cukor to Charles Higham, *Time-Life History of the Movies,* 6/22/71, Columbia University.

640   "going along well": ST to Garson Kanin, 12/21/52 (LOC).

640   "pretty deep stuff": Garson Kanin to ST, 9/25/52, Gordon-Kanin Papers/SW.

640   "organized my hotel": Dally-Watkins, *The Secrets Behind My Smile,* p. 104.

641   "Talk about people": Lambert, *On Cukor,* p. 212.

641   "He loved": Schickel, *The Men Who Made the Movies,* p. 177.

642   "In the play": George Cukor to Ruth Gordon and Garson Kanin, 9/26/52 (LOC).

642   "devastating": Richard Burton to Dick Cavett, September 1980.

643   "Evelyn Keyes": Garson Kanin to ST, 1/1/53, Gordon-Kanin Papers/SW.

643   "stinkin' ": Leland Hayward to Ernest Hemingway, 3/10/53 (EH).

643   "disturbing element": Lawrence Weingarten to George Cukor, 2/25/53 (AMPAS).

643   clashed bitterly: Cukor's objections are outlined in a letter to Weingarten, 3/2/53 (AMPAS).

644   "At first they think": George Cukor to Ruth Gordon and Garson Kanin, 4/24/53 (LOC).

644   "Hollywood people": Leland Hayward to Ernest Hemingway, 12/3/52 (NYPL).

645   "he looks great": Leland Hayward to Ernest Hemingway, 1/16/53 (NYPL).

645   The deal: Details of the agreement to film *The Old Man and the Sea* are contained in a letter to Leland Hayward from Robert M. Coryell of the William Morris Agency, 3/2/53 (NYPL); and in an M-G-M meeting memorandum by F. L. Hendrickson, 8/12/53, Turner Entertainment/SW.

645   "talk things over": Ernest Hemingway to Leland Hayward, 3/15/53 (EH).

646   "Hemingway . . . was afraid": *Dallas Morning News,* 11/13/55.

646   "big fight": Carlos Baker, ed., *Ernest Hemingway: Selected Letters, 1917–1961* (New York: Scribner, 1981), p. 817.

646   "practical time": Ernest Hemingway to Leland Hayward, 4/23/53 (NYPL).

646   "He believes": Faith Service, "His Son Made Spencer Tracy What He Is Today!" *Movie Classic,* August 1933.

646   "people thought": Ardmore, "John," n.d.

646   "I only saw him": Seymour Gray to Selden West.

647   "I went to Las Vegas": Susie Tracy to the author, Brentwood, 1/28/05.

648   "STILL HERE": ST to Ruth Gordon, 4/13/53, Gordon-Kanin Papers/SW.

648   "he was joking": Gottfried Reinhardt to Garson Kanin, 4/27/53, Gordon-Kanin Papers/SW.

649   "on a European train": Lambert, *On Cukor,* p. 217.

650   "real, honest story": Schickel, *The Men Who Made the Movies,* p. 235.

650   "absolutely convinced": Garson Kanin to Robert E. Sherwood, 7/16/53, Gordon-Kanin Papers/SW.

650   "long and happy": *Los Angeles Examiner,* 8/10/53.

650   "co-starring days": *Los Angeles Times,* 8/13/53.

650   "one word of French": Garson Kanin, "I Remember Spence and Kate," Center for Cassette Studies, West Hollywood.

650   "Old Florentine": ST to Louise Tracy, n.d. (SLT).

651   "shocking routine": Garson Kanin to George Cukor, 9/17/53 (AMPAS). Where Kanin's account of Tracy's visit to Cap Ferrat differs in his book *Tracy and Hepburn,* I have chosen to regard this letter, written within days of the actual events, as likely the more accurate of the two.

CHAPTER 27   A GRANITE-LIKE WEDGE OF A MAN

652   "That film": Lawrence Weingarten, AFI seminar.

652   "I have a hunch": *Los Angeles Times,* 5/9/52.

653   "For the vitality": *New York Times,* 10/25/53.

654   a loss: The Mannix ledger shows a cost of $1,424,000 for *The Actress,* and domestic billings of just $594,000. It was the first Tracy picture since *Whipsaw* to post total billings of under $1 million.

654   "Failure . . . is a more common": Schary, *Heyday,* p. 258.

654   "adhered too closely": Darryl F. Zanuck to Sol Siegel and Richard Murphy, 8/21/53 (USC).

655   "STARTED NEW YEAR": ST to Ruth Gordon and Garson Kanin, 1/11/54, Gordon-Kanin Papers/SW.

655   "not going": Emily Torchia to Selden West.

655   "newest admirer": *Lowell Sun,* 2/5/54.

656   "beginning of the end": Eyman, "Clarence Brown: Garbo and Beyond."

656   "disgusted, upset": Tornabene, *Long Live the King,* p. 345.

657   "He saw me": Robert Wagner to the author, Brentwood, 8/29/05.

658   "He'd agonize": "Edward Dmytryk," *Films in Review,* December 1985.

659   "Spence did everything": Edward Dmytryk, *It's a Hell of a Life But Not a Bad Living* (New York: Times Books, 1978), p. 182.

659   "pissed off": Hugh O'Brien to the author, via telephone, 5/1/05.

659   "down-to-earth": Ronald Neame (with Barbara Roisman Cooper), *Straight from the Horse's Mouth* (Lanham, Md.: Scarecrow Press, 2003), p. 145.

660   "diffident at working": Dmytryk, *It's a Hell of a Life,* p. 185.

660   "I told Tracy": "Richard Widmark Part II," *Films in Review,* May 1986.

661   "one thing pleased me": *Hollywood Citizen-News,* 4/14/52.

662   Tracy's guests: Tracy made careful note of his drug and alcohol intake in his 1955 date-book.

662   "she and Tracy": Sandy Sturges to the author, via telephone, 3/30/04.

662   "our first evening": Dmytryk, *It's a Hell of a Life,* p. 201. In his book Dmytryk has this taking place in August 1955, when he and Tracy were on their way to France to make *The Mountain.* But Tracy's datebooks show that he flew directly to Paris for the start of that film and that Hepburn was still touring Australia at the time. Dmytryk dined with Tracy and Hepburn on May 11, 1954.

664   "Years ago": *Los Angeles Times,* 1/31/54.

664   "go to London": Jane Feely Desmond to the author, via telephone, 3/29/04.

666   "granite-like wedge": *Bad Day at Parma,* incomplete screenplay by Millard Kaufman, 8/26/53 (MGM).

666   "Daddy loves": Jill Schary Zimmer, *With a Cast of Thousands* (New York: Stein and Day, 1963), p. 50.

666   "liked the idea": Millard Kaufman to the author.

668   "We simplified it": Dore Schary, Oral History with Mr. and Mrs. Robert C. Franklin, Columbia University, November 1958.

669   "his opinion": Ibid.

669   "people at Metro": John Sturges commentary track, *Bad Day at Black Rock,* laserdisc edition, Criterion Collection, 1991.

670   "an idea": Joseph J. Cohn Oral History with Rudy Behlmer, August–November 1987 (AMPAS).

670   "new boy": Schary, *Heyday,* p. 279. Schary describes this exchange as taking place the Friday before the start of shooting, which would have been July 16, 1954. However, Tracy's datebook shows their last meeting as having occurred a week earlier, on July 9, 1954.

670   "I anticipated": John Sturges to Heeley and Kramer.

670   "hardly had it altered": Millard Kaufman to the author.

671 " 'I figure' ": John Sturges to Heeley and Kramer.

671 "My first scene": Ernest Borgnine to Scott Eyman, via telephone, 3/4/08 (courtesy of Scott Eyman).

671 "form of torture": Anne Francis, interviewed in *Spencer Tracy: Triumph and Turmoil,* Peter Jones Productions/A&E Network, 1999.

672 "He said that Katie": Anne Francis, quoted in Glenn Lovell, *Escape Artist: The Life and Films of John Sturges* (Madison: University of Wisconsin Press, 2008), p. 103.

672 "disturbing observation": Millard Kaufman, "A Vehicle for Tracy: The Road to Black Rock," *Hopkins Review,* Winter 2008.

672 "never rehearsed": Ernest Borgnine to Scott Eyman.

672 "on the porch": John Ericson to the author, via telephone, 6/24/05.

672 "Ryan is bristling": Millard Kaufman to the author.

673 "great script": John Ericson to the author.

674 "a grownup CinemaScope": *Variety,* 7/28/54.

674 "my old man": Marshall, *Blueprint on Babylon,* p. 252.

674 "almost no film": Sturges commentary track.

674 "rather apologetic": Millard Kaufman to the author.

675 "I wondered": Ernest Borgnine to Scott Eyman.

676 "We were interested": John Sturges to Heeley and Kramer.

676 "He listened": Millard Kaufman to the author.

677 " 'ideas in your head' ": John Ericson to the author.

678 "a smoker": Millard Kaufman to the author.

679 "winning streak": Leo Durocher (with Ed Lynn), *Nice Guys Finish Last* (New York: Simon and Schuster, 1975), p. 327.

679 "been on the trip": King Vidor to Selden West.

680 "Perfect!": Spencer Tracy, 1954 datebook (SLT).

680 "I was there": Susie Tracy to the author, via telephone, 1/31/08.

680 " 'wonderful place' ": Ardmore, "Tracy," n.d.

681 "firm offer": Bert Allenberg to Eddie Mannix, 1/7/55, Turner Entertainment/SW.

682 "one of the finest": John O'Hara, "Appointment with O'Hara," *Collier's,* 3/18/55.

683 "selling me": Robert Wise to Selden West, via telephone, 4/30/96 (SW).

683 "not trying to be difficult": *Los Angeles Times,* 3/8/55.

683 "Poor Spence": Constance Collier to Katharine Hepburn, 4/2/55 (KHLA).

684 "talked to Spence": Constance Collier to Katharine Hepburn, 4/16/55 (KHNY).

684 "almost impossible": Kevin Brownlow, *David Lean* (New York: St. Martin's Press, 1996), p. 486.

686 "Wonderful set": Spencer Tracy, 1955 datebook (SLT).

686 "no merit": Katharine Hepburn to Phyllis Wilbourn, n.d. (KHLA).

686 "in a better position": F. L. Hendrickson, memorandum, 6/14/55, Turner Entertainment/SW.

687 "arranged our shooting": Sergio Leemann, *Robert Wise on His Films* (Los Angeles: Silman-James Press, 1995), p. 131.

688 "That's crazy": Dore Schary to Selden West.

689 "take it down": Joseph J. Cohn Oral History.

CHAPTER 28   THE MOUNTAIN

690 "I bet": Interview with Ardmore, 7/5/72.

691 "interested in working": "Cagney": James Cagney, *Cagney by Cagney* (Garden City, N.Y.: Doubleday, 1976), p. 146.

691 "Who cares?": Spencer Tracy, 1955 datebook (SLT).

691 "Is there a romance": *Sydney Sun,* 6/5/55 (courtesy of Kerrie Tickner).

691 "I saw a report": *Sun Herald,* 8/5/55 (courtesy of Kerrie Tickner).

691 "first waking thought": *Brisbane Telegraph,* 7/18/55.

691   "We miss Constance": Theresa Helburn to Katharine Hepburn, 6/29/55 (TGC).

692   "the next day": Jane Feely Desmond to the author, via telephone, 4/6/04.

694   "simple story": Harry Mines, draft press release, n.d. (AMPAS).

694   "a primal contest": Marshall, *Blueprint on Babylon,* p. 308.

695   "a good relationship": Dmytryk, *It's a Hell of a Life,* p. 200.

695   "extraordinary": Robert Wagner to the author.

695   "I can't do it": Dmytryk, *It's a Hell of a Life,* p. 201.

695   "He wore it": Robert Wagner, "My Hat's Off to Spencer Tracy," *Movie Mirror,* July 1956.

695   "He was leaving": Bert Allenberg to Katharine Hepburn, 8/22/55 (KHLA).

696   "very unhappy": Harry Caplan to Hugh Brown, 8/20/55 (AMPAS).

696   "Our unit": Harry Caplan to Hugh Brown, 8/22/55 (AMPAS).

697   "giving them trouble": Robert Wagner to the author.

697   "short line": Margaret Shipway to Katharine Hepburn, 8/29/55 (KHLA).

698   "Those damn things": Dmytryk, *It's a Hell of a Life,* p. 204.

698   "From our viewpoint": Frank Westmore (with Muriel Davidson), *The Westmores of Hollywood* (New York: Lippincott, 1976), p. 188.

698   "Conditions": Harry Caplan to Hugh Brown, 9/3/55 (AMPAS).

700   "the word 'job' ": Lloyd Shearer, "Spencer Tracy: Hollywood's Least-Known Star," *Parade,* 12/11/55.

701   "Young man": Edward Dmytryk, as quoted in *Close Up: The Contract Director* (Metuchen, N.J.: Scarecrow Press, 1976), p. 365.

702   "Only parts": Fisher, *Spencer Tracy: A Bio-Bibliography,* p. 56.

702   "quite a wingding": Dmytryk, *It's a Hell of a Life,* p. 205.

702   "first inkling": Susie Tracy to the author.

702   "next six days": Dmytryk, *It's a Hell of a Life,* p. 206. Tracy's datebook indicates three days "on the town," not six as Dmytryk remembered it. On day four (not seven) Tracy was under a doctor's care. He did, however, resume work on the fourteenth, just as Dmytryk has it in his book.

703   "an old bastard": Jack Hirshberg, questionnaire for Spencer Tracy (AMPAS).

703   "prompted the tops": Carle, "Magnificent Katharine Hepburn."

703   "I'm not retiring": Shearer, "Spencer Tracy: Hollywood's Least-Known Star."

704   "whole thing evaporated": Frank Tracy to Selden West.

704   "terrible picture": Gallagher, "Claire Trevor."

704   "older brother": "Edward Dmytryk."

704   "long scene": Dmytryk, *It's a Hell of a Life,* p. 205.

707   "What's the matter?": Rosemary Clooney, *Girl Singer* (New York: Doubleday, 1999), p. 141.

707   "good feeling": Fred Zinnemann to Ernest Hemingway, 12/23/55 (AMPAS).

707   "some sort of shape": Ernest Hemingway to Fred Zinnemann, 1/3/56 (NYPL).

707   "near Katharine Hepburn": Fred Zinnemann to Ernest Hemingway, 12/23/55 (AMPAS).

707   "disappointed": Spencer Tracy, 1956 datebook (SLT).

710   "He said he didn't know": Don Page to Charles Greenlaw, 4/17/56, Jack Warner Collection, Cinematic Arts Library, University of Southern California.

710   "behaving fairly well": Fred Zinnemann to Ernest Hemingway, 4/24/56 (AMPAS).

710   "LOOKED EXCELLENT": Jack L. Warner to Fred Zinnemann, 5/1/56, Jack Warner Collection, University of Southern California.

711   "We notify you": Leland Hayward to ST, 5/12/56 (NYPL).

712   "BYGONES": Leland Hayward, ST, and Fred Zinnemann to Steve Trilling, 5/14/56, Jack Warner Collection.

712   "triumph of man's spirit": Fred Zinnemann, *A Life in Movies: An Autobiography* (New York: Scribner, 1992), p. 148.

712   "Hemingway hated it": Ibid, p. 150.

712 "tadpole": Viertel, *Dangerous Friends*, p. 279.

712 "some difficulty": Baker, *Ernest Hemingway: Selected Letters*, p. 855.

712 "most certainly a problem": Fred Zinnemann to Selden West, 5/20/92 (SW).

713 "He seemed malevolent": Fred Zinnemann to Selden West, 9/9/92 (SW).

713 "SAW DAILIES": Jack L. Warner to Fred Zinnemann, 6/15/56 (AMPAS).

714 "studio tank": Zinnemann, *A Life in Movies*, p. 150.

714 "argument had nothing": *Los Angeles Examiner*, 6/23/56.

715 "One time at Romanoff's": Jean Porter Dmytryk to the author, Encino, 11/17/04.

715 "one damned thing": Kanin, *Tracy and Hepburn*, p. 108.

715 "My elusive tenant": George Cukor to Katharine Hepburn, 2/26/54 (AMPAS).

715 "He knew the way": Katharine Hepburn, at "A Tribute to Spencer Tracy," Majestic Theatre, New York, 3/3/86 (courtesy of American Academy of Dramatic Arts).

716 "Kate very attractive": Joseph L. Mankiewicz to Selden West.

717 "little wop": Rex Harrison, *Rex* (London: Macmillan, 1974), p. 173.

717 "lifted a few": Frank Sinatra, at "A Tribute to Spencer Tracy."

718 "in a sailor suit": Frank Sinatra to David Heeley and Joan Kramer, Los Angeles, 12/12/85 (TH).

718 "he did love her": Seymour Gray to Selden West.

CHAPTER 29 THE LAST HURRAH

720 "no more than adequate": *Daily Variety*, 9/27/56.

720 "an actor": Dmytryk, *It's a Hell of a Life*, p. 206.

721 "hard to determine": *New York Times*, 11/15/56.

721 "We made inquiries": Carle, "Magnificent Katharine Hepburn."

721 "It is regrettable": *Los Angeles Times*, 8/26/56.

722 "That morning": Henry Ephron, *We Thought We Could Do Anything* (New York: Norton, 1977), p. 184.

722 "great with Bogie": Lauren Bacall to the author.

723 "For one thing": *Los Angeles Times*, 11/25/56.

723 "the whole scene": Ephron, *We Thought We Could Do Anything*, p. 188.

724 "desperately ill": Katharine Hepburn in *Bacall on Bogart*, Educational Broadcasting Corporation/Turner Entertainment Co., 1988.

725 "deliver the eulogy": Lauren Bacall to the author.

725 "blocking and rehearsing": Dina Merrill to Scott Eyman, 4/12/05 (courtesy of Scott Eyman).

726 "remarkable example": Katharine Hepburn to Heeley and Kramer.

726 "You don't know": Joel Greenberg, "The Other Lang," *Focus on Film*, summer 1974.

726 "reading a magazine": Dina Merrill commentary track, *Desk Set*, DVD edition, 20th Century-Fox Home Entertainment, 2004.

727 "Shut your mouth": Greenberg, "The Other Lang."

727 "gave it to her": Dina Merrill to Scott Eyman.

727 "mischievous kid": Ephron, *We Thought We Could Do Anything*, p. 191.

727 "didn't even go": *Nashua* (N.H.) *Telegraph*, 2/27/57.

727 obvious jab: Ingrid Bergman did indeed win the Best Actress Oscar for *Anastasia*.

728 "felt he was too old": Greenberg, "The Other Lang."

728 "schoolgirl crush": Henry Ephron to Charles Higham, circa 1975 (USC).

730 "They got mixed up": Paul Mayersberg, *Hollywood, the Haunted House* (London: Penguin, 1967), p. 93.

731 "powerful generators": James Wong Howe, "Necessary to Hide Evidences of 'Fixed Light' in Film on Sea," *Film and A-V World*, August 1960.

732 "my life's work": *Dallas Morning News*, 7/29/57.

732 "make money": Ernest Hemingway to Leland Hayward, 7/5/57 (EH).

733 "very appealing": Leland Hayward to Ernest Hemingway, 8/9/57 (NYPL).

733 "Maybe Zinnemann": *New York Post*, 8/12/57.

734 "Tracy's performance": Leland Hayward to Ernest Hemingway, 8/9/57 (NYPL).

734 "repulsed her": *Fresno Bee*, 8/29/57. See also *Los Angeles Times*, 8/29/57.

735 "She spoke of him": John Houseman, *Final Dress* (New York: Simon and Schuster, 1983), p. 81.

736 "sensed an affinity": Laurence Olivier to Katharine Hepburn, 7/10/67 (KHLA).

736 "a party to celebrate": *London Sunday Express*, 5/21/61.

738 "first citizen": Philip Dunne, n.d., Philip Dunne Collection, University of Southern California.

738 "out of the black": Katharine Hepburn to Ella Winter, 11/13/57, Ella Winter Collection, Columbia University.

739 "There were giants": *Los Angeles Examiner*, 11/1/57.

739 "BRILLIANT DIRECTOR": ST to Leland Hayward, 6/28/54 (NYPL).

741 "theory about acting": Shearer, "Spencer Tracy."

742 "The wake is as obsolete": *Los Angeles Examiner*, 5/4/58.

743 "strong habits": Katharine Hepburn to Dan Ford, n.d., John Ford Collection.

744 voice of the Old Man: John Sturges didn't want Tracy to attempt an accent. "We used Hemingway's trick, which is to drop in a Spanish word once in a while, but when a Spanish person or Cuban speaks to another Cuban, they don't have an accent. And that was Hemingway's approach to doing that." John Sturges to Heeley and Kramer.

744 "Worth all the agony": Louise Tracy to Mary Kennedy Taylor, 1/12/58, Taylor Collection, Beinecke Rare Book and Manuscript Library, Yale University.

744 "emotional quality": Leland Hayward as reported to Jack L. Warner by Steve Trilling, 3/10/58, Jack Warner Collection, University of Southern California.

745 "went to the preview": Lauren Bacall to the author.

745 "twenty-eight years": *New York Times*, 3/16/58.

CHAPTER 30 OUR GREATEST ACTOR

746 "Irish revolutionary": John Sturges to Heeley and Kramer.

747 Gersten reported: Houseman, *Final Dress*, p. 123.

747 "meek and motherly": Graham, *Confessions of a Hollywood Columnist*, p. 38.

747 "*utterly* dependent": Betsy Drake to the author, via telephone, 10/29/05.

747 "She was *abject*": Sally Erskine to Selden West, 12/5/91 (SW).

748 "Spence was down": Chester Erskine to Katharine Hepburn, 5/27/58 (KHNY).

748 "He would come up": Eddie Lawrence to Selden West.

748 "a beautiful piece": *Hollywood Reporter*, 5/19/58.

748 "remarkable achievements": *Daily Variety*, 5/21/58.

749 "pay was low": Donald Spoto, *Stanley Kramer, Film Maker* (New York: Putnam, 1978), p. 23.

750 vacationing in Europe: After March's turndown, Shumlin got Melvyn Douglas to fill in for Paul Muni.

751 "enough trouble": Stanley Kramer to Selden West, Los Angeles, n.d. (SW).

751 "Everyone identified": George Stevens, Jr., *Conversations with the Great Moviemakers of Hollywood's Golden Age*, p. 569.

751 "Kramer said": William Weber Johnson, rough notes of an unpublished Tracy interview for *Time*, 10/14/58 (KHLA).

751 price tag: To be exact, the negative cost of *The Old Man and the Sea* was $5,487,000.

752 "arrange for someone": Johnson, notes for *Time*.

752 "all that schmaltz": Jane Feely Desmond to the author.

752 "getting old": Johnson, notes for *Time*.

752 " 'Kate' ": Dina Merrill to Scott Eyman, 4/12/05. In her column of March 28, Dorothy

Kilgallen erroneously reported that Hepburn and her "long-time Great Love" had been "making the scene on the tropical island of Martinique."

753 "new low": *New York Herald Tribune,* 12/29/59.

754 "I earn": *Dallas Morning News,* 1/8/60.

754 "The young actors": Johnson, notes for *Time.*

755 "really gifted": Higham and Greenberg, *The Celluloid Muse,* p. 56.

755 "a sort of slightly affected": Cukor to Higham, *Time-Life History of the Movies.*

755 "Our company": Dmytryk, *It's a Hell of a Life,* p. 205.

755 "He covers up": Ezra Goodman, *The Fifty Year Decline and Fall of Hollywood* (New York: Simon and Schuster, 1961), p. 269.

755 "an actor is normally trained": Laraine Day to Barbara Hall.

755 "easy to imitate": John McCabe, *Cagney* (New York: Knopf, 1997), p. 256.

756 "the kind of actor": Truman Capote, "The Duke in His Domain," *New Yorker,* 11/9/57.

756 back to the original: First published by the National Book Company of Cincinnati in 1925, the transcripts of "the world's most famous court trial" were readily available.

757 "improve and sharpen": Stanley Kramer to Fredric March, 9/8/59, Fredric March Papers, Wisconsin State Historical Society, Madison.

757 "more topical": Walter Wagner, *You Must Remember This* (New York: Putnam, 1975), pp. 289–90.

757 supporting cast: Dick York was a last-minute choice for the role of Cates. Kramer originally envisioned Anthony Perkins in the part, later Roddy McDowell.

757 "first exchange": *New York Times,* 11/1/59.

758 "We were rehearsing": Stanley Kramer, unpublished interview with Pete Martin, December 1960 (USC).

759 "doing waltzes": Donna Anderson to the author, Los Angeles, 1/16/05.

759 "fine powder": Stanley Kramer, Southern Methodist University Oral History with Ronald L. Davis.

759 "I had been warned": Stanley Kramer to Pete Martin.

760 "sort of petrified": Jimmy Boyd to the author, via telephone, 8/27/05.

760 "extras as spectators": Stanley Kramer to Pete Martin.

761 "Better stand up": *New York Herald Tribune,* 12/29/59.

761 "fucking fan": Robert Wagner to Scott Eyman.

761 "lot of fun": ST to Pete Martin.

761 "I could understand": Clive Hirschhorn, *Gene Kelly* (New York: St. Martin's Press, 1984), p. 229.

762 "quite a system": Stanley Kramer to Pete Martin.

763 "Tracy was so *good* ": Elliott Reid to the author, Los Angeles, 10/21/03.

763 "very funny": Stanley Kramer to Pete Martin.

764 "At one performance": Lauren Bacall, *By Myself* (New York: Knopf, 1979), p. 301.

764 "a pair of hands": Martin Gottfried to Selden West.

765 "struck me as fantastic": Abby Mann, *Judgment at Nuremberg* (London: Cassell, 1961), p. v.

765 "Kate . . . was out": Philip Langner to the author, via telephone, 3/31/05.

765 "tremendous responsibility": *New York Times,* 1/31/60.

766 "our greatest actor": *Newsweek,* 6/13/60.

766 "the thing she didn't admire": William Self to the author.

767 "Mervyn LeRoy said to me": Frank Sinatra to Heeley and Kramer.

768 "a certain amount": Bertha Calhoun to the author.

768 "ringing phrases": *Hollywood Reporter,* 6/28/60.

768 "casting genius": *Daily Variety,* 6/29/60.

768 "reviews I could have written": Stanley Kramer to Heeley and Kramer.

769 "enjoyed the movie": John T. Scopes and James Presley, *Center of the Storm* (New York: Holt, Rinehart and Winston, 1967), p. 270.

769   "reprehensible": *Los Angeles Times,* 2/9/60.

770   "The first day": Kerwin Matthews to the author, 2/26/04.

770   "never interfered": Mervyn LeRoy, *Mervyn LeRoy: Take One* (New York: Hawthorn Books, 1974), p. 211.

770   "near perfect": Gregoire Aslan, unpublished interview with Pete Martin, December 1960 (USC).

770   "Tracy's turn": Bob Yager, unpublished interview with Pete Martin, December 1960 (USC).

771   "The problem": Jean-Pierre Aumont, *Sun and Shadow* (New York: Norton, 1977), p. 198.

771   "particularly horny": George Jacobs and William Stadiem, *Mr. S: My Life with Frank Sinatra* (New York: Harper Entertainment, 2003), p. 212.

771   "brilliant and engrossing": *New York Times,* 10/13/60.

771   "first run houses": Stanley Kramer to Pete Martin.

772   "double disappointment": Stanley Kramer, American Film Institute Seminar with James Powers, 2/1/77 (AFI).

772   flop: According to records in the Stanley Kramer collection at UCLA, *Inherit the Wind* had a domestic gross of $1,100,000. In April 1962 it became one of the recent releases acquired by the American Broadcasting Company for its new Sunday night movie slot.

772   "good reporter": Joe Hyams to Selden West, via telephone, 12/15/93.

772   "thought about directing": *New York Times,* 11/3/60.

772   "rare exception": *Beverly Hills Citizen,* 6/11/59.

773   "wonderful people": *Los Angeles Mirror,* 12/5/60.

773   "By the end": Kerwin Matthews to the author, 3/14/05.

773   "a lovely set": LeRoy, *Mervyn LeRoy: Take One,* p. 211.

773   "I called him": Stanley Kramer to Pete Martin.

774   "the boy's big chance": ST to Pete Martin.

776   "half a million": Despite Kate Buford's assertion in her biography of Lancaster that he was paid his usual fee of $750,000 for *Judgment at Nuremberg,* the actor's contract in the Stanley Kramer collection shows that he was paid $500,000 and a percentage of the gross. Tracy's compensation was adjusted to $375,000 to accommodate Lancaster's percentage. Kramer himself took a producer's fee of $75,000, deferring the $50,000 he was due as director of the picture.

776   "Frank wasn't there": ST to Pete Martin.

CHAPTER 31   THE VALUE OF A SINGLE HUMAN BEING

777   "Dorothy and Louise were two": Frank Tracy to Selden West.

777   "Being Mrs. Spencer Tracy publicly": Larry Swindell to the author.

778   "a saint": Jane Feely Desmond to Selden West.

778   "trailing the Clinic": Louise Tracy to Mary Kennedy Taylor, 1/12/58, Taylor Collection.

778   "very gratified": Dr. Edgar Lowell to Jane Ardmore, 8/2/71 (JKA).

779   "absorb my life": Ardmore, "Clinic," 7/20/72.

780   "first person": A kinescope of Louise Tracy's remarks is at John Tracy Clinic.

780   "go to the back": Ardmore, "Clinic."

780   "art director": William Self to the author.

780   "a lot of things": Ruthie Thompson to the author.

780   "his eye trouble": Ardmore, "John." Although John Tracy Clinic was strictly oralist during Louise Tracy's lifetime, many graduates of the program went on to learn American Sign Language (ASL), using speech and lipreading to communicate with the hearing world and ASL to talk with their deaf friends (and those hearing friends who knew ASL). Sign is almost universally regarded as more precise than lipreading.

781   "distribution objection": Steven Bach, *Marlene Dietrich: Life and Legend* (New York: Morrow, 1992), p. 407.

781   "Tracy's no lodestone": Abby Mann to the author, via telephone, 1/23/05.

781   "character was guilty": Kate Buford, *Burt Lancaster: An American Life* (New York: Knopf, 2000), p. 212.

782   "single scene": Patricia Bosworth, *Montgomery Clift* (New York: Harcourt Brace Jovanovich, 1978), p. 359. According to his friend Jack Larson, Clift was offered $200,000 to play Colonel Lawson, the part subsequently played in the film by Richard Widmark. Evidently Clift found the role of Petersen more interesting from an actor's perspective and agreed to do it for expenses alone. "He had a car and driver on call twenty-four hours a day," Larson recalled. "I'm sure they ended up spending more than $10,000 on his expenses."

782   " 'pace-setting' ": *Daily Variety,* 2/20/61.

782   "hard ticket": *Variety,* 3/8/61.

782   "still in use": Spoto, *Stanley Kramer, Film Maker,* p. 229.

783   "Max Schell arrived": Marshall Schlom to the author, Brea, Calif., 8/11/05.

784   "I acted less": *New York Herald Tribune,* 12/6/60.

784   "An actor's personality": James Zunner, "Tracy: The Great Stone Face," *Cue,* 7/12/58.

784   "what he really meant": Erskine, *Spencer Tracy: A Biographical and Interpretive Symposium,* p. 15.

784   "he could play anything": John Ford to Katharine Hepburn, n.d., John Ford Collection.

785   "Everyone in the crew": Spoto, *Stanley Kramer, Film Maker,* p. 231.

785   "All you can do": *New York Times,* 4/30/61.

785   "She was nice": "Richard Widmark Part II," *Films in Review,* May 1986.

786   "good character shots": Bob Yager to Pete Martin.

786   "Cook County": ST to Fredric March, 3/3/61, Fredric March Papers.

786   "I care about": ST to Pete Martin.

787   "I can't really answer": *Los Angeles Times,* 3/19/61.

788   "very low point": Richard Widmark to David Heeley and Joan Kramer, Los Angeles, 12/17/85 (TH).

789   "greatest reactor": Bosworth, *Montgomery Clift,* p. 360.

789   "If I remember": Erskine, *Spencer Tracy: A Biographical and Interpretive Symposium,* p. 60.

790   adjusted his dialogue: The blue pages for *Judgment at Nuremberg* are in the Montgomery Clift Collection at New York Public Library.

790   "a better job": Marshall Schlom to the author, via e-mail, 4/10/09.

790   "Julie Harris": *Hollywood Citizen News,* 3/22/61.

790   "cliché come true": Ibid.

791   "It meant a lot": "Richard Widmark Part II."

791   "a performance!": *Hollywood Citizen News,* 3/22/61.

791   "almost a symbol": *New York Times,* 4/30/61.

792   "laughed a lot": Marlene Dietrich, *Marlene* (New York: Grove Press, 1989), p. 110.

792   "not my type": Bach, *Marlene Dietrich: Life and Legend,* p. 408.

792   "very lonely man": Dietrich, *Marlene,* p. 242.

792   dissenting opinion: It's interesting to note that Judge Kenneth Norris, the third member of the tribunal, was played by actor-director Kenneth MacKenna. In 1928 MacKenna was, very briefly, Katharine Hepburn's leading man in *The Big Pond.* For years he was also head of the Story and Scenario Department at M-G-M. In 1941 it was MacKenna who handled the purchase of *Woman of the Year.*

792   "During rehearsals": *Los Angeles Times,* 8/28/61.

794   Lancaster approached: Erskine, *Spencer Tracy: A Biographical and Interpretive Symposium,* p. 71.

794   "almost conked": *Ft. Pierce* (Fla.) *News Tribune,* 5/15/61.

795   "What a bore": *Sunday Express,* 5/21/61.

796   " 'look at these pictures' ": Interview with Ardmore, 7/5/72.

796   "Every writer ought": Abby Mann to ST, 7/10/61, Abby Mann Collection, USC.

796   "AFTER FINISHING NUREMBERG": ST to Abby Mann, 7/18/61 (courtesy of
       Abby Mann).

797   set a budget: Cost figures on *The Devil at 4 O'Clock* are from the Mervyn LeRoy Col-
       lection (AMPAS).

797   "Kate's the lunatic": Higham, *Kate,* p. 191.

798   "I wanted Spencer": Ibid., p. 188.

798   "she got him set up": Stanley Kramer to Heeley and Kramer.

798   press conference: Details of the world premiere in Berlin are from *Los Angeles Times,*
       12/14 and 12/24/61; *New York Times,* 12/15/61; and *Variety,* 12/27/61. See also Bob Con-
       sidine, " 'Judgment' is Potent," *New York Journal American,* 12/18/61.

798   "There was a buffet": Stanley Kramer to Heeley and Kramer. "At the end of the
       screening the applause came almost exclusively from the foreign element in the the-
       ater," Harold Myers reported in *Variety,* "and it seemed as if the locals were stunned
       into silence."

799   "fair and human": *Variety,* 12/27/61.

799   "reservations": *Variety,* 10/18/61.

800   "raw force": Arthur Schlesinger, Jr., "Movies: *Judgment at Nuremberg," Show,* Decem-
       ber 1961.

800   "I had a friend": Frank Tracy to Selden West.

801   "quite disturbed": Eddie Lawrence to Selden West.

801   "Tracy is ornery": Bill Davidson, "Spencer Tracy," *Look,* 1/30/62.

802   "Kate, my Kate": Bill Davidson, *Spencer Tracy: Tragic Idol* (New York: Dutton, 1988),
       p. 145. Tracy did indeed submit to an interview with Bill Davidson (likely in 1960,
       rather than 1959 as the author states). However, Davidson used very few direct quotes
       from Tracy in his *Look* profile, and the "interview" recounted in his book is fascinat-
       ing in its clumsy inventions. The suggestion that Tracy would sit for an on-the-record
       interview with an unfamiliar journalist and refer to Hepburn as "Kate, my Kate" is, in
       itself, ridiculous. Davidson quotes Tracy (supposedly in 1959) on the subject of his
       daughter, Susie: "Would you believe it but that little button wrote herself the cutest
       little book about a little girl teaching a deaf cat to cope, and she got it published. And
       she's also turning into one helluva little photographer." In reality, Susie Tracy never
       picked up a camera until two years after her father's death. Moreover, the book Tracy
       allegedly refers to, *Pritt,* wasn't published until 1982—more than twenty years after
       Davidson's one interview with Tracy occurred. Indeed, the cat the book is about
       hadn't even been born yet.

802   no memory: Pat Newcomb to Selden West, via telephone, 7/16/93 (SW). Newcomb
       said that she would have remembered any talk of Hepburn "because everyone was
       interested in that."

802   "local reporters": Joe Hyams to Selden West.

802   "You son of a bitch!": Newquist, *A Special Kind of Magic,* p. 153.

803   Produced on a budget: Figures on *Judgment at Nuremberg* are from the Stanley
       Kramer Collection. As of May 11, 1966, United Artists was showing a loss of
       $1,585,900 for the picture.

       CHAPTER 32   SOMETHING A LITTLE LESS SERIOUS

804   "tired of controversy": *Newsweek,* 10/17/60.

804   "less serious": According to Karen Kramer, it was Bosley Crowther who made the sug-
       gestion.

805   "monster chase story": *New York Times,* 11/17/63.

805   "weeks and weeks": Tania Rose to Stanley Kramer, n.d. (SK).
805   "From the onset": *New York Times,* 11/17/63.
806   "The script and the casting": *New York Times,* 11/17/63.
807   "I am eager": Stanley Kramer to William Rose, 6/14/62, (SK).
807   "Tracy has never appeared": Stanley Kramer to William Rose, 7/11/62 (SK).
807   "staring contest": *New York Times,* 11/17/63.
807   "too much, too strenuous": Ardmore, "Tracy," n.d.
807   The deal: According to production records, Milton Berle and Ethel Merman were the highest-paid cast members apart from Tracy—each got $155,000 for doing the film. Sid Caesar was paid $135,000, Buddy Hackett and Mickey Rooney $105,000 each.
807   "We didn't know": *Los Angeles Times,* 3/29/01.
808   "The comedians": Marshall Schlom to the author.
808   "made me flash back": Sid Caesar (with Eddy Friedfeld), *Caesar's Hours* (New York: Public Affairs, 2003), p. 276.
808   "Everyone knew": Dorothy Provine to the author, via telephone, 11/17/05.
808   "Monroe had died": Caesar, *Caesar's Hours,* p. 276.
808   "We had rubber masks": *Los Angeles Times,* 12/3/63.
809   "During the filming": Deschner, *The Films of Spencer Tracy,* p. 17.
809   "The people whose memories": ST to Pete Martin.
810   "It had been budgeted": Marshall Schlom to the author, via e-mail, 12/16/07.
810   Youngstein: In Berlin, Max Youngstein told the assembled press that Kramer possessed the simple idea that a picture could be good and yet be successful. "We are a world-wide industry," he said. "We must get smart and back the Stanley Kramers of the world, who have more guts and talent than the others put together."
811   "get rid of the comics": *Los Angeles Times,* 11/18/62.
811   "a project": According to clinic records, Tracy donated $32,650 for the year 1962. In the years 1963 and 1964—years in which he did not work—his contributions amounted to $16,800 and $19,300, respectively.
811   "He smiled": Hepburn, *Me,* pp. 56–57.
812   "specific memories": Katharine Houghton to the author, via e-mail, 4/11/09.
812   "enjoying the rain": Katharine Hepburn to Ella Winter, "Christmas" [1962], Ella Winter Collection, Columbia University.
813   "read a great deal": Katharine Hepburn to Heeley and Kramer.
813   "greatly calmed": Brownlow, *David Lean,* pp. 485–86.
813   "should have quit": Ardmore, "Tracy."
813   "It was so hard": Kennedy, "Spencer Called Her Kath."
814   "I would appreciate": John Ford to ST, 6/10/63 (SLT).
814   "very quiet": Katharine Hepburn to Ella Winter, 6/2/63, Ella Winter Collection.
814   "Be calm": Details of Tracy's edema attack are from *Los Angeles Times,* 7/22, 7/23, 7/24, and 8/3/63; *Los Angeles Herald-Examiner,* 7/22 and 8/2/63; and Selden West's interview with Sally Erskine.
815   "SEE WHAT HAPPENS": George Cukor to ST, 7/23/63 (SLT).
816   "thinking about Spencer": Tim Durant to Katharine Hepburn, 8/7/63 (KHLA).
816   "have her choice": *New Castle News,* 9/14/63.
816   "It wouldn't do": James Prideaux, *Knowing Hepburn* (Boston: Faber and Faber, 1996), p. 23.
816   "soccer players": Frank Sinatra, at "A Tribute to Spencer Tracy," Majestic Theatre, New York, 3/3/86 (courtesy of American Academy of Dramatic Arts).
817   "Mr. Tracy is funny": *New York Times,* 11/19/63.
819   "director's chair": *Los Angeles Herald-Examiner,* 6/24/64.
820   "dropped 35 pounds": *Yuma Daily Sun,* 7/7/64.
820   "good or better": *Newark Evening News,* 7/14/64.
820   "I'm from M-G-M": Marshall Schlom to the author, via e-mail, 8/15/06.

820   "feel of a western": David Weddle, *If They Move . . . Kill 'Em!* (New York: Grove Press, 1994), p. 257.
821   "in his dressing gown": Ring Lardner, Jr., to Charles Higham.
821   "bellyache": Spencer Tracy, 1964 datebook (in Katharine Hepburn's hand) (SLT).
821   "disquieting": George Cukor to Katharine Hepburn, 9/30/64 (KHLA).
822   "hard to know": Tracy, 1964 datebook (in Katharine Hepburn's hand).
822   "Spence very thrown": Ibid.
823   "Don't EVER do this": Susie Tracy to the author.
823   "always some reason": Dr. Mitchel Covel to Selden West, 8/18/92 (SW).
824   "familiar grin": Jared Brown, *Alan J. Pakula: His Films and His Life* (New York: Back Stage Books, 2005), pp. 64–65.
825   "tiny little life": Hepburn, *Me,* pp. 405–06.
826   Tracy was groggy: Dr. Covel consulted his notes to provide details on Tracy's worsening condition.

CHAPTER 33   A LION IN A CAGE

827   "We needed prayers": Louise Tracy to Mary Kennedy Taylor, 9/22/65, Taylor Collection.
827   "When Louise would come": Dr. Mitchel Covel to Selden West.
827   "hated to be sick": Interview with Ardmore, 7/5/72.
827   "bumped into her": Virginia Thielman to Jane Ardmore, 8/1/72 (JKA).
828   "shake hands": John Tracy to Selden West, via fax, 3/23/98 (SW).
828   "If I hadn't known": Frank Tracy to Selden West, via telephone, October 1995 (SW).
829   "sort of an invalid": Katharine Houghton to the author, via e-mail, 8/12/08.
829   "all major problems": Dr. Mitchel Covel to Selden West. It should be noted that Dr. Covel did not consider his patient a hypochondriac. "A hypochondriac is somebody who imagines they have illness," he said. "He *had* illness, and would react violently to some of his symptoms. But, mind you, he had a lot of problems, a lot of physical problems. His heart, diabetes."
829   "Bullshit": McCabe, *Cagney,* p. 330.
830   "Your letter": Eugene Cullen Kennedy, "Just Above Sunset, Off Doheny," unpublished manuscript (courtesy of Eugene Kennedy).
830   "The substance": Deposition of Stanley Kramer in *Joseph Than and Elick Moll* v. *Columbia Pictures Corp., etc., Stanley Kramer, Sidney Poitier, William Rose, et al.,* 1/20/69, (SK).
830   "they budgeted it": Stanley Kramer to Heeley and Kramer.
831   "I pointed out": Deposition of William Arthur Rose in *Joseph Than and Elick Moll* v. *Columbia Pictures Corp., etc., Stanley Kramer, Sidney Poitier, William Rose, et al.*
832   "He took the ball": Stanley Kramer deposition.
832   "Stanley, who was in California": William Arthur Rose deposition.
833   "My suggestions": Stanley Kramer deposition.
833   "One of the things": William Arthur Rose deposition.
834   "first 'live' time": ST to William Dozier, 8/26/66.
834   "I'll do a *Batman*": *Los Angeles Herald-Examiner,* 9/26/66.
834   "now president of Fox": William Self to the author.
834   "no thought of going": Swindell, *Spencer Tracy,* p. 263.
836   "The anticipation": Stanley Kramer deposition.
837   "I feel great": Details of the news conference are from *Los Angeles Times,* 9/26/66; *Los Angeles Herald-Examiner,* 9/26/66; and *Long Beach Independent,* 9/26/66.
837   "a gasp": Laraine Day to Barbara Hall.
838   "taken aback": Susie Tracy to the author, Brentwood, 5/13/05.
838   "see my niece": Newquist, *A Special Kind of Magic,* pp. 42–43.
838   "my trepidation": Stanley Kramer deposition.

838 " 'can she act?' ": Karen Kramer to the author, North Hollywood, 7/21/04.

839 "lucky girl": *Los Angeles Times*, 2/3/67.

839 "pretty well controlled": Dr. Mitchel Covel to Selden West.

840 "When I arrived": Sidney Poitier, *The Measure of a Man* (San Francisco: Harper San Francisco, 2000), pp. 121–22.

840 "colored person": Newquist, *A Special Kind of Magic*, pp. 91–92.

840 "decent folks": Poitier, *The Measure of a Man*, pp. 122–23.

840 "delicious meal": Sidney Poitier, *This Life* (New York: Knopf, 1980), pp. 285–86.

840 "once-over": Katharine Houghton to the author, via e-mail, 5/29/09.

841 "chopping block": Higham, *Kate*, p. 198.

841 "His idea": Marshall Schlom to the author.

841 makeup test: According to Michael Blake, this was a common practice in color film-making through the mid-1970s, when film speeds got faster and less light was necessary to bring out the features of darker skin. Without makeup, lighter-skinned actors would typically wash out. "As for the correct term, we would say 'bump up their color,' which means take them a bit darker than their natural skin tone." Cinematographer Sam Leavitt, who had shot the black-and-white *Defiant Ones* for Kramer, favored TV-style lighting for much of the picture, possibly to minimize problems of skin tone and contrast, possibly to shoot more quickly at times when Tracy was available. A trade item in the *Reporter* noted that Leavitt, at Kramer's request, had suspended all the lighting needed to illuminate the set from above—no floor lamps or fill lights—so that Kramer could make circular shots if he wished.

842 "In the rehearsals": Higham, *Kate*, p. 200.

842 "My aunt": Katharine Houghton to the author, Sherman Oaks, 3/1/05.

843 "The key to Spencer": Jack Hamilton, "A Last Visit with Two Undimmed Stars," *Look*, 7/11/67.

843 "all the words": Sidney Poitier to David Heeley and Joan Kramer, Los Angeles, 1986 (TH).

843 "quite a few scenes": Katharine Hepburn to Heeley and Kramer. In his autobiography Poitier remembers asking Kramer to send them home, and the production report for that day appears to bear that out: Tracy and Hepburn finished at 4:50 p.m., while Poitier remained on the set until 6:45.

844 "play tennis": Leah Bernstein to the author, Los Angeles, 9/14/04.

844 "strange relationship": Higham, *Kate*, p. 201.

845 "Your job": Katharine Houghton to the author.

846 "he was embarrassed": Marshall Schlom to the author.

847 "tried to work him": Katharine Houghton to the author.

847 "Milkman": Hamilton, "A Last Visit with Two Undimmed Stars."

847 "best actor": *Los Angeles Herald-Examiner*, 4/30/67.

848 "my last picture": *Los Angeles Herald-Examiner*, 5/10/67.

848 "I miss M-G-M": Spencer Tracy interview with Roy Newquist, cassette tape, n.d. (courtesy of Susie Tracy).

849 "Uncle Spencer?": Bobs Watson to Selden West, via telephone, 7/9/91 (SW).

849 "go visit him": Jean Simmons to the author.

849 "Please wait": A. C. Lyles to the author.

849 "love of your life": Katharine Houghton in *A Special Kind of Love*, Sony Home Entertainment, 2007.

849 "One night": Katharine Houghton to the author.

850 "Watch out for Kate": Katharine Houghton to the author, New York, 4/25/08.

851 "walked into this house": Katharine Houghton to the author, New York, 3/1/05.

851 "the summation": Stanley Kramer to Heeley and Kramer.

851 "tenser than tense": Mark Harris, *Pictures at a Revolution* (New York: Penguin, 2008), p. 322.

851 after some preliminaries: Tracy may well have delivered the entire speech on set before

any film got exposed, as there are witnesses who recall that he did it straight through. "As I remember it," said Katharine Houghton, "he did the whole damn thing from beginning to end." An examination of the film establishes, however, that it could not have been shot in one take, and the daily production reports clearly show the scene took five days to complete.

852 "first day's work: Details of the production of *Guess Who's Coming to Dinner* are from the daily production reports in the Stanley Kramer Collection at UCLA.

853 "I came to visit": Karen Kramer to the author.

853 "Our reaction shots": Katharine Houghton to the author, via e-mail, 7/24/05.

854 "superb, moving": *Los Angeles Times*, 6/12/67.

854 "Every person": Poitier, *This Life*, pp. 286–87.

854 "very relieved": Katharine Houghton to the author, via e-mail, 7/24/05.

855 "You know, Kiddo": Wagner, *You Must Remember This*, p. 293.

855 "He didn't know": Tina Smith to the author, Milwaukee, 7/9/06.

856 "I rehearsed": Katharine Hepburn to Heeley and Kramer.

856 "shot the scene": Marshall Schlom to the author, via e-mail, 4/10/09.

856 "rehearsed quite a bit": D'Urville Martin to Selden West, 12/27/77 (SW).

858 Ivan Volkman: Details of Tracy's last shot on the picture are from Marshall Schlom. It was customary for the assistant director to make such an announcement, but Marshall Schlom remembered that Volkman, who had been Kramer's A.D. until he was promoted to production manager on *Ship of Fools,* claimed the privilege for himself on this occasion.

858 "made me wild": Katharine Hepburn to Heeley and Kramer.

858 "The party": Details of the party are from *Daily Variety,* 5/29/67; *Los Angeles Times,* 6/12/67; and Bob Thomas' AP dispatch, 5/31/67.

859 "Finished!": *New York Times,* 6/25/67.

859 "very pleased": Interview with Ardmore, 7/5/72.

859 "No bunk": Miscellaneous handwritten notes for Chester Erskine's proposed documentary on Tracy, evidently made between June and December 1967 (KHLA).

860 "Eddie Leonard": *Los Angeles Times,* 6/12/67.

860 "I went to see him": Dr. Mitchel Covel to Selden West.

860 "He would wear": Susie Tracy to the author.

860 "Sometimes he would carry": Interview with Ardmore, 7/5/72.

861 "give it a push": Hepburn, *Me,* p. 402.

861 the phone rang: Susie Tracy to the author, Brentwood, 5/13/05.

862 "peculiar spot": Hepburn, *Me,* p. 404.

863 "Some idiot called": Jean Simmons to the author.

863 "up to par": Jean Porter Dmytryk to the author.

864 "state of shock": *Milwaukee Journal,* 6/11/67.

864 "true to himself": *Dallas Morning News,* 6/15/67.

CHAPTER 34   A HUMBLE MAN

866 "seen his face": Hepburn, *Me,* p. 408.

866 "Nobody gets out": Frank Tracy to Selden West.

866 "don't like anything": *Newsweek,* 6/19/67.

866 "strong and vibrant": *New York Times,* 6/18/67.

867 "I can't explain": Stanley Kramer, "He Could Wither You With a Glance," *Life,* 6/30/67.

868 "fine example": Katharine Hepburn to William O. Douglas, 6/18/67 (LOC).

868 "What can one say": Katharine Hepburn to Joan Blondell, 6/23/67 (courtesy of Judy Samelson).

868 "unique creature": Katharine Hepburn to Anne Pearce Kramer, 6/17/67 (courtesy of Judy Samelson).

868   "there is silence": Katharine Hepburn to Jack Hamilton, 6/27/67 (courtesy of Judy Samelson).

868   "Do you remember": Dorothy Gopadze to Katharine Hepburn, 6/14/67 (KHLA).

868   "DEAREST GIRL": Vivien Leigh to Katharine Hepburn, 6/10/67 (KHLA).

868   "blinded with sorrow": Vivien Leigh to Katharine Hepburn, Saturday (KHLA).

868   "wholehearted devotion": J. J. Cohn to Katharine Hepburn, 6/13/67 (KHLA).

869   "Your letter": Katharine Hepburn to J. J. Cohn, 6/12/67 (courtesy of Judy Samelson).

869   "The estate": Details of the Tracy estate are from Los Angeles Probate File P523809.

869   "terrible shock": Carroll Tracy to Katharine Hepburn, 3/11/68 (KHLA).

871   "run out of gas": Robert C. Jones to the author, via telephone, 5/20/09.

872   "How possible": Sidney Poitier, in *AFI's 100 Years 100 Cheers* (Gary Smith Company), 2006.

872   "Who says": Spoto, *Stanley Kramer, Film Maker,* p. 277.

872   "I'm getting nicer": *New York Times,* 10/27/67.

873   "one of the finest": *Los Angeles Times,* 11/26/67.

873   "HOW WONDERFUL": Barry Day, ed., *The Letters of Noël Coward* (New York: Knopf, 2007), p. 747.

873   "torrid b.o.": *Variety,* 12/6/67.

873   "glisten with style": *Harper's Magazine,* January 1968.

873   "faultless": *New Yorker,* 12/16/67.

873   "gives his blessings": *Newsweek,* 12/25/67.

874   "repeats the charge": *Village Voice,* 12/6/67.

874   "I liked him": Interview with Ardmore, 7/5/72.

875   "pat on the back": Katharine Hepburn to Lewis W. Douglas, 5/5/68, Lewis W. Douglas Collection, University of Arizona, Tucson.

875   "disgusted": Katharine Hepburn to Ella Winter, n.d., Ella Winter Collection.

875   "I think": Stanley Kramer to Katharine Hepburn, 5/7/68 (KHLA).

875   "can be friends": Details of the call are from Hepburn, *Me,* p. 407; and Susie Tracy, who remembered her mother's account of it.

876   "straighten things out": Hepburn, *Me,* p. 407.

876   "Spencer's faith": Eugene Kennedy to the author, via e-mail, 2/3/10.

876   "always thrilled": Katharine Houghton to the author, via e-mail, 2/18/10.

877   "enormously vulnerable": Anthony Harvey to the author, via phone, 10/25/07.

877   "fulfilled something deep": Katharine Houghton to the author.

877   "last speech": Katharine Houghton to the author, via e-mail, 10/4/05.

877   "Is anyone coming?": Hepburn, *Me,* p. 409.

878   "fuss": In interviews, Katharine Hepburn always maintained that she never had any intention of attending Tracy's funeral. Within days of his death, however, she told Bill Self that she and Phyllis had indeed started for the church "and then decided not to go. She didn't want any fuss, she said. No doubt her appearance would have caused one."

Selected Bibliography

BOOKS

Andersen, Christopher. *An Affair to Remember.* New York: Morrow, 1997. A dual biography of Tracy and Hepburn, focusing on their twenty-six-year relationship. Relying heavily on the Bill Davidson book (see below), Andersen falls for every outlandish fabrication and ends up making a muddle of Tracy's life. (See notes for pages 38 and 271 for additional commentary.)

Davidson, Bill. *Spencer Tracy: Tragic Idol.* New York: Dutton, 1988. A blatant fraud of a book, presumably written for quick money after *The Spencer Tracy Legacy* appeared on public television in 1986. Davidson's M.O. was to take legitimate interviews (Don Taylor, Robert Wagner, Walter Seltzer), cook the quotes to make them as sensational as possible, then intermix them with "interviews" that were entirely—and obviously—fictional. (See notes for pages 46, 252, 271, 302, 429, 518, and 802 for particularly egregious examples.) Edward Everett Horton is quoted describing the preview of *Six Cylinder Love* at the Loyola Theater in Westchester a full fifteen years before that theater was built. Louise Tracy is quoted as saying it was *she* who was offered a job with Stuart Walker's company in Cincinnati, not Spencer, and that it was *she* who subsequently told Walker she "wanted Spencer Tracy as my leading man." Gene Kelly describes his friend Spence as a "right wing conservative" when Kelly would certainly have known better. Davidson also quotes from interviews he supposedly conducted with the likes of Clark Gable, Humphrey Bogart, Eddie Mannix, Charles Jehlinger, and a host of other figures who died years—if not decades—prior to the book's appearance. According to Davidson, Tracy discovered his son's deafness in Brooklyn, not Grand Rapids, and he disappeared into the Hotel St. George as a result. Toots Shor, a bouncer at Billy LaHiff's, is quoted as telling Davidson that Tracy got "loaded" and beat up one of the girls at a neighborhood whorehouse called

Lu's—but Shore didn't even arrive in New York until 1930, the year Tracy filmed *Up the River* and relocated to California. Though every page brings a fresh distortion, this crude exercise in biography has been regarded as a primary resource on Tracy for more than twenty years.

Deschner, Donald. *The Films of Spencer Tracy.* New York: Citadel Press, 1968. The first book-length study of Tracy's career.

Fisher, James. *Spencer Tracy: A Bio-Bibliography.* Westport, Conn.: Greenwood Press, 1994. An academic approach to Tracy's life and career, admirably balanced.

Hepburn, Katharine. *Me.* New York: Knopf, 1991.

Kanin, Garson. *Tracy and Hepburn.* New York: Viking, 1971. A self-described "intimate memoir" derived from "written records + journals and memorandums of telephone conversations + of correspondence" kept by the author over a period of some thirty years. Though Kanin's memoir, on the whole, is remarkably accurate, Katharine Hepburn considered it a betrayal of their friendship—as did many of their mutual friends—and refused to speak to him for a number of years. "[T]aking detailed notes on private conversations . . . then publishing them . . . and not very accurately I'm afraid . . . is hardly the act of a friend," she wrote. "I think had I been dead and S[pence] alive he would not have dared."

Kartseva, Elena Nikolaevna. *Spenser Tresi.* Moscow: Isdatelstvo Iskustvo, 1970.

King, Alison. *Spencer Tracy.* New York: Crescent, 1992.

Newquist, Roy. *A Special Kind of Magic.* Skokie, Ill.: Rand McNally, 1967. Interviews with Spencer Tracy, Katharine Hepburn, Sidney Poitier, Katharine Houghton, Stanley Kramer, and George Glass on the set of *Guess Who's Coming to Dinner.*

Packer, Eleanor. *Private Lives of Movie Stars.* Los Angeles: Bantam, 1940. Tracy is one of ten stars whose biographies are accorded a chapter apiece in this early paperback.

Swindell, Larry. *Spencer Tracy.* Cleveland: NAL/World, 1969. The first book-length Tracy biography, admirably written yet sketchy in places, due, no doubt, to the tight deadline on which the book was produced. Nevertheless, Swindell's book has been the gold standard on Tracy for over forty years.

Tozzi, Romano. *Spencer Tracy.* New York: Pyramid Publications, 1973.

PERIODICALS

Albert, Dora. "Hollywood's Most Enduring Triangle." *Modern Screen,* November 1963.

Ardmore, Jane. "Mrs. Spencer Tracy's Own Story." *Ladies' Home Journal,* December 1972.

Back, J. Gunner. "What You Should Know About Spencer Tracy." *Modern Screen,* May 1932. Tracy's first fan magazine profile.

Bangs, Bee. "He's an Actor's Actor." *Movie Show,* July 1945.

Biery, Ruth. "Worry! Who Me? Say!" *Photoplay,* December 1932.

Black, Peggy Hoyt. "That Tough Tracy Kid." *Picture Play,* February 1937.

Bruce, Carter. "Fated for Unhappiness." *Modern Screen,* November 1934.

———. "I'm Glad I Married Before I Came to Hollywood." *Modern Screen,* October 1933.

Callahan, Kitty. "Spencer Tracy." *Family Circle,* June 5, 1942.

Carroll, Jean. "Finally! The Facts About Spencer Tracy and Katharine Hepburn." *Confidential,* November 1963.

Chapman, John. "Once There Were Two Irishmen." *Chicago Sunday Tribune,* April 6, 1941.

Coons, Robin. "Plain Guy." *Screen Guide,* February 1948.

Craig, Carol. "Hollywood Goes to Sea Again." *Motion Picture,* March 1937.

Crawford, Jed. "It's Simple—It's Modest—It's Spencer Tracy." *Our Home,* Volume 3, Number 3. A photo tour of the Tracy home in Encino.

Darnton, Charles. "Down with Romance!" *Screenland,* February 1937.

Davidson, Bill. "Spencer Tracy." *Look,* January 30, 1962.

Davidson, Judith. "Once There Were Two Irishmen . . ." *Movies,* May 1940.

De Vane, Tom. "Hollywood's New Bogey Man." *Hollywood,* July 1941.

Dillon, Franc. "Meet Father Tracy." *Picture Play,* December 1938.

Dufy, Lisette. "That Tracy-Hepburn Affair." *Inside Story,* October 1956.

English, Richard T. "I'm a Mug[g] and Proud of It!" *Hollywood,* September 1934.

Erskine, Chester. "Spencer Tracy: The Face of Integrity." *The Movie* No. 7 (UK), 1980.

Erskine, John. "The Private Mind of Spencer Tracy." *Liberty,* August 24, 1940.

Flanagan, Monsignor E. J. "I Meet Myself in Spencer Tracy." *Liberty,* October 8, 1938.

———. "The Story Behind *Boys Town.*" *Photoplay,* November 1938.

"Flood Tide for Spencer Tracy." *Hollywood,* January 1937.

French, William. "The Greatest Friendship in Hollywood." *Modern Movies,* February 1938.

Friedman, F. "The Gal Who Loves to Be Hated." *Motion Picture,* August 1957. A profile of Katharine Hepburn which alludes to her relationship with Tracy.

Frings, Kay. "Because She Loved Him So Much." *Modern Screen,* August 1938.

Gable, Clark, as told to James Reid. "My Pal, Spencer Tracy." *Screen Life,* July 1940. Derived from a fascinating interview with Gable on the subject of Tracy.

Gammie, John. "The Two Tracys." *Film Weekly,* July 23, 1934.

Goldbeck, Elizabeth. "Some New Evidence About Spencer Tracy." *Movie Classic,* December 1932.

Grant, Jack. "Why Loretta Young Broke Up Her Romance." *Movie Mirror,* October 1934.

Hall, Gladys. "Good Advice from Spencer Tracy." *Screenland,* July 1940.

———. "I Have No Regrets." *Movie Classic,* September 1936.

———. "Spencer Tracy Faces Forty." *Photoplay,* March 1938.

———. "Spencer Tracy's Love Confession." *Movie Mirror,* March 1934.

———. "Spencer Tracy Speaks His Mind." *Modern Screen,* December 1935.

———. "Spencer Tracy Tells 'Why My Wife and I Are Together Again.'" *Movie Mirror,* May 1935.

———. "We Know Tracy." *Modern Screen,* May 1940.

———. "You Can Only Defeat Yourself." *Motion Picture,* July 1940.

———. "You Can't Put Spencer Tracy into Words." *Motion Picture,* November 1937.

Hamilton, Jack. "Last Visit with Two Undimmed Stars." *Look,* July 11, 1967.

Hasso, Signe. "Spencer Tracy." *Movies,* October 1944.

Hersey, Captain J. M. "The Log of the *We're Here.*" *Woman's Home Companion,* April 1937.

James, Antony. "The Untold Story of Spencer Tracy and Katharine Hepburn." *Inside Story,* March 1964.

Janisch, Arthur. "Fighting Irishman." *Hollywood,* July 1937.

Johnson, Van. "Spencer Tracy." *Screenland,* May 1948.

Keene, Harold. "How Spencer Tracy's Love Survived the Greatest Test." *Movie Mirror,* October 1937.

Keethe, Larry. "I Call It Heart." *Photoplay,* September 1948.

———. "Tracy the 4 AM Man." Photoplay, June 1953.

Kramer, Stanley. "He Could Wither You With a Glance." *Life,* June 30, 1967.

Lang, Harry. "Good Guy of the Movies." *Screenplay,* April 1937.

Lewis, Frederick. "Spencer Tracy Conquers Himself." *Liberty,* October 9, 1937

Magee, Ted. "It's Undeclared War." *Hollywood,* February 1938.

Marshal, Flo. "Six Characters in Search of Spencer Tracy." *Movies,* November 1940.

McEvoy, J. P. "Will They Get Wise to Him?" *This Week,* May 24, 1942.

Moak, E. R. "We Actors are Overpaid!" *New Movie,* November 1933.

Mook, S. R. "Checking Up on Spencer Tracy." *Screenland,* April 1942.

———. "Every-Day Tracy." *Silver Screen,* January 1933.

———. "For More Than Money." *Screenland,* May 1938

———. "He's Often Been Hungry." *Movie Mirror,* August 1932.

———. "The Man Who's Had Everything." *Screenland,* October 1943.

———. "Master Mugg." *Screenland,* April 1933.

———. "Spencer Tracy as I Know Him." *Screen Book,* March 1938.

——. "Spencer Tracy's Home Life." *Screenland,* March 1940.

——. "Spencer Tracy Talks About His Past." *Screen Book,* April 1936.

——. "Tough to You." *Picture Play,* September 1932.

——. "Tracy Fights Through." *Screenland,* May 1935.

——. "Tracy Talks." *Screenland,* January 1934.

——. "The Truth About the Tracy Separation." *Movie Mirror,* November 1933.

Moore, Jim. "This Guy Tracy." *Hollywood,* August 1932.

"The Movie Life of Spencer Tracy." *Movie Life,* September 1942.

"Mr. and Mrs. Spencer Tracy: Hollywood's Prize Love Story." *True Experiences,* October 1938. A largely fictionalized account of the Tracy marriage with manufactured quotes throughout.

O'Brien, Pat. "Himself." *Modern Screen,* November 1947.

——. "Spencer Tracy As Is." *Screenland,* November 1951.

——, as told to S. R. Mook. "My Pal, Spencer Tracy." *Screen Book,* March 1939.

Parkes, Mary. "Never Out of Character." *Modern Screen,* November 1938.

Peter, Michael. "It Seems There Were Two Irishmen." *Modern Screen,* March 1935.

Proctor, Kay. "Ex-Bad Boy." *Screen Guide,* April 1937.

——. "Fame Makes You Behave." *Picture Play,* March 1940.

——. " 'Northwest Passage'—Tracy's Toughest Assignment." *Screen Life,* March 1940.

Ramsey, Walter. "The Life Story of a Real Guy." *Modern Screen,* June and July 1934.

Rathbone, A. D., IV. "Out of Spencer Tracy's Yesterdays." *Photoplay,* October 1940.

——. "Spencer Tracy Learns His Lines." *Outdoors,* April 1941.

Reid, James. "Even Barrymore Calls Him the Best." *Motion Picture,* November 1938.

Reynolds, Colin. "He's Afraid of Women." *Screenland,* July 1932.

Rooney, Mickey, as told to Marian Rhea. "Uncle Spence." *Movie Mirror,* October 1940.

St. Johns, Adela Rogers. "Man of Conflict." *Photoplay,* February 1945.

Samuels, Charles. "Spencer Tracy—Nothing But the Best." *Motion Picture,* July 1946.

Service, Faith. "His Son Made Spencer Tracy What He Is Today." *Movie Classic,* August 1933.

Shane, Ted. "He Should Worry." *Liberty,* December 15, 1945.

Sharpe, Howard. "The Adventurous Life of Spencer Tracy." *Photoplay,* February, March, April 1937.

——. "The Startling Story Behind Spencer Tracy's Illness." *Movie Mirror,* July 1937.

Shawell, Julia. "Tellin' on Tracy." *Modern Screen,* September 1939.

Shearer, Lloyd. "Spencer Tracy: Hollywood's Least Known Star." *Parade,* December 11 and 18, 1955.

Skolsky, Sidney. "Things I Never Knew About Spencer Tracy." *Motion Picture,* April 1944.

Smith, Frederick James. "Courageous Irishman." *Picture Play,* March 1938.

"Spencer Tracy Meets the Press." *Film Weekly,* May 6, 1939.

"Spencer Tracy's Fight for Life!" *Motion Picture,* December 1965.

Steele, Joseph Henry. "Portrait of a Man Who Has What He Wants." *Photoplay,* May 1939.

Sullivan, Ed. "The Best Bet of the Year." *Silver Screen,* September 1936.

——. "A Prediction That Came Doubly True." *Silver Screen,* April 1940.

Thompson, Jerry. "Spencer Tracy's Lost Weekend in Havana." *Uncensored,* May 1957.

Tracy, Carroll. "My Kid Brother Spence." *Photoplay,* August 1943.

Tracy, John. "My Complicated Life." *Volta Review,* June 1946 and July 1946.

Tracy, Louise Treadwell. "The Women Take to Polo." *Polo,* June 1935.

Tracy, Spencer. "Deflating Your Ego." *Movies in Review,* September 1946.

——. "Dress Suit." *American Magazine,* December 1942.

——. "Film War Too Real to Suit Private Tracy." *New York Daily Mirror,* May 8, 1937.

——. "For Relaxation, Spencer Tracy Will Take Polo." *Oakland Tribune,* January 31, 1937.

——. "The Grand Guy Cohan." *Modern Screen,* December 1932.

——. "A Great Graduation Message." *Movie Mirror,* July 1939.

——. "I Arrive in Hollywood." *Picturegoer,* June 11, 1938.

——. "I Learned About Life from Them." *Picturegoer,* April 10, 1937.

——. "I've Been to Boys Town." *Screen Guide,* November 1938.

——. "The Log of the *We're Here.*" *Picturegoer,* December 11, 1937.

——. "Long Runs Wear." *New York Telegraph,* April 6, 1930.

——. "My Modest Friend." *American Magazine,* March 1945.

——. "My Pal, Will Rogers." *Picture Play,* December 1935.

——. "Professor Boody Pointed My Nose Toward the Stage." *The Forensic,* January 1936.

——. "The Secret Deal I Made with Hemingway." *Photoplay,* November 1956.

——. "There Was a Guy . . ." *Screen and Radio Weekly,* December 1937.

——. "This Is My Life Story." *Picturegoer,* May 28, 1938.

——. "The Unknown Will Rogers I Know." *New Movie,* December 1933.

——. "Van Johnson." *Screenland,* May 1948.

——. "When I Shared Pat O'Brien's Dress Suit." *Picturegoer,* June 4, 1938.

——, as told to James Reid. "My Pal, Clark Gable." *Screen Life,* May 1940.

——, as told to Frank Whitbeck. "The Power of the Pass." *Ringling Bros. and Barnum & Bailey Circus Magazine and Program,* 1949.

Tully, Jim. "Spencer Tracy." *The Scribbler,* February 1937.

——. "Tough Guy—Huh?" *Picturegoer,* November 7, 1938.

Van Dyke, W. S. "They've Got Location Blues." *Screen Book,* July 1937.

Wagner, Robert. "My Hat's Off to Spencer Tracy." *Movie Mirror,* July 1956.

Walsh, Larry. "Virtue's Victim." *Screen Book,* October 1939.

Waterbury, Ruth. "Anything You Can Do I Can Do Better." *Modern Screen,* May 1956.

Weller, Helen Hover. "Gratefully Yours, Spencer Tracy." *Movieland,* January 1948.

Wilcox, Grace. "Injuns!" *Detroit Free Press Sunday Magazine,* February 4, 1940.

Wolfenden, John. "Spencer Tracy as Seen by His Friends." *Australian Women's Weekly,* January 6, 1940.

Worth, Sheila. "Spencer Tracy's Brother and Keeper." *Movie Mirror,* September 1938. A heavily embellished account of Carroll Tracy's relationship with his brother, probably derived mostly from previous articles; it's doubtful the author talked with either Spencer or Carroll Tracy.

Wright, Tom. "When Spencer Tracy Was Seventeen." *Movies,* August 1941.

Yates, Eva. "New Hope for the Deaf Child." *Collier's,* July 14, 1945.

Zeitlin, Ida. "Manuel the Lovable." *Modern Screen,* October 1937.

——. "That Tracy-Gable Feud." *Movie Mirror,* February 1938.

Zunner, Jesse. "Tracy: The Great Stone Face." *Cue,* July 12, 1958.

Index

Page numbers in *italics* refer to illustrations.

Abbott and Costello, 422, 423, 590
Abbott, Richard, 125
Abe Lincoln in Illinois, 519
Abraham Lincoln, 169
Ace, The, 242
Actress, The, 614, 616, 637–44, 645, 650, 653–4, 655, 756
Adams, Edie, 806
Adams, Maude, 43
Adam's Rib, 572–9, 582, 584, 586–7, 588, 590, 599, 602, 621, 636, 756
Addams, Dawn, 623–4
Adelman, Joseph, 67
Adler, Buddy, 721, 722, 723, 728, 738, 739
Advise and Consent, 786
Affair to Remember, An, 728
Affairs of Cellini, The, 217
African Queen, The, 610, 611, 615, 633, 663, 692
After the Rain, see Painted Woman, The
Ager, Cecelia, 422, 423
Akins, Zoë, 16
Albertson, Frank, 179
Albertson, Lillian, 278
Albiez, Harry, 314

Aldrich, Winthrop, 251
Alexander's Ragtime Band, 365
Alessandro, Jose, 16
Alexander, Dan, 506
Alexander, John, 551–2
Alexander, Katherine, 133–4, *136*
Algiers, 358, 359, 362
Alibi Ike, 118
Alice Adams, 433
Alice in Wonderland, 807
All About Eve, 608n
Allan, Elizabeth, 199
Alldredge, Charles, 564
Allen, Adrianne, 572
Allen, Gracie, 231
Allen, H. H., 56
Allenberg, Bert, 588, 603, 631, 645, 664, 670, 680–1, 682, 686, 688, 689, 691, 692, 695, 711, 717, 719, 722, 736, 738, 739–40, 751, 752, 753
All the World Wondered, see Last Mile, The
Allvine, Glendon, 257
Allwyn, Astrid, 255
Allyson, June, 623, 820
Alpert, Don, 787

Ameche, Don, 609
American, The, 192, 197–8, 200
American in Paris, An, 600
Americanization of Emily, The, 819
Amigo, 614
Amos 'n Andy, 853
Anders, Merry, 724
Anderson, Donna, 757, *758*, 759, 761, 762
Anderson, Maxwell, 519, 520, 527, 569
Anderson, Richard, 609
Andersonville, 831
Andersonville Trial, The, 831
Angels in the Outfield, 614
Angels With Dirty Faces, 361, 362
Anhalt, Edward, 750
Anna Christie, 76, 415, 474
Another Language, 224
Any Number Can Play, 570
Apartment, The, 791
Apron Strings, 133
Ardmore, Jane Kesner, 383, 588, 870, 876
Are You a Mason? 22
Arlen, Michael, 507
Arlen, Richard, 247, 695
Arliss, George, 178, 182, 217, 298, 709
Arness, James, 609–10
Arnold, Edward, 115, 276
Arnstein, Nicky, 233
Around the World in 80 Days, 727
Arsenic and Old Lace, 552
Arthur, Jean, 574
Ashley, Edward, 410
Ashley, Elizabeth, 819, 820
Aslan, Gregoire, 770
Astaire, Fred, 65, 111, 407, 516, 595, 626, 681, 723, 738
Astaire, Phyllis, 595
Astor, Mary, 191, 551
As You Like It, 512, 544, 584, 586, 587, 594, 599, 600, 601, 606
Atchley, Dr. Dana Winslow, 682
Atkinson, J. Brooks, 115, 131, 635
Auchincloss, Louis, 821
August, Joseph, 153, 161
Aumont, Jean-Pierre, 771
Austin, Frank, 584
Awful Truth, The, 481
Aylmer, Felix, 567
Ayres, Lew, 157

Baby Cyclone, The (film), 165
Baby Cyclone, The (play), 101, 103–4, 106, 107, 108, 109, 111, 119, 132, 273, 503

Bacall, Lauren, 615, 634, 640, 706–7, 722–5, 745, 764, 815, 863
Bachelor Father, 760
Backer, George, 527
Backus, Georgia, 76
Bacon, James, 634
Bad and the Beautiful, The, 685 and *n*
Bad Day at Black Rock, 643, 650, 654, 664, 665, 666–73, 674–8, 680, 681, 682, 708, 719, 751, 756, 786
Bad Girl, 173
Bad Time at Honda, see Bad Day at Black Rock
Baggott, King, 154
Bagnall, George, 192
Bailey, Pearl, 703
Baker, Belle, 263
Baker, Carroll, 821
Baker, Reginald "Snowy," 156, 168, *169*, 184, 237, 239
Bakewell, William, 232
Balcon, Michael, 661, 804
Balderston, John L., 410
Ball, Lucille, 508, 511, 820
Ballard, Lucinda, 613
Balmat, Charles, 696
Balmat, Jacques, 696
Bannister, Harry, 91
Bannon, 680
Bara, Theda, 150
Barabbas, 631, 632
Barcellona, Marie, 455
Barnes, George, 161
Barnes, Howard, 422
Barnes, Nancy, 490
Barrat, Robert, *262*
Barrie, Elaine, 271
Barrie, Mona, 551
Barrie, Wendy, 256
Barry, Ellen, 509, 512
Barry, Philip, 431–2, 442, 453, 457, 462, 472, 473, 507, 509, 512, 755
Barrymore, Ethel, 16, 40, 224, 426, 489, 752, 754, 784
Barrymore, John, 72, 116, 163, 194, 207, 224, 271, 408, 409, 414, 467, 513, 596, 723, 739, 754, 795, 811, 812
Barrymore, Lionel, 42, 63, *64*, 224, 300, 302, 307, 310, 332, 347, 390, 407, 548, 572, 820
Barter, Theodore, 117
Bartholomew, Freddie, 300, 302, 303, 304, 306, 307, 311–12, 316, 317, 324, 343, 412, 434, 808

Bartlett, Sy, 614
Bastian, Dr. Carl, 717
Bat, The, 76, 77
Batista, Fulgencio, 713
Batman, 834 and *n*
Battleground, 610
Bavu, 67
Baxter, Warner, 150, 178
Beal, Mrs. Carl, 237
Bearman, Joe, 36
Beast of Berlin, The, 44
Beauchamp, Clem, 763
Beaudry, Yvonne, 308–9, 312–13, 344, 352
Beaumont, Lucy, 171
Beck, Meyer, 769
Becket, 775
Beery, Wallace, 224, 259, 272, 372, 390, 479, 548, 614, 820
Before the Sun Goes Down, 555
Beggers of Life, 256
Beginning or the End, The, 531
Begley, Ed, 756
Behar, Carolyn Rothstein, 229
Behind the Front, 165
Behrman, S. N., 152, 374, 512, 520, 526
Beilinson, Lawrence, 711
Belasco, David, 111
Bell, James, 124, 127, *128*
Bellamy, Ralph, 168, 170, 176, 200, 214, 387, 553
Belser, Lee, 772
Belzer, Gladys, 208, 271
Benchley, Robert, 259, 820
Beneath the 12-Mile Reef, 657
Ben-Hur, 388
Bennett, Constance, 163
Bennett, Joan, 161, 163–4, 169, 170, 172, 173, 179, 180, 182–3, 199, 200, 211, 590, 592, 593, 594, 601, 602, 717
Benny, Jack, 589–90, 809, 866
Benthall, Michael, 662, 682
Beresford, Harry, 89
Berg, A. Scott, 510
Berg, Phil, 681
Bergman, Ingrid, 410–11, 412–14, 415, 421, 422, 426, 436, 440, 451, 452–3, 497, *498*, 568, 570, 682, 717, 727
Berkeley, Busby, 155
Berkeley, Reginald, 242
Berkeley Square (film), 210
Berkeley Square (play), 120
Berle, Milton, 806
Berlin, Irving, 5, 111, 341, 507

Berman, Pandro S., 495, 496, 538, 542, 589–90, 598, 600
Bernhardt, Sarah, 43, 860
Bernstein, Leah, 844
Bertha the Sewing Machine Girl, 150
Best People, The, 87
Best Years of Our Lives, The, 531 and *n*
Betjeman, John, 231
B.F.'s Daughter, 554, 555
Bickford, Charles, 294
Big City, 321–2, 323–4, 339
Big Deal, 754, 764, 766
Bigelow, Joe, 296
Big House, The, 134, 138, 180
Big Show, The, 607
Big Town, 749
Big Trail, The, 147
Bill of Divorcement, A, 468
Bishoff, Samuel, 179*n*
Black Fury, 301
Blake, Michael, 140*n*
Blake, Robert, 122, 123
Blandick, Clara, 224, 225
Blankfort, Michael, 682, 683, 750
Blashfield, Edwin, 68
Block, Ralph, 151
Blondell, Joan, 725, 728, 868
Bloomingdale, Hiram, 114
Blossom Time, 5
Blue Angel, The, 738, 739
Blue Heaven, 120
Blum, Edwin Harvey, 365
Blystone, John G., 163, 164, 170, 176, 199
Bob Cummings Show, The, 724
Boehnel, William, 292, 374, 457
Bogart, Humphrey, 136, 138 and *n*, *141*, 407, 548, 558, 610, 615, 633–4, 640, 644, 680, 681, 694, 706, 719, 722–5, 755, 784, 795, 864
Bogdanovich, Peter, 138, 288
Bohlman, Meta, *59*
Boland, Bridget, 753, 766
Bolin, Erik, 606
Bolton, Guy, 261
Bolton, Whitney, 131
Bombers B-52, 337
Bonaventure, Mother, 30
Bond, Johnny, 490
Bond, Ward, 558
Bondi, Beulah, 14, 323
Boody, Henry Phillips, 50, 53, 56, 57, 58–9, 62, 63, 403, 405, *406*
Boom Town, 397, 399–402, 403, 404, 406, 444, 553

Booth, Earle, 85, 86
Booth, Shirley, 639, 721
Bootleggers, The, 19, 20, 22
Borden, Lizzie, 12
Borgnine, Ernest, 671, 672, 674–6
Born Yesterday, 533, 574
Borzage, Frank, 150, 151, 173, 174, 175, 185,
　　200–1, 202–3, *207*, 208, 217, 218, 314,
　　321, 322, *323*, 326, 359, 608
Borzage, Ray, 175
Bosworth, Halliam, 20, 79
Bottoms Up, 220, 222, 223, 232, 249
Bought and Paid For, 23–4
Boundry Line, The, 133
Bow, Clara, 189, 242
Bowron, Fletcher, 628
Boyd, Jimmy, 760, 763
Boyd, William, 158
Boyd, William "Stage," 113, 165
Boyer, Charles, 220, 340, 358, 362, 390, 568
Boyer, Cliff, 19
Boys Town, 343–6, 349–52, 353–6, 358, 361–2,
　　364, 372, 373, 374, 376, 390, 393, 402,
　　408, 604, 767, 830, 849, 866
Brackett, Charles, 340, 721–2, 738
Bradford, Jack, 772
Brady, Alice, 65
Branch, Dr. William, 327
Brandt, Willy, 798
Brando, Marlon, 750, 756
Brandt, Harry, 431
Breen, Joseph I., 468, 494, 500
Breen, Tommy, 506
Breese, Edmund, 89
Bremer, Edward G., 227 and *n*
Bren, Milton, 702
Brendel, El, 170, 172, 176, 179
Brennan, Walter, 366, 377, 379, 671, 672,
　　677
Brent, George, 136
Brent, Olga, 4
Breslin, Howard, 666
Brice, Fannie, 307, 543
Brick Foxhole, The, see Crossfire
Bridge on the River Kwai, The, 813 and *n*
Bridges, Lloyd, 625
Briskin, Irving, 749
Briskin, Sam, 217–18, 554, 562, 753, 768
Britton, Layne, 265
Broadhurst, George, 18, 23
Broadway, 96
Broken Lance, 654–5, 656–9, 660–1, 673–4,
　　680, 684, 685, 695
Bronson, Arthur, 533

Brooks, Phyllis, 459
Brooks, Richard, 666–7
Brophy, Edward, 741, 742, 743, 756, 865
Brower, Otto, 365
Brown, Abigail, 27, 34, 35–6
Brown, Caleb Wescott, 27
Brown, Caroline, *see* Tracy, Caroline
Brown, Chamberlain, 96 and *n*, 97, 98, 100,
　　101, 102, 103, 115, 117
Brown, Clarence, 397, 548, 615, 624, 625,
　　626, 627, 630, 636, 637, 656, 738
Brown, Emma, 27, 31, 35, 113, 360, 456, 503,
　　522, 608, 768
Brown, Edward S., 27, 28, 34, 456
Brown, Frank, 27
Brown, George, 707, 708, 709
Brown, John Mason, 131
Brown, Johnny Mack, 185
Brown, Katherine, 415, 452
Brown, Nicholas, 27
Brown, Rowland, 152–3, 155, 188
Brown, Sam, 152–3
Browne, Florence, 478
Browning, Geraldine, 99
Bruce, Carter, 206
Bruce, Virginia, 261, *262*
Brush, Katharine, 326
Bryan, William Jennings, 750, 756, 757, 762,
　　769
Bryant, Lester, 113
Buck, Gene, 407
Buckingham, Tom, 159, 164
Bucquet, Harold, 508
Buddies, 6, 12, 87
Budge, Don, 620
Bullard, Donna, 606
Bulldog Drummond Strikes Back, 217, 228
Bumby, J. Harold, 63, 64, 65, 404, 405, 866
Burke, Billie, 738
Burke, Edwin, 229–30, 233
Burns, Bob, 136, 138, 340
Burns, George, 231, 754, 866
Burns, Marion, 199
Burns, Robert, *see* Burns, Bob
Butler, Dan, 350
Butler, David, 161, 222
Butler, Hugo, 343, 393
Butler, Jimmy, 350
Byington, Spring, 14
Byron, Arthur, 180
By the People, 479

Caesar and Cleopatra, 595, 611
Caesar, Sid, 805, 806, 808, 810

Cagney, James, 157, 179, 214, 254, 294, 362, 363, 374, 387, *388*, 391, 407, 413, 462, 488, 489, 502, 608, 681, 691, 739, 755, 770, 828–9 and *n*, 864

Cahn, Sammy, 770

Cain, Andrew, 346

Caine Mutiny, The, 658, 685, 750

Caldwell, Audrey, 237, 238, 257, 383, 426, 430, 439, 487, 493

Caldwell, David, 383, 430

Caldwell, June, 358, 565

Caldwell, Orville, 257, 383, 430

Calhern, Louis, 180, 637

Calhoun, Bertha, 34, 35, 503, 768, 869

Calleia, Joseph, 125

Call Me Madame, 722

Call of the Wild, 269

Callow, Ridgeway "Reggie," 158, 159, 625–6, 627

Camel Caravan, 297

Camelot, 874

Camille, 682

Campbell, Maurice, 10

Campbell, Stan, 335

Campbell, William, 609

Cannon, Jimmy, 430

Cantinflas, 727

Cantor, Eddie, 231, 243, 558

Caplan, Harry, 696–7, 699, 701, 703

Capote, Truman, 756

Capp, Raymond, 12

Capra, Frank, 202, 255, 310, 341, 553, 554, 555–6, 557, 558, 561, 562, 564, 752, 764, 766

Captains Courageous, 300–1, 302–7, 310–13, 314, 316–18, 324, 325, 332, 339, 349, 374, 412, 422, 429, 430, 434, 445, 569, 761, 774, 808, 875

Captain's Table, The, 680, 681

Carey, Harry, 135

Carle, Cecil "Teet," 265, 703, 721

Carnegie, Andrew, 68

Carnegie, Dale, 67

Carney, Alan, 810

Carr, Joe, 647

Carr, Nadine, 646–7, 679–80, 708, 734–5

Carradine, John, 311, 741

Carré, Ben, 161, 252

Carrie, 736

Carrigan, Tom, 60*n*

Carrillo, Leo, 137, 276

Carroll, Harrison, 250, 316, 359, 366, 500

Carroll, Leo G., 866

Cassini, Oleg, 616

Cass Timberlane, 530, 547, 549–52, 553, 559, 561, 564, 565, 599, 756

Cat and Mouse, 649, 651

Cat and the Canary, The, 83, 101

Cat on a Hot Tin Roof, 751, 753

Cavalcade, 190, 191, 210, 242, 249

Ceccarini, Olindo, 411

Ceiling Zero, 332

Cermak, Anton, 192

Chains of Dew, 10

Champ, The, 261

Champion, 750

Champlin, Charles, 854, 858

Chaney, Lon, 207, 678

Chaplin, Charles, 225, 231, 451, 554, 581

Chaplin, Oona, 554

Chapman, John, 412, 437, 531

Charisse, Cyd, 606

Charley's Aunt, 22, 69

Chase and Sanborn Hour, The, 749

Chase, Clarence, 125

Chase, Ilka, 138

Chasen, Dave, 866

Chauvent, Virginia, 16

Chayefsky, Paddy, 819, 821

Cheever, John, 824

Chennault, Gen. Claire, 489*n*

Chevalier, Maurice, 178, 243, 259

Cheyenne Autumn, 814, 818

Chicago, 134, 138

Chicken Feed, 76

"Child Is Waiting, A," 765

Chorpenning, Charlotte, 86

Christie, Audrey, 461, 465

Christie, Gus, 41, 404

Christopher Strong, 542

Christy, Eileen, 606

Church, Frederick E., 68

Churchill, Douglas, 185, 264

Churchill, Winston, 475, 630

Cincinnati Kid, The, 819, 820–1, 822

Cinerama Holiday, 682

Citadel, The, 362, 377

Citizen Kane, 426, 465

City of Little Men, 352

Clark, Bobby, 307

Clark, Tom, 555

Clarke, Donald Henderson, 229

Clarke, Harley, 166–7, 172

Clarke, Mae, 137

Clatworthy, Robert, 841

Claw, The, 63

Clemens, Paul, 796

Clifford, Ruth, 741

Clift, Montgomery, 521, 680, 753, 781, 782, 783, 787–90, 798, *799*
Clooney, Rosemary, 706–7
Close, Adelaide Brevoort, 451
Cobb, Lee J., 770
Cock-Eyed World, The, 150
Coffee, Lenore, 588
Cohan, George M., 20, 76, 77, 87, 90, 91–2, 93–4, 96, 100–1, 102, 103 and *n*, 103, 104, 106–7, 108, 109, 110, 111, 117, 301, 331, 342, 474, 533, 596, 621, 754, 784, 848
Cohan, Helen Costigan, 110*n*
Cohen, George, 686
Cohn, Harry, 201, 218, 574, 740
Cohn, Joseph J., 460, 669–70, 821, 868
Colbert, Claudette, 400–1, 500*n*, 548, 553, 554, 555–6
Collier, Constance, 513, 522, 584, 601, 606, 608, 610, 611, 612–13, 635, 662, 683, 684, 691–2, 717
Collier, William Sr., 138, 139, 146, 179
Colman, Ronald, 163, 178, 572
Come Back, Little Sheba, 721
Command Performance, 505
Common Clay, 21
Conflict, 114–15, 177, 278
Conlon, Tommy, 175
Connolly, Mike, 626
Connolly, Miles, 187
Connolly, Walter, 276
Conquest, 340, 624
Conselman, William, 214
Considine, Bob, 501, 531
Considine, John W., Jr., 168–9, 170, 172, 182, 343–4, 348–9, 393, 407–8
Conway, Jack, 299, 310, 389, 508
Conway, Peggy, 89
Cooke, Joe, 350
Coons, Robbin, 311
Cooper, Gary, 254, 260, 294, 310, 360, 407, 487, 553, 659 and *n*, 681, 795, 864
Cooper, George, 158, 159, 165
Cooper, Jackie, 259, 857
Copland, Aaron, 512
Corbaley, Kate, 343
Cornell, Katharine, 83, 525
Cornered, 22
Cortese, Valentina, 572
Cortez, Ricardo, 741
Costello, Dolores, 812
Costello, Don, 125, 128, 130
Cotten, Joseph, 568, 734

Country Girl, The, 681, 682
Courtright, Hernando, 589
Covel, Dr. Mitchel, 823, 825–6, 827, 828, 829, 839, 851, 855, 860, 861, 862, 863
Cowan, Sada, 63
Coward, Noël, 308, 370, 801, 873
Cowl, Jane, 21, 43
Cramer, Duncan, 161
Crandall, Edward H., 7
Craven, Frank, 77, 115, 469
Crawford, Cheryl, 458
Crawford, Joan, 224, 302, 324, 325, 326–7, *328*, 330, 431
Creelman, Eileen, 422
Crewe, Regina, 146, 209
Crime Does Not Pay series, 261
Criminal Code, The (play), 124, 134
Crisp, Donald, 411, 741
Crocker, Harry, 451
Cromwell, John, 96–7, 98, 100, 101, 102, 103 and *n*, 156, 168, 185, 557
Cromwell, Lincoln, 196, 246–7, 309, 373, 490–2, 493
Cronin, A. J., 479
Cronyn, Hume, 495, 496–7, 498, 499
Crosby, Bing, 197, 360, 407, 502, 548, 695, 806*n*
Crosman, Henrietta, 8–9, 10
Crossfire, 669 and *n*
Crouse, Russel, 552
Crow, James Francis, 340–1
Crowe, Dr. Samuel, 464
Crowther, Bosley, 457, 500, 564, 579, 599, 636, 653, 721, 771, 817, 866
Crusades, The, 269
Cukor, George, 113, 412, 433, 465, 466, 467, 468–9, 470, 471, 474, 479, 522, 563, 566, 567, 568, 572, 573, 574, 575, 577, 578, 579, 600*n*, 601, 606, 608, 616–17, 618, 619, 621, 622, 626, 633, 634, 635, 637–44, 648, 649, 655, 659, 662, 715, 717, 736, 754–5, 777, 800, 815, 821–22, 830, 834, 862, 863, 864, 866, 873, 875, 877
Cumberland, John, 111
Cummings, Irving, 215, 218, 255
Curie, Eve, 399
Curie, Marie, 399
Curie, Pierre, 399
Curley, James Michael, 740
Currie, George, 67
Curtis, Tony, 753
Curtiz, Michael, 180

Cushing, Dr. Harvey, 105
Cyrano de Bergerac, 16, 750

Daddy Long Legs, 173
Daigneau, Kenneth, 20, 22
Dally-Watkins, June, 632–3, 634–5, 640
Dalrymple, Jean, 115
Daly, John, 118
Damien, 545
Daniels, Bebe, 10
Daniels, William, 623
Dante's Inferno, 248–9, 251–2, 256, 263, 264
Darkness at Noon, 607
Darrow, Barbara, 695
Darrow, Clarence, 756, 757, 762, 769
Dart, Justin, 779
Darwell, Jane, 741
Da Silva, Howard, 469
Davey, William Melvin, 629
Davidson, Bill, 772, 774, 800–2
Davidson, Royal Page, 47
Davies, John, 51–2, 53, 57
Davis, Bette, 180, *181*, 182, 200, 211, 363, *364*, 390, 453, 548
Davis, Edith "Lucky," 503–5
Davis, Johnnie "Scat," 429
Davis, Dr. Loyal, 503–5, 866
Davis, Nancy, 504
Davis, Owen, 117, 118
Davis, Richard, 504–5
Davy, 804
Dawn, Jack, 394, 411, 422
Day, Laraine, 337, 359, 395–6, 678, 745, 755, 837–8, 866
Dead End, 307
Dean, Clarence, 20, 21, 22, 79, 80, 90
Death of a Salesman, 750
Death Takes a Holiday, 132
Defiant Ones, The, 750, 751, 753, 756, 757, 769
de Havilland, Olivia, 451
Dehner, John, 624
Dekker, Albert, *114*, 115, 551
De Laurentiis, Dino, 813
De Liagre, Alfred, Jr., 581
Delicious, 173
Del Rio, Dolores, 656, 659
Deluge, The, 67
Demarest, William, 695, 810, 811, 812*n*
de Medicis, Rodrigo, 305
DeMille, Cecil B., 67, 269, *329*, 341
DeMille, William, 10
Deming, Emily, 79–80, 81, 82, 83, 86, 90
Dempsey, Jack, 768

Dennis, Dr. Howard O., 193, 196, 246, 310, 332, 346, 347, 376, 492, 586, 723
Dere Mabel, 589
De Sica, Vittorio, 707
Desire Under the Elms, 545
Desk Set, 721–2, 723, 724 and *n*, 725–9, 738, 740
Desperate Hours, The, 680
Destry Rides Again, 785
DeSylva, B. G. "Buddy," 222
Deutsch, Helen, 495, 496, 615
Devil at 4 O'Clock, The, 752, 753, 754, 764, 766, 767–8, 769–71, 773, 780, 786, 787, 796–7, 798
Devil's Disciple, The, 375, 436, 520, 545
Devil with Women, A, 138*n*
Dial M for Murder, 682
Diary of Anne Frank, The, 782
Dietrich, Marlene, 316, 359, 431, 738, 781, 782, 785–6, 792
Dietz, Howard, 295, 408, 459, 516–17, 533, 613
Digby, see Highland Fling
Dillon, Josephine, 416
Dinehart, Allan, 170
Dinner at Eight, 210, 224
Dirty Dozen, The, 860
Disch, Mrs. Henry, 31–2
Disney, Diane, 630
Disney, Lillian, 237, 319, 413
Disney, Roy, 487
Disney, Walt, 237, 288, *291* and *n*, 319, 324, 353, 407, 413, 426, 434, 485, 487, 535, 558, 559, 608, 630, 779, 780, 800, 863
Disorderly Conduct, 167, 168, 169–72, 173, 174, 176
Dmytryk, Edward, 658–9, 660–1, 662–3, 694, 695–6, 697–8, 702–3, 704–5, *706*, 714–15, 720, 750, 755, 863
Dmytryk, Jean, 714–15
Dr. Jekyll and Mr. Hyde (film, 1920), 408, 410, 723
Dr. Jekyll and Mr. Hyde (film, 1931), 408, 409, 410, 411, 723
Dr. Jekyll and Mr. Hyde (film, 1941), 408–15, 416 and *n*, 420–3, 434, 436, 444, 457, 723, 756, 761
Dodsworth, 310, 545
Dolan, Frank, 163
Donat, Robert, 362, 408, 566
Don Juan in Hell, 644
Donlevy, Brian, 501
Doolittle, Lt. Col. Jimmy, 501

Doorway to Hell, 152
Double Life, A, 572, 573
Douglas, Kirk, 558, 626–7, 636, 750
Douglas, Lewis W., 630, 658, 659, 662, 815, 866
Douglas, Melvyn, 300, 502, 543, 756
Douglas, Nathan E., *see* Young, Nedrick
Douglas, Peg, 630, 662
Douglas, William O., 607, 792, 868
Dowling, Rev. Michael P., 41
Doyle, Adelaide, 635*n*
Doyle, Miriam, 117
Doyle, Sir Arthur Conan, 18
Dozier, William, 834
Dracula, 410
Dragon Seed, 490, 496, 507, 508, 539
Drake, Alfred, 765
Drake, Betsy, 747
Dread, 117–19, 120, 211, 224
Dregs, The, 56
Dressler, Marie, 224
Dreyfus, Henry, 127
Dudley, Charles, 194
Dull, O. O. "Bunny," 350
Duncan, Isadora, 651
Dunham, June, 509–10
Dunn, Eddie, 91
Dunn, James, 173, 176, 178
Dunn, Red, 864
Dunne, Irene, 191, 390, 407, 472, *498*, 481–2, *483*, 484, 488, 489, 494, *498*, 500, 806*n*, 820
Dunne, Philip, 365, 366, 738
Dunnigan's Daughter, 539
Dunstan, Clifford, 89
Durant, Thomas W. "Tim," 451–2, 461, 581, 582, 599, 816, 866
Durant, Will, 679
Durante, Jimmy, 231, 371, 738
Durbin, Deanna, 390
Durnin, Fr. Patrick, 25
Durocher, Leo, 678–9, 745, 752, 837
Dwan, Allan, 300

Eames, Clare, 96
Ebert, Roger, 873
Ebsen, Buddy, 330
Eckman, Gene, 416, 417, 418, *419*, 420, 479
Eddy, Nelson, 259, 333
Edgers, Kenneth B., 47–9, 51, 53, 54–5, 58*n*, *59*, 60, 61, 66, 490–1
Edgers, Lois, 54–55, 490
Edison, Charles, 393, 397, 402

Edison, Mina, 393, 402
Edison, the Man, 393–4, 397, 399, 402, 403, 404, 425, 443, 444, 756
Edward, My Son (film), 562–3, 566, 567–8, 579–80, 630, 813
Edward, My Son (play), 562, 567, 579
Edwards, Alan, 224
Edwards, Ralph, 870
Eggar, Samantha, 833
Eichmann, Adolf, 800
Eilers, Sally, 170, 172, 173, 179, 200
Elderson, Don, 647
Eldridge, Florence, 65, 637, 750, 757
Elias, Hal, 493–4
Ellis, Edward, 280
Ellis, John, 19, 20, 21, 22, 79
Elmer Gantry, 781, 791
Elsey, Pat, 376, 379, 384, 699
Emerson, George, 416
Emerson, Hope, 579
Emerson, John, 276, 284
Engelbracht, Evelyn, *59*
Enright, Elizabeth, 631
Enright, Ray, 179, 180
Enter Laughing, 838
Entertainer, The, 791
Ephron, Henry, 722, 723, 724, 727, 729
Ephron, Phoebe, 722, 723, 727, 729
Ericson, John, 671, 672, 677–8
Erskine, Chester, 124, 125, 126, 127, 129, 143, 520, 748, 784, 789*n*, 814, 866, 876–7
Erskine, John, 402–3, 446–7
Erskine, Sally, 747–8, 814
Erstwhile Susan, 9
Erwin, Stu, 188
Esmond, Carl, 508
Evans, Harry, 400
Evans, Madge, 117, 118, 211, 224, *232*, 247
Evans, Maurice, 458, 506
Evans, Ross, 588–9, 863
Evans, Silas, 55, 62, 404, 405, *406*
Eve of St. Mark, The, 507
Ewell, Tom, 574, 577, 578
Exodus, 782

Face in the Sky, 183, 187–8, 189
Fadiman, William, 433
Fairbanks, Douglas, 111, 206, 341
Fairbanks, Douglas, Jr., 316, 407, 434
Fame and Fortune, see Actress, The
Family Upstairs, The, 89
Fantasia, 426
Farewell to Arms, A, 188, 254, 744

Farmer, Frances, 420
Farmer, Milton, 213
Farmer Takes a Wife, The, 257
Farrell, Charles, 178, 185
Farrow, Mia, 833
Father and the Actress, see Actress, The
Father Brown, Detective, 276
Father of the Bride, 589–94, 598, 599–600,
    602, 603, 604, 607, 609, 644, 756, 798
Father's Little Dividend, 600, 601, 602,
    603–4, 606, 609, 736, 751
Faulkner, William, 569
Faversham, William, 89
Fay, Frank, 65, 271
Faye, Alice, 233, 407
Feely, Bernard, 39, 165, 205
Feely, Jane, 27, 34, 37–8, 46, 109, 110–11, 165,
    204–5, 210, 211, 212–13, 319–21, 361,
    386, 522, 549, 566, 587, 611, 629, 664–5,
    692–3, 705–6, 752, 778
Feely, Jenny, 26, 27, 29–30, 32, 39, 110, 165,
    184, 204, 205, 211, 212, 213, 361, 386,
    427, 566, 587, 594, 664, 692–3
Feely, Patrick, 39, 165
Fenton, Frank, 569
Fenton, Leslie, 350
Ferguson, Elsie, 21
Ferrer, José, 606, 707, 819
Fetchit, Stepin, 138
Fields, Madalynne, 455
Fields, Marguerite, 19
Fields, W. C., 297, 341, 443, 696
Fields, William, 534
Filkas, Det. Lt. Joseph, 230
Fine, Larry, 136
Firestone, Leonard, 779
First Year, The, 77, 87
Fitzmaurice, Margaret, 330–1
Fitzpatrick, Ken, 324
5,000 Fingers of Dr. T, The, 750
Fixer, The, 837
Flanagan, Fr. Edward J., 343–6, 348–52, 353,
    354, 355, 356, 358–9, 361, 362, 363, 364,
    370, 393, 407–8, 565–6, 570, 701
Flapper, The, 17
Flavin, Martin, 134
Fleming, George, 79
Fleming, Victor, 289, 300, 302, 303, 304,
    307, 310–12, 314, 317, 321, 330, 331,
    332–3, 334, 335–6, 337–8, 383, 408, 409,
    410, 411, 412, 414, 415, 416 and *n*, 417,
    418, 420, 421, 443, 446, 453, 460–1,
    481–3, 494, 569–70, 608

Flesh, 188
Flight to the Islands, 631, 643, 645, 648–9,
    651, 654
Flim Flam Man, The, 831
Flynn, Errol, 360, 390
Foat, Olive Lorraine, 54, 55–6, 57–8, 59,
    61–2, 65, 66–7, 68, 71, 108, 203, 406
Folger, Gertrude, 639
Folsey, George, 326
Fonda, Henry, 257, 558
Fontaine, Joan, 612
Fontanne, Lynn, 22, 194, 402, 525
Fonteyn, Margot, 632
Foote, Bradbury, 343, 393
Ford, Glenn, 749
Ford, Henry, 393, 397, 465
Ford, John, 135, 136 and *n*, 137–8, 139–41,
    146, 150, 151, 153, 155, 156, 264, 450, 539,
    707, 739–40, 741–4, 745, 748, 784, 791,
    797, 806*n*, 814, 818, 859, 866
Ford, Mary, 151
Ford, Wallace, 164, 348, 741, 756, 865
Foreman, Carl, 750
Forgotten Village, The, 444–5
Forrest, Sam, 91, 104
Forry, Bertha, *see* Calhoun, Bertha
Forry, Clarence, 35
Foster, Preston, 179*n*, 198
Fowler, Gene, 407
Fox, Sidney, 154
Fox, William, 136, 149, 150, 167
Foy, Eddie, 111
Francis, Anne, 671, 672
Francis, Robert, 685, 687
Frank, Sally, 163
Franken, Rose, 249
Frankenstein, 410
Frankfurter, Felix, 527
Franklin, Chester, 417
Franklin, Harold B., 178
Franklin, Sidney, 326, 340, 416, 417, 420,
    488, 643
Frankovich, Mike, 832, 839, 841
Frazee, Henry H., 71
Freeland, Thornton, 155
Freeman, Y. Frank, 719–20, 779
Freund, Karl, 495, 499, 506
Frings, Kurt, 639
Frohman, Daniel, 70
Front Page, The, 173
Fury, 272–4, 277, 279–82, 283, 286–9, 290,
    291, 292, 293, 296, 297, 298, 302, 308,
    310, 326, 339, 374, 495, 756

Gabin, Jean, 372–3
Gable, Clark, 114, 224, 259, 269–71, 272, 275–6, 277–8, 279, *281*, 282, 283, 286, 289, 291*n*, 294, 295, 297, 316, 318*n*, 330, 332–8, 339, 346, 363, 384, 390, 392, 394, 397, 399, 400–2, 416, 433, 450 and *n*, 453, 454–5, 463, 502, 548, 553, 558, 568, 569, 570–1, 572, 588, 613, 623–4, 626, 627, 630, 633, 655–6, 657, 659, 681, 691, 695, 751, 764, 770, 772–3, 795, 809, 820, 863, 864
Gable, Ria, 270, 454
Gabriel, Gilbert, 129
Gain, Jack J., 190, 241, 247, 248, 255
Galbraith, W. W., 16
Gallian, Ketti, 242, 243–4
Galsworthy, John, 10
Ganter, Ernest, 19
Garbo, Greta, 178, 224, 292, 329, 398, 399, 472, 503, 564
Gardner, Ava, 453, 613
Gardner, Jack, 144
Garfield, John, 446
Garland, Judy, 271, 330, 339, 781, 782, 783, 790–1, 798, *799*, 815
Garmes, Lee, 199
Garnier, Philippe, 152
Garrett, Oliver H. P., 273
Garrick Gaieties, The, 89
Garson, Greer, 467, 626, 820
Gaslight, 497
Gaynor, Janet, 150, 178, 187, 257
Gebler, Ernest, 613
Gehman, Richard, 601
Geist, Kenneth L., 289
Genevieve, 804
Genn, Leo, 623, 637
George, Gladys, 314
George White's Scandals, 249
Georgy Girl, 860
Gerasimov, Sergei, 864
Germain, Larry, *304*
Gershwin, George, 600
Gershwin, Ira, 600
Gersten, Bernie, 747
Getting Gertie's Garter, 13
Gheczy, Ida, 830, 861, 863
Gheczy, Willie, 861
Giant, 682
Gibbons, Cedric, 334*n*
Gibbons, Irene, 556
Gielgud, John, 766

Gilbert, John, 153
Gilbert, Walter, 115
Gill, Brendan, 873
Gillespie, Arnold "Buddy," 284, 625
Gilmore, Helen, 320
Girl in Every Port, A, 156
Girl Who Came Back, The, 19
Glass, George, 847, 851
Glass Menagerie, The, 528
Gleason, James, 86, 185, 741, 742, 742–3, 756, 865
Glenn, Roy, Sr., 853
Glenville, Peter, 753, 766
Glory for Me, see Best Years of Our Lives, The
Godfrey, Peter, 411
Goetz, Edie, 612, 834
Goetz, William, 612, 834
Golden, John, 115, 203
Golden, Sam, 124 and *n*
Golden Boy, 331
Goldie, 156–7, 158, 159, 180
Goldwyn, Samuel, 60*n*, 261, 324, 394, 430, 531, 681
Gombel, Minna, 179
Gone With the Wind, 252, 376, 380, 383, 387, 388, 390, 398, 399, 406, 410, 416*n*, 553, 656, 736
Goodbye, Charley, 764
Good Earth, The, 314, 317, 321, 328
Goodman, Edward, 10, 67
Goodman, Jules Eckert, 4
Goodman, Olga, 68
Good News of 1938, 329, 333, 354
Goodrich, Frances, 590, 598, 602, 723
Goodwin, Nat, 92
Goosson, Stephen, 203
Gopadze, Dorothy, *see* Griffith, Dorothy
Gordon, Billy, 724
Gordon, Leon, 474, 479, 507
Gordon, Max, 257
Gordon, Richard, 680
Gordon, Ruth, 522, 572–3, 574, 576, 577, 600*n*, 602, 608, 614, 615, 616, 617, 618, *619*, 627, 632, 633, 634–5, 636, 637, 638–9, 641, 642, 643, 648, 650–1, 655, 662, 683, 724, 735, 749, 764
Gorgeous Hussy, The, 326
Gorlay, Logan, 663–4
Gottfried, Martin, 510
Gough, Peggy, 352, 428–9, 453, 455, 539
Grable, Betty, 407, 507
Graduate, The, 874

Grady, Billy, 339, 348, 357, 359, 398, 416, 488, 866

Graham, Billy, 665, 779

Graham, James Clark, 52, 58, 61, 62, 404, 405, *406*

Graham, Sheilah, 299, 360–1, 368, 396, 398, 451, 484, 495, 638, 663, 691, 747, 754

Granger, Stewart, 401, 460–1, 605, 638, 752

Granger, Tracy Stewart, 719

Grant, Cary, 201, 434, 633, 681, 703, 728, 756

Grant, Jack, 243

Grant, James Edward, 268

Grant, Katharine Houghton, *see* Houghton, Katharine

Grapes of Wrath, The, 374, 403, 443

Grapewin, Charley, 307, 310

Graves, Dolores, 69, 71

Gray, David, 87

Gray, Dr. Seymour, 586, 594, 646–7, 718

Great Divide, The, 56

Greatest Story Ever Told, The, 797, 812 and n

Great God Brown, The, 520

Great Ziegfeld, The, 292, 315, 321

Greed, 670

Green, Abel, 263, 292, 533

Green, Carolyn, *see* Behar, Carolyn Rothstein

Green Dolphin Street, 516

Green Hat, The, 82, 85

Greenstreet, Sidney, 572, 582

Griffin, Arvid, 686, 687

Griffin, Eleanore, 343, 349, 362, 393

Griffin, Dr. Francis, 494

Griffith, D. W., 262

Griffith, Dorothy "Miss G," 539, 540–2, 546, 589, 592, 625, 855, 868

Griffith, Raymond, 185

Groesse, Paul, 446

Ground Hogs, see Sky Devils

Grounds for Divorce, 80

Guardsman, The, 194

Guernsey, Otis, 637

Guess Who's Coming to Dinner, 830–4, 836–45, 846–8, 850–9, 868, 870–5, 877

Guhin, Mary, *see* Tracy, Mary Guhin

Guinness, Alec, 770, 813 and n

Guitry, Lucien, 92

Gunderson, Coleman, 60

Gunga Din, 607

Guns of Navarone, The, 797

Guy Named Joe, A, 481–4, 487, 488, 489–90, 494, 497, 499–500, 502, 506, 512, 535, 569, 820, 868

Gypsy Trail, The, 14, 15

Hackett, Albert, 14, 590, 598, 602, 723

Hackett, Buddy, 805, 807–8, 809, 815

Hackett, Walter C., 67

Hagen, Jean, 574

Hagen, Uta, 639

Haines, Donald, 350

Haircut, 118

Half Gods, 133

Hall, David S., *252*

Hall, Gladys, 220, 253, 317, 368, 374, 397

Hall, Mordaunt, 157, 209

Hall, Porter, 99

Hamilton, Bernie, 774, 776

Hamilton, Hale, 91

Hamilton, Jack, 847, 868

Hamilton, Neil, 160

Hamilton, Patrick, 497

Hamlet, 72, 596

Hamman, Dr. Louis V., 463–4

Hammerstein, Oscar II, 581

Hammett, Dashiell, 159

Hammid, Alexander, 444

Hampden, Walter, 16, 75

Hanemann, H. W., 265

Hanna, Betty, 83, 85

Happiness, 10, 90

Hard Guy, The, 135, *136*, 143

Harding, Ann, 83, 214, 637

Harding, Laura, 527, 661, 709

Harding, Warren G., 703

Hardwicke, Sir Cedric, 363, 367, 595

Harlow, Jean, 156–7, 161, 224, 259, 265, *266*, 268, 269, 272, 293, 299, 314, 315, 320, 326, 429, 821, 863

Harrell, Hattie, 536

Harris, Julie, 790

Harris, Mitchell, 138

Harris, Orville, 125

Harris, Sam, 117, 118, 224, 533

Harris, Southard, 8

Harrison, Geneva, 21

Harrison, Rex, 717

Hart, William S., 57, 111

Hartford, Huntington, 684

Hartley, Mariette, 838

Hartman, Don, 694

Hartmann, Edmund, 244

Harvey, Anthony, 877

Hasso, Signe, 499, 510

Hathaway, Henry, 657

Hatton, Fanny, 133

Hatton, Frederick, 133

Hawks, Howard, 633

Hawks, Kenneth, 152
Hay, Alexandra, 856
Hayes, Helen, 21, 65, 224, 308, 323, 371, 412, 419–20, 525, 639
Hays, Will, 192
Hayward, Leland, 449–50, 644–5, 649, 662, 666, 681, 690, 707, 709, 710, 711–14, 730, 732, 733, 734–5, 736, 739, 744–5
Hayworth, Rita, 446, 558, 636
Hazard, Lawrence, 326
Hearst, William Randolph, 465
Heath, Percy, 409
Heberlein, Lois, *see* Edgers, Lois
Hecht, Ben, 119, 394
Hecht, Harold, 551, 750
Heeley, Ted, 136, 295, 330
Heflin, Van, 502
Heil, Julius, 403
Helburn, Teresa, 375, 471, 472, 473–4, 508, 561, 692
Held, Anna, 315
Hell Divers, 332
Helldorado, 247, 255
Hellinger, Mark, 776
Hellman, Sam, 365–6
Hell's Angels, 156, 157–8
Hellzapoppin', 371
Helpmann, Robert, 643, 662, 664, 682, 691, 764
Heming, Violet, 65
Hemingway, Ernest, 644, 645–6, 650, 655, 666, 680, 707, 708–9, 711, 712, 713, 730, 732, 734–5, 753
Hendrickson, Floyd, 686
Hendrix, Wanda, 638
Hendry, Whitey, 517, 772
Henie, Sonja, 333, 366, 390
Henreid, Paul, 548, 557
Henry, Bill, 562
Henry—Behave, 95
Hepburn, Katharine Houghton, 431–9, 440–3, 448–50, 451–2, 456, 457–9, 460, 461, 462–3, 464, 465–6, 467–9, 471–5, 479–80, 481, 487–8, 489, 490, 492–3, 495–8, 502–3, 504, 507–15, 516, 517, 519, 520, 521, 522, 523, 526, 527, 528–9, 538–9, 542, 543, 544–5, 546–9, 550, 554–6, 557–9, 561, 562, 563, 564, 567, 568, 569, 572, 573, 574–9, 581–3, 584–7, 588–9, 594–7, 599, 600–1, 606, 607–8, 610, 611, 612–13, 615–23, 626, 627, 630, 631, 632, 633, 634, 635–6, 640, 643, 649, 650, 651, 655, 660, 661–6, 669*n*, 671–2, 679, 682, 684 and *n*, 686, 688,

690, 691–2, 697, 701–2, 705 and *n*, 707, 708, 709, 710, 714–17, 718, 719, 720, 721, 722, 723, 724, 725–9, 735, 736, 738, 739–40, 743, 747–9, 751, 752, 753, 755, 764, 765, 766, 770, 771, 785, 795, 795–6, 797, 798–9, 801–2, 811–17, 818, 820, 821, 822, 823, 824–5, 826, 827, 828, 830, 831–2, 833–7, 838–46, 847–61, 862–3, 864, 865–6, 867–9, 870, 871, 872–4, 875–8
Hepburn, Katharine Martha Houghton, 448–9, 463, 584, 586, 610, 635 and *n*, 692, 866
Hepburn, Margaret Houghton, 509
Hepburn, Marion Houghton, 585, 850*n*
Hepburn, Richard Houghton, 585 and *n*
Hepburn, Dr. Robert, 507, 515
Hepburn, Rev. Sewell Stavely, 448
Hepburn, Dr. Thomas Norval, 448, 449, 463, 584, 585, 586, 633, 747, 785, 811–12, 866
Here Comes Mr. Jordan, 481
Hersey, Capt. J. M., 303, 306, 307
Hershfield, Harry, 422
Hersholt, Jean, 194
Her Unborn Child, 19, 20
Herzog, Buck, 503, 601
Heston, Charlton, 694
Heywood, Herbert, 125
Hibbard, Edna, 113
Hickman, Darryl, 469–71, 525, 570, 607
Higginbottom, Walter, 427
Higgins, John C., 261
High and the Mighty, The, 650
Highjacker, The, 18
Highland Fling, 654, 659–60, 661, 664, 668
High Noon, 645, 659, 680, 682, 750, 795
High Sierra, 670
Hirshberg, Jack, 703
Hitchcock, Alfred, 567, 682
Hitchcock, Tommy, 239*n*
Hitler, Adolf, 453, 788, 800
Hobart, Rose, 136, 137, 551
Hodiak, John, 572
Hoffenstein, Samuel, 242, 409
Hoffman, Herman, 667, 681
Hoffman, John, 286, 295
Hohl, Arthur, 203
Holden, Fay, 349
Holden, William, 695
Holiday, 755
Holiday for Lovers, 864
Holliday, Judy, 574, 577, 621
Holloway, Sterling, 70, 71

Holly and the Ivy, The, 653
Hollywood Hotel, 269
Holmes, Brown, 179
Holt, Sir Herbert, 567
Holt, Jack, 185, 295
Holtz, Lou, 231, 263
Homecoming, 582*n*
Home of the Brave, 750
Hondo, 666
Honors Are Even, 20
Hoover, Herbert, 16
Hope, Bob, 502, 548, 695, 707, 809
Hopkins, Arthur, 16, 519, 526
Hopkins, Miriam, 214, 410
Hopkins, Robert E. "Bob," 274–5, 276, 284
Hopper, Hedda, 472, 491*n*, 510, 555, 588, 627, 650, 754, 812 and *n*
Hopwood, Avery, 87
Horan, Fr. W. A., 28
Hornblow, Arthur Jr., 299, 550, 551
Horne, Harry, 99
Hottentot, 90
Houdini, Harry, 43
Houghton, Katharine, 449, 452, 497, 510, 514, 576–7, 584, 585–6, 612, 649, 812, 829, 838–9, 840*n*, 841, 842, 845–6, 847, *848*, 849–51, 853, 854, 855, 872, 874, 876, 877
Houghton, Katharine Martha, *see* Hepburn, Katharine Martha Houghton
Houseman, John, 413, 415, 631, 680, 685, 735
House of Rothschild, 217
House of Strangers, 654
Howard, Harry, *see* Howard, Moe
Howard, Leslie, 362
Howard, Moe, 136
Howard, Shemp, 136
Howard, Sidney, 96, 98, 100, 133, 520
Howard, Trevor, 791
Howard, William K., 151, 189, 191, 193, 194, 195, 197, 242, 264
Howe, James Wong, 193, 224, 359, 731, 732, 733
How the West Was Won, 791, 806 and *n*, 814
Hubbard, Lucien, 224, 332
Hudkins, John, 808
Hudson, Rock, 802
Hughes, Howard, 156, 157–8, 159, 164, 165, 173, 179, 432, 449–50, 569, 638, 659, 663
Hughes, Shirley, 269, 336
Hull, Henry, 65, 120, 350
Hunt, Helen, 497
Hunt, Margaret, 427, 537

Hunter, Ian, 567
Hunter, Jeffrey, 654, 657, 741, 755
Hurley, Arthur, 135
Hurray for What!, 331
Hussey, Ruth, 420
Hustler, The, 819
Huston, John, 610, 611, 615, 666, 725, 770
Huston, Walter, 207, 310, 725
Hutchinson, Josephine, 551
Hyams, Joe, 761, 772, 775, 784, 786, 801
Hyman, Bernard H., 276, 282, 284, 286, 295, 340, 394
Hymer, John B., 156
Hymer, Warren, 138, 140, *141*, 147, 156, 159, 164, 176, 180–1

I Am a Fugitive from a Chain Gang, 179, 183
Icebound, 118
Iceman Cometh, The, 436, 561
Idiot's Delight, 308, 390, *519*
I'd Rather Be Right, 331
Importance of Being Earnest, The, 71
Ince, Thomas, 262
Informer, The, 297, 495
Ingram, Rex, 188, 357
Inherit the Wind (film), 750–1, 753, 756–63, 766, 768–9, 770, 771, 774, 782, 784, 786, 798, 800, 811
Inherit the Wind (play), 690
In Love with Love, 22
In Old Chicago, 365
Intermezzo, 410
In the Heat of the Night, 872, 875
In the Reign of Rothstein, 229
Intruder in the Dust, 569
Invisible Man, The, 188
I Remember Mama, 564
Iron Man, 157
Irving, George, 158
Is Zat So? 85
I Take This Woman, 358–61, 366, 368, 384, 390, 394–6, 398, 399, 407, 444
It Happened One Night, 255, 400
It's a Boy, 6
It's a Mad, Mad, Mad, Mad World, 804–11, 812, 813, 817–18, 819, 824, 830, 831, 839
It's a Small World, 251, 255–6, 257, 263
It's a Wise Child, 120
Ivancich, Gianfranco, 712

Jackpot, The, 722
Jackson, Doris, 484
Jacobowsky and the Colonel, 512
Jacobs, George, 771

Jacobs, Morris E., 345–6
Jagger, Dean, 671
James, Det. Lt. Frank "Lefty," 228
Jamison, Han, 325
Janis, Elsie, 7
Jannings, Emil, 738
Jarman, Claude, Jr., 569
Jarrico, Paul, 431
Jay, Ernest, 567
Jealousy, 614
Jefferson Sellick, 643
Jehlinger, Charles, 67, 70–1
Jenkins, Allen, 125, 143, 387
Jennings, Talbot, 377, 380, 382, 386, 393
Jeremy Rodock, see Tribute to a Bad Man
Jergens, Diane, 724
Jessup, Richard, 819
Jewell, Austin, 810
Jewell, Isabel, 377
Jezebel, 363
Joan of Lorraine, 569
Johannsen, Bland, 209
John Brown's Body, 644
Johnny O'Hara's Life, see People Against O'Hara, The
Johns, Florence, 97
Johns, Mervyn, 567
Johnson, Kay, 70
Johnson, Nunnally, 507
Johnson, Osa, 365
Johnson, Rita, 402
Johnson, Van, 482–4, 488, 489, 494, 500, 501, 522, 548, 553, 570, 585, 637, 738, 820
Johnson, William Weber, 754
John XXIII, 825
Jolson, Al, 809
Jones, Allan, 330
Jones, Barry, 623
Jones, Clifford, 195
Jones, Jennifer, 550, 684, 685
Jones, Newton, 63
Jones, Robert C., 871
Josephs, Lemuel, 67
Josephson, Julien, 366
Journey, The, 273
Journey of a Soul, 825
Journey's End, 124
Journey to a Star, see Actress, The
Joy, Helen, 88, 89
Judgment at Nuremberg, 765–6, 768, 769, 773, 774, 775–6, 781–6, 787–94, 795, 796, 798, 800, 802–3, 804, 805, 806n, 810, 811, 817, 819, 846

Julius Caesar, 563
June Moon, 120
June, Ray, 170
Jurado, Katy, 659, 685
Just Imagine, 147

Kael, Pauline, 871
Kahn, Prince Aly, 636
Kane, Whitford, 11
Kanin, Fay, 503
Kanin, Garson, 430–1, 436, 450, 458, 516, 521, 522, 523–4, 525, 527, 528, 529, 533, 572–3, 574, 576, 577, 600n, 602, 608, 611, 615, 616, 617, 618, 619, 621, 627, 631, 632, 633, 634–5, 636, 637–8, 639, 640, 643, 648–9, 650–1, 655, 662, 683, 714, 715, 724, 735, 749, 751, 754, 764, 766, 795, 827, 829n, 838, 859, 866
Kanin, Michael, 431–3, 439, 503
Kantor, MacKinlay, 831
Kaplan, Marvin, 578, 579
Karloff, Boris, 214, 422
Katz, Sam, 280, 288, 302, 432, 442
Kaufman, Lori, 510, 666
Kaufman, Millard, 510, 666–9, 670–1, 672–3, 674–5, 676–7, 678, 831
Kaye, Danny, 681, 752
Kazan, Elia, 539, 542, 543, 544, 545, 550
Keating, Elizabeth, 136, 138
Keating, Helen, 136, 138
Keaton, Buster, 158, 225, 808, 809
Keeper of the Flame, 461, 465–71, 474, 477, 479–80, 483, 494, 507, 587
Keethe, Larry, 376, 400, 540, 541, 553, 592–3, 607, 629, 685, 730, 763
Keighley, Cyril, 16
Keith, Robert, 531
Kellaway, Cecil, 845, 847, 857
Keller, Helen, 538
Kellogg, Phil, 819, 821, 822
Kelly, Edward J., 505
Kelly, Gene, 718, 757, 758, 761–2
Kelly, George, 223, 225, 231 and n
Kelly, Grace, 655 and n, 656, 681–2, 683
Kelly, Gregory, 15
Kelly, Nancy, 368
Kelly, Paul, 86
Kennedy, Eugene Cullen, 497, 830, 876
Kennedy, Eunice, 372
Kennedy, John F., 773, 818
Kennedy, Joseph P., 339, 346, 372
Kennedy, Madge, 60n
Kennedy, Pat, 372
Kennedy, Robert F., 859, 866

Kent, Elsie, 156
Kent, Sidney R., 190–1, 192, 244, 247, 248, 249–50, 255, 257, 661
Kentucky, 366
Kenyon, Doris, 175
Kerr, Deborah, 566, 567, 568, 728
Kert, Larry, 764
Keyes, Evelyn, 643
Keys of the Kingdom, 479
Kid Boots, 17
Kilbride, Percy, 469
Kilgallen, Dorothy, 459, 518, 608, 630, 635, 655, 663, 794, 816
Kim, 324
Kimbrell, Marketa, 790
King and I, The, 722
King, Henry, 241, 242, 243, 244, 366, 367
King Kong, 199
Kingsley, Dorothy, 511
Kingsley, Sidney, 550
Kinkead, Eugene, 530
Kipling, Rudyard, 300, 305, 324
Kirkland, Muriel, 70
Kirkland, Patricia, 637
Kirkland, William, 15
Kirkwood, James, 163, 164
Kiss of Death, 602
Klaw & Erlanger, *18*
Klein, Anna, 59
Klein, Herbert, 444
Klein, Philip, 249
Klemperer, Werner, 783
Klumpf, Helen, 178
Knapp, Evelyn, 134
Kneubuhl, John, 545
Knight, Eric, 249
Knight, Goodwin, 628
Knopf, Edwin, 554, 562, 563, 566, 633
Knopf, Mildred, 563
Knox, Alexander, 557
Knut at Roeskilde, 4, 71
Kober, Arthur, 183
Kohl, Arthur, 76
Kohlmar, Fred, 753, 754, 764, 767
Korda, Alexander, 408, 644
Kotlowitz, Robert, 873
Kramer, Anne Pearce, 868
Kramer, Earl, 815, 844
Kramer, Karen, 838, 853, 862, 863
Kramer, Larry, 863
Kramer, Stanley, 658, 682, 749–51, 753, 756–63, 765–6, 768–9, 771–2, 773, 775–6, 781–5, 786, 788, 790, 791, 792–4, 797–9, 800, 803, 804–10, 811,

815, 817, 818, 819–20, 822, 824, 830–3, 836–7, 838–45, 847, *848*, 849, 851–2, 853–9, 861, 862, 863, 864, 866, 867, 870–2, 873, 875
Krasna, Norman, 272–3, 298
Kress, Harold, 420–1
Krim, Arthur, 805
Krizman, Serge, 780
Krug, Karl, 462
Kruger, Harold, 731
Kruger, Stubby, 307
Kuehn, Louis, 34
Kupferberg, Herbert, 720–1

Lachman, Harry, 188, 249, 251, 252, 253
Ladd, Alan, 668
Ladies in Distress, 344
Lady Comes to Burkburnett, A, see Boom Town
Ladykillers, The, 804
Lady Lies, The, 117
Lady of the Tropics, 395
Laff That Off, 99
Lagerkvist, Pär, 631 and *n*
Laing, Dr. Gordon, 405
Lait, Jack, 505*n*
Lake, The, 436
La Marr, Barbara, 358
Lamarr, Hedy, 358–9, 360–1, 368, 384, 394–5, 400, 401, 446, 554, 820
Lambert, Gavin, 649
Lancaster, Burt, 710, 721, 736, 750, 775–6, 781, 783, 788, *789*, 790, 791, 793, 794, 797, 800
Landau, Ely, 797
Landau, Jack, 735
Lane, Lola, 158
Lanfield, Sidney, 161
Lang, Fritz, 273–4, 279, 280–1, 283–4, 286, 287–9, 292, 314, 322
Lang, Walter, 722, 725, 727, 728
Langdon, Harry, 153
Langley, Noel, 562
Langner, Lawrence, 472, 473, 520, 539, 544–5, 547, 561, 562, 563, 569, 584, 765
Langner, Philip, 765, 794
Lansburgh, Larry, 559
Lansbury, Angela, 553, 554, 556, 557
Lardner, Foster, 116–17, 526 and *n*
Lardner, Ring, 118, 750
Lardner, Ring, Jr., 430, 431, 433 and *n*, 436, 439, 441, 442, 555, 821
Larimore, Earle, 97
Larrimore, Francine, 4

Lasky, Jesse L., 189, 190, 191, 198, 201, 247, 703, 729
Last Hurrah, The, 733, 739–44, 745, 747, 748, 751–2, 753, 755, 756
Last Mile, The (film), 179n
Last Mile, The (play), 120–1, 123, 124, 125–31, 132, 133, 134, 135, 136, 137, 138, 141, 143, 145, 147, 177, 179, 278, 323, 434, 568, 569, 596
Last of Mrs. Cheyney, The, 328
Lastfogel, Abe, 681, 721, 722, 739, 753, 754, 764, 766, 781, 796, 814, 818, 821, 822, 835–6, 839, 866
Laughton, Charles, 259, 298, 590
Laurel and Hardy, 443
Lauter, Harry, 810
Laveau, William, 22, 79, 89
Law Takes Its Toll, The, 122–3
Lawes, Joan Marie "Cherie," 137, 140
Lawes, Lewis E., 135, 137, 179–80
Lawford, Peter, 624
Lawrence, D. H., 672
Lawrence, Eddie, 265–6, 334, 417, 418–20, 460, 482, 484, 748, 801, 802
Lawrence, Gertrude, 308
Lawrence, Jerome, 750, 756
Lawrence of Arabia, 813
Lawrence, Vincent, 21, 114, 333, 538
Lawrence, Warren, 114
Lawson, Capt. Ted, 501
Lazarus Laughed, 520
Leach, George, 125, 128
Lead Harvest, see Mad Game, The
Lean, David, 664, 684, 697, 707, 813 and n
Leavitt, Sam, 847, 858
Lee, Anna, 741
Lee, Harper, 786
Lee, Robert E., 750, 756
Le Gallienne, Eva, 10
Leigh, Janet, 606
Leigh, Vivien, 431, 601, 612, 736, 819, 868
Leighton, Margaret, 544
Lejeune, Caroline, 372
Lemmon, Jack, 791
Leonard, Eddie, 860
Leopard, The, 797
LeRoy, Kitty, 770
LeRoy, Mervyn, 340, 542, 615, 767, 770, 773
Leslie, Lawrence, 138 and n
Levien, Sonya, 163, 242, 550, 551
Levigne, Emil, 527
Levine, Joseph E., 821
Lewin, Albert, 749, 750
Lewis, David, 265

Lewis, Frederick, 202
Lewis, Jerry, 695
Lewis, Judy, 232
Lewis, Dr. Karl, 814, 815
Lewis, Sinclair, 550, 599
Lewton, Val, 749
Libeled Lady, 299, 300, 305, 308, 310, 320, 339
Lichtman, Al, 354
Life Begins at 40, 249
Life in the Raw, 199
Life of Christ, The, 35
Life of Emile Zola, The, 340
Life With Father, 552
Lighton, Louis D. "Bud," 300, 538, 539, 542
Lili, 653
Lillie, Beatrice, 137, 371
Lincoln Portrait, 512
Lindsay, Howard, 67, 552
Lindsay, Margaret, 551
Lindstrom, Petter, 436, 440
Lindstrom, Pia, 415, 436
Lion in Winter, The, 877
Lipsky, Eleazar, 602–3
Listening Eyes, 559–60, 606
Litel, John, 551
Littell, Robert, 131
Little Caesar, 152, 157
Little Colonel, The, 249
Little Me, 810
Little Women, 431, 456
Lloyd, Frank, 185
Lloyd, Harold, 262
Lloyd, Norman, 451
Lockridge, Richard, 131
Loeb, Philip, 67
Loew, Arthur, 640
Loew, David, 750
Loew, Marcus, 262
Loftin, Carey, 808n
Logan, Josh, 666
Lombard, Carole, 234, 293–4, 316, 392, 434, 454–5, 772, 863
London, Jack, 269
Lone Star, 613
Long Day's Journey into Night, 797, 812
Looking for Trouble, 217, 218, 265, 269, 366
Loos, Anita, 265, 275, 284, 712
Lord, Pauline, 21, 474
Loren, Sophia, 754, 764, 766
Loring, Jane, 496
Lorne, Marion, 67
Lorre, Peter, 289
Louis, Joe, 768

Louise, Anita, 201
Love, Elmer, 456
Love, Josephine, 456
Love Finds Andy Hardy, 350
Love Is Legal, see Adam's Rib
Love Story, A, see Song of Love
Love Test, The, 19
Love with the Proper Stranger, 824
Lowe, Edmund, 150, 156, 161, 168, 243, 244, 741
Lowell, Dr. Edgar L., 778–9, 780, 870
Loy, Myrna, 268–9, 272, 293, 299, 329, 332, 333, 335–6, 337, 338, 366, 390, 399, 400, 407, 413, 455, 459–60, 538, 548, 558
Lubitsch, Ernst, 507
Luce, Claire, 138, 139, 140
Luckett, Edith, *see* Davis, Edith "Lucky"
Lueck, Clemens E., 53 and *n*
Luft, Friedrich, 799
Lumet, Sidney, 797
Lunt, Alfred, 194, 402, 525
Lux Radio Theatre, 327, 368, 452
Lycan, Bryan, 4
Lydon, Jimmy, 608
Lyles, A. C., 696, 849
Lynn, Diana, 606, 609
Lystad, Eleanor, 113, 427

MacArthur, Charles, 119, 371, 394
Macbeth, 458
MacDonald, Jeanette, 274–6, 277–8, 286, 295, 330, 333, 390, 738
MacDougall, Curtis, 62–4, 65
MacDougall, Ranald, 694 and *n*, 704, 720
MacFadden, Bernarr, 320
Macgowan, Kenneth, 367, 389
MacGrath, Leureen, 567
Mack, Arthur, 19
MacKeller, Helen, 203
MacKenna, Kenneth, 432, 648
MacLoon, Louis, 278
MacMurray, Fred, 294
Madame Bovary, 589
Madame Currie, 472, 520
Mad Game, The, 214–15, 218, 223, 227, 300
Mad Honeymoon, The, 87
Maggie, The, 804
Magnani, Anna, 877
Magnificent Seven, The, 676
Magnificent Yankee, The, 603, 637
Mahin, John Lee, 305, 310, 311, 332–3, 334, 400, 409, 410, 414, 416, 442–3, 445
Malamud, Bernard, 837
Malaya, 569, 570, 571–2, 573, 582, 588

Malleson, Miles, 242, 544
Mamoulian, Rouben, 411
Man and Wife, see Adam's Rib
Manhattan Melodrama, 276
Man in the Sky, 804
Mankiewicz, Christopher, 608
Mankiewicz, Herman J., 224, 231, 275, 282, 513
Mankiewicz, Joseph L., 272–3, 280, 281, 283, 286, 288, 289, 326, 337–8, 340, 349, 432, 434–5, 442, 443, 450, 469, 493, 497 and *n*, 513, 608 and *n*, 633, 654, 716–17, 753, 877
Mann, Abby, 765, 775, 781–2, 784, 791, 796, 800, 818, 831
Mann, Hank, 741
Mann, Roderick, 795
Mannequin, 324, 326–7, 330, 339
Manners, Dorothy, 848
Manners, J. Hartley, 90
Mannix, Alice, 330
Mannix, Bernice, 330
Mannix, Edgar J. "Eddie," 255, 275, 283, 288, 289, 294, 302, 307, 316, 326, 330–1, 339, 344–5, 357, 358, 359, 360, 377, 380, 385, 386, 395, 396, 399, 407, 408, 420, 444, 454–5, 460, 481, 500, 501, 545, 554, 562, 565, 570, 614, 645, 648, 649, 650, 664, 670, 680–1, 683, 688, 689, 690–1, 739, 758
Man's Castle, 200–1, 202–3, 206, 207, 208, 214, 217–18, 220–1, 223, 741
Mansfield, Richard, 408
Mantle, Burns, 129
Mantz, Paul, 810
Man Who Came Back, The (film), 173
Man Who Came Back, The (play), 4, 5–6
March, Eve, 577, 578
March, Fredric, 194, 340, 408, 411, 414, 590, 614, 637, 723, 750–1, 757 and *n*, 760–1, 772, 786
March, Joseph Moncure, 158
Marco Millions, 520
Maree, Morgan, 723
Marie Antoinette, 326, 366
Marie Galante, 189, 234, 241, 242–4, 246, 251, 255, 367
Marin, Ned, 152
Marion, Frances, 138, 259, 265
Markey, Gene, 182, 368
Markovin, Dr. Boris, 476–8
Marquand, John P., 554
Marrying Kind, The, 621
Marsh, Mae, 741

Marshall, Armina, 765
Marshall, E. G., 701–2, 705
Marshall, Gen. George C., 521
Marsters, Jim, 647
Martelle, Tommy, 89
Martin, Dean, 695
Martin, D'Urville, 856–8
Martin, Pete, 774–6, 786, 801
Marvin, Lee, 671, 819
Marx Brothers, The, 146, 259, 696
Marx, Harpo, 302, 590
Marx, Sam, 272
Marx, Zeppo, 320
Mary of Scotland, 450
Mary's Ankle, 22
Massey, Emily, *see* Perkins, Emily
Massey, Raymond, 572
Matchmaker, The, 683
Matinee Theatre, 765
Mating Call, The, 158
Matthews, Kerwin, 770, 773
Mature, Victor, 801
Maugham, W. Somerset, 22, 412
Maxwell, Marilyn, 490, 820
Mayer, Louis B., 262, 272–3, 292, 294, 326,
   328, 340, 341, 354, 356–7, 358, 394–5,
   396, 407, 431, 432, 433, 442, 453, 480,
   482, 484, 509, 546, 554, 557, 570, 600,
   612, 613–14, 626, 627, 661, 688, 738–9,
   820
Mays, Willie, 837
McAvoy, Earl, 510
McCabe, John, 277, 829*n*
McCall, Mary, 237
McCarey, Leo, 558, 728
McCarthy, Gus, 354
McCarthy, Neil, 244, 407, 487
McClintic, Guthrie, 374
McCrea, Joel, 450, 752
McDonald, Thomas, 757
McDowell, Roddy, 479, 847
McGarry, Bill, 699, 703
McGill, Barney, 180
McGowan, Jack, 91, 117
McGraw, Charles, 810
McGuinness, James Kevin, 151, 359, 408
McGuire, Don, 666
McGuire, Dorothy, 639, 685
McGuire, William Anthony, 154, 163,
   169–70
McHugh, Dorothy, 387, 489
McHugh, Frank, 113, 115, 139, 159, 164, 387,
   388, 409, 488, 608, 609, 741, 756, 865
McIntyre and Heath, 43

McKneally, Martin B., 769
McKnight, Robert, 450
McLaglen, Victor, 150, 156, 161, 168, 202,
   297, 422
McNally, Horace, 469
McNicol, Forrest, 38
McPhail, Angus, 661
McQueen, Steve, 819, 822 and *n*
Me and My Gal, 181, 183, 186, 188, 199, 592
Meanest Man in the World, The, 20, 21
Measure for Measure, 682
Meehan, John, 91, 117, 349, 350, 362
Meek, Donald, 469
Meeker, George, 70, 115
Meet Danny Wilson, 666
Member of the Wedding, A, 645, 750
Men, The, 750
Menace, The, 180
Mencken, H. L., 10, 757, 769
Men in White, 309
Menjou, Adolphe, 553, 556, 557, 558, 671
Men of Boys Town, 370, 407–8, 410, 411, 415,
   417, 600
Menzies, William Cameron, 170, 416*n*
Merchant of Venice, 682, 728
Meredith, Burgess, 444
Merkel, Una, 163, 164
Merman, Ethel, 371, 805
Merrill, Dina, 724, 725, 726, 727, 738,
   752–3
Merrill, Sherburn S., 25, 29, 31
Merry Malones, The, 104, 106
Merry Widow, The, 7, 275
Mescall, John J., 161
Methot, Mayo, 133
Mich, Dan, 801, 802
Michael and Mary, 120
Michelangelo, 679, 748
Middleton, George, 151
Mielziner, Jo, 527
Milestone, Lewis, 158, 444
Milland, Ray, 553
Miller, Alice Duer, 488
Miller, Arthur, 255
Miller, Marilyn, 65
Miller, Seton I., 242
Miller, Sidney, 350, 351
Millhauser, Bertram, 332
Millionairess, The, 618, 622–3, 627, 630, 632,
   633, 634, 635, 636, 640, 643, 655, 661
Million Pound Note, The, 659
Milne, A. A., 71, 120
Min and Bill, 261
Mines, Harry, 699–701

Minnelli, Vincente, 589, 590, 591, 592, 600, 601

Mintz, Jack, 349, 350, 351

Mishkin, Leo, 263

Mister Roberts, 578, 666

Mitchell, Grant, 103, 104, 139, 180, 214, 224

Mitchell, Julian, 91

Mitchell, Thomas, 138, 143, 407

Mitchum, Robert, 569, 866

Mix, Tom, 57, 153

Mizner, Wilson, 179, 275

M'Laren, L. W., 94

Moak, E. R., 43

Mob Rule, see Fury

Mockridge, Norton, 422

Moffitt, Jack, 748

Mogambo, 653, 655, 682

Monahan, Kaspar, 462

Monfried, Walter, 406

Monroe, Marilyn, 513, 738, 739, 772, 808 and *n*

Monsky, Henry, 349

Montgomery, Goodie, 138

Montgomery, Robert, 160, 214, 224, 259, 291*n*, 340, 340, 407, 502, 548

Montgomery and Stone, 7

Moody, William Vaughn, 56

Mook, S. R. "Dick," 160, 173–5, 176, 178, 179, 183, 184, 187, 197, 206, 215–16, 240, 247, 248, 254, 290, 307, 319, 324, 357, 374, 375, 423, 424–6, 565, 570

Moon, Susan, 876

Moon and Sixpence, The, 749

Moon for the Misbegotten, A, 561

Moon Is Down, The, 520

Moore, Gov. A. Harry, 402

Moore, Colleen, 191, 194–5, 197, 210, 434

Moore, Dickie, *171*

Moorhead, Natalie, 103

Moran, Gertrude "Gussie," 620

Moran, Polly, 231

Morgan, Byron, 479

Morgan, Frank, 387

Morgan, Harry, 757

Morgan, Ralph, 170, 199, 214

Morgenstern, Joe, 873–4

Morison, Patricia, 508, 509

Morley, Robert, 340, 374, 377, 562, 563, 567, 579–80

Morning Glory, 209, 431, 558, 727

Morris, Chester, 91, 92, 214

Morrison, Leo, 137, 149, 152, 184, 248, 255, 257, 384, 385, 396, 397, 460, 490, 545, 562, 563, 588–9

Mortimer, Lee, 422

Moses, Anna Mary Robertson "Grandma," 796

Mother Goose Goes Hollywood, 434

Mother Machree, 150

Mountain, The, 680, 681, 686, 687, 690, 693–702, 707–8, 719, 723, 741, 755, 778

Mourning Becomes Electra, 503

Mr. Deeds Goes to Town, 310

Mrs. Parkington, 552

Mrs. Wiggs of the Cabbage Patch, 17

Much Ado About Nothing, 735, 747, 797

Mulligan, Robert, 824–5

Muni, Bella, 568

Muni, Paul, 183, 301, 306, 310, 315, 340, 568, 690, 756

Munsel, Warren, 471

Murder Man, The, 261, 262–3, 264, 293, 811

Murnau, F. W., 153

Murphy, George, 330, 558, 606, 866

Murphy, Richard, 654, 674

Murray, James J., 67

Murray, Jim, 633

Mutiny on the Bounty, 317

My Fair Lady, 717

My Man Godfrey, 299, 310

Nash, Mary, 5

Nathan, George Jean, 10, 404

Naughty Marietta, 275

Navarro, Ramon, 153

Neal, Tom, 741

Neame, Ronald, 659–60

Ned McCobb's Daughter, 96–7, 98, 99

Neilan, Marshall, 300

Nelson, Barry, 483, 489

Nelson, Harman, 182

Nervous Wreck, The, 79

New, Mary, 486

Newcomb, Pat, 802

Newhill, Charles, 512, 517, 518

Newman, Joseph, 278, 282

Newman, Paul, 753, 781

Newquist, Roy, 848

New York Cinderella, A, see I Take This Woman

Ney, Richard, 502

Nice People, 4, 5

Nichols, Dudley, 165, 242

Nichols, Lewis, 529

Nickolaus, John, 411

Nigger Rich, 117

Night of 100 Stars, 754

Night Must Fall, 340

Ninotchka, 400
Nishi, Baron Takeichi, 185
Nissen, Greta, 176
Niven, David, 753
Nixon, Marian, 179, 187
Nixon, Richard M., 558, 779, 800
Nolte, Nick, 840*n*
Noonan, Tommy, 350
Norcross, Hale, 125, 130
Northwest Passage, 366, 372, 375–82, 384, 386, 387–9, 390, 396, 398–9, 403, 404, 417, 580, 599, 697, 756
Norton, Patrick, 566
Not As a Stranger, 781
Not So Long Ago, 10
"Now I'll Tell" by Mrs. Arnold Rothstein, 228, 232, 233–4, 245
Nugent, Elliott, 457, 461, 462, 473
Nugent, Frank, 297, 362, 741, 756
Nugent, J. C., 89

Oakie, Jack, 217, 269
Ober, Harold, 326
Oberon, Merle, 569
O'Brien, Bill, *see* O'Brien, Pat
O'Brien, Eloise, 256, 319, 864
O'Brien, George, 179, 199
O'Brien, Hugh, 657, 659
O'Brien, Liam, 770
O'Brien, Margaret, 548, 638
O'Brien, Pat, 42–3, 46, 47, 59, 69, 70, 71–2, 73, 95–6, 105–6, 111, 112, 113, 119, 120, 159, 176, 180, 256, 277, 294, 319, 361*n*, 373, 387, *388*, 391, 407, 430, 481, 608–9, 610, 741, 742, 770, 828, 864, 870
O'Brien, Terry, 481
O'Brien-Moore, Erin, 247
O'Connor, Donald, 703
O'Connor, Edwin, 739, 740, 742
Odets, Clifford, 322
O'Donnell, Msgr. John, 866
Of Mice and Men, 348, 444
O'Hara, John, 550, 682, 737, 738
O'Hara, Maureen, 606
O'Hara, Shirley, 549
Old Homestead, The, 77
Old Man and the Sea, The, 644–6, 649, 650, 654, 680, 681, 703, 707, 708–14, 729–34, 735, 736, 739, 740, 744–5, 746, 748, 750, 751–2, 753, 774, 786
Oliver, Edna May, 259
Oliver Twist, 343

Olivier, Laurence, 431, 544, 566–7, 601, 612, 727, 736, *737*, 753, 761, 764, 766, 775 and *n*, 791
Olsen and Johnson, 370–1
Olson, Nancy, 606
On Borrowed Time, 416
O'Neil, Nance, 89
O'Neill, Carlotta, 569
O'Neill, Eugene, 436, 474, 503, 520, 545, 561, 562, 563, 569
O'Neill, Henry, 125
O'Neill, James, 43
Only Saps Work, 152
On the Beach, 753, 757–8, 765
On the Waterfront, 683
On Your Toes, 308
Operation Malaya, see Malaya
Orry-Kelly, 577, 632
Osborn, Paul, 416, 472, 520, 666, 732, 733
Oscar Wilde, 374, 376
O'Sullivan, Maureen, 355, 356, 358
Othello, 735
Othman, Frederick, 499
Oursler, Fulton, 797
Out of Hell, see Rugged Path, The
Overman, Lynne, 65, 387, 409
Over the Hill, 150
Owen, Reginald, 259
Owsley, Monroe, 70

Page, Don, 708, 709–12
Page, Jennings, 57
Page, Dr. John, 88
Page, Joy, 712
Page, William, 19
Painted Woman, The, 176, 177, 178, 184, 187, 242
Pakula, Alan, 824
Palmer, Ernest, 161
Palmy Days, 173
Pangborn, Franklin, 231*n*
Pankhurst, Emmeline, 449
Papas, Irene, 685
Parade, see Nigger Rich
Paramore, Earl, 538
Parker, Austin, 199
Parker, Dorothy, 866
Parker, Frank, *596*, 620
Parker, Suzy, 738
Parnell, 333, 339, 399, 571
Parsons, Louella, 201, 210, 220, 259–60, 261, 265, 269, 316, 374, 491*n*, 501, 506, 516, 542, 560, 563, 565, 630, 650, 714
Party's Over, The, 215

Pascal, Ernest, 365
Pascal, Gabriel, 375
Pasteur, Louis, 229
Pat and Mike, 602, 611, 614–22, 627, 633, 637, 651, 756
Patch of Blue, A, 871
Patsy, The, 99–100
Patterson, Pat, 220
Paulee, Mona, 493
Payson, George, 647
Payton, Corse, 75, 600n
Pazos, Felipe, Jr., 710, 711, 712, 732–3
Peabody, Eddie, 176
Pearson, Virginia, 150
Pease, Dr. Charles, 148–9
Peck, Gregory, 558, 640, 659, 691, 797, 866
Peckinpah, Sam, 820–2
Pendleton, Nat, 136, 377
People Against O'Hara, The, 602–3, 604, 607, 609–10, 615
People in Love, 614
People on Sunday, 495n
Perkins, Emily, 508, 634
Perpetua, Sister Mary, 361, 460
Peters, Bess, 454
Peters, Jean, 657, 659
Peters, Ken, 810
Peterson, Dorothy, 163
Pevney, Joseph, 666
Peyton Place, 838
Philadelphia Story, The (film), 432, 433, 456, 457, 465
Philadelphia Story, The (play), 431–2, 436, 442, 450, 473, 599
Phillips, Howard, 124, 127
Phillips, West, 4
Pickford, Mary, 206
Pidgeon, Walter, 334n, 590, 626, 820, 870
Pier 13, see Me and My Gal
Pigeon, The, 10
Pitts, Zasu, 810
Playhouse 90, 765, 783
Plough and the Stars, The, 293, 300, 739
Plowright, Joan, 775n
Plugge, Domis, 72
Plunkett, Walter, 542, 638
Plymouth Adventure, The, 613, 614–15, 616, 618, 623–7, 629, 636–7, 640, 641, 644, 798
Pogany, Willie, 251
Poitier, Sidney, 753, 766, 830, 831, 832, 833, 838, 839–40, 841, 843–4, *848*, 853, 854, 855, 871–2, 874, 875
Polly of the Circus, 89

Poor Aubrey, 231n
Poppy, 297
Porgy and Bess, 458
Porter, Cole, 574 and n, *575*
Porter, Jean, *see* Dmytryk, Jean
Post, C. W., 189, 190
Post, Marjorie Merriweather, 451
Post, Wiley, 264, 491
Powell, Dick, 185
Powell, Eleanor, 330, 738
Powell, William, 67, 259, 268, 272, 299, 310, 333, 346, 347, 820
Power and the Glory, The, 189–90, 191–2, 193–6, 197, 198, 199, 200, 201, 202, 204, 208–10, 214, 223, 224, 258, 737, 744, 756
Power, Tyrone, 331, 333, 360, 365, 366 and n, 390
Power, Tyrone, Sr., 136
Powers, James, 768, 864
Praskins, Leonard, 274
Preminger, Otto, 782, 786
Pressure Point, 830
Prince There Was, A, 77
Prince Valiant, 657
Prisoner, The, 753
Proctor, Mrs. Gilbert, 237
Provine, Dorothy, 808
Pryor, Roger, 133
Pryor, Tom, 687, 745
Public Enemy, The, 157, 179
Putnam, H. Phelps, 449
Putnam, Wellington, 67
Pygmalion, 362, 375

Quick Millions, 152–4, 157, 161, 170, 258
Quinn, Anthony, 797

Racket, The, 158
Rackety Rax, 176, 179
Raft, George, 153–4, 214, 609
Rage in Heaven, 410
Rainer, Luise, 315, 321, 322 and n, 323, 341, 358
Raines, Halsey, 119
Rainmaker, The, 692, 714, 718, 721, 727
Rains Came, The, 366
Rains, Claude, 607, 765
Raker, Lorin, 154–5
Rambeau, Marjorie, 203
Ramsaye, Terry, 150
Ramsey, Walter, 226
Rand, Ayn, 557
Randall, Sue, 724, 725

Ransohoff, Martin, 819, 820–1, 822
Rapf, Harry, 261, 262, 263, 268, 316, 330
Rapf, Maurice, 316
Raphaelson, Samson, 507, 511
Rasinen, Frances, 429
Rathbone, A. D., 79
Rathbone, Basil, 741
Rattigan, Terence, 736
Rau, Neil, 772
Rawlings, Marjorie Kinnan, 415, 417, 418
Ray, Aldo, 621, 622
Razor's Edge, The, 522
Reade, Walter, 86
Reagan, Nancy, *see* Davis, Nancy
Reagan, Ronald, 564, 800
Rear Window, 682
Rebecca of Sunnybrook Farm, 187
Rector of Justin, The, 821, 822
Red, Hot and Blue, 308
Red, White & Blue, The, 825
Red Headed Woman, 326
Red Mill, The, 7
Red Pony, The, 398, 443, 444
Reed, Donna, 820
Reid, Elliott, 757, 763
Reiner, Carl, 838
Reinhardt, Gottfried, 275, 643, 648–9
Reinhardt, Max, 275, 358
Reinsch, Emil, 51
Remey, Ethel, 86, 87–8, 95
Remington, Mary, 20
Revere, Anne, 417, 418, *419*
Reynolds, Debbie, 632, 637–8
Reynolds, Gene, 350, 351, 352, 415, 416
Rhue, Madlyn, 810
Rice, Alfred, 644, 646
Rice, E. W., Jr., 394
Rice, Elmer, 520, 527
Richardson, Ralph, 544, 566, 801
Richter, Conrad, 530, 538, 539
Ricketts, Ed, 444
Riesner, Charles F. "Chuck," 224–5
Riffraff, 259, 265, 266, 267, 268, 269, 272,
   273, 292, 293, 302, 320, 344, 349, 420
Riley, James Whitcomb, 18
Rinehart, Mary Roberts, 77
Ring of Steel, 458
Ripon College Story, The, 824
Riskin, Everett, 481, 494
Riskin, Robert, 481
Ritchie, Bob, 278
Rittenberg, Saul, 686
Ritter, Thelma, 70
Roach, Hal, 444

Road to Rome, The, 519
Roark, Capt. C. T. I. "Pat," 382–3
Robards, Jason, Jr., 863
Robe, The, 653, 674
Roberts, Kenneth, 376, 377, 398–9, 599
Roberts, Marguerite, 539
Roberts, Valli, *136*
Robeson, Paul, 557, 590
Robinson, Edward G., 16, 67, 70, 214, 301,
   554, 609, 749, 752, 818, 866
Robinson Crusoe, 569
Robson, Flora, 417
Rockett, Al, 199
Rogers, Betty, 479
Rogers, Henry H., 47, 48
Rogers, Howard Emmett, 507
Rogers, Roy, 548, 549, 659
Rogers, Will, 111, 150, 178, 184–5, 237, 239*n*,
   249, 264–5, 479, 491
Roland, Gilbert, 572
Romanoff, Mike, 570, 634, 866
Romeo and Juliet, 126, 273, 315
Room Service, 331
Rooney, Mickey, 303–4, 330, 343, 344, 346,
   349, 350, 351, 352, 354, 355, 356, 357, *363*,
   390, 393, 398, 413, 453, 502, 548, 609,
   791, 805, 820
Roosevelt, Betsey Cushing, 451
Roosevelt, Eleanor, 430, 511
Roosevelt, Franklin D., 192, 406–7, 453, 465,
   474, 475, 505, 511, 515, 516, 563
Roosevelt, Jimmy, 492
Rope, 567
Roper, Elmo, 390
Rose, Harold, 517
Rose, Tania, 805
Rose, William, 804–5, 806–7, 810, 817, 830,
   831–3, 837, 840, 842, 852, 871, 875
Rosenstein, Arthur, 302
Rossellini, Roberto, 568
Rosson, Hal, 303, 311
Rothstein, Arnold, 228–9, 230, 233
Rothstein, Carolyn, *see* Behar, Carolyn
   Rothstein
Royal Family, The, 116
Royal Fandango, A, 16
Royal Gelatin Hour, The, 308
Royle, Edwin Milton, 21, 85, 89
Royle, Josephine, 85
Royle, Selena, 21–3, 75, 76, 77, 79, 80, 82–3,
   85, 89, 90, 91, 92–3, 115–16, 347, 552
Rub, Christian, 303
Ruben, J. Walter, *266*, 324, 344, 346, 349
Rubin, J. Robert, 521, 524, 525

Rugged Path, The, 520–34, 536, 538, 550, 552–3, 562, 601

Runyon, Damon, 229, 445

R.U.R., 4, 72, 73–4

Russell, Rosalind, 297, 400, 434

Russians Are Coming, The Russians Are Coming, The, 831

Ruttenberg, Joseph, 283–4, 286, 421, 577

Ruysdael, Basil, 741

Ryan, Bishop James H., 353, 354, 355, 358, 370

Ryan, Robert, 72, 671–3

Sacco and Vanzetti, 273

Sadie Thompson, 176

Sagor, Frederica, 162

Saint, Eva Marie, 683, 685

Saint Joan, 436

Sally, 65

Salt Water, 115

Samrock, Victor, 524–5, 527, 528, 529, 530, 531, 533, 534

Sanders, John Monk, 201

Sanford, Isobel, 841

San Francisco, 274–9, 282–3, 284–6, 288*n*, 289, 290, 294–7, 298, 302, 308, 310, 315, 339, 343, 361, 374, 500, 830

Sanger, Margaret, 449

Santley, Joseph, 117

Sargent, Franklin Haven, 61, 63, 65–6, 67, 69, 70, 71, 73, 404

Sarris, Andrew, 874

Saturday's Children, 297

Savage, Henry W., 18, 75

Saville, Victor, 399, 408, 409, 410–11, 412–13, 414, 421, 465, 466, 467, 468, 474, 479

Sax, Sam, 135

Scaramouche, 624

Scarface, 183

Scars, see Conflict

Schaefer, Jack, 682

Schallert, Edwin, 259, 277, 362, 390, 546–7, 721

Schary, Dore, 145, 323, 343–4, 346, 348, 349, 353, 362, 393, 568–9, 570, 571, 573, 589–90, 598, 602, 603, 610, 613–14, 615, 618, 623, 625, 626, 627, 631, 636, 637, 638, 641, 644, 648, 652, 654, 656, 664, 666–70, 673, 675, 680, 681, 683, 685, 686, 688

Schary, Jill, 666

Schell, Maximilian, 781, 783, 785, 788, 789, 790, 798, 802, 864

Schenck, Joseph, 169, 170, 217, 257, 294, 330

Schenck, Nicholas, 172, 294, 332, 396, 415, 422–3, 613, 631, 668, 670, 673, 680, 691

Scheuer, Philip K., 317, 436–7, 723, 753, 817

Schlesinger, Arthur, Jr., 800

Schlitz Playhouse of Stars, The, 780

Schlom, Marshall, 783–4, 785, 788–90, 791, 792–4, 808, 811, 819, 820, 841, 843, 846–7, 851, 855, 856, 858

Schlosser, Herb, 835–6

Schnee, Charles, 648, 666–7

Schreiber, Lew, 739

Schultz, Lola, 50–1

Schumach, Murray, 772

Schumacher, Jerry, 350, 376

Schumann, Clara, 547

Schurz, Carl, 814

Schuster, Harold, 253

Scopes, John T., 769

Scott, Audrey, 237

Scott, Randolph, 294

Scott, Vernon, 772, 847

Sea of Cortez, 444*n*

Sea of Grass, The, 530, 538–9, 542, 543, 544, 546, 547, 548–9, 550

Seaton, George, 779

Second Man, The, 116

Sedgwick, Edward, 158–9, 165, 215

Seghers, Anna, 494–5

Seitz, John F., 161, 163

Self, Peggy, 595, 606

Self, William "Bill," 492, 546, 581–2, 594–8, 606, 607, 618, 621, 623–4, 625, 635, 699, 766–7, 780, 794, 834–6, 860, 866, 877, 878

Selig, Col. William, 262

Selznick, David O., 273, 387, 399, 410, 412, 434, 453, 506, 550, 684, 825

Selznick, Irene, 527, 546, 581, 608, 643, 662, 738, 747

Sennett, Mack, 262

Separate Tables, 736, 753

Serlin, Oscar, 520

Sersen, Fred, 252

Set Free, 85

Set to Music, 370

Seuss, Dr., 750

Seven Days in May, 813

Seven Keys to Baldpate, 76, 88

Seventeen, 15

Seventh Cross, The, 494–6, 498–9, 500, 501, 503, 503, 505–6, 512

7th Heaven, 150, 205

Shaffer, Rosalind, 505

Shakespeare, William, 405, 512, 544, 584, 599, 766
Shamroy, Leon, 728
Shane, 682
Shanghai, 271
Shanghai Madness, 176, 198, 199–200, 214, 215
Shannon, Frank, 76, 117
Shannon, Peggy, 173, 176, 178, 200
Sharpe, Howard, 315
Sharpe, Karen, *see* Kramer, Karen
Shatner, William, 783
Shaw, George Bernard, 375, 618
Shaw, Irwin, 764
Shawn, Dick, 806
She Stoops to Conquer, 21
She Wanted a Millionaire, 161, 162–4, 169, 172, 173, 183
Shearer, Lloyd, 626, 699–701, 703
Shearer, Norma, 298, 315, 326–7, 329, 340, 390
Sheehan, Winfield R., 136 and *n*, 137, 138, 141, 146, 149–51, 152, 157, 161–2, 163, 164, 166, 168, 170, 172–3, 176, 178, 179, 188, 190, 192, 201, 214, 215, 216, 220, 229, 231, 233, 242, 244, 247, 249–50, 252, 254, 255, 257, 259, 356, 365, 661
Sheepman, The, 86
Shepherd of the Hills, The, 19
Sherman, Vincent, 613
Sherman, Gen. William T., 791
Sherwood, Madeline, 521, 522
Sherwood, Robert Emmet, 475, 512, 515–16, 519, 520–2, 523, *524*, 526, 527, 528, 529, 530–1, 532, 533, 534, 601, 649
Shino, Baron, 185
Ship of Fools, 818, 819, 831, 838, 871
Shipway, Margaret, 697
Shipwrecked, 87
Shore, Dinah, 800
Show-Off, The (film), 223–6, 230–1, *232*, 258, 261, 262, 298, 756
Show-Off, The (play), 231
Shubert, Lee, 117
Shumlin, Herman E., 123–4, 125, 127, 130, 131, 132, 137, 138, 143, 144, 148, 533, 690, 750
Shumow, H. J., 354
Siddens, Sarah, 513
Sidney, George, 550, 551, 650
Sidney, Sylvia, 279, 280, 283, *284*, 288, 292, 293, 323, 435
Siegel, Sol, 654, 661, 680

Signoret, Simone, 819
Silent House, 116
Silver Cord, The, 96, 97
Silver Theatre, 453
Silvers, Phil, 724, 806, 808
Simmons, Jean, 638–44, 653, 849, 863
Simon, Mrs. Richard, 477
Sinatra, Frank, 666, 717–18, 719, 754, 767–8, 771, 773–4, 776, 781, 798, 816–17, 833, 866, 867
Since You Went Away, 506
Singer, Paris, 651
Sin of Madelon Claudet, The, 261
Sintram of Skagerrak, 63, 66
Siodmak, Curt, 495*n*
Siodmak, Robert, 495*n*
Sisk, Robert, 430
Sitgreaves, Beverly, 16
Six Cylinder Love (film), 154–5, 157, 161, 169
Six Cylinder Love (play), 65, 163
Sjöberg, Alf, 631*n*, 632
Skall, William V., 380*n*
Skelly, Hal, 231
Skelton, Red, 502, 738, 820
Skidding, 116
Skinner, Richard Dana, 131
Skinner, Otis, 40, 43
Skin of Our Teeth, The, 539
Skolsky, Sidney, 299, 323, 387, 552, 790–1
Skouras, Spyros, 728
Sky Devils, 158, 160, 164–5, 166, 173
Sky Line, see Quick Millions
Sleeper, Martha, 523
Sligh, Charles R., Jr., 89, 90, 106, 107, 108–9, 144, 427, 583–4, 866
Smallest Show on Earth, The, 804
Smith, Al, 331
Smith, Dr. Alathena, 547, 565, 588
Smith, Bernard, 814
Smith, Bright, 7–8, 10, 588
Smith, Harold Jacob, 756–7
Smith, Louisa, 21, 81
Smith, Ludlow Ogden, 449
Smith, Tina Gopadze, 546, 855
Smith, Wingate, 241
Society Girl, 176, 178, 242
So Ends Our Night, 749
So Many Thieves, see It's a Mad, Mad, Mad, Mad World
Something a Little Less Serious, see It's a Mad, Mad, Mad, Mad World
Sommers, Harry G., 76, 82
Sondheim, Stephen, 764
Song and Dance Man, The, 87

Song of Love, 547–8, 555
Son of the Sheik, 169
Sons and Lovers, 791
Sothern, Ann, 548
So This Is New York, 750, 807
Sousa, John Philip, 44, 111
Spencer, Daisy, 30 and *n*
Sperry, Ray, 303
Spiegel, Sam, 610, 753, 813
Spiegelgass, Leonard, 614
Spirit of St. Louis, The, 666
Spurin-Calleia, Joseph, *see* Calleia, Joseph
Squaw Man, The, 21, 89
Stage Door, 308, 434
Stallings, Lawrence, 364, 377, 380
Stanislavsky, Constantin, 322, 789*n*
Stanley and Livingstone, 365–9, 370, 372, 384, 389–90
Stanwyck, Barbara, 333, 555
Stapleton, Maureen, 639
Star Is Born, A, 340, 782
Stars in Your Eyes, 371
Starr, Jimmy, 272
State of the Union (film), 553–9, 561, 562, 563, 564, 570, 584–5
State of the Union (play), 552–3
Steamboat Bill, Jr., 225
Steamboat Round the Bend, 264
Stebbins, Abigail, *see* Brown, Abigail
Stebbins, Warren, 34
Steele, Marjorie, 684, 738
Steiger, Rod, 875
Steinbeck, Carol, 444
Steinbeck, John, 398, 443–5, 520
Sten, Anna, 394
Sterling, Ford, 231
Stern, Phil, 786
Stevens, George, 433, 435, 437–8, 442–3, 449, 508, 555, 633, 682, 797, 812*n*
Stevens, Inger, 738
Stevenson, Robert Louis, 408
Stewart, Donald Ogden, 465, 466 and *n*, 467, 468, 479–80, 507, 509, 511, 550–1, 563, 566, 662
Stewart, Gloria, 665, 779
Stewart, James, 459, 502, 570, 572, 644, 665, 681, 738, 779, 781, 820, 866, *867*
Stewart, Rosalie, 133
Stirling, Jack, 311
St. Johns, Adela Rogers, 397, 399, 409, 454, 490, 506–7
Stock, Dr. Richard, 718, 735
Stolen Fruit, 89
Stoloff, Benjamin, 157, 161

Stone, Lewis, 346, 349, 553, 820
Story of G. I. Joe, The, 224
Story of John, The, 439–40, 452, 477
Story of Louis Pasteur, The, 310
Stowitts, Hubert Julian, 251
Strange, Hugh, 163
Strange Interlude, 474, 520
Strasberg, Lee, 789*n*
Straus, Ann, 358
Strauss, Ted, 422
Streeter, Edward, 589, 590, 598, 599, 603
Street Scene (film), 173
Street Scene (play), 132
Strickling, Gail, 402, 566
Strickling, Howard, 299, 315, 316, 330, 334 and *n*, 357–8, 374, 393, 402, 429, 455, 459, 489, 493, 510, 558–9, 564, 566, 568, 655, 656, 662, 683, 686, 687, 738, 862, 863, 866, *868*, 870
Strictly Dishonorable, 120, 188, 191
Stromberg, Hunt, 330, 340, 377, 380, 382, 386, 396
Struggle Everlasting, The, 89
Studio One, 765
Stulberg, Gordon, 836, 839, 841
Sturges, John, 603, 610, 669–70, 671, *673*, 674–8, 707, 714, 730, 732–3, 744, 745, 746, 748, 755–6
Sturges, Preston, 188–9, 191, 192, *195*, 655, 661
Sturges, Sandy, 662
Suddenly, Last Summer, 753–4
Sullavan, Margaret, 749, 820, 834*n*
Sullivan, "Big Tim," 150
Sullivan, Dorothy, *see* Tracy, Dorothy
Sullivan, Ed, 231, 297–8, 298, 331, 333, 373–4
Sullivan, Gene, 404, 601, 704
Sullivan, "Little Tim," 150
Sullivan, Wallace, 299
Summertime, 664, 671, 697, 708, 721, 813
Sunderland, Nan, 103
Sunny Side Up, 150
Sunrise, 153
Surles, Gen. Alexander D., 527
Surtees, Robert, 499
Suskind, David, 774
Sutherland, A. Edward "Eddie," 164–5
Swanson, Gloria, 259
Swan Song, 118
Swerling, Flo, 219
Swerling, Jo, 201, 202, 211, 217, 219, 614
Swor, John, 136, 138
Sydney, Basil, 375

Take the High Ground, 666
Talbot, Lyle, 180
Taliaferro, Edith, 89
Tallman, Frank, 810
Talmadge, Norma, 153, 294
Taming of the Shrew, The, 682
Tandy, Jessica, 495, 499
Tannen, Julius, 741
Tasker, Robert, 138, 331
Taste of Honey, A, 776n
Tate, Sharon, 821
Taurog, Norman, 349, 350, 351, 362
Taxi Talks, 132, 133–4, 135
Taylor, Don, 591–2, 601
Taylor, Elizabeth, 590, 591, 592, 593–4, 602, 753
Taylor, Laurette, 65, 90 and n, 528–9, 872
Taylor, Mary Kennedy, 778
Taylor, Robert, 259, 329, 333, 346, 360, 372, 453, 502, 738, 773, 866
Taylor, Sam, 822
Teahouse of the August Moon, 655
Tempest, 169
Temple, Shirley, 202, 249, 292, 297, 333, 390, 640
Ten North Frederick, 733, 736–8, 739
Tenny, Jack B., 555
Tenth Avenue, 113
Terrett, Courtenay, 152, 179
Terry-Thomas, 806
Test Pilot, 330, 332–8, 339, 340, 345, 347, 362, 399, 459, 538
Tevis, Walter, 819
Thalberg, Irving G., 224, 258, 259–60, 261, 262, 265, 266, 273, 275, 294, 302, 356, 357, 568, 570, 603, 688, 863
That Broader Outlook, 239–41
Thau, Benny, 259, 336, 345, 396–7, 407, 432, 459, 460, 500, 538, 545, 570, 586, 600, 610, 611, 613–14, 624, 640, 665, 683, 686, 689, 690–1, 717, 752, 866
Thaxter, Phyllis, 552
Theodora Goes Wild, 481
Theodore, Ralph, 125
There Shall Be No Night, 402, 515
There's No Business Like Show Business, 722
They Gave Him a Gun, 314, 315–16, 318, 339
They Were Expendable, 488, 516
Thielman, Virginia, 827–8
Thimig, Helene, 506
Thin Man, The, 268
Thirty Seconds Over Tokyo, 501, 506, 512, 552, 559

This Is the Army, 507
This Is Your Life, 870
Thomas, Bob, 254, 558, 661, 727, 733, 820, 864
Thomas, Frank, 350
Thomas, J. Parnell, 558
Thompson, Dave, 208
Thompson, Dorothy, 430
Thompson, Ruthie, 780
Thompson, Sam, 198, 428
Thompson, Dr. William Paul, 823
Thomson, Polly, 538
Thorpe, Richard, 572
Three on a Match, 214
Three Rooms in Heaven, see Mannequin
Three Time Loser, see You Only Live Once
Thunderbolt, 138
Thursby, Dave, 311
Tibbett, Lawrence, 522
Tierney, Belle, 630–1, 635
Tierney, Gene, 548, 616, 623, 624, 626–7, 630–1, 632, 635, 636, 637, 649
Tight Little Island, 653
Tilden, Bill, 615
Time, 15
Time of the Cuckoo (film), *see Summertime*
Time of the Cuckoo (play), 639
Tinker, Edward R., 172, 173, 190
To Kill a Mockingbird, 786, 824
Toland, Dr. Clarence, 315, 346
Toler, Sidney, 158, 159, 165
Tom, Dick and Harry, 430, 431
Tomorrow, John Jones, 505
Tone, Franchot, 259, 327
Tonight or Never, 173
Too Many Husbands, 22
Topping, Henry J. "Bob," Jr., 560
Topping, Dr. Norman, 779
Torchia, Emily, 450, 468, 482, 558, 560, 655
Torch Song, 653
Torres, Raquel, 176
Tortilla Flat, 407, 443, 444–6, 453, 455, 456, 459, 461, 471, 479, 488, 506
Toscanini, Arturo, 372
To Sir, With Love, 872
To the Ladies, 65, 67
Touch and Go, 804
Touch of the Poet, 561, 563, 569
Toulouse-Lautrec, Henri de, 615
Tovarich, 308
Towell, Sidney, 248
Tracy, Andrew B., 26, 29, 34, 35, 36, 110, 198, 257, 361, 455, 503, 522, 529, 587, 608, 703–4, 705, 746, 777

Tracy, Caroline "Carrie," 14, 20, 27, 28–30, 32–3, 36, 37, 38, 39, 40, 44, 45, 47, 48, 52, 61, 77, 80, 86, 87, 90, 107, 110, 112, 113, 119, 139, 141, 148, 151, 160, 164, 167, 186, 187, 197, 204, 211, 220, 227, 228, 230, 236, 239, 247, 256, *285*, 317–18, 340, 353, 360, 386, 373, 376, 392, 394, 440, 453, 455–6

Tracy, Carroll Edward, 13, 15, 29, 31, 32, 33, 34, 35, 36, 40–1, 43, 44, 45, 46, 47, 69, 109, 112, 139, 160, 186, 187, 197, 198, 199, 203, 205, 210, 211, 212, 219–20, 246, 247, 248, 256, 272, *296*, 348, 350, 353, 360, 386, 392, 397, 404, 427–8, 439, 440, 451, 453, 455, 460, 465, 475, 503, 522, 524–5, 528, 533, 540, 587–8, 594, 626, 635, 684, 692–3, 703–4, 715, 718, 745, 746, 763, 768, 777, 800, 814, 816, 817, 822, 826, 862, 863, 869, 874, 876, 877

Tracy, Catherine, *see* Bonaventure, Mother

Tracy, Dorothy, 198, 199, 205, 360, 392, 453, 455, 588, 626, 763, 777, 862, 863, 865, 866, 869, 874

Tracy, Frank, 26, 39, 109, 139, 198, 256, 272, 384, 427–8, 429–30, 529, 587–8, 607, 624, 693, 704, 777, 800–1, 828–9

Tracy, Frank J., 35, 37, 110, 503

Tracy, Jane "Jenny," *see* Feely, Jenny

Tracy, John D., 26–8, 29, 30

Tracy, John Edward, 13, 14, 20, 21, 26, 27, 28–9, 30, 31, 32, 33–4, 39, 41, 44, 45, 47, 48, 52, 61, 65, 69, 77, 86, 90, 94, 95, 107, 108, 109–10, 111, 113, 143, 198, 346, 456, 540, 642, 665

Tracy, John Ten Broeck, 21, 22, 76, 78, 80–1, 82, 83, 86, 87, 88, 90, 91, 94, 95, 96, 98–9, 100, 103, 104, 105, 107–8, 109, 112, 113, 116, 117, 139, 140, 141–2, 144–6, 147, 148–9, 151–2, 159, 160–1, *162*, 164, 165–6, 167, 177–8, 181–2, 184, 185–7, 188, 192, 193, 197, *204*, 205, 211, 213, 221, 222–3, 226, 228, 236, 241, 245–6, 253–4, 256, 260, 266–8, 269, *270*, 301–2, 309, 315, 319, 320–1, 324, 334, 338, 341, 352–3, *354*, 360, 369, 383, 386, 392, 394, 408, 411, 413, 425, 427, 430, 439–40, 452, 453, 458, 461, 467, 476, 477, 478, 485, 493, *511*, 523, 530, 536, 537–8, 552, 559, 560, 565, 580, 582, 583, 588, 598, 605, 606, 618, 625, 628, 646–7, 673–4, 679, 690, 706, 708, 714, 725, 729, 730–1,

734–5, 743, 763, 780, 800, 802, 828, 837, 860, 861, 864, 869, 874, 875, 876

Tracy, Joseph Spencer, 690, 708, 734

Tracy, Lee, 138, 208, 224 and *n*

Tracy, Letitia, 26, 30

Tracy, Louise Treadwell, 3, 4, 5–11, 13, 14–15, 17–18, 20–1, 22, 24, 76–7, 78, 79, 80–1, 82, 83–5, 86, 87, 88, 89–90, 91, 93, 94–5, 98–100, 101, 102, 103, 104–5, 107, 108–9, 110, 112, 116, 119–20, 124, 133, 139, 140, 141–2, 144, 145–6, 147, 148–9, 151, 152, 155–6, 159, 160–1, 164, 166, 167, 174–5, 177–8, 181–2, 184, 185–7, 188, 192–3, 196, 197, 204, 205, 206–8, 211, 212, 213, 215–16, 221, 222–3, 226, 227–8, 236–41, 245–6, 247, 250–1, 253, 254, 256–7, 260, 264, 266–7, 268, 271, 272, 277, 290, 298, 300, 301, 302, 305, 307–8, 309, 310, 315, 318–19, 320, 322, 324, 325, 330, 331–2, 337, 338, 340, 341–2, 344–5, 346, 348, 352–3, 360, 363, 369, 372, 373, 375, 376, 383 and *n*, 384, 386, 391, 392, 394, *395*, 401, 402, 404, 408, 411, 413, 424–6, 427, 429*n*, 430, 439–40, 444, 452, 453, 455, 456, 458, 461, 467, 471, 476–8, 484–7, 489–90, 492, 493, 501, 509, *511*, 516, 528, 529, 535–7, 543, 546, 547, 549, 552, 559–60, 582–4, 587, 588, 598, 601, 605–6, 608, 612, 618, 626, 628–9, 636, 646, 647, 651, 674, 679–80, 690, 702, 705–6, 708, 714–15, 717, 718, 720*n*, 725, 729, 734, 736, 743, 744, 746, 763, 777–80, 796, 800, 802, 807, 811, 813, 814, 816, 817, 823, *824*, 825, 826, 827–8, 837–8, 859, 860, 861–3, 865, 866, *868*, 869–70, 874–6, 877, 878

Tracy, Louise Treadwell "Susie," 177–8, 186, 177–8, 204, 221, 226, 228, 253, 254, 260, 302, 309, 315, 319, 324, 341, *354*, 360, 369, 383, 386, 392, 394, *395*, 425, 427, 452, 458, 461, *462*, 467, 493, 503, *511*, 537, 570, 580, 582, 583, 598, 605, 606, 611, 618, *629*, 630, 636, 647, 680, 690, 702 and *n*, 708, 714, 725, 743, 763, 802, 828, 837–8, 851, 860, 861–3, 864, 865, 869, 870, 874, 875, 876

Tracy, Mary Ann, *see* Perpetua, Sister Mary

Tracy, Mary Guhin, 26, 29, 36

Tracy, Mary "Mame," 35, 110, 386, 503, 608, 746

Tracy, Nadine, *see* Carr, Nadine

Tracy, Spencer Bernard, *see* Tracy, Spencer
    Bonaventure
Tracy, Spencer Bonaventure: and the
    Academy Awards, 310, 314–15, 339–42,
    355, 356, 362–4, 366, 374, 423, 430, 604,
    606, 708, 727, 736, 753, 786–7, 802,
    874–5; acting technique of, 57, 60, 73,
    76–7, 104, 125, 126, 129, 194, 223, 345,
    351, 389, 401, 414, 419, 420, 435, 436,
    440, 469, 489, 498, 524, 528, 529–30,
    567, 578–9, 591, 594, 621, 641, 658,
    676–8, 741, 754–6, 759, 761–2, 784,
    789n, 794, 847, 872; and alcoholism,
    79, 159, 160, 170, 174, 198–9, 201, 213,
    219–20, 231–2, 235, 241–2, 244, 245,
    247, 252–3, 254, 256–7, 265, 272, 308,
    319, 322, 325–6, 327, 334, 335–6, 348–9,
    391, 396, 402, 409, 453, 459–61, 463–4,
    492–3, 494, 502, 503–5, 509–11, 512–15,
    516–17, 518–19, 546, 565–6, 568, 596,
    603, 609, 612, 687, 698–9, 702–3,
    708–9, 710, 717–18, 728, 794, at the
    American Academy of Dramatic Arts,
    61, 65–6, 67–73; birth of, 29; and
    Catholicism, 32, 37, 64, 84–5, 208,
    212–13, 221, 234, 277, 279, 309, 429–30,
    471–2, 515, 646–7, 830, 846; and
    childhood love of movies, 35, 36, 38–9,
    40; and deafness of his son, 84, 95–6,
    182, 211, 338, 492–3, 646–7, 802; death
    of, 860–1; education of, 32, 36–7, 46–9;
    and father's alcoholism, 33–4, 39–40,
    79; funeral of, 865–6; and insomnia,
    266, 338–9, 384, 385–6, 411, 463–4,
    471–2, 474, 508–9, 808, 813, 859; and
    John Tracy Clinic, 485, 486, 536, 546,
    547, 559–60, 564–5, 580, 628–30,
    746–7, 778–80, 800, 807, 811, 870; and
    kidnapping threat, 227–8, 230;
    marriage of, 12, 14–15, 206, 213, 215–16,
    226, 236, 250–1, 254, 320–1, 426–7, 452,
    493, 546, 556, 583–4, 636, 714–15, 717;
    military service of, 44–6; and polo, 156,
    168, 184–5, 236, 237, *238*, 269, 291n, 324,
    327, 332, 350, 369, 382–3, 404; on the
    Ripon debate team, 62–5; and his son's
    battle with polio, 145–6, 148, 160, 164,
    182
Tracy, William, 26, 27, 28, 29, 34
Treadwell, Allienne, 7, 81, 88, 105, 139, 588,
    869
Treadwell, Eleanor, 874
Treadwell, George Edwards, 7

Treadwell, Louise Ten Broeck, *see* Tracy,
    Louise Treadwell
Treasure of the Sierra Madre, The, 694
Treat, Earl, 504
Treat, Katie, 504
Tree Grows in Brooklyn, A, 539
Treitel, Herbert, 79
Trevor, Claire, 199, 215, 223, 249, 251, 450–1,
    695, 701–2, 704
Tribute to a Bad Man, 681–9, 690, 691, 694,
    829n
Trilling, Steve, 712
Trouble Shooter, The, *see Looking for
    Trouble*
Trowbridge, Charles, 259
Troyat, Henri, 693
True Colors, see Nigger Rich
Truex, Ernest, 86
Truman, Bess, 607
Truman, Harry S., 521, 531, 555–6,
    607
Truman, Margaret, 607
Trumbo, Dalton, 481, 494, 821
Truth, The (film), 60 and *n*
Truth, The (play), 51, 52–4, 56, 59–61, 63
Tucker, Forrest, 469
Tucker, Sophie, 330, 565
Tugboat Annie, 209
Tully, Hugh, 256–7, 427, 537
Tully, Jim, 256
Tunberg, Karl, 614
Turman, Lawrence, 831
Turnbull, Hector, 188, 189, 191
Turner, Lana, 412, 551, 559, 560
Twain, Mark, 18
Twelfth Night, 767
Twentieth Century, 299
Twenty Thousand Years in Sing Sing (book),
    179
20,000 Years in Sing Sing (film), 180–1, 182,
    202, 213
Two Arabian Knights, 158
Two Weeks in Another Town, 764
Tyler, Jeri, 730–1
Tynan, Kenneth, 574, 577

Uggams, Leslie, 768
Ulmer, Edgar G., 495n
Ulric, Lenore, 43, 65
Uncle Tom's Cabin, 77
Under Capricorn, 568
Undercurrent, 538, 539
United States Steel Hour, The, 765

Up in Mabel's Room, 11, 12
Up the River, 135, 137, 138 and *n*, 140, 143, 145, 146, 153, 160, 176, 177, 179, 725
Urban, Joseph, 161

Valiant, The, 54, 56–8, 71
Valiant Is the Word for Carrie, 314
Valiant Lady, 724
Vallee, Rudy, 308, 749
Valley of the Dolls, 874
Van Dekker, Albert, *see* Dekker, Albert
Vandenberg, Arthur, 527
Van Dyke, W. S. "Woody," 276, 277, 278, 279, 282, 285, 314, 315, 319, 321, 330, 340, 377, 395–6, 398
Veitch, John, 819
Veneer, 120, 163
Vernon, Margaret, 91
Very Rich Woman, A, 838
Victoria Regina, 308
Vidor, King, 340, 376, 377, 379–82, 386, 388–9, 415, 420, 479, 679
Viertel, Peter, 633, 666, 707, 713, 732
Viertel, Salka, 550
Virginian, The, 300
Visconti, Luchino, 797
Viva Villa, 224
Vogel, Paul, 411
Vogel, Robert M. W., 539
Volkman, Ivan, 839, 858
Von Hagen, Dr. Karl, 813–14
von Kleinschmid, Dr. Rufus, 478, 628
von Sternberg, Josef, 359
Vorkapich, Slavko, 286

Wadsworth, Henry, 224
Wagner, Elmer "Red," 59, 61
Wagner, Max, 444
Wagner, Robert, 657–8, 694–9, *700*, 701–2, 704, 745, 802, 866
Wagner, Sid, 380*n*
Wait Until Dark, 874
Walburn, Raymond, 231
Waldo, Rhinelander, 150
Wales, Carol Lee, 486, *487*
Walker, David, 661
Walker, James J., 112
Walker, Robert, 553
Walker, Stuart, 13, 15, 108
Wallace, Henry, 554, 555, 587, 672
Wallis, Hal, 692
Walsh, Raoul, 150, 183, 454
Walters, Eugene, 17

Wanger, Walter, 185, 292, 299, 358, 570, 821, 822
Wapshot Chronicle, The, 824
Wapshot Scandal, The, 824
Warfield, David, 43
Waring, Fred, 173
Warner, Ann, 712
Warner, Jack L., 179, 185, 291*n*, 407, 557, 710, 711, 713, 733
Warren, Ruth, 136, 137
Wasson, George, 241–2, 263
Waterloo Bridge, 519
Watkins, Maurine, 134–5, 138, 140, 146
Watson, Bobs, 350, 351–2, 364, 849
Watson, Minor, 203
Way Down East, 77
Wayne, David, 348, 574, 578, 579
Wayne, John, 219, 220, 231, 232, 558, 570, 650, 666
Wayne, Josephine, 219, 220, 231, 243
Wead, Frank, 332, 333
Webb, Clifton, 516
Wedding Guests, The, 71
Weeks, Keith, 172
Weigel, Helene, 506
Weinberger, Harrold, 378
Weingarten, Lawrence, 261, 340, 394, 396, 507, 508, 509, 573, 587, 604, 621, 630, 631, 643, 648, 652, 654, 659, 866
Weismuller, Johnny, 305
Weiss, Milton, 516–17
Welles, Orson, 436, 740, 770
Wellman, Dorothy "Dottie," 271
Wellman, William A., 179, 224, 269, 270, 271–2, 615, 650
Wells, H. G., 188
Wengraf, John, 785
We're No Angels, 694
Wertheimer, Al, 330
West, Albert, 125
West, Mae, 431
Westcott, Gordon, 291*n*
Westmore, Ern, 194
Westmore, Frank, 698–9
Weston, Kendal, 4, 11, 17
Wexley, John, 122, 123, 124, 125, 127, 134, 135, 143, 278
Wharton, John, 525, 526
What Price Glory? (film), 150, 156, 158, 176, 179
What Price Glory? (play), 88, 165
What's Your Wife Doing? 17
What the Doctor Ordered, 100, 103*n*

Wheeler, John, 451

Wheelwright, Ralph, 454

Whelan, Tim, 261, 262, 399

When in Rome, 614

Whipple, Sidney, 418

Whipsaw, 268–9, 271, 272, 293, 334

Whiskey Galore, 661

Whispering Friends, 109, 110, 112

Whitbeck, Frank, 266, 350, 352, 353–4, 361, 370, 385, 404, 539

White, Les, 263

White Cliffs of Dover, The, 488

White Parade, The, 247

White Sister, The, 276

Whitman, Ernest, 125

Whitney, Dorothy, 572

Whitney, William Dwight, 572

Whoopie, 155

Whorf, Richard, 469

Widmark, Richard, 657, 660–1, 775, 781, 783, 785, 788–9, 790–1, 798

Wilbourn, Phyllis, 612, 817, 821, 822, 861, 863, 877–8

Wilde, Cornel, 548

Wilder, Billy, 495n

Wilder, Thornton, 586, 649

Wilding, Michael, 568

Wild One, The, 750

Wilkerson, W. R. "Billy," 198, 200, 201, 218, 223, 224, 271, 357

Will, Wolfgang, 799

Williams, Bert, 43, 809

Williams, Esther, 606, 820

Williams, Ethyl, 52–4, 59, 61, 63, 203

Williams, Guinn "Big Boy," 191

Williams, Jesse Lynch, 263

Williams, Kay, 772

Williams, Rex, 533

Williams, Tennessee, 753

Willits, Ann, 503

Willits, Kathleen, 522

Willits, Henry, 522

Willkie, Wendell, 407

Wilson, Earl, 515, 543, 544, 816n

Wilson, Dr. John C., 148, 149, 152, 160, 182, 186

Wilson, Lois, 224

Winchell, Walter, 505n, 515, 518, 618, 635, 663, 866

Wingate, Dr. James, 191–2, 217–18

Wings, 224, 332

Wings of Tomorrow, see Test Pilot

Winkler, Otto, 340, 454

Winninger, Charles, 136

Winston, Archer, 422

Winston, Matie E., 94–5, 458, 467, 476

Winter, Ella, 466 and n, 550, 551, 662

Winter, Wales, 96

Winters, Jonathan, 806

Winwood, Estelle, 65

Wise, Robert, 682–3, 684, 685–7, 688

Wise, Walter, 343

Witching Hour, The, 51

Within the Law, 17, 91

Without Love (film), 505–10, 511, 512, 515, 531

Without Love (play), 453, 457, 459, 460, 461, 464, 465, 471, 472–5, 479

Wolfe, John, 619

Wolfe, Edwin R., 67

Wolheim, Louis, 158

Woman of the Year, 430–9, 440–3, 450, 452, 456–7, 465, 469, 479, 479, 480, 505, 547, 603, 633, 663, 756, 821

Wood, Judith, 265

Wood, Leonard Jr., 3–4, 6, 11, 13, 74

Wood, Marjorie, 91, 92, 93

Wood, Natalie, 745, 754, 802

Wood, Peggy, 6

Wood, Sam, 557

Woodward, Ernest, 4, 5–6, 70

Woodward, Joanne, 781

Wooing of Eve, The, 71

Woolf, Edgar Allan, 232

Woollcott, Alexander, 131, 132

Wray, Fay, 199–200, 201, 329

Wright, Jean, 331

Wright, Teresa, 639, 640n, 653

Wright, W. H., 18–19, 20, 21–2, 75, 76, 77, 82, 86, 87, 88–9, 90, 98, 99, 102

Wurtzel, Sol M., 141, 144, 145, 151, 152, 157, 161, 163, 169, 170, 173, 176, 177, 190, 192, 248, 249, 256, 264, 298, 356

Wurzburg, William, 82

Wurzel-Flummery, 71

Wycherly, Margaret, 474

Wyler, William, 278, 558, 680, 736

Wylie, I. A. R., 465, 466

Wyman, Jane, 639

Wynn, Ed, 331

Wynn, Keenan, 508, 510

Yager, Bob, 770–1, 773, 786

Yankees in Texas, 614

Yeaman, Elizabeth, 295, 323

Yearling, The, 372, 397, 398, 399, 407, 415–18, 420, 433, 443, 444, 479, 481, 569

Years Ago, see Actress, The

Yellen, Jack, 242

Yellow, 91–4, 95, 96, 103
Yordan, Philip, 654
York, Dick, 757, *758*
Yost, Robert, 249
You Can't Take It With You, 584
You for Me, 624
Young, Freddie, 567–8
Young, Gig, 728
Young, Loretta, 201, 203, 206–8, 210–12, 213, 215, 216, 217, 218, 219–222, 226, 228, 231–2, 233, 234–5, 243, 246, 247, 269–72, 277, 321, 333, 356, 439, 450, 452
Young, Nedrick, 756–7, 769
Young, Robert, 330, 377, 378, 379, 386, 695, 779, 800
Young, Roland, 65
Young, Waldemar, 333
Young America, 173, 175–6
Young Bess, 638
Youngstein, Max, 810
Young Tom Edison, 393

You Only Live Once, 293n
Yurka, Blanche, 14, 65

Zagon, Samuel S., 805
Zaharias, Mildred Ella "Babe" Didrikson, 616, 620
Zanuck, Darryl F., 153, 185, 217, 257, 291n, 365, 366, 367, 374, 389, 654, 655, 656, 657, 659, 661
Zavits, Lee, 252
Zeidler, Carl, 405
Zeitlin, Ida, 301, 317–18
Ziegfeld Follies, 161, 307
Zimbalist, Efrem, Jr., 533–4
Zimbalist, Sam, 400, 445, 501, 650, 681, 683, 684, 685, 687, 694
Zimmermann, Jerry, 800–1
Zimring, Mike, 805
Zinn, John, 242
Zinnemann, Fred, 495–6, 498, 499, 506, 508, 645, 707, 708–14, 730, 733
Zolotow, Sam, 528